Canadian 7th edition

Marketing Management

Analysis, Planning, Implementation, and Control

works

thought process

Philip Kotler
*Northwestern
University*

Ronald E. Turner
*Queen's
University*

Prentice Hall Canada Inc., Scarborough, Ontario

This book is dedicated
to Nancy and Caroline
with love

Canadian Cataloguing in Publication Data

Kotler, Philip
    Marketing management : analysis, planning, implementation and control

Canadian 7th ed.
ISBN 0-13-561630-1

1. Marketing - Management. I. Turner, Ronald E.,
1931-   . II. Title.

HF5415.13.K67 1992   658.8'02   C92-094407-8

Prentice Hall, Inc., Englewood Cliffs, New Jersey
Prentice-Hall International, Inc., London
Prentice-Hall of Australia, Pty., Ltd., Sydney
Prentice-Hall of India Pvt., Ltd., New Delhi
Prentice-Hall of Japan, Inc., Tokyo
Prentice-Hall of Southeast Asia (Pte.) Ltd., Singapore
Editora Prentice-Hall do Brasil Ltda., Rio de Janeiro
Prentice-Hall Hispanoamericana, S.A., Mexico

ISBN 0-13-561630-1

Acquisitions Editor: Jacqueline Wood
Developmental Editor: David Jolliffe
Copy Editor: Heather McClune
Production Editor: Valerie Adams
Production Coordinator: Florence Rousseau
Cover Design: Monica Kompter
Technical Artist: Phillip Allen
Page Layout: Hermia Chung
Cover Image: "Ascending Forms" by Bertram Brooker

1 2 3 4 5 RRD 97 96 95 94 93

Printed and bound in the U.S.A. by R.R. Donnelley

Table of Contents

PREFACE   XIV
CLASSIFICATION OF EXHIBITS   XIX

PART I UNDERSTANDING MARKETING MANAGEMENT   2

1 UNDERSTANDING THE CRITICAL ROLE OF MARKETING IN ORGANIZATIONS AND SOCIETY   2

THE CORE CONCEPTS OF MARKETING   4
Needs, Wants, and Demands   5   Products   6
Value, Cost, and Satisfaction   6   Exchange, Transactions, and Relationships   7
Markets   9   Marketing and Marketers   10

MARKETING MANAGEMENT   11
Marketing Concepts and Tools 1-1: Demand States and Marketing Tasks   12

COMPANY ORIENTATIONS TOWARD THE MARKETPLACE   13
The Production Concept   13   The Product Concept   14
The Selling Concept   15   The Marketing Concept   17
Marketing Strategies 1-1: The Secret of L. L. Bean's Profitability—Customer Satisfaction   20
Marketing Strategies 1-2: How Jan Carlzon "Marketized" SAS   23
Companies and Industries 1-1: Five Stages in the Slow Learning of Bank Marketing   26
The Societal Marketing Concept   28

THE RAPID ADOPTION OF MARKETING MANAGEMENT   29
In the Business Sector   29   In the Nonprofit Sector   29
In the International Sector   30

SUMMARY   30

2 LAYING THE GROUNDWORK THROUGH STRATEGIC PLANNING   34

CORPORATE STRATEGIC PLANNING   36
Corporate Mission   37   Strategic Business Unit Identification   39
Evaluating the Current Business Portfolio   40   Corporate New-Business Plan   47

BUSINESS STRATEGIC PLANNING   49
Business Mission   50   External Environment Analysis (Opportunity and Threat Analysis)   50
Marketing Strategies 2-1: Which Company Should Produce an Electric Car?   52
Internal Environment Analysis (Strengths/Weaknesses Analysis)   53
Marketing Concepts and Tools 2-1: Assessing Interdepartmental Strengths and Weaknesses   55
Goal Formulation   56   Strategy Formulation   57
Program Formulation   58   Implementation   58
Marketing Concepts and Tools 2-2: Strategic Groups in the Truck-Manufacturing Industry   59
Feedback and Control   60

SUMMARY   61

3 MANAGING THE MARKETING PROCESS AND MARKETING PLANNING   64

THE MARKETING PROCESS   65
Analyzing Market Opportunities   66   Researching and Selecting Target Markets and Positioning

the Offer   68   Designing Marketing Strategies   69   Planning Marketing Programs   70
Organizing, Implementing, and Controlling the Marketing Effort   73

THE NATURE AND CONTENTS OF A MARKETING PLAN   75
Executive Summary   76   Current Marketing Situation   76
Opportunity and Issue Analysis   78   Objectives   79
Marketing Strategy   80   Action Programs   81
Projected Profit-and-Loss Statement   82   Controls   82

SUMMARY   82

**APPENDIX: THE THEORY OF EFFECTIVE
MARKETING-RESOURCE ALLOCATION**   **85**

PART II ANALYZING MARKETING OPPORTUNITIES   **99**

**4 MARKETING INFORMATION SYSTEMS
AND MARKETING RESEARCH**   **100**
CONCEPT AND COMPONENTS OF A MARKETING INFORMATION SYSTEM   101

INTERNAL RECORDS SYSTEM   102
The Order-Shipping-Billing System   102   The System of Sales Reporting   103
Designing a User-Oriented Reports System   103

MARKETING INTELLIGENCE SYSTEM   104

MARKETING RESEARCH SYSTEM   105
Suppliers of Marketing Research   105   Marketing Strategies 4-1: A New Answer to Information
Needs—Information Centers   106   The Scope of Marketing Research   106
The Marketing Research Process   108   Marketing Concepts and Tools 4-1: A "Questionable"
Questionnaire   113   Marketing Concepts and Tools 4-2: The Marketer's Dream—Measuring Consumer
Response to Ads   118   Characteristics of Good Marketing Research   119
Management's Use of Marketing Research   120

MARKETING DECISION SUPPORT SYSTEM   120
Marketing Strategies 4-2: The 1990s Marketing Manager Uses Information Power   121

SUMMARY   122

APPENDIX: MARKETING DECISION SUPPORT SYSTEMS   **125**

5 ANALYZING THE MARKETING ENVIRONMENT   **135**
ACTORS IN THE COMPANY'S MICROENVIRONMENT   136
Company   137   Suppliers   137   Marketing Intermediaries   138
Customers   140   Competitors   140   Publics   141
Marketing Environment and Trends 5-1: The Impact of Consumerism on Marketing Practices   143

FORCES IN THE COMPANY'S MACROENVIRONMENT   144
Demographic Environment   144   Marketing Environment and Trends 5-2: Age-Group Growth
Trends and Their Marketing Implications   146   Economic Environment   149
Natural Environment   150   Marketing Environment and Trends 5-3: Impact of Environmentalism
on Marketing Decision Making   151   Technological Environment   152
Political Environment   154   Cultural Environment   158

SUMMARY   160
Marketing Environment and Trends 5-4: Ten "Megatrends" of Great Import to Marketers   161

APPENDIX: MAPPING A COMPANY'S MARKETING ENVIRONMENT, MARKETING SYSTEM, AND MARKETING STRATEGY 164

6 ANALYZING CONSUMER MARKETS AND BUYER BEHAVIOR 170

A MODEL OF CONSUMER BEHAVIOR 170
Marketing Environment and Trends 6-1: Three Market Segments— French-Canadian, Teenage-Student, and Older Consumer 171
MAJOR FACTORS INFLUENCING CONSUMER BEHAVIOR 172
Cultural Factors 173   Social Factors 174
Marketing Environment and Trends 6-2: Women Become a More Important Market for Car Buying 178
Personal Factors 179   Psychological Factors 181
Marketing Concepts and Tools 6-1: How Lifestyles Are Identified 182
THE BUYING DECISION PROCESS 188
Buying Roles 188   Types of Buying Behavior 188
Researching the Buying Decision Process 190   Stages in the Buying Decision Process 191
SUMMARY 199

APPENDIX: SOME ALTERNATIVE DECISION PROCESSES USED BY CONSUMERS TO EVALUATE ALTERNATIVE BRANDS 204

7 ANALYZING BUSINESS MARKETS AND ORGANIZATIONAL BUYER BEHAVIOR 207

THE INDUSTRIAL MARKET 208
Who Is in the Industrial Market? 208   What Buying Decisions Do Industrial Buyers Make? 210
Who Participates in the Industrial Buying Process? 212   What Are the Major Influences on Industrial Buyers? 213   How Do Industrial Buyers Make Their Buying Decisions? 215
Marketing Strategies 7-1: Just-in-Time Production Changes the Face of Organizational Buying 216
Marketing Strategies 7-2: Adapting Marketing Strategy to the Type of Industrial Buyer Segment: The Case of Microprocessors 222
THE RESELLER MARKET 223
Who Is in the Reseller Market? 223   What Buying Decisions Do Resellers Make? 223
Who Participates in the Reseller Buying Process? 224   What Are the Major Influences on Reseller Buyers? 225   How Do Resellers Make Their Buying Decisions? 225
THE GOVERNMENT MARKET 225
Who Is in the Government Market? 225   Marketing Concepts and Tools 7-1: A New Tool for Resellers: Direct Product Profitability (DPP) 226   What Buying Decisions Do Government Buyers Make? 227   Who Participates in the Government Buying Process? 227
Companies and Industries 7-1: The Institutional Market 227   What Are the Major Influences on Government Buyers? 228   How Do Government Buyers Make Their Buying Decisions? 228
SUMMARY 229

8 ANALYZING COMPETITORS 233

IDENTIFYING THE COMPANY'S COMPETITORS 234
Industry Concept of Competition 234   Marketing Concept and Tools 8-1: Five Industry Structure Types 236   Market Concept of Competition 237
IDENTIFYING THE COMPETITOR'S STRATEGIES 238
DETERMINING THE COMPETITORS' OBJECTIVES 239
ASSESSING THE COMPETITORS' STRENGTHS AND WEAKNESSES 242

Marketing Concepts and Tools 8-2: Du Pont Profitability Chart   244

ESTIMATING THE COMPETITORS' REACTION PATTERNS   245

DESIGNING THE COMPETITIVE INTELLIGENCE SYSTEM   246
Marketing Concepts and Tools 8-3: Intelligence Gathering—Snooping on Competitors   247

SELECTING COMPETITORS TO ATTACK AND AVOID   247
Marketing Concepts and Tools 8-4: Customer Value Analysis: The Key to Competitive Advantage   249

BALANCING CUSTOMER AND COMPETITOR ORIENTATIONS   250

SUMMARY   252

PART III   RESEARCHING AND SELECTING TARGET MARKETS   255

9   MEASURING AND FORECASTING MARKET DEMAND   256

MAJOR CONCEPTS IN DEMAND MEASUREMENT   256
A Multitude of Measures of Market Demand   257   Which Market to Measure?   257
A Vocabulary for Demand Measurement   259

ESTIMATING CURRENT DEMAND   262
Total Market Potential   262   Area Market Potential   263
Estimating Industry Sales and Market Shares   266

ESTIMATING FUTURE DEMAND   266
Marketing Concepts and Tools 9-1: Geodemographic Analysis: A New Tool for Identifying Market
Targets   267   Survey of Buyers' Intentions   268
Marketing Concepts and Tools 9-2: Methods of Environmental Forecasting   269
Composite of Salesforce Opinions   270   Expert Opinion   270
Market-Test Method   271   Time-Series Analysis   271   Statistical-Demand Analysis   272

SUMMARY   273

APPENDIX: DETERMINANTS OF COMPANY MARKET SHARE   276

10   IDENTIFYING MARKET SEGMENTS AND SELECTING TARGET MARKETS   278

MARKET SEGMENTATION   280
The General Approach to Segmenting a Market   280   Marketing Strategies 10-1: Customized
Marketing: It's Coming Back   281   Markets and Niches 282
Patterns of Market Segmentation   282   Market-Segmentation Procedure   283
Bases for Segmenting Consumer Markets   285   Bases for Segmenting Industrial Markets   293
Developing the Customer Segment Profile   295   Requirements for Effective Segmentation   295

MARKET TARGETING   296
Evaluating the Market Segments   297   Selecting the Market Segments   299
Additional Considerations in Evaluating and Selecting Segments   303

SUMMARY   304

PART IV DESIGNING MARKETING STRATEGIES 307

11 MARKETING STRATEGIES FOR DIFFERENTIATING AND POSITIONING THE MARKETING OFFER 308

HOW BUYERS DEFINE VALUE AND CHOOSE SUPPLIERS   308

IDENTIFYING POTENTIAL COMPETITIVE ADVANTAGES THROUGH VALUE-CHAIN ANALYSIS   311

TOOLS FOR COMPETITIVE DIFFERENTIATION   313
Product Differentiation   313   Services Differentiation   317
Marketing Strategies 11-1: Turbomarketing: Using Quick Response Time as a Competitive Tool   318
Personnel Differentiation   319   Image Differentiation   320

DEVELOPING A POSITIONING STRATEGY   321
Marketing Concepts and Tools 11-1: Positioning a Beer Brand Using Compatible Advertising   322
How Many Differences to Promote?   324   Marketing Strategies 11-2: "Positioning" According to Ries and Trout   325   Which Differences to Promote?   326

COMMUNICATING THE COMPANY'S POSITIONING   327

SUMMARY   328

12 DEVELOPING, TESTING, AND LAUNCHING NEW PRODUCTS AND SERVICES 330

THE NEW-PRODUCT-DEVELOPMENT DILEMMA   332

EFFECTIVE ORGANIZATIONAL ARRANGEMENTS   333
Marketing Concepts and Tools 12-1: Key Findings on New-Product-Management Activity   334
Companies and Industries 12-1: 3M's Approach to Innovation   336

IDEA GENERATION   337
Sources of New-Product Ideas   337   Idea-Generating Techniques   338

IDEA SCREENING   341
Product-Idea Rating Devices   342

CONCEPT DEVELOPMENT AND TESTING   342
Concept Development   344   Concept Testing   345
Marketing Concepts and Tools 12-2: Measuring Consumer Preferences   346

MARKETING-STRATEGY DEVELOPMENT   348

BUSINESS ANALYSIS   349
Estimating Sales   349   Estimating Costs and Profits   350
Marketing Concepts and Tools 12-3: Estimating First-Time Purchases of New Products   351

PRODUCT DEVELOPMENT   353
Marketing Concepts and Tools 12-4: Methods for Measuring Consumer Preferences   354

MARKET TESTING   355
Consumer-Goods Market Testing   355   Marketing Concepts and Tools 12-5: Decisions Facing Management in Setting Up Test Markets   358   Industrial-Goods Market Testing   358
Marketing Strategies 12-1: Not "Whether to Test" But "How to Test"—The Case of New Coke   359

COMMERCIALIZATION   361
When (Timing)   361   Where (Geographical Strategy)   361
To Whom (Target-Market Prospects)   362   How (Introductory Market Strategy)   362

THE CONSUMER-ADOPTION PROCESS   362
Concepts in Innovation, Diffusion, and Adoption   364   Stages in the Adoption Process   364
Individual Differences in Innovativeness   365   Role of Personal Influence   366
Influence of Product Characteristics on the Rate of Adoption   366
Influence of Organizational Buyers' Characteristics on the Rate of Adoption   367
SUMMARY   367

13

MANAGING PRODUCTS THROUGH THEIR PRODUCT LIFE CYCLE   370

THE PRODUCT LIFE CYCLE   370
Demand/Technology Life Cycle   370   Stages in the Product Life Cycle   372
Product-Category, Product-Form, and Brand Life Cycles   373   Other Shapes of the Product Life
Cycle   374   Marketing Concepts and Tools 13-1: Forecasting the Shape and Duration of the Product
Life Cycle   375   Rationale for the Product Life Cycle   376

INTRODUCTION STAGE   377
Market Strategies in the Introduction Stage   377   Marketing Strategies 13-1: The Market Pioneer
"Advantage"   379

GROWTH STAGE   380
Marketing Strategies in the Growth Stage   381

MATURITY STAGE   381
Marketing Strategies in the Mature Stage   382   Marketing Strategies 13-2: Breaking Through the
"Mature-Product" Syndrome   385

DECLINE STAGE   386
Marketing Strategies During the Decline Stage   387

SUMMARY AND CRITIQUE OF THE PRODUCT LIFE-CYCLE CONCEPT   388

THE CONCEPT OF MARKET EVOLUTION   391
Stages in Market Evolution   391   Dynamics of Attribute Competition   393

SUMMARY   394

14

DESIGNING MARKETING STRATEGIES FOR MARKET LEADERS, CHALLENGERS, FOLLOWERS, AND NICHERS   398

MARKET-LEADER STRATEGIES   399
Expanding the Total Market   400   Defending Market Share   401
Marketing Strategies 14-1: Defensive Strategies According to the Defender Model   402
Expanding Market Share   406   Marketing Concepts and Tools 14-1: The Impact of Different
Marketing-Mix Variables on Market Share   409

MARKET-CHALLENGER STRATEGIES   409
Companies and Industries 14-1: How Procter & Gamble and Caterpillar Maintain Their Market
Leadership   410   Defining the Strategic Objective and Opponent(s)   412
Choosing an Attack Strategy   412   Marketing Strategies 14-2: Some Specific Attack Strategies
Available to Challengers   417

MARKET-FOLLOWER STRATEGIES   418

MARKET-NICHER STRATEGIES   419
Marketing Strategies 14-3: Specialist Roles Open to Market Nichers   420
Marketing Strategies 14-4: Strategies for Entering Markets Held by Incumbent Firms   421
SUMMARY   422

15

DESIGNING STRATEGIES FOR THE GLOBAL MARKETPLACE   425

Market Environment and Trends 15-1: The Challenge of Free Trade   426
Marketing Strategies 15-1: Global Marketing Blunders   428
APPRAISING THE GLOBAL MARKETING ENVIRONMENT   429

The International Trade System   429   Economic Environment   430
Political-Legal Environment   432   Marketing Environment and Trends 15-2: How Nations Have
Been Moving Back to Barter   433   Cultural Environment   433
Marketing Strategies 15-2: Megamarketing: Breaking into Blocked Markets   434
Business Environment   434

DECIDING WHETHER TO GO ABROAD   435
Marketing Environment and Trends 15-3: The International Product Life Cycle   436

DECIDING WHICH MARKETS TO ENTER   436
Marketing Strategies 15-3: Should Multinationals Restrict Their Trade to the Triad Markets?   438
Marketing Concepts and Tools 15-1: Assessing Country Risk   439

DECIDING HOW TO ENTER THE MARKET   440
Indirect Export   440   Direct Export   441
Licensing   441   Joint Ventures   442
Direct Investment   442   The Internationalization Process   443

DECIDING ON THE MARKETING PROGRAM   443
Product   444   Marketing Strategies 15-4: Global Standardization or Adaptation?   445
Promotion   447   Price   448
Distribution Channels   449

DECIDING ON THE MARKETING ORGANIZATION   450
Export Department   450   International Division   450
Global Organization   451   Companies and Industries 15-1: The World's Champion Marketers: The
Japanese?   452

SUMMARY   453

PART V PLANNING MARKETING PROGRAMS   457

16 MANAGING PRODUCT LINES, BRANDS, AND PACKAGING   458

WHAT IS A PRODUCT?   458
Five Levels of a Product   459   Product Hierarchy   460
Product Classifications   461   Marketing Concepts and Tools 16-1: Product Classifications and
Their Marketing-Strategy Implications   461

PRODUCT-MIX DECISIONS   464

PRODUCT-LINE DECISIONS   465
Product-Line Analysis   465   Product-Line Length   467
Line-Stretching Decision   467   Line-Filling Decision   469
Line-Modernization Decision   470   Line-Featuring Decision   470
Line-Pruning Decision   470

BRAND DECISIONS   471
Branding Decision   472   Brand-Sponsor Decision   473
Marketing Strategies 16-1: Licensing Brand Names for Royalties   474   Family-Brand Decision   475
Brand-Extension Decision   477   Multibrand Decision   477
Brand-Repositioning Decision   478

PACKAGING AND LABELING DECISIONS   479

SUMMARY   481

17 MANAGING SERVICE BUSINESSES AND ANCILLARY SERVICES   484

NATURE AND CLASSIFICATION OF SERVICES   485

CHARACTERISTICS OF SERVICES AND THEIR MARKETING IMPLICATIONS   486
Intangibility   487   Inseparability   487

Variability 488 Perishability 488

MARKETING STRATEGIES FOR SERVICE FIRMS 490

Marketing Strategies 17-1: Motivating Employees to Care for the Customer: The Challenge Facing Canada's Hospitals 492 Managing Differentiation 493
Managing Service Quality 494 Marketing Concepts and Tools 17-1: Market-Performance Analysis 497 Companies and Industries 17-1: Walt Disney Enterprises—A Highly Responsive Organization 498 Managing Productivity 499

MANAGING PRODUCT SUPPORT SERVICES 499

Presale Service Strategy 500 Postsale Service Strategy 501

SUMMARY 502

18 DESIGNING PRICING STRATEGIES AND PROGRAMS 505

SETTING THE PRICE 506

Selecting the Pricing Objective 507 Marketing Concepts and Tools 18-1: Finding the Profit-Maximizing Price 508 Determining Demand 509
Estimating Costs 512 Analyzing Competitors' Prices and Offers 514
Selecting a Pricing Method 514 Marketing Concepts and Tools 18-2: Methods of Estimating Perceived Value—An Illustration 518 Marketing Concepts and Tools 18-3: Methods for Establishing a Price Around a Perceived Value 519 Selecting the Final Price 520

ADAPTING THE PRICE 522

Geographical Pricing 522 Marketing Strategies 18-1: Five Geographical Pricing Strategies 522
Price Discounts and Allowances 523 Promotional Pricing 524
Discriminatory Pricing 525 Product-Mix Pricing 526

INITIATING AND RESPONDING TO PRICE CHANGES 527

Initiating Price Cuts 528 Marketing Strategies 18-2: Analyzing the Marketing-Mix Alternatives Facing a Firm in an Economic Recession 528 Initiating Price Increases 530
Customers' Reactions to Price Changes 532 Competitors' Reactions to Price Changes 532
Marketing Concepts and Tools 18-4: How a Large Chemical Company Used Decision Theory to Assess Probable Competitors' Reactions to a Contemplated Price Cut 533
Responding to Price Changes 534

SUMMARY 535

19 SELECTING AND MANAGING MARKETING CHANNELS 539

THE NATURE OF MARKETING CHANNELS 540

Why Are Marketing Intermediaries Used? 540 Marketing-Channel Functions and Flows 541
Number of Channel Levels 543 Channels in the Service Sector 544

CHANNEL-DESIGN DECISIONS 545

Analyzing Service Output Levels Desired by Customers 545 Establishing the Channel Objectives and Constraints 546 Identifying the Major Channel Alternatives 547
Evaluating the Major Channel Alternatives 549

CHANNEL-MANAGEMENT DECISIONS 550

Selecting Channel Members 550 Companies and Industries 19-1: Building a Distributor Team for Epson Products 551 Motivating Channel Members 552
Marketing Concepts and Tools 19-1: Five Bases of Power for Managing Channel Relationships 553
Evaluating Channel Members 554 Marketing Strategies 19-1: Turning Industrial Distributors into Business Partners 554 Modifying Channel Arrangements 555

CHANNEL DYNAMICS 555

Marketing Strategies 19-2: How Companies Change Their Marketing Channels Over the Product Life Cycle 556 Marketing Concepts and Tools 19-2: Modifying Existing Distribution Systems Toward the Ideal 557 Growth of Vertical Marketing Systems 558
Growth of Horizontal Marketing Systems 560 Growth of Multichannel Marketing Systems 561

Roles of Individual Firms in a Channel   561   Marketing Strategies 19-3: The Case for Multichannel
Marketing   562

CHANNEL COOPERATION, CONFLICT, AND COMPETITION   563
Types of Conflict and Competition   563   Causes of Channel Conflict   564
Managing Channel Conflict   564

SUMMARY   565

20

MANAGING RETAILING, WHOLESALING, AND PHYSICAL-DISTRIBUTION SYSTEMS   568

RETAILING   568
Nature and Importance of Retailing   568   Types of Retailers   569
Marketing Environment and Trends 20-1: Major Retailer Types   569
Retailer Marketing Decisions   577   Marketing Strategies 20-1: Does an "Everyday-Low-Prices"
Strategy Make More Sense Than a "Promotional-Pricing" Strategy?   581
Trends in Retailing   582

WHOLESALING   583
Nature and Importance of Wholesaling   583   Growth and Types of Wholesaling   584
Marketing Environment and Trends 20-2: Major Wholesaler Types   584   Wholesaler Marketing
Decisions   587   Trends in Wholesaling   588

PHYSICAL DISTRIBUTION   588
Marketing Strategies 20-2: Strategies of High-Performance Wholesaler-Distributors   589
Nature of Physical Distribution   590   The Physical-Distribution Objective   590
Order Processing   592   Warehousing   593
Inventory   594   Transportation   594
Organizational Responsibility for Physical Distribution   595
Marketing Environment and Trends 20-3: Five Major Transportation Modes   596

SUMMARY   597

21

DESIGNING COMMUNICATION AND PROMOTION-MIX STRATEGIES   600

THE COMMUNICATION PROCESS   601

STEPS IN DEVELOPING EFFECTIVE COMMUNICATIONS   604
Identifying the Target Audience   604   Determining the Communication Objectives   607
Marketing Concepts and Tools 21-1: Determining the Target Audience and Sought Response   609
Designing the Message   610   Marketing Strategies 21-1: Do Fear Appeals Work?   611
Selecting the Communication Channels   613   Companies and Industries 21-1: Dentists Use Word of
Mouth to Draw Mouths to Their Practice   614   Establishing the Total Promotion Budget   615
Deciding on the Promotion Mix   617   Marketing Strategies 21-2: The Promotional Mix of
Business-to-Business Marketers   618   Marketing Strategies 21-3: Role of Corporate Advertising in
Industrial Marketing   621   Marketing Concepts and Tools 21-2: The Advisor Project Probes into
How Industrial Marketers Set Their Marketing Budgets   622   Measuring Promotion's Results   625
Managing and Coordinating the Marketing Communication Process   626

SUMMARY   626

22

DESIGNING EFFECTIVE ADVERTISING PROGRAMS   629

SETTING THE ADVERTISING OBJECTIVES   630
Companies and Industries 22-1: How Does an Advertising Agency Work?   631

DECIDING ON THE ADVERTISING BUDGET   633

DECIDING ON THE MESSAGE   635
Message Generation   635   Message Evaluation and Selection   636
Message Execution   637   Marketing Strategies 22-1: Celebrity Endorsements as a Strategy   639

DECIDING ON THE MEDIA   640
Deciding on Reach, Frequency, and Impact   640   Choosing among Major Media Types   642
Marketing Environment and Trends 22-1: The Ceaseless Search for New Media   644
Selecting Specific Media Vehicles   644   Deciding on Media Timing   645

EVALUATING ADVERTISING EFFECTIVENESS   648
Communication-Effect Research   648   Marketing Concepts and Tools 22-1: Some Advertising
Research Techniques   649   Sales-Effect Research   650
SUMMARY   652

23 DESIGNING DIRECT MARKETING, SALES-PROMOTION, AND PUBLIC-RELATIONS PROGRAMS   655

DIRECT MARKETING   655
Nature, Growth, and Advantages of Direct Marketing   656   Marketing Concepts and Tools 23-1:
Major Tools of Direct Marketing   657   The Development of Integrated Direct Marketing   661
Developing a Marketing Database System   661   Marketing Concepts and Tools 23-2: The
"Maximarketing" Model for Integrated Marketing   662   Major Decisions in Direct Marketing   663

SALES PROMOTION   666
Rapid Growth of Sales Promotion   666   Purpose of Sales Promotion   667
Major Decisions in Sales Promotion   668   Marketing Concepts and Tools 23-3: Major Consumer-
Promotion Tools   669   Marketing Concepts and Tools 23-4: Major Trade-Promotion Tools   671
Marketing Concepts and Tools 23-5: Major Business-Promotion Tools   674

PUBLIC RELATIONS   677
Major Decisions in Marketing PR   678
Marketing Concepts and Tools 23-6: Major Tools in Marketing PR   679
SUMMARY   682

24 MANAGING THE SALESFORCE   686

DESIGNING THE SALESFORCE   687
Salesforce Objectives   688   Salesforce Strategy   689
Salesforce Structure   689   Companies and Industries 24-1: Building a Salesforce from Scratch: The
Case of Wilkinson   690   Marketing Strategies 24-1: National Account Management—What It Is
and How It Works   693   Salesforce Size   694   Salesforce Compensation   695
Marketing Concepts and Tools 24-1: Sales Plans and Components   696

MANAGING THE SALESFORCE   697
Recruiting and Selecting Sales Representatives   697   Training Sales Representatives   698
Directing Sales Representatives   700   Marketing Environment and Trends 24-1: How Efficiently
Do Companies Manage Their Salesforces?   701   Motivating Sales Representatives   703
Marketing Environment and Trends 24-2: Salespeople Use Computers as a Productivity Tool   703
Evaluating Sales Representatives   705

PRINCIPLES OF PERSONAL SELLING   708
Selling   708   Marketing Concepts and Tools 24-2: The Variety of Selling Styles and Buying
Styles   710   Negotiation   712   Marketing Concepts and Tools 24-3: The Principled-
Negotiation Approach to Bargaining   715   Marketing Strategies 24-2: Some Classic Bargaining
Tactics   716   Relationship Management   716   Marketing Strategies 24-3: When—and How—
to Use Relationship Marketing   718
SUMMARY   719

PART VI ORGANIZING, IMPLEMENTING, AND CONTROLLING MARKETING EFFORT   723

25 ORGANIZING AND IMPLEMENTING MARKETING PROGRAMS   724

COMPANY ORGANIZATION   724

MARKETING ORGANIZATION   726
The Evolution of the Marketing Department   726   Ways of Organizing the Marketing Department   728   Marketing Environment and Trends 25-1: Regionalization—A Passing Fad or the New Marketing Era?   730   Market Management Organization   734
Marketing Environment and Trends 25-2: What's the Future of Brand Management?   735
Marketing's Relations with Other Departments   738   Strategies for Building a Companywide Marketing Orientation   742

MARKETING IMPLEMENTATION   744
Diagnostic Skills   745   Company Levels   745 Marketing Implementation Skills   745
Implementation-Evaluation Skills   746

SUMMARY   746

26 EVALUATING AND CONTROLLING MARKETING PERFORMANCE   749

ANNUAL-PLAN CONTROL   750
Sales Analysis   751   Market-Share Analysis   751
Marketing Concepts and Tools 26-1: Defining and Measuring Market Share   752
Marketing Expense-to-Sales Analysis   754   Financial Analysis   755
Customer-Satisfaction Tracking   756   Corrective Action   757

PROFITABILITY CONTROL   757
Methodology of Marketing-Profitability Analysis   758   Determining the Best Corrective Action   760   Direct versus Full Costing   761

EFFICIENCY CONTROL   762
Salesforce Efficiency   762   Advertising Efficiency   763
Sales-Promotion Efficiency   763   Distribution Efficiency   763

STRATEGIC CONTROL   764
Marketing-Effectiveness Rating Review   764   The Marketing Audit   767
THE MARKETING CONTROLLER CONCEPT   773
SUMMARY   775

CASE STUDIES   778
NAME INDEX   819
COMPANY/BRAND INDEX   824
SUBJECT INDEX   828

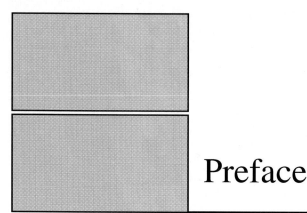

Preface

The 1990s represent the last decade of the last century before the next millennium. Many changes have been taking place in the global economy: the rising power of the Far East in global markets; the development of a European Common Market of 324 million consumers; the disillusionment with state-operated economies and the turn to market-driven economies; the political reforms in Eastern Europe, South Africa, and elsewhere; the giant advances in technology; and so on.

All this means that old business road maps cannot be trusted. Companies are learning that it is hard to build a reputation and easy to lose it. Companies that focus inward become blind to seismic changes in markets, competition, distribution, media, and technology that are occurring outside. Mass markets are fragmenting into micromarkets; multiple channels of distribution are replacing single channels; customers are buying direct through catalogs and telemarketing; price discounting and sales promotion are eroding brand loyalty; conventional advertising media are delivering less and costing more. These and other changes mean that companies must reexamine and sometimes reverse the very premises on which they built their business.

In the end, the companies that best satisfy their customers will be the winners. It is the special responsibility of marketers to understand the needs and wants of the marketplace and to help their companies translate them into solutions that win customers' approval. Today's smart managers are not merely looking for sales; they are investing in long-term, mutually satisfying customer relationships based on delivering quality, service, and value.

Marketing is the business function that identifies unfulfilled needs and wants, defines and measures their magnitude, determines which target markets the organization can best serve, decides on appropriate products, services, and programs to serve these markets, and calls upon everyone in the organization to "think and serve the customer." From a societal point of view, marketing is the force that harnesses a nation's industrial capacity to meet the society's material wants.

Marketing must not be seen narrowly as the task of finding clever ways to sell the company's products. Many people confuse marketing with some if its subfunctions, such as advertising and selling. Authentic marketing is not the art of selling what you make but knowing what to make! It is the art of identifying and understanding customer needs and creating solutions that deliver satisfaction to the customers, profits to the producers, and benefits for the stakeholders. Market leadership is gained by creating customer satisfaction through product innovation, product quality, and customer service. If these are absent, no amount of advertising, sales promotion, or salesmanship can compensate.

William Davidow observed: "While great devices are invented in the laboratory, great products are invented in the marketing department." There is a wide chasm between an invention and an innovation. Too many wonderful laboratory products are greeted with yawns or laughs. The job of marketers is to "think customer" and to guide companies and nonprofit organizations into developing offers that are meaningful and attractive to target customers.

The Current Marketing Environment

Market-oriented thinking is a necessity in today's competitive world. In many places, there are too many goods chasing too few customers. There are global gluts of steel, agricultural produce, automobiles, and many other products and services. Some companies are trying to expand the size of the market, but most are competing to enlarge their share of the existing market. As a result, there are winners and losers. The losers are those who bring nothing special to the market. We believe that if you can't bring something special to a market, you don't belong in it. The winners are those who carefully analyze needs, identify opportunities, and create value-laden offers for target customer groups that competitors can't match. These are anxious times for many Canadian companies. The economy is still suffering from a prolonged recession. Chronic budget deficits are driving taxes up and consumers are rebelling against rising prices by crossing the border to do their shopping. The dismantling of tariff barriers is creating opportunities in distant markets, but also subjecting the domestic market to increased competition.

Company marketers face several tough market challenges:

1. The low economic growth rates throughout the world with many major industries in the mature or decline stage of the product life cycle

2. The growing power of global competitors from Europe and the Far East who are capable of making high-quality products at lower costs

3. An international market that is moving toward greater protectionism in some industries and geographical areas

4. Foreign companies that receive subsidies from their government and use them to win business through lower prices

5. Many nations that are so debt-ridden and/or politically unstable that it is risky to do business with them

6. A great amount of price cutting and discounting in all industries, resulting in an increasing number of buyers who "shop" for prices

7. Too much short-term focus by management and a fixation on buying other businesses rather than on building their existing businesses

8. Growing power of large retail chains to dictate terms to manufacturers

9. The splintering of the mass market into many micromarkets requiring tailored marketing
10. Increasing marketing costs owing to the declining effectiveness of mass media and the rising costs of personal selling

Problems, properly analyzed, are also opportunities. Companies such as McDonald's, Procter & Gamble, Campbell's, and IBM have shown a capacity to adapt by staying close to their markets and reading the signs. They know that the marketplace, not the factory, ultimately determines which companies will succeed. Too many of our major auto companies, steel companies, electronics companies, and others didn't have their ears to the market and paid dearly—along with the rest of us—for their "marketing myopia." Marketing thinking obviously isn't easy, or it would be applied more successfully. Although it takes only a semester to learn marketing, it takes a lifetime to master it. Marketing problems, it turns out, do not exhibit the neat quantitative properties of many problems in the production, accounting, and finance areas. Psychological forces play a large role; marketing expenditures affect demand and costs simultaneously; marketing plans shape and interact with other business-function plans. Marketing decisions must be made in the face of insufficient information about processes that are dynamic, lagged, stochastic, interactive, and downright difficult. However, this is not an argument for intuitive decision making. Rather it is an argument for improved strategic theory and sharper tools of analysis.

The Nature of This Book

Marketing Management has several major features:

1. *A managerial orientation.* This book focuses on the major decisions that marketing managers and top management face in their efforts to harmonize the objectives and resources of the organization with the needs and opportunities in the marketplace.

2. *An analytical approach.* This book presents a framework for analyzing recurrent problems in marketing management. Marketing principles are frequently illustrated by real company examples and a set of teaching cases about Canadian companies.

3. *A basic disciplines perspective.* This book draws on economics, behavioral science, and mathematics. *Economics* provides fundamental concepts and tools for seeking optimal results in the use of scarce resources. *Behavioral science* provides fundamental concepts and tools for understanding consumer and organizational buying behavior. *Mathematics* provides an exact language for expressing relationships among important variables.

4. *A universal approach.* This book applies marketing thinking to products and services, consumer and industrial markets, profit and nonprofit organizations, domestic and foreign companies, small and large firms, manufacturing and middlemen businesses, and low-tech and high-tech industries.

5. *Comprehensive and balanced coverage.* This book covers all the topics that an informed marketing manager needs to know. It covers the main issues faced in strategic, tactical, and administrative marketing.

MARKETING MANAGEMENT   This seventh edition is organized into six parts. *Part I* develops the societal, managerial, and strategic underpinnings of marketing theory and practice. *Part II* presents concepts and tools for analyzing any market and marketing environment to discern opportunities. *Part III* presents principles for measuring and forecasting markets and carrying out segmenting and targeting. *Part IV* examines issues in designing marketing strategies for companies in different market positions, global positions, and stages in the product life cycle. *Part V* deals with tactical marketing and how companies handle, or should handle, each element of the marketing mix—product, price, place, and promotion. Finally, *Part VI* examines the administrative side of marketing, namely, how firms organize, implement, and control marketing efforts.

Changes in the Seventh Edition

The seventh edition has the following objectives:

1. To update the statistics and analyze new trends and developments in the environment
2. To strengthen the discussion of strategic marketing
3. To introduce recent company examples of creative market-focused and customer-driven thinking
4. To describe new developments in marketing planning, organization, implementation, and control
5. To describe the growing use of computers, telecommunications, and other new technologies in improving marketing planning and performance

These objectives led to the following distinctive features:

1. A new Chapter 11, "Marketing Strategies for Differentiating and Positioning the Market Offer."
2. A whole new section on direct marketing introduced into Chapter 23.
3. A reordering of chapters in Part IV. Specifically, new-product development is introduced earlier, because the problem involves many strategic issues. The chapter is followed naturally by the product-life-cycle chapter, because new strategies are called for as the product matures.
4. Theoretical material has been removed in some chapters and transferred to appendices so as not to encumber the basic message.
5. New exhibits have been added, and all exhibits have been classified into four groups: Marketing Strategies, Marketing Concepts and Tools, Marketing Environment and Trends, and Companies and Industries.
6. Writing has been made smoother and tighter.
7. Several parts of chapters have been substantially revised.
8. New and expanded material has been added on local marketing, global marketing, turbomarketing, customized marketing, telemarketing, service-marketing theory, category management, customer value analysis, geodemographic analysis, maximarketing, marketing decision support systems, direct product profitability, total-quality-improvement programs, relationship marketing, offer differentiation, benefit positioning, multi-channel conflict, trade shows, sales contests, specialty advertising, cause-related marketing, and building a marketing culture.
9. A new set of Canadian-based cases has been included.

Improved Pedagogical Aids

Pedagogical Aids for this edition of *Marketing Management* include

☐ A comprehensive, extensively revised Instructor's Manual which contains teaching formats, suggested syllabi, case solutions, and transparency masters, as well as a complete section on integrating supplementary material into the course such as cases, casebooks, readings, videos, and computer-based material. It is available to adopters on request.

☐ A Test Item File containing over 2000 questions; a computerized version in IBM PC and compatible formats is also available. Both are available to adopters on request.

Acknowledgments

The Canadian seventh edition bears the imprint of many people at Northwestern University, Queen's University, and elsewhere. In addition to those who contributed to the U.S. seventh edition, special mention should be made of the following:

☐ Dean Donald Jacobs and Dean David Anderson who provided support for research and secretarial services

☐ Our marketing colleagues at Northwestern University and Queen's University

☐ Wendy LeBlanc and Carolyn Koch for their help in the preparation of the manuscript

☐ Colleagues at other universities who reviewed the manuscript and provided many helpful suggestions, in particular Tony Schellinck and Bob Isotalo

☐ People at Prentice-Hall who contributed, especially Jacqueline Wood, Judith Dawson, Heather McClune, and Valerie Adams

Our overriding debt is to our wives, Nancy and Caroline, to whom this book is dedicated.

Philip Kotler   Ronald E. Turner
Northwestern University Queen's University
Evanston, Illinois   Kingston, Ontario
U.S.A.   Canada

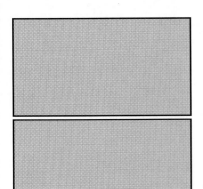

Classification of Exhibits

Marketing Strategies

1-1 The Secret of L.L. Bean's Profitability: Customer Satisfaction 20
1-2 How Jan Carlzon "Marketized" SAS 23
2-1 Which Company Should Produce an Electric Car? 52
4-1 A New Answer to Information Needs—Information Centers 106
4-2 The 1990s Marketing Manager Uses Information Power 121
7-1 Just-In-Time Production Changes the Face of Organizational Buying 216
7-2 Adapting Marketing Strategy to the Type of Industrial Buyer Segment: The Case of Microprocessors 222
10-1 Customized Marketing: It's Coming Back 281
11-1 Turbomarketing: Using Quick Response Time as a Competitive Tool 318
11-2 "Positioning" According to Ries and Trout 325
12-1 Not "Whether to Test" but "How to Test"—The Case of New Coke 359
13-1 The Market Pioneer "Advantage" 379
13-2 Breaking Through the "Mature Product" Syndrome 385
14-1 Defensive Strategies According to the Defender Model 402
14-2 Some Specific Attack Strategies Available to Challengers 417
14-3 Specialist Roles Open to Market Nichers 420
14-4 Strategies for Entering Markets Held by Incumbent Firms 421
15-1 Global Marketing Blunders 428
15-2 Megamarketing: Breaking into Blocked Markets 434
15-3 Should Multinationals Restrict Their Trade to the Triad Markets? 438
15-4 Global Standardization or Adaptation? 445
16-1 Licensing Brand Names for Royalties 474

17-1 Motivating Employees to Care for the Customer: The Challenge Facing Canada's Hospitals   492

18-1 Five Geographical Pricing Strategies   522

18-2 Analyzing the Marketing-Mix Alternatives Facing a Firm in an Economic Recession   528

19-1 Turning Industrial Distributors into Business Partners   554

19-2 How Companies Change Their Marketing Channels Over the Product Life Cycle   556

19-3 The Case for Multichannel Marketing   562

20-1 Does an "Everyday-Low-Prices" Strategy Make More Sense than a "Promotional-Pricing" Strategy?   581

20-2 Strategies of High-Performance Wholesaler-Distributors   589

21-1 Do Fear Appeals Work?   611

21-2 The Promotional Mix of Business-to-Business Marketers   618

21-3 Role of Corporate Advertising in Industrial Marketing   621

22-1 Celebrity Endorsements as a Strategy   639

24-1 National Account Management—What It Is and How It Works   693

24-2 Some Classic Bargaining Tactics   716

24-3 When—and How—to Use Relationship Marketing   718

Marketing Concepts and Tools

1-1 Demand States and Marketing Tasks   12

2-1 Assessing Interdepartmental Strengths and Weaknesses   55

2-2 Strategic Groups in the Truck-Manufacturing Industry   59

3-1 Marketing-Mix Interactions Need to Be Watched   93

4-1 A "Questionable" Questionnaire   113

4-2 The Marketer's Dream: Measuring Consumer Response to Ads   118

6-1 How Lifestyles Are Identified   182

7-1 A New Tool for Resellers: Direct Product Profitability (DPP)

8-1 Five Industry Structure Types   236

8-2 Du Pont Profitability Chart   244

8-3 Intelligence Gathering: Snooping on Competitors   247

8-4 Customer Value Analysis: The Key to Competitive Advantage   249

9-1 Geodemographic Analysis: A New Tool for Identifying Market Targets   267

9-2 Methods of Environmental Forecasting   269

11-1 Positioning a Beer Brand Using Compatible Advertising   322

12-1 Key Findings on New-Product-Management Activity   334

12-2 Measuring Consumer Preferences   346

12-3 Estimating First-Time Purchases of New Products   351

12-4 Methods for Measuring Consumer Preferences   354

12-5 Decisions Facing Management in Setting Up Test Markets   358

13-1 Forecasting the Shape and Duration of the Product Life Cycle   375

14-1 The Impact of Different Marketing-Mix Variables on Market Share   409

15-1 Assessing Country Risk   439

16-1 Product Classifications and Their Marketing-Strategy Implications   461

17-1 Market-Performance Analysis   497

18-1 Finding the Profit-Maximizing Price   508

18-2 Methods of Estimating Perceived Value—An Illustration   518

18-3 Methods for Establishing a Price Around a Perceived Value   519

18-4 How a Large Chemical Company Used Decision Theory to Assess Probable Competitors' Reactions to a Contemplated Price Cut   533
19-1 Five Bases of Power for Managing Channel Relationships   553
19-2 Modifying Existing Distribution Systems Toward the Ideal   557
21-1 Determining the Target Audience and Sought Response   609
21-2 The Advisor Project Probes into How Industrial Marketers Set Their Marketing Budgets   622
22-1 Some Advertising Research Techniques   649
23-1 Major Tools of Direct Marketing   657
23-2 The "Maximarketing" Model for Integrated Marketing   662
23-3 Major Consumer-Promotion Tools   669
23-4 Major Trade-Promotion Tools   671
23-5 Major Business-Promotion Tools   674
23-6 Major Tools in Marketing PR   679
24-1 Sales Plans and Components   696
24-2 The Variety of Selling Styles and Buying Styles   710
24-3 The Principled-Negotiation Approach to Bargaining   715
26-1 Defining and Measuring Market Share   752

Marketing Environment and Trends

5-1 Impact of Consumerism on Marketing Practices   143
5-2 Age-Group Growth Trends and Their Marketing Implications   146
5-3 Impact of Environmentalism on Marketing Decision Making   151
5-4 Ten "Megatrends" of Great Import to Marketers   161
6-1 Three Market Segments: French-Canadian, Teenage-Student and Older Consumer   171
6-2 Women Become a More Important Market for Car Buying   178
15-1 The Challenge of Free Trade   426
15-2 How Nations Have Been Moving Back to Barter   433
15-3 The International Product Life Cycle   436
20-1 Major Retailer Types   569
20-2 Major Wholesaler Types   584
20-3 Five Major Transportation Modes   596
22-1 The Ceaseless Search for New Media   644
24-1 How Efficiently Do Companies Manage Their Salesforces?   701
24-2 Salespeople Use Computers as a Productivity Tool   703
25-1 Regionalization—A Passing Fad or the New Marketing Era?   730
25-2 What's the Future of Brand Management?   735

Companies and Industries

1-1 Five Stages in the Slow Learning of Bank Marketing   26
7-1 The Institutional Market   227
12-1 3M's Approach to Innovation   336
14-1 How Procter & Gamble and Caterpillar Maintain Their Market Leadership   410
15-1 The World's Champion Marketers: The Japanese?   452
17-1 Walt Disney Enterprises—A Highly Responsive Organization   498
19-1 Building a Distributor Team for Epson Products   551
21-1 Dentists Use Word of Mouth to Draw Mouths to Their Practice   614
22-1 How Does an Advertising Agency Work?   631
24-1 Building a Salesforce from Scratch: The Case of Wilkinson   690

PART I

Understanding Marketing Management

1

Understanding the Critical Role of Marketing in Organizations and Society

Marketing is so basic that it cannot be considered a separate function. It is the whole business seen from the point of view of its final result, that is, from the customer's point of view.

Peter Drucker

The decade of the 1990s is one of great promise and great uncertainty. On the one hand, great opportunities lie before us. The thawing of the Cold War will release resources to build up badly needed capital goods and infrastructure. Western Europe is moving rapidly toward becoming the world's largest common market with 324 million consumers. Eastern Europe is emerging as a promising market for Western goods. Asian economies continue to expand their internal markets and their global market share. Add to this several promising new technologies of the 1990s: high-definition television, new wonder drugs, superconductivity, genetic engineering, and other miracles of science.

On the other hand, the problems are also great. Hunger, disease, and illiteracy continue to plague most of the world's population. Environmental quality continues to deteriorate because of unabated pollution. Many nations are paralyzed by internal strife and corrupt leadership and saddled with enormous internal and external debt. The gap between the wealthier and poorer nations keeps widening.

The supreme irony is that the underdeveloped world has a crying need for food, clothing, shelter, and basic goods but lacks purchasing power. The developed world has enormous industrial capacity to satisfy these needs but will sell only to those with purchasing power. Thus the companies in the industrial West fight fiercely for market share in the triad markets—Western Europe, North America, and the Far East—while the rest of the world languishes.

The last decade taught a humbling lesson to business firms everywhere. Domestic companies can no longer ignore foreign competitors, foreign markets, and foreign sources of supply. Companies cannot allow their wage and material costs to get far out of line with the rest of the world. Companies cannot ignore emerging technologies, materials, equipment, and new ways of organizing.

Many small companies fail because they ignore these trends, but large size does not provide immunity. RCA in manufacturing and Simpsons in retailing are examples of large companies that have failed in some aspect of marketing. RCA was unable to transform its many patents into winning products, and now has to rely on imports from Japan and South Korea. Simpsons lost the battle for the "carriage trade," and even retrenching into a more youthful high-fashion niche did not save it.

Although these companies can easily blame outside events and forces, such as bad government decisions, unfair foreign competition, corporate raiders, and the short-term mentality of capital markets, their failures are largely failures in management. Too many corporate leaders focused their attention on the stock market but ignored the product market. They failed to define their target markets carefully and study their needs. They relied on selling, not marketing. They pursued profits first and customer satisfaction second.

Beginning in the 1980s, several business writers began to expound on what makes a company excellent. Tom Peters and Bob Waterman interviewed forty-three high-performing companies—companies like Hewlett-Packard, Procter & Gamble, 3M, McDonald's, Marriott—to find out what made them tick. They wrote up the results in what was to become the best-selling business book of all times—*In Search of Excellence*.[1] And what they found was that all of these companies shared a set of basic operating principles, among them a deep respect for the customer ("stay close to the customer"), a keen sense of the appropriate market ("stick to your knitting"), and an admirable capacity to motivate their employees to produce high quality and value for the customers. Many of their findings supported what marketers call the *marketing concept*.

Since then, Tom Peters has published *A Passion for Excellence*, and *Thriving on Chaos*, offering further stories about companies doing wonderful and smart things to improve their customers' satisfaction.[2] An important ingredient in these companies' success stories is their commitment to obtaining feedback from their customers about how they can increase customer satisfaction. At Marriott, J. Willard Marriott Sr. continued for fifty-seven years to personally read guest suggestion cards. At Stew Leonard's supermarket, the owner sat down with eight customers each Saturday to talk about ways to improve service.

In 1986, Frank "Buck" Rodgers wrote *The IBM Way* in which he described the steps IBM takes to ensure that the customer is king.

> At IBM, *everybody sells!* . . . Walk into the IBM building in New York or into any of its offices throughout the world and you'll get the idea. Every employee has been trained to think that the customer comes first—everybody from the CEO, to the people in finance, to the receptionists, to those who work in manufacturing.
>
> When I am asked, "What products does IBM sell?" I answer, "IBM doesn't sell products. It sells solutions." . . . An IBM marketing rep's success depends totally on his ability to understand a prospect's business so well that he can identify and analyze its problems and then come up with a solution that makes sense to the customer.[3]

Other business writers presented their views of the attitudes and strategies that make companies great, bearing such titles as *The Customer is Key*, *Delivering Quality Service*, and *The Winning Performance*.[4] While they recognize several factors that make a business successful—great strategy, good information systems, dedicated workers, excellent implementation—they all emphasize the central importance of dedicating the business to sensing, serving, and satisfying the customers in a well-understood target market. It is not enough for a company to be product driven or technology driven. Steve Jobs, the brilliant young founder of Apple Computer, learned the hard way that he could not manage Apple as strictly a high-tech, engineering-oriented firm. He scurried to hire the best marketing professional he could find, who turned out to be John Scully, then at Pepsi-Cola Company. Scully came to Apple and brought the company to new heights.

A growing number of companies are recognizing the utter necessity of turning from a product and selling mentality to one of strategic marketing. In a recent study, 250 senior managers of major corporations identified their number-one planning challenge to be "developing, improving, and implementing competitive marketing strategies." "Controlling costs" and "improving human resources" ran second and third.[5] Russell Reynolds Associates reported a 52 percent increase in demand for top executives with marketing backgrounds.[6] And Heidrick and Shruggles found that more top executives have come out of marketing than out of any other field.[7]

The emphasis on marketing is appropriate for Canadian companies, whose domestic market is too small to sustain a world-class competitive advantage. Today's companies survive by competing successfully in a global marketplace, not simply in their domestic market. Their domestic market is being invaded by skillful players such as Sony, Hitachi, Toshiba, Daimler-Benz, Unilever, Beecham, Philips, Erickson, and other major players from the Far East, Western Europe, and elsewhere. And these players are capturing other markets around the world. Canadian companies must increasingly play an international game where the stakes are high and the prizes go to those who can best read customer wants and deliver the highest value to their target markets. It will be marketing skills that distinguish the amateur from the professional players in the global market.

We believe that stronger company marketing skills can potentially launch a new era of high economic growth and rising living standards. One marketing scholar defined *marketing* as "the creation and delivery of a standard of living." We take this as an inspired and insightful view of the marketing job.

This first chapter will describe the major concepts and philosophies underlying marketing thinking and practice, and we will come back to them again and again throughout the book. This chapter will answer the following specific questions:

☐ What are the core concepts that underlie the discipline of marketing?

☐ What are the basic tasks performed by marketing managers?

☐ What is the marketing philosophy, and how does it contrast with other philosophies of doing business?

☐ What role does marketing play in different industries, in nonprofit organizations, and in different countries?

THE CORE CONCEPTS OF MARKETING

Marketing has been defined in various ways by different writers.[8] We like the following definition of marketing:

> Marketing *is a social and managerial process by which individuals and groups obtain what they need and want through creating, offering, and exchanging products of value with others.*

This definition of marketing rests on the following core concepts: *needs, wants, and demands; products; value, cost, and satisfaction; exchange, transactions, and relationships; markets; and marketing and marketers.* These concepts are illustrated in Figure 1-1 and discussed on the next page.

FIGURE 1-1

The Core Concepts of Marketing

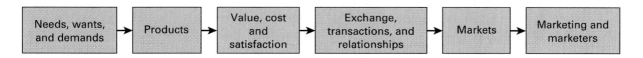

| Needs, wants, and demands | → | Products | → | Value, cost and satisfaction | → | Exchange, transactions, and relationships | → | Markets | → | Marketing and marketers |

Needs, Wants, and Demands

The starting point for the discipline of marketing lies in human needs and wants. People need food, air, water, clothing, and shelter to survive. Beyond this, people have a strong desire for recreation, education, and other services. They have strong preferences for particular versions and brands of basic goods and services.

There is no doubt that people's needs and wants today are staggering. In a recent year, 26.8 million Canadians purchased one million autos, eight million cable TV services, two billion litres of beer, and 609 thousand enrolments in colleges and universities.

In turn, these consumer goods and services contributed to even more demand: 33 billion litres of gasoline for car drivers, $1450 million of TV advertising, $14.2 billion of restaurant, caterer, and tavern income, and $298 million of bookstore services for college and university students. These are only a few of the many wants and needs that are satisfied by Canada's $654 billion economy.[9]

A useful distinction can be drawn between needs, wants, and demands. A *human need is a state of felt deprivation of some basic satisfaction.* People require food, clothing, shelter, safety, belonging, esteem, and a few other things for survival. These needs are not created by their society or by marketers; they exist in the very texture of human biology and the human condition.

Wants are desires for specific satisfiers of these deeper needs. A Canadian needs food and wants a hamburger, needs clothing and wants a Pierre Cardin suit, needs esteem and buys a Cadillac. In another society, these needs are satisfied differently: The Balinese satisfy their hunger with mangoes, their clothing needs with a loincloth, their esteem with a shell necklace. While people's needs are few, their wants are many. Human wants are continually shaped and reshaped by social forces and institutions, such as churches, schools, families, and business corporations.

Demands are wants for specific products that are backed up by an ability and willingness to buy them. Wants become demands when backed up by purchasing power. Many people want a Cadillac; only a few are able and willing to buy one. Companies must therefore measure not only how many people want their product but, more important, how many would actually be willing and able to buy it.

These distinctions shed light on the frequent charge by marketing critics that "marketers create needs" or "marketers get people to buy things they don't want." Marketers do not create needs; needs preexist marketers. Marketers, along with other influencers in the society, influence wants. They suggest to consumers that a Cadillac would satisfy a person's need for social status. Marketers do not create the need for social status but try to point out that a particular product would satisfy that need. Marketers try to influence demand by making the product attractive, affordable, and easily available.

Products

People satisfy their needs and wants with products. We will define products broadly to cover *anything that can be offered to someone to satisfy a need or want.* Normally the word *product* brings to mind a physical object, such as an automobile, a television set, or a soft drink. And we normally use the expression *products and services* to distinguish between physical objects and intangible ones. But in thinking about physical products, their importance lies not so much in owning them as in using them to satisfy our wants. We don't buy a car to look at but because it supplies transportation service. We don't buy a microwave oven to admire but because it supplies a cooking service. Thus physical products are really vehicles that deliver services to us.

In fact, services are also supplied by other vehicles, such as *persons, places, activities, organizations,* and *ideas.* If we are bored, we can go to a nightclub and watch an entertainer (person); travel to a warm vacationland like Florida (place); engage in some physical exercise (activity); join a lonely hearts club (organization), or adopt a different philosophy about life (idea). In other words, services can be delivered through physical objects and other vehicles. We will use the term *product* to designate either tangible goods or intangible services that are capable of delivering satisfaction of a want or need. Occasionally we will use other terms for product, such as *offers, satisfiers, or resources.*

Manufacturers get into a lot of trouble by paying more attention to their physical products than to the services produced by these products. Manufacturers love their products but forget that customers buy them because they satisfy a need. People do not buy physical objects for their own sake. A tube of lipstick is bought to supply a service: helping the person look better. A drill bit is bought to supply a service: producing a hole. A physical object is a means of packaging a service. The marketer's job is to sell the benefits or services built into physical products rather than just describe their physical features. Sellers who concentrate on the product instead of the customer's need are said to suffer from "marketing myopia."[10]

Value, Cost, and Satisfaction

How do consumers choose among the many products that might satisfy a given need? Suppose Tom Jones needs to travel six kilometres to work each day. Jones can visualize a number of products that will satisfy this need: roller skates, a bicycle, a motorcycle, an automobile, a taxicab, and a bus. These alternatives constitute his *product choice set.* Assume that Jones would like to satisfy different needs in traveling to work, namely speed, safety, ease, and economy. We call these his *need set.* Now each product has a different capacity to satisfy his various needs. Thus a bicycle will be slower, less safe, and more effortful than an automobile, but it will be more economical. Somehow Tom Jones has to decide on which product delivers the most satisfaction.

The guiding concept is *value.* Tom Jones will form an estimate of the value of each product in satisfying his needs. He might rank the products from the most need-satisfying to the least need-satisfying. Value is the consumer's estimate of the product's overall capacity to satisfy his or her needs.

We can ask Jones to imagine the characteristics of an *ideal product* for this task. Jones might answer that the *ideal product* would get him to his place of work in a split second with absolute safety, no effort, and zero cost. Then the value of each actual product would depend on how close it came to this ideal product.

Suppose Jones is primarily interested in the speed and ease of getting to work. If Jones were offered any of these products at no cost, we would predict that he would choose the automobile. But now comes the rub. Since each product involves a *cost,* he will not necessarily buy the automobile. The automobile costs substantially more than, say, a bicycle. Jones will have to give up more of other things (represented by the cost) to obtain the car. Therefore he will consider the product's value and price before making a choice. He will choose the product that will produce the most value per dollar.

Today's consumer-behavior theorists have gone beyond narrow economic assumptions of how consumers form value in their mind and make product choices. We will look at modern theories of consumer-choice behavior in Chapter 6. These theories are important to marketers because the whole marketing plan rests on assumptions about how customers make choices. Therefore the concepts of value, cost, and satisfaction are crucial to the discipline of marketing.

Exchange, Transactions, and Relationships

The fact that people have needs and wants and can place value on products does not fully define marketing. Marketing emerges when people decide to satisfy needs and wants through exchange. Exchange is one of four ways people can obtain products they want.

The first way is *self-production*. People can relieve hunger through hunting, fishing, or fruit gathering. They need not interact with anyone else. In this case, there is no market and no marketing.

The second way is *coercion*. Hungry people can wrest or steal food from others. No benefit is offered to the others except that of not being harmed.

The third way is *begging*. Hungry people can approach others and beg for food. They have nothing tangible to offer except gratitude.

The fourth way is *exchange*. Hungry people can approach others and offer some resource in exchange, such as money, another good, or some service.

Marketing arises from this last approach to acquiring products. *Exchange is the act of obtaining a desired product from someone by offering something in return*. Exchange is the defining concept underlying marketing. For exchange to take place, five conditions must be satisfied:

1. There are at least two parties.

2. Each party has something that might be of value to the other party.

3. Each party is capable of communication and delivery.

4. Each party is free to accept or reject the offer.

5. Each party believes it is appropriate or desirable to deal with the other party.

If these conditions exist, there is a potential for exchange. Whether exchange actually takes place depends upon whether the two parties can agree on *terms of exchange* that will leave them both better off (or at least not worse off) than before the exchange. This is the sense in which exchange is described as a value-creating process; that is, exchange normally leaves both parties better off than before the exchange.

Exchange must be seen as a process rather than as an event. Two parties are said to be engaged in exchange if they are negotiating and moving toward an agreement. If an agreement is reached, we say that a *transaction* takes place. Transactions are the basic unit of exchange. *A transaction consists of a trade of values between two parties*. We must be able to say: A gave X to B and received Y in return. Jones gave $400 to Smith and obtained a television set. This is a classic *monetary transaction*. Transactions, however, do not require money as one of the traded values. A *barter transaction* would consist of Jones giving a refrigerator to Smith in return for a television set. A barter transaction can also consist of the trading of services instead of goods, as when lawyer Jones writes a will for dentist Smith in return for a dental examination.

A transaction involves several dimensions: at least two things of value, agreed-upon conditions, a time of agreement, and a place of agreement. Usually a legal system arises to support and enforce compliance on the part of the transactors. Transactions can easily give rise to conflicts based on misinterpretation or malice. Without a "law of contracts," people would approach transactions with some distrust, and everyone would lose.

Businesses maintain records of their transactions and sort them by item, price, customer, location, and other variables. Sales analsysis is the act of analyzing where the company's sales are coming from by product, customer, territory, and so on.

A *transaction* differs from a *transfer*. In a transfer, A gives X to B but does not receive anything tangible in return. When A gives B a gift, a subsidy, or a charitable contribution, we call this a transfer, not a transaction. It would seem that marketing should be confined to the study of transactions and not transfers. However, transfer behavior can also be understood through the concept of exchange. Typically, the transferer has certain expectations upon giving a gift, such as getting back gratitude or seeing good behavior in the recipient. Professional fund raisers are acutely aware of the "reciprocal" motives underlying donor behavior and try to provide benefits to the donors, such as thank-you notes, donor magazines, and special invitations to events. Marketers have recently broadened the concept of marketing to include the study of transfer behavior as well as transaction behavior.

In the most generic sense, the marketer is seeking to elicit some *behavioral response* from another party. A business firm wants a response called buying, a political candidate wants a response called voting, a church wants a response called joining, a social-action group wants a response called adopting the idea. Marketing consists of actions undertaken to elicit desired responses to some object from a target audience.

To effect successful exchanges, the marketer analyzes what each party expects to give and get. Simple exchange situations can be mapped by showing the two actors and the wants and offers flowing between them. Suppose Caterpillar, the world's largest manufacturer of earth-moving equipment, researches the benefits that a typical construction company wants in buying earth-moving equipment. These benefits are listed at the top of the exchange map in Figure 1-2. A construction company wants high-quality equipment, a fair price, on-time delivery, good financing, and good service. This is the buyer's *want list*. The wants are not all equally important and may vary from buyer to buyer. One of Caterpillar's tasks is to discover the importance of these different wants of the buyer. At the same time, Caterpillar has a want list that is shown below the Caterpillar arrow in Figure 1-2. Caterpillar wants a good price for the equipment, on-time payment, and good word of mouth. If there is a sufficient match or overlap in the want lists, there is a basis for a transaction. Caterpillar's task is to formulate an offer that motivates the construction company to buy Caterpillar equipment. The construction company might in turn make a counteroffer. The process of trying to arrive at mutually agreeable terms is called *negotiation*. Negotiation leads to either mutually acceptable terms or a decision not to transact.

FIGURE 1-2
Two-Party Exchange Map Showing
Want Lists of Both Parties

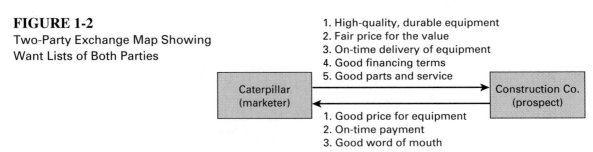

1. High-quality, durable equipment
2. Fair price for the value
3. On-time delivery of equipment
4. Good financing terms
5. Good parts and service

Caterpillar (marketer) → Construction Co. (prospect)

1. Good price for equipment
2. On-time payment
3. Good word of mouth

So far, we have explained the nature of *transaction marketing*. Transaction marketing is part of a larger idea, that of *relationship marketing*. Smart marketers try to build up long-term, trusting, "win-win" relationships with customers, distributors, dealers, and suppliers. That is accomplished by promising and delivering high quality, good service, and fair prices to the other party over time. It is accomplished by strengthening the economic, technical, and social ties between members of the two organizations. The two parties grow more trusting, more knowledgeable, and more interested in helping each other. Relationship marketing cuts down on transaction costs and time; in the best cases, transactions move from being negotiated each time to being routinized.

The ultimate outcome of relationship marketing is the building of a unique company asset called a *marketing network*. A marketing network consists of the company and the firms with which it has built solid, dependable business relationships. Increasingly, marketing is shifting from trying to maximize the profit on each individual transaction to maximizing beneficial relationships with other parties. The operating principle is, build good relationships, and profitable transactions will follow.

Markets

The concept of exchange leads to the concept of a market.

> A market *consists of all the potential customers sharing a particular need or want who might be willing and able to engage in exchange to satisfy that need or want.*

Thus the size of the market depends upon the number of persons who exhibit the need, have resources that interest others, and are willing to offer these resources in exchange for what they want.

Originally the term *market* stood for the place where buyers and sellers gathered to exchange their goods, such as a village square. Economists use the term market to refer to a collection of buyers and sellers who transact over a particular product or product class; hence the housing market, the grain market, and so on. Marketers, however, see the sellers as constituting the *industry* and the buyers as constituting the market. The relationship between the industry and the *market* is shown in Figure 1-3. The sellers and the buyers are connected by four flows. The sellers send goods and services and communications to the market; in return they receive money and information. The inner loop shows an exchange of money for goods; the outer loop shows an exchange of information.

Businesspeople use the term *markets* colloquially to cover various groupings of customers. They talk about *need markets* (such as the diet-seeking market); *product markets* (such as the shoe market); *demographic markets* (such as the youth market); and *geographic markets* (such as the Quebec market). Or they extend the concept to cover noncustomer groupings as well, such as *voter markets, labor markets*, and *donor markets*.

The fact is that modern economies operate on the principle of division of labor where each person specializes in the production of something, receives payment, and buys needed things

FIGURE 1-3
A Simple Marketing System

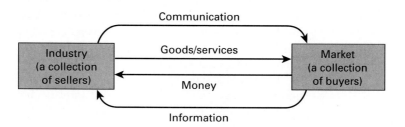

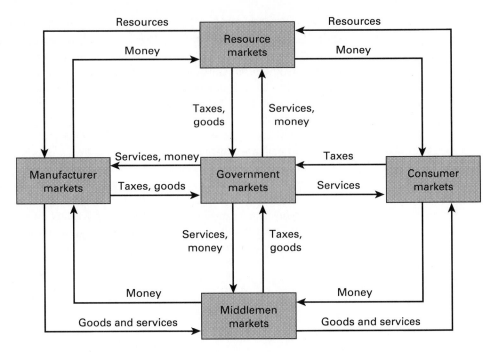

FIGURE 1-4
Structure of Flows in a Modern Exchange Economy

with this money. Thus modern economies abound in markets. The basic kinds of markets and the flows connecting them are shown in Figure 1-4. Essentially, manufacturers go to resource markets (raw-material markets, labor markets, money markets, and so on), buy resources, turn them into goods and services, sell them to middlemen, who sell them to consumers. The consumers sell their labor, for which they receive money income to pay for the goods and services they buy. The government is another market that plays several roles. It buys goods from resource, manufacturer, and middlemen markets; it pays them; it taxes these markets (including consumer markets); and it returns needed public services. Thus each nation's economy and the whole world economy consist of complex interacting sets of markets that are linked through exchange processes.

Marketing and Marketers

The concept of markets brings us full circle to the concept of marketing. Marketing means human activity taking place in relation to markets. Marketing means working with markets to actualize potential exchanges for the purpose of satisfying human needs and wants.

If one party is more actively seeking an exchange than the other party, we call the first party a *marketer* and the second party a *prospect*. *A marketer is someone seeking a resource from someone else and willing to offer something of value in exchange.* The marketer is seeking a response from the other party, either to sell something or to buy something. The marketer, in other words, can be a seller or a buyer. Suppose several persons want to buy an attractive house that has just became available. Each would-be buyer will try to market himself or herself to be the one the seller selects. These buyers are doing the marketing. In the event that both parties actively seek an exchange, we say that both of them are marketers and call the situation one of reciprocal marketing.

In the normal situation, the marketer is a company serving a market of end users in the face of competitors (see Figure 1-5). The company and the competitors send their respective products and messages directly and/or through marketing intermediaries (middlemen and

FIGURE 1-5
Main Actors and Forces in a Modern Marketing System

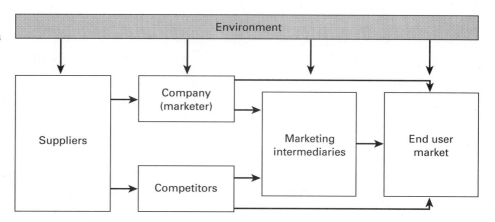

facilitators) to the end users. Their relative effectiveness is influenced by their respective suppliers as well as major environmental forces (demographic, economic, physical, technological, political/legal, social/cultural). Thus Figure 1-5 represents the main elements in a modern marketing system.

Having reviewed these concepts, we are ready to repeat our definition of marketing: *marketing is a social and managerial process by which individuals and groups obtain what they need and want through creating, offering, and exchanging products of value with others.*

MARKETING MANAGEMENT

Coping with exchange processes calls for a considerable amount of work and skill. *Persons* become fairly adept at buying to meet their household needs. Occasionally they also undertake selling—selling their car, selling personal services. *Organizations* are more professional in handling exchange processes. They must attract resources from one set of markets, convert them into useful products, and sell them in another set of markets. *Nations* also plan and manage exchange relations with others. They search for beneficial trade relations with other nations. In this book we will focus on *organizational marketing* rather than on *person* or *nation* marketing.

Marketing management takes place when at least one party to a potential exchange gives thought to objectives and means of achieving desired responses from other parties. We will use the following definition of marketing (management) approved in 1985 by the American Marketing Association:

> Marketing *(management) is the process of planning and executing the conception, pricing, promotion, and distribution of ideas, goods, and services to create exchanges that satisfy individual and organizational objectives.*[11]

This definition recognizes that marketing management is a process involving analysis, planning, implementation, and control; that it covers ideas, goods, and services; that it rests on the notion of exchange; and that the goal is to produce satisfaction for the parties involved.

Marketing management can occur in an organization in connection with any of its markets. Consider an automobile manufacturer. The vice-president of personnel deals in the *labor market*; the vice-president of purchasing, the *raw-materials market*; and the vice-president of finance, the *money market*. They must set objectives and develop strategies for achieving

Marketing Concepts and Tools 1-1

DEMAND STATES AND MARKETING TASKS

1. *Negative demand*: A market is in a state of negative demand if a major part of the market dislikes the product and may even pay a price to avoid it. People have a negative demand for vaccinations, dental work, vasectomies, and gall bladder operations. Employers feel a negative demand for ex-convicts and alcoholics as employees. The marketing task is to analyze why the market dislikes the product and whether a marketing program consisting of product redesign, lower prices, and more positive promotion can change the market's beliefs and attitudes.

2. *No demand*: Target consumers may be uninterested or indifferent to the product. Thus farmers may not be interested in a new farming method, and college students may not be interested in foreign-language courses. The marketing task is to find ways to connect the benefits of the product with the person's natural needs and interests.

3. *Latent demand*: Many consumers may share a strong need that cannot be satisfied by any existing product. There is a strong latent demand for harmless cigarettes, safer neighborhoods, and more fuel-efficient cars. The marketing task is to measure the size of the potential market and develop effective goods and services that would satisfy the demand.

4. *Falling demand*: Every organization, sooner or later, faces falling demand for one or more of its products. Churches have seen their memberships decline, and community colleges have seen their applications fall. The marketer must analyze the causes of market decline and determine whether demand can be restimulated by finding new target markets, changing the product's features, or developing more effective communication. The marketing task is to reverse the declining demand through creative remarketing of the product.

5. *Irregular demand*: Many organizations face demand that varies on a seasonal, daily, or even hourly basis, causing problems of idle capacity or overworked capacity. In mass transit, much of the equipment is idle during the off-peak hours and insufficient during the peak travel hours. Museums are undervisited on weekdays and overcrowded on weekends. Hospital operating rooms are overbooked early in the week and underbooked toward the end of the week. The marketing task, called synchromarketing, is to find ways to alter the same pattern of demand through flexible pricing, promotion, and other incentives.

6. *Full demand*: Organizations face full demand when they are pleased with their volume of business. The marketing task is to maintain the current level of demand in the face of changing consumer preferences and increasing competition. The organization must maintain or improve its quality and continually measure consumer satisfaction to make sure it is doing a good job.

7. *Overfull demand*: Some organizations face a demand level that is higher than they can or want to handle. Thus, in good skiing weather, skiers must queue up to use the lifts at Whistler, and summer crowds at Peggy's Cove tend to spoil the experience. The marketing task, called *demarketing*, requires finding ways to reduce the demand temporarily or permanently. General demarketing seeks to discourage overall demand and consists of such steps as raising prices and reducing promotion and service. Selective demarketing consists of trying to reduce the demand coming from those parts of the market that are less profitable or less in need of the service. Demarketing aims not to destroy demand but only to reduce its level, temporarily or permanently.

8. *Unwholesome demand*: Unwholesome products will attract organized efforts to discourage their consumption. Unselling campaigns have been conducted against cigarettes, alcohol, hard drugs, handguns, X-rated movies, and large families. The marketing task is to get people who like something to give it up, using such tools as fear communication, price hikes, and reduced availability.

Source: For a fuller discussion, see Philip Kotler, "The Major Tasks of Marketing Management," *Journal of Marketing*, October 1973, pp. 42-49; and Philip Kotler and Sidney J. Levy, "Demarketing, Yes, Demarketing," *Harvard Business Review*, November-December 1971, pp. 74-80.

satisfactory results in these markets. Traditionally, however, these executives have not been called marketers, nor have they trained in marketing. Instead, marketing management is historically identified with tasks and personnel dealing with the *customer market*. We will follow this convention, although what we say about marketing applies to all markets.

Marketing work in the customer market is formally carried out by *sales managers, salespeople, advertising and promotion managers, marketing researchers, customer-service managers, product managers, market managers, and the marketing vice-president*. Each job carries well-defined tasks and responsibilities. Many of these jobs involve managing particular *marketing resources* such as advertising, salespeople, or marketing research. On the other hand, product managers, market managers, and the marketing vice-president manage *programs*. Their job is to analyze, plan, and implement programs that will produce a desired level and mix of transactions with target markets.

The popular image of the marketing manager is someone whose task is primarily to stimulate demand for the company's products. However, this is too limited a view of the diversity of marketing tasks performed by marketing managers. *Marketing management has the task of influencing the level, timing, and composition of demand in a way that will help the organization achieve its objectives.* Marketing management is essentially *demand management*.

The organization presumably forms an idea of a *desired level of transactions* with a target market. At times, the *actual demand level* may be below, equal to, or above the desired demand level. That is, there may be no demand, weak demand, adequate demand, excessive demand, and so on, and marketing management has to cope with these different states. The Marketing Concepts and Tools 1-1 exhibit distinguishes eight different states of demand and the corresponding tasks facing marketing managers.

Marketing managers cope with these tasks by carrying out *marketing research, planning, implementation, and control*. Within marketing planning, marketers must make decisions on target markets, market positioning, product development, pricing, channels of distribution, physical distribution, communication, and promotion. These marketing tasks will be analyzed in subsequent chapters of the book. Suffice it to say that marketing managers must acquire several skills to be effective in the marketplace.

COMPANY ORIENTATIONS TOWARD THE MARKETPLACE

We have described marketing management as the conscious effort to achieve desired exchange outcomes with target markets. Now the question arises, What philosophy should guide these marketing efforts? What weights should be given to the interests of the *organization*, the *customers*, and *society*? Very often these interests conflict. Clearly, marketing activities should be carried out under some well-thought-out philosophy of efficient, effective, and responsible marketing.

There are five competing concepts under which organizations conduct their marketing activity.

The Production Concept

The production concept is one of the oldest concepts guiding sellers.

> *The* production concept *holds that consumers will favor those products that are widely available and low in cost. Managers of production-oriented organizations concentrate on achieving high production efficiency and wide distribution coverage.*

The assumption that consumers are primarily interested in product availability and low price holds in at least two types of situations. The first is where the demand for a product exceeds supply, as is the case in many Third World countries. Here consumers are more interested in obtaining the product than in its fine points. The suppliers will concentrate on finding ways to increase production. The second situation is where the product's cost is high and has to be brought down through increased productivity to expand the market. Texas Instruments provides a contemporary example of the production concept:

> Texas Instruments is the leading exponent of the "get-out-production, cut-the-price" philosophy that Henry Ford pioneered in the early 1900s to expand the automobile market. Ford put all of his talent into perfecting the mass production of automobiles to bring down their costs so that people could afford them. Texas Instruments puts all of its efforts into building production volume and improving technology in order to bring down costs. It uses its lower costs to cut prices and expand the market size. It goes after and usually achieves the dominant position in its markets. To Texas Instruments, marketing means one thing: bringing down the price to buyers. This orientation has also been a key strategy of many Japanese companies.[12] ∎

Some service organizations also follow the production concept. Many medical and dental practices are organized on assembly-line principles, as are some government agencies such as unemployment offices and license bureaus. While it results in handling many cases per hour, this management orientation is open to charges of impersonality and questionable service quality.

The Product Concept

Other sellers are guided by the product concept.

> *The* product concept *holds that consumers will favor those products that offer the most quality or performance. Managers in these product-oriented organizations focus their energy on making good products and improving them over time.*

These managers assume that buyers admire well-made products and can appraise product quality and performance. These managers are caught up in a love affair with their product and fail to appreciate that the market may be less "turned on" and may even be moving in a different direction. They say, "We make the finest men's tailored suits" or "We make the finest television sets" and wonder why the market doesn't appreciate this.

The Elgin National Watch Company provides a dramatic example of product-centered, rather than market-centered, thinking:

> Since its founding in 1864, the Elgin National Watch Company had enjoyed a reputation as one of the finest watchmakers. Elgin placed its major emphasis on maintaining a superior product and merchandising it through a large network of leading jewelry and department stores. Its sales rose continuously until 1958, and thereafter its sales and market share began to slip. What happened to undermine Elgin's dominant position?

> Essentially, Elgin's management was so enamored with fine, traditionally styled watches that it didn't notice the major changes taking place in the consumer watch market. Many consumers were losing interest in the idea that a watch needed superior timekeeping accuracy, had to carry a prestigious name, and last a lifetime. They expected a watch to tell time, look attractive, and not cost too much. Consumers had a growing desire for convenience (self-winding watches), durability (waterproof and shockproof watches), and economy (pin-lever watches). As for *channels*, an increasing number of watches were being sold through mass-distribution outlets and

discount stores. Many people wanted to avoid the higher markups of the local jeweler, and also often bought on impulse when exposed to inexpensive watch displays. As for *competitors*, many had added lower-priced watches to their line and had begun to sell them through mass-distribution channels. Elgin's problem was that it had riveted its attention on a set of products instead of adapting to a rapidly changing market. ■

One of the most common manifestations of the product concept occurs with new products that a company invents. Management becomes enamored of the product and often loses perspective. It falls into the "better-mousetrap" fallacy, believing that a better mousetrap will cause people to beat a path to its door.[13] Consider the following example:

In 1972, Du Pont researchers invented Kevlar, which it considers its most important new fiber since nylon. Kevlar has the same strength as steel with only one-fifth the weight. Du Pont asked its divisions to find applications for this new miracle fiber. Du Pont's executives imagined a huge number of applications and a billion-dollar market. Now, years later, Du Pont is still waiting for the bonanza. True, Kevlar is a very good fiber for bulletproof vests, but there isn't a big demand for bulletproof vests, so far. Kevlar is a promising fiber for sails, cords, and tires, and manufacturers are beginning to nibble. Eventually Kevlar may prove to be a miracle fiber, but it is taking longer than Du Pont expected.[14] ■

Product-oriented companies go about designing their product in the wrong way. A General Motors executive said some years ago: "How can the public know what kind of car they want until we've invented it?" GM's perspective was that the company's designers and engineers would create a car, with emphasis on styling and durability. Then manufacturing would make it. Then the finance department would price it. Finally, marketing and sales would be called on to sell it. No wonder the car required such hard selling by the dealers GM failed to ask customers what they wanted and never brought in the marketing people at the beginning to help figure out what kind of car would sell.

The product concept leads to "marketing myopia," an undue concentration on the product rather than the need. Railroad management thought that users wanted trains rather than transportation and overlooked the growing challenge of the airlines, buses, trucks, and automobiles. Slide-rule manufacturers thought that engineers wanted slide rules rather than the calculating capacity and overlooked the challenge of pocket calculators. Churches, symphonies, and the post office all assume that they are offering the public the right product and wonder why their sales falter. These organizations too often are looking into a mirror when they should be looking out of the window.

The Selling Concept

The selling concept (or sales concept) is another common approach many firms take to the market.

The selling concept *holds that consumers, if left alone, will ordinarily not buy enough of the organization's products. The organization must therefore undertake an aggressive selling and promotion effort.*

The concept assumes that consumers typically show buying inertia or resistance and have to be coaxed into buying more, and that the company has available a whole battery of effective selling and promotion tools to stimulate more buying.

The selling concept is practiced most aggressively with "unsought goods," those goods that buyers normally do not think of buying, such as insurance, encyclopedias, and funeral plots.

These industries have perfected various sales techniques to locate prospects and hard-sell them on the benefits of their product.

Hard selling also occurs with sought goods, such as automobiles:

> From the moment the customer walks into the showroom, the auto salesperson "psychs him out." If the customer likes the floor model, he may be told that there is another customer about to buy it and that he should decide now. If the customer balks at the price, the salesperson offers to talk to the manager to get a special concession. The customer waits ten minutes and the salesperson returns with "the boss doesn't like it but I got him to agree." The aim is to "work up the customer" and "close the sale."[15] ■

The selling concept is also practiced in the nonprofit area, by fund raisers, college admissions offices, and political parties. A political party will vigorously sell its candidate to the voters as being a fantastic person for the job. The candidate stomps through voting precincts from early morning to late evening shaking hands, kissing babies, meeting donors, making breezy speeches. Countless dollars are spent on radio and television advertising, posters, and mailings. Any flaws in the candidate are concealed from the public because the aim is to make the sale, not worry about postpurchase satisfaction. After the election, the new official continues to take a sales-oriented view toward the citizens. There is little research into what the public wants and a lot of selling to get the public to accept policies that the politician or party wants.[16]

Most firms practice the selling concept when they have overcapacity. *Their aim is to sell what they make rather than make what they can sell.* In modern industrial economies, productive capacity has been built up to a point where most markets are buyer markets (i.e., the buyers are dominant), and sellers have to scramble hard for customers. Prospects are bombarded with television commercials, newspaper ads, direct mail, and sales calls. At every turn, someone is trying to sell something. As a result, the public identifies marketing with hard selling and advertising.

Therefore people are surprised when they are told that the most important part of marketing is not selling! Selling is only the tip of the marketing iceberg. Peter Drucker, one of the leading management theorists, puts it this way:

> There will always, one can assume, be need for some selling. *But the aim of marketing is to make selling superfluous.* The aim of marketing is to know and understand the customer so well that the product or service fits him and sells itself. Ideally, marketing should result in a customer who is ready to buy. All that should be needed then is to make the product or service available. . . .[17]

Thus selling, to be effective, must be preceded by several marketing activities such as needs assessment, marketing research, product development, pricing, and distribution. If the marketer does a good job of identifying consumer needs, developing appropriate products, and pricing, distributing, and promoting them effectively, these products will sell very easily. When Eastman Kodak designed its Instamatic camera, when Atari designed its first video game, and when Mazda introduced its RX-7 sports car, these manufacturers were swamped with orders because they had designed the "right" product based on careful marketing homework.

Indeed, marketing based on hard selling carries high risks. It assumes that customers who are coaxed into buying the product will like it; and if they don't, they won't bad-mouth it to friends or complain to consumer organizations. And they will possibly forget their disappointment and buy it again. These are indefensible assumptions to make about buyers. One study showed that disappointed customers bad-mouth the product to eleven acquaintances, while satisfied customers may good-mouth the product to only three.

The Marketing Concept

The marketing concept is a business philosophy that arose to challenge the previous concepts. Although it has a long history, its central tenets did not fully crystallize until the mid-1950s.[18]

> *The* marketing concept *holds that the key to achieving organizational goals consists in determining the needs and wants of target markets and delivering the desired satisfactions more effectively and efficiently than competitors.*

The marketing concept has been expressed in many colorful ways:

- "Find wants and fill them."
- "Make what will sell instead of trying to sell what you can make."
- "Love the customer and not the product."
- "Have it your way."
- "You're the boss."
- "To do all in our power to pack the customer's dollar full of value, quality, and satisfaction."

Theodore Levitt drew a perceptive contrast between the selling and marketing concepts.

> Selling focuses on the needs of the seller; marketing on the needs of the buyer. Selling is preoccupied with the seller's need to convert his product into cash; marketing with the idea of satisfying the needs of the customer by means of the product and the whole cluster of things associated with creating, delivering and finally consuming it.[19]

The marketing concept rests on four main pillars, namely a *market focus, customer orientation, coordinated marketing, and profitability*. These are shown in Figure 1-6, where they are contrasted with a selling orientation. The selling concept takes an *inside-out* perspective. It starts with the factory, focuses on the company's existing products and calls for heavy selling and promoting to produce profitable sales. The marketing concept takes an *outside-in* perspective. It starts with a well-defined market, focuses on customer needs, coordinates all the activities that will affect customers, and produces profits through creating customer satisfaction. In essence, the *marketing concept* is a *market-focused, customer-oriented,*

FIGURE 1-6
The Selling and Marketing Concepts Contrasted

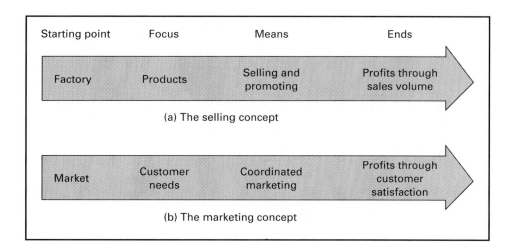

Starting point	Focus	Means	Ends
Factory	Products	Selling and promoting	Profits through sales volume

(a) The selling concept

Starting point	Focus	Means	Ends
Market	Customer needs	Coordinated marketing	Profits through customer satisfaction

(b) The marketing concept

coordinated marketing effort aimed at generating *customer satisfaction* as the key to satisfying *organizational goals*.

Here we examine how each pillar of the marketing concept contributes to more effective marketing.

Market Focus   No company can operate in every market and satisfy every need. Nor can it even do a good job within one broad market: Even mighty IBM cannot offer the best customer solution for every computer need. Companies do best when they define their target markets carefully. They do best when they prepare a tailored marketing program for each target market.

> An auto manufacturer can think of designing passenger cars, station wagons, sports cars, and luxury cars. But this thinking is less precise than defining a market target. One Japanese car maker is designing a car for the career woman, and it will have many features that male-dominated cars don't have. Another Japanese car maker is designing a car for the "town man," the young person who needs to get about town and park easily. In each case, the company has clarified a market target, and this will greatly influence the design of the car.   ■

Customer Orientation   A company can define its market carefully and still fail at customer-oriented thinking. Consider the following example:

> The chemists in a major chemical company invented a new substance that hardened into a pseudomarble. Looking for an application, the marketing department thought that the substance could be used to produce elegant-looking bathtubs. They went ahead and created a few model bathtubs and rented space at a bathroom furnishing trade show. They were hoping to convince bathtub manufacturers to produce bathtubs with the new material. Although manufacturers thought the new bathtubs were attractive, none signed up. The reason became obvious. The bathtub would have to be priced at $2000; for this price, consumers could buy bathtubs made out of real marble or onyx. In addition, the bathtubs were so heavy that the bathroom floor would have to be reinforced at additional cost. Furthermore, most bathtubs were sold in the $500 range, and few people were ready to spend $2000. The chemical company had succeeded in developing a market focus but had failed to understand the customers.   ■

Customer-oriented thinking requires the company to define customer needs from the *customer point of view*, not from its own point of view. Every product involves tradeoffs, and management cannot know what these are without talking to and researching customers. Thus a car buyer would like a high-performance car that never breaks down, that is safe, attractively styled, and cheap. Since all of these virtues cannot be combined in one car, the car designers must make hard choices not on what pleases them but rather on what customers prefer or expect. The aim, after all, is to make a sale through meeting the customer's needs.

Why is it supremely important to satisfy the customer? Basically because a company's sales each period come from two groups: *new customers* and *repeat customers*. It always costs more to attract new customers than to retain current customers. Therefore *customer retention* is more critical than *customer attraction*. The key to customer retention is *customer satisfaction*. A satisfied customer:

1. Buys again

2. Talks favorably to others about the company

3. Pays less attention to competing brands and advertising

4. Buys other products from the same company

One Japanese businessman recently told the author: "Our aim goes beyond satisfying the customer. Our aim is to *delight* the customer." In fact, this is a higher standard and a deeper quest and may be the secret of the great marketers. They go beyond meeting the mere expectations of the customer. When they delight a customer, the customer talks to even more acquaintances about the fine company. The delighted customers are more effective advertisers than are advertisements placed in the media.

Now let us consider what happens when the company creates a dissatisfied customer. Whereas, as we have pointed out, a satisfied customer tells three people about a good product experience, a dissatisfied customer gripes to eleven people. In fact, in one study, 13 percent of the people who had a problem with an organization complained about the company to more than twenty people.[20] Suppose each person who heard the bad story told eleven people, who told another eleven, and so on. Clearly, bad word of mouth travels farther and faster than good word of mouth and can easily poison the public's attitude about the company.

Thus a company would be wise to regularly measure customer satisfaction. It cannot rely just on voluntary complaints from customers when they are dissatisfied. In fact, 96 percent of unhappy customers never tell the company.[21] Companies should set up suggestion and survey systems to *maximize the customer's opportunity to complain.* In this way, the company will learn how well it is doing. It is also a major way for the company to learn how to do better. The 3M company claims that over two-thirds of its innovation ideas come from listening to customer complaints.

Listening is not enough. The company must respond constructively to the complaints.

> Of the customers who register a complaint, between 54 and 70 percent will do business again with the organization if their complaint is resolved. The figure goes up to a staggering 95 percent if the customer feels that the complaint was resolved quickly. Customers who have complained to an organization and had their complaints satisfactorily resolved tell an average of five people about the treatment they received.[22]

When a company realizes that a loyal customer may account for a substantial sum of revenue over the years, it seems foolish to risk losing the customer by ignoring a grievance or quarreling over a small matter. For example, IBM makes every salesperson write a full report on each lost customer and all the steps taken to restore satisfaction.

A customer-oriented company would track its customer-satisfaction level each period and set improvement goals. For example, the Chevrolet division of General Motors achieved a dealer/service satisfaction index of 79 (maximum 100) in 1984 and hoped to reach 90 by 1990. Its owner-repurchase loyalty stood at 38 in 1984, and it wants to move this figure to 55 by 1990. If Chevrolet manages to increase customer satisfaction and loyalty, it does not have to worry even if its profits are down in a particular year: It is on the right track. If, on the other hand, its profits rise but its customer satisfaction keeps falling, it is on the wrong track. Profits could go up or down in a particular year for many reasons, including rising costs, falling prices, major new investments, and so on, but the ultimate sign of a healthy company is that its customer-satisfaction index is high and keeps rising. Customer satisfaction is the best indicator of the company's future profits. (See Marketing Strategies 1-1.)

Coordinated Marketing   Unfortunately, not all the employees in a company are trained or motivated to pull together for the customer. An engineer at one company complained that the salespeople were "always protecting the customer and not thinking of the company's interest"! He went on to blast customers for "asking for too much." The following situation highlights the coordination problem:

The marketing vice-president of a major airline wants to build up the airline's traffic share. Her strategy is to build up customer satisfaction through providing better food, cleaner cabins, and better trained cabin crews. Yet she has no authority in these matters. The catering department chooses food that keeps down food costs; the maintenance department uses cleaning services that keep down cleaning costs; and the personnel department hires people without regard to whether they are friendly and inclined to serve other people. Since these departments generally take a cost or production point of view, she is stymied in creating a high level of customer satisfaction. ■

Coordinated marketing means two things. First, the various marketing functions—sales-force, advertising, product management, marketing research, and so on—must be coordinated among themselves. Too often the salesforce is mad at the product managers for setting "too high a price" or "too high a volume target"; or the advertising director and a brand manager cannot agree on the best advertising campaign for the brand. These marketing functions must be coordinated from the customer point of view.

Second, marketing must be well coordinated with the other company departments. Marketing does not work when it is merely a department; it only works when all employees appreciate the effect they have on customer satisfaction. As David Packard of Hewlett Packard put it: "Marketing is too important to be left to the marketing department!" IBM goes so far as to include in every one of its four hundred thousand job descriptions an explanation of how that job relates to serving the customer. An IBM factory manager knows that customer visits to the factory can help sell a potential customer if the factory is clean and efficient. An IBM accountant knows that customer attitudes toward IBM are affected by the accuracy

Marketing Strategies 1-1

THE SECRET OF L.L. BEAN'S PROFITABILITY: CUSTOMER SATISFACTION

One of the most successful mail-order houses is L.L. Bean, Inc., which specializes in clothing and equipment for rugged living. L.L. Bean has carefully blended its external and internal marketing programs. To its customers, it offers the following:

100% GUARANTEE

All of our products are guaranteed to give 100% satisfaction in every way. Return anything purchased from us at any time if it proves otherwise. We will replace it, refund your purchase price or credit your credit card, as you wish. We do not want you to have anything from L.L. Bean that is not completely satisfactory.

To motivate its employees to serve the customers well, it prominently displays the following poster around its offices:

WHAT IS A CUSTOMER?

A Customer is the most important person ever in this office . . . in person or by mail.

A Customer is not dependent on us . . . we are dependent on him.

A Customer is not an interruption of our work . . . he is the purpose of it. We are not doing a favor by serving him . . . he is doing us a favor by giving us the opportunity to do so.

A Customer is not someone to argue or match wits with. Nobody ever won an argument with a Customer.

A Customer is a person who brings us his wants. It is our job to handle them profitably to him and to ourselves.

Source: Brochure and poster material from L.L. Bean, Inc.

of the billing procedure and the promptness and courtesy with which customer calls are answered.

For this reason, the marketing concept requires the company to carry out *internal marketing* as well as *external marketing. Internal marketing is the task of successfully hiring, training, and motivating able employees to serve the customers well.* In fact, internal marketing must precede external marketing. It makes no sense to promise excellent service before the company's staff is ready to provide excellent service. A story is told about how Bill Marriott, Jr., chairman of the Marriott hotels, interviews prospective managers:

> Bill Marriott, tells the job candidate that the hotel chain wants to satisfy three groups: *customers, employees*, and *stockholders*. While all the groups are important, he asks, in which order the groups should be satisfied? Most candidates say first satisfy the customers. Bill Marriott, however, reasons differently. First, the hotel must satisfy its employees. If the employees love their jobs and feel a sense of pride in the hotel, they will serve the customers well. Satisfied customers will return frequently to the Marriott. This repeat business, in turn, yields a level of profits that satisfy the Marriott stockholders. ∎

Bill Marriott is still saying that the customer is the key to profitability. He and others consider the typical organization chart—a pyramid with the president at the top, management in the middle, and front-line people (sales and service people, telephone operators, receptionists) at the bottom—to be obsolete. Master marketing companies know better; they invert the chart, as shown in Figure 1-7. At the top of the organization are the customers. Next in importance are the front-line people who meet, serve, and satisfy the customers. Under them are the middle managers whose job it is to support the front-line people so they can serve the customers better. And finally, at the base is top management whose job it is to support the middle managers so that they can support the front-line people who make all the difference in whether the customers end up feeling satisfied with the company. We have added customers along the sides of the figure to indicate that all the managers in the company are personally involved in knowing, meeting, and serving customers.

Profitability   The purpose of the marketing concept is to help organizations achieve their goals. In the case of private firms, the major goal is profit; in the case of nonprofit and public organizations, it is surviving and attracting enough funds to perform their work. Now the

FIGURE 1-7
The "Correct" View of the Company Organization Chart

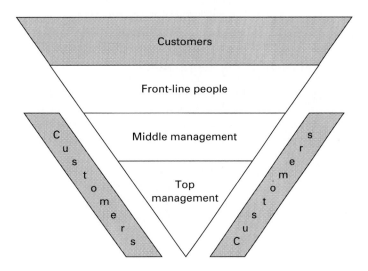

key is not to aim for profits as such but to achieve them as a byproduct of doing the job well. The General Motors executive who said, "We're in the business of making money, not cars," is misplacing the emphasis. A company makes money by satisfying customer needs better than competitors can. The job is not making money or cars but finding a profitable way to satisfy some target group's wants for personal transportation.

> The importance of satisfying customers is dramatically illustrated by Perdue Farms, a one-billion-dollar chicken business whose margins are substantially above the industry average and whose market shares in its major markets reach 50 percent. And the product is chicken—a commodity if there ever was one. Yet its colorful founder, Frank Perdue, does not believe that "a chicken is a chicken is a chicken," nor do his customers. His theme is, "It takes a tough man to make a tender chicken," and he offers a money-back guarantee to dissatisfied customers. He is so devoted to producing quality chickens that his customers pay a price premium to buy them. His attitude is that if one works toward superior product quality and business integrity, the profits, market share, and growth will take care of themselves. ∎

This is not to say that marketers are unconcerned with profits. Quite the contrary, they are highly involved in analyzing the profit potential of different marketing opportunities. Whereas salespeople focus on achieving sales-volume goals, marketing people focus on identifying profit-making opportunities. The following story vividly clarifies the difference between an order taker, a salesperson, and a marketer:

> A shoe company sent its financial officer to an African country to see if the company could sell its shoes there. In a few days, the officer wired back: "The people here don't wear shoes. There is no market."

> The shoe company president decided to send its best salesman to the country to doublecheck on this. After a week, the salesman wired back: "The people here don't wear shoes. There is a tremendous market"

> The shoe company president next sent the marketing vice-president to assess the situation. After two weeks, the marketing vice-president wired back: "The people here don't wear shoes. However, they have bad feet and could benefit from wearing shoes. We would have to redesign our shoes, however, because they have smaller feet. We would have to invest in educating the people about the benefits of wearing shoes. We would need to gain the tribal chief's cooperation before we could begin. The people don't have any money, but they grow the sweetest pineapples I've ever tasted. I've estimated the potential sales over a three-year period and all of our costs, including selling the pineapples to a European supermarket chain that can pay us in dollars, and concluded that we could make a 30 percent return on our money. I say that we should go ahead." ∎

Clearly, the marketing vice-president not only wore a marketing hat—he noticed a need and a way to satisfy it—but also wore a financial hat. He is in the business of creating profitable customers.

All four pillars of the marketing concept—market focus, customer orientation, coordinated marketing, and profitability—are admirably illustrated in the story of how Scandinavian Airlines recovered its fortunes through the marvelous market-oriented leadership provided by its new president, Jan Carlzon (see Marketing Strategies 1-2).

But how many companies have actually implemented the marketing concept? The answer is, too few. Only a handful of companies really stand out as master practitioners of the marketing concept: Procter & Gamble, IBM, Hewlett-Packard, Avon, McDonald's, Marriott Hotels, and Caterpillar, as well as some Japanese and European companies.

How Jan Carlzon "Marketized" SAS

When Jan Carlzon took over as president of SAS, now Scandinavian Airlines, in 1980, the airline was losing money. For some previous years, management had faced this problem by cutting costs. Carlzon saw that as the wrong solution: the airline needed to find new ways to compete and build its revenue. SAS had been pursuing all travelers with no focus and no superior advantage to offer to anyone; in fact, it was seen as one of the least punctual carriers in Europe. Competition had increased so much that Carlzon had to figure out:

- Who are our customers?
- What are their needs?
- What must we do to win their preference?

Carlzon decided that the answer was to focus SAS's services on *frequent-flying business people* and their needs. But he recognized that other airlines were trying to attract the same segment. They were offering wider seats, free drinks, and other amenities. SAS had to find a way to do this better if it was to be the preferred airline for the frequent business traveler. The starting point was market research to find out what frequent business travelers wanted and expected in the way of airline service. His goal was to find ways to be 1 percent better in one hundred details rather than 100 percent better in only one detail.

The market research showed that the number-one priority of business travelers was on-time arrival. Business travelers also wanted to check in fast and be able to retrieve their luggage fast. Carlzon appointed dozens of task forces to come up with ideas for improving these and other services. They came back with hundreds of projects, of which 150 were selected at an implementation cost of $40 million.

One of the key projects was to train a total customer orientation into all SAS's personnel. Carlzon figured that the average passenger came into contact with five SAS employees on an average trip. Each interaction created "a moment of truth" about SAS. Given the five million passengers per year flying SAS, this amounted to twenty-five million moments of truth where the airline either satisfied or dissatisfied its customers. To create the right customer attitudes within the company, the airline sent ten thousand front-line staff to service seminars for two days and twenty-five thousand managers to three-week courses. Carlzon regarded the front-line people who met the customers as the most important people in the company. As for managers, their role was to help the front-line people do their job well. And his role as president was to help the managers support the front-line employees.

The result: within four months, SAS achieved the record as the most punctual airline in Europe, and it has maintained this record since. Check-in systems are much faster, including a service where travelers who are staying at Scandinavian Airlines hotels can have their luggage sent directly to the airport and airplane for loading. Scandinavian Airlines does a much faster job of unloading luggage upon landing. Another innovation is that it sells all tickets as business class unless the traveler wants economy class. The airline's improved reputation among business flyers led to an increase in its European full-fare traffic of 8 percent and its full-fare intercontinental travel of 16 percent, quite an accomplishment considering that price cutting and zero growth were taking place in the air travel market.

Carlzon's impact on Scandinavian Airlines illustrates the customer satisfaction and profits that a corporate leader can achieve when he or she creates a vision and mission for the company that excites and gets the personnel to all swim in the same direction—namely toward satisfying the target customers.

These companies focus on the customer and are organized to respond effectively to changing customer needs. Not only do they have well-staffed marketing departments, but their other departments—manufacturing, finance, research and development, personnel, purchasing—all accept the concept that the customer is king. These organizations have a marketing culture that has deep roots in all of their departments and divisions.

Most companies have not arrived at full marketing maturity. They *think* they have marketing because they have a marketing vice-president, product managers, a salesforce, advertising budgets, and so on. *But a marketing department does not assure a market-oriented company.* The company has marketing operations, and yet it may fail to see the big picture and adapt to changing customer needs and changing competiton. International Harvester was on the verge of bankruptcy; Chrysler almost collapsed; and companies like Harley Davidson, Xerox, Singer, and Zenith, one-time leaders in their respective fields, all lost substantial market shares to Japanese competitors.

Most companies do not really grasp or embrace the marketing concept until driven to it by circumstances. Any of the following developments might prod them:

☐ *Sales decline*: When companies experience falling sales, they panic and look frantically for answers. For example, newspapers have experienced falling circulation as more people turn to television news. Some publishers are realizing that they know very little about why people read newspapers and what they want out of newspapers. These publishers are commissioning consumer research and attempting to redesign newspapers to be contemporary, relevant, and interesting to readers.

☐ *Slow growth*: Slow sales growth will lead some companies to cast about for new markets. They realize that they need marketing know-how if they are to identify, evaluate, and select new opportunities successfully. Dow Chemical, wanting new sources of revenue, decided to enter consumer markets and invested heavily in acquiring marketing expertise to perform well in the markets.

☐ *Changing buying patterns*: Many companies operate in markets characterized by rapidly changing customer wants. These companies need more marketing know-how if they are to continue producing value for buyers.

☐ *Increasing competition*: Complacent companies may suddenly be attacked by powerful marketing companies and forced to learn marketing to meet the challenge. Bell Canada remained a regulated monopoly until the 1970s when competing equipment producers were permitted to connect their equipment to Bell's lines. Faced with the new competition, Bell brought out new equipment, opened retail stores, and reorganized to facilitate the development of new non-regulated enterprises.

☐ *Increasing marketing expenditures*: Companies may find their expenditures for advertising, sales promotion, marketing research, and customer service getting out of hand. Management then decides it is time to undertake a *marketing performance assessment* and to improve their marketing.[23]

In the course of converting to a market-oriented company, a company will face three hurdles—organized resistance, slow learning, and fast forgetting.

Organized Resistance   Some company departments, often manufacturing, finance, and R&D, do not like to see marketing built up because it threatens their power in the organization. The nature of the threat is illustrated in Figure 1-8. Initially, the marketing function is seen as one of several equally important business functions in a check-and-balance relationship (Fig. 1-8[a]). A dearth of demand then leads marketers to argue that their function is somewhat more important than the others (Fig. 1-8[b]). A few marketing enthusiasts go further and say marketing is the major function of the enterprise, for without customers, there would be no company. They put marketing at the center, with other business functions serving as support functions (Fig. 1-8[c]). This view incenses the other managers, who do not want to think of themselves as working for marketing. Enlightened marketers clarify the issue by putting the customer rather than marketing at the center of the company (Fig. 1-8[d]). They argue for a *customer orientation* in which all functions work together to sense, serve, and satisfy the customer. Finally, some marketers say that marketing still needs to command a central company position if customers' needs are to be correctly interpreted and efficiently satisfied (Fig. 1-8[e]).

The marketer's argument for the business view shown in Figure 1-8(e) is as follows:

1. The assets of the firm have little value without the existence of customers.
2. The key task of the firm is therefore to attract and retain customers.
3. Customers are attracted through competitively superior offers and retained through satisfaction.
4. Marketing's task is to define a superior offer to the customer and to ensure the delivery of satisfaction.
5. The satisfaction actually received by the customer is affected by the performance of the other departments.
6. Marketing needs influence or control over these other departments if customers are to receive the expected satisfaction.

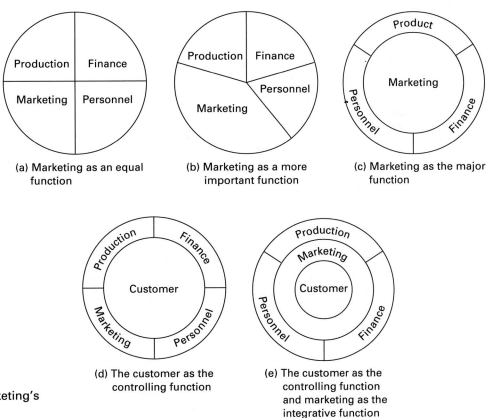

(a) Marketing as an equal function

(b) Marketing as a more important function

(c) Marketing as the major function

(d) The customer as the controlling function

(e) The customer as the controlling function and marketing as the integrative function

FIGURE 1-8
Evolving Views of Marketing's Role in the Company

FIVE STAGES IN THE SLOW LEARNING OF BANK MARKETING

Years ago, bankers had little understanding of or regard for marketing. Banks were supplying needed services. Bankers did not have to make a case for checking accounts, savings, loans, or safe-deposit boxes. The bank building was created in the image of a Greek temple, calculated to impress the public with the bank's importance and solidity. The interior was austere, and the tellers rarely smiled. One lending officer arranged his office so that a prospective borrower would sit across from his massive desk on a lower chair than his own. The office window was located behind the officer's back, and the sun would pour in on the hapless customer, who tried to explain why he or she needed a loan. This was the bank's posture before the age of marketing.

1. Marketing Is Advertising, Sales Promotion, and Publicity

Marketing came into banks not in the form of the "marketing concept" but in the form of the "advertising and promotion concept." Banks were facing increased competition for savings. A few banks started to do heavy advertising and sales promotion. They offered umbrellas, radios, and other "come-ons" and attracted new customer accounts. Their competitors were forced to adopt the same measures and scurried out to hire advertising agencies and sales-promotion experts.

2. Marketing Is Smiling and a Friendly Atmosphere

The banks that first initiated advertising and sales promotion soon found their advantage dissipated by the rush of imitators. They also learned that attracting people to a bank is easy; converting them into loyal customers is hard. These banks began to formulate programs to please the customer. Bankers learned to smile. The bars were removed from the tellers' windows. The bank interior was redesigned to produce a warm, friendly atmosphere. Even the outside Greek-temple architecture was changed.

These banks began to outperform their competitors in attracting and holding new customers. Their competitors, however, quickly launched similar programs of friendliness training and decor improvement. Soon all banks were so friendly that friendliness lost its decisiveness as a factor in bank choice.

3. Marketing Is Innovation

Banks found a new differential advantage when they realized that they were in the business of meeting the changing financial needs of their customers. They began to innovate new banking products, such as credit cards, Christmas savings plans, and automatic bank loans. Today, Canadian banks offer their customers dozens of financial products. But financial services are easily copied, so the innovating bank's advantage is short-lived. Only by innovating continuously can a bank stay ahead of its competition.

4. Marketing Is Positioning

What happens when all banks advertise, smile, and innovate? Clearly they begin to look alike. They are forced to find a new basis for distinction. They begin to realize that no bank can offer all products and be the best bank for all customers. A bank must choose. It must examine its opportunities and "take a position" in the market.

Positioning goes beyond image making. The image-making bank seeks to cultivate an image in the customer's mind as a large, friendly, or efficient bank. It may develop a symbol such as the Royal Bank's lion, to dramatize its personality in a distinctive way. Yet the customer may see the competing banks as basically alike, except for the chosen symbols.

Positioning is an attempt to distinguish the bank from its competitors in terms of service attributes that really matter. By helping consumers to recognize the relevant differences between banks, the positioning bank hopes to become the preferred bank.

In spite of this argument, marketing is still resisted in many quarters. The resistance is especially strong in industries where marketing is being introduced or proposed for the first time, for instance, in law offices, colleges, hospitals, or government agencies. Colleges have to face the hostility of professors, and hospitals have to face the hostility of doctors, because each group thinks that "marketing" their service would be degrading. In the newspaper industry, the hostility of oldtimers is shown by one newspaper editor who wrote a diatribe entitled "Beware the 'Market' Thinkers."[24] This editor warned newspapers not to let marketers in because they do not understand the function of newspapers, which is to print news. Marketing is not the solution, he feels, to the national decline in newspaper readership. Marketers would destroy all that is good about today's newspapers.

Slow Learning   In spite of some resistance, many companies manage to build up the marketing function in their organization. The company president gives enthusiastic support to the function; new job positions are created; outside marketing talent is hired; key members of management attend marketing seminars to gain a deeper understanding of marketing; the marketing budget is substantially increased; marketing planning and control systems are introduced. Even with these steps, however, the learning as to what marketing really is comes slowly. In the typical company, marketing enlightenment tends to pass through five stages. These stages are described for the banking industry in the exhibit Companies and Industries 1-1.

Fast Forgetting   Even after effective marketing is installed in an organization and matures through the various stages, management must fight a strong tendency to forget basic marketing principles. Management tends to forget marketing principles in the wake of marketing success. For example, a number of major companies entered European markets in the 1950s and 1960s expecting to achieve outstanding success with their sophisticated products and marketing capabilities. A number of them failed, and a major reason is that they forgot the marketing maxim: *Know your target market and know how to satisfy it*. The companies came into these markets with their current products and advertising programs instead of redesigning them on the basis of what each market needed. For example, General Mills went into the British market with its Betty Crocker cake mixes only to have to withdraw a short time later. Their angel cake and devil's food cake sounded too exotic for British homemakers. And many potential customers felt that such perfect-looking cakes as those pictured on the Betty Crocker packages must be hard to make. The marketers failed to appreciate the major cultural variations between and even within European countries and the need to start where the target consumers were, not where their products were.

The Societal Marketing Concept

In recent years, some people have questioned whether the marketing concept is an appropriate organizational philosophy in an age of environmental deterioration, resource shortages, explosive population growth, world hunger and poverty, and neglected social services.[25] The question is whether companies that do an excellent job of sensing, serving, and satisfying individual consumer wants are necessarily acting in the best long-run interests of consumers and society. The marketing concept sidesteps the potential conflicts between *consumer wants, consumer interests*, and *long-run societal welfare*.

Consider the following criticisms:

> The fast-food hamburger industry offers tasty but not nutritious food. The hamburgers have a high fat content, and the restaurants promote fries and pies, two products high in starch and fat. In satisfying consumer wants, they may be hurting consumer health. ∎

> The auto industry traditionally catered to the demand for large automobiles, but meeting this desire resulted in high fuel consumption, heavy pollution, more fatal accidents to those in small cars, and higher auto purchase and repair costs. ∎

> The soft-drink industry has catered to the consumer's desire for convenience by increasing the share of one-way disposable bottles. However, the one-way bottle represents a great waste of resources in that approximately seventeen bottles are necessary where formerly one two-way bottle made seventeen trips before it was damaged; many one-way bottles are not biodegradable; and these bottles often litter the environment. ∎

> The detergent industry catered to the consumer's passion for cleaner clothes by offering a product that polluted rivers and streams, killed fish, and injured recreational opportunities. ∎

These situations called for a new concept that revised or replaced the marketing concept. Among the proposals are "the human concept," "the intelligent consumption concept," and "the ecological imperative concept," all of which get at different aspects of the same problem.[26] We propose calling it the societal marketing concept.

> *The* societal marketing concept *holds that the organization's task is to determine the needs, wants, and interests of target markets and to deliver the desired satisfactions more effectively and efficiently than competitors in a way that preserves or enhances the consumer's and the society's well-being.*

The societal marketing concept calls upon marketers to balance three considerations in setting their marketing policies, namely, *company profits, consumer want satisfaction*, and *public interest*. Originally, companies based their marketing decisions largely on immediate company profit calculations. Then they began to recognize the long-run importance of satisfying consumer wants, and this introduced the marketing concept. Now they are beginning to factor in society's interests in their decision making. The societal marketing concept calls for balancing all three considerations. A number of companies have achieved notable sales and profit gains through adopting and practicing the societal marketing concept. Here is an example:

> Giant Food, Inc., a leading supermarket chain took the initiative during the consumerist era in the seventies and introduced unit pricing, open dating, and nutritional labeling. The company assigned

home economists to its stores to help consumers buy and prepare food more intelligently. It invited Esther Peterson, an advisor on consumer affairs, to join the board of directors and provide guidance on consumer-oriented retailing. According to a spokesman for the company, "These actions have improved Giant's goodwill immeasurably and have earned the admiration of leaders of the consumer movement." ■

THE RAPID ADOPTION OF MARKETING MANAGEMENT

Marketing management today is a subject of growing interest in all sizes and types of organizations within and outside the business sector in all kinds of countries.

In the Business Sector

In the business sector, marketing entered the consciousness of different companies at different times. General Electric, General Motors, Procter & Gamble, and Coca-Cola were among the early leaders. Marketing spread most rapidly in consumer packaged-goods companies, consumer durables companies, and industrial-equipment companies—in that order. Producers of commodities like steel, chemicals, and paper came later to marketing consciousness, and many still have a long way to go. Within the past decade consumer-service firms, especially airlines and banks, have moved toward modern marketing. Marketing is beginning to attract the interest of insurance and stock-brokerage companies, although they also have a long way to go in applying marketing effectively.

The most recent business groups to take an interest in marketing are professional service providers, such as lawyers, accountants, physicians, and architects.[27] Professional societies until recently, prohibited their members from engaging in price competition, client solicitation, and advertising. But these restraints are being gradually relaxed, and professionals are increasingly showing an interest in marketing.

> The fierce competition engendered by the new limits on corporate growth is forcing accounting firms into aggressive new postures. . . . The accountants insist on referring to their efforts to drum up business as "practice development." But many of the activities that fall under this euphemism are dead ringers for what is called "marketing" in other fields. . . . Accountants speak of "positioning" their firms and of "penetrating" unexploited new industries. They compile "hit lists" of prospective clients and then "surround" them by placing their firms' partners in close social contact with the top executives of the target companies.[28]

In the Nonprofit Sector

Marketing is increasingly attracting the interest of nonprofit organizations such as colleges, hospitals, museums and orchestras. These organizations have marketplace problems. Their administrators are struggling to keep them functioning in the face of changing consumer attitudes and diminishing financial resources.

Consider the following examples:

□ St. Lawrence College analyzed the continuing education needs of the Kingston area to design new course offerings. During a subsequent province-wide downturn in college registrations, St. Lawrence was one of the few colleges that continued to grow.

□ Via Rail conducted on-board surveys of travelers needs and wants. The subsequent introduction of a complimentary snack was accompanied by a significant increase in patronage.

☐ The Vancouver Symphony surveyed its audience. The resulting information enabled management to reappraise its marketing mix, including programming, concert scheduling, ticket pricing and distribution, and promotional messages and media.

In the International Sector

Many international companies are investing heavily in improving their marketing skills. In fact, several European and Japanese multinationals—companies like Nestlé, Beecham, Volvo, Olivetti, Unilever, Nixdorf, Toyota, and Sony—have in many cases understood marketing better and outperformed their domestic competitors. Multinationals have introduced and spread modern marketing practices throughout the world. This trend has prodded smaller domestic companies in various countries to start looking into ways to strengthen their marketing muscle so they can compete effectively with the multinationals.

In socialist economies, marketing has traditionally had a bad name, even though some public-sector agencies carried on some limited marketing research and advertising. But total public ownership and control produced economic stagnation. Mikhail Gorbachev recognized this problem and initiated two revolutionary policies, namely *perestroika* (economic restructuring) and *glasnost* (political openness). These policies spread to the other Eastern Bloc countries, and they undertook a major effort to convert their centrally planned economies into market-driven economies. The challenge is enormous and this conversion will take years if not decades to achieve. Countries in the West and the Far East—notably the U.S., Japan, and West Germany—are giving economic aid, and individual companies in the West are exploring the potentially large market opportunities that lie in trading and investing in Eastern European countries.[29]

SUMMARY

Companies cannot survive today by simply doing a good job. They must do an excellent job if they are to succeed in markets characterized by slow growth and fierce competition at home and abroad. Consumer and business buyers face an abundance of suppliers in seeking to satisfy their needs and therefore look for excellence in quality, value, or cost when they choose their suppliers. Recent studies have demonstrated that the key to profitable company performance is knowing and satisfying target customers with competitively superior offers. And marketing is the company function charged with defining customer targets and the best way to satisfy their needs and wants competitively and profitably.

Marketing has its origins in the fact that humans are creatures of needs and wants. Needs and wants create a state of discomfort, which is resolved through acquiring products that satisfy these needs and wants. Since many products can satisfy a given need, product choice is guided by the concepts of value, cost, and satisfaction. These products are obtainable in several ways: self-production, coercion, begging, and exchange. Most modern societies work on the principle of exchange, which means that people specialize in producing particular products and trade them for the other things they need. They engage in transactions and relationship building. A market is a group of people who share a similar need. Marketing encompasses those activities involved in working with markets, that is, in trying to actualize potential exchanges.

Marketing management is the conscious effort to achieve desired exchange outcomes with target markets. The marketer's basic skill lies in influencing the level, timing, and composition of demand for a product, service, organization, place, person, or idea.

Five alternative philosophies can guide organizations in carrying out their marketing work. The production concept holds that consumers will favor products that are affordable and available, and therefore management's major task is to improve production and distribution efficiency and bring down prices. The product concept holds that consumers favor quality products that are reasonably priced, and therefore little promotional effort is required. The selling concept holds that consumers will not buy enough of the company's products unless they are stimulated through a substantial selling and promotion effort. The marketing concept holds that the main task of the company is to determine the needs, wants, and preferences of a target group of customers and to deliver the desired satisfactions. Its four principles are market focus, customer orientation, coordinated marketing, and profitability. The societal marketing concept holds that the main task of the company is to generate customer satisfaction and long-run consumer and societal well-being as the key to satisfying organizational goals and responsibilities.

Interest in marketing is intensifying as more organizations in the business sector, the non-profit sector, and the international sector recognize how marketing contributes to improved performance in the marketplace.

■ QUESTIONS

1. A managing director of a large company made the following statement: "To be successful in business, all you need is a customer. You don't need any of those tight little academic concepts of how to manage. You don't even need to solve all of your problems or be efficient. All you need is to find out what you do right for the customer you've already got and do more of it." Assess the validity of this statement.

2. How does relationship marketing differ from "conventional" marketing? Does L.L. Bean practice relationship marketing? (See Marketing Concepts and Tools 1.1)

3. Discuss the difference between a *need* and a *want* as they might be expressed for computers. Why is such a distinction important to a computer manufacturer?

4. During the early 1980s many auto dealerships went out of business. William Turnbull, president of the National Automobile Dealers Association, stated that if the remaining dealers were to survive, they must change their orientation toward consumers. What might he have meant by that statement?

5. Does the marketing concept imply that marketers should confine themselves only to those wants and needs that consumers say they want to satisfy?

6. Is there a contradiction between marketing something that has negative demand and practicing the marketing concept?

7. Do all companies need to practice the marketing concept? Could you cite companies that do not need this orientation? Which companies need it most?

8. "Marketing is the science of actualizing the buying potentials of a market for a specific product." Does this definition reflect a product, selling, or marketing concept?

9. "Marketing is not simply the job of a group of people in the company who are responsible for selling the company's products. Every member of the firm should function as a marketer." What does it mean for a company recruiter, for example, to function as a marketer?

10. The five stages through which organizations pass as they develop an understanding of marketing were discussed in connection with the banking industry. Discuss them in the context of four-year liberal arts faculties that are facing declining enrolment.

■ NOTES

1. Thomas J. Peters and Robert H. Waterman, Jr., *In Search of Excellence: Lessons from America's Best-Run Companies* (New York: Harper & Row, 1982).

2. Thomas J. Peters and Nancy Austin, *A Passion for Excellence: The Leadership Difference* (New York: Random House, 1985); and Peters, *Thriving on Chaos* (New York: Knopf, 1987).

3. *The IBM Way: Insights into the World's Most Successful Marketing Organization* (New York: Harper & Row, 1985).

4. Milind M. Lele with Jagdish N. Sheth, *The Customer Is Key: Gaining an Unbeatable Advantage through Customer Satisfaction* (New York: John Wiley, 1987); Valarie A. Zeithaml, A. Parasutaman, and Leonard J. Berry, *Delivering Quality Service* (New York: Free Press, 1990); and Donald K. Clifford, Jr., and Richard E. Cavanaugh, *The Winning Performance: How America's High-Growth Midsize Companies Succeed* (New York: Bantam Books, 1985).

5. "Business Planning in the Eighties: The New Competitiveness of American Corporations," a study conducted by Yankelovich, Skelly & White for Coopers and Lybrand, 1984.

6. See E. S. Ely, "Room at the Top: American Companies Turn to Marketers to Lead Them through the '80s," *Madison Avenue*, September 1984, p. 57.

7. *Ibid.*

8. For various definitions, see note 10.

9. The above statistics were taken from several sources, including: *Canadian Economic Observer*, Statistics Canada, April 1991, p. 11.1; *Canada Yearbook 1990*, Statistics Canada (Supply and Services Canada); *Annual Radio & Television Broadcasting 1989*, Statistics Canada, Cat. 56-204; *National Income & Expenditure Accounts*, Quarterly estimates 1983 Q1-1990 Q4, Ottawa, April 1991.

10. See Theodore Levitt's classic article, "Marketing Myopia," *Harvard Business Review*, July-August 1960, pp. 45-56.

11. Here are some other useful definitions of marketing (management):
Marketing is the process by which an organization relates creatively, productively, and profitably to the marketplace.
Marketing is the art of creating and satisfying customers at a profit.
Marketing is getting the right goods and services to the right people at the right places at the right time at the right price with the right communications and promotion.

12. See "Texas Instruments Shows U.S. Business How to Survive in the 1980s," *Business Week*, September 18, 1978, pp. 66 ff. But TI was not entirely successful with this strategy, especially in launching watches and personal computers in the consumer market. See "When Marketing Failed at Texas Instruments," *Business Week*, June 22, 1981, pp. 91-94.

13. Emerson originated this advice: "If a man . . . makes a better mousetrap . . . the world will beat a path to his door." Several companies, however, have built better mousetraps—one was a laser mousetrap costing $1500—and most of these companies failed. People do not automatically

14. See Lee Smith, "A Miracle in Search of a Market," *Fortune*, December 1, 1980, pp. 92-98.

15. See Irving J. Rein, *Rudy's Red Wagon: Communication Strategies in Contemporary Society* (Glenview, Ill.: Scott, Foresman, 1972).

16. See Joseph McGinniss, *The Selling of the President* (New York: Trident Press, 1969); and the special political advertising issue of the *Journal of Advertising* 13, no. 3 (1984).

17. *Management: Tasks, Responsibilities, Practices* (New York: Harper & Row, 1973), pp. 64-65.

18. See John B. McKitterick, "What Is the Marketing Management Concept?" *The Frontiers of Marketing Thought and Action* (Chicago: American Marketing Association, 1957), pp. 71-82; Fred J. Borch, "The Marketing Philosophy as a Way of Business Life," *The Marketing Concept: Its Meaning to Management*, marketing series, no. 99 (New York: American Management Association, 1957), pp. 3-5; and Robert J. Keith, "The Marketing Revolution," *Journal of Marketing*, January 1960, pp. 35-38.

19. Levitt, "Marketing Myopia," p. 50.

20. See Karl Albrecht and Ron Zemke, *Service America!* (Homewood, Ill.: Dow-Jones-Irwin, 1985), pp. 6 -7.

21. *Ibid.*

22. *Ibid.*

23. For a discussion of the instrument, see Thomas V. Bonoma and Bruce H. Clark, *Marketing Performance Assessment* (Boston: Harvard Business School Press, 1988).

24. William H. Hornby, "Beware the 'Market' Thinkers," *The Quill*, 1976, pp. 14 ff.

25. See Lawrence P. Feldman, "Societal Adaptation: A New Challenge for Marketing," *Journal of Marketing*, July 1971, pp. 54-60; and Martin L. Bell and C. William Emery, "The Faltering Marketing Concept," *Journal of Marketing*, October 1971, pp. 37-42; and Franklin S. Houston, "The Marketing Concept: What It Is and What It Is Not," *Journal of Marketing*, April 1986, pp. 81-87.

26. Leslie M. Dawson, "The Human Concept: New Philosophy for Business," *Business Horizons*, December 1969, pp. 29-38; James T. Rothe and Lissa Benson, "Intelligent Consumption: An Attractive Alternative to the Marketing Concept," *MSU Business Topics*, Winter 1974, pp. 29-34; and George Fisk, "Criteria for a Theory of Responsible Consumption," *Journal of Marketing*, April 1973, pp. 24-31.

learn about new products, believe in their superiority, or willingly pay a higher price.

27. See Philip Kotler and Paul Bloom, *Marketing Professional Services* (Englewood Cliffs, N.J.: Prentice-Hall, 1984).

28. Deborah Rankin, "How C.P.A.'s Sell Themselves," *New York Times*, September 25, 1977.

29. See Padma Desia, *Perestroika in Perspective: The Design and Dilemmas of Soviet Reform* (Princeton, N.J.: Princeton University Press, 1989); and Wolfgang J. Koschnick, "Russian Bear Bullish on Marketing," *Marketing News*, November 21, 1988, p. 1.

Laying the Groundwork Through Strategic Planning

There are three types of companies: those who make things happen; those who watch things happen; those who wonder what happened.

Anonymous

In Chapter 1, we raised the question: "What makes a company excellent?" We found that a large part of the answer is that the company's employees are committed to creating satisfied customers. We can now add a second part to the answer, namely that excellent companies know how to adapt and respond to a continuously changing marketplace. They practice the art of *market-oriented strategic planning*. We define strategic planning as follows:

> Strategic planning *is the managerial process of developing and maintaining a viable fit between the organization's* objectives *and* resources *and its changing* market opportunities. *The aim of strategic planning is to shape and reshape the company's businesses and products so that they combine to produce satisfactory profits and growth.*

Strategic planning and its collection of concepts and tools did not surface until the early 1970s. In the fifties and sixties, Canadian management could pretty much get by with operations planning. With the steady growth of total demand, it was hard for even poor management to make a mess of a business. Then the turbulent seventies erupted. There was a succession of crises: Oil prices shot up following the Yom Kippur war; material and energy shortages ensued, along with double-digit inflation; then economic stagnation and rising unemployment set in. Low cost, high-quality foreign goods from Japan and elsewhere started to pour into North America, taking share away from several Canadian industries, such as steel, autos, office copiers, and cameras. Still later, business firms had to cope with a growing wave of deregulation in such key industries as telecommunications, transportation, and some professional associations. Firms that had played by the old rules now faced intense competition at home and abroad that challenged their time-honored business practices.

This succession of shock waves called for a new management planning process that would keep firms healthy in spite of upsets occurring in any one of their businesses or product lines. Three key ideas defined the new planning process. The first called for managing a company's businesses as an *investment portfolio*. The question became, Which business entities deserve to be *built, maintained, phased down* (harvested, milked), or *terminated*? This question is especially critical when a company no longer commands enough funds to finance all of its current businesses, as happened to many firms in the seventies. In this situation, it does not make sense for a company to reduce its support proportionately to all businesses. Each business has a different profit potential. The company should reallocate its resources to its more promising businesses.

The second key idea is to assess accurately the *future profit potential* of each business. The firm can no longer build forecasts by naively extrapolating past business trends. The firm has to develop more analytical scenarios of future conditions in each market. It is not sufficient to use current sales or profits as a guide to which businesses the company should support. For example:

> If the Ford Motor Company used current profits as a guide to investment in the seventies, it would have continued to pour money into large cars, since that was where it made its money. But Ford's analysis showed that the profits on large cars would dry up, and therefore Ford needed to reallocate its funds to improving its compact cars, even though the company was losing money on compact cars at the time. ■

The third key idea underlying strategic planning is that of *strategy*. For each of its businesses, the company must develop a "game plan" for achieving its long-run objectives. Furthermore, there is no one strategy that is optimal for all competitors in that business. Each company must determine what makes the most sense in the light of its *industry position* and its *objectives, opportunities*, and *resources*. Here are vastly different game plans of four major companies operating in the rubber-tire industry:[1]

> Goodyear Tire & Rubber Co., the world's number one tire maker, is pouring money into this industry in spite of the industry's slow growth, overcapacity, and price wars. Goodyear is investing heavily in plant modernization to lower costs and improve quality, in R&D to develop more advanced tires, and in marketing to build up consumer and dealer preference. Goodyear is the world leader in tire sales with 23 percent of the market. It has had to defend its share in the face of Michelin's purchase of Uniroyal Goodrich and Bridgestone's purchase of Firestone. ■

> The French tire company Michelin rose to its high place by leading the industry in innovation. Michelin introduced the steelbelted radial tire, a tire that lasted longer than its competitors. Michelin's continuous innovation of better tires won it a high-quality image and allowed it to charge premium prices. Michelin recently purchased Uniroyal Goodrich Tire Company in its drive to challenge Goodyear for the number one position. ■

> Uniroyal Goodrich has chosen the route of diversification to reduce its dependence on the tire industry. Its strongest push is in two nontire businesses, agricultural chemicals and fabricated plastic products. ■

> Armstrong Rubber has decided to make tires for specialty markets. It has shown great skill in picking and exploiting specialized niches—tires for recreational vehicles and for farm equipment. "When you really excel in a market segment, you get paid for it," said Frank R. O'Keefe Jr., Armstrong's president. O'Keefe has sharpened Armstrong's strategic-planning process through which Armstrong identifies profitable market segments and prepares marketing programs to capture leadership in the chosen market segments. ■

All of these companies exhibit different adaptations to a rapidly changing environment. Each has adopted a different game plan: Goodyear is pressing for *cost reduction*; Michelin is

FIGURE 2-1
The Strategic Planning, Implementation, and Control Process

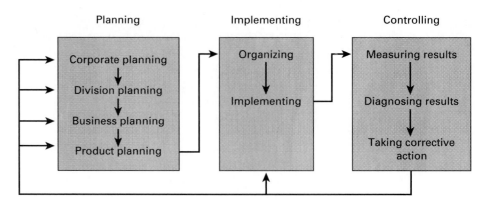

pursuing *innovation*; Uniroyal prefers *diversification*; and Armstrong is practicing *niche-manship*. Each strategy can be successful under the right circumstances.

Marketing plays a critical role in the company's strategic-planning process. According to a strategic-planning manager at General Electric:

> . . . the marketing manager is the most significant functional contributor to the strategic- planning process, with leadership roles in defining the business mission; analysis of the environmental, competitive, and business situations; developing objectives, goals, and strategies; and defining product, market, distribution, and quality plans to implement the business' strategies. This involvement extends to the development of programs and operating plans that are fully linked with the strategic plan.[2]

To understand strategic planning, we have to remember how the modern corporation is structured. Most large corporations consist of four organizational levels: the *corporate level, division level, business level,* and *product level*.[3] Corporate headquarters is responsible for designing a *corporate strategic plan* to guide the whole enterprise into a profitable future; it makes decisions on how much resource support to allocate to each division as well as which new businesses to start. Each division establishes *a division plan* covering the allocation of funds to each business unit within the division. Each business unit in turn develops a *business unit strategic plan* to carry that business unit into a profitable future. Finally, each product level (product line, brand) within a business unit develops a *marketing plan* for achieving its objectives in its product market. These plans are then implemented at the various levels of the organization, results are monitored and evaluated, and corrective actions are taken. The whole planning, implementation, and control cycle is shown in Figure 2-1.

In this chapter, we will examine the major concepts and tools for carrying out corporate strategic planning and business strategic planning. In the next chapter, we will focus on marketing planning and the overall marketing management process.

CORPORATE STRATEGIC PLANNING

Corporate headquarters has the responsibility for setting into motion the whole planning process. By preparing broad statements of mission, policy, and strategy, headquarters establishes the framework within which the individual business units prepare their business-level plans. Some corporations give a lot of freedom to their individual business units to set their own sales and profit goals and strategies; they require only that these business units deliver

FIGURE 2-2
The Corporate Strategic-
Planning Process

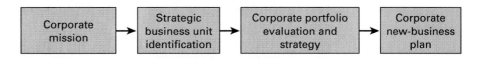

the promised performance. Other corporations set goals for their business units but let them develop their own strategies for achieving these goals. Still other corporations set the goals and get heavily involved in the strategies of the individual business units.[4]

Regardless of which management style the corporation pursues, all corporations must carry out the following four planning activities (see Figure 2-2):

□ Defining the corporate mission

□ Identifying the company's strategic business units (SBUs)

□ Analyzing and evaluating the current portfolio of businesses

□ Identifying new business arenas to enter

Corporate Mission

An organization exists to accomplish something in the larger environment. Its specific mission or purpose is usually clear at the beginning. Over time the mission may remain clear, but some managers may lose interest in it. Or the mission may remain clear but lose its relevance to the new conditions in the environment. Or the mission may become unclear as the organization grows and adds new products and markets. For example, Uniroyal is gradually moving out of the tire business and evidently redefining its mission.

When management senses that the organization is drifting, it must renew its search for purpose. According to Peter Drucker, it is time to ask some fundamental questions.[5] *What is our business? Who is the customer? What is value to the customer? What will our business be? What should our business be?* These simple-sounding questions are among the most difficult the company will ever have to answer. Successful companies continuously raise these questions and answer them thoughtfully and thoroughly.

The company's mission is shaped by five elements. The first is its *history*. Every company has a history of aims, policies, and achievements. In redefining its purpose, the organization must not depart too radically from its past history. It would not make sense for the University of Toronto, for example, to open vocational trade schools even if such schools represented a growth opportunity. The second consideration is the *current preferences* of the management and owners. Those who direct the company have their personal goals and visions. If Zenith's current management wants to get out of the television-receiver business, this is going to influence Zenith's mission statement. Third, *the market environment* influences the organization's mission. The market environment defines the main opportunities and threats that must be taken into account. The Girl Guides would not get far in today's environment with their former purpose of preparing young girls for traditional motherhood duties. Fourth, the organization's *resources* determine which missions are possible. Air Ontario would be deluding itself if it adopted the mission to become the world's largest airline. Finally, the organization should base its mission on its *distinctive competences*. McDonald's could probably enter the solar energy business, but that would not use its main competence— providing low-cost food and fast service to large groups of customers.

Organizations develop mission statements in order to share them with their managers, employees, and in many cases, customers and other publics. A well-worked-out mission statement provides company personnel with a shared sense of purpose, direction, and opportunity. The company mission statement acts as an "invisible hand" that guides geographically dispersed employees to work independently and yet collectively toward realizing the organization's goals.

Writing a formal mission statement is not easy. Some organizations spend a year or two trying to prepare a satisfactory statement about the purpose of their firm. In the process, they generally discover a lot about themselves and their potential opportunities.

Good mission statements embody a number of characteristics. They should focus on a limited number of goals rather than embracing everything. The statement "We want to produce the highest-quality products, offer the most service, achieve the widest distribution, and sell at the lowest prices" claims too much. It fails to supply guidelines when management faces difficult decisions.

The mission statement should define the major *competitive scopes* within which the corporation will operate.

- *Industry scope*: The range of industries that the corporation will consider. Some corporations will operate only in one industry, some in only a set of related industries, some in only industrial goods, consumer goods, or services, and finally some in any industry. For example, Du Pont prefers to operate in the industrial market whereas Dow is willing to operate in the industrial and consumer markets. 3M will get into almost any industry where it can make money.

- *Market-segment scope*: The type of market or customers the corporation will serve. Some corporations will serve only the upscale market in all their businesses (for example, Porsche makes only expensive cars, sunglasses, and other accessories). Gerber, for a long time, served only the baby market with its line of products.

- *Vertical scope*: The degree to which the corporation will produce its own needed supplies internally. At one extreme are corporations that produce many of their supplies internally, such as Ford, which owns its own rubber plantations, glass manufacturing plants, and some steel foundries. At the other extreme are corporations with low vertical integration, such as the "hollow corporation" or "pure marketing company," which consists of a person with a phone and a desk who contracts outside for every service including design, manufacture, marketing, and physical distribution.[6]

- *Geographical scope*: The range of regions, countries, or country groups where the corporation will operate. At one extreme are companies that operate in a specific city and at the other extreme are multinationals like Unilever or Caterpillar, which operate in almost every one of the world's 150-plus countries.

The company's mission statement should be *motivating*. Employees need to feel that their work is significant and contributes to people's lives. The mission should not be "to make profits." Profits are the result of accomplishing something useful *outside* the organization. When the prosaic task of producing fertilizer is reshaped into the larger idea of improving agricultural productivity to feed the world's hungry, a new sense of purpose is felt by the employees. When the task of selling vacuum cleaners is transformed into the larger idea of creating a cleaner and healthier home environment, salespeople feel more challenged. Profits are the reward for companies that do their basic job well.

The corporate mission statement should stress major *policies* that the company wants to honor. Policies define how employees should deal with customers, suppliers, distributors, competitors, and other important groups. Policies narrow the range of individual discretion, so that employees act consistently on important issues.

The company's mission statement should provide a vision and direction for the company for the next ten to twenty years. Missions are not revised every few years in response to every new turn in the economy. On the other hand, a company must redefine its mission if that mission has lost credibility or no longer defines an optimal course for the company.[7]

Strategic Business Unit Identification

Most companies, even small ones, operate several businesses. But these businesses may not all be obvious. A corporation with twelve operating divisions is not necessarily in twelve businesses. One division may in fact contain several businesses, as when the division produces different products for different customer groups. Sometimes two divisions may be so inter-related that they form a single business. Therefore companies must take the important step of identifying the businesses they are in, and managing each as a business.

Companies too often define their business in terms of a product they make. They will say they are in the "auto business" or the "slide-rule business," and so on. But this definition of a business is myopic. In his "Marketing Myopia," Levitt advanced the thesis that market definitions of a business were superior to product definitions of a business.[8] He argued that a business must be viewed as a *customer-satisfying process*, not a *goods-producing process*. Products are transient, but basic needs and customer groups endure forever. A horse-car-riage company will go out of business soon after the automobile is invented. But the same company, if it defines its purpose as that of providing transportation, will switch from making horse carriages to making cars. Levitt encouraged companies to shift their business-domain definition from a product to a market focus. Several examples are given in Table 2-1.

In developing a market-based business definition, management should avoid a definition that is too narrow or too broad. Consider a lead-pencil manufacturer. If it sees itself as a *small-writing-instruments company*, it might expand into the production of pens and other small writing instruments. If it sees itself as a *writing-equipment company*, then it might also consider making typewriters and word-processing equipment. The broadest concept of its business is that it is a *communication company*, but this would be stretching things too far for a lead-pencil manufacturer.

> Holiday Inns, Inc., the world's largest hotel chain with over 300 000 rooms, fell into this trap. Some years ago it broadened its business definition from the "hotel business" to the "travel indus-try," of which hotels are only a part. It implemented this by acquiring a bus compnay and a steamship line. But after failing to manage its acquisitions well, the company decided to divest

Table 2-1 Product-Oriented Versus Market-Oriented Definitions of a Business

Company	Product-Oriented Definition	Market-Oriented Definition
Revlon	We make cosmetics	We sell hope.
Canadian Pacific	We run a railroad	We are a people-and-goods mover
Xerox	We make copying equipment	We help improve office productivity
Massey-Ferguson	We sell farm machinery	We help improve agricultural productivity
Imperial Oil	We sell gasoline	We supply energy
Encyclopedia Britannica	We sell encyclopedias	We are in the information-production and distribution business
Carrier	We make air conditioners and furnaces	We provide a comfortable climate in the home

them in 1978. Holiday Inns decided to stick to the "hospitality industry" and blanket this industry with alternative room and food systems.[9] ∎

A business can be defined, according to Abell, in terms of three dimensions: the *customer groups* that will be served, the *customer needs* that will be met, and the *technology* that will satisfy these needs.[10] Consider, for example, a small company that designs incandescent lighting systems for television studios. Its customer group is television studios; the customer need is lighting; and the technology is incandescent lighting. The company's business domain is defined by the floating cell in Figure 2-3. This diagram gives a very clear picture of the company's business.

The company might want to expand into additional businesses. For example, it could make lighting for other customer groups, such as homes, factories, and offices. Or it could supply other services needed by television studios, such as heating, ventilation, or air conditioning. Or it could design other lighting technologies for television studios, such as infrared or ultraviolet lighting. Each business is defined by the intersection of the three dimensions. If this company expands into other cells, we say that it has widened its business domain.

Companies have to identify their businesses in order to manage them strategically. General Electric went through this grueling exercise some years ago and identified forty-nine *strategic business units* (SBUs). An SBU has three characteristics:

1. It is a single business or collection of related businesses that can be planned separately from the rest of the company.

2. It has its own competitors, which it is trying to equal or surpass.

3. It has a responsible manager who is responsible for strategic planning and profit performance and who controls most of the factors affecting profit.

FIGURE 2-3
A Small Lighting
Company's Current
Definition of Its Business
Domain

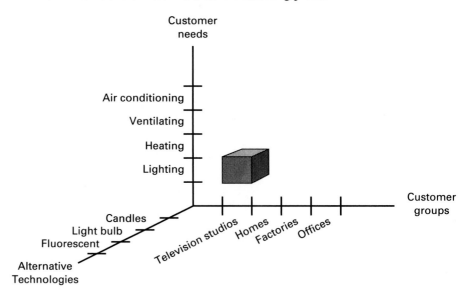

Evaluating the Current Business Portfolio

The purpose of identifying the corporation's strategic business units is to assign to these units strategic-planning goals and appropriate funding. These units send their plans to the corporation, which approves them or sends them back for revision. The corporation reviews these plans in order to decide which of its SBUs to *build, maintain, harvest,* and *divest.* Senior management knows that its portfolio of businesses includes a number of "yesterday's has beens" as well as "tomorrow's breadwinners." But it cannot rely just on impressions; it needs analytical tools for classifying its businesses by profit potential. In the past decade, several portfolio-evaluation models have come into widespread use. Two of the best known are the Boston Consulting Group model and the General Electric model.[11]

Boston Consulting Group Approach   The Boston Consulting Group (BCG), a leading management consulting firm, developed and popularized an approach known as the *growth-share matrix* shown in Figure 2-4. The eight circles represent the current sizes and positions of eight businesses making up a hypothetical company. The dollar-volume size of each business is proportional to the circle's area; thus the two largest businesses are 5 and 6. The location of each business indicates its market growth rate and relative market share.

Specifically, the *market growth rate* on the vertical axis indicates the annual growth rate of the market in which the business operates; in the figure, it ranges from 0 percent to 20 percent, although a larger range could be shown. A market growth rate above 10 percent is considered high.

The horizontal axis, *relative market share*, refers to the SBU's market share relative to that of the largest competitor. It serves as a measure of the company's strength in the relevant market. A relative market share of 0.1 means that the company's SBU sales volume is only 10 percent of the leader's sales volume; and 10 means that the company's SBU is the leader and has ten times the sales of the next-strongest company in the market. Relative market share is divided into high and low share, using 1.0 as the dividing line. Relative market share is drawn in log scale, so that equal distances represent the same percentage increase.

The growth-share matrix is divided into four cells, each indicating a different type of business:

FIGURE 2-4

The Boston Consulting Group's Growth-Share Matrix

Source: B. Heldey, "Strategy and the Business Portfolio," *Long Range Planning,* February 1977, p. 12. Reprinted with permission from *Long Range Planning,* copyright © 1977, Pergamon Press, Ltd.

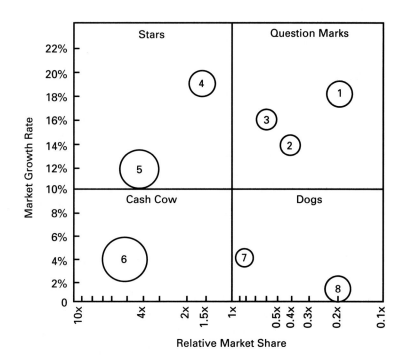

- *Question marks*: Question marks are company businesses that operate in high-growth markets but have low relative market shares. Most businesses start off as a question mark in that the company tries to enter a high-growth market in which there is already a market leader. A question mark requires a lot of cash, since the company has to keep adding plants, equipment, and personnel to keep up with the fast-growing market, and additionally, it wants to overtake the leader. The term question mark is well chosen because the company has to think hard about whether to keep pouring money into this business. The company in Figure 2-4 operates three question-mark businesses, and this may be too many. The company might be better off investing more cash in one or two of these businesses instead of spreading its cash thinly over all three businesses.

- *Stars*: If the question-mark business is successful, it becomes a star. A star is the market leader in a high-growth market. This does not necessarily mean that the star produces a positive cash flow for the company. The company must spend substantial funds to keep up with the high market growth and fight off competitors' attacks. Stars are usually profitable and become the company's future cash cows. In the illustration, the company has two stars. The company would justifiably be concerned if it had no stars.

- *Cash cows*: When a market's annual growth rate falls to less than 10 percent, the star becomes a cash cow if it still has the largest relative market share. A cash cow produces a lot of cash for the company. The company does not have to finance a lot of capacity expansion because the market's growth rate has slowed down. And since the business is the market leader, it enjoys economies of scale and higher profit margins. The company uses its cash-cow businesses to pay its bills and support the stars, question marks, and dogs, which tend to be cash hungry. In the illustration, however, the company has only one cash-cow business and is therefore highly vulnerable. In the event this cash cow starts losing relative market share, the company has to pump enough money back into its cash cow to maintain market leadership. If instead it uses the throw-off cash to support its other businesses, its strong cash cow may transform into a dog business.

- *Dogs*: Dogs are company businesses that have weak market shares in low-growth markets. They typically generate low profits or losses, although they may throw off some cash. The company in the illustration manages two dog businesses, and this may be two too many. The company should consider whether it is holding on to these dog businesses for good reasons (such as an expected turn-around in the market growth rate or a new chance at market leadership) or out of sentimental reasons. Dog businesses often consume more management time than they are worth and need to be phased down or out.

Having plotted its various businesses in the growth-share matrix, the company then determines whether its business portfolio is healthy. An unbalanced portfolio would have too many dogs or question marks and/or too few stars and cash cows.

The company's next task is to determine what objective, strategy, and budget to assign to each SBU. Four alternative objectives can be pursued:

- *Build*: Here the objective is to increase the SBU's market share, even foregoing short-term earnings to achieve this objective. "Building" is appropriate for question marks whose shares have to grow if they are to become stars.

- *Hold*: Here the objective is to preserve the SBU's market share. This objective is appropriate for strong cash cows if they are to continue to yield a large positive cash flow.

- *Harvest*: Here the objective is to increase the SBU's short-term cash flow regardless of the long-term effect. This strategy is appropriate for weak cash cows whose future is dim and from whom more cash flow is needed. Harvesting can also be used with question marks and dogs.

□ *Divest*: Here the objective is to sell or liquidate the business because resources can be better used elsewhere. That is appropriate for dogs and question marks that are acting as a drag on the company's profits.

As time passes, SBUs change their position in the growth-share matrix. Successful SBUs have a life cycle. They start as question marks, become stars, then cash cows, and finally dogs toward the end of their life cycle. For this reason, companies should examine not only the current positions of their businesses in the growth-share matrix (as in a snapshot) but also their moving positions (as in a motion picture). Each business should be reviewed as to where it was last year, the year before, and so on, and where it will probably move next year, the year after, and so on. If the expected trajectory of a given business is not satisfactory, the company should ask its business's manager to propose a new strategy and the likely resulting trajectory. Thus the growth-share matrix becomes a planning framework for the strategic planners at company headquarters. They use it to try to assess each business and assign the most reasonable objective.

Although the portfolio in Figure 2-4 is basically healthy, wrong objectives or strategies could be assigned. The worst mistake would be to require all the SBUs to aim for the same growth rate or return level; the very point of SBU analysis is that each business has a different potential and requires its own objective. Additional mistakes would include:

1. Leaving cash-cow businesses with too little in retained funds, in which case they grow weak; or leaving them with too much in retained funds, in which case the company fails to invest enough in new growth businesses.

2. Making major investments in dogs hoping to turn them around but failing each time.

3. Maintaining too many question marks and underinvesting in each; question marks should either receive enough support to achieve segment dominance or be dropped.

General Electric Approach   The appropriate objective to assign to an SBU cannot be determined solely on the basis of its position in the growth-share matrix. If additional factors are introduced, the growth-share matrix can be seen as a special case of a multifactor portfolio matrix that General Electric (GE) pioneered. This model is shown in Figure 2-5A, and seven businesses of a disguised company are plotted. This time the size of the circle represents the size of the relevant market rather than the size of the company's business. And the shaded part of the circle represents that business's market share. Thus the company's clutch business operates in a moderate-size market and enjoys approximately a 30 percent market share.

Each business is rated in terms of two major dimensions, *market attractiveness* and *competitive position*. These two factors make excellent marketing sense for rating a business. Companies will be successful to the extent that they go into attractive markets and possess the required competitive business strengths to succeed in those markets. If one or the other is missing, the business will not produce outstanding results. Neither a strong company operating in an unattractive market nor a weak company operating in an attractive market will do very well.

The real issue, then, is to measure these two dimensions. To do so, the strategic planners must identify the factors underlying each dimension and find a way to measure them and combine them into an index. Table 2-2 illustrates sets of factors making up the two dimensions. (Each company has to decide on its list of factors.) Thus market attractiveness varies with the market's size, annual market growth rate, historical profit margins, and so on. And competitive position varies with the company's market share, share growth, product quality, and so on. Note that the two BCG factors, market growth rate and market share, are subsumed under the two major variables of the GE model. The GE model leads strategic

FIGURE 2-5

Market Attractiveness—
Competitive-Position
Portfolio Classification and
Strategies

Source: Slightly modified and
adapted with permission from
Analysis for Strategic Marketing
Decisions by George S. Day
(St. Paul, Minn.: West
Publishing, 1986),
pp. 202 and 204.

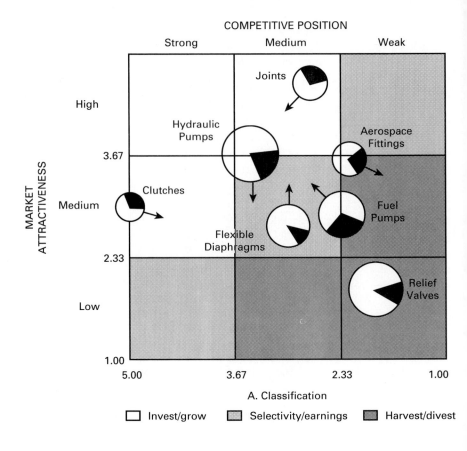

A. Classification

☐ Invest/grow   ▨ Selectivity/earnings   ▨ Harvest/divest

	Strong	Medium	Weak
High	PROTECT POSITION • invest to grow at maximum digestible rate • concentrate effort on maintaining strength	INVEST TO BUILD • challenge for leadership • build selectively on strengths • reinforce vulnerable areas	BUILD SELECTIVELY • specialize around limited strengths • seek way to overcome weaknesses • withdraw if indications of sustainable growth are lacking
Medium	BUILD SELECTIVELY • invest heavily in most attractive segments • build up ability to counter competition • emphasize profitability by raising productivity	SELECTIVITY/MANAGE FOR EARNINGS • protect existing program • concentrate investments in segments where profitability is good and risk is relatively low	LIMITED EXPANSION OR HARVEST • look for ways to expand without high risk; otherwise minimize investment and rationalize operations
Low	PROTECT AND REFOCUS • manage for current earnings • concentrate on attractive segments • defend strengths	MANAGE FOR EARNINGS • protect position in most profitable segments • upgrade product line • minimize investment	DIVEST • sell at time that will maximize cash value • cut fixed costs and avoid investment meanwhile

B. Strategies

planners to look at more factors in evaluating an actual or potential business than the BCG model.

Table 2-2 shows a hypothetical rating for the hydraulic-pumps business. Management rates each factor from 1 (very unattractive) to 5 (very attractive) to reflect how the business stands on that factor. In the illustration, the hydraulic-pumps business is rated 4.00 on over-all market size, indicating that the market size is pretty large (a 5.00 would be very large). Clearly, these factors require data and assessment from marketing and other company per-sonnel. The ratings are then multiplied by weights reflecting the factors' relative importance to arrive at the values, which are summed for each dimension. The hydraulic-pumps business scored a 3.70 on market attractiveness and a 3.40 on competitive position, out of a maxi-mum possible score of 5.00 for each. The analyst places a point in the multifactor matrix in Figure 2-5A representing this business and draws a circle around it whose size is propor-tional to the size of the relevant market. The company's market share of approximately 14 per-cent is shaded in. Clearly, the hydraulic-pumps business is in a fairly attractive part of the matrix.

Table 2-2 Factors Underlying Market Attractiveness and Competitive Position in GE Multifactor Portfolio Model: Hydraulic-Pumps Market

		Weight	Rating (1-5)	Value
	Overall market size	0.20	4.00	0.80
	Annual market growth rate	0.20	5.00	1.00
	Historical profit margin	0.15	4.00	0.60
Market	Competitive intensity	0.15	2.00	0.30
Attractiveness	Technological requirements	0.15	4.00	0.60
	Inflationary vulnerability	0.05	3.00	0.15
	Energy requirements	0.05	2.00	0.10
	Environmental impact	0.05	3.00	0.15
	Social/political/legal	Must be acceptable		
		1.00		3.70

		Weight	Rating (1-5)	Value
	Market share	0.10	4.00	0.40
	Share growth	0.15	2.00	0.30
	Product quality	0.10	4.00	0.40
	Brand reputation	0.10	5.00	0.50
	Distribution network	0.05	4.00	0.20
Competitive	Promotional effectiveness	0.05	3.00	0.15
Position	Productive capacity	0.05	3.00	0.15
	Productive efficiency	0.05	2.00	0.10
	Unit costs	0.15	3.00	0.45
	Material supplies	0.05	5.00	0.25
	R&D performance	0.10	3.00	0.30
	Managerial personnel	0.05	4.00	0.20
		1.00		3.40

Source: Slightly modified from La Rue T. Hormer, Strategic Management (Englewood Cliffs, N.J.: Prentice-Hall, 1982), p. 310.

In fact, the GE matrix is divided into nine cells, which in turn fall into three zones. The three cells at the upper left indicate strong SBUs in which the company should *invest/grow*. The diagonal cells stretching from the lower left to the upper right indicate SBUs that are medium in overall attractiveness: The company should pursue *selectivity/earnings*. The three cells at the lower right indicate SBUs that are low in overall attractiveness: The company should give serious throught to *harvest/divest*. For example, the relief-values business represents an SBU with a small market share in a fair-size market that is not very attractive and in which the company has a weak competitive position: it is a fit candidate for harvest/divest.[12]

Management should also forecast the expected position of each SBU in the next three to five years given the current strategy. This involves analyzing where each product is in its product life cycle, as well as expected competitor strategies, new technologies, economic events, and so on. The results are indicated by the length and direction of the vectors in Figure 2-5A. For example, the hydraulic-pumps business is expected to decline slightly in market attractiveness, and the clutches business is expected to decline strongly in the company's competitive position.

The final step is for management to decide what it wants to do with each business. Figure 2-5B outlines plausible strategy options for businesses in each cell. The strategy for each business has to be discussed and debated. The intent is for business and corporate management to agree on the objectives and strategies for each business and the funds necessary to achieve these objectives.

Marketing managers will find that their objective is not always to build sales in each SBU. Their job might be to maintain the existing demand with fewer marketing dollars or to take cash out of the business and allow demand to fall. *Thus the task of marketing management is to manage demand or revenue to the target level negotiated with the corporate management.* Marketing contributes to assessing each SBU's sales and profit potential, but once the SBU's objective and budget are set, marketing's job is to carry out the plan efficiently and profitably.

Critique of Portfolio Models   Other portfolio models have been developed and used, particularly the Arthur D. Little model and the Shell directional-policy model.[13] The use of portfolio models has produced a number of benefits. The models have helped managers to think more futuristically and strategically, to understand the economics of their businesses better, to improve the quality of their plans, to have better communication between business and corporate management, to pinpoint information gaps and important issues, and to eliminate weaker businesses and strengthen their investment in more promising businesses.

On the other hand, portfolio models must be used cautiously. They may lead the company to place too much emphasis on market-share growth and entry into high-growth businesses, to the neglect of managing the current businesses well. The results are sensitive to the ratings and weights and can be manipulated to produce a desired location in the matrix. Furthermore, since an averaging process is occurring, two or more businesses may end up in the same cell position but differ greatly in the underlying ratings and weights. A lot of businesses will end up in the middle of the matrix owing to compromises in ratings, and this makes it hard to know what the appropriate strategy should be. Finally, the models fail to accommodate the synergies between two or more businesses, which means that making decisions for one business at a time might be risky. Overall, however, portfolio models have improved the analytical and strategic capabilities of managers and permitted them to make tough decisions on a more data-oriented and hard-nosed basis than mere impressions would permit.

FIGURE 2-6
The Strategic-Planning Gap

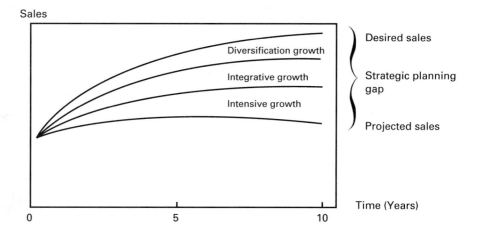

Corporate New-Business Plan

The company's plans for its existing businesses will allow it to project total sales and profits. Often, however, projected sales and profit will be less than what corporate management wants to achieve over the planning horizon. After all, the portfolio plan will include divesting some businesses, and these will need replacement. If there is a gap between future desired sales and projected sales, corporate management will have to develop or acquire new businesses to fill this strategic planning gap.

Figure 2-6 illustrates this strategic planning gap for a major manufacturer of cassette tape called Musicale (name disguised). The lowest curve projects the expected sales over the next ten years from the company's current portfolio of businesses. The highest curve describes the corporation's desired sales over the next ten years. Evidently the company wants to grow much faster than its current businesses will permit; in fact, it wants to double its size in ten years. How can it fill the strategic-planning gap?

A company can fill the gap in three ways. The first is to identify further opportunities to achieve growth within the company's current businesses (*intensive growth opportunities*). The second is to identify opportunities to build or acquire businesses that are related to the company's current businesses (*integrative growth opportunities*). The third is to identify opportunities to add attractive businesses that are unrelated to the company's current businesses (*diversification growth opportunities*). The specific opportunities within each broad class are listed in Table 2-3 and discussed below.

Intensive Growth Corporate management should first review whether there are any further opportunities for improving the performance of its existing businesses. Ansoff has proposed a useful framework for detecting new intensive growth opportunities. Called a

Table 2-3 Major Classes of Growth Opportunities

Intensive Growth	Integrative Growth	Diversification Growth
• Market penetration	• Backward integration	• Concentric diversification
• Market development	• Forward integration	• Horizontal diversification
• Product development	• Horizontal integration	• Conglomerate diversification

product/market expansion grid, it is shown in Figure 2-7.[14] Management first considers whether it could gain more market share with its current products in their current markets (*market-penetration strategy*). Next it considers whether it can find or develop new markets for its current products (*market-development strategy*). Then it considers whether it can develop new products of potential interest to its current markets (*product-development strategy*). (Later it will also review opportunities to develop new products for new markets—*diversification strategy*.) Let us examine the three major intensive growth strategies further.

Market-Penetration Strategy Here management looks for ways to increase the market share of its current products in their current markets. There are three major ways. A company like Musicale could try to encourage its current customers to buy more cassette tapes per period. This would make sense if most of its customers were infrequent buyers of tape and could be shown the benefits of using more tape for music recording or dictation. Or Musicale could try to attract the competitors' customers to switch to its brand. This would make sense if Musicale noticed a lot of weaknesses in the competitors' product or marketing program that it could exploit. Finally, Musicale could try to convince nonusers of cassette tapes who resemble current users to start using tapes. This would make sense if there were still many people who did not own tape recorders or tape players.

Market-Development Strategy Management should also look for new markets whose needs might be met by its current products. First, Musicale might try to identify potential user groups in the current sales areas whose interest in cassette tapes might be stimulated. If Musicale had been selling cassette tapes only to consumer markets, it might go after office and factory markets. Second, the company might seek additional distribution channels in its present locations. If it has been selling its tape only through stereo-equipment dealers, it might add mass merchandising channels. Third, the company might consider selling in new locations here or abroad. Thus if Musicale sold only in Quebec and Ontario, it could consider adding the provinces or opening markets in Europe.

Product-Development Strategy Next, management should consider some new-product development possibilities. It could develop new cassette-tape features, such as a longer-playing tape and a tape that buzzes at the end of its play. It could develop other quality levels of tape, such as a higher quality tape for fine-music listeners and a lower-quality tape for the mass market. Or it could research an alternative technology to cassette tape such as compact discs and digital audio tape.

By examining all of these intensive growth strategies—deeper market penetration, broader market development, and new-product development—it is hoped that management will discover several ways to grow. Still, that may not be enough, in which case management must also examine integrative growth possibilities.

FIGURE 2-7

Three Intensive Growth Strategies: Ansoff's Product/Market Expansion Grid

Source: Adapted from Igor Ansoff, "Strategies for Diversification," *Harvard Business Review*, September-October 1957, p. 114.

	Current Products	New Products
Current Markets	1. Market penetration strategy	2. Product development strategy
New Markets	3. Market development strategy	(Diversification strategy)

FIGURE 2-8
Core Marketing-System
Map for a Cassette-Tape
Manufacturer

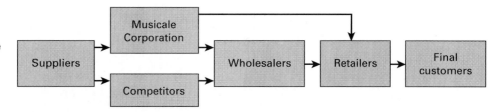

Integrative Growth Management should review each of its businesses to identify integrative growth possibilities. Often a business's sales and profits can be increased through integrating backward, forward, or horizontally within that business's industry. Figure 2-8 shows Musicale's core marketing system. Musicale might acquire one or more of its suppliers (such as plastic-material producers) to gain more profit or control (*backward integration strategy*). Or Musicale might acquire some wholesalers or retailers, especially if they are highly profitable (*forward integration strategy*). Finally, Musicale might acquire one or more competitors, provided that the government does not bar this move (*horizontal integration strategy*).

Through investigating possible integration moves, the company will possibly discover additional sources of sales-volume increases over the next ten years. These new sources may still not be enough to achieve the desired sales-growth level. In that case, the company must consider diversification moves.

Diversification Growth Diversification growth makes sense when good opportunities can be found outside the present businesses. A good opportunity, of course, is one where the industry is highly attractive and the company has the mix of business strengths needed to be successful. Three types of diversification can be considered. The company could seek new products that have technological and/or marketing synergies with existing product lines, even though the products may appeal to a new class of customers (*concentric diversification strategy*). For example, Musicale might start a computer-tape manufacturing operation based on knowing how to manufacture audio cassette tape, well aware that it will be entering a new market and selling to a different class of customers. Second, the company might search for new products that could appeal to its current customers though technologically unrelated to its current product line (*horizontal diversification strategy*). For example, Musicale might go into the production of cassette holding trays, even though they require a different manufacturing process. Finally, the company might seek new businesses that have no relationship to the company's current technology, products, or markets (*conglomerate diversification strategy*). Musicale might want to consider such new-business areas as personal computers, real-estate office franchising, or fast-food services.

Thus we see that a company can systematically identify new business opportunities by using a marketing-systems framework, first looking at ways to intensify its position in current product markets, then considering ways to integrate backward, forward, or horizontally in relation to its current businesses, and finally searching for profitable opportunities outside of its current businesses.

BUSINESS STRATEGIC PLANNING

Having examined the strategic-planning tasks of corporate management, we can now look more closely at the strategic-planning tasks facing business unit managers. The business

FIGURE 2-9
The Business Strategic-Planning Process

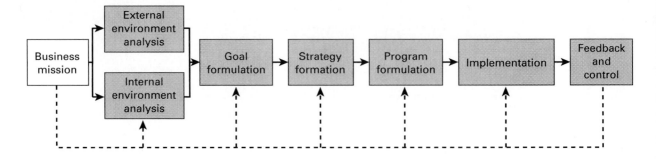

strategic-planning process consists of the eight steps shown in Figure 2-9. We shall now examine these steps.

Business Mission

Each business unit within the corporation needs to define its specific mission within the broader corporate mission. To illustrate, let us return to the business illustrated in Figure 2-3 that designed incandescent lighting systems for television studios. This business is clearly defined in terms of its *market-segment scope*, namely, lighting systems for television studios. But it may need additional definition of its market scope. With regard to customer groups, will it go after all television studios or only those that can afford the most advanced lighting systems? With regard to customer needs, will it install and service the systems or merely sell them? With regard to *vertical scope*, will it manufacture its own lighting equipment or contract out the manufacturing to someone else? And will it sell the lighting through a direct salesforce or through distributors? With regard to *geographical scope*, will it sell in one region, the whole country, or certain groups of countries in the world? Obviously, the business unit will need to spell out its business scope in more detail.

In addition, the mission statement should indicate the broad goals and policies of the business unit, going beyond the corporate goals and policies. Does this television-lighting-equipment business want to pursue growth, short-term profit, technological leadership, and so on? What policies does it want to have regarding customers, employees, and other stakeholders? All of these matters require clarification in the mission statement.

External Environment Analysis
(Opportunity and Threat Analysis)

The mission statement will help the business define its *environmental scanning* needs. The business manager now knows the parts of the environment to monitor and understand if the business is to achieve its objectives. For example, the television-lighting-equipment company needs to watch:

☐ The growth rate in the number of television studios.

☐ The level of television viewing as it affects the financial health of television studios and their ability to buy new equipment.

☐ The strategies of current competitors as well as the entry of new competitors.

□ New technological developments that might affect present and future equipment.

□ Changes in laws and regulations that might affect equipment design or marketing.

□ New or changing distribution channels for selling lighting equipment.

□ Increases in supplier costs that might be passed on to equipment manufacturers

In general, the company has to monitor key *macroenvironment forces* (demographic/economic, technological, political/legal, and social/cultural) that affect its business. And it must monitor significant *microenvironment actors* (customers, competitors, distribution channels, suppliers) that affect its ability to earn profits in this marketplace.

The business unit needs to categorize these environmental factors and set up a *marketing intelligence system* to track trends and important developments. Then, for each trend or development, the marketer should identify the implied opportunities and threats.

Opportunities One of the major purposes of environmental scanning is to discern new opportunities. We define a company marketing opportunity as follows:

> A company marketing opportunity *is an attractive arena for company marketing action in which the company would enjoy a competitive advantage.*

These opportunities should be classified according to their *attractiveness* and the *success probability* that the company would have with each opportunity (Figure 2-10). The company's success probability with a particular opportunity depends on whether its *business strengths* (i.e., distinctive competences) not only match the *key success requirements* for operating in the target market but also exceed those of its competitors. The best-performing company will be the one that can generate the *greatest customer value and sustain it over time*. Having competence is not enough. The company must bring superior competence in order to attain a *sustainable competitive advantage* (see Marketing Strategies 2-1).

Looking at Figure 2-10, the best opportunities facing a TV-lighting-equipment company are those in the upper-left cell, and management should prepare plans to pursue one or more of these opportunities. The opportunities in the lower-right cell are too minor to consider. The opportunities in the upper-right cell and lower-left cell should be monitored in the event that any of them improve in their attractiveness and success probability.

Threats Some of the developments in the external environment represent threats. We define an environmental threat as follows:

FIGURE 2-10
Opportunity Matrix

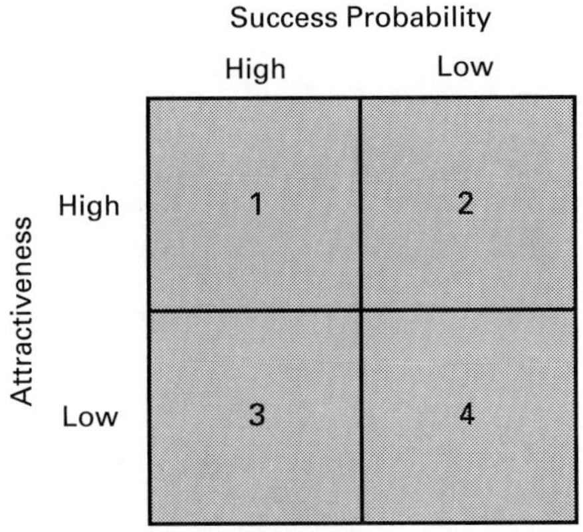

Opportunities

1. Company develops a more powerful lighting system
2. Company develops a much lower cost lighting system
3. Company develops a software disc to teach lighting fundamentals to TV studio personnel
4. Company develops a device for measuring the energy efficiency of any lighting system

WHICH COMPANY SHOULD PRODUCE AN ELECTRIC CAR?

Suppose General Motors, General Electric, and Sears all became interested in developing and marketing an electric car. Which firm would enjoy the greatest competitive advantage? First consider the success requirements. The success requirements would include (1) having good relations with suppliers of metal, rubber, plastic, glass, and other materials needed to produce an automobile; (2) having skill at mass production and mass assembly of complicated pieces of equipment; (3) having a strong distribution capacity to store, show, and deliver automobiles to the public; and (4) having the confidence of buyers that the company is able to produce and service a good auto product.

Now General Motors has distinctive competences in all four of these areas. General Electric has distinctive competences in (1) supply and (2) production but not in (3) distribution or (4) automobile reputation. It does have great know-how in electrical and electronic technology. Sears's major distinctive competence is its extensive retailing system, and it has some of the other competences through its wholly owned subsidiaries. All said, General Motors would enjoy the greatest differential advantage in the production and marketing of electric cars.

An environmental threat *is a challenge posed by an unfavorable trend or development in the environment that would lead, in the absence of purposeful marketing action, to the erosion of the company's position.*

The various identified threats should be classified according to their *seriousness* and *probability of occurrence*. Figure 2-11 shows a threat matrix and the location of several threats facing a TV-lighting-equipment company. The threats in the upper-left cell are major threats, since they can seriously hurt the company and have a high probability of occurrence. For these threats, the company needs to prepare a contingency plan that spells out in advance what changes the company can make before or during the threat's occurrence. The threats in the lower-right cell are very minor and can be ignored. The threats in the upper-right and lower-

FIGURE 2-11
Threat Matrix

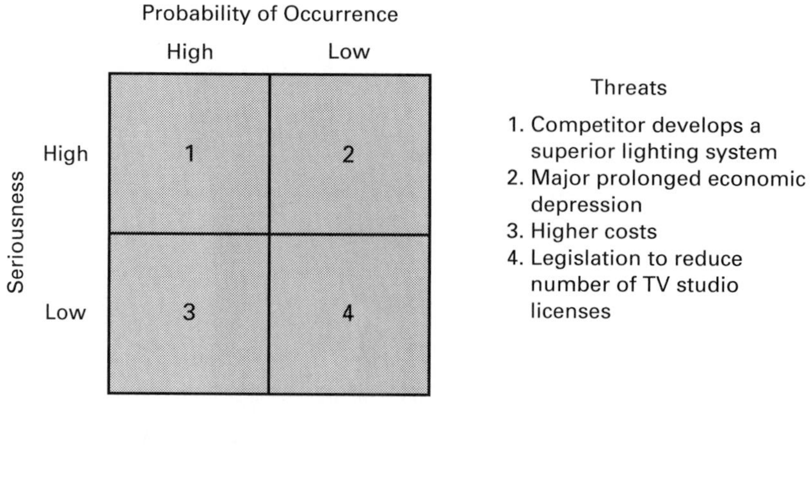

Probability of Occurrence

	High	Low
High	1	2
Low	3	4

Seriousness

Threats

1. Competitor develops a superior lighting system
2. Major prolonged economic depression
3. Higher costs
4. Legislation to reduce number of TV studio licenses

left cells do not require contingency planning but need to be carefully monitored in the event they grow more critical.

By assembling a picture of the major threats and opportunities facing a specific business, it is possible to characterize its overall attractiveness. Four outcomes are possible. An *ideal business* is one that is high in major opportunities and low in major threats. A *speculative business* is high in both major opportunities and threats. A *mature business* is low in major opportunities and threats. Finally, a *troubled business* is low in opportunities and high in threats.

Internal Environment Analysis (Strengths/Weaknesses Analysis)

It is one thing to discern attractive opportunities in the environment; it is another to have the necessary competencies to succeed in these opportunities. Each business needs to evaluate its strengths and weaknesses periodically. This can be done by using a form such as the one shown in Figure 2-12. Management—or an outside consultant—reviews the business's marketing, financial, manufacturing, and organizational competencies. Each factor is rated as to whether it is a major strength, minor strength, neutral factor, minor weakness, or major weakness. A company with strong marketing capability would show up with the ten marketing factors all rated as major strengths. By connecting the ratings vertically for a specific business, we can easily identify the business's major strengths and major weaknesses.

Of course, not all factors are equally important for succeeding in a business or succeeding with a new marketing opportunity. It is also necessary to rate the importance of each factor—high, medium, or low—for that opportunity. When combining performance and importance levels, four possibilities emerge. They are illustrated in Figure 2-13. In cell A fall important factors where the business is performing poorly, and therefore the business must strengthen these factors; hence "concentrate here." In cell B fall important factors where the business is already strong; hence "keep up the good work." In cell C fall unimportant factors where the business is performing poorly; these factors consequently are of "low priority." In cell D fall unimportant factors where the business is strong; perhaps it is overinvesting in these factors at the cost of "possible overkill." An application of the analysis is shown in Chapter 17, Marketing Concepts and Tools 17-1.

This analysis tells us that even when a business has a major strength in a certain factor (i.e., a *distinctive competence*), that strength does not necessarily create a *competitve advantage*. First, it may not be a competence of any importance to the customers in that market. Second, even if it is, competitors may have the same strength level in that factor. What becomes important, then, is for the business to have relatively greater strength in that important factor than its competitors. Thus two competitors may both enjoy low manufacturing costs; but the one with the lower of the manufacturing costs has a competitive advantage.

In examining its pattern of strengths and weaknesses, clearly the business does not have to correct all of its weaknesses (some are unimportant) nor gloat about all of its strengths (again, some are unimportant). The big question is whether the business should limit itself to those opportunities where it now possesses the required strengths or consider possibly better opportunities where it might have to acquire or develop certain strengths. For example, managers in Texas Instruments (TI) split between those who wanted TI to stick to industrial electronics where it had clear strength and those who urged the company to go into digital watches, personal computers, and other consumer products where it did not have the required marketing strengths. As it turned out, TI did poorly in these consumer areas but perhaps its mistake was not so much in going into consumer products as in failing to acquire the marketing strengths to do the job right.

FIGURE 2-12

Strengths/Weaknesses
Analysis

	Performance					Importance		
	Major strength	**Minor strength**	**Neutral**	**Minor Weakness**	**Major Weakness**	**Hi**	**Med**	**Low**
Marketing								
1. Company reputation	___	___	___	___	___	___	___	___
2. Market share	___	___	___	___	___	___	___	___
3. Quality reputation	___	___	___	___	___	___	___	___
4. Service reputation	___	___	___	___	___	___	___	___
5. Manufacturing costs	___	___	___	___	___	___	___	___
6. Distribution costs	___	___	___	___	___	___	___	___
7. Promotion effectiveness	___	___	___	___	___	___	___	___
8. Salesforce effectiveness	___	___	___	___	___	___	___	___
9. R&D and innovation	___	___	___	___	___	___	___	___
10. Geographical coverage	___	___	___	___	___	___	___	___
Finance								
11. Cost/availability of capital	___	___	___	___	___	___	___	___
12. Profitability	___	___	___	___	___	___	___	___
13. Financial stability	___	___	___	___	___	___	___	___
Manufacturing								
14. Facilities	___	___	___	___	___	___	___	___
15. Economies of scale	___	___	___	___	___	___	___	___
16. Capacity	___	___	___	___	___	___	___	___
17. Able dedicated workforce	___	___	___	___	___	___	___	___
18. Ability to deliver on time	___	___	___	___	___	___	___	___
19. Technical manufacturing skill	___	___	___	___	___	___	___	___
Organization								
20. Visionary capable leadership	___	___	___	___	___	___	___	___
21. Dedicated employees	___	___	___	___	___	___	___	___
22. Entrepreneurial orientation	___	___	___	___	___	___	___	___
23. Flexible/responsive	___	___	___	___	___	___	___	___

FIGURE 2-13

Performance-
Importance Matrix

Performance

	Low	High
High (Importance)	A. Concentrate here	B. Keep up the good work
Low	C. Low priority	D. Possible overkill

Sometimes a business does poorly not because its departments lack the required strengths but because they do not work together as a team. In one major electronics company, the engineers look down upon the salespeople as "engineers who couldn't make it," and the salespeople look down upon the service people as "salespeople who couldn't make it." It is critically important to assess the quality of the interdepartmental working relationships as part of the internal environmental audit.

A computer company has solved this problem by conducting a survey each year asking each department to rate itself and every other department on its strengths and weaknesses. The findings in the last survey are shown in Marketing Concepts and Tools 2-1. Note that each department was seen as having some positive strengths, but there was also concern about some major weaknesses. Following these findings, the company undertakes programs to correct the departmental weaknesses and improve interdepartmental teamwork. ∎

Marketing Concepts and Tools 2-1

ASSESSING INTERDEPARTMENTAL STRENGTHS AND WEAKNESSES

A major computer manufacturer undertook an audit of its strengths and weaknesses by department. It asked each department (engineering, manufacturing, marketing, field sales, etc.) to evaluate the strengths and weaknesses of every other department. Here is what the company learned:

	Strengths	Weaknesses
Engineering	Skilled engineers Up to date in CADC/AM	Overcosting Overdelays
Manufacturing	Produces good quality Can customize equipment Responsive to field needs	High cost Lack of cost-reduction programs Union is inflexible
Field Sales	Good customer relations	Focus on big orders, neglecting small orders Need more training in benefit selling Conflict between home office and branches
Marketing	Competent Good programs for segments	Has not provided long-run strategy Planning is done in September instead of continuously Slow in filling product gaps

Goal Formulation

After the business unit has defined its mission and examined its external and internal environments, it can proceed to develop specific objectives and goals for the planning period. This stage is called *goal formulation*.

Very few businesses pursue only one objective. Most business units pursue a mix of objectives including *profitability, sales growth, market-share improvement, risk containment, innovativeness, reputation*, and so on. The business unit sets these objectives and *manages by objectives*. For this system to work, the business unit's various objectives should be hierarchical, quantitative, realistic, and consistent.

Instead of just developing a long list of objectives for the planning period, which vary in importance, the business unit should strive to arrange them *hierarchically*, from the most to the least important. An excellent example of hierarchical objectives is provided by Interprovincial Telephone (name disguised), a strategic business unit of a larger company. This business unit has been earning only a 7.5 percent return on investment, too low to support its plans to expand and provide better service and equipment to customers. The business unit's mission is to provide good service to customers. Its current major objective is to increase its return on investment. From this objective follows a whole hierarchy of further objectives (see Figure 2-14). Thus a major business objective can be ultimately translated into specific objectives for all employees.

FIGURE 2-14

Hierarchy of Objectives for the Interprovincial Telephone Company

Source: Adapted from Leon Winer, "Are You Really Planning Your Marketing?"
Journal of Marketing, January 1965, p. 3. Published by the American Marketing Association.

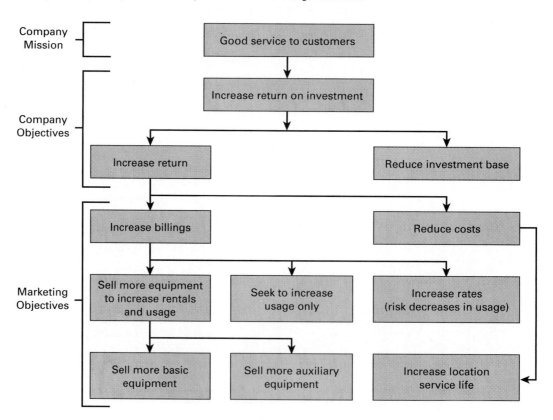

To the extent possible, objectives should be stated *quantitatively*. The objective "increase the return on investment" is not as satisfactory as "increase the return on investment to 15 percent" or, even better, "increase the return on investment to 15 percent within two years." Managers use the term goals to describe objectives that are specific with respect to *magnitude* and *time*. Turning the objectives into concrete goals facilitates the process of management planning, implementation, and control.

A business has to choose *realistic* target levels for its objectives. The levels should come out of an analysis of its opportunities and competitive strengths, not out of wishful thinking.

Finally, the company's objectives need to be *consistent*. It is not possible to "maximize both sales and profits," or "achieve the greatest sales at the least cost," or "design the best product in the shortest possible time." These objectives are in a *tradeoff* relationship. Here are some important tradeoffs:

☐ High profit margins versus high market share

☐ Deep penetration of existing markets versus developing new markets

☐ Profit goals versus nonprofit goals

☐ High growth versus high stability

A business has to adopt consistent goals, or else there will be confusion. Too often Canadian CEOs tell their managers to invest for "long-run market-share growth" and then put pressure on them to achieve "high current profits." Meanwhile Japanese CEOs clearly tell their managers to pursue higher market shares and worry about profits later. Each choice in the above set of goal tradeoffs will call for quite a different marketing strategy.

Strategy Formulation

Goals indicate where a business wants to go; strategy answers how to get there. Every business must tailor a strategy for achieving its goals. The strategy must then be refined into specific programs that are implemented efficiently and corrected if they are failing to achieve the objectives.

We saw at the beginning of this chapter that competitors within an industry (here rubber tires) might pursue quite different strategies that are all reasonable, given that these competitors have different objectives, opportunities, and resources. Although one can list many types of strategies, Porter has condensed them into three generic types that provide a good starting point for strategic thinking:

☐ *Overall Cost Leadership*: Here the business works hard to achieve the lowest costs of production and distribution, so that it can price lower than its competitors and win a large market share. Firms pursuing this strategy must be good at engineering, purchasing, manufacturing, and physical distribution and need less skill in marketing. Texas Instruments is a leading practitioner of this strategy. The problem with this strategy is that other firms will usually emerge with still lower costs (from the Far East, for example) and hurt the firm that rested its whole future on being low cost. The real key is for the firm to achieve the lowest costs among those competitors adopting a similar differentiation or focus strategy.

☐ *Differentiation*: Here the business concentrates on achieving superior performance in some important customer benefit area valued by the market as a whole. It can strive to be the service leader, the quality leader, the style leader, the technology leader, and so on; but it is hardly possible to be all of these things. The firm cultivates those strengths that will give it a differential performance advantage along some benefit line. Thus the firm seeking quality leadership must make or buy the best components, put them together expertly, inspect them carefully, and so on. This has been Canon's strategy in the copy-machine field.

- [ ] *Focus*: Here the business focuses on one or more narrow market segments rather than going after the whole market. The firm gets to know the needs of these segments and pursues either cost leadership or some form of differentiation within the target segment. Thus Armstrong Rubber has specialized in making superior tires for farm-equipment vehicles and recreational vehicles and keeps looking for new niches to serve.[15]

According to Porter, those firms pursuing the same strategy directed to the same market or market segment constitute a *strategic group*. The firm that carries off that strategy best will make the most profits. Thus the lowest-cost firm among those pursuing a low-cost strategy will do the best. Porter suggests that firms that do not pursue a clear strategy—middle-of-the-roaders—do the worst. Thus Chrysler and International Harvester both came upon hard times because in their respective industries neither stood out as either lowest in cost, highest in perceived value, or best in serving some market segment. Middle-of-the-roaders try to be good on all strategic dimensions, but since strategic dimensions require different and often inconsistent ways to organize the firm, these firms end up being not particularly excellent at anything. (Marketing Concepts and Tools 2-2 illustrates these principles for the truck-manufacturing industry.)

Program Formulation

Once the business has developed its principal strategies for attaining its goals, it must work out supporting programs for carrying out these strategies. Thus if the business has decided to attain technologicial leadership, it must run programs to strengthen its research-and-development department, gather intelligence on the newest technologies that might affect the business, develop leading-edge products, train the salesforce to understand the products and educate the customers, develop an advertising program to communicate its position as the technological leader, and so on. Since we will say much more about these programs later in the book, we will now turn to implementation.

Implementation

Even if the firm has developed a clear strategy and well-thought-out supporting programs, they may not be enough. The firm may fail at implementation. According to McKinsey & Company, a leading consulting firm, strategic planning is not enough. Strategy is only one of seven elements that the best-managed companies exhibit.[16] The McKinsey 7-S framework is shown in Figure 2-15. The first three elements—strategy, structure, and systems—are considered the "hardware" of success. The next four—style, staff, skills, and shared values—are the "software."

Consultants at McKinsey added the four software elements as a result of studying a large sample of excellently managed companies—IBM, P&G, Caterpillar, McDonald's, Levi Strauss, and so on—and discovering that their strengths went beyond strategy, structure, and systems. These organizations have four additional elements. The first is *style*, which means that employees in that company share a common style of behaving and thinking. Thus everyone at McDonald's smiles at the customer, and employees of IBM are very professional in their customer dealings. The second element is *skills*, which means that employees have mastered the skills needed to carry out the company's strategy. The third element is *staffing*, in that the company has hired able people, trained them well, and assigned the right jobs to exercise their talents. The fourth element is *shared values*, in that the employees

Marketing Concepts and Tools 2-2

STRATEGIC GROUPS IN THE TRUCK-MANUFACTURING INDUSTRY

The role of generic strategies and strategic groups can be illustrated by William Hall's research in the truck-manufacturing industry. The accompanying figure shows how seven truck manufacturers were positioned some years ago in terms of their *relative delivered cost* (i.e., being a low-cost firm) and their *relative performance* (i.e., offering the most differentiated or desirable product and service). The percentages in the figure represent each manufacturer's rate of return on investment (ROI) in this industry.

Ford clearly has the lowest relative delivered cost, followed by General Motors. Although its trucks are average, Ford's low-cost leadership gives it the highest ROI (i.e., 25 percent) in its strategic group. Paccar, on the other hand, is the leader in the high-performance truck strategic group and commands a 31 percent ROI, compared with Mack's 20 percent.

At the other extreme is White Motor, whose trucks were below average in performance and high in manufacturing cost. Not surprisingly, its rate of return was 4.7 percent, and White was subsequently purchased by Volvo, whose intent is to reposition it and strengthen its competitive effectiveness.

The four companies in the middle box are "middle-of-the-roaders" that try to be good at performance and cost but are not superior at either. Their rates of return are lower than those of the two leading firms, Ford and Paccar. As it turns out, Freightliner was subsequently purchased by Mercedes, and International Harvester's truck line was later reborn as Navistar.

In order for a middle-of-the-roader to improve its ROI, the company must make a clearer commitment to one of the three winning strategies. For example, International Harvester (IH) had three options. IH could invest in a more modern plant in a drive to become the low-cost firm. In this case, its major competitors would be Ford and General Motors, both of which make up the strategic group pursuing cost leadership. Alternatively, IH could try to improve the quality of its trucks and services so that it competed with Paccar and Mack, the strategic group pursuing profitability through product differentiation. This would be harder for IH because it takes years to build a better product and reputation, and Paccar is too well entrenched. Finally, IH might go after multiple niches within the trucking industry (this cannot be shown in the figure), becoming a leader in each niche through either low costs, product differentiation or both. As it turned out, IH adopted the third strategy, and it has been successful.

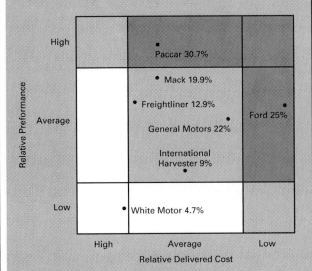

FIGURE 2-15

McKinsey 7-S Framework

Source: Thomas J. Peters and Robert H. Waterman, Jr., *In Search of Excellence: Lessons from America's Best Run Companies.* Copyright © 1982 by Thomas J. Peters and Robert H. Waterman, Jr. Reprinted by permission of Harper & Row, Publishers.

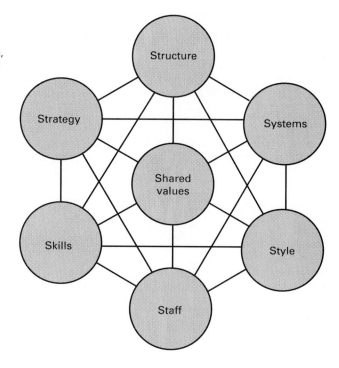

share the same guiding values and missions. Successful companies exhibit widely shared cultures that fit their strategy.[17]

Feedback and Control

The "software" of management will affect the firm's ability to implement its strategies and programs successfully. As the implementation occurs, the business needs to track the results and monitor new developments in the environment. The company can count on one thing: that the environment will change during the planning period. And when it does, the company will be pressed to make appropriate adjustments in one or more steps of the planning process if it is to achieve its objectives.

The extent of the required adjustments depends on the magnitude and speed of environmental change. Some environments are fairly stable from year to year in their economics, technology, law, culture, consumer wants, and competitive behavior. Other environments evolve slowly in a fairly predictable way. Still other environments are turbulent and change rapidly in major and unpredictable ways.

In turbulent environments, business units have to be ready to revise their programs, strategies, goals or even mission in some cases. Some companies carry on continuous strategic planning in that they keep adapting their programs to changing conditions while holding to their core objectives and strategies. On the other hand, some dominant producers fail to recognize when their demand environment has changed from a stable to a turbulent one, and they do not respond quickly enough. Consider what happened at GE's vacuum-tube division:

> The president of General Electric called in the general manager of the vacuum-tube division. The general manager expected to be congratulated because he had increased vacuum-tube sales by 20 percent. Instead, he was berated for keeping GE too long in the wrong business. GE's

sales had risen because some competitors had left the vacuum-tube business, not because of GE's competitive edge. In addition, transistor technology had just appeared and was making headway against vacuum tubes and bringing in new players such as Texas Instruments, Fairchild, and Transitron. In fact, the total market for devices that amplified weak electrical signals had grown by 30 percent during the same period, which meant that GE's market share of the total market had actually fallen. The manager was guilty of marketing myopia, focusing on vacuum tubes instead of the total range of technologies competing to serve the particular need. Some businesses are dead without management's really knowing it. ■

A company's *strategic fit* with the environment will evitably erode because the market environment will almost always change faster than the company's 7-S's. It is possible for a company to remain efficient while it becomes ineffective. Peter Drucker pointed out that it is more important to *do the right thing* (being effective) than *to do things right* (being efficient). Excellent companies excel at both.

Once an organization starts losing its market position through failure to respond to critical events in its environment, it has a limited number of options:

> General Motors was slow in recognizing the rapidly growing market for small cars. Small cars were a new opportunity for car manufacturers in a mature market. A new opportunity is a *strategic window* that stays open for only a short time.[18] As Volkswagens and small Japanese cars increased their market share, GM finally responded with a poorly made car called the Vega. GM's blindness was the result of operating in the 1970s and 1980s with the leftovers of 1960s strategy, structure, systems, style, staff, skills, and shared values. GM's leadership needs to realize that competitiveness requires drastic steps, including reducing bloated management and labor costs, sourcing parts from abroad, partnering with foreign car manufacturers, and improving product quality and service. ■

Organizations, especially large ones, have much inertia. They are set up as efficient machines, and it is difficult to change one part without adjusting everything else. Yet organizations can be changed through leadership, probably in advance of a crisis but certainly in the midst of a crisis. The key to organizational survival is the organization's willingness to examine the changing environment and to adopt appropriate new goals and behaviors. Adaptable organizations continuously monitor the environment and attempt through flexible planning to maintain a strategic fit with the evolving environment.

SUMMARY

Excellent companies know how to adapt and respond to a continuously changing marketplace through the practice of market-oriented strategic planning. They know how to develop and maintain a viable fit between their objectives, resources, and opportunities. They carry out the strategic-planning process at the corporate level, business level, and product level. The objectives developed at the corporate level move down to lower levels where business strategic plans and marketing plans are prepared to guide the company's activities. Strategic planning involves repeated cycles of analysis, planning, implementation, and control.

Corporate strategic planning involves four planning activities. The first is developing a clear sense of the company's mission in terms of its industry scope, market-segment scope, vertical scope, and geographical scope. A well-developed mission statement provides employees with a shared sense of purpose, direction, and opportunity.

The second activity calls for identifying the company's strategic business units (SBUs). A business is defined by its customer groups, customer needs, and technologies. SBUs are business units that can benefit from separate planning, face specific competitors, and be managed as profit centers.

The third activity calls for allocating resources to the various SBUs based on their market attractiveness and company competitive strength. Several portfolio models, including those by the Boston Consulting Group and General Electric, are available to help corporate management determine the SBUs that should be built, maintained, harvested, or divested.

The fourth activity calls for expanding present businesses and developing new ones to fill the strategic-planning gap. The company can identify opportunities by considering intensive growth (market penetration, market development and product development); integrative growth (backward, forward, and horizontal integration); and diversification growth (concentric, horizontal, and conglomerate diversification).

Each SBU conducts its own business strategic planning, which consists of eight steps: defining the business's mission, analyzing the external environment, analyzing the internal environment, choosing business objectives and goals, developing business strategies, preparing program plans, implementing program plans, and gathering feedback and exercising control. All of these steps keep the SBU close to its environment and alert to new opportunities and problems. Furthermore, the SBU strategic plan provides the context for preparing market plans for specific products and services, which we will examine in the next chapter.

■ QUESTIONS

1. Define the competitive domain for a consumer packaged goods company by discussing each of the four statements of scope for the company.

2. Joint venturing has become a popular method used by corporate strategists for competing in selected markets. What strategic motivations are behind the formation of joint ventures? Cite two examples of joint ventures to illustrate these motivations.

3. Portfolio models can be helpful to managers seeking to know whether the objective for an SBU should be to build, to hold, to harvest, or to divest. However, research has shown that SBU managers tend to invest more than one might expect on the basis of such models. What could account for this deviation from these prescriptive decision models?

4. Select a company in the personal computer industry and conduct a SWOT (strength/weaknesses, opportunities/threats) analysis of that firm.

5. A local high school has operated a night school program with only marginal success for several years. Due to a recent tax referendum, the school board has decided it must either significantly increase night school enrolments or cancel the entire program. Suggest a statement of purpose for the night school program and a hierarchy of objectives based on the intention to increase enrolments.

6. An industrial-equipment company consists of the five strategic business units (SBUs) shown in the table. Using the Boston Consulting Group portfolio analysis, determine whether the company is in a healthy condition. What future strategies should it consider?

SBU	Dollar Sales (in millions)	Number of Competitors	Dollar Sales of the Top 3 (in millions)	Market-Growth Rate
A	.5	8	7, .7, .5	15%
B	1.6	22	1.6, 1.6, 1.0	18%
C	1.8	14	1.8, 1.2, 1.0	7%
D	3.2	5	3.2, .8, .7	4%
E	.5	10	2.5, 1.8, 1.7	4%

7. What is the major distinctive competence of (a) Sears; (b) Procter & Gamble; (c) Polaroid Company.

8. "With more than 80 percent of the market already in its grasp, Campbell Soup Co. really doesn't need to increase its share of the $1.2 billion of condensed soup sold annually in food stores. What the company does is to make folks hungrier for soup." What intensive growth strategy is being pursued, and how might the company accomplish this objective?

9. After decades as a marketer of personal-care products to men, Gillette began to move into the women's personal-care market with such products as Silkience hair products and Apri skin products. Describe Gillette's strategy, using Table 2-3 (Major Classes of Growth Opportunities) and Figure 2-7 (Intensive-Growth Strategies).

10. Cite examples of recent concentric, horizontal, and conglomerate diversification. Give reasons for your choice.

■ NOTES

1. See Zachary Schiller, "Goodyear Feels the Heat," Business Week, March 7, 1988, pp. 26-28.

2. Steve Harrell, in a speech at the plenary session of the American Marketing Association's Educators' Meeting, Chicago, August 5, 1980.

3. Two points need to be made. First, these distinctions are not limited to corporations. Most organizations, including partnerships and nonprofit organizations, have three levels. There is a command center or group (headquarters), two or more businesses, and two or more products within each business. For example, a law firm may do corporate and personal work (two businesses) and within corporate, handle franchising and antitrust work (two product lines). Second, large corporations may even have more organizational levels, such as groups, sectors, and divisions, all of which do planning. However, the most basic types of planning are done at the corporate, business, and product/market levels.

4. Currently, many companies are shrinking their corporate planning staffs and shifting strategic planning responsibilities to their operating-division managers. Planning works best when it is done by line people who have to carry out the plans; and the line people have picked up a lot of training in strategic planning in the last decade. See "The New Breed of Strategic Planning," Business Week, September 7, 1984.

5. See Drucker, Management: Tasks, Responsibilities and Practices (New York: Harper & Row, 1973), Chap. 7.

6. See "The Hollow Corporation," Business Week, March 3, 1986, pp. 57-59.

7. For more discussion, see Laura Nash, "Mission Statements—Mirrors and Windows," Harvard Business Review, March-April 1988, pp. 155-56.

8. Theodore Levitt, "Marketing Myopia," Harvard Business Review, July-August 1960, pp. 45-56.

9. See "Holiday Inns: Refining Its Focus to Food, Lodging and More Casinos," Business Week, July 21, 1980, pp. 100-104.

10. Derek Abell, Defining the Business: The Starting Point of Strategic Planning (Englewood Cliffs, N.J.: Prentice-Hall, 1980), Chap. 3.

11. See Roger A. Kerin, Vijay Mahajan, and P. Rajan Varadarajan, Contemporary Perspectives on Strategic Planning (Boston: Allyn & Bacon, 1990).

12. A hard decision must be made between harvesting and divesting a business. Harvesting a business will strip it of its long-run value, in which case it will be difficult to find a buyer. Divesting, on the other hand, is facilitated by maintaining a business in a fit condition in order to attract a buyer.

13. See Peter Patel and Michael Younger, "A Frame of Reference for Strategy Development," Long Range Planning, April 1978, pp. 6-12; and S. J. Q. Robinson et al., "The Directional Policy Matrix—Tool for Strategic Planning," Long Range Planning, June 1978, pp. 8-15.

14. The same matrix can be expanded into nine cells by adding modified products and modified markets. See S. C. Johnson and Conrad Jones, "How to Organize for New Products," Harvard Business Review, May-June 1957, pp. 49-62.

15. See Michael E. Porter, Competitive Strategy: Techniques for Analyzing Industries and Competitors (New York: Free Press, 1980), Chap. 2.

16. See Thomas J. Peters and Robert H. Waterman, Jr., In Search of Excellence: Lessons from America's Best-Run Companies (New York: Harper & Row, 1982), pp. 9-12. The same framework is used in Richard Tanner Pascale and Anthony G. Athos, The Art of Japanese Management: Applications for American Executives (New York: Simon and Schuster, 1981).

17. See Terrence E. Deal and Allan A. Kennedy, Corporate Cultures: The Rites and Rituals of Corporate Life (Reading, Mass.: Addison-Wesley, 1982); "Corporate Culture," Business Week, October 27, 1980, pp. 148-60; and Stanley M. Davis, Managing Corporate Culture (Cambridge, Mass.: Ballinger, 1984).

18. See Derek F. Abell, "Strategic Windows," Journal of Marketing, July 1978, pp. 21-26.

3

Managing the Marketing Process and Marketing Planning

Think then and plan; no more of this indecision; let action take the place of hesitation.

Frances Griffiths

We saw in Chapters 1 and 2 that the *marketing concept* and *strategic planning* form the principal basis for managing the modern company in highly competitive markets. We saw that *corporate headquarters* has to evaluate its strategic business units continuously and assign appropriate objectives and funds to each. We saw that each *strategic business unit* in turn must carefully monitor its external and internal environments and develop a strategic business unit plan. Since each strategic business unit typically handles a number of products destined to a number of market segments, it must prepare marketing plans for each.

Marketing plans differ from *strategic business unit plans* in focusing more narrowly on a product/market and developing more detailed marketing strategies and programs for achieving the business unit's objectives in that product market. *The marketing plan is the central instrument for directing and coordinating the marketing effort.* Companies that want to improve their marketing effectiveness and efficiency must learn how to create and implement sound marketing plans.

Our discussion of marketing planning will seek to answer these questions:

☐ What are the major steps in the marketing process?

☐ What are the major contents of a marketing plan?

☐ What are the main theoretical tools for describing how various types of marketing efforts affect the company's sales and profits?

After this overview of marketing management and planning, we will examine more thoroughly in the subsequent chapters the steps involved in analyzing, planning, implementing, and controlling the marketing process.

THE MARKETING PROCESS

The relationship between marketing and strategic planning is shown in Figure 3-1. Marketing supplies information and strategic recommendations (step 1) to the strategic planners for the latter's analysis and evaluation (step 2). The strategic planners then negotiate goals and resources (step 3). Marketing then formulates marketing plans based on these goals (step 4) and carries them out (step 5). The results are evaluated by the strategic planners and the process recycles.

Thus the first step in business planning is the marketing step, where the target market and product-positioning strategy are defined and sales goals and needed resources are established for achieving these goals. The role of the finance, purchasing, manufacturing, physical distribution, and personnel departments is to make sure that the proposed marketing plan can be supported with enough money, materials, machines, and personnel.

To carry out their responsibilities, marketing managers go through a marketing process. We define it as follows:

> *The* marketing process *consists of analyzing marketing opportunities, researching and selecting target markets, designing marketing strategies, planning marketing programs, and organizing, implementing, and controlling the marketing effort.*

These steps are listed in Figure 3-2, along with the chapters in this book that will describe each step in detail. The steps will be illustrated here in connection with the following situation:

> Zeus, Inc. (name disguised) is a large company that operates in several industries, including chemicals, energy, typewriters, and some consumer goods. Each area is organized as an SBU. Corporate management is considering what to do with its Atlas typewriter division. At present, Atlas produces standard office electric typewriters that are comparable to the highly popular IBM Selectric typewriters but sell for less. The market for standard electric typewriters is showing slow growth, and this company's brand is dwarfed by the leader. On a growth-share matrix, this business would be called a dog. Zeus's corporate management wants Atlas's marketing group to produce a strong turnaround plan for this product line or else face being dropped as a division. Marketing management has to come up with a convincing marketing plan, sell corporate management on the plan, and then implement and control it. ■

FIGURE 3-1

Relationship between Marketing and Strategic Planning

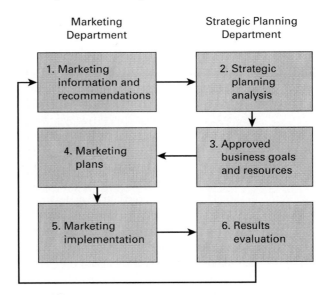

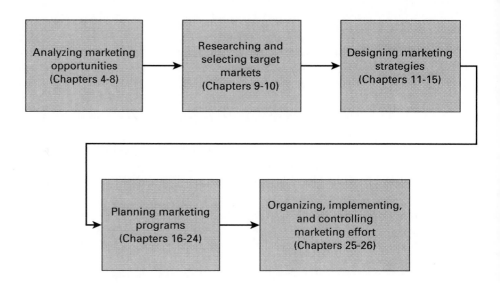

FIGURE 3-2
The Marketing
Management Process

Analyzing marketing
opportunities
(Chapters 4-8)

Researching and
selecting target
markets
(Chapters 9-10)

Designing marketing
strategies
(Chapters 11-15)

Planning marketing
programs
(Chapters 16-24)

Organizing, implementing,
and controlling
marketing effort
(Chapters 25-26)

Analyzing Market Opportunities

The first task facing Atlas's marketing management is to analyze the long-run opportunities in this market for improving its performance as a business division of Zeus, Inc. These managers recognize the abundance of opportunities in the burgeoning business-office-equipment field. The *office of the future* is a major investment frontier in the coming decades, just as the factory was the frontier in the past (the new robotic factory is another frontier). The Canadian economy is increasingly becoming a service economy, and there are more office workers than factory workers. Yet offices are often poorly organized for such elementary tasks as typing, filing, storing, and transmitting information, especially in terms of the latest available technologies. Many manufacturers are active in this market and are seeking to provide integrated systems of typewriters, microcomputers, copying and duplicating machines, facsimile transmission machines, electronic message systems, and the like. Among them are IBM, Xerox, Olivetti, and several Japanese companies. They are all engaged in developing office hardware and software that will increase office productivity, which is the chief buying motive of office-equipment purchasing agents. Xerox, in fact, sees itself not as a copying-machine company but as an office-productivity-improvement company.

Atlas's marketing management's long-run goal is to become a complete office-equipment manufacturer. At the present time, however, it must come up with a plan to improve its typewriter product line. Even within typewriters, there are many opportunities. Atlas, for example, can scale down its office typewriter to a version for the home market and advertise it as an "office-quality" home typewriter. But even larger opportunities lie in incorporating certain technological advances. Just as typing productivity increased greatly in the past when typewriters evolved from manual machines to electric machines, they are now evolving further. Atlas could design an electronic or "smart" typewriter, one of the hottest new products in the office-equipment field. An electronic typewriter has only twenty-four moving parts compared with the roughly one thousand levers, springs, gears, and screws inside an electric typewriter; offers more characters; has a memory; can make automatic corrections; does not jam; and has a number of other useful features. Electronic typewriters are priced from several hundred to several thousand dollars and now include such entries as Smith Corona's Typetronic, Royal's 5010, Olivetti's ET121, and IBM's electronic Selectric. Atlas can also consider designing a word processor, which would have more memory and text-editing capability than an electronic typewriter and sell for a few thousand dollars. Or Atlas can develop a whole computer work station like IBM's Displaywriter system that performs a large number of functions. Ultimately, Atlas can work on voice-activated typewriters, which only require oral dictation.

To identify and evaluate its opportunities, Atlas needs to build and operate a reliable marketing information system (Chapter 4). Marketing research is an indispensable ingredient of the modern marketing concept, in that companies can serve their customer markets well only by researching their needs and wants, their locations, their buying practices, and so on. There are different degrees of formal research that can be carried on by Atlas. At the very least, Atlas needs a good internal accounting system that speedily and accurately reports current sales by typewriter model, customer, industry and size, customer location, salesperson, and channels of distribution. In addition, Atlas's executives should be collecting continuous market intelligence on customers, competitors, dealers, and so on. The marketing people should conduct formal research by looking up information in secondary sources; running focus groups; and conducting telephone, mail, and personal surveys. If the collected data are well analyzed using advanced statistical methods and models, the company will probably gain useful information on how sales are affected by various marketing forces.

The purpose of Atlas's research is to gather significant and continuous information about Atlas's relevant marketing environment (Chapter 5). The marketing environment consists of a microenvironment and a macroenvironment. The company's *microenvironment* consists of all the actors who help or affect the company's ability to produce and sell typewriters, namely, suppliers, marketing intermediaries, customers, competitors, and publics of various sorts. Such questions arise as: What do customers want and look at in buying typewriters? What channels of distribution are growing and shrinking? Which suppliers are most efficient at making components? What are competitors doing?

Atlas's management also must stay on top of broad trends in the *macroenvironment*, namely, demographic, economic, physical, technological, political/legal, and social/cultural developments. It would be myopic to confine attention to the microenvironment and ignore larger changing forces in the society. Such questions arise as: What areas of the country are growing and shrinking? What is the economic outlook, and how will it affect sales of typewriters and the models purchased? What new technologies can be applied to improve typewriter efficiency? The large-scale forces can have a profound effect on Atlas's market.

To the extent that Atlas considers manufacturing a typewriter for the home, it needs to understand *consumer markets* and how they function (Chapter 6). It needs to know: How many households plan to buy new typewriters? Who buys and why do they buy? What are they looking for in the way of features and prices? Where do they shop? What are their images of existing competitors? What is the potential influence of price, advertising, sales promotion, personal selling, and so forth, on consumer brand choice decisions?

Atlas also sells to *business markets*, including large corporations, professional firms, retailers, government agencies, and so on (Chapter 7). Large organizations are staffed with professional purchasing agents who are skilled at evaluating equipment and value. Major equipment decisions are also made by buying committees consisting of different company personnel with different objectives and different degrees of influence on the final vendor decision. Selling to organizations usually involves personal selling through a salesforce that is well trained to present the product and show how it can meet the customer's needs. Atlas needs to gain a full understanding of how organizational buyers buy.

Atlas must also pay close attention to identifying and monitoring its competitors (Chapter 8). Atlas can expect such surprise moves from its competitors as sudden price cuts, improved products, and new selling and promotion methods, all of which might cut into its market share. Atlas must anticipate its competitors' possible moves and know how to react quickly and decisively. Atlas may want to initiate some surprise moves of its own, in which case it needs to anticipate how its competitors will respond. The key lies in developing and maintaining a well-thought-out, up-to-date, competitive intelligence system.

Researching and Selecting Target Markets and Positioning the Offer

Now the firm is ready to research and select target markets. It needs to know how to measure and forecast the attractiveness of any given market (Chapter 9). This requires estimating the market's overall size, growth, and profitability. Marketers must understand the major techniques for measuring market potential and forecasting future demand. Each technique has certain advantages and limitations that must be carefully understood by marketers to avoid their misuse.

These market measures and forecasts become key inputs into deciding which markets and new products to focus on. Modern marketing practice calls for dividing the market into major market segments, evaluating them, and selecting and targeting those market segments that the company can best serve (Chapter 10).

Market segmentation—the task of breaking the total market (which is typically too large to serve) into segments that share common properties—can be done in a number of ways. Atlas can segment the typewriter market by *customer size* (large, medium, small), *customer buying criteria* (quality, price, service), *customer industry* (banks, professional firms, manufacturing companies), and so on.

Market segments can also be formed by combining two or more variables. Figure 3-3 shows a segmentation of the typewriter market by two broad variables, namely, customer groups and customer needs (represented by different products). This particular framework is called a *product/market grid*. Marketing management can estimate, for each of the nine cells, the degree of market segment attractiveness and the company's degree of business strength. Essentially, Atlas seeks to determine which product/market cells, if any, best match the company's objectives and resources.

Suppose the most attractive segment for Atlas is the "small customer, electronic typewriter market" that is shaded in Figure 3-3. Even this market segment may be larger than the company can serve effectively, in which case *subsegmentation* can be undertaken. For example, Atlas might decide that its best opportunity lies in designing an inexpensive electronic typewriter whose features will have great appeal to small professional firms. In this way, Atlas will arrive at a clear idea of its *target market*.

FIGURE 3-3
Product/Market Grid for Typewriters

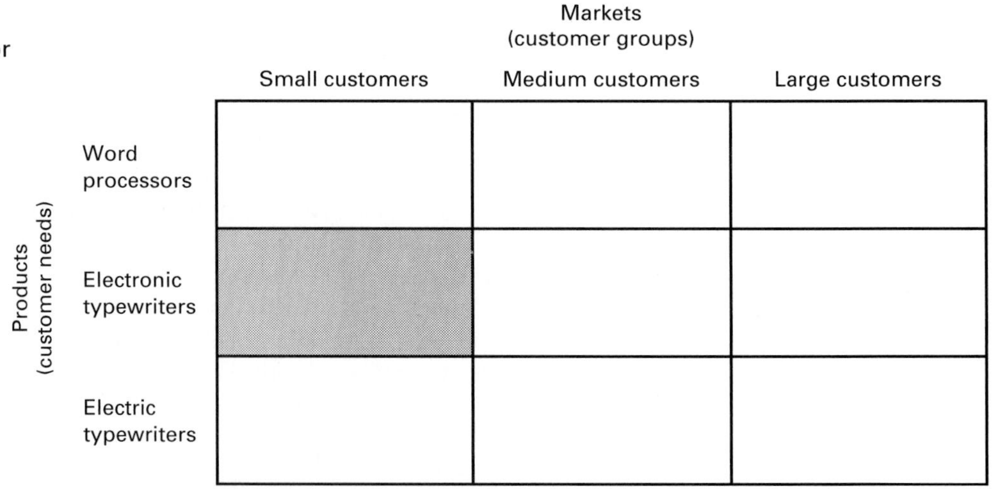

Designing Marketing Strategies

Given that Atlas wants to pursue the "small customer, electronic typewriter market," it needs to develop a *differentiating and positioning strategy* for that target market (Chapter 11). Atlas needs to define how it will differ from its significant competitors and how it wants to come across to its target buyers. Should it be the "Cadillac" firm offering a superior product at a premium price with excellent service that is well advertised and aimed at the more affluent buyers? Or should Atlas build a simple low-price electronic typewriter aimed at the more price-conscious market?

Atlas needs to study carefully the positions taken by its major competitors in the same target market. Suppose companies position themselves in terms of their product quality and price. We can develop a *product-positioning map* (Figure 3-4) to describe the positions of four competitors currently selling to this market. The four competitors, A, B, C, and D, differ in sales volume as reflected by the sizes of the circles. Competitor A occupies the high-quality/high-price position in this market. Competitor B is perceived by the market to produce an average-quality product at an average price. Competitor C is known to sell a slightly below-average-quality product for a low price. Competitor D is perceived as a "rip-off artist" because it sells a low-quality product for a high price.

Where should Atlas position itself in entering this market? It normally would not make sense to position itself against competitor A because then it would have to fight a well-established company for the limited number of customers who want the best electronic typewriter money can buy. However, if competitor A is rendering poor service or underpromoting, Atlas may decide to attack A. Most marketing-oriented companies generally prefer not to attack an existing competitor (unless it is a weak one) but to find some important customer needs that competitors are not filling. For example, Atlas might give serious consideration to positioning itself in the high-quality/medium-price quadrant (shown by the dotted circle). In this way, it would be "filling a hole" in the market. It must satisfy itself about three things, however. First, Atlas must find out from its engineers if they can build a high-quality typewriter

FIGURE 3-4

A Product-Positioning Map
Showing Perceived Offers of
Four Competitors and a
Possible Position for Atlas

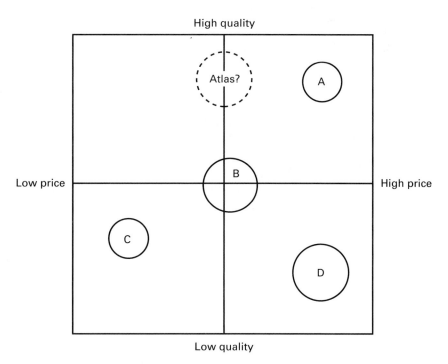

that could sell at a medium price and still make money. Second, Atlas must check whether there are a sufficient number of buyers who want a high-quality machine at a medium price. Formally yes, but price might contribute to snob appeal. Finally, Atlas must be able to convince buyers that its typewriter's quality and service are comparable to A's. Many buyers do not believe that medium-price units can be as good as higher-priced units, so heavy promotional expenditures may be required.

The main point is that companies today must carefully choose not only their consumer targets but also their competitor targets. In an era of slow-growth markets, planning for the competitors is as important as planning for the consumers.

Once Atlas decides on its product positioning, it has to undertake the difficult work of new-product development, testing, and launching (Chapter 12). The new-product-development process is a road strewn with land mines and booby traps. Too many products never come out of the laboratory, and of those that do, many fail in the marketplace, causing great expense to the company and a loss to society. The art of new-product development calls for organizing this process effectively and using distinct decision tools and controls at each stage of the process. Atlas, in designing a new electronic typewriter, will have to pay close attention to the various pitfalls involved in developing a successful new product.

After launch, the new product's strategy will have to be modified at the different stages in the product life cycle: introduction, growth, maturity, and decline (Chapter 13). Furthermore, strategy choice will depend on whether the firm plays the role of a market leader, challenger, follower, or nicher (Chapter 14). Finally, strategy will have to take into account changing global marketing opportunities and challenges (Chapter 15).

Planning Marketing Programs

Company planners must not only formulate the broad business strategies to help the company achieve its objectives but also must plan marketing strategies and tactics for specific products. We define marketing strategy as follows:

> Marketing strategy *comprises the broad principles by which marketing management expects to achieve its business and marketing objectives in a target market. It consists of basic decisions on marketing expenditures, marketing mix, and marketing allocation.*

Marketing management must decide what level of *marketing expenditures* is necessary to achieve its marketing objectives. Companies typically establish their marketing budget at some conventional percentage of the sales goal. Companies entering a market try to learn what the *marketing budget-to-sales ratio* is for competitors. A particular company may spend more than the normal ratio in the hope of achieving a higher market share. Ultimately the company should analyze the marketing work required to attain a given sales volume or market share and then cost out this work; the result is the required marketing budget.

The company also has to decide how to divide the total marketing budget among the various tools in the marketing mix. Marketing mix is one of the key concepts in modern marketing theory.

> Marketing mix *is the set of marketing tools that the firm uses to pursue its marketing objectives in the target market.*

There are literally dozens of marketing-mix tools. McCarthy popularized a four-factor classification of these tools called the four Ps: *product, price, place* (i.e., distribution), and *promotion*.[1] The particular marketing variables under each P are shown in Figure 3-5.

FIGURE 3-5
The Four Ps of the
Marketing Mix

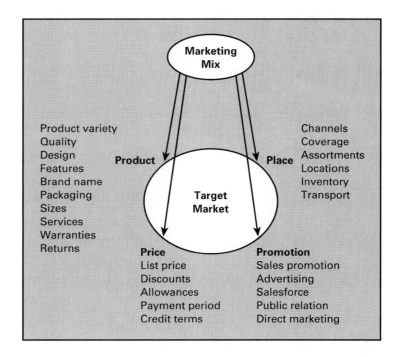

The company's marketing mix at time t for a particular product can be represented by the vector

$$(P_1, P_2, P_3, P_4)_t$$

where

$$P_1 = \text{product quality, } P_2 = \text{price, } P_3 = \text{place, and } P_4 = \text{promotion.}$$

If Atlas develops product quality at 1.2 (with 1.00 = average), prices it at $1000, and spends $30 000 a month on distribution and $20 000 a month on promotion, its marketing mix at time t is

$$(1.2, \$1000, \$30\,000, \$20\,000)_t$$

One can see that a marketing mix is selected from a great number of possibilities. If product quality could take on one of two values, and product price is constrained to lie between $500 and $1500 (to the nearest $100), and distribution and advertising expenditures are constrained to lie between $10 000 and $50 000 (to the nearest $10 000), then 550 (= $2 \times 11 \times 5 \times 5$) marketing-mix combinations are posssible.

To complicate matters further, marketing-mix decisions must be made for both the distribution channels and the final consumers. Figure 3-6 shows the company preparing an *offer mix* of products, services, and prices, and utilizing a *promotion mix* of sales promotion, advertising, salesforce, public relations, direct mail, and telemarketing to reach the distribution channels and the target consumers.

Not all marketing-mix variables can be adjusted in the short run. They vary in their adjustability. Typically, the firm can change its price, salesforce size, and advertising expenditures

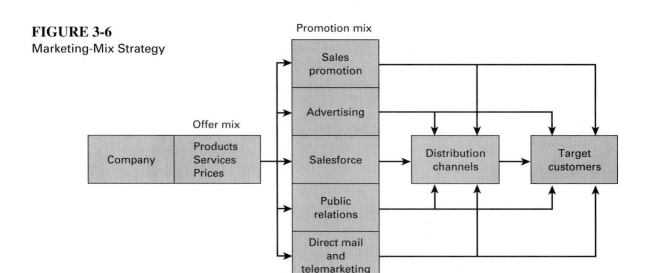

FIGURE 3-6
Marketing-Mix Strategy

in the short run. It can only develop new products and modify its distribution channels in the long run. Thus the firm typically makes fewer period-to-period marketing-mix changes in the short run than the number of marketing-mix variables suggests.

Finally, marketers must decide on the *allocation* of the marketing dollars to the various products, channels, promotion media, and sales areas. How many dollars should support Atlas's electric versus electronic typewriters? Direct versus distributor sales? Direct-mail advertising versus trade-magazine advertising? East Coast markets versus West Coast markets? We can represent a distinct allocation in the following way: Suppose management sets product quality at 1.2, price at $1000, a monthly distribution budget of $5 000, and a monthly advertising budget of $10 000 for product *i* selling to customer-type *j* in area *k* at time *t*. This is represented by the vector

$$(1.2, \$1000, \$5000, \$10\ 000)_{i,j,k,t}$$

To make these strategic allocations, marketing managers use the notion of *sales-response functions* (see the Appendix at the end of this chapter) that show how sales would be affected by marketing expenditure levels.

The most basic marketing-mix tool is *product*, which stands for the firm's tangible offer to the market, including the product quality, design, features, branding, and packaging (Chapter 16). Thus Atlas manages a product line of typewriters that differ in features, quality, styling, and packaging. Atlas also provides various services, such as delivery, repair, and training, as well as running a financial leasing business (Chapter 17).

A critical marketing-mix tool is *price*, namely, the amount of money that customers have to pay for the product (Chapter 18). Atlas has to decide on wholesale and retail prices, discounts, allowances, and credit terms. Its price should be commensurate with the perceived value of the offer, or else buyers will turn to competitors in choosing their products.

Place, another key marketing-mix tool, stands for the various activities the company undertakes to make the product easily accessible and available to target customers (Chapters 19 and 20). Atlas must identify, recruit, and link various middlemen and marketing facilitators so that its products and services are efficiently supplied to the target market. It must understand the various types of retailers, wholesalers, and physical-distribution firms and how they make their decisions.

Promotion, the fourth marketing-mix tool, stands for the various activities the company undertakes to communicate its products' merits and to persuade target customers to buy them (Chapters 21-24). Thus Atlas has to hire, train, and motivate salespeople to promote its products to middlemen and other buyers. It has to set up communication and promotion programs consisting of advertising, direct marketing, sales promotion, and public relations.

Organizing, Implementing, and Controlling the Marketing Effort

The final step in the marketing management process is organizing the marketing resources and implementing and controlling the marketing plan. A plan is nothing "unless it degenerates into work."[2] Therefore the company must build a marketing organization that is capable of *implementing* the marketing plan (Chapter 25). In a small company, one person might carry out all the marketing tasks: marketing research, selling, advertising, customer servicing, and so on. In large companies, several marketing specialists will be found. Thus Atlas has salespeople, sales managers, marketing researchers, advertising personnel, product and brand managers, market-segment managers, and customer-service personnel.

Marketing organizations are typically headed by a marketing vice-president, who performs two tasks. The first is to coordinate the work of all of the marketing personnel. Atlas's marketing vice-president must make sure, for example, that the advertising manager works closely with the salesforce manager, so that the salesforce is ready to handle customer leads generated by ads that are placed by the advertising department.

The marketing vice-president's other task is to work closely with the vice-presidents of finance, manufacturing, research and development, purchasing, and personnel to coordinate company efforts to satisfy customers. Thus if Atlas's marketing people advertise its new electronic typewriter as a quality product, but R&D does not design a quality product or manufacturing fails to manufacture it carefully, then marketing will not deliver on its promise. The marketing vice-president's job is to make sure that all the company departments collaborate to fulfill the company's marketing promise to the customers.

The marketing department's effectiveness depends not only on how it is structured but also on how well its personnel are selected, trained, directed, motivated, and evaluated. There is a vast difference in the performance of a "turned-on" versus "turned-off" marketing group. The marketing personnel need constructive feedback on their marketing performance. Managers must meet with their subordinates periodically to review their performance, praise their strengths, point out their weaknesses, and suggest ways to improve.

There are likely to be many surprises as marketing plans are implemented by the marketing organization. The company needs feedback and control procedures to make sure that the marketing objectives will be achieved (Chapter 26). Various managers will have to exercise control responsibilities in addition to their analysis, planning, and implementing responsibilities. Three types of marketing control can be distinguished: annual-plan control, profitability control, and strategic control.

Annual-plan control is the task of making sure that the company is achieving the sales, profits, and other goals that it established in its annual plan. The task breaks into four steps. First, management must state well-defined goals in the annual plan for each month, quarter, or other period during the year. Second, management must have ways to measure its ongoing performance in the marketplace. Third, management must determine the underlying causes of any serious gaps in performance. Fourth, management must decide on the best corrective action to take to close the gaps between goals and performance. It may call for improving the ways the plan is being implemented or changing the programs, strategy, or even the goals.

Companies need to analyze periodically the actual *profitability* of their various products, customer groups, trade channels, and order sizes. This is not a simple task. A company's accounting system is seldom designed to report the real profitability of different marketing entities and activities. To measure the profit on different typewriter models, for example, Atlas's accountants have to estimate how much time the salesforce spends promoting each model, how much advertising supports each model, and so on. *Marketing profitability analysis* is the tool used to measure the profitability of different marketing activities. *Marketing efficiency studies* also need to be undertaken to study how various marketing activities could be carried on more efficiently. From time to time, Atlas must stand back and critically reexamine its overall marketing game plan and decide whether it continues to make good *strategic* sense. Marketing is one of the major areas where rapid obsolescence of objectives, policies, strategies, and programs is a constant possibility. Giant companies such as Chrysler, International Harvester, Singer, and A&P all fell on hard times because they did not watch the changing marketplace and make the proper adaptations. Because of the rapid changes in the marketing environment, each company needs to reassess periodically its marketing effectiveness through a control instrument known as the *marketing audit*.

Figure 3-7 presents a grand summary of the marketing management process and the forces shaping the company's marketing strategy. The target customers stand in the center, and the company focuses its effort on serving and satisfying them. The company develops a marketing mix made up of the factors under its control, the four Ps. To arrive at its marketing mix, the company manages four systems: a marketing information system, marketing planning system, marketing organizational system, and marketing control system. These systems are interrelated in that marketing information is needed to develop marketing plans; the plans in turn are implemented by the marketing organization; and the results of this implementation are reviewed and controlled.

Through these systems, the company monitors and adapts to the marketing environment. The company adapts to its microenvironment, consisting of marketing intermediaries, suppliers,

FIGURE 3-7
Factors Influencing Company
Marketing Strategy

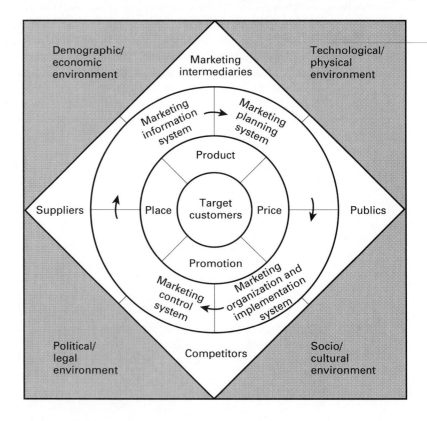

competitors, and publics. And it adapts to the macroenvironment, consisting of demographic/economic forces, political/legal forces, technological/physical forces, and social/cultural forces. The company takes into account the actors and forces in the marketing environment in developing its strategy to serve the target market.

THE NATURE AND CONTENTS OF A MARKETING PLAN

We have seen that one of the most important outputs of the marketing process is the *marketing plan*. We may now ask, What does a marketing plan look like?

Marketing plans will have several sections, varying with how much detail top management wants from its managers. Most marketing plans, particularly product and brand plans, will have the following sections: *executive summary, current marketing situation, opportunity and issue analysis, objectives, marketing strategy, action programs, projected profit-and-loss statement*, and *controls*. These sections and their purposes are listed in Table 3-1 and discussed in the following paragraphs. The plan sections will be illustrated with the following case:

> Zenith Corporation is a major producer of electronic consumer products, including television receivers, radios, stereo equipment, and personal computers. Each product line is the responsibility of a product manager, who must prepare a long-range plan and an annual plan that would meet the financial objectives of the Zenith Corporation. ∎
>
> Currently Jane Melody is the product manager of Zenith's line of modular stereo systems, called the Allegro line. Each system consists of an AM-FM tuner/amplifier plus phonograph plus tape deck and separate speakers. Zenith offers thirteen different models that sell in the $150-$400

Table 3-1 Contents of a Marketing Plan

Section	Purpose
I. Executive summary	Presents a brief overview of the proposed plan for quick management skimming.
II. Current marketing situation	Presents relevant background data on the market, product, competition, distribution, and macroenvironment.
III. Opportunity and issue analysis	Identifies the main opportunities/threats, strengths/weaknesses, and issues facing the product.
IV. Objectives	Defines the goals the plan wants to reach in the areas of sales volume, market share, and profit.
V. Marketing strategy	Presents the broad marketing approach that will be used to meet the plan's objectives.
VI. Action programs	Answers: **What** will be done? **Who** will do it? **When** will it be done? and **How much** will it cost?
VII. Projected profit-and-loss statement	Forecasts the expected financial outcomes from the plan.
VIII. Controls	Indicates how the plan will be monitored.

range. A modular stereo system differs on the one hand from stereo consoles, in which all of the components are built into one cabinet, and on the other hand from audio component systems, where consumers select unrelated but compatible components to make up the systems they want. Zenith also produces a line of stereo console units, but the console market is in a state of decline as consumers switch to smaller sound systems. Zenith does not produce audio components but has considered it from time to time. Zenith's main goal is to increase its market share and profitability in the modular-stereo-system market. As product manager, Jane Melody has to prepare a marketing plan to improve the performance of the Allegro line.[3] ■

Executive Summary

The planning document should open with a short summary of the main goals and recommendations to be found in the body of the plan. Here is an abbreviated example:

The 1988 Allegro marketing plan seeks to generate a significant increase in company sales and profits over the preceding year. The profit target is set at $180 000. The sales-revenue target is set at $1.8 million, which represents a planned 9 percent sales gain over last year. This increase is seen as attainable through improved pricing, advertising, and distribution effort. The required marketing budget will be $229 000, a 14 percent increase over last year. . . . [More details follow.] ■

The executive summary permits higher management to grasp quickly the major thrust of the plan. A table of contents should follow the executive summary.

Current Marketing Situation

This section of the plan presents relevant background data on the market, product, competition, distribution, and macroenvironment. Many of the data will be drawn from a *product fact book* kept and updated by the product or brand manager.

Market Situation   Here data are presented on the target market. The size and growth of the market (in units and/or dollars) are shown for several past years in total and by market and geographical segments. Data are also presented on customer needs, perceptions, and buying-behavior trends.

The modular stereo market accounts for approximately $40 million, or 20 percent of the home stereo market. Sales are expected to be stable or declining over the next few years. . . . The primary buyers are upscale people who want to listen to good music but do not want to invest in expensive component equipment. They want to buy a complete system produced by a name they can trust. They want a system with good sound and whose looks fit the decor primarily of family or living rooms. ■

Product Situation   Here the sales, prices, contribution margins, and net profits are shown for each major product in the line for several past years.

Table 3-2 shows an example of how product data might be presented for the modular stereo line. Row 1 shows the total industry sales in units growing at 5 percent annually until 1990, when demand declined slightly. Row 2 shows Zenith's market share hovering around 3 percent, although it reached 4 percent in 1989. Row 3 shows the average price for an Allegro stereo rising about 10 percent a year except the last year, when it rose 4 percent. Row 4 shows variable costs—materials, labor, energy—rising each year. Row 5 shows that the gross contribution margin per unit—the difference between price (row 3) and unit variable cost (row 4)—rose the first few years and remained at $100 in the latest year. Rows 6 and 7 show sales volume in units and dollars, and row 8 shows the total gross contribution margin, which rose until the latest year, when it fell. Row 9 shows that overhead remained constant during 1987 and 1988 and increased to a high level during 1989 and 1990, owing to an explosion of manufacturing capacity. Row 10 shows net contribution margin, that is, gross contribution margin less overhead. Rows 11, 12, and 13 show marketing expenditures on advertising and promotion, sales force and distribution, and marketing research. Finally, row 14 shows net operating profit after marketing expenses. The picture is one of increasing profits until 1990, when they fell to about one-third of the 1989 level. Clearly Zenith's product manager needs to find a strategy for 1991 that will restore healthy growth in sales and profits to the product line. ■

Competitive Situation   Here the major competitors are identified and are described in terms of their size, goals, market share, product quality, marketing strategies, and other characteristics that are appropriate for understanding their intentions and behavior.

Zenith's major competitors in the modular-stereo-system market are Panasonic, Sony, Magnavox, General Electric, and Electrophonic. Each competitor has a specific strategy and niche in the market. Panasonic, for example, offers thirty-three models covering the whole price range, sells primarily in department stores and discount stores, and is a heavy advertising spender. It is out to dominate the market through product proliferation and price discounting. . . . [Similar descriptions are prepared for the other competitors.] ■

Distribution Situation   This section presents data on the number of stereo units sold in each distribution channel and the changing importance of each channel. Changes are noted

Table 3-2 Historical Product Data

Variable	Columns	1987	1988	1989	1990
1. Industry sales—in units		200 000	210 000	220 500	220 000
2. Company market share		0.03	0.03	0.04	0.03
3. Average price per unit $		200	220	240	250
4. Variable cost per unit $		120	125	140	150
5. Gross contribution margin per unit $	(3 − 4)	80	95	100	100
6. Sales volume in units	(1 × 2)	6 000	6 300	8 820	6 600
7. Sales revenue $	(3 × 6)	1 200 000	1 386 000	2 116 800	1 650 000
8. Gross contribution margin $	(5 × 6)	480 000	598 500	882 000	660 000
9. Overhead $		200 000	200 000	350 000	350 000
10. Net contribution margin $	(8 − 9)	280 000	398 500	532 000	310 000
11. Advertising and promotion $		80 000	100 000	100 000	90 000
12. Salesforce and distribution $		70 000	100 000	110 000	100 000
13. Marketing research $		10 000	12 000	15 000	10 000
14. Net operating profit $	(10 − 11 − 12 − 13)	120 000	186 500	307 000	110 000

in the power of distributors and dealers as well as in the prices and trade terms necessary to motivate them.

> Modular stereo sets are sold through a variety of distribution channels: department stores, radio/TV stores, appliance stores, discount stores, furniture stores, music stores, audio specialty stores, and mail order. Zenith sells 37 percent of its sets through appliance stores, 23 percent through radio/TV stores, 10 percent through furniture stores, 3 percent through department stores, and the remainder through other channels. Zenith dominates in channels that are declining in importance, while it is a weak competitor in the faster-growing channels, such as discount stores. Zenith gives about a 30 percent margin to its dealers, which is similar to what other competitors give. ■

Macroenvironment Situation   This section describes broad macroenvironment trends—demographic, economic, technological, political/legal, social/cultural—that bear on this product line's future.

> About 50 percent of households now have stereo equipment. As the market approaches saturation, effort must be turned to convincing consumers to upgrade their equipment. . . . The economy is expected to be weak, which means people will postpone consumer-durables purchases. . . . The Japanese have designed new and more compact audio systems that pose a challenge to conventional stereo systems. ■

Opportunity and Issue Analysis

On the basis of the data describing the current marketing situation, the product manager needs to identify the major *opportunities/threats, strengths/weaknesses*, and *issues* the company faces with this product over the term of the plan.

Opportunities/Threats Analysis (O/T Analysis)   Here the manager identifies the main opportunities and threats facing the business. Opportunities and threats refer to outside factors that can affect the future of the business. They are written so as to suggest some possible actions that might be taken. The manager should rank the opportunities and threats so that the more important ones receive special attention.

The main *opportunities* facing Zenith's Allegro line follow.

☐ Consumers are showing increased interest in more compact modular stereo systems, and Zenith should consider designing one or more compact models.

☐ Two major national department store chains are willing to carry the Allegro line if we will give them extra advertising support.

☐ A major national discount chain is willing to carry the Allegro line if we will offer a special discount for their higher purchase volume.

The main *threats* facing Zenith's Allegro line follow.

☐ An increasing number of consumers who choose modular stereo systems are buying them in mass-merchandise and discount stores, in which we have weak representation.

☐ An increasing number of upscale consumers are showing a preference for component systems, and we do not have an audio component line.

☐ Some of our competitors have introduced smaller speakers with excellent sound quality, and consumers are favoring these smaller speakers.

- The federal government may pass a more stringent product-safety law, which would entail some product redesign work on our part.

Strengths/Weaknesses Analysis (S/W Analysis)   The manager needs to identify product strengths and weaknesses. Strengths and weaknesses are inside factors, in contrast with opportunities and threats, which are outside factors. Company strengths point to certain strategies the company might be successful in using, while company weaknesses point to certain things the company needs to avoid or correct.

The main *strengths* of Zenith's Allegro line follow.

- Zenith's name has excellent brand awareness and an image of high quality.
- Dealers who sell the Allegro line are knowledgeable and well trained in selling.
- Zenith has an excellent service network, and consumers know they will get quick repair service if needed.

The main *weaknesses* of Zenith's Allegro line follow.

- The sound quality of Allegro is not demonstrably better than the sound quality of competing sets, and yet sound quality can make a big difference in brand choice.
- Zenith is budgeting only 5 percent of its sales revenue for advertising and promotion, while some major competitors are spending at twice that level.
- Zenith's Allegro line is not clearly positioned compared with Magnavox ("quality") and Sony ("innovation"). Zenith needs a unique selling proposition. The current advertising campaign is not particularly creative or exciting.
- Zenith's brand is priced higher relative to other brands without being supported by a real perceived difference in quality. The brand loses the price-conscious buyer. The pricing strategy should be reevaluated.

Issues Analysis   In this section, the company uses the findings of the O/T and S/W analyses to define the main issues that must be addressed in the plan. Decisions on these issues will lead to the subsequent setting of objectives, strategies, and tactics.

Zenith must consider the following basic *issues* with respect to the Allegro line.

- Should Zenith stay in the stereo-equipment business? Can it compete effectively? Or should it harvest or divest this product line?
- If Zenith stays in, should it continue with its present products, channels of distribution, and price and promotion policies, making further refinements where possible?
- Or should Zenith switch to high-growth channels (such as discount stores), and can it do this and yet retain the loyalty of its traditional channel partners?
- Should Zenith increase its advertising and promotion expenditures to match competitors' expenditures, and will this move lead to sufficient increases in market share and profitability?
- Should Zenith pour money into R&D to develop advanced features, sound, and styling?

Objectives

At this point, management knows the issues and is faced with making some basic decisions about the objectives. These objectives will guide the subsequent research for strategies and action programs.

Two types of objectives must be set: financial and marketing.

Financial Objectives   Every company seeks certain financial objectives. The owners will be looking for a specific long-run rate of return on investment and will know the profits they would like to achieve in the current year.

Zenith's management wants each business unit to deliver a certain rate of profit and return on investment. Furthermore, it wants the Allegro line to grow stronger. The product manager sets the following financial objectives for the Allegro line:

☐ Earn an average rate of return on investment over the next five years of 20 percent after taxes.

☐ Produce net profits of $180 000 in 1991.

☐ Produce a cash flow of $200 000 in 1991.

Marketing Objectives   The financial objectives must be converted into marketing objectives. For example, if the company wants to earn $180 000 profit, and its target profit margin is 10 percent on sales, then it must set a goal of $1.8 million in sales revenue. If the company sets an average price of $260, it must sell 6923 units. If it expects total industry sales to reach 230 000 units, that is a 3 percent market share. To maintain this market share, the company will have to set certain goals for consumer awareness, distribution coverage, and so on. Thus the *marketing objectives* might read:

☐ Achieve total sales revenue of $1 800 000 in 1988, which represents a 9 percent increase from last year.

☐ Therefore, achieve a sales volume in units of 6923, which represents an expected market share of 3 percent.

☐ Expand consumer awareness of the Allegro brand from 15 percent to 30 percent over the planning period.

☐ Expand the number of distribution outlets by 10 percent.

☐ Aim for an average realized price of $260.

The set of objectives should meet certain criteria. First, each objective should be stated in an unambiguous and measurable form with a stated time period for accomplishment. Second, the various objectives should be internally consistent. Third, the objectives should be stated hierarchically, if possible, with lower objectives being derived from higher objectives. Fourth, the objectives should be attainable but sufficiently challenging to stimulate maximum effort.

Marketing Strategy

The manager now outlines the broad marketing strategy, or "game plan." In developing a marketing strategy, a manager faces a multitude of possible choices. Each objective can be achieved in a number of ways. For example, the objective *increase the sales revenue by 9 percent* can be achieved by increasing the average price on all units, increasing the overall sales volume, and/or selling more of the higher-price units. Each of these objectives can in turn be achieved in a number of ways. The *overall sales volume* can be increased by increasing market growth and/or increasing market share. In turn, *increased market growth* can come about by convincing people to own more stereo systems per household or to replace their old systems more frequently. By going down the path of each objective, the manager can identify the major strategy alternatives facing the product line.

Strategy formulation calls for making basic choices among these strategy alternatives. The manager can write up a basic strategy statement in verbal form, like the following:

Zenith's basic strategy for Allegro is to aim at the upscale family, with particular emphasis on the female buyer. The product line will be expanded by adding lower-price and higher-price units. The average price of the line will be raised 4 percent. A new and intensified advertising campaign will be developed to increase the perceived reliability of our brand in the consumer's mind. We will schedule a strong sales-promotion program to attract increased consumer and dealer attention to our line. We will expand distribution to cover department stores but will avoid discount stores. We will put more funds into restyling the Allegro line so that it projects an image of high-quality sound and reliability. ■

Alternatively, the strategy statement can be presented in list form covering the major marketing tools:

STRATEGY STATEMENT

Target market:	Upscale households, with particular emphasis on female buyer.
Positioning:	The best-sounding and most reliable modular stereo system.
Product line:	Add one lower-price model and two higher-price models.
Price:	Price somewhat above competitive brands.
Distribution outlets:	Heavy in radio/TV stores and appliance stores; increased efforts to penetrate department stores.
Salesforce:	Expand by 10 percent and introduce a national account-management system.
Service:	Widely available and quick service.
Advertising:	Develop a new advertising campaign, directed at the target market, that supports the positioning strategy; emphasize higher-price units in the ads; increase the advertising budget by 20 percent.
Sales promotion:	Increase the sales-promotion budget by 15 percent to develop a point-of-purchase display and to participate to a greater extent in dealer trade shows.
Research and development:	Increase expenditures by 25 percent to develop better styling of Allegro line.
Marketing research:	Increase expenditures by 10 percent to improve knowledge of consumer-choice process and to monitor competitor moves.

In developing the strategy, the manager needs to discuss it with others whose cooperation will make the difference between failure and success. The product manager will see the purchasing and manufacturing people to make sure they are able to buy enough material and produce enough units to meet the planned sales-volume levels, the sales manager to obtain the planned salesforce support, and the financial officer to make sure enough funds will be available.

Action Programs

The strategy statement represents the broad marketing thrusts that the manager will use to achieve the business objectives. Each element of the marketing strategy must now be elaborated to answer: *What* will be done? *When* will it be done? *Who* will do it? *How much* will it cost? Here is an example for the sales-promotion program:

> Zenith's sales-promotion program will be divided into two parts, one directed at dealers and the other at consumers. The dealer-promotion program will consist of:
>
> *April.* Zenith will participate in the Consumer Electronics Trade Show. John Smith, dealer promotion director, will make the arrangements. The expected cost is $4000.
>
> *August.* A sales contest will be conducted, which will award three Hawaiian vacations to the three dealers producing the greatest percentage increase in sales of Allegro units. The contest will be handled by John Smith at a planned cost of $8000. ∎
>
> The consumer promotion program will consist of:
>
> *February.* Zenith will advertise in the newspapers that a free Anne Murray record album will be given to everyone buying an Allegro unit this month. Ann Morris, consumer promotion director, will handle this project at a planned cost of $3000.
>
> *September.* A newspaper advertisement will announce that consumers who listen to an Allegro store demonstration in the second week of September will have their names entered in a sweepstakes, the grand prizes to be ten Allegros. Ann Morris will handle this project at a planned cost of $2000. ∎

Projected Profit-and-Loss Statement

The action plans allow the product manager to assemble a supporting budget that is essentially a projected profit-and-loss statement. On the revenue side, it shows the forecasted sales volume in units and the average realized price. On the expense side, it shows the cost of production, physical distribution, and marketing, broken down into finer categories. The difference is projected profit. Higher management will review the budget and approve or modify it. If the requested budget is too high, the product manager will have to make some cuts. Once approved, the budget is the basis for developing plans and schedules for material procurement, production scheduling, employee recruitment, and marketing operations.

Controls

The last section of the plan outlines the controls that will be applied to monitor the plan's progress. Typically the goals and budget are spelled out for each month or quarter. Higher management can review the results each period and spot businesses that are not attaining their goals. Managers of lagging businesses must explain what is happening and the actions they are taking to improve plan fulfillment.

Some control sections include contingency plans. A contingency plan outlines the steps that management would implement in response to specific adverse developments that might occur, such as a price war or a strike. The purpose of contingency planning is to encourage managers to give prior thought to some difficulties that might lie ahead.

SUMMARY

Marketing plans focus on a product/market and consist of the detailed marketing strategies and programs for achieving the product's objectives in the market. Marketing plans are the central instrument for directing and coordinating the marketing effort.

The marketing planning process consists of five steps: analyzing market opportunities; researching and selecting target markets; designing marketing strategies; planning marketing programs; and organizing, implementing and controlling the marketing effort. Each step is briefly described in this chapter and examined in the following chapters.

Marketing planning results in a marketing-plan document that contains the following sections: executive summary, current market situation, opportunity and issue analysis, objectives, marketing strategy, action programs, projected profit-and-loss statement, and controls.

To plan effectively, marketing managers must understand the key relationship between types of marketing-mix expenditures and their sales and profit consequences. These relationships are explained in the appendix to Chapter 3.

■ QUESTIONS

1. An automotive-parts manufacturer produces three products: mufflers, filters, and silencers. The company is seeking new growth opportunities. Develop a product-market matrix showing some potential expansion opportunities for this manufacturer.

2. Various models have been developed to aid marketing managers in determining the marketing mix for their products. What properties should be included in the design of these models?

3. Marketing planning is difficult for toy companies because toys tend to be fads, and toy companies must replace roughly 60 percent of their volume every year. Given the nature of this market, what would you do as a marketing manager for a toy company to generate long-term growth?

4. John Smith, Heinz's ketchup product manager, prepared the following marketing plan. Critique his procedure. What improvements can you suggest?

   1) *Forecast of total market*
     This year's total market
     (2 358 000 cases) × recent
     growth rate (6%)   2 500 000 cases
   2) *Forecast of market share*   28%
   3) *Forecast of sales volume*   700 000 cases
     (1 × 2)
   4) *Price to distributor* $4.45 per case
   5) Estimate of sales revenue $3 115 000
     (3 × 4)
   6) *Estimate of variable costs*
     Tomatoes and spices ($0.50) +
     bottles and caps ($1.00) +
     labor ($1.10) + physical
     distribution ($0.15) $2.75 per case
   7) *Estimate of contribution margin*
     to cover fixed costs, profits,
     and marketing (3 × [4 − 6]) $1 190 000

   8) *Estimate of fixed costs*
     Fixed charge $1 per case × 700 000
     cases $ 700 000
   9) .*Estimate of contribution margin*
     to cover profits and marketing
     (7 − 8) $ 490 000
   10) *Estimate of target profit goal* $ 190 000
   11) *Amount available for marketing*
     (9 − 10) $ 300 000
   12) *Split of the marketing budget*
     Advertising $ 200 000
     Sales Promotion $ 90 000
     Marketing Research $ 10 000

5. Opportunities/threats analysis, an important part of the marketing plan, is designed to let management see what external factors it is facing and the possible action it might take. Develop an O/T analysis for the Export cigarette brand of RJR-Macdonald Inc.

6. One marketing theorist maintains that "value rigidity" on the part of marketing managers poses a serious problem in the development of marketing plans. What does he mean by this assertion?

7. A marketer evaluates two marketing strategies and estimates their expected rates of return to be 8 percent and 12 percent, respectively. Which strategy should be chosen if this decision is to be made many times? Which strategy should be chosen if this decision is to be made only once?

8. Suppose the quantity sold (Q) of an item depends on the price charged (P), the level of advertising expenditure (A), and the level of distribution expenditure (D). Develop a sales-response equation (a) where the marginal effect of each marketing variable is uninfluenced by the levels of the other marketing variables; (b) where the marginal effect of each marketing variable is influenced by the levels of the other variables (see the following Appendix).

9. Suggest some equation forms that might be used to represent (a) a sales-response function when sales increase at a decreasing rate with marketing expenditures; (b) a sales-response function when sales increase at an increasing and then decreasing rate (see the following Appendix).

10. A firm wants to decide how much quality to build into a new machine tool. Illustrate diagrammatically the logic of determining the optimal quality level.

11. The brand manager in charge of a dry breakfast cereal has the following sales and expense statement:

Net sales		100%
Manufacturing and shipping costs		
Fixed	12.9%	
Variable	39.6	
Total		52.5
All other expenses (excluding advertising and merchandising expenses)		
Distribution and delivery expenses	5.4	
Administrative and general expenses	4.0	
Salespeoples' expenses	3.5	
Market research	0.5	
Total		13.4
Available for advertising, merchandising, and profit		34.1

List several ways the brand manager can try to increase profits.

■ NOTES

1. E. Jerome McCarthy, *Basic Marketing: A Managerial Approach* (Homewood, Ill.: Richard D. Irwin, 1981), now in its ninth edition. Two alternative classifications are worth noting. Frey proposed that all marketing-decision variables could be categorized into two factors: the *offering* (product, packaging, brand, price, and service) and *methods and tools* (distribution channels, personal selling, advertising, sales promotion, and publicity). See Albert W. Frey, *Advertising*, 3rd ed., (New York: Ronald Press, 1961), p. 30. Lazer and Kelly proposed a three-factor classification: *goods and service mix, distribution mix*, and *communications mix*. See William Lazer and Eugene J. Kelly, *Managerial Marketing: Perspectives and Viewpoints*, rev. ed. (Homewood, Ill.: Richard D. Irwin, 1962), p. 413.

2. Peter F. Drucker, *Management: Tasks, Responsibilities, Practices* (New York: Harper & Row, 1973), p. 128.

3. This example is adapted with several changes and additions from "Zenith Radio Corporation; Allegro," a Harvard Business School case 9-575-062 prepared by Ed Popper under the supervision of Scott Ward, 1975.

appendix

THE THEORY OF EFFECTIVE MARKETING-RESOURCE ALLOCATION

Having examined how actual marketing plans are constructed, we will now describe some important tools and concepts that managers can use to improve their marketing planning. Planning can now be done on microcomputers using tailored computer programs and spreadsheets. At companies such as Quaker Oats and General Mills, brand managers develop and estimate the cost of different marketing strategies, using computer programs in searching for the best plan. These computer programs utilize simple sales-and-profit equations and make assumptions on how sales and profits would respond to different marketing-mix expenditures. We will illustrate these concepts in the following paragraphs.

The Profit Equation

Every marketing-mix strategy will lead to a certain level of profit. The profit can be estimated through a profit equation. Profits (Z) by definition are equal to the product's revenue (R) less its costs (C):

$$Z = R - C \tag{3-1}$$

Revenue is equal to the product's net price (P') times its unit sales (Q):

$$R = P'Q \tag{3-2}$$

But the product's net price (P') is equal to its list price (P) less any allowance per unit (k) representing freight allowances, commissions, and discounts:

$$P' = P - k \tag{3-3}$$

The product's costs can be conveniently classified into unit variable nonmarketing costs (c), fixed costs (F), and marketing costs (M):

$$C = cQ + F + M \tag{3-4}$$

Substituting equations (3-2), (3-3), and (3-4) into (3-1) and simplifying,

$$Z = [(P - k) - c]\, Q - F - M \tag{3-5}$$

where:

Z = total profits
P = list price
k = allowance per unit (such as freight allowances, commissions, discounts)
c = production and distribution variable cost (such as labor costs, delivery costs)
Q = number of units sold
F = fixed costs (such as salaries, rent, electricity)
M = discretionary marketing costs

The expression $[(P - k) - c]$ is the *gross contribution margin per unit*—the amount the company realizes on the average unit after deducting allowances and the variable costs of producing and distributing the average unit. The expression $[(P - k) - c]\, Q$ is the *gross contribution margin*—the net revenue available to cover the fixed costs, profits, and discretionary marketing expenditures.

The Sales Equation

In order to use the profit equation for planning purposes, the product manager needs to model the determinants of sales volume (Q). The relation of sales volume to its determinants is specified in a sales equation (also called the sales-response function):

$$Q = f(X_1, X_2 \ldots, X_n, Y_1, Y_2, \ldots, X_m) \tag{3-6}$$

where:

$$(X_1, X_2, \ldots, X_n) = \text{sales variables under the control of the firm}$$
$$(Y_1, Y_2, \ldots, Y_m) = \text{sales variables not under the control of the firm}$$

Y variables include such things as the cost-of-living index and the size and income of the target market. As these variables change, so does the market's buying rate. The manager has no influence over the Y variables but needs to estimate them for use in forecasting. We will assume that the manager has estimated Y variables and their effect on sales volume, which is conveyed by

$$Q = f(X_1, X_2, \ldots, X_n \mid Y_1, Y_2, \ldots, Y_m) \tag{3-7}$$

which says that sales volume is a function of the X variables, for given levels of the Y variables.

The X variables are the variables that the manager can set to influence the sales level. The X variables include the list price (P), allowances (k), variable cost (c) (to the extent that high variable costs reflect improved product quality, delivery time, and customer service), and marketing expenditures (M). Thus sales, as a function of the manager's controllable variables, is described by

$$Q = f(p, k, c, M) \tag{3-8}$$

We can make one additional refinement. The marketing budget, M, can be spent in several ways, such as advertising (A), sales promotion (S), sales force (D), and marketing research (R). The sales equation is now

$$Q = f(P, k, c, A, S, D, R) \tag{3-9}$$

where the elements in the parentheses represent the marketing mix.

Profit-Optimization Planning

Suppose the manager wants to find a marketing mix that will maximize profits in the coming year. This requires having some idea of how each element in the marketing mix will affect sales. We will use the term *sales-response function* to describe the relationship between sales volume and a particular element of the marketing mix. Specifically, *the sales-response function forecasts the likely sales volume during a specified time period associated with different possible levels of a marketing-mix element, holding constant the other marketing-mix elements*. It should not be thought of as describing a relationship over time between the two variables. To the extent that managers have a good intuition for the relevant sales-response functions, they are in a position to formulate more effective marketing plans.

What are the possible shapes of sales-response functions? Figure 3A-1 shows several possibilities. Figure 3A-1(a) shows the well-known relationship between price and sales volume, known as the law of demand. The relationship states that more sales will occur, other things being equal, at lower prices. The illustration shows a curvilinear relationship, although a linear relationship is also possible.

Figure 3A-1(b) shows four possible function relationships between sales volume and marketing expenditures. Marketing expenditure function (*A*) is the least plausible: It states that sales volume is not affected by the level of marketing expenditures. It would mean that the number of customers and their purchasing rates are not affected by sales calls, advertising, sales promotion, or marketing research. Marketing expenditure function (*B*) states that sales volume grows linearly with marketing expenditures. In the illustration, the intercept is 0, but this is inaccurate if some sales would take place even in the absence of marketing expenditures.

Marketing expenditure function (*C*) is a concave function showing sales volume increasing throughout at a decreasing rate. It is a plausible description of sales response to salesforce-size increases. The rationale is as follows: If a field salesforce consisted of one sales representative, that representative would call on the best prospects, and the marginal rate of sales response would be highest. A second sales rep would call on the next best prospects, and the marginal rate of sales response would be somewhat less. Successively hired sales reps would call on successively less responsive prospects, resulting in a diminishing rate of sales increase.

Marketing expenditure function (*D*) is an S-shaped function showing sales volume initially increasing at an increasing rate and then increasing at a decreasing rate. It is a plausible description of sales response to increasing levels of advertising expenditure. The rationale is as follows: Small advertising budgets do not buy enough advertising to create more than minimal brand awareness. Larger budgets can produce high brand awareness, interest, and preference, all of which might lead to increased purchase response. Very large budgets, however, may not produce much additional response because the target market is already highly familiar with the brand.

FIGURE 3A-1
Sales-Response Functions

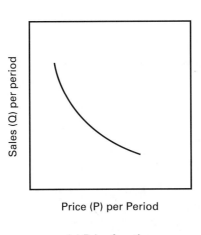

Price (P) per Period

(a) Price function

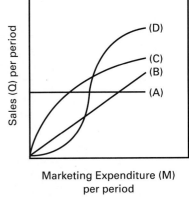

Marketing Expenditure (M) per period

(b) Market expenditure functions

The relation of eventually diminishing returns to increases in marketing expenditures is plausible for the following reasons. First, there is an upper limit to the total potential demand for any particular product. The easier sales prospects buy almost immediately, leaving the more recalcitrant sales prospects. As the upper limit is approached, it becomes increasingly expensive to attract the remaining buyers. Second, as a company steps up its marketing effort, its competitors are likely to do the same, with the net result that each company experiences increasing sales resistance. And third, if sales were to increase at an increasing rate throughout, natural monopolies would result. A single firm would take over each industry. Yet we do not see this happening.

How can marketing managers estimate the sales-response functions that apply to their business? Three methods are available. The first is the *statistical method*, where the manager gathers data on past sales and levels of marketing-mix variables and estimates the sales-response functions through statistical techniques. Several researchers have used this method with varying degrees of success, depending on the quantity and quality of available data and the stability of the underlying relationships.[1] The second is the *experimental method*, which calls for varying the marketing expenditure and mix levels in matched samples of geographical or other units and noting the resulting sales volume.[2] The experimental method produces the most reliable results but is not used extensively because of its complex requirements, high cost, and inordinate level of management resistance. The third is the *judgmental method*, where experts are asked to make intelligent guesses about the needed magnitudes. This method requires a careful selection of the experts and a defined procedure for gathering and combining their estimates, such as the Delphi method.[3] The judgmental method is often the only feasible one and can be quite useful. We believe that using the estimates of experts is better than forgoing formal analysis of profit optimization.

In estimating sales-response functions, some cautions have to be observed. The sales-response function assumes that other variables remain constant over the range of the function. Thus the company's price and competitors' prices are assumed to remain unchanged no matter what the company spends on marketing. Since this assumption is unrealistic, the sales-response function has to be modified to reflect competitors' probable responses. The sales-response function also assumes a certain level of company efficiency in spending marketing dollars. If the spending efficiency rises or falls, the sales-response function has to be modified. Also, the sales-response function has to be modified to reflect delayed impacts of expenditures on sales beyond one year. These and other characteristics of sales-response functions are spelled out in more detail elsewhere.[4]

Profit Optimization

Once the sales-response functions are estimated, how are they used in profit optimization? Graphically, we introduce some further curves to find the point of optimal marketing expenditure. The analysis is shown in Figure 3A-2. The sales-response function shown here is S shaped, although the same analysis applies to any shape. First the manager subtracts all nonmarketing costs from the *sales-response function* to derive the *gross profit function*. Next, the marketing expenditure function is represented as a straight line starting at the origin and rising at the rate of one dollar of marketing expenditure for every ten dollars of the vertical axes. The marketing expenditure function is then subtracted from the *gross profit curve* to derive the *net profit curve*. The net profit curve shows positive net profits with marketing expenditures between M_L and M_U, which could be defined as the rational range of marketing expenditure. The net profit curve reaches a maximum of M. Therefore the marketing expenditure that would maximize net profit is M.

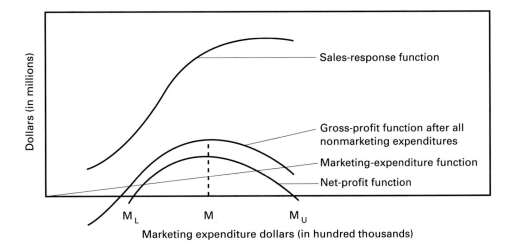

FIGURE 3A-2
Relationship between
Sales Volume,
Marketing
Expenditures, and
Profits

Dollars (in millions)

Sales-response function

Gross-profit function after all
nonmarketing expenditures

Marketing-expenditure function

Net-profit function

M_L M M_U

Marketing expenditure dollars (in hundred thousands)

The graphical solution can also be carried out numerically or algebraically; indeed it has to be if sales volume is a function of more than one marketing-mix variable. Here we will present a numerical example of how it is done.

A Numerical Example   Jane Melody, the Allegro product manager at Zenith, also handles a small phonograph-record-cleaning machine that sells for $16. For some years, she has been using a low-price, low-promotion strategy. Last year she spent $10 000 on advertising and another $10 000 on sales promotion. Sales were 12 000 units, and profits were $14 000. Her boss thinks more profits could be made on this item. Ms. Melody is anxious to find a better strategy to increase profits.

Her first step is to visualize some alternative marketing-mix strategies. She imagines the eight strategies shown in the first three columns of Table 3A-1 (the first strategy is the current one). They were formed by assuming a high and a low level for each of three marketing variables and elaborating all the combinations ($2^3 = 8$).

Her next step is to estimate the likely sales that would be attained with each marketing mix. She feels that the needed estimates are unlikely to be found through fitting historical data or through conducting experiments. She decides to ask the sales manager for his estimates, since he has shown an uncanny ability to be on target. Suppose he provides the sales estimates shown in the last column in Table 3A-1.

The final step calls for determining which marketing mix maximizes profits, assuming the sales estimates are reliable. This calls for introducing a profit equation and inserting the different marketing mixes into this equation to see which maximizes profits.

Suppose fixed costs, F, are $38 000; unit variable costs, c, are $10; and the contemplated allowance off list price, k, is $0. Then profit equation (3-5) reads:

$$Z = (P - 10) \, Q - 38 \, 000 - A - S \qquad (3\text{-}10)$$

Thus profits are a function of the chosen price and advertising and sales-promotion budgets.

At this point, the manager can insert each marketing mix and estimated sales level (from Table 3A-1) into this equation. The resulting profits are #1($16 400), #2($13 000), #3(−$7400), #4(−$2400), #5($19 000), #6($16 800), #7(−$4200), and #8($2000). Marketing mix #5, calling for a price of $24, advertising of $10 000, and promotion of $10 000, yields the highest expected profits ($19 000).

Table 3A-1 Marketing Mixes and Estimated Sales

Marketing Mix No.	Price (P)	Advertising (A)	Promotion (S)	Sales (Q)
1	$16	$10 000	$10 000	12 400
2	16	10 000	50 000	18 500
3	16	50 000	10 000	15 100
4	16	50 000	50 000	22 600
5	24	10 000	10 000	5 500
6	24	10 000	50 000	8 200
7	24	50 000	10 000	6 700
8	24	50 000	50 000	10 000

The manager can take one more step. Some marketing mix not shown might yield a still higher profit. To check that possibility, the product manager can fit a sales equation to the data shown in Table 3A-1. The sales estimates can be viewed as a sample from a larger universe of expert judgments concerning the sales equation $Q = f(P, A, S)$. A plausible mathematical form for the sales equation is the multiple exponential:

$$Q = bP^p A^a S^s \tag{3-11}$$

where:

b = a scale factor
p, a, s = price, advertising, and promotion elasticity, respectively

Using least-squares regression estimation (not shown), the manager finds the fitted sales equation to be

$$Q = 100\ 000P^{-2}A^{1/8}S^{1/4} \tag{3-12}$$

This fits the sales estimates in Table 3A-1 extremely well. Price has an elasticity of –2; that is, a 1 percent reduction in price, other things being equal, tends to increase unit sales by 2 percent. Advertising has an elasticity of 1/8, and promotion has an elasticity of 1/4. The coefficient 100 000 is a scale factor that translates the dollar magnitudes into sales-volume units.

The product manager now substitutes this sales equation for Q in the profit equation (3-10). This yields, when simplified:

$$Z = 100\ 000\ A^{1/8}S^{1/4}[P^{-1} - 10P^{-2}] - 38\ 000 - A - S \tag{3-13}$$

Profits are shown to be strictly a function of the chosen marketing mix. The manager can insert any marketing mix (including those not shown in Table 3A-1) and derive an estimate of profits. To find the profit-maximizing marketing mix, she applies standard calculus. The optimal marketing mix (P, A, S) is ($20, $12 947, $25 894). Twice as much is spent on promotion as on advertising because its elasticity is twice as great. The product manager would forecast a sales volume of 10 358 units and profits of $26 735. While other marketing mixes can produce higher sales, no other marketing mix can produce higher profits. Using this equation, the product manager has solved not only the optimum marketing mix but also the optimum marketing budget ($A + S = $38 841$).

To facilitate profit-optimization planning, several companies have designed computer programs for use by marketing managers to identify and assess the impact of alternative marketing plans on profits and sales. The marketing manager sits at a computer terminal, requests the particular program, and proceeds to build and test a marketing expenditure plan. One computer program consists of four subprograms.[5] First the marketing manager retrieves the major statistics on the product for the past several years. This material is called the *historical base* and is similar to Table 3-2. She then instructs the computer to produce a *straightforward projection* of the major statistics for the next several years, using extrapolation. She then modifies any projections based on her knowledge, and the result is called the *profit-and-loss planning base*. This shows a normal "extrapolated" level of marketing expenditures, price, and sales and the resulting profits. If the projected profits are satisfactory, the marketing manager can stop here. However, a fourth subprogram called a *marketing-plan simulator* is available for trying out alternative marketing plans and estimating their sales and profits. The simulator incorporates an estimated sales equation. The marketing manager tests alternative marketing plans until she finds a satisfactory one.

Marketing-Mix Optimization

The theory of profit optimization leads to finding the optimal total marketing expenditure level. Now we want to examine the issue of optimally dividing the marketing budget over the tools of the marketing mix. Clearly, the tools of the mix are partially substitutable for each other. A company that is seeking increased sales can achieve them by lowering the price or increasing the salesforce, advertising budget, or promotion budget. The challenge is to find the optimal marketing mix.

Assume that a product manager has identified advertising and sales promotion dollars as the two major elements of the marketing budget. In principle, the marketing budget can be divided in an infinite number of ways on these two items. This is shown in Figure 3A-3(a). If there are no constraints on the level of advertising and sales promotion, then every point in the $A - S$ plane shown in Figure 3A-3(a) is a possible marketing mix. An arbitrary line drawn from the origin, called a constant-mix line, shows the set of all marketing mixes where the two tools are in a fixed ratio but where the budget varies. Another arbitrary line, called a constant-budget line, shows a set of varying mixes that would be affordable with a fixed marketing budget.

Associated with every possible marketing mix is a resulting sales level. Three sales levels are shown in Figure 3A-3(a). The marketing mix (A_1S_2)—calling for a small budget divided approximately equally between advertising and sales promotion—is expected to produce sales of Q_1. The marketing mix (A_2S_1) involves the same budget with more expenditure on advertising than on sales promotion; this is expected to produce slightly higher sales, Q_2. The mix (A_3S_3) calls for a larger budget but a relatively equal splitting between advertising and sales promotion and is expected to yield Q_3. Given the many possibilities, the marketer's job is to find the sales equation that predicts the Q_s.

For a given marketing budget, the money should be divided among the various marketing tools in a way that gives the same marginal profit on the marginal dollar spent on each tool. A geometrical version of the solution is shown in Figure 3A-3(b). Here we are looking down at the $A - S$ plane shown in Figure 3A-3(a). A constant-budget line is shown, indicating all the alternative marketing mixes that could be achieved with this budget. The curved lines are called *iso-sales curves*. An iso-sales curve shows the different mixes of advertising and sales promotion that would produce a given level of sales. It is a projection into the $A - S$ plane of the set of points resulting from horizontal slicing of the sales function shown in Figure 3A-3(a) at a given level of sales. Figure 3A-3(b) shows iso-sales curves for three

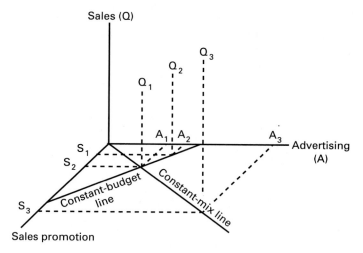

(a) Relation of sales to different
marketing mixes of advertising
and promotion

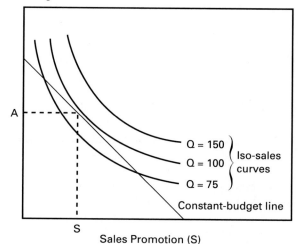

(b) Finding the optimal marketing
mix for a given marketing
budget

different sales levels: 75, 100, and 150 units. Given the budget line, it is not possible to attain sales of more than 100 units. The optimum marketing mix is shown at the point of tangency between the budget line and the last-touching iso-sales curve above it. Consequently, the marketing mix $(A*S*)$, which calls for somewhat more advertising than promotion, is the sales-maximizing (and in this case profit-maximizing) marketing mix.

This analysis could be generalized to more than two marketing tools. Ferber and Verdoorn stated that "In an optimum position the additional sales obtained by a small increase in unit costs are the same for all nonprice instruments. . ."[6]

Dorfman and Steiner went further and formalized the conditions under which price, promotion, and product quality would be optimized.[7] More recently, marketing scientists have investigated how various marketing-mix variables interact in their impact on sales, as the Marketing Concepts and Tools 3-1 exhibit shows.

Marketing Concepts and Tools 3-1

MARKETING-MIX INTERACTIONS NEED TO BE WATCHED

Marketing managers carry beliefs in their heads about how specific pairs of marketing variables interact. Here are some of the more popular beliefs:

- *Higher advertising expenditures reduce buyers' price sensitivity. Thus a company wishing to charge a higher price should spend more on advertising.*

- *Advertising expenditures have a greater sales impact on low-price products than on high-price products.*

- *Better positioning of advertising copy reduces buyers' price sensitivity.*

- *Higher advertising expenditures reduce the total cost of selling. The advertising expenditures presell the customer, and sales representatives can spend their time answering objections and closing the sale.*

- *Higher product quality allows the company to charge a disproportionately higher price.*

- *Higher prices lead buyers to impute higher product quality.*

- *Price cuts or increased sales effort places a strain on the distribution system and may require its enlargement or revision.*

- *Tighter credit terms require greater selling and advertising effort to move the same volume of goods.*

While these relationships hold true for many products, managers of particular products should be cautious. For example, Sasieni showed data on advertising elasticities for a number of brands and found that while some showed a more sensitive response at high prices, others were more sensitive at lower prices. He concluded that without a clear understanding of the nature of the advertising appeal and the structure of the market, a clear direction for such interactions could not be predicted in advance (Maurice Sasieni, "Pricing and Advertising for Profit," paper presented at Pennsylvania State University, October 1981).

Marketing-mix variables interact not only with each other but also with nonmarketing variables in the firm. The chart below shows that the product's price and product quality are dependent upon nonmarketing variables. Japanese companies are especially sensitive to the dependence of marketing variables on nonmarketing variables. The price they can charge depends upon the company's productivity, which is influenced by personnel policies as well as investment decisions. Similarly, product quality is influenced by production reliability and technology, which in turn are influenced by personnel management and R&D investment. Thus marketers must not take price and product for granted but must influence those nonmarketing variables that will enable the company to drive down costs and produce higher-quality products.

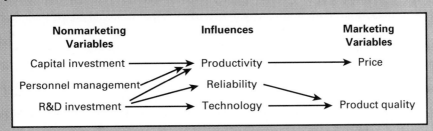

Nonmarketing Variables	Influences	Marketing Variables
Capital investment	Productivity	Price
Personnel management	Reliability	
R&D investment	Technology	Product quality

Marketing-Allocation Optimization

A final issue facing the marketing planner is to optimally allocate a given marketing budget to the various *target markets* (TMs). The TMs could be different sales territories, customer groups, or other market segments. With a given marketing budget and mix, it may be possible to increase sales and profits by shifting funds among different markets.

Most marketing managers allocate their marketing budgets to the various TMs on the basis of some percentage of actual or expected sales. Consider the following example:

> The marketing manager at the Guardian Oil Company (name disguised) estimates total gasoline sales volume (which combines regular and premium gasoline) and adds premium sales volume back to this figure to yield "profit gallons" (thus giving double weight to premium gasoline sales). The manager then takes the ratio of the advertising budget to the profit gallons to establish a figure for advertising dollars per profit gallon. This is called the prime multiplier. Each market receives an advertising budget equal to its previous year's profit gallons sold multiplied by the prime multipler. Thus the advertising budget is allocated largely on the basis of last year's company sales in the territory.[8] ∎

Unfortunately, size rules for allocating funds lead to inefficient allocations. They confuse "average" and "marginal" sales response. Figure 3A-4(a) illustrates the difference between the two and indicates that there is no reason to assume they are correlated. The two dots in the figure show current marketing expenditures and company sales in two TMs. The company spends $3 million on marketing in both TMs. Company sales are $40 million in TM 1 and $20 million in TM 2. The average sales response to a dollar of marketing effort is thus greater in TM 1 than in TM 2; it is 40/3 as opposed to 20/3, respectively. It might seem desirable to shift funds from TM 2 to TM 1, where the average response is greater. Yet the real issue is one of the marginal response. The marginal response is represented by the *slope* of the sales function through the points. A higher slope has been drawn for TM 2 than for TM 1. The respective slopes show that another $1 million in marketing expenditure would produce a $10 million sales increase in TM 2 and only a $2 million sales increase in TM 1. Evidently marginal response, not average response, should guide the allocation of marketing funds.

Marginal response is indicated along the sales-response function for each territory. Assume that a company is able to estimate TM sales-response functions. Suppose the sales-response functions for two TMs are those shown in Figure 3A-4(b). The company wishes to allocate a budget of B dollars between the two TMs to maximize profits. When costs are identical for the two TMs, then the allocation that will maximize profits is the one that will maximize sales. The funds are optimally allocated when they exhaust the budget, and the marginal sales response is the same in both TMs. Geometrically, this means that the slopes of the tangents to the two sales-response functions at the optimal allocations will be equal. Figure 3A-4(b) shows that a budget of $6 million would be allocated in the amounts of approximately $4.6 million to TM 1 and $1.4 million to TM 2 to produce maximum sales of approximately $180 million. The marginal sales response would be the same in both TMs.

The principle of allocating funds to TMs to equalize the marginal response is used in the planning technique called *zero-based budgeting*.[9] The manager of each TM is asked to formulate a marketing plan and estimate the expected sales for (say) three levels of marketing expenditure, such as 30 percent below the normal level, the normal level, and 30 percent above the normal level. An example is shown in Table 3A-2, outlining what the Zenith marketing manager would do with each budget level and her estimate of Allegro sales volume. Then higher management reviews this response function against those of other product managers and gives serious consideration to shifting funds from TMs with low marginal responses to TMs with higher marginal responses.

FIGURE 3A-4

Sales-Response Functions in Two
Target Markets (TMs)

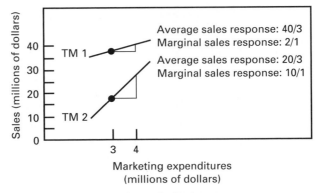

(a) Average and marginal sales response
in two target markets (TMs)

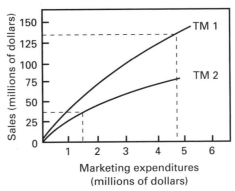

(b) Sales response functions in two
target markets (TMs)

Table 3A-2 Illustration of Zero-Based Marketing Budgeting

Budget (M)	Marketing Plan	Sales Forecast (Q)
$140 000	Maintain sales and market share in the short term by concentrating sales effort on largest chain stores, advertising only on TV, sponsoring two promotions a year, and carrying on only limited marketing research	6000 units
$200 000	Implement a coordinated effort to expand market share by contacting 80 percent of all retailers, adding magazine advertising, adding point-of-purchase displays, and sponsoring three promotions during the year.	7000 units
$260 000	Seek to expand market size and share by adding two new product sizes, enlarging the salesforce, increasing research, and expanding the advertising budget.	9000 units

Measuring sales-response functions can lead to substantial shifts in company marketing strategy. A major oil company had located its service stations in every large city.[10] In many markets, it operated only a small percentage of the total stations. Company management began to question this broad location strategy. It decided to estimate how the company's market share in each city varied with its percentage share of marketing expenditures in each city (as measured by the share of outlets). A curve was fitted showing the share of outlets and share of markets in different cities. The resulting curve was S shaped (see Figure 3A-5). This showed that having a low percentage of stations in a city yielded an even lower percentage of market volume. The practical implication was clear: The company should either withdraw from its weak markets or build them up to, say, 15 percent of the competitive outlets. Instead of establishing a few outlets in each of many cities, the oil company should establish a large number of outlets in a smaller number of cities. In fact, that is what is happening. Most of the major oil companies in the past tried to be national companies. Today, each is concentrating regionally and trying to be the regional leader.

FIGURE 3A-5

Share of Market as a Function of Share of Outlets

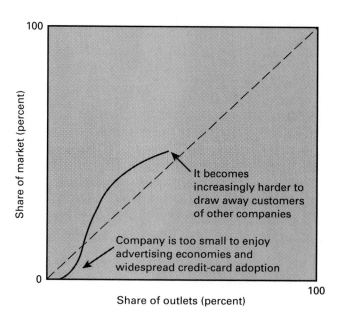

◼ NOTES

1. For examples of empirical studies using fitted sales-response functions, see Doyle L. Weiss, "Determinants of Market Share," *Journal of Marketing Research*, August 1968, pp. 290-95; Donald E. Sexton, Jr., "Estimating Marketing Policy Effects on Sales of a Frequently Purchased Product," *Journal of Marketing Research*, August 1970, pp. 338-47; and Jean-Jacques Lambin, "A Computer On-Line Marketing Mix Model," *Journal of Marketing Research*, May 1972, pp. 119-26. More recent studies are reviewed in Dominique M. Hanssens, Leonard J. Parsons, and Randall L. Schultz, *Market Response Models: Econometric and Time Series Analysis* (Boston: Kluwer Academic Publishers, 1990), Chap. 6.

2. See Russell Ackoff and James R. Emshoff, "Advertising Research at Anheuser-Busch," *Sloan Management Review*, Winter 1975, pp. 1-15.

3. See Philip Kotler, "A Guide to Gathering Expert Estimates," *Business Horizons*, October 1970, pp. 79-87.

4. See Gary L. Lilien and Philip Kotler, *Marketing Decision Making: A Model Building Approach*, 2nd ed. (New York: Harper & Row, 1983).

5. See "Concorn Kitchens," in *Marketing Management Casebook*, ed. Harper W. Boyd, Jr., and Robert T. Davis (Homewood, Ill.: Richard D. Irwin, 1971), pp. 125-36.

6. Robert Ferber and P. J. Verdoorn, *Research Methods in Economics and Business* (New York: Macmillan, 1962), p. 535.

7. Robert Dorfman and Peter O. Steiner, "Optimal Advertising and Optimal Quality," *American Economic Review*, December 1954, pp. 826-36.

8. Donald C. Marschner, "Theory versus Practice in Allocating Advertising Money," *Journal of Business*, July 1967, pp. 286-302.

9. See Paul J. Stonich, *Zero-Base Planning and Budgeting: Improved Cost Control and Resource Allocation* (Homewood, Ill.: Dow-Jones-Irwin, 1977).

10. See John J. Cardwell, "Marketing and Management Science—A Marriage on the Rocks?" *California Management Review*, Summer 1968, pp. 3-12.

PART II

Analyzing Marketing Opportunities

4 Marketing Information Systems and Marketing Research

When you cannot measure what you are speaking about, when you cannot express it in numbers, your knowledge is of a meager and unsatisfactory kind; it may be the beginning of knowledge, but you have scarcely in your thoughts advanced to the stage of a science, whatever the matter may be.

Lord Kelvin

We have seen the importance of starting marketing and strategic planning with an outside-inside point of view. Management needs to monitor the larger forces in the marketing environment if it is to keep its products and marketing practices current. But how can management learn about changing customer wants, new competitor initiatives, new modes of distribution, and so on? The answer is clear: Management must develop and maintain a marketing information system and have the skills to carry out sound marketing research. This chapter will show how marketers collect and use marketing information. The next four chapters will describe what marketers have learned about the marketing environment and the behavior of consumers, organizational buyers, and competitors.

In the long history of business enterprise, management devoted most of its attention to managing *money, materials, machines*, and *men*. Management has paid less attention to the fifth critical resource of the firm: *information*. It is hard to find company managers who are highly satisifed with their marketing information. Their complaints include not knowing where the information is located in the company; getting too much information that they can't use and too little that they really need; getting important information too late; and doubting the accuracy of the information. Here is one example:

> A computer salesperson wanted to prepare a quote for a customer who wanted to buy an upgraded computer system. The customer was planning to choose between her company and a major competitor. The salesperson, however, couldn't locate the prices for some components on her computer and in other cases got contradictory prices. It took her three days to prepare the quote. Meanwhile her major competitor prepared the quote in one day and was working to close the sale. ∎

The irony is that this salesperson's company was selling computer information systems but lacked a well-run computer information system of its own.

Many companies have not yet adapted to the intensified information requirements for effective marketing in the 1990s. Three developments render the need for marketing information stronger than at any time in the past:

□ *From local to national to global marketing*: As companies expand their geographical market coverage, their managers need more market information than ever before.

□ *From buyer needs to buyer wants*: As buyers' incomes increase, they become more selective in their choice of goods. Sellers find it harder to predict buyers' response to different features, styles, and other attributes, unless they turn to marketing research.

□ *From price to nonprice competition*: As sellers increase their use of branding, product differentiation, advertising, and sales promotion, they require information on the effectiveness of these marketing tools.

The explosive information requirements have been met on the supply side by impressive new information technologies. The past thirty years have witnessed the emergence of the computer, microfilming, cable television, copy machines, fax machines, tape recorders, video recorders, videodisc players, and other devices that have revolutionized information handling. Nevertheless, most business firms lack information sophistication. Many firms do not have a marketing research department. Many other firms have small marketing research departments whose work is limited to routine forecasting, sales analysis, and occasional surveys. Only a few firms have developed advanced marketing information systems that provide company management with up-to-date marketing information and analysis.

CONCEPT AND COMPONENTS OF A MARKETING INFORMATION SYSTEM

Every firm must organize the flow of marketing information to its marketing managers. Companies are studying their managers' information needs and designing *marketing information systems* (MIS) to meet these needs. We define a marketing information system as follows:

> A marketing information system *(MIS) consists of people, equipment, and procedures to gather, sort, analyze, evaluate, and distribute needed, timely, and accurate information to marketing decision makers.*

The marketing-information-system concept is illustrated in Figure 4-1. The marketing managers, in order to carry out their analysis, planning, implementation, and control responsibilities (shown at the far left), need information about developments in the marketing environment (shown at the far right). The role of the MIS is to assess the manager's information needs, develop the needed information, and distribute the information in a timely fashion to the marketing managers. The needed information is developed through internal company records, marketing intelligence activities, marketing research, and marketing decision support analysis. We will now describe each major subsystem of the company's MIS.

FIGURE 4-1
The Marketing Information System

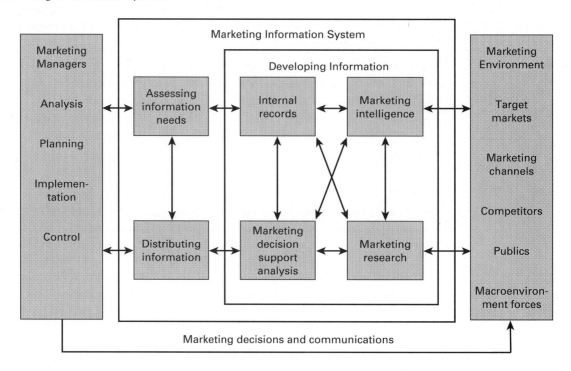

INTERNAL RECORDS SYSTEM

The most basic information system used by marketing managers is the internal records system. Included are reports on orders, sales, prices, inventory levels, receivables, payables, and so on. By analyzing this information, marketing managers can spot important opportunities and problems.

The Order-Shipping-Billing System

The heart of the internal records system is the order-shipping-billing cycle. Sales representatives, dealers, and customers dispatch orders to the firm. The order department prepares invoices and sends copies to various departments. Out-of-stock items are back ordered. Shipped items are accompanied by shipping and billing documents that are also multicopied and sent to various departments.

Today's companies need to perform these steps quickly and accurately. Customers favor those firms that can deliver their goods on time. Sales representatives need to send in their orders every evening, in some cases immediately. The order-fulfillment department must process these orders quickly. The warehouse must send the goods out as soon as possible. And bills should go out as soon as possible. Alert firms are now applying *total quality-improvement programs* to improve the speed and accuracy of workflows between departments, and many report substantial gains in efficiency.[1]

The System of Sales Reporting

Marketing managers receive sales reports some time after the sales have taken place. In consumer-food companies, warehouse-withdrawal reports are issued with fair regularity, but actual retail-purchase reports take about two months, based on special store or consumer-panel audits. In the auto industry, executives wait about ten days for their sales report; if sales are down, they will have to work harder and face ten sleepless nights until the next report. Many marketing executives complain that sales are not reported fast enough in their company.

Companies that do produce timely sales information have a competitive edge. Canadian Tire is one such company whose marketing information system has made it a leader in retail distribution. Each sale that goes through a checkout counter in one of the 364 stores is recorded automatically at central distribution warehouses in Toronto, Brampton, or Edmonton. The computer automatically allocates inventory and prints price tags and routing sheets for the replacement stock. Management has access to sales information on a daily basis to monitor the effectiveness of local promotions. Emergency orders to replenish promotions can be filled in half a day.

Designing a User-Oriented Reports System

In designing an advanced sales information system, the company should avoid certain pitfalls. First, it is possible to create a system that delivers too much information. The managers arrive at their offices each morning to face voluminous sales statistics, which they either ignore or spend too much time on. Second, it is possible to create a system that delivers information that is too current! Managers may end up overreacting to minor sales reversals.

The company's marketing information system should represent a cross between what managers think they need, what managers really need, and what is economically feasible. A useful step is the appointment of an *internal marketing-information-systems committee*, which interviews a cross-section of marketing executives—product managers, sales managers, sales representatives, and so on—to discover their information needs. A useful set of questions is shown in Table 4-1. The MIS committee will want to pay special attention to strong desires and complaints. At the same time, the committee will wisely discount some of the

Table 4-1 Questionnaire for Determining Marketing Information Needs

1. What types of decisions are you regularly called upon to make?
2. What types of information do you need to make these decisions?
3. What types of information do you regularly get?
4. What types of special studies do you periodically request?
5. What types of information would you like to get that you are not getting now?
6. What information would you want daily? Weekly? Monthly? Yearly?
7. What magazines and trade reports would you like to see routed to you on a regular basis?
8. What specific topics would you like to be kept informed of?
9. What types of data-analysis programs would you like to see made available?
10. What do you think would be the four most helpful improvements that could be made in the present marketing information system?

information requests. Managers with a strong appetite for information will list many needs, failing to distinguish between *what is nice to know and what they need to know*. Other managers will be too busy to give the questionnaire serious thought and will omit many things they ought to know. That is why the information planning committee must take another step, that of determining what managers *need to know* to be able to make responsible decisions. For example, what do brand managers need to know in order to set the size of the advertising budget? Suppose they should know the degree of market saturation, the rate of sales decay in the absence of advertising, and the spending plans of competitors. The information system should be designed to provide the data needed for making the key marketing decisions.

MARKETING INTELLIGENCE SYSTEM

While the internal records system supplies managers with *results data*, the marketing intelligence system supplies managers with *happenings data*. We define a marketing intelligence system as follows:

> A marketing intelligence system *is a set of procedures and sources used by managers to obtain their everyday information about pertinent developments in the marketing environment.*

Managers scan the environment in four ways:

☐ *Undirected viewing*: General exposure to information where the manager has no specific purpose in mind

☐ *Conditioned viewing*: Directed exposure, not involving active search, to a more or less clearly identified area or type of information

☐ *Informal search*: A relatively limited and unstructured effort to obtain specific information or information for a specific purpose

☐ *Formal search*: A deliberate effort—usually following a preestablished plan, procedure, or methodology—to secure specific information or information relating to a specific issue.[2]

Marketing managers carry on marketing intelligence mostly on their own by reading books, newspapers, and trade publications; talking to customers, suppliers, distributors, and other outsiders; and talking with other managers and personnel within the company. Yet this system is quite casual, and valuable information could be lost or arrive too late. Managers might learn of a competitive move, a new-customer need, or a dealer problem too late to make the best response.

Well-run companies take additional steps to improve the quality and quantity of marketing intelligence. First, they train and motivate the salesforce to spot and report new developments. Sales representatives are the company's "eyes and ears." They are in an excellent position to pick up information missed by other means. Yet they are very busy and often fail to pass on significant information. The company must "sell" its salesforce on their importance as intelligence gatherers and must emphasize this importance through their sales bonuses. The salesforce should be provided with easy reports to fill out. Sales representatives should know which types of information to send to different managers.

Second, the company motivates distributors, retailers, and other middlemen to pass along important intelligence. Consider the following example:

> Parker Hannifin Corporation, a major fluid-power-products manufacturer, has arranged with each distributor to forward to Parker's marketing research division a copy of all the invoices

containing sales of their products. Parker analyzes these invoices to learn about end-user characteristics and to help its distributors improve their marketing programs.[3] ■

Some companies appoint specialists to gather marketing intelligence. They send out "ghost shoppers" to monitor the presentations of retail personnel. Much can be learned about competitors through purchasing their products; attending open houses and trade shows; reading competitors' published reports and attending stockholders' meetings; talking to their former employees and present employees, dealers, distributors, suppliers, and freight agents; collecting competitors' ads; and reading *The Financial Post, The Globe and Mail,* and trade association papers (see Marketing Concepts and Tools 8-3, in Chapter 8).

Third, the company purchases information from outside suppliers such as the A. C. Nielsen Company and Information Resources, Inc. (see Table 4-5, part 4). These research firms can gather store and consumer-panel data at much less cost than if each company carried on its own panel operations.

Fourth, some companies have established an internal *marketing information center* to collect and circulate marketing intelligence. The staff scans major publications, abstracts relevant news, and disseminates a news bulletin to marketing managers. It collects and files relevant information. The staff assists managers in evaluating new information. These services greatly improve the quality of information available to marketing managers (see Marketing Strategies 4-1).

MARKETING RESEARCH SYSTEM

Besides information from internal reports and marketing intelligence, marketing managers often need focused studies of specific problems and opportunities. They may need a market survey, a product-preference test, a sales forecast by region, or an advertising-effectiveness study. The managers themselves normally do not have the skill or time to obtain this information. They need to commission formal marketing research. We define *marketing research* as follows:

> Marketing research *is the systematic design, collection, analysis, and reporting of data and findings relevant to a specific marketing situation facing the company.*

Suppliers of Marketing Research

A company can obtain marketing research in a number of ways. Small companies can ask students or professors at a local college to design and carry out the project, or they can hire a marketing research firm. Large companies, in fact over 85 percent of them, have their own marketing research departments.[4] Marketing research departments consist of anywhere from one to several dozen researchers. The marketing research manager normally reports to the marketing vice-president and acts as a study director, administrator, company consultant, and advocate.

> Procter & Gamble assigns marketing researchers to conduct research for existing brands. There are two separate in-house research groups, one in charge of overall company advertising research and the other in charge of market testing. The staff of each group consists of marketing research managers, supporting specialists (survey designers, statisticians, behavioral scientists), and in-house field representatives to conduct and supervise interviewing. Each year, Procter & Gamble calls or visits thousands of people in connection with dozens of research projects. ■

Marketing Strategies 4-1

A NEW ANSWER TO INFORMATION NEEDS— INFORMATION CENTERS

Although the concept of an integrated management information system was widely discussed in the 1960s, few companies did anything to centralize and coordinate their information flows. Many managers complained that needed information was somewhere in the company but that it would take too long to find. There would be no one place to find a list of the data files available in the company.

Beginning in 1979, IBM recommended that its clients establish information centers as adjuncts of existing data-processing departments. Many of IBM's larger clients have now done this. Travelers Insurance Company, for example, opened its information center in December 1981 with ten consultants answering two hundred calls for assistance a month. A year later, Travelers had twenty consultants handling four thousand calls a month.

Managers have found these information centers to be real time savers. In one case, an insurance manager needed to know why customers in a certain part of the country were not renewing their insurance policies. The information center quickly drew data, analyzed these data, and demonstrated that the company's rates had become uncompetitive.

One of the main advantages of establishing an information center is that it leads the company for the first time to compile a list of what data files exist and where they are located, as well as what data gaps exist in terms of questions frequently asked by managers. In addition, these centers often provide a higher level of data analysis than busy executives can achieve by themselves. Montgomery and Weinberg see these centers performing many functions including data evaluation, data transformation into information, data transmission, data accumulation, data analysis, and pattern recognition.

Sources: See "Helping Decision Makers Get at Data," *Business Week*, September 13, 1982, p. 118; and David B. Montgomery and Charles B. Weinberg, "Toward Strategic Intelligence Systems," *Journal of Marketing*, Fall 1979, pp. 41-57.

Companies normally budget marketing research at anywhere from 1 to 2 percent of company sales. Between 50 percent and 80 percent of this money is spent directly by the department, and the remainder is spent in buying the services of outside marketing research firms. Marketing research firms fall into three groups:

- *Syndicated-service research firms*: These firms gather periodic consumer and trade information, which they sell for a fee to clients. Examples: A. C. Nielsen, SAMI/Burke.
- *Custom marketing research firms*: These firms are hired to carry out specific research projects. They participate in designing the study, and the report becomes the client's property.
- *Specialty-line marketing research firms*: These firms provide a specialized service to other marketing research firms and company marketing research departments. The best example is the field-service firm, which sells field interviewing services to other firms.

The Scope of Marketing Research

Although marketing research has been practised in Canada for decades, its scope was quite limited prior to the eighties. Early estimates of spending were $41 million in 1966 and

Table 4-2 Research Activities of Canadian Companies

	% of all companies 1966	% of all companies 1984
Number of companies	302	202
ADVERTISING RESEARCH	16	47
Motivation research	8	25
Copy research	6	33
Studies of effectiveness	8	42
Studies of competitive advertising		38
Media research	4	36
BUSINESS ECONOMICS AND CORPORATE RESEARCH	16	56
Short-range forecasting		51
Long-range forecasting		50
Studies of business trends	9	49
Pricing, profit and/or value analysis	8	50
Location studies	3	35
Acquisition/diversification studies		41
Export and international studies		33
MIS		41
Operations Research		34
Internal employee studies		39
CORPORATE RESPONSIBILITY RESEARCH		35
Consumers' "right to know" studies		16
Ecological impact studies		16
Studies of legal constraints		29
Social values and policies studies		18
PRODUCT RESEARCH	17	59
New product modelling/optimization	11	48
Competitive product studies	6	54
Product testing (existing products)	8	52
Packaging research design char.	7	41
SALES AND MARKET RESEARCH	32	62
Measurement of market potential	17	59
Market share analysis	19	61
Determination of market char.	18	60
Sales analysis	15	58
Establishment of sales quotas, etc.	7	54
Distribution channels and costs	7	49
Test markets, store audits	5	35
Consumer panel studies	4	33
Sales compensation studies		37
Studies of premiums, coupons, etc.	3	28

Sources: Joyce Cheng, David Conway, and George Haines Jr., "Marketing Research in Canada: A 1985 Update," ASAC 1986 Conference, Whistler, BC; see also W. H. Mahatoo, *Marketing Research in Canada*, (Toronto: Thomas Nelson and Sons) 1968, and Kenneth Hardy and Joseph Fry, "Marketing Research in Canada: What's Going On?," in *Canadian Marketing: Problems and Prospects*, Donald W. Thompson and David S. Leighton (eds.) (Toronto: John Wiley and Sons), 1973.

$74 million in 1973. By 1984, spending on marketing research had mushroomed to $1710 million.[5] This dramatic growth was accompanied by corresponding increases in the percentages of companies that perform specific types of marketing research. As Table 4-2 shows, the most common research activities are market measurement, sales analysis, product studies, pricing analysis, and forecasting.

These studies have benefited from increasingly sophisticated techniques. Table 4-3 shows the approximate decade in which various techniques came into consideration or use in marketing research. Many of them—such as questionnaire construction and area sampling—came along early and were quickly and widely applied by marketing researchers. Others—such as motivation research and mathematical methods—came in uneasily, with prolonged and heated debates among practitioners over their practical usefulness. But they, too, settled in the corpus of marketing research methodology.

The Marketing Research Process

Marketing research is undertaken to understand a marketing problem better. A brand manager at Procter & Gamble will commission three or four major marketing research studies annually. Marketing managers in smaller companies will order fewer marketing research studies. Nonprofit organizations increasingly find that they need marketing research. A hospital wants to know whether people in its service area have a positive attitude toward the hospital and its services. A college wants to determine what kind of image it has among high school counselors. A political organization wants to find out what voters think of the candidates.

Effective marketing research involves five steps: *defining the problem and research objectives, developing the research plan, collecting the information, analyzing the information*, and *presenting the findings* (see Figure 4-2). We will illustrate these steps with the following situation:

> Via Rail Canada was concerned about ways to improve its participation in the intercity passenger market in the Windsor-Quebec corridor. Management recognized that many travelers preferred other means of travel, including the automobile, airplane, and bus. Although travel by rail had declined substantially since the 1950s, a minority of Canadian travelers still preferred to take the train. Management wanted to determine the most appropriate travel services to offer, in order to expand from this base of loyal rail travelers. ∎

Defining the Problem and Research Objectives   The first step in research calls for the marketing manager and marketing researcher to define the problem carefully and agree on the research objectives. Hundreds of things can be researched in any problem. Unless the problem is well defined, the cost of information gathering may well exceed the value of the findings. An old adage says, "A problem well defined is half solved."

Management must steer between defining the problem too broadly and defining it too narrowly. If the marketing manager tells the marketing researcher, "Find out everything you can about train travelers' needs," the manager will get much unneeded information and may not get the information he or she really needs. On the other hand, if the marketing manager

FIGURE 4-2
The Marketing Research Process

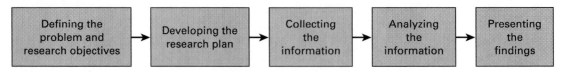

Table 4-3 Evolving Techniques in Marketing Research

Decade	Technique
Prior to 1910	First-hand observation Elementary surveys
1910-20	Sales analysis Operating cost analysis
1920-30	Questionnaire construction Survey technique
1930-40	Quota sampling Simple correlation analysis Distribution-cost analysis Store-auditing techniques
1940-50	Probability sampling Regression methods Advanced statistical inference Consumer and store panels
1950-60	Motivation research Operations research Multiple regression and correlation Experimental design Attitude-measuring instruments Analysis of variance (ANOVA)
1960-70	Factor analysis and discriminant analysis Mathematical models Bayesian statistical analysis and decision theory Scaling theory Computer data processing and analysis Marketing simulation Information storage and retrieval
1970-80	Multidimensional scaling Econometric models Comprehensive marketing planning models Test-marketing laboratories Multiattribute-attitude models
1980-90	Conjoint analysis and tradeoff analysis Causal analysis Computer-controlled interviewing Uniform product code and optical scanners Canonical correlation

said, "Find out what additional services the passengers on our Toronto-Montreal trains would like," this would be too narrow a view of the problem. Many potential users of new Via services would not be users of the present services.

Further reflection about the problem brought the realization that people take trips for various reasons. Some travel on business, some for recreation, and others to visit relatives or friends. It seemed plausible that the travel services which people would like to receive might depend on the purpose of the trip. This line of thought led to the following specific research questions:

1. What are the main reasons why people aged 18 or more take intercity trips in the Windsor-Quebec corridor?
2. What are the characteristics of the people who travel for each purpose?
3. What are the travel service characteristics which differentiate the train from the automobile, the airplane, and the bus?
4. Which of these service characteristics should management try to provide with Via's service?

Not all research projects can be made this specific in its objectives. Three types of research projects can be distinguished. Some research is *exploratory*, i.e., to gather preliminary data to shed light on the real nature of the problem and possibly suggest some hypotheses or new ideas. Some research is *descriptive*, i.e., to describe certain magnitudes, such as how many people would pay a premium fare for Via club-car service. Some research is *causal*, i.e., to test a cause-and-effect relationship, such as that a 20 percent reduction of the price premium would lead to an increase of at least 20 percent in club-car usage.

Developing the Research Plan   The second stage of marketing research calls for developing the most efficient plan for gathering the needed information. The marketing executive cannot simply say to the marketing researcher, "Find some passengers and ask them what kinds of travel services they would like on the train." The research plan should be designed professionally. At the same time, the marketing manager should know enough about marketing research to approve the research plan and know how to interpret its findings.

The marketing manager should ask the marketing researcher to estimate the cost of the research plan before approving it. The purpose of the marketing research project is to help the company reduce its risks and improve its profits. Suppose the company estimates that introducing a new train service without any marketing research would yield a long-term profit of $50 000. The manager also believes that the research will help him improve the promotional plan and make a long-term profit of $90 000. In this case, he should be willing to spend up to $40 000 on this research. If the research design would cost more than $40 000, he should decline it.[6]

Data Sources   The research plan can call for gathering secondary data, primary data, or both. Secondary data consist of information that already exists somewhere, having been collected

Table 4-4 Constructing the Research Plan

Data Sources:	Secondary Data	Primary Data		
Research Approaches:	Observation	Focus groups	Survey	Experiment
Research Instruments:	Questionnaire	Mechanical instruments		
Sampling Plan:	Sampling unit	Sample size	Sampling procedure	
Contact Methods:	Telephone	Mail	Personal	

for another purpose. Primary data consist of original information gathered for the specific purpose at hand.

SECONDARY DATA Researchers usually start their investigation by examining secondary data to see whether their problem can be partly or wholly solved without collecting costly primary data. The secondary data available to company researchers can come from internal sources, such as company financial statements, sales-call reports, and prior market studies. A rich variety of secondary data is also available from external sources, such as government publications, on-line data banks, periodicals, books, and commercial services. Table 4-5 lists some external sources of secondary data.[7]

For the Via Rail study, researchers will find data covering travel behavior in government sources such as the Census of Population. Relevant industry data include the schedules and fares of the bus lines and air lines which serve the corridor. Internal sources include Via's ticket sales and the results obtained from past "on-board" surveys.

Secondary data provide a starting point for research and offer the advantages of lower cost and quicker availability. On the other hand, the data needed by the researcher might not exist, or the existing data might be dated, inaccurate, incomplete, or unreliable. In this case, the researcher will have to collect primary data at greater cost and longer delay but probably with more relevance and accuracy.

Table 4-5 Secondary Sources of Data

1. General Sources
    1.1 Newspapers and periodicals
        The Financial Post, The Globe & Mail, Report on Business, Business Quarterly, Canadian Banker, Canada Commerce, Financial Times of Canada, Canadian Consumer, Consumer Interest, Marketing
    1.2 Indexing services
        Canadian Periodicals Index, Business Periodicals Index, Marketing Abstracts (Journal of Marketing)

2. Bibliographies
    2.1 *A Bibliography of Canadian Bibliographies*, American Marketing Association bibliographies, *Consumer Information: An Annotated Catalogue*

3. Government Catalogues
    Statistics Canada Catalogue, *Market Research Handbook*, Annual Catalogue of Government Publications

4. Directories
    4.1 Telephone and city directories
    4.2 Trade directories
        Canadian Trade Index, Fraser's Canadian Trade Directory, Scott's Directory, Directory of Canadian Trade Directories
    4.3 Media directories
        Canadian Advertising Rates and Data, National List of Advertisers, Canadian Serials Directory

5. Compendiums of Statistics
    Canada Yearbook, Handbook of Canadian Consumer Markets, Financial Post Survey of Markets, Canadian Statistical Review

Source: Ronald Rotenberg and Beth Hutton, "Sources of Marketing Information in Canada." *The Canadian Marketer*, Spring, 1974, p. 35.

PRIMARY DATA Most marketing research projects involve some primary-data collection. Primary-data collection is more costly, but the data are usually more relevant to the issue at hand. The normal procedure is to interview some people individually and/or in groups to get a preliminary sense of how people feel about air carriers and particular carrier services and, on the basis of the findings, develop a more formal and extensive interviewing approach and research instrument, debug it, and then carry it into the field. Here we present a fuller picture of the possible research approaches.

Research Approaches Primary data can be collected in four broad ways: observation, focus groups, surveys, and experiments.

OBSERVATIONAL RESEARCH One way to gather fresh data is to observe the relevant actors and settings. The Via Rail researchers might linger around airports, bus depots, and travel agencies to hear how travelers talk about the different carriers and how agents handle the flight arrangement process. The researchers can travel by bus and by air to observe the quality of service and hear consumer reactions. Their observations might yield some useful hypotheses about how travelers choose their carriers.

FOCUS-GROUP RESEARCH A focus group is a gathering of six to ten persons who spend a few hours with a skilled interviewer to discuss a project, service, organization, or other marketing entity. The interviewer needs objectivity, knowledge of the subject matter and industry, and knowledge of group dynamics and consumer behavior; otherwise the results can be misleading. The participants are normally paid a small sum for attending. The meeting is typically held in pleasant surroundings (a home for example), and refreshments are served to increase the informality.

In the Via Rail example, the group interviewer may start with a broad question, such as "What factors influence what carrier you use for trips between Toronto and Montreal?" Questions then move to how people feel about different services that they would want when traveling by air, by bus, or by train. The interviewer encourages free and easy discussion among the participants, hoping that the group dynamics will reveal deep feelings and thoughts that are new to the researcher. At the same time, the interviewer "focuses" the discussion, and hence the name *focus-group interviewing*. The discussion is recorded through note taking or on audio or video tape and is subsequently studied to understand consumer attitudes and behavior.

Focus-group research is a useful exploratory step to take before designing a large-scale survey. It yields insights into consumer perceptions, attitudes, and satisfaction that help define the issues to be researched more formally. Consumer-goods companies have been using focus groups for many years, and an increasing number of newspapers, law firms, hospitals, and public-service organizations are discovering their value. Yet however useful they are, researchers must avoid generalizing the reported feelings of the focus-group participants to the whole market, since the sample size is too small and the sample is not drawn randomly.[8]

SURVEY RESEARCH Survey research stands midway between the exploratory nature of observational and focus group research and the rigor of experimental research. Generally speaking, observation and focus groups are best suited for exploratory research, surveys are best suited for descriptive research, and experiments are best suited for causal research. Companies undertake surveys to learn about people's knowledge, beliefs, preferences, satisfaction, and so on, and to measure these magnitudes in the population. Thus, Via Rail researchers might want to survey how many people know Via, have taken a train, prefer it, and so on. We will say more about survey research when we move to research instruments, sampling plan, and contact methods.

EXPERIMENTAL RESEARCH The most scientifically valid research is experimental research. Experimental research calls for selecting matched groups of subjects, subjecting them to different treatments, controlling extraneous variables, and checking whether observed response differences are statistically significant. To the extent that extraneous factors are eliminated or controlled, the observed effects can be related to the variations in the stimuli. The purpose of experimental research is to capture cause-and-effect relationships by eliminating competing explanations of the observed findings.

An example of an experimental research design would be the setting up by Via of a special car where travelers can watch movies for a nominal surcharge. The amount of the surcharge can be varied on consecutive trips, and the numbers of travelers paying the various amounts can be recorded. This would permit Via to determine the effect of the amount of the surcharge on the use of the new service.

The experimental method supplies the most convincing information when the proper controls are exercised. For example, if the traffic on some days is not typical of the rest of the week, it is necessary to control this source of variation by taking all measurements on comparable days.

Research Instruments Marketing researchers have a choice of two main research instruments in collecting primary data: the questionnaire and mechanical devices.

QUESTIONNAIRES The questionnaire is by far the most common instrument in collecting primary data. Broadly speaking, a questionnaire consists of a set of questions presented to respondents for their answers. The questionnaire is very flexible in that there are any number of ways to ask questions. Questionnaires need to be carefully developed, tested, and debugged before they are administered on a large scale. One can usually spot several errors in a casually prepared questionnaire (see Marketing Concepts and Tools 4-1).

Marketing Concepts and Tools 4-1

A "QUESTIONABLE" QUESTIONNAIRE

Suppose an airline asked passengers the following questions. What do you think of each question? (Answer before reading the comment supplied.)

1. What is your income to the nearest hundred dollars?

   People don't necessarily know their income to the nearest hundred dollars, nor do they want to reveal their income that closely, if at all. Furthermore, a questionnaire should never open with such a personal question.

2. Are you an occasional or a frequent flyer?

   How do you define frequent versus occasional flying?

3. Do you like this airline?

   Yes ( ) No ( )
   "Like" is a relative term. Besides, will people answer this honestly? Furthermore, is yes-no the best way to allow a response to the question? Why is the question being asked in the first place?

4. How many airline ads did you see on television last April? This April?

   Who can remember?

5. What are the most salient and determinant attributes in your evaluation of air carriers?

   What are "salient" and "determinant" attributes? Don't use big words on me.

6. Do you think it is right for the government to tax air tickets and deprive a lot of people of the chance to fly?

   Loaded question. How can one answer this biased question?

In preparing a questionnaire, the professional marketing researcher carefully chooses the questions and their form, wording, and sequence.

A common type of error occurs in the *questions asked*, that is, in including questions that cannot, would not, or need not be answered and in omitting questions that should be answered. Each question should be checked to determine whether it contributes to the research objectives. Questions that are merely interesting should be dropped because they lengthen the time required and try the respondent's patience.

The *form of the question* can influence the response. Marketing researchers distinguish between closed-end and open-end questions. *Closed-end questions* prespecify all the possible answers, and respondents make a choice among them. Table 4-6, section A, shows the most common forms of closed-end questions.

Open-end questions allow respondents to answer in their own words. These questions take various forms; the main ones are shown in Table 4-6, section B. Generally speaking, open-end questions often reveal more because respondents are not constrained in their answers. Open-end questions are especially useful in the exploratory stage of research where the

Table 4-6 Types of Questions

A. Close-End Question		
Name	*Description*	*Example*
Dichotomous	A question offering two answer choices.	"In arranging this trip, did you personally phone Air Canada?" Yes ☐ No ☐
Multiple Choice	A question offering three or more answer choices.	"With whom are you travelling on this flight?" No one ☐ Children only ☐ Spouse ☐ Business associatates/ Spouse and friends/relatives ☐ children ☐ An organized tour group ☐
Likert scale	A statement with which the respondent shows the amount of agreement/disagreement.	"Small airlines gererally give better service than large ones." Strongly disagree Disagree Neither agree nor disagree Agree Strongly agree 1 ☐ 2 ☐ 3 ☐ 4 ☐ 5 ☐
Semantic differential	A scale is inscribed between two bipolar words, and the respondent selects the point that represents the direction and intensity of his or her feelings.	Air Canada Large __ .__ .__ .__ .__ .__ .__ Small Experienced__ .__ .__ .__ .__ .__ .__ Inexperienced Modern __ .__ .__ .__ .__ .__ .__ Old-fashioned
Importance scale	A scale that rates the importance of some attribute from "not at all important" to "extremely important."	"Airline food service to me is" Extremely important Very important Somewhat important Not very important Not at all important 1 ____ 2 ____ 3 ____ 4 ____ 5 ____
Rating scale	A scale that rates some attribute from "poor" to "excellent."	"Air Canada's food service to me is" Excellent Very good Good Fair Poor 1 ____ 2 ____ 3 ____ 4 ____ 5 ____
Intention-to-buy scale	A scale that describes the respondent's intention to buy.	"If an inflight telephone was available on a long flight, I would" Definitely buy Probably buy Not sure Probably not buy Definitely not buy 1 ____ 2 ____ 3 ____ 4 ____ 5 ____

Table 4-6 Types of Questions

B. Open-End Question		
Name	*Description*	*Example*
Completely unstructured	A question that respondents can answer in an almost unlimited number of ways.	"What is your opinion of Air Canada?"
Word association	Words are presented, one at a time, and respondents mention the first word that comes to mind.	"What is the first word that comes to your mind when you hear the following?" Airline_____ Air Canada_____ Travel_____
Sentence completion	Incomplete sentences are presented, one at a time, and respondents complete the sentence.	"When I choose an airline, the most important consideration in my decision is_____ _____
Story completion	An incomplete story is presented, and respondents are asked to complete it.	"I flew Air Canada a few days ago. I noticed that the exterior and interior of the plane had very bright colors. This aroused in me the following thoughts and feelings." Now complete the story.
Picture completion	A picture of two characters is presented, with one making a statement. Respondents are asked to identify with the other and fill in the empty balloon.	Example WELL HERE'S THE FOOD. Fill in the empty balloon.
Thematic Apperception Tests (TAT)	A picture is presented, and respondents are asked to make up a story about what they think is happening or may happen in the picture.	Make up a story about what you see.

researcher is looking for insight into how people think rather than in measuring how many people think in a certain way. Closed-end questions, on the other hand, provide answers that are easier to interpret and tabulate.

Care should be exercised in the *wording of questions*. The researcher should use simple, direct, unbiased wording. The questions should be pretested with a sample of respondents before they are formally included.

Care should also be exercised in the *sequencing of questions*. The lead question should create interest when possible. Difficult or personal questions should be asked toward the end of the interview so that respondents do not become defensive. The questions should come up in a logical order. Classificatory data on the respondent are put last because they are more personal and less interesting to the respondent.

MECHANICAL INSTRUMENTS Mechanical devices are less frequently used in marketing research. Galvanometers are used to measure the strength of a subject's interest or emotions aroused by an exposure to a specific ad or picture. The galvanometer picks up the minute degree of sweating that accompanies emotional arousal. The tachistoscope is a device that flashes an ad to a subject with an exposure interval that may range from less than one-hundredth of a second to several seconds. After each exposure, the respondent describes everything he or she recalls. Eye cameras are used to study respondent's eye movements to see at what points their eyes land first, how long they linger on a given item, and so on. The "people meter" is an electronic device that is attached to television sets in participating homes to record when the set is on and to which channel it is tuned.[9]

Sampling Plan The marketing researcher must design a sampling plan, which calls for three decisions:

1. *Sampling Unit:* This answers *Who is to be surveyed?* The proper sampling unit is not always obvious. In the Via Rail survey, should the sampling unit be business travelers, pleasure travelers, or both? Should travelers under twenty-one be interviewed? Should both husbands and wives be interviewed?

2. *Sample Size:* This answers *How many people should be surveyed?* Large samples give more reliable results than small samples. However, it is not necessary to sample the entire target or even a substantial portion to achieve results. Samples of less than 1 percent of a population can often provide good reliability, given a creditable sampling procedure.

3. *Sampling Procedure:* This answers *How should the respondents be chosen?* To obtain a representative sample, a probability sample of the population should be drawn. Probability sampling allows the calculation of confidence limits for sampling error. Thus one could conclude after the sample is taken that "the interval 10-12 trips per year has 95 chances in 100 of containing the true number of trips taken annually by travelers in the Windsor-Quebec corridor." Three types of probability sampling are described in Table 4-7A. When the cost or time involved in probability sampling is too high, marketing researchers will take nonprobability samples. Table 4-7B describes three types of nonprobability sampling. Some marketing researchers feel that nonprobability samples can be very useful in many circumstances, even though the sampling error cannot be measured.

Contact Methods This answers *How should the subject be contacted?* The choices are mail, telephone, or personal interviews.

The *mail questionnaire* is the best way to reach individuals who would not give personal interviews or whose responses might be biased or distorted by the interviewers. On the other hand, mail questionnaires require simple and clearly worded questions, and the response rate is usually low and/or slow.

Telephone interviewing is the best method for gathering information quickly; the interviewer is also able to clarify questions if they are not understood. The response rate is typically higher than in the case of mailed questionnaires. The two main drawbacks are that only people with telephones can be interviewed, and the interviews have to be short and not too personal.

Personal interviewing is the most versatile of the three methods. The interviewer can ask more questions and can record additional observations about the respondent, such as dress and body language. Personal interviewing is the most expensive method and requires more administrative planning and supervision. It is also subject to interviewer bias or distortion.

Personal interviewing takes two forms, *arranged interviews* and *intercept interviews*. In arranged interviews, respondents are randomly selected and are either telephoned or approached at their homes or offices and asked to grant an interview. Often a small payment or incentive

Table 4-7 Types of Probability and Nonprobability Samples

A. Probability Sample

Simple random sample	Every member of the population has a known and equal chance of selection.
Stratified random sample	The population is divided into mutually exclusive groups (such as age groups), and random samples are drawn from each group.
Cluster (area) sample	The population is divided into mutually exclusive groups (such as blocks), and the researcher draws a sample of the groups to interview.

B. Nonprobability Sample

Convenience sample	The researcher selects the most accessible population members from which to obtain information.
Judgment sample	The researcher uses his or her judgment to select population members who are good prospects for accurate information
Quota sample	The researcher finds and interviews a prescribed number of people in each of several categories.

is presented to respondents in appreciation of their time. Intercept interviews involve stopping people at a shopping mall or busy street corner and requesting an interview. Intercept interviews have the drawback of being nonprobability samples, and the interviews must be quite short.

Collecting the Information   The researcher must now arrange for collecting the data. This phase is generally the most expensive and the most liable to error. In the case of surveys, four major problems arise. Some respondents will not be at home and must be recontacted or replaced. Other respondents will refuse to cooperate. Still others will give biased or dishonest answers. Finally, some interviewers will occasionally be biased or dishonest.

In the case of experimental research, the researchers have to worry about matching the experimental and control groups, not influencing the participants by their presence, administering the treatments in a uniform way, and controlling for extraneous factors.

Data-collection methods are rapidly changing under the impact of modern telecommunications and electronics. Computers and electronic-communication hardware are causing a quiet revolution in marketing research. Some research firms now conduct their interviewing from a centralized location using a combination of *WATS lines, cathode-ray tubes* (CRT), and *data-entry terminals*. Professional telephone interviewers sit in separate booths and draw telephone numbers at random from somewhere in the nation. In dialing the person whose number has been selected, the interviewers use WATS lines, which means that the research firm has prepaid the telephone company so that it can make a large number of long-distance calls at a low cost. When the phone is answered, the interviewer asks the person a set of questions, reading them from the cathode-ray tube. The interviewer types the respondents' answers right into a computer, using the data-entry terminal. This procedure eliminates editing and coding, reduces the number of errors, saves time, and produces all the required statistics.

Other research firms have set up *interactive terminals* in shopping centers. Persons willing to be interviewed sit down at a terminal, read the questions from the CRT, and type in their answers. Most respondents enjoy this form of "robot" interviewing.[10] Marketing Concepts and Tools 4-2 describes an even more recent and revolutionary breakthrough in electronic marketing research.

Analyzing the Information   The next step in the marketing research process is to extract pertinent findings from the data. The researcher tabulates the data and develops one-way and two-way frequency distributions. Averages and measures of dispersion are computed for the major variables. The researcher will attempt to apply some of the advanced statistical techniques and decision models in the analytical marketing system in the hope of discovering additional findings (see the Appendix to this chapter).

Presenting the Findings   The researcher should not try to overwhelm management with lots of numbers and fancy statistical techniques—these will lose them. The researcher should present major findings that are relevant to the major marketing decisions facing

---

Marketing Concepts and Tools 4-2

THE MARKETER'S DREAM: MEASURING CONSUMER RESPONSE TO ADS

Several technical advances have recently permitted marketers to test the sales impact of ads and sales promotions. The advances include (1) the universal code on packages, (2) optical scanners, (3) electronic cash registers, (4) smart cards, (5) cable television, and (6) television viewing monitors. Here is how they work in concert.

A research firm, Information Resources, Inc., recruits a panel of supermarkets that are equipped with optical scanners and electronic cash registers. The store clerk passes the customer's goods over a light beam that reads the *universal code* on each package and records the brand, size, and price. Meanwhile the research firm has also recruited a panel of customers of these stores who have agreed to charge their grocery purchases with a special Shopper's Hotline ID card that not only has their name and bank account number but also personal information on household characteristics, lifestyle, income, and so on. These customers have also agreed to let their television-viewing habits be monitored by a black box in their television sets that records what is being watched, when, and by whom. All consumer panelists receive their programs through cable television. Now, the key is that Information Resources, Inc., controls the advertising messages being sent out to the consumer-panel members. The company can beam different messages, headlines, or promotions to different panel members. The research firm can then capture through the store purchase data which ads led to more purchasing and by what kinds of consumers. This research service, which Information Resources, Inc., calls BehaviorScan, makes it possible to evaluate consumer responses to various marketing stimuli with greater precision than ever.

Aside from this advanced service for advertisers, the retailers themselves have benefited greatly from using optical scanner equipment. Retailers can more quickly analyze the movement of goods for the purposes of improved inventory control and shelf space allocation, thus helping them improve the profitability of their store operations.

Sources: See "Big Brother Gets a Job in Market Research," *Business Week*, April 8, 1985, pp. 96-97; "Wired Consumers: Market Researchers Go Hi-Tech to Hone Ads, Weed Out Flops," *Wall Street Journal*, January 23, 1986; and "High-Tech Shocks in Ad Research," *Fortune*, July 7, 1986, pp. 58-62.

management. The study is useful when it reduces management's uncertainty concerning the right move to make.

Suppose the results obtained from Via's experimental use of a special car where travelers can watch movies, were as follows:

- About ten passengers out of an average trainload of two hundred watched movies at a price of eight dollars, but forty were willing to pay five dollars. Thus, the lower price generated more revenue ($200) than the higher price ($80).

- Suppose further that the results of Via's survey indicated that offering the movie service would add five passengers to the average train, bringing in additional ticket revenues of $60 per passenger or $300 in total.

- Based on the above findings, if the extra cost of offering the movie service were less than $500 per train (i.e., $200 + $300), it would be profitable for Via to offer the service. The findings should be checked for various sources of error, such as sampling error (resulting from having drawn an unrepresentative sample). But it seems clear that the marketing research has helped Via's management to make a better decision than would have resulted from "seat-of-the-pants" decision making.

Characteristics of Good Marketing Research

Having examined the major steps in the marketing research process, we can highlight five characteristics of good marketing research.

Scientific Method   Effective marketing research uses the principles of the scientific method: careful observation, formulation of hypotheses, prediction, and testing. An example follows.

> A mail-order house was suffering from a high rate (30 percent) of returned merchandise. Management asked the marketing research manager to investigate the causes of the high return rate. The marketing researcher examined the characteristics of returned orders, such as the geographical locations of the customers, the sizes of the returned orders, and the merchandise categories. One hypothesis was that the longer the customer waited for ordered merchandise, the greater the probability of its return. Statistical analysis confirmed this hypothesis. The researcher estimated how much the return rate would drop for a specific speed up of service. The company did this, and the prediction proved correct.[11]   ■

Research Creativity   At its best, marketing research develops innovative ways to solve a problem. A classic example of research creativity is described below.

> When instant coffee was first introduced, housewives complained that it did not taste like real coffee. Yet in blindfold tests, many of these same housewives could not distinguish between a cup of instant coffee and real coffee. This indicated that much of their resistance was psychological. The researcher decided to design two almost identical shopping lists, the only difference being that regular coffee was on one list and instant coffee on the other. The regular-coffee list was given to one group of housewives and the instant-coffee list was given to a different, but comparable, group. Both groups were asked to guess the social and personal characteristics of the woman whose shopping list they saw. The comments were pretty much the same with one significant difference: a higher proportion of the housewives whose list contained instant coffee described the subject as "lazy, a spendthrift, a poor wife, and failing to plan well for her family." These women obviously were imputing to the fictional housewife their own anxieties and negative images about the use of instant coffee. The instant-coffee company now knew the nature of the resistance and could develop a campaign to change the image of the housewife who serves instant coffee.[12]   ■

Multiple Methods Competent marketing researchers shy away from overreliance on any one method, preferring to adapt the method to the problem rather than the other way around. They also recognize the desirability of gathering information from multiple sources to give greater confidence.

Interdependence of Models and Data Competent marketing researchers recognize that the facts derive their meaning from models of the problem. These models guide the type of information sought and therefore should be made as explicit as possible.

Value and Cost of Information Competent marketing researchers show concern for measuring the value of information against its cost. Value/cost helps the marketing research department determine which research projects to conduct, which research designs to use, and whether to gather more information after the initial results are in. The costs of research are typically easy to quantify, while the value is harder to anticipate. The value depends on the reliability and validity of the research findings and management's willingness to accept and act on its findings.

Management's Use of Marketing Research

In spite of the rapid growth of marketing research, many companies still fail to use it sufficiently or correctly. Several factors stand in the way of its greater utilization.

☐ *A narrow conception of marketing research*: Many managers see marketing research as only a fact-finding operation. The marketing researcher is supposed to design a questionnaire, choose a sample, conduct interviews, and report results, often without being given a careful definition of the problem or of the decision alternatives facing management. As a result, some of the fact finding fails to be useful. This reinforces management's idea of the limited usefulness of some marketing research.

☐ *Uneven caliber of marketing researchers*: Some managers view marketing research as little better than a clerical activity and reward it as such. Less-able marketing researchers are hired, and their weak training and deficient creativity lead to unimpressive results. The disappointing results reinforce management's prejudice against expecting too much from marketing research. Management continues to pay low salaries, perpetuating the basic difficulty.

☐ *Late and occasional erroneous findings by marketing research*: Managers want early results that are accurate and conclusive. But good marketing research takes time and money. Managers become disappointed, and they lower their opinion of the value of marketing research.

☐ *Intellectual differences*: Intellectual divergences between the mental styles of line managers and marketing researchers often get in the way of productive relationships. The marketing researcher's report may seem abstract, complicated, and tentative, while what the line manager wants is concreteness, simplicity, and certainty. Yet in the more progressive companies, marketing researchers are increasingly being included as members of the product management team, and their influence on marketing strategy is growing.

MARKETING DECISION SUPPORT SYSTEM

A growing number of organizations have added a fourth information service to help their marketing managers—a marketing decision support system—which is defined as follows:

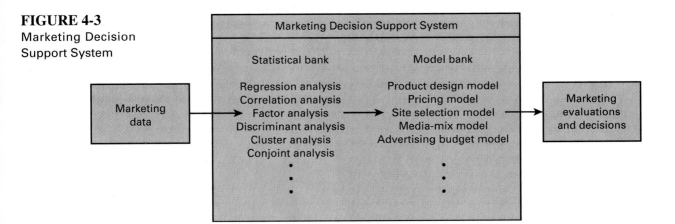

FIGURE 4-3
Marketing Decision
Support System

A marketing decision support system *(MDSS) is a set of statistical tools and decision models with supporting hardware and software available to marketing managers to assist them in analyzing data and making better marketing decisions* (see Figure 4-3).

Given the complex nature of modern markets and marketing activities, marketing managers need a basic familiarity with sophisticated tools for analyzing markets and making informed

---

Marketing Strategies 4-2

THE 1990S MARKETING MANAGER USES INFORMATION POWER

Envision the working day of a 1990s marketing manager. On arriving at work, the manager turns to a desk terminal and reads any message that arrived during the night, reviews the day's schedule, checks the status of an ongoing computer conference, reads several intelligence alerts, and browses through abstracts of relevant articles from the previous day's business press. To prepare for a late-morning meeting of the new-products committee, the manager calls up a recent marketing research report from microfilm storage to the screen, reviews relevant sections, edits them into a short report, sends copies electronically to other committee members who are also connected to the information network, and has the computer file a copy on microfilm. Before leaving for the meeting, the manager uses the terminal to make lunch reservations at a favorite resturant for an important distributor and to buy airline tickets for next week's sales meeting.

The afternoon is spent preparing sales and profit forecasts for the new product. The manager obtains test market data from company data banks and information on market demand, sales of competing products, and expected economic conditions from external data bases to which the company subscribes. These data are used as inputs for the sales forecasting model stored in the company's model bank. The manager "plays" with the model to see how different assumptions affect predicted results.

At home later that evening, the manager uses a laptop computer to contact the network, prepare a report on the product, and send copies to the terminals of other involved managers, who can read them first thing in the morning. When the manager logs off, the computer automatically sets an alarm clock for a wake-up call the next morning.

decisions. (The main tools are described and illustrated in the appendix to this chapter.) Because these managers will receive studies from marketing researchers and others who have employed advanced tools—multiple regression analysis, optimization analysis, and so on—they will need enough understanding to review these results critically. Furthermore, as many companies add *computer workstations* to their *information network*, marketing managers will be able to perform their own sophisticated analysis. They or their assistants can carry out critical analyses as needed. The computer work station will be to the marketing manager what the cockpit controls are to the pilot—arming the manager with the means of "flying" the business in the right direction.[13]

A growing number of software programs will help marketing managers analyze, plan, and control their operations. *Marketing News* of April 24, 1989, lists over ninety-two different software programs. They provide support for designing marketing research studies, segmenting markets, setting prices and advertising budgets, analyzing media, planning salesforce activity, and so on. One software system, Metaphor, promises to improve the management of internal and external databases and lead to quicker and better decisions by brand management.[14] New software programs are appearing that employ expert systems and/or artificial intelligence. One system helps advertisers select the best advertising theme for frequently purchased consumer packaged goods;[15] another helps managers plan more effective sales promotions.[16]

The 1990s will usher in newer dramatic software programs. Those companies that supply superior information power to their marketing managers will gain a competitive edge. Marketing Strategies 4-2 describes a day in the life of the 1990s marketing manager.

SUMMARY

Marketing information is a critical element in effective marketing as a result of the trend toward national and international marketing, the transition from buyer needs to buyer wants, and the transition from price to nonprice competition. All firms have a marketing information system connecting the external environment with its managers, but the systems vary greatly in the level of sophistication. In too many cases, information is not available or comes too late or cannot be trusted. An increasing number of companies are now taking steps to improve their marketing information system.

A well-designed market information system consists of four subsystems. The first is the internal records system, which provides current data on sales, costs, inventories, cash flows, and accounts receivable and payable. Many companies have developed advanced computer-based internal records systems to allow for speedier and more comprehensive information.

The second is the marketing intelligence system, which supplies marketing managers with everyday information about developments in the external marketing environment. Here a well-trained salesforce, purchased data from syndicated sources, and a marketing information center can improve the marketing intelligence available to company marketing managers.

The third system is marketing research, which involves collecting information that is relevant to a specific marketing problem facing the company. The marketing research process consists of five steps: defining the problem and research objectives, developing the research plan, collecting the information, analyzing the information, and presenting the findings. Good marketing research is characterized by the scientific method, creativity, multiple methodologies, model building, and cost/benefit measures of the value of information.

The fourth system is the marketing decision support system, which consists of statistical techniques and decision models to assist marketing managers in making better analyses and decisions.

QUESTIONS

1. The market for selling electronic data (e.g., Reuters selling commodities and securities quotes, and Dun and Bradstreet selling credit checks and business information to customers who access information on terminals and personal computers) is extremely competitive. What do you think are the "success requirements" that must be met by firms competing in this market?

2. A mail panel consists of large and nationally representative samples of households that have agreed to periodically participate in mail questionnaires, product tests, and telephone surveys. Under what circumstances would you use mail panels as part of the marketing research process described in this chapter?

3. Some research plans call for specifying in the design stage of the plan the multivariate statistical tools that will be used to analyze the data after they have been collected. Why would it be necessary to indicate these statistical techniques before the research approach and instruments have been designed?

4. For a model to prove useful to a marketing decision maker it first must be calibrated—values must be assigned to the model's parameters (the unknowns). What are some ways of calibrating models?

5. The uses of the computer for analyzing market research data are well known. What are some ways the computer can be helpful in collecting marketing research information?

6. Read Marketing Concepts and Tools 4-2. Do you agree with social activists that this type of research violates the privacy of consumers?

7. What might some research tasks be for the following areas: distribution decisions, product decisions, advertising decisions, personal-selling decisions, pricing decisions?

8. You are a marketing director. Your boss wants to know how many stores carry your dry cereal. Because you sell through food brokers, you don't know the answer. She wants the answer in two days. What would you do?

9. (a) Suggest how a liquor company might estimate liquor consumption in a legally dry town. (b) Suggest how a research organization might estimate the number of people who read a specific magazine in doctor's offices. (c) Suggest six ways in which male respondents can be interviewed on their usage of hair tonics.

10. A manufacturer of automobiles is testing a new direct-mail approach B versus a standard approach A. An experiment is conducted in which each approach is tried out on random samples of size n (sample size $2n$ in total) from a large national mailing list. Suppose that $n = 100\ 000$, also that $200\ 000$ is the total sample size of the experiment. During a three-month period, approach B has 761 sales and A has 753. What decision should be made? List the alternatives and the rationale of each.

11. Evaluate the following questions found in a consumer survey: (a) What is your husband's favorite brand of golf balls? (b) What TV programs did you watch last Monday? (c) How many pancakes did you make for your family last year? (d) Tell me your exact income. (e) Can you supply a list of your grocery purchases this month?

12. In obtaining estimates from company salespeople, product managers, and other personnel, one must discourage estimates that are self-serving. Give some examples of self-serving estimates, and suggest how to combat this problem.

13. Some marketers are hostile toward mathematical model building in marketing. They will make the following statements: (a) We don't use models; (b) Models are unrealistic; (c) Anyone can build a model; (d) A model is useless unless you can get the data. How would you answer each objection?

NOTES

1. See "The Payoff from Teamwork: The Gains in Quality Are Substantial—So Why Isn't It Spreading Faster?" *Business Week*, July 10, 1989, pp. 56-62.

2. Francis Joseph Aguilar, *Scanning the Business Environment* (New York: Macmillan, 1967).

3. James A. Narus and James C. Anderson, "Turn Your Industrial Distributors into Partners," *Harvard Business Review*, March-April 1986, pp. 66-71.

4. Dik Warren Twedt, ed., *1983 Survey of Marketing Research:* *Organization, Functions, Budget, Compensation* (Chicago: American Marketing Association, 1983). Updated statistics are taken from 1988 *Survey of Marketing Research*, Thomas Kinnear and Ann Root, eds. (Chicago: American Marketing Association, 1988).

5. In constant dollars, this represented a twelve-fold increase from 1966 to 1984. Joyce Cheng, David Conway, and George Haines Jr., "Marketing Research in Canada: A 1985 Update," ASAC 1986 Conference, Whistler, B.C.

6. For a discussion of the decision-theory approach to the

value of research, see Donald R. Lehmann, *Market Research and Analysis*, 3rd ed. (Homewood, Ill: Richard D. Irwin, 1989), Chap. 2.

7. For an excellent annotated reference to major secondary sources of business and marketing data, see M.D. Beckman, "A Guide to Locating Secondary Data," Holt, Rinehart and Winston of Canada Ltd. (undated pamphlet).

8. Herbert I. Abelson, "Focus Groups in Focus," *Marketing Communications*, February 1989, pp. 58-61.

9. An overview of mechanical devices is presented in Roger D. Blackwell, James S. Hensel, Michael B. Phillips, and Brian Sternthal, *Laboratory Equipment for Marketing Research* (Dubuque, Iowa: Kendall/Hunt Publishing Co., 1970), pp. 7-8. For newer devices, see Wally Wood, "The Race to Replace Memory," *Marketing and Media Decisions*, July 1986, pp. 166-67.

10. Selwyn Feinstein, "Computers Replacing Interviewers for Personnel and Marketing Tasks," *Wall Street Journal*, October 9, 1986, p. 35.

11. Horace C. Levinson, "Experiences in Commercial Operations Research," *Operations Research*, August 1953, pp. 220-39.

12. Mason Haire, "Projective Techniques in Marketing Research," *Journal of Marketing*, April 1950, pp. 649-56.

13. See "Information Power: How Companies Are Using New Technologies to Gain a Competitive Edge," *Business Week*, October 14, 1985, pp. 108-14; and Valerie Free, "Ready, Aim, Computer . . . The Marketing War Gets Automated," *Marketing Communications*, June 1988, p. 41 ff.

14. See Bob Goligoski, "Brand Leaders: Clorox Product Managers, Aided by Decision Support Systems, Won a $1.1 Billion Share . . ." *Business Computer Systems*, June 1986.

15. Arvind Rangaswamy, Raymond Burke, Jerry Wind, and Jehoshua Eliashberg, "Expert Systems for Marketing," working paper no. 86-036, Wharton School, University of Pennsylvania, November 1986.

16. John W. Keon and Judy Bayer, "An Expert Approach to Sales Promotion Management," *Journal of Advertising Research*, June-July 1986, pp. 19-26.

appendix

MARKETING DECISION SUPPORT SYSTEMS

Today's marketing managers in such companies as General Foods and General Mills can sit down at their computer terminals and answer many questions based on stored data that were formerly inaccessible. Their computers store a bank of linked statistical techniques and marketing decision models that make up a *marketing decision support system.*

The Statistical Bank

The *statistical bank is a collection of statistical procedures for extracting meaningful information from data.* It contains the usual statistical routines for calculating averages, measures of dispersion, and cross-tabulations of the data. In addition, the researcher can use various *multivariate statistical techniques* to discover important relationships in the data. The most important multivariate techniques are described below.[1]

Multiple Regression Analysis Every marketing problem involves a set of variables. The marketing researcher is typically interested in one of these variables, such as sales, and seeks to understand the cause(s) of its variation over time and/or space. This variable is called the dependent variable. The researcher hypothesizes about other variables, called independent variables, whose variations over time or space might contribute to the variations in the dependent variable. Regression analysis is the technique of estimating an equation that shows the contribution of independent variables to variations in the dependent variable. When one independent variable is involved, the statistical procedure is called simple regression; when two or more independent variables are involved, the procedure is called multiple regression. An example of multiple regression is presented at the end of Chapter 9 in equation 9-5.

Discriminant Analysis In many marketing situations, the dependent variable is classificatory rather than numerical. Consider the following situations:

An automobile company wants to identify consumer traits associated with brand preferences for Chevrolet versus Ford.

A detergent company wants to determine what consumer traits are associated with heavy, medium, and light usage of its brand.

A retailing chain wants to be able to discriminate between potentially successful and unsuccessful store sites. ∎

In these cases, the analyst visualizes two or more groups to which a person or object may belong. The challenge is to find discriminating variables that could be combined in a predictive equation to produce better-than-chance assignment of the entities to the groups. The technique for solving this problem is known as discriminant analysis. This analysis has been useful to identify profiles of innovators, develop relevant criteria for market segmentation, and examine consumer brand preference behavior.[2]

Factor Analysis   One of the problems faced in many regression and discriminant studies is a high intercorrelation among the explanatory variables, which leads to biased estimates of the effect of these variables on the dependent variable(s). The ideal in multiple regression is to use variables that are truly independent, both in the sense that they influence, but are not influenced by, the dependent variable and in the sense that each independent variable is independent of the others. The simple correlation coefficients for all pairs of variables will reveal which variables are highly correlated. Factor analysis is a statistical procedure for trying to discover a few basic factors that may underlie and explain the correlations among a larger number of variables. In the marketing area, factor analysis has been used to determine the basic factors underlying attitudes toward air travel, alcoholic beverages, and television programs.

Cluster Analysis   Many marketing problems require the researcher to sort a set of objects into subgroups or clusters. The objects may be products, people, places, and so on. Thus the researcher might want to sort several automobile makes into major groups with as much likeness within groups and as much difference between groups as possible; automobiles within a group can be assumed to be most competitive with each other. Or the researcher might want to cluster people into subgroups, which is essentially what we mean by market segmentation. Or the researcher might want to cluster cities into groups so that test cities could be drawn that resemble each other. In all cases, the objects are described by multidimensional data, and the chosen clustering technique sorts the objects into a prespecified number of groups.[3]

Conjoint Analysis   Conjoint analysis is used by marketers to determine how to design an appealing product for a target market. The marketer wants to decide what attributes to build in the product at what levels. Consumers are shown a set of product concepts (differing in attributes) and are asked to express their preferences. From these rankings, the researcher can determine the importance of each attribute and the most effective combination of attributes. Conjoint analysis has proved to be an increasingly useful marketing research tool with more than one thousand reported applications to date.[4]

The Model Bank

The *model bank is a collection of models that will help marketers develop better marketing decisions.* A model itself is a *set of variables and their interrelationships designed to represent some real system or process.* Models are built by management scientists (also called operations researchers), who apply scientific methodology to achieve understanding, prediction, or control of some management problem.

Although management science is a relative latecomer in marketing, it has already yielded useful models for new-product sales forecasting,[5] site selection,[6] sales-call planning,[7] media mix,[8] and marketing-mix budgeting.[9] Several models are being used by some large companies.[10] Although marketing managers often lack the training to understand the mathematics of the more complex models, they certainly can grasp the central idea behind each type of model and can judge its relevance to their work. The major types of models are listed in Table 4A-1 and discussed in the following paragraphs.

Descriptive Models   Descriptive models are designed to communicate, explain, or predict. They can be built at three levels of detail. A *macromodel* consists of a few variables and a set of relationships among them. An example would be a sales model consisting of a single equation with total sales as the dependent variable and national income, average price, and

Table 4A-1 A Classification of Models

I. According to Purpose	II. According to Techniques

A. Descriptive Models
   1. Markov-process model
   2. Queuing model
B. Decision Models
   1. Differential calculus
   2. Mathematical programming
   3. Statistical decision theory
   4. Game theory
	A. Verbal Models
	B. Graphical Models
	   1. Logical-flow model
	   2. Network-planning model
	   3. Causal model
	   4. Decision-tree model
	   5. Functional-relationship model
	   6. Feedback-systems model
	C. Mathematical Models
	   1. Linear vs. nonlinear model
	   2. Static vs. dynamic model
	   3. Deterministic vs. stochastic model

company advertising expenditures as the independent variables. They are derived by fitting the "best" possible equation to the set of variables.

A *microanalytic model* specifies more links between a dependent variable and its determinants. A good example is the DEMON model, in which the effect of advertising expenditures on sales is explained through a set of successive links between advertising expenditure, gross number of exposures, reach and frequency, advertising awareness, consumer trial, usage, and usage rate.[11]

A *microbehavioral model* creates hypothetical entities (consumers, dealers, and so on) who interact and produce a record of behavior, which is then analyzed. A good example is a consumer model built by Amstutz, in which a population of potential purchasers is exposed to weekly marketing stimuli, and some fraction of them purchase the product.[12]

Two descriptive models in the management-science literature are particularly germane to marketing-type problems. The first is the *Markov-process model*, which describes the probabilities of moving from any current state to any new state. Suppose there are three coffee brands, A, B, and C. Of those consumers who bought brand A last time, suppose 70 percent buy it again, 20 percent buy B, and 10 percent buy C. This information is represented in row 1 of Figure 4A-1, along with probabilities associated with brands B and C. The brand-switching matrix provides information about the following:

FIGURE 4A-1
A Brand-Switching Matrix
(Markov-Process Model)

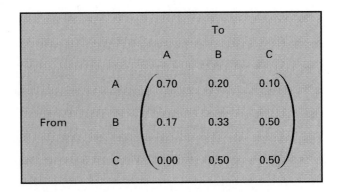

□ The *repeat-purchase rate* for each brand, indicated by the numbers in the diagonal starting at the upper left. Under certain assumptions, the repeat-purchase rate can be interpreted as a measure of brand loyalty.

□ The *switching-in* and *switching-out* rate for each brand, represented by the off-diagonal numbers.

If the switching rates remain constant, the matrix can be used to predict the ultimate brand shares.[13]

Queuing models are also of interest to marketers. Queuing models describe waiting-line situations and answer two questions: What waiting time can be expected in a particular system? How will this waiting time change if the system is altered?

These questions are of interest to supermarkets, gasoline stations, airline ticket offices, and so on. Wherever customers wait, there is the danger that waiting time will become excessive, leading some customers to switch to competitors.

If the current system breeds long queues, the analyst can simulate the effects of different queue-handling arrangements. In the case of a supermarket, four possible attacks are possible. The supermarket can influence its customers to shop on less-busy days. The supermarket can employ baggers to aid the cashiers and thus reduce waiting time. More service channels can be added. Finally, some service channels can be specialized to handle small orders.

Decision Models   Decision models assist managers in evaluating alternatives and finding a good solution. An *optimization model* is one for which mathematical routines exist for finding the best solution. A *heuristic model* is one for which computational routines exist to find a pretty good solution. The heuristic model may involve a more complex statement of the problem. The analyst applies heuristics, defined as rules of thumb that shorten the time or work required to find a reasonably good solution. For example, in a model to determine good warehouse locations, the heuristic might be, consider locations only in large cities. This may exclude a perfectly good location in a small city, but the savings in having to check far fewer cities may compensate for the omission.

Four optimization-type decision models are of particular relevance to marketing. The first is *differential calculus*, which is applied to well-defined mathematical functions to find the maximum or minimum value. Suppose a marketing analyst has determined the profit equation shown in Figure 4A-2(a). The task is to find the best price—that is, the value of P that will maximize the value of Z. One approach is to graph the equation and examine it for the profit-maximizing price, here $150. A quicker procedure is to apply differential calculus to this equation without bothering to draw a graph.

The second type of decision model is *mathematical programming*. Here the decision maker's objective is expressed as some variable to be optimized subject to a set of explicitly expressed constraints. Consider the problem in Figure 4A-2(b). It shows a profit function relating profits to the amount of funds spent on advertising and distribution. A dollar of advertising contributes $10 of profit, and a dollar of distribution contributes $20. A set of policy constraints is also introduced. First the marketing budget, as divided between advertising and distribution, should not exceed $100 (constraint 1). Of this, advertising should receive at least $40 (constraint 2) and no more than $80 (constraint 3); and distribution should receive at least $10 (constraint 4) and no more than $70 (constraint 5). Because of the simplicity of this problem, the best marketing program can be found without invoking higher mathematics. Since distribution dollars are twice as effective as advertising dollars, it would make sense to spend all that is permitted within the constraints on distribution. This would be $70, leaving $30 for advertising. However, advertising must receive at least $40, according to

FIGURE 4A-2
Four Decision Models

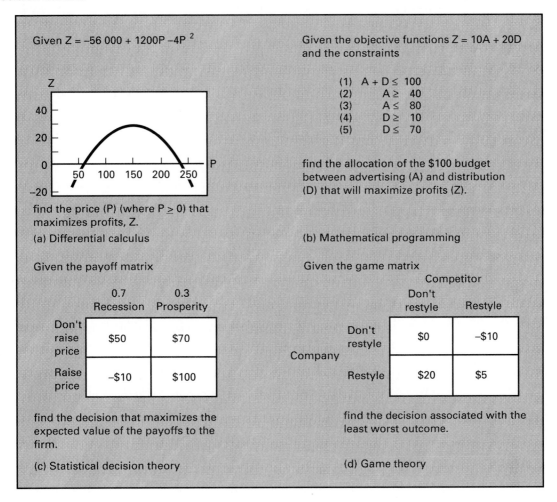

Given $Z = -56\,000 + 1200P - 4P^2$

Z

40

20

0

−20

50 100 150 200 250 P

find the price (P) (where $P \geq 0$) that maximizes profits, Z.

(a) Differential calculus

Given the objective functions $Z = 10A + 20D$ and the constraints

(1) $A + D \leq 100$
(2) $A \geq 40$
(3) $A \leq 80$
(4) $D \geq 10$
(5) $D \leq 70$

find the allocation of the $100 budget between advertising (A) and distribution (D) that will maximize profits (Z).

(b) Mathematical programming

Given the payoff matrix

	0.7 Recession	0.3 Prosperity
Don't raise price	$50	$70
Raise price	−$10	$100

find the decision that maximizes the expected value of the payoffs to the firm.

(c) Statistical decision theory

Given the game matrix

	Competitor Don't restyle	Restyle
Company Don't restyle	$0	−$10
Restyle	$20	$5

find the decision associated with the least worst outcome.

(d) Game theory

constraint 2. Therefore, the optimal marketing-mix allocation would be $40 for advertising and $60 for distribution; and with this solution, profits will be $10($40) + $20($60) = $1600. In larger problems, the analyst would have to use specific mathematical procedures.

The third type of decision model is called *statistical decision theory* (or Bayesian decision theory). This model calls for (1) identifying major decision alternatives facing the firm, (2) distinguishing the events (states of nature) that might, with each possible decision, bring about a distinct outcome, (3) estimating the probability of each state of nature, (4) estimating the value (payoff) of each outcome to the firm, (5) determining the expected value of each decision, and (6) choosing the decision with the highest expected value. Consider this in relation to the problem in Figure 4A-2(c). Suppose a product manager is trying to decide between raising a price or leaving it alone. The outcome will be affected by whether the economy slides into a recession, of which the product manager believes there is a 0.7 chance. If a recession occurs and the price is not raised, profits will be $50; but if the price is raised, there will be a loss of $10. On the other hand, if the economy is prosperous and prices are unchanged, the profits will be $70; and if prices had been raised, profits would have been $100. These estimates are summarized in the payoff matrix.

Statistical decision theory calls for the product manager to estimate the expected value of each decision. Expected value is the weighted mean of the payoffs, with the probabilities serving as the weights. The expected value associated with not raising the price is 0.7($50) + 0.3($70) = $56, while the expected value of raising the price is 0.7(–$10) + 0.3($100) = $23. Clearly, the extra gain with the best thing happening (a raised price and prosperity) is not worth the risk, and the product manager is better off leaving the price alone. This assumes that expected value is a satisfactory criterion for the firm to maximize. This criterion is sensible for a large firm that makes repeated decisions of this kind. It makes less sense for a smaller firm facing a major one-shot decision that could ruin it if things went wrong.[14] For more-complex problems, the options are represented in a decision tree (see Figure 4A-3[d]).

Game theory is a fourth approach to evaluating decision alternatives. Like statistical decision theory, it calls for identifying the decision alternatives, uncertain variables, and the value of different outcomes. It differs from statistical decision theory in that the major uncertain variable is assumed to be a competitor, nature, or some other force that is malevolent. The probability is 1.00 that each actor will do what is in its best interest. Consider the example in Figure 4A-2(d). An auto manufacturer is deciding whether to restyle its car. It knows that the competitor is also facing the same decision. The company estimates that if neither restyles, neither will gain anything over the normal rate of profit. If the company restyles and the competitor does not, the company will gain $20 over the competitor. (We will assume the competitor loses $20—that is, the gain to one company is a loss to the other.) If the company does not restyle and the competitor does, the company loses $10. Finally, if they both restyle, the company gains $5, and the competitor loses $5, because the company is assumed to be better at restyling.

A solution is possible if we assume that both opponents will want to take the course of action that will leave them *least worst off*. Called the *minimax criterion* (minimizing the maximum loss), it assumes that both opponents are conservative. This criterion would lead the company to prefer the restyling alternative. If it does not restyle, it might lose as much as $10; if it does restyle, it will make at least $5. The competitor would also prefer to restyle. If it does not restyle, it might lose as much as $20; if it does restyle, it cannot lose more than $5. Hence, both opponents will decide to restyle, which leads to a $5 gain for the company and a $5 loss for the competitor. Neither opponent can gain by switching unilaterally to a different strategy.[15]

Verbal Models   Models in which the variables and their relationships are described in prose are verbal models. Most of the great theories of individual, social, and societal behavior—theories such as those of Freud, Darwin, and Marx—are cast in verbal terms. Many models of consumer behavior are essentially in verbal-model form. Consider ". . . advertising should move people from *awareness* . . . to *knowledge* . . . to *liking* . . . to *preference* . . . to *conviction* . . . to *purchase*."[16]

Graphical Models   Graphical models represent a useful step in the process of symbolizing a verbal model. Six graphical models can be distinguished.

Figure 4A-3(a) shows a *logical-flow diagram*. A logical-flow diagram is a visual representation of a logical process or operation. The boxes in the diagram are connected in a sequential-flow pattern and related through two operations. One of these is *branching*.

FIGURE 4A-3
Six Graphical Models for Marketing Analysis

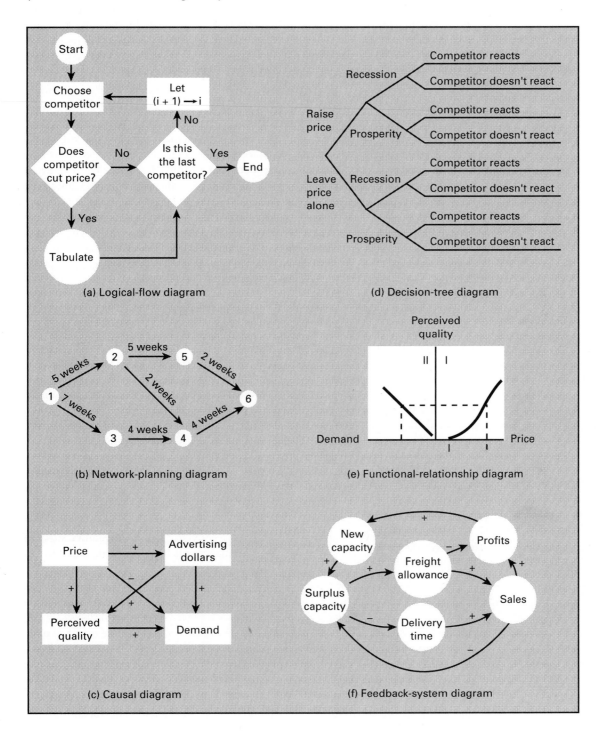

(a) Logical-flow diagram

(b) Network-planning diagram

(c) Causal diagram

(d) Decision-tree diagram

(e) Functional-relationship diagram

(f) Feedback-system diagram

Branching takes place when a question is posed at a certain step of the process, and its possible answers are depicted as alternative branches leading away from the box. The other operation is *looping*. Looping takes place if certain answers return the flow to an earlier stage. The logical-flow diagram in Figure 4A-3(a) describes a firm's efforts to determine how many competitors will cut their prices. The firm first considers competitor *i* and asks whether it is likely to cut its price. If the answer is yes, this result is tabulated, and then the firm asks whether there are any additional competitors to consider. If the answer is no, the firm goes directly to the next question. If there are more competitors to consider, the logical flow loops back to the first box; otherwise, the flow ends. Logical-flow diagrams are coming into increasing use in marketing because of the clarity with which they illustrate a logical process.

Figure 4A-3(b) shows a *network-planning diagram* (also called a critical-path diagram), which portrays the events that must occur to complete a project. The events, shown as circles, are connected by arrows indicating precedent relationships. In Figure 4A-3(b), event 6 cannot occur until events 4 and 5 are completed; event 5 cannot occur until event 2 is completed; event 4 cannot occur until events 2 and 3 are completed; and so on. By estimating the completion time of each task (and sometimes the optimistic and pessimistic completion times), the analyst can find the earliest date to completion of the entire project. The network will contain a critical path that defines the earliest possible completion time; here it is fifteen weeks. Unless this critical path is shortened, there is no way to complete the project earlier. This diagram is the basis of planning, scheduling, and controlling projects, such as the development of a new product.

Figure 4A-3(c) shows a *causal diagram*, which is used to portray the directions of influence of specific variables on each other. This diagram shows that price has a direct (negative) influence on demand and an indirect influence also through its positive effects on advertising dollars and perceived quality. A high price leads to high perceived quality and leads the company to spend more on advertising. Both of these—high perceived quality and advertising—in turn have a positive effect on demand. (Not shown is the fact that the resulting demand will have a feedback influence on advertising expenditures as well as on the perceived quality.) The value of causal diagrams is in exposing the complex relationships that the analyst must take into account. They remind us that single-equation relationships between variables may fail to capture the true causal relations among variables.

Figure 4A-3(d) shows a *decision-tree diagram*, which portrays the decision alternatives and consequences found in a decision situation. A manager is trying to decide between raising the price and leaving it alone. The outcome will be influenced by whether the economy moves toward recession or prosperity and further by whether competitors react. The tree could be extended to show other contingencies related to buyer reactions, inventory situations, and so on. By adding payoffs and probabilities to the various branches of the tree, the best decision can be found by using statistical decision theory.

Figure 4A-3(e) is a *functional-relationship diagram*, which portrays functional relationship(s) between two or more variables. Quadrant I shows a positive relationship between price and perceived quality. Quadrant II shows a positive relationship between perceived quality and demand. The two quadrants enable the analyst to trace the effect of a particular price, through perceived quality, on a particular demand level. Thus one can generate a demand function from knowledge of two other functions. Functional graphs can be used to portray sales-response functions, probability distributions, and many other relationships.

Figure 4A-3(f) shows a *feedback-system diagram*, which portrays any system whose outputs return and influence subsequent outputs. This process should not be confused with looping in logical-flow diagrams, which merely returns the procedure to an earlier point without implying any influence on that point. The example shows the interactions among sales, profits, capacity, and marketing variables. Surplus capacity leads the company to offer higher freight allowances to customers and faster delivery time. These lead to higher sales. Increased sales lead to increased profits while drawing down surplus capacity. In the meantime, the higher freight allowances reduce profits. If the net effect is a gain in profits, that leads to additional investment in capacity; and the cycle continues. Thus feedback-system diagrams are useful devices for representing variables that have interactive properties and feedbacks.[17]

Graphical models have all the virtues that are found in "pictures." A graph strips the phenomenon of non-essentials; it allows a viewer to grasp the whole and select which relationships to examine. For marketing analysts, graphs improve exposition, facilitate discussion, and guide analysis.

Mathematical Models   Mathematical models can be classified in many ways. One distinction is between *linear* and *nonlinear models*. In a linear model, all the relationships between variables are expressed as straight lines. This means that a unit change in one variable has a constant marginal impact on a related variable. The advertising-sales relationship would be linear if every $100 increase in advertising created a $1000 increase in sales, no matter how much had already been spent. This kind of increase is unlikely, however, because diminishing returns to advertising can be expected. It is also likely that other marketing inputs, such as price and sales-call time, do not relate to sales in a thoroughly linear way. The assumption of linearity is useful as a first approximation for mathematical convenience. A second distinction can be drawn between *static* and *dynamic models*. A *static* model centers on the ultimate state (or solution) of a system, independent of time. A dynamic model brings time explicitly into its framework and allows the state of the system to be observed over time. The demand-supply diagram in beginning economics courses represents a static model of price determination in that it indicates where price and output will be in equilibrium without indicating the path of adjustment through time. Brand-switching models are dynamic in that they predict period-to-period changes in customer brand choices.

A third distinction can be drawn between *deterministic* and *stochastic* models. A *deterministic model* is one in which chance plays no role. The solution is determined by a set of exact relationships. The linear-programming model for determining blends (oils, animal feeds, candies) is deterministic because the relationships are exact and the cost data are known. A *stochastic model*, on the other hand, is one where chance or random variables are introduced explicitly. Brand-switching models are stochastic in that customers' brand choices are regulated by probabilities.

As management scientists enter more companies, they will provide a set of statistical procedures and decision models that will greatly enhance the marketing manager's skill in making better-informed decisions. The main need is that marketing managers and management scientists move rapidly toward understanding each other's needs and capabilities.[18]

■ NOTES

1. For an overview, see Kinnear and Taylor, *Marketing Research*, pp. 517-65.

2. William R. Dillon, Matthew Goldstein, and Leon G. Schiffman, "Appropriateness of Linear Discriminant and Multinomial Classification Analysis in Marketing Research," *Journal of Marketing Research*, February 1978, pp. 103-12; and Edward R. Bruning, Mary L. Kovacic, and Larry E. Oberdick, "Segmentation Analysis of Domestic Airline Passenger Markets," *Journal of Academy of Marketing Science*, Winter 1985, pp. 17-31.

3. Girish Punj and David W. Stewart, "Cluster Analysis in Marketing Research: Review and Suggestions for Application," *Journal of Marketing Research*, May 1983, pp. 134-48.

4. Philippe Cattin and Dick R. Wittink, "Commercial Use of Conjoint Analysis: A Survey," *Journal of Marketing*,

Summer 1982, pp. 44-53; and Thomas W. Leigh, David B. MacKay, and John O. Summers, "Reliability and Validity of Conjoint Analysis and Self-Explicated Weights: A Comparison," *Journal of Marketing Research*, November 1984, pp. 456-62.

5. See Glen L. Urban and John R. Hauser, *Design and Marketing of New Products* (Englewood Cliffs, N.J.: Prentice-Hall, 1980); and Glen L. Urban and Gerald M. Katz, "Pre-Test-Market Models: Validation and Managerial Implications," *Journal of Marketing Research*, August 1983, pp. 221-34; and Fred S. Zufryden, "PROD II: A Model for Predicting from Tracking Studies," *Journal of Advertising Research*, April-May 1985, pp. 45-51.

6. T. E. Hlavac, Jr., and J. D. C. Little, "A Geographic Model of an Automobile Market," working paper no. 186-66 (Cambridge: Massachusetts Institute of Technology, Alfred P. Sloan School of Management, 1966); and Philippe A. Naert and Alain V. Bultez, "A Model of a Distribution Network Aggregate Performance," *Management Science*, June 1975, pp. 1102-12.

7. Leonard M. Lodish, "Callplan: An Interactive Salesman's Call Planning System," *Management Science*, December 1971, pp. 25-40; Arthur Meidan, "Optimizing the Number of Industrial Salespersons," *Industrial Marketing Management*, February 1982, pp. 63-74; and Andris A. Zoltners and Prabhakant Sinha, "Sales Territory Alignment: A Review and Model," *Management Science*, November 1983, pp. 1237-56.

8. See John D. C. Little and Leonard M. Lodish, "A Media Planning Calculus," *Operations Research*, January-February 1969, pp. 1-35.

9. John D. C. Little, "BRANDAID: A Marketing Mix Model, Structure, Implementation, Calibration, and Case Study," *Operations Research*, July-August 1975, pp. 628-73.

10. Applications of marketing models are examined in Jean-Claude Lerreche and David B. Montgomery, "A Framework for the Comparison of Marketing Models: A Delphi Study,"

Journal of Marketing Research, November 1977, pp. 487-98; and Randall L. Schultz and Andris A. Zoltners, eds., *Marketing Decision Models* (New York: Elsevier North-Holland, 1981).

11. David B. Learner, "Profit Maximization through New-Product Marketing Planning and Control," in *Applications of the Sciences to Marketing Management*, ed. Frank M. Bass et al. (New York: John Wiley, 1968), pp. 151-67.

12. Arnold E. Amstutz, *Computer Simulation of Competitive Market Response* (Cambridge, Mass.: MIT Press, 1967).

13. David B. Montgomery and Adrian B. Rejans, "Stochastic Models of Consumer Choice Behavior," in *Consumer Behavior: Theoretical Sources*, ed. S. Ward and T. S. Robertson (Englewood Cliffs, N.J.: Prentice-Hall, 1973), pp. 521-76.

14. See Frank M. Bass, "Marketing Research Expenditures: A Decision Model," *Journal of Business*, January 1963, pp.77-90; and Rex V. Brown, "Do Managers Find Decision Theory Useful?" *Harvard Business Review*, May-June 1970, pp. 78-89.

15. R. Duncan Luce and Howard Raiffa, *Games and Decisions* (New York: John Wiley, 1957), pp. 453-55.

16. Robert J. Lavidge and Gary A. Steiner, "A Model for Predictive Measurements of Advertising Effectiveness," *Journal of Marketing*, October 1961, pp. 59-62.

17. See Jay W. Forrester, "Modeling of Market and Company Interactions," in *Marketing and Economic Development*, ed. Peter D. Bennett (Chicago: American Marketing Association, 1965), pp. 353-64.

18. For an overview of statistical and decision models in marketing, see Gary L. Lilien and Philip Kotler, *Marketing Decision Making: A Model-Building Approach*, 2nd ed. (New York: Harper & Row, 1983). For an overview of computer applications in marketing, see John M. McCann, *The Marketing Workbench: Using Computers for Better Performance* (Homewood, Ill.: Dow Jones-Irwin, 1986).

5

Analyzing the Marketing Environment

Canada could have enjoyed English government, French culture, and American know-how. Instead it ended up with English know-how, French government, and American culture.

John Robert Colombo

We have repeatedly emphasized that excellent companies take an *outside-inside* view of their business. These companies monitor the changing environment and continuously adapt their businesses to their best opportunities. In this and the next three chapters, we examine the world outside the firm and consider how to monitor and analyze it. In this chapter, we address two questions: Who are the *key outside actors* that the company interacts with in carrying on its marketing activities? and What are the *key outside forces* that affect the company's performance?

To the company's marketers falls the major responsibility for identifying major changes in the environment. The marketing environment is constantly spinning out new opportunities, in bad as well as in good years. Table 5-1 shows some of the great marketing success stories in the 1960s, 1970s, and 1980s. Although the 1970s and 1980s were years of slow growth, there were enough enterprising people around to create marvelous new businesses out of ideas that seem obvious in retrospect.

The marketing environment also spins out new threats—such as foreign competition, a military crisis, a deep recession—and firms find their markets collapsing. Recent times have been marked by many sudden changes in the marketing environment, leading Drucker to dub it an *Age of Discontinuity* and Toffler to describe it as a time of *Future Shock.*[1]

Company marketers use marketing intelligence and marketing research to track the changing environment. By erecting early warning systems, marketers will be able to revise marketing strategies in time to meet new challenges and opportunities in the environment.

What do we mean by the marketing environment? The marketing environment comprises the "noncontrollable" actors and forces that impact on the company's markets and marketing. Specifically:

Table 5-1 Great Marketing Successes

1990s		1970s	1980s
McDonald's	Lite beer	Boeing 747	Atari videogames
Honda motorcycles	Perrier water	H&R Block	Apple computers
Playboy	Charlie perfume	Intel's "Chip"	Computerland stores
Avon cosmetics	Club Mediterranée	Disposable diapers	Pocket TV
Levi jeans	Nautilus	Pac Man	Compact disc players
Crest toothpaste	Pocket calculators	Rubik's cube	Telephone-answering machines
Convenience stores	Prince tennis racquets	Tylenol	Automatic teller machines
BIC pens	Adidas and Nike shoes	L'eggs hosiery	Camcorders
K-mart	Softsoap	Microwace ovens	
Bombardier Ski-doo		Videorecorders	

A company's marketing environment *consists of the actors and forces that affect the company's ability to develop and maintain successful transactions and relationships with its target customers.*

The actors and forces in a company's marketing environment are shown in Figure 5-1. We can distinguish between the company's microenvironment and macroenvironment. The *microenvironment* consists of the actors in the company's immediate environment that affect its ability to serve its markets: the company, suppliers, market intermediaries, customers, competitors, and publics. The *macroenvironment* consists of the larger societal forces that affect all of the actors in the company's microenvironment: the demographic, economic, natural, technological, political, and cultural forces. We will first examine the company's microenvironment and then its macroenvironment.

ACTORS IN THE COMPANY'S MICROENVIRONMENT

Every company's primary goal is to profitably serve and satisfy specific needs of chosen target markets. To carry out this task, the company links itself with a set of suppliers and a set of marketing intermediaries to reach its target customers. The *suppliers/company/marketing intermediaries/customers* chain comprises the *core marketing system* of the company.

FIGURE 5-1
Major Actors and
Forces in the
Company's Marketing
Environment

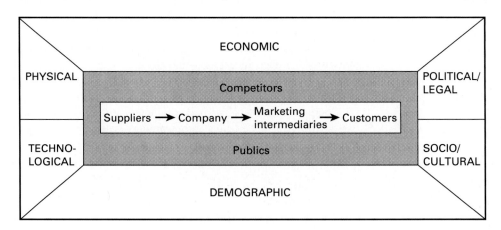

The company's success will be affected by two additional groups, namely, a set of competitors and a set of publics. All the actors are shown in Figure 5-1. We will illustrate the roles of these actors in the case of Hershey Canada Inc., the Canadian subsidiary of a major U.S. candy manufacturer. We shall look at the company's candy line and its suppliers, marketing intermediaries, competitors, and publics, in that order.

Company

Hershey Canada is part of an organization based in Pennsylvania which makes over $1.8 billion in chocolate and confection sales each year. Its product line includes Hershey's Chocolate Bars, Hershey Kisses, Reese's candy, and several other items. Its marketing is handled by a large marketing and sales department consisting of brand managers, marketing researchers, advertising and sales promotion specialists, sales managers and sales representatives, and so on. The marketing department is responsible for developing marketing plans for all the existing products and brands as well as developing new products and brands.

Marketing management at Hershey, in formulating marketing plans, takes into account the other groups in the company, such as top management, finance, R&D, purchasing, manufacturing, and accounting. All of these groups constitute the *company's internal microenvironment*.

Hershey's top management consists of the president, the executive committee, and the board of directors. These higher levels of management set the company's mission, objectives, broad strategies, and policies. Marketing managers must make decisions within the context set by top management. Furthermore, their marketing proposals must be approved by top management before they can be implemented.

Marketing managers must also work closely with the functional departments. *Financial management* is concerned with the availability of funds to carry out the marketing plan; the efficient allocation of these funds to different products, brands, and marketing activities; the likely rates of return that will be realized; and the level of risk in the sales forecast and marketing plans. *Research-and-development management* focuses on researching and developing successful new products. *Purchasing* worries about obtaining sufficient supplies of raw materials (cocoa, sugar, and so on) as well as other items required to run this company. *Manufacturing* is responsible for acquiring sufficient productive capacity and personnel to meet production targets. *Accounting* has to measure revenues and costs to help marketing know how well it is achieving its profit objectives.

All of these departments have an impact on the marketing department's plans and actions. The various brand managers have to sell the R&D, manufacturing, and finance departments on their plans before presenting them to top management. If the manufacturing vice-president will not allocate enough production capacity or the financial vice-president will not allocate money, the brand managers will have to revise their sales targets or bring the issue before top management. The many potential conflicts between marketing and the other functions mean that marketing has to negotiate with internal company groups in the course of designing and implementing its marketing plans (see Chapter 25).

Suppliers

Suppliers are business firms and individuals who provide resources needed by the company and its competitors to produce goods and services. For example, Hershey must obtain cocoa, sugar, cellophane, paper, and various other materials to produce and package its candies. In addition, it must obtain labor, equipment, fuel, electricity, computers, and other factors of production. Hershey's purchasing department must decide which resources to make and which to buy outside. For "buy" decisions, Hershey's purchasing agents must develop specifications, search for suppliers, qualify them, and choose those who offer the best mix of quality, delivery reliability, credit, warranties, and low cost.

Developments in the "suppliers" environment can have a substantial effect on the company's marketing operations. Marketing managers need to watch price trends of their key inputs. Rising costs of sugar or cocoa may force Hershey to raise its prices or shrink its candy-bar sizes, either step probably hurting Hershey's sales. Marketing managers are equally concerned with supply availability. Supply shortages, labor strikes, and other events can prevent fulfilling delivery promises and lose sales in the short run and damage customer goodwill in the long run. Many companies prefer to buy from multiple sources to avoid depending on a single supplier who might raise prices or limit supply. Company purchasing agents try to build long-term relationships with key suppliers. In times of shortage, purchasing agents find that they have to "market" their company to suppliers in order to obtain preferential supplies.[2]

Supply planning has become more important and sophisticated in recent years. To the extent that companies can lower their supply costs and/or increase their product quality, they can gain a competitive advantage. Some companies are integrating backward so that they can make and control some of their key supplies. Other companies are requiring their suppliers to move closer to their plants and practice "just-in-time production," that is, produce as the supplies are needed rather than for inventory. In this case, the suppliers must deliver the required quality, and this has led companies to work more closely with their suppliers on quality assurance programs taking place at the suppliers' sites. Companies are looking for suppliers whose quality, reliability, and efficiency they can trust.

The marketing manager is a direct purchaser of certain services to support the marketing effort, such as advertising, marketing research, sales training, and marketing consulting. In going outside, the marketing manager evaluates different advertising agencies, marketing research firms, sales-training consultants, and marketing consultants. The manager has to decide which services to purchase outside and which to produce inside by adding specialists to the staff.

Marketing Intermediaries

Marketing intermediaries are firms that aid the company in promoting, selling, and distributing its goods to final buyers. They include middlemen, physical-distribution firms, marketing service agencies, and financial intermediaries.

Middlemen   Middlemen are business firms that help the company find customers or close sales with them. They fall into two types, agent middlemen and merchant middlemen. *Agent middlemen*—such as agents, brokers, and manufacturers' representatives—find customers or negotiate contracts but do not take title to merchandise. Hershey, for example, might hire agents to find retailers in various South American countries and pay commission to these agents based on their success. The agents do not buy the candy; Hershey ships directly to the retailers. *Merchant middlemen*—such as wholesalers, retailers, and other resellers—buy, take title to, and resell merchandise. Hershey's primary method of marketing candy is to sell candy to wholesalers, large supermarket chains, and vending-machine operators, who in turn resell the candy to consumers at a profit.

Why does Hershey use middlemen at all? The answer is that middlemen are able to perform several marketing tasks more efficiently than Hershey can. As a manufacturer, Hershey is primarily interested in producing and rolling out large quantities of candy from its factory doors. The customer, on the other hand, is interested in finding one bar of candy in a convenient location, at a convenient time, with a related assortment of other goods sought by the consumer, and with an easy payment mechanism. The gap between the large quantities of candy that Hershey rolls out and the consumer's preferred way of buying candy must be overcome. Middlemen come into being to help overcome the discrepancies in quantities, place, time, assortment, and possession that would otherwise exist.

Specifically, middlemen create *place utility* by stocking Hershey candy where customers are located. They create *time utility* by staying open long hours so that customers can shop at their convenience. They create *quantity utility* by making candy available in single-bar purchases. They create *assortment utility* by collecting in one point other goods that consumers may seek on the same shopping trip. They create *possession utility* by transferring the candy bar to the consumer in an easy transaction format, namely, for a simple cash payment without the need for any billing. Hershey, to create the same utilities, would have to establish, finance, and operate a far-flung network of national stores and vending machines. Hershey, of course, finds it more efficient to work through established marketing channels.

Selecting and working with middlemen, however, is not a simple task. At one time the manufacturer had to contact and sell to numerous small independent middlemen. Today, the manufacturer deals with fewer but larger middlemen organizations. An increasing share of all food distribution is in the hands of large corporate retail chains (such as Loblaws and Steinberg), large wholesalers, and franchise-sponsored voluntary chains (such as Mac's and Becker's). To cite an extreme case, in Switzerland 70 percent of all food distribution is in the hands of two giant middlemen, Migros and the Coop. These groups have great power to dictate terms or else shut the manufacturer out of some large-volume markets. The manufacturer must work hard to get and maintain "shelf space." The manufacturer has to learn how to manage and satisfy members of its marketing channel or face diminishing support and maybe even exclusion.

Physical-Distribution Firms   Physical-distribution firms assist the company in stocking and moving goods from their original locations to their destinations. *Warehousing firms* store and protect goods before they move to the next destination. Every company has to decide how much storage space to build for itself and how much to rent from warehousing firms. *Transportation firms* consist of railroads, truckers, airlines, barges, and other freight-handling companies that move goods from one location to another. Every company has to decide on the most cost-effective modes of shipment, balancing such considerations as cost, delivery, speed, and safety (see Chapter 19).

Marketing Service Agencies   Marketing service agencies—marketing research firms, advertising agencies, media firms, and marketing consulting firms—assist the company in targeting and promoting its products to the right markets. The company faces a "make or buy" decision with respect to each of these services. Some large companies—such as Du Pont and Quaker Oats—operate their own in-house advertising agencies and marketing research departments. But most companies contract for the services of outside agencies. When a firm decides to buy outside services, it must carefully choose whom to hire, since the agencies vary in their creativity, quality, service, and price. The company has to review their performance periodically and must consider replacing those that no longer perform at the expected level.

Financial Intermediaries   Financial intermediaries include banks, credit companies, insurance companies, and other companies that help finance and/or insure risk associated with the buying and selling of goods. Most companies and customers depend on financial intermediaries to finance their transactions. The company's marketing performance can be seriously affected by rising credit costs and/or limited credit. Each time the company needs major capital, it must develop a business plan and convince financial intermediaries of the plan's soundness. For these reasons, the company has to develop strong relationships with outside financial intermediaries.

Customers

A company links itself with suppliers and middlemen so that it can efficiently supply appropriate products and services to its target market. Its target market can be one (or more) of the following five types of customer markets:

□ *Consumer markets*: Individuals and households that buy goods and services for personal consumption

□ *Industrial markets:* Organizations that buy goods and services needed for producing other products and services for the purpose of making profits and/or achieving other objectives

□ *Reseller markets:* Organizations that buy goods and services in order to resell them at a profit

□ *Government and nonprofit markets:* Government and nonprofit agencies that buy goods and services in order to produce public services or transfer these goods and services to others who need them

□ *International markets:* Buyers found abroad, including foreign consumers, producers, resellers, and governments

Hershey sells its products to all these customer markets. Its main customer market is resellers, which in turn sell Hershey candy to consumers. Another important group is institutional customers, namely, factories, hospitals, schools, government agencies, and other organizations that run cafeterias for their employees. Hershey also sells a substantial volume to foreign consumers, producers, resellers, and governments. Each customer market exhibits specific characteristics that warrant careful study by the seller. The major characteristics of *consumer markets* and *business markets* (producers, resellers, and government and nonprofit agencies) will be examined in the following two chapters; and foreign markets will be examined in Chapter 15.

Competitors

A company rarely is alone in selling to a given customer market. The company vies with a host of competitors. These competitors have to be identified, monitored, and outmaneuvered to capture and maintain customer loyalty.

The competitive environment consists not only of other companies but also of more basic things. The best way for a company to grasp the full range of its competition is to take the viewpoint of a buyer. What does a buyer think about that eventually leads to purchasing something? Suppose a person has been working hard and needs a break. The person asks, "What do I want to do now?" Among the possibilities that pop into his or her mind are socializing, exercising, and eating (see Figure 5-2). We will call these *desire competitors*. Suppose the person's most immediate need is to eat something. Then the question becomes, "What do I want to eat?" Different foods come to mind, such as potato chips, candy, crackers, and fruit. These can be called *generic competitors* in that they represent different basic ways to satisfy the same need. At this point, the person decides on candy and asks, "What type of candy do I want?" Different candy forms come to mind, such as chocolate bars, licorice, and sugar drops. They all represent *product-form competitors* in that they are different forms for satisfying a desire for candy. Finally, the consumer decides on a chocolate bar and faces several brands besides Hershey, such as Neilson's Crispy Crunch or Sweet Marie. These are brand competitors.

FIGURE 5-2
Four Types of
Competition

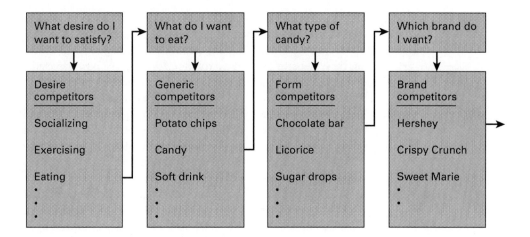

In this way, Hershey's marketers can determine all of the competitors standing in the way of selling more Hershey chocolate bars. Unfortunately, company executives tend to focus primarily on the brand competitors and on the task of building brand preference. Hershey wants to be thought of as the leading candy-bar producer, and its executives spend their time trying to position its candy as the quality leader and a good value for the money. Hershey relies primarily on product quality, advertising, sales promotion, and universal distribution to build up its brand preference. Its competitive stance against Crispy Crunch, Sweet Marie and so on may range from "live and let live" most of the time to occasional attacks on competitor positions. More often, however, the leading candy-bar company is on the defensive against smaller companies that aggressively attack its position.

Candy-bar companies are myopic if they focus only on their brand competitors. The real challenge is to expand their primary market, namely, the candy market, rather than simply fight for a larger share in a fixed-size market. Candy companies have to be concerned about mega-trends in the environment, such as the trend toward eating less in general and eating less candy in particular or even switching to such forms as dietetic candy. In too many industries, companies focus on the brand competitors and fail to exploit opportunities to expand the whole market or at least prevent it from eroding.

A basic observation about the task of competing effectively can now be summarized. A company must keep four basic dimensions in mind, which can be called the four Cs of market positioning. It must consider the nature of the *customers*, *channels*, and *competition*, and its own characteristics as a *company*. Successful marketing is a matter of achieving an effective alignment of the company with customers, channels, and competitors.

Publics

Not only does a company have to contend with competitors in seeking to satisfy a target market, but it must also acknowledge a large set of interested publics. We define a public as follows:

> A public *is any group that has an actual or potential interest or impact on a company's ability to achieve its objectives.*

A public can facilitate or impede a company's ability to achieve its objectives. The wise manager takes concrete steps to manage successful relations with the company's key publics

Most companies operate public-relations departments to plan constructive relations with various publics. These departments monitor the attitudes of the organization's publics and distribute information and communications to build goodwill. When negative publicity breaks out, these departments act as trouble-shooters. The best departments spend time counseling top management to adopt positive programs and to eliminate questionable practices so that negative publicity does not arise in the first place.

A company must not leave public relations entirely in the hands of the public-relations department. All the organization's employees are involved in public relations, from the chief executive officer who makes headlines in the press to the financial vice-president who addresses the financial community to the field sales representatives who call on customers to the telephone operators who answer the phones.

We believe that public relations is a broad marketing operation rather than a narrow communication operation.[3] A public is a group from which an organization wants some response, such as goodwill, favorable mentions, or donations of time or money. The organization must ask what that public is seeking that it could satisfy. It then plans a benefit bundle that builds goodwill.

Every company faces several important publics:

☐ *Financial publics*: Financial institutions—banks, investment houses, stock-brokerage firms, insurance companies—affect the company's ability to obtain funds. Hershey seeks the confidence of these groups by issuing upbeat annual reports, answering financial questions, and managing its money conservatively.

☐ *Media publics:* Companies must cultivate the goodwill of media organizations, specifically newspapers, magazines, and radio and television stations. Hershey seeks more and better media coverage in the form of favorable news, features, and editorial comment.

☐ *Government publics:* Companies need to take government developments into account in formulating marketing plans. Hershey's marketers must consult the company's lawyers about possible issues of product safety, truth in advertising, and so on. Hershey will join with other candy manufacturers to lobby against legislation that would hurt their interests.

☐ *Citizen-action publics:* A company's marketing practices may be questioned by consumer organizations, environmental groups, minority groups, and others. For example, some consumerists have attacked candy as having little nutritional value, as causing tooth decay, because it is high in calories, and so on. Hershey must choose between remaining silent or counterattacking with positive statements about candy's benefits. (See Marketing Environment and Trends 5-1, which describes how consumerism affects company marketing practices.)

☐ *General public:* A company needs to be concerned with the general public's attitude toward its products and practices. While the general public does not act in an organized way toward the company, the public's image of the company affects its patronage. To build a strong "corporate citizen" image, Hershey will lend its officers to community fund drives, make substantial contributions to charity, and set up systems of consumer-complaint handling.

☐ *Internal publics:* A company's internal publics include blue-collar workers, white-collar workers, managers, and the board of directors. Large companies develop newsletters and other forms of communication to inform and motivate its internal publics. When employees feel good about their company, this positive attitude spills over to external publics.

Although companies must put their primary energy into effectively managing their relationships with their customers, distributors, and suppliers, their overall success will be

Marketing Environment and Trends 5-1

THE IMPACT OF CONSUMERISM ON MARKETING PRACTICES

Starting in the 1960s, business firms found themselves the target of a growing consumer movement. Consumers had become better educated; products had become increasingly complex and hazardous; discontent with institutions was widespread; influential writings by John Kenneth Galbraith, Vance Packard, and Rachel Carson accused big business of wasteful and manipulative practices; early consumer advocates argued that consumers had the right to safety, to be informed, to choose, and to be heard; investigations of certain industries proved embarrassing; and, finally, Ralph Nader appeared on the scene to crystalize many of the issues.

Since these early stirrings, many private consumer organizations have emerged, several pieces of consumer legislation have been passed, and several government offices of consumer affairs have been created. Furthermore, the consumer movement has acquired an international character, with much strength in Scandinavia and the Low Countries and a growing presence in France, Germany, and Japan.

But what is consumerism? *Consumerism is an organized movement of citizens and government to strengthen the rights and power of buyers in relation to sellers.* Consumerists' groups seek to increase the amount of consumer information, education, and protection. Consumerists have advocated—and in many cases won—such proposals as the right to know the true interest cost of a loan (*truth-in-lending*), the true cost per standard unit of competing brands (*unit pricing*), the basic ingredients in a product (*ingredient labeling*), the nutritional quality of food (*nutritional labeling*), the freshness of products (*open dating*), and the true benefits of a product (*truth-in-advertising*). They want the government to check on the safety of products that are potentially hazardous and to penalize companies that are careless. Some consumerists want companies to elect consumer representatives to their boards to introduce consumer considerations into business decision making.

The most successful consumer group is Ralph Nader's *Public Citizen*. Nader lifted consumerism into a major social force, first with his successful attack on unsafe automobiles. In Canada, the Automobile Protection Association has promoted the rights of new-car buyers, but so far, only Quebec and Saskatchewan have passed the legislation to ensure those rights.

At first a number of companies balked at the consumer movement. They resented the power of strong consumer leaders to point an accusing finger at their products and cause their sales to plummet, such as when Ralph Nader called the Corvair automobile unsafe, when Robert Choate accused breakfast cereals of providing "empty calories," and when Herbert S. Denenberg published a list showing the wide variation in premiums that different insurance companies were charging for the same protection. Businesses resented consumer proposals that appeared to increase business costs more than they helped the consumer. They also felt that most consumers would not pay attention to unit pricing or ingredient labeling and that the doctrines of advertising substantiation, corrective advertising, and counter advertising would stifle advertising creativity.

Many other companies took no stand and simply went about their business. A few companies undertook a series of bold initiatives to show their endorsement of consumer aims. For example:

> The Cadillac division of General Motors responded to consumerism at the dealership level by implementing a system of customer response cards called "Satisfaction Plus." Using criteria of courtesy, commitment, and excellence, customers rated the service which they received from their Cadillac dealer. ∎

Several companies took the initiative in showing "we care" and on several cases enjoyed increased profits. Competitors were forced to emulate them, without, however, achieving the same impact enjoyed by these firms.

Currently, most companies have accepted consumerism in principle. They recognize the consumers' right to information and protection. Those who take a leadership role recognize that consumerism involves a total commitment by top management, new company policy guidelines, and training programs for all personnel. Several companies have established consumer-affairs departments to help formulate policies and deal with "consumerist" problems.

Product managers today have to spend more time checking product ingredients and product features for safety, preparing safe packaging and informative labeling, substantiating their advertising claims, reviewing their sales promotion, developing clear and adequate product warranties, and so on. They have to work more closely with company lawyers.

Consumerism is actually the ultimate expression of the marketing concept. It compels company marketers to consider things from the consumers' point of view. It suggests consumer needs and wants that may have been overlooked by the firms in the industry. The resourceful manager will look for the positive opportunities created by consumerism rather than brood over its restraints.

For an appraisal of the consumer movement see Paul N. Bloom, and Stephen A. Greyser, "The Maturity of Consumerism," *Harvard Business Review*, November-December 1981, pp. 130-39.

affected by how other publics in the society view their activity. Managers would be wise to spend time monitoring all of the company's publics, understanding their needs and opinions, and dealing with them constructively.

FORCES IN THE COMPANY'S MACROENVIRONMENT

The company and its suppliers, marketing intermediaries, customers, competitors, and publics all operate in a larger macroenvironment of forces and megatrends that shape opportunities and pose threats to the company. These forces represent "uncontrollables," which the company must monitor and respond to. There are six major forces, namely, demographic, economic, natural, technological, political, and cultural. As an illustration, we will describe the major forces and megatrends affecting the Canadian marketplace. The major forces and megatrends would have to be assessed separately for each country.

Demographic Environment

The first environmental fact of interest to marketers is population because people make up markets. Marketers are keenly interested in the size of the world's population; its geographical distribution and density; mobility trends; age distribution; birth, marriage, and death rates; and racial, ethnic, and religious structure. We will examine the major demographic trends and their implications for marketing planning.[4]

Worldwide Explosive Population Growth   The world population is showing "explosive" growth. It totaled 5.0 billion in 1986 and is growing at 1.7 percent per year. At this rate, the world's population will reach 6.2 billion by A.D. 2000.[5]

The world population explosion has been a major concern of governments and various groups throughout the world. Two factors underlie this concern. The first is the possible finiteness of the earth's resources to support this much human life, particularly at living standards that represent the aspiration of most people. *The Limits to Growth* presented an impressive array of evidence that unchecked population growth and consumption would eventually result in insufficient food supply, depletion of key minerals, overcrowding, pollution, and an overall deterioration in the quality of life.[6] One of its strong recommendations is the worldwide *social marketing* of birth control and family planning.[7]

The second cause for concern is that population growth is highest in countries and communities that can least afford it. The less-developed regions of the world currently account for 76 percent of the world population and are growing at 2 percent per year, whereas the population in the more-developed regions of the world is growing at only 0.6 percent per year. In less-developed economies, the death rate has been falling as a result of modern medicine, while the birthrate has remained fairly stable. For these countries to feed, clothe, and educate the children and also provide a rising standard of living is out of the question. Furthermore, the poorer families have the most children, and this reinforces the cycle of poverty. The explosive world population growth has great implications for business. A growing population means growing human needs, but it does not mean growing markets unless there is sufficient purchasing power. If the growing population presses too hard against the available food supply and resources, costs will shoot up and profit margins will be depressed.

Slowdown of Canada's Birthrate   A "birth dearth" has replaced the former "baby boom" in Canada. The 1991 Canadian population is 26.8 million, an annual increase of only 314 200 or less than 1.2 percent. This rate has slowed considerably since the fifties, when it reached a peak of 479 000 or nearly 3 percent of the 1959 population. Low population growth is expected to continue near 1.2 percent for the next few years. By the year 2011, Canada's population is forecasted to reach 30.8 million. Factors contributing to smaller families are the desire to improve personal living standards, the increasing desire of women to work outside the home, and the improved technology and knowledge of birth control.[8]

The declining birthrate is a threat to some industries, a boon to others. It has created sleepless nights for executives in such businesses as children's toys, clothes, furniture, and food. For many years, the Gerber Company advertised "Babies are our business—our only business" but quietly dropped this slogan some time ago. Gerber now sells life insurance to older folks, using the theme "Gerber now babies the over-50's." Johnson & Johnson responded to the declining birthrate by wooing adults to switch to its baby powder, baby oil, and baby shampoo. Meanwhile, industries such as hotels, airlines, and restaurants have benefited from the fact that young childless couples have more time and income for travel and dining out.

Aging of Canada's Population   Recent generations have been blessed with a declining mortality rate. From 1961 to 1985, the life expectancy of females at birth increased by eight years to 79, while that of men increased six years to 72. The combination of longer lives and fewer births, means that the average age of the Canadian population is increasing. In 1961, the median age was 26.3 years, in 1986, it was 32 years, and by 2006, it is expected to become 38 years.[9]

The changing age structure of the population will result in different growth rates for various age groups over the decade, and these differences will strongly affect marketers' targeting strategies. (See Marketing Environment and Trends 5-2).

The Changing Canadian Household   The Canadian ideal of the two-children, two-car suburban family has been losing some of its lustre. Two of the many reasons for this are that people have been marrying later and having fewer children. In 1986, 60 percent of females aged 20-24 years were still single, compared with only 40 percent in 1961. By 1989, the number of births had declined 14.5 per thousand of the population, barely half of the 27.5 per thousand in 1961. Nowhere has this trend caused more concern than in the province of

Quebec, which has offered generous financial incentives for couples having two or more children.

There has also been an increase in the number of women working outside the home. By 1986, the proportion of "working wives" exceeded 50 percent, about double the levels of the early sixties. They contributed 40 percent of household income. Such dual-income households are able to purchase better goods and services. Marketers of tires, automobiles, insurance, travel, and financial services are increasingly directing their advertising to working

---

Marketing Environment and Trends 5-2

AGE-GROUP GROWTH TRENDS AND THEIR MARKETING IMPLICATIONS

Children

The number of pre-schoolers and children increased through the eighties because of the "baby boom echo." However, the rate of increase tapered off as the original boomers left the child-bearing years. By 1990 the number had actually decreased by one percent. Markets for children's toys, clothes and furniture also enjoyed a brief boom after several years of bust. Specialty toy retailers like Toys-R-Us benefited, and Sears joined with McDonald's to market McKids clothing.

Youths

Teenagers decreased in number during the eighties, but are expected to increase by 10 percent in the nineties. That means first a slow-down then an increase for manufacturers of jeans, recordings, and cosmetics, as well as providers of fast foods and movies.

Young Adults

The number of 20-34-year-olds declined by two percent during 1985-1990, and the trend will continue through the nineties as the "birth dearth" generation moves on. Marketers of furniture and life insurance can no longer rely on an incrasing market size for sales growth. They will have to work for bigger shares of shrinking markets.

Early Middle Age

As the baby-boom generation moves into middle age, this group is experiencing rapid growth, for example, a sixteen percent increase of 30 to 49-year-olds during 1985-90. This group is a major market for larger homes, new automobiles, quality clothing, entertainment, and investments.

Late Middle Age

The number of 50-60-year-olds grew less than two percent during 1985-90, but the growth rate will pick up by the late nineties as the boomers move on. As they become empty-nesters, their homes tend to be down-sized. But this group contains heavy users of services, including travel, recreation, and investments.

Retirees

From 1961 to 1986, the number of Canaidans over 65 nearly doubled to 2.7 million, and they are expected to add another million by the year 2011. With a 1985-90 growth rate of sixteen percent, they are a compelling feature of the Canadian demographic mosaic. This group provides considerable demand for retirement accomodation, small-portion food packaging, healthcare products and travel services.

Thus the changing age structure of the Canadian population will create many opportunities and threats for marketers. The challenge is to anticipate the primary and secondary impacts of demographic changes on consumption behavior.

women. These changes are accompanied by a shift in the traditional roles and values of husbands and wives, with the husband assuming more domestic functions, such as shopping and child care. As a result, husbands are becoming more of a target market for food and household appliance marketers.

Finally, the number of nontraditional households is increasing. More young adults are living away from their families in cooperative or cohabitor relationships. Among those who marry, divorce splits one in three Canadian marriages, thus contributing to the 882 000 single-parent families in Canada. Many divorced parents remarry, producing "blended families" of children from previous marriages. The needs of nontraditional households justify special attention by marketers. For example, the SSWD group (single, separated, widowed, divorced) need smaller apartments, inexpensive furniture and appliances, and food packaged in smaller portions.

Geographical Shifts in Population   Canadians are a mobile people, with approximately one out of five moving each year. Among the major mobility trends are:

1. *Movement of people westward*: The Atlantic provinces have experienced a longterm migration of their people into Canada's industrial heartland. The traditional reason has been economic—the job opportunitites were less attractive at home than they were in the more industrialized parts of Quebec and Ontario. In recent years a second wave of migration to the Western provinces has occurred. Whereas there had always been some westward migration because of the milder climate of the West coast, this has increased as the impact of the West's energy resources on its economic growth has been realized. Marketers are interested in population migration because of its impact on the demand for housing and household goods in the local markets.

2. *Movement from rural to urban areas*: This movement has been going on for half a century. In 1911, approximately 54 percent of the nation's population lived in rural areas; now approxiamtely 76 percent live in urban areas. Cities are characterized by a faster pace of living, more commuting, typically higher incomes, and a greater variety of goods and services than the small towns and rural areas of Canada. The largest cities, such as Montreal, Toronto and Vancouver, account for most of the sales of expensive furs, perfumes, luggage, and works of art, and they still boast most of what there is of opera, ballet, and other forms of "high culture." Recently, there has been a slight shift of population back to rural areas on the part of some people who have grown tired of the big city.

3. *Movement from the city to the suburbs*: Many persons have moved far away from their places of work, owing largely to the development of automobiles, major highways, and rapid rail and bus transit. Cities have become surrounded by suburbs, and these suburbs in turn by "exurbs." Canada's 25 largest Census metropolitan Areas (CMA) contain 59 percent of the total population and 87 percent of the urban population. It is the CMAs rather than the cities proper that are the primary market focus of firms.

    Firms normally distinguish between the city and the suburban segments of the metropolitan areas. About 60 percent of the total metropolitan population now live in suburbs. Suburban areas are frequently marked by a style of living different from that in the cities. Suburbs tend to be characterized by casual, outdoor living, greater neighbor interaction, higher incomes, and younger families. Suburban dwellers are the source of much of the demand for station wagons, home workshop equipment, garden furniture, lawn and gardening tools and supplies, and outdoor cooking equipment. Retailers have recognized the importance of convenience and have brought their goods out to the suburbs through the development of branch department stores and suburban shopping centers.

At the same time, marketers should recognize a recent countermove back to the central city, especially in cities where urban renewal has been successful. Young adults and older adults whose children have grown up are attracted by the superior cultural and recreational opportunities and less interested in suburban commuting and gardening. This means strong opportunities for new high-rise apartment construction and new retail outlets within the central city.

Marketers must proceed cautiously when they develop their geographical marketing plans. Marketing researchers use several schemes to segment geographical markets—census tracts, standard metropolitan areas, Neilsen regions, media markets, and so forth. Garreau recently proposed a suggestive new segmentation scheme, which he calls "The Nine Nations of North America."[10]

A Better-Educated and White-Collar Population The average number of years of formal education has increased significantly in Canada, from 10.6 years in 1971 to 12.2 years in 1986. The proportion of adults who were graduates of universities or colleges rose to 22.4 percent in 1986 from 17.6 percent five years earlier. Mirroring this increase in education, there was an increasing emphasis on white-collar occupations: 138 percent more in the social sciences, 118 percent more in management, 105 percent more in recreation and the arts, and 72 percent more in science and mathematics.

These changes present both opportunities and challenges to marketers. A greater white-collar and educated work force will mean increased affluence and demand for quality products, books, magazines, and travel. It will also mean a decline in television viewing because educated consumers tend to watch less than the population at large.

A Cultural Mosaic Many cultural and ethnic backgrounds are represented in the Canadian population, particularly in the larger cities. Thus, there is a significant Italian community in Toronto, and Vancouver has many residents of Asian origin. Government policy is to maintain the essential differences in this "cultural mosaic," in contrast to the "melting pot" policy in the United States. Most cultural minorities have a local, or possibly a regional significance for marketers. Retailers especially should be aware of specific wants and buying habits of such groups. But the French-Canadian minority deserves special attention because of its size and dispersion in several provinces. Comprising 83 percent of Quebec households and 23 percent of Canadian households, this minority cannot be ignored by national marketers.

Canada is officially a bicultural country, and Canadian marketers need to be sensitive to cultural differences. French-Canadians have traditionally emphasized family, home, and Church (See also Marketing Environment and Trends 6-1 in Chapter 6). But since the "Quiet Revolution" of the sixties, a growing secularism has weakened these ties in favor of materialism and nationalism. The question whether Quebec consumers are becoming more like other Canadians has been debated by various researchers. Most marketers would agree however, that existing differences make it hazardous to employ a uniform promotional strategy across Canada. Differences in lifestyle, attitudes, and product usage make separate copy strategy and media decisions essential.

Shift from a Mass Market to Micromarkets The effect of all these changes is to transform the Canadian marketplace from a *mass market* into more fragmented *micromarkets*, differentiated by age, sex, geography, lifestyle, ethnic background, education, and so on. Each group has strong preferences and consumer characteristics and is reached through increasingly targeted media. Companies are abandoning the "shotgun" approach that aimed at a mythical "average" consumer and are increasingly designing their products and marketing programs for specific micromarkets.

Demographic trends are highly reliable for the short and intermediate run. There is little excuse for a company's being suddenly surprised by demographic developments. The Singer Company should have known for years that its sewing machine business would be negatively affected by small families and more working wives; yet it was slow in responding. Companies can list the major demographic trends, then spell out what the trends mean for them.

Economic Environment

The economic environment consists of factors that affect consumer purchasing power and spending patterns. Markets require purchasing power as well as people. Total purchasing power depends on current income, prices, savings, and credit. Marketers should be aware of major trends in income and of changing consumer spending patterns.

Changes in Income   Real income per capita declined during the early 1980s, as inflation, high unemployment, and increased taxes reduced the amount of money people had to spend. As a result, many Canadians turned to more cautious buying. They bought more store brands and fewer national brands, to save money. Many companies introduced economy versions of their products and turned to price appeals in their advertising. Some consumers postponed purchases of durable goods, while others purchased them out of fear that prices would be 10 percent higher the next year. Many families began to feel that a large home, two cars, foreign travel, and and a university education were beyond their reach.

In recent years, however, economic conditions improved. And current projections suggest that real income will increase modestly through the mid-1990s. This increase will largely result from rising income in certain important segments. The baby-boom generation will be moving into its prime wage-earning years, and the number of small families headed by dual-career couples will increase greatly. These more affluent groups will demand higher quality and better service, and they will be willing to pay for it. These consumers will buy more time-saving products and services, more travel and entertainment, more physical-fitness products, more cultural activities, and more continuing education.

Marketers must pay attention to income distribution as well as average income. Income distribution in Canada is still very skewed. At the top are upper-class consumers, who are a major market for luxury goods. The comfortable middle class has to be somewhat careful about its spending but can still afford the good life some of the time. The working class must stick close to the basics of food, clothing, and shelter and must try hard to save. Finally, the underclass (people on welfare, the homeless, and many retirees) have to count their pennies when making even the most basic purchases.

Some observers have described the Canadian marketplace as a bipolar market. During a recession, some people continue to buy luxury goods while many other people patronize low-price merchants. Retailers who offer medium-price goods seem to suffer the most.

Changing Consumer Spending Patterns   Consumer spending in major goods and services categories has been changing over the years. Food, housing, household operations, and transportation consume two-thirds of household income. Over time, however, the food, clothing, and personal-care bills of households have been declining percentagewise while the housing, transportation, medical-care, and recreational bills have been increasing. Some of these changes were observed over a century ago by Ernest Engel, a German statistician who studied how families shifted their expenditures as their income rose. He observed that as *family income rises, the percentage spent on food declines, the percentage spent on housing and household operations remains constant, and the percentage spent on other categories (clothing, transportation, recreation, health, and education) and the percentage put into savings increase.* Engel's "laws" have generally been supported by later studies.

Many Canadian consumers have also changed their geographic spending patterns. The retail phenomenon of "out-shopping" from city core to suburban mall, and from small town to big city, is becoming routine for cross-border shoppers. Same-day car trips to the U.S. in 1991 increased 21 percent over 1990 volume, as the Canadian exchange rate strengthened and the Goods and Services Tax bit into recession-bound family budgets. Consumers in Toronto, a full two-hour drive from the border, are expected to spend $181 million in U.S. stores in 1991.[11]

Low Rate of Savings and High Debt   Consumer expenditures are affected by consumer savings and debt. As savings decline in response to a reduction in interest rates, a reserve of spending power is released that helps to sustain a high level of economic activity. That happened in Canada when declining interest rates brought the rate of personal savings from a peak of 17.8 percent in 1982 down to 9.6 percent in 1987.

Canadians hold their savings in the form of bank savings accounts, bonds and stocks, real estate, insurance, money market funds, and other assets. These savings are an important source of funds for financing major purchases.

Consumers can increase their purchasing power through borrowing. Consumer credit has been a major contributor to the rapid growth of the Canadian economy, enabling people to buy more than their current income and savings allowed, thus creating more jobs and still more income and more demand. In 1989, outstanding consumer credit stood at $92.7 billion, or $3458 for every man, woman, and child in Canada. Conversely, when interest rates are high, consumers spend their discretionary income by paying off consumer credit. Shrinking credit retards the growth of housing and other "big ticket" durables that are dependent on the availability of credit.

Natural Environment

The deteriorating condition of the natural environment is bound to be one of the major issues facing business and the public in the 1990s. In many world cities, air and water pollution have reached dangerous levels. There is great concern about some by-products that cause on overheating of the atmosphere called the "greenhouse effect," and others that cause acid rain or destroy the ozone layer that protects us from the sun's harmful radiation. Writers such as Kenneth Boulding, Rachel Carson, the Erlichs, and the Meadows, have documented the amount of ecological deterioration. Watchdog groups like Pollution Probe and Greenpeace have raised public awareness. Political pressure for governments to act against pollution has been urged by various "green" parties. (See Marketing Environment and Trends 5-3).

Marketers need to be aware of the threats and opportunities associated with four trends in the natural environment.

Shortage of Raw Materials   The earth's materials consist of the infinite, the finite renewable, and the finite nonrenewable. An *infinite resource*, such as air, poses no immediate problem, although some groups see a long-run danger. Environmental groups have lobbied for a ban of certain propellants used in aerosol cans because of their potential damage to the ozone layer of air. Water is already a major problem in some parts of the world.

Finite renewable resources, such as forests and food, have to be used wisely. Forestry companies are required to reforest timberlands in order to protect the soil and to ensure sufficient wood to meet future demand. Food supply can be a major problem in that the amount of arable land is relatively fixed, and urban areas are constantly encroaching on farmland.

Finite nonrenewable resources—oil, coal, platinum, zinc, silver—will pose a serious problem as their time of depletion approaches. Firms making products that require these increasingly scarce minerals face substantial cost increases. They may not find it easy to

Marketing Environment and Trends 5-3

IMPACT OF ENVIRONMENTALISM ON MARKETING DECISION MAKING

Whereas consumerists focus on whether companies are efficiently serving consumer material wants, environmentalists focus on the costs imposed on the environment in serving these needs and wants. *Environmentalism is an organized movement of concerned citizens and government to protect and enhance people's living environment.* Environmentalists are concerned with smoke that causes acid rain, liquid waste that pollutes water, deforestation that destroys topsoil, litter that defaces scenery, and food additives that cause illness.

Environmentalists are not against marketing and consumption; they simply want businesses and consumers to operate on more ecological principles. They think the goal of the marketing system should be to maximize life quality. And *life quality* means not only the quantity and quality of consumer goods and services but also the quality of the environment.

Environmentalists want environmental costs included in producer and consumer decision making. They favor taxes and regulations to limit the social costs of antienvironmental behavior. Requiring business to invest in antipollution devices, taxing nonreturnable bottles, and banning high-phosphate detergents are viewed as necessary to induce businesses and consumers to act in environmentally sound ways.

Environmentalists are more critical of marketing than are consumerists. They complain of too much wasteful packaging, whereas consumerists like the convenience of modern packaging. Environmentalists feel that advertising leads people to consume more than they need, whereas consumerists worry more about deception in advertising. Environmentalists dislike shopping centers, whereas consumerists welcome more stores.

Environmentalism has hit certain industries hard. Steel companies and public utilities have had to invest billions of dollars in pollution-control equipment and costlier fuels. The auto industry has had to introduce expensive emission controls in cars. The soap industry has had to develop ways to reduce litter and increase biodegradability in its products. The gasoline industry has had to formulate low-lead and no-lead gasolines. These industries resent environmental regulations, especially when imposed too rapidly to allow the companies to make the proper adjustments. These companies have absorbed large costs and have passed them on to buyers.

Marketers' lives have become more complicated. Marketers have to check into the environmental consequences of the product, its packaging, and its production processes. They have to raise prices to cover environmental costs, even though this makes the product harder to sell. At the same time, many managers recognize the validity of respecting the environment and have introduced environmental criteria in their decision making on product ingredients, design, and packaging. Some companies introduced environmentally friendly products that became industry standards. Sears pioneered a phosphate-free detergent, and Pepsi-Cola was first with a biodegradable bottle. Loblaws introduced a broad line of "green" products in several categories.

---

pass these cost increases on to customers. Firms engaged in research and development face an excellent opportunity to develop new substitute materials.

Increased Cost of Energy   Oil is a finite nonrenewable form of energy whose supply has already caused problems. The creation of the OPEC cartel caused the price of a barrel of crude oil to rise from $3 in 1970 to $40 a decade later. Although Canada is self-sufficient in energy, this increased consumers' costs significantly, because Canadians are among the world's heaviest users of energy. An urgent search for alternative energy sources produced innovations in solar, tidal, and wind technology, plus improvements in alternatives like coal, natural gas, and nuclear energy. Combined with efforts to conserve energy, these developments resulted in a worldwide excess which led to a decline in oil prices by the mid-eighties.

But many oil-dependent firms were hurt in the meantime. The airlines suffered cost increases at a time when excess capacity and deregulation prevented them from passing on the costs in higher fares. Automobile producers also had to scramble to respond to consumers' increased demand for smaller fuel-efficient vehicles. Importers of small Asian and European cars were winners, while producers like Chrysler whose product line featured big cars, suffered. It can be fatal for companies to misjudge the impact of energy costs on consumer behavior.

Increased Levels of Pollution   Some industrial activity will inevitably damage the quality of the natural environment. Consider the disposal of chemical and nuclear wastes, the dangerous mercury levels in the ocean, the quantity of DDT and other chemical pollutants in the soil and food supply, and the littering of the environment with nonbiodegradable bottles, plastics, and other packaging materials.

The public's concern creates a marketing opportunity for alert companies. It creates a large market for pollution-control solutions, such as scrubbers, recycling centers, and land-fill systems. It leads to a search for alternative ways to produce and package goods that do not cause environmental damage.[12]

Role of Government in Environment Protection   Federal, provincial and municpal agencies play an active role in the protection of the physcial environment by establishing regualtions, monitoring compliance, and punishing offenders. Private agencies like Pollution Probe publicize issues and lobby for government action. But the existence of these public and private institutions does not ensure that the physical environment will be protected. The reason is that when businesses are forced to buy expensive pollution-control equipment they may be unable to make other plant investments that are necessary to remain competitive and maintain employment levels. The situation is further complicated by the contribution of U.S. industry to Canadian pollution in the form of acid rain. The U.S. administration is predisposed to letting the most efficient use of business resources be determined by market forces rather than by government regulation. The Canadian authorities are reluctant to impose regulations that would handicap Canadian businesses, especially when much of the pollution problem is beyond Canadian jurisdiction.

Managers need to pay attention to the physical environment, in terms of obtaining needed resources and also of avoiding damage to the physical environment. Business can still expect strong influence from both government and pressure groups. Instead of opposing all forms of regulation, business should help develop acceptable solutions to the material and energy problems facing the nation.

Technological Environment

The most dramatic force shaping people's lives is technology. Technology has released such wonders as penicillin, open-heart surgery, and the birth-control pill. It has released such horrors as the hydrogen bomb, nerve gas, and the submachine gun. It has also released such mixed blessings as the automobile, video games, and white bread. One's attitudes toward technology depend on whether one is more enthralled with its wonders or its horrors.

Every new technology is a force for "creative destruction." Transistors hurt the vacuum-tube industry, xerography hurts the carbon-paper business, autos hurt the railroads, and television hurts the movies. Instead of old industries moving into the new, many fought or ignored them, and their businesses declined.

The economy's growth rate is affected by how many major new technologies are discovered. Unfortunately, technological discoveries do not arise evenly through time—the railroad industry created a lot of investment, and then there was a dearth until the auto industry emerged; later radio created a lot of investment, and then there was a dearth until television appeared. In the time between major innovations, the economy can stagnate. Some economists believe that the current economic flatness of the world economy will continue until a sufficient number of new major innovations emerge.

In the meantime, minor innovations fill the gap. Freeze-dried coffee probably made no one happier, and antiperspirant deodorants probably made no one wiser, but they do create new markets and investment opportunities.

Each technology creates major long-run consequences that are not always foreseeable. The contraceptive pill, for example, led to smaller families, more working wives, and larger discretionary incomes—resulting in higher expenditures on vacation travel, durable goods, and other things.

The marketer should watch the following trends in technology.

Accelerating Pace of Technological Change   Many of the products we take for granted today were not even present one hundred years ago. Canadians of 100 years ago did not know of automobiles, airplanes, or the electric light. Canadians of 50 years ago did not know of television, antibiotics, or electronic computers. Canadians of 25 years ago did not know of xerography, tape recorders, word processors, or laser surgery.

Alvin Toffler, in *Future Shock*, sees an accelerative thrust in the invention, exploitation, and diffusion of new technologies.[13] More ideas are being worked on; the time lag between new ideas and their successful implementation is decreasing rapidly; and the time between introduction and peak production is shortening considerably.

In Toffler's later book, The Third Wave, he forecasts the emergence of the electronic cottage as a new way that work and play will be organized in society.[14] The advent of word-processing typewriters, telecopiers, personal computers and audio and video links make it possible for many people to work at home instead of traveling to offices that may be thirty or more minutes away. Eventually people will find that the cost of installing and operating telecommunications equipment in the home will fall below the cost of commuting. As seen by Toffler, the electronic-cottage revolution will reduce auto pollution, bring the family closer together as a work unit, and create more home-centered entertainment and activity. It will have substantial impact on consumption patterns and marketing systems.

Unlimited Innovational Opportunities   Scientists today are working on a startling range of new technologies that will revolutionize our products and production processes. The most exciting work is being done in biotechnology, solid state electronics, robotics, and material sciences.[15] Scientists today are working on cancer cures, lung and liver cures, chemical control of mental illness, happiness pills, practical solar energy, practical electric cars, household robots, totally safe contraceptives, and nutritious foods that are nonfattening and tasty. In addition, scientists also speculate on fantasy products, such as small flying cars, single-person rocket belts, three-dimensional television, space colonies, and human clones. The challenge in each case is not only technical but commercial, namely, to develop affordable versions of these products.

High R&D Budgets   The principal reason for the rapid growth of technology is the increase in research and development expenditures in the industrialized countries. Many

Canadian branch plants have imported technology developed by their foreign affiliates, particularly those in the U.S. Perhaps because of this, Canadian R&D expenditures, at roughly one percent of the GNP, have been substantially less than the corresponding rates in the other industrialized countries. Since R&D expenditures seem to aid export activity,[16] some analysts are delighted with the expected increase to over $5 billion or 1.4 percent of GNP.[17] Others have questioned this strategy and, more fundamentally, the feasibility of increasing industrial innovation by aggregate government spending.[18] However, at the level of the individual company, a recent study showed a high correlation between R&D expenditures and company profitability.[19]

Managing company scientists is a major challenge. They resent too much cost control. They are often more interested in solving scientific problems than in coming up with marketable products. Companies are adding marketing people to R&D research teams, hoping to achieve a stronger marketing orientation.

Concentration on Minor Improvements   As a result of the high cost of R&D, many companies are pursuing minor product improvements rather than gambling on major innovations. Even basic-research companies like Bell Northern Research, and DuPont are proceeding cautiously. Many companies are content to put their money into copying competitors' products and making minor feature and style improvements. Much of the research is defensive rather than offensive. Increasingly, research directed toward major breakthroughs is being conducted by consortiums of companies rather than by single companies.

Increased Regulation of Technological Change   Technological change is encountering more regulations and opposition than ever before. As products get more complex, the public needs assurance of their safety. Government agencies have responded by expanding their powers to investigate and ban new products that might be directly harmful or have questionable side effects. The Health Protection branch of Health and Welfare Canada has been involved in various regulations that constrain R&D activities and increase their cost. Health regulations have substantially increased in areas such as food, automobiles, clothing, electrical appliances, and construction. Marketers must know these regulations and consider them seriously when proposing, developing, and launching new products.

Technological change is opposed by those who see it as threatening nature, privacy, simplicity, and even the human race. Various groups have opposed the construction of nuclear plants, high-rise buildings, and recreational facilities in national parks. They have called for *technological assessment* of new technologies before allowing their commercialization.

Marketers need to understand the changing technological environment and how new technologies can serve human needs. They need to work closely with R&D people to encourage more market-oriented research. They must be alert to undesirable side effects of any innovation that might harm the users and create consumer distrust and opposition.

Political Environment

Marketing decisions are strongly affected by developments in the political environment. This environment is composed of *laws, government agencies, and pressure groups* that influence and limit various organizations and individuals in society. The main political trends and their implications for marketing management are discussed below.

Substantial Amount of Legislation Regulating Business   Legislation affecting business has increased steadily over the years, partly in reaction to the growing complexity of technology and business practices. The legislation seeks to accomplish any of three purposes.

The first is to protect companies form each other. Business executives all praise competition in the abstract but try to neutralize it when it touches them. So laws are passed to define and prevent unfair competition. The principal federal legislation is the *Competition Act.* Several sections of the Act should interest marketers in topics such as mergers (Section 33), pricing (Sections 34 and 38), and advertising (Section 36). The authorities can hold hearings and issue orders prohibiting unfair practices, whereas formerly it was necessary to contest such offences in court under criminal law. The *Competition Act* now applies to the fast-growing service industries, and the enforcement procedures permit the necessary flexibility to deal with this dynamic sector.

Marketing Boards   One method for limiting competition which is used extensively in Canada is the marketing board. Marketing boards for agricultural products have become a controversial type of government agency for wielding influence over the market. The number of provincial marketing boards for specific commodities ranges from one in Newfoundland to 26 in Quebec. In addition, national marketing boards exist for eggs, turkeys, broiler chickens, wheat, and dairy products.

Proponents of marketing boards argue that they are necessary to smooth the inherent fluctuations in the supply of agricultural products, and to ensure "orderly marketing" including the maintainence of the producers' prices. The Consumers Association of Canada has opposed the creation of marketing boards on the grounds that consumers pay inflated prices and are denied access to lower-priced imports. Some marketing boards have even tried to control the advertising by retail grocery stores of loss-leader specials. While marketing boards have the potential to increase marketing efficiency through centralization, the possibilities for abusing their monopoly position necessitate a careful monitoring of their activities.

Foreign Competition   The government of Canada, like governments in other countries, traditionally protected its domestic industries from foreign competition by erecting a wall of tariffs and regulations that limited imports. But in recent decades the barriers have been gradually reduced. Canada has participated in mutual tariff reductions under the General Agreement on Tariffs and Trade, and in sectoral agreements like the Canada-U.S. Auto Pact and the deregulation of the transportation industry. The rationale of such changes was that they forced domestic producers to be competitive, which benefited consumers, while opening up export opportunities for enterprising firms (See also Chapter 15).

The most ambitious of these changes is the recent Free Trade Agreement, which will progressively eliminate all tariffs between Canada and the U.S. during the nineties. Some industries like textiles will be subjected to more foreign competition; others like construction will benefit from more foreign opportunities. Still on the horizon is the possibility of an extension of the free trade area to Mexico. At the very least, management should closely monitor the potential impact of such developments in the political environment.

The second purpose of government regulation is to protect consumers from business firms. Protection is required for consumers because a few disreputable businesses are willing to mislead prospective buyers by adulterating their products, packaging deceptively, advertising false claims, or employing bait pricing. Unfair consumer practices must be defined and governmental agencies established to enforce appropriate regulations. The principal federal legislation is embodied in the *Competition Act* which makes it an offence to make a representation to the public that is false or misleading in a material respect. This is broad enough to include packaging, point-of-purchase displays, and spoken claims in sales interviews, as well as broadcast and print advertising. Provincial legislation, such as Ontario's *Business Practices Act*, is also intended to protect consumers from businesses making misleading claims.

Differences between the consumerists pursuing their goals and the businessmen and investors pursuing their goals have focused on three consumer rights, which consumerists claim are not being given sufficient recognition. These rights are

1. the right to be adequately informed about the more important aspects of the products;
2. the right to be protected against questionable products and marketing practices;
3. the right to influence products and marketing practices in directions that will enhance the "quality of life."

Each of these rights leads to a whole series of specific proposals by consumerists. The *right to be informed* includes such things as the right to know the true interest cost of a loan (*truth-in-lending*), the true cost per standard unit of competing brands (*unit pricing*), the basic ingredients in a product (*ingredient labeling*), the nutritional quality of foods (*nutritional labeling*), the freshness of products (*open dating*), and the true benefits of a product (*truth-in-advertising*).

Proposals related to additional *consumer protection* include strengthening consumers' position in cases of business fraud, requiring more safety to be designed into products, and issuing greater powers to existing government agencies.

Proposals relating to *quality-of-life* considerations include regulating the ingredients that go into certain products (detergents, gasoline) and packaging (soft-drink containers), reducing the level of advertising and promotional "noise," and creating consumer representation on company boards to introduce consumers welfare considerations in business decision making.

Whether the protection the consumer is receiving has increased commensurately is not clear. On the one hand, the number of prosecutions against misleading advertising has certainly increased; on the other, this increase may have been at the expense of large structural investigations involving price fixing, mergers, and monopolies.[20]

The marketing manager who has to propose specific marketing programs will find that the demands of the job continue to change as a result of consumerism. Increasingly, he will have to check that product ingredients are safe, that labeling is informative, that advertising claims are substantiated, that warranties are understood, and so on. While these tasks may make his job more difficult, they also provide the stimulus to an understanding of the consumer's viewpoint in a way that will strengthen his market position.

The third purpose of government regulation is to protect the larger interest of society against unbridled business behavior. People have become aware in recent years that economic growth is often accompanied by social costs. The contamination of air and water and the replacement of traditional surroundings by urban sprawl are only the more obvious consequences of this trade off. Typically business costs or production do not include these social costs, so selling prices are artificially low. Faced with government demands to protect society form such unwanted by-products, businesses have to weigh carefully the possibility of passing on the increased costs to the firm's customers.

The societal protection function involves government in a wide range of activities and regulations at the federal, provincial, and municipal levels. The Health Protection branch of Health and Welfare Canada is one of the more active agencies, being involved in various prohibitions concerning the treatment, processing, packaging, labeling, advertising, and selling of foods, drugs, and other devices. Provincial agencies control the sale of liquor, the censorship of movies, and the issuance of insurance and securities.

The marketing executive cannot plan intelligently without a working knowledge of the major laws and regulations that exist to protect consumers, competition, and society. The principal federal laws are listed in Table 5-2. In addition, the marketing executive should be aware of the laws of those provinces in which he does business, as well as the implications of the principal regulations associated with the various laws.

Simply to list the various Acts, as in Table 5-2, fails to convey the complexity of the legislated constraints on the marketer who tries to put together a national marketing program. The basic problem is that the laws and regulations are fragmented by the individual provincial jurisdictions. The control of advertising best illustrates the marketer's dilemma. There are over one hundred federal and provincial statutes concerning advertising. Nova Scotia has nineteen of them for example.[21]

Since the requirements differ across the various jurisdictions, the marketer must decide how many forms of the advertisement to produce. If only one form can be justified, then the most stringent requirement may govern. However, these may not be the requirements of the provinces containing the largest market areas. Thus, Ontario and Quebec permit the advertising of alcoholic beverages on TV and radio, whereas New Brunswick does not permit such advertising.[22] Should the advertiser use newspaper advertising, which is permitted in all three provinces, or should the form of the advertising be adapted to the media that are permissible in each province?

Control of the content of the advertising may also vary across provincial jurisdictions. An Alberta court ruled in 1970 that an Imperial Tobacco advertisement was misleading on the basis of *credulous* man concept. However, an Ontario court based its 1975 ruling that the advertising of Viceroy homes could be misleading on the concept of the *average* man.

Several countries have gone further than Canada in the passage of strong consumerist legislation. Norway banned several forms of sales promotion, such as trading stamps, contests, and premiums, as being inappropriate or "unfair" instruments for the sellers to use in promoting products. Thailand requires food processors selling national brands to market low-price brands also so that low-income consumers can also find economy brands on the shelves. In India, food companies need special approval to launch brands that duplicate what already exists on the market, such as another cola drink or brand of rice. These and other legislative developments have not surfaced prominently in Canada, but they suggest how far regulations could be pushed to constrain marketing practice.

Table 5-2 Major Federal Legislation Affecting Marketing

1. **Trade practices:**	*Competition Act*
	Small Loans Act
	Broadcasting Act
	Patent Act
	Trade Marks Act
	Copyright Act
	Criminal Code
2. **Product standards and grades:**	*Canada Agriculture Products Standards Act*
	Consumer Packaging and Labeling Act
	Weights and Measures Act
	Industrial Design and Union Label Act
	Precious Metals Marketing Act
3. **Health and safety:**	*Food and Drugs Act*
	Narcotic Control Act
	Hazardous Products Act
	Meat and Canned Food Act

The real issue raised by business legislation is, Where is the point reached when the costs of regulation exceed the benefits? The laws are not always administered fairly by those responsible for enforcing them. They may hurt many legitimate business firms and discourage new investment and market entry. They may also increase consumer costs. Although each new law may have a legitimate rationale, their totality may sap initiative and slow down economic growth.

Growth of Public-Interest Groups   Public-action committees (PACs) have increased in number and power during the past two decades. These groups lobby government officials and put pressure on business executives to pay more attention to consumer rights, women's rights, senior citizen rights, minority rights, and so on. Many companies have established public-affairs departments to study and deal with these groups and issues.

New laws and growing numbers of pressure groups have put more restraints on marketers. Marketers have to clear their plans with the company's legal, public-relations, and public-affairs departments. Private marketing transactions have moved into the public domain. Salancik and Upah put it this way:

> There is some evidence that the consumer may not be king, nor even queen. The consumer is but a voice, one among many. Thus, insurance companies directly or indirectly affect the design of smoke detectors; scientific groups affect the design of spray products by condemning aerosols; minority activist groups affect the design of dolls by requesting representative figures. Legal departments also can be expected to increase their importance in firms, affecting not only product design and promotion but also marketing strategies. At a minimum, marketing managers will spend less time with their research departments asking, "What does the consumer want?" and more and more time with their production and legal people asking, "What can the consumer have?"[23]

Cultural Environment

The society that people grow up in shapes their basic beliefs, values, and norms. People absorb, almost unconsciously, a world view that defines their relationship to themselves, to others, to nature, and to the universe. Here are some of the main cultural characteristics and trends of interest to marketers.

Core Cultural Values have High Persistence   The people living in a particular society hold many core beliefs and values that tend to persist. Thus most Canadians still believe in work, in getting married, in giving to charity, and in being honest. Core beliefs and values are passed on from parents to children and are reinforced by major social institutions— schools, churches, business, and government.

People's secondary beliefs and values are more open to change. Believing in the institution of marriage is a core belief; believing that people ought to get married early is a secondary belief. Family-planning marketers could make more headway arguing that people should get married later than that they should not get married at all. Marketers have some chance of changing secondary values but little chance of changing core values.

Each Culture Consists of Subcultures   Each society contains subcultures, that is, various groups with shared values emerging from their special life experiences or circumstances. Anglicans, teenagers, and Hell's Angels all represent subcultures whose members share common beliefs, preferences, and behaviors. To the extent that subcultural groups exhibit different wants and consumption behavior, marketers can choose subcultures as their target markets.

Secondary Cultural Values Undergo Shifts Through Time   Although core values are fairly persistent, cultural swings do take place. The advent in the 1960s of the "hippies," the Beatles, Elvis Presley, *Playboy* magazine, and other cultural phenomena had a major impact on young people's hair styles, clothing, sexual norms, and life goals. Today's young people are influenced by new heroes and fads; older symbols, such as the *playboy*, seem to be dying. One of the major new symbols is the "yuppies"—young urban professionals, who represent the much more careerist and conservative leanings of today's youth.

Marketers have a keen interest in spotting cultural shifts that might auger new marketing opportunities or threats. Several firms offer social/cultural forecasts in this connection. One of the best known is the *Yankelovich Monitor*. The *Monitor* interviews twenty-five hundred people each year and tracks thirty-five social trends, such as "antibigness," "mysticism," "living for today," "away from possessions," and "sensuousness." It describes the percentage of the population who share the attitude as well as the percentage who are antitrend. For example, the percentage of people who value physical fitness and well-being has risen steadily over the years, especially in the under-thirty group, the young women and upscale group, and people living in the West. Marketers of health foods and exercise equipment cater to this trend with appropriate products and communications.

The major cultural values of a society are expressed in people's views of themselves, others, organizations, society, nature, and the cosmos.

People's Views of Themselves   People vary in the relative emphasis they place on self-gratification versus serving others. The move toward self-gratification was especially strong during the 1960s and 1970s. *Pleasure seekers* sought fun, change, and escape. Others sought *self-realization* and joined therapeutic or religious groups. The marketing implications of a "me society" were many. People bought products, brands, and services as a means of self-expression. They bought "dream cars" and "dream vacations." They spent more time in health activities (jogging, tennis), in introspection, and in arts and crafts. The leisure industry (camping, boating, arts and crafts, sports) benefited from the growing number of self-gratifiers.

People's Views of Others   Some observers have pointed to a countermovement from a "me society" to a "we society." They think that more people want serious and long-lasting relationships with others. Some recent advertising features people in groups sharing things with others. A Doyle Dane Bernbach survey showed a widespread concern among adults about social isolation and a strong desire for human contact.[24] This portends a bright future for "social support" products and services that promote direct relations between human beings, such as health clubs, vacations, and games. It also suggests a growing market for "social surrogates," things that allow people who are alone to feel that they are not, such as television, home video games, and computers.

People's Views of Organizations   People vary in their attitudes toward corporations, government agencies, trade unions, and other organizations. Most people are willing to work for these organizations, although they may be critical of particular ones. There appears to be a decline in *organizational loyalty*. People are giving a little less to these organizations and trusting them less. The work ethic is eroding. Many see work not as a source of satisfaction but as a necessary pursuit to earn the means to enjoy their nonwork hours.

Several marketing implications follow from this outlook. Companies need to find new ways to win consumer confidence. They need to review their advertising communications to make sure their messages are honest. They need to review their various activities to make sure they are being "good corporate citizens." More companies are turning to *social audits*[25] and to *public relations* to improve their image with their publics.

People's Views of Society People vary in their attitudes toward their society, from those who defend it (preservers), to those who run it (makers), to those who take what they can from it (takers), to those who want to change it (changers), to those who are looking for something deeper (seekers), to those who want to leave it (escapers).[26] Often peoples' consumption patterns will reflect their social attitude. Makers are high achievers, who eat, dress, and live well, while changers live more frugally by driving smaller cars, wearing simpler clothes, and so on. Escapers and seekers are a major market for movies, music, surfing, and camping.

People's Views of Nature People vary in their attitude toward the natural world. Some feel subjugated by it, others feel harmony with it, and still others seek mastery over it. A long-term trend has been people's growing mastery over nature through technology and the attendant belief that nature is bountiful. More recently, however, people have awakened to nature's fragility and finite supplies. People recognize that nature can be spoiled and destroyed by human activities.

People's love of nature is leading to more camping, hiking, boating, and fishing. Business has responded with hiking boots, tenting equipment, and other gear for nature enthusiasts. Tour operators are packaging more tours to wilderness areas. Food producers have found growing markets for "natural" products, such as natural cereal, natural ice cream, and health foods. Marketing communicators are using more scenic backgrounds in advertising their products.

People's Views of the Universe People vary in their beliefs about the origin of the universe and their place in it. Most Canadians are monotheistic, although their religious conviction and practice have been waning through the years. Church attendance has fallen steadily, with the exception of certain evangelical movements that reach out to bring people back into organized religion. Some of the religious impulse has not been lost but has been redirected into an interest in Eastern religions, mysticism, the occult, and the human-potential movement.

As people lose their religious orientation, they seek more of the "good life" here on earth. Self-fulfillment and immediate gratification are rising cultural values. At the same time, every trend seems to breed a counterforce. From time to time, a "futurist" will announce a new list of trends that warrant attention. Marketing Environment and Trends 5-4 describes the ten "megatrends" identified by John Naisbitt.

SUMMARY

The marketing environment is the place where the company must start its search for opportunities and possible threats. It consists of all the actors and forces that affect the company's ability to transact effectively with its target market. We can distinguish between the company's microenvironment and macroenvironment.

The company's microenvironment consists of the actors in the company's immediate environment that affect its ability to serve its markets; specifically, the company itself, suppliers, market intermediaries, customers, competitors, and publics. The company itself consists of several interacting departments, all of which influence marketing management's decision making. Suppliers, through their influence on the cost and availability of productive inputs, also have an influence on marketing decisions. The company converts these supplies into useful products and services and uses marketing intermediaries (middlemen, physical-distribution facilitators, marketing service agencies, financial intermediaries) to find customers and deliver the goods. The target market itself will consist of consumers, producers, resellers, or government agencies, here or abroad. In carrying out its marketing task, the

Marketing Environment and Trends 5-4

TEN "MEGATRENDS" OF GREAT IMPORT TO MARKETERS

For the past eighteen years, John Naisbitt has been publishing *Trend Report,* and several major corporations each pay over $15 000 a year to receive these reports. Naisbitt and his staff spot the trends through content analysis, namely, by counting the number of times hard-news items appear in major newspapers. The items fall into thirteen broad categories and over two hundred subcategories. In 1982, Naisbitt published a book based on his findings called *Megatrends: Ten New Directions Transforming Our Lives.* Here are the ten megatrends Naisbitt found:

1. The economy is experiencing a "megashift" from an industrial-based society to an information-based society, with an increase in the proportion of the workforce in occupations which convey information (e.g., teachers, clerks, secretaries, accountants, stockbrokers, lawyers, and managers).

2. The tendency towards "high-tech" is creating a need for "high-touch" reactions. Thus, the hospice movement is a "high-touch" reaction to medical "high-tech," just as user-friendly software is a "high-touch" reaction to computer "high-tech."

3. Global interdependence is forcing companies and governments at all levels to think internationally.

4. Managers are beginning to plan for the long term as well as the next quarter.

5. Corporate organizations are relaxing the need for workers to go to a centralized location. In an information society many work activities can be decentralized.

6. People are returning to self-reliance rather than depending on institutions.

7. Workers and consumers are more knowledgeable, and are demanding a greater voice in government, in business, and in the marketplace.

8. People who have access to information are increasing their influence in organizations. The resulting information-sharing networks may disrupt organizational hierarchies.

9. Workers are migrating to the areas of growing opportunity in the information society.

10. People are demanding a greater variety in products and in lifestyles.

Naisbitt summed it up with the last statement in his book, "My God what a fantastic time to be alive."

Source: John Naisbitt, Megatrends: Ten New Directions Transforming Our Lives (New York: Warner Books, 1982).

---

company faces several types of competitors: desire competitors, generic competitors, product-form competitors, and brand competitors. The company also has to deal with various publics that have an actual or potential interest in or impact on the company's ability to achieve its objectives: financial; media; government; citizen action; and general and internal publics. All of these actors make up the company's microenvironment.

The company's macroenvironment consists of six major forces: demographic, economic, natural, technological, political, and cultural. The demographic environment shows a worldwide explosive population growth, a Canadian birthrate slowdown, an aging population, a changing family, a rise of nonfamily households, geographical poplation shifts, a more-educated and white-collar population, a changing ethnic and racial population, and a shift from a mass market to micromarkets. The economic environment shows a slowdown in real-income growth, low savings and high debt, and changing consumer expenditure patterns. The natural environment shows potential shortages of certain raw materials, unstable cost of energy, increased pollution levels, and a changing role of government in environment protection. The technological environment exhibits accelerating technological change, unlimited innovational opportunities, concentration on minor improvements rather than on major discoveries, and increased regulation of technological change. The political environment shows substantial business regulation, strong government agency enforcement, and the growth of public-interest groups. The cultural environment shows long-run trends toward self-fulfillment, immediate gratification, and a more secular orientation.

The Appendix to this chapter illustrates techniques for mapping the interaction of a company's marketing environment, marketing system, and marketing strategy, using a major candy company as an example.

■ QUESTIONS

1. The social environment is a major environmental force influencing marketing activities. How can marketing managers measure change in the social environment?

2. Counterfeit trade—the selling of illegal copies of a licensed product—costs legitimate businesses billions of dollars annually in lost sales. What steps can businesses take to reduce losses due to counterfeiting?

3. Market data can be purchased on the number and composition of Canadian households. How might such data be useful to marketers?

4. Teenagers spend over $6 billion annually on goods and services in the Canada. In what ways is marketing to teenage consumers different from marketing to adult consumers?

5. Develop a diagram showing the major publics of a privately owned art gallery.

6. Videotex, also called Viewdata, is a two-way interactive system that allows a user to view a presentation over cable TV and then communicate a response via a home terminal to a computer over telephone lines. What implications does this new technology have for marketers?

7. Tell whether you would support or not support each of the following new legislative proposals (give your reasoning):

(a) a bill that requires companies in concentrated industries to go through federal hearings before each price boost; (b) a bill that allows auto makers to prevent dealers from selling outside their territories; (c) a bill that requires manufacturers to grant wholesalers a bigger discount than they give to large retail chains; (d) a bill that protects independent retailers from price competition from a manufacturerer that does its own retailing.

8. Lifestyle studies have shown a positive trend in the attitude that "meal preparation should take as little time as possible." How might this attitude affect the sales of frozen vegetables?

9. A major alcoholic-beverage marketer is considering introducing an "adult" soft drink that would be a socially acceptable substitute for alcohol. What cultural factors could influence the introduction decision and subsequent marketing mix?

10. Discuss in some depth how the six macroenvironmental forces discussed in this chapter may affect the marketing of Coca-Cola in 1995.

11. Develop a comprehensive marketing system map of some company of your choice. Be sure to show the marketing-mix elements and the channels of distribution.

■ NOTES

1. Peter Drucker, *Age of Discontinuity* (New York: Harper & Row, 1969); and Alvin Toffler, *Future Shock* (New York: Bantam Books, 1970), p. 28.

2. This point is elaborated in Philip Kotler and Sidney J. Levy, "Buying Is Marketing, Too," *Journal of Marketing*, January 1973, pp. 54-59.

3. The interrelations between marketing and public relations are examined in Philip Kotler and William Mindak,

"Marketing and Public Relations: Partners or Rivals?" *Journal of Marketing*, October 1978, pp. 13-20.

4. For a discussion on use of demographic data in structuring marketing strategy, see Louis G. Pol, "Marketing and the Demographic Perspective," *Journal of Consumer Marketing*, Winter 1986, pp. 57-64.

5. Much of the statistical data in this chaper are drawn from the *Statistical Abstract of the United States*, 1988. Also see

"America at Mid-Decade," *American Demographics*, January 1986, pp. 24-29.

6. Donella H. Meadows, Dennis L. Meadows, Jorgen Randers, and William W. Behrens III, *The Limits to Growth* (New York: New American Library, 1972), p. 41.

7. Philip Kotler and Eduardo Roberto, *Social Marketing: Strategies for Changing Public Attitudes* (New York: Free Press, 1989).

8. *Canadian Social Trends*, Winter 1990, No. 19, p. 31. *Marketing Research Handbook*, Statistics Canada, p. 545.

9. *Canada Yearbook*, Supply and Services, Government of Canda, 1986, pp. 2-5, 3-2.

10. Garreau, *The Nine Nations of North America* (Boston: Houghton Mifflin Co., 1981).

11. Kenneth Kidd, "Born to shop in the U.S.A.," *The Globe and Mail*, November 1, 1990; and Marilyn Ronald, "U.S. trips accelerate," *The Globe and Mail*, August 15, 1991, p. B6.

12. See Karl E. Henion II, *Ecological Marketing* (Columbus, Ohio: Grid, 1976).

13. Toffler, *Future Shock*, pp. 25-30.

14. Toffler, *The Third Wave* (New York: Bantam Books, 1980).

15. For an excellent and comprehensive list of possible future products, see Charles Panat, *Breakthroughs* (Boston: Houghton Mifflin Co., 1980); and "Technologies for the '80s," *Business Week*, July 6, 1981, pp. 48 ff.

16. Peter Haneland and Kristian S. Palda, "The Export Connection to Innovativeness Among Canadian Manufacturers," *Marketing*, Administrative Sciences Association of Canada, Vol. 3, Part 3, 1982, pp. 90-97.

17. Robert Steklasa, "R&D Spending Is Up as Renovation of Economy Starts to Take Hold": *The Financial Post*, December 10, 1983, p. 24.

18. Kristian S. Palda and Bohumir Pazderka, *Approaches to an International Comparison of Canada's R&D Expenditures*, Economic Council of Canada, 1982.

19. "Corporate Growth, R&D, and the Gap Between," *Technology Review*, March-April 1978, p. 39.

20. W.T. Stanbury, *Business Interests and the Reform of Canadian Competition Policy 1971-1975*, (Toronto: Methuen Publications, 1977) p. 1983.

21. Robert W. Sweitzer, Paul Temple and John H. Burnett, "The Political Dimensions of Canadian Advertising Regulations," *The Canadian Marketer,* Vol. 10, No. 2, Fall 1979, pp. 3-8.

22. *Marketing*, September 3, 1979, pp. 26-28.

23. "Corporate Growth, R&D, and the Gap Between," *Technology Review*, March-April 1978, p. 39.

24. See Bill Abrams, "'Middle Generation' Growing More Concerned with Selves," *Wall Street Journal*, January 21, 1982, p. 25.

25. See Raymond A. Bauer and Dan H. Fenn, Jr., "What Is a Corporate Social Audit?" *Harvard Business Review*, January-February 1973, pp. 37-48.

26. Arnold Mitchell of the Stanford Research Institute, private publication.

appendix

MAPPING A COMPANY'S MARKETING ENVIRON-MENT, MARKETING SYSTEM, AND MARKETING STRATEGY

This chapter has described how a company must forge links with various parties to carry out its marketing work, and how these parties are all affected by major forces in the environment. We shall use the Hershey Food Company to pull these ideas together and show the relationship between the company's marketing environment, marketing system, and marketing strategy.

Figure 5A-1 shows the major components and flows in a candy company's marketing system. The diagram is divided into six elements:

1. The forces in the *environment* that affect candy demand and supply, such as population growth, per capita income, attitudes toward candy, and raw material availability and cost.

2. The *company's* and *competitors' marketing strategies.*

3. The *major marketing decision variables*—product characteristics, price, salesforce, physical distribution and service, and advertising and sales promotion.

4. The *major marketing channels* that the company uses for this product.

5. The *buyer-behavior model*, which shows consumer responses to manufacturers, distribution channels, and the environment.

6. The total *industry sales, company sales*, and *company costs*.

The arrows show key flows in the marketing system. Let us select one element in Figure 5A-1, the company marketing strategy, and list on the right side of this box the major marketing decisions made by the company (see Figure 5A-2). The company makes trade decisions and consumer decisions. To influence the trade, the company sets the wholesale price, trade allowances, credit policy, and delivery policy. To influence consumers, the company decides on product characteristics, packaging characteristics, retail price, consumer deals, and consumer advertising.

The next step is to list on the left side of the box the inputs and influences on these decisions, which fall into three groups:

1. The company's long- and short-range goals for sales growth, return on sales, and return on investment

2. Forecastable factors in the environment, such as population growth, disposable personal income, cultural factors, and the cost and supply outlook

3. Assumptions about the sales effectiveness of different marketing instruments as well as expectations concerning competition.

Any input can be elaborated further. For example, it is possible to isolate four cultural factors that will have a significant effect on future candy consumption:

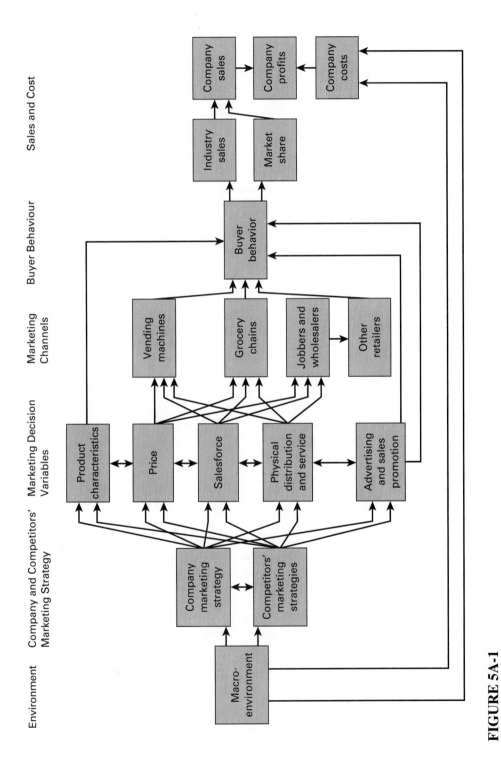

Environment | Company and Competitors' Marketing Strategy | Marketing Decision Variables | Marketing Channels | Buyer Behaviour | Sales and Cost

FIGURE 5A-1
Comprehensive Marketing-System Map: Candy Company

FIGURE 5A-2

Input-Output Map of Company Marketing Decisions: Candy Company

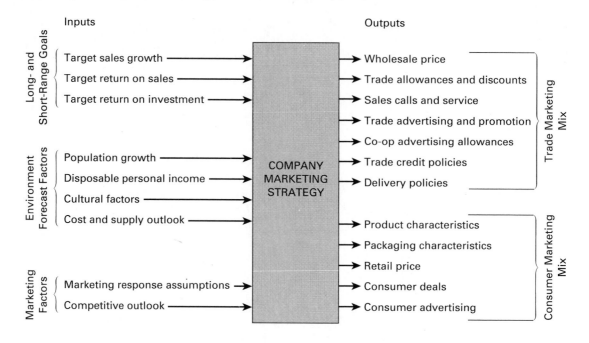

- *Weight consciousness*: If people start abandoning the idea that "thin is beautiful," candy sales will rise substantially.

- *Cavity consciousness*: As better toothpastes are developed, people will worry less about how sugar affects their teeth; on the other hand, some companies see cavity consciousness as an opportunity to develop a tasty, sugarless candy.

- *Nutrition consciousness*: If publicity on the negative effects of refined sugar on human metabolism continues to grow, more people will steer away from candy.

- *Cigarette consumption*: If people reduce their cigarette smoking, we can expect that candy, gum, and other oral gratifiers will replace cigarettes.

We can now trace how the company marketing strategy outputs feed into other parts of the system. Consider the trade marketing mix. This output becomes input into each distribution channel—for example, the grocery-chain model (see Figure 5A-3). The trade marketing mix is the manufacturer's tool for influencing retailers to provide favorable shelf facings and location, special displays and promotions, advertising, and in-stock maintenance.

The influence of the retailers' decisions on the final consumers is shown in Figure 5A-4 along with influences coming from other parts of the marketing system. The influences are classified into product and promotion factors (outputs coming from the company's marketing decisions), distribution-channels factors, and environmental factors (outputs coming from the environment). These factors influence consumers' buying behavior and lead to a certain level of industry sales, company sales, and company profits.

Ultimately, the marketing planner must estimate the quantitative relationships between various key elements. Figure 5A-5 shows the estimated effect of a product characteristic—chocolate-weight percentage—on the sales of one of its soft-center candy bars. The company would like to keep this percentage down because chocolate is expensive compared with

FIGURE 5A-3
Input-Output Map of Grocery-Chain Decisions: Candy Company

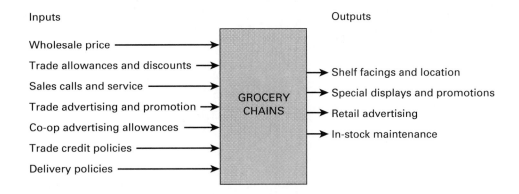

the other ingredients that make up the soft center. Consumer tests, however, reveal that as the bar's chocolate content is reduced, the candy bar loses its appeal, and sales decline. The soft center begins to appear through the chocolate and leads consumers to feel that the candy bar is poorly made. Furthermore, consumers desire more chocolate to offset the soft center. When the layer of chocolate gets too thick (above 35 percent of the bar's weight), consumer preference for the bar also falls. The consumers begin to think of it not as a soft-centered chocolate candy bar but as a chocolate bar with "some stuff in it." They compare it to pure chocolate bars, and it suffers by comparison. Thus Figure 5A-5 shows management's best estimate of how sales are affected by a specific product characteristic, "percentage chocolate." Any function that shows how sales are affected by a marketing variable under management's control is known as a *sales-response function.*

Given this sales-response function, what is the optimum percentage of chocolate? If the company wants to maximize sales, chocolate should constitute 35 percent of the candy bar's weight. Since the company is primarily interested in maximizing profit, however,

FIGURE 5A-4
Input-Output Map of Buyer Behavior: Candy Company

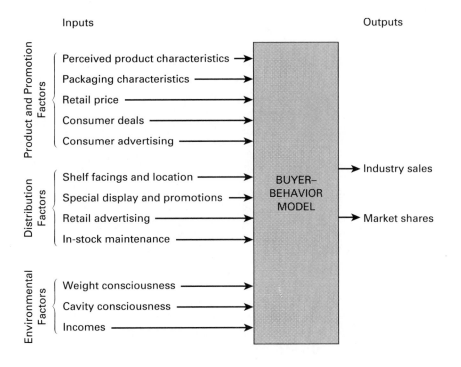

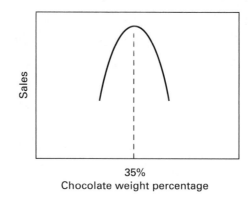

management needs the ingredient-cost functions, as well as the sales-response function, to determine the profit-maximizing amounts of chocolate.

Other functional relationships should be studied—the relationship between advertising expenditure and sales, the number of sales representatives and sales, and so on. At some point, the various functional relationships must be put together into a model for analyzing the sales and profit consequences of a proposed marketing plan. A useful device is shown in Figure 5A-6.

Quadrant 1 shows the assumed relationship between population and the total sales of chocolate-covered, soft-centered candy bars. The relationship shows that sales increase with population but at a decreasing rate. The curve indicates that a population of 26 million consumes approximately $11 million of soft-centered candy bars.

The second quadrant shows the relationship between total sales of soft-centered candy bars and company sales. When industry sales are $11 million, the company enjoys sales of $5 million—that is, a market share of approximately 45 percent. The line indicates that the company expects its market share to fall slightly as total sales increase. For example, when industry sales are $14 million, the expectation of company sales is $6 million, or an estimated market share of 43 percent, as compared with 45 percent now.

The third quadrant shows a linear relationship between company sales and company profits. Current profits are $0.5 million on company sales of approximately $5 million, or 10 percent. If company sales rise to $7 million, the company expects profits of approximately $1 million—that is, 14 percent.

This graphical device allows the marketer to visualize the effect of a particular environment factor and marketing program on company sales and profits. Suppose the company expects a new antismoking campaign to favor candy-bar sales and shift the curve in the first quadrant higher (see Figure 5A-6). Furthermore, suppose the company plans to intensify its marketing effort to capture more market share. The anticipated effect on company market share can be seen by shifting the function in the second quadrant to the right, as shown in Figure 5A-6. At the same time, the company's marketing costs increase and shift the sales-profit curve to the right, as shown in the third quadrant of Figure 5A-6. What is the net effect of this complicated set of shifts? The result is that although sales have increased, profits have fallen. Apparently, the cost to the company of attaining a higher market share exceeds the profits on the extra sales. The company would be wise not to intensify its marketing effort unless such a move would have a stronger effect on sales and profits.

The graphical model assists management in visualizing the impact of specific environmental assumptions and marketing plans on final sales and profits. It can be improved further by introducing more variables and representing their relationships in an overall mathematical model of the candy company's marketing system.

FIGURE 5A-6

Profit-Forecasting and Planning Map: Candy Company

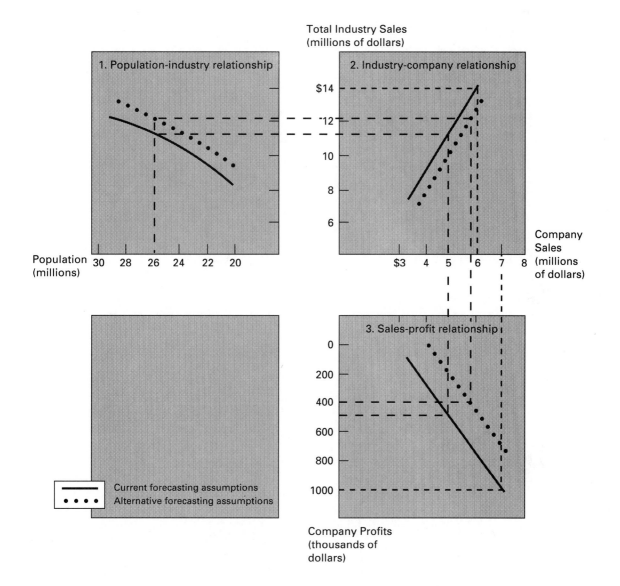

6

Analyzing Consumer Markets and Buyer Behavior

There is an old saying in Spain: To be a bullfighter, you must first learn to be a bull.

Anonymous

Understanding the buying behavior of the target market is the essential task of marketing managers under the marketing concept. This chapter will explore the buying dynamics of consumers, and the next chapter will explore the buying dynamics of business buyers.

The consumer market consists of all the individuals and households that acquire goods and services for personal consumption. In 1991, the Canadian consumer market consisted of 26.8 million people in 6.7 million family units, having an average family income of $40 356—the equivalent of $10 089 for every man, woman, and child. With a current growth rate of 314 200 new Canadians each year, this market is both affluent and growing.[1]

Consumers vary tremendously in age, income, educational level, mobility patterns, and taste. Marketers find it useful to distinguish different consumer groups or segments and to develop products and services tailored to their needs. If a market segment is large enough, some companies will set up a special marketing program to serve this market segment. Marketing Environment and Trends 6-1 describes three consumer groups—French-Canadians, teenage-students, and older consumers—that managers are currently focusing on as important and growing market segments. Marketers are also focusing on other market segments such as young urban professionals and women.[2] The 26.8 million Canadian consumers buy an incredible variety of goods and services. We will try to understand how consumers make their purchase choices among these goods and services.

A MODEL OF CONSUMER BEHAVIOR

In earlier times, marketers could understand consumers through the daily experience of selling to them. But the growth in the size of firms and markets has removed many marketing

Marketing Environment and Trends 6-1

THREE MARKET SEGMENTS: FRENCH-CANADIAN, TEENAGE-STUDENT, AND OLDER CONSUMERS

French-Canadian Consumers

Canadians whose mother tongue is French number 6.2 million or 23 percent of the population. They constitute 83 percent of the population in Quebec, 34 percent in New Brunswick, and lesser percentages in Ontario and Manitoba. Marketers who would appeal to these consumers need to do more than communicate in French. Research has revealed differences in the activities, interests, opinions, and consumption of French-Canadian versus English-Canadian consumers. French-Canadian women are more family-oriented and fashion conscious and serve more home-made soup than canned soup, for example. Such differences are partly derived from culture; their Latin roots may make French-Canadians more emotional and impulsive. Demographic and socioeconomic differences also exist; education and income are both lower in Quebec than in Ontario. The legal environment also differs for marketers in Quebec; besides strict language laws, there are stronger restrictions on advertising to children, for example. To be successful in French Canada, marketers must develop appeals and strategies that take these differences into account.

Teenage-Student Consumers

There are 2.5 million Canadians aged 13-19 years, most of them high-school students. Their numbers declined in the eighties, but in the nineties they are expected to increase by 10 percent, thanks to the "baby-boom echo." Teenages have more discretionary income per capita than many adults. Their weekly spending ranges upward from $25 per week for 13- and 14-year-olds, to $75 per week for 18- and 19-year-olds. Collectively, that amounts to a $6 billion market which is forecast to reach $10 billion in the next decade. Most of their money is spent on clothing, personal-care products, snacks, and entertainment, with lesser amounts spend on recordings, transportation, hobbies, books, and magazines.

Marketers who want to tap that market must first understand how teenagers differ from adults. Convenience is important because they are incredibly active, with many holding one or more part-time jobs. Music is a big part of their lifestyle; currently rap is in. Social acceptance and peer approval are important. Teenagers tend to be idealistic, with strong ideas about issues like the environment. To reach them, marketers should consider TV and AM radio, as well as specialized publications like *TG Magazine*.

Older Consumers

"Old age" typically begins for Canadians at their sixty-fifth birthday when retirement from work occurs and Old Age Security and other pensions begin. Older Canadians constitute 11 percent of the population. They are growing at double the overall rate and are expected to make up one-sixth of the population by the year 2011. Many own their homes as well as other assets, and have higher discretionary income than some younger age groups. Older consumers are far from being homogeneous: they can be segmented into the "go-gos" (active), the "go-slows" (frail), and the "no-gos" (nursing dependent). But many older consumers think of themselves as years younger and resent the sedentary image. Effective marketing to this group must avoid old-age stereotyping, and recognize their market potential. Many older consumers maintain an active lifestyle, traveling, shopping, and eating out. They are consumers of large cars, clothes, and jewelry, and have positive attitudes towards fitness and nutrition. Many are indulgent grandparents who lavish expensive toys and designer clothing on their grandchildren.

Sources: See the *Canada Yearbook 1986*, p. 2-5; *The Globe and Mail, Report on Business*, Tuesday, March 5, 1991, "Teen pockets run deep"; *The Globe and Mail*, April 17, 1991, p. B1 "Grocers miss hungry teens"; "Employment Patterns of Elderly Canadians," *Canadian Social Trends*, Statistics Canada, Autumn 1987; "Chasing the over-50 market," *Marketing*, April 4, 1988, p. 25.

decision makers from direct contact with customers. Increasingly, managers have had to turn to consumer research for answers to the most important questions about any market, called the seven O's of the marketplace:

Who constitutes the market?	*Occupants*
What does the market buy?	*Objects*
Why does the market buy?	*Objectives*
Who participates in the buying?	*Organizations*
How does the market buy?	*Operations*
When does the market buy?	*Occasions*
Where does the market buy?	*Outlets*

Of central interest is the question, How do consumers respond to various marketer-controlled stimuli? The company that understands how consumers will respond to different product features, prices, advertising appeals, and so on, will have an enormous advantage over its competitors. Therefore, business and academic marketing researchers have invested much energy in researching the relationship between marketing stimuli and consumer response.

Their starting point is the stimulus-response model shown in Figure 6-1. This figure shows marketing and other stimuli entering the buyer's "black box" and producing the buyer's responses. The stimuli on the left are of two types. Marketing stimuli consist of the Four Ps: product, price, place, and promotion. Environmental stimuli consist of major forces and events in the buyer's macroenvironment: economic, technological, political, and cultural. All these stimuli pass through the buyer's black box and produce the buyer's purchase decisions shown on the right: product choice, brand choice, dealer choice, purchase timing, and purchase amount.

The marketer's task is to understand what happens in the buyer's black box between outside stimuli and the buyer's purchase decisions. We will address two questions:

□ How does the buyer's background—cultural, social, personal and psychological—influence the buyer's buying behavior?

□ How does the buyer move through a decision process to make purchasing choices?

MAJOR FACTORS INFLUENCING CONSUMER BEHAVOR

Figure 6-1 indicates that a buyer's purchase decisions are highly influenced by the buyer's cultural, social, personal, and psychological factors. These factors are further elaborated in Figure 6-2. For the most part, they are "noncontrollable" by the marketer but must be taken into account. We want to examine each factor's influence on buying behavior. We will illustrate these influences for a hypothetical consumer named Linda Brown:

Linda Brown is thirty-five, married, and a brand manager in a leading consumer-packaged-goods company. She received an M.B.A. some years before computers became available. Linda wants to expand her skill base and use a computer in her work and home. She is considering buying a personal computer but faces a great number of brand choices: IBM, Radio Shack, Apple, Compaq, and so on. Her choice will be influenced by many factors. ■

FIGURE 6-1
Model of Buyer
Behavior

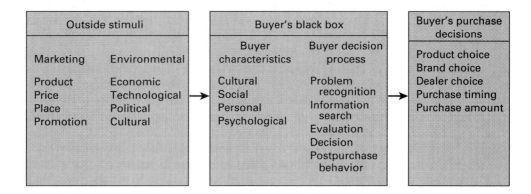

Outside stimuli		Buyer's black box		Buyer's purchase decisions
Marketing	Environmental	Buyer characteristics	Buyer decision process	Product choice
Product	Economic	Cultural	Problem recognition	Brand choice
Price	Technological	Social	Information search	Dealer choice
Place	Political	Personal	Evaluation	Purchase timing
Promotion	Cultural	Psychological	Decision	Purchase amount
			Postpurchase behavior	

Cultural Factors

Cultural factors exert the broadest and deepest influence on consumer behavior. We will look at the role played by the buyer's culture, subculture, and social class.

Culture   Culture is the most fundamental determinant of a person's wants and behavior. Whereas lower creatures are governed by instinct, human behavior is largely learned. The growing child acquires a set of values, perceptions, preferences, and behaviors through a process of socialization involving the family and other key institutions. A child growing up in Canada is exposed to the following values: achievement and success, activity, efficiency and practicality, progress, material comfort, individualism, freedom, external comfort, humanitarianism, and youthfulness.[3]

Linda Brown's interest in computers reflects her upbringing in an advanced technological society. Computers presuppose a whole set of consumer learnings and values. Linda knows what computers are; she knows how to read instructions on how to operate a computer; she knows that the society values computer expertise. In another culture, say a remote tribe in central Africa, a computer would mean nothing. It would simply be a curious piece of hardware, and there would be no buyers.

FIGURE 6-2
Detailed Model of
Factors Influencing
Behavior

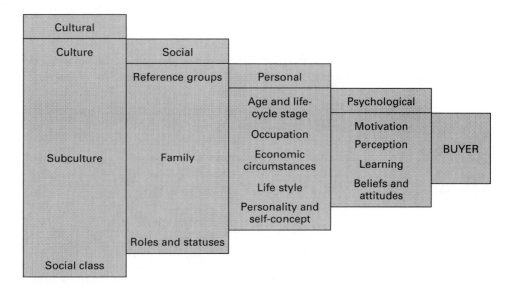

Subculture   Each culture consists of smaller subcultures that provide more specific identification and socialization for its members. Four types of subcultures can be distinguished. *Nationality groups* such as Toronto's Italian Canadians are found within large communities and exhibit distinct ethnic tastes and proclivities. *Religious groups* such as the Catholics, Presbyterians, and Jews represent subcultures with specific cultural preferences and taboos. *Racial groups* from Asia and other parts of the third world have distinct cultural styles and attitudes. *Geographical areas* such as the Maritimes and the Prairies are distinct subcultures with characteristic lifestyles.

Linda Brown's interest in various goods will be influenced by her nationality, religion, race, and geographical background. These factors will influence her food preferences, clothing choices, recreation, and career aspirations. Her subculture identifications may influence her interest in a personal computer. She may come from a subculture that places a high value on being an "educated person," and this helps explain her interest in computers.

Social Class   Virtually all human societies exhibit social stratification. Stratification sometimes takes the form of a caste system where the members of different castes are reared for certain roles and cannot change their caste membership. More frequently, stratification takes the form of social classes. *Social classes are relatively homogeneous and enduring divisions in a society, which are hierarchically ordered and whose members share similar values, interests, and behavior.* Social scientists have identified the seven social classes shown in Table 6-1.

Social classes have several characteristics. First, persons within each social class tend to behave more alike than persons from two different social classes. Second, persons are perceived as occupying inferior or superior positions according to their social class. Third, a person's social class is indicated by a number of variables, such as occupation, income, wealth, education, and value orientation, rather than by any single variable. Fourth, individuals can move from one social class to another—up or down—during their lifetime. The extent of this mobility varies according to the rigidity of social stratification in a given society.

Social classes show distinct product and brand preferences in such areas as clothing, home furnishings, leisure activities, and automobiles. Some marketers focus their efforts on one social class. Thus Winston's restaurant focuses on upper-class diners whereas McDonald's focuses on the middle-class family market. The social classes differ in their media preferences, with upper-class consumers having greater exposure to magazines and newspapers than lower-class consumers. Even within a media category, the social classes differ in their preferences. Upper-class consumers prefer news and drama, and lower-class consumers prefer soap operas and quiz shows. There are also language differences among the social classes. The advertiser has to compose copy and dialogue that ring true to each social class.

Linda Brown comes from a middle-class background. Her family places a lot of value on education and becoming a professional, such as a manager, lawyer, accountant, or physician. As a result, Linda has acquired good verbal and mathematical skills and is not daunted by computers, as someone from a less-educated background might be.

Social Factors

A consumer's behavior is also influenced by such social factors as reference groups, family, and social roles and statuses.

Reference Groups   Many groups influence a person's behavior. A person's *reference groups* consist of *all the groups that have a direct (face-to-face) or indirect influence on the person's attitudes or behavior.* Groups having a direct influence on a person are called

Table 6-1 Characteristics of Seven Major Social Classes

1. UPPER UPPERS (LESS THAN 1 PERCENT)	Upper uppers are the social elite who live on inherited wealth and have well-known families. They give large sums to charity, run the debutante balls, maintain more than one home, and send their children to the finest schools. They are a market for jewelry, antiques, homes, and vacations. They often buy and dress conservatively, not being interested in ostentation. While small as a group, they serve as a reference group for others to the extent that their consumption decisions trickle down and are imitated by the other social classes.
2. LOWER UPPERS (ABOUT 2 PERCENT)	Lower uppers are persons who have earned high income or wealth through exceptional ability in the professions or business. They usually come from the middle class. They tend to be active in social and civic affairs and seek to buy the symbols of status for themselves and their children, such as expensive homes, schools, yachts, swimming pools, and automobiles. They include the nouveaux riches, whose pattern of conspicuous consumption is designed to impress those below them. The ambition of lower uppers is to be accepted in the upper-upper stratum, a status that is more likely to be achieved by their children than themselves.
3. UPPER MIDDLES (12 PERCENT)	Upper middles possess neither family status nor unusual wealth. They are primarily concerned with "career." They have attained positions as professionals, independent businesspersons, and corporate managers. They believe in education and want their children to develop professional or administrative skills so that they will not drop into a lower stratum. Members of this class like to deal in ideas and "high culture." They are joiners and highly civic minded. They are the quality market for good homes, clothes, furniture, and appliances. They seek to run a gracious home, entertaining friends and clients.
4. MIDDLE CLASS (32 PERCENT)	The middle class are average-pay white- and blue-collar workers who live on "the better side of town" and try to "do the proper things." Often, they buy products that are popular "to keep up with the trends." Twenty-five percent own imported cars, while most are concerned with fashion, seeking "one of the better brand names." Better living means "a nicer home" in "a nice neighborhood on the better side of town" with "good schools." The middle class believes in spending more money on "worthwhile experiences" for their children and aiming them toward a college education.
5. WORKING CLASS (38 PERCENT)	Working class consists of average-pay blue-collar workers and those who lead a "working-class lifestyle," whatever their income, school background, or job. The working class depends heavily on relatives for economic and emotional support, for tips on job opportunities, for advice on purchases, and for assistance in times of trouble. A working-

	class vacation means "staying in town," and "going away" means to a lake or resort no more than two hours away. The working class main tains sharp sex-role divsion and stereotyping. Car preferences include standard size and larger cars, rejecting domestic and foreign compacts.
6. UPPER LOWERS (9 PERCENT)	Upper lowers are working, not on welfare, although their living standard is just above poverty. They perform unskilled work and are very poorly paid, although they are striving toward a higher class. Often, upper lowers are educationally deficient. Although they fall near the poverty line financially, they manage to "present a picture of self-discipline" and "maintain some effort at cleanliness."
7. LOWER LOWERS (7 PERCENT)	Lower lowers are on welfare, visibly poverty stricken, and and usually out of work or have "the dirtiest jobs." Some are not interested in finding a permanent job and most are dependent on public aid or charity for income. Their homes, clothes, and possessions are "dirty," "raggedy," and "broken-down."

Source: Richard P. Coleman, "The Continuing Significance of Social Class to Marketing," *Journal of Consumer Research*, December, 1983, pp. 265-80; and Richard P. Coleman and Lee P. Rainwater, *Social Standing in America: New Dimension of Class* (New York: Basic Books, 1978).

membership groups. These are groups to which the person belongs and interacts. Some are *primary groups* with which there is fairly continuous interaction, such as family, friends, neighbors, and coworkers. Primary groups tend to be informal. A person also belongs to *secondary groups*, which tend to be more formal and where there is less continuous interaction: They include religious, professional, and trade-union groups.

People are also influenced by groups in which they are not members. Groups to which a person would like to belong are called *aspirational groups*. For example, a teenager may hope one day to play for the Edmonton Oilers. A *dissociative group* is one whose values or behavior an individual rejects. The same teenager may want to avoid any relationship with the Hare Krishna cult group.

Marketers try to identify the reference groups of their target customers. People are significantly influenced by their reference groups in at least three ways. Reference groups expose an individual to new behaviors and lifestyles. They also influence the person's attitudes and self-concept because he or she normally desires to "fit in." And they create pressures for conformity that may affect the person's actual product and brand choices.

The importance of reference-group influence varies among products and brands. Hendon asked two hundred consumers to specify which of their product and brand choices were strongly influenced by others.[4] He found that reference groups had a strong influence on both product and brand choice in the case of automobiles and color television. Reference groups had a strong influence in brand choice only in such items as furniture and clothing. And reference groups had a strong influence on product choice only in such items as beer and cigarettes.

Hendon also observed that reference-group influence changes as products go through the product life cycle. When a product is first introduced, the decision to buy it is heavily influenced by others, but the brand chosen is less influenced by others. In the market growth stage, group influence is strong on both product and brand choice. In the product maturity stage, brand choice but not product choice is heavily influenced by others. In the decline stage, group influence is weak in both product and brand choice.

Manufacturers of products and brands where group influence is strong must determine how to reach and influence the *opinion leaders* in these reference groups. At one time, sellers thought that opinion leaders were primarily community social leaders whom the mass market imitated because of "snob appeal." But opinion leaders are found in all strata of society, and a specific person can be an opinion leader in certain product areas and an opinion follower in other areas. The marketer tries to reach the opinion leaders by identifying demographic and psychographic characteristics associated with opinion leadership, identifying the media read by opinion leaders, and directing messages at the opinion leaders.

Group influence is strong for products that are visible to others whom the buyer respects. Linda Brown's interest in a computer and her attitudes toward various brands will be strongly influenced by some of her membership groups. Her coworkers' attitudes and brand choices will influence her. The more cohesive the group is, the more effective its communication process is, and the higher the person esteems it, the more influential it will be in shaping the person's product and brand choices.[5]

Family Family members constitute the most influential primary reference groups shaping a buyer's behavior. We can distinguish between two families in the buyer's life. The *family of orientation* consists of one's parents. From parents a person acquires an orientation toward religion, politics, and economics and a sense of personal ambition, self-worth, and love.[6] Even if the buyer no longer interacts very much with his or her parents, the parents' influence on the unconscious behavior of the buyer can be significant. In countries where parents continue to live with their grown children, their influence can be substantial.

A more direct influence on everyday buying behavior is one's *family of procreation*, namely, one's spouse and children. The family is the most important consumer-buying organization in society, and it has been researched extensively.[7] Marketers are interested in the roles and relative influence of the husband, wife, and children in the purchase of a large variety of products and services.

Husband-wife involvement varies widely by product category. The wife has traditionally acted as the family's main purchasing agent, especially for food, sundries, and staple-clothing items. This is changing with the increased number of working wives and the husbands doing more family shopping. Convenience-goods marketers would therefore make a mistake to think of women as the main or only purchasers of their products.

In the case of expensive products and services, husbands and wives engage in more joint decision making. The marketer needs to determine which member normally has the greater influence in choosing various products. Often it is a matter of who has more power or expertise than being husband or wife per se. The husband may be more dominant, or the wife may be, or they may have equal influence. Here are typical product patterns:

❑ *Husband dominant*: Life insurance, automobiles, television

❑ *Wife dominant*: Washing machines, carpeting, non-living-room furniture, kitchenware

❑ *Equal*: Living-room furniture, vacation, housing, outside entertainment

At the same time, a family member's influence can vary with different subdecisions made within a product category. Davis found that the decision of "when to buy an automobile" was influenced primarily by the husband in 68 percent of the cases, primarily by the wife in 3 percent of the cases, and equally in 29 percent of the cases.[8] On the other hand, the decision on "what color automobile to buy" was influenced primarily by the husband in 25 percent of the cases, by the wife in 25 percent of the cases, and equally in 50 percent of the cases. An automobile company would take these varying decision roles into account in designing and promoting its cars (see Marketing Environment and Trends 6-2 for more recent data on the influence of women car buyers).

In the case of Linda Brown's purchase of a personal computer, her husband will play an influencer role. He may have initiated the suggestion. He may offer advice on the brand and features. His influence will depend on how strongly he makes the case for buying a computer and how much Linda values his opinion.

Roles and Statuses   A person participates in many groups throughout life—family, clubs, organizations. The person's position in each group can be defined in terms of *role* and *status*. With her parents, Linda Brown plays the role of daughter; in her family, she plays wife; in her corporation, she plays brand manager. A role consists of the activities that a person is expected to perform according to the persons around him or her. Each of Linda's roles will influence some of her buying behavior.

Each role carries a status reflecting the esteem accorded to it by society. A Supreme Court justice has more status than a brand manager, and a brand manager has more status than an office clerk. People choose products that communicate their role and status in society. Thus company presidents drive Mercedes, wear expensive custom-tailored suits, and drink Chivas Regal Scotch. Marketers are aware of the *status symbol* potential of products and brands. However, status symbols vary for social classes and also geographically. Jogging, cross-country skiing, and hang-gliding are activities which hold different symbolic meanings for Montrealers and Vancouverites.[9]

Marketing Environment and Trends 6-2

WOMEN BECOME A MORE IMPORTANT MARKET FOR CAR BUYING

Laurie Ashcraft made the following observations at a marketing and research conference:

> Women in car ads have typically been shown sitting on the hood rather than behind the wheel. . . . (Top management) is always trying to catch up to changes in consumer demands. . . . And now, they're trying to catch up in their marketing to women. In 1980, women influenced 80 percent of new-car purchases and actually made 40 percent of these purchases. And the increase in car ownership by women has been a steady trend, jumping to 40 percent from 21 percent in 1972. . . . Some auto manufacturers are frantically trying to change their advertising to reflect the reality that women do more than pick out the color of the upholstery. . . . A study . . . revealed that 47 percent of women feel they are not being communicated with effectively in car ads. The women said car ads assume women to be primarily interested in appearance, underestimate women's car sense, and overestimate male influence on women drivers. . . . For example, 60 percent of service contracts are bought by women, and surveys have found that they should be approached differently than men, since women are interested in aspects such as safety to a greater degree.

> . . . .Top management suffers from inertia and cannot be easily persuaded that change is occurring. . . . Marketing decision makers are bringing too much of their own mind-set to the party.

Sources: Laurie Ashcraft, "Marketers Miss Their Target When They Eschew Research," *Marketing News*, January 7, 1983, p. 10. Also see J. Gilbert, "Marketing Cars to Women," *Madison Avenue*, August 1985, pp. 52-56.

Personal Factors

A buyer's decisions are also influenced by personal characteristics, notably the buyer's age and life-cycle stage, occupation, economic circumstances, lifestyle, and personality and self-concept.

Age and Life-Cycle Stage   People buy different goods and services over their lifetime. They eat baby food in the early years, most foods in the growing and mature years, and special diets in the later years. People's taste in clothes, furniture, and recreation is also age related.

Consumption is also shaped by the stage of the *family life cycle*. Nine stages of the family life cycle are listed in Table 6-2, along with the financial situation and typical product interests of each group. Marketers often choose life-cycle groups as their target market.

Some recent work has identified *psychological life-cycle stages*. Adults experience certain *passages* or *transformations* as they go through life.[10] Thus Linda Brown may move from being a satisfied brand manager and wife to being a dissatisfied person searching for a new career. This search may have stimulated her interest in computers. Marketers should pay attention to changing life circumstances—divorce, widowhood, remarriage—and their effect on consumption behavior.

Occupation   A person's consumption pattern is also influenced by his or her occupation. A blue-collar worker will buy work clothes, work shoes, lunch boxes, and bowling recreation. A company president will buy expensive suits, air travel, country club membership, and a large sailboat. Marketers try to identify the occupational groups that have above-average interest in their products and services. A company can even specialize their products for certain occupational groups. Thus computer software companies will design different computer software for brand managers, engineers, lawyers, and physicians.

Economic Circumstances   Product choice is greatly affected by one's economic circumstances. People's economic circumstances consist of their *spendable income* (its level, stability, and time pattern), savings and assets (including the percentage that is liquid), *borrowing power*, and *attitude toward spending versus saving*. Thus Linda Brown can consider buying a personal computer if she has enough spendable income, savings, or borrowing power and prefers spending to saving. Marketers of income-sensitive goods pay constant attention to trends in personal income, savings, and interest rates. If economic indicators point to a recession, marketers can take steps to redesign, reposition, and reprice their products so they continue to appeal to target customers.

Lifestyle   People coming from the same subculture, social class, and occupation may lead quite different lifestyles. Linda Brown, for example, can choose to live a "belonging" lifestyle, which is reflected in wearing conservative clothes, spending a lot of time with her family, helping her church. Or she can choose an "achiever" lifestyle, marked by working long hours on major projects and playing hard when it comes to travel and sports.

A person's *lifestyle* is the person's *pattern of living in the world as expressed in the person's activities, interests, and opinions*. Lifestyle portrays the "whole person" interacting with his or her environment. Lifestyle reflects something beyond the person's social class, on the one hand, or personality, on the other. If we know someone's social class, we can infer several things about the person's likely behavior but fail to see the person as an individual. If we know someone's personality, we can infer distinguishing psychological characteristics but not

Table 6-2 An Overview of the Family Life Cycle and Buying Behavior

Stage in Family Life Cycle	Buying or Behavioral Pattern
1. Bachelor stage: young, single people not living at home.	Few financial burdens. Fashion opinion leaders. Recreation oriented. Buy: basic kitchen equipment, basic furniture, cars, equipment for the mating game, vacations.
2. Newly married couples: young, no children.	Better off financially than they will be in near future. Highest purchase rate and highest average purchase of durables. Buy: cars, refrigerators, stoves, sensible and durable furniture, vacations.
3. Full nest I: youngest child under six.	Home purchasing at peak. Liquid assets low. Dissatisfied with financial position and amount of money saved. Interested in new products. Like advertised products. Buy: washers, dryers, TV, baby food, chest rubs and cough medicines, vitamins, dolls, wagons, sleds, skates.
4. Full nest II: youngest child six or over.	Financial position better. Some wives work. Less influenced by advertising. Buy larger-size packages, multiple-unit deals. Buy: many foods, cleaning materials, bicycles, music lessons, pianos.
5. Full nest III: older married couples with dependent children.	Financial position still better. More wives work. Some children get jobs. Hard to influence with advertising. High average purchase of durables. Buy: new, more tasteful furniture, auto travel, unnecessary appliances, boats, dental services, magazines.
6. Empty nest I: older married couples, no children living with them, head in labor force.	Home ownership at peak. Most satisfied with financial position and money saved. Interested in travel, recreation, self-education. Make gifts and contributions. Not interested in new products. Buy: vacations, luxuries, home improvements.
7. Empty nest II: older married. No children living at home, head retired.	Drastic cut in income. Keep home. Buy: medical appliances, medical-care products that aid health, sleep, and digestion.
8. Solitary survivor, in labor force.	Income still good but likely to sell home.
9. Solitary survivor, retired.	Same medical and product needs as other retired group; drastic cut in income. Special need for attention, affection, and security.

Sources: William D. Wells and George Gubar, "Life-Cycle Concepts in Marketing Research," *Journal of Marketing Research*, November 1966, pp. 355-63, here p. 362. Also see Patrick E. Murphy and William A. Staples, "A Modernized Family Life Cycle," *Journal of Consumer Research*, June 1979, pp. 12-22; and Frederick W. Derrick and Alane E. Linfield, "The Family Life Cycle: An Alternative Approach," *Journal of Consumer Research*, September 1980, pp. 214-17.

much about actual activities, interests, and opinions. Lifestyle attempts to profile a person's way of being and acting in the world (see Marketing Concepts and Tools 6-1).

Marketers will search for relationships between their products and lifestyle groups. A personal-computer manufacturer might find that most buyers fit the VALS description of achievers. The marketer may then aim the brand more clearly at the achiever lifestyle. Ad copywriters can then draw on symbols that appeal to achievers:

> He lives in one of those modern high-rise apartments and the rooms are brightly colored. He has modern, expensive furniture, but not Danish modern. He buys his clothes at Brooks Brothers. He owns a good hi-fi. He skis. He has a sailboat. He eats Limburger and any other prestige cheese with his beer. He likes and cooks a lot of steak and would have a filet mignon for company. His liquor cabinet has Jack Daniels bourbon, Beefeater gin, and a good Scotch.[11]

The implications of the lifestyle concept are well stated by Boyd and Levy:

> Marketing is a process of providing customers with parts of a potential mosaic from which they, as artists of their own lifestyles, can pick and choose to develop the composition that for the time seems the best. The marketer who thinks about his products in this way will seek to understand their potential settings and relationships to other parts of consumer lifestyles, and thereby to increase the number of ways they fit meaningfully into the pattern.[12]

Personality and Self-Concept   Each person has a distinct personality that will influence his or her buying behavior. By *personality*, we mean the *person's distinguishing psychological characteristics that lead to relatively consistent and enduring responses to his or her environment*. Personality is usually described in terms of such traits as self-confidence, dominance, autonomy, deference, sociability, defensiveness, and adaptability.[13] Personality can be a useful variable in analyzing consumer behavior provided that personality types can be classified and that strong correlations exist between certain personality types and product or brand choices. For example, a personal-computer company might discover that many prospects have high self-confidence, dominance, and autonomy. This suggests using these appeals in advertising personal computers.

Many marketers use a concept related to personality—a person's *self-concept* (or self-image). All of us carry a complex mental picture of ourselves. For example, Linda Brown may see herself as highly accomplished and deserving the best. To that extent, she will favor a computer that projects the same qualities. If the IBM personal computer is promoted as a computer for those who want the best, then its brand image will match her self-image. Marketers should try to develop brand images that match the self-image of the target market.

The theory, admittedly, is not that simple. Linda's actual *self-concept* (how she views herself) differs from her *ideal self-concept* (how she would like to view herself) and from her *others-self-concept* (how she thinks others see her). Which self will she try to satisfy with the choice of a computer? Some marketers feel that buyers' choices will correspond more to their actual self-concepts; others think the ideal self-concept will dominate; and still others think the others-self-concept will win out. As a result, self-concept theory has had a mixed record of success in predicting consumer responses to brand images.[14]

Psychological Factors

A person's buying choices are also influenced by four major psychological factors—motivation, perception, learning, and beliefs and attitudes. We will explore each factor's role in the buying process.

Marketing Concepts and Tools 6-1

HOW LIFESTYLES ARE IDENTIFIED

Researchers have worked hard to develop a lifestyle classification, based on *psychographic* measurements. A number of classifications have been proposed, two of which will be described here, namely, the AIO framework and the VALS framework.

The AIO Framework

In this approach, respondents are presented with long questionnaires seeking to measure their activities, interests, and opinions (AIO). The table below shows the major dimensions used to measure the AIO elements, as well as respondents' demographics.

Activities	Interests	Opinions	Demographics
Work	Family	Themselves	Age
Hobbies	Home	Social issues	Education
Social events	Job	Politics	Income
Vacation	Community	Business	Occupation
Entertainment	Recreation	Economics	Family size
Club membership	Fashion	Education	Dwelling
Community	Food	Products	Geography
Shopping	Media	Future	City size
Sports	Achievements	Culture	Stage in cycle

Source: Joseph T. Plummer, "The Concept and Application of Life-Style Segmentation," *Journal of Marketing*, January 1974, p. 34.

Many of the questions are in the form of agreeing or disagreeing with such statements as

- I would like to become an actor.
- I enjoy going to concerts.
- I usually dress for fashion, not for comfort.
- I often have a cocktail before dinner.

The data are analyzed on a computer to find distinctive lifestyle groups. Using this approach, the advertising agency Needham, Harper and Steers identified several major lifestyle groups. Here are the five male groups:

- Ben, the self-made businessman (17%)
- Scott, the successful professional (21%)
- Dale, the devoted family man (17%)
- Fred, the frustrated factory worker (19%)
- Herman, the retiring homebody (26%)

When developing an advertising campaign, the marketers state the target lifestyle group, and the ad people develop an ad appealing to the AIO characteristics of the group(s).

The VALS Framework

Arnold Mitchell of SRI International classified the public into nine value lifestyle groups (VALS) based on analyzing the answers of 2713 respondents to over eight hundred questions. The nine groups are described below.

- Survivors (4 percent) are disadvantaged people who tend to be "despairing, depressed, withdrawn."
- Sustainers (7 percent) are disadvantaged people who are valiantly struggling to get out of poverty.
- Belongers (33 percent) are people who are conventional, conservative, nostalgic, and unexperimental, and who would rather fit in than stand out.
- Emulators (10 percent) are ambitious, upwardly mobile, and status conscious; they want to "make it big."
- Achievers (23 percent) are the nation's leaders, who make things happen, work within the system, and enjoy the good life.
- "I-am-me" (5 percent) are people who are typically young, self-engrossed, and given to whim.
- Experientials (7 percent) are people who pursue a rich inner life and want to experience directly what life has to offer.
- Societally conscious (9 percent) people have a high sense of social responsibility and want to improve conditions in society.

□ Integrateds (2 percent) are people who have fully matured psychologically and combine the best elements of inner directedness and outer directedness.

The classification is based on the idea that individuals pass through a number of developmental stages, with each stage affecting the person's attitudes, behavior, and psychological needs. People pass from a need-driven stage (survivors and sustainers) into either an outer-directed hierarchy of stages (belongers, emulators, and achievers) or an inner-directed hierarchy of stages (I-am-me, experientials, societally conscious), with a few reaching an integrated stage.

Marketers pay little attention to need-driven segments of the population because the latter lack economic resources. The other groups are of greater interest and have some distinct demographic, occupational, and media characteristics. Thus a manufacturer of expensive luggage will want to know more about the characteristics of achievers and how to advertise effectively to them; a manufacturer of hot tubs will want to focus on the experientials. A manufacturer of garbage disposals will direct different appeals to belongers and societally conscious people. Over forty major corporations now subscribe to VALS and use the data to reach lifestyle groups more effectively.

Sources: For further discussion of AIO, see William D. Wells, "Psychographics: A Critical Review," *Journal of Marketing Research*, May 1975, pp. 196-213; and Peter W. Bernstein, "Psychographics Is Still an Issue on Madison Avenue," *Fortune*, January 16, 1978, pp. 78-84. For further discussion of VALS, see Arnold Mitchell, *The Nine American Life Styles* (New York: Macmillan, 1983).

Motivation   We saw that Linda Brown became interested in buying a computer. Why? What is she really seeking? What needs is she trying to satisfy?

A person has many needs at any given time. Some needs are *biogenic*. They arise from physiological states of tension such as hunger, thirst, discomfort. Other needs are *psychogenic*. They arise from psychological states of tension such as the need for recognition, esteem, or belonging. Most psychogenic needs are not intense enough to motivate the person to act on them immediately. A need becomes a motive when it is aroused to a sufficient level of intensity. A motive (or drive) is a need that is sufficiently pressing to drive the person to act. Satisfying the need reduces the felt tension.

Psychologists have developed theories of human motivation. Three of the best known—the theories of Sigmund Freud, Abraham Maslow, and Frederick Herzberg—carry quite different implications for consumer analysis and marketing strategy.

Freud's Theory of Motivation   Freud assumes that the real psychological forces shaping people's behavior are largely unconscious. Freud sees the person as repressing many urges in the process of growing up and accepting social rules. These urges are never eliminated or perfectly controlled; they emerge in dreams, in slips of the tongue, in neurotic behavior.

Thus a person cannot fully understand his or her own motivations. If Linda Brown wants to purchase a personal computer, she may describe her motive as wanting a hobby or furthering her career. At a deeper level, she may be purchasing a computer to impress others. At a still deeper level, she may be buying the computer because it helps her feel smart and sophisticated.

When Linda looks at a particular computer, she will react not only to its stated capabilities but also to other cues. The computer's shape, size, weight, material, color, and brand name can all trigger certain emotions. The manufacturer, in designing the computer, should be aware of the impact of visual, auditory, and tactile elements in triggering consumer emotions that could stimulate or inhibit purchase.

The leading modern exponent of Freudian motivation theory in marketing is Ernest Dichter, who for over three decades has been interpreting buying situations and product choices in terms of underlying unconscious motives. Dichter calls his approach *motivational research*, and it consists of collecting "in-depth interviews" with a few dozen consumers to uncover their deeper motives triggered by the product. He uses various "projective techniques" to throw the ego off guard—techniques such as word association, sentence completion, picture interpretation, and role playing.[15]

Motivation researchers have produced some interesting and occasionally bizarre hypotheses as to what may be in the buyer's mind regarding certain products. They have suggested that

☐ Consumers resist prunes because prunes are wrinkled looking and remind people of old age.

☐ Men smoke cigars as an adult version of thumb sucking. They like their cigars to have a strong odor in order to prove their masculinity.

☐ Women prefer vegetable shortening to animal fats because the latter arouse a sense of guilt over killing animals.

☐ A woman is very serious when baking a cake because unconsciously she is going through the symbolic act of giving birth. She dislikes easy-to-use cake mixes because the easy life evokes a sense of guilt.

Maslow's Theory of Motivation Abraham Maslow sought to explain why people are driven by particular needs at particular times.[16] Why does one person spend considerable time and energy on personal safety and another on pursuing the esteem of others? His answer is that human needs are arranged in a hierarchy, from the most pressing to the least pressing. Maslow's hierarchy of needs is shown in Figure 6-3. In their order of importance, they are *physiological* needs, *safety* needs, *social* needs, *esteem* needs, and *self-actualization* needs. A person will try to satisfy the most important needs first. When a person succeeds in satisfying an important need, it will cease being a current motivator, and the person will try to satisfy the next-most-important need.

For example, a starving man (need 1) will not take an interest in the latest happenings in the art world (need 5), nor in how he is viewed or esteemed by others (need 3 or 4), nor even in whether he is breathing clean air (need 2). But as each important need is satisfied, the next-most-important need will become salient.

Maslow's theory helps the marketer understand how various products fit into the plans, goals, and lives of potential consumers. What light does Maslow's theory throw on Linda Brown's interest in buying a computer? We can guess that Linda has satisfied her physiological, safety, and social needs; they do not motivate her interest in computers. Her computer interest might come from a strong need for more esteem from others or from a higher need for self-actualization. She wants to actualize her potential as a creative person through learning to master the computer.

Herzberg's Theory of Motivation Frederick Herzberg developed a "two-factor theory" of motivation, which distinguishes dissatisfiers (factors that cause dissatisfaction) and satisfiers (factors that cause satisfaction).[17] For example, if an Apple computer did not come with a warranty, that would be a dissatisfier. Yet the presence of a product warranty would not act as a satisfier or motivator of Linda's purchase, since it is not a source of intrinsic satisfaction with the Apple computer. The Apple computer's fine color graphics would be a satisfier and enhance Linda's enjoyment of the computer.

This theory of motivation has two implications. First, sellers should do their best to avoid dissatisfiers such as a poor training manual or a poor service policy. While these things will not sell the computer, they might easily unsell the computer. Second, the manufacturer should identify the major satisfiers or motivators of purchase in the computer market and be sure to

FIGURE 6-3
Maslow's Hierarchy of Needs

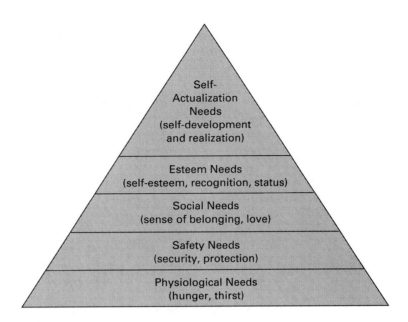

supply them. These satisfiers will make the major difference as to which computer brand the customer buys.

Perception   A motivated person is ready to act. How the motivated person actually acts is influenced by his or her perception of the situation. Two people in the same motivated state and objective situation may act quite differently because they perceive the situation differently. Linda Brown might see a fast-talking computer salesperson as aggressive and insincere. Another shopper might see the same salesperson as intelligent and helpful.

Why do people have different perceptions of the same situation? We start with the notion that all of us experience a stimulus object through *sensations*, that is, flows of information through our five senses: sight, hearing, smell, touch, and taste. However, each of us notices, organizes, and interprets this sensory information in an individual way. *Perception* can be defined as "the process by which an individual selects, organizes, and interprets information inputs to create a meaningful picture of the world."[18] Perception depends not only on the character of the physical stimuli but also on the relation of the stimuli to the surrounding field (the Gestalt idea) and on conditions within the individual.

People can emerge with different perceptions of the same stimulus object because of three perceptual processes: selective attention, selective distortion, and selective retention.

Selective Attention   People are exposed to a tremendous number of stimuli each day. Looking at commercial stimuli alone, the average person may be exposed to over fifteen hundred ads a day. It is impossible for a person to notice all of these stimuli. Most stimuli will be screened out. The real challenge is to explain what stimuli people will notice. Here are some findings:

☐ *People are more likely to notice stimuli that relate to a current need.* Linda Brown will notice most computer ads because she is motivated to buy one; she will probably not notice stereo-equipment ads.

☐ *People are more likely to notice stimuli that they anticipate.* Linda Brown is more likely to notice computers than radios in a computer store because she did not expect the store to carry radios.

□ *People are more likely to notice stimuli whose deviations are large in relation to the normal size of the stimuli.* Linda Brown is more likely to notice an ad offering $100 off the list price of an Apple computer than one offering $5 off the list price.

Selective attention means that marketers have to work hard to attract consumer attention. Their messages will be lost on most people who are not in the market for the product. Even people who are in the market may not notice a message unless it stands out from the surrounding sea of stimuli. Ads that are larger in size or that use four colors or are novel and provide contrast are more likely to be noticed.

Selective Distortion   Even stimuli that consumers note do not necessarily come across in the predicted way. Each person attempts to fit incoming information into his or her existing mind-set. Selective distortion describes the tendency of people to twist information into personal meanings. Thus Linda Brown may hear the salesperson mention some good and bad points about an IBM computer. If Linda has a strong leaning toward IBM, she is likely to discount the negative statements in order to justify buying an IBM. People interpret information in a way that will support rather than challenge their preconceptions.

Selective Retention   People will forget much that they learn. They will tend to retain information that supports their attitudes and beliefs for chosen alternatives. Because of selective retention, Linda is likely to remember good points mentioned about the IBM and forget good points mentioned about competing computers. She remembers IBM's good points because she "rehearses" them more whenever she thinks about choosing a computer.

These perceptual factors—selective exposure, distortion, and retention—mean that marketers have to work hard to get their messages across. That explains why marketers use drama and repetition in sending messages to their market.

Learning   When people act, they learn. *Learning* describes *changes in an individual's behavior arising from experience.* Most human behavior is learned.

Learning theorists say that a person's learning is produced through the interplay of *drives, stimuli, cues, responses,* and *reinforcement.*

We have seen that Linda Brown has a drive toward self-actualization. A *drive* is defined as a strong internal stimulus impelling action. Her drive becomes a motive when it is directed toward a particular drive-reducing *stimulus object,* in this case a computer. Linda's response to the idea of buying a computer is conditioned by the surrounding cues. Cues are minor stimuli that determine when, where, and how the person responds. Her husband's encouragement of her interest, seeing a computer in a friend's home, seeing computer ads and articles, hearing about a special sales price are all cues that can influence Linda's response to the impulse to buy a computer.

Suppose Linda buys a computer and chooses an IBM. If her experience is *rewarding,* she will continue to use the computer. Her response to computers will be reinforced. Later on, Linda may want a portable typewriter. She notices several brands, including one by IBM. Since she knows that IBM makes good computers, she infers that IBM also makes good typewriters. We say that she *generalizes* her response to similar stimuli.

A countertendency to generalization is *discrimination.* When Linda examines a typewriter made by Olivetti, she sees that it is lighter and more compact than IBM's typewriter. Discrimination means she has learned to recognize differences in sets of similar stimuli and can adjust her responses accordingly.

Learning theory teaches marketers that they can build up demand for a product by associating it with strong drives, using motivating cues, and providing positive reinforcement.

A new company can enter the market by appealing to the same drives that competitors use and providing similar cue configurations because buyers are more likely to transfer loyalty to similar brands than to dissimilar brands (generalization). Or the company might design its brand to appeal to a different set of drives and offer strong cue inducements to switch (discrimination).

Beliefs and Attitudes   Through acting and learning, people acquire beliefs and attitudes. These in turn influence their buying behavior.

A *belief* is *a descriptive thought that a person holds about something.* Linda Brown may believe that an IBM personal computer has a larger memory, stands up well under rugged usage, and costs $2000. These beliefs may be based on knowledge, opinion, or faith. They may or may not carry an emotional charge. For example, Linda Brown's belief that an IBM personal computer is heavier than an Apple might not matter to her decision.

Manufacturers, of course, are very interested in the beliefs that people carry in their heads about their products and services. These beliefs make up product and brand images, and people act on their images. If some of the beliefs are wrong and inhibit purchase, the manufacturer will want to launch a campaign to correct these beliefs.[19]

An *attitude* describes a person's *enduring favorable or unfavorable cognitive evaluations, emotional feelings, and action tendencies toward some object or idea.*[20] People have attitudes toward almost everything: religion, politics, clothes, music, food, and so on. Attitudes put them into a frame of mind of liking or disliking an object, moving toward or away from it. Thus Linda Brown may hold such attitudes as, "Buy the best," "IBM makes the best computers in the world," and "Creativity and self-expression are among the most important things in life." The IBM computer is therefore salient to Linda because it fits well into her preexisting attitudes. A computer company can benefit greatly from researching the attitudes people hold toward the product and the company's brand.

Attitudes lead people to behave in a fairly consistent way toward similar objects. People do not have to interpret and react to every object in a fresh way. Attitudes economize on energy and thought. For this reason, attitudes are very difficult to change. A person's attitudes settle into a consistent pattern, and to change a single attitude may require major adjustments in other attitudes.

Thus a company would be well advised to fit its product into existing attitudes rather than to try to change people's attitudes. There are exceptions, of course, where the great cost of trying to change attitudes might pay off.

> Honda entered the motorcycle market facing a major decision. It could either sell its motorcycles to a small number of people already interested in motorcycles or try to increase the number interested in motorcycles. The latter would be more expensive because many people had negative attitudes toward motorcycles. They associated motorcycles with black leather jackets, switchblades, and crime. Honda took the second course and launched a major campaign based on the theme "You meet the nicest people on a Honda." Its campaign worked and many people adopted a new attitude toward motorcycles. ∎

We can now appreciate the many forces acting on consumer behavior. A person's purchase choice is the result of the complex interplay of cultural, social, personal, and psychological factors. Many of these factors cannot be influenced by the marketer. They are useful, however, in identifying the buyers who might have the most interest in the product. Other factors are subject to marketer influence and clue the marketer on how to develop product, price, place, and promotion to attract strong consumer response.

THE BUYING DECISION PROCESS

Marketers have to go beyond the various influences on buyers and develop an understanding of how consumers actually make their buying decisions. Marketers must identify who makes the buying decision, the type of buying decision that is involved, and the steps in the buying process.

Buying Roles

For many products, it is fairly easy to identify the buyer. Men normally choose their tobacco, and women choose their pantyhose. On the other hand, other products involve a *decision-making unit* consisting of more than one person. Consider the selection of a family automobile. The suggestion to buy a new car might come from the oldest child. A friend might advise the family on the kind of car to buy. The husband might choose the make. The wife might have definite desires regarding the car's appearance. The husband might make the final decision. The wife might end up using the car more than the husband does.

Thus we can distinguish five roles people might play in a buying decision:

□ *Initiator*: A person who first suggests the idea of buying the particular product or service
□ *Influencer*: A person whose views or advice carry some weight in making the final decision
□ *Decider*: A person who decides on any component of a buying decision: whether to buy, what to buy, how to buy, or where to buy
□ *Buyer*: The person who makes the actual purchase
□ *User*: A person who consumes or uses the product or service

A company needs to identify these roles because they have implications for designing the product, determining messages, and allocating the promotional budget. If the husband decides on the car make, then the auto company will direct advertising to reach husbands. The auto company might design certain car features to please the wife. Knowing the main participants and their roles helps the marketer fine-tune the marketing program.

Types of Buying Behavior

Consumer decision making varies with the type of buying decision. There are great differences between buying toothpaste, a tennis racket, a personal computer, and a new car. Complex and expensive purchases are likely to involve more buyer deliberation and more participants. Assael distinguished four types of consumer buying behavior based on the degree of buyer involvement and the degree of differences among brands.[21] The four types are named in Table 6-3 and described below.

Complex Buying Behavior   Consumers go through complex buying behavior when they are highly involved in a purchase and aware of significant differences among brands. Consumers are highly involved in a purchase when it is expensive, bought infrequently, risky, and highly self-expressive. Typically the consumer does not know much about the product category and has much to learn. For example, a person buying a personal computer may not even know what attributes to look for. Many of the product features carry no meaning: "16K memory," "disc storage," "screen resolution," "BASIC language," and so on.

This buyer will pass through a learning process characterized by first developing beliefs about the product, then attitudes, and then making a thoughtful purchase choice. The marketer

Table 6-3 Four Types of Buying Behavior

	High Involvement	Low Involvement
Significant Differences between Brands	Complex buying behavior	Variety-seeking buying behavior
Few Differences between Brands	Dissonance-reducing buying behavior	Habitual buying behavior

Source: Modified from Henry Assael, *Consumer Behavior and Marketing Action* (Boston: Kent Publishing Co., 1987), p. 87. Copyright © 1987 by Wadsworth, Inc. Printed by permission of Kent Publishing Co., a division of Wadsworth, Inc.

of a high-involvement product must understand the information-gathering and evaluation behavior of high-involvement consumers. The marketer needs to develop strategies that assist the buyer in learning about the attributes of the product class, their relative importance, and the high standing of the company's brand on the more important attributes. The marketer needs to differentiate the brand's features, use mainly print media and long copy to describe the brand's benefits, and motivate store sales personnel and the buyer's friends to influence the final brand choice.

Dissonance-Reducting Buying Behavior   Sometimes the consumer is highly involved in a purchase but sees little difference in the brands. The high involvement is again based on the fact that the purchase is expensive, infrequent, and risky. In this case, the buyer will shop around to learn what is available but will buy fairly quickly because brand differences are not pronounced. The buyer may respond primarily to a good price or to purchase convenience. For example, carpet buying is a high-involvement decision because it is expensive and self-expressive; yet the buyer may consider most carpeting in a given price range to be the same.

After the purchase, the consumer might experience dissonance that stems from noticing certain disquieting features of the carpet or hearing favorable things about other carpets. The consumer is alert to more information that might justify his or her decision to reduce the dissonance. In this example, the consumer first acted, then acquired some new beliefs, and ended up with a set of attitudes. Here marketing communications should aim to supply beliefs and evaluations that help the consumer feel good about his or her brand choice.

Habitual Buying Behavior   Many products are bought under conditions of low consumer involvement and the absence of significant brand differences. Consider the purchase of salt. Consumers have little involvement in this product category. They go to the store and reach for the brand. If they keep reaching for the same brand, it is out of habit, not strong brand loyalty. There is good evidence that consumers have low involvement with most low-cost, frequently purchased products.

Consumer behavior in these cases does not pass through the normal belief/attitude/behavior sequence. Consumers do not search extensively for information about the brands, evaluate their characteristics, and make a weighty decision on which brand to buy. Instead, they are passive recipients of information as they watch television or see print ads. Ad repetition creates *brand familiarity* rather than *brand conviction*. Consumers do not form a strong attitude toward a brand but select it because it is familiar. After purchase, they may not even evaluate the choice because they are not highly involved with the product. So the buying process is: brand beliefs formed by passive learning, followed by purchase behavior, which may be followed by evaluation.

Marketers of low-involvement products with few brand differences find it effective to use price and sales promotions as an incentive to product trial, since buyers are not highly committed to any brand. In advertising a low-involvement product, a number of things should be observed. The ad copy should stress only a few key points. Visual symbols and imagery are important because they can easily be remembered and associated with the brand. The ad campaigns should go for high repetition with short-duration messages. Television is more effective than print media because it is a low-involvement medium that is suitable for passive learning.[22] Advertising planning should be based on classical conditioning theory where the buyer learns to identify a certain product by a symbol that is repeatedly attached to it.

Marketers can try to convert the low-involvement product into one of higher involvement. This can be accomplished by linking the product to some involving issue, as when Crest toothpaste is linked to avoiding cavities. Or the product can be linked to some involving personal situation, for instance, by advertising a coffee brand early in the morning when the consumer wants to shake off sleepiness. Or the advertising might seek to trigger strong emotions related to personal values or ego defense. Or an important product feature might be added to a low-involvement product, such as by fortifying a plain drink with vitamins. These strategies at best raise consumer involvement from a low to a moderate level; they do not propel the consumer into highly involved buying behavior.

Variety-Seeking Buying Behavior   Some buying situations are characterized by low consumer involvement but significant brand differences. Here consumers are often observed to do a lot of brand switching. An example occurs in purchasing cookies. The consumer has some beliefs, chooses a brand of cookies without much evaluation, and evaluates it during consumption. But next time, the consumer may reach for another brand out of boredom or a wish for a different taste. Brand switching occurs for the sake of variety rather than dissatisfaction.

The marketing strategy is different for the market leader and the minor brands in this product category. The market leader will try to encourage habitual buying behavior by dominating the shelf space, avoiding out-of-stock conditions, and sponsoring frequent reminder advertising. Challenger firms will encourage variety seeking by offering lower prices, deals, coupons, free samples, and advertising that presents reasons for trying something new.

Researching the Buying Decision Process

Companies need to research the buying decision process involved in their product category. They need to ask consumers when they first became acquainted with the product category and brands, what their brand beliefs are, how involved they are with the product, how they make their brand choices, and how much satisfaction they feel after purchase.

Consumers, of course, vary in the way they buy a given product. In buying a personal computer, some consumers will spend a great deal of time seeking information and making comparisons; others will go straight to a computer store and buy any recommended brand. Thus consumers can be segmented in terms of *buying styles*—for instance, deliberate versus impulsive buyers—and different marketing strategies can be directed at each segment.

How can marketers learn about the typical stages in the buying process for any given product? They can think about their own probable behavior, although this is of limited usefulness (*introspective method*). They can interview a small number of recent purchasers, asking them to recall the events leading to the purchase of the product (*retrospective method*). They can find some consumers who are contemplating buying the product and ask them to think out loud about going through the buying process (*prospective method*). Or they can ask a group of consumers to describe the ideal way to go about buying the product (*prescriptive method*). Each method results in a consumer-generated report of the steps in the buying process.

Table 6-4 shows a retrospective report by a consumer who bought a computer. The consumer is a married male, who first got interested when his neighbor purchased a computer. He then developed reasons to justify purchasing one. A few days later, he saw an ad for an Apple computer. Two weeks later he dropped into a computer store just to browse. He liked the salesperson, felt that he could afford a computer, and purchased one. The computer did not satisfy him completely, and an ad for a competitive brand made him feel a little dissonance. He was annoyed a few days later when his salesperson did not seem very cooperative in answering some questions. The marketing analyst should collect reports from other consumers and identify one or more typical buying processes for that product.[23]

Stages in the Buying Decision Process

Based on examining many consumer reports of buying episodes, proposals have been made by consumer-behavior researchers for "stage models" of the buying process. Stage models are mostly relevant to complex decision making, i.e., buying expensive, high-involvement products. We will use the model shown in Figure 6-4, which shows the consumer as passing through five stages: *need recognition, information search, evaluation of alternatives, purchase decision*, and *postpurchase behavior*. This model emphasizes that the buying process starts long before the actual purchase and has consequences long after the purchase. It encourages the marketer to focus on the *buying process* rather than on the *purchase decision*.[24]

This model implies that consumers pass through all five stages in buying a product. We saw that this is not the case, especially in low-involvement purchases. Consumers may skip or

Table 6-4 Report of a Particular Consumer's Involvement in Buying a Computer

3/17	My neighbor just bought a computer. He says he finds it challenging. It would be nice to have a computer; I could keep my financial records on it.
3/19	Here's an ad for an Apple computer showing several applications that I would find interesting.
4/2	I don't have any plans this evening. I'll go over to Computerland and learn something about these computers.
	Here comes a salesperson.
	He's very helpful. I'm pleased that he is not pressuring me to buy one.
	I don't think I can afford a computer.
	How much would it cost a month to finance?
	I can afford it.
	My wife also wants me to buy one. I'm impressed with the Apple. I'll buy it and take it home.
4/5	I didn't realize how much time it takes to master.
	I wish the screen had eighty columns instead of forty.
4/6	Here's the new IBM advertised. It looks like it has some neat features.
4/8	My other neighbor wants to buy a computer. I told him the good and bad points about the Apple.
4/11	I phoned the computer salesperson for some information about a sticky key. He wasn't helpful. He told me to call the service department.

reverse some of these stages. Thus a woman buying her regular brand of toothpaste goes directly from the need for toothpaste to the purchase decision, skipping information search and evaluation. However, we will use the model in Figure 6-4 because it shows the full range of considerations that arise when a consumer faces a highly involving new purchase. We will allude again to Linda Brown and try to understand how she became interested in buying a personal computer and the stages she went through to make her final choice.

Need Recognition   The buying process starts when the buyer recognizes a problem or need. The buyer senses a difference between his or her actual state and a desired state. The need can be triggered by internal or external stimuli. In the former case, one of the person's normal needs—hunger, thirst, sex—rises to a threshold level and becomes a drive. From previous experience, the person has learned how to cope with this drive and is motivated toward a class of objects that will satisfy the drive.

Or a need can be aroused by an external stimulus. A person passes a bakery and sees freshly baked bread that stimulates her hunger; she admires a neighbor's new car; or she watches a television commercial advertising a Jamaican vacation. All these stimuli can trigger a problem or need.

The marketer needs to identify the circumstances that trigger a particular need. In Linda Brown's case, she might answer that her "busy season" at work had tapered off; she felt a need for a new hobby; and she was led to think of computers when a coworker bought one. By gathering information from a number of consumers, the marketer can identify the most frequent stimuli that spark an interest in a product category. The marketer can then develop marketing strategies that trigger consumer interest.

Information Search   An aroused consumer will be inclined to search for more information. We can distinguish between two levels. The milder search state is called *heightened attention*. Here Linda Brown simply becomes more receptive to information about computers. She pays attention to computer ads, computers purchased by friends, and conversation about computers.

Or Linda may go into *active information search* where she looks for reading material, phones friends, and engages in other search activities to learn about computers. How much search she undertakes depends upon the strength of her drive, the amount of information she initially has, the ease of obtaining additional information, the value she places on additional information, and the satisfaction she gets from search. Normally the amount of consumer search activity increases as the consumer moves from situations of *limited problem solving* to *extensive problem solving*.

Of key interest to the marketer are the major information sources that the consumer will turn to and the relative influence each will have on the subsequent purchase decision. *Consumer information sources fall into four groups*:

☐ Personal sources: Family, friends, neighbors, acquaintances

☐ *Commercial sources*: Advertising, salespersons, dealers, packaging, displays

☐ *Public sources*: Mass media, consumer-rating organizations

FIGURE 6-4
Five-Stage Model of the Buying Process

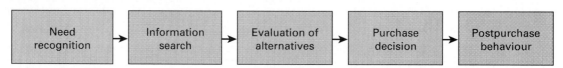

☐ *Experiential sources*: Handling, examining, using the product

The relative amount and influence of these information sources varies with the product category and the buyer's characteristics. Generally speaking, the consumer receives the most information exposure about a product from commercial sources, that is, marketer-dominated sources. On the other hand, the most effective exposures come from personal sources. Each information source performs a somewhat different function in influencing the buying decision. Commercial information normally performs an informing function, and personal sources perform a legitimizing and/or evaluation function. For example, physicians often learn of new drugs from commercial sources but turn to other doctors for evaluation information.

Through gathering information, the consumer learns about competing brands and their features. The first box in Figure 6-5 shows the *total set* of brands available to the consumer. Linda Brown will become acquainted with only a subset of these brands, the *awareness set*. A few of these brands will meet Linda's initial buying criteria and make up the *consideration set*. As Linda gathers more information, only a few will remain as strong choices and make up the *choice set*. The brands in the choice set might all be acceptable. Linda makes her final choice from this set.[25]

The practical implication is that a company must develop a strategy to get its brand into the prospect's awareness set, consideration set, and choice set. Otherwise the company has lost its opportunity to sell to the customer. The company must go further and learn which other brands remain in the consumer's choice set so that it knows its competition and can plan its appeals.

As for the consumer's information sources, the marketer should identify them and evaluate their relative importance. Consumers should be asked how they first heard about the brand, what information came in later, and the relative importance of the different information sources. The answers will help the company prepare effective communications for the target market.

Evaluation of Alternatives   How does the consumer process the information about brand choices to make the final choice? It turns out that there is no simple and single evaluation process used by all consumers or even by one consumer in all buying situations. There are several decision evaluation processes. Most current models of the consumer evaluation process are cognitively oriented—that is, they see the consumer as forming product judgments largely on a conscious and rational basis.

Certain basic concepts will help us understand consumer evaluation processes. We see the consumer as trying to satisfy some *need*. The consumer is looking for certain *benefits* from the product solution. The consumer sees each product as a *bundle of attributes* with varying capabilities of delivering the sought benefits and satisfying this need. The attributes of interest to buyers in some familiar product classes are the following.

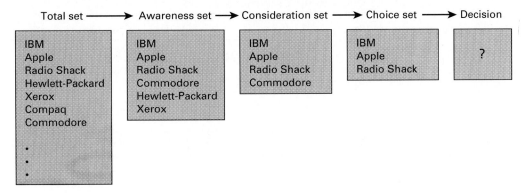

FIGURE 6-5
Successive Sets Involved in Consumer Decision Making

Total set ⟶ Awareness set ⟶ Consideration set ⟶ Choice set ⟶ Decision

Total set	Awareness set	Consideration set	Choice set	Decision
IBM	IBM	IBM	IBM	?
Apple	Apple	Apple	Apple	
Radio Shack	Radio Shack	Radio Shack	Radio Shack	
Hewlett-Packard	Commodore	Commodore		
Xerox	Hewlett-Packard			
Compaq	Xerox			
Commodore				
.				
.				
.				

- □ *Cameras*: Picture sharpness, camera speeds, camera size, price
- □ *Hotels*: Location, cleanliness, atmosphere, cost
- □ *Mouthwash*: Color, effectiveness, germ-killing capacity, price, taste/flavor
- □ *Tires*: Safety, tread life, ride quality, price

Consumers will differ as to which product attributes are seen as relevant or salient. They will pay the most attention to the ones that will deliver the sought benefits. The market for a product can often be segmented according to the attributes that are salient to different consumer groups.

The most salient attributes may not be the most important ones. Some may be salient, because the consumer was recently exposed to an ad mentioning them, hence making these attributes "top-of-the-mind." Furthermore, nonsalient attributes might include some that the consumer forgot but whose importance would be recognized when mentioned. Marketers should be more concerned with the importance of attributes than with their salience. They should measure the *importance weights* that consumers attach to the various attributes.[26]

The consumer is likely to develop a set of *brand beliefs* about where each brand stands on each attribute. The brand beliefs make up the *brand image*. The consumer's brand beliefs will vary with his or her experiences and the effect of selective perception, selective distortion, and selective retention.

The consumer is assumed to establish her overall satisfaction or *utility* for a brand according to her *utility function*,[27] which determines how satisfaction varies with different levels of each attribute. For example, Linda Brown's satisfaction may increase with a computer's memory capacity, graphics capability, and software availability; and decrease with its price. If we combine the attribute levels where the utilities are highest, they make up Linda's ideal computer. The expected utility from actual computers in the marketplace will be less than the maximum utility that would be derived from an ideal computer.

The consumer arrives at attitudes (judgments, preferences) toward the brand alternatives through some *evaluation procedure*. Consumers have been found to apply different evaluation procedures to make a choice among multiattribute objects.[28]

We will illustrate these concepts in connection with Linda Brown's purchase of a computer. Suppose she has narrowed her choice set to four computers (A, B, C, D). Assume that she is interested in four attributes: memory capacity, graphics capability, software availability, and price. Table 6-5 shows her beliefs about how each brand rates on the four attributes. Linda rates brand A as follows: memory capacity, 10 on a 10-point scale; graphics capability, 8; software availability, 6; and price, 4 (somewhat expensive). Similarly, she has beliefs about how the other three computers rate on these attributes. The marketer would like to be able to predict which computer Linda will buy.

Table 6-5 A Consumer's Brand Beliefs about Computers

Computer	Attribute			
	Memory Capacity	Graphics Capability	Software Availability	Price
A	10	8	6	4
B	8	9	8	3
C	6	8	10	5
D	4	3	7	8

Note: Each attribute is rated from 0 to 10, where 10 represents the highest level on that attribute. Price, however, is indexed in a reverse manner, with a 10 representing the lowest price, since a consumer prefers a low price to a high price.

Clearly, if one computer dominated the others on all the criteria, we could predict that Linda would choose it. But her choice set consists of brands that vary in their appeal. If Linda wants the best memory capacity, she should buy A; if she wants the best graphics capability, she should buy B; if she wants the best software availability, she should buy C; if she wants the lowest-price computer, she should buy D. Some buyers will buy on only one attribute, and we can easily predict their choice.

Most buyers will consider several attributes but place different weights on them. If we knew the importance weights that Linda Brown attached to the four attributes, we could more reliably predict her computer choice.

Suppose Linda assigned 40 percent of the importance to the computer's memory capacity, 30 percent to its graphics capability, 20 percent to its software availability, and 10 percent to its price. To find Linda's perceived value for each computer, her weights are multiplied by her beliefs about each computer. This leads to the following perceived values:

$$\text{Computer A} = 0.4(10) + 0.3(8) + 0.2(6) + 0.1(8) = 8.0$$

$$\text{Computer B} = 0.4(8) + 0.3(9) + 0.2(8) + 0.1(3) = 7.8$$

$$\text{Computer C} = 0.4(6) + 0.3(8) + 0.2(10) + 0.1(5) = 7.3$$

$$\text{Computer D} = 0.4(4) + 0.3(3) + 0.2(7) + 0.1(8) = 4.7$$

We would predict that Linda will favor computer A.

This model is called the *expectancy-value model* of consumer choice.[29] It is one of several possible models describing how consumers go about evaluating alternatives. (See the appendix to this chapter for a technical description of alternative consumer decision models).

Suppose most computer buyers say they form their preferences using the expectancy-value process described above. Knowing this, a computer manufacturer can do a number of things to influence buyer decisions. The marketer of computer C, for example, could apply the following strategies to influence people like Linda Brown to show a greater interest in brand C:

☐ *Modify the computer*: The marketer could redesign brand C so that it offers more memory or other characteristics that the buyer desires. This is called *real repositioning*.

☐ *Alter beliefs about the brand*: The marketer could try to alter buyers' beliefs about where his brand stands on key attributes. This tactic is especially recommended if buyers underestimate brand C's qualities. It is not recommended if buyers are accurately evaluating brand C; exaggerated claims would lead to buyer dissatisfaction and bad word of mouth. Attempting to alter beliefs about the brand is called *psychological repositioning*.

☐ *Alter beliefs about the competitors' brands*: The marketer could try to change buyers' beliefs about where competitive brands stand on different attributes. That would make sense where buyers mistakenly believe a competitor's brand has more quality than it actually has. It is called *competitive depositioning* and is often accomplished by running a comparison ad.

☐ *Alter the importance weights*: The marketer could try to persuade buyers to attach more importance to the attributes in which the brand excels. The marketer of brand C can tout the benefits of choosing a computer with great software availability, since C is superior in this attribute.

☐ *Call attention to neglected attributes*: The marketer could draw the buyer's attention to neglected attributes. If brand C is a highy portable computer, the marketer might tout the benefit of portability.

☐ *Shift the buyer's ideals*: The marketer could try to persuade buyers to change their ideal levels for one or more attributes. The marketer of brand C might try to convince buyers that computers with a large memory are more complex and that a moderate-size memory is more desirable.[30]

Purchase Decision   In the evaluation stage, the consumer forms preferences among the brands in the choice set. The consumer may also form a purchase intention to buy the most preferred brand. However, two factors can intervene between the purchase intention and the purchase decision. These factors are shown in Figure 6-6.[31]

The first factor is the *attitudes of others*. Suppose Linda Brown's husband feels strongly that Linda should buy the lowest-priced computer (D). As a result, Linda's "purchase probability" for computer A will be somewhat reduced and for computer D will be somewhat increased. The extent to which another person's attitude reduces one's preferred alternative depends upon two things: (1) the intensity of the other person's negative attitude toward the consumer's preferred alternative and (2) the consumer's motivation to comply with the other person's wishes.[32] The more intense the other person's negativism, and the closer the other person is to the consumer, the more the consumer will adjust his or her purchase intention. The converse is also true: A buyer's preference for a brand will increase if someone he or she likes favors the same brand. The influence of others becomes complex when several people close to the buyer hold contradictory opinions and the buyer would like to please them all.

Purchase intention is also influenced by *unanticipated situational factors*. The consumer forms a purchase intention on the basis of such factors as expected family income, expected price, and expected product benefits. When the consumer is about to act, *unanticipated situational factors* may erupt to change the purchase intention. Linda Brown might lose her job, some other purchase might become more urgent, a friend might report disappointment in that computer brand, or a store salesperson may affect her negatively. Thus preferences and even purchase intentions are not completely reliable predictors of purchase behavior.

A consumer's decision to modify, postpone, or avoid a purchase decision is heavily influenced by *perceived risk*. Expensive purchases involve some *risk taking*.[33] Consumers cannot be certain about the purchase outcome. This produces anxiety. The amount of perceived risk varies with the amount of money at stake, the amount of attribute uncertainty, and the amount of consumer self-confidence. A consumer develops certain routines for reducing risk, such as decision avoidance, information gathering from friends, and preference for national brand names and warranties. The marketer must understand the factors that provoke a feeling of risk in consumers and provide information and support that will reduce the perceived risk.

A consumer who decides to execute a purchase intention will be making up to five *purchase subdecisions*. Thus Linda Brown will make a *brand decision* (brand A), vendor decision (dealer 2), *quantity decision* (one computer), *timing decision* (weekend), and *payment-method decision* (credit card). On the other hand, purchases of everyday products

FIGURE 6-6
Steps between Evaluation of Alternatives and a Purchase Decision

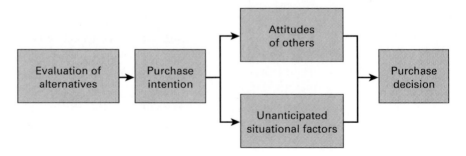

involve fewer decisions and less buyer deliberation. In buying sugar, Linda gives little thought to the vendor or payment method. We deliberately chose a product that involved extensive problem solving—here personal computers—to illustrate the full range of behavior that might arise in buying something.

Postpurchase Behavior   After purchasing the product, the consumer will experience some level of satisfaction or dissatisfaction. The consumer will also engage in postpurchase actions and product uses of interest to the marketer. The marketer's job does not end when the product is bought but continues into the postpurchase period.

Postpurchase Satisfaction   After purchasing a product, a consumer may detect a flaw. Some buyers will not want the flawed product, others will be indifferent to the flaw, and some may even see the flaw as enhancing the value of the product.[34] Some flaws can be dangerous to consumers. Companies making automobiles, toys, and pharmaceuticals must quickly recall any product that has the slightest chance of injuring users.

What determines whether the buyer will be highly satisfied, somewhat satisfied, or dissatisfied with a purchase? The buyer's satisfaction is a function of the closeness between the buyer's product *expectations* and the product's *perceived performance*.[35] If the product's performance falls short of customer expectations, the customer is disappointed; if it meets expectations, the customer is satisfied; if it exceeds expectations, the customer is delighted. These feelings make a difference in whether the customer buys the product again and talks favorably or unfavorably about the product to others.

Consumers form their expectations on the basis of received messages from sellers, friends, and other information sources. If the seller exaggerates the benefits, consumers will experience *disconfirmed expectations*, which lead to dissatisfaction. The larger the gap between expectations and performance, the greater the consumer's dissatisfaction. Here the consumer's coping style comes into play. Some consumers magnify the gap when the product is not perfect, and they are highly dissatisfied. Other consumers minimize the gap and are less dissatisfied.[36]

This theory suggests that the seller must make product claims that faithfully represent the product's likely performance so that buyers experience satisfaction. Some sellers might even understate performance levels so that consumers experience higher-than-expected satisfaction with the product.

Festinger and Bramel believe that most nonroutine purchases will involve some postpurchase dissonance:

> When a person chooses between two or more alternatives, discomfort or dissonance will almost inevitably arise because of the person's knowledge that while the decision he has made has certain advantages, it also has some disadvantages. That dissonance arises after almost every decision, and further, the individual will invariably take steps to reduce this dissonance.[37]

Postpurchase Actions   The consumer's satisfaction or dissatisfaction with the product will influence subsequent behavior. If the consumer is satisfied, then he or she will exhibit a higher probability of purchasing the product again.

> Data on automobile brand choice show a high correlation between being *highly satisfied* with the last brand bought and the intention to rebuy the brand. For example, 75 percent of Toyota buyers were highly satisfied and about 75 percent intended to buy a Toyota again; 35 percent of Chevrolet buyers were highly satisfied and about 35 percent intended to buy a Chevrolet again.   ■

The satisfied customer will also tend to say good things about the brand to others. Marketers say: "Our best advertisement is a satisfied customer."[38]

A dissatisifed consumer responds differently. The dissatisfied consumer will try to reduce the dissonance because a human being strives "to establish internal harmony, consistency, or congruity among his opinions, knowledge, and values."[39] Dissonant consumers will resort to one or two courses of action. They may try to reduce the dissonance by *abandoning* or *returning* the product, or they may try to reduce the dissonance by seeking information that might *confirm* its high value (or avoiding information that might confirm its low value). In the case of Linda Brown, she might return the computer, or she might seek information that would make her feel better about the computer.

Marketers should be aware of the full range of ways consumers handle dissatisfaction (see Figure 6-7). Consumers have a choice between taking and not taking any action. If the former, they can take public action or private action. Public actions include complaining to the company, going to a lawyer, or complaining to other groups that might help the buyer get satisfaction, such as business, private, or government agencies. Or the buyer might simply stop buying the product, utilizing the *exit option*. Alternatively, the consumer may choose to use the *voice option*.[40] In all these cases, the seller loses something in having done a poor job of satisfying the customer.[41]

Marketers can take steps to minimize the amount of consumer postpurchase dissatisfaction. Computer companies can send a letter to new computer owners congratulating them on having selected a fine computer. They can place ads showing satisfied brand owners. They can solicit customer suggestions for improvements and list the location of available services. They can write instruction booklets that are dissonance reducing. They can send owners a magazine containing articles describing new computer applications. Postpurchase communications to buyers have been shown to result in fewer product returns and order cancellations.[42] In addition, they can provide good channels for customer complaints and for speedy redress of customer grievances. In general, marketers should provide consumers with maximum channels for venting complaints to the company. Smart marketers will welcome customer feedback as a way to continually improve their offer and performance.

FIGURE 6-7
How Customers Handle
Dissatisfaction

Source: Ralph L. Day and E. Laird Landon, Jr., "Toward a Theory of Consumer Complaining Behavior," in *Consumer and Industrial Buying Behavior*, ed. Arch G. Woodside, Jagdish N. Sheth, and Peter D. Bennett (New York: Elsevier North-Holland, 1977), p. 432.

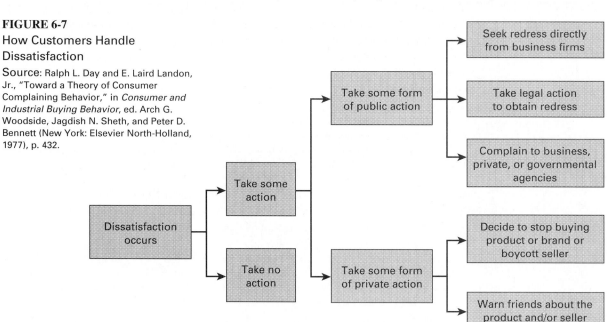

FIGURE 6-8
How Customers Use or Dispose of Products

Source: Jacob Jacoby, Carol K. Berning, and Thomas F. Dietvorst,
"What about Disposition?" *Journal of Marketing*, July 1977, p. 23.

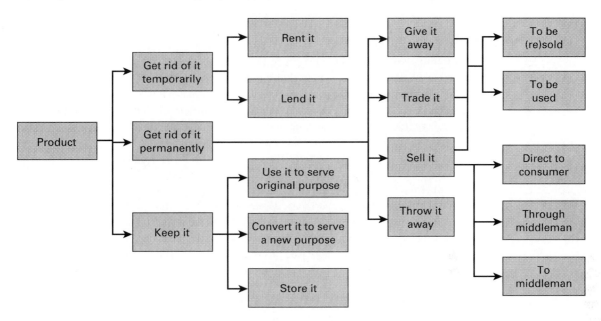

Postpurchase Use and Disposal Marketers should also monitor how the buyers use and dispose of the product (see Figure 6-8). If consumers find a new use for the product, that should interest the marketer because this use can be advertised. If consumers store the product in their closet, that indicates that the product is not very satisfying, and word of mouth would not be strong. If they sell or trade the product, new-product sales will be depressed. If they throw the product away, the marketer needs to study how they dispose of it, especially if it can hurt the environment, as is the case with beverage containers and disposable diapers. All said, the marketer needs to study product use and disposal for clues to possible problems and opportunities.[43]

Understanding consumer needs and buying processes is essential to building effective marketing strategies. By understanding how buyers go through need recognition, information search, evaluation of alternatives, the purchase decision, and postpurchase behavior, marketers can pick up clues as to how to meet buyer needs. By understanding the various participants in the buying process and the major influences on their buying behavior, marketers can design effective marketing programs for their target markets.

SUMMARY

Consumer markets and consumer buying behavior have to be understood before sound marketing plans can be developed.

The consumer market buys goods and services for personal consumption. It is the ultimate market for which economic activities are organized. The market consists of many submarkets, such as French-Canadians, teenage-students, and older consumers. In analyzing a consumer market, one needs to know the occupants, the objects, and the buyers' objectives, organization, operations, occasions, and outlets.

The buyer's behavior is influenced by four major factors: cultural (culture, subculture, and social class), social (reference groups, family, and roles and statuses), personal (age and life-cycle stage, occupation, economic circumstances, lifestyle, and personality and self-concept), and psychological (motivation, perception, learning, and beliefs and attitudes). All of these provide clues as to how to reach and serve buyers more effectively.

Before planning its marketing, a company needs to identify its target consumers and their decision processes. While many buying decisions involve only one decision maker, other decisions may involve several participants, who play such roles as initiator, influencer, decider, buyer, and user. The marketer's job is to identify the other buying participants, their buying criteria, and their influence on the buyer. The marketing program should be designed to appeal to and reach the other key participants as well as the buyer.

The amount of buying deliberateness and the number of buying participants increase with the complexity of the buying situation. Marketers must plan differently for four types of consumer buying behavior: complex buying behavior, dissonance-reducing buying behavior, habitual buying behavior, and variety-seeking buying behavior. These four types are based on whether the consumer has high or low involvement in the purchase and whether brands exhibit many or few significant differences.

In complex buying behavior, the buyer goes through a decision process consisting of need recognition, information search, evaluation of alternatives, purchase decision, and postpurchase behavior. The marketer's job is to understand the buyer's behavior at each stage and what influences are operating. This understanding allows the marketer to develop an effective and efficient marketing program for the target market.

■ QUESTIONS

1. Discuss and compare marketing applications of the following: (a) demographics; (b) psychographics; (c) culture and subculture; (d) social class. How would the first two differ from the last two?

2. Using the model of buyer behavior (Figure 6-1) in the chapter, show how the model explains the following consumer behaviors: (a) bird's nest soup made from dried bird spittle is not generally viewed as a delicacy in Canada but honey, which is regurgitated nectar, is highly esteemed; (b) some consumers shop in a broad variety of stores while others stick to a few known stores; (c) some products are purchased after extensive searching, others are bought at a moment's notice; (d) two people are exposed to the same ad—one notices and processes the ad, the other is unaware of its existence.

3. Some car companies are trying to design "chameleon cars," or cars that will change "personality" to fit the personality of the consumer who is using the car. In what ways can a car adapt to its driver, and will consumers desire such a feature?

4. Although technological advances have resulted in "better sound for less money" for home audio equipment, the fastest-growing segment of the market is the "high-end"—the most-expensive equipment. What explains this phenomenon?

5. Some marketers are studying consumer behavior by using a form of ethnographic research—observing the behavior of consumers in their own homes. How might such an approach provide more valuable insights to consumer behavior than survey methods? Give three examples of products that might benefit from such research, citing specific observational techniques to be used.

6. Many marketers use taste tests to help predict the behavior of consumers regarding a new food product. What are some of the dangers of using taste-test information as a predictor of consumer behavior?

7. "A person will tend to buy the brand in the product class whose image is most congruent with his or her self-image." Is a person's self-image a highly reliable predictor of his or her brand choice?

8. Identify who played each of the five buying roles in your choice of a university. How would the knowledge of these roles influence the university's marketing strategy?

9. Your friend plans to buy a new car. He prefers foreign makes and his choice has narrowed down to Volkswagen, Toyota, and Volvo. He looks for three things in a car: economy, quality, and roominess, and he values them at .5, .3, and .2, respectively. On a scale of 1-10 (10 being best), he rates Volkswagen at 8, 8, and 2 on the three attributes; Toyota, 3, 5, 9; and Volvo, 5, 8, 7. Predict which car he is most likely to buy and which least likely to buy if he evaluates cars according to the expectancy-value model. Which attribute change has potentially the biggest impact on the overall evaluation of Toyota's product? What strategies might Toyota use to influence consumer choice of its product?

10. Suppose Linda Brown, the consumer discussed in this chapter, purchased a personal computer. How might her information search for computer software change over time as she gains more experience and knowledge. (Hint: consider Figures 6-4 and 6-5.)

11. Outline the successive steps potential buyers of paint might go through in making a purchase decision. Indicate how a paint company such as Glidden can determine at which points in the decision process the company's advertising might favorably influence its share of market.

12. Describe the consumer market for briefcases, using the "Seven Os" framework described in this chapter.

■ NOTES

1. See *Canadian Social Trends*, Statistics Canada, Winter 1990, p. 31; also *Canada Yearbook* 1986, Statistics Canada (Supply and Services Canada) 5-34.

2. On young urban professionals, see Stephen Kindel, "The Last Yuppie Story You Will Ever Have to Read," *Forbes*, February 25, 1985, pp. 134-36; and Stewart Alter, "Yuppie Pursuit: It's Too Trivial for Marketers," *Advertising Age*, July 18, 1985, p. 3; on women, see "Special Report: Marketing to Women," *Advertising Age*, April 2, 1984, pp. 9-36; and Alladi Venkatesh, "Changing Roles of Women: A Life-Style Analysis," *Journal of Consumer Behavior*, September 1980, pp. 189-97.

3. See Leon G. Schiffman and Leslie Lazar Kanuk, *Consumer Behavior*, 3rd ed. (Englewood Cliffs, N.J.: Prentice-Hall, 1987), pp. 495-503.

4. See Donald W. Hendon, "A New Empirical Look at the Influence of Reference Groups on Generic Product Category and Brand Choice: Evidence from Two Nations," in *Proceedings of the Academy of International Business: Asia-Pacific Dimension of International Business* (Honolulu: College of Business Administration, University of Hawaii, December 18-20, 1979), pp. 752-61.

5. See Linda L. Price and Lawrence F. Feick, "The Role of Interpersonal Sources in External Search: An Informational Perspective," in *Advances in Consumer Research*, vol. 11, ed. Thomas C. Kinnear (Ann Arbor, Mich.: Association for Consumer Research, 1984), p. 250; and David Brinberg and Linda Plimpton, "Self-Monitoring and Product Conspicuousness on Reference Group Influence," in *Advances in Consumer Research*, vol. 13, ed. Richard Lutz (1986), pp. 297-300.

6. See George Moschis, "The Role of Family Communication in Consumer Socialization of Children and Adolescents," *Journal of Consumer Research*, March 1985, pp. 898-913.

7. See Rosann L. Spiro, "Persuasion in Family Decision Making," *Journal of Consumer Research*, March 1983, pp. 393-402; Lawrence H. Wortzel, "Marital Roles and Typologies as Predictors of Purchase Decision Making for Everyday Household Products: Suggestions for Research," in *Advances in Consumer Research*, vol. 7, ed. Jerry C. Olson (1980), pp. 212-15.

8. See Harry L. Davis, "Dimensions of Marital Roles in Consumer Decision-Making," *Journal of Marketing Research*, May 1970, pp. 168-77.

9. See "Flaunting Wealth: It's Back in Style," *U.S. News & World Report*, September 21, 1981, pp. 61-64; John Brooks, *Showing Off in America: From Conspicuous Consumption to Parody Display* (Boston: Little, Brown, 1978).

10. See Lawrence Lepisto, "A Life Span Perspective of Consumer Behavior," in *Advances in Consumer Research*, ed. Elizabeth Hirshman and Morris Holbrook, vol. 12 (Provo, Utah: Association for Consumer Research, 1985), p. 47.

11. Sidney J. Levy, "Symbolism and Life Style," in *Toward Scientific Marketing*, ed. Stephen A. Greyser (Chicago: American Marketing Association, 1964), pp. 140-50.

12. Harper W. Boyd, Jr., and Sidney J. Levy, *Promotion: A Behavioral View* (Englewood Cliffs, N.J.: Prentice-Hall, 1967), p. 38.

13. See Harold H. Kassarjian and Mary Jane Sheffet, "Personality and Consumer Behavior: An Update," in *Perspectives in Consumer Behavior*, ed. Harold H. Kassarjian and Thomas S. Robertson (Glenview, Ill.: Scott, Foresman, 1981), pp. 160-80.

14. See M. Joseph Sirgy, "Self-Concept in Consumer Behavior: A Critical Review, *Journal of Consumer Research*, December 1982, pp. 287-300.

15. See Dichter, *Handbook of Consumer Motivations* (New York: McGraw-Hill, 1964).

16. Maslow, *Motivation and Personality* (New York: Harper & Row, 1954, pp. 80-106.

17. See Herzberg, *Work and the Nature of Man* (Cleveland: William Collins, 1966); and Henk Thierry and Agnes M. Koopman-Iwerna, "Motivation and Satisfaction," in *Handbook of Work and Organizational Psychology*," ed. P. J. Drenth (New York: John Wiley, 1984), pp. 141-42.

18. Bernard Berelson and Gary A. Steiner, *Human Behavior: An Inventory of Scientific Findings* (New York: Harcourt Brace Jovanovich, 1964), p. 88.

19. See Alice M. Tybout, Bobby J. Calder, and Brian Sternthal, "Using Information Processing Theory to Design Marketing Strategies," *Journal of Marketing Research*, February 1981, pp. 73-79.

20. See David Krech, Richard S. Crutchfield, and Egerton L. Ballachey, *Individual in Society* (New York: McGraw-Hill, 1962), Chap. 2.

21. See Henry Assael, *Consumer Behavior and Marketing Action* (Boston: Kent, 1987), Chap. 4 for a full discussion of these four types of consumer buying behavior. An earlier classification of three types of consumer buying behavior—extensive problem solving, limited problem solving, and routinized response behavior—is found in John A. Howard and Jagdish N. Sheth, *The Theory of Buyer Behavior* (New York: John Wiley, 1969), pp. 27-28.

22. Herbert E. Krugman, "The Impact of Television Advertising: Learning without Involvement," *Public Opinion Quarterly*, Fall 1965, pp. 349-56.

23. See James R. Bettman, *Information Processing Theory of Consumer Behavior* (Reading, Mass.: Addison-Wesley, 1979).

24. Marketing scholars have developed several models of the consumer buying process. The most prominent models are those of John A. Howard and Jagdish N. Sheth, *The Theory of Buyer Behavior* (New York: John Wiley, 1969); Francesco M. Nicosia, *Consumer Decision Processes* (Englewood Cliffs, N.J.: Prentice-Hall, 1966); and James F. Engel, Roger D. Blackwell, and Paul W. Miniard, *Consumer Behavior*, 5th ed. (New York: Holt, Rinehart & Winston, 1986).

25. Originally, Howard and Sheth suggested the term "evoked set" to describe the set of alternatives that the buyer considers. (See their *Theory of Buyer Behavior*, p. 26). We believe that the set of brands of interest to the consumer keeps changing as information comes in, and it is more useful to distinguish different sets as he or she goes through the buying decision process. See Chem L. Narayana and Rom J. Markin, "Consumer Behavior and Product Performance: An Alternative Conceptualization," *Journal of Marketing*, October 1975, pp. 1-6.

26. James H. Myers and Mark, L. Alpert, "Semantic Confusion in Attitude Research: Salience vs. Importance vs. Determinance," in *Advances in Consumer Research*, Proceedings of the Seventh Annual Conference of the Association of Consumer Research, October 1976, pp 106-10.

27. Some progress has been made in attempting to measure individual and market utility functions. See Table 12-2.

28. See Paul E. Green and Yoram Wind, *Multiattribute Decisions in Marketing: A Measurement Approach* (Hinsdale, Ill.: Dryden Press, 1973), Chap. 2; Leigh McAlister, "Choosing Multiple Items from a Product Class," *Journal of Consumer Research*, December 1979, pp. 213-24.

29. This model was developed by Martin Fishbein in "Attitudes and Prediction of Behavior," in *Readings in Attitude Theory and Measurement*, ed. Martin Fishbein (New York: John Wiley, 1967), pp. 477-92. For a critical review of this model, see Paul W. Miniard and Joel B. Cohen, "An Examination of the Fishbein-Ajzen Behavioral-Intentions Model's Concepts and Measures, *Journal of Experimental Social Psychology*, May 1981, pp. 309-39.

30. See Harper W. Boyd, Jr., Michael L. Ray, and Edward C. Strong, "An Attitudinal Framework for Advertising Strategy," *Journal of Marketing*, April 1972, pp. 27-33; and Richard E. Petty and John T. Cacioppo, *Attitudes and Persuasion: Classic and Contemporary Approaches* (Dubuque, Iowa: W. C. Brown Co., 1981), pp. 60-86.

31. See Jagdish N. Sheth, "An Investigation of Relationships among Evaluative Beliefs, Affect, Behavioral Intention, and Behavior," in *Consumer Behavior: Theory and Application*, ed. John U. Farley, John A. Howard, and L. Winston Ring (Boston: Allyn & Bacon, 1974), pp. 89-114.

32. See Fishbein, "Attitudes and Prediction."

33. See Raymond A. Bauer, "Consumer Behavior as Risk Taking," in *Risk Taking and Information Handling in Consumer Behavior*, ed. Donald F. Cox (Boston: Division of Research, Harvard Business School, 1967); James W. Taylor, "The Role of Risk in Consumer Behavior," *Journal of Marketing*, April 1974, pp. 54-60; and Arniram Gafin and George W. Torrance, "Risk Attitude and Time Preference in Health," *Management Science*, April 1981, pp. 440-51.

34. See Philip Kotler and Murali K. Mantrala, "Flawed Products: Consumer Responses and Marketer Strategies," *Journal of Consumer Marketing*, Summer 1985, pp. 27-36.

35. See Priscilla A. La Barbera and David Mazursky, "A Longitudinal Assessment of Consumer Satisfaction/ Dissatisfaction: The Dynamic Aspect of the Cognitive Process," *Journal of Marketing Research*, November 1983, pp. 393-404.

36. See Ralph L. Day, Modeling Choices among Alternative Responses to Dissatisfaction," in *Advances in Consumer Research*, vol. 11 (1984), pp. 496-99.

37. Leon Festinger and Dana Bramel, "The Reactions of Humans to Cognitive Dissonance," in *Experimental Foundations of Clinical Psychology*, ed. Arthur J. Bachrach (New York: Basic Books, 1962), pp. 251-62.

38. See Barry L. Bayus, "Word of Mouth: The Indirect Effects of Marketing Efforts," *Journal of Advertising Research*, June/July 1985, pp. 31-39.

39. Leon Festinger, A Theory of Cognitive Dissonance (Stanford, Calif.: Stanford University Press, 1957), p. 260; Everett M. Rogers, *Diffusion of Innovations* (New York: Free Press, 1983), pp. 185-88.

40. See Albert O. Hirschman, *Exit, Voice, and Loyalty* (Cambridge, Mass.: Harvard University Press, 1970).

41. See Mary C. Gilly and Richard W. Hansen, "Consumer Complaint Handling as a Strategic Marketing Tool," *Journal of Consumer Marketing*, Fall 1985, pp. 5-16.

42. See James H. Donnelly, Jr., and John M. Ivancevich, "Post-Purchase Reinforcement and Back-Out Behavior," *Journal of Marketing Research*, August 1970, pp. 399-400.

43. See Jacob Jacoby, Carol K. Berning, and Thomas F. Dietvorst, "What about Disposition?" *Journal of Marketing*, July 1977, p. 23.

appendix

SOME ALTERNATIVE DECISION PROCESSES USED BY CONSUMERS TO EVALUATE ALTERNATIVE BRANDS

The text described the *expectancy-value model* of how consumers might evaluate alternatives. It can be stated more formally as follows:

$$A_{jk} = \sum_{i=1}^{n} W_{ik} B_{ijk} \qquad (6\text{-}1)$$

where:

A_{jk} = consumer k's attitude score for brand j

W_{ik} = the importance weight assigned by consumer k to attribute i

B_{ijk} = consumer k's belief as to the amount of attribute i offered by brand j

n = the number of important attributes in the selection of a given brand

Essentially, a consumer's beliefs about a brand's attributes are multiplied by the respective importance weights and summed to derive an attitude score. Here are some other models.

Ideal-Brand Model   This model says that a consumer compares actual brands to her ideal brand. The closer an actual brand comes to this ideal, the more it will be preferred.

Suppose Linda Brown does not value memory capacity beyond a certain point because she has no use for it, and it adds to cost. And suppose she has a certain price in mind as ideal. Suppose her ideal levels of the four attributes are not (10, 10, 10, 10) as in the expectancy value model but (6, 10, 10, 5). We would calculate how dissatisfied she would be with each brand according to the formula

$$D_{jk} = \sum_{i=1}^{n} W_{ik} \left| B_{ijk} - I_{ik} \right| \qquad (6\text{-}2)$$

where D_{jk} is consumer k's *dissatisfaction* with brand j, and I_{ik} is consumer k's *ideal ideal level* of attribute i. Other terms remain the same. The lower the D, the more favorable consumer k's *attitude* toward brand j. For example, if a brand was ideal, the term $\left| B_{ijk} - I_{jk} \right|$ would disappear, and the dissatisfaction would be zero. Here is Linda Brown's dissatisfaction score with each brand:

Computer A $= 0.4 \left| 10 - 6 \right| + 0.3 \left| 8 - 10 \right| + 0.2 \left| 6 - 10 \right| + 0.1 \left| 4 - 5 \right| = 3.1$

Computer B $= 0.4 \left| 8 - 6 \right| + 0.3 \left| 9 - 10 \right| + 0.2 \left| 8 - 10 \right| + 0.1 \left| 3 - 5 \right| = 1.7$

Computer C $= 0.4 \left| 6 - 6 \right| + 0.3 \left| 8 - 10 \right| + 0.2 \left| 10 - 10 \right| + 0.1 \left| 5 - 5 \right| = 0.6$

Computer D $= 0.4 \left| 4 - 6 \right| + 0.3 \left| 3 - 10 \right| + 0.2 \left| 7 - 10 \right| + 0.1 \left| 8 - 5 \right| = 3.8$

In this case, Linda Brown would have the strongest preference (i.e., least dissatisfaction) with computer C.

To use the ideal-brand model, the marketer would interview a sample of buyers and ask them to describe their ideal brand. The marketer will obtain three classes of response. Some consumers will have clear pictures of their ideal brand. Other consumers will mention two or more ideals that would satisfy them. The remaining consumers will have trouble defining an ideal brand and would find a wide range of brands equally acceptable.

Conjunctive Model   Some consumers will evaluate alternatives by establishing minimum attribute levels that acceptable brands must possess. They will consider only the brands that exhibit a *conjunction* of all the minimum requirements. Thus Linda Brown might consider only computers that score better than (7, 6, 7, 2) on memory, graphics, software, and price, respectively. These cutoffs eliminate brands A, C, D from further consideration. Conjunctive evaluation in the extreme could eliminate all brands. A consumer might not purchase any computer because no brand meets his or her minimal requirements. Note that conjunctive evaluation does not pay attention to how high an attribute level is as long as it exceeds the minimum. A high level of one attribute does not compensate for a below-minimum level of another attribute.

Disjunctive Model   Linda Brown might want to consider only computers that exceed specified levels on one or a few attributes, regardless of their standing on the other attributes. She might decide that she will consider only computers that have strong memory (> 9) *or* graphics (> 9). According to Table 6-5, Linda is left with computers A and B as choices. The model is noncompensatory in that high scores on the other variables have no bearing on keeping them in the choice set.

Lexicographic Model   Another noncompensatory process occurs if Linda Brown arranges the attributes in order of importance and compares the brands on the first important attribute. If one brand is superior on the most important attribute, it becomes her choice. If two or more brands are tied on this attribute, Linda considers the second most important attribute; she continues this process until one brand remains. Suppose Linda "prioritizes" the attributes in the following order: price, software, memory, graphics. She looks at price and finds brand D dominates. At this point she has determined that brand D is her preferred computer.

Determinance Model   This model says that an attribute might be important to the customer but will not influence his or her choice if all the products possess the same amount of that attribute. Thus Linda Brown might highly value computer speed, but if all four computers are equally fast, it will not help decide among them. Ironically, many products are at parity on the important attributes, and it is the less important attributes that often determine product choice. The marketing researcher must identify the determinant attributes, not simply the important ones.

Marketing Implications   The preceding models indicate that buyers can form their product preferences in several ways. A particular buyer, on a particular buying occasion, facing a particular product class, might be a conjunctive buyer, disjunctive buyer, or some other type. The same buyer might be a conjunctive buyer for large-ticket purchases and a disjunctive buyer for small-ticket items. Or the same buyer, in buying a large-ticket item, might behave first like a conjunctive buyer to eliminate many alternatives and then make a final choice as an ideal brand buyer. When we realize that a market is made up of many buyers, we need to identify the major buying styles.

The marketer might find that the majority of consumers in that market use one particular evaluation procedure. The marketer can then try to make this brand salient to consumers who are using that evaluation procedure.

Source: For additional discussion of these models, see Paul E. Green and Yoram Wind, *Multiattribute Decisions in Marketing: A Measurement Approach* (Hinsdale, Ill.: Dryden Press, 1972), Chap. 2. Also see James H. Myers and Mark I. Alpert, "Determinant Buying Attitudes: Meaning and Measurement," *Journal of Marketing*, October 1968, pp. 13-20.

7

Analyzing Business Markets and Organizational Buyer Behavior

Companies don't make purchases; they establish relationships.

Charles S. Goodman

Business organizations not only sell; they also buy vast quantities of raw materials, manufactured products, accessories, supplies, and services. In the food industry, for example, in 1987, 4846 hotels and 5306 food stores bought bakery products from 473 manufacturers which were served by 6211 trucking firms. Companies selling steel, computers, business services, and other products need to understand business buyers' needs and buying procedures. They must take into account several considerations not normally found in consumer marketing.

☐ Organizations buy goods and services to satisfy a variety of goals: making profits, reducing costs, meeting employee needs, and satisfying legal obligations.

☐ More persons typically participate in organizational buying decisions than in consumer buying decisions, especially in procuring major items. The decision participants usually have different organizational responsibilities and apply different criteria to the purchase decision.

☐ The buyers must heed formal purchasing policies, constraints, and requirements established by their organizations.

☐ The buying instruments, such as requests for quotations, proposals, and purchase contracts, add another dimension not typically found in consumer buying.

Webster and Wind define *organizational buying* as "the decision-making process by which formal organizations establish the need for purchased products and services and identify, evaluate, and choose among alternative brands and suppliers.[1] No two companies buy in the same way, yet the seller hopes to identify enough uniformities in organizational buying behavior to improve the task of marketing strategy planning.

In this chapter, we will look at three organizational markets: industrial markets, reseller markets, and government markets. Industrial buyers buy goods and services to aid them in producing other goods and services. Resellers buy goods and services to resell at a profit. Government agencies buy goods and services to carry out mandated governmental functions.

We will examine five questions about each market: *Who is in the market? What buying decisions do buyers make? Who participates in the buying process? What are the major influences on the buyers? How do the buyers make their buying decisions?*

THE INDUSTRIAL MARKET

Who Is in the Industrial Market?

The *industrial market* (also called the producer or business market) consists of all the individuals and organizations that acquire goods and services to use in the production of other products or services that are sold, rented, or supplied to others. The major industries making up the industrial market are agriculture, forestry, and fisheries; mining; manufacturing; construction; transportation; communication; public utilities; banking, finance, and insurance; and services.

More dollars and items are involved in sales to industrial buyers than to consumers. To produce and sell a simple pair of shoes, hide dealers must sell hides to tanners, who sell leather to shoe manufacturers, who sell shoes to wholesalers, who sell shoes to retailers, who finally sell them to consumers. Each party in the production-and-distribution chain has to buy many other goods and services, and this explains why there is more industrial buying than consumer buying.

Industrial markets have several characteristics that contrast sharply with consumer markets.[2]

Fewer Buyers   The industrial marketer normally deals with far fewer buyers than the consumer marketer does. The fate of a tire manufacturer, such as Goodyear, critically depends on getting an order from one of only a few automakers. But when Goodyear sells replacement tires to consumers, it faces a potential market of 12.1 million Canadian car owners.

Larger Buyers   Many industrial markets are characterized by a high buyer-concentration ratio in that a few large buyers do most of the purchasing. In such industries as motor vehicles, telephones, cigarettes, aircraft engines, and organic fibers, the top four manufacturers account for over 70 percent of total production.

Close Supplier-Customer Relationship   Because of the smaller customer base and the importance and power of the larger customers over the suppliers, we observe a close relationship between customers and sellers in industrial markets. Suppliers are frequently expected to customize their offerings to individual customer needs. Sales go to those suppliers who cooperate with the buyer on technical specifications and delivery requirements such as just-in-time production. Suppliers are expected to attend special seminars held by the industrial customer to become familiar with the buyer's quality and procurement requirements.

Geographically Concentrated Buyers   More than half of the nation's industrial buyers are concentrated in eight metropolitan areas between Windsor and Quebec. Industries such as petroleum, rubber, and steel, show even greater geographic concentration. Most agricultural output comes from a relatively small number of provinces. This geographical concentration of producers helps to reduce the costs of selling to them. Industrial marketers will want to watch any tendencies toward or away from further geographic concentration.

Derived Demand   The demand for industrial goods is ultimately derived from the demand for consumer goods. Thus animal hides are purchased because consumers buy shoes, purses, and other leather goods. If the demand for these consumer goods slackens, so will the demand for all the industrial goods entering into their production. For this reason, the industrial marketer must closely monitor the buying patterns of ultimate consumers and those environmental factors that affect them.[3]

Inelastic Demand   The total demand for many industrial goods and services is not much affected by price changes. Shoe manufacturers are not going to buy much more leather if the price of leather falls. Nor are they going to buy much less leather if the price of leather rises unless they can find satisfactory leather substitutes. Demand is especially inelastic in the short run because producers cannot make quick changes in their production methods. Demand is also inelastic for industrial goods that represent a small percentage of the item's total cost. For example, an increase in the price of metal eyelets for shoes will barely affect the total demand for metal eyelets. At the same time, producers may switch their eyelets supplier in response to price differences.

Fluctuating Demand   The demand for industrial goods and services tends to be more volatile than the demand for consumer goods and services. That is especially true of the demand for new plants and equipment. A given percentage increase in consumer demand can lead to a much larger percentage increase in the demand for plants and equipment necessary to produce the additional output. Economists refer to this as the *acceleration principle*. Sometimes a rise of only 10 percent in consumer demand can cause as much as a 200 percent rise in industrial demand in the next period; and a 10 percent fall in consumer demand may cause a complete collapse in the demand for investment goods. This sales volatility has led many industrial marketers to diversify their products and markets to achieve more balanced sales over the business cycle.

Professional Purchasing   Industrial goods are purchased by professionally trained purchasing agents, who spend their work lives learning how to buy better. Many belong to the Purchasing Management Association of Canada, which seeks to improve the effectiveness and status of professional buyers. Their professional approach and greater ability to assimilate technical details leads to a more rational buying decision. This means that industrial marketers have to provide a greater amount of specific performance and technical data about their products.

Several Buying Influences   More people typically influence business buying decisions than consumer buying decisions. Buying committees consisting of technical experts and even senior management are common in the purchase of major goods. Consequently, industrial marketers have to hire well-trained sales representatives and often use sales teams to deal with the well-trained buyers. Although advertising, sales promotion, and publicity play an important role in the industrial promotional mix, personal selling serves as the main selling tool.

Miscellaneous Characteristics   Here are some additional characteristics of industrial buying:

☐ *Direct Purchasing:* Industrial buyers often buy directly from producers rather than through middlemen, especially those items that are technically complex and/or expensive.

□ *Reciprocity:* Industrial buyers often select suppliers who also buy from them. An example would be a paper manufacturer who buys chemicals from a chemical company that buys a considerable amount of its paper. Reciprocity is illegal if there is coercive use of pressure by one of the parties and it results in reduced competition. Noncoercive reciprocity is legal provided it is supported by elaborate records of purchases and sales to and from other parties.[4]

□ *Leasing:* Many industrial buyers lease their equipment instead of buying it. This happens with computers, shoe machinery, packaging equipment, heavy-construction equipment, delivery trucks, machine tools, and company automobiles. The lessee gains a number of advantages: conserving capital, getting the seller's latest products, receiving better service, and gaining some tax advantages. The lessor often ends up with a larger net income and the chance to sell to customers who could not afford outright purchase.[5]

What Buying Decisions Do Industrial Buyers Make?

The industrial buyer faces many decisions in making a purchase. The number of decisions depends on the type of buying situation.

Major Types of Buying Situations   Robinson and others distinguish three types of buying situations, which they call *buyclasses*.[6] They are the straight rebuy, modified rebuy, and new task.

Straight Rebuy   The straight rebuy describes a buying situation where the purchasing department reorders on a routine basis (e.g., office supplies, bulk chemicals). The buyer chooses from suppliers on its "approved list," giving weight to its past buying satisfaction with the various suppliers. The "in-suppliers" make an effort to maintain product and service quality. They often propose automatic reordering systems so that the purchasing agent will save reordering time. The "out-suppliers" attempt to offer something new or to exploit dissatisfaction so that the industrial buyer will consider buying some amount from them. Out-suppliers try to get a foot in the door with a small order and then try to enlarge their "purchase share" over time.

Modified Rebuy   The modified rebuy describes a situation where the buyer wants to modify product specifications, prices, delivery requirements or other terms. The modified rebuy usually involves additional decision participants on both the buyers' and the sellers' sides. The in-suppliers become nervous and have to put their best foot forward to protect the account. The out-suppliers see an opportunity to propose a "better offer" to gain some business.

New Task   The new task describes a purchaser buying a product or service for the first time (e.g., custom-built office building, new weapon system). The greater the cost and/or risk, the larger the number of decision participants, and the greater their information seeking, the longer the time to decision completion.[7] The new-task situation is the marketer's greatest opportunity and challenge. The marketer tries to reach as many key buying influences as possible and provide helpful information and assistance. Because of the complicated selling involved in the new task, many companies use a special salesforce, called a *missionary salesforce*, consisting of their best salespeople.

New-task buying passes through several stages, each with its own requirements and challenges to the marketer. Ozanne and Churchill have applied an innovation diffusion perspective to the new task, identifying the stages as *awareness, interest, evaluation, trial,* and *adoption.*[8] They found that information sources varied in effectiveness at each stage. Mass media were most important during the initial awareness stage, whereas salespeople had their greatest impact at the interest stage. Technical sources were the most important during the evaluation stage. These findings provide clues to the marketer as to efficient communications to use at different stages of the new-task buying process.

Major Subdecisions Involved in the Buying Decision   The buyer makes the fewest decisions in the straight rebuy and the most in the new-task situation. In the new-task situation, the buyer has to determine *product specifications, price limits, delivery terms and times, service terms, payment terms, order quantities, acceptable suppliers*, and the *selected supplier*. Different decision participants influence each decision, and the order varies in which these decisions are made.

The Role of Systems Buying and Selling   Many buyers prefer to buy a total solution to their problem and not make many separate decisions. This is called *systems buying*; it originated in government buying of major weapons and communication systems. Instead of making separate purchases and putting all the components together, the government would solicit bids from prime contractors, who would assemble the package or system. The winning prime contractor would be responsible for bidding and assembling the subcomponents. The prime contractor would thus provide a *turnkey solution*, so called because the buyer simply had to turn one key to get everything that was wanted.

Sellers have increasingly recognized that buyers like to purchase in this way and have adopted the practice of *systems selling* as a marketing tool. Systems selling can take different forms. The supplier might sell a set of interlocking products; thus a glue supplier sells not only glue but glue applicators and dryers as well. The supplier might sell a system of production, inventory control, distribution, and other services to meet the buyer's need for a smooth-running operation. Another variant is systems contracting where a single supply source provides the buyer with his entire requirement of MRO (maintenance, repair, operating) supplies. The customer benefits from reduced costs as the inventory is maintained by the seller. Savings also result from reduced time spent on supplier selection and from price protection over the term of the contract. The seller benefits from lower operating costs because of a steady demand and reduced paperwork.[9]

Systems selling is a key industrial marketing strategy in bidding to build large-scale industrial projects, such as dams, steel factories, irrigation systems, sanitation systems, pipelines, utilities, and even new towns. Project engineering firms such as Lavalin and Bechtel must compete on price, quality, reliability, and other attributes to win awards. The award often goes to the firm that best meets the customer's real needs. Consider the following:

> The Indonesian government requested bids to build a cement factory near Jakarta. One firm made a proposal that included choosing the site, designing the cement factory, hiring the construction crews, assembling the materials and equipment, and turning over the finished factory to the Indonesian government. A second firm, in outlining its proposal, included all of these services plus hiring and training the workers to run the factory, exporting the cement through its trading companies, using the cement to build some needed roads out of Jakarta, and using the cement to build some new office buildings in Jakarta. Although the second proposal involved more money, its appeal was greater and they won the contract. Clearly, the second firm viewed the problem not as one of just building a cement factory (the narrow view of systems selling) but of running it in a way that would contribute to the country's economy. It saw itself not as an engineering project firm but as an economic development agency. It took the broadest view of the customer's needs. This is true systems selling. ∎

Who Participates in the Industrial Buying Process?

Who does the buying of the billions of dollars' worth of goods and services needed by the industrial market? Purchasing agents are influential in straight rebuy and modified rebuy situations, whereas other organizational members are more influential in new-buy situations. Engineering personnel usually have greatest influence over product selection, whereas purchasing agents dominate the supplier-selection decision.[10] Thus in new-buy situations, the industrial marketer must first direct product information to the engineering personnel. In rebuy situations and at supplier-selection time in new-buy situations, communications should be directed primarily at the purchasing agent.

Webster and Wind call the decision-making unit of a buying organization the *buying center*, defined as "all those individuals and groups who participate in the purchasing decision-making process, who share some common goals and the risks arising from the decisions."[11]

The buying center includes all members of the organization who play any of six roles in the purchase decision process.[12]

☐ *Users:* Users are those who will use the product or service. In many cases, the users initiate the buying proposal and help define the product specifications.

☐ *Influencers:* Influencers are persons who influence the buying decision. They often help define specifications and also provide information for evaluating alternatives. Technical personnel are particularly important as influencers.

☐ *Deciders:* Deciders are persons who decide on product requirements and/or on suppliers.

☐ *Approvers:* Approvers are persons who authorize the proposed actions of deciders or buyers.

☐ *Buyers:* Buyers are persons with formal authority for selecting the supplier and arranging the terms of purchase. Buyers may help shape product specifications, but they play their major role in selecting vendors and negotiating. In more complex purchases, the buyers might include high-level officers participating in the negotiations.

☐ *Gatekeepers:* Gatekeepers are persons who have the power to prevent sellers or information from reaching members of the buying center. For example, purchasing agents, receptionists, and telephone operators may prevent salespersons from contracting users or deciders.

Within any organization, the buying center will vary in the number and type of participants for different classes of products. More decision participants will be involved in buying a computer than in buying paper clips. The industrial marketer has to figure out: *Who are the major decision participants? What decisions do they influence? What is their level of influence? What evaluation criteria does each participant use?* Consider the following example:

> A distributor of hospital supplies sells nonwoven disposable surgical gowns to hospitals. It tries to identify the hospital personnel who participate in this buying decision. The decision participants turn out to be the vice-president of purchasing, the operating-room administrator, and the surgeons. Each party plays a different role. The vice-president of purchasing analyzes whether the hospital should buy disposable gowns or reusable gowns. If the findings favor disposable gowns, then the operating-room administrator compares various competitor's products and prices and makes a choice. This administrator considers the gown's absorbency, antiseptic quality, design, and cost and normally buys the brand that meets the functional requirements at the lowest cost. Finally, surgeons influence the decision retroactively by reporting their satisfaction with the particular brand. ∎

When a buying center includes many participants, the seller will not have the time or resources to reach all of them. Smaller sellers concentrate on reaching the *key buying influences*. Larger sellers go for *multilevel in-depth selling* to reach as many buying participants as possible. Their salespeople virtually "live" with their high-volume customers.

Industrial marketers must periodically review their assumptions on the roles and influence of different decision participants. For example, for years, Kodak's strategy for selling X-ray film to hospitals was to sell through lab technicians. The company did not notice that the decision was increasingly being made by professional administrators. As its sales declined, Kodak finally grasped the change in buying practices and hurriedly revised its market targeting strategy.

What Are the Major Influences on Industrial Buyers?

Industrial buyers are subject to many influences when they make their buying decisions. Some marketers assume that the most important influences are economic. They see the buyers as favoring the supplier who offers the lowest price, or best product, or most service. This view suggests that industrial marketers should concentrate on offering strong economic benefits to buyers.

Other marketers see buyers responding to personal factors such as favors, attention, or risk avoidance. A study of buyers in ten large companies concluded that

> corporate decision-makers remain human after they enter the office. They respond to "image"; they buy from companies to which they feel "close"; they favor suppliers who show them respect and personal consideration, and who do extra things "for them"; they "over-react" to real or imagined slights, tending to reject companies which fail to respond or delay in submitting requested bids.[13]

Industrial buyers actually respond to both economic and personal factors. Where there is substantial similarity in supplier offers, industrial buyers have little basis for rational choice. Since they can satisfy the purchasing requirements with any supplier, these buyers will place more weight on the personal treatment they receive. Where competing products differ substantially, industrial buyers are more accountable for their choice and pay more attention to economic factors.

Webster and Wind have classified the various influences on industrial buyers into four main groups: environmental, organizational, interpersonal, and individual.[14] These groups are shown in Figure 7-1 and described below.

Environmental Factors Industrial buyers are heavily influenced by factors in the current and expected economic environment, such as the level of primary demand, the economic outlook, and the cost of money. In a recession economy, industrial buyers reduce their investment in plant, equipment, and inventories. Industrial marketers can do little to stimulate total demand in this environment. They can only fight harder to increase or maintain their share of demand.

Companies that fear a shortage of key materials are willing to buy and hold large inventories. They will sign long-term contracts with suppliers to ensure a steady flow of materials. Du Pont, Ford, Chrysler, and several other major companies regard *supply planning* as a major responsibility of their purchasing executives.

Industrial buyers are also affected by technological, political, and competitive developments in the environment. The industrial marketer has to monitor all of these environmental forces, determine how they will affect buyers, and try to turn problems into opportunities.

FIGURE 7-1

Major Influences on Industrial Buying Behavior

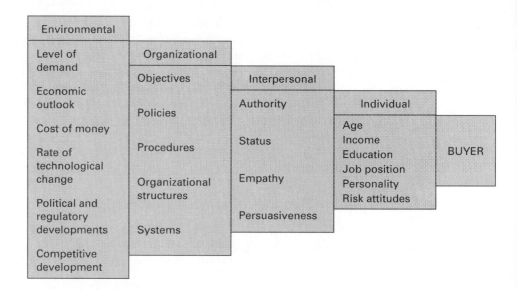

Organizational Factors   Each buying organization has specific objectives, policies, procedures, organizational structures, and systems. The industrial marketer has to be as familiar with them as possible. Such questions arise as: How many people are involved in the buying decision? Who are they? What are their evaluation criteria? What are the company's policies and constraints on the buyers?

Industrial marketers should be aware of the following organizational trends in the purchasing area:

☐ *Purchasing-department upgrading:* Purchasing departments often occupy a low position in the management hierarchy, in spite of managing often more than half of the company's costs. However, recent bouts with inflation and shortages have led many companies to upgrade their purchasing departments and elevate their heads to vice-presidential status. These departments have been changed from old-fashioned *purchasing departments* with their emphasis on buying at the lowest cost to *procurement departments* with their mission to seek the best value from fewer and better suppliers. Some multinationals have elevated them into *strategic materials departments* with responsibility for sourcing around the world and working with strategic partners. At Caterpillar, functions such as purchasing, inventory control, production scheduling, and traffic have been combined in their strategic materials department. Many companies are looking for top talent, hiring M.B.A.s, and offering higher compensation. This means that industrial marketers must correspondingly upgrade their sales personnel to match the caliber of the new buyers.

☐ *Centralized purchasing:* In multidivisional companies, most purchasing is carried out by separate divisions because of their differing needs. Recently companies have started to recentralize some of the purchasing. Headquarters identifies materials purchased by several divisions and considers buying them centrally. This gives the company more purchasing clout. The individual divisions can buy from another source if they can get a better deal, but in general, centralized purchasing produces substantial savings for the company. For the industrial marketer, this development means dealing with fewer and higher-level buyers. Instead of the seller's regional salesforces selling at separate plant locations, the seller may use a *national account salesforce* to deal with the corporate buyer. National account selling is challenging and demands a sophisticated salesforce and marketing planning effort.[15]

□ *Long-term contracts:* Industrial buyers are increasingly initiating or accepting long-term contracts with trusted suppliers. For example, General Motors wants to buy from fewer suppliers who are willing to locate close to its plants and produce high-quality components. Another aspect involves companies supplying *electronic order exchange* systems to their customers. The customer can type orders directly on the computer, and these go by modem to the supplier.

□ *Purchasing-performance evaluation*: More companies are setting up incentive systems to reward purchasing managers for good buying performance, in much the same way that sales personnel receive bonuses for good selling performance. These systems will lead purchasing managers to increase their pressure on sellers for the best terms.

The emergence of just-in-time production systems promises to have a major impact on organizational purchasing policies. Its ramifications are described in Marketing Strategies 7-1.

Interpersonal Factors   The buying center usually includes several participants with differing interests, authority, and persuasiveness. The industrial marketer is not likely to know what kind of group dynamics will take place during the buying decision process, although whatever information he or she can discover about the personalities and interpersonal factors would be useful.

Individual Factors   Each participant in the buying decision process has personal motivations, perceptions, and preferences. These are influenced by the participant's age, income, education, professional identification, personality, and attitudes toward risk. Buyers definitely exhibit different buying styles. There are "keep-it-simple" buyers, "own-expert" buyers, "want-the-best," buyers, and "want-everything-done" buyers. Some younger, highly educated buyers are "computer freaks" and make rigorous analyses of competitive proposals before choosing a supplier. Other buyers are "tough guys" from the "old school" and play off the sellers:

> For example, the purchasing manager of a large brewery punishes any supplier who gets out of line. When the sales representative of one of his suppliers of metal cans started talking about a price rise, the manager ". . . punished them for talking about it" by diverting orders for millions of cans to a competitor.[16]

Industrial marketers must know their customers and adapt their tactics to known environmental, organizational, interpersonal, and individual influences on the buying situation.

How Do Industrial Buyers Make Their Buying Decisions?

Industrial buyers do not buy goods and services for personal consumption or utility. They buy goods and services to make money, or to reduce operating costs, or to satisfy a social or legal obligation. A steel company will add another furnace if it sees a chance to make more money. It will computerize its accounting system to reduce the costs of doing business. It will add pollution-control equipment to satisfy legal requirements. To buy the needed goods, industrial buyers move through a purchasing or procurement process. Robinson, et al., have identified eight stages of the industrial buying process and called them *buyphases*.[17] These stages are shown in Table 7-1. All eight stages apply to a new-task buying situation, and some of them to the other two types of buying situations. This model is called the *buygrid* framework. We will describe the eight steps for the typical new-task buying situation.

JUST-IN-TIME PRODUCTION CHANGES
THE FACE OF ORGANIZATIONAL BUYING

Over the past two decades, domestic markets have been bombarded with foreign products. Japanese market-share gains have been especially pronounced in such industries as steel, office equipment, electronics, and automobiles. As domestic companies started studying the reasons for Japanese success in manufacturing, it discovered several concepts including just-in-time (JIT), early supplier involvement, value analysis, quality circles, total quality control, and flexible manufacturing.

JIT in particular promises to produce significant change in the relationship between suppliers and their industrial customers. The goal of JIT is zero inventory with 100 percent quality. It means that materials arrive at the customer's factory exactly at the time they are needed. It does not mean that the customer shifts inventory to the supplier, as this would not reduce total system costs; instead it calls for a synchronization between supplier and customer production schedules so that inventory buffers are unnecessary. Effective implementation of JIT should result in reduced inventory and lead times, and increased quality, productivity, and adaptability to changes.

In a survey of two thousand purchasing executives in 1986, 59 percent indicated that their firm had used or planned to use JIT. General Motors, through its JIT programs, reduced inventory-related costs from $8 billion to $2 billion.

Industrial marketers need to be aware of the changes that JIT will bring about in the purchasing practices of organizations. They must position themselves to exploit the opportunities that JIT will create. The following are the major features and implications of JIT:

- *Strict quality control*: Maximum cost savings from JIT are achieved if preinspected goods are received by the buyer. The buyers thus expect that suppliers have strict quality-control procedures such as SPC (statistical process control) or TQC (total quality control). This means that suppliers need to work closely with the industrial

customer and satisfy the latter that they can ship products that meet the quality standards.

- *Frequent and reliable delivery*: Daily delivery is frequently the only way to avoid inventory buildup. Increasingly, customers are specifying delivery dates rather than shipping dates, with penalties for not meeting them. Apple even penalizes for early delivery, while Kasle Steel has around-the-clock deliveries to the General Motors Buick plant. This means that suppliers must develop reliable transportation arrangements.

- *Closer location*: Since JIT involves frequent delivery, a location closer to the customer can be an advantage for the supplier. A close location results in more efficiency in delivering smaller lots and greater reliability in inclement weather. Kasle Steel set up its blanking mill in the same city as the Buick plant. This means that an industrial marketer may have to make large commitments to major customers.

- *Telecommunication*: New technologies of communication permit suppliers to establish computerized purchasing systems that are hooked up to their customers. One large customer requires that suppliers make their inventory figures and prices available on the system. It allows for just-in-time on-line ordering as the computer looks for the lowest prices where inventory is available. This reduces transaction costs but puts pressure on industrial marketers to keep prices very competitive.

- *Stable production schedule*: Under JIT, customers provide their production schedule to the supplier as the materials are required. International Harvester provides one of its suppliers with a six-month forecast and a firm twenty-day order. If any last-minute changes are made, International Harvester is billed for the additional costs. This will help reduce the uncertainty and costs faced by the industrial suppliers.

- *Single sourcing*: JIT implies that the buying and selling organizations work closely together to reduce costs. This often translates into the industrial customer's awarding a long-term contract to only one supplier who can be trusted. This makes payoffs high for the winning supplier, and very difficult for other competitors to subsequently get the contract. Contracts are almost automatically renewed provided the supplier met delivery schedules and maintained quality. Single sourcing is increasing rapidly under JIT. Thus while General Motors still uses more than 3500 suppliers, Toyota which has totally adopted JIT, uses less than 250. Harley Davidson reduced its supplier base from 320 to 180 in two years.

□ *Value analysis*: The major objectives of JIT are to reduce costs and improve quality, and value analysis is critical to accomplishing these objectives. To reduce costs of its product, a customer must not only reduce its own costs but also get its suppliers to reduce their costs. Thus some large manufacturers hold VA seminars for their suppliers. Suppliers with a strong VA program have a competitive edge, as they can contribute to their customers' VA program.

□ *Early supplier involvement*: Industrial buyers are increasingly realizing that industrial marketers are experts in their field and should be brought into the design process. Industrial marketers must have qualified personnel who can participate in customers' design teams. In 1986, a survey of one thousand purchasing executives found that the major criteria for selecting suppliers to participate in design teams were quality, prior delivery performance, recommendations by the customer's engineering department, and prior value-analysis assistance.

□ *Close relationship*: All the above features of JIT help to forge a close relationship between the industrial customer and the industrial marketer. To make JIT successful, they coordinate their efforts to maximally satisfy the customer's needs. Under JIT, the supplier is viewed as a work station that is located away from the customer's manufacturing site. To be successful, the supplier has to customize its offering for the particular industrial customer. In return, the supplier wins the contract for a specific term. Because of the time invested by the parties, locational decisions, and telecommunication hookups, the transaction-specific investments are high. Since switching costs for the industrial customer are high, these customers are extremely selective in choosing suppliers. A major implication is that industrial marketers must improve their skill in *relationship marketing* as compared with *transaction marketing*. Profit maximization over the entire relationship rather than over each transaction should be the objective. Otherwise the supplier may lose the customer for good.

For further information, see G. H. Manoochehri, "Suppliers and the Just-In-Time Concept," *Journal of Purchasing and Materials Management*, Winter 1984, pp. 16-21; Somerby Dowst, "Buyers Say VA Is More Important Than Ever," *Purchasing*, June 26, 1986, pp. 64-83; Ernest Raia, "Just-In-Time USA," *Purchasing*, February 13, 1986, pp. 48-62; Eric K. Clemons and F. Warren McFarlan, "Telecom: Hook Up or Lose Out," *Harvard Business Review*, July-August 1986, pp. 91-97; and Somerby Dowst and Ernest Raia, "Design Team Signals for More Supplier Involvement," *Purchasing*, March 27, 1986, pp. 76-83.

Problem Recognition The buying process begins when someone in the company recognizes a problem or need that can be met by acquiring a good or a service. Problem recognition can occur as a result of internal or external stimuli. Internally, the most common events leading to problem recognition are the following:

□ The company decides to develop a new product and needs new equipment and materials to produce this product.

□ A machine breaks down and requires replacement or new parts.

□ Some purchased material turns out to be unsatisfactory, and the company searches for another supplier.

□ A purchasing manager senses an opportunity to obtain lower prices or better quality.

Externally, the buyer may get some new ideas at a trade show, or see an ad, or receive a call from a sales representative who offers a better product or a lower price. Industrial marketers can therefore stimulate problem recognition by developing ads, calling on prospects, and so on.

General Need Description Having recognized a need, the buyer proceeds to determine the general characteristics and quantity of the needed item. For standard items, this is not much of a problem. For complex items, the buyer will work with others—engineers, users,

Table 7-1 Major Stages (Buyphases of the Industrial Buying Process in Relation to Major Buying Situations (Buyclasses)

		Buy Classes		
		New Task	Modified Rebuy	Straight Rebuy
	1. Problem recognition	Yes	Maybe	No
	2. General need description	Yes	Maybe	No
	3. Product specification	Yes	Yes	Yes
BUY	4. Suppliers' search	Yes	Maybe	No
PHASES	5. Proposal solicitation	Yes	Maybe	No
	6. Supplier selection	Yes	Maybe	No
	7. Order-routine specification	Yes	Maybe	No
	8. Performance review	Yes	Yes	Yes

Source: Adapted from Patrick J. Robinson, Charles W. Faris, and Yoram Wind, *Industrial Buying and Creative Marketing* (Boston: Allyn & Bacon, 1967), p. 14.

and so on—to define the general characteristics. They will want to rank the importance of reliability, durability, price, and other attributes desired in the item.

The industrial marketer can render assistance to the buyer in this phase. Often the buyer is not aware of the benefits of different product features. An alert marketer can help buyers define their companies' needs.

Product Specifications   The buying organization next develops the item's technical specifications. A *product-value-analysis* engineering team is assigned to the project. *Product value analysis is an approach to cost reduction in which components are carefully studied to determine if they can be redesigned or standardized or made by cheaper methods of production.* The team will examine the high-cost components in a given product—usually 20 percent of the parts account for 80 percent of the costs. The team will also identify overdesigned product components that last longer than the product itself. Table 7-2 lists the major questions raised in product-value analysis. The team will decide on the optimal product characteristics. Tightly written specifications will allow the buyer to refuse merchandise that fails to meet the intended standards.

Suppliers, too, can use product-value analysis as a tool for positioning themselves to win an account. By getting in early and influencing buyer specifications, the supplier has a good chance of being chosen in the supplier-selection stage.

Supplier Search   The buyer now tries to identify the most appropriate vendors. The buyer can examine trade directories, do a computer search, or phone other companies for recommendations. Vendors who lack the required production capacity or suffer from a poor reputation will be rejected. Those who qualify may be visited to examine their production facilities and meet their personnel. The buyer will end up with a short list of qualified suppliers.

The newer the buying task and the more complex and expensive the item, the greater the amount of time buyers will spend in searching for, and qualifying, suppliers. A survey of purchasing managers in the electronics industry found that their major information sources, in order of importance, were

1. Internal information such as purchasing records, other departments, and purchasing directories

2. Salespersons' telephone calls and personal visits

Table 7-2 Questions Asked in Product-Value Analysis

1. Does the use of the item contribute value?
2. Is its cost proportionate to its usefulness?
3. Does it need all its features?
4. Is there anything better for its intended use?
5. Can a usable part be made by a lower-cost method?
6. Can a standard product be found that will be usable?
7. Is the product made on proper tooling, considering the quantities that are used?
8. Will another dependable supplier provide it for less?
9. Is anyone buying it for less?

Source: Albert W. Frey, *Marketing Handbook*, 2nd ed. (New York: Ronald Press, 1965), section 27, p. 21. Copyright by John Wiley & Sons.

3. External information, such as investigations of vendors' facilities, outside purchasing managers, credit and financial reports, and members of the local purchasing chapter
4. External information, such as journal advertisements, journal articles, mail advertisements, catalogs, telephone directories, and trade shows[18]

The supplier's task is to get listed in major directories, develop a strong advertising and promotion program, build a good reputation in the marketplace, and identify buyers who are looking for new suppliers.

Proposal Solicitation   The buyer will now invite qualified suppliers to submit proposals. Some suppliers will send only a catalog or a sales representative. Where the item is complex or expensive, the buyer will require a detailed written proposal from each potential supplier. The buyer will eliminate some and invite the remaining suppliers to make formal presentations.

Thus industrial marketers must be skilled in researching, writing, and presenting proposals. Their proposals should be marketing documents, not just technical documents. Their oral presentations should inspire confidence. They should position their company's capabilities and resources so that they stand out from the competition.

Supplier Selection   In this stage, the members of the buying center will review the proposals and move toward supplier selection. They will perform a vendor analysis to select supplier(s). They will consider not only the suppliers' technical competence but also their ability to deliver on time and provide necessary services. The buying center will often specify desired supplier attributes and indicate their relative importance. A survey of purchasing managers listed the following eight attributes in order of importance: delivery capability, quality, price, repair service, technical capability, performance history, production facilities, and aid and advice.[19] The buying center will rate suppliers against these attributes and identify the most attractive suppliers. They often use a supplier-evaluation model such as the one shown in Table 7-3.

Lehmann and O'Shaughnessy found that the relative importance of different attributes varies with the type of buying situation.[20] For *routine-order products*, they found that delivery reliability, price, and supplier reputation are highly important. For *procedural-problem products*, such as a copying machine, the three most important attributes are technical service, supplier flexibility, and product reliability. Finally, for *political-problem products* that stir rivalries in the organization, such as a computer system, the most important attributes are price, supplier reputation, product reliability, service reliability, and supplier flexibility.

Table 7-3 An Example of Vendor Analysis

Attributes	Rating Scale				
	Unacceptable (0)	Poor (1)	Fair (2)	Good (3)	Excellent (4)
Technical and production capabilities					×
Financial strength			×		
Product reliability					×
Delivery reliability			×		
Service capability					×
Total score: 4 + 2 + 4 + 2 + 4 = 16					
Average score: 16/5 = 3.2					

Note: This vendor shows up as strong, except on two attributes. The purchasing agent has to decide how important the two weaknesses are. The analysis could be redone using importance weights for the five attributes.
Source: Adapted from Richard Hill, Ralph Alexander, and James Cross, *Industrial* Marketing, 4th ed. (Homewood, Ill.: Richard D. Irwin, Copyright 1975), pp. 101-4.0

The buying center may attempt to negotiate with the preferred suppliers for better prices and terms before making the final selection. The marketer can counter the request for a lower price in a number of ways. The marketer can cite the value of the services the buyer now receives, especially where these services are superior to those offered by competitors. The marketer may be able to show that the "life-cycle cost" of using its product is lower than that of competitors, even if its purchase price is higher. Other more innovative ways may also be used to counter intense price competition. Consider the following example:

> Lincoln Electric has instituted the Guaranteed Cost Reduction Program for its distributors. Whenever a customer requests a distributor to lower prices on Lincoln equipment to match Lincoln's competitors, the company and the particular distributor guarantee that during the coming year, they will find cost reductions in the customer's plant that meet or exceed the price difference between Lincoln's products and the competition's. Lincoln sales representative and the distributor then get together and after surveying the customer's operations, identify and propose specific cost reductions. If an independent audit at the end of the year does not reveal the promised cost reductions, Lincoln Electric and the distributor compensate the customer for the difference, with Lincoln paying 70 percent and the distributor paying the rest.[21] ■

Buying centers must also decide how many suppliers to use. Many buyers prefer multiple suppliers so that they will not be totally dependent on one supplier in case something goes wrong and also so that they will be able to compare the prices and performance of the various suppliers. The buyer will normally place most of the order with one supplier, and the rest with other suppliers. For example, a buyer using three suppliers may buy 60 percent of the needed quantity from the prime supplier and 30 and 10 percent, respectively, from the two other suppliers. The *prime supplier* will make an effort to protect its prime position, while the *secondary suppliers* will try to expand their supplier share. In the meantime, *out-suppliers* will seek to get their foot in the door by making an especially low price offer and then work hard to increase their share of the customer's business.

Order-Routine Specification The buyer now writes the final order with the chosen supplier(s), listing the technical specifications, the quantity needed, the expected time of delivery, return policies, warranties, and so on. In the case of MRO items (maintenance, repair, and operating items), buyers are increasingly moving toward *blanket contracts* rather than *periodic purchase orders*. Writing a new purchase order each time stock is needed is expensive. Nor does the buyer want to write fewer and larger purchase orders because that means carrying more inventory. A blanket contract establishes a long-term relationship where the supplier promises to resupply the buyer as needed on agreed price terms over a specified period of time. The stock is held by the seller; hence the name *stockless purchase plan*. The buyer's computer automatically sends an order to the seller when stock is needed. Blanket contracting leads to more single-source buying and ordering more items from that single source. This locks the supplier in tighter with the buyer and makes it difficult for out-suppliers to break in unless the buyer becomes dissatisfied with the in-supplier's prices, quality, or service.[22]

Performance Review In this stage, the buyer reviews the performance of the particular supplier(s). Three methods are used. The buyer may contact the end users and ask for their evaluations. Or the buyer may rate the supplier on several criteria using a weighted point method. Or the buyer might aggregate the cost of poor performance to come up with an

FIGURE 7-2

Organizational Buying Behavior in Japan: Packaging-Machine Purchase Process

Source: "Japanese Firms Use Unique Buying Behavior," *The Japan Economic Journal*, December 23, 1980, p. 29. Reprinted by permission.

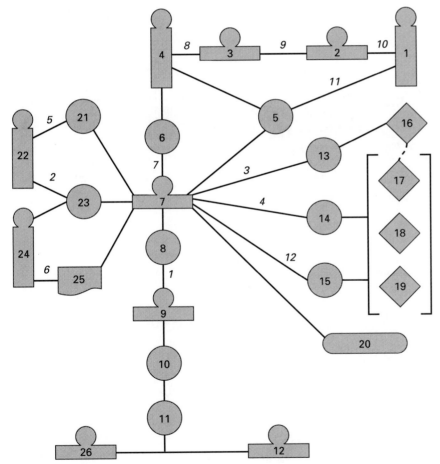

1 President
2 Financial Dept.
3 Sales headquarters
4 Production chief
5 Decision
6 Discussion of production and sales plans
7 Production Dept.
8 Production of packing process plan
9 New Products Development Committee
10 Request for consultation
11 Production of new product marketing plan
12 Product Development Dept.
13 Discussion on design of prototype machines
14 Prototype machine
15 Placement of orders
16 Makers design and technical staff
17 Supplier A
18 Supplier B
19 Supplier C
20 Overseas machine exhibitions
21 Request for testing of prototype machines
22 Research staff
23 Production of basic design
24 Foreman
25 Production of draft plans
26 Marketing Dept.

adjusted cost of purchase, including price.[23] The performance review may lead the buyer to continue, modify, or drop the supplier. The supplier should monitor the same variables that buyers and end users use.

We have described the buying stages that would operate in a new-task buying situation. In the modified rebuy or straight rebuy situation, some of these stages would be compressed or bypassed. For example, in a straight rebuy situation, the buyer normally has a favorite supplier or an ordered list of suppliers. Each stage represents a narrowing of the number of supplier alternatives. Cardozo has used the buying stages to come up with a model to yield the probability that a supplier will get the order for a product from a particular buyer. To use the model, industrial marketers must:

1. Specify the decisions to be included in the sequence for a particular situation
2. Estimate probabilities of outcomes favorable to them for each decision in the sequence
3. Multiply those probabilities together to compute the overall probability of purchase or repurchase[24]

The eight-stage buyphase model represents the major steps in the industrial buying process. In any real situation, further steps can occur. The industrial marketer needs to model each situation individually. Each buying situation involves a particular flow of work, and this *buyflow* can provide many clues to the marketer. A buyflow map for the purchase of a packaging machine in Japan is shown in Figure 7-2. The numbers within the icons are defined at the right. The italicized numbers between icons show the flow of events.

Over twenty people in the purchasing company were involved, including the production manager and staff, new-product committee, company laboratory, the marketing department,

---

Marketing Strategies 7-2

ADAPTING MARKETING STRATEGY TO THE TYPE OF INDUSTRIAL BUYER SEGMENT: THE CASE OF MICROPROCESSORS

The market for microprocessors consists of three submarkets: military, industrial, and commercial. Each group buys quite differently.

The military buyer attaches the utmost importance to the adequacy of the producer's quality standards and plant facilities.

Only after these two considerations have been realized does price become a factor.

Quality is also of great importance to industrial customers, such as computer manufacturers. Loyalties can be established in this segment through high quality and good service. Price itself is not a critical factor unless it gets completely out of line.

Commercial buyers, such as pocket-radio manufacturers, are in the most competitive user market and consequently buy their components mostly on price and delivery. Little loyalty to suppliers exists, and quality requirements are seldom high.

Because of these differences, marketing strategies vary. To sell microprocessors in the military market, firms must make a considerable investment in R&D, use salespeople who know military buying procedures, and specialize in limited-line products. To sell in the industrial market, firms must make a modest investment in R&D, use salespeople who have technical knowledge concerning the product, and offer a broad line. To sell to the commercial market, firms need little or no R&D effort, can use salespeople who are relatively nontechnical, and can offer common mass-produced items.

---

and the department for market development. The entire decision-making process took 121 days.

Clearly, industrial marketing is a challenging area. The key is to know the user's needs, the buying participants, the buying criteria, and the buying procedures. With this knowledge, the industrial marketer can design marketing plans for selling to different types of customers (see Marketing Strategies 7-2).

THE RESELLER MARKET

Who Is in the Reseller Market?

The reseller market consists of all the individuals and organizations which acquire goods for the purpose of reselling or renting them to others at a profit. Instead of producing form utility, resellers provide time, place, and possession utility. There are two main types of resellers: wholesale merchants, (including agents and brokers), and retailers (including chains and independents). In Canada in 1987, there were 64 542 wholesalers of all kinds which sold goods worth $210 billion. Some of those goods were subsequently sold by retailers, whose sales amounted to $154 billion. The total number of retailers was 53 000, including 1187 chains having 35 300 stores. Located in cities and towns, resellers are more geographically dispersed than producers, but more concentrated than consumers.

Resellers purchase goods for resale and goods and services for conducting their operations. The latter are bought by resellers in their role as "producers." We will confine the discussion here to the goods they purchase for resale.

Resellers handle a vast variety of products for resale, indeed everything except goods that producers sell directly to final customers, such as heavy or complex machinery, customized products, and products sold on a direct-mail or a door-to-door basis. With these exceptions, most products are sold to final buyers through selling intermediaries.

Suppliers should view resellers as purchasing agents for their customers, not selling agents for the suppliers. Suppliers will be successful to the extent they can help resellers serve their customers better.

What Buying Decisions Do Resellers Make?

Resellers must make the following purchasing decisions: *What assortment to carry? What vendors to buy from?* and *What prices and terms to negotiate?* The assortment decision is primary and positions the reseller in the marketplace. Wholesalers and retailers can choose one of four assortment strategies:

☐ Exclusive assortment: Carrying the line of only one manufacturer

☐ *Deep assortment:* Carrying a product family in depth, drawing on many producers' outputs

☐ *Broad assortment:* Carrying several product lines that fall within the normal scope of the reseller's type of business

☐ *Scrambled assortment:* Carrying many unrelated product lines

Thus a camera store may carry only Kodak cameras (exclusive assortment); many brands of cameras (deep assortment); cameras, tape recorders, radios, and stereophonic equipment (broad assortment); or the last plus stoves and refrigerators (scrambled assortment). The reseller's chosen assortment will influence its customer mix, marketing mix, and supplier mix.

Resellers confront three types of buying situations.

The *new-item situation* describes the situation where the reseller is offered a new item. The reseller will give a yes-no answer depending on how profitable the item looks. This differs from the new-task situation faced by producers who definitely have to purchase the needed item from someone.

The *best-vendor situation* faces the reseller who needs an item and must determine the best supplier. This occurs (1) when the reseller does not have the space to carry all the available brands and (2) when the reseller is seeking someone to produce a private brand. Resellers such as Sears and A&P sell a substantial number of items under their own name; therefore much of their buying operation consists of vendor selection.

The *better-terms situation* arises when the reseller wants to obtain better terms from current suppliers. Legally, suppliers are prevented, under *The Competition Act*, from granting different terms to different resellers in the same reseller class unless they reflect cost differences, distress sales, or other special conditions. Nevertheless, resellers will press their suppliers for preferential treatment, such as more service, easier credit terms, and larger-volume discounts.

Who Participates in the Reseller Buying Process?

Who does the buying for wholesale and retail organizations? In small "mom and pop" firms, the owner usually handles merchandise selection and buying. In large firms, buying is a specialized function and full-time job. Buying is carried out in different ways by department stores, supermarkets, drug wholesalers, and so on, and differences can even be found within each reseller type.

Consider supermarkets. In the corporate headquarters of a supermarket chain, specialist buyers (sometimes called merchandise managers) will be responsible for developing brand assortments and listening to new-brand presentations by salespersons. In some chains, these buyers have the authority to accept or reject new items. In other chains, they are limited to screening "obvious rejects" and "obvious accepts"; they bring other items to the chain's buying committee for approval. Borden found that the buyer's recommendation carries a lot of influence in the committee decision.[25]

Even when an item is accepted by a chain-store buying committee, individual stores in the chain may not carry it. According to one supermarket chain executive: "No matter what the sales representatives sell or buyers buy, the person who has the greatest influence on the final sale of the new item is the store manager." In the nation's chain and independent supermarkets, two-thirds of the new items accepted at the warehouse are ordered on the store manager's own decision, and only one-third represent forced distribution.

Thus producers face a major challenge trying to get new items into stores. They offer the nation's supermarkets between 150 and 250 new items each week, and store space does not permit more than 10 percent to be accepted.

Several studies have attempted to rank the acceptance criteria used by buyers, buying committees, and store managers. A. C. Nielsen Company asked store managers to rank on a three-point scale the importance of different elements in influencing their decision to accept a new item. They found that buyers are most influenced, in order of importance, by strong evidence of consumer acceptance, a well-designed advertising and sales-promotion plan, and generous financial incentives to the trade. The seller who passes these tests may still face charges called *listing fees*, for getting the brand on a list of products approved for stores to order. Some buyers also try to extract *exit fees* for removing failed products.

The role of supermarket buyers, buying committees, and store managers characterize, with some variation, the buying organizations of other reseller enterprises. Large department-store chains use buyers who specialize by line of merchandise and have a lot of authority to select the merchandise to be featured. The buyers are aided by assistant buyers who assist in demand forecasting, stock control, and merchandising. Individual store managers then make future decisions with respect to which goods to order and which to display prominently.

What Are the Major Influences on Reseller Buyers?

Resellers are influenced by the same factors—environmental, organizational, interpersonal, and individual—shown earlier in Figure 7-1. The seller has to note these influences and develop strategies that help resellers improve their sales or reduce their costs.

The reseller's buying style should be taken into account. Dickinson has distinguished seven buyer types:[26]

- □ *Loyal buyer:* This buyer remains loyal to a source year after year.
- □ *Opportunistic buyer:* This buyer selects those vendors who will further his or her long-term interests and drives a hard bargain.
- □ *Best-deal buyer:* This buyer selects the best deal available at the time.
- □ *Creative buyer:* This buyer tells the seller what he or she wants in the way of a product, services, and prices.
- □ *Advertising buyer:* This buyer attempts to obtain advertising money as part of every deal.
- □ *The chiseler:* This buyer constantly negotiates extra concessions in price.
- □ *Nuts-and-bolts buyer:* This buyer selects the merchandise offering the best value.

How Do Resellers Make Their Buying Decisions?

For new items, resellers use roughly the same buying process described for the industrial buyer. For standard items, resellers simply reorder goods when the inventory gets low. The orders are placed with the same suppliers as long as their terms, goods, and services are satisfactory. Resellers will try to renegotiate prices if their margins erode owing to rising operating costs. In many retail lines, the profit margin is so low (1 to 2 percent on sales in supermarkets, for example) that a sudden drop in sales or a rise in operating costs will drive profits into the red.

Resellers are improving their buying skills over time. They are mastering the principles of demand forecasting, merchandise selection, stock control, space allocation, and display. They are using computers to track inventory, compute economic order quantities, prepare orders, and generate printouts of dollars spent on vendors and products. They are learning to measure direct product profitability (see Marketing Concepts and Tools 7-1).

Thus vendors are facing increasingly sophisticated reseller buyers, and this accounts for some of the shifting of power from manufacturers to resellers. Vendors need to understand the resellers' changing requirements and to develop competitively attractive offers that help resellers serve their customers better. Table 7-4 lists several marketing tools used by vendors to improve their attractiveness to resellers.

THE GOVERNMENT MARKET
Who Is in the Government Market?

The government market consists of governmental units—federal, provincial, municipal—that purchase or rent goods and services for carrying out the main functions of government.

Marketing Concepts and Tools 7-1

A NEW TOOL FOR RESELLERS: DIRECT PRODUCT PROFITABILITY (DPP)

Resellers are making increased use of a tool to evaluate new-product profits, called *direct product profitability* (DPP). DPP enables resellers to measure a product's handling costs from the time it reaches their warehouse until a customer buys it and takes it out of their retail store. DPP measures only the direct costs associated with handling the product—receiving, moving to storage, paperwork, selecting, checking, loading, and space cost. Resellers who have adopted DPP learn to their surprise that the gross margin on a product often has little correlation with the direct product profit. For example, some high-volume products may have such high handling costs that they are less profitable and deserve less shelf space than some low-volume products.

The Food Marketing Institute (FMI) is standardizing this tool and promoting its widespread use. DPP can make a number of contributions. First, DPP can help resellers improve the management of their space. Second, DPP will bring about joint manufacturer/reseller actions to lower handling costs, for instance, improving package and case design and size or changing delivery methods. Third, DPP permits testing the profitability of alternative store-shelving plans and locations.

Some manufacturers feel threatened by this tool because it gives resellers a powerful argument for selecting or rejecting existing or new products. Smart manufacturers, however, are studying this tool and using it to help resellers reduce their costs, and thus gaining greater trade acceptance in the process.

In 1990, governmental units purchased $136.9 billion worth of goods and services, or 20.9 percent of the gross national product. That volume made it the nation's largest customer.

Table 7-4 Vendor Marketing Tools Used with Resellers

Cooperative advertising, where vendor agrees to pay a portion of the retailer's advertising costs for the vendor's product

Preticketing, where the vendor places a tag on each product listing its price, manufacturer, size, identification number, and color; these tags help the reseller reorder merchandise as it is sold

Stockless purchasing, where the vendor carries the inventory and delivers goods to the reseller on short notice

Automatic reordering systems, where the vendor supplies forms and computer links for the automatic reordering of merchandise by the reseller

Advertising ads, such as glossy photos, broadcast scripts

Special prices for storewide promotion

Return and exchange privileges for the reseller

Allowances for merchandise markdowns by the reseller

Sponsorship of in-store demonstrations

What Buying Decisions Do Government Buyers Make?

Government buying is based on acquiring products and services that the voters establish as necessary to carry out public objectives. What kinds of products does government buy? Practically everything! One alphabetical list starts with advertising services and aerial photography and ends with vehicles and white goods.[27] Approximately 20 000 commodity groups are kept on file by federal buying units. Although purchases may be worth millions of dollars, 95 percent of federal contracts are for less than $10 000.[28] Provincial and municipal purchases tend to be even smaller. Thus, most of the objects governments buy involve transactions which could be handled by small businesses. No wonder the government market represents a tremendous market for any producer or reseller.

Each good that the government buys requires further decisions on how much to buy, where to buy it, how much to pay, and what services to require. These decisions are made on the basis of trying to minimize *taxpayer cost*. Normally government buyers will favor lowest-cost bidders that can meet the stated specifications. Parenthetically, the institutional market—which we have not described—overlaps with the government market and has many of the same buying characteristics. (See the Companies and Industries 7-1 exhibit.)

Who Participates in the Government Buying Process?

Who does the buying of the billions of dollars worth of goods and services? Government buying organizations are found at the federal, provincial, and municipal levels. Each of the federal departments has some purchasing power, but the Department of Supply and Services is probably the best organized from the viewpoint of potential suppliers. DSS buys nationally and also regionally from its 17 field offices. The national buys are typically bulk purchases, for which sellers may be approached from coast to coast. Regional buys are for standard commercial items, such as fresh foods and snow removal, that can be purchased better at the local level. The Canadian Commercial Corporation is a crown corporation that also reports to the DSS Minister. It is an import-export organization which functions as the purchasing agent for for-

---

Companies and Industries 7-1

THE INSTITUTIONAL MARKET

The institutional market consists of schools, hospitals, nursing homes, prisons and other institutions that must provide goods and services to people in their care. Included also are companies that must feed their employees. Many of these institutions are characterized by low budgets and captive clienteles. A hospital purchasing agent has to decide on the quality of food to buy for the patients. The buying objective is not profit, since the food is provided to the patients as part of the total service package. The basic objective is not cost minimization either, because patients served with poor food in a hospital will complain to others and hurt the hospital's reputation. The hospital purchasing agent has to find institutional-food vendors whose quality meets or exceeds a certain minimum standard and whose prices are low. Many food vendors set up a separate division to sell to institutional buyers because of their special buying needs and characteristics.

---

eign governments. Since its inception in 1946, the Corporation has signed purchasing agreements with 78 foreign countries, and has had a total turnover of $6 billion.[29]

Other federal departments purchase substantial amounts from Canadian sources. In addition, provincial and municipal governments maintain their own buying organizations. Typically these are centralized and located within the respective government administrative offices.

What Are the Major Influences on Government Buyers?

Government buying is premised on a different fundamental objective than is found in the other sectors of the economy. Government does not pursue a personal consumption or a profit-making standard: rather it buys a level and mix of products and services that it or the voters establish as necessary or desirable for the maintenance of society.

Government purchasing of specific goods and services largely follows the objective of *minimizing taxpayer cost*. Government buyers are supposed to buy from the lowest-cost bidders providing that their goods meet the stated specifications. Increasingly, however, the buyers will relax low-cost purchasing rules in the pursuit of other objectives, such as favoring depressed business firms or areas, small business firms, and business firms that do not practice racial, sex, or age discrimination. Sellers need to keep these factors in mind when deciding whether to pursue government business.

How Do Government Buyers Make Their Buying Decisions?

Government buying practices appear complex and often frustrating to suppliers. In a recent survey, suppliers registered a variety of complaints about government purchasing procedures. These complaints included excessive paperwork, bureaucracy, needless regulations, emphasis on low bid prices, decision-making delays, frequent shifts in procurement personnel, and excessive policy changes. Yet the ins and outs of selling to the government can be mastered in a short time. The government is generally helpful in diffusing information about its buying needs and procedures. Government is often as anxious to attract new suppliers as the suppliers are to find customers. For example, the Department of Supply and Services prints the *Weekly Bulletin of Business Opportunities*, which lists the unclassified contracts awarded to Canadian firms on behalf of federal government departments and agencies.[30] In addition, large meetings sponsored by government agencies are held in principal cities to familiarize business representatives with the government's buying needs. Regional offices provide information about DSS buying procedures, including descriptive literature that can be mailed to interested persons.

Government buying procedures fall into two types: the *open bid* and the *negotiated contract*. Open-bid buying means that the government procurement office invites bids from qualified suppliers for carefully described items, generally awarding a contract to the lowest bidder. The supplier must consider whether it can meet the specifications and accept the terms. For commodities and standard items, such as fuel or school supplies, the specifications are not a hurdle. They may be a hurdle, however, for nonstandard items. The government procurement office is usually required to award the contract to the lowest bidder on a winner-take-all basis. In some cases, allowance is made for the supplier's superior product or reputation for completing contracts.

In negotiated-contract buying, the agency works with one or more companies and directly negotiates a contract covering the project and terms. This type of buying occurs primarily with complex projects, often involving major research-and-development costs and risks and/or where there is little effective competition. Contracts can have countless variations, such as *cost-plus pricing, fixed price*, and *fixed price-and-incentive* (the supplier earns more if costs are reduced). Contract performance is open to review and renegotiation if the supplier's profits appear excessive.

Government contracts won by large companies give rise to substantial subcontracting opportunities for small companies. Thus government purchasing activity creates derived demand in the producer market. Subcontracting firms, however, must be willing to place performance bonds with the prime contractor, thereby assuming some of the risk.

Many companies that sell to the government have not manifested a marketing orientation—for a number of reasons. Total government spending is determined by elected officials rather than by marketing effort to develop this market. The government's procurement policies have emphasized price, leading the suppliers to invest considerable effort in bringing their costs down. Where the product's characteristics are carefully specified, product differentiation is not a marketing factor. Nor are advertising and personal selling of much consequence in winning bids on an open-bid basis.

More companies, however, are now establishing separate government marketing departments. Kodak and Goodyear now do so. These companies are preparing their bids more scientifically, initiating projects that anticipate government needs rather than just responding to government initiatives, gathering competitive intelligence, and producing stronger communications to describe the company's competence.

SUMMARY

Business markets consist of individuals and organizations that buy goods for purposes of further production, resale, or redistribution. Businesses (including government and nonprofit organizations) are a market for raw and manufactured materials and parts, installations, accessory equipment, and supplies and services.

The industrial market buys goods and services for the purpose of increasing sales, cutting costs, or meeting social and legal requirements. Compared with the consumer market, the industrial market consists of fewer buyers, larger buyers, and more geographically concentrated buyers; the demand is derived, relatively inelastic, and more fluctuating; and the purchasing is more professional, and more buying influences are involved. Industrial buyers make decisions that vary with the buying situation or buyclass. Buyclasses consist of three types: straight rebuys, modified rebuys, and new tasks. The decision-making unit of a buying organization, the buying center, consists of persons who play any of six roles: users, influencers, buyers, deciders, approvers and gatekeepers. The industrial marketer needs to know: Who are the major participants? In what decisions do they exercise influence? What is their relative degree of influence? and What evaluation criteria does each decision participant use? The industrial marketer also needs to understand the major environmental, organizational, interpersonal, and individual influences operating in the buying process. The buying process itself consists of eight stages called buyphases: problem recognition, general need description, product specification, supplier search, proposal solicitation, supplier selection, order-routine specification, and performance review. As industrial buyers become more sophisticated, industrial marketers must upgrade their marketing capabilities.

The reseller market consists of individuals and organizations that acquire and resell goods produced by others. Resellers have to decide on their assortment, suppliers, prices, and terms. They face three types of buying situations: new items, new vendors, and new terms. In small wholesale and retail organizations, buying may be carried on by one or a few individuals; in larger organizations, by a whole purchasing department. In a modern supermarket chain, the major participants include headquarters buyers, storewide buying committees, and individual store managers. With new items, the buyers go through a buying process similar to the one shown for industrial buyers; and with standard items, the buying process consists of routines for reordering and renegotiating contracts.

The government market is a vast one that annually purchases $80 billion worth of products and services—for the pursuit of defense, education, public welfare, and other public needs. Government buying practices are highly specialized and specified, with open bidding and/or negotiated contracts characterizing most of the buying. Government buyers operate under the watchful eye of Parliament, the Auditor-General and several private watchdog groups. Hence they tend to fill out more forms, require more signatures, and respond more slowly in placing orders.

■ QUESTIONS

1. Would the buying needs and buying procedures of institutional markets such as hospitals and educational institutions differ significantly from those of manufacturing and construction industries?

2. How do the following buying situations affect the purchasing agent's buying-decision process? (a) Purchase of a custom-designed machine to manufacture steering columns for vehicles. (b) Purchase of brake systems from a regular supplier. (c) Improved and updated circuit-board for a personal computer from a recognized and well respected supplier.

3. How would the assortment strategies of the following businesses differ? Give reasons for these differences. (a) A manufacturer of carburetion systems for motor vehicles. (b) A Caterpillar dealer. (c) A reseller of personal computer memory chips and parts. (d) A manufacturer of generic pharmaceutical and automotive parts.

4. A research lab discovered a new method of detecting minute vibrations in objects. A venture capital firm was considering financing the development of this new technique into a production model but required that market research be undertaken to (a) determine the market for application of the technique, and (b) develop specifications for the equipment that would fit the needs of customers in the market. Develop a research plan that accomplishes these objectives.

5. How might the buying decision for a computer system differ between a university and a private individual buying a personal computer?

6. You are a wholesale-distributor for chemicals. What types of concerns would you have in distributing products for manufacturers like Polysar or DuPont Canada?

7. Discuss the major influences affecting how airlines buy airplane seats.

8. General Electric has begun to market a factory automation planning service along with CAD/CAM and robotic products in an attempt to sell fully automated factories-of-the-future to other manufacturers. Using the model in Figure 7-1 discuss the factors that will determine the success or failure of such a venture.

9. How do the buying influences on the government buyer differ from those on the producer or reseller buyer?

10. Describe some of the major characteristics of commercial-services firms (finance, insurance, and real estate) as a market for goods and services.

11. A home-decorating service plans to buy a paint-mixing machine. Four machines are available:

Evoked Set	Price	Number of Speeds	Size (in Grams)	Quietness Level*
1	$30	10	960	3
2	$22	7	900	4
3	$25	5	1440	5
4	$22	5	900	4

* A score of 5 represents the least noise.

Which machine(s) would this company prefer if its decision making could be explained by: (a) a conjunctive model using cut-off points of less than $28, with at least 5 speeds, weighing 960 grams, and with a quietness level equal to or greater than 4; (b) a disjunctive model based upon criteria of at least 8 speeds or at least 1440 grams; and (c) a lexicographic model with an importance ordering of least cost, size, speeds, and quietness. (See Chapter 6 Appendix for discussion of these models.)

■ NOTES

1. Frederick E. Webster, Jr., and Yoram Wind, *Organizational Buying Behavior* (Englewood Cliffs, N.J.: Prentice-Hall, 1972), p. 2.

2. However, for an argument that consumer and industrial marketing do not differ substantially, see Edward F. Fern and James R. Brown, "The Industrial/Consumer Marketing Dichotomy: A Case of Insufficient Justification," *Journal of Marketing*, Spring 1984, pp. 68-77.

3. See William S. Bishop, John L. Graham, and Michael H. Jones, "Volatility of Derived Demand in Industrial Markets and Its Management Implications," *Journal of Marketing*, Fall 1984, pp. 95-103.

4. See Louis W. Stern and Thomas L. Eovaldi, *Legal Aspects of Marketing Strategy* (Englewood Cliffs, N.J.: Prentice-Hall, 1984).

5. See Russell Hindin, "Lease Your Way to Corporate Growth," *Financial Executive*, May 1984, pp. 20-25.

6. Patrick J. Robinson, Charles W. Faris, and Yoram Wind, *Industrial Buying and Creative Marketing* (Boston: Allyn & Bacon, 1967).

7. See Peter Doyle, Arch G. Woodside, and Paul Mitchell, "Organizational Buying in New Task and Rebuy Situations," *Industrial Marketing Management*, February 1979, pp. 7-11.

8. Urban B. Ozanne and Gilbert A. Churchill, Jr., "Five Dimensions of the Industrial Adoption Process," *Journal of Marketing Research*, 1971, pp. 322-28.

9. Marsha A. Schiedt, Fredrick T. Trawick, and John E. Swan, "Impact of Purchasing Systems Contracts on Distributors and Producers," *Industrial Marketing Management*, October 1982, pp. 283-89.

10. See Donald W. Jackson, Jr., Janet E. Keith, and Richard K. Burdick, "Purchasing Agents' Perceptions of Industrial Buying Center Influence: A Situational Approach," *Journal of Marketing*, Fall 1984, pp. 75-83.

11. Webster and Wind, *Organizational Buying Behavior*, p. 6.

12. *Ibid.*, pp. 78-80.

13. See Murray Harding, "Who Really Makes the Purchasing Decision?" *Industrial Marketing*, September 1966, p. 76. This point of view is further developed in Ernest Dichter, "Industrial Buying Is Based on Same 'Only Human' Emotional Factors that Motivate Consumer Market's Housewife," *Industrial Marketing*, February 1973, pp. 14-16.

14. Webster and Wind, *Organizational Buying Behavior*, pp. 33-37.

15. See Thomas H. Stevenson and Albert L. Page, "The Adoption of National Account Marketing by Industrial Firms," *Industrial Marketing Management* 8 (1979), 94-100; and Benson P. Shapiro and Rowland T. Moriarty, *National Account Management: Emerging Insights* (Cambridge, Mass.: Marketing Science Institute, March 1982).

16. Walter Guzzardi, Jr., "The Fight for 9/10 of a Cent," *Fortune*, April 1961, p. 152.

17. Robinson, Faris, and Wind, *Industrial Buying*.

18. See William A. Dempsey, "Vendor Selection and the Buying Process," *Industrial Marketing Management* 7 (1978), 257-67.

19. *Ibid.*

20. See Donald R. Lehmann and John O'Shaughnessy, "Difference in Attribute Importance for Different Industrial Products," *Journal of Marketing*, April 1974, pp. 36-42.

21. See James A. Narus and James C. Anderson, "Turn Your Industrial Distributors into Partners," *Harvard Business Review*, March-April 1986, pp. 66-71.

22. See Leonard Groeneveld, "The Implications of Blanket Contracting for Industrial Purchasing and Marketing," *Journal of Purchasing*, November 1972, pp. 51-58; and H. Lee Mathews, David T. Wilson, and Klaus Backhaus, "Selling to the Computer Assisted Buyer," *Industrial Marketing Management* 6 (1977), 307-15.

23. See C. David Wieters and Lonnie L. Ostrom, "Supplier Evaluation as a New Marketing Tool," *Industrial Marketing Management* 8 (1979), 161-66.

24. See Richard N. Cardozo, "Modelling Organizational Buying as a Sequence of Decisions," *Industrial Marketing Management* 12 (1983), 75-81.

25. Neil H. Borden, Jr., *Acceptance of New Food Products by Supermarkets* (Boston: Division of Research, Graduate School of Business Administration, Harvard University, 1968).

26. Roger A. Dickinson, *Buyer Decision Making* (Berkeley, Calif.: Institute of Business and Economic Research, 1967), pp. 14-17.

27. *How to do Business with the Department of Supply and Services* (Ottawa: Information Canada, 1976) p. 7

28. "Biggest Buyer of All," *Financial Post*, October 23, 1976, p. 6.

29. Notes for a speech by the Honorable Jean-Pierre Goyer, Minister of Supply and Services at "Operation Access," Place Bonaventure, Montreal, October 27, 1976.

30. *Weekly Bulletin of Business Opportunities*, Department of Supply and Services, Government of Canada.

8

Analyzing Competitors

Marketing is merely a civilized form of warfare in which most battles are won with words, ideas, and disciplined thinking.

Albert W. Emery

Understanding one's customers is not enough. True, companies could ignore their competitors in the Soaring Sixties because most markets were growing. But in the Turbulent Seventies and Flat Eighties, company growth increasingly depended on wresting share away from competitors. The nineties will be a decade of intensified competition, foreign and domestic. Many national economies are deregulating and encouraging market forces to operate. The European Common Market is removing trade barriers between Western European countries. Multinationals are aggressively moving into new markets and practicing global marketing. The result is that companies have no choice but to cultivate "competitiveness." They must start paying as much attention to their competitors as to their target customers.

This explains the current talk about "marketing warfare," "competitive intelligence systems," and similar themes.[1] Yet not all companies are investing enough in monitoring their competitors. Some marketers think they know all about their competitors because they compete with them. Other marketers think they can never know enough about their competitors, so why bother? Sensible marketers, however, design and operate systems for gathering continuous information about their competitors.

Knowing one's competitors is critical to effective marketing planning. A company must constantly compare its products, prices, channels, and promotion with its close competitors. In this way, it can identify areas of competitive advantage and disadvantage. The company can launch more precise attacks on its competitors as well as prepare stronger defenses against attacks.

But what do marketers need to know about their competitors? They need to know five things: *Who are our competitors? What are their strategies? What are their objectives? What are their strengths and weaknesses? What are their reaction patterns?* We will examine how this information helps the company shape its marketing strategy.

IDENTIFYING THE COMPANY'S COMPETITORS

Normally, it would seem a simple task for a company to identify its competitors. Coca-Cola knows that Pepsi-Cola is its major competitor; and General Motors knows that Ford is a major competitor. But the range of a company's actual and potential competitors is much broader. Companies must avoid "competitor myopia." A company is more likely to be "buried" by its latent competitors than by its current ones. Here are two vivid examples:

> Kodak has been worrying about the growing competition from Fuji, the Japanese film maker. But Kodak faces a much greater threat from the recent invention of the "filmless camera." This camera, sold by Canon and Sony, takes video still pictures that can be shown on a TV receiver, turned into hard copy, and even erased. What greater threat is there to a film business than a filmless camera! ∎

> Procter & Gamble and other detergent manufacturers are nervous about research being done on an ultrasonic washing machine. If perfected, this machine would wash clothes in water without any detergent. So far, it can clean only certain kinds of dirt and fabrics. What greater threat to the detergent business than an ultrasonic washing machine! ∎

We can distinguish four levels of competitors, based on the concept of *product substitution*:

1. A company can see its competitors as other companies offering a similar product and services to the same customers at similar prices. Thus Buick might see its major competitors to be Ford, Toyota, Honda, Renault, and other manufacturers of moderate-price automobiles. But it would not see itself as competing with Mercedes, on the one hand, or Yugo automobiles, on the other.

2. A company can see its competitors more broadly as all companies making the same product or class of products. Here Buick would see itself as competing against all other automobile manufacturers.

3. A company can see its competitors even more broadly as all companies manufacturing products that supply the same service. Here Buick would see itself competing against not only other automobile manufacturers but also manufacturers of motorcycles, bicycles, and trucks.

4. A company can see its competitors still more broadly as all companies that compete for the same consumer dollars. Here Buick would see itself competing with companies that sell major consumer durables, foreign vacations, new homes, major home repairs, and so on.

More specifically we can identify a company's competitors from an *industry* point of view and a *market* point of view.

Industry Concept of Competition

An *industry* is defined as *a group of firms that offer a product or class of products that are close substitutes for each other.* We talk about the auto industry, the oil industry, the pharmaceutical industry, and so on. Economists define "close substitutes" as products with a *high cross-elasticity of demand.* If the price of one product rises and causes the demand for another product to rise, the two products are close substitutes. If the price of coffee rises and people switch to tea, coffee and tea are substitutes, even though they are physically different products.

Economists have formulated the framework shown in Figure 8-1 to understand industry dynamics. Essentially, it must start with understanding the basic conditions underlying *demand and supply.* These conditions in turn influence the *industry structure.* Industry structure in

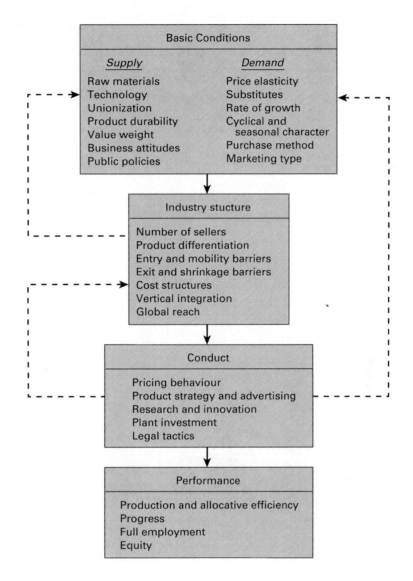

FIGURE 8-1

A Model of Industrial-Organization Analysis

Source: Adapted from F.M. Scherer, *Industrial Market Structure and Economic Performance*, 2nd ed. (Chicago: Rand McNally, 1980), p. 4.

turn influences *industry conduct* in such areas as product development, pricing, and advertising strategy. Industry conduct then shapes *industry performance*, for instance, the industry's efficiency, growth, and employment.

Here we focus on the main factors determining industry structure.

Number of Sellers and Degree of Differentiation   The starting point for describing an industry is to specify whether there are one, few, or many sellers and whether the product is homogeneous or highly differentiated. These characteristics are extremely important and give rise to five well-known industry structure types, those shown in the exhibit Marketing Concepts and Tools 8-1.

The competitive structure of an industry can change over time. Consider the case where Sony innovated the Walkman. Sony is a monopolist at first, but soon many other companies enter, offering different versions of the product, leading to a monopolistically competitive structure. When demand growth slows down, a "shakeout" occurs, and the industry structure might turn into a differentiated oligopoly. Eventually the products might be seen as

Marketing Concepts and Tools 8-1

FIVE INDUSTRY STRUCTURE TYPES

- *Pure monopoly:* A pure monopoly exists when only one seller provides a product in a market area (e.g., Canada Post, Ontario Hydro). This monopoly might be the result of a regulatory edict, a patent, license, scale economies, or other factors. An unregulated monopolist that sought to maximize profits would charge a high price, do little or no advertising, and offer minimal service, since customers have to buy its product in the absence of close substitutes. If there are partial substitutes and some danger of imminent competition, the pure monopolist might invest in more service and technology to act as entry barriers to new competition. A regulated monopoly, on the other hand, would be required to charge a lower price and provide more service as a matter of public interest.

- *Pure oligopoly:* A pure oligopoly consists of a few companies producing essentially the same commodity (oil, steel, and so on). A company would find it hard to charge anything more than the going price unless it can differentiate its services. If the competitors match on services, then the only way to gain a competitive advantage is through achieving lower costs. Lower costs are achieved through pursuing a higher volume strategy.

- *Differentiated oligopoly:* A differentiated oligopoly consists of a few companies producing partially differentiated products (autos, cameras, and so on). The differentiation can occur along lines of quality, features, styling, or services. Each competitor may seek leadership along one of these major attributes, attract the customers favoring that attribute, and charge a premium for that attribute.

- *Monopolistic competition:* A monopolistic competitive industry consists of many competitors able to differentiate their offers in whole or part (restaurants, beauty shops). Many of the competitors focus on market segments where they can meet customer needs in a superior way and command a price premium.

- *Pure competition:* A pure competitive industry consists of many competitors offering the same product and service (stock market, commodity market). Since there is no basis for differentiation, competitors' prices will be the same. No competitor will advertise unless advertising can create psychological differentiation (cigarettes, beer); in this case, it would be more proper to describe the industry as monopolistically competitive. Sellers will enjoy different profit rates only to the extent that they achieve lower costs of production or distribution.

	One Seller	Few Sellers	Many Sellers
Undifferentiated Product	Pure monopoly	Pure oligopoly	Pure Competition
Differentiated Product		Differentiated oligopoly	Monopolistic competition

highly similar with price being the only characteristic of buyer interest; in this case, the industry is now virtually a pure oligopoly.

Entry and Mobility Barriers   Ideally, firms should be free to enter industries that show attractive profits. Their entry would lead to more supply and ultimately bring down profits to a normal rate of return. Ease of entry prevents current firms from extracting long-run excess profits. However, industries differ greatly in the ease with which they can be entered. It is easy to open a new restaurant but difficult to enter the auto industry. The major barriers to entry include *high capital requirements; economies of scale; patents and licensing requirements; scarce locations, raw materials, or distributors; reputational requirements; and so on.* Some barriers are intrinsic to certain industries, and others are erected by the single or combined actions of the incumbent firms. Even after a firm enters an industry, it might face mobility barriers when it tries to enter more attractive market segments.

Exit and Shrinkage Barriers   Ideally, firms should be free to leave industries in which profits are unattractive, but they often face exit barriers.[2] Among the exit barriers are *legal or moral obligations to customers, creditors, and employees; government restrictions; low-asset salvage value due to overspecialization or obsolescence; lack of alternative opportunities; high vertical integration; emotional barriers*; and so on. Many firms persevere in an industry as long as they cover their variable costs and some or all of their fixed costs. Their presence, however, dampens profits for everyone. Companies that want to stay in the industry should lower the exit barriers for others. They can offer to buy competitors' assets, meet customer obligations, and so on. Even if some firms will not exit, they might be induced to shrink their size. Here, too, there are *shrinkage barriers* that the more aggressive firms can try to remove.[3]

Cost Structures   Each industry will have a certain cost mix that will drive much of its strategic conduct. For example, steelmaking involves large manufacturing and raw-material costs, whereas toy manufacturing involves large distribution and marketing costs. Astute managers concentrate on the largest costs and develop strategies to reduce these costs. Thus the steel company with the most modern plant will have a great advantage over the other steel companies.

Vertical Integration   In some industries, companies will find it advantageous to integrate backward and/or forward. A good example is the oil industry where major oil producers carry on oil exploration, oil drilling, oil refining, and chemical manufacturing as part of their operation. Vertical integration often effects lower costs and also more control over the value-added stream. In addition, these firms can manipulate their prices and costs in different segments of their business to earn profits where taxes are lowest. Firms that are not able to integrate vertically operate at a disadvantage.

Global Reach   Some industries are highly local (such as lawn care) and others are *global industries* (such as oil, aircraft engines, cameras). Companies in global industries need to compete on a global basis if they are to achieve economies of scale and keep up with the latest advances in technology.[4]

Market Concept of Competition

Instead of looking at companies making the same product (the industry approach), we can look at companies that satisfy the same customer need or serve the same customer group. A typewriter manufacturer normally sees its competition as other typewriter manufacturers. From a customer-need point of view, however, the customer really wants "writing ability." This need can be satisfied by pencils, pens, computers, and so on. In general, market concept of competition opens the company's eyes to a broader set of actual and potential competitors and stimulates more long-run strategic market planning.

The key to identifying competitors is to link industry and market analysis through mapping the *product/market battlefield.* Figure 8-2 illustrates the product/market battlefield in the

FIGURE 8-2

Product/Market
Battlefield Map
for Toothpaste

Source: William A. Cohen,
*Winning on the Marketing
Front: The Corporate
Manager's Game Plan*
(New York: John Wiley &
Sons, Inc., 1986), p. 63.

	Children/Teens	Age 19-35	Age 36+
Plain toothpaste	Colgate-Palmolive Procter & Gamble	Colgate-Palmolive Procter & Gamble	Colgate-Palmolive Procter & Gamble
Toothpaste with fluoride	Colgate-Palmolive Procter & Gamble	Colgate-Palmolive Procter & Gamble	Colgate-Palmolive Procter & Gamble
Gel	Colgate-Palmolive Procter & Gamble Lever Bros.	Colgate-Palmolive Procter & Gamble Lever Bros.	Colgate-Palmolive Procter & Gamble Lever Bros.
Striped	Beecham	Beecham	
Smoker's toothpaste		Topol	Topol

Customer segmentation

toothpaste market according to product types and customer age groups. We see that P&G and Colgate-Palmolive occupy nine segments; Lever Brothers, three; Beecham, two; and Topol, two. If Topol wanted to enter other segments, it would need to estimate each segment's market size, competitors' market shares in each segment, and their competitors' capabilities, objectives, and strategies as well as the entry barriers in each segment.

IDENTIFYING THE COMPETITORS' STRATEGIES

A company's closest competitors are those pursuing the same target markets with the same strategy. *A strategic group is a group of firms following the same strategy in a given market.*[5]

To illustrate, suppose a company wants to enter the major appliance industry. Suppose the two important strategic dimensions of this industry are quality image and *vertical integration.* It develops the chart shown in Figure 8-3 and discovers that there are four strategic groups. Strategic group A consists of one competitor (Maytag). Strategic group B consists of three major competitors (General Electric, Whirlpool, and Sears). Strategic group C consists of four competitors, and strategic group D consists of two competitors.

Some important insights emerge from this strategic-group identification. First, the height of the entry barriers differs for each strategic group. A new company would find it easier to enter group D because it requires minimal investment in vertical integration and in quality components and reputation. Conversely, the company would find it hardest to enter group A or group B. Second, if the company successfully enters one of the groups, the members of that group become its key competitors. Thus if the company enters group B, it will need strength primarily against General Electric, Whirlpool, and Sears. It needs to enter with some competitive advantage if it hopes to succeed.

Although competition is most intense within a strategic group, there is also rivalry between the groups as well. First, some strategic groups may appeal to overlapping customer groups. For example, major appliance manufacturers with different strategies might nevertheless all go after apartment home builders. Second, the customers might not see much difference in all the offers. Third, each group might want to expand its market segment scope, especially if the companies are fairly equal in size and power and the mobility barriers between groups are low.

FIGURE 8-3
Strategic Groups
in the Major
Appliance Industry

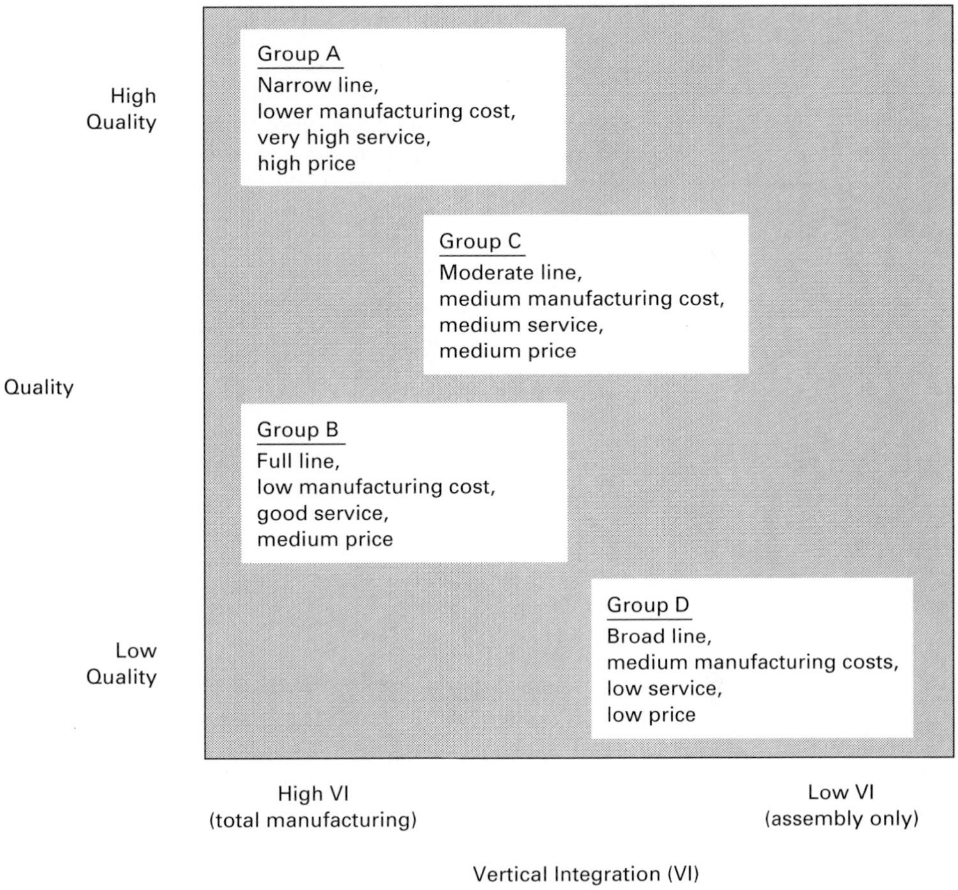

High
Quality

Quality

Low
Quality

Group A
Narrow line,
lower manufacturing cost,
very high service,
high price

Group C
Moderate line,
medium manufacturing cost,
medium service,
medium price

Group B
Full line,
low manufacturing cost,
good service,
medium price

Group D
Broad line,
medium manufacturing costs,
low service,
low price

High VI
(total manufacturing)

Low VI
(assembly only)

Vertical Integration (VI)

Figure 8-3 used only two dimensions to identify strategic groups within an industry. Other dimensions would include level of technological sophistication, geographical scope, manufacturing methods, and so on. In fact, each competitor should be more fully profiled than the two dimensions would suggest. Table 8-1 contrasts two major electronics firms, Texas Instruments and Hewlett-Packard. Clearly, each has a different strategic makeup and therefore appeals to somewhat different customer segments. A company needs even more detailed information about each competitor. It should know each competitor's product quality, features, and mix; customer services; pricing policy; distribution coverage; salesforce strategy; advertising and sales-promotion programs, R&D, manufacturing, purchasing, financial, and other strategies.

DETERMINING THE COMPETITORS' OBJECTIVES

Having identified the main competitors and their strategies, we must ask: What is each competitor seeking in the marketplace? What drives each competitor's behavior?

A useful initial assumption is that competitors strive to maximize their profits. Even here, companies differ in the weights they put on short-term versus long-term profits. Furthermore, some companies orient their thinking around "satisficing" rather than "maximizing." They set target profit goals and are satisfied in achieving them, even if more profits could have been produced by other strategies and exertions.

Table 8-1 Comparison of Strategic Profiles of Texas Instruments and Hewlett-Packard

	Texas Instruments	*Hewlett-Packard*
BUSINESS STRATEGY	Competitive advantage in large standard markets based on long run low cost position	Competitive advantage in selected, small markets based on unique, high-value products
MARKETING	High volume/low price Rapid growth	High value/high price Controlled growth
MANUFACTURING	Experience curve cost-driven Vertical integration	Delivery and quality Limited vertical integration
R & D	Design to cost	Features and quality Design to performance
FINANCIAL	Aggressive Full utilization	Conservative No debt
HUMAN RESOURCES	Competitive Individual incentives	Cooperative Companywide incentives

An alternative assumption is that each competitor has a mix of objectives with different weights. We would want to know the relative weights a competitor places on current profitability, market-share growth, cash flow, technological leadership, service leadership, and so on. Knowing a competitor's weighted mix of objectives allows us to know whether the competitor is satisfied with its current financial results, how it might react to different types of competitive attack, and so on. For example, a competitor pursuing low-cost leadership will react more strongly to a manufacturing process breakthrough by a competitor than to an advertising budget increase by the same competitor.

That competitors' goals can differ sharply is well illustrated by contrasting Canadian and Japanese firms:

> Canadian firms operate largely on a short-run profit maximization model, largely because their current performance is judged by stockholders who might lose confidence, sell their stock, and cause the company's cost of capital to rise. Japanese firms operate largely on a market-share maximization model. They need to provide employment for more than 100 million people in a resource-poor country. Japanese firms have lower profit requirements because most of the capital comes from banks that seek regular interest payments rather than high returns at somewhat higher risks. As a result, Japanese firms can charge lower prices and show more patience in building and penetrating markets. Thus, competitors who are satisfied with lower profits have an advantage over their opponents. ∎

A competitor's objectives are shaped by many things, including its size, history, current management, and economics. If the competitor is part of a larger company, we would like to know whether it is being run for growth or cash or being milked by the parent firm. If the business unit is not central to the parent's enterprise (for example, if it is a dumping ground for excess capacity or is used to exploit distribution channels), we could attack it more readily than if it were the centerpiece in the competitor's empire. Rothschild contends that the worst competitor to attack is the competitor for whom this is the only or major business and who has a global operation.[6] The situation is illustrated in the product/market battlefield map in

FIGURE 8-4
Market Battlefield Map for Microcomputers

Source: William Rothschild, *How to Gain (and Maintain) the Competitive Advantage* (New York: McGraw-Hill, 1984), p. 72.

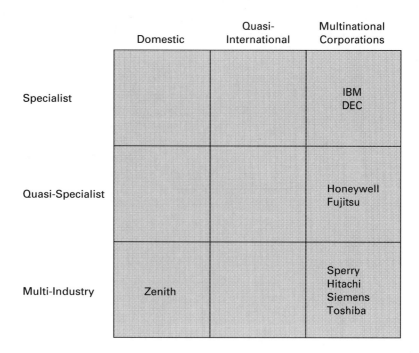

	Domestic	Quasi-International	Multinational Corporations
Specialist			IBM DEC
Quasi-Specialist			Honeywell Fujitsu
Multi-Industry	Zenith		Sperry Hitachi Siemens Toshiba

Figure 8-4. It would make no sense to attack IBM in the microcomputer business because it is a multinational specialist; but attacking Zenith would make sense because computers are only one of the company's businesses, and Zenith operates only domestically.

A company must also monitor its competitors' expansion plans. Figure 8-5 shows a product/market battlefield map for the television industry. It shows the present locations of major competitors as well as their possible moves into other segments. It appears that Zenith will move into television accessories for individual users, and that Radio Shack will move its accessories business into the commercial market. The incumbents in these segments are therefore forewarned and, it is hoped, forearmed.

FIGURE 8-5
The Changing Television Scene

Source: Rothschild, *How to Gain (and Maintain) the Competitive Advantage*, p. 23.

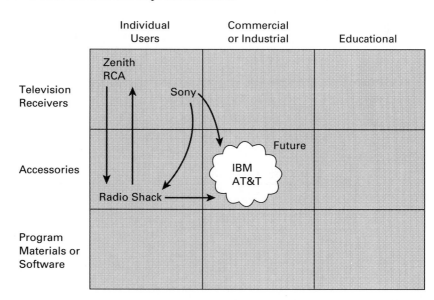

ASSESSING THE COMPETITORS' STRENGTHS AND WEAKNESSES

Can the various competitors carry out their strategies and reach their goals? That depends on each competitor's resources and capabilities. The company needs to identify each competitor's strengths and weaknesses. As a first step, a company should gather key recent data on each competitor's business, particularly (1) *sales*, (2) *market share*, (3) *profit margin*, (4) *return on investment*, (5) *cash flow*, (6) *new investment*, and (7) *capacity utilization*. Some information will be difficult to collect. For example, industrial-goods companies find it hard to estimate competitors' market shares because they do not have syndicated data services that are available to consumer-packaged-goods companies (such as Nielsen). Nevertheless, any information will help them form a better estimate of each competitor's strengths and weaknesses. This kind of information helped a company decide who to attack in the programmable-controls market:

> A company recently made a decision to enter the programmable-controls market. It faced three entrenched competitors, Allen Bradley, Texas Instruments, and Gould. Its research showed that Allen Bradley enjoyed an excellent reputation for technological leadership; Texas Instruments enjoyed low costs and engaged in bloody battles for market share; and Gould did a good job but not a distinguished job. The company concluded that its best target was Gould. ■

Companies normally learn about their competitors' strengths and weaknesses through secondary data, personal experience, and hearsay. They can augment their knowledge by conducting primary marketing research with customers, suppliers, and dealers. Table 8-2 shows the results of a company asking customers to rate its three competitors, A, B, and C, on five attributes. Competitor A turns out to be well-known and viewed as producing high-quality products sold by a good salesforce. However, competitor A is poor in providing product availability and technical assistance. Competitor B is good across the board and excellent in product availability and salesforce. Competitor C rates poor to fair on most attributes. This information suggests that our company could attack competitor A on product availability and technical assistance and competitor C on almost anything, but competitor B has no glaring weakness.

The research findings summarized in Table 8-2 need to be expanded. First, the company's strengths and weaknesses must be included in the ratings. One company's management was shocked to learn that customers rated it in the bottom third on most attributes. Second, the cell ratings should show more detail. Obviously, not every customer thought competitor B had good quality; this was an average perception. Behind it might lie the finding that 20 percent said excellent, 40 percent said good, 30 percent said fair, and 10 percent said poor. It would be interesting to know which customer types did not share the general view of competitor B's product quality. Third, customers should also rate other variables, such as price, management quality, and manufacturing capability.

Table 8-2 Customers' Ratings of Competitors on Key Success Factors

	Customer Awarness	Product Quality	Product Availability	Technical Assistance	Selling Staff
A	E	E	P	P	G
B	G	G	E	G	E
C	F	P	G	F	F

Note: E = excellent, G = good, F = fair, P = poor

There are three other variables that should be competitively tracked:

- *Share of Market:* A measure of the sales share that the competitor has of the relevant market.

- *Share of Mind:* A measure of the percentage of customers who named the competitor in answering the question, "Name the first company that comes to mind in this industry."

- *Share of Heart:* A measure of the percentage of customers who named the competitor in answering the question, "Name the company from whom you would prefer to buy the product."

There is an interesting relationship among these three measures. Table 8-3 shows these numbers for the three competitors listed in Table 8-2. Competitor A enjoys the highest market share, but it is falling. A partial explanation is provided by the fact that its mind share and its heart share are also falling. This slip in customer awareness and preference is probably because competitor A, although providing a good product, is not providing good product availability and technical assistance. Competitor B, on the other hand, is steadily gaining in market share, and that is probably due to strategies that are increasing its mind share and heart share. Competitor C seems to be stuck at a low level of market share, mind share, and heart share, given its poor product and marketing attributes. We could generalize as follows: *Companies that make steady gains in mind share and heart share will inevitably make gains in market share and profitability.* What is important, then, is not whether the company made high or low profits in a particular year (so many factors could affect this) but *whether the company has been steadily building up customer awareness and customer preference over time.*

Among the other measures that a company should track about its competitors are their financial strengths and weaknesses. The financial situation of a competitor is revealed by examining five key ratios:

1. *Liquidity Ratio:* Indicates whether the competitor can easily meet short-term financial obligations when they fall due.

2. *Leverage-Capital-Structure Ratio:* Indicates whether the competitor has the ability to fulfill its long-term commitments to its debtholders. This could be a problem if the competitor's capital structure has too much long-term debt in relation to shareholders' equity.

3. *Profitability Ratio:* Indicates whether the competitor is generating a reasonable level of profits. It can be tracked by such measures as return on total assets, return on equity, or profit margin.

4. *Turnover Ratio:* Indicates whether the competitor is utilizing its assets efficiently. It is measured by dividing its sales by its average assets during the period. A low turnover would dampen the profitability ratio.

5. *Common-Stock Security Ratio:* Tells us whether the stock market has high or low confidence in the competitor. It is measured by movements in earnings per share or market-to-book value.[7]

Table 8-3 Market Share, Mind Share, and Heart Share

	Market Share			Mind Share			Heart Share		
	1988	1989	1990	1988	1989	1990	1988	1989	1990
A	50%	47%	44%	60%	58%	54%	45%	42%	39%
B	30%	34%	37%	30%	31%	35%	44%	47%	53%
C	20%	19%	19%	10%	11%	11%	11%	11%	8%

The profitability and turnover ratios can be combined in a chart that shows the financial profile of the key competitors—specifically, how much money is coming from operating margin versus asset turnover (see Marketing Concepts and Tools 8-2).

Finally, in searching for competitors' weaknesses, we should identify any assumptions they make about their business and the market that are no longer valid. Some companies believe they produce the best quality in the industry when that is no longer true. Many com-

---

Marketing Concepts and Tools 8-2

Du Pont Profitability Chart

A company's return on operating assets (ROA) is a function of its *operating margin* and its *operating asset turnover*. It is possible for companies to earn the same ROA in vastly different ways. The accompanying figure below shows three competitors, A, B, and C, and their ROAs. Competitors A and B both earn a 20 percent ROA but in quite different ways. Competitor A earns it through a low margin but a high turnover; competitor B earns it through a high margin and a low turnover. Competitor C turns over its assets at approximately the same rate as competitor A but has a much lower margin, thereby achiev-

ing only a 10 percent ROA. The industry as a whole averages 15 percent, consisting of a 15 percent margin and an asset turnover of 1.00.

A company must increase its margin and/or its turnover in order to increase its ROA. The figure shows company C as hoping to move to C' (a higher ROA) through increasing its operating margin by more than the decline in its asset turnover.

Source: Adapted from William L. Sammon, Mark A. Kurland, and Robert Spitalnic, *Business Competitor Intelligence* (New York: John Wiley, 1984).

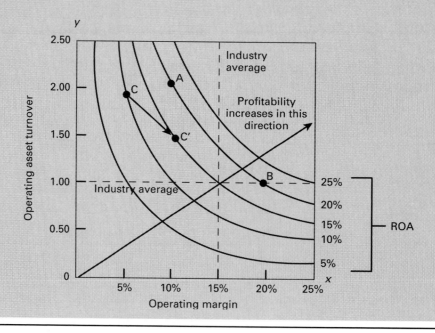

panies are victims of conventional wisdom like "Customers prefer full-line companies," "The salesforce is the only important marketing tool," "Customers value service more than price." If we know that a competitor is operating on a major wrong assumption, we can take advantage of it.

ESTIMATING THE COMPETITORS' REACTION PATTERNS

A competitor's objectives and strengths/weaknesses go a long way toward predicting its likely moves and reactions to company moves such as a price cut, a promotion step-up, or a new-product introduction. In addition, each competitor has a certain philosophy of doing business, a certain internal culture, and certain guiding beliefs. One needs a deep understanding of a given competitor's mind-set to have hope of anticipating how the competitor might act or proact.

Here are some common reaction profiles of competitors:

1. *The Laid-Back Competitor:* Some competitors do not react quickly or strongly to a given competitor move. They may feel their customers are loyal; they may be milking the business; they may be slow in noticing the initiative; they may lack the funds to react. The firm must try to assess the reasons for the competitors' laid-back behavior.

2. *The Selective Competitor:* A competitor might react only to certain types of attacks and not to others. It might respond to price cuts in order to signal that they are futile. But it might not respond to advertising expenditure increases, believing them to be less threatening. Knowing what a key competitor reacts to gives the company a clue as to the most feasible lines of attack.

3. *The Tiger Competitor:* This company reacts swiftly and strongly to any assault on its terrain. Thus P&G does not let a new detergent come easily into the market. A tiger competitor is signaling that another firm had better avoid any attack because the defender is going to fight to the finish if attacked. It is always better to attack a sheep than a tiger.

4. *The Stochastic Competitor:* Some competitors do not exhibit a predictable reaction pattern. Such a competitor might or might not retaliate on any particular occasion, and there is no way to foresee what it will do based on its economics, history, or anything else.

Some industries are characterized by relative accord among the competitors, and others by constant fighting. Bruce Henderson, founder of the Boston Consulting Group, thinks that much depends on the industry's "competitive equilibrium." Here are some of his observations about the likely state of competitive relations:[8]

1. *If competitors are nearly identical and make their living in the same way, then their competitive equilibrium is unstable:* There is likely to be perpetual conflict in industries where competitive ability is at parity. This would describe "commodity industries" where sellers have not found any major way to differentiate their costs or their offers. In such cases, the competitive equilibrium would be upset if any firm lowers its price—a strong temptation, especially for a competitor with overcapacity. This explains why price wars frequently break out in these industries.

2. *If a single major factor is the critical factor, then competitive equilibrium is unstable:* This would describe industries where cost-differentiation opportunities exist through economies of scale, advanced technology, experience curve learning, and so on. In such industries, any company that achieves a cost breakthrough can cut its price and win market share at the

expense of other firms who could only defend their market shares at great cost. Price wars frequently break out in these industries as a result of cost breakthroughs.

3. *If multiple factors may be critical factors, then it is possible for each competitor to have some advantage and be differentially attractive to some customers. The more the multiple factors that may provide an advantage, the more the number of competitors who can coexist. Competitors all have their competitive segment, defined by the preference for the factor tradeoffs that they offer:* This would describe industries where many opportunities exist to differentiate quality, service, convenience, and so on. If customers also place different values on these factors, then many firms can coexist through niching.

4. *The fewer the number of competitive variables that are critical, the fewer the number of competitors:* If only one factor is critical, then no more than two or three competitors are likely to coexist. Conversely, the larger the number of competitive variables, the larger the number of competitors, but each is likely to be smaller in its absolute size.

5. *A ratio of 2 to 1 in market share between any two competitors seems to be the equilibrium point at which it is neither practical nor advantageous for either competitor to increase or decrease share.*

Henderson goes on to give the following advice to a firm. Be sure that the rival is fully aware of what would be gained through cooperation and what otherwise would be lost. Convince the rival that you are emotionally dedicated to your position and completely convinced that it is reasonable. Avoid actions that will arouse your competitor's emotions.

DESIGNING THE COMPETITIVE INTELLIGENCE SYSTEM

We have described the main types of information that company decision makers need to know about their competitors. This information must be collected, interpreted, disseminated, and used. While the cost in money and time of gathering competitive intelligence is high, the cost of not gathering it is higher. Yet the company must design its competitive intelligence system in a cost-effective way. There are four main steps:

1. *Setting up the System:* The first step calls for identifying vital types of competitive information, identifying the best sources of this information and assigning a person who will manage the system and its services.

2. *Collecting the Data:* Here the data are collected on a continuous basis from the field (salesforce, channels, suppliers, market research firms, trade associations) and from published data (government publications, speeches, articles). The company has to develop effective ways of acquiring needed information about competitors without violating legal or ethical standards (see Marketing Concepts and Tools 8-3).

3. *Evaluating and Analyzing:* In this step, the data are checked for validity and reliability, interpreted, and organized in an appropriate way.

4. *Disseminating and Responding:* Here key information is sent to relevant decision makers, and managers' inquiries about competitors are answered.

With this system, company managers will receive timely information about competitors through phone calls, bulletins, newsletters, and reports. Managers can also contact the department when they need an interpretation of a sudden move by a competitor, or when they need to know a competitor's weaknesses and strengths or how a competitor will respond to a contemplated company move. The competitive information can be organized in a form like that

Marketing Concepts and Tools 8-3

INTELLIGENCE GATHERING: SNOOPING ON COMPETITORS

Competitive intelligence gathering has grown dramatically as more companies need to know what their competitors are doing. An article in *Fortune* lists over twenty techniques companies use to collect their intelligence. The techniques fall into four major categories.

□ *Getting Information from Recruits and Competitors' Employees:* Companies can obtain intelligence through job interviews or from conversations with competitors' employees. Companies send engineers to conferences and trade shows to question competitors' technical people. They sometimes advertise and hold interviews for jobs that don't exist in order to pump competitors' employees for information. Companies hire key executives from competitors to find out what they know.

□ *Getting Information from People Who Do Business with Competitors:* Key customers can keep the company informed about competitors—they might even be willing to request and pass along information on competitors' products. Companies may provide their engineers free of charge to customers. The close, cooperative relationship that the engineers on loan cultivate with the customer's design staff often enables them to learn what new products competitors are pitching.

□ *Getting Information from Published Materials and Public Documents:* Keeping track of seemingly meaningless published information can provide competitor intelligence. For example, the types of people sought in help-wanted ads can indicate something about a competitor's technological thrusts and new product development. Although it is illegal for a company to photograph a competitor's plant from the air, aerial photos often are on file with government departments like the Ontario Ministry of Natural Resources.

□ *Getting Information by Observing Competitors or Analyzing Physical Evidence:* Companies increasingly buy competitors' products and take them apart to determine costs of production and even manufacturing methods. Some companies even buy their competitors' garbage. Once it has left the competitor's premises, refuse is legally considered abandoned property.

Though most techniques are legal, many involve questionable ethics. The company should take advantage of publicly available information, but responsible companies avoid practices that might be considered illegal or unethical. A company does not have to break the law or violate accepted codes of ethics to collect intelligence, and the benefits gained from using such techniques are not worth the risks.

Source: Based on Steven Flax, "How to Snoop on Your Competitors," *Fortune*, May 14, 1984, pp. 29-33.

shown in Table 8-4. This table shows what each manager should know about each competitor in each product market.

In smaller companies that cannot afford to set up a formal competitive intelligence office, a useful step would be to assign specific executives to watch specific competitors. Thus a manager who used to work for a competitor would closely follow all developments connected with that competitor; he or she would be the "in-house" expert on that competitor. In this way, any manager who needs to know the thinking of a specific competitor could contact the corresponding in-house expert.

SELECTING COMPETITORS TO ATTACK AND AVOID

Given good competitive intelligence, managers will find it easier to formulate their competitive strategies. They will have a better sense of whom they can effectively compete with

Table 8-4 Competitor Profile Information

	Competitor A	Competitor B	Competitor C
Descriptors (product line, market segments, sales, market shares, profit margin, ROI, new investment, capacity utilization, etc.)			
Strategies (R&D, manufacturing, marketing, financial, personnel) (Within marketing: products, price, distribution, and promotion strategies)			
Objectives (marketing, financial, etc.)			
Strengths/weaknesses			
Reaction patterns			
Marketing implications			

in the market. The manager must decide which competitors to compete against most vigorously. This manager's choice is aided by conducting a *customer value analysis*, which will reveal the company's strengths and weaknesses relative to various competitors (Marketing Concepts and Tools 8-4 describes the methodology of customer value analysis). The company can focus its attack on one of several classes of competitors as described below.

Strong Versus Weak Competitors Most companies aim their shots at their weak competitors. This requires fewer resources and time per share point gained. But in the process, the firm may achieve little in the way of improved capabilities. The firm should also compete with strong competitors because, by competing with them, the firm will have to keep up with the state of the art. Furthermore, even strong competitors have some weaknesses, and the firm may prove to be a worthy competitor.

Close Versus Distant Competitors Most companies compete with competitors who resemble them the most. Thus Chevrolet competes with Ford, not with Jaguar. At the same time, the company should avoid trying to "destroy" the close competitor. Porter cites two examples of counterproductive "victories":

> Bausch and Lomb in the late 1970s moved aggressively against other soft-lens manufacturers with great success. However, this led each weak competitor to sell out to larger firms, such as Revlon, Johnson & Johnson, and Schering-Plough, with the result that Bausch and Lomb now faced much larger competitors.

> A specialty rubber manufacturer attacked another specialty rubber manufacturer and took away share. The damage to the other company allowed the specialty divisions of the large tire companies to move more quickly into specialty rubber markets, using them as a dumping ground for excess capacity.[9]

In each case, the company's success in hurting its closest rival brought in tougher competition to contend with.

"Good" Versus "Bad" Competitors Porter argues that every industry contains "good" and "bad" competitors.[10] A marketer would be smart to support the good competitors and attack

Marketing Concepts and Tools 8-4

CUSTOMER VALUE ANALYSIS: THE KEY TO COMPETITIVE ADVANTAGE

In the search for competitive advantage, one of the most important steps is to carry out a *customer value analysis*. The aim of a customer value analysis is to determine the benefits that customers in a target market segment want and how they perceive the relative value of competing suppliers' offers. The major steps in customer value analysis are described below.

1. *Identify the major attributes that customers value:* Various company employees will have their ideas on what customers value. Senior management will say quality and service, salespeople will say price, and so on. Their lists will generally be short and not in full agreement. Therefore it is essential to ask the customers themselves what functions and performance levels they look for in choosing a product and vendors. Different customers will mention different features/benefits. If the list gets overly long, the researcher can remove redundant attributes. Still, the final list of attributes that customers value may run as high as ten or twenty items.

2. *Assess the quantitative importance of the different attributes:* Here again company personnel will have varying opinions on the importance that customers attach to the different attributes. R&D will see design as important, manufacturing will see cost as important, and salespeople will see price as important. But it is the customers who must supply their ratings or rankings of the importance of the different attributes. If the customers diverge much in their ratings, they should be clustered into different customer segments.

3. *Assess the company's and competitors' performances on the different customer values against their rated importance:* Here the customers are asked where they see each competitor's performance on each attribute. Ideally, the company's own performance should be high on the attributes the customers value most and low on the attributes customers value least. Two pieces of bad

news would be (a) the company performs high on some minor attributes—a case of "overkill," and (b) the company performs low on some major attributes—a case of "underkill." The company must also examine how each competitor ranks on the attributes which are important to customers.

4. *Examine how customers in a specific segment rate the company's performance against a specific major competitor on an attribute-by-attribute basis:* The key to gaining competitive advantage is to take each customer segment and examine how the company's offer compares to that of its major competitor. If the company's offer exceeds the competitor's offer on all important attributes, the company can charge a higher price, thereby earning higher profits, or it can charge the same price and gain more market share. However, if the company finds that it performs at a lower level on some important attributes than its major competitor does, it must invest in strengthening those attributes or finding other important attributes where it can build even more of a lead on the competitor. Investments can take two forms. If the company's performance is really inferior on an important attribute, it needs to improve it in real terms. If the company's attribute standing is on par with the competitor's but it has not been adequately or persuasively communicated to customers, the company must improve its marketing communication program rather than the attribute.

5. *Monitor customer values over time:* Although customer values are fairly stable in the short run, they will most probably change as competing technologies and features become available and as customers face different economic climates. A company that assumes that customer values will remain stable is flirting with danger. The company must periodically redo its studies of customer values and competitors' standings if it wants to be strategically effective.

the bad competitors. Good competitors have a number of characteristics: They play by the rules of the industry; they make realistic assumptions about the industry's growth potential; they set prices in a reasonable relation to costs; they favor a healthy industry; they limit themselves to a portion or segment of the industry; they motivate others to lower costs or improve differentiation; and they accept the general level of their share and profits. Bad competitors violate the rules: They try to buy share rather than earn it; they take large risks; they invest in overcapacity; and in general, they upset the industrial equilibrium. For example, IBM finds Cray Research to be a good competitor because it plays by the rules, sticks to its segment, and does not attack IBM's core markets; but IBM finds Fujitsu a bad competitor because it attacks IBM in its core markets with subsidized prices and little differentiation. The implication is that the "good" companies in an industry should try to configure an industry that consists of only good competitors. Through careful licensing, selective retaliation, and coalitions, they can shape the industry so that (1) the competitors are not seeking to destroy each other and behave irrationally; (2) they follow the rules; (3) each differentiates somewhat; and (4) they each try to earn share rather than buy it.

Behind this is a larger point, that a company really needs and benefits from competitors. The existence of competitors confers several strategic benefits: (1) They lower the antitrust risk; (2) they increase total demand; (3) they lead to more differentiation; (4) they provide a cost umbrella for the less-efficient producers; (5) they share the cost of market development and legitimatize a new technology; (6) they improve bargaining power vis-à-vis labor unions or regulators; and (7) they may serve less attractive segments.

BALANCING CUSTOMER AND COMPETITOR ORIENTATIONS

We have stressed the importance of a company's watching its competitors closely. The question now arises, Is it possible to spend too much time and energy tracking competitors, to the detriment of a customer orientation? The answer is yes! A company can become so competitor centered that it loses its customer focus.[11]

A *competitor-centered company* is one whose moves are basically dictated by competitors' actions and reactions. The company spends a great deal of time tracking competitors' moves and market shares on a market-by-market basis. It sets its course based on data like the following:

COMPETITOR-CENTERED COMPANY

Situation

☐ Competitor W is going all out to crush us in Calgary.

☐ Competitor X is improving its distribution coverage in Vancouver and hurting our sales.

☐ Competitor Y has cut its price in Montreal and we lost three share points.

☐ Competitor Z has introduced a new service feature in Toronto and our customers are starting to switch their business to this competitor.

Solutions

☐ We will withdraw from the Calgary market because we cannot afford to fight this battle.

☐ We will increase our advertising expenditure level in Vancouver.

☐ We will meet competitor Y's price cut in Montreal.

☐ We will increase our sales-promotion budget in Toronto.

Now this mode of strategy planning has some pluses and minuses. On the positive side, the company develops a fighter orientation. It trains its marketers to be on a constant alert, watching for weaknesses in its own position, and watching for competitors' weaknesses. On the negative side, the company exhibits too much of a reactive pattern. Rather than carrying out a consistent customer-oriented strategy, it determines its moves based on its competitors' moves. As a result, it does not move in a predetermined direction toward a goal. It does not know where it will end up, since so much depends on what the competitors decide to do.

A *customer-centered company*, in contrast, would focus more on customer developments in formulating its strategies. It would pay more attention to the following types of data:

CUSTOMER-CENTERED COMPANY

Situation

- □ The total market is growing at 4 percent annually.
- □ The fastest-growing segment is the quality-sensitive segment; it is growing at 8 percent annually.
- □ The deal-prone customer segment is also growing, but these customers do not stay with any supplier very long.
- □ A growing number of customers have expressed an interest in a twenty-four-hour hotline, which no one in the industry offers.

Solutions

- □ We will focus more effort on reaching and satisfying the quality segment of the market; our plan will be to buy better components, improve our quality control, and shift our advertising theme to quality.
- □ We will avoid cutting prices and making deals, because we do not want the kind of customer that buys this way.
- □ We will investigate the costs and share-gain potential of a twenty-four-hour hotline and install it if it looks promising.

Clearly, the customer-centered company is in a better position to identify new opportunities and set a strategy course that makes long-run sense. By watching customer needs evolve, it can decide what customer groups and what emerging needs are the most important to serve, given its resources and objectives.

In practice, today's companies must watch both customers and competitors. The caution is that they must not let competitor watching blind them to customer focusing. Figure 8-6 shows that companies have moved through four orientations over the years. In the first stage, companies paid little attention to either customers or competitors; they were *product oriented.* In the second stage, they started to pay attention to customers; they were *customer oriented.* In the third stage, they started to pay attention to competitors; they became *competitor oriented.* In today's stage, they need to pay balanced attention to both, and we say they are *market oriented.*

FIGURE 8-6
Shifting Company Orientations

		Competitor Centered: No	Competitor Centered: Yes
Customer Centered	No	Product orientation	Customer orientation
	Yes	Competitor orientation	Market orientation

SUMMARY

To prepare an effective marketing strategy, a company must consider its competitors as well as its actual and potential customers. That is especially necessary in slow-growth markets because sales can be gained only by winning them away from competitors.

A company's competitors include those seeking to satisfy the same customers and customer needs and making similar offers to them. A company should also pay attention to its latent competitors, who may offer new or other ways to satisfy the same needs. The company should try to identify its competitors by using both an industry and a market-based analysis.

A company needs to gather information on competitors' strategies, objectives, strengths/weaknesses, and reaction patterns. The company needs to know each competitor's strategies in order to identify its closest competitors and take the proper steps. The company should know the competitor's objectives in order to anticipate further moves and reactions. Knowing the competitor's strengths and weaknesses permits the company to refine its strategy to take advantage of the competitor's limitations while avoiding engagement where the competitor is strong. Knowing the competitor's typical reaction pattern helps the company choose and time its moves.

Competitive intelligence needs to be collected, interpreted, and disseminated continuously. Company marketing executives should be able to obtain full and reliable information about any competitor that has a bearing on a decision.

As important as a competitive orientation is in today's markets, companies should not overdo their focus on competitors. Companies are more likely to be hurt by changing customer needs and latent competitors than by their existing competitors. Companies that manage in a good balance of consumer and competitor considerations are practicing a true market orientation.

■ QUESTIONS

1. Discuss the four levels of competition for Pepsi based on a broadening of the concept of product substitution.

2. Contrast the industry and market concept of competition for the category "lawn care." Design and discuss a product/market battlefield map for this category.

3. Mobility barriers are factors that protect members of a strategic group from incursion by firms inside the group. What are some sources of mobility barriers? That is, what factors can deter movement between strategic groups in an industry by making such movement costly for invading firms?

4. Why is the concept of strategic groups useful to marketing strategists?

5. Set up a chart similar to Table 8-2 to compare the Shouldice Hospital (which specializes in hernia operations) with its full-service "competitor" the Toronto General Hospital. (a) How would you determine the appropriate criteria for comparison and (b) each hospital's ratings on the criteria? (c) Devise a strategy for the hospital that you believe has a competitive advantage.

6. Competition in the pasta market is primarily on a regional, instead of a national, basis. What explanation would you give for this phenomenon? If you were a marketing manager for one of these pasta companies, what would you do to try to make your brand nationally dominant?

7. Despite being the first entrant in the home videocassette recorder market, having several technological advantages, and an overall cost/benefit advantage, Sony's Beta format is no longer a major force in the market. What happened? Use relevant concepts of competition discussed in this chapter in your analysis.

8. Listed below are several company strengths, as might be seen by a manager conducting an internal audit. How might these strengths be translated into customer benefits that would give the company a competitive advantage?
   a) Innovative product features
   b) Broad distribution
   c) Lower costs and prices
   d) Broad product line
   e) Strong technical service

9. A headline for an article in *Business Week* read "Forget Satisfying the Consumer—Just Outfox the Other Guy." Debate the merits of this advice.

10. In what ways does competition at the domestic level differ from that at the international level? Consider the auto industry. What are the keys to success in this battle of the giants? Who are the beneficiaries?

■ NOTES

1. See Al Ries and Jack Trout, *Marketing Warfare* (New York: McGraw-Hill, 1986); William L. Sammon, Mark A. Kurland, and Robert Spitalnic, *Business Competitor Intelligence* (New York: Ronald Press, 1984); and Leonard M. Fuld, *Monitoring the Competition* (New York: John Wiley, 1988).

2. See Kathryn Rudie Harrigan, "The Effect of Exit Barriers upon Strategic Flexibility," *Strategic Management Journal 1* (1980), pp. 165-76.

3. See Michael E. Porter, *Competitive Advantage* (New York: Free Press, 1985), pp. 225, 485.

4. See Michael E. Porter, *Competitive Strategy* (New York: Free Press, 1980), Chap. 13.

5. George Foster, *Financial Statement Analysis* (Englewood Cliffs, N.J.: Prentice-Hall, 1978).

6. William E. Rothschild, *How to Gain (and Maintain) the Competitive Advantage* (New York: McGraw-Hill, 1984), Chap. 5.

7. Porter, *Competitive Strategy*, Chap. 7.

8. The following has been drawn from various Bruce Henderson writings, including "The Unanswered Questions, The Unsolved Problems" (paper delivered in a speech at Northwestern University in 1986); *Henderson on Corporate Strategy* (New York: Mentor, 1982); and "Understanding the Forces of Strategic and Natural Competition," *Journal of Business Strategy*, Winter 1981, pp. 11-15.

9. Porter, *Competitive Advantage*, pp. 226-27.

10. *Ibid.,* Chap. 6.

11. See Alfred R. Oxenfeldt and William L. Moore, "Customer or Competitor: Which Guidelines for Marketing?" *Management Review*, August 1978, pp. 43-48.

PART III

Researching and Selecting Target Markets

9

Measuring and Forecasting Market Demand

Forecasting is hard, particularly of the future.

Anonymous

Forecasting is like trying to drive a car blindfolded and following directions given by a person who is looking out of the back window.

Anonymous

Having examined the tools for analyzing customer markets and competitive forces, we are now ready to consider how the company can choose *attractive markets* and develop *winning strategies* in these markets. Companies face many market opportunities and must carefully evaluate them before choosing their target markets. They need skill in measuring and forecasting the size, growth, and profit potential of various market opportunities.

Once in a market, the company needs to prepare accurate demand projections. These projections are used by the finance department to raise the needed cash for investment and operations; by the manufacturing department to establish capacity and output levels; by purchasing to acquire the right amount of inventory; and by personnel to hire the needed number of workers. Marketing is responsible for making these estimates. If their forecast is far off the mark, the company either will be saddled with excess capacity and inventory or will have lost money because it was out of stock.

This chapter will address three broad questions: *What are the main concepts in demand measurement and forecasting? How can current demand be estimated? How can future demand be forecasted?*

MAJOR CONCEPTS IN DEMAND MEASUREMENT

Managers need to define carefully what they mean by market demand. We will present several distinctions that will help managers talk more precisely about market demand.

A Multitude of Measures of Market Demand

As part of their ongoing planning, companies prepare a great number of market-size estimates. Figure 9-1 shows *ninety* different types of demand estimates that a company can make. Demand can be measured for six different *product levels* (product item, product form, product line, company sales, industry sales, national sales), five different space levels (customer, territory, province, Canada, world), and three different *time levels* (short range, medium range, and long range).

Each type of demand measurement serves a specific purpose. Thus a company might make a short-range forecast of the total demand for a particular product item to provide a basis for ordering raw materials, planning production, and scheduling short-run financing. Or it might make a long-range forecast of regional demand for its major product line to provide a basis for considering market expansion.

Which Market to Measure?

Marketers talk about *potential markets, available markets, served markets*, and *penetrated markets*. To clarify these terms, let us start with the notion that a *market* is *the set of all actual and potential buyers of a product*. The *size* of a market then hinges on the number of buyers who might exist for a particular market offer. Those who are in the market would have three characteristics: *interest, income*, and *access*.

Let us apply this to the motorcycle market. We will ignore companies that purchase motorcycles and concentrate on the consumer market. We must first estimate the number of consumers who have a potential *interest* in owning a motorcycle. To do this, we can contact a random sample of consumers and pose the following question: "Would you have a strong interest in owning a motorcycle?" If one person out of ten says yes, we can assume that 10 percent of the total number of consumers would constitute the potential market for motorcycles. The *potential market* is the set of consumers who profess a sufficient level of interest in a defined market offer.

FIGURE 9-1

Ninety Types of Demand Measurement (6 × 5 × 3)

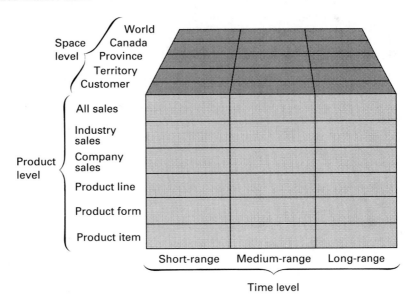

Consumer interest is not enough to define a market. Potential consumers must have enough *income* to afford the product. They must be able to answer the following question positively: "Can you afford to purchase a motorcycle?" The higher the price, the fewer the number of people who can answer this question positively. The size of a market is a function of both interest and income.

Access barriers further reduce market size. If motorcycles are not distributed in the far north because the driving season is short, potential consumers in that area are not available to marketers. The *available market* is the set of consumers who have interest, income, and access to a particular market offer.

For some market offers, the company or government may restrict sales to certain groups. Some provinces might ban motorcycle sales to anyone under twenty-one years of age. The remaining adults constitute the *qualified available market*—the set of consumers who have interest, income, access, and qualifications for the particular market offer.

The company now has the choice of going after the whole qualified available market or concentrating on certain segments. The *served market* (also called the *target market*) is the part of the qualified available market the company decides to pursue. The company, for example, might decide to concentrate its marketing and distribution effort in Ontario and Quebec. These provinces become its served market.

The company and its competitors will end up selling a certain number of motorcycles in its served market. The *penetrated market* is the set of consumers who have already bought the product.

Figure 9-2 brings the preceding concepts together with some hypothetical numbers. The bar on the left illustrates the ratio of the potential market—all interested persons—to the total population, here 10 percent. The bar on the right illustrates several breakdowns of the potential market. The available market—those who have interest, income, and access—is 40 percent of the potential market. The qualified available market—those who can meet the legal requirements—is 20 percent of the potential market (or 50 percent of the available market). The company is concentrating its efforts on 10 percent of the potential market (or 50 percent of the qualified available market). Finally, the company and its competitors have already penetrated 5 percent of the potential market (or 50 percent of the served market).

These definitions of a market are a useful tool for marketing planning. If the company is not satisfied with current sales, it can consider a number of actions. It can try to attract a

FIGURE 9-2
Levels of Market Definition

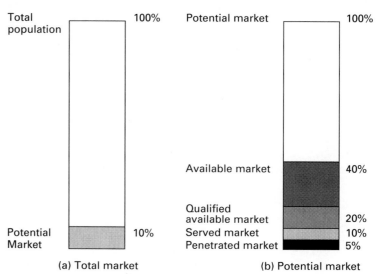

(a) Total market

(b) Potential market

larger percentage of buyers from its served market. It can lower the qualifications of potential buyers. It can expand to other available markets, for instance, the Atlantic provinces. It can lower its price to expand the size of the available market. Ultimately, the company can try to expand the potential market by a major advertising campaign to convert uninterested consumers into interested consumers. That is what Honda did when it ran its successful campaign on the theme, "You meet the nicest people on a Honda."

A Vocabulary for Demand Measurement

The field of demand measurement is filled with a confusing number of terms. Company executives talk of forecasts, predictions, potentials, estimates, projections, goals, targets, quotas, and budgets. Many of these terms are redundant. The major concepts in demand measurement are *market demand* and *company demand*. Within each, we distinguish between a *demand function*, a *forecast*, and a *potential*.

Market Demand   In evaluating marketing opportunities, the first step is to estimate total market demand. It is not a simple concept, however, as the following definition makes clear:

> Market demand *for a* product *is the* total volume *that would be* bought *by a defined* customer group *in a defined* geographical area *in a defined* time period *in a defined* marketing environment *under a defined* marketing program.

Thus market demand requires specifying how the product is defined; whether demand is measured in physical or dollar volume; whether *bought* means the volume ordered, shipped, or paid for; the assumptions made about the marketing environment and marketing program; and so on.

The most important thing about total market demand is that it is not a fixed number but a function of the stated conditions. For this reason, it can be called the *market demand function or market response function*. The dependence of total market demand on underlying conditions is illustrated in Figure 9-3(a). The horizontal axis shows different possible levels of industry marketing expenditure in a given time period. The vertical axis shows the resulting demand level. The curve represents the estimated market demand associated with varying levels of industry marketing expenditure. Some base sales (called the *market minimum*) would take place without any demand-stimulating expenditures. Higher levels of industry marketing expenditures would yield higher levels of demand, first at an increasing rate, then at a decreasing rate. Marketing expenditures beyond a certain level would not stimulate much further demand, thus suggesting an upper limit to market demand called the *market potential*.

The distance between the market minimum and the market potential shows the overall *marketing sensitivity of demand*. We can think of two extreme types of markets, the *expansible* and the *nonexpansible*. An expansible market, such as the market for racquetball playing, is quite affected in its total size by the level of industry marketing expenditures. In terms of Figure 9-3(a), the distance between Q_1 and Q_2 is relatively large. A nonexpansible market, for example, the market for opera, is not much affected by the level of marketing expenditures; the distance between Q_1 and Q_2 is relatively small. Organizations selling in a nonexpansible market can accept the market's size (the level of *primary demand*) and direct their marketing resources to winning a desired market share (the level of *selective demand*).

It is important to emphasize that the *market demand function* is *not* a picture of market demand over *time*. Rather, the curve shows alternative current forecasts of market demand associated with alternative possible levels of industry marketing effort in the current period.

FIGURE 9-3
Market Demand

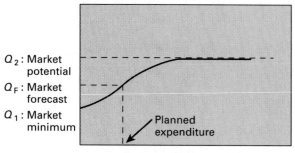

Q_2: Market potential

Q_F: Market forecast

Q_1: Market minimum

Planned expenditure

Market demand in the specific period

Industry marketing expenditure

(a) Marketing demand as a function of industry marketing expenditure (assumes a particular marketing environment)

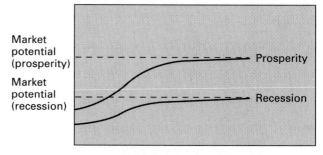

Market demand in the specific period

Market potential (prosperity)

Market potential (recession)

Prosperity

Recession

Industry marketing expenditure

(a) Marketing demand as a function of industry marketing expenditure (two different environments assumed)

Market Forecast   Only one level of industry marketing expenditure will actually occur. The market demand corresponding to this level is called the *market forecast*.

Market Potential   The market forecast shows expected market demand, not maximum market demand. For the latter, we have to visualize the level of market demand for a very "high" level of industry marketing expenditure, where further increases in marketing effort would have little effect in stimulating further demand. *Market potential is the limit approached by market demand as industry marketing expenditures approach infinity, for a given environment.*

The phrase "for a given environment" is crucial in the concept of market potential. Consider the market potential for automobiles in a period of recession versus a period of prosperity. The market potential is higher during prosperity. In other words, market demand is income elastic. The dependence of market potential on the environment is illustrated in Figure 9-3(b). Thus the analyst distinguishes between the position of the market demand function and movement along it. Companies cannot do anything about the position of the market demand function; that is determined by the marketing environment. However, companies influence their particular location on the function when they decide how much to spend on marketing.

Company Demand   We are now ready to define company demand. *Company demand* is the company's *share of market demand*. In symbols:

$$Q_i = s_i Q \qquad (9\text{-}1)$$

where:

$$Q_i = \text{company } i\text{'s demand}$$
$$s_i = \text{company } i\text{'s market share}$$
$$Q = \text{total market demand}$$

Company demand, like market demand, is a function—called the *company demand function* or *sales-response function*—and is subject to all the determinants of market demand plus the determinants of *company market share*. The determinants of company market share are described in the appendix.

Company Forecast   Company demand describes estimated company sales at alternative levels of company marketing effort. It remains for management to choose one of the levels.[1] The chosen level of marketing effort will produce an expected level of sales, called the company sales forecast.

> *The* company sales forecast *is the expected level of company sales based on a chosen marketing plan and an assumed marketing environment.*

The company sales forecast is represented graphically in the same way as the market forecast was in Figure 9-3(a): substitute company sales for the vertical axis and company marketing effort for the horizontal axis.

Too often the sequential relationship between the company forecast and the company marketing plan is confused. One frequently hears that the company should develop its marketing plan on the basis of its sales forecast. The forecast-to-plan sequence is valid if *forecast* means an estimate of national economic activity or if company demand is nonexpansible. The sequence is not valid, however, where market demand is expansible, or where *forecast* means an estimate of company sales. The company sales forecast does not establish a basis for deciding what to spend on marketing; quite the contrary, the sales forecast is the *result* of an assumed marketing expenditure plan.

Two other concepts are worth mentioning in relation to the company forecast.

> A sales quota *is the sales goal set for a product line, company division, or sales representative. It is primarily a managerial device for defining and stimulating sales effort.*

Management sets sales quotas on the basis of the company forecast and the psychology of stimulating its achievement. Generally, sales quotas are set slightly higher than estimated sales to stretch the salesforce's effort.

The other concept is a *sales budget*.

> A sales budget *is a conservative estimate of the expected volume of sales and is used primarily for making current purchasing, production, and cash-flow decisions.*

The sales budget considers the sales forecast and the need to avoid excessive risk. Sales budgets are generally set slightly lower than the company forecast.

Company Potential   Company sales potential is *the limit approached by company demand as company marketing effort increases relative to competitors*. The absolute limit of company demand is, of course, the market potential. The two would be equal if the company achieved 100 percent of the market—that is, if the company became a monopolist. In most cases, company sales potential is less than market potential, even when company marketing expenditures increase considerably relative to competitors. The reason is that each competitor has a hard core of loyal buyers who are not very responsive to other companies' efforts to woo them away.

ESTIMATING CURRENT DEMAND

We are now ready to examine practical methods for estimating current market demand. Marketing executives will want to estimate *total market potential, area market potential,* and *total industry sales and market shares.*

Total Market Potential

Total market potential is the maximum amount of sales (in units or dollars) that might be available to all the firms in an industry during a given period under a given level of industry marketing effort and given environmental conditions. A common way to estimate it is as follows:

$$Q=nqp \tag{9-2}$$

where:

Q = total market potential

n = number of buyers in the specific product/market under the given assumptions

q = quantity purchased by an average buyer

p = price of an average unit

Thus if there are ten million buyers of books each year, and the average book buyer buys three books a year, and the average price is $5, then the total market potential for books is $150 million (i.e., 10 000 000 × 3 × $5).

The most difficult component to estimate in (9-2) is n, the number of buyers in the specific product/market. One can always start with the total population in the nation, say 26.8 million people. This can be called the *suspect pool.* The next step is to eliminate groups that obviously would not buy the product. Let us assume that illiterate people, children under twelve, and persons with poor eyesight do not buy books, and they constitute 20 percent of the population. Then only 80 percent of the population, or 21.4 million people, would be in the *prospect pool.* We might do further research and find that persons of low income and low education do not buy books, and they constitute over 30 percent of the prospect pool. Eliminating them, we arrive at a *hot prospect pool* of approximately 15 000 000 book buyers. We would use this number of potential buyers in formula (9-2) for calculating total market potential.

A variation on formula (9-2) is known as the *chain-ratio method.* This method involves multiplying a base number by several adjusting percentages. Suppose a brewery is interested in estimating the market potential for a new dietetic beer. An estimate can be made by the following calculation:[2]

$$
\begin{matrix}
\text{Demand for} \\
\text{the new} \\
\text{dietetic beer}
\end{matrix}
\Biggr\}
\; - - - - - \;
\Biggl\{
\begin{matrix}
\text{Population} \times \text{personal discretionary income per capita} \times \text{average} \\
\text{percentage of discretionary income spent on food} \times \text{average} \\
\text{percentage of amount spent on food that is spent on beverages} \times \\
\text{average percentage of amount spent on beverages that is spent on} \\
\text{alcoholic beverages} \times \text{average percentage of amount spent on} \\
\text{alcoholic beverages that is spent on beer} \times \text{expected percentage of} \\
\text{amount spent on beer that will be spent on dietetic beer.}
\end{matrix}
$$

Area Market Potential

Companies face the problem of selecting the best territories and allocating their marketing budget optimally among these territories. Therefore they need to estimate the market potential of different territories. Two major methods are available: the *market-buildup method*, which is used primarily by business marketers, and the *multiple-factor index method*, which is used primarily by consumer marketers.

Market-Buildup Method   The market-buildup method calls for identifying all the potential buyers in each market and estimating their potential purchases. It is straightforward if we have a list of all potential buyers *and* a good estimate of what each will buy. Unfortunately, one or both are usually lacking.

Consider a machine-tool company that wants to estimate the area market potential for its wood lathe in the Quebec City metropolitan area.

The first step is to identify all potential buyers of lathes in the Quebec area. The lathe is of no purchase interest to households and many other types of buyers, such as hospitals, retailers, and farmers. The market consists primarily of manufacturing establishments, specifically, those that have to shape or ream wood as part of their operation.

The company could compile a list from a directory of all manufacturing establishments in the metropolitan Quebec area. Then it might estimate the number of lathes each industry might purchase based on the number of lathes per thousand employees or per $1 million of sales in that industry.

An efficient method of estimating area market potentials makes use of the Standard Industrial Classification System (SIC). The SIC designations for a large number of industry types are defined and listed by Statistics Canada. The classification is based on the product made or the operation performed. The manufacturing industries are classified into twenty groups using a basic two-digit number; thus 08 designates the wood industries and 14 designates the machinery industries. These industry groups are further subdivided into more than 200 industry types by three-digit and four-digit numbers. For example, among the wood industries are sawmills (SIC 251) and shingle mills (SIC 2511).

For each SIC number, Statistics Canada provides several industry statistics such as number of establishments, expenditures on labor and materials, and outputs such as value added and value of shipments.

To use the SIC, the lathe manufacturer first must determine the SIC codes that represent products whose manufacturer is likely to require lathe machines. For example, lathes will be used by manufacturers in SIC 261 (wood household furniture), and so on. To get a full picture of all four-digit SIC industries that might use lathes, the company can use three methods. It can determine the SIC codes of past customers. It can go through the SIC manual and check off all the four-digit industries that in its judgment would have an interest in lathes. It can mail questionnaires to a wide range of companies inquiring about their interest in wood lathes.

The company's next task is to determine an appropriate base for estimating the number of lathes that will be used in each industry. Suppose customer industry sales are the most appropriate base. For example, in SIC 2513, one lathe may be used for every $1 million worth of sales. Once the company estimates the rate of lathe ownership relative to the customer industry's sales, it can compute the market potential.

Table 9-1 shows a hypothetical computation for the Quebec area involving two SIC codes. In SIC 254 there are four establishments with annual sales of $1 million and one

Table 9-1 Market Build-up Method Using SIC Numbers (Hypothetical Lathe Manufacturer, Quebec Area)

SIC Number	Value of Shipments (In Millions $)	Number of Establishments	Potential Number of Lathe Sales Per $1 Million Value of Shipments	Market Potential (1 × 2 × 3)
254	$1	4	2	8
	$3	1	2	6
2513	$1	3	1	3
	$3	1	1	3
				20

establishment with annual sales of $3 million. It is estimated that two lathes can be sold in this SIC code for every $1 million in customer sales. Since there are four establishments with annual sales of $1 million, they account for $4 million in sales, which is a potential of 8 lathes (4 × 2). The other figures in the table are similarly computed. Altogether, it appears that the metropolitan Quebec area has a market potential for 20 lathes.

The company can use the same method to estimate the market potential for other areas in the country. Suppose the market potentials for all the markets add to 400 lathes. Then the Quebec market contains 5 percent of the total market potential. This might warrant the company's allocating 5 percent of its marketing expenditures to the Quebec market. Before doing this, the lathe manufacturer needs additional information about each market, such as the extent of market saturation, the number of competitors, the market growth rate, and the average age of existing equipment.

If the company decides to sell lathes in Quebec it must know how to identify the best-prospect companies. In the old days, sales reps called on companies door to door; this was called *bird-dogging* or *smokestacking*. "Cold calls" are far too costly today. The company should get a list of the companies in Quebec, qualify them, and then use direct mail or phone calls to reach the best prospects. The lathe manufacturer can use *Dun's Market Identifiers*, which lists twenty-seven key facts for over 3 250 000 establishments in the U.S. and Canada.[3]

Multiple-Factor Index Methods Consumer companies also have to estimate area market potentials. Because their customers are so numerous, they cannot list them. The method most commonly used is a straightforward *index method*. A drug manufacturer, for example, might assume that the market potential for drugs is directly related to population. If the province of British Columbia has 10.79 percent of the Canadian population, the company might assume that British Columbia would be a market for 10.79 percent of total drugs sold.

A single factor, however, is rarely a complete indicator of sales opportunity. Regional drug sales are also influenced by per capita income and the number of physicians per 10 000 people. This makes it desirable to develop a multiple-factor index with each factor assigned a specific weight.

One of the best-known multiple-factor indices of area demand is provided by the "Annual Survey of Buying Power" published by *Sales and Marketing Management*.[4] The index reflects the relative consumer buying power in the different regions, provinces, and metropolitan areas of the nation. *Sales and Marketing Management's* index of the relative buying power of an area is given by:

$$B_i = 0.5y_i + 0.3r_i + 0.2p_i \qquad (9\text{-}3)$$

where:

B_i = percentage of total national buying power found in area i

y_i = percentage of national disposable personal income originating in area i

r_i = percentage of national retail sales in area i

p_i = percentage of national population located in area i

For example, suppose British Columbia has 12.04 percent of the Canadian disposable personal income, 11.71 percent of Canadian retail sales, and 10.79 percent of the Canadian population. The buying-power index for British Columbia would be:

$$0.5(12.04) + 0.3(11.71) + 0.2(10.79) = 11.69$$

Thus, 11.69 percent of the nation's drug sales might be expected to take place in British Columbia.

The manufacturer recognizes that the weights used in the buying-power index are somewhat arbitrary. They apply mainly to consumer goods that are neither low-priced staples nor high-priced luxury goods. Other weights can be assigned if more appropriate. Furthermore, the manufacturer would want to adjust the market potential for additional factors, such as competitor's presence in that market, local promotional costs, seasonal factors, and local market idiosyncrasies.

Many companies will compute additional area indices as a guide to allocating marketing resources. Suppose the company is reviewing the eight cities listed in Table 9-2. The first three columns show the percentage of total population, category sales, and brand A sales, respectively, in these eight cities. Column 4 shows the *category development index*, which is the ratio of consumption intensity to population intensity. Montreal, for example, has a category development index of 142 because it accounts for 15.3 percent of the nation's consumption of this category, while it has 10.8 percent of the nation's population. Column 5 shows the *brand*

Table 9-2 Indices of Category Development, Brand Development, and Market Opportunity

Territory	Percent of Total Population (1)	Percent of Total Sales of Product Category (2)	Percent of Total Sales of Brand A (3)	Category Development Index (4) = (2 ÷ 1)	Brand Development Index (5) = (3 ÷ 1)	Market Opportunity (6) = (4 ÷ 5)
Montreal	10.8	15.3	16.5	142	153	0.93
Toronto	10.6	19.6	17.2	185	162	1.14
Vancouver	5.0	8.3	7.7	166	154	1.08
Ottawa	2.8	4.2	5.1	150	182	0.82
Edmonton	2.8	5.8	6.3	207	225	0.92
Winnipeg	2.5	4.2	3.9	168	156	1.08
Quebec	2.3	3.2	4.0	139	174	0.80
Calgary	2.2	4.5	6.4	205	291	0.70

development index, which is the ratio of brand consumption intensity to population intensity. For Montreal, the brand development index is 153 because Montreal consumes 16.5 percent of this brand and has 10.8 percent of the nation's population. Column 6 shows the *market opportunity index*, which is the ratio of category development to brand development. This ratio is 0.93 for Montreal, indicating that the company's brand is more developed in Montreal than in other cities. Montreal is an area of low (incremental) opportunity in that the company brand is highly developed in Montreal. In Toronto, the market opportunity index stands at 1.14, indicating a high opportunity in that area. Companies do not necessarily put all of their money in the high market opportunity areas.

After the company decides on the city-by-city allocation of its budget, it can refine each city allocation down to enumeration areas or postal-code centers. Enumeration areas are small areas about the size of a neighborhood, and postal-code centers (which were designed by the Post Office) are even smaller areas, often individual office buildings. Information on population size, median family income, and other characteristics is available for each type of unit. Marketers have found these data extremely useful for identifying high-potential retail areas within large cities or for buying mailing lists to use in direct-mail campaigns.[5]

Marketing Concepts and Tools 9-1 describes how government census data are now incorporated into geocoding systems for improving customer targeting.

Estimating Industry Sales and Market Shares

Besides estimating total potential and area potential, a company needs to know the actual industry sales taking place in its market. This means identifying its competitors and estimating their sales.

The industry's trade association will often collect and publish total industry sales, although not listing individual company sales separately. In this way, each company can evaluate its performance against the whole industry. Suppose a company's sales are increasing 5 percent a year, and industry sales are increasing 10 percent. This company is actually losing its relative standing in the industry.

Another way to estimate sales is to buy reports from a marketing research firm that audits total sales and brand sales. For example, A. C. Nielsen Company audits retail sales in various product categories in supermarkets and drug stores and sells this information to interested companies. In this way, a company learns total product-category sales as well as brand sales. It can compare its performance to the total industry and/or any particular competitor to see whether it is gaining or losing share.

Industrial-goods marketers typically have a harder time estimating industry sales and market shares than do consumer-goods marketers. The former have no Nielsens or other regular syndicated services to rely on. Distributors typically will not supply information about how much of competitors' products they are selling. Industrial-goods marketers therefore have to live with less knowledge of their market-share results. Some industrial-goods marketers simply want to know their share relative to their leading competitor rather than relative to the whole market. They can then concentrate on estimating only their leading competitor's sales and comparing results.

ESTIMATING FUTURE DEMAND

We are now ready to examine methods of estimating future demand. Very few products or services lend themselves to easy forecasting. Cases of easy forecasting generally involve a product whose absolute level or trend is fairly constant and where competition is nonexistent

Marketing Concepts and Tools 9-1

GEODEMOGRAPHIC ANALYSIS: A NEW TOOL FOR IDENTIFYING MARKET TARGETS

In recent years, several new business information services have been offered to marketing planners that link Census data on a postal-code basis with lifestyle patterns. A geocoding service based on Canadian Census data is available from Compusearch. But the following example is based on the PRIZM service available from the U.S. firm Claritas Corp.

The designers have picturesquely classified all postal-code markets into forty clusters, such as "blue blood estates," "money and brains," "furs and station wagons," "shotguns and pickups," and "tobacco roads." The clusters were formed by manipulating eight characteristics. For example, "blue blood estates" are characterized by

- A medium household density per square mile
- A suburban complexion
- A high degree of homogeneity of the residents
- A white ethnicity
- A heavy family orientation
- A college graduate makeup
- A white-collar makeup
- A single-unit housing pattern

On the other hand, the cluster "single city blues" is characterized by a high household density, city location, mixed population, white with minorities, many singles and couples, some college, white/blue collar mix, and multiunit housing. Each of the other thirty-eight clusters has a unique combination of characteristics.

To illustrate how geocoding works, we can draw from a recent publication of the Seventh Day Adventists who are seeking to identify the best areas for recruiting new members. Their working hypothesis is that they would have the best chance attracting new members from areas that resemble the ones that now contain most current members. Using their home addresses, all Seventh Day Adventists were coded into one of the forty clusters. In examining the data, the researchers found that the "Hispanic mix" cluster had the highest *index of concentration* of Seventh

Day Adventists. Specifically, while the Hispanic mix cluster accounted for only 3.393 percent of the population, it accounted for 12.706 percent of all Seventh Day Adventists. By dividing the latter number by the former, and multiplying by 100, they found that the "Hispanic mix" cluster had an index of concentration of 375. This suggests that this type of area has a high potential for further members and deserves focused marketing, including the opening in these areas of new Seventh Day Adventist churches, door-to-door recruitment, and direct-mail campaigns. On the other hand, the cluster with the lowest potential for Seventh Day Adventist recruitment was "nonmobile married couples, old homes, farm areas," whose index of concentration was only 16. Using this methodology, all forty areas could be ranked, and those whose index of concentration exceeded 100 would be the most attractive areas for recruitment.

The areas are also linked with other data banks showing product preferences, lifestyle characteristics, and so on. For example, the "Hispanic mix" cluster had product preferences for high-quality dresses, tequila, nonfilter cigarettes, lip gloss, and so on, and this information, plus lifestyle information, can help the religious marketers in their communication and recruitment efforts.

We have deliberately illustrated the geocoding methodology in an unusual application: religious recruitment. More normally, geocoding is used by manufacturers, retailers, and others to identify the best clusters to target based on where their current customers live.

Source: Thomas Moore, "Different Folks, Different Strokes," *Fortune*, September 16, 1985, pp. 65-68; "PRIZM-Guided Retail Plan Yields Dynamic Results," *Direct Marketing*, November 1985, p. 116; Hugh M. Cannon and Gerald Linda, "Beyond Media Imperatives: Geodemographic Media Selection," *Journal of Advertising Research*, June/July 1982, pp. 31-36; and "Marketing Firm Slices U.S. into 240,000 Parts to Spur Clients' Sales," *Wall Street Journal*, November 3, 1986, p. 1. The illustration was taken from *The North American Division Marketing Program*, Vol. 1: *Profiling Adventist Members and Baptisms*, published in mimeograph form, 1986.

(public utilities) or stable (pure oligopolies). In most markets, total demand and company demand are not stable, and good forecasting becomes a key factor in company success. Poor forecasting can lead to overly large inventories, costly price markdowns, or lost sales due to out-of-stock conditions. The more unstable the demand, the more critical is forecast accuracy, and the more elaborate is forecasting procedure.

Forecasting methods range from the crude to the highly sophisticated. Marketing managers need to be familiar with the major forecasting methods. They need to understand each method's strengths and weaknesses.

Companies commonly use a three-stage procedure to prepare a sales forecast. They make an *environmental forecast*, followed by an *industry forecast*, followed by a *company sales forecast*. The environmental forecast calls for projecting inflation, unemployment, interest rates, consumer spending and saving, business investment, government expenditures, net exports, and other environmental magnitudes and events of importance to the company (see Marketing Concepts and Tools 9-2). The end result is a forecast of *gross national product*, which is then used, along with other environmental indicators, to forecast industry sales. Then the company derives its sales forecast by assuming that it will win a certain market share.

All forecasts are built on one of three information bases: *what people say, what people do*, or *what people have done*. The first basis—*what people say*—involves surveying the opinions of buyers or those close to them, such as salespeople or outside experts. It encompasses three methods: surveys of buyer intentions, composites of salesforce opinions, and expert opinion. Building a forecast on *what people do* involves another method, that of putting the product into a market test to measure buyer response. The final basis—*what people have done*—involves analyzing records of past buying behavior or using time-series analysis or statistical demand analysis.

Survey of Buyers' Intentions

Forecasting is the art of anticipating what buyers are likely to do under a given set of conditions. This suggests that the buyers should be surveyed. Surveys are especially valuable if the buyers have clearly formulated intentions, will carry them out, and will describe them to interviewers.

In regard to *major consumer durables*, several research organizations conduct periodic surveys of consumer buying intentions. These organizations ask questions like the following:

Do you intend to buy an automobile within the next six months?					
0.00	0.20	0.40	0.60	0.80	1.00
No chance	Slight possibility	Fair possibility	Good possibility	High possibility	Certain

This is called a *purchase probability scale*. For example, an Index of Consumer Attitudes is computed each quarter by the Conference Board in Canada. It is based on survey responses by consumers regarding their present and expected finances, their attitudes toward the job market, and whether now is an appropriate time to make a major purchase. Consumer durable-goods producers subscribe to such indices in the hope of anticipating major shifts in consumer buying intentions so that they can adjust their production and marketing plans accordingly.[6]

In the realm of *industrial buying*, it is necessary to survey business organizations to determine their buying plans and attributes towards the economic environment. For large corporations,

Many companies buy economic and industry forecasts from well-known economic-forecasting firms, such as Data Resources, Wharton Econometric, and Chase Econometric. These forecasting specialists are able to prepare better economic forecasts than the company because they have more data available and more forecasting expertise.

Occasionally companies will assemble an invited group of experts to make a particular forecast. The experts exchange views and produce a group estimate (*group-discussion methods*). Or they supply their estimates individually, and the analyst combines them in a single estimate (*pooling of individual estimates*). Or they supply individual estimates and assumptions that are reviewed by a company analyst, revised, and followed by further rounds of estimating (*Delphi method*).[9]

An interesting variant of the expert-opinion method brings experts together in a "decision lab" setting. The experts' judgments are input in a series of stages using individual computer terminals. The results are then combined and displayed on a common monitor, and discussed by the group before the next set of judgments is made. This process is both efficient and, because of its anonymity, less prone to social pressure and "bandwagon" bias.

Market-Test Method

Where buyers do not plan their purchases carefully or are erratic in carrying out their intentions or where experts are not good guessers, a direct market test is desirable. A direct market test is especially desirable in forecasting the sales of a new product or of an established product in a new channel of distribution or territory. Market testing is discussed in Chapter 12.

Time-Series Analysis

Many firms prepare their forecasts on the basis of past sales. The assumption is that past data capture causal relations that can be uncovered through statistical analysis. These causal relations can be used to predict future sales.

A time series of a product's past sales (Y) can be analyzed into four major components.

The first component, *trend* (T), is the result of basic developments in population, capital formation, and technology. It is found by fitting a straight or curved line through past sales.

The second component, *cycle* (C), captures the wavelike movement of sales. Many sales are affected by swings in general economic activity, which tends to be somewhat periodic. The cyclical component can be useful in intermediate-range forecasting.

The third component, *season* (S), refers to a consistent pattern of sales movements within the year. The term *season* broadly describes any recurrent hourly, weekly, monthly, or quarterly sales pattern. The seasonal component may be related to weather factors, holidays, and trade customs. The season pattern provides a norm for forecasting short-range sales.

The fourth component, *erratic events* (E), includes strikes, blizzards, fads, riots, fires, war scares, and other disturbances. These erratic components are by definition unpredictable and should be removed from past data to discern the more normal behavior of sales.

Time-series analysis consists of decomposing the original sales series, Y, into the components, T, C, S, and E. Then these components are recombined to produce the sales forecast.[10] Here is an example:

> An insurance company sold 12 000 new ordinary life-insurance policies this year. It would like to predict next year's December sales. The long-term trend shows a 5 percent sales growth rate per year. This suggests sales next year of 12 600 (= 12 000 × 1.05). However, a business recession is expected next year and will probably result in total sales achieving only 90 percent of the

expected trend-adjusted sales. Sales next year will more likely be 11 340 (= 12 600 × 0.90). If sales were the same each month, monthly sales would be 945 (= 11 340/12). However, December is an above-average month for insurance-policy sales, with a seasonal index standing at 1.30. Therefore December sales may be as high as 1228.5 (= 0.945 × 1.3). No erratic events, such as strikes or new insurance regulations, are expected. Therefore the best estimate of new policy sales next December is 1228.5. ∎

For a company that has hundreds of items in its product line and wants to produce efficient and economical short-run forecasts, a simpler time-series technique called *exponential smoothing* is available. In its simplest form, exponential smoothing requires only three pieces of information: this period's actual sales, Q_t; this period's smoothed sales, $\overline{Q}_t$; and a smoothing parameter, α. The sales forecast for next period's sales is given by

$$\overline{Q}_{t+1} = \alpha Q_t + (1 - \alpha)\overline{Q}_t \qquad (9\text{-}4)$$

where:

$\overline{Q}_{t+1}$ = sales forecast for next period

α = the smoothing constant, where $0 \leq \alpha \leq 1$

Q_t = current sales in period t

$\overline{Q}_t$ = smoothed sales in period t

Suppose the smoothing constant is 0.4, current sales are $50 000, and smoothed sales are $40 000. Then the sales forecast is

$$\overline{Q}_{t+1} = 0.4(\$50\ 000) + 0.6(\$40\ 000) = \$44\ 000$$

In other words, the sales forecast is always between current sales and smoothed sales. The relative influence of current and smoothed sales depends on the smoothing constant, here 0.4. Thus the sales forecast "tracks" actual sales.

For each product, the company determines an initial level of smoothed sales and a smoothing constant. The initial level of smoothed sales can simply be average sales for the last few periods. The smoothing constant is derived by trial-and-error testing of different smoothing constants between 0 and 1 to find the constant that produces the best fit of past sales. The method can be refined to reflect seasonal and trend factors by adding two more constants.[11]

Statistical-Demand Analysis

Time-series analysis treats past and future sales as a function of time rather than of any real demand factors. Yet numerous real factors affect the sales of any product. *Statistical-demand analysis* is a set of statistical procedures designed to discover the most important real factors affecting sales and their relative influence. The factors most commonly analyzed are price, income, population, and promotion.

Statistical-demand analysis consists of expressing sales (Q) as a dependent variable and trying to explain sales as a function of a number of independent demand variables $X_1, X_2, \ldots, X_n$; that is,

$$Q = f(X_1, X_2, \ldots, X_n)$$

Using multiple regression analysis, various equation forms can be statistically fitted to the data in search of the best predicting variables and equation.

For example, Palda found that the following demand equation gave a fairly good fit to the historical sales of Lydia Pinkham's Vegetable Compound between the years 1908 and 1960:[12]

$$Y = -3649 + 0.665X_1 + 1180 \log X_2 + 774X_3 + 32X_4 - 2.83X_5 \qquad (9\text{-}5)$$

where:

Y = yearly sales in thousands of dollars

X_1 = yearly sales (lagged one year) in thousands of dollars

X_2 = yearly advertising expenditures in thousands of dollars

X_3 = a dummy variable, taking on the value of 1 between 1908 and 1925 and 0 from 1926 on

X_4 = year (1908 = 0, 1909 = 1, and so on)

X_5 = disposable personal income in billions of current dollars

The five independent variables on the right account for 94 percent of the yearly variation in the sale of Lydia Pinkham's Vegetable Compound between 1908 and 1960. To use it as a sales-forecasting equation for 1961, it would be necessary to insert numbers for the five independent variables. Sales in 1960 should be put in X_1; the log of the company's planned advertising expenditures for 1961 should be put in X_2; 0 should be put in X_3; the numbered year corresponding to 1961 should be put in X_4; and estimated 1961 disposable personal income should be put in X_5. Multiplying these numbers by the respective coefficients and summing them gives a sales forecast (Y) for 1961.

Computers have rendered statistical-demand analysis an increasingly popular approach to forecasting. The user, however, should be wary of five problems that might diminish the validity or usefulness of a statistical-demand equation: too few observations, too much correlation among the independent variables, violation of normal distribution assumptions, two-way causation, and emergence of new variables not accounted for.

SUMMARY

To carry out their responsibilities, marketing managers need estimates of current and future demand. Quantitative measurements are essential for the analysis of market opportunity, the planning of marketing programs, and the control of marketing effort. The firm usually prepares several estimates of demand, varying in the level of product aggregation, the time dimension, and the space dimension.

A market consists of the set of actual and potential purchasers of a market offer. The size of the market depends on how many people have interest, income, and access to the market offer. Marketers must know how to distinguish between the potential market, available market, qualified available market, served market, and penetrated market.

Marketers must also distinguish between market demand and company demand, and within these, between potentials and forecasts. Market demand is a function, not a single number, and as such is highly dependent on the level of other variables.

A major task is estimating current demand. Total demand can be estimated through the chain-ratio method, which involves multiplying a base number by successive percentages. Area market demand can be estimated by the market-buildup method (for industrial markets) and the multiple-factor index method (for consumer markets). In the latter case, geodemographic coding systems are proving a boon to marketers. Actual industry sales require identifying the relevant competitors and estimating the sales of each. Finally, companies are interested in estimating the market shares of competitors to judge their relative performance.

For estimating future demand, the company can use seven major forecasting methods: buyer intention surveys, composite of salesforce opinion, expert opinion, market tests, time-series analysis, and statistical-demand analysis. These methods vary in their appropriateness with the purpose of the forecast, the type of product, and the availability and reliability of data.

■ QUESTIONS

1. Compare and contrast the concepts of demand and potential as they apply to the firm and the market. Illustrate your answer with an example from industry.

2. A manager has several options available to estimate future demand. Create a comparison matrix that shows the advantages and disadvantages of each technique.

3. What kinds of information can be derived from standard industrial classifications for demand forecasting? What are some limitations of SIC analysis?

4. What evaluative dimensions would you use to compare the various forecasting methods?

5. Using the dimensions you developed in Question 2, compare the following forecasting methods: salesforce-composite opinions, market testing, exponential smoothing, regression models.

6. One use of forecasts is as input for the development of marketing strategy. However, integrating forecasts, goals, and strategies can be a complex and politicized process. Suggest some guidelines to achieve a better link between forecasts, goals, and strategies.

7. Describe the difference between the potential market, the available market, the served market, and the penetrated market for a Rolls Royce Silver Spirit.

8. A manufacturer of women's hair products (home permanents, hair rinses, shampoos, and so on) wants to determine the relative market potential for its products in each county in Canada. What factors are most likely to belong in a weighted index of potential?

9. A chemical company wants to estimate the demand for sulfur next year. One use of sulfur is in manufacturing sulfuric acid. Another use of sulfur is in polishing new cars. Auto maker C is a customer of this manufacturer. What ratios have to be linked to go from auto maker C's new-car production to its impact on the chemical company's sulfur sales?

10. An automotive manufacturer is developing its sales forecast for next year. The company forecaster has estimated sales

for six different environment-strategy combinations:

Sales Forecast

	High Marketing Budget	Medium Marketing Budget	Low Marketing Budget
Recession	15	12	10
Normal	20	16	14

The forecaster believes that there is a 0.20 probability of recession and an 0.80 probability of normal times. She also believes the probabilities of a high, medium, and low company marketing budget are 0.30, 0.50, and 0.20, respectively. How might she arrive at a single point forecast? What assumptions are being made?

11. A motorboat company plans to open additional retail outlets in several counties. Using market opportunity indexes, recommend in which counties the outlets should be located.

County	Population	Industry Sales of Motorboats (in Dollars)	Sales of Company's Boats (in Dollars)
A	161 300	2 800 000	186 200
B	13 400	140 000	38 000
C	72 000	455 000	72 000
D	261 700	2 835 000	361 000
E	16 200	1 750 000	836 000
F	56 200	2 310 000	155 000
Total in Counties	580 000	10 290 000	1 649 000
Market Total	3 583 400	3 500 000	3 800 000

12. Suppose a company's past sales are: 10, 12, 15, 12, 11, 13, 18, 20. The company forecaster uses an exponential smoothing equation with $\alpha = 0.4$ and initial $Q_t = 10$. Estimate the exponentially smoothed sales that would be predicted for the third period on.

13. A beverage company wants to use multiple regression to explain province-to-province variations in the consumption

of soft drinks. (a) What independent variable should be tested? (b) If the fitted regression equation explains most of the province-to-province variation in sales, does it follow that it indicates relative market potential by province?

14. A marketing researcher sought a multiple-regression equation to explain past sales in an industry. Industry data on the dependent and independent variables went back only five years. The following equation was fitted:

$$Y = 5241 + 31X_1 + 12X_2 + 50X_3$$

where:

Y = yearly sales in thousands of dollars

X_1 = disposable personal income in billions of dollars

X_2 = population in millions of households

X_3 = time, in years (1983 = 0)

The marketing researcher was pleased that this equation accounted for 98 percent of the yearly variations in industry sales. List any reservations you have about using this equation to forecast industry sales.

NOTES

1. The theory of choosing the best level of marketing effort is described in the appendix to Chapter 3.

2. See Russell L. Ackoff, *A Concept of Corporate Planning* (New York: Wiley-Interscience, 1970), pp. 36-37.

3. Dun's Market Identifiers (DMI), Dun & Bradstreet, New York, 1982.

4. For a helpful exposition on using this survey and three other surveys published by *Sales and Marketing Management*, see "Putting the Four to Work," *Sales Management*, October 28, 1974, pp. 13ff.

5. See Bob Stone, *Successful Direct Marketing Methods*, 4th ed. (Lincolnwood, Ill.: NTC Business Books, 1988).

6. The consumer pollsters include the Survey Research Center at the University of Michigan; Sindlinger & Company of Norwood, Pa.; the Conference Board; and the Commercial Credit Corporation.

7. Adapted from *Forecasting Sales*, business policy study no. 106 (New York: National Conference Board, 1963), pp. 31-32.

8. See Jacob Gonik, "Tie Salesmen's Bonuses to Their Forecasts," *Harvard Business Review*, May-June 1978, pp. 116-23.

9. See Norman Dalkey and Olaf Helmer, "An Experimental Application of the Delphi Method to the Use of Experts," *Management Science*, April 1963, pp. 458-67. Also see Roger J. Best, "An Experiment in Delphi Estimation in Marketing Decision Making," *Journal of Marketing Research*, November 1974, pp. 447-52.

10. See Ya-Lun Chou, *Statistical Analysis with Business and Economic Applications*, 2nd ed. (New York: Holt, Rinehart & Winston, 1975), Chap. 2. For computer programs, see Julius Shiskin, *Electronic Computers and Business Indicators* (New York: National Bureau of Economics Research, 1957). For an application, see Robert L. McLaughlin, "The Breakthrough in Sales Forecasting," *Journal of Marketing*, April 1963, pp. 46-54.

11. See S. Makridakis and S. C. Wheelwright, *The Handbook of Forecasting* (New York: John Wiley, 1987).

12. Kristian S. Palda, *The Measurement of Cumulative Advertising Effects* (Englewood Cliffs, N.J.: Prentice-Hall, 1964), pp. 67-68.

appendix DETERMINANTS OF COMPANY MARKET SHARE

What influences company market share? The most popular theory is that the *market shares* of various competitors will be proportional to their *marketing-effort shares*. This normal expectation can be called the *fundamental theorem of market-share determination* and is expressed:

$$s_i = \frac{M_i}{\sum M_i} \qquad (9\text{-}6)$$

where:

$$M_i = \text{company } i\text{'s marketing effort}$$

Consider the simple case where two identical firms are selling the same product but spending different amounts on marketing: \$60 000 and \$40 000, respectively. Using equation (9-6), company 1's market share is predicted to be 60 percent:

$$s_1 = \frac{\$60\,000}{\$60\,000 + \$40\,000} = 0.60$$

If company 1 is not enjoying a 0.60 market share, additional factors must be operating. Suppose the companies differ in the *effectiveness* with which they spend marketing dollars. Then equation (9-6) can be revised to read

$$s_i = \frac{\alpha_i M_i}{\sum \alpha_i M_i} \qquad (9\text{-}7)$$

where:

α_i = marketing effectiveness of a dollar spent by company i (with $\alpha = 1.00$ for average effectiveness)
$\alpha_i M_i$ = company i's effective marketing effort

Suppose that company 1 spends its marketing funds less effectively than company 2, with $\alpha_1 = 0.90$ and $\alpha_2 = 1.20$. Then company 1's market share would be 53 percent:

$$s_1 = \frac{0.90(\$60\,000)}{0.90(\$60\,000) + 1.20(\$40\,000)} \cong 0.53$$

Equation (9-7) assumes a strict proportionality between market share and effective marketing-effort share. Yet if there are grounds for expecting diminishing returns as one firm's effective effort increases relative to the industry's effective effort, equation (9-7) should be modified to reflect this expectation. One way to reflect diminishing returns is through the use of a marketing-effort elasticity exponent that is less than unity:

$$s_i = \frac{(\alpha M_i)^{e_{m_i}}}{\sum(\alpha_i M_i)^{e_{m_i}}} \quad \text{where } 0 < e_{m_i} < 1 \tag{9-8}$$

where:

e_{m_i} = elasticity of market share with respect to company i's effective marketing effort

Assume that the marketing-effort elasticity is 0.8 for all companies. As a result, company 1's market share would be

$$s_1 = \frac{[(0.90)(\$60\ 000)]^{0.8}}{[(0.90)(\$60\ 000)^{0.8} + [(1.20)(\$40\ 000)]^{0.8}} \cong 0.50$$

Thus company 1's estimated market share is revised to reflect diminishing returns. Although company 1 is spending 60 percent of the marketing funds in the industry, its market share is only 50 percent because of lower spending efficiency and diminishing returns.

A further improvement can be introduced by breaking up each company's marketing effort into its major components and separately expressing the effectiveness and elasticity of each marketing component. The equation becomes

$$s_{it} = \frac{R_{it}^{e_{Ri}} P_{it}^{-e_{Pi}} (\alpha_{it} A_{it})^{e_{Ai}} (d_{it} D_{it})^{e_{Di}}}{\sum [R_{it}^{e_{Ri}} P_{it}^{-e_{Pi}} (\alpha_{it} A_{it})^{e_{Ai}} (d_{it} D_{it})^{e_{Di}}]} \tag{9-9}$$

where:

s_{it} = company i's estimated market share at time t

R_{it} = quality rating of company i's product in year t

P_{it} = price of company i's product in year t

A_{it} = advertising and promotion costs of company i in year t

D_{it} = distribution and salesforce costs of company i in year t

α_{it} = advertising effectiveness index for company i at time t

d_{it} = distribution effectiveness index for company i at time t

$\left.\begin{matrix} e_{Ri}, e_{Pi}, \\ e_{Ai}, e_{Di} \end{matrix}\right\}$ = elasticities of quality, price, advertising, and distribution, respectively, of company i

Thus equation (9-9) reflects four major influences on a company's market share: *marketing expenditures, marketing mix, marketing effectiveness*, and *marketing elasticity*. Although this would seem to be a great deal, the expression could be further refined (we will not do it here) to take into account (1) *geographical allocation of marketing expenditures*, (2) *carry-over effects of past marketing expenditures*, and (3) *synergistic effects of marketing-mix variables*.

Source: For further discussion, see Gary Lilien and Philip Kotler, *Marketing Decision Making: A Model-Building Approach* (New York: Harper & Row, 1983). Also see David E. Bell, Ralph L. Keenye, and John D. C. Little, "A Market Share Theorem," *Journal of Marketing Research*, May 1975, pp. 136-41

10

Identifying Market Segments and Selecting Target Markets

There isn't any one Canada, any average Canadian, any average place, any type.

Marian Chapin

A company that decides to operate in some broad market—whether consumer, industrial, reseller, or government—recognizes that it normally cannot serve all customers in that market. The customers are too numerous, dispersed, and varied in their buying requirements. Some competitors will be in a better position to serve particular customer segments of that market. The company instead of competing everywhere, often against superior odds, needs to identify the most attractive market segments that it can serve effectively.

The heart of modern *strategic marketing* can be described as *STP* marketing—namely, *segmenting, targeting, and positioning*. This does not negate the importance of *LGD* marketing—lunch, golf, and dinner—but rather provides the broader framework for strategic success in the marketplace.

Sellers have not always held this view of market strategy. Their thinking passed through three stages:

☐ *Mass Marketing:* Here the seller engages in the mass production, mass distribution, and mass promotion of one product for all buyers. This market strategy was epitomized by Henry Ford, who offered the Model T Ford to all buyers. They could have the car "in any color as long as it is black." The traditional argument for mass marketing is that it will lead to the lowest costs and prices and create the largest potential market.

☐ *Product-Variety Marketing:* Here the seller produces several products that exhibit different features, styles, qualities, sizes, and so on. They are designed to offer variety to buyers rather than to appeal to different market segments. General Motors practices this market strategy in that many of its cars go under different names—Pontiac, Buick, Oldsmobile—and exhibit only slight differences in features and style. The traditional argument for product-variety marketing is that customers have different tastes and their tastes change over time. Customers seek change and variety.

☐ *Target Marketing:* Here the seller distinguishes the major market segments, targets one or more of these segments, and develops products and marketing programs tailored to each selected segment. Hyundai, Mercedes, and Porsche have targeted clear automobile-customer segments. Ford, with its larger product line, nevertheless creates concept cars—such as the Mustang and Thunderbird—that are often targeted to specific types of customers. Target marketing is increasingly taking on the character of *micromarketing* where marketing programs are tailored to the needs and wants of customer groups on a *local basis* (trading area, neighborhood, even individual stores). The ultimate form of target marketing is *customized marketing*, where the product and marketing program is adapted to the needs and wants of a distinct consumer or buying organization. Thus Ford may change the features on police cars for the cities of Toronto versus Montreal.

Today's companies are finding it increasingly unrewarding to practice mass marketing or product-variety marketing. Mass markets are becoming "demassified." They are dissolving into hundreds of *micromarkets* characterized by different lifestyle groups pursuing different products in different distribution channels and listening to different communication channels. According to Arbeit:

> All advertisers will be forced to design products that fit with the multiplicity of channels, with a multiplicity of retail outlets, and with a multiplicity of discrete consumer target audiences . . . McDonald's understands the great lesson of the 1980's—that marketing in the 80's is guerrilla warfare. You can no longer fly over in your network B-52's and drop coherent, heavy messages, saturating communities with what you want to say, and hope for a response. Guerrilla warfare marketing in the 80's means that the battles for the heart and mind and pocketbook of the consumer will be won on a block-by-block, store-by-store, purchase-by-purchase basis.[1]

Companies are increasingly embracing target marketing. Target marketing helps sellers identify marketing opportunities better. The sellers can develop the right offer for each target market. They can adjust their prices, distribution channels, and advertising to reach the target market efficiently. Instead of scattering their marketing effort ("shotgun" approach), they can focus it on the buyers whom they have the greatest chance of satisfying ("rifle" approach).

Target marketing calls for three major steps (Figure 10-1). The first is *market segmentation*, the act of dividing a market into distinct groups of buyers who might require separate products and/or marketing mixes. The company identifies different ways to segment the market and develops profiles of the resulting market segments. The second step is *market targeting*, the act of developing measures of segment attractiveness and selecting one or more market segments to enter. The third step is *product positioning*, the act of establishing a viable competitive positioning of the firm and its offer in each target market. Positioning will be discussed in the next chapter. In this chapter, we will address two questions: How can distinct market segments be identified? How can the company evaluate and select the best market segments to pursue?

FIGURE 10-1
Steps in Market Segmentation, Targeting, and Positioning

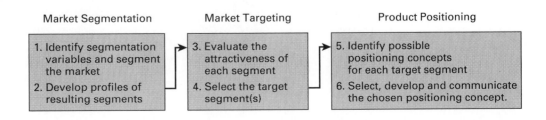

MARKET SEGMENTATION

Markets consist of buyers, and buyers differ in one or more respects. They may differ in their wants, purchasing power, geographical locations, buying attitudes, and buying practices. Any of these variables can be used to segment a market.

The General Approach to Segmenting a Market

Figure 10-2(a) shows a market of six buyers. Each buyer is potentially a separate market because of unique needs and wants. A seller might design a separate product and/or marketing program for each buyer. For example, companies like Bombardier and UTDC that make rapid transit trains, have few major customers, and customize their product for each. This ultimate degree of market segmentation, called *customized marketing*, is illustrated in Figure 10-2(b) and Marketing Strategies 10-1.

Most sellers will not find it profitable to "customize" their product for each buyer. It would cost the organization too much to adjust their offer each time. Instead the seller identifies classes of buyers who differ in their broad product requirements and/or marketing responses. For example, the seller might discover that income groups differ in their wants. In Figure 10-2(c), a number (1, 2, or 3) is used to identify each buyer's income class. Lines are drawn around buyers in the same income class. Segmentation by income results in three segments, the most numerous segment being income class 1.

On the other hand, the seller might discover pronounced differences between younger and older buyers. In Figure 10-2(d), a letter (A or B) is used to indicate each buyer's age. Segmentation by age class results in two segments, each with three buyers.

Now both income and age might influence the buyer's behavior toward the product. In this case, the market can be divided into five segments: 1A, 1B, 2B, 3A, and 3B. Figure 10-2(e) shows that segment 1A contains two buyers, and the other segments each contain one buyer.

FIGURE 10-2
Different Segmentations of a Market

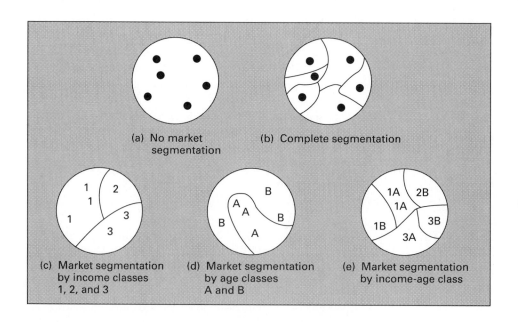

(a) No market segmentation

(b) Complete segmentation

(c) Market segmentation by income classes 1, 2, and 3

(d) Market segmentation by age classes A and B

(e) Market segmentation by income-age class

CUSTOMIZED MARKETING: IT'S COMING BACK

In early markets, many sellers designed their goods for each customer. Tailors made garments for the individual man and woman; and shoemakers custom made shoes. These craftspeople did not produce for inventory but for order, because they did not know in advance what size or materials their customers would require. Even today, some people order customized suits, shirts, and shoes to fit their individual requirements. But generally, the advent of mass production led producers to produce standard sizes of goods for inventory, thus ending many "job shops."

Today, customized marketing is coming back, in a form that Stanley Davis calls *mass customization*. This apparent contradiction of terms, like "jumbo shrimp," or "permanent change," well describes new marketing possibilities opened up by advances in manufacturing technology. *Mass customization is the ability to prepare on a mass basis individually designed products to meet each customer's requirements.* Here are some examples.

The aim of General Motors's Saturn project was to enable car buyers to walk into a GM dealership, sit down at a computer terminal, and select the car's color, engine, seat material, radio, and so on. Their order would be transmitted to the auto plant, which would then produce the desired car.

In Japan, home buyers can sit down at a computer terminal with a sales representative and design their future home. They can choose from twenty thousand different standardized parts, make the rooms as large or small as they want, and design the overall layout. The information is sent electronically to the factory where the walls, ceilings, and floors are prepared on an assembly line that stretches hundreds of meters. The prefabricated modules are delivered to the site within thirty days, and the rooms and walls are assembled in a few days. The finishing touches take several more days, and the family can then move into its customized home.

Today, there are clothing stores experimenting with new ways to make custom-fitted clothes:

> It may seem too good to be true, but it's already at eighteen stores across the country. It is a camera linked to a computer that calculates your measurements and prints out a custom-fitted pattern for a bathing suit.
>
> The video screen shows how the new suit will look from the front and side. You choose the fabric from about one hundred and fifty samples; tailors stitch it up. The minimum cost: about fifty-six dollars. ■

Customization permits people to participate in producing exactly what they want. That people enjoy this is demonstrated in a number of situations. Salad bars are becoming increasingly popular in restaurants because they permit people to "compose" their own salads. Similarly, certain ice-cream parlors allow people to make their own ice-cream concoctions.

Services as well as products can be customized. Jack Whittle predicts the following scenario for financial services:

> The customer will enter an institution, sit down at a selling module, and be counseled by a highly qualified professional. . . . The counselor and the customer will work together from a computer terminal to build and price a financial relationship. For example, the customer might inquire about opening up a deposit relationship. The counselor asks a number of basic questions: Does the customer want to earn interest? Write checks? Transfer money between accounts occasionally? Obtain a loan? Depending on the customer's responses, the desired services will be configured and priced based upon the customer's individualized needs. ■

Business-to-business marketers are more familiar with customization. The Beckton-Dickenson Company, supplier of medical supplies, offers the following options to hospitals: custom-designed labeling; bulk packaging option; customized quality-control recommendations; customized computer software; and customized billing program.

Markets and Niches

As the seller subdivides a market by introducing more characteristics, the seller is moving beyond segments into niches. A *market segment* is a gross slice of the market, such as high-income car buyers. A *market niche* is a smaller, specially formed segment, such as high-income car buyers who want high-performance sports cars. Whereas a segment usually attracts several competitors, a niche typically attracts fewer competitors.

Ideally, a company would like to define its target market so carefully that it is the only company serving that niche. For example, Porsche believes that it "owns" a niche, that Porsche buyers wouldn't get the same set of satisfactions from any other expensive sports car. The major problem with niches is that the more narrowly they are defined, the fewer the remaining number of buyers, and the less the profit potential.

Patterns of Market Segmentation

In the preceding illustration, the market was segmented by income and age, resulting in different *demographic segments*. Suppose, instead, buyers are asked how much they want of two product attributes (say, *sweetness* and *creaminess* in the case of ice cream). The result is the identification of different *preference segments* in the market. Three different patterns can emerge.

□ *Homogeneous Preferences:* Figure 10-3(a) shows a market where all the consumers have roughly the same preference. The market shows no natural segments, at least as far as the two attributes are concerned. We would predict that existing brands would be similar and located in the center of the preferences.

□ *Diffused Preferences:* At the other extreme, consumer preferences may be scattered throughout the space [Figure 10-3(b)], showing that consumers vary greatly in their preferences. If one brand enters the market, it is likely to be positioned in the center to appeal to the most people. A brand in the center minimizes the sum of total consumer dissatisfaction. A new competitor could locate next to the first brand and fight for market share. Or the competitor could locate in a corner to win over a customer group that was not satisfied with the center brand. If several brands are in the market, they are likely to be positioned throughout the space and show real differences to match consumer-preference differences.

□ *Clustered Preferences:* The market might reveal distinct preference clusters, called *natural market segments* [Figure 10-3(c)]. The first firm in this market has three options. It might position itself in the center hoping to appeal to all groups (undifferentiated marketing). It might position itself in the largest market segment (concentrated marketing). It might develop several brands, each positioned in a different segment (differentiated marketing). Clearly, if the first firm developed only one brand, competitors would enter and introduce brands in the other segments.

FIGURE 10-3
Basic Market-
Preference Patterns

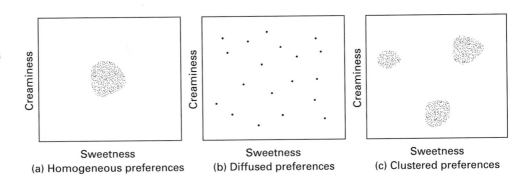

Creaminess | Creaminess | Creaminess

Sweetness
(a) Homogeneous preferences

Sweetness
(b) Diffused preferences

Sweetness
(c) Clustered preferences

Market-Segmentation Procedure

We have seen that market segments can be identified by applying successive variables to subdivide a market. As an illustration:

> An airline is interested in attracting nonflyers (segmentation variable: *user status*). Nonflyers consist of those who fear flying, those who are indifferent, and those who are positive toward flying (segmentation variable: *attitude*). Among those who feel positive are people with higher incomes who can afford to fly (segmentation variable: *income*). The airline may decide to target higher-income people who have a positive attitude toward flying but simply have not flown. ∎

The question arises, Is there a formal procedure for identifying the major segments in a market? The answer is yes, and several research firms regularly conduct formal segmentation studies in which the major market segments are systematically revealed. The procedure consists of three steps:

1. *Survey Stage:* The researcher conducts informal interviews and focus groups with consumers to gain insight into their motivations, attitudes, and behavior. Using these findings, the researcher prepares a formal questionnaire, which is administered to a sample of consumers to collect data on

   □ Attributes and their importance ratings

   □ Brand awareness and brand ratings

   □ Product-usage patterns

   □ Attitudes toward the product category

   □ Demographics, psychographics, and mediagraphics of the respondents

   The sample should be large in order to gather enough data to profile each segment accurately. If the researcher guesses that there are, say, four segments, and generally two hundred interviews are desired per segment, then the questionnaire might be administered to eight hundred consumers.

2. *Analysis Stage:* Factor analysis is used to identify combinations of characteristics (called factors) that differentiate consumers from each other. Then cluster analysis groups the consumers into maximally different clusters. The members of each cluster are similar to each other, but different from other clusters.

3. *Profiling Stage*: Each cluster is now profiled in terms of its distinguishing attitudes, behavior, demographics, psychographics, and media-consumption habits. Each segment can be

given a name based on a dominant distinguishing characteristic. Thus in a study of the leisure market, Andreasen and Belk found six market segments:[2]

☐ The passive homebody

☐ The active sports enthusiast

☐ The inner-directed self-sufficient

☐ The culture patron

☐ The active homebody

☐ The socially active

They found, for example, that the culture patron is the best target for both theater and symphony subscriptions. The socially active can also be drawn to symphonies (but not theaters) in order to satisfy social needs.

This market-segmentation procedure must be reapplied periodically because market segments change. The companies in an industry have always operated on an assumed segmentation. For example, Henry Ford assumed that only price mattered. General Motors later outpaced Ford because it started to design cars that recognized different income and preference groups in the market. Still later, Volkswagen and the Japanese auto makers recognized the growing importance of car size and fuel economy as consumer-choice attributes. Very often, the way in which a new company successfully breaks into an entrenched market is by discovering new segmentation possibilities in the market. The company transcends the current segmentation thinking assumed by the incumbents.

One way to discover new segments is to investigate the hierarchy of attributes that consumers look at on their way to choosing a brand. In the 1960s, most car buyers first decided on the manufacturer and then on one of its car divisions. This is shown in Figure 10-4(a) as a *brand-dominant hierarchy*. Thus a buyer might favor General Motors cars and, within this set, Pontiac. Today, many buyers decide first on the nation from which they want to buy a car [see Figure 10-4(b)]. Thus a growing number of buyers first decide that they want to buy a Japanese car, and then they may have a second-level preference for, say, Toyota followed by a third-level preference for the Cressida model of Toyota. Now behind the emergence of a *nation-dominant hierarchy* is a deeper attribute, namely, quality, and the perception that

FIGURE 10-4

Hierarchy of Attributes in the Auto Market

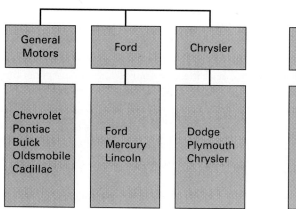

(a) Brand-dominated hierarchy (1960s)

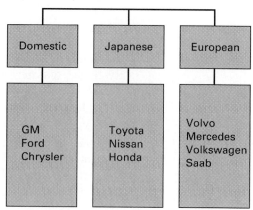

(b) Source-dominated hierarchy (1980s)

nations differ in the quality of cars they produce. Had domestic automakers understood that the switch to Japanese cars was based on the growing importance of quality and value to the car-buying public, they would not have relied on "Buy Canadian" campaigns so much as on more rapidly improving the quality of their cars. The lesson is that a company must be alert to changes in the consumers' hierarchy of attributes in order to move with changing consumer priorities.

The hierarchy of attributes also reveals customer segments. Those buyers who first decide on price are price dominant; those who first decide on the type of the car (e.g., sports, passenger, station wagon) are type dominant; those who first decide on the car brand are brand dominant; and so on. One can go further and identify those who are type/price/brand dominant, in that order, as making up a segment; those who are quality/service/type dominant as making up another segment; and so on. Each segment may have distinct demographics, psychographics, and mediagraphics. This reasoning is called *market-partitioning theory*. The Hendry Corporation has built a successful brand-forecasting system based on identifying the primary partitioning attributes used by buyers.[3]

Bases for Segmenting Consumer Markets

Here we want to look at variables that are commonly used to segment consumer markets (later we will look at industrial markets). The variables fall into two broad groups. Some researchers try to form segments by looking at *consumer characteristics*. They commonly use geographic, demographic, and psychographic characteristics. Then they see whether these customer segments show different responses to the product. For example, they might examine the differing attitudes of "professionals," "blue collars," and other groups toward Canadian-built cars.

Other researchers try to form segments by looking at *consumer responses* to the particular product, such as benefits sought, use occasions, brand, and loyalties. Once the segments are formed, the researcher sees whether different consumer characteristics are associated with each segment. For example, the researcher might examine whether people who want "quality" versus "low price" in buying an automobile differ in their geographic, demographic, and psychographic makeup.

We will now comment on the major variables shown in Table 10-1 and describe how they are used to segment markets.

Geographic Segmentation   Geographic segmentation calls for dividing the market into different geographical units such as nations, provinces, regions, counties, cities, or neighborhoods. The company can decide to operate in one or a few geographic areas or operate in all but pay attention to local variations in geographic needs and preferences. For example, *The Globe and Mail* positions itself as "Canada's national newspaper," but part of its content is adapted to regional interests. Thus, Ontario readers receive more news about Toronto-based happenings than B.C. readers do.

Demographic Segmentation   Demographic segmentation consists of dividing the market into groups on the basis of demographic variables such as age, sex, family size, family life cycle, income, occupation, education, religion, race, and nationality. Demographic variables are the most popular bases for distinguishing customer groups. One reason is that consumer wants, preferences, and usage rates are often highly associated with demographic variables. Another is that demographic variables are easier to measure than most other types of variables. Even when the target market is described in nondemographic terms (say, a personality type), the link back to demographic characteristics is necessary in order to know the size of the target market and how to reach it efficiently.

Table 10-1 Major Segmentation Variables for Consumer Markets

Variable	Typical Breakdowns
Geographic Region	Maritimes, Central Canada, Western Provinces
County Size	A, B, C, D
City or CMA size	Under 5000; 5000-20 000; 20 000-50 000; 50 000-100 000; 100 000-250 000; 250 000-500 000; 500 000-1 000 000; 1 000 000 or over
Density	Urban, suburban, rural
Demographic Socioeconomic	
Age	Under 6, 6-11, 12-19, 20-34, 35-49, 50-64, 65+
Sex	Male, female
Family size	1-2, 3-4, 5+
Family life cycle	Young, single; young, married, no children; young, married, youngest child under 6; young, married, youngest child 6 or over; older, married, with children; older, married, no children under 18; older, single; other
Income	Under $10 000; $10 000-$15 000; $15 000-$20 000; $20 000-$30 000; $30 000-$50 000; $50 000 and over
Occupation	Professional and technical; managers, officials, and proprietors; clerical, sales; craftsmen, foremen; operatives; farmers; retired; students; homemakers; unemployed
Education	Grade school or less; some high school; high school graduate; community college, university
Religion	Catholic, Protestant, Jewish, other
Ethnicity	French, English, Indian, Inuit
Nationality	Canadian, British, French, German, Scandinavian, Italian, American, Middle Eastern, Japanese, Chinese
Psychographic	
Social class	Lower lowers, upper lowers, lower middles, upper middles, lower uppers, upper uppers
Lifestyle	Straights, swingers, counter-culture
Personality	Compulsive, gregarious, authoritarian, ambitious
Behavioral	
Use occasion	Regular occasion, special occasion
Benefits sought	Quality, service, economy
User status	Nonuser, ex-user, potential user, first-time user, regular user
Usage rate	Light user, medium user, heavy user
Loyalty status	None, medium, strong, absolute
Readiness stage	Unaware, aware, informed, interested, desirous, intending to buy
Attitude toward product	Enthusiastic, positive, indifferent, negative, hostile

Here we will illustrate how certain demographic variables have been applied to market segmentation.

Age and Life-Cycle Stage Consumer wants and capacities change with age. Even six-month-old infants differ from three-month-old infants in their consumption potential. Alabe Products, a toy manufacturer, realized this and designed different toys for babies as they move through various stages from three months to one year. Crib Jiminy is used when babies begin to reach for things, Talky Rattle when they first grasp things, and so on. This segmentation strategy means that parents and gift givers can more easily find the appropriate toy by considering the baby's age.

General Foods applied age segmentation strategy to dog food. Many dog owners know that their dog's food needs change with age. So General Foods formulated four types of canned dog food: Cycle 1 for puppies, Cycle 2 for adult dogs, Cycle 3 for overweight dogs, and Cycle 4 for older dogs. General Foods managed to grab a large market share through this creative segmentation strategy.

Nevertheless, age and life cycle can be tricky variables. For example, the Ford Motor Company used buyers' ages in developing its target market for its Mustang automobile; the car was designed to appeal to young people who wanted an inexpensive sporty automobile. But Ford found that the car was being purchased by all age groups. It then realized that its target market was not the chronologically young but the psychologically young.

The Neugartens' research indicates that age stereotypes need to be guarded against:

> Age has become a poor predictor of the timing of life events, as well as a poor predictor of a person's health, work status, family status, and therefore, also, of a person's interests, preoccupations, and needs. We have multiple images of persons of the same age: there is the 70-year-old in a wheelchair and the 70-year-old on the tennis court. Likewise, there are 35-year-olds sending children off to college and 35-year-olds furnishing the nursery for newborns, producing in turn, first-time grandparenthood for persons who range in age from 35 to 75.[4] ■

Sex Sex segmentation has long been applied in clothing, hairdressing, cosmetics, and magazines. Occasionally other marketers will notice an opportunity for sex segmentation. The bar soap market provides an excellent example. Lux and Camay are positioned for women who are concerned about skin care, while Irish Spring is positioned as "manly." An industry that is beginning to recognize the potential for sex segmentation is the automobile industry. In the past, cars were designed to appeal primarily to males. With more women car owners, however, some manufacturers are studying the opportunity to design cars with features appealing to women.

Income Income segmentation is another longstanding practice in such product and service categories as automobiles, boats, clothing, cosmetics, and travel. Other industries occasionally recognize its possibilities. For example, Suntory, the Japanese liquor company, introduced a scotch selling for $75 to attract drinkers who want to think that they are drinking the very best.

Income does not always predict the best customers for a given product. We would guess that manual workers would buy Chevrolets and managers would buy Cadillacs. Yet many Chevrolets are bought by managers (often as a second car), and some Cadillacs are bought by manual workers (such as highly paid plumbers and carpenters). Manual workers were among the first purchasers of color television sets; it was cheaper for them to buy these sets than to go to movies and restaurants. Coleman drew a distinction between the "underprivileged" segments and the "overprivileged" segments of each social class.[5] The most economical cars are not bought by the really poor, he said, but rather by "those who think of themselves as poor relative to their status aspirations and to their needs for a certain level of clothing, furniture, and housing which they could not afford if they bought a more expensive car." On the other hand, medium-price and expensive cars tend to be purchased by the overprivileged segments of each social class.

Multiattribute Demographic Segmentation Most companies will segment a market by combining two or more demographic variables. For example, a major bank identified age and income as the two major demographic variables for segmenting its retail customers. Figure 10-5 shows three age breakdowns and three income breakdowns. A number of things should be noted. First, the age breakdowns could be finer: People in their early forties can differ substantially from those in their late fifties with respect to financial needs, yet they are lumped together. The fact that the middle cell is subdivided into two cells acknowledges that differences exist between young middle-aged people and preretired people. Second, income must be supplemented by an asset category. For example, some retired people have low incomes but high assets, and others have high incomes but low assets. Nevertheless, this demographic segmentation scheme provides a starting point by which the bank can create different offers and programs for different customer groups.

The "young, high-income" segment shown at the lower left of Figure 10-5 would include the so-called yuppie segment, namely *young urban professionals*. Defined demographically, yuppies are aged twenty-five to thirty-nine, high income, upscale professional, city address. Defined psychographically, they are thought to favor tennis, skiing, and sailing as sports; gourmet foods and wines; fashion, art, and cultural events; and foreign travel. However, demographics and psychographics are not always tightly linked. It turns out that many yuppies living in the West as opposed to the East favor golf, hunting, and fishing; prefer "junk" food and beer; and score low in art and cultural interests. Thus a bank would have to decide whether it wants to reach demographically defined yuppies or psychographically defined yuppies; it makes a big difference in the bank's offer-and-communication mix.

Psychographic Segmentation   In psychographic segmentation, buyers are divided into different groups on the basis of social class, lifestyle, and/or personality characteristics. People within the same demographic group can exhibit very different psychographic profiles.

Social Class We described the seven social classes in Chapter 6, and showed that social class has a strong influence on the person's preference in cars, clothing, home furnishings,

FIGURE 10-5
Age and Income
Segmentation of a
Bank's Retail
Customers

		Age		
		Under 40	40–65	Over 65
Income	Below $16 000	Young, low income	Middle-aged, lower income		Retired, low income
	$16 000–44 000	Young, middle income	Middle-aged, middle income	Preretired, middle income	Retired, middle income
	Above $44 000	Young, high income	Middle-aged, high income		Retired, high income

leisure activities, reading habits, retailers, and so on. Many companies design products and/or services for specific social classes.

Lifestyle We also saw in Chapter 6 that people's product interests are influenced by their lifestyles. In fact, the goods they consume express their lifestyle. Marketers of various products and brands are increasingly segmenting their markets by consumer lifestyles.

> Volkswagen has designed lifestyle automobiles: a car for "the good citizen" emphasizing economy, safety, and ecology; and a car for the "car freak" emphasizing handling, maneuverability, and sportiness. A research firm classified auto buyers into six types: "auto philes," "sensible centrists," "comfort seekers," "auto cynics," "necessity drivers," and "auto phobes." ∎

> Manufacturers of women's clothing have followed Du Pont's advice and are designing different clothes for the "plain woman," the "fashionable woman," and the "manly woman." ∎

> Cigarette companies develop brands for the "defiant smoker," the "casual smoker," and the "careful smoker." ∎

Companies making cosmetics, alcoholic beverages, and furniture are seeking opportunities in lifestyle segmentation. At the same time, lifestyle segmentation does not always work; Nestlé introduced a special brand of decaffeinated coffee for "late nighters," and it failed.

Personality Marketers have used personality variables to segment markets. They endow their products with *brand personalities* that correspond to *consumer personalities*. In the late fifties, Fords and Chevrolets were promoted as having different personalities. Ford buyers were identified as "independent, impulsive, masculine, alert to change, and self-confident, while Chevrolet owners were conservative, thrifty, prestige-conscious, less masculine, and seeking to avoid extremes."[6] Evans investigated the validity of these descriptions by subjecting Ford and Chevrolet owners to the Edwards Personal Preference test, which measured needs for achievement, dominance, change, aggression, and so on. Except for a slightly higher score on dominance, Ford owners' scores were not significantly different from those of Chevrolet owners. Evans concluded that "the distributions of scores for all needs overlap to such an extent that [personality] discrimination is virtually impossible." Work subsequent to Evans on a wide variety of products and brands has occasionally revealed personality differences. Westfall found some evidence of personality differences between the owners of convertibles and nonconvertibles, with owners of the former appearing to be more active, impulsive and sociable.[7] Shirley Young, the director of research for a leading advertising agency, reported developing successful market segmentation strategies based on personality traits in such product categories as women's cosmetics, cigarettes, insurance, and liquor.[8]

Behavioral Segmentation In behavioral segmentation, buyers are divided into groups on the basis of their knowledge, attitude, use, or response to a product. Many marketers believe that behavioral variables are the best starting point for constructing market segments.

Occasions Buyers can be distinguished according to occasions when they develop a need, purchase a product, or use a product. For example, air travel is triggered by occasions related to business, vacation, or family. An airline can specialize in serving people for whom one of these occasions dominates. Thus charter airlines serve people who fly for a vacation.

Occasion segmentation can help firms expand product usage. For example, orange juice is most usually consumed at breakfast. An orange juice company can try to promote drinking orange juice on other occasions—lunch, dinner, midday. Certain holidays—Mother's

Day and Father's Day for example—were promoted partly to increase the sale of candy and flowers. Candy companies make miniature candy bars for the "trick-or-treat" custom at Halloween, so every home can dispense candy to eager little callers knocking at their doors.

Instead of looking for product-specific occasions, a company can look at the major occasions that mark life's passages to see whether they are accompanied by certain needs that can be met by product and/or service bundles. Sometimes called critical-event segmentation, the occasions include marriage, separation, divorce; acquisition of a home; injury or illness; change in employment or career; retirement; death of a family member; and so on. Among the providers that have emerged to offer services on these critical occasions are marriage counselors, employment counselors, and bereavement counselors.

Benefits A powerful form of segmentation is the classification of buyers according to the different benefits they seek from the product. Yankelovich applied benefit segmentation to the purchase of watches. He found that "approximately 23 percent of the buyers bought for lowest price, another 46 percent bought for durability and general product quality, and 31 percent bought watches as symbols of some important occasion."[9] The better-known watch companies at the time focused almost exclusively on the third segment by producing expensive watches, stressing prestige, and selling through jewelry stores. Timex decided to focus on the first two segments by creating inexpensive, rugged watches and selling them through mass merchandisers. This segmentation strategy led to its becoming one of the world's largest watch companies.

Benefit segmentation calls for identifying the major benefits that people look for in the product class, the kinds of people who look for each benefit, and the major brands that deliver each benefit. One of the most successful benefit segmentations was reported by Haley, who studied the toothpaste market (see Table 10-2). Haley's research uncovered four benefit segments, seeking economy, protection, cosmetic, and taste benefits, respectively. Each benefit-seeking group had particular demographic, behavioristic, and psychographic characteristics. For example, decay-prevention seekers had large families, were heavy toothpaste users, and were conservative. Each segment also favored certain brands. A toothpaste company can use these findings to clarify which benefit segment it is appealing to, the characteristics of that segment, and the major competitive brands. The company can also search for a new benefit and launch a brand that delivers it.

Table 10-2 Benefit Segmentation of the Toothpaste Market

Benefit Segments	Demographics	Behavioristics	Psychographics	Favored Brands
Economy (low price)	Men	Heavy users	High autonomy, value oriented	Brands on sale
Medicinal (decay prevention)	Large families	Heavy users	Hypochondriac, conservative	Crest
Cosmetic (bright teeth)	Teens, young adults	Smokers	High sociability, active	Maclean's, Ultra Brite
Taste (good tasting)	Children	Spearmint lovers	High self-involvement, hedonistic	Colgate, Aim

Source: Adapted from Russell J. Haley, "Benefit Segmentation: A Decision Oriented Research Tool," *Journal of Marketing*, July 1963, pp. 30-35.

Benefit segmentation usually implies that a company should focus on satisfying one benefit group. Thus Crest toothpaste offered the benefit of "anticavity protection" and became extremely successful. "Anticavity protection" became its *unique selling proposition*. A unique selling proposition (USP) is stronger than just a unique proposition (UP). Too many companies develop a unique proposition and forget selling. For example, a purple toothpaste is unique, but it probably won't sell.

User Status Many markets can be segmented into nonusers, ex-users, potential users, first-time users, and regular users of a product. High-market-share companies are particularly interested in converting potential users into actual users, while smaller firms will try to attract users of competitive brands to switch to their brand. Potential users and regular users require different marketing approaches.

Social agencies pay close attention to user status. Drug rehabilitation agencies sponsor talks by ex-users to discourage young people from trying drugs. They also sponsor rehabilitation programs to help regular users quit the habit.

Usage Rate Markets can also be segmented into light-, medium-, and heavy-user groups of the product (called *volume segmentation*). Heavy users are often a small percentage of the market but account for a high percentage of total consumption. Some data on usage rates for popular consumer products are shown in Figure 10-6. Using beer as an example, the chart shows that 68 percent of the people did not drink beer. The 32 percent who did were divided into two groups. The lower 16 percent were light users and accounted for only 12 percent of total beer consumption. The heavy half accounted for 88 percent of the total consumption—that is, for over seven times as much consumption as the light users. Thus a beer company would prefer to attract one heavy user to its brand over several light users. Most beer companies target the heavy beer drinker, using appeals such as "The one beer to have when you're having more than one."

A product's heavy users often have common demographics, psychographics, and media habits. The profile of heavy beer drinkers shows the following characteristics: More of them

FIGURE 10-6

Annual Purchase Concentration in Several Product Categories

Source: Dik Warren Twedt, "How Important to Marketing Strategy Is the 'Heavy User'?" *Journal of Marketing*, January 1974, p. 72.

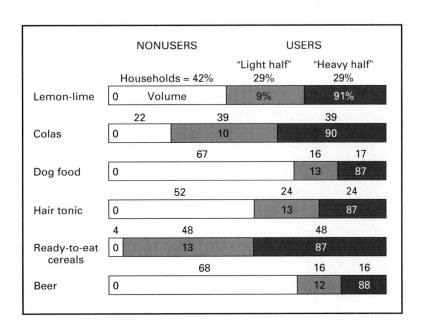

are in the working class; they concentrate in the ages of twenty-five to fifty; they watch television more than three and one-half hours per day; and they prefer sports programs.[10] These profiles can assist marketers in developing price, message, and media strategies.

Social marketing agencies often face a heavy-user dilemma. A family-planning agency would normally target families who have many children, but these families are also the most resistant to birth control messages. The Construction Safety Association of Ontario would like to target unsafe workers but these workers are the most resistant to safe-working appeals. The agencies must consider whether to go after a few highly resistant heavy offenders or many less-resistant light offenders.

Loyalty Status A market can be segmented by consumer-loyalty patterns. Consumers can be loyal to brands (Molson), stores (Sears), and other entities. Suppose there are five brands: A, B, C, D, and E. Buyers can be divided into four groups according to their loyalty status:

□ *Hard-Core Loyals:* Consumers who buy one brand all the time. Thus a buying pattern of A, A, A, A, A, A, might represent a consumer with undivided loyalty to brand A.

□   *Soft-Core Loyals:* Consumers who are loyal to two or three brands. The buying pattern A, A, B, B, A, B represents a consumer with a divided loyalty between A and B.

□ *Shifting Loyals:* Consumers who shift from favoring one brand to another. The buying pattern A, A, A, B, B, B would suggest a consumer who is shifting brand loyalty from A to B.

□ *Switchers:* Consumers who show no loyalty to any brand. The buying pattern A, C, E, B, D, B would suggest a nonloyal consumer who is either *deal prone* (buys the brand on sale) or *variety prone* (wants something different each time).[11]

Each market consists of different numbers of the four types of buyers. A brand-loyal market is one with a high percentage of hard-core brand-loyal buyers. Thus the toothpaste market and the beer market are fairly high brand-loyal markets. Companies selling in a brand-loyal market have a hard time gaining more market share, and companies that enter such a market have a hard time getting in.

A company can learn a great deal by analyzing loyalty in its market. It should study the characteristics of its own hard-core loyals. Colgate finds that its hard-core loyals are more middle class, have larger families, and are more health conscious. This pinpoints the target market for Colgate.

By studying its soft-core loyals, the company can pinpoint which brands are most competitive with its own. If many Colgate buyers also buy Crest, Colgate can attempt to improve its positioning against Crest, possibly using direct-comparison advertising.

By looking at customers who are shifting away from its brand, the company can learn about its marketing weaknesses. As for nonloyals, the company can attract them by running frequent sales.

One caution: what appear to be brand-loyal purchase patterns might reflect *habit, indifference,* a *low price,* or the *nonavailability* of other brands. The company must examine what is behind the observed purchase patterns.

Buyer-Readiness Stage At any time, people are in different stages of readiness to buy a product. Some people are unaware of the product; some are aware; some are informed; some are interested; some are desirous of buying; and some intend to buy. The relative numbers make a big difference in designing the marketing program. Suppose a health agency wants women to take an annual Pap test to detect possible cervical cancer. At the beginning, most women are unaware of the Pap test. The marketing effort should go into high-awareness-building advertising using a simple message. If successful, the advertising should then dramatize the benefits of the Pap test and the risks of not taking it, in order to move more women into the stage of desire. Facilities should be readied for handling the large number of women who now might be motivated to have the examination. In general, the marketing program must be adjusted to the changing number of people in each buyer-readiness stage.

Attitude People in a market can be classified by their degree of enthusiasm for the product. Five attitude classes can be distinguished: enthusiastic, positive, indifferent, negative, and hostile. Door-to-door workers in a political campaign use the voter's attitude to determine how much time to spend with the voter. They thank enthusiastic voters and remind them to vote; they reinforce those who are positively disposed; they try to win the votes of indifferent voters; they spend no time trying to change the attitudes of negative and hostile voters. To the extent that attitudes are correlated with demographic descriptors, the organization can increase its efficiency in locating the best prospects.

Bases for Segmenting Industrial Markets

Industrial markets can be segmented using many of the same variables employed in consumer market segmentation, such as geography, benefits sought, and usage rate. Yet there are also some new variables. Bonoma and Shapiro proposed the classification of segmentation variables for the industrial market shown in Table 10-3. They suggest that the demographic variables are the most important, followed by the operating variables—down to the personal characteristics of the buyer.

The table lists major questions that industrial marketers should ask in determining which segments and customers to serve. In going after segments instead of the whole market, the company can deliver more real value than competitors and charge a premium for this value. Thus a rubber-tire company should decide which *industries* it wants to serve, noting the following differences:

> Automobile manufacturers seeking original-equipment tires vary in their requirements, with luxury-car manufacturers wanting a much higher grade tire than standard car manufacturers. And the tires needed by aircraft manufacturers have to meet much higher safety standards than tires needed by farm tractor manufacturers. ∎

Within a chosen target industry, a company can further segment by *customer size*. The company might set up separate programs for dealing with large and small customers. Steelcase, a major manufacturer of office furniture, divides its customers into two groups:

☐ *Major accounts:* Accounts such as IBM are handled by national account managers working with field district managers.

☐ *Dealer accounts:* Smaller accounts are handled through field sales personnel working with franchised dealers who sell Steelcase products.

Within a certain target industry and customer size, the company can segment by *purchase criteria*:

> Government laboratories, university laboratories, and industrial laboratories typically differ in their purchase criteria for scientific instruments. Government laboratories need low prices (because they have difficulty getting funds to buy instruments) and service contracts (because they can easily get money to maintain instruments). University laboratories need equipment that requires little continuous service because they do not have service people on their payroll. Industrial laboratories need equipment that is highly reliable because they cannot afford downtime. ∎

Table 10-3 Major Segmentation Variables for Industrial Markets

DEMOGRAPHIC

□ *Industry:* Which industries that buy this product should we focus on?

□ *Company size:* What size companies should we focus on?

□ *Location:* What geographical areas should we focus on?

OPERATING VARIABLES

□ *Technology:* What customer technologies should we focus on?

□ *User/nonuser status:* Should we focus on heavy, medium, light users or nonusers?

□ *Customer capabilities:* Should we focus on customers needing many services or few services?

PURCHASING APPROACHES

□ *Purchasing-function organization:* Should we focus on companies with highly centralized or decentralized purchasing organizations?

□ *Power structure:* Should we focus on companies that are engineering dominated, financially dominated, etc.?

□ *Nature of existing relationships:* Should we focus on companies with which we have strong existing relationships or simply go after the most desirable companies?

□ *General purchase policies:* Should we focus on companies that prefer leasing? service contracts? systems purchases? sealed bidding?

□ *Purchasing criteria:* Should we focus on companies that are seeking quality? service? price?

SITUATIONAL FACTORS

□ *Urgency:* Should we focus on companies that need quick and sudden delivery or service?

□ *Specific application:* Should we focus on certain applications of our product rather than all applications?

□ *Size of order:* Should we focus on large or small orders?

PERSONAL CHARACTERISTICS

□ *Buyer-seller similarity:* Should we focus on companies whose people and values are similar to ours?

□ *Attitudes toward risk:* Should we focus on risk-taking or risk-avoiding customers?

□ *Loyalty:* Should we focus on companies that show high loyalty to their suppliers?

Source: Adapted from Thomas V. Bonoma and Benson P. Shapiro, *Segmenting the Industrial Market* (Lexington, Mass.: Lexington Books, 1983).

In general, industrial companies do not focus on one segmentation variable but generally apply multiattribute segmentation. This is illustrated in Figure 10-7 for an aluminum company:

> The aluminum company first undertook macrosegmentation consisting of three steps.[12] It looked at which end-use market to serve: automobile, residential, or beverage containers. Choosing the residential market, it determined the most attractive product application: semifinished material, building components, or aluminum mobile homes. Deciding to focus on building components, it next considered the best customer size and chose large customers. ■

> The second stage consisted of *microsegmentation* within the large-customer building-components market. The company saw customers falling into three groups—those who bought on price, those who bought on service, and those who bought on quality. Because the aluminum company had a high-service profile, it decided to concentrate on the service-motivated segment of the market. ■

FIGURE 10-7

Three-Step Segmentation of the Aluminum Market

Source: Based on an example in E. Raymond Corey, "Key Options in Market Selection and Product Planning," *Harvard Business Review*, September-October 1975, pp. 119-28.

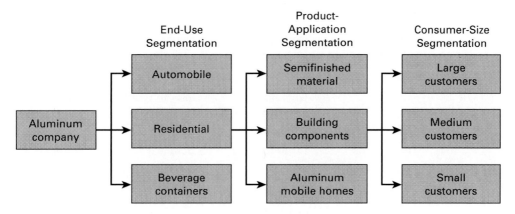

Developing the Customer Segment Profile

Each customer segment that a company considers should be profiled in more detail. It is not enough to consider, say, price-sensitive customers versus quality-sensitive customers. We need further segment descriptors, such as their demographics, psychographics, mediagraphics, attitudes, and behavior. As an example, Smythe reported a benefit segmentation study of coffee drinkers.[13] Coffee drinkers were asked to assign importance ratings to twenty-five product attributes. The data were factor analyzed, and three clear segments emerged based on different needs for coffee. The segments were named decaffeinated, nondecaffeinated, and ground. Table 10-4 shows a partial profile of the three customer segments. They were approximately equal in size but quite different in benefits desired, use frequency, and demographics. The finding, for example, that decaffeinated-coffee drinkers were older, widowed, and so on, did not mean that no decaffeinated-coffee drinkers were younger, married, and so on. It only meant that decaffeinated-coffee drinkers were on the average older, widowed, and so on. In fact, if there were no demographic differences among the three groups, then demographic characteristics would be omitted from the profiles.

Clearly, the marketer hopes to discover different profiles for the segments. In the best case, the segments will differ psychographically and have different demographics and mediagraphics. Thus the results would indicate that a decaffeinated-coffee brand such as Sanka should be placed into heavy distribution where people who are older, widowed, and so on are found, and the brand should be advertised mostly in print media read by people who are older, widowed, and so on.

Requirements for Effective Segmentation

There are many ways to segment a market. Not all segmentations, however, are effective. For example, buyers of table salt could be divided into blond and brunet customers. But hair color is not relevant to the purchase of salt. Furthermore, if all salt buyers buy the same amount of salt each month, believe all salt is the same, and want to pay the same price, this market would be minimally segmentable from a marketing point of view.

Table 10-4 Coffee-Market-Segment Profiles

Name	Segment		
	Decaffeinated	Nondecaffeinated	Ground
Size	35%	33%	32%
Distinguishing benefits desired	Decaffeinated Not make me nervous Prepared quickly Not wake up Concentrated form	Not decaffeinated Wake up Convenient package Well-known brand Easy to prepare	Not prepared quickly Not convenient package Not easy to prepare Special equipment Not concentrated form
Frequency of use	Light users	Medium users	Heavy users
Type usage	Instant	Both	Ground
Brand usage	Sanka Brim Taster's Choice Nescafé High Point	Maxwell House Folger's	Hills Bros. All others
Demographics	Older Widowed Lower Income More minorities	Average age Divorced Average income More minorities	Younger Married Higher income Fewer minorities

Source: Robert J. Smythe, *Market Segmentation*, a pamphlet published by NFO Research, Inc.

To be maximally useful, market segments must exhibit four characteristics:

☐ *Measurability:* The degree to which the size and purchasing power of the segments can be measured. Certain segmentation variables are difficult to measure. An illustration would be the size of the segment of teenage smokers who smoke primarily to rebel against their parents.

☐ *Substantiality:* The degree to which the segments are large and/or profitable enough. A segment should be the largest possible homogeneous group worth going after with a tailored marketing program. It would not pay, for example, for an automobile manufacturer to develop cars for persons who are shorter than four feet.

☐ *Accessibility:* The degree to which the segments can be effectively reached and served. Suppose a perfume company finds that heavy users of its brand are single women who are out late at night and frequent bars. Unless this groups lives or shops at certain places and is exposed to certain media, they will be difficult to reach.

☐ *Actionability:* The degree to which effective programs can be formulated for attracting and serving the segments. A small airline, for example, identified seven market segments, but its staff was too small to develop separate marketing programs for each segment.

MARKET TARGETING

Market segmentation reveals the market-segment opportunities facing the firm. The firm now has to evaluate the various segments and decide how many and which ones to serve. We will now look at the tools for segment evaluation and selection.

Evaluating the Market Segments

In evaluating different market segments, the firm must look at three factors, namely segment size and growth, segment structural attractiveness, and company objectives and resources.

Segment Size and Growth   The first question that a company should ask is whether a potential segment has the right size and growth characteristics. The "right size" is a relative matter. Large companies prefer segments with large sales volumes and often overlook or avoid small segments. Small companies in turn avoid large segments because they require too many resources.

Segment growth is normally a desirable characteristic, since companies generally want growing sales and profits. At the same time, competitors will rapidly enter growing segments and depress their profitability.

Segment Structural Attractiveness   A segment might have desirable size and growth and still not be attractive from a profitability point of view. Porter has identified five forces that determine the intrinsic long-run attractiveness of a whole market or any segment within it.[14] His five-force model is shown in Figure 10-8. The company has to appraise the impact on long-run profitability of five groups: *industry competitors, potential entrants, substitutes, buyers,* and *suppliers*. The five threats they pose are as follows:

1. *Threat of Intense Segment Rivalry*: A segment is unattractive if it already contains numerous, strong or aggressive competitors. The picture is even worse if the segment is stable or declining, if capacity additions are done in large increments, if fixed costs are high, if

FIGURE 10-8
Five Forces Determining Segment Structural Attractiveness

Source: Adapted with permission of the Free Press, a Division of Macmillan, Inc. from *Competitive Advantage: Creating and Sustaining Superior Performance* by Michael E. Porter, p. 235. Copyright © 1985 by Michael E. Porter.

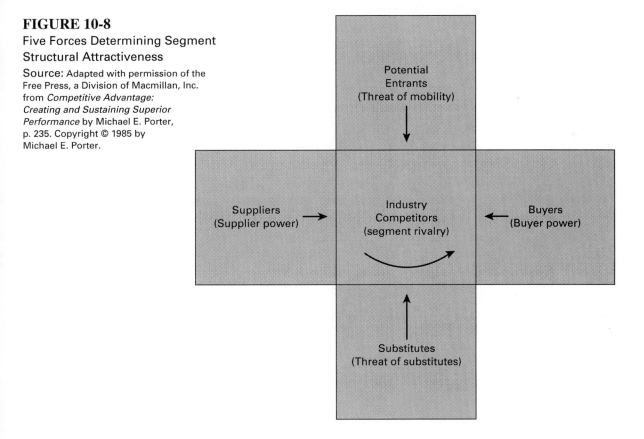

exit barriers are high, or if competitors have high stakes in staying in the segment. These conditions will lead to frequent price wars, advertising battles, and new-product introductions and will make it expensive for the companies to compete.

2. *Threat of New Entrant:* A segment is unattractive if it is likely to attract new competitors who will bring in new capacity, substantial resources, and a drive for market-share growth. The question boils down to whether new entrants can easily get in. They will find it hard if there are high barriers to entry coupled with sharp retaliation from incumbent firms. The lower the barriers to entry or willingness to retaliate, the less attractive the segment.

   A segment's attractiveness varies with the height of the entry and exit barriers.[15] The most attractive segment from the viewpoint of industry profits is one in which entry barriers are high and exit barriers are low (see Figure 10-9). Few new firms can enter the industry, and poor-performing firms can easily exit. When both entry and exit barriers are high, profit potential is high but is usually accompanied by more risk because poorer-performing firms stay in and fight it out. When entry and exit barriers are both low, then firms easily enter and leave the industry, and the returns are stable and low. The worst case is when entry barriers are low and exit barriers are high: here firms enter during good times but find it hard to leave during bad times. The result is chronic overcapacity and depressed earnings for all.

3. *Threat of Substitute Products:* A segment is unattractive if there exist actual or potential substitutes for the product. Substitutes place a limit on the potential prices and profits that can be earned in a segment. The company has to watch closely the price trends in the substitutes. If technology advances or competition increases in these substitute industries, prices and profits in the segment are likely to fall.

4. *Threat of Growing Bargaining Power of Buyers:* A segment is unattractive if the buyers possess strong or increasing bargaining power. Buyers will try to force prices down, demand more quality or services, and set competitors against each other, all at the expense of seller profitability. Buyers' bargaining power grows when they become more concentrated or organized, when the product represents a significant fraction of the buyers' costs, when the product is undifferentiated, when the buyers' switching costs are low, when the buyers are price sensitive because of low profits, or when the buyers can integrate backward. In defense, sellers might select buyers who possess the least power to negotiate or switch suppliers. A better defense consists of developing superior offers that buyers cannot refuse.

5. *Threat of Growing Bargaining Power of Suppliers:* A segment is unattractive if the company's suppliers—raw-material and equipment suppliers, public utilities, banks, trade unions, and the like—are able to raise prices or reduce the quality or quantity of ordered goods and services. Suppliers tend to be powerful when they are concentrated or organized, when there are few substitutes, when the supplied product is an important input, when

FIGURE 10-9
Barriers and Profitablity

		Exit Barriers	
		Low	High
Entry Barriers	Low	Low, stable returns	Low, risky returns
	High	High, stable returns	High, risky returns

the switching costs are high, and when the suppliers can integrate forward. The best defense is to build good relations with suppliers and have multiple supply sources.

Company Objectives and Resources   Even if a segment has positive size and growth and is structurally attractive, the company needs to consider its own objectives and resources in relation to that segment. Some attractive segments could be dismissed because they do not mesh with the company's long-run objectives. They may be tempting segments in themselves, but they do not move the company forward toward its goals. At worst, they would divert the company's energy from its main goals.

Even if the segment fits the company's objectives, the company must consider whether it possesses the requisite skills and resources to succeed in that segment. Each segment has certain success requirements. The segment should be dismissed if the company lacks one or more necessary competences and is in no position to acquire the necessary competences. But even if the company possesses the requisite competences, that is not enough. If it is really to win in that market segment, it needs to develop some superior advantages to the competition. It should not enter markets or market segments where it cannot produce some form of superior value.

Selecting the Market Segments

As a result of evaluating different segments, the company hopes to find one or more market segments worth entering. The company must decide which and how many segments to serve. That is the problem of *target market selection*. A *target market* consists of a set of buyers sharing common needs or characteristics that the company decides to serve. The company can consider five patterns of target market selection, shown in Figure 10-10.

Single-Segment Concentration   In the simplest case, the company selects a single segment. The company might have a natural match to this segment's key success requirements; it might have very limited funds and can operate only in one segment; it might be a segment with no other competitor; it might be a segment that is a logical launching pad for further segment expansion.

Several examples of *concentrated marketing* can be cited. Volkswagen has concentrated on the small-car market, Hewlett-Packard on the high-price calculator market, and Richard

FIGURE 10-10

Five Patterns of Target Market Selection

Source: Adapted from Derek F. Abell, *Defining the Business: The Starting Point of Strategic Planning* (Englewood Cliffs, N.J.: Prentice-Hall, 1980), Chap. 8, pp. 192-96.

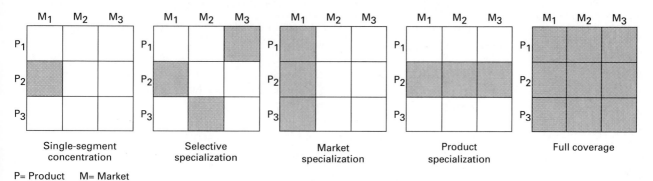

P= Product   M= Market

D. Irwin on the economics and business texts market. Through concentrated marketing, the firm achieves a strong market position in the segment owing to its greater knowledge of the segment's needs and the special reputation it builds. Furthermore, the firm enjoys many operating economies through specializing its production, distribution, and promotion. If it niches well in the segment, the firm can earn a high return on its investment.

At the same time, concentrated marketing involves higher than normal risks. The particular market segment can turn sour; for example, the end of the baby boom caused considerable concern at Gerber because of the company's concentration on baby foods. Or a competitor may decide to enter the same segment. For these reasons, many companies prefer to diversify in several market segments.

Selective Specialization   Here the firm selects a number of segments, each of which is objectively attractive and matches the firm's objectives and resources. There may be little or no synergy between the segments, but each segment promises to be a money maker. This strategy of *multisegment coverage* has the advantage over *single-segment coverage* of diversifying the firm's risk. Even if one segment becomes unattractive, the firm can continue to earn money in other segments.

Product Specialization   Here the firm concentrates on making a certain product that it sells to several segments. An example would be a microscope manufacturer that sells microscopes to university laboratories, government laboratories, and commercial laboratories. The firm is prepared to make different microscopes for these different customer groups but avoids getting into the production of any other instruments that laboratories might use. Through this strategy, the firm builds up a strong reputation in the specific product area. The downside risk would occur if the product—here microscopes—were supplanted by an entirely new technology for magnifying small objects.

Market Specialization   Here the firm concentrates on serving many needs of a particular customer group. An example would be a firm that carries an array of products for university laboratories, including microscopes, oscilloscopes, bunsen burners, chemical flasks, and so on. The firm gains a strong reputation for specializing in serving this customer group and becomes a channel agent for all new products that this customer group could feasibly use. The downside risk would occur if this customer group—here university laboratories—suddenly had their budgets cut, and they reduced their purchases from this market-specialized firm.

Full Market Coverage   Here a firm attempts to serve all customer groups with all the products that they might need. Only large firms can undertake a full market coverage strategy. Examples would include IBM (computer market), General Motors (vehicle market), and Coca-Cola (drink market).

Large firms can cover a whole market in two broad ways, namely, through undifferentiated marketing or differentiated marketing.

Undifferentiated Marketing The firm might ignore market-segment differences and go after the whole market with one market offer. It focuses on what is common in the needs of buyers rather than on what is different. It designs a product and a marketing program that will appeal to the broadest number of buyers. It relies on mass distribution and mass advertising. It aims to endow the product with a superior image in people's minds. An example of undifferentiated marketing is the Coca-Cola Company's early marketing of only one drink in one bottle size in one taste to suit everyone.

Undifferentiated marketing is defended on the grounds of cost economies. It is seen as "the marketing counterpart to standardization and mass production in manufacturing."[17] The narrow product line keeps down production, inventory, and transportation costs. The undifferentiated advertising program keeps down advertising costs. The absence of segment-marketing research and planning lowers the costs of marketing research and product management. Presumably, the company can turn its lower costs into lower prices to win the price-sensitive segment of the market.

Nevertheless, a growing number of marketers have expressed strong doubts about this strategy. Gardner and Levy, while acknowledging that "some brands have very skillfully built up reputations of being suitable for a wide variety of people," noted that

> in most areas audience groupings will differ, if only because there are deviants who refuse to consume the same way other people do. . . . It is not easy for a brand to appeal to stable lower-middle-class people and at the same time to be interesting to sophisticated, intellectual upper-middle-class buyers. . . . It is rarely possible for a product or brand to be all things to all people.[18]

The firm practicing undifferentiated marketing typically develops an offer aimed at the largest segments in the market. When several firms do this, the result is intense competition for the largest segments and undersatisfaction of the smaller ones. Thus the domestic auto industry for a long time produced only large automobiles. The further result is that the larger segments may be less profitable because they attract disproportionately heavy competition. Kuehn and Day have called this tendency to go after the largest market segment the "majority fallacy."[19] The recognition of this fallacy has led firms to show increased interest in the smaller market segments.

Differentiated Marketing Here the firm operates in most market segments but designs different programs for each segment. General Motors claims to do this when it says that it produces a car for every "purse, purpose, and personality." And IBM offers many hardware and software packages for different segments in the computer market.

A growing number of firms have adopted differentiated marketing. Here is an excellent example:

> Dylex is Canada's largest specialty retailer with 1990 sales of $1.84 billion. In the men's clothing market, its Harry Rosen chain provides superior service and elegant ambience for upscale customers; its Tip Top chain offers moderate prices for men with conservative tastes; and its Steel chain emphasizes fashion and leisure wear for younger men. Similarly, Dylex covers the major segments of the women's clothing market through its Suzy Shier, Fairweather, and Braemar chains. In the family market, Dylex chains include BiWay, Thrifty's, and Club Monaco. This differentiated approach seems to work. In only two decades, the company has grown from 70 to 1352 stores, and claims to have ten percent of the Canadian retail clothing market.[20]

Differentiated marketing typically creates more total sales than undifferentiated marketing. "It is ordinarily demonstrable that total sales may be increased with a more diversified product line sold through more diversified channels."[21] However, it also increases the costs of doing business. The following costs are likely to be higher:

☐ *Product Modification Costs:* Modifying a product to meet different market segment requirements usually involves some R&D, engineering, and/or special tooling costs.

☐ *Production Costs:* It is usually more expensive to produce, say, ten units of ten different products than one hundred units of one product. The longer the production setup time for each product and the smaller the sales volume of each product, the more expensive it becomes. On the other hand, if each model is sold in sufficiently large volume, the higher costs of setup time may be quite small per unit.

☐ *Administrative Costs:* The company has to develop separate marketing plans for the separate segments of the market. This requires extra marketing research, forecasting, sales analysis, promotion, planning, and channel management.

☐ *Inventory Costs:* It is generally more costly to manage inventories of differentiated products than an inventory of only one product. The extra costs arise because more records must be kept, and more auditing must be done. Furthermore, each product must be carried at a level that reflects basic demand plus a safety factor to cover unexpected variations in demand. The sum of the safety stocks for several products will exceed the safety stock required for one product.

☐ *Promotion Costs:* Differentiated marketing involves trying to reach different market segments with different advertising. This strategy leads to lower usage rates of individual media and the loss of quantity discounts. Furthermore, since each segment might require separate creative advertising planning, promotion costs are increased.

Since differentiated marketing leads to both higher sales and higher costs, nothing can be said in advance regarding the profitability of this strategy. Some firms find that they have *oversegmented* their market and offer too many brands. They would like to manage fewer brands, each appealing to a broader customer group. This approach is called countersegmentation or broadening the base. It seeks a larger volume for each brand.[22] Johnson & Johnson, for example, broadened its target market for its baby shampoo to include adults. And Beecham launched its Aquafresh toothpaste to attract three benefit segments, those seeking (1) fresh breath, (2) whiter teeth, and (3) cavity protection.

FIGURE 10-11
Three Alternative Market
Selection Strategies

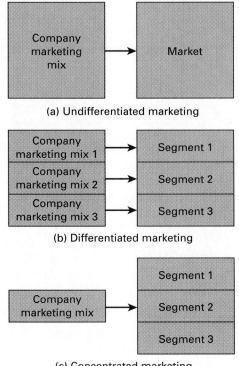

(a) Undifferentiated marketing

(b) Differentiated marketing

(c) Concentrated marketing

Figure 10-11 summarizes the differences between undifferentiated marketing, differentiated marketing, and concentrated marketing.

Additional Considerations in Evaluating and Selecting Segments

Two other considerations must be taken into account in evaluating and selecting segments.

Segment Interrelationships and Supersegments   In selecting more than one segment to serve, the company should pay close attention to *segment interrelationships* on the cost, performance, and technology side. A company carrying a fixed cost (its salesforce, store outlets, and so on) will add products to absorb and share some of the cost. Thus a salesforce will be given additional products to sell, and a fast-food outlet will offer additional dishes. This is a search for *economies of scope*, which can be just as important as economies of scale.

Companies should also identify and try to operate in *supersegments* rather than in isolated segments. Figure 10-12 shows how twelve single segments can be regrouped into five supersegments based on certain synergies, such as using the same raw materials, manufacturing facilities, or distribution channels. The firm would be wise to choose a supersegment rather than a single segment within the supersegment; otherwise, it might be at a competitive disadvantage with those firms that have locked into that supersegment.

Segment-by-Segment Invasion Plans   Even if the firm plans to move into a supersegment, it is wise to enter one segment at a time and conceal its grand plan. The competitors must not know to what segment(s) the firm will move next. This situation is illustrated in Figure 10-13. Three firms, A, B, and C, have specialized in adapting computer systems to the needs of transportation companies—specifically, airlines, railroads, and trucking companies. Company A has specialized in meeting all the computer needs of airlines. Company B has specialized in selling large computer systems to all three transportation sectors. Company C recently entered this market and has specialized in tailoring and selling value-added microcomputers to trucking companies. The question is, Where should company C move next? The arrows have been added to the chart to show the planned sequence of market-segment inva-

FIGURE 10-12
Segments and Supersegments

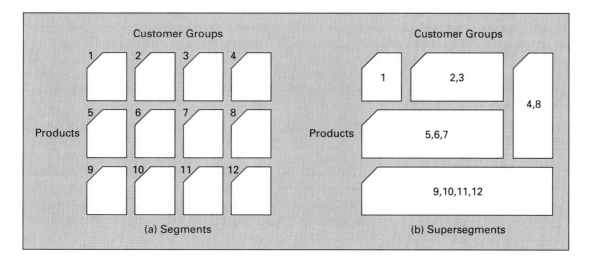

FIGURE 10-13
A Segment-by-Segment
Invasion Plan

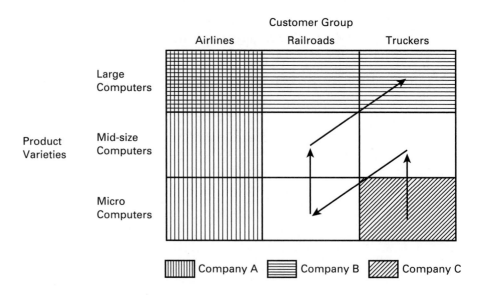

sions unknown to company C's competitors. Company C will start offering midsize computers to trucking companies; then to allay company B's concern about its large computer business in the face of the attack on trucking companies, company C moves into offering microcomputers tailored to railroad needs. Later, it offers midsize computers to railroads. Finally, it launches a full attack on company B's large computer position in trucking companies. Of course, its planned sequence is provisional in that much depends on the segment moves of the other competitors over time.

Unfortunately, too many companies fail to develop a long-term invasion plan in which they have plotted the sequence and timing of market-segment entries. Pepsi-Cola is an exception in that its attack on Coca-Cola was thought through in grand-plan terms, first attacking Coca-Cola in the grocery market, then in the vending-machine market, then in the fast-food market, and so on. Japanese firms also plot their invasion sequence. They first gain a foothold in a market—say Toyota brings in a small car into the market—and then they expand with more cars, then larger cars, and eventually luxury cars. Managers of domestic firms know that when a Japanese firm enters their market, it will not stop at the first segment, but will use that beachhead as a launching pad for successive invasions.

The question of who will dominate a segment is also raised by Figure 10-13. For example, both company A and company B compete in selling large computers to airlines. Company A is a specialist in large computers and probably enjoys lower costs through its higher volume. Company B specializes in all the computer needs of airlines and has the advantage of knowing airlines and their people better. The issue boils down to which is a greater advantage for operating in that segment.

SUMMARY

Sellers can take three approaches to a market. Mass marketing is the decision to mass produce and mass distribute one product and attempt to attract all kinds of buyers. Product-variety marketing is the decision to produce two or more market offers differentiated in style, features, quality, sizes, and so on, and designed to offer variety to the market and distinguish the seller's products from competitors' products. Target marketing is the decision to distinguish the different groups that make up a market and to develop corresponding products and marketing mixes for each target market. Sellers today are moving away from mass marketing and product differentiation toward target marketing because the latter is more helpful in spotting market opportunities and developing effective products and marketing mixes.

The key steps in target marketing are market segmentation, market targeting, and product positioning. Market segmentation is the act of dividing a market into distinct groups of buyers who might merit separate products and/or marketing mixes. The marketer tries different variables to see which reveal the best segmentation opportunities. For each segment, a customer-segment profile is developed. The effectiveness of the segmentation analysis depends on arriving at segments that are measurable, substantial, accessible, and actionable.

Next, the seller has to target the best market segment(s). To do so, the seller must first evaluate the profit potential of each segment, which is a function of segment size and growth, segment structural attractiveness, and company objectives and resources. Then the seller must decide how many segments to cover. The seller can ignore segment differences (undifferentiated marketing), develop different market offers for several segments (differentiated marketing), or go after one or a few market segments (concentrated marketing). In choosing target segments, marketers need to consider segment interrelationships and potential segment roll-out plans.

■ QUESTIONS

1. "Creating market segments is only part of the process." Do you agree? What further steps must be taken for a market segment to be maximally useful?

2. Think of the market for denim jeans. Imagine you are going through a formal procedure for segmenting this market. Describe what you are likely to find in each of the three steps.

3. Evaluate the pros and cons of "regionalized" marketing, or segmenting markets on a geographic basis.

4. Use Porter's five forces for determining segment structural attractiveness to evaluate the "light" beer segment of the beer market.

5. How might the personal computer market be segmented? Develop a segment-by-segment invasion plan for Compaq, a manufacturer of IBM-compatible personal computers. Develop a position strategy statement for Compaq.

6. The choice of a base for segmenting consumer markets depends on its relevance for differentiating the buying patterns of consumer groups in a particular market. What might be the relevant base(s) for segmenting the market for banking and other financial services?

7. By making slight changes in the product and its packaging, cigarette manufacturers have been able to make what

is essentially the same product appeal to a wide variety of consumer segments. In what ways has the smoking public been segmented?

8. Choose a consumer service and discuss how the market for such a service is segmented.

9. Market segments can be developed by cross-classifying pertinent variables. What problems arise in trying to cross-classify more than a few variables?

10. Suggest a useful way to segment the markets for the following products: (a) household detergents, (b) animal feeds, (c) household coffee, (d) automobile tires.

11. A camera manufacturer wants to develop a benefit segmentation of the camera market. Suggest some major benefit segments.

12. The Quaker Oats Company produces a dry breakfast cereal called Life. Life's brand manager wants to identify different market segments for the cereal. The segments are formed by using wife's age, family size, and city size. Rank the segments from the most important to the least important.

13. A clock manufacturer recognizes that it is basically in the time-measurement business. It wants to segment the time-measurement market in order to identify new opportunities. Identify the major segments in this market.

■ NOTES

1. Stephen P. Arbeit, "Confronting the Crisis in Mass Marketing," *Viewpoint* 2 (1982), pp. 2, 9.

2. Alan R. Andreasen and Russell W. Belk, "Predictors of Attendance at the Performing Arts," *Journal of Consumer Research*, September 1980, pp. 112-20.

3. See Manohar U. Kalwani and Donald G. Morrison, "A Parsimonious Description of the Hendry System," *Management Science*, January 1977, pp. 467-77.

4. *American Demographics*, August 1986.

5. Richard P. Coleman, "The Significance of Social Stratification in Selling," in *Marketing: A Maturing Discipline*, ed. Martin L. Bell (Chicago: American Marketing Association, 1961), pp. 171-84.

6. Quoted in Franklin B. Evans, "Psychological and Objective Factors in the Prediction of Brand Choice; Ford versus Chevrolet," *Journal of Business*, October 1959, pp. 340-69.

7. Ralph Westfall, "Psychological Factors in Predicting Product Choice," *Journal of Marketing*, April 1962, pp. 34-40.

8. Shirley Young, "The Dynamics of Measuring Unchange," in *Attitude Research in Transition*, ed. Russell I. Haley (Chicago: American Marketing Association, 1972), pp. 61-82.

9. See Daniel Yankelovich, "New Criteria for Market Segmentation," *Harvard Business Review*, March-April 1964, pp. 83-90, here p. 85.

10. Frank M. Bass, Douglas J. Tigert, and Ronald T. Lonsdale, "Market Segmentation: Group versus Individual Behavior," *Journal of Marketing Research*, August 1968, p. 276.

11. This classification was adapted from George H. Brown, "Brand Loyalty—Fact or Fiction?" *Advertising Age*, June 1952-January 1953, a series.

12. Wind and Cardozo suggest that industrial segmentation should proceed by first developing macrosegments and then microsegments. See Yoram Wind and Richard Cardozo, "Industrial Market Segmentation," *Industrial Marketing Management* 3 (1974), pp. 153-66. For other views, see Thomas V. Bonoma and Benson P. Shapiro, *Segmenting the Industrial Market* (Lexington, Mass.: Lexington Books, 1983); and James D. Hlavacek and B. C. Ames, "Segmenting Industrial and High-Tech Markets," *Journal of Business Strategy*, Fall 1986, pp. 39-50.

13. Robert J. Smythe, *Market Segmentation*, a pamphlet published by NFO Research, Toledo, Ohio (no date).

14. Michael E. Porter, *Competitive Advantage* (New York: Free Press, 1985), pp. 4-8 and pp. 234-36.

15. Michael E. Porter, *Competitive Strategy* (New York: Free Press, 1980), pp. 22-23.

16. See Wendell R. Smith, "Product Differentiation and Market Segmentation as Alternative Marketing Strategies," *Journal of Marketing*, July 1956, pp. 3-8; and Alan A. Roberts, "Applying the Strategy of Market Segmentation," *Business Horizons*, Fall 1961, pp. 65-72.

17. Smith, "Product Differentiation," p. 4.

18. Burleigh Gardner and Sidney Levy, "The Product and the Brand," *Harvard Business Review*, March-April 1955, p. 37.

19. Alfred A. Kuehn and Ralph L. Day, "Strategy of Product Quality," *Harvard Business Review*, November-December 1962, pp. 101-2.

20. John Heinzl, "Dylex upsurge distant," *The Globe and Mail*, Thursday, June 27, 1991.

21. Roberts, "Applying the Strategy of Market Segmentation," p. 66.

22. Alan J. Resnik, Peter B. B. Turney, and J. Barry Mason, "Marketers Turn to 'Countersegmentation,'" *Harvard Business Review*, September-October, 1979, pp. 100-106.

PART IV

Designing
Marketing Strategies

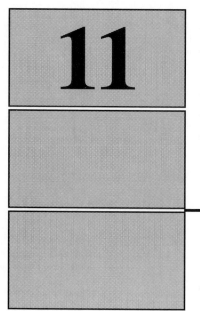

11 Marketing Strategies for Differentiating and Positioning the Marketing Offer

Fill a need, keep things simple, buck the trend, messy sells better than neat.

Ed Mirvish

Suppose a company has researched and selected its target market. If it is the only company serving this target market, it will probably be able to charge a price that will yield a reasonable profit. If it charges too high a price and there are no substantial entry barriers, competitors will enter this market and bring the price down. If several firms pursue this target market and their products are undifferentiated, then most buyers will buy from the lowest price firm. Other firms will be forced to lower their price. The only alternative for the original firm is to differentiate its market offer from the competitors. If it can effectively differentiate its offer, it can charge a price premium. Differentiation allows the firm to get a price premium based on the extra value perceived by the customers.

This chapter will explore the ways a company can effectively differentiate its offer to target customers and thereby secure a competitive advantage and price premium in its target market. We will address the following questions:

☐ How do buyers define value and choose among suppliers?

☐ How can the firm proceed to identify sources of potential competitive advantage?

☐ What are the major differentiating attributes available to firms?

☐ How can the firm choose the most effective differences for positioning itself in the market?

☐ How can the firm communicate its positioning to the market?

HOW BUYERS DEFINE VALUE AND CHOOSE SUPPLIERS

The key to winning long-term customers is to understand their needs and buying behavior better than competitors do. We examined the buying process for consumers and business buyers in Chapters 6 and 7, respectively. Here we will recast buyer choice as being directed toward value maximization.

Our premise is that buyers will buy from the firm that offers the highest delivered value. *Delivered value* is the difference between *total customer value* and *total customer price* (see Figure 11-1).

We will explain delivered value in terms of an example. The buyer for a large construction company wants to buy a tractor. He will buy it from either Caterpillar or Komatsu. The competing salespeople carefully describe the terms of their respective offers.

Now the buyer has a particular application in mind, namely employing the tractor in residential construction work. He evaluates the two tractors for the intended application and places a higher value on the Caterpillar tractor. He also perceives differences in the accompanying services—delivery, training, and maintenance—and places a higher value on Caterpillar's services. He sees a difference in the personnel of the two companies and places a higher value on Caterpillar. He also sees a difference in the images of the two companies and places a higher value on Caterpillar's image. He adds all the values from these four sources—product, services, personnel, and image—and perceives Caterpillar as offering more *total customer value*.

Does he buy the Caterpillar tractor? Not necessarily. He also examines the *total customer price* of transacting with each seller. The total customer price consists of more than the *monetary price*. As Adam Smith observed over two centuries ago, "The real price of everything is the toil and trouble of acquiring it." It includes the anticipated time, energy, and psychic costs. These costs are evaluated and included with the monetary price into a picture of total customer price.

FIGURE 11-1
Determinants of Customer Added Value

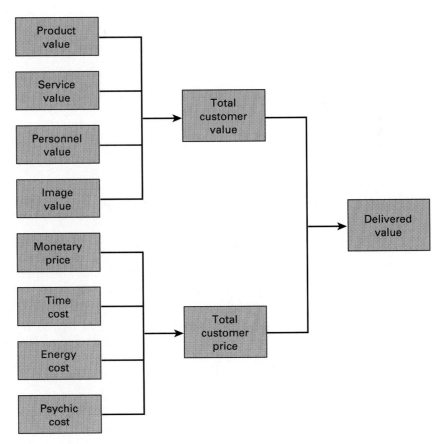

The buyer must now consider whether Caterpillar's total customer price is too high in relation to Caterpillar's total customer value. If it is, the buyer might buy the Komatsu tractor. The buyer will favor the firm that offers the highest delivered value.

Now let's use this buyer theory to help Caterpillar succeed in selling its tractor to this buyer. Caterpillar can improve its offer in three ways. First, Caterpillar can augment total customer value by improving product, services, personnel, and/or image benefits. Second, Caterpillar can reduce the buyer's nonmonetary costs by simplifying the buyer's time, energy, and psychic costs. Third, Caterpillar can reduce its monetary price to the buyer.

Suppose Caterpillar carries out a *customer value assessment* and concludes that the buyer sees Caterpillar's offer as worth $20 000. Further suppose Caterpillar's cost of producing the tractor is $14 000. This means that Caterpillar's offer potentially generates $6000 ($20 000 – $14 000) of *total added value*.

Caterpillar needs to charge a price between $14 000 and $20 000. If it charges less than $14 000, it won't cover its costs. If it charges more than $20 000, it would exceed the total customer value. The price Caterpillar charges will determine how much of the *total added value* will be delivered to the buyer and how much will flow to Caterpillar. For example, if Caterpillar charges $16 000, it is granting $4000 of total added value to the customer and keeping $2000 for itself as profit. If Caterpillar charges $19 000, it is granting only $1000 of total added value to the customer and keeping $5000 for itself as profit. Naturally, the lower Caterpillar sets its price, the higher is the delivered value and, therefore, the customer's *incentive to purchase* from Caterpillar. Delivered value should be looked at as the "profit" to the customer.

Given that Caterpillar wants to win the sale, it must offer more delivered value than does Komatsu. Delivered value can be measured either as a difference or a ratio. If total customer value is $20 000 and total customer price is $16 000, then the delivered value is $4000 (measured as a difference) or 1.25 (measured as a ratio). When ratios are used to compare offers, they are often called *value/price ratios*.

Some marketers might argue that this is too rational a theory of how buyers choose suppliers. They will cite examples where buyers didn't choose the offer with the highest delivered value. Consider the following situation:

> The Caterpillar salesperson convinces the buyer that taking into account the purchase price and the benefits in use and disposal, Caterpillar's tractor offers a higher delivered value to the buyer's company. The salesperson points out that the Komatsu tractor uses more fuel and has more breakdowns. Yet the buyer decides to buy the Komatsu tractor.

How can we explain this appearance of non-value-maximizing behavior? Here are three possible explanations:

1. The buyer might be under company orders to buy at the lowest price because of a current cash-flow problem. The buyer is explicitly prevented from making a choice based on delivered value. The salesperson's task is to convince the buyer's management that buying on price will damage the customer's long-run profitability.

2. The buyer will retire before the company realizes that the Komatsu tractor is more expensive to operate than the Caterpillar tractor. The buyer will look good in the short run and is maximizing personal benefit and placing no weight on company benefit. The salesperson's task is to convince other members of the customer company that Caterpillar's offer creates greater delivered value.

3. The buyer enjoys a long-term friendship with the Komatsu salesperson. Caterpillar's salesperson needs to show the buyer that the Komatsu tractor will draw complaints from

the tractor operators when they discover the high fuel cost and frequent repairs associated with this tractor.

Clearly, buyers operate under various constraints and furthermore make occasional choices that give more weight to their personal benefit than to the company benefit. However, we feel that delivered-value maximization is a useful interpretative framework that applies to many situations and that yields rich insights. Here are its implications. First, the seller must assess the total customer value and total customer price associated with each competitor to know where his own offer will stand. Second, the seller who is at a delivered-value disadvantage has two alternatives. This seller can try to increase the total customer value or decrease the total customer price. The former calls for strengthening or augmenting the product, services, personnel, and/or image benefits of the offer. The latter calls for reducing the buyer's costs. The seller can reduce the price, simplify the ordering and delivery process, or absorb some buyer risk by offering a warranty.

IDENTIFYING POTENTIAL COMPETITIVE ADVANTAGES THROUGH VALUE-CHAIN ANALYSIS

Assuming that buyers choose the supplier who offers the greatest added value, how can the supplier identify sources of value enhancement that will give it a competitive advantage? Porter proposed the *value chain* as the major tool for identifying potential sources of value enhancement (see Figure 11-2).[1] Every firm is a collection of activities that are performed to design, produce, market, deliver, and support its product. The value chain disaggregates a firm into nine strategically relevant activities in order to understand the behavior of costs in the specific business and industry and the existing and potential sources of differentiation. The nine value activities consist of five primary activities and four support activities.

The primary activities represent the sequence of bringing materials into the business, operating on them, sending them out, marketing them, and servicing them. The support activities occur throughout all of these primary activities. Thus procurement represents the purchasing of various inputs for each primary activity, only a fraction of which are handled by

FIGURE 11-2
The Generic Value Chain

Source: Michael E. Porter, *Competitive Advantage*, (New York: Free Press, 1985), p. 37.

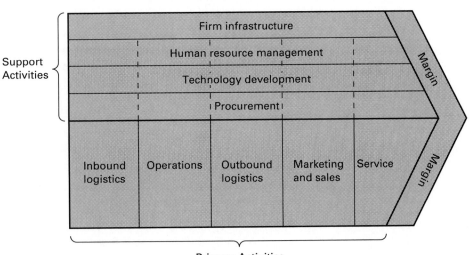

the purchasing department. Technology development occurs in every primary activity, only a fraction of which are done in the R&D department. Human-resource management also occurs in all departments. The firm's infrastructure covers the overhead of general management, planning, finance, accounting, and legal and government affairs that are borne by all the primary and support activities.

The firm's task is to examine its costs and performance in each value-creating activity and to look for improvements. The firm should estimate its competitors' costs and performances as benchmarks. To the extent that it can do better than its competitors, it has achieved a competitive advantage.

The firm needs to look for competitive advantages beyond its own value chain, into the value chains of its suppliers, distributors, and ultimately, customers. Thus the company might help a major supplier reduce its costs and thereby pass on savings to the supplier; or it might help customers perform some activity better or cheaper and win their loyalty.

Clearly, the value chain provides the firm with a comprehensive framework for systematically searching for ways to provide superior value to customers. Whether it produces few or many ideas depends upon the nature of the industry.

The Boston Consulting Group distinguished four types of industries based on the number of competitive advantages and their size (see Figure 11-3). The four industry types are as follows:

☐ *Volume Industry:* A volume industry is one in which companies can gain only a few, but rather large, advantages. An example would be the construction-equipment industry where a company can strive for the low-cost position or the highly differentiated position and win "big" on either basis. Here profitability is correlated with company size and market share.

☐ *Stalemated Industry:* A stalemated industry is one in which there are few potential advantages and each is small. An example would be the steel industry where it is hard to differentiate the product or its manufacturing cost. The companies can try to hire better salespeople, entertain more lavishly, and the like, but these are small advantages. Here profitability is unrelated to company market share.

☐ *Fragmented Industry:* A fragmented industry is one in which companies face many opportunities for differentiation, but each opportunity is small. A restaurant, for example, can differentiate in many ways but end up not gaining a large market share. Profitability is not related to restaurant size: Both small and large restaurants can be profitable or unprofitable.

☐ *Specialized Industry:* A specialized industry is one in which companies face many differentiation opportunities, and each differentiation can have a high payoff. An example would be companies making specialized machinery for selected market segments. Some small companies can be as profitable as some large companies.

FIGURE 11-3
The New BCG Matrix

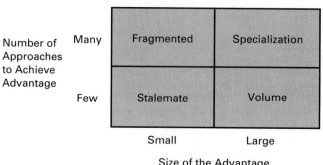

Thus not every company faces a plethora of cost-reducing or benefit-building opportunities for gaining competitve advantage. Some companies will find many minor advantages available, but all are highly imitable and therefore perishable. One solution for these companies is to continually identify new potential advantages and continually move them out one by one to keep the competitors off balance. These companies need to "routinize" the innovation process, expecting not so much to achieve a major sustainable advantage but rather to discover many little differences that can build up market share over time.

TOOLS FOR COMPETITIVE DIFFERENTIATION

Here we ask, "What are the ways a company can differentiate its offer from competitors?" We saw earlier that a company or market offer can be differentiated along lines of product, services, personnel or image. Let us look at these categories more closely.

Product Differentiation

Here we will identify bases for differentiating a physical product. At one extreme we find highly standardized products that allow little variation: salt, steel, aspirin. Yet even here, some variation is possible. Morton established brand preference by claiming that its salt runs more freely under humid conditions ("When it rains, it pours"). Steel can vary in its properties and consistency. And Bayer claims that its aspirin "gets into the bloodstream faster."

At the other extreme are products capable of high differentiation, such as automobiles, commercial buildings, and furniture. Here the seller faces an abundance of design parameters. The main ones are discussed below.[2]

Features   *Features are characteristics that supplement the product's basic functioning.* Most products can be offered with varying features. The starting point is a stripped-down, or "barebones," version of the product. The company can create additional versions by adding extra features. Thus an automobile manufacturer can offer optional features, such as electric windows, automatic transmission, and air conditioning. The automobile manufacturer needs to decide which features to make standard and which to make optional. Each feature has a chance of capturing the fancy of additional buyers.

Features are a competitive tool for differentiating the company's product. Some companies are extremely innovative in adding new features to their product. One of the key factors in the success of Japanese companies is that they continuously enhance the features in their watches, cameras, automobiles, motorcycles, calculators, videorecorders, and so on. Being first in introducing valued new features is one of the most effective ways to compete.

How can a company identify and select appropriate new features? The answer is that the company should contact recent buyers and ask them a series of questions:

> How do you like the product? Any bad features? Good features? Are there any features that could be added that would improve your satisfaction? What are they? How much would you pay for each feature? How do you feel about the following features that other customers mentioned? ∎

This will provide the company with a fresh list of potential features. The next task is to decide which ones are worth adding. For each potential feature, the company should calculate its *customer value* versus *company cost*. Suppose an auto manufacturer is considering the three possible improvements shown in Table 11-1. "Rear window defrosting" would cost the company $10 per car to add at the factory level. And the average customer said this feature was worth $20. The company could therefore generate $2 of incremental customer satisfaction for $1 in incremental company cost. Looking at the other two features, it appears that "power steering" would create the most customer satisfaction per dollar of company cost.

These criteria are only a starting point. The company will also consider how many people want each feature, how long it would take to introduce each feature, whether competitors could copy the feature, and so on.

Performance   *Performance refers to the levels at which the product's primary characteristics operate.* Thus a Cadillac performs better than a Chevrolet if the drive is smoother, the handling is better, and the acceleration is faster. A Digital Equipment midsize computer performs better than a Data General computer if it has speedier processing and a larger memory. Buyers of expensive products normally compare the performance characteristics of different brands. They will pay more for better performance as long as the higher price does not exceed the higher perceived value.

Most products are established initially at one of four performance levels: low, average, high, and superior. The question is, Does higher product performance produce higher profitability? The Strategic Planning Institute studied the impact of higher relative product quality (which is a surrogate for performance and other value-adding factors) and found a significantly positive correlation between relative product quality and return on investment [see Figure 11-4(a)]. In a subsample of 525 midsize business units, those with low relative product quality earned about 17 percent; medium quality, 20 percent; and high quality, 27 percent. Thus the high-quality business units earned 60 percent more than the low-quality business units. They earned more because their premium quality enabled them to charge a premium price, they benefited from more repeat purchasing, consumer loyalty, and positive word of mouth, and their costs of delivering more quality were not much higher than for business units producing low quality.

At the same time, this does not mean that the firm should design the highest quality possible. There are diminishing returns to still higher quality in that fewer buyers are willing to pay for it. Certain products are "overengineered." A person who drives ten blocks to work does not need a Rolls-Royce. The manufacturer must choose a quality level appropriate to the target market and the positions of competitors.

A company must also decide how to manage product quality through time. Three strategies are illustrated in Figure 11-4(b). The first, where the manufacturer continuously improves the product, often produces the highest return and market share. Procter & Gamble is a major practitioner of product-improvement strategy, which combined with the high initial product performance, helps explain its leading position in many markets. The second strategy is to maintain product quality. Many companies leave their quality unaltered after its initial formulation unless glaring faults or opportunities occur. The third strategy is to reduce product quality through time. Some companies cut the quality to offset rising costs, hoping the buyers

Table 11-1 Measuring Customer Effectiveness Value

Feature	Company Cost (1)	Customer Value (2)	Customer Effectiveness (3) = (2) ÷ (1)
Rear window defrosting	$10	$20	2
Cruise control	$60	$60	1
Power steering	$60	$180	3

FIGURE 11-4
Brand-Quality
Strategies and
Profitability

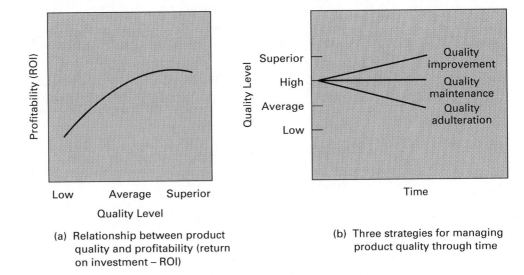

(a) Relationship between product
quality and profitability (return
on investment – ROI)

(b) Three strategies for managing
product quality through time

will not notice any difference. Others reduce the quality deliberately in order to increase their current profits, although this often hurts their long-run profitability.

Conformance *Conformance is the degree to which a product's design and operating characteristics come close to the target standard.* This is called conformance to specifications. Suppose a Porsche is designed to accelerate to sixty miles (100 km) an hour within ten seconds. If every Porsche coming off the assembly line does this, the automobile is said to have high conformance. However, if Porsches vary greatly in their acceleration time, they have low conformance on this criterion. The problem with low conformance is that the product's promised performance will not be fulfilled for many buyers and they will be disappointed. One of the major reasons for the high-quality reputation enjoyed by Japanese manufacturers is that their products have high conformance. Their automobiles are praised for having good "fit and finish," and people pay for this gladly.

Durability *Durability is a measure of the product's expected operating life.* For example, Volvo advertises that it has the highest mean life of automobile makes and this justifies its higher price. Buyers will pay more for a more durable product. However, this is subject to some qualifications. The extra price must not be excessive. Furthermore, the product must not be subject to high fashion or technological obsolescence in which case the buyer may not pay more for longer-lived products. Thus advertising that a personal computer or videocamera has the highest durability may have little appeal because their features and performance levels are undergoing rapid change.

Reliability *Reliability is a measure of the probability that a product will not malfunction or fail within a specified time period.* Thus a Cadillac has more reliability than a Chevrolet if its chance of not malfunctioning in some important way within a month is 90 percent compared to 60 percent. Buyers pay a premium for products with a reputation for more reliability. They want to avoid the cost of breakdowns and repair time. Here again the Japanese have been especially successful in improving the reliability of their products. Here are two examples:

> A Japanese firm imported Oster blenders and sold them through twenty-five hundred stores in Japan. The Japanese firm complained about receiving 2 percent returns, because the agitator

blade rusted within two years. It told Sunbeam, the manufacturer, that it would not accept more than 1/2 of 1 percent returns and that the manufacturer needed to use a higher grade of stainless steel for Japan. The manufacturer acceded and in time introduced the better blade in its domestic market as well. ■

The Mitsubishi company acquired Motorola's Quasar division, which manufactured television receivers. Motorola had experienced 141 defects in every hundred sets; Mitsubishi reduced this to 6 per hundred. Buyer complaints fell to one-tenth their previous level and the company's warranty liability also dropped to one-tenth. ■

Repairability   *Repairability is a measure of the ease of fixing a product that malfunctions or fails.* Thus an automobile made with standard parts that are easily replaced has higher repairability. Ideal repairability would exist if users could fix the product themselves with little or no cost or time lost. The buyer might simply remove the defective part and insert a replacement part. As the next best thing, some products include a diagnostic feature that allows service people to correct it over the telephone from a distant location or advise the user how to correct it. The worst situation is when a product breaks down and requires a service call, and much time elapses before the service people and parts are available.

Style   *Style describes how well the product looks and feels to the buyer.* Thus many car buyers pay a premium for Jaguar automobiles because of their extraordinary look, even though Jaguar's record of reliability is poor. General Motors's Cadillac division hired Pininfarina, an Italian automobile-design firm, to design its new Avanti, to give it European styling. Some companies have outstanding styling reputations, such as Herman Miller in modern furniture, Olivetti in office machines, Bang & Olufsen in home stereo equipment, and Nissan and Mazda in sports cars. Style has the advantage of creating product distinctiveness that is difficult to copy. Therefore it is surprising that more companies have not invested in better styling. Many products are yawn-producing rather than eye-catching. For example, most small kitchen appliances lack styling distinctiveness, with the exceptions of some coffee makers and other small appliances made by Italian and German firms. At the same time, a strong style does not necessarily promise high performance. A chair may look sensational but be extremely uncomfortable.

Under style differentiation, we must include *packaging* as a styling weapon, especially in food products, cosmetics, toiletries, and small consumer appliances. The package provides the buyer's first encounter with the product and is capable of turning the buyer "on" or "off." Packaging is discussed in detail in Chapter 12.

Design: The Integrating Force   All of the foregoing qualities are design parameters. They suggest how difficult the product-design task is, given all the tradeoffs that can be made. The designer has to figure out how much to invest in feature development, performance, conformance, reliability, repairability, style, and so forth. From the company's point of view, a well-designed product would be easy to manufacture and distribute. From the customer's point of view, a well-designed product would be pleasant to look at, and also easy to open, install, learn how to use, use, repair, and dispose of. The designer has to take all of this into account and follow the maxim, "form follows function." The designer has to compromise some of the desirable characteristics. Much depends on knowing how the target market perceives and weighs the different benefits and costs.

Unfortunately, too many companies fail to invest in good design. Some companies confuse design with styling and think that design is a matter of making a product and then putting some fancy casing around it. Or they think that reliability is something to catch during inspections rather than designing it into the manufacturing process. They may think of designers as people who pay insufficient attention to cost or who produce designs that are too novel for the market to accept. A design audit instrument to measure a company's design sensitivity and effectiveness would help management gauge whether it is adding sufficient value through design.[3]

Several companies are now waking up to design's importance. Ford is an excellent example of a company that improved its process and product design and quality. In Britain, the British Design Council reports that some of its design projects not only have helped British companies increase their sales by more than 100 percent and cut manufacturing costs by 50 percent, but have also helped nearly bankrupt companies turn around and vigorously compete with Japanese and West German firms. All said, good design can attract attention, improve performance, cut costs, and communicate value to the intended target market.

Services Differentiation

In addition to differentiating its physical product, the firm can also differentiate the accompanying services. When the physical product cannot easily be differentiated, the key to competitive success often lies in services augmentation and quality. The main service variables are described below.

Delivery   Delivery refers to how well the product or service is delivered to the customer. It includes the speed, accuracy, and care attending the delivery process. Deluxe Check Printers, Inc., for example, has built an impressive reputation for shipping out its checks one day after receiving the order—without being late once in twelve years. Buyers will often choose the supplier who has a better reputation for on-time delivery. The choice among rail carriers often hinges on their perceived differences in delivery speed and reliability. (See Marketing Strategies 11-1).

Installation   Installation refers to the work that has to be done to make a product operational in its planned location. Buyers of heavy equipment expect good installation service from the vendor. Vendors can differ in the quality of their installation service. IBM, for example, delivers all of the purchased equipment to the site at the same time rather than sending in different components at different times, to sit waiting for everything else to arrive. When IBM is asked to move IBM equipment to another location, it is willing to move competitors' equipment and furniture as well.

Customer Training   Customer training refers to training the customer's employees to use the vendor's equipment properly and efficiently. Thus General Electric not only sells and installs expensive x-ray equipment in hospitals but takes responsibility for training the users on this equipment. McDonald's requires its new franchisees to attend Hamburger University for two weeks to learn how to properly manage their franchise.

Consulting Service   Consulting service refers to the various kinds of advice, information, and related services a seller offers to buyers of its products. Although the service may appear to be free, the costs are typically incorporated into the selling price. Alternatively, they may be "unbundled" and offered as optional extras.

The use of consulting service is common in the marketing of technical products to business organizations. IBM uses consulting service effectively in selling its mainframe computers. Consulting service is also used in marketing consumer products to channel intermediaries. The Procter & Gamble sales representative offers grocery store managers

TURBOMARKETING: USING QUICK RESPONSE TIME AS A COMPETITIVE TOOL

A company can try to win its competitive battle in four ways: It can make a better offer, a different offer, a cheaper offer, or a faster offer. Many smart managers are placing their bet today on being faster. They are becoming *turbomarketers*, learning the art of *time compression* or *time speedup*. They are applying turbomarketing to three areas: innovation, distribution, and retailing.

Speeding up innovation is essential in an age of shorter product life cycles. Competitors in many industries learn about new technologies and new market opportunities at about the same time. For example, several companies are racing today to achieve a breakthrough treatment for AIDS, to exploit the promising application of superconductivity, and to develop high-definition television. Those companies that first reach practical solutions will enjoy "first-mover" advantages in the market. In auto manufacture, the Japanese have achieved a considerable competitive advantage in being able to design and introduce new car models within three years. Ford is catching up, having designed the 1986 Taurus in four years, while GM still seems to need five years. Being early rather than late pays off. A McKinsey and Company study found that products that came out six months late but on budget earned an average of 33 percent less profit in their first five years; products that came out on time but 50 percent over budget cut profit only 4 percent.

The key to innovation speedup is to eliminate unnecessary delays in the company's new-product-development process. Is the company too slow at gathering new research ideas, screening them, developing and testing new concepts and prototypes, or launching the product? By examining each step of the product development process, the company can usually find ways to reduce innovation time.

Distribution is a second area begging for time compression. Buyers don't like to wait several days, weeks, or months for an out-of-stock product. Alert manufacturers are working hard to develop faster resupply systems. Here are some examples:

The Levi Strauss Company knows each night which style and size jeans have sold that day throughout the country. Levi uses this information to manufacture replacement stock and order replacement material. ∎

The ultimate rapid response is to be there before the customer is aware of the need for service. Using remote sensing, Bell Canada is able to provide that service now. Some photocopier manufacturers are working on it. ∎

Federal Express's huge success is the result of recognition by its founder, Fred Smith, of the importance that households and businesses place on fast and reliable mail delivery. Smith implemented a brilliant logistical hub-and-spoke system that enabled Federal Express to deliver letters and small packages picked up before 5 p.m. to anywhere in the country before 11 a.m. the next day, or money back. He is now extending this system to worldwide delivery of mail. ∎

Speeding up distribution calls for finding ways to reduce the time that passes between the retail sale, after which the order is sent to the manufacturer (*sales-order reporting time*); the receipt of the order by the manufacturer, who then starts production (*manufacturing time*); and the completion of production and shipment of the goods to the retailer (*delivery time*). These steps are expedited by nightly reporting of orders, flexible factories with just-in-time production and low resetup time, and faster shipment modes.

Retailing speedup is a third frontier for competitive advantage. Years ago, customers waited a week to have a roll of film developed or to receive a new pair of glasses. Today, film is developed in one hour, and a new pair of glasses can be produced in an hour. The key concept has been to turn the retail store into a minifactory. Black's and other photo stores operate film-developing equipment. Lens Crafters and and other optician retailers operate mini-laboratories in their stores. The same factory principle is applied by specialty fast food stores like Mmmarvelous Mmmuffins and others who bake the goods as needed in their stores.

various inventory-management services as well as the latest Nielsen data on product movements.

Maple Leaf Mills provides a number of services to farmers who use their feeds for chickens and other livestock. Besides offering advice on the proper temperature, ventilation, and medication for ailing chicks, the Maple Leaf sales representative will even take chicks to the veterinarian for regular examinations. For their contract growers, Maple Leaf also supplies both chicks and feed, and designates the best processing plants to receive the farmer's output.

Repair   Repair describes the quality of repair service available to buyers of the company's product. Caterpillar claims to offer better and faster repair service for its heavy-construction equipment anywhere in the world. Automobile buyers are quite concerned with the quality of repair service that they can expect from any dealer from whom they buy.

Miscellaneous Services   Companies can find many other ways to add value through differentiated services. The company can offer a better product warranty or maintenance contract than its competitors. The company can establish patronage awards as the airlines have done with their frequent-flyer programs. There are virtually an unlimited number of specific services and benefits that companies can offer to differentiate themselves from their competitors.

Personnel Differentiation

Companies can gain a strong competitive advantage through hiring and training better people than their competitors do. Thus Singapore Airlines enjoys an excellent reputation in large part because of the beauty and grace of their cabin crew. The McDonald's people are courteous, the IBM people are professional, and the Disney people are upbeat.

Many companies in the service sector consider personnel to be the "fifth P" of their marketing mix (recall Figure 3-5), because of the importance of having well qualified people in contact with their customers.[4] Management should not only recruit and train the right kind of people, but they should also acknowledge the importance of their roles and empower them to make customer-service decisions on the spot, rather than having to wait for a supervisor's approval.

Qualified personnel exhibit six characteristics:

☐ Competence: The employees possess the required skill and knowledge.

- □ *Courtesy:* The employees are friendly, respectful, and considerate.
- □ *Credibility:* The employees are trustworthy.
- □ *Reliability:* The employees perform the service with consistency and accuracy.
- □ *Responsiveness:* The employees respond quickly to customers' requests and problems.
- □ *Communication:* The employees make an effort to understand the customer and communicate clearly.[5]

Image Differentiation

Even when the competition looks similar, consumers may perceive a difference in the image of the company or its brand. One of the best ways to differentiate in the retail sector is on the basis of service. Eaton's department stores have accomplished that by their promise of unconditionally accepting the return of any merchandise that is not completely satisfactory. Several generations of loyal Canadian shoppers have grown up with that image.

Marketers seek to achieve certain characteristics in an image. It must convey a *singular message* that establishes the product's major virtue and positioning. It must convey this message in a *distinctive* way so that it is not confused with similar messages from competitors. It must deliver *emotional power* so that it stirs the heart as well as the mind of the buyer.

Developing a strong image for a brand or company calls for creativity and hard work. The image cannot be implanted in the public's mind overnight nor seeded by one media vehicle alone. The image must be carried out in every communication vehicle available to the company and carried out repeatedly. If "IBM means service," this singular message must be expressed in symbols, written and audiovisual media, atmosphere, events, and personnel. Here we review these major media for image communication.

Symbols   Recognition of company or a brand image can be triggered by the use of a symbol. The symbol's physical form or "logo" should be an instant reminder of the company or brand. It can be an object, for example, the Royal Bank's lion, which symbolizes some quality of the organization. Or the symbol can be a celebrity such as Johnny Cash who represents Canada Trust, or Anne Murray who represents the Canadian Imperial Bank of Commerce. The image conveyed by a symbol can be enhanced by the use of sound (Avon's door chime) or colour (Toronto Dominion's Green Line investment service).[6]

Written and Audiovisual Media   The chosen symbols must be worked into *advertisements* that convey the personality of the company or brand. The ads will attempt to establish a storyline, a mood, a performance level-something distinctive. The message should be replicated in other *publications*, such as annual reports, brochures, catalogs. The company's *stationery and business cards* should reflect the same image tone that the company wants to convey.

Atmosphere   The physical space where customers receive the product or service can reinforce or destroy an otherwise strong image. Lawyer's offices display law books and diplomas in subdued settings, while pediatricians' offices are bright and cheerfully decorated with cartoon characters. A bank that wants to look friendly must choose the right building design, interior design, layout, colors, materials, and furnishings.

Events   A company can create an image through the type of events it sponsors. Xerox sponsored sporting events while introducing its "marathon" line of copiers and promoting the service provided by "Team Xerox." STP, the automobile engine additive, is a regular sponsor of auto racing events. Cultural events like symphonies and jazz concerts are sponsored by du Maurier, a cigarette targeted at an upscale segment. Still other organizations support popular causes, such as General Foods contributing to MADD (Mothers Against Drunk Drivers).

DEVELOPING A POSITIONING STRATEGY

We have seen that any company or brand can be differentiated. There is no such thing as a *commodity*. Instead of thinking it is selling a "commodity," the company must see itself as handling an "undifferentiated product" waiting to be turned into a "differentiated offer." Dermot Dunphy, whose company pioneered plastic bubble wrap, puts it emphatically:

> The lesson to be learned is that no matter how commonplace a product may appear, it does not have to become a commodity. Every product, every service can be differentiated.[7]

Levitt and others have pointed out dozens of ways to differentiate an offer.[8] Part of the answer lies in recognizing that buyers have different needs and are therefore attracted to different offers.

At the same time, not all brand differences are meaningful or worthwhile. Not every difference is a differentiator. Each difference has the potential to create company costs as well as customer benefits. Therefore the company must carefully select the ways in which it will distinguish itself from competitors. A difference is worth establishing to the extent that it satisfies the following criteria:

□ *Important:* The difference delivers a highly valued benefit to a sufficient number of buyers.

□ *Distinctive:* The difference either isn't offered by others or is offered in a more distinctive way by the company.

□ *Superior:* The difference is superior to other ways to obtain the same benefit.

□ *Communicable:* The difference is communicable and visible to buyers.

□ *Preemptive:* The difference cannot be easily copied by competitors.

□ *Affordable:* The buyer can afford to pay for the difference.

□ *Profitable:* The company will find it profitable to introduce the difference.

Many companies have introduced differentiations that failed on one or more of these tests. The Westin Stamford hotel in Singapore advertises that it is the world's tallest hotel; actually this isn't important to many tourists and in fact turns many off. Picturevision phones were distinctive but they bombed, according to Bell Northern, because the two images are not in a "shared space," in the sense that two people can share a conversation. Polaroid's Polarvision was a new way of producing instant home movies, but it was considered inferior to video recording by consumers who wanted the flexibility of being able to re-record and edit.

Suppose a heavy-duty-truck manufacturer, say Volvo, worried that truck buyers saw most truck brands as similar and therefore chose their brand mainly on price. Table 11-2 describes this hypothetical situation. In this case, the buyer sees no differences among the trucks. Every truck has an excellent ride (score 9 out of 10), and every truck has only average living features (score 6). Realizing this, Volvo and its three competitors decide to differentiate their truck's physical characteristics.

> Differentiation *is the act of designing a set of meaningful differences to distinguish the company's offer from competitors' offers.*

Table 11-2 Purchase Decision by Customer for Heavy-Duty Trucks

No Differentiation

		Performance Rating			
Attribute	*Weight*	*Navistar*	*Paccar*	*Volvo*	*Mack*
Durability	35	7	7	7	7
Fuel economy	25	8	8	8	8
Living features	20	6	6	6	6
Ride	20	9	9	9	9

Substantial Differentiation

Attribute	*Weight*	*Navistar*	*Paccar*	*Volvo*	*Mack*
Durability	35	7	7	8	[9]
Fuel economy	30	[9]	8	7	7
Living features	20	6	[9]	7	6
Ride	15	5	7	[8]	6

Hypothetical examples.

Source: Robert D. Buzzell and Bradley T. Gale, *The PIMS Principles: Linking Strategy to Performance* (New York: Free Press, 1987), p. 122.

The results are shown in Table 11-2. No truck is superior to all of its competitors on all attributes. Navistar is best at fuel economy, but that entailed cutting down its investment in ride quality. Mack is superior in durability (the most important concern of buyers, accounting for 35 percent of the importance weight), but it is less distinguished on the other attributes.

We conclude that each truck now appeals differently to different buyers. If it wishes, any truck manufacturer can show this *comparison chart* to potential buyers. Sometimes these charts are prepared by others, such as customers and product-evaluation agencies. The column under each brand, if it represents all the dimensions of the offer, describes the brand's *total positioning strategy*. The brand's total positioning strategy can also be displayed using perceptual maps instead of tables, as shown in the Marketing Concepts and Tools 11-1 exhibit.

Marketing Concepts and Tools 11-1

POSITIONING A BEER BRAND USING COMPATIBLE ADVERTISING

As an example of product positioning using perceptual mapping, consider a brewery which is attempting to develop an advertising program for one of its beer brands. To do this successfully, management must understand how the target market segments perceive its brand relative to the major competing brands. The basis for these comparisions is a set of attributes, of which it is assumed that at least some are relevant to the brands, the consumers, and the beer-drinking occasions.

To reposition a brand through advertising, it is necessary to alter consumers' perceptions or preferences or both. The advertising which accomplishes this in a cost-effective manner must be believable. This means that the beer-drinking occasion and the people portrayed in the advertisement must not seem incompatible with the brand. Even the media vehicle which is used should seem appropriate.

Darmon has proposed a method for portraying all of these elements of the repositioning challenge.[9] The figure shows his joint space for one segment of the Quebec beer-drinking market represented by a sample of English-speaking MBA students. This was derived from a series of judgments elicited from the students, using Johnson's multiple discriminant analysis technique.[10]

The positions of six brands of beer are shown beside their respective boxes. The various attributes are represented by the arrows pointing out from the origin. The relative amount of an attribute possessed by a brand can be estimated by projecting a perpendicular line from it to the appropriate arrow. Thus, Brador is perceived as being stronger than Molson or Labatt.

Also shown in the figure are several potential spokespersons (Guy Lafleur, Bobby Orr, Frank Sinatra, and Tex Lecor), and several potential print media vehicles (*The Gazette, Le Devoir, Playboy*, and *The Financial Post*). The relative positions in the figure suggest, for example, that if the management of Brador wanted to position it as an expensive beer, it would be appropriate to employ Frank Sinatra as spokesperson and buy advertising space in *Playboy*.

But it seems unlikely that this would be an appropriate strategy, given consumers' preferences. These are implied by the location of the "ideal" brand, which would be less expensive and less strong than Brador is perceived to be. To reposition Brador in the "ideal" direction, it would be more appropriate to employ Guy Lafleur as spokesperson and buy advertising in *The Gazette*.

Before adopting any advertising program, it is advisable to perform similar analyses for other significant market segments. Indeed, Darmon's analysis of the French-speaking segment produced a mapping which was similar but not identical.

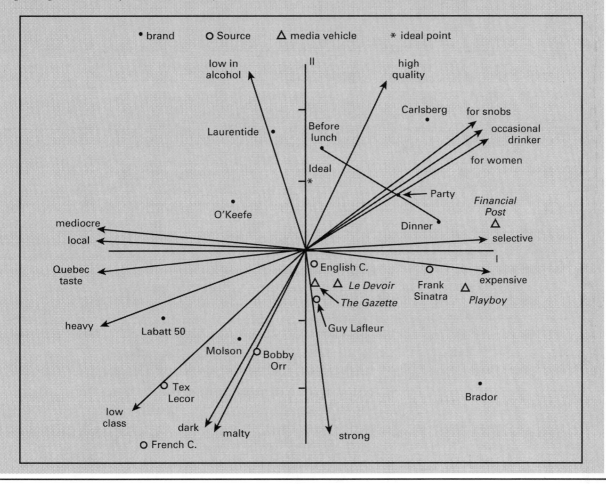

Not all buyers will notice or be interested in all the ways one brand differs from another. Nor is it useful for a company to describe exhaustively to each prospect every detail of difference. Each firm will want to promote those few differences that will appeal most strongly to its target market. The firm will want to develop a *focused positioning strategy.* We will simply call this *positioning* and define it as follows:

> Positioning *is the act of communicating the company's offer so that it occupies a distinct and valued place in the target customers' minds.*

Positioning calls for the company to decide how many differences and which differences to promote to the target customers.

How Many Differences to Promote?

Many marketers advocate aggressively promoting only one benefit to the target market. Rosser Reeves, for example, said a company should develop a *unique selling proposition* (USP) for each brand and stick to it.[11] Thus Crest toothpaste consistently promotes its anticavity protection, and Mercedes promotes its great automotive engineering. Ries and Trout also favor one consistent positioning message.[12] Each brand should pick an attribute and tout itself as "number one" on that attribute. Buyers tend to remember "number one" better than other messages, especially in an overcommunicated society. (See Marketing Strategies 11-2, for more on Ries and Trout's views on positioning.)

What are some of the "number-one" positions to promote? The major ones are "best quality," "best service," "lowest price," "best value," and "most advanced technology." If a company hammers away at one of these positionings and convincingly delivers on it, it will probably be best known and recalled for this strength.

Not everyone agrees that *single benefit positioning* is always best. The company can try for *double benefit positioning.* This may be necessary if two or more firms are claiming to be best on the same attribute. To gain a competitive advantage it is necessary to make a claim for a second attribute without giving ground on the first attribute. Thus, Volvo positions its automobiles as "safest" and "most durable." Fortunately, these two benefits are compatible. One would expect that a very safe car would also be very durable.

There are even cases of successful *triple benefit positioning.* For example, Beecham promotes its Aquafresh toothpaste as offering three benefits: "anticavity protection," "better breath," and "whiter teeth." Clearly, many people want all three benefits, and the challenge is to convince them that the brand delivers all three. Beecham hit upon the solution by creating a toothpaste that squeezed out of the tube in three colors, thus visually confirming the three benefits. In doing this, Beecham "countersegmented"; that is, it attracted three segments instead of one. In a time when segments are becoming very small, companies are trying to broaden the positioning strategy to appeal to more segments.

However, as companies increase the number of claims for their brand, they risk disbelief and a loss of clear positioning. In general, a company must avoid four major positioning errors:

- ☐ *Underpositioning:* Some companies discover that buyers have only a vague idea of the brand. Buyers don't really know anything special about it.

- ☐ *Overpositioning:* Buyers may have too narrow a picture of the brand. Thus a consumer might think that the Steuben company makes only fine glass in the range of $1000 and up when in fact it makes affordable fine glass starting at around $50.

"Positioning" According to Ries and Trout

The word *positioning* was popularized in 1972 by two advertising executives, Al Ries and Jack Trout, in a series of articles in *Advertising Age* called "The Positioning Era." Later they wrote a book called *Positioning: The Battle for Your Mind*. Ries and Trout see positioning as a creative exercise done with an existing product. Here is their definition:

> Positioning starts with a product. A piece of merchandise, a service, a company, an institution, or even a person. . . . But positioning is not what you do to a product. Positioning is what you do to the mind of the prospect. That is, you position the product in the mind of the prospect.

Ries and Trout argue that current products generally have a position in the minds of consumers. Thus Hertz is thought of as the world's largest auto-rental agency, Coca-Cola as the world's largest soft-drink company, Porsche as one of the world's best sports cars, and so on. These brands own those positions and it would be hard for a competitor to steal these positions. A competitor has only three strategy options.

One strategy is to strengthen and leverage its own current position in the mind of consumers. Thus Avis took its second position in the auto rental business and made a strong point about it: "We're number two. We try harder." This is believable to the consumer. And 7-Up capitalized on the fact that it was not a cola soft drink by advertising itself as the Uncola.

The second strategy is to search for a new unowned position that is valued by enough consumers and to grab it. They call it "Cherchez le creneau," or "Look for the hole." Find the hole in the market and fill it. Thus Milky Way candy wanted to strengthen its market share against Hershey. Its marketers noticed that most candy bars were eaten within a minute once they were opened, but Milky Way lasted longer. So they went after the position "lasts longer," which no competitor owned.

The third strategy is to deposition or reposition the competition. Most buyers of dinnerware thought that Lenox china and Royal Doulton both came from England. Royal Doulton put out ads showing that Lenox china was made in New Jersey, but theirs came from England.

Essentially, Ries and Trout outline how similar brands can acquire some distinctiveness in an "overcommunicated society" where there is so much advertising that consumers screen out most of the messages. A consumer may know only about seven soft drinks even though there are many more on the market. Even then, the mind often knows them in the form of a *product ladder*, such as Coke/Pepsi/RC Cola or Hertz/Avis/National. Ries and Trout note that the second firm usually enjoys half the business of the first firm, and the third firm enjoys half the business of the second firm. Furthermore, the top firm is remembered best.

People tend to remember *number one*. For example, when asked, "Who was the first person to successfully fly alone over the Atlantic Ocean?" we will answer "Charles Lindbergh." When we are asked, "Who was the second person to do this?" we draw a blank. This is why companies fight for the number-one position. But Ries and Trout point out that the "size" position can be held by only one brand. What counts is to achieve a number-one position along some valued attribute, not necessarily "size." Thus 7-Up is the number-one Uncola, Porsche is the number-one small sports car, and Dial is the number-one deodorant soap. The marketer should identify an important attribute or benefit that can convincingly be won by the brand. In this way, brands get hooked into the mind in spite of the incessant advertising bombardment reaching consumers.

A fourth strategy that Ries and Trout do not mention can be called the "exclusive-club strategy." It can be developed by a company when a number one position along some meaningful attribute cannot be achieved. A competitor can promote the idea that it is one of the Big Three, Big Eight, and so on. The Big Three idea was invented by the third-largest auto firm, Chrysler, and the Big Eight idea was invented by the eighth-largest accounting firm. (The market leader never invents this concept.) The implication is that those in the club are the "best."

Ries and Trout essentially deal with the psychology of positioning or repositioning a current brand in the consumer's mind. They acknowledge that the positioning strategy might call for changes in the product's name, price, and packaging, but these are "cosmetic changes done for the purpose of securing a worthwhile position in the prospect's mind." Other marketers would add more emphasis to *real positioning* where they work up every tangible aspect of a new product to capture a position. Psychological positioning must be supported by real positioning; it is not just a mind game.

Source: See Al Ries and Jack Trout, *Positioning: The Battle for Your Mind* (New York: Warner Books, 1982).

□ *Confused Positioning:* Buyers could have a confused image of the brand. This confusion might result from making too many claims or changing the brand's positioning too frequently.

□ *Doubtful Positioning:* Buyers may find it hard to believe the brand claims in view of the product's features, price, or manufacturer.

The advantage of solving the *positioning problem* is that it enables the company to solve the *marketing-mix problem*. The marketing mix—product, price, place, and promotion—is essentially the working out of the tactical details of the positioning strategy. Thus a firm that seizes upon the "high-quality position" knows that it must produce high-quality products, charge a high price, distribute through high-class dealers, and advertise in high-quality magazines. That is the only way to project a consistent and believable high-quality image.

Which Differences to Promote?

We suggested that a company should promote its major strengths provided that the target market values these strengths. The company should also recognize that differentiation is a continuous process. Suppose a company compares its current positioning on four attributes—technology, cost, quality, and service—with its major competitor's positioning (see Table 11-3). Both companies stand at 8 on technology (1 = low score, 10 = high score), which means they both have good technology. The company cannot gain much by improving its technology further, especially given the cost of doing so. The competitor has a better standing on cost (8 instead of 6), and this can hurt the company if the market becomes more price sensitive. The company offers higher quality than its competitors (8 instead of 6). Finally, both companies offer below-average service.

It would seem that the company should go after cost or service to improve its market appeal relative to the competitor. However, other considerations arise. The first is, How important to the target customers are improvements in each of these attributes? Column 4 indicates that improvements in cost and service would be of high importance to customers. Next, "Can the company afford to make the improvements, and how fast can it complete them?" Column 5 shows that improving service would have high affordability and speed. But would the competitor also be able to improve service if the company started to do so? Column 6 shows that the competitor's ability to improve service is low, perhaps because the competitor does not believe in service or is strapped for funds. Column 7 then shows the appropriate actions to take with respect to each attribute. The one that makes the most sense is for the company

Table 11-3 Method for Competitive-Advantage Selection

(1) Competitive Advantage	(2) Company Standing (1-10)	(3) Competitor Standing (1-10)	(4) Importance of Improving Standing (H-M-L)*	(5) Affordability and Speed (H-M-L)	(6) Competitor's Ability to Improve Standing (H-M-L)	(7) Recommended Action
Technology	8	8	L	L	M	Hold
Cost	6	8	H	M	M	Monitor
Quality	8	6	L	L	H	Monitor
Service	4	3	H	H	L	Invest

• H = High; M = Medium; L = Low

to improve its service and promote the improvement as a secondary benefit. Service is important to customers; the company can afford to improve its service and do it fast; and the competitor probably cannot catch up.

> This was the conclusion that Monsanto reached in one of its chemical markets. Monsanto immediately hired additional technical service people and when they were trained and ready, Monsanto promoted itself as the "technical service leader." ■

Thus this type of reasoning can help the company choose or add genuine competitive advantages.

COMMUNICATING THE COMPANY'S POSITIONING

The company must not only develop a clear positioning strategy; it must also communicate it effectively. Suppose a company chooses the "best-in-quality" positioning strategy. It must then make sure that it can communicate this claim convincingly. Quality is communicated by choosing those physical signs and cues that people normally use to judge quality. Here are some examples:

> A designer of fine fur coats sews in expensive silk linings, knowing that women will judge the quality of the fur partly by the quality of the lining. ■

> A lawn-mower manufacturer claims its lawn mower is "powerful" and uses a noisy motor, because buyers think noisy lawn mowers are more powerful. ■

> A truck manufacturer undercoats the chassis not because it needs undercoating but because undercoating suggests concern for quality. ■

> A car manufacturer makes cars with good-slamming doors because many buyers slam the doors in the showroom as a test of how well the car is built. ■

> Ford designed its Mustang to be a "sports car" and communicated this by the car's styling, bucket seats, and leather steering wheel. Yet it was not a true sports car in terms of performance. On the other hand, the BMW is a true sports car but is not designed to look like one. ■

Quality is also communicated through other marketing elements. A high price usually signals a premium-quality product to buyers. The product's quality image is also affected by the packaging, distribution, advertising and promotion. Here are some cases where a brand's quality image was hurt:

A well-known frozen-food brand lost its prestige image by being on sale too often. ∎

A premium beer's image was hurt when it switched from bottles to cans. ∎

A highly regarded television receiver lost its quality image when mass-merchandise outlets began to carry it. ∎

Thus the quality of the brand's packaging, channels, promotion, and so on, must collectively communicate and support the brand's image.

The manufacturers' reputation also contributes to the perception of quality. Certain companies are sticklers for quality; consumers expect P&G products and IBM products to be good. Consumers' perceptions are also affected by the product's country of origin. Japanese products, at one time considered shoddy, today are widely perceived as having high quality even when the perception is not justified. Italian clothing is assumed to be well made and stylish. On the other hand, Chrysler had a problem selling its Mexican-made cars because of a perception that products manufactured in Mexico would not be built to the same standards as those built by domestic manufacturers. Ironically, the Mexican cars were better made because the factory was newer and the newly trained workers were more careful.

To make a quality claim credible, the surest way is to offer "satisfaction or your money back." Smart marketers communicate this by reassuring buyers that there is no risk in trying the product.

SUMMARY

Positioning is the act of designing the company's offer and image so that the target market understands and appreciates what the company stands for in relation to its competitors. The company's positioning must be rooted in an understanding of how the target market defines value and makes choices among vendors. The positioning tasks consist of three steps. First, the company has to identify possible product, services, personnel, and image differences that might be established in relation to competition. Second, the company has to apply criteria to select the most important differences. Third, the company has to effectively signal to the target market how it differs from its competition. The company's product-positioning strategy will then enable it to take the next step, namely, plan its competitive marketing strategies.

∎ QUESTIONS

1. How is positioning different from segmentation? Give illustrations from industry to support your answer.

2. Discuss the following concepts showing their relationship to each other:
   Image   Product features

Position	Competitive advantage
Customer perception	Positioning strategy

3. A positioning strategy can be developed and implemented in one of several different ways. List and discuss at least four of these approaches.

4. You are invited to a planning session to develop a positioning strategy for a small business. Your task is to guide the committee through a series of planning steps for developing the positioning strategy. Suggest what these steps might be and give reasons for your answer.

5. In what ways has the smoking public been segmented? How have cigarette makers positioned their products to these markets via product and package design and advertising messages?

6. Four brands of washing machines have been compared on the following seven dimensions. (The highest positive score indicates the best position on the given dimension.) Create a two dimensional map for brands A, B, C, and D.

	A	B	C	D
Variable wash and spin	-2	2	2	3
Wash water temperature control	-1	2	1	3
Frequency of repair record	2	3	2	-1
Detergent requirement	-3	1	1	2
Repair service availability	1	2	1	-2
Guarantee	1.5	2.5	2	-1
Maximum load capacity	-2	3	1	2

7. Assume marketing research for washing machines yields the evaluations shown in Question 6. Where would you position a new brand of washing machine?

8. Identify some attributes of universities and colleges that might be used for positioning them. Discuss the positioning of some universities and/or colleges that you are familiar with, using a positioning map.

9. Select one of the institutions you reviewed in Question 8 and suggest what strategies you would employ to position it more advantageously.

10. Find an example of a company which has used "Turbomarketing" (see Marketing Strategies 11-1) and report on the following issues: (a) In what ways is the firm applying turbomarketing? (b) How does the increased speed translate into a competitive advantage in this industry? (c) In your opinion, will the firm be capable of sustaining a competitive advantage from this source? Why or why not?

11. What are some industries which fit the BCG classification (Figure 11-3)? Select a firm in each of these industries and describe how the firm gains a competitive advantage by providing superior value to its customers. To what do you attribute the differences in strategies among these firms?

■ NOTES

1. Michael Porter, *Competitive Analysis* (New York: Free Press, 1985), p. 37. Also see George S. Day and Robin Wensley, "Assessing Advantage: A Framework for Diagnosing Competitive Superiority," *Journal of Marketing*, April 1988, pp. 1-20.

2. Some of the following bases are discussed in David A. Garvin, "Competing on the Eight Dimensions of Quality," *Harvard Business Review*, November-December, 1987, pp. 101-9.

3. See Philip Kotler, "Design: A Powerful but Neglected Strategic Tool," *Journal of Business Strategy*, Fall 1984, pp. 16-21. Also see Christopher Lorenz, *The Design Dimension* (New York: Basil Blackwell Inc., 1986).

4. A.J. Magrath, "When Marketing Services, 4P's Are Not Enough," *Business Horizons*, May-June 1986.

5. Adapted from A. Parasuraman, V. A. Zeithaml, and L. L. Berry, "A Conceptual Model of Service Quality and Its Implications for Future Research," *Journal of Marketing*, Fall 1985, pp. 41-50.

6. Brian Milner, "TD denied injunction against CT's use of green," *The Globe and Mail*, July 5, 1991.

7. Speech to a sales meeting of Sealed Air Corporation, March 19, 1984.

8. Theodore Levitt, "Marketing Success through Differentiation— of Anything," *Harvard Business Review*, January-February, 1980.

9. Rene Y. Darmon, "Multiple Joint Space for Improved Advertising Strategy," *Canadian Marketer*, Vol. 10, No. 1, 1979, pp. 10-14.

10. Richard M. Johnson, "Market Segmentation: A Strategic Management Tool," *Journal of Marketing Research*, Vol. 9, Feb. 1971, pp. 13-18.

11. Rosser Reeves, *Reality in Advertising* (New York: Knopf, 1960).

12. See Al Ries and Jack Trout, *Positioning: The Battle for Your Mind* (New York: Warner Books, 1982).

12

Developing, Testing, and Launching New Products and Services

Nothing in this world is so powerful as an idea whose time has come.

Victor Hugo

Once a company has carefully segmented the market, chosen its target customer groups, and determined the desired market positioning, it is ready to develop and launch appropriate and, it is hoped, successful products. The marketing management group plays a key role in this process. Rather than leave it to the R&D department to develop the specified products, marketing actively participates with the other departments in every stage of the new-product-development process.

Every company must carry on new-product development, if for no other reason than that some existing company products will enter the decline stage. Replacement products and businesses must be found in order to maintain or build the company's sales. Furthermore, customers want new products, and competitors will do their best to supply them. A Booz, Allen & Hamilton survey reported that seven hundred companies expected that 31 percent of their profits would come from new products introduced in the next five years.[1]

A company can add new products through *acquisition* and/or *new-product development*. The acquisition route can take three forms. The company can buy other companies; it can buy selected patents from other companies; or it can buy a license or franchise from another company. In these cases, the company does not develop new products but acquires the rights to existing ones.

The new-product route can take two forms. The company can develop new products in its own laboratories. Or it can contract with independent researchers or new-product-development firms to develop specific products for the company.

Many companies pursue growth through both acquisition and new-product development. Their management feels that the best opportunities might lie in acquisition at certain times and new-product development at other times, and they want to be skilled at both.

What do we mean by new products? "New products" for our purposes will include *original products, improved products, modified products,* and *new brands* that the firm develops through its own R&D efforts. We will also be concerned with whether consumers see them as "new."

Booz, Allen & Hamilton identified six categories of new products in terms of their newness to the company and to the marketplace.[2] Figure 12-1 shows the percentage of products appearing in each category over the past five years. The categories are

☐ *New-to-the-World Products:* New products that create an entirely new market

☐ *New-Product Lines:* New products that allow a company to enter an established market for the first time

☐ *Additions to Existing Product Lines:* New products that supplement a company's established product lines

☐ *Improvements or Revisions to Existing Products:* New products that provide improved performance or greater perceived value and replace existing products

☐ *Repositionings:* Existing products that are targeted to new markets or market segments

☐ *Cost Reductions:* New products that provide similar performance at lower cost

FIGURE 12-1
Types of New Products

Source: New Products Management for the 1980s (New York: Booz, Allen & Hamilton, 1982), p. 9.

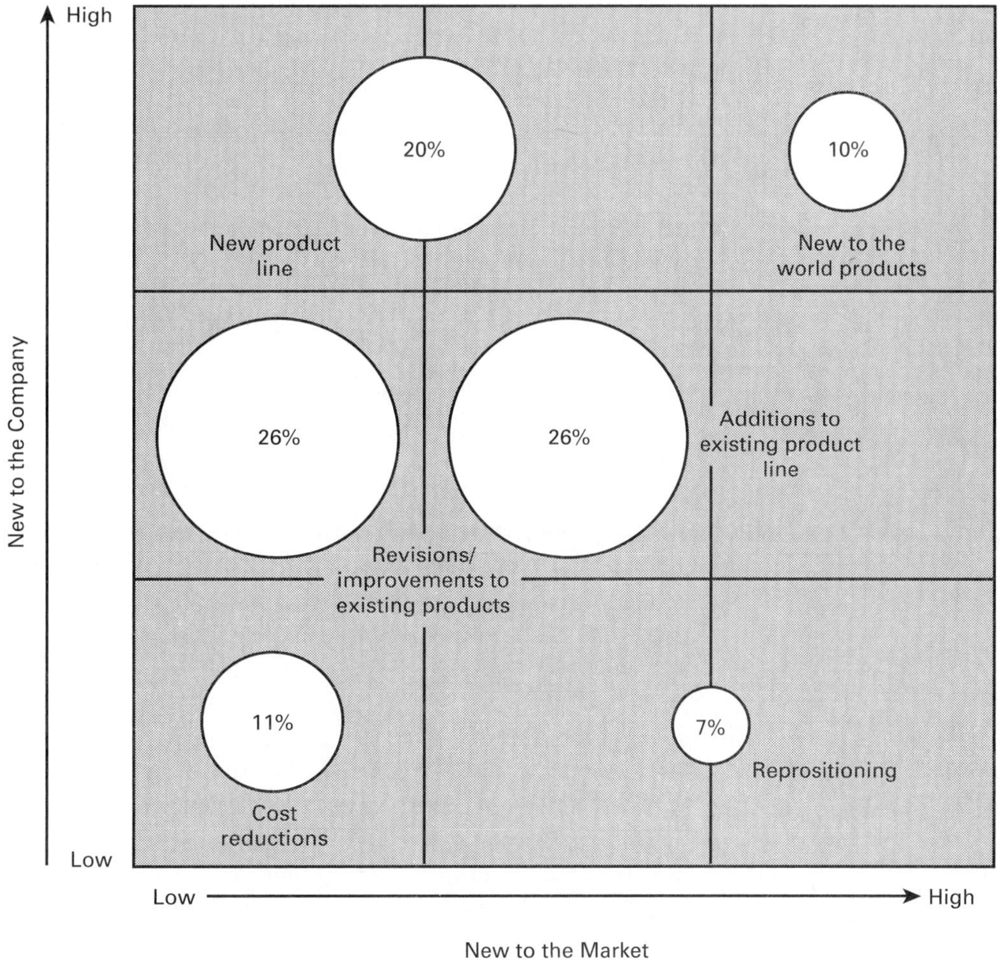

The product introductions of most companies fall into more than one of the above categories. But an important finding is that only 10 percent of all new products are truly innovative and new to the world. Such products involve the greatest cost and risk because they are new to both the company and the marketplace.

This chapter will examine the following questions:

☐ What are the main risks in developing new products?

☐ What organizational structures are used in managing new-product development?

☐ How can the stages of the new-product-development process be better managed?

☐ After product launch, what factors affect the rate of consumer adoption and new-product diffusion?

THE NEW-PRODUCT-DEVELOPMENT DILEMMA

Given the intense competition in most markets today, companies that fail to develop new products are exposing themselves to great risk. Their existing products are vulnerable to changing consumer needs and tastes, new technologies, shortened product life cycles, and increased domestic and foreign competition.

At the same time, new-product development is risky. Texas Instruments lost $660 million before withdrawing from the home computer business; RCA lost $575 million on its ill-fated videodisc players; Ford lost $350 million on its ill-fated Edsel; Du Pont lost an estimated $100 million on its synthetic leather called Corfam; and the French Concorde aircraft will never recover its investment.

One study found that the new-product failure rate was 40 percent for consumer products, 20 percent for industrial products, and 18 percent for services.[3] The failure rate for new consumer products is especially disturbing.

Why do many new products fail? There are several factors. A high-level executive might push a favorite idea through in spite of negative marketing research findings. Or the idea is good, but the market size is overestimated. Or the actual product is not well designed. Or it is incorrectly positioned in the market, not advertised effectively, or overpriced. Often new-product-development costs are higher than expected, or the competitors fight back harder than expected.

Successful new-product development is hindered by many factors:

☐ *Shortage of Important New-Product Ideas in Certain Areas:* There may be few ways left to improve some basic products such as steel, detergents, and so forth.

☐ *Fragmented Markets:* Keen competition is leading to market fragmentation. Companies have to aim their new products at similar market segments, and this means lower sales and profits for each product.

☐ *Social and Governmental Constraints:* New products have to satisfy public criteria such as consumer safety and ecological compatibility. Government requirements have slowed down innovation in the drug industry and have complicated product-design and advertising decisions in industries such as industrial equipment, chemicals, automobiles, and toys.

☐ *Costliness of the New-Product-Development Process:* A company typically has to generate many new-product ideas in order to finish with a few good ones. Furthermore, the company has to face rising R&D, manufacturing, and marketing costs.

☐ *Capital Shortage:* Some companies with good ideas cannot raise the funds needed to research them.

□ *Faster Development Time:* Many competitors are likely to get the same idea at the same time, and the victory often goes to the swiftest. Alert managers have to compress development time by using computer-aided design and manufacturing techniques, joint partners, early concept tests, and advanced marketing planning. Japanese companies see the challenge as "achieving better quality at a cheaper price at a faster speed than competitors."[4]

□ *Shorter Product Life Cycle:* When a new product is successful, rivals are so quick to copy it that the new product's life cycle is considerably shortened. Sony used to enjoy a three-year lead time on its new products before they were copied extensively by competitors. Now Matsushita and other competitors can copy the product within six months, hardly leaving enough time for Sony to recoup its investment.

Yet some common elements characterize successful products. Madique found that successful companies spend a lot of time studying the needs of target customers and getting their reactions and suggestions as the product moved through development. They make the customer part of the development team. Successful new products typically have the support of a high company officer and advocate. And successful companies spend a lot to announce the new product, not leaving this step to chance.

Successful new-product development requires the company to establish an effective organization for managing the new-product-development process. The company must also apply the best analytical tools and concepts in each stage of the new-product-development process. We will look at each in turn.

EFFECTIVE ORGANIZATIONAL ARRANGEMENTS

Top management is ultimately accountable for the new-product success record. It cannot simply ask the new-product manager to come up with great ideas. New-product-development work requires top management to define the business domains and product categories that the company wants to emphasize. In one food company, the new-product manager spent thousands of dollars researching a new snack idea only to hear the president say, "Drop it. We don't want to be in the snack business."

Top management must establish specific criteria for acceptance of new-product ideas, especially in large multidivisional companies where all kinds of projects bubble up as favorites of various managers. The criteria can vary with the specific *strategic role* the product is expected to play. Booz, Allen & Hamilton identified six major strategic roles that companies set for their new products (figures show the percentage of recent products playing each role):

□ Maintain position as a product innovator (46 percent)

□ Defend a market-share position (44 percent)

□ Establish a foothold in a future new market (37 percent)

□ Preempt a market segment (33 percent)

□ Exploit technology in a new way (27 percent)

□ Capitalize on distribution strengths (24 percent)[5]

For example, at Gould, a producer of electrical equipment, a new product that exploits technology in a new way must satisfy the following: (1) the product can be introduced within five years; (2) the product has a market potential of at least $50 million and a 15 percent growth rate; (3) the product will provide at least 30 percent return on sales and 40 percent on investment; and (4) the product will achieve technical or market leadership.

A major decision facing top management is how much to budget for new-product development. R&D outcomes are so uncertain that it is difficult to use normal investment criteria for budgeting. Some companies solve this problem by encouraging and financing as many projects as possible, hoping to achieve a few winners. Other companies set their R&D budget by applying a conventional percentage-of-sales figure or by spending what the competition spends. Still other companies decide how many successful new products they need and work backwards to estimate the required R&D investment.

Booz, Allen & Hamilton conducted studies of how many new-product ideas it takes to yield one successful product (see Marketing Concepts and Tools 12-1). In 1968, it took fifty-eight new-product ideas to yield one good one. Booz, Allen & Hamilton's latest study shows that companies are now able to turn one out of seven new-product ideas into a successful new product. Figure 12-2 shows the decay curve for new-product ideas. Booz, Allen & Hamilton concluded that many companies have learned to handle prescreening and planning more effectively and to budget on the best ideas instead of using a shotgun approach.

Table 12-1 shows how a company can calculate the investment cost of new-product development. The new-products manager at a large consumer-packaged-goods company reviewed the results of sixty-four new-product ideas his company considered. Only one in four ideas, or sixteen, passed the idea-screening stage, and it cost $1000 per idea reviewed at this stage. Half of these ideas, or eight, survived the concept-testing stage, at a cost of $20 000 each. Half of these, or four, survived the product development stage, at a cost of $200 000 each. Half of these, or two, did well in the test market, at a cost of $500 000 each.[6] When these two ideas were launched, at a cost of $5 000 000 each, only one was highly successful. Thus the one successful idea had cost the company $5 721 000 to develop. In the process, sixty-three other ideas

---

Marketing Concepts and Tools 12-1

KEY FINDINGS ON NEW-PRODUCT-MANAGEMENT ACTIVITY

Here are some key findings from a Booz, Allen & Hamilton study of new-product-management activity. Their information comes from a mail survey of seven hundred consumer and industrial companies and lengthy interviews with 150 new-product executives.

1. Management achieved success with 65 percent of their product launches.

2. Companies developed one successful product for every seven they researched.

3. Ten percent of the new products were "new to the world," and 20 percent were "new-product lines." Yet these high-risk products represented 60 percent of the "most successful" new products.

4. New-product spending had become more efficient, in that successful entries accounted for 54 percent of total new-product expenditures, up from 30 percent in 1968.

5. Successful new-product companies don't spend more on R&D and marketing, as a percentage of sales, than unsuccessful ones.

6. The median company introduced five new products in the period 1976-81; that number is expected to double over the next five years.

7. Managers expect new products to increase company sales growth by one-third over the next five years, while the portion of total company profits generated by new products is expected to be 40 percent.

Source: *New Products Management for the 1980s* (New York: Booz, Allen & Hamilton, 1982).

FIGURE 12-2

Mortality of New-Product Ideas

Source: New Products Management for the 1980s (New York: Booz, Allen & Hamilton, 1982), p. 3.

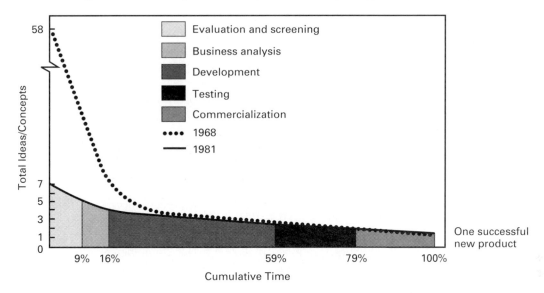

fell by the wayside. Therefore the total cost for developing one successful new product was $13 984 400. Unless the company can improve the pass ratios and reduce the costs at each stage, it will have to budget nearly $14 000 000 for each successful new idea it hopes to find. If top management wants four successful new products in the next few years, it will have to budget at least $56 000 000 (= 4 × $14 000 000) for new-product development.

A key factor in new-product-development work is to establish effective organizational structures. Companies handle new-product development in several ways:[7]

☐ *Product Managers:* Many companies assign responsibility for new-product ideas to their product managers. In practice, this system has several faults. Product managers are usually so busy managing their product lines that they give little thought to new products other than brand modifications or extensions; they also lack the specific skills and knowledge needed to critique and develop new products.

☐ *New-Product Managers:* General Foods and Johnson & Johnson have new-product managers who report to group product managers. This position professionalizes the new-product

Table 12-1 Estimated Cost of Finding One Successful New Product (Starting with Sixty-Four New Ideas)

Stage	Number of Ideas	Pass Ratio	Cost per Product Idea	Total Cost
1. Idea screening	64	1:4	$1 000	$64 000
2. Concept test	16	1:2	20 000	320 000
3. Product development	8	1:2	200 000	1 600 000
4. Test marketing	4	1:2	500 000	2 000 000
5. National launch	2	1:2	5 000 000	10 000 000
			$5 721 000	$13 984 000

function; on the other hand, new-product managers tend to think in terms of product modifications and line extensions limited to their product market.

- □ *New-Product Committees:* Most companies have a high-level management committee charged with reviewing and approving new-product proposals.
- □ *New-Product Departments:* Large companies often establish a new-product department headed by a manager who has substantial authority and access to top management. The department's major responsibilities include generating and screening new ideas, working with the R&D department, and carrying out field testing and commercialization.
- □ *New-Product Venture Teams:* The 3M Company, Dow, Westinghouse, and General Mills often assign major new-product-development work to venture teams. A venture team is a group brought together from various operating departments and charged with developing a specific product or business. They are "intrapreneurs" relieved of their other duties, given a budget, a time frame, and an informal bureaucracy-free environment (see Companies and Industries 12-1).

Where companies have poor records of new-product success, the cause often is a lack of organizational teamwork. The traditional model of innovation calls for the R&D department to get a bright idea and research it, then have an engineering team design, which they throw over to the manufacturing department to produce, and then over to sales to sell. But this "serial" model of innovation creates many problems. The manufacturing people often send the design back to the engineers saying they could not produce it at the targeted cost; the engineers then spend time redesigning the product. When the salesforce later shows the product to customers, they find that it cannot be sold at the targeted price, since consumer needs

---

Companies and Industries 12-1

3M'S APPROACH TO INNOVATION

Certain companies have earned an outstanding reputation for successful and continuous innovation. Heading most lists is the 3M Company, whose ambitious goal is for each of its forty divisions to generate at least 25 percent of its income from products introduced within the preceding five years! And more astonishing, they succeed. Each year the company launches more than one hundred new products.

On 3M's innovation-driven corporate culture: 3M encourages everyone, not just its engineers, to become "product champions." Anyone who is hot about an idea is encouraged to do some homework to find out what knowledge exists, where the product would be developed in the company, whether it is patentable, and how profitable it might be. If the idea finds support, a venture team is formed with representatives

from R&D, manufacturing, sales, marketing, and legal. Each team is headed by an "executive champion," who nurtures the team and protects it from bureaucratic intrusion. If a "healthy-looking product" is developed, the team stays with it and markets it. If the product fails, each team member returns to his or her previous level. Some teams have tried three or four times to make a success out of an idea and, in several cases, have succeeded.

Each year 3M hands out its Golden Step awards to venture teams whose new product earned more than $2 million in domestic sales or $4 million in export sales within 3 years of its introduction. "Intrapreneurship" is the name of the game at 3M, a game that more companies are seeking to play.

---

and wants are not met. The salespeople are mad at the engineers, the R&D people call the salespeople incompetent, and everyone blames the other person.

The solution is clear. Effective product development requires closer *teamwork* among R&D, engineering, manufacturing, purchasing, marketing, and finance from the beginning. The product idea must be researched from a marketing point of view, and a marketing team must advise on the idea throughout its development. Design engineers and manufacturing people must work together so that the design passes smoothly into manufacture. Studies of Japanese companies show that their new-product success is due in large part to building in much more teamwork. Also of great importance is that Japanese companies bring customers in at an early stage to get their views of what is developing.

According to the Booz, Allen & Hamilton study, the most successful innovating companies have made a consistent commitment of resources to new-product development, have designed a new-product strategy that is linked to their strategic planning process, and have established formal and sophisticated organizational arrangements for managing the new-product-development process.[8]

We are now ready to look at the major marketing challenges at each stage of the new-product-development process. Eight stages are involved: *idea generation, screening, concept development and testing, marketing strategy, business analysis, product development, market testing, and commercialization.*

IDEA GENERATION

The new-product-development process starts with the search for ideas. The search should not be casual. Top management should define the products and markets to emphasize. It should state the new-product objective, whether it is high cash flow, market-share domination, or some other objective. It should state how much effort should be devoted to developing original products, modifying existing products, and copying competitors' products.

Sources of New-Product Ideas

New-product ideas can come from many sources: customers, scientists, competitors, employees, channel members, and top management.

The marketing concept holds that *customers' needs and wants* are the logical place to start in the search for new-product ideas. Hippel has shown that the highest percentage of ideas for new industrial products originate with customers.[9] Technical companies can learn a great deal by studying a special set of their customers, the *lead users*, namely, those customers who make the most advanced use of the company's product and who recognize needed improvements ahead of other customers. Companies can identify customers' needs and wants through customer surveys, projective tests, focus-group discussion, and suggestion and complaint letters from customers. Many of the best ideas come from asking customers to describe their problems with current products. Thus an automobile company can ask recent buyers what they like and dislike about the car; what improvements could be made; and how much they would pay for each improvement. This survey will yield a large set of ideas for future improvements of the product.

Companies also rely on their *scientists, engineers, designers*, and other *employees* for new-product ideas. Successful companies have established a company culture that encourages every employee to seek new ideas for improving the company's production, products, and services. Toyota claims that its employees submit two million ideas annually, about thirty-five suggestions per employee, and over 85 percent of them are implemented. Kodak is one of many firms that give monetary and recognition awards to the employees who submit the best ideas during the year.

Companies can find good ideas by examining their *competitors'* products and services. They can learn from distributors, suppliers, and sales representatives what competitors are doing. They can find out what customers like and dislike in their competitors' new products. They can buy their competitors' products, take them apart, and build better ones. Their competitive strategy is one of *product imitation and improvement* rather than *product innovation*. The Japanese are masters of this strategy, in that they have licensed or copied many Western products and found ways to improve them. Domestic companies such as Ford and Xerox are increasingly doing the same thing:

> Using a tactic called benchmarking, Ford now buys competing autos and takes them apart to see how they are made. The successful Taurus came about when Ford realized that its automobiles were losing sales to Japanese and European cars. Don Peterson, chairman of Ford, instructed his engineers and designers to build a new car that utilized the best features of the competitive cars. If Saab made the best seats, then Ford should copy Saab's seats, and so on. Peterson went further: he asked his engineers to "better the best" where possible. When the Taurus was finished, Peterson claimed that his engineers had improved upon the competition in 350 of the 500 components making up the Taurus. ∎

Company *sales representatives* and *middlemen* are a particularly good source of new-product ideas. They have firsthand exposure to customers' needs and complaints. They often learn first of competitive developments. An increasing number of companies train and reward their sales representatives, distributors, and dealers for finding new ideas. For example: Bill Keefer, chairman of Warner Electric Brake and Clutch, requires his salesforce to list on each monthly call report the three best product ideas they heard on customer visits. He reads these ideas each month and pens notes to his engineers, manufacturing executives, and so on, to follow up the better ideas.

Top management can be another major source of new-product ideas. Some company leaders, like Edwin H. Land, former CEO of Polaroid, take personal responsibility for technological innovation in their companies. That is not always constructive, as when a top executive pushes through a pet idea without thoroughly researching market size or interest. When Land pushed forward his Polarvision project (instantly developed movies), it ended as a major product failure, because the market became more interested in videotapes as a way to film action.

New-product ideas can come from other sources as well, including inventors, patent attorneys, university and commercial laboratories, industrial consultants, advertising agencies, marketing research firms, and industrial publications.

While ideas can flow in from many sources, their chance of receiving serious attention often depends on someone in the organization taking the role of *product champion*. Unless someone strongly advocates the product idea, it is not likely to receive serious consideration.

Idea-Generating Techniques

Really good ideas come out of inspiration, perspiration, and techniques. A number of "creativity" techniques can help individuals and groups generate better ideas.

Attribute Listing This technique calls for listing the major attributes of an existing product and then modifying each attribute in the search for an improved product. Consider a screwdriver.[10] Its attributes: a round, steel shank; a wooden handle, manually operated; and torque provided by twisting action. Now a group considers ways to improve product performance or appeal. The round shank could be made hexagonal so that a wrench could be applied to increase the torque; electric power could replace manual power; the torque could be produced by pushing. Osborn suggested that useful ideas can be found by addressing the following questions to an object and its attributes: *put to other uses? adapt? magnify? minify? substitute? rearrange? reverse? combine?*[11]

Forced Relationships　　Here several objects are listed, and each project is considered in relation to every other object. Recently an office-equipment manufacturer wanted to design a new desk for executives. Several objects were listed—a desk, television set, clock, computer, copying machine, bookcase, and so on. The result was a fully electronic desk with a console resembling that found in an airplane cockpit.

Morphological Analysis　　Morphology means structure, and this method calls for identifying the structural dimensions of a problem and examining the relationships among them. Suppose the problem is that of "getting something from one place to another via a powered vehicle." The important dimensions are the type of vehicle (cart, chair, sling, bed); the medium in which the vehicle operates (air, water, oil, hard surface, rollers, rails); the power source (compressed air, internal-combustion engine, electric motor, steam, magnetic fields, moving cables, moving belt). Then the imagination is let loose on every combination. A cart-type vehicle powered by an internal-combustion engine and moving over hard surfaces is the automobile. The hope is to find some novel combinations.[12]

Need/Problem Identification　　The preceding creativity techniques do not require consumer input to generate ideas. Need/problem identification, on the other hand, starts with the consumer. Consumers are asked about needs, problems, and ideas. For example, they can be asked about their problems in using a particular product or product category. Here is an illustration:

> The Landis Group, a marketing research firm, uses this technique. For a given product category, it interviews about one thousand respondents and asks whether they are "completely satisfied," "slightly dissatisfied," "moderately dissatisfied," or "extremely dissatisfied." If they have any degree of dissatisfaction, the respondents describe their problems and complaints in their own words. For example, in a study of users of English muffins, 15 percent expressed some dissatisfaction, and the largest problems were muffins that were not precut, were too dry or soft, or had poor taste. The demographics revealed that the most dissatisfied users were in the 19-29 age group with low incomes. This information can be used by an existing competitor or a new entrant to improve the product and target the most dissatisfied groups. The various problems would be rated for their *seriousness, incidence*, and *cost of remedying* to determine which product improvements to make.　■

The above techniques can be used in reverse. Consumers receive a list of problems and tell which products come to mind as having each problem.[13] Thus the problem: "The package of _____ doesn't fit well on the shelf" might lead consumers to name dog foods and dry breakfast cereals. A food marketer might think of entering these markets with a smaller-size package.

Hippel recommends that industrial marketers can identify new-product ideas best by working with *lead users* rather than *average users* of the product class. Lead users are individuals and companies that have more-advanced needs and face them years before the majority of the other users. Thus the Allen-Bradley Company, a leading programmable-controls manufacturer, would pick up "breakthrough" ideas by researching the needs of its most advanced customers.[14]

Brainstorming   Group creativity can be stimulated through brainstorming, a technique developed by Alex Osborn. Brainstorming sessions are held when a company needs to generate many ideas related to a need or object. The usual group consists of six to ten people. It is not a good idea to include too many experts in the group because they tend to look at a problem in a rigid way. The problem should be specific. The sessions, preferably held in the morning, should last about an hour. The chairman starts with, "Remember, we want as many ideas as possible—the wilder the better—and remember, no *evaluation*." The ideas start flowing, one idea sparks another, and within an hour over a hundred or more new ideas may find their way into the tape recorder. For the conference to be maximally effective, Osborn laid down four guidelines:

☐ *Criticism Is Ruled Out:* Negative comments on ideas must be withheld until later.

☐ *Freewheeling Is Welcomed:* The wilder the idea, the better; it is easier to tame down than to think up.

☐ *Quantity Is Encouraged:* The greater the number of ideas, the more the likelihood of useful ideas.

☐ *Combining and Improving Ideas Is Encouraged:* Participants should suggest how ideas of others can be joined into still newer ideas.[15]

Synectics   William J.J. Gordon felt that Osborn's brainstorming session produced solutions too quickly, before a sufficient number of perspectives had been developed. Gordon decided to define the problem so broadly that the group would have no inkling of the specific problem.

> One problem was to design a method of closing vaporproof suits worn by workers who handled high-powered fuels.[16] Gordon kept the specific problem a secret and led a discussion on the general problem of "closure," which led to images of different closure mechanisms, such as birds' nests, mouths, or thread. As the group exhausted the initial perspectives, Gordon gradually introduced facts that refined the problem further. When the group was getting close to a good solution, Gordon described the problem. Then the group started to refine the solution. These sessions would last a minimum of three hours, for Gordon believed that fatigue played an important role in unlocking ideas.   ■

Gordon described five principles underlying the synectics method:

☐ *Deferment:* Look first for viewpoint rather than solutions.

☐ *Autonomy of Object:* Let the problem take on a life of its own.

☐ *Use of the Commonplace:* Take advantage of the familiar as a springboard to the strange.

☐ *Involvement/Detachment:* Alternate between entering into the particulars of the problem and standing back from them, in order to see them as instances of a universal.

☐ *Use of Metaphor:* Let apparently irrelevant, accidental things suggest analogies that are sources of new viewpoints.[17]

The main point about idea generation is that any company can attract good ideas by organizing properly. The company should motivate groups to submit ideas. They should be sent to an *idea chairman* whose name and phone number are well-known. The ideas should be put in written form and reviewed each week by an *idea committee*. The idea committee should sort the ideas into three groups: promising ideas, marginal ideas, and rejects. Each promising idea should be briefly researched by a committee member who reports back. The surviving promising ideas then move into a full-scale screening process.

IDEA SCREENING

The purpose of idea generation is to create a large number of ideas. The purpose of the succeeding stages is to *reduce* the number of ideas to an attractive, practicable few. The first idea-pruning stage is screening.

In screening the ideas, the company must avoid two types of errors. A DROP-error occurs when the company dismisses an otherwise good idea. The easiest thing to do is to find fault with other people's ideas (see Figure 12-3). Managers at some companies must shudder when they recall certain ideas that they dismissed.

> Xerox saw the novel promise of Chester Carlson's copying machine; IBM and Eastman Kodak did not see it at all. RCA was able to envision the innovative opportunity of radio; the Victor Talking Machine Company could not. Henry Ford recognized the promise of the automobile; yet

FIGURE 12-3
Forces Fighting New Ideas

Source: Adapted from Jerold Panas, Young & Partners, Inc.

"I've got a great idea."

"It won't work here."

"We've tried it before."

"This isn't the right time."

"It can't be done."

"It's not the way we do things."

"We've done all right without it."

"It will cost too much."

"Let's discuss it at our next meeting."

only General Motors realized the need to segment the automobile market into price and performance categories, with a model for every classification, if the promise was to be fully achieved. And so it has gone.[18]

If a company makes too many DROP-errors, its standards are too conservative.

A GO-error occurs when the company permits a poor idea to move into development and commercialization. We can distinguish three types of product failures that ensue. An *absolute product failure* loses money; its sales do not cover variable costs. A *partial product failure* loses money, but its sales cover all the variable costs and some of the fixed costs. A *relative product failure* yields a profit but one that is less than the company's normal or target rate of return.

The purpose of screening is to spot and drop poor ideas as early as possible. The rationale is that product-development costs rise substantially with each successive development stage. When products reach later stages, management feels that they have invested so much in developing the product that it should be launched to recoup some of the investment. But this is letting good money chase bad money, and the real solution is to not let poor product ideas get this far.

Product-Idea Rating Devices

Most companies require new-product ideas to be written up on a standard form that can be reviewed by a new-product committee. The write-up describes the product idea, the target market, and the competition, and it roughly estimates the market size, product price, development time and costs, manufacturing costs, and rate of return.

The executive committee then reviews each new-product idea against a set of criteria. In the case of the Kao Company of Japan, the committee considers such questions as: Is the product truly useful to consumers and society? Is its cost performance superior to competitive products? Is it easy to advertise and distribute? Figure 12-4 shows a detailed set of questions about whether a product idea meshes well with the company's objectives, strategies, and resources. Ideas that do not satisfy one or more of these questions are dropped.

The surviving ideas can be rated using the weighted-index method shown in Table 12-2. The first column lists factors required for successful product launches. In the next column, management assigns weights to these factors to reflect their relative importance. Thus management believes marketing competence will be very important (0.20) and purchasing and supplies competence of minor importance (0.05). The next task is to rate the company's competence on each factor on a scale from 0.0 to 1.0. Here management feels that its marketing competence is very high (0.9) and its location and facilities competence low (0.3). The final step is to multiply the importance of each success factor by the company competence level to obtain an overall rating of the company's ability to launch this product successfully into the market. Thus if marketing is an important success factor, and this company is very good at marketing, the overall product rating of the product idea will be increased. In the example, the product idea scored 0.72, which places it at the high end of the "fair idea" level.

This basic rating device can be refined further.[19] Its purpose is to promote systematic product-idea evaluation and discussion—it is not supposed to make the decision for management.

CONCEPT DEVELOPMENT AND TESTING

Attractive ideas must be refined into testable product concepts. We can distinguish between a product idea, a product concept, and a product image. A *product idea* is a possible product

FIGURE 12-4
Evaluating a Market
Opportunity in Terms
of the Company's
Objectives and
Resources

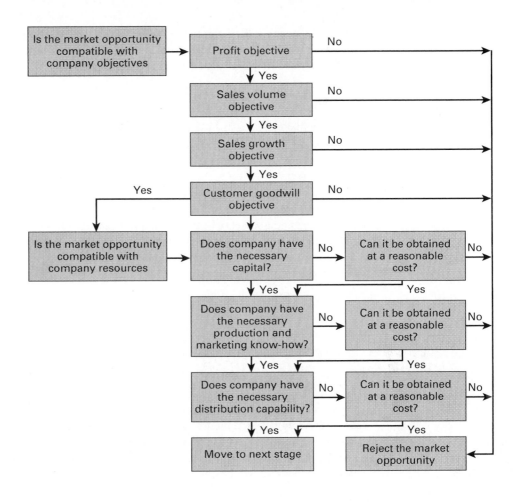

Table 12-2 Product-Idea-Rating Device

Product Success Requirements	Relative Weight (A)	Company Competence Level (B)											Rating (A × B)
		0.0	0.1	0.2	0.3	0.4	0.5	0.6	0.7	0.8	0.9	1.0	
Company personality and goodwill	0.20							√					0.120
Marketing	0.20										√		0.180
Research and development	0.20								√				0.140
Personnel	0.15							√					0.090
Finance	0.10										√		0.090
Production	0.05									√			0.040
Location and facilities	0.05			√									0.015
Purchasing and supplies	0.05										√		0.045
Total	1.00												0.720*

*Rating scale: 0.00-0.40 poor; 0.41-0.75 fair; 0.76-1.00 good. Present minimum acceptance rate: 0.70

Source: Adapted with modifications from Barry M. Richman, "A Rating Scale for Product Innovation," *Business Horizons*, Summer 1962, pp. 37-44.

that the company might offer to the market. A *product concept* is an elaborated version of the idea expressed in meaningful consumer terms. A *product image* is the particular picture that consumers acquire of an actual or potential product.

Concept Development

We shall illustrate concept development with the following situation. A large food processor gets the idea of producing a powder to add to milk to increase its nutritional value and taste. This is a product idea. Consumers, however, do not buy product ideas; they buy product concepts.

Any product idea can be turned into several product concepts. First, the question, Who is to use this product? The powder can be aimed at infants, children, teenagers, or young or middle-aged adults. Second, What primary benefit should be built into this product? Taste, nutrition, refreshment, energy? Third, What is the primary occasion for this drink? Breakfast, midmorning, lunch, midafternoon, dinner, late evening? By asking these questions, a company can form several concepts:

☐ *Concept 1:* An instant breakfast drink for adults who want a quick nutritious breakfast without preparing a breakfast.

☐ *Concept 2: A tasty snack drink* for children to drink as a midday refreshment.

☐ *Concept 3: A health supplement* for older adults to drink in the late evening before retiring.

These represent *category concepts*; that is, they position the idea within a category. An *instant breakfast drink* would compete against bacon and eggs, breakfast cereals, coffee and pastry, and other breakfast alternatives. A *tasty snack drink* would compete against soft drinks, fruit juices, and other tasty thirst quenchers. The category concept and not the product idea defines the product's competition.

Suppose the instant-breakfast-drink concept looks best. The next task is to show where this powdered product would stand in relation to other breakfast products. This is shown in the *product-positioning map*, Figure 12-5(a), using the two dimensions of cost and preparation time. An instant breakfast drink offers the buyer low cost and quick preparation. Its nearest competitor is cold cereal; its most distant competitor is bacon and eggs. These contrasts can be utilized in communicating and promoting the concept to the market.

FIGURE 12-5
Product and
Brand Positioning

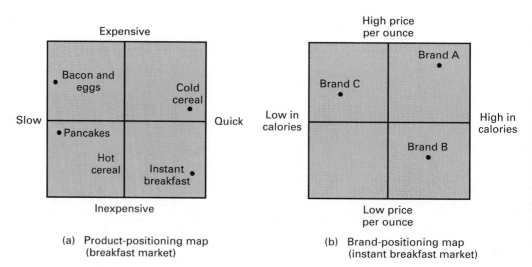

(a) Product-positioning map
(breakfast market)

(b) Brand-positioning map
(instant breakfast market)

Next, the product concept has to be turned into a *brand concept*. Figure 12-5(b) is a *brand-positioning map* showing the current positions of three existing brands of instant breakfast drinks. The company needs to decide how much to charge and how calorific to make its drink. The new brand could be positioned in the medium-price, medium-calorie market or in the low-price, low-calorie market. The new brand would gain distinctiveness in either position, as opposed to positioning next to another brand name and fighting for share of market. This decision requires researching the size of alternative preference segments in the market.

Concept Testing

Concept testing calls for testing these competing concepts with an appropriate group of target consumers. The concepts can be presented symbolically or physically. At this stage, a word and/or picture description suffices, although the reliability of a concept test increases, the more concrete and physical the stimulus is. The consumers are presented with an elaborated version of each concept. Here is concept 1:

> A powdered product that is added to milk to make an instant breakfast that gives the person all the breakfast nutrition needed along with good taste and high convenience. The product would be offered in three flavors, chocolate, vanilla, and strawberry and would come in individual packets, six to a box, at 79¢ a box. ∎

Consumers are asked to respond to the following questions about the concept:

1. Are the benefits clear to you and believable?

   This measures the concept's *communicability* and *believability*. If the scores are low, the concept must be refined or revised.

2. Do you see this product as solving a problem or filling a need for you?

   This measures the *need level*. The stronger the need, the higher the expected consumer interest.

3. Do other products currently meet this need and satisfy you?

   This measures the *gap level* between the new product and existing products. The greater the gap, the higher the expected consumer interest. The need level can be multiplied by the gap level to produce a *need-gap score*. The higher the need-gap score, the higher the expected interest. A high need-gap score means that the consumer sees the product as filling a strong need *and* is not satisfied with available alternatives.

4. Is the price reasonable in relation to the value?

   This measures *perceived value*. The higher the perceived value, the higher the expected consumer interest.

5. Would you (definitely, probably, probably not, definitely not) buy the product?

   This measures *purchase intent*. We would expect it to be high for consumers who answered the previous three questions positively.

6. Who would use this product, and how often would it be used?

   This provides a measure of *user targets* and *purchase frequency*.

The marketer now summarizes the respondents' answers to judge whether the concept has a broad and strong consumer appeal. The need-gap levels and purchase-intent levels can be checked against norms for the product category to see whether the concept appears to be a winner, a long shot, or a loser. One food manufacturer rejects any concept that draws a definitely-will-buy score of less than 40 percent. If the concept looks good, the information also tells the company what products this new product would replace, what consumers are the best targets, and so on.

Concept development and testing methodology applies to any product, service, or idea, such as an electric car, a new machine tool, a new banking service, or a new health plan. Too many managers think their job is done when they get a product idea. They think the task is to turn the idea into a physical product and sell it. But as Theodore Levitt put it, "Everybody sells intangibles in the marketplace, no matter what is produced in the factory." They forget that all selling is *concept selling*.[20] Later the product encounters all kinds of problems in the marketplace that would have been avoided if the company had done a good job of concept development and testing. (For some advanced methods of concept development and testing, see Marketing Concepts and Tools 12-2.)

Marketing Concepts and Tools 12-2

MEASURING CONSUMER PREFERENCES

Consumer preferences for alternative product concepts can be measured through conjoint analysis. Two approaches to data collection can be used, the full-profile approach and the pairwise approach. We will illustrate these methods below.

Full-Profile Approach

Green and Wind have illustrated the full-profile approach in connection with developing a new carpet-cleaning agent for home use. Suppose the new-product marketer is considering the following five design elements:

- Three package designs (a, b, c—see figure)
- Three brand names (K2R, Glory, Bissell)
- Three prices ($1.19, $1.39, $1.59)
- A possible Good Housekeeping seal (yes, no)
- A possible money-back guarantee (yes, no)

EXPERIMENTAL DESIGN USED IN SPOT-REMOVER PRODUCT EVALUATION Altogether, the marketer can form 108 possible product concepts ($3 \times 3 \times 3 \times 2 \times 2$), but it would be too much to ask consumers to rank or rate all of these concepts. A sample of, say, 18 contrasting product concepts can be chosen, and con-sumers would find it easy enough to rank them from the most preferred to the least preferred. The accompanying chart shows how one consumer ranked the 18 product concepts. This consumer ranked product concept 18 the highest, thus preferring package design C, the name Bissell, a price of $1.19, a Good Housekeeping seal, and a money-back guarantee.

Now suppose one hundred consumers provide their rankings. A statistical program will analyze these rankings and derive a utility function measured for each attribute. Suppose the derived utility functions are those shown in the following illustration.

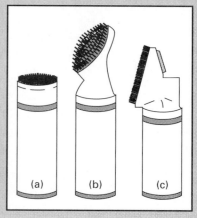

(a)   (b)   (c)

One Consumer's Ranking of Eighteen Stimulus Combinations

Card	Package Design	Brand Name	Price	Good Housekeeping Seal?	Money-Back Guarantee?	Respondent's Evaluation (Rank Number)
1	A	K2R	$1.19	No	No	13
2	A	Glory	1.39	No	Yes	11
3	A	Bissell	1.59	Yes	No	17
4	B	K2R	1.39	Yes	Yes	2
5	B	Glory	1.59	No	No	14
6	B	Bissell	1.19	No	No	3
7	C	K2R	1.59	No	Yes	12
8	C	Glory	1.19	Yes	No	7
9	C	Bissell	1.39	No	No	9
10	A	K2R	1.59	Yes	No	18
11	A	Glory	1.19	No	Yes	8
12	A	Bissell	1.39	No	No	15
13	B	K2R	1.19	No	No	4
14	B	Glory	1.39	Yes	No	6
15	B	Bissell	1.59	No	Yes	5
16	C	K2R	1.39	No	No	10
17	C	Glory	1.59	No	No	16
18	C	Bissell	1.19	Yes	Yes	1*

• Highest ranked

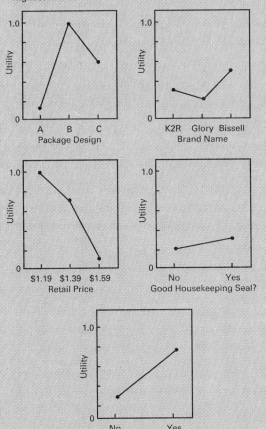

RESULT OF COMPUTER ANALYSIS OF EXPERIMENTAL DATA From these utility functions, we can derive a number of conclusions. Package B is the most favored, followed by C and then A; in fact, A has hardly any utility. The preferred names are Bissell, K2R, and Glory, in that order. The consumer's utility varies inversely with price. A Good Housekeeping seal is preferred, but it does not add that much utility and may not be worth the bother of obtaining it. A money-back guarantee is strongly preferred. Putting these results together, we can see that the most desirable offer would be package design B, with the brand name Bissell, selling at the price of $1.19, with a Good Housekeeping seal and a money-back guarantee. Thus we see how conjoint analysis can help the new product researcher develop and test the attractiveness of alternative product concepts.

Pairwise Approach

An alternative approach to data collection is the pairwise approach (also called tradeoff approach).

Consumers are asked to indicate their preferences for attribute levels, with two attributes taken at a time. The following table shows how a consumer filled in six tradeoff matrices:

One Respondent's Tradeoff Data
(Rank Orders of Preference)

	Top Speed Kilometers/Hour			Seating Capacity			Months of Warranty		
	210	160	110	2	4	6	60	12	3
Price									
$8 000	1	2	5	2	1	3	1	3	4
$12 000	3	4	6	5	4	6	2	5	6
$16 000	7	8	9	8	7	9	7	8	9
Top speed									
210 km/h				2	1	3	1	2	5
160 km/h				5	4	6	3	4	6
110 km/h				8	7	9	7	8	9
Seating capacity									
2							2	5	8
4							1	4	7
6							3	6	9

Look at the matrix on the left, which shows three car prices and three top car speeds. The consumer placed a *1* in the most preferred cell; here it is for a car priced at $8000 with a top speed of 210 km/h. The consumer placed a *2* in the next preferred cell, showing that she would prefer to pay $8000 and give up some top speed. The consumer ranked the remaining combinations, each time showing the tradeoff she would make. The other matrices were similarly filled in by the consumer. By collecting the numbers from many consumers, the researcher can derive the utility functions for each attribute: price, top speed, seating capacity, and months of warranty. These utility functions will help the researcher figure out the most appropriate car to design.

Source: The full-profile example was taken from Paul E. Green and Yoram Wind, "New Ways to Measure Consumers' Judgments," *Harvard Business Review* (July-August, 1975), pp. 107-17. Copyright © 1975 by the President and Fellows of Harvard College; all rights reserved. The pairwise example was adapted from Richard M. Johnson, "Tradeoff Analysis of Consumer Values," *Journal of Marketing Research*, May 1974, pp. 121-27.

MARKETING-STRATEGY DEVELOPMENT

The new-product manager must now develop a marketing-strategy plan for introducing this product into the market. The marketing strategy will undergo further refinement in subsequent stages.

The marketing-strategy plan consists of three parts. The first part describes the size, structure, and behavior of the target market, the planned product positioning, and the sales, market share, and profit goals sought in the first few years. Thus:

> The target market for the instant breakfast drink is families with children who are receptive to a new, convenient, nutritious, and inexpensive form of breakfast. The company's brand will be positioned at the higher-price, higher-quality end of the market. The company will aim initially to sell 500 000 cases or 10 percent of the market, with a loss in the first year not exceeding $1.3 million. The second year will aim for 700 000 cases or 14 percent of the market, with a planned profit of $2.2 million. ∎

The second part of the marketing strategy outlines the product's planned price, distribution strategy, and marketing budget for the first year:

> The product will be offered in a chocolate flavor in individual packets of six to a box at a retail price of 79¢ a box. There will be forty-eight boxes per case, and the case's price to distributors will be $24. For the first two months, dealers will be offered one case free for every four cases bought, plus cooperative-advertising allowances. Free samples will be distributed door to door. Coupons with 20¢ off will be advertised in newspapers. The total sales-promotional budget will be $2 900 000. An advertising budget of $6 million will be split between national and local 50:50. Two-thirds will go into television and one-third into newspapers. Advertising copy will emphasize the benefit concepts of nutrition and convenience. The advertising-execution concept

will revolve around a little boy who drinks instant breakfast and grows strong. During the first year, $100 000 will be spent on marketing research to buy store audits and consumer-panel information to monitor the market's reaction and buying rates. ∎

The third part of the marketing-strategy plan describes the long-run sales and profit goals and marketing-mix strategy over time:

The company intends to ultimately capture 25 percent market share and realize an aftertax return on investment of 12 percent. To achieve this return, product quality will start high and be improved over time through technical research. Price will initially be set at a skimming level and lowered gradually to expand the market and meet competition. The total promotion budget will be boosted each year about 20 percent, with the initial advertising/sales promotion split of 63:37 evolving eventually to 50:50. Marketing research will be reduced to $60 000 per year after the first year. ∎

BUSINESS ANALYSIS

After management develops the product concept and marketing strategy, it can evaluate the business proposal's attractiveness. Management needs to prepare the sales, cost, and profit projections to determine whether they satisfy the company's objectives. If they do, the product concept can move to the product-development stage. As new information comes in, the business analysis will undergo further revision.

Estimating Sales

Management needs to estimate whether sales will be high enough to yield a satisfactory profit. Sales-estimation methods depend on whether the product is a one-time-purchase product, an infrequently purchased product, or a frequently purchased product. Figure 12-6(a) illustrates the product life-cycle sales that can be expected for one time-purchased products. Sales rise at the beginning, peak, and later approach zero as the number of potential buyers is exhausted. If new buyers keep entering the market, the curve will not go down to zero.

Infrequently purchased products, such as automobiles, toasters, and industrial equipment, exhibit replacement cycles dictated by either their physical wearing out or their obsolescence associated with changing styles, features, and tastes. Sales forecasting for this product

FIGURE 12-6
Product Life-Cycle Sales for Three Types of Products

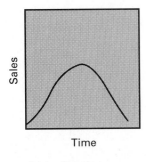

(a) One-time purchased product

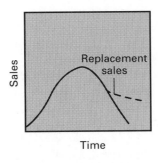

(b) Infrequently purchased product

(c) Frequently purchased product

category calls for separately estimating first-time sales and replacement sales [see Figure 12-6(b).]

Frequently purchased products, such as consumer and industrial nondurables, have product life-cycle sales resembling Figure 12-6(c). The number of first-time buyers initially increases and then decreases as fewer are left (assuming a fixed population). Repeat purchases occur soon, providing that the product satisfies some fraction of people who become steady customers. The sales curve eventually falls to a plateau representing a level of steady repeat-purchase volume; by this time, the product is no longer in the class of new products.

Estimating First-Time Sales   The first task is to estimate first-time purchases of the new product in each period. Three examples of methods for estimating first-time purchases are shown in Marketing Concepts and Tools 12-3.

Estimating Replacement Sales   To estimate replacement sales, management has to research the *survival-age distribution* of its product. The low end of the distribution indicates when the first replacement sales will take place. The actual timing of replacement will be influenced by the customer's economic outlook, cash flow, and product alternatives as well as the company's prices, financing terms, and sales effort. Since replacement sales are difficult to estimate before the product is in actual use, some manufacturers base their decision to launch a new product solely on their estimate of first-time sales.

Estimating Repeat Sales   For a frequently purchased new product, the seller has to estimate repeat sales as well as first-time sales. That is because the unit value of frequently purchased products is low, and repeat purchases take place soon after the introduction. A high rate of repeat purchasing means that customers are satisfied; sales are likely to stay high even after all first-time purchases take place. The seller should note the percentage of repeat purchases that take place in each *repeat-purchase class*: those who buy once, twice, three times, and so on. Some products and brands are bought a few times and dropped. It is important to estimate whether the repeat-purchase ratio is likely to rise or fall, and at what rate, with deeper repeat-purchase classes.[21]

Estimating Costs and Profits

After preparing the sales forecast, management can estimate the expected costs and profits of this venture. The costs are estimated by the R&D, manufacturing, marketing, and finance departments. Table 12-3 illustrates a five-year projection of sales, costs, and profits for the instant-breakfast-drink product.

Row 1 shows the projected sales revenue over the five-year period. The company expects to sell $11 889 000 (approximately 500 000 cases at $24 per case) in the first year. Sales are expected to rise around 28 percent in each of the next two years, increase by 47 percent in the fourth year, and then slow down to 15 percent growth in the fifth year. Behind this sales projection is a set of assumptions about the rate of market growth, the company's market share, and the factory-realized price.

Row 2 shows the *cost of goods sold*, which hovers around 33 percent of sales revenue. This cost is found by estimating the average cost of labor, ingredients, and packaging per case.

Row 3 shows the expected *gross margin*, which is the difference between sales revenue and cost of goods sold.

Row 4 shows anticipated *development costs* of $3.5 million. The development costs consist of three components. The first is the *product-development cost* of researching, developing, and testing the physical product. The second is the *marketing research costs* of fine

Marketing Concepts and Tools 12-3

ESTIMATING FIRST-TIME PURCHASES OF NEW PRODUCTS

Medical Equipment

A medical-equipment manufacturer developed a new instrument for analyzing blood specimens. The company identified three market segments—hospitals, clinics, and unaffiliated laboratories. For each segment, management defined the minimum-size facility that would buy this instrument. Then it estimated the number of facilities in each segment. It reduced the number by the estimated purchase probability, which varied from segment to segment. It then summed the remaining number of potential customers and called this the *market potential. Market penetration* was then estimated, based on the planned advertising and personal selling per period, the rate of favorable word of mouth, the price of the machine, and the activity of competitors. These two estimates were multiplied to estimate new product sales.

Room Air Conditioners

Models of epidemics (sometimes called contagion models) provide a useful analogy to the new-product diffusion process. Bass has used an epidemic equation to forecast sales of new appliances, including room air conditioners, refrigerators, home freezers, black-and-white television, and power lawn movers.[*] He used sales data for the first few years of product introduction to estimate sales for the subsequent years, until replacement demand became a major factor. His sales projection for room air conditioners fit the pattern of actual sales with a coefficient of determination, $R^2 = 0.92$. The predicted time of peak was 8.6 years as against an actual time of peak of 7.0 years. The predicted magnitude of peak was 1.9 million as against in actual peak of 1.8 million.

Consumer Nondurables

Fourt and Woodlock developed a first-time sales model that they tested with several new consumer-nondurable products.[†] Their observation of new-

product market-penetration rates showed that (1) cumulative sales approached a limiting penetration level of less than 100 percent of all households and (2) the successive increments of gain declined. Their equation is

$$q_t = r\bar{q}(1 - r)^{t-1} \qquad (12\text{-}1)$$

where:

q_t = percentage of total households expected to try the product in period t

r = rate of penetration of untapped potential

$\bar{q}$ = percentage of total households expected to eventually try the new product

t = time period

Assume that it is estimated that 40 percent of all households will eventually try a new product ($\bar{q} = 0.4$). Furthermore, in each period 30 percent of the remaining new-buyer potential is penetrated ($r = 0.3$). The percentages of households trying the product in the first four periods are

$$q_1 = r\bar{q}(1 - r)^{1-1} = (0.3)(0.4)(0.7^0) = 0.120$$
$$q_2 = r\bar{q}(1 - r)^{2-1} = (0.3)(0.4)(0.7^1) = 0.084$$
$$q_3 = r\bar{q}(1 - r)^{3-1} = (0.3)(0.4)(0.7^2) = 0.059$$
$$q_4 = r\bar{q}(1 - r)^{4-1} = (0.3)(0.4)(0.7^3) = 0.041$$

As time moves on, the incremental trial percentage moves toward zero. To estimate dollar sales from new buyers in any period, the estimated trial rate for any period is multiplied by the total number of households times the expected first-purchase expenditure per household of the product.

[*] Frank M. Bass, "A New Product Growth Model for Consumer Durables," *Management Science*, January 1969, pp. 215-17.

[†] Louis A. Fourt and Joseph N. Woodlock, "Early Prediction of Market Success for New Grocery Products," *Journal of Marketing*, October 1960, pp. 31-38.

Table 12-3 Projected Five-Year Cash-Flow Statement (in thousands of dollars)

	Year 0	Year 1	Year 2	Year 3	Year 4	Year 5
1. Sales revenue	0	11 889	15 381	19 654	28 253	32 491
2. Cost of goods sold	0	3 981	5 150	6 581	9 461	10 880
3. Gross margin	0	7 908	10 231	13 073	18 792	21 611
4. Development costs	−3 500	0	0	0	0	0
5. Marketing costs	0	8 000	6 460	8 255	11 866	13 646
6. Allocated overhead	0	1 189	1 538	1 965	2 825	3 249
7. Gross contribution	−3 500	−1 281	2 233	2 853	4 101	4 716
8. Supplementary contribution	0	0	0	0	0	0
9. Net contribution	−3 500	−1 281	2 233	2 853	4 101	4 716
10. Discounted contribution (15%)	−3 500	−1 113	1 691	1 877	2 343	2 346
11. Cumulative discounted cash flow	−3 500	−4 613	−2 922	−1 045	1 298	3 644

tuning the marketing program and assessing the market's likely response. It covers the estimated costs of package testing, in-home placement testing, name testing, and test marketing. The third is the *manufacturing-development costs* of new equipment, new or renovated plant, and inventory investment.

Row 5 shows the estimated *marketing costs* over the five-year period to cover advertising, sales promotion, and marketing research and an amount allocated for salesforce coverage and marketing administration. In the first year, marketing costs stand at 67 percent of sales and by the fifth year are estimated to run at 42 percent of sales.

Row 6 shows the *allocated overhead* to this new product to cover its share of the cost of executive salaries, heat, light, and so on.

Row 7, the *gross contribution*, is found by subtracting the preceding three costs from the gross margin. Years 0 and 1 involve losses, and thereafter the gross contribution becomes positive and is expected to run as high as 15 percent of sales by the fifth year.

Row 8, *supplementary contribution*, is used to list any change in income from other company products caused by the introduction of the new product. It has two components. *Dragalong income* is additional income on other company products resulting from adding this product to the line. *Cannibalized income* is the reduced income on other company products resulting from adding this product to the line.[22]

Row 9 shows the *net contribution*, which in this case is the same as the gross contribution.

Row 10 shows the *discounted contribution*, namely, the present value of each future contribution discounted at 15 percent per annum. For example, the company will not receive $4 716 000 until the fifth year, which means that it is worth only $2 346 000 today if the company can earn 15 percent on its money.[23]

Finally, row 11 shows the *cumulative discounted cash flow*, which is the cumulation of the annual contributions in row 10. This cash flow is the key series on which management bases its decision on whether to go forward into product development or drop the project. Two things are of central interest. The first is the *maximum investment exposure*, which is the highest loss that the project can create. We see that the company will be in a maximum loss position of $4 613 000 in year 1; this will be the company's loss if it terminates the project. The second is the *payback period*, which is the time when the company recovers all of its investment including the built-in return of 15 percent. The payback period here is approximately three and a half years. Management therefore has to decide whether to risk a maximum investment loss of $4.6 million and a payback period of three and a half years.

Companies use other financial measures to evaluate the merit of a new-prospect proposal. The simplest is *break-even analysis*, where management estimates how many units of the product the company would have to sell to break even with the given price and cost structure. If management believed that the company could sell at least the break-even number, it would normally move the project into product development.

The most complex method is *risk analysis*. Here three estimates (optimistic, pessimistic, and most likely) are obtained for each uncertain variable affecting profitability under an assumed marketing environment and marketing strategy for the planning period. The computer simulates possible outcomes and computes a rate-of-return probability distribution, showing the range of possible rates of returns and their probabilities.[24]

PRODUCT DEVELOPMENT

If the product concept passes the business test, it moves to R&D and/or engineering to be developed into a physical product. Up to now it has existed only as a word description, a drawing, or a very crude mockup. This step calls for a large jump in investment, which dwarfs the idea-evaluation costs incurred in the earlier stages. This stage will answer whether the product idea can be translated into a technically and commercially feasible product. If not, the company's accumulated project cost will be lost except for any useful information gained in the process.

The R&D department will develop one or more physical versions of the product concept. It hopes to find a prototype that satisfies the following criteria: (1) the consumers see it as embodying the key attributes described in the product-concept statement; (2) the prototype performs safely under normal use and conditions; (3) the prototype can be produced for the budgeted manufacturing costs.

Developing a successful prototype can take days, weeks, months, or even years. Designing a new commercial aircraft, for example, will take several years of development work. Even developing a new taste formula can take time. For example, the Maxwell House Division of General Foods discovered that consumers wanted a brand of coffee that was "bold, vigorous, deep tasting." Its laboratory technicians spent over four months working with various coffee blends and flavors to formulate a corresponding taste. It turned out to be too expensive to produce, and the company "cost reduced" the blend to meet the target manufacturing cost. The change compromised the taste, however, and the new coffee brand did not sell well in the market.

The lab scientists must not only design the required functional characteristics but also know how to communicate the psychological aspects through *physical cues*. This requires knowing how consumers react to different colors, sizes, weights, and other physical cues. In the case of a mouthwash, a yellow color supports an "antiseptic" claim (Listerine), a red color supports a "refreshing" claim (Lavoris), and a green color supports a "cool" claim (Micrin). Or to support the claim that a lawn mower is powerful, the lab people have to design a heavy frame and a fairly loud engine. Marketers need to supply lab people with information on what attributes consumers seek and how consumers judge whether these attributes are present.

When the prototypes are ready, they must be put through rigorous functional and consumer tests. The *functional tests* are conducted under laboratory and field conditions to make sure that the product performs safely and effectively. The new aircraft must fly; the new snack food must be shelf stable; the new drug must not create dangerous side effects. Functional product testing of new drugs now takes years of laboratory work with animal subjects and then human subjects before the drugs obtain government approval. In the case of equipment testing, consider the Bissell Company's experience testing a combination electric vacuum cleaner and floor scrubber:

> . . . four were left with the research and development department for continued tests on such things as water lift, motor life, effectiveness in cleaning, and dust bag design. The other eight were sent to the company's advertising agency for tests by a panel of fifty housewives. The research and development department found some serious problems in their further tests of the product. The life of the motor was not sufficiently long, the filter bag did not fit properly, and the scrubber

---

Marketing Concepts and Tools 12-4

METHODS FOR MEASURING CONSUMER PREFERENCES

Suppose a consumer is shown three items—*A*, *B*, and *C*. They might be three automobiles or advertisements or names of political candidates. There are three methods—simple rank ordering, paired comparison, and monadic rating—for measuring an individual's preference for these items.

The *simple-rank-order* method asks the consumer to rank the three items in order of preference. The consumer might respond with $A > B > C$. This method does not reveal how intensely the consumer feels about each item. The consumer may not like any one of them very much. Nor does it indicate how much the consumer prefers one object to another. Also, this method is difficult to use when there are many objects.

The *paired-comparison* method calls for presenting a set of items to the consumer, two at a time, asking which one is preferred in each pair. Thus the consumer could be presented with the pairs *AB*, *AC*, and *BC* and say that he or she prefers *A* to *B*, *A* to *C*, and *B* to *C*.

Then we could conclude that $A > B > C$. Paired comparisons offer two major advantages. First, people find it easy to state their preference between items taken two at a time. The second advantage is that the paired-comparison method allows the consumer to concentrate intensely on the two items, noting their differences and similarities.

The *monadic-rating* method asks the consumer to rate his or her liking of each product on a scale. Suppose the following seven-point scale is used.

Suppose the consumer returns the following ratings: $A = 6$, $B = 5$, $C = 3$. This yields more information than the previous methods. We can derive the individual's preference order (i.e., $A > B > C$) and even know the qualitative levels of his or her preference for each and the rough distance between preferences. This method is also easy for respondents to use, especially when there is a large set of objects to evaluate.

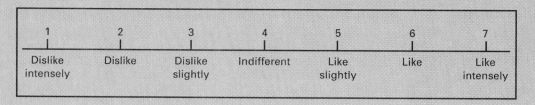

1	2	3	4	5	6	7
Dislike intensely	Dislike	Dislike slightly	Indifferent	Like slightly	Like	Like intensely

---

foot was not correct. Similarly, the consumer tests brought in many consumer dissatisfactions that had not been anticipated; the unit was too heavy, the vacuum did not glide easily enough, and the scrubber left some residue on the floor after use.[25]

Consumer testing can take a variety of forms, from bringing consumers into a laboratory to giving them samples to use in their homes. *In-home product placement tests* are common with products ranging from ice-cream flavors to new appliances. When Du Pont developed its new synthetic carpeting, it installed free carpeting in several homes in exchange for the homeowners' willingness to report their likes and dislikes about synthetic carpeting. Consumer-preference testing draws on a variety of techniques, such as simple ranking, paired comparisons, and rating scales, each with its own advantages and limitations (see Marketing Concepts and Tools 12-4).

MARKET TESTING

After management is satisfied with the product's functional and psychological performance, the product is ready to be dressed up with a brand name, packaging, and a preliminary marketing program to test it in more authentic consumer settings. (Branding and packaging decisions are discussed in Chapter 16.) The purpose of market testing is to learn how consumers and dealers react to handling, using, and repurchasing the actual product and how large the market is.

Not all companies choose the route of market testing. A company officer of Revlon, Inc., stated:

> In our field—primarily higher-priced cosmetics not geared for mass distribution—it would be unnecessary for us to market test. When we develop a new product, say an improved liquid makeup, we know it's going to sell because we're familiar with the field. And we've got 1500 demonstrators in department stores to promote it.

Most companies, however, know market testing can yield valuable information about buyers, dealers, marketing program effectiveness, market potential, and other matters. The main issues are, How much market testing and what kind?

The amount of market testing is influenced by the *investment cost* and *risk* on the one hand, and the *time pressure* and *research cost* on the other. High investment/risk products deserve to be market tested so as not to make a mistake; the cost of the market tests will be an insignificant percentage of the total project cost. High-risk products—those that create new-product categories (first instant breakfast) or have novel features (first fluoride toothpaste)—warrant more market testing than modified products (another toothpaste brand). But the amount of market testing may be severely reduced if the company is under great time pressure because the season is just starting or because competitors are about to launch their brands. The company may prefer the risk of a product failure to the risk of losing distribution or market penetration on a highly successful product. The cost of market testing will also affect how much is done and what kind.

Market-testing methods differ in testing consumer versus industrial products.

Consumer-Goods Market Testing

In testing consumer products, the company seeks to estimate four variables, namely, *trial, first repeat, adoption*, and *purchase frequency*. The company hopes to find these variables at high levels. In some cases, it will find many consumers trying the product but few rebuying it, showing a lack of product satisfaction. Or it might find high first-time repurchase but then a rapid wear out in the repeat purchase rate. Or it might find high permanent adoption but low purchase frequency (as with "gourmet" frozen foods) because the buyers use the product only on special occasions.

In testing the trade, the company wants to learn how many and what types of dealers will handle the product, under what terms, and with what shelf-position commitments.

The major methods of consumer-goods market testing, from the least to the most costly, are described in the following paragraphs.

Sales-Wave Research   In sales-wave research, consumers who initially try the product at no cost are reoffered the product, or a competitor's products, at slightly reduced prices. They might be reoffered the product as many as three to five times (sales waves), the company noting how many customers selected that company's product again and their reported level of satisfaction. Sales-wave research can also include exposing consumers to one or more advertising concepts in rough form to see what impact the advertising has on repeat purchase.

Sales-wave research enables the company to estimate the repeat-purchase rate under conditions where consumers spend their own money and choose among competing brands. The company can also gauge the impact of alternative advertising concepts on producing repeat purchases. Finally, sales-wave research can be implemented quickly, conducted under relative competitive security, and carried out without needing to develop final packaging and advertising.

On the other hand, sales-wave research does not indicate the trial rates that would be achieved with different sales-promotion incentives, since the consumers are preselected to try the product. Nor does it indicate the brand's power to gain distribution and favorable shelf position from the trade.

Simulated Store Technique   The simulated store technique (also called laboratory test markets, purchase laboratories, or accelerated test marketing) calls for finding thirty to forty shoppers (at a shopping center or elsewhere) and inviting them to a brief screening of some television commercials. Included are a number of well-known commercials and some new ones, covering a range of products. One commercial advertises the new product, but it is not singled out for attention. The consumers receive a small amount of money and are invited into a store where they may buy any items or keep the money. The company notes how many consumers buy the new product and competing brands. This provides a measure of the commercial's relative effectiveness in stimulating trial against competing commercials. The consumers are reconvened and asked the reasons for their purchases or nonpurchases. Some weeks later, they are reinterviewed by phone to determine product attitudes, usage, satisfaction, and repurchase intention and are offered an opportunity to repurchase any products.

This method has several advantages, including the measuring of advertising effectiveness and trial rates (and repeat rates if extended), speedy results, and competitive security. The results are usually incorporated into mathematical models to project ultimate sales levels. Marketing research firms report surprisingly accurate predictions of sales levels of products that are subsequently launched in the market.[26]

Controlled Test Marketing   Several research firms manage a panel of stores that have agreed to carry new products for a certain fee. The company with the new product specifies the number of stores and geographical locations it wants. The research firm delivers the product to the participating stores and controls shelf location, number of facings, displays and point-of-purchase promotions, and pricing, according to plans. Sales results can be audited both from shelf movement and from consumer diaries. The company can also test small-scale advertising in local newspapers during the test.

Controlled testing (also called minimarket testing) allows the company to test the impact of in-store factors and limited advertising on consumer's buying behavior without involving consumers directly. A sample of consumers can be interviewed later to gather their impressions of the product. The company does not have to use its own salesforce, give trade allowances, or "buy" distribution. On the other hand, controlled test marketing does not challenge the company to sell the trade on carrying the new product. This technique also exposes the product to competitors.

Test Markets   Test markets are the ultimate way to test a new consumer product in a situation resembling the one that would be faced in a full-scale launching of the product. The company usually works with an outside research firm to locate a few representative test cities in which the company's salesforce will try to sell the trade on carrying the product and giving it good shelf exposure. The company will put on a full advertising and promotion campaign in these markets similar to the one that would be used in national marketing. It is a chance to do a dress rehearsal of the total plan. Test marketing can cost the company several hundred thousand dollars, depending on the number of cities tested, the duration of the test, and the amount of data the company wants to collect. Marketing Concepts and Tools 12-5 shows the major decisions called for in test marketing.

Test marketing can yield several benefits. Its primary benefit is to make a *more reliable forecast of future sales*. If product sales fall below target levels in the test market, the company must drop or modify the product or the marketing program.

A second benefit is the *pretesting of alternative marketing plans*. Some years ago Colgate-Palmolive used a different marketing mix in each of four cities to market a new soap product. The four approaches were (1) an average amount of advertising coupled with free samples distributed door to door, (2) heavy advertising plus samples, (3) an average amount of advertising linked with mailed redeemable coupons, and (4) an average amount of advertising with no special introductory offer. The third alternative generated the best profit level, although not the highest sales level.

Through test marketing, the company may discover a product fault that escaped attention in the product-development stage. The company picks up valuable clues to distribution-level problems. And the company may gain better insight into the behavior of different market segments.

In spite of the benefits of test marketing, some experts question its value. Achenbaum lists the following concerns:

□ There is the problem of obtaining a set of markets that is reasonably representative of the country as a whole.

□ There is the problem of translating national media plans into local equivalents.

□ There is the problem of estimating what is going to happen next year based on what has happened in this year's competitive environment.

□ There is the problem of competitive knowledge of your test and of deciding whether any local counteractivities are representative of what competition will do nationally at a later date.

□ There is the problem of extraneous and uncontrollable factors such as economic conditions and weather.[27]

DECISIONS FACING MANAGEMENT IN SETTING UP TEST MARKETS

1. *How many test cities?* Many test markets use two or more cities. A large number of cities should be used, (1) the greater the maximum possible loss and/or the probability of loss from going national, (2) the greater the number of contending marketing strategies and/or the greater the uncertainty surrounding which is best, (3) the greater the regional differences, and (4) the greater the chance of calculated test market interference by competitors.

2. *Which cities?* No single Canadian city is a perfect microcosm of the nation. The bicultural characteristics of the national market provide a strong reason for using more than one test market in situations where culture is expected to be an important factor. However, some cities represent regional characteristics better than others, and consequently have been used for test marketing. Peterborough and London are two such Ontario cities that were used extensively until the growth of cable TV complicated the problem of monitoring their exposure to the mass media. When General Foods developed Crispy Fry, they decided that television would be the prime medium if the product were to be commercialized. Test marketing took place in Alberta, where Calgary and Edmonton are relatively isolated from other major Canadian markets.

3. *Length of test?* Test markets last anywhere from a few months to several years. The longer the product's *average repurchase period*, the longer the test period nec-

essary to observe repeat-purchase rates. On the other hand, the period should be cut down if competitors are rushing to the market.

4. *What information?* Management must decide on the type of information to collect in relation to its value and cost. *Warehouse shipment data* will show gross inventory buying but will not indicate weekly sales at retail. *Store audits* will show actual retail sales and competitors' market shares but will not reveal the characteristics of the buyers of the different brands. *Consumer panels* will indicate which people are buying which brands and their loyalty and switching rates. *Buyer surveys* will yield in-depth information about consumer attitudes, usage, and satisfaction. Among other things that can be researched are trade attitudes, retail distribution, and the effectiveness of advertising, promotion, and point-of-sale material.

5. *What action to take?* If the test markets show a high trial and high repurchase rate, this indicates a GO-decision. If the test markets show a high trial and a low repurchase rate, the customers are not satisfied, and the product should be redesigned or dropped. If the test markets show a low trial and a high repurchase rate, the product is satisfying, but more people have to try it. This means increasing advertising and sales promotion. Finally, if the trial and repurchase rates are both low, then the product should be dropped.

Achenbaum contends that test marketing's main value lies not in sales forecasting but in learning about unsuspected problems and opportunities connected with the new product. He points to the large number of products that failed after successful test-market results. Some large companies are skipping the test-marketing stage and relying on other market-testing methods.[28] (However, see Marketing Strategies 12-1.)

Industrial-Goods Market Testing

New industrial goods typically undergo extensive *product testing* in the labs to measure performance, reliability, design, and operating cost. Following satisfactory results, many companies will commercialize the product by listing it in the catalog, advertising it in trade journals, and turning it over to the salesforce. Today, however, an increasing number of

NOT "WHETHER TO TEST" BUT "HOW TO TEST"— THE CASE OF NEW COKE

In May 1985, the Coca-Cola Company made what appears to have been a spectacular marketing blunder. After ninety-nine successful years, it set aside its longstanding rule—"Don't mess with Mother Coke"—and dropped its original formula Coke! In its place came New Coke, with a sweeter, smoother taste. The company boldly announced the "exciting" new taste with a flurry of advertising and publicity.

At first, New Coke sold well. But sales soon went flat. Coke began receiving more than fifteen hundred phone calls and many sacks of mail each day from angry consumers. A group called Old Cola Drinkers staged protests, handed out T-shirts, and threatened to start a class-action suit unless Coca-Cola brought back the old formula or made it public. Business analysts and the media debated the decision, and some marketing experts predicted that New Coke would be the "Edsel of the Eighties."

In mid-July 1985, after just two months, the Coca-Cola Company brought old Coke back. Called Coke Classic, it was sold side by side with New Coke on supermarket shelves. The company said that New Coke would remain its "flagship" brand, but consumers had a different idea. By the end of 1985, Classic was outselling New Coke in supermarkets by two to one. By mid-1986, the company's two largest fountain accounts, McDonald's and Kentucky Fried Chicken, had returned to serving Coke Classic in their restaurants. Thus Coke Classic again became the company's main brand, and New Coke became the also-ran.

But why was New Coke introduced in the first place? And what went wrong? Many analysts blame the blunder on poor marketing research.

In the early 1980s, though Coke was still the leading soft drink, it was slowly losing market share to Pepsi. For years, Pepsi had successfully mounted the "Pepsi Challenge," a series of televised taste tests showing that consumers preferred the sweeter taste of Pepsi. By early 1985, although Coke led in the overall market, Pepsi led in share of supermarket sales by 2 percent. (That doesn't sound like much, but 2 percent of the huge soft-drink market amounts to $600 million in retail sales!) Coca-Cola had to do something to stop the erosion of its market share. The solution appeared to be a change in Coke's taste.

Coca-Cola began the largest new-product research project in the company's history. It spent over two years and $4 million on research before settling on a new formula. It conducted some two hundred thousand taste tests—thirty thousand on the final formula alone. In the blind tests, 60 percent of consumers chose the new Coke over the old, and 52 percent chose it over Pepsi. Research showed that New Coke would be a winner and the company introduced it with confidence. So what happened?

Looking back, Coke's marketing research appears to have been too narrowly focused. The research looked only at taste; it did not explore how consumers felt about dropping the old Coke and replacing it with a new version. As one expert noted, the research consisted mostly of "blind comparisons, which took no account of the total product . . . name, history, packaging, cultural heritage, image—a rich mix of tangible and intangible." To many people, Coke stands beside baseball, hotdogs, and apple pie as a national institution in the United States. It represents the very fabric of the nation. The company failed to measure these deep emotional ties, but Coke's symbolic meaning was more important to many consumers than its taste. More complete concept testing would have detected these strong emotions.

Coke's managers may also have used poor judgment in interpreting the research findings and planning strategies around them. For example, they took the finding that 60 percent of consumers preferred New Coke's taste to mean that the new product would win in the marketplace. But test results also showed that 40 percent still wanted the old Coke. By dropping the old Coke, the company trampled on the taste buds of its large core of loyal Coke drinkers who did not want a change. The company might have been wiser to leave the old Coke alone and introduce New Coke as a brand extension, as was later done successfully with Cherry Coke.

Furthermore, the New Coke should not have gone national immediately. Too much was at stake. New Coke should have been introduced regionally to see how well it did in repeat sales.

Some observers thought that Coke's managers had pulled off a smart move rather than a marketing blunder. Supermarket chains would have resisted adding another Coke flavor on their shelves. By first withdrawing its original Coke and then reintroducing it, the company got two brands on the shelf, quite a coup in the bitter struggle for shelf space.

Source: Based on numerous sources, including Betsy D. Gelb and Gabriel M. Gelb, "New Coke's Fizzle—Lessons for the Rest of Us," *Sloan Management Review*, Fall 1986; "Coke 'Family' Sales Fly as New Coke Stumbles," *Advertising Age*, January 17, 1986, pp. 1ff; and Scott Scredon and Marc Frons, "Coke's Man on the Spot: The Changes Goizueta Is Making Outweigh the Spectacular Blunder," *Business Week*, July 29, 1985, pp. 56-61. The quoted material is from Jack Honomichl, "Missing Ingredients in 'New' Coke's Research," *Advertising Age*, July 22, 1985, pp. 1ff.

industrial companies are turning to *market testing* as an intermediate step. Market testing can indicate the product's performance under actual operating conditions; the key buying influences; how different buying influences react to alternative prices and sales approaches; the market potential; and the best market segments.

Test marketing is not typically used in the case of industrial products. It is too expensive to produce a sample of Concordes or new mainframe computers, let alone put them up for sale in a select market to see how well they sell. Industrial buyers will not buy durable goods without assurances of service and parts. Furthermore, marketing research firms have not built the test-market systems that are found in consumer markets. Therefore industrial-goods manufacturers have to use other methods to research the market's interest in a new industrial product.

The most common method is a *product-use test*, similar to the in-home use test for consumer products. The manufacturer selects some potential customers, who agree to use the new product for a limited period. The manufacturer's technical people observe how these customers use the product, a practice that often exposes unanticipated problems of safety and servicing and clues the manufacturer about customer training and servicing requirements. After the test, the customer is asked to express purchase intention and other reactions.

A second common market-test method is to introduce the new industrial product at *trade shows*. Trade shows draw a large number of buyers, who view new products in a few concentrated days. The manufacturer can observe how much interest buyers show in the new product, how they react to various features and terms, and how many express purchase intentions or place orders. The disadvantage is that trade shows reveal the product to competitors; therefore the manufacturer should be ready to launch the product at that point.

The new industrial product can also be tested in *distributor and dealer display rooms*, where it may stand next to the manufacturer's other products and possibly competitors' products. This method yields preference and pricing information in the normal selling atmosphere for the product. The disadvantages are that the customers might want to place orders that cannot be filled, and those customers who come in might not represent the target market.

Controlled, or *test marketing*, has been used by some manufacturers. They produce a limited supply of the product and give it to the salesforce to sell in a limited set of geographical areas that will be given promotional support, printed catalog sheets, and so on. In this way, management can learn what might happen under full-scale marketing and make a more informed decision about launching.

COMMERCIALIZATION

Market testing presumably gives management enough information to decide about whether to launch the new product. If the company goes ahead with commercialization, it will face its largest costs to date. The company will have to contract for manufacture or build or rent a full-scale manufacturing facility. The size of the plant will be a critical decision variable. The company can build a plant smaller than called for by the sales forecast, to be on the safe side. That is what Quaker Oats did when it launched its 100 Percent Natural breakfast cereal. The demand so exceeded the company's sales forecast that for about a year it could not supply enough product to the stores. Although Quaker Oats was gratified with the response, the low forecast cost it a considerable amount of lost profits.

Another major cost is marketing. To introduce a major new consumer packaged good into the national market, the company may have to spend in excess of $1 million on advertising and promotion in the first year. In the introduction of new food products, marketing expenditures typically represent 57 percent of sales during the first year.

When (Timing)

In commercializing a new product, *market-entry timing* can be critical. Suppose a company has almost completed the development work on its new product and hears about a competitor nearing the end of its development work. The company faces three choices:

1. *First Entry.* The first firm entering a market usually enjoys "first mover advantages" consisting of locking up some key distributors and customers and gaining reputational leadership. On the other hand, if the product is rushed to the market before it is thoroughly debugged, the company can acquire a flawed image.

2. *Parallel Entry.* The firm might time its entry with the competitor. If the competitor rushes to launch, the company does the same. If the competitor takes its time, the company also takes time, using the extra time to refine its product. The company might want the promotional costs of launching to be borne by both of them.

3. *Late Entry.* The firm might delay its launch until after the competitor has entered. There are three potential advantages. The competitor will have borne the cost of educating the market. The competitor's product may reveal faults that the late entrant can avoid. And the company can learn the size of the market.

The timing decision involves additional considerations. If the new product replaces the company's older product, the company might delay the introduction until the old product's stock is drawn down. If the product is highly seasonal, it might be held back until the right season. All said, market-entry timing deserves careful thought.[29]

Where (Geographical Strategy)

The company must decide whether to launch the new product in a *single locality*, a *region,* *several regions*, the *national market*, or the *international market.* Few companies have the confidence, capital, and capacity to launch new products into full national distribution. They will develop a *planned market rollout* over time. Small companies, in particular, will select an attractive city and put on a blitz campaign to enter the market. They will enter other cities one at a time. Large companies will introduce their product into a whole region and then move to the next region. Companies with national distribution networks, such as auto companies, will launch their new models in the national market.

In rollout marketing, the company has to rate the alternative markets for their attractiveness. A rating table can be prepared in which the rows are the candidate markets, and the columns are attractiveness criteria, such as market potential, company reputation, cost of obtaining distribution, quality of research data, influence of adjacent areas, and competitive penetration. The resulting ratings allow the company to rank-order the prime markets and develop the sequence for a geographic rollout plan.

The factor of competitive presence is very important. Ultimately, it may be necessary to rate each local market to determine whether to introduce the product in the market. Mother's Pizza introduced their new Taco Pizza selectively, depending on the local competition. If a local manager felt that the competitive situation would more than cover the logistical costs of the extra product line, then the Taco Pizza could be added to that restaurant.

To Whom (Target-Market Prospects)

Within the rollout markets, the company must target its distribution and promotion to the best prospect groups. Presumably, the company has already profiled the prime prospects on the basis of earlier market testing. Prime prospects for a new consumer product would ideally have the following characteristics: They would be early adopters; they would be heavy users; they would be opinion leaders and would talk favorably about the product; and they could be reached at a low cost.[30] Few groups have all of these characteristics. The company can rate the various prospect groups on these characteristics and target to the best prospect group. The aim is to generate strong sales as soon as possible to motivate the salesforce and attract further prospects.

How (Introductory Market Strategy)

The company must develop an action plan for introducing the new product into the rollout markets. It must allocate the marketing budget to the marketing-mix tools and schedule the various activities. For example:

> In May 1986, Polaroid launched its new Spectra instant camera with a $40 million first-year advertising budget. Billboard ads were put up in twenty-five markets as part of a teaser campaign, followed by a saturation print and television campaign aiming to generate twenty-five exposures for 90 percent of Spectra's target audience. ∎

To sequence and coordinate the many activities involved in launching a new product, management can use network-planning techniques such as critical path scheduling (see Chapter 4).

A summary of the various steps and decisions in the new-product-development process is presented in Figure 12-7.

THE CONSUMER-ADOPTION PROCESS

The *consumer-adoption process* begins where the firm's *innovation process* leaves off. It describes how potential customers learn about new products, try them, and adopt or reject them. Management must understand this process in order to build an effective strategy for early market penetration. The *consumer-adoption process* is later followed by the *consumer-loyalty process*, which is the concern of the established producer.

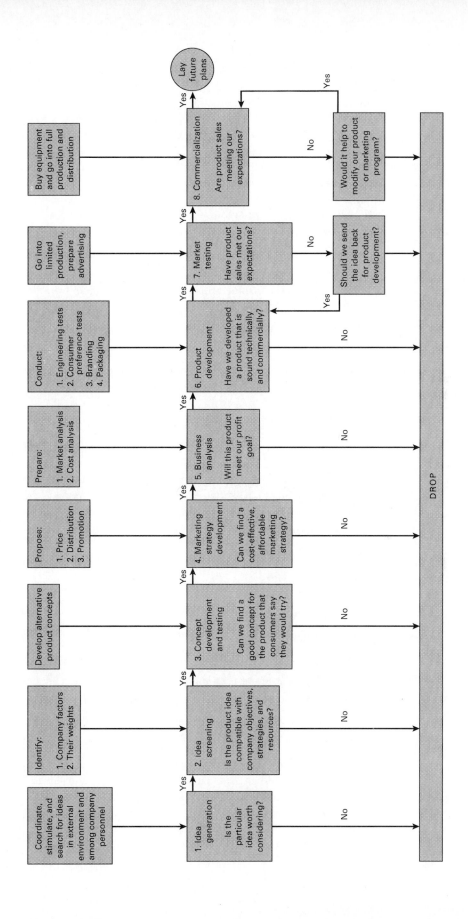

FIGURE 12-7
Summary of the New-Product-Development Decision Process

Years ago, new-product marketers used a *mass-market approach* in launching their product. They would distribute the product everywhere and advertise it to everyone on the assumption that most people are potential buyers. The mass-market approach, however, has two drawbacks: It calls for heavy marketing expenditures, and it involves many wasted exposures to people who are not potential consumers. These drawbacks led to a second approach, *heavy-user target marketing*, where the product is initially aimed at the heavy users. This approach makes sense, provided that heavy users are identifiable and are early adopters. But even within the heavy-user group, consumers differ in their interest in new products and brands; many heavy users are loyal to their existing brands. Some heavy users are earlier adopters than others. Many new-product marketers now aim at those consumers who are earlier adopters. According to *early-adopter theory*:

□ Persons within a target market differ in the amount of elapsed time between their exposure to a new product and their trial.

□ Early adopters share some traits that differentiate them from late adopters.

□ Efficient media exist for reaching early-adopter types.

□ Early adopters tend to be opinion leaders and helpful in "advertising" the new product to other potential buyers.

We now turn to the theory of innovation diffusion and consumer adoption, which provides clues to identifying early adopters.

Concepts in Innovation, Diffusion, and Adoption

An *innovation* refers to any good, service, or idea that is *perceived* by someone as new. The idea may have a long history, but it is an innovation to the person who sees it as new.

Innovations take time to spread through the social system. Rogers defines the *diffusion process* as "the spread of a new idea from its source of invention or creation to its ultimate users or adopters."[31] The *adoption process*, on the other hand, focuses on "the mental process through which an individual passes from first hearing about an innovation to final adoption." *Adoption* is the decision of an individual to become a regular user of a product.

We will now examine the main generalizations drawn from hundreds of studies of how people accept new ideas.

Stages in the Adoption Process

Adopters of new products have been observed to move through the following five stages:

□ *Awareness:* The consumer becomes aware of the innovation but lacks information about it.

□ *Interest:* The consumer is stimulated to seek information about the innovation.

□ *Evaluation:* The consumer considers whether to try the innovation.

□ *Trial:* The consumer tries the innovation to improve his or her estimate of its value.

□ *Adoption:* The consumer decides to make full and regular use of the innovation.

This progression suggests that the new-product marketer should aim to facilitate consumer movement through these stages. A portable electric-dishwasher manufacturer might discover that many consumers are stuck in the interest stage; they do not buy because of their uncertainty and the large investment cost. But these same consumers would be willing to use an electric dishwasher on a trial basis for a small monthly fee. The manufacturer should consider offering a trial-use plan with option to buy.

Individual Difference in Innovativeness

People differ markedly in their readiness to try new products. Rogers defines a person's *innovativeness* as "the degree to which an individual is relatively earlier in adopting new ideas than the other members of his social system." In each product area, there are "consumption pioneers" and early adopters. Some women are the first to adopt new clothing fashions or new appliances; some doctors are the first to prescribe new medicines; and some farmers are the first to adopt new farming methods.

Other individuals adopt new products much later. People can be classified into the adopter categories shown in Figure 12-8. The adoption process is represented as a normal distribution when plotted over time. After a slow start, an increasing number of people adopt the innovation, the number reaches a peak, and then it diminishes as fewer nonadopters remain. Innovators are defined as the first 2 1/2 percent of the buyers to adopt a new idea; the early adopters are the next 13 1/2 percent who adopt the new idea; and so forth.

Rogers sees the five adopter groups as differing in their value orientations. Innovators are *venturesome*; they are willing to try new ideas at some risk. Early adopters are guided by *respect*; they are opinion leaders in their community and adopt new ideas early but carefully. The early majority are *deliberate*; they adopt new ideas before the average person, although they rarely are leaders. The late majority are *skeptical*; they adopt an innovation only after a majority of people have tried it. Finally, laggards are *tradition bound*; they are suspicious of changes, mix with other tradition-bound people, and adopt the innovation only when it takes on a measure of tradition itself.

This adopter classification suggests that an innovating firm should research the demographic, psychographic, and media characteristics of innovators and early adopters and direct communications specifically to them. Identifying early adopters is not always easy. No one has demonstrated the existence of a general personality trait called innovativeness. Individuals tend to be innovators in certain areas and laggards in others. We can think of a businessperson who dresses conservatively but who delights in trying unfamiliar cuisines. The marketer's challenge is to identify the characteristics of likely early adopters in its product area. For example, innovative farmers are likely to be better educated and more efficient than noninnovative farmers. Innovative homemakers are more gregarious and usually higher in social status than noninnovative homemakers. Certain communities have a high share of early adopters. Rogers offers the following hypotheses about early adopters:

FIGURE 12-8
Adopter
Categorization
on the Basis of
Relative Time of
Adoption
of Innovations

Source: Redrawn from
Everett M. Rogers,
Diffusion of Innovations
(New York: Free Press,
1962), p. 162.

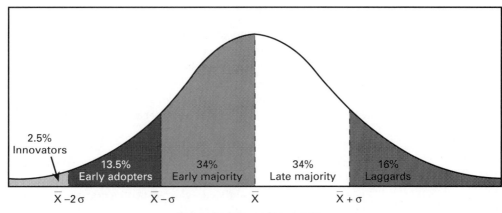

The relatively earlier adopters in a social system tend to be younger in age, have higher social status, a more favorable financial position, more specialized operations, and a different type of mental ability from later adopters. Earlier adopters utilize information sources that are more impersonal and cosmopolite than later adopters and that are in closer contact with the origin of new ideas. Earlier adopters utilize a greater number of different information sources than do later adopters. The social relationships of earlier adopters are more cosmopolite than for later adopters, and earlier adopters have more opinion leadership.[32]

Role of Personal Influence

Personal influence plays a large role in the adoption of new products. Personal influence describes the effect of product statements made by one person on another's attitude or purchase probability. According to Katz and Lazarsfeld:

> About half of the women in our sample reported that they had recently made some change from a product or brand to which they were accustomed to something new. The fact that one third of these changes involved personal influences indicates that there is also considerable traffic in marketing advice. Women consult each other for opinions about new products, about the quality of different brands, about shopping economies and the like.[33]

Although personal influence is an important factor, its significance is greater in some situations and for some individuals than for others. Personal influence is more important in the evaluation stage of the adoption process than in the other stages. It has more influence on late adopters than early adopters. And it is more important in risky situations than in safe situations.

Influence of Product Characteristics on the Rate of Adoption

The characteristics of the innovation affects its rate of adoption. Some products catch on immediately overnight (e.g., frisbees), whereas others take a long time to gain acceptance (e.g., diesel-engine autos). Five characteristics are especially important in influencing the rate of adoption of an innovation. We will consider these characteristics in relation to the rate of adoption of personal computers for home use.

The first is the innovation's *relative advantage*—the degree to which it appears superior to existing products. The greater the perceived relative advantage of using a personal computer, say, in preparing income taxes and keeping financial records, the more quickly personal computers will be adopted.

The second characteristic is the innovation's *compatibility*—the degree to which it matches the values and experiences of the individuals in the community. Personal computers, for example, are highly compatible with the lifestyles found in upper-middle-class homes.

Third is the innovation's *complexity*—the degree to which it is relatively difficult to understand or use. Personal computers are complex and will therefore will take a longer time to penetrate into home use.

Fourth is the innovation's *divisibility*—the degree to which it can be tried on a limited basis. The availability of rentals of personal computers with an option to buy increases their rate of adoption.

The fifth characteristic is the innovation's *communicability*—the degree to which the results of its use are observable or describable to others. The fact that personal computers lend themselves to demonstration and description helps them diffuse faster in the social system.

Other characteristics influence the rate of adoption, such as initial costs, ongoing costs, risk and uncertainty, scientific credibility, and social approval. The new-product marketer has to research all these factors and give the key ones maximum attention in designing the new-product and marketing program.[34]

Influence of Organizational Buyers' Characteristics on the Rate of Adoption

Organizations can also be classified as to their readiness to try and adopt a new product. Thus the producer of a new teaching method would want to identify the schools that have a high adoption probability. The producer of a new piece of medical equipment would want to identify hospitals that have a high adoption probability. Adoption is associated with variables in the organization's environment (community progressiveness, community income), the organization itself (size, profits, pressure to change), and the administrators (education level, age, cosmopoliteness). Once a set of useful indicators are found, they can be used to identify the best target organizations.

SUMMARY

Organizations are increasingly recognizing the necessity and advantages of regularly developing new products and services. Their more mature and declining products must be replaced by newer products.

New products, however, can fail. The risks of innovation are as great as the rewards. The key to successful innovation lies in developing better organizational arrangements for handling new-product ideas and developing sound research and decision procedures at each stage of the new-product-development process.

The new-product-development process consists of eight stages: idea generation, idea screening, concept development and testing, marketing-strategy development, business analysis, product development, market testing, and commercialization. The purpose of each stage is to decide whether the idea should be further developed or dropped. The company wants to minimize the chances that poor ideas will move forward and good ideas will be rejected.

With regard to new products, consumers respond at different rates, depending on the consumer's characteristics and the product's characteristics. Manufacturers try to bring their new products to the attention of potential early adopters, particularly those with opinion-leader characteristics.

■ QUESTIONS

1. The declining pool of eligible youth has led to a decreasing enrolment for a Maritimes university. The institution offers a liberal arts program at the undergraduate level with professional schools in business and in education at the graduate and undergraduate levels. What new-product services might be developed? How might the university test and launch these new services?

2. Seek out examples of new services development in one of the following areas and discuss its success or failure in light of the concepts presented in this chapter: (a) financial services, (b) health-care delivery, (c) electronic or rapid mail delivery.

3. Consider the chapter's list of sources for new-product ideas. Is there a correspondence between these sources and the orientation discussed in Chapter 1 (production, product, selling, marketing orientation)?

4. Devise a list of questions that management should answer prior to developing a new product or service. Organize the questions according to the following areas: market

opportunity, competition, production, patents, distribution, finance. Would the development and testing of a new service differ from that of a new product?

5. A food company develops a new salad-dressing powder that is mixed with water. The company is trying to compete against another company that has a powdered dressing that is mixed with oil and vinegar. Discuss different methods of concept testing this new product.

6. Polaroid, an acknowledged leader in photographic technology, introduced an "instant movie" system, Polavision, to retailers and consumers with substantial promotion expenditures. Polaroid spent $60 million the first two years after introduction of the product, yet the product never gained wide acceptance. Given Polaroid's previous record of new-product successes, how can you explain Polavision's failure?

7. A candy-store chain is seeking ideas for a new sales promotion campaign. Show how morphological analysis might be used to generate a large number of ideas for a campaign.

8. Consider the following four test marketing problems: (a) Expected profit and risk are two dimensions for determining whether to introduce a new product nationally. Can you develop a diagram using these two dimensions to show how critical limits might be set up by a firm before a market test to guide its decision after the test? (b) Suppose a firm finds that test-market results are borderline and concludes that the product would probably yield a below-average return. It has sunk a lot of money into the development of the product. Should the firm introduce the product nationally or drop it? (c) State the two opposing risks that a firm faces when it bases its new-product decision on test-market results. How can it reduce these risks? (d) In the test marketing of Colgate's new soap (described in the text), the third marketing mix yielded the best profit level. Does this mean that that mix should be adopted when the product is launched nationally?

9. A school-furniture manufacturer wants to develop a line of lightweight chairs for elementary school classrooms. Recommend steps for researching, developing, and testing these chairs.

10. A company president asked the new-product manager what a proposed new product would earn if launched. "Profits of three million dollars in five years." Then the president asked whether the product might fail. "Yes." "What would we lose if the product fails?" "One million dollars." "Forget it," said the president. Do you agree with the president's decision?

■ NOTES

1. *New Products Management for the 1980s* (New York: Booz, Allen & Hamilton, 1982).

2. *Ibid.*

3. David S. Hopkins and Earl L. Bailey, "New Product Pressures," *Conference Board Record*, June 1971, pp. 16-24.

4. See "High-Speed Management for the High-Tech Age," *Fortune*, March 5, 1984, pp. 62-68.

5. *New Products Management for the 1980s.*

6. In a sample of 228 frequently purchased consumer products that were test marketed in 1977, 64.5 percent were not launched nationally. See Nielsen Marketing Service, "New Product Success Ratios," *Nielsen Researcher*, 1979, pp. 2-9.

7. See David S. Hopkins, *Options in New-Product Organization* (New York: Conference Board, 1974).

8. A good review of other studies of factors associated with new-product success is found in Modesto A. Maidique and Billie Jo Zirger, "A Study of Success and Failure in Product Innovation: The Case of the U.S. Electronics Industry," *IEEE Transactions on Engineering Management*, November 1984, pp. 192-203.

9. Eric A. von Hippel, "Users as Innovators," *Technology Review*, January 1978, pp. 3-11.

10. See John E. Arnold, "Useful Creative Techniques," in *Source Book for Creative Thinking*, ed. Sidney J. Parnes and Harold F. Harding (New York: Scribner's, 1962), p. 255.

11. See Alex F. Osborn, *Applied Imagination*, 3rd ed. (New York: Scribner's, 1963), pp. 286-87.

12. See Edward M. Tauber, "HIT: Heuristic Ideation Technique—A Systematic Procedure for New Product Search," *Journal of Marketing*, January 1972, pp. 58-70; and Charles L. Alford and Joseph Barry Mason, "Generating New Product Ideas," *Journal of Advertising Research*, December 1975, pp. 27-32.

13. See Edward M. Tauber, "Discovering New Product Opportunities with Problem Inventory Analysis," *Journal of Marketing*, January 1975, pp. 67-70.

14. Eric von Hippel, "Learning from Lead Users," in *Marketing in an Electronic Age*, ed. Robert D. Buzzell (Cambridge, Mass.: Harvard Business School Press, 1985), pp. 308-317.

15. Osborn, *Applied Imagination*, p. 156.

16. John W. Lincoln, "Defining a Creativeness in People," in *Source Book for Creative Thinking*, pp. 274-75.

17. *Ibid.*, p. 274.

18. Mark Hanan, "Corporate Growth through Venture Management," *Harvard Business Review*, January-February 1969, p. 44.

19. See John T. O'Meara, Jr., "Selecting Profitable Products," *Harvard Business Review*, January-February 1961, pp. 110-18.

20. Theodore Levitt, "Marketing Intangible Products and Product Intangibles," *Harvard Business Review*, May-June, 1981, p. 95.

21. See Robert Blattberg and John Golanty, "Tracker: An Early Test Market Forecasting and Diagnostic Model for New Product Planning," *Journal of Marketing Research*, May 1978, pp. 192-202.

22. See Roger A. Kerin, Michael G. Harvey, and James T. Rothe, "Cannibalism and New Product Development," *Business Horizons*, October 1978, pp. 25-31.

23. The present value (V) of a future sum (I) to be received t years from today and discounted at the interest rate (r) is given by $V = I_t/(1 + r)^t$. Thus $4716/(1.15)^5 = 2346$.

24. See David B. Hertz, "Risk Analysis in Capital Investment," *Harvard Business Review*, January-February 1964, pp. 96-106.

25. Ralph Westfall and Harper W. Boyd, Jr., *Cases in Marketing Management* (Homewood, Ill.: Richard D. Irwin, 1961), p. 365.

26. The best-known systems are Yankelovich's "Laboratory Test Market," Elrick and Lavidge's "Comp," and Management Decision Systems's "Assessor." For a description of "Assessor," see Alvin J. Silk and Glen L. Urban, "Pre-Test Marketing Evaluation of New Packaged Goods: A Model and Measurement Methodology," *Journal of Marketing Research*, May 1978, pp. 171-91. For a recent assessment, see Allan D. Shocker and William G. Hall, "Pretest Market Models: A Critical Evaluation," *Journal of Product Innovation Management* 3 (1986), pp. 86-107.

27. Alvin A. Achenbaum, "The Purpose of Test Marketing," in *The Marketing Concept in Action*, ed. Robert M. Kaplan (Chicago: American Marketing Association, 1964), p. 582.

28. See "Spotting Competitive Edges Begets New Product Success," *Marketing News*, December 21, 1984, p. 4. Also see "Testing Time for Test Marketing," *Fortune*, October 29, 1984, pp. 75-76; and Jay E. Klompmaker, G. David Hughes, and Russell I. Haley, "Test Marketing in New Product Development," *Harvard Business Review*, May-June 1976, pp. 128-38.

29. See Robert J. Thomas, "Timing—The Key to Market Entry," *Journal of Consumer Marketing*, Summer 1985, pp. 77-87.

30. Philip Kotler and Gerald Zaltman, "Targeting Prospects for a New Product," *Journal of Advertising Research*, February 1976, pp. 7-20.

31. The following discussion leans heavily on Everett M. Rogers, *Diffusion of Innovations* (New York: Free Press, 1962). Also see his third edition, published in 1983.

32. Rogers, *Diffusion of Innovations*, p. 192.

33. Elihu Katz and Paul F. Lazarsfeld, *Personal Influence* (New York: Free Press, 1955), p. 234.

34. For a recent summary of the literature, see Hubert Gatignon and Thomas S. Robertson, "A Propositional Inventory for New Diffusion Research," *Journal of Consumer Research*, March 1985, pp. 849-67.

13

Managing Products Through Their Product Life Cycle

It's funny how you tire of yesterday's dreams.

Randy Bachman

During a product's life, a company will normally reformulate its marketing strategy several times. Not only do economic conditions change, and competitors launch new assaults, but in addition, the product passes through new stages of buyer interest and requirements. Consequently a company must plan successive strategies appropriate to each stage in the product's life cycle. The company hopes to extend the product's life and profitability even knowing that the product will not last forever.

We will answer three questions in this chapter: What is a product life cycle? What marketing strategies are appropriate at each stage of the product life cycle? How do whole markets evolve, and what marketing strategies are appropriate?

THE PRODUCT LIFE CYCLE

The product life cycle (PLC) is an important concept in marketing that provides insights into a product's competitive dynamics. At the same time, the concept can prove misleading if not carefully used. To fully understand PLC, we will first describe its parent concept, the *demand/technology life cycle*.[1]

Demand/Technology Life Cycle

Marketing thinking should not begin with a product, or even a product class, but rather with a need. The product exists as one solution among many to meet a need. For example, the human race has a need for "calculating power," and this need has grown over the centuries with the expansion of trade. The changing need level is described by a *demand life-cycle*

FIGURE 13-1
Demand-Technology-Product Life Cycles

Source: H. Igor Ansoff, Implanting Strategic Management (Englewood Cliffs, N.J.: Prentice-Hall, 1984), p. 41.

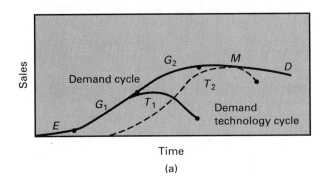

(a)

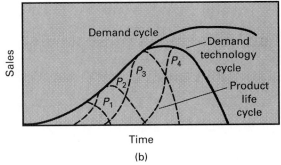

(b)

curve, the highest curve shown in Figure 13-1(a). There is a stage of *emergence* (*E*), followed by stages of *accelerating growth* (*G*1), *decelerating growth* (*G*2), *maturity* (*M*), and *decline* (*D*). In the case of "calculating power," the maturity and decline stage might not have set in yet. In the case of another need, say the need for "personal transportation," the need may be in a mature or declining stage in certain advanced countries.

Now a need is satisfied by some technology. The need for "calculating power" was first satisfied by finger counting; then by abacuses; still later by slide rules, adding machines, hand calculators, and computers. Each new technology normally satisfies the need in a superior way. Each exhibits a *demand-technology life cycle*, shown by the curves (T_1 and T_2) under the demand-cycle curve in Figure 13-1(a). Each demand-technology life cycle shows an emergence, rapid growth, slower growth, maturity, and then decline.

Within a given demand-technology cycle, there will appear a succession of product forms that satisfy the specific need at the time. Thus the hand calculator provided a new technology offering "calculating power." Initially, it took the product form of a large plastic box with a small screen and numerical keys, and it could perform only four tasks: adding, subtracting, multiplying, and dividing. This form lasted a few years and was succeeded by smaller hand calculators that could perform even more mathematical operations. Today's product forms include hand calculators no larger than the size of a business card. Figure 13-1(b) shows a succession of *product-forms life cycles*, P_1, P_2, P_3, P_4. Later we will show that each product form contains a set of brands with their own *brand life cycles*.

These distinctions suggest that if a company concentrates only on its own brand life cycle, it is missing the bigger picture and might wake up one day to find its whole business destroyed. Thus a manufacturer of slide rules might have considered its competitors to be other manufacturers of slide rules (brand competitors), but it should actually have worried about a new technology (hand calculators), destroying the slide-rule market.

The same point can be made about vacuum tubes. Vacuum tubes met the need for "amplifying weak electrical signals," and many improvements appeared over the years. Yet vacuum tubes were ended by the innovation of a solid-state technology. The leading vacuum-tube companies, such as General Electric and RCA, failed to convert to the new technology, and that was how Texas Instruments, Fairchild, and Transitron got their start.

Companies must decide what demand technology to invest in and when to transit to a new demand technology. Ansoff calls a demand technology a *strategic business area (SBA)*, namely "a distinctive segment of the environment in which the firm does or may want to do business."[2] Today's companies face many changing technologies but cannot invest in all of them. They have to bet on which demand technology will win. They can bet heavily on one new technology or bet lightly on several. If the latter, they are not likely to become the leader. The pioneering firm that bets heavily on the winning technology is likely to capture leadership. Thus firms must carefully choose the strategic business areas in which they will operate.

Stages in the Product Life Cycle

We can now focus on the product life cycle. The product life cycle portrays *distinct stages* in the *sales history* of a product. Corresponding to these stages are distinct opportunities and problems with respect to marketing strategy and profit potential. By identifying the stage that a product is in, or may be headed toward, companies can formulate better marketing plans.

To say that a product has a life cycle is to assert four things:

☐ Products have a limited life.

☐ Product sales pass through distinct stages, each posing different challenges to the seller.

☐ Profits rise and fall at different stages of the product life cycle.

☐ Products require different marketing, financial, manufacturing, purchasing, and personnel strategies in each stage of their life cycle.

Most discussions of product life cycle (PLC) portray the sales history of a typical product as following an S-shaped curve (see Figure 13-2). This curve is typically divided into four stages, known as *introduction, growth, maturity*, and *decline*:[3]

☐ *Introduction:* A period of slow sales growth as the product is introduced in the market. Profits are nonexistent in this stage because of the heavy expenses of product introduction.

☐ *Growth:* A period of rapid market acceptance and substantial profit improvement.

☐ *Maturity:* A period of a slowdown in sales growth because the product has achieved acceptance by most potential buyers. Profits stabilize or decline because of increased marketing outlays to defend the product against competition.

☐ *Decline:* The period when sales show a downward drift and profits erode.

Designating where each stage begins and ends is somewhat arbitrary. Usually the stages are marked where the rates of sales growth or decline become pronounced. Polli and Cook

FIGURE 13-2
Sales and Profit Life Cycles

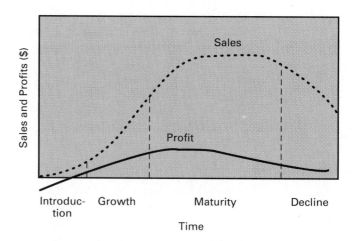

proposed an operational measure based on a normal distribution of percentage changes in real sales from year to year.[4]

Studies by Buzzell of grocery food products and Polli and Cook of consumer nondurables showed that the S-shaped PLC concept holds up well for many product categories.[5] Those planning to use this concept must investigate the extent to which the PLC concept describes product histories in their industry. They should check the normal sequence of stages and the average duration of each stage. Cox found that a typical ethical drug spanned an introductory period of one month, a growth stage of six months, a maturity stage of fifteen months, and a very long decline stage—the last because of manufacturers' reluctance to drop drugs from their catalogs. These stage lengths must be reviewed periodically. Intensifying competition is leading to shorter PLCs over time, which means that products must earn their profits in a shorter period.

Product-Category, Product-Form, and Brand Life Cycles

The PLC concept can be used to analyze a product category (cigarettes), a product form (plain filter cigarettes), or a brand (Export regular nonfilter). (See Figure 13-3.) The PLC concept has a different degree of applicability in each case:

☐ *Product categories* have the longest life cycles. Many product categories stay in the mature stage for an indefinite duration, since they are highly population related. Some major product categories—cigars, newspapers, coffee, movies—seem to have entered the decline stage of the PLC.[6] Meanwhile some others—microcomputers, videocassettes, cordless telephones—are clearly in the introductory or growth stage.

☐ *Product forms* exhibit the standard PLC histories more faithfully than do product categories. Thus manual typewriters passed through the stages of introduction, growth, maturity, and decline; now electric typewriters are showing a similar fate as electronic typewriters start replacing them.

☐ *Brands* tend to show the shortest PLC history. A Nielsen study found that in the past the life expectancy of a new brand was approximately three years, and the signs are that it is

FIGURE 13-3

PLCs for a Product Category, Product Form, and Brand

Source: Rolando Polli and Victor Cook, "Validity of the Product Life Cycle," *Journal of Business*, October 1969, p. 389. The University of Chicago Press. Copyright © 1969 by The University of Chicago Press.

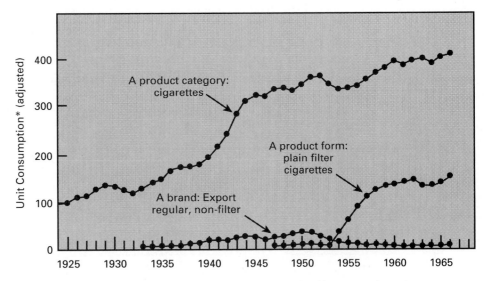

*Number of cigarettes per $100 of constant dollar nondurable consumption

growing shorter.[7] At the same time, some very old brands—such as Arm & Hammer Baking Soda, Ivory Soap, Jell-O—are still going strong.

Other Shapes of the Product Life Cycle

Not all products exhibit an S-shaped PLC. Researchers have identified from six to seventeen different PLC patterns.[8] Three common patterns are shown in Figure 13-4. Figure 13-4(a) shows a "growth-slump-maturity" pattern, often characteristic of small kitchen appliances. For example, the sales of slow cookers grew rapidly between 1970 and 1976, then slid to half their 1976 level by 1979, and thereafter stabilized or "petrified" at that level. The petrified level is held up by late adopters buying the product for the first time and early adopters replacing the product.

The "cycle-recycle" pattern in Figure 13-4(b) often describes the sales of new drugs. The pharmaceutical company aggressively promotes its new drug, and this produces the first cycle. Later sales start declining, and the company gives the drug another promotion push, which produces a second cycle usually of smaller magnitude and duration.

Still another common pattern is the "scalloped" PLC in Figure 13-4(c). Here sales pass through a succession of life cycles based on the discovery of new-product characteristics, uses, or users. Nylon's sales, for example, show a scalloped pattern because of the many new uses—parachutes, hosiery, shirts, carpeting—discovered over time.[9] Marketing Concepts and Tools 13-1 describes some of the major factors that shape the PLC for a specific product.

Style, Fashion, and Fad Life Cycle   There are three special categories of product life cycles that should be distinguished, those pertaining to styles, fashions, and fads (see Figure 13-5).

A *style* is a basic and distinctive mode of expression appearing in a field of human endeavor. For example, styles appear in homes (colonial, ranch, split level); clothing (formal, casual, funky); and art (realistic, surrealistic, abstract). Once a style is invented, it can last for generations, going in and out of vogue. A style exhibits a cycle showing several periods of renewed interest.

A *fashion* is a currently accepted or popular style in a given field. For example, jeans are a fashion in today's clothing, and "country western" is a fashion in today's popular music. Fashions pass through four stages.[10] In the *distinctiveness stage*, some consumers take an interest in something new to set themselves apart from other consumers. The products may be custom made or produced in small quantities by some manufacturer. In the *emulation stage*, other consumers take an interest out of a desire to emulate the fashion leaders, and

FIGURE 13-4
Some Common Product Life-Cycle Patterns

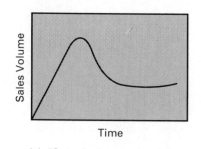

(a) "Growth-slump-maturity" pattern

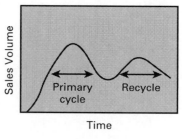

(b) "Cycle-recycle" pattern

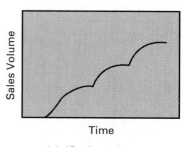

(c) "Scalloped" pattern

Marketing Concepts and Tools 13-1

FORECASTING THE SHAPE AND DURATION OF THE PRODUCT LIFE CYCLE

Goldman and Muller have presented some interesting observations on factors influencing the shape and duration of product-specific life cycles. First consider the shape of an ideal product life cycle:

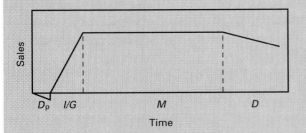

This shape is ideal. The product-development period (D_p) is short, and therefore the product-development costs are low. The introduction/growth period (I/G) is short, and therefore sales reach their peak quite soon, which means early maximum revenue. The maturity period (M) lasts quite long, which means the company enjoys an extended period of profits. The decline (D) is very slow, which means that profits fall gradually rather than suddenly.

A firm launching a new product should forecast the PLC shape based on factors that influence the length of each stage:

☐ Development time is shorter and less costly for routine products than for high-tech products. Thus new perfumes, new snacks, and so on, do not involve much development time, whereas high-tech products require much R&D and engineering time and cost.

☐ *Introduction and growth time* will be short under the following conditions:

The product does not require setting up a new infrastructure of distribution channels, transportation, services, or communication.

The dealers will readily accept and promote the new product.

Consumers have an interest in the product, will adopt it early, and will give it favorable word of mouth.

These conditions apply to many familiar consumer products. They are less valid for many high-tech products, which therefore require longer introduction/growth periods.

☐ *Maturity time* will last long to the extent that consumer tastes and product technology are fairly stable and the company maintains leadership in the market. Companies make the most money by riding out a long maturity period. If the maturity period is short, the company might not recover its full investment.

☐ *The decline time* is long if consumer tastes and product technology change only slowly. The more brand loyal the consumers, the slower the rate of decline. The lower the exit barriers, the faster some firms will exit, and this will slow down the rate of decline for the remaining firms.

Given these factors, we can see why many high-tech firms fail. They face highly unattractive PLCs. The worst type of PLC would look like this:

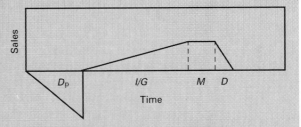

The development time is long, and the development cost is steep; the introduction/growth time is long; the maturity period is short; and the decline is fast. Many high-tech firms must invest a great amount of time and cost to develop their product; they find that it takes a long time to introduce it to the market; the market does not last long; and the decline is steep, owing to the rapid technological change.

Source: Arieh Goldman and Eitan Muller, "Measuring Shape Patterns of Product Life Cycles: Implications for Marketing Strategy," paper, August 1982, Hebrew University of Jerusalem,

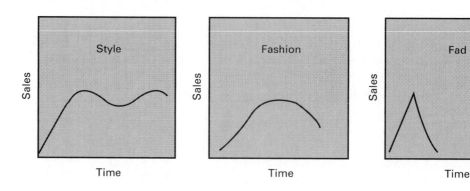

FIGURE 13-5
Style, Fashion, and Fad Life Cycles

Style · Sales · Time

Fashion · Sales · Time

Fad · Sales · Time

additional manufacturers begin to produce larger quantities of the product. In the *mass-fashion stage*, the fashion has become extremely popular, and manufacturers have geared up for mass production. Finally, in the *decline stage*, consumers start moving toward other fashions that are beginning to catch their attention.

Thus fashions tend to grow slowly, remain popular for a while, and decline slowly. The length of a fashion cycle is hard to predict. Wasson believes that fashions come to an end because they represent a purchase compromise, and consumers start looking for missing attributes. For example, as automobiles become smaller, they become less comfortable, and then a growing number of buyers start wanting larger cars. Furthermore, too many consumers adopt the fashion, thus turning others away. Reynolds suggests that the length of a particular fashion cycle depends on the extent to which the fashion meets a genuine need, is consistent with other trends in the society, satisfies societal norms and values, and does not meet technological limits as it develops.[11] Robinson, however, sees fashions as living out inexorable cycles regardless of economic, functional, or technological changes in society.[12] Sproles has reviewed and compared several theories of fashion cycles.[13]

Fads are fashion that come quickly into the public eye, are adopted with great zeal, peak early, and decline very fast. Their acceptance cycle is short, and they tend to attract only a limited following. They often have a novel or capricious aspect, as when people start buying "pet rocks" or run naked and "streak." Fads appeal to people who are searching for excitement or who want to distinguish themselves from others or have something to talk about to others. Fads do not survive because they do not normally satisfy a strong need or do not satisfy it well. It is difficult to predict whether something will be only a fad, or how long it will last—a few days, weeks, or months. The amount of media attention, along with other factors, will influence the fad's duration.

Rationale for the Product Life Cycle

Earlier we described the S-shaped PLC concept without providing a rationale in marketing terms. The theory of the diffusion and adoption of innovations provides the underlying rationale. (See Chapter 12). When a new product is launched, the company has to stimulate awareness, interest, trial, and purchase. This takes time, and in the introductory stage only a few persons ("innovators") will buy it. If the product is satisfying, larger numbers of buyers ("early adopters") are drawn in. The entry of competitors into the market speeds up the adoption process by increasing the market's awareness and by causing prices to fall. More buyers come in ("early majority") as the product is legitimized. Eventually, the growth rate decreases as the number of potential new buyers approaches zero. Sales become steady at the replacement-purchase rate. Eventually sales decline as new-product classes, forms, and brands appear and divert buyer interest from the existing product. Thus the product life cycle is explained by normal developments in the diffusion and adoption of new products.

The PLC concept provides a useful framework for formulating marketing strategies in different stages of the product life cycle. We now turn to these stages and consider the appropriate marketing strategies.

INTRODUCTION STAGE

The introduction stage starts when the new product is launched. It takes time to roll out the product in several markets and to fill the dealer pipelines, so sales growth is apt to be slow. Such well-known products as instant coffee, frozen orange juice, and powdered coffee creamers lingered for many years before they entered a stage of rapid growth. Buzzell identified several causes for the slow growth of many processed food products: delays in the expansion of production capacity; technical problems ("working out the bugs"); delays in obtaining adequate distribution through retail outlets; and customer reluctance to change established behaviors.[14] In the case of expensive new products, sales growth is retarded by additional factors, for one thing, the small number of buyers who can afford the new product.

In this stage, profits are negative or low because of the low sales and heavy distribution and promotion expenses. Much money is needed to attract distributors and "fill the pipelines." Promotional expenditures are at their highest ratio to sales "because of the need for a high level of promotional effort to (1) inform potential consumers of the new and unknown product, (2) induce trial of the product, and (3) secure distribution in retail outlets."[15]

There are only a few competitors, and they produce basic versions of the product, since the market is not ready for product refinements. The firms focus their selling on those buyers who are the readiest to buy, usually higher-income groups. Prices tend to be on the high side because "(1) costs are high due to relatively low output rates, (2) technological problems in production may have not yet been fully mastered, and (3) high margins are required to support the heavy promotional expenditures which are necessary to achieve growth."[16]

Marketing Strategies in the Introduction Stage

In launching a new product, marketing management can set a high or a low level for each marketing variable, such as price, promotion, distribution, and product quality. Considering only price and promotion, management can pursue one of the four strategies shown in Figure 13-6.

FIGURE 13-6
Four Introductory Marketing Strategies

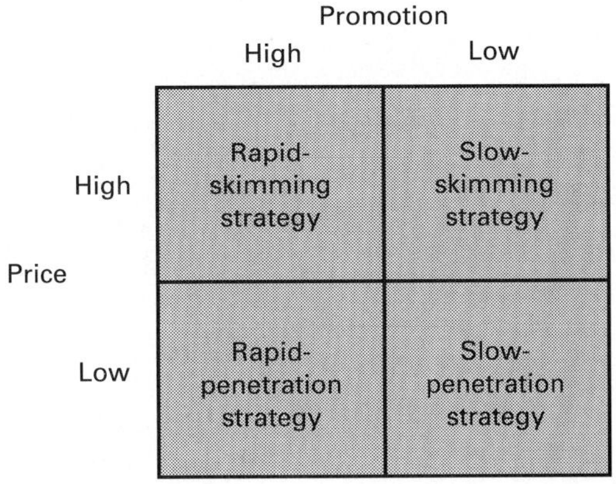

	Promotion	
	High	**Low**
Price High	Rapid-skimming strategy	Slow-skimming strategy
Price Low	Rapid-penetration strategy	Slow-penetration strategy

A *rapid-skimming strategy* consists of launching the new product at a high price and a high promotion level. The firm charges a high price in order to recover as much gross profit per unit as possible. It spends heavily on promotion to convince the market of the product's merits even at the high price level. The high promotion acts to accelerate the rate of market penetration. This strategy makes sense under the following assumptions: (1) a large part of the potential market is unaware of the product; (2) those who become aware are eager to have the product and can pay the asking price; (3) the firm faces potential competition and wants to build up brand preference.

A *slow-skimming strategy* consists of launching the new product at a high price and low promotion. The high price helps recover as much gross profit per unit as possible, and the low level of promotion keeps marketing expenses down. This combination is expected to skim a lot of profit from the market. This strategy makes sense when (1) the market is limited in size; (2) most of the market is aware of the product; (3) buyers are willing to pay a high price; and (4) potential competition is not imminent.

A *rapid-penetration* consists of launching the product at a low price and spending heavily on promotion. This strategy promises to bring about the fastest market penetration and the largest market share. This strategy makes sense when (1) the market is large; (2) the market is unaware of the product; (3) most buyers are price sensitive; (4) there is strong potential competition; and (5) the company's unit manufacturing costs fall with the scale of production and accumulated manufacturing experience.

A *slow-penetration strategy* consists of launching the new product at a low price and low level of promotion. The low price will encourage rapid product acceptance; and the company keeps its promotion costs down in order to realize more net profit. The company believes that market demand is highly price elastic but minimally promotion elastic. This strategy makes sense when (1) the market is large; (2) the market is highly aware of the product; (3) the market is price sensitive; and (4) there is some potential competition.

A company, especially the *market pioneer*, must not choose one of these launch strategies arbitrarily; rather the launch strategy should be the first step in a grand plan for life-cycle marketing. If the pioneer chooses its launch strategy to make a "killing," it will be sacrificing long-run revenue for the sake of short-run gain. Market pioneers have the best chance of retaining market leadership if they play their cards right (see Marketing Strategies 13-1). The pioneer should visualize the various product markets it could initially enter, knowing that it cannot enter all of them. Suppose market-segmentation analysis reveals the product market segments shown in Figure 13-7. The pioneer should analyze the profit potential of each product market singly and in combination and decide on a market expansion strategy. Thus the pioneer in Figure 13-7 plans to launch its initial product in product market P_1M_1, then move the product into a second market (P_1M_2), then surprise competition by developing a

FIGURE 13-7
Long-Range Product/Market
Expansion Strategy
(P_i = product *i*; M_j = market *j*)

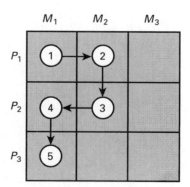

THE MARKET PIONEER "ADVANTAGE"

Firms that pioneer new markets typically develop sustainable competitive advantages. One has only to think of Campbell's, Coca-Cola, Eastman Kodak, Hallmark, and Xerox. Of course there are exceptions such as Bowmar (hand calculators); Reynolds (ballpoint pens), and Osborne (portable computers); which were quickly overtaken by later entrants.

William Robinson and Claes Fornell studied a broad range of mature consumer and industrial-goods businesses, and found that market pioneers generally enjoy a substantially higher market share than late entrants do.

Average Market Share

	Consumer Goods	Industrial Goods
Pioneer	29%	29%
Early follower	17%	21%
Late entrant	13%	15%

In the PIMS data, a business is classified as (1) one of the *pioneers* in first developing such products or services, or (2) an *early follower* of the pioneer(s) in a still-growing dynamic market, or (3) a *later entrant* into a more established market position.

Why do market pioneers gain a sustainable competitive advantage? First, pioneers tend to have higher product quality and broader product lines than late entrants. Second, they gain a brand-name advantage because being first is an effective way to secure a position in the consumer's mind. That is especially important in markets where consumers buy out of habit.

Pioneers are *not* found to have important direct cost savings. While cost savings are roughly 1 to 2 percent, the associated market-share impact is less than one share point. In these mature markets, patents and trade secrets do not benefit pioneers. Thus these sustainable competitive advantages are typically developed in the marketplace and not in the patent office.

Source: William T. Robinson and Claes Fornell, "Sources of Market Pioneer Advantages in Consumer Goods Industries," *Journal of Marketing Research*, August 1985, pp. 305-17; and Robinson and Fornell, "Market Pioneering and Sustainable Market Share Advantages," PIMSletter No. 39, Strategic Planning

second product for the second market (P_2M_2), then take the second product back into the first market (P_2M_1), and then launch a third product for the first market (P_3M_1). If this game plan works, the market-pioneer firm will own a good part of the first two market segments and serve them with two or three products. Naturally, this game plan may be altered as time passes and new factors emerge. But at least the firm has planned ahead how to evolve in this new market.

By looking ahead, the pioneer knows that competition will eventually enter and cause prices and its market share to fall. The questions are, When will this happen? and What should the pioneer do at each stage? Frey has described five stages of the competitive cycle that the pioneer has to anticipate (see Figure 13-8).[17] Initially, the pioneer is the sole supplier, with 100 percent of the production capacity and, of course, all the sales of the product. The second stage, competitive penetration, starts when a new competitor has built production capacity and begins commercial sales. Other competitors enter as well, and the leader's share of production capacity and share of sales fall.

FIGURE 13-8
Stages of the
Competitive Cycle
Source: John B. Frey,
"Pricing Over the
Competitive Cycle,"
speech presented
at the 1982
Marketing Conference,
© 1982, The Conference
Board, New York.

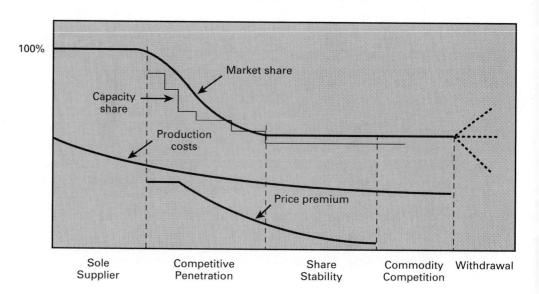

Subsequent competitors often enter the market charging a lower price than the leader's, because the buyers are uncertain about their performance. As time goes on, the perceived relative value of the leader's offer declines, forcing a decline in the leader's price premium.

Capacity tends to be overbuilt during the rapid growth stage, so that when a cyclical slow-down occurs, industry overcapacity drives down margins to more "normal" levels. New competitors decide not to enter, and existing competitors try to solidify their positions. This leads to the third stage, share stability, in which capacity shares and market shares stabilize.

This period of share stability is followed by a stage when the product has turned into a commodity, buyers no longer pay a price premium, and the suppliers earn only an average rate of return. At this point, one or more firms withdraw. The pioneer, which is still likely to own the dominant share, might decide to build share further as others leave or might give up share and gradually withdraw. As the pioneer moves through the various stages of this competitive cycle, it must continuously formulate new pricing and marketing strategies.

GROWTH STAGE

The growth stage is marked by a rapid climb in sales. The early adopters like the product, and middle-majority consumers start buying the product. New competitors enter the market, attracted by the opportunities for large-scale production and profit. They introduce new product features, and this move further expands the market. The increased number of competitors leads to an increase in the number of distribution outlets, and factory sales jump to fill the distribution pipeline.

Prices remain where they are or fall slightly insofar as demand is increasing quite rapidly. Companies maintain their promotional expenditures at the same or at a slightly increased level to meet competition and to continue to educate the market. Sales rise much faster, causing a decline in the promotion-sales ratio.

Profits increase during this stage as promotion costs are spread over a larger volume, and unit manufacturing costs fall faster than price declines owing to the "experience-curve" effect.

The rate of growth eventually changes from an accelerating rate to a decelerating rate. Firms have to watch for the onset of the decelerating rate in order to prepare new strategies.

Marketing Strategies in the Growth Stage

During this stage, the firm uses several strategies to sustain rapid market growth as long as possible:

- ☐ The firm improves product quality and adds new product features and improved styling.
- ☐ The firm adds new models and flanker products.
- ☐ It enters new market segments.
- ☐ It enters new distribution channels.
- ☐ It shifts some advertising from building product awareness to bringing about product conviction and purchase.
- ☐ It lowers prices at the right time to attract the next layer of price-sensitive buyers.

The firm that pursues these market-expanding strategies will strengthen its competitive position. But this improvement comes at additional cost. The firm in the growth stage faces a tradeoff between high market share and high current profit. By spending money on product improvement, promotion, and distribution, it can capture a dominant position. It forgoes maximum current profit in the hope of making even greater profits in the next stage.

MATURITY STAGE

At some point, a product's rate of sales growth will slow down, and the product will enter a stage of relative maturity. This stage normally lasts longer than the previous stages, and it poses formidable challenges to marketing management. *Most products are in the maturity stage of the life cycle, and therefore most of marketing management deals with the mature product.*

The maturity stage can be divided into three phases. In the first phase, *growth maturity*, the sales growth rate starts to decline. There are no new distribution channels to fill, although some laggard buyers still enter the market. In the second phase, *stable maturity*, sales flatten on a per capita basis because of market saturation. Most potential consumers have tried the product, and future sales are governed by population growth and replacement demand. In the third phase, *decaying maturity*, the absolute level of sales now starts to decline, and customers start switching to other products and substitutes.

The slowdown in the rate of sales growth creates overcapacity in the industry. This overcapacity leads to intensified competition. Competitors scramble to find and enter niches. They engage in frequent markdowns and off-list pricing. They increase their advertising and trade and consumer deals. They increase their R&D budgets to develop product improvements and flanker products. They make deals to supply private brands. These steps spell some profit erosion. A shakeout period begins, and weaker competitors withdraw. The industry eventually consists of well-entrenched competitors whose basic drive is to gain competitive advantage.

These competitors are of two types (see Figure 13-9). Dominating the industry are a few giant firms that produce a large proportion of the industry's output. These firms serve the whole market and make their profits mainly through high volume and low cost. They are somewhat differentiated in terms of reputations for low cost, high quality, high service, and

FIGURE 13-9
Companies in a Mature
Industry

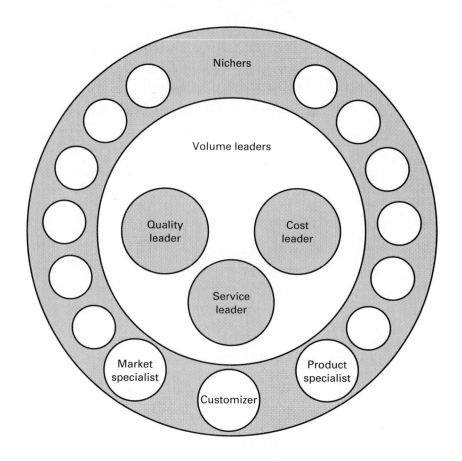

the like. Surrounding these dominant firms are a multitude of niching firms. The nichers include market specialists, product specialists, and customizing firms. The nichers serve and satisfy their small target markets very well and command a price premium. The issue facing a firm in a mature market is whether to struggle to become one of the "big three" and achieve profits through high volume and low cost or to pursue a niching strategy and achieve profits through high margin.

Marketing Strategies in the Mature Stage

In the mature stage, some companies abandon their weaker products, believing there is little they can do. They think the best thing is to conserve their money and spend it on newer products in the development pipeline. This ignores the low success rate of new products and the high potential that many old products still have. Many industries widely thought to be mature—autos, motorcycles, television, watches, cameras—were proved otherwise by the Japanese, who found ways to offer new values to customers. Seemingly moribund brands like Jell-O, Ovaltine, and Arm & Hammer baking soda have had major sales revivals several times, through the exercise of marketing imagination. Marketing managers should not ignore or passively defend aging products. A good offense is the best defense. Marketers should systematically consider strategies of market, product, and marketing-mix modification.

Market Modification　　The company might try to expand the market for its brand by working with the two factors that make up sales volume:

$$\text{Volume} = \text{number of brand users} \times \text{usage rate per user}$$

The company can try to expand the number of brand users in three ways:

- *Convert Nonusers:* The company can try to attract nonusers to the product. For example, the key to the growth of air freight service is the constant search for new users to whom air carriers can demonstrate the benefits of using air freight over ground transportation.

- *Enter New Market Segments:* The company can try to enter new market segments—geographic, demographic, and so on—that use the product but not the brand. For example, Johnson & Johnson successfully promoted its baby shampoo to adult users.

- *Win Competitors' Customers:* The company can attract competitors' customers to try or adopt the brand. For example, Pepsi-Cola is constantly coaxing Coca-Cola users to switch to Pepsi-Cola, throwing out one challenge after another.

Volume can also be increased by getting current brand users to increase their annual usage of the brand. Here there are three strategies:

- *More Frequent Use:* The company can try to get customers to use the product more frequently. For example, orange-juice marketers try to get people to drink orange juice on occasions other than breakfast time.

- *More Usage per Occasion:* The company can try to interest users in using more of the product on each occasion. Thus a shampoo manufacturer might indicate that the shampoo is more effective with two rinsings than one.

- *New and More Varied Uses:* The company can try to discover new product uses and convince people to use the product in more varied ways. Food manufacturers, for example, list several recipes on their packages to broaden the consumers' awareness of all the uses of the product.

Product Modification   Managers also try to stimulate sales by modifying the product's characteristics. This can take several forms.

A strategy of *quality improvement* aims at increasing the functional performance of the product—its durability, reliability, speed, taste. A manufacturer can often overtake its competition by launching the "new and improved" machine tool, automobile, television set, or detergent. Grocery manufacturers call this a "plus" launch and promote a new additive or advertise something as "stronger," "bigger," or "better." This strategy is effective to the extent that the quality is improved, buyers accept the claim of improved quality, and a sufficient number of buyers want higher quality.

A strategy of *feature improvement* aims at adding new features (e.g., size, weight, materials, additives, accessories) that expand the product's versatility, safety, or convenience. For example, adding electric power to hand lawn mowers increased the speed and ease of cutting grass. Lawn-mower manufacturers then worked on designing better safety features. Some manufacturers have added conversion features so that a power lawn mower doubles as a snow plow.

A strategy of feature improvement has several advantages. New features build an image of company progressiveness and leadership. They win the loyalty of certain market segments who seek these features. They can be adopted or dropped quickly and made optional to the buyer. They provide an opportunity for free publicity and they typically generate salesforce and distributor enthusiasm. The chief disadvantage is that feature improvements are highly imitable; unless there is a permanent gain from being first, the feature improvement might not pay.

A strategy of *style improvement* aims at increasing the aesthetic appeal of the product. The periodic introduction of new car models amounts to style competition rather than quality or feature competition. In the case of packaged-food and household products, companies introduce color and texture variations and often restyle the package, treating it as an extension of the product. The advantage of a style strategy is that it might confer a unique market identity and secure a loyal following. Yet style competition has some problems. First, it is difficult to predict whether people—and which people—will like a new style. Second, a style change usually requires discontinuing the old style, and the company risks losing some customers who liked the old style.

Marketing-Mix Modification   Product managers might also try to stimulate sales by modifying one or more marketing-mix elements. They should ask the following questions about the nonproduct elements of the marketing mix in searching for ways to stimulate a mature product's sales:

- *Prices:* Would a price cut attract new triers and users? If so, should the list price be lowered, or should prices be lowered through price specials, volume or early-purchase discounts, freight absorption, or easier credit terms? Or would it be better to raise the price to signal higher quality?

- *Distribution:* Can the company obtain more product support and display in the existing outlets? Can more outlets be penetrated? Can the company introduce the product into some new types of distribution channels?

- *Advertising:* Should advertising expenditures be increased? Should the advertising message or copy be changed? Should the media-vehicle mix be changed? Should the timing, frequency, or size of ads be changed?

- *Sales Promotion:* Should the company step up sales promotion—trade deals, cents-off, rebates, warranties, gifts, and contests?

- *Personal Selling:* Should the number or quality of salespeople be increased? Should the basis for salesforce specialization be changed? Should sales territories be revised? Should salesforce incentives be revised? Can sales-call planning be improved?

- *Services:* Can the company speed up delivery? Can it extend more technical assistance to customers? Can it extend more credit?

Marketers often debate which tools are more effective in the mature stage. For example, would the company gain more by increasing its advertising or sales-promotion budget? Some say that sales promotion has more impact at this stage because consumers have reached an equilibrium in their buying habits and preferences, and psychological persuasion (advertising) is not as effective as financial persuasion (sales-promotion deals). In fact, many consumer-packaged-goods companies spend over 60 percent of their total promotion budget on sales promotion to support mature products. Yet other marketers say that brands should be managed as capital assets and supported by advertising. Advertising expenditures should be treated as a capital investment, not a current expense. Brand managers, however, use sales promotion because its effects are quicker and more visible to their superiors. Unfortunately, excessive use of sales promotion rather than advertising can hurt the brand's long-run performance.

A major problem with marketing-mix modifications is that they are highly imitable by competition, especially price reductions and additional services. The firm may not gain as much as expected, and all firms might experience profit erosion as they step up their marketing attacks on each other.

Marketing Strategies 13-2 presents a framework for finding ideas for rebuilding the sales of mature products.

BREAKING THROUGH THE "MATURE-PRODUCT" SYNDROME

Managers of mature products need a systematic framework for identifying possible "breakthrough ideas. Professor John A, Weber of Notre Dame developed the following framework, which he calls "Gap Analysis," to guide the search for growth opportunities:

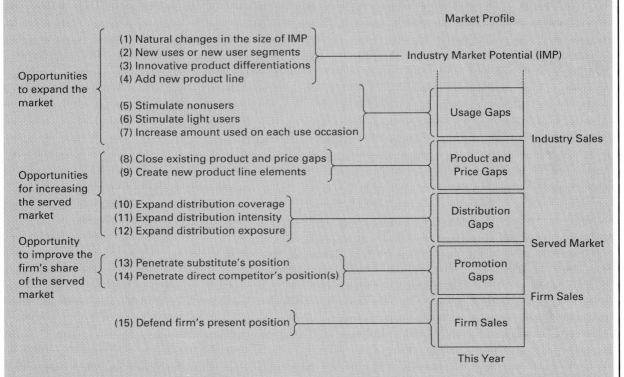

Opportunities to expand the market
(1) Natural changes in the size of IMP
(2) New uses or new user segments
(3) Innovative product differentiations
(4) Add new product line
(5) Stimulate nonusers
(6) Stimulate light users
(7) Increase amount used on each use occasion

Opportunities for increasing the served market
(8) Close existing product and price gaps
(9) Create new product line elements
(10) Expand distribution coverage
(11) Expand distribution intensity
(12) Expand distribution exposure

Opportunity to improve the firm's share of the served market
(13) Penetrate substitute's position
(14) Penetrate direct competitor's position(s)
(15) Defend firm's present position

Market Profile — Industry Market Potential (IMP) — Usage Gaps — Industry Sales — Product and Price Gaps — Distribution Gaps — Served Market — Promotion Gaps — Firm Sales — Firm Sales — This Year

The key idea is to identify possible gaps in the product line, distribution, usage, competition, and so on. Market structure analysis would prompt the following questions about a product like General Foods' Kool-Aid:

1. *Natural changes in the size of industry market potential:* Will current birthrates and demographics favor more consumption of Kool-Aid? How will the economic outlook affect Kool-Aid consumption?

2. *New uses or new user segments:* Can Kool-Aid be made to appeal to teenagers, young adult singles, young adult parents, etc?

3. *Innovative product differentiations:* Can Kool-Aid be made in different versions such as low-cal, super-sweet, etc.?

4. *Add new product lines:* Can the Kool-Aid name be used to launch a new soft-drink line?

5. *Stimulate nonusers:* Can children who have not tried Kool-Aid be convinced to try it?

6. *Stimulate light users:* Can children be reminded to drink Kool-Aid daily?

7. *Increase amount used on each use occasion:* Can more Kool-Aid be put in each package at a higher price?

8. *Close existing product and price gaps:* Should new sizes of Kool-Aid be introduced?

9. *Create new product line elements:* Should Kool-Aid create new flavors?

10. *Expand distribution coverage:* Can Kool-Aid distribution coverage be expanded to other countries?

DECLINE STAGE

The sales of most product forms and brands eventually decline. The sales decline might be slow, as in the case of oatmeal; or rapid, as in the case of the Edsel automobile. Sales may plunge to zero, or they may petrify at a low level.

Sales decline for a number of reasons, including technological advances, consumer shifts in tastes, and increased domestic and foreign competition. All lead to overcapacity, increased price cutting, and profit erosion.

As sales and profits decline, some firms withdraw from the market. Those remaining may reduce the number of product offerings. They may withdraw from smaller market segments and weaker trade channels. They may cut the promotion budget and reduce their prices further.

Unfortunately, most companies have not developed a well-thought-out policy for handling their aging products. Sentiment plays a role:

> But putting products to death—or letting them die—is a drab business, and often engenders much of the sadness of a final parting with old and tried friends. The portable, six-sided pretzel was the first product The Company ever made. Our line will no longer be our line without it.[18]

Logic also plays a role. Management believes that product sales will improve when the economy improves, or when the marketing strategy is revised, or when the product is improved. Or the weak product may be retained because of its alleged contribution to the sales of the company's other products. Or its revenue may cover out-of-pocket costs, and the company has no better use for the money.

Unless strong reasons for retention exist, carrying a weak product is very costly to the firm. The cost is not just the amount of uncovered overhead and profit. Financial accounting cannot adequately convey all the hidden costs: The weak product might consume a disproportionate amount of management's time; it often requires frequent price and inventory adjustment; it generally involves short production runs in spite of expensive setup times; it requires both advertising and salesforce attention that might be better used to make the "healthy" products more profitable; its very unfitness can cause customer misgivings and cast a shadow on the company's image. The biggest cost might well lie in the future. Failing to eliminate weak products delays the aggressive search for replacement products; the weak products create a lopsided product mix, long on "yesterday's breadwinners" and short on "tomorrow's breadwinners"; they depress current profitability and weaken the company's foothold on the future.

Marketing Strategies During the Decline Stage

A company faces a number of tasks and decisions to handle its aging products.

Identify the Weak Products   The first task is to establish a system for identifying weak products. The company appoints a product-review committee with representatives from marketing, R&D, manufacturing, and finance. This committee develops a system for identifying weak products. The controller's office supplies data for each product showing trends in market size, market share, prices, costs, and profits. This information is analyzed by a computer program that identifies dubious products. The criteria include the number of years of sales decline, market-share trends, gross-profit margin, and return on investment. The managers responsible for dubious products fill out rating forms showing where they think sales and profits will go, with and without any changes in marketing strategy. The product-review committee examines this information and makes a recommendation for each dubious product—leave it alone, modify its marketing strategy, or drop it.[19]

Determing Marketing Strategies   Some firms will abandon declining markets earlier than others. Much depends on the level of the *exit barriers*.[20] The lower the exit barriers, the easier it is for firms to leave the industry, and the more tempting it is for the remaining firms to remain and attract the customers of the withdrawing firms. The remaining firms will enjoy increased sales and profits. For example, Procter & Gamble stayed in the declining liquid-soap business and improved its profits as the others withdrew.

In a study of company strategies in declining industries, Harrigan distinguished five decline strategies available to the firm:

- [ ] Increasing the firm's investment (to dominate or strengthen its competitive position)
- [ ] Maintaining the firm's investment level until the uncertainties about the industry are resolved
- [ ] Decreasing the firm's investment level selectively, by sloughing off unprofitable customer groups, while simultaneously strengthening the firm's investment in lucrative niches
- [ ] Harvesting (or milking) the firm's investment to recover cash quickly
- [ ] Divesting the business quickly by disposing of its assets as advantageously as possible[21]

The appropriate decline strategy depends on the industry's relative attractiveness and the company's competitive strength in that industry. For example, a company in an unattractive industry but possessing competitive strength should consider shrinking selectively. However, if the company is in an attractive industry and has competitive strength, it should consider strengthening its investment. Procter & Gamble on a number of occasions has taken disappointing brands that were in strong markets and *restaged* them.

> P&G launched a "not oily" hand cream called Wondra that was packaged in an inverted bottle so the cream would flow out from the bottom. Although initial sales were high, repeat purchases were disappointing. Consumers complained that the bottom got sticky and that "not oily" suggested it wouldn't work well. P&G carried out two restagings: First, it reintroduced Wondra in an upright bottle, and later reformulated the ingredients so they would work better. Sales then picked up. ■

P&G prefers restaging to abandoning brand names. P&G spokespersons like to claim that there is no such thing as a product life cycle, and they point to Ivory, Camay, and many other "dowager" brands that are still thriving.

If the company were choosing between *harvesting* and *divesting*, its strategies would be quite different. Harvesting calls for gradually reducing a product or business's costs while trying to maintain its sales. The first costs to cut are R&D costs and plant and equipment investment. The company might also reduce product quality, salesforce size, marginal services, and advertising expenditures. It would try to cut these costs without tipping off customers, competitors, and employees that it is slowly pulling out of the business. If customers knew that, they would switch suppliers; if competitors knew it, they would tell customers; if employees knew it, they would seek new jobs elsewhere. Thus harvesting is an ethically ambivalent strategy, and it is also difficult to execute. Yet many mature products warrant this strategy. Harvesting can substantially increase the company's cash flow, provided that sales do not collapse.[22]

Harvesting eventually makes a business worthless. On the other hand, if the firm had decided instead to divest the business, it would have first looked for a buyer. It would have tried to increase the attractiveness of the business, not run it down. Therefore the company must think carefully about whether to harvest or divest the weakening business unit.

The Drop Decision　When a company decides to drop a product, it faces further decisions. If the product has strong distribution and residual goodwill, the company can probably sell it to a smaller firm.

> Jeffrey Martin, Inc., bought several "worn-out" brands from Purex Corporation, including Cuticura, Bantron, and Doan's Pills and turned them around. Two businessmen bought the *Ipana* toothpaste name and formula from Bristol-Myers; with no promotion, they sold $250 000 in the first seven months of operation. ∎

If the company can't find any buyers, it must decide whether to liquidate the brand quickly or slowly. It must also decide on how much parts inventory and service to maintain for past customers.

SUMMARY AND CRITIQUE OF THE PRODUCT LIFE-CYCLE CONCEPT

Table 13-1 summarizes the characteristics, marketing objectives, and marketing strategies of the four stages of the PLC.

Some marketers have prescribed more specific strategies during each stage of the PLC. Figure 13-10 displays life-cycle strategies for grocery-product marketing.

The PLC concept is used by marketing managers to interpret product and market dynamics. As a *planning tool*, the PLC concept characterizes the main marketing challenges in each stage and poses major alternative marketing strategies. As a *control tool*, the launched PLC concept allows the company to measure product performance against similar products launched in the past. As a *forecasting tool*, the PLC concept is less useful because sales histories exhibit diverse patterns, and the stages vary in duration.

PLC theory has its share of critics. They claim that life-cycle patterns are too variable in their shape and duration. PLCs lack what living organisms have, namely, a fixed sequence of stages and a fixed length of each stage. Critics charge that marketers can seldom tell what stage the product is in. A product may appear to be mature when actually it has only reached a temporary plateau prior to another upsurge. They charge that the PLC pattern is the result of marketing strategies rather than an inevitable course that sales must follow:

Table 13-1 Summary of Product Life-Cycle Characteristics, Objectives, and Strategies

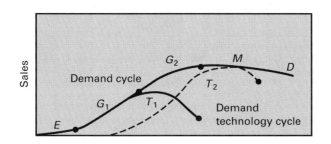
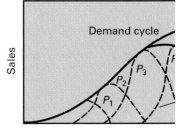

CHARACTERISTICS

Sales	Low sales	Rapidly rising sales	Peak sales	Declining sales
Costs	High cost per customer	Average cost per customer	Low cost per customer	Low cost per customer
Profits	Negative	Rising profits	High profits	Declining profits
Customers	Innovators	Early adopters	Middle majority	Laggards
Competitors	Few	Growing number	Stable number beginning to decline	Declining number

MARKETING OBJECTIVES

	Create product awareness and trial	Maximize market share	Maximize profit while defending market share	Reduce expenditure and milk the brand

STRATEGIES

Product	Offer a basic product	Offer product extensions, service, warranty	Diversify brands and models	Phase out weak items
Price	Use cost-plus	Price to penetrate market	Price to match or beat competitors	Cut price
Distribution	Build selective distribution	Build intensive distribution	Build more intensive distribution	Go selective: phase out unprofitable outlets
Advertising	Build product awareness among early adopters and dealers	Build awareness and interest in the mass market	Stress brand differences and benefits	Reduce to level needed to retain hardcore loyals

	Sales Promotion	Use heavy sales promotion to entice trial	Reduce to take advantage of heavy consumer demand	Increase to encourage brand switching	Reduce to minimal level

Sources: This table was assembled from several sources: Chester R. Wasson, *Dynamic Competitive Strategy and Product Life Cycles* (Austin, Tex; Austin Press, 1978); John A. Weber, "Planning Corporate Growth with Inverted Product Life Cycles," *Long Range Planning*, October 1976, pp. 12-29; and Peter Doyle, "The Realities of the Product Life Cycle," *Quarterly Review of Marketing*, Summer 1976, pp. 1-6.

Suppose a brand is acceptable to consumers but has a few bad years because of other factors—for instance, poor advertising, delisting by a major chain, or entry of a "me-too" competitive product backed by massive sampling. Instead of thinking in terms of corrective measures, management begins to feel that its brand has entered a declining stage. It therefore withdraws funds from the promotion budget to finance R&D on new items. The next year the brand does even worse, panic increases . . . Clearly, the PLC is a dependent variable which is determined by marketing actions; it is not an independent variable to which companies should adapt their marketing programs.[23]

In other words, if a brand's sales are declining, management should not conclude that the brand is inevitably in the decline stage. If management withdraws funds from the brand, it will create a self-fulfilling prophecy that will continue the brand's decline. Instead, management should examine all the ways it could stimulate sales: modifying the customer mix, the brand's positioning, or the marketing mix. Only when management cannot identify a promising turnaround strategy might it conclude that the brand is in the decline stage of its life cycle. Then it must decide what to do.

FIGURE 13-10
Marketing for Grocery Products

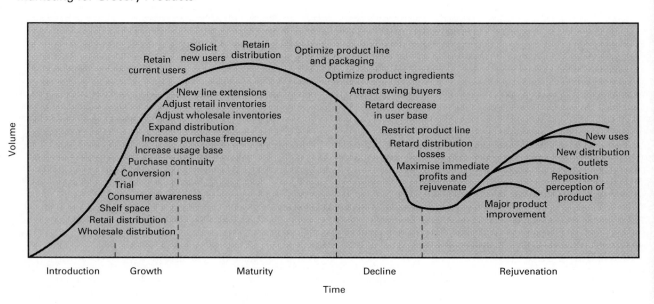

THE CONCEPT OF MARKET EVOLUTION

The PLC focuses on what is happening to a particular product or brand rather than on what is happening to the overall market. It yields a product-oriented picture rather than a market-oriented picture. The demand/technology life cycle mentioned earlier reminds us to take a broader look at the whole market. Firms need to anticipate the evolutionary path of a market as it is affected by new needs, competitors, technology, channels, and other developments.

Stages in Market Evolution

A market evolves through four stages: emergence, growth, maturity, and decline. We will describe and illustrate these stages.

Emergence Stage   Before a market materializes, it exists as a *latent market*. A latent market consists of people who share a similar need or want for something that does not yet exist. For example, people have wanted a means of more rapid calculation than can be provided by a paper and pencil. Until recently, this need was imperfectly satisfied through abacuses, slide rules, and large adding machines.

Suppose an entrepreneur recognizes this need and imagines a technological solution in the form of a small, hand-size electronic calculator. He now has to determine the product attributes, specifically *physical size* and *number of arithmetic functions*. Being market oriented, he interviews potential buyers and asks them to state their preferred levels on each attribute.

Suppose consumer preferences are represented by the dots in Figure 13-11(a). Evidently target customers vary greatly in their preferences. Some want a four-function calculator (adding, subtracting, multiplying, and dividing) and others want more functions (calculating percentages, square roots, logs, and so forth). Some want a small hand calculator and others want a large one. When buyer preferences scatter evenly in a market, it is called a *diffused-preference market*.

The entrepreneur's problem is to design an optimal product for this market.[24] He has three options:

☐ The new product can be designed to meet the preferences of one of the corners of the market (*a single-niche strategy*).

FIGURE 13-11
Market-Space Diagrams

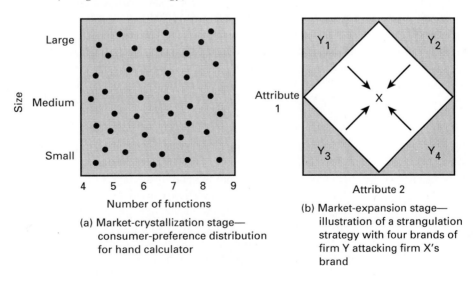

(a) Market-crystallization stage—
    consumer-preference distribution
    for hand calculator

(b) Market-expansion stage—
    illustration of a strangulation
    strategy with four brands of
    firm Y attacking firm X's
    brand

□ Two or more products can be simultaneously launched to capture two or more parts of the market (*a multiple-niche strategy*).

□ The new product can be designed for the middle of the market (*a mass-market strategy*).

For small firms, a single-niche market strategy makes the most sense. A small firm has insufficient resources for capturing and holding the mass market. Larger firms would enter and outsell the small firm. Its best bet is to develop a specialized product and capture a corner of the market that will not attract competitors for a long time.

A large firm might go after the mass market by designing a product that is "medium" in size and number of functions. A product in the center minimizes the sum of the distances of existing preferences from the actual product. A hand calculator designed for the mass market will minimize total dissatisfaction. Assume that the pioneer firm is large and designs its product for the mass market. On launching the product, the *emergence stage* begins.

Growth Stage   If sales are good, new firms will enter the market, ushering in a *market growth stage*. An interesting question is, Where will a second firm enter the market, assuming that the first firm established itself in the center? The second firm has three options:

□ It can locate its brand in one of the corners (*a single-niche strategy*).

□ It can locate its brand next to the first competitor (*a mass-market strategy*).

□ It can launch two or more products in different unoccupied corners (*a multiple-niche strategy*).

If the second firm is small, it will avoid head-on competition with the pioneer and launch its brand in one of the market corners. If the second firm is large, it might launch its brand in the center against the pioneer firm. The two firms can easily end up sharing the mass market almost equally. Or a large second firm can implement a multiniche strategy.

> Procter & Gamble will occasionally enter a market containing a large, entrenched competitor, and instead of launching a me-too product or single-segment product, it introduces a succession of products aimed at different segments. Each entry creates a loyal following and takes some business away from the major competitor. Soon the major competitor is surrounded, its revenue is weakened, and it is too late to launch new brands in outlying segments. P&G, in a moment of triumph, then launches a brand against the major segment. This is called an encirclement strategy and is illustrated in Figure 13-11(b). ∎

Maturity Stage   Each firm entering the market will go after some position, locating either next to a competitor or in some unoccupied segment. Eventually, the competitors cover and serve all the major market segments. In fact, they go further and invade each other's segments, reducing everyone's profits in the process. As the market's growth slows down, the market splits into finer segments and a condition of high market fragmentation occurs. This is illustrated in Figure 13-12(a), the letters representing different companies supplying various segments. Note that two segments are unserved because they are too small to yield a profit.[25]

This, however, is not the end of the market's evolution. Market fragmentation is often followed by market consolidation, caused by the emergence of a new attribute that has strong market appeal. Market consolidation took place in the toothpaste market when P&G introduced its new fluoride toothpaste, Crest, which effectively retarded dental decay. Suddenly toothpaste brands that claimed whitening power, cleaning power, sex appeal, taste, and mouthwash effectiveness were pushed into the corners because consumers primarily wanted a dental-protection toothpaste. P&G's Crest won a lion's share of the market, as shown by the X territory in Figure 13-12(b).

But even a consolidated market condition will not last. Other companies will copy the successful brand, and the market will eventually splinter again. Mature markets swing between market fragmentation and market consolidation. The fragmentation is brought about by competition, and the consolidation is brought about by innovation.

Decline Stage   Eventually, the market demand for the present products will begin to decline. Either the total need level declines or a new technology starts replacing the old. Thus an entrepreneur might invent a mouth-spray substitute that is superior to toothpaste. In this case, the old technology will eventually disappear and a new demand-technology life cycle will emerge.

Dynamics of Attribute Competition

Thus markets emerge and evolve through several stages. Consider the evolution of the paper-towel market. Originally, homemakers used cotton and linen dish cloths and towels in their kitchens. A paper company, looking for new markets, developed paper towels to compete with cloth towels. This development crystallized a new market. Other paper manufacturers entered and expanded the market. The number of brands proliferated and created market fragmentation. Industry overcapacity led manufacturers to search for new features. One manufacturer, hearing consumers complain that paper towels were not absorbent, introduced "absorbent" paper towels and increased its market share. This market consolidation did not last long because competitors came out with their versions of absorbent paper towels. The market became fragmented again. Then another manufacturer heard consumers express a wish for a "superstrength" paper towel and introduced one. It was soon copied by other manufacturers. This innovation-emulation cycle was repeated for "lint-free" paper towels, and for "environmentally friendly" paper towels made from recycled paper. Thus, the paper towel market evolved from one simple product to several products having various absorbencies, strengths and other features. Market evolution was driven by the forces of innovation and competition.

Competition produces a continuous round of newly discovered product attributes. If a new attribute succeeds, then several competitors soon offer it, and it loses its determinance. To the extent that most banks are now "friendly," friendliness no longer influences consumer choice of a bank. To the extent that most airlines serve in-flight meals, meals are no longer a basis for air-carrier choice. *Customer expectations are progressive.* This underlines

FIGURE 13-12
Market-Fragmentation and
Market-Reconsolidation
Stages

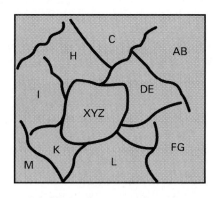

(a) Market-fragmentation stage

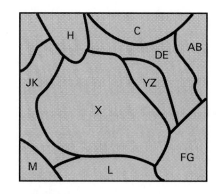

(b) Market-reconsolidation stage

the strategic importance of a company's maintaining the lead in innovating other attributes. Each new attribute, if successful, creates a competitive advantage for the firm, leading to temporarily higher-than-average market share and profits. The market leader must learn to *routinize* the innovation process.

A crucial question is, Can a firm look ahead and anticipate the succession of attributes that are likely to be high in demand and technologically feasible over time? How can the firm discover new attributes? There are four approaches.

The first approach employs an *empirical process* to identify new attributes. The company asks consumers what benefits they would like added to the product and their desired level for each. The firm also examines the cost of developing each new attribute and likely competitive responses. It chooses those attributes promising the highest incremental profit.

The second approach sees attribute search as an intuitive process. Producers base their product development on hunches rather than marketing research. The producer who chose an attribute that the market wants is considered smart, but the choice may have been mostly good luck. Unfortunately, this theory offers no guidance on how to choose winning attributes.

A third approach says that new attributes emerge through a *dialectical process*. Any valued attribute gets pushed to an extreme form through the competitive process. Thus blue jeans, starting out as an inexpensive clothing article, over time became fashionable and more expensive. This unidirectional movement, however, contains the seeds of its own destruction. Eventually some manufacturer introduces a cheaper material for pants, and consumers flock to buy it. Dialectical theory says that innovators should not march with the crowd but rather in the opposite direction toward market segments that are suffering from increasing neglect.

A fourth approach holds that new attributes emerge through a *needs-hierarchy* process (see Maslow's theory in Chapter 6). Based on this theory, we would predict that the first automobiles would provide basic transportation and be designed for safety. At a later time, automobiles would start appealing to social acceptance and status needs. Still later, automobiles would be designed to help people "fulfill" themselves. The innovator's task is to assess when the market is ready to satisfy a higher-order need.

The actual unfolding of new attributes in a market is more complex than any simple theories would suggest. We should not underestimate the role of technological and societal processes in influencing the emergence of new attributes. For example, the strong consumer interest in compact-size television sets remained unmet until miniaturization technology was sufficiently developed. Technological forecasting attempts to predict the timing of future technological developments that will permit new-attribute offers to consumers. The societal factor also plays a major role in shaping attribute evolution. Developments such as inflation, shortages, environmentalism, consumerism, and new lifestyles create consumer disequilibrium and lead consumers to reevaluate product attributes. For example, inflation increases the desire for a smaller car, and car safety increases the desire for a heavier car. The innovator must use marketing research to gauge the demand potency of different attributes in order to determine the company's best move vis-à-vis competition.

SUMMARY

Products and markets have life cycles that call for changing marketing strategies over time. Every new need follows a demand life cycle that passes through the stages of emergence, accelerating growth, decelerating growth, maturity, and decline. Each new technology that emerges to satisfy that need exhibits a demand-technology life cycle. Particular product forms of a given technology also show a life cycle, as do brands within that product form.

The sales history of many products follow an S-shaped curve consisting of four stages. The *introduction* stage is marked by slow growth and minimal profits as the product is pushed into distribution. During this stage, the company has to decide between strategies of rapid skimming, slow skimming, rapid penetration, or slow penetration. If successful, the product enters a *growth* stage marked by rapid sales growth and increasing profits. The company attempts to improve the product, enter new market segments and distribution channels, and reduce its prices slightly. There follows a *maturity* stage in which sales growth slows down and profits stabilize. The company seeks innovative strategies to renew sales growth, including market, product, and marketing-mix modification. Finally, the product enters a *decline* stage in which little can be done to halt the deterioration of sales and profits. The company's task is to identify the truly weak product; develop for each one a strategy of continuation, focusing, or milking; and finally phase out weak products in a way that minimizes the hardship to company profits, employees, and customers.

Not all products pass through an S-shaped PLC. Some products show a growth-slump-maturity pattern, others a cycle-recycle shape, and still others a scalloped shape. Researchers have discovered over a dozen PLC shapes, including those describing styles, fashions, and fads. PLC theory has been criticized on the grounds that companies cannot predict the shapes in advance, or know what stage they are in within a given shape, or predict the duration of the stages. Also, PLCs are the result of chosen marketing strategies rather than of an inevitable sales history that is independent of the chosen marketing strategies.

Product life-cycle theory must be broadened by a theory of market evolution. The theory of market evolution holds that new markets *emerge* when a product is created to satisfy an unmet need. The innovator usually designs a product for the mass market. Competitors enter the market with similar products leading to *market growth*. Growth eventually slows down and the market enters *maturity*. The market undergoes increasing *fragmentation* until some firm introduces a powerful new attribute that *consolidates* the market into fewer and larger segments. This stage does not last, because competitors copy the new attributes. There is a cycling back and forth between market consolidation based on innovation and fragmentation based on competition. The market for the present technology will ultimately *decline* upon the discovery of super technologies.

Companies must try to anticipate new attributes that the market wants. Profits go to those who introduce new and valued benefits early. The search for new attributes can be based on empirical work, intuition, dialectical reasoning, or needs-hierarchy reasoning. Successful marketing comes through creatively visualizing the market's evolutionary potential.

■ QUESTIONS

1. Discuss the demand/technology life cycle for home entertainment.

2. Conduct a "gap-analysis" (see Marketing Strategies 13-2) for Ocean Spray Cranberry Juice.

3. Select a personal-care product that you believe is in the maturity stage of its product life cycle (PLC). Discuss the competitive strategies used by the brands in this product category. Have all the strategies been equally effective? Why or why not?

4. Packaging strategies were not included in Table 13-1 as one of the marketing areas where changes would be made over the course of a PLC. Would you expect changes in packaging to coincide with PLC stages? If so, what would they be? If not, why not?

5. If the denim jean market is in the mature stage of its PLC, what might Levi Strauss do to achieve corporate growth objective?

6. What should be the focus for marketing research studies at each stage of the PLC?

7. Develop a long-range marketing plan for a new line of

electric can openers, indicating for each stage in the product life cycle the major objective and the likely policy on price, quality, advertising, personal selling, and channels.

8. As a product passes through the successive stages of its product life cycle, both its rate of sales growth and its rate of return on investment change. Using these two variables as axes, develop a diagram showing the typical trajectory of these variables over the product life cycle.

9. Discuss the changes in the promotion level and mix in the different stages of the product life cycle.

10. Select an actual fad and a fashion product and plot their respective product life-cycle patterns on one graph. How do they differ from each other?

11. What is the difference between a product life-cycle analysis of the product class "paper towels" and the market-evolution analysis of them found in the chapter?

■ NOTES

1. This discussion of demand/technology cycles is drawn from H. Igor Ansoff, *Implanting Strategic Management* (Englewood Cliffs, N.J.: Prentice-Hall, 1984), pp. 37-44.

2. *Ibid.*, p. 38.

3. Some authors distinguish additional stages. Wasson suggested a stage of competitive turbulence between growth and maturity. See Chester R. Wasson, *Dynamic Competitive Strategy and Product Life Cycles* (Austin, Texas: Austin Press, 1978). *Maturity* describes a stage of sales growth slowdown and *saturation* a stage of flat sales after sales have peaked.

4. Rolando Polli and Victor Cook, "Validity of the Product Life Cycle," *Journal of Business*, October 1969, pp. 385-400.

5. Robert D. Buzzell, "Competitive Behavior and Product Life Cycles," in *New Ideas for Successful Marketing*, ed. John S. Wright and Jac L. Goldstucker (Chicago: American Marketing Association, 1966), pp. 46-68; and Polli and Book, "Product Life Cycle."

6. For some prescriptions, see Richard G. Hamermesh and Steven B. Silk, "How to Compete in Stagnant Industries," *Harvard Business Review*, September-October 1979, pp. 161-68.

7. *Nielsen Researcher*, no. 1 (Chicago: A. G. Nielsen Co., 1968).

8. See William E. Cox, Jr., "Product Life Cycles as Marketing Models," *Journal of Business*, October 1967, pp. 375-84; John E. Swan and David R. Rink, "Fitting Market Strategy to Varying Product Life Cycles," *Business Horizons*, January-February 1982, pp. 72-76; and Gerald J. Tellis and C. Merle Crawford, "An Evolutionary Approach to Product Growth Theory," *Journal of Marketing*, Fall 1981, pp. 125-34.

9. Jordan P. Yale, "The Strategy of Nylon's Growth," *Modern Textiles Magazine*, February 1964, pp. 32 ff. Also see Theodore Levitt, "Exploit the Product Life Cycle," *Harvard Business Review*, November-December 1965, pp. 81-94.

10. Chester R. Wasson, "How Predictable Are Fashion and Other Product Life Cycles?" *Journal of Marketing*, July 1968, pp. 36-43.

11. William H. Reynolds, "Cars and Clothing: Understanding Fashion Trends," *Journal of Marketing*, July 1968, pp. 44-49.

12. Dwight E. Robinson, "Style Changes: Cyclical, Inexorable and Foreseeable," *Harvard Business Review*, November-December 1975, pp. 121-31.

13. George B. Sproles, "Analyzing Fashion Life Cycles—Principles and Perspectives," *Journal of Marketing*, Fall 1981, pp. 116-24.

14. Buzzell, "Competitive Behavior," p. 51.

15. *Ibid.*

16. *Ibid.*, p. 52.

17. John B. Frey, "Pricing over the Competitive Cycle," speech presented at the 1982 Marketing Conference, Conference Board, New York.

18. R. S. Alexander, "The Death and Burial of 'Sick Products'," *Journal of Marketing*, April 1964, p. 1.

19. See Philip Kotler, "Phasing Out Weak Products," *Harvard Business Review*, March-April 1965, pp. 107-18; Paul W. Hamelman and Edward M. Mazze, "Improving Product Abandonment Decisions," *Journal of Marketing*, April 1972, pp. 20-26; and Richard T. Hise, A. Parasuraman, and R. Viswanathan, "Product Elimination: The Neglected Management Responsibility," *Journal of Business Strategy*, Spring 1984, pp. 56-63.

20. See Kathryn Rudie Harrigan, "The Effect of Exit Barriers upon Strategic Flexibility," *Strategic Management Journal*, 1 (1980), pp. 165-76.

21. Kathryn Rudie Harrigan, "Strategies for Declining Industries," *Journal of Business Strategy*, Fall 1980, p. 27.

22. See Philip Kotler, "Harvesting Strategies for Weak Products," *Business Horizons*, August 1978, pp. 15-22; and Laurence P. Feldman and Albert L. Page, "Harvesting: The Misunderstood Market Exit Strategy," *Journal of Business Strategy*, Spring 1985, pp. 79-85.

23. Nariman K. Dhalla and Sonia Yuspeh, "Forget the Product Life Cycle Concept" *Harvard Business Review*, January-February 1976, pp. 102-12, here p. 105.

24. This problem is trivial if consumers' preferences are concentrated at one point. If there are distinct clusters of preference, the entrepreneur can design a product for the largest cluster or for the cluster that the company can serve best.

25. The product space is drawn with two attributes for simplicity. Actually, more attributes come into being as the market evolves. The product space grows from a two-dimensional to an *n*-dimensional space.

14

Designing Marketing Strategies for Market Leaders, Challengers, Followers, and Nichers

The biggest things are always the easiest to do because there is no competition.

Sir William Van Horne

We will now examine, in this and the next two chapters, the problem of designing winning marketing strategies that take into account competitors' strategies, changing stages of the product life cycle, and global opportunities and challenges.

Competitors in a particular target market will differ in their objectives and resources, and hence in their strategies. Some firms will be large, others small. Some will have great resources, others will be strapped for funds. Some will go for leadership, others for followership. In general, firms will occupy different competitive positions in the target market.

The Arthur D. Little management consulting firm sees firms as occupying one of six competitive positions in their industry:[1]

- □ *Dominant:* This firm controls the behavior of other competitors and has a wide choice of strategic options.

- □ *Strong:* This firm can take independent action without endangering its long-term position and can maintain its long-term position regardless of competitors' actions.

- □ *Favorable:* This firm has a strength that is exploitable in particular strategies and has more than average opportunity to improve its position.

- □ *Tenable:* This firm is performing at a sufficiently satisfactory level to warrant continuing in business, but it exists at the sufferance of the dominant company and has a less-than-average opportunity to improve its position.

- □ *Weak:* This firm has unsatisfactory performance but an opportunity exists for improvement and it must change or else exit.

- □ *Nonviable:* This firm has unsatisfactory performance and no opportunity for improvement.

FIGURE 14-1
Hypothetical Market Structure

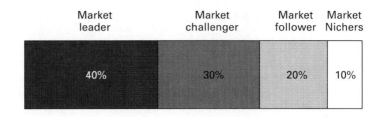

Market leader	Market challenger	Market follower	Market Nichers
40%	30%	20%	10%

Every firm or business unit can recognize itself in one of these competitive positions. The business unit's competitive position, along with its stage in the product life cycle, will help it decide whether to invest, maintain, harvest, or exit from the industry.

We will develop a different classification of competitive positions in this chapter. Much can be gained by classifying firms by the role they play in the target market, that of leading, challenging, following, or niching. Suppose a market is occupied by the firms shown in Figure 14-1. Forty percent of the market is in the hands of a *market leader*, the firm with the largest market share. Another 30 percent is in the hands of a *market challenger*, a runner-up firm that is fighting hard for an increased market share. Another 20 percent is in the hands of a *market follower*, another runner-up firm that is willing to maintain its market share and not rock the boat. The remaining 10 percent is in the hands of *market nichers*, firms that serve small market segments not being served by larger firms.

We will argue on the following pages that different marketing challenges and strategies face market leaders, challengers, followers, and nichers.

MARKET-LEADER STRATEGIES

Most industries contain one firm that is the acknowledged market leader. This firm has the largest market share in the relevant product market. It usually leads the other firms in price changes, new-product introductions, distribution coverage, and promotional intensity. The leader may or may not be admired or respected, but other firms acknowledge its dominance. The leader is an orientation point for competitors, a company to either challenge, imitate, or avoid. Some of the best-known market leaders are General Motors (autos), Kodak (photography), IBM (computers), Xerox (copying), Procter & Gamble (consumer packaged goods), Caterpillar (earth-moving equipment), Coca-Cola (soft drinks), Sears (retailing), McDonald's (fast food), Gillette (razor blades), and Canadian Pacific (transportation).

Unless a dominant firm enjoys a legal monopoly, its life is not altogether easy. It must maintain a constant vigilance. Other firms keep challenging its strengths or trying to take advantage of its weaknesses. The market leader can easily miss a turn in the road and plunge into second or third place. A product innovation may come along and hurt the leader (e.g., Tylenol's nonaspirin painkiller taking over the lead from Bayer Aspirin). The leader might spend conservatively, while a challenger spends liberally (Stelco stayed with existing products while Dofasco invested in new steel-making technology). The leader might look old-fashioned against new and peppier rivals (as Mother's Pizza was overtaken by Domino's).

Dominant firms want to remain number one. This calls for action on three fronts. First, the firm must find ways to expand total market demand. Second, the firm must protect its current market share through good defensive and offensive actions. Third, the firm can try to increase its market share further, even if market size remains constant.

Expanding the Total Market

The dominant firm normally gains the most when the total market expands. If people increase their picture taking, Kodak stands to gain the most because it sells over 70 percent of the country's film. If Kodak can convince more people to buy cameras and take pictures, or to take pictures on other occasions besides holidays, or to take more pictures on each occasion, Kodak will benefit considerably. In general, the market leader should look for *new users, new uses*, and *more usage* of its products.

New Users   Every product class has the potential of attracting buyers who are unaware of the product or who are resisting it because of its price or lack of certain features. A manufacturer can search for new users among three groups. For example, a perfume manufacturer can try to convince women who do not use perfume to use perfume (*market-penetration strategy*), or convince men to start using perfume (*new-market strategy*), or sell perfume in other countries (*geographical-expansion strategy*).

One of the great success stories in developing a new class of users is that of Johnson & Johnson's baby shampoo, the leading brand of baby shampoo. As we mentioned earlier, the company became concerned about future sales growth when the birthrate slowed down. Their marketers noticed that other family members occasionally used the baby shampoo for their own hair. Management decided to develop an advertising campaign aimed at adults. In a short time, Johnson & Johnson baby shampoo became the leading brand in the total shampoo market.

New Uses   Markets can be expanded through discovering and promoting new uses for the product. For example, the average person eats dry breakfast cereal three mornings a week. Cereal manufacturers would gain if they could promote cereal eating on other occasions during the day. Thus some cereals are promoted as snacks to increase their use frequency.

Du Pont's nylon provides a classic story of new-use expansion. Every time nylon became a mature product, Du Pont discovered a new use. Nylon was first used in parachutes; then as a fiber for women's stockings; later, a major material in women's blouses and men's shirts; still later, it entered automobile tires, seat upholstery, and carpeting.[2] Each new use started the product on a new life cycle. Credit goes to Du Pont's continuous R&D program to find new uses.

In even more cases, customers deserve credit for discovering new uses. Vaseline petroleum jelly started out as a lubricant in machine shops, and over the years, users have reported many new uses for the product, including use as a skin ointment, a healing agent, and a hair dressing.

Arm & Hammer, the baking-soda manufacturer, had a product whose sales had been on a downward slide for 125 years! Baking soda had a number of uses, but no single use was advertised. Then the company discovered some consumers who used it as a refrigerator deodorant. It launched a heavy advertising and publicity campaign focusing on this single use and succeeded in getting half of the homes in America to place an open box of baking soda in their refrigerator. A few years later, Arm & Hammer discovered consumers who used it to quell kitchen grease fires, and it promoted this use with great results.

The company's task is to monitor customers' uses of the product. This applies to industrial products as well as consumer products. Von Hippel's studies show that most new industrial products were originally suggested by customers rather than by company R&D laboratories.[3] This highlights the importance of systematically collecting customer needs and suggestions to guide new-product development.

More Usage   A third market-expansion strategy is to convince people to *use more of the product per use occasion*. If a cereal manufacturer convinces consumers to eat a full bowl of cereal instead of half a bowl, total sales will increase. Procter & Gamble advises users that its Head & Shoulders shampoo is more effective with two applications instead of one per shampoo.

A creative example of a company that stimulated higher usage per occasion is the Michelin, the French tire company. Michelin wanted French car owners to drive their cars more kilometres per year—thus leading to more tire replacement. It conceived the idea of rating French restaurants on a three-star system. They reported that many of the best restaurants were in the South of France, leading many Parisians to consider weekend drives to Provence and the Riviera. Michelin also published guidebooks with maps and sights along the way to further entice travel.

Defending Market Share

While trying to expand total market size, the dominant firm must continuously defend its current business against rival attacks. The leader is like a large elephant being attacked by a swarm of bees. The largest and nastiest bee keeps buzzing around the leader. Coca-Cola must constantly guard against Pepsi-Cola; Gillette against Bic; Kodak against Fuji; Hertz against Avis; McDonald's against Burger King; General Motors against Ford.

What can the market leader do to defend its terrain? Twenty centuries ago, Sun Tsu told his warriors: "One does not rely on the enemy not attacking, but relies on the fact that he himself is unassailable." The most constructive response is *continuous innovation*. The leader refuses to be content with the way things are and leads the industry in developing new-product ideas, customer services, distribution effectiveness, and cost cutting. It keeps increasing its competitive effectiveness and value to customers. The leader applies the military principle of the offensive: The commander exercises initiative, sets the pace, and exploits enemy weaknesses. The best defense is a good offense.

The dominant firm, even when it does not launch offensives, must guard all fronts and not leave any exposed flanks. It must keep its costs down, and its prices must be consonant with the value the customers see in the brand. The leader must "plug holes" so that attackers do not jump in. Thus a consumer-packaged-goods leader will produce its brands in several sizes and forms to meet varying consumer preferences and hold on to as much scarce dealer shelf space as possible. IBM decided to produce personal computers partly in order to block others from getting entrenched and stronger.

The cost of "plugging holes" can be high. But the cost of abandoning a losing product/market segment can be higher. General Motors did not want to lose money by making small cars; but it is losing more now because it allowed Japanese car makers to get established in its domestic market. Kodak abandoned the 35mm camera market because its 35mm camera was losing money, but the Japanese figured out a way to make these cameras easy to operate, and they are now replacing cheaper Kodak cameras at a fast rate. Xerox didn't want to lose money on making small copier machines but now has lost more as a result of the Japanese entry into the domestic copier market.

The real answer is that the market leader must consider carefully which terrains are important to defend even at a loss and which can be given up with little risk. The leader cannot defend all of its positions in the market; it must concentrate its resources where they count. The aim of defensive strategy is to reduce the probability of attack, divert attacks to less threatening areas, and lessen their intensity. Any attack is likely to hurt profits. But the defender's form and speed of response can make an important difference in the profit consequences. Researchers are currently exploring the most appropriate forms of response to price and other attacks (see Marketing Strategies 14-1 for an interesting model called Defender).

The intensified competition that has taken place worldwide in recent years has sparked management's interest in models of military warfare, particularly as described in the writings of Sun Tsu, Mushashi, von Clausewitz, and Liddell-Hart.[4] Leader companies, like leader nations, have been advised to protect their interests with such strategies as "brinkmanship," "massive

---

Marketing Strategies 14-1

DEFENSIVE STRATEGIES ACCORDING TO THE DEFENDER MODEL

Professors Hauser, Shugan, and Gaskin have built and tested a model called Defender. The model makes the following assumptions:

1. Consumers share the same product perceptions. (Thus all consumers see Tylenol as high in gentleness per dollar and low in effectiveness per dollar, Excedrin as high in effectiveness but low in gentleness, and so on.)

2. Consumers differ in their preferences for various product characteristics. (Thus some consumers value gentleness more than effectiveness, others show the reverse preference.)

3. Consumers vary in the number of brands they know and will consider.

4. Consumers' choices are affected by product features, price, distribution, advertising and promotion. (Each marketing tool's effect on sales response is plausibly represented.)

The Defender model can be illustrated with the history of *Datril's* price attack on the market leader, *Tylenol*. Tylenol had gained a large market share based on its perceived gentleness (no stomach upsets) and was achieving outstanding profits. Along came Bristol-Myers, which introduced the same product, Datril, and advertised is as "just as good as Tylenol, only cheaper." If consumers believed this, Datril would make deep inroads into Tylenol's market share. How should Tylenol defend itself?

The researchers examined the possible defensive measures available to Tylenol, using the Defender model, and came to the following conclusions:

1. The defender should lower its prices, especially if the market is unsegmented. If the market is segmented, the price might be raised in some of the less vulnerable segments. (The best pricing strategy is independent of what should be done with distribution and advertising; once chosen, however, the pricing strategy will affect distribution and advertising.)

2. The defender should reduce its expenditures on distribution; specifically, it should drop marginal retailers who no longer are profitable to serve.

3. The defender should improve its strong product features even more rather than try to improve along the lines of the attacker's strong product features.

4. The defender should spend less on awareness-building advertising and direct more on repositioning-building advertising.

These conclusions are subject to further qualifications given the restrictive assumptions on which the model was based. For example, price and positioning are interrelated strategically. In some cases, price cuts encourage price wars. To avoid such destructive competition, it is often best to differentiate products in order to compete on product benefits, not price.

What did Tylenol actually do to defend itself from Datril's attack? Tylenol quickly cut its price to match Datril's, and later added the Extra Strength Tylenol brand to capture consumers' interest in effectiveness. Through these steps, Tylenol preserved its position as market leader and prevented Datril from making much of an inroad.

Source: John R. Hauser and Steve M. Shugan, "Defensive Marketing Strategy," *Marketing Science*, Fall 1983, pp. 319-60; John R. Hauser and S. P. Gaskin, "Application of the 'DEFENDER' Consumer Model," *Marketing Science*, Fall 1984, pp. 327-51.

---

retaliation," "limited warfare," "graduated response," "diplomacy of violence," and "threat systems." There are, in fact, six military defense strategies that a dominant firm can use. They are illustrated in Figure 14-2 and described below.[5]

Position Defense   The most basic idea of defense is to build an impregnable fortification around one's territory. The French built the famous Maginot line in peacetime to protect its territory against possible future German invasion. But this fortification, like all static defense maneuvers, failed. Simply defending one's current position or products is a form of *marketing myopia*. Henry Ford's myopia about his Model-T brought an enviably healthy company with $1 billion in cash reserves at its zenith to the brink of financial ruin. Even such death-defying brands as Coca-Cola and Bayer aspirin cannot be relied on by their companies as the main sources of future growth and profitability. Coca-Cola today, in spite of producing nearly half the soft drinks of the world, has aggressively moved into the wine market, has acquired fruit-drink companies, and has diversified into desalinization equipment and plastics. Clearly, leaders under attack would be foolish to put all their resources into building fortifications around their current product.

Flanking Defense   The market leader should not only guard its territory but also erect some flanks or outposts to serve as a defensive corner to protect a weak front or possibly as an invasion base for counterattacking if necessary. Here is a good example of a flanking defense:

> The defensive stance taken by Loblaws, Canada's largest food distributor, is instructive. The company believes that the supermarket will continue to remain a dominant force but is flanking

FIGURE 14-2
Defense Strategies

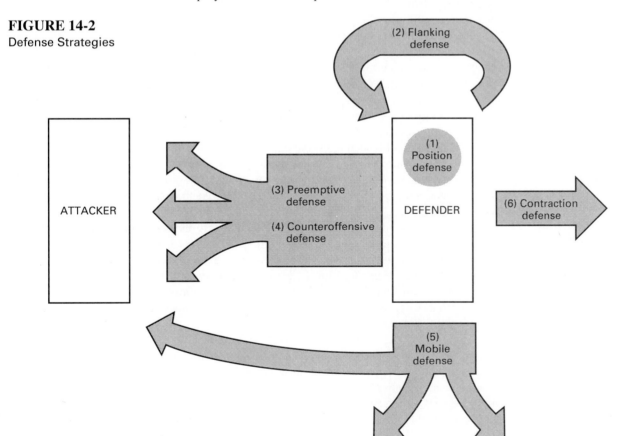

its position by strengthening its food-retailing-assortment mix to meet new challenges. The fast-food boom has been met by offering a wide assortment of instant and frozen meals, and the discount-food challenge by promoting the No-Name line of generic products. Additional defense against the food discounters is provided by the company's No-Frills "box" stores. But Loblaws has also positioned itself to appeal to upscale shoppers. In-store Ziggy's delicatessens provide "Fantastic Foods" in some stores. Premium merchandise has been available since 1985 under the President's Choice private label. Finally, Loblaws also enjoys a strong position with regard to costs and sources of supply. As part of the George Weston food conglomerate, Loblaws can gain access to bakeries, biscuit factories, and other food processors. The recent addition of dozens of "super-combination" stores promises lower costs from economies of scale, as well as the opportunity to participate in higher-margin non-food sales. ∎

The flanking position is of little value if it is so lightly defended that an attacker could control it with a small force while its main formations march forward. This was precisely General Motors's and Ford's mistake when they half-heartedly designed the Vega and Pinto compacts some years ago to ward off the small-car attacks launched by the Japanese and European car makers. The domestic compacts were poorly made, and they failed to retard the sale of the foreign compact cars. A careful assessment of any potential threat must be made, and if warranted, a relatively serious commitment should be made to flanking the threat.

Preemptive Defense   A more aggressive defense maneuver is to launch an attack on the enemy *before* it starts its offense against the company. Preemptive defense assumes that an ounce of prevention is worth more than a pound of cure. When Chrysler's market share began rising from 12 to 18 percent some years ago, one rival marketing executive was overheard to say, "If they [Chrysler] go to 20 percent, it will be over our dead bodies."

Or a company could wage guerrilla action across the market—hitting one competitor here, another there—and keep everyone off balance. Or the preemptive defense could assume the proportions of a grand market envelopment, as practiced by Seiko with its twenty-three hundred watch models distributed worldwide. Or it could resemble the sustained price attack that Texas Instruments practiced. Sustained, high-pressure strategies aim at retaining the initiative at all times and keeping the competition always on the defensive.

Sometimes the preemptive strike is waged psychologically rather than actually implemented. The market leader sends out *market signals* to dissuade competitors from attacking.[6] A major pharmaceutical firm is the leader in a certain drug category. Every time it learns that a competitor might build a factory to produce that drug, the company leaks the news that it is considering cutting the drug price and building another plant. This intimidates the competitor, who decides against entering that product arena. Meanwhile the leader never gets to cutting its price or adding another plant. Of course, this bluff can work only a few times.

Companies fortunate enough to enjoy strong market assets have the capacity to weather some punishment and may even entice the opponents into costly attacks that will not pay off in the long run. Heinz let Hunt's carry out its massive attack in the ketchup market without much counteroffensive; and in the end, this strategy proved very costly to Hunt's.[7] Not reacting to a strong attack, however, calls for great confidence in the ultimate superiority of the company's market offer.

Counteroffensive Defense   When a market leader is attacked in spite of its flanking and even preemptive maneuvers, it must respond with a counterattack on the opponent. The leader cannot remain passive in the face of a competitor's price cut, promotion blitz, product improvement, or sales-territory invasion. The leader has the strategic choice of meeting the attacker frontally, or maneuvering against the attacker's flank, or launching a pincer movement to cut off the attacking formations from their base of operation.

Clearasil, the market leader in the acne medications market, suddenly found itself under a powerful promotional attack by Oxy-5. Clearasil retaliated with a stepped-up counterpromotion of its own. ∎

Sometimes market-share erosion is so rapid that a head-on counterattack is necessary. But a defender enjoying some strategic depth can often weather the initial attack and riposte effectively at the opportune moment. In many situations, it may be worth some minor setbacks to allow the offensive to develop fully (and be understood) before counterattacking. This may seem a dangerous strategy of "wait and see," but there are sound reasons for not barreling into a counteroffensive.

A better retort to an offensive is for the defender to pause and identify a chink in the attacker's armor, namely, a segment gap in which a viable counteroffensive can be launched. Cadillac designed its Seville as an alternative to the Mercedes and pinned its hope on offering a smoother ride and more creature comforts than Mercedes was willing to design.

Mobile Defense   Mobile defense involves more than the leader aggressively defending its territory. In mobile defense, the leader stretches its domain over new territories that can serve as future centers for defense and offense. It spreads to these new territories not so much through normal brand proliferation as through innovation activity on two fronts, namely, market broadening and market diversification. These moves generate strategic depth for the firm, enabling it to weather continual attacks and launch retaliatory strikes.

Market broadening calls upon a company to shift its focus from the current product to the underlying generic need and get involved in R&D across the whole range of technology associated with that need. Thus "petroleum" companies sought to recast themselves into "energy" companies. Implicitly, this demands that they dip their research fingers into the oil, coal, nuclear, hydroelectric, and chemical industries. But this market-broadening strategy should not be carried too far or it would fail two fundamental military principles—the *principle of the objective* (pursue a clearly defined and attainable objective) and the *principle of mass* (concentrate your efforts at a point of the enemy's weakness). The objective of being in the energy business is too broad. The energy business is not a single need but a whole range of needs (heating, lighting, propelling, and so on). That leaves very little in the world that is not potentially the energy business. Furthermore, too much broadening would dilute the company's mass in the competitive theater today, and survival today surely must take precedence over the grand battles imagined for some tomorrow. The error of *marketing myopia* would be replaced by *marketing hyperopia*, a condition where vision is better for distant than for near objects.

Reasonable broadening, however, makes sense. Armstrong Cork exemplified a successful market-broadening strategy by redefining its domain from "floor covering" to "decorative room covering" (including walls and ceilings). By recognizing the customer's need to create a pleasant interior through various covering materials, Armstrong Cork expanded into neighboring businesses that were synergistically balanced for growth and defense.

Market diversification into unrelated industries is the other alternative to generating "strategic depth." Imperial Tobacco produces half of the cigarettes sold in Canada, and further strengthening of its position in the tobacco industry is hampered by government constraints. So its parent firm Imasco has been diversifying by buying the 440-store Shoppers Drug Mart and the 598-store Peoples Drug Stores. Imasco already owns 2000 Hardee's fast-food restaurants, and made an unsuccessful bid to buy Canadian Tire.

Contraction Defense   Large companies sometimes recognize that they can no longer defend all of their territory. Their forces are spread too thin, and competitors are nibbling away on several fronts. The best course of action then appears to be planned contraction (also called strategic withdrawal). Planned contraction is not market abandonment but rather giving up the weaker territories and reassigning forces to stronger territories. Planned contraction is a move to consolidate one's competitive strength in the market and concentrate mass at pivotal positions. General Motors standardized its auto engines and now offers fewer options. Westinghouse left the home appliance business to concentrate on its various industrial markets. Campbell's Soup, Heinz, General Mills, and Del Monte are only a few of the packaged-goods companies that have pruned their product lines in recent years.

Expanding Market Share

Market leaders can also try to improve their profitability through increasing their market share further. In many markets, one share point is worth tens of millions of dollars. No wonder normal competition has turned into marketing warfare.

Some years ago, the Strategic Planning Institute launched a study called *Profit Impact of Market Strategy (PIMS)*, which sought to identify the most important variables affecting profits. It gathered data from hundreds of business units in a variety of industries and identified the most important variables associated with profitability. The key variables included market share, product quality, and a few others.

They found that a company's *profitability* (measured by pretax ROI) rises with its *relative market share* of its served market,[8] as shown in Figure 14-3(a).[9] According to a PIMS report, "The average ROI for business with under 10 percent market share was about 9 percent. . . . On the average, a difference of ten percentage points in market share is accompanied by a difference of about five points in pretax ROI." The PIMS study shows that businesses with market shares above 40 percent earn an average ROI of 30 percent, or three times that of those with shares under 10 percent.[10]

These findings have led many companies to adopt market-share expansion as their objective, assuming that would produce not only more *profit dollars* but also more *profitability* (return on investment). General Electric, for example, has decided that it wants to be at least number one or two in each of its markets or else get out. GE divested its computer business and its air-conditioning business because it could not achieve top-dog position in these industries. Cynics have concluded that GE does not really want to stay in markets where it has to compete!

Various critics have attacked the PIMS study as either weak or spurious. Hammermesh reported finding numerous successful low-share businesses.[11] Woo and Cooper identified forty low-share businesses that enjoyed pretax ROIs of 20 percent or more; they were characterized as having high relative product quality, medium-to-low prices relative to high-quality, narrow product lines, and low total costs.[12] Most of these companies produced industrial components or supplies and seldom changed their products.

Some industry studies have yielded a V-shaped relationship between market share and profitability. Figure 14-3(b) shows a V-curve for agricultural-equipment firms. The industry leader, Deere & Company, earns a high return. However, Hesston and Sperry-New Holland, small specialty firms, also earn high returns. J. I. Case and Massey-Ferguson are trapped in the valley, and International Harvester commands substantial market share but earns lower returns. Thus such industries have one or a few highly profitable large firms, several profitable small and more-focused firms, and several medium-sized firms with poorer profit performance. According to Roach:

> The large firms on the V-curve tend to address the entire market, achieving cost advantages and high market share by realizing economies of scale. The small competitors reap high profits by

FIGURE 14-3

Relationship between Market Share and Profitability

Source: Strategic Planning Institute, (The PIMS Program), 955 Massachusetts Avenue, Cambridge, Mass. 02139.

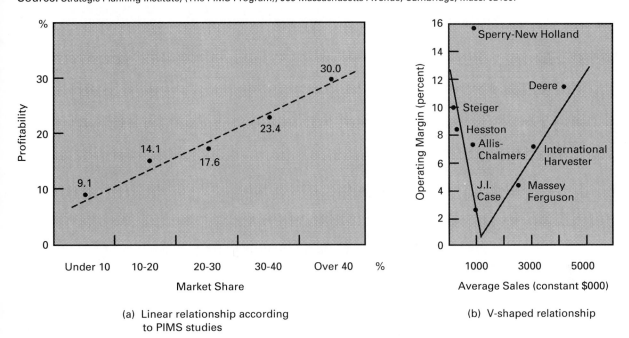

(a) Linear relationship according to PIMS studies

(b) V-shaped relationship

focusing on some narrower segment of the business and by developing specialized approaches to production, marketing, and distribution for that segment. Ironically, the medium-sized competitors at the trough of the V-curve are unable to realize any competitive advantage and often show the poorest profit performance. Trapped in a strategic "No Man's Land," they are too large to reap the benefits of more focused competition, yet too small to benefit from the economies of scale that their larger competitors enjoy.[13]

How can the two graphs in Figure 14-3 be reconciled? The PIMS findings argue that profitability increases as a business gains share relative to its competitors in its *served market*. The V-shaped curve ignores market segments and looks at a business's profitability relative to its size in the total market. Thus Mercedes earns high profit because it is a high-share company in its served market of luxury cars even though it is a low-share company in the total auto market. And it has achieved this high share in its served market because it does other things right, such as producing high relative product quality and achieving high asset turnover and good cost control.

Companies must not think, however, that gaining increased market share will automatically improve their profitability. Much depends on their strategy for gaining increased market share. The cost of buying higher market share may far exceed its revenue value. The company should consider three factors before blindly pursuing increased market share.

The first factor is the possibility of provoking anti-combines action. Jealous competitors are likely to cry "monopolization" if a dominant firm makes further inroads on market share. This rise in risk would cut down the attractiveness of pushing market-share gains too far. Thus IBM would have to carefully consider the anti-combines implications of plotting further market-share gains. Yet IBM is very tempted to attack DEC's strong position in the minicomputer market. According to a former IBM marketing strategist:

IBM's management committee approved plans for a so-called competitive-analysis task force that . . . targeted DEC. IBM even set up a "war room" at marketing headquarters . . . with maps and lists of target areas. The management committee authorized a specially trained force of up to 1300 salespeople . . . to win the scientific and engineering accounts that favor midrange machines.[14]

The second factor is economic cost. Figure 14-4 shows the possibility that profitability might begin to fall with further market-share gains after some level. In the illustration, the firm's *optimal market share* is 50 percent, and if the firm pursues a larger share, this move might come at the expense of profitability. That is consistent with the PIMS findings in that PIMS did not show what happens to profitability for different levels within the over-40-percent category. Basically, the cost of gaining further market share might exceed the value. A company that has, say, 60 percent of the market must recognize that the "holdout" customers may dislike the company, be loyal to competitive suppliers, have unique needs, or prefer dealing with smaller suppliers. Furthermore, the competitors are likely to fight harder to defend their falling market share. The cost of legal work, public relations, and lobbying rises with market share. In general, pushing for higher market share is less justified when there are few scale or experience economies, unattractive market segments exist, buyers want multiple sources of supply, and exit barriers are high. The leader might be better off concentrating on expanding market size rather than fighting for further increases in market share. Some dominant marketers have even gained by selectively decreasing their market share in weaker areas.[15]

The third factor is that companies might pursue the wrong marketing-mix strategy in their bid for higher market share and therefore not increase their profit. While certain marketing-mix variables are effective in building market share, not all lead to higher profits (see Marketing Concepts and Tools 14-1). Higher shares tend to produce higher profits under two conditions:

☐ *Unit costs fall with increased market share:* Unit costs fall because the leader enjoys cost economies by running larger plants and because it goes down the cost-experience curve faster. This means that one effective marketing strategy for gaining profitable increases in market share is to fanatically pursue the lowest costs in the industry and pass the cost savings to customers through lower prices. That was Henry Ford's strategy for selling autos in the 1920s and Texas Instruments' strategy for selling transistors in the 1960s.

☐ *The company offers a superior-quality product and charges a premium price that more than covers the cost of offering higher quality:* Crosby, in his book *Quality Is Free*, claims that building more quality into a product does not cost the company much more because the company saves in less scrappage, aftersales servicing, and so on.[16] Furthermore, its

FIGURE 14-4
The Concept of an Optimal Market Share

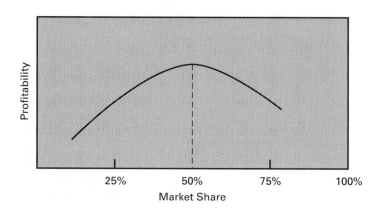

THE IMPACT OF DIFFERENT MARKETING-MIX VARIABLES ON MARKET SHARE

Some light on the impact of different marketing variables on market share was shed by Buzzell and Wiersema, drawing on the PIMS (Profit Impact of Management Strategies) data base. They found that companies showing market-share gains typically outperformed their competitors in three areas: new-product activity, relative product quality, and marketing expenditures. Specifically:

1. Share-gaining companies typically developed and added more new products to their line.

2. Companies that increased their product quality relative to competitors' enjoyed greater share gains than those whose quality ratings remained constant or declined.

3. Companies that increased their marketing expenditures faster than the rate of market growth typically achieved share gains. Increases in salesforce expenditures were effective in producing share gains for both industrial and consumer markets. Increased advertising expenditures produced share gains mainly for consumer-goods companies. Increased sales-promotion expenditures were effective in producing share gains for all kinds of companies.

4. Companies that cut their prices more deeply than competitors did not achieve significant market-share gains, contrary to expectations. Presumably, enough rivals met the price cuts partly, and others offered other values to the buyers, so that buyers did not switch as much to the price cutter.

The reported study did not investigate whether the market-share gains were worth the cost of achieving them. Evidently companies are able to "buy" a higher market share, but the real issue is whether it will lead to higher profits sooner or later.

Source: Based on Robert D. Buzzell and Frederik D. Wiersema, "Successful Share-Building Strategies," *Harvard Business Review*, January-February, 1981, pp. 135-44.

products are so desired that consumers pay a large premium over cost. This strategy for profitable market-share growth is pursued by IBM, Caterpillar, and Michelin, among others.

All said, market leaders who stay on top have learned the art of expanding the total market, defending their current territory, and increasing their market share profitably. The Companies and Industries 14-1 exhibit details the specific principles that two great companies—Procter & Gamble and Caterpillar—use to maintain and expand their leadership in their respective markets.

MARKET-CHALLENGER STRATEGIES

The firms that occupy second, third, and lower ranks in an industry can be called runner-up, or trailing, firms. Some are quite large in their own right, such as Colgate, Ford, Westinghouse, Eaton's, and Pepsi-Cola. These runner-up firms can adopt one of two postures. They can attack the leader and other competitors in an aggressive bid for further market share (market challengers). Or they can play ball and not rock the boat (market followers). Dolan found that competitive rivalry is most intense in industries with high fixed costs, high inventory costs, and stagnant primary demand.[17] We will now examine the competitive attack strategies available to market challengers.[18]

HOW PROCTER & GAMBLE AND CATERPILLAR MAINTAIN THEIR MARKET LEADERSHIP

The principles of maintaining market leadership are admirably illustrated by companies such as Procter & Gamble, Caterpillar, IBM, and McDonald's, all of which have shown a remarkable ability to protect their market shares against repeated attacks by able challengers. Their success is based not on doing one thing well but on doing everything well. They do not allow any weaknesses to develop. We will examine the basics behind Procter & Gamble's and Caterpillar's success.

Procter & Gamble: P&G is widely regarded as the nation's most skilled marketer of consumer packaged goods. It sells the number-one brand in several important categories: automatic dishwashing (Cascade), detergent (Tide), toilet tissue (Royale), fabric softener (Downy), toothpaste (Crest), and shampoo (Head & Shoulders). Its market leadership rests on several principles:

- *Customer Knowledge:* P&G studies its customers—both final consumers and the trade—through continuous marketing research and intelligence gathering. It provides a toll-free 800 number so consumers can call P&G directly with any comments or complaints about P&G products.

- *Long-Term Outlook:* P&G takes its time to analyze an opportunity and prepare the best product and then commits itself for the long-run to make this product a success. It struggled with Pringles potato chips for almost a decade before achieving marketplace success.

- *Product Innovation:* P&G is an active product innovator and benefit segmenter. It launches brands offering new consumer benefits rather than me-too brands backed by heavy advertising. P&G spent ten years researching and developing the first effective anticavity toothpaste, Crest. It spent several years researching the first effective over-the-counter antidandruff shampoo, Head & Shoulders. P&G found that new parents wanted relief from handling and washing diapers and innovated Pampers, an affordable disposable paper diaper. The company thoroughly tests its new products with consumers, and only when real preference is indicated does it launch them in the national market.

- *Quality Strategy:* P&G designs products of above average quality. Once launched, the product is continuously improved. When P&G announces "new and improved," they mean it. This is in contrast to some companies that, after establishing the quality level, rarely improve it, and to other companies that reduce the quality in an effort to squeeze out more profit.

- *Product Flanking:* P&G produces its brands in several sizes and forms to satisfy varying consumer preferences. This gives its brand more shelf space and prevents competitors from moving in to satisfy unmet market needs.

- *Multibrand Strategy:* P&G originated the art of marketing several brands in the same product category. For example, it produces ten laundry-detergent brands, each positioned differently in the consumer's mind. The aim is to design brands that meet different consumer wants and that compete against specific competitors' brands. Each brand manager runs the brand independently and competes for company resources. Having several brands on the shelf, the company "locks up" shelf space and gains more clout with distributors.

- *Brand-Extension Strategy:* P&G will often use its strong brand names to launch new products. For example, the Ivory brand has been extended from a soap to include liquid soap, a dishwashing detergent, and a shampoo. Launching a new product under a strong existing brand name gives the new brand more instant recognition and credibility with much less advertising outlay.

- *Heavy Advertising:* P&G is Canada's fourth largest advertiser. Its 1990 spending of $67 million was well ahead of other packaged-goods marketers. P&G never stints on spending to create strong consumer awareness and preference.

- *Aggressive Salesforce:* P&G has a top-flight field salesforce, which is very effective in working with key retail customers to gain shelf space and cooperation in point-of-purchase displays and promotions.

- *Effective Sales Promotion:* P&G has a sales-promotion department to counsel its brand managers on the most effective promotions to achieve particular objectives. The department studies the results of consumer and trade deals and develops an expert sense of their effectiveness under varying circumstances. At the same time, P&G tries to minimize the use of sales promotion, preferring to rely on advertising to build long-term consumer preference.

- *Competitive Toughness:* P&G carries a big stick when it comes to constraining aggressors. P&G is willing to spend large sums of money to outpromote new competitive brands and prevent them from gaining a foothold in the market.

- *Manufacturing Efficiency:* P&G's reputation as a great marketing company is matched by its greatness as a manufacturing company. P&G spends large sums of money developing and improving production operations to keep its costs among the lowest in the industry.

- *Brand-Management System:* P&G originated the brand-management system, in which one executive is responsible for each brand. The system has been copied by many competitors but frequently without the success that P&G has achieved through perfecting its system over the years. In a recent development, P&G modified its general management structure so that each brand category is now run by a general manager with volume and profit responsibility. While this does not replace the independent brand-management system, it helps to sharpen strategic focus on the key consumer needs and competition in the category.

Thus P&G's market leadership is not based on doing one thing well but on the successful orchestration of myriad factors that contribute to market leadership. In 1985, P&G suffered its first profit decline in thirty-three years, as a result of successful attacks by Colgate, Lever Brothers, Beecham, and Kimberly-Clark on some of its key brands. But P&G bounced back with new innovations and product improvements and continues to lead the pack.

Caterpillar: Since the 1940s, Caterpillar has dominated the construction-equipment industry. Its tractors, crawlers, and loaders, painted in the familiar yellow, are a common sight at any construction area and account for 50 percent of the world's sales of heavy construction equipment. Caterpillar has managed to retain leadership in spite of charging a premium price for its equipment and being challenged by a number of able competitors, including John Deere, Massey-Ferguson, J. I. Case, and Komatsu. Several principles combine to explain Caterpillar's success:

- *Premium-Product Quality:* Caterpillar produces high-quality equipment known for its reliability. Reliability is a key buyer consideration in the purchase of heavy industrial equipment. Caterpillar designs its equipment with a heavier gauge of steel than necessary, to convince buyers of its superior quality.

- *Extensive-and-Efficient-Dealership System:* Caterpillar maintains the largest number of independent construction-equipment dealers in the industry. Its 260 dealers throughout the world carry a complete line of Caterpillar equipment. Caterpillar dealers focus their attention on Caterpillar equipment and do not carry other lines. Competitors' dealers, on the other hand, normally lack a full line and carry complementary, noncompeting lines. Caterpillar can choose the best dealers (a new Caterpillar dealership costs the franchisee $5 million) and spends the most money in training, servicing, and motivating them.

- *Superior Service:* Caterpillar has built a worldwide parts and service system second to none in the industry. Caterpillar can deliver replacement parts and service anywhere in the world within a few hours of equipment breakdown. Competitors cannot match this without making a substantial investment. Any competitor duplicating this service level would only neutralize Caterpillar's advantage rather than score a new advantage.

- *Superior Parts Management:* Thirty percent of Caterpillar's sales volume and over 50 percent of its profit come from the sale of replacement parts. Caterpillar has developed a superior parts-management system to keep margins high in this end of the business.

- *Premium Price:* Caterpillar charges a 10-to-20-percent premium over comparable competitors' equipment because of the extra value perceived by buyers.

- *Full-Line Strategy:* Caterpillar produces a full line of construction equipment to enable customers to do one-stop buying.

- *Good Financing:* Caterpillar arranges generous financial terms to customers buying its equipment. This is important because of the high purchase cost.

Recently Caterpillar experienced difficulties because of the depressed global-construction-equipment market and cutthroat competition. Their specific problem has been Komatsu, Japan's number-one construction firm, which adopted the internal slogan "Encircle Caterpillar." Komatsu studies and attacks market niches, continuously enlarges its product line and improves its product quality, and prices its equipment sometimes as much as 40 percent lower. Caterpillar tells buyers that Komatsu's lower prices reflect lower quality, but not all buyers accept this or are willing to pay more for higher quality.

Caterpillar has fought back by cutting its costs by 27 percent and meeting Komatsu's prices and sometimes even initiating price cutting. The price wars drove competitors like International Harvester and Clark Equipment near the brink of ruin, and Caterpillar itself lost almost $1 billion in the years 1982-84. But Caterpillar has rebounded strongly, winning back share and profits in its world markets. Komatsu, in the meantime, has had to raise its prices seven times in the last three years, and its market share, which was 12 percent in 1986, has now dropped to 9 percent. The long and damaging price wars appear to be coming to an end, with both sides settling for peaceful coexistence and improved profits.

Sources: Faye Rice, "The King of Suds Reigns Again," *Fortune,* August 4, 1986, pp. 130-34; Bill Kelley, "Komatsu in Cat Fight," *Sales & Marketing Management,* April 1986, pp. 50-53; and Ronald Henkoff, "This Cat Is Acting Like a Tiger," *Fortune,* December 19, 1988, pp. 71-76.

Defining the Strategic Objective and Opponent(s)

A market challenger must first define its strategic objective. The military *principle of objective* holds that "every military operation must be directed toward a clearly defined, decisive, and attainable objective." The strategic objective of most market challengers is to increase their market shares, thinking that this will lead to greater profitability. Deciding on the objective, whether it is to crush the competitor or reduce its share, interacts with the question of who the competitor is. Basically, an aggressor can choose to attack one of three types of firms:

☐ *It can attack the market leader:* This is a high-risk but potentially high-payoff strategy and makes good sense if the leader is a "false leader" and not serving the market well. The "terrain" to examine is consumer need or dissatisfaction. If a substantial segment is unserved or poorly served, it provides an excellent strategic target. Miller's "lite beer" campaign was successful because it pivoted on discovering many consumers who wanted a "lighter" beer. The alternative strategy is to out-innovate the leader across the whole segment. Thus Xerox took the copy market away from 3M by developing a better copying process (dry instead of wet copying).

☐ *It can attack firms of its own size that are not doing the job and are underfinanced:* Consumer satisfaction and innovation potential need to be examined minutely. Even a frontal attack might work if the other firm's resources are limited.

☐ *It can attack small local and regional firms that are not doing the job and are underfinanced:* Several of the major beer companies grew to their present size not by stealing each other's customers but by gobbling up the small regional brewers.

Thus the issue of choosing the competitors and choosing the objective interact. If the attacking company goes after the market leader, its objective might be to wrest a certain share. Thus Bic is under no illusion that it could topple Gillette in the razor market—it is simply seeking a larger share. If the attacking company goes after a small local company, its objective might be to drive that company out of existence. The important principle remains: Every military operation must be directed toward a clearly defined, decisive, and attainable objective.

Choosing an Attack Strategy

Given clear opponents and objectives, how do military strategists view their major options in attacking an enemy? The starting point is known as the principle of mass, which holds that "superior combat power must be concentrated at the critical time and place for a decisive purpose." We can make progress by imagining an opponent who occupies a certain market territory. We distinguish among five attack strategies shown in Figure 14-5.

Frontal Attack   An aggressor is said to launch a frontal (or "head-on") attack when it masses its forces right up against its opponent. It attacks the opponent's strengths rather than its weaknesses. The outcome depends on who has more strength and endurance. In a pure frontal attack, the attacker matches its opponent's product, advertising, price, and so on. Recently the runner-up razor-blade manufacturer in Brazil decided to attack Gillette, the market leader. Management was asked if it was offering the consumer a better blade. "No," was the reply. "A lower price?" "No." "A better package?" "No." "A cleverer advertising campaign?" "No." "Better allowances to the trade?" "No." "Then how do you expect to take share away from Gillette?" "Sheer determination" was the reply. Needless to say, its offensive failed.

For a pure frontal attack to succeed, the aggressor needs a strength advantage over the competitor. The *principle of force* says that the side with the greater manpower (resources) will win the engagement. This rule is modified if the defender has greater firing efficiency through enjoying a terrain advantage (such as holding a mountain top). The military dogma is that for a frontal attack to succeed against a well-entrenched opponent or one controlling the "high ground," the attacking forces must deploy at least a 3:1 advantage in combat firepower. If the aggressor has a smaller force or poorer firepower than the defender, a frontal attack amounts to a suicide mission and makes no sense. RCA, GE, and Xerox learned this the hard way when they launched frontal attacks on IBM, overlooking its superior defensive position.

FIGURE 14-5
Attack Strategies

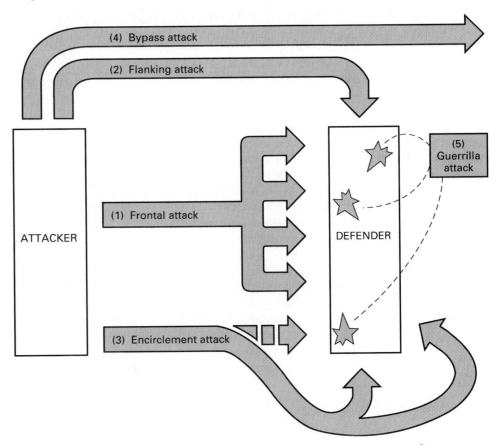

As an example of a successful pure frontal attack and the resources it required, consider S. C. Johnson & Son's entry into the shampoo market with its new Agree brand.[19] In 1977, with what Forbes described as "almost Japanese-like thoroughness," S. C. Johnson first raided Colgate and others for experienced executives. Then it blitzed the market with a $14 million promotion that included thirty million sample bottles of its new hair conditioner, Agree. That about equaled the industry's total promotion on hair conditioners. It grabbed 15 percent of the market in its first year, wrested from such giants as Gillette's Toni, Breck, and Clairol. (By 1979, its share was 20 percent.) Then, in 1978, it invaded the shampoo market, reportedly spending $30 million in marketing costs in the summer of that year. It ended up with a 6 percent share of that market.   ∎

As an alternative to a pure frontal attack, the aggressor can launch a modified frontal attack, the most common being to cut its price vis-à-vis the opponent's. Such attacks can take two forms. The more usual ploy is to match the leader's offer on other counts and beat it on price. This can work if the market leader does not retaliate by cutting price, and if the competitor convinces the market that its product is equal to the competitor's or that at a lower price, it is a real value.

Helene Curtis is a master practitioner of the somewhat risky strategy of convincing the market that its product is equal in quality to the higher-priced products of competitors.[20] Curtis makes no bones about its approach—making budget imitations of leading high-priced brands and promoting them with blatant comparative-advertising campaigns: "We do what theirs does for less than half the price," is the message. In 1972 Curtis had a meager 1 percent share of the shampoo market for its five Suave shampoos. It launched its new strategy in 1973. By 1976, it had overtaken Procter & Gamble's Head & Shoulders and Johnson & Johnson's Baby Shampoo to lead the market in volume. Its share hit 16 percent in 1979.   ∎

The other form of price-aggressive strategy involves a heavy investment in research by the attacker to achieve lower production costs and then an attack on competitors on a price basis. Texas Instruments has had brilliant success in using the price weapon strategically. It invests heavily in R&D and moves rapidly down the experience curve. The Japanese, too, launch frontal attacks involving price and cost cutting.

Flank Attack   An enemy's army is strongest where it expects to be attacked. It is necessarily less secure in its flanks and rear. Its weak spots (blind sides), therefore, are natural targets for attack by the enemy. The major principle of modern offensive warfare is *concentration of strength against weakness*. The aggressor may attack the strong side to tie up the defender's troops but will launch the real attack at the side or rear. This "turning" maneuver catches the defending army off guard. Flank attacks make excellent marketing sense and are particularly attractive to the aggressor possessing fewer resources than the opponent. If the aggressor cannot overwhelm the defender with brute strength, it can outmaneuver the defender with subterfuge.

A flank attack can be directed along two strategic dimensions—geographical and segmental. In a geographical attack, the aggressor spots areas where the opponent is underperforming. For example, some of IBM's rivals chose to set up strong sales branches in medium- and smaller-size cities that were relatively neglected by IBM. According to a Honeywell field sales manager:

Out in the rural areas, we are relatively better off than in the cities. We have been quite successful in these areas because our sales force does not meet the ten plus to one ratio it hits in the cities where IBM concentrates its people. Thus, ours must be a concentration game.[21]

The other flanking strategy is to spot uncovered market needs not being served by the leaders:

> German and Japanese automakers chose not to compete with domestic automakers by producing large, flashy, gas-guzzling automobiles, even though these were supposedly the preference of buyers. Instead they recognized an unserved consumer segment that wanted small, fuel-efficient cars. They moved vigorously to fill this hole in the market, and to their satisfaction, buyers' tastes for smaller, fuel-efficient cars grew to be a substantial part of the market. ∎

> "Discovering," so to speak, the "light" beer segment, Miller Brewing Company pivoted on this unserved gap in the market and vigorously developed it into a huge breach across the whole industry's front and propelled itself from seventh place in the industry to a very close second in five years. ∎

A flanking strategy is another name for identifying shifts in market segments—which are causing gaps to develop that are not being served by the industry's product profile—and rushing in to fill the gaps and develop them into strong segments. Instead of a bloody battle between two or more companies trying to serve the same market, flanking leads to a fuller coverage of the market's varied needs. Flanking is in the best tradition of modern marketing philosophy, which holds that the purpose of marketing is to "discover needs and satisfy them." Flank attacks are more likely to be successful than frontal attacks. That is also borne out in military history. In his penetrating analysis of the thirty most important conflicts of the world from the Greek wars up to World War I, Liddell-Hart concluded that in only six campaigns did decisive results follow strategies of direct head-on assault.[22] The strategy of "the indirect approach" has overwhelming support from history as the most effective and economic form of strategy.

Encirclement Attack   The pure flanking maneuver was defined as pivoting on a market need neglected by competitors. The encirclement maneuver, on the other hand, is an attempt to capture a wide slice of the enemy's territory through a comprehensive "blitzkrieg" attack. Encirclement involves launching a grand offensive on several fronts, so that the enemy must protect its front, sides, and rear simultaneously. The aggressor may offer the market everything the opponent offers and more, so that the offer is unrefusable. Encirclement makes sense where the aggressor commands superior resources and believes that a swift encirclement will break the opponent's will. Here are two examples:

> Seiko's attack on the watch market illustrates an encirclement strategy.[23] For several years, Seiko has been acquiring distribution in every major watch outlet and overwhelming its competitors and consumers with an enormous variety of constantly changing models. Its marketing clout is backed by the some twenty-three hundred models it makes and sells worldwide. "They hit the mark on fashion, features, user preferences, and everything else that might motivate the consumer," says an admiring vice-president of a competitor. ∎

> An encirclement attack does not always work, as Hunt's found out when it tried to blitz Heinz's brand of ketchup in a grab for increased market share. In 1963 Hunt's, with a 19 percent market share, launched a major encirclement attack to go after Heinz's 27 percent market share. Hunt's rolled out a number of marketing attacks simultaneously. It introduced two new flavors of ketchup (pizza and hickory) to disrupt the consumers' traditional taste preference for Heinz and also to capture more retail shelf space. It lowered its price to 70 percent of Heinz's price. It offered heavy trade allowances to retailers. It raised its advertising budget to over twice the level of Heinz's. This marketing program meant that Hunt's would lose money while the battle raged but would make it up if it attracted enough brand switchers. The strategy failed to work.

The Heinz brand continued to enjoy consumer preference; as a result, not enough Heinz users tried the Hunt's brand, and most who did try returned to the Heinz brand. By the mid-1970s, Heinz had increased its share to over 40 percent. ■

Hunt's debacle underscores our core proposition that segmentation opportunity should be a fundamental basis for attack. If empty niches do not now exist or cannot be created by segment diffusion tactics, then what if a flank attack in the mind of the aggressor peters out into a plain frontal attack in the marketplace. As such, it would require the three-to-one advantage in combat firepower to succeed.

Bypass Attack   The bypass is the most indirect of assault strategies and eschews any belligerent move directed against the enemy's existing territory. It means bypassing the enemy and attacking easier markets to broaden one's resource base. This strategy offers three lines of approach: diversifying into *unrelated products*, diversifying into new *geographical markets* for existing products, and leapfrogging into *new technologies* to supplant existing products.

> Colgate's impressive turnaround utilized the first two principles.[24] Colgate has always struggled in Procter & Gamble's shadow. In heavy-duty detergents, P&G's Tide routed Colgate's Fab by almost 5:1. In dishwashing liquids, P&G had almost twice Colgate's share. In soaps, too, Colgate trailed far behind. When David Foster took over as CEO in 1971, despite its $1.3 billion in sales, Colgate still had the reputation as a stodgy marketer of soap and detergent. By 1979 Foster had transformed the company into a $4.3 billion conglomerate, capable of challenging P&G if necessary. Foster's real achievement was in recognizing that any head-on battle with P&G was futile. "They outgunned us 3 to 1 at the store level," said Foster, "and had three research people to our one." Foster's strategy was simple—increase Colgate's lead abroad and bypass P&G at home by diversifying into non-P&G markets. A string of acquisitions followed in textiles and hospital products, cosmetics, and a range of sporting goods and food products. The outcome: In 1971, Colgate was underdog to P&G in about half of its business. By 1976, in three-fourths of its business, it was either comfortably placed against P&G or did not face it at all. ■

Technological leapfrogging is a bypass strategy used often in high-tech industries. Instead of copying the competitor's product and waging a costly frontal attack, the challenger patiently researches and develops the next technology and, when satisfied about its superiority, launches an attack, thus shifting the battleground to its territory, where it has an advantage. Intellevision's attack strategy on Atari in the video-game market was precisely to bypass Atari's state of the art and attack it with a superior technology.

Guerrilla Attack   Guerrilla attack is another option available to market aggressors, especially smaller undercapitalized ones. Guerrilla warfare consists of waging small, intermittent attacks on different territories of the opponent, with the aim of harassing and demoralizing the opponent and eventually securing permanent footholds. Liddell-Hart stated the military rationale:

> The more usual reason for adopting a strategy of limited aim is that of awaiting a change in the balance of force—a change often sought and achieved by draining the enemy's force, weakening him by pricks instead of risking blows. The essential condition of such a strategy is that the drain on him should be disproportionately greater than on oneself. The object may be sought by raiding his supplies; by local attacks which annihilate or inflict disproportionate loss on parts of his force; by bringing him into unprofitable attacks; by causing an excessively wide distribution of his force; and, not least, by exhausting his moral and physical energy.[25]

The guerrilla aggressor will use both conventional and unconventional means to attack the opponent. These would include selective price cuts, intense promotional bursts, and occasional legal actions. The key is to focus the attack on a narrow territory:

> Diamond Crystal Salt had less than a 5 percent share of the national salt market compared with Morton's 50 percent. There was no way that it could compete with Morton on a broad front. Diamond decided to focus its attack against Morton in its own core regional market and launched an aggressive marketing campaign. They managed to build a three-to-one lead over Morton. ∎

Normally, guerrilla warfare is practiced by a smaller firm against a larger one. It is a case of David attacking Goliath. Not able to mount a frontal or even an effective flanking attack, the smaller firm launches a barrage of short promotional and price attacks in random corners of the larger opponent's market in a manner calculated to gradually weaken the opponent's market power. Even here, the attacker has to decide between launching a few major attacks or a continual stream of minor attacks. Military dogma holds that a continual stream of minor attacks usually creates more cumulative impact, disorganization, and confusion in the enemy than a few major ones. In line with this, the guerrilla attacker would find it more effective to attack small, isolated, weakly defended markets rather than major stronghold markets, where the defender is better entrenched and more willing to retaliate quickly and decisively.

It would be a mistake to think of a guerrilla campaign as only a "low-resource" strategy alternative available to financially weak challengers. Conducting a continual guerrilla campaign can be expensive, although admittedly less expensive than a frontal, encirclement, or even flanking attack. Furthermore guerrilla war is more a preparation for war than a war itself. Ultimately it must be backed by a stronger attack if the strategy hopes to "beat" the opponent. Hence in terms of resources, guerrilla warfare is not necessarily a cheap operation.

The preceding attack strategies are very broad. The challenger must put together a total strategy consisting of several specific strategies. Marketing Strategies 14-2 lists several specific marketing strategies for attacking competitive positions.

Marketing Strategies 14-2

SOME SPECIFIC ATTACK STRATEGIES AVAILABLE TO CHALLENGERS

Several specific attack strategies are available to the market challenger who is seeking an advantage vis-à-vis competition:

1. *Price-Discount Strategy:* A major attack strategy for challengers is to offer buyers a product comparable to the leader's at a lower price. (See Chapter 18, Fig. 18-1, Leader in cell 1, challenger in cell 2.) The Fuji Corporation used this strategy to attack Kodak's preeminence in the photographic-paper field. Its paper is of comparable quality and is priced 10 percent lower than Kodak's. Kodak chose not to lower its price, with the result that Fuji achieved strong market-share inroads. Texas Instruments is the prime practitioner of price cutting. It will offer a comparable-quality product and cut its price progressively to gain market share and still lower costs of production. Texas Instruments willingly forgoes profits in the first few years in a drive to gain unchallenged market leadership. It did this with transistors and hand calculators and seemed bent on doing this in the personal computer market. For a price-discount strategy to work, three assumptions must be fulfilled. First, the challenger must convince buyers that its product and service are comparable to the leader's.

Second, the buyers must be sensitive to the price difference and feel comfortable about turning their back on existing suppliers. Third, the market leader must refuse to cut its price in spite of the competitor's attack.

2. *Cheaper-Goods Strategy:* Another strategy is to offer the market an average- or low-quality product at a much lower price. (See Chapter 18, Fig. 18-1, Leader in cell 1, challenger in cell 5 or 9.) This works when there is a sufficient segment of buyers who are interested only in price. Firms that get established through this strategy, however, may be attacked by "cheaper-goods" firms whose prices are even lower. In defense, they try to upgrade their quality gradually over time.

3. *Prestige-Goods Strategy:* A market challenger can launch a higher-quality product and charge a higher price than the leader. (See Chapter 18, Fig. 18-1, Leader in cell 1, challenger goes to northwest of cell 1.) Mercedes gained on Cadillac in the American market by offering a car of even higher quality and higher price. Some prestige-goods firms later roll out lower-price products to take advantage of their charisma.

4. *Product-Proliferation Strategy:* The challenger can go after the leader by launching a large number of product versions, thus giving buyers more options. Hunt went after Heinz's leadership in the ketchup market by creating several new ketchup flavors and bottle sizes in contrast with Heinz's reliance on one flavor of ketchup, sold in a limited number of bottle sizes.

5. *Product-Innovation Strategy:* The challenger may pursue product innovation to attack the leader's position. Polaroid and Xerox are companies whose success is based on continuously introducing outstanding innovations in the camera and copying fields respectively. Miller rose to second place in the beer industry by successfully launching a light beer and introducing "pony-sized" bottles for lighter beer drinkers. The public often gains most from challenger strategies oriented toward product innovation.

6. *Improved-Services Strategy:* The challenger might find ways to offer new or better services to customers. IBM achieved its success by recognizing that customers were more interested in the software and the service than in the hardware. Avis's famous attack on Hertz, "We're only second. We try harder," was based on promising and delivering cleaner cars and faster service than Hertz.

7. *Distribution-Innovation Strategy:* A challenger might discover or develop a new channel of distribution. Avon became a major cosmetics company by perfecting door-to-door selling instead of battling other cosmetic firms in conventional stores. Timex achieved great success by selling its low-price watches through mass-merchandise channels instead of jewelry stores.

8. *Manufacturing-Cost-Reduction Strategy:* The challenger might seek to achieve lower manufacturing costs than its competitors through more efficient purchasing, lower labor costs, and more modern production equipment. The company can use its lower costs to price more aggressively in order to gain market share. This strategy has been the key to the successful Japanese invasion of various world markets.

9. *Intensive Advertising Promotion:* Some challengers attack the leader by increasing their expenditures on advertising and promotion. When Hunt's went after Heinz in the ketchup market, it built its annual spending level to $6.4 million as against Heinz's $3.4 million. Substantial promotional spending, however, is usually not a sensible strategy unless the challenger's product or advertising message exhibits some superiority over competition.

A challenger rarely succeeds in improving its market share by relying on only one strategy element. Its success depends on designing a total strategy that will improve its position over time.

MARKET-FOLLOWER STRATEGIES

Some years ago, Professor Levitt wrote an article entitled "Innovative Imitation" in which he argued that a strategy of *product imitation* might be as profitable as a strategy of *product innovation*.[26] After all, the innovator bears the huge expense of developing the new product, getting it into distribution, and informing and educating the market. The reward for all this work and risk is normally market leadership. However, another firm can come along, copy or improve the new product, and launch it. Although this firm probably will not overtake the leader, the follower can achieve high profits because it did not bear any of the innovation expense.

Not all runner-up companies will challenge the market leader. The effort to draw away the leader's customers is never taken lightly by the leader. If the challenger's lure is lower prices, improved service, or additional product features, the leader can quickly match these to diffuse the attack. The leader probably has more staying power in an all-out battle. A hard fight might leave both firms worse off, and this means the challenger must think twice before attacking. Unless the challenger can launch a preemptive strike—in the form of a substantial product innovation or distribution breakthrough—it often prefers to follow rather than attack the leader.

Patterns of "conscious parallelism" are common in capital-intensive homogeneous-product industries, such as steel, fertilizers, and chemicals. The opportunities for product differentiation and image differentiation are low; service quality is often comparable; price sensitivity runs high. Price wars can erupt at any time. The mood in these industries is against short-run grabs for market share, because that strategy only provokes retaliation. Most firms decide against stealing each other's customers. Instead, they present similar offers to buyers, usually by copying the leader. Market shares show a high stability.

This is not to say that market followers lack strategies. A market follower must know how to hold current customers and win a fair share of new customers. Each follower tries to bring distinctive advantages to its target market—location, services, financing. The follower is a major target of attack by challengers. Therefore, the market follower must keep its manufacturing costs low and its product quality and services high. It must also enter new markets as they open up. Followership is not the same as being passive or a carbon copy of the leader. The follower has to define a growth path, but one that does not invite competitive retaliation. Three broad followership strategies can be distinguished:

- □ *Cloner:* The cloner emulates the leader's products, distribution, advertising, and so on. The cloner doesn't originate anything but parasitically lives off the market leader's investments. In the extreme, the cloner is a *counterfeiter* who produces "knockoffs" of the leader's product. Firms such as Apple Computer and Rolex are plagued with the counterfeiter problem, especially in the Far East, and are seeking ways to defeat or police the counterfeiters.

- □ *Imitator:* The imitator copies some things from the leader but maintains some differentiation in terms of packaging, advertising, pricing, and so on. The leader doesn't mind the imitator as long as the imitator doesn't attack the leader aggressively. The imitator even helps the leader avoid the charge of monopoly.

- □ *Adapter:* The adapter takes the leader's products and adapts and often improves them. The adapter may choose to sell to different markets to avoid direct confrontation with the leader. But often the adapter grows into the future challenger, as many Japanese firms have done after adapting and improving products developed elsewhere.

MARKET-NICHER STRATEGIES

Almost every industry includes firms that specialize in serving market niches. Instead of pursuing the whole market, or even large segments of the market, these firms target segments within segments, or niches. This is particularly true of smaller firms because of their limited resources. But business units of larger firms have also pursued niching strategies. In fact, here are two large companies that have been very profitable as a result of pursuing niching strategies:

> Johnson & Johnson is a large health-care marketer that practices a "grow-and-divide" philosophy. It consists of 170 affiliates and subsidiaries. Each operation is headed by a president. Many

of the business units pursue niche markets and more than half of the company's products are in leadership positions in their respective markets. ∎

EG&G is a large industrial-equipment-and-components company consisting of over 175 distinct and autonomous business units, many with less than $10 million in sales in markets worth $25 million. Many business units have their own R&D, manufacturing, and salesforce. EG&G is currently the market or technical leader in 80 percent of its markets. More astonishing, EG&G ranked second in earnings per share and first in profitability in the *Fortune 1000*. EC&G illustrates how niche marketing may pay larger dividends than mass marketing. ∎

The main point is that firms with low shares of the total market can be highly profitable through smart niching. Recently Clifford and Cavanagh carefully identified over two dozen highly successful midsize companies and studied their success factors.[27] They found that virtually all these companies were nichers. One example is A. T. Cross, which niched itself in the high-price pen-and-pencil market with its famous gold writing instruments that most executives own or want to own. Instead of manufacturing all types of writing instruments, it has stuck to the high-price niche and enjoyed great sales growth and profit. The consultants discovered other common factors shared by successful midsize companies, including offering high value, charging a premium price, creating new experience curves, and shaping a strong corporate culture and vision.

Marketing Strategies 14-3

SPECIALIST ROLES OPEN TO MARKET NICHERS

- *End-User Specialist:* The firm specializes in serving one type of end-use customer. For example, a law firm can specialize in the criminal, civil, or business-law markets.

- *Vertical-Level Specialist:* The firm specializes at some vertical level of the production-distribution cycle. For example, a copper firm may concentrate on producing raw cooper, copper components, or finished copper products.

- *Customer-Size Specialist:* The firm concentrates on selling to either small, medium-size or large customers. Many nichers specialize in serving small customers who are neglected by the majors.

- *Specific-Customer Specialist:* The firm limits its selling to one or a few major customers. Many firms sell their entire output to a single company, such as Sears or General Motors.

- *Geographic Specialist:* The firm sells only in a certain locality, region, or area of the world.

- *Product or Product-Line Specialist:* The firm produces only one product line or product. Within the laboratory-equipment industry are firms that produce only microscopes, or even more narrowly, only lenses for microscopes.

- *Product-Feature Specialist:* The firm specializes in producing a certain type of product or product feature. Rent-a-Wreck, for example, is a car-rental agency that rents only "beat-up" cars.

- *Job-Shop Specialist:* The firm manufactures customized products as ordered by the customer.

- *Quality/Price Specialist:* The firm operates at the low or high end of the market. For example, Hewlett-Packard specializes in the high-quality, high-price end of the hand-calculator market.

- *Service Specialist:* The firm offers one or more services not available from other firms. An example would be a bank that takes loan requests over the phone and hand delivers the money to the customer.

- *Channel Specialist:* The firm specializes in serving only one channel of distribution. For example, a soft-drink company decided to make a very large size soft-drink available only in gas stations.

Why is niching profitable? The main reason is that the market nicher ends up knowing the target customer group so well that he meets their needs better than other firms that are casually selling to this niche. As a result, the nicher can charge a substantial markup over costs because of the added value. The nicher achieves *high margin*, whereas the mass marketer achieves *high volume*.

What characterizes an ideal niche? An ideal market niche would have the following characteristics:

□ The niche is of sufficient size and purchasing power to be profitable.

□ The niche has growth potential.

□ The niche is of negligible interest to major competitors.

□ The firm has the required skills and resources to serve the niche effectively.

□ The firm can defend itself against an attacking major competitor through the customer goodwill it has built up.

The key idea in nichemanship is specialization. Marketing Strategies 14-3 describes several specialist roles open to nichers. Consider, for example, end-user specialization:

> Computer companies are among the newest converts to "end user" specialization, except they call it *vertical marketing*. For years, computer companies sold general hardware and software systems across many markets and the price battles got rough. Smaller companies started to specialize by vertical slices—law firms, medical practices, banks, etc.—studying the specific hardware and software needs of their target group and designing high value-added products that had a competitive advantage over more general products. Their salesforces were trained to understand and service the particular vertical market. Computer companies also worked with independent

---

Marketing Strategies 14-4

STRATEGIES FOR ENTERING MARKETS HELD BY INCUMBENT FIRMS

What marketing strategies do companies use to enter a market that is already occupied by incumbent firms? Biggadike examined the strategies of forty firms that had recently entered a market occupied by incumbents. He found that ten market entrants came in at a lower price, nine matched the incumbents' prices, and twenty-one entered at a higher price. He also found that twenty-eight claimed superior quality, five matched incumbents' quality, and seven reported inferior product quality. Most of the entrants offered a specialist product line and served a narrower market segment. Less than 20 percent managed to innovate a new channel of distribution. Over half the entrants claimed to offer a higher level of customer service. And over half the entrants spent less than incumbents on salesforce, advertising, and promotion. Thus the modal marketing mix of entrants was

□ Higher prices and higher quality

□ Narrower product line

□ Narrower market segment

□ Similar distribution channels

□ Superior service

□ Lower expenditure on salesforce, advertising, and promotion

Source: Ralph Biggadike, *Entering New Markets: Strategies and Performance* (Cambridge, Mass: Marketing Science Institute, September 1977), pp. 12-20.

---

value-added resellers (VARS) who customized the computer hardware and software for individual clients or customer segments and earned a price premium in the process.[28]

Niching carries a major risk in that the market niche might dry up or be attacked. That is why *multiple niching* is preferable to *single niching*. By developing strength in two or more niches, the company increases its chances for survival. One law firm has achieved national prominence by specializing in only three areas of the law—mergers and acquisitions, bankruptcies, and prospectus development—and does little else.

Firms seeking to enter a market should aim at a niche initially rather than the whole market. Marketing Strategies 14-4 describes the major entry strategies used by several firms that entered markets occupied by incumbents. Most of them chose a niching strategy.

SUMMARY

Marketing strategies are highly dependent on whether the company is a market leader, challenger, follower, or nicher.

A market leader faces three challenges: expanding the total market, protecting market share, and expanding market share. The market leader is interested in expanding the total market because it is the chief beneficiary of any increased sales. To expand market size the leader looks for new users, new uses, and more usage. To protect its existing market share, the market leader has several defenses: position defense, flanking defense, preemptive defense, counteroffensive defense, mobile defense, and contraction defense. The most sophisticated leaders cover themselves by doing everything right, leaving no openings for competitive attack. Leaders can also try to increase their market share. This makes sense if profitability increases at higher market-share levels, and the company's tactics do not invite anti-combines action.

A market challenger is a firm that aggressively tries to expand its market share by attacking the leader, other runner-up firms, or smaller firms in the industry. The challenger can choose from a variety of attack strategies, including a frontal attack, flanking attack, encirclement attack, bypass attack, and guerrilla attack.

A market follower is a runner-up firm that chooses not to rock the boat, usually out of fear that it stands to lose more than it might gain. The follower is not without a strategy, however, and seeks to use its particular competences to participate actively in the growth of the market. Some followers enjoy a higher rate of return on equity than the industry leaders.

A market nicher is a smaller firm that chooses to operate in some specialized part of the market that is unlikely to attract the larger firms. Market nichers often become specialists in some end use, vertical level, customer size, specific customer, geographic area, product or product line, product feature, job-shop approach, quality/price level, service, or channel. Multiple niching is preferable to single niching in order to reduce risk. Many of the most profitable small and medium-size firms owe their success to a niching strategy.

■ QUESTIONS

1. Briefly discuss the strategies used by market leaders, challengers, followers, and nichers in the personal computer market.

2. What is the difference between market niche and market segment? Describe a market-nicher strategy for a small firm competing in the home refrigerator market. Show the difference between the two strategies.

3. Describe how Coca-Cola or McDonald's has used and

could use the market-leader strategies listed in this chapter.

4. Describe how Pepsi-Cola or Burger King has used and could use the market-challenger strategies listed in this chapter.

5. Hewlett-Packard, a market leader in the top end of the hand-held calculator market, has found itself in a squeeze between aggressively promoted portable computers and less-expensive calculators with increasingly sophisticated features. What market-leader strategy would you recommend for Hewlett-Packard?

6. What are some of the marketing principles that General Motors used to maintain its four decades of leadership in the auto industry?

7. IBM is one of the best marketing companies in the world. List the principles upon which its market leadership rests.

8. Although Caterpillar is an extremely strong company, it has some vulnerabilities. Name some potential threats to Caterpillar.

9. Briefly critique the following marketing strategy statement: "The company will offer the best product and best service at the lowest price."

10. Suggest a strategy for a new small firm entering the photocopying market.

11. Comment on the following statements made about the appropriate marketing strategy of smaller firms: (a) "The smaller firm should concentrate on pulling away the larger firm's customers, while the larger firm should concentrate on stimulating new customers to enter the market." (b) "Larger firms should pioneer new products, and smaller ones should copy them."

12. What are some of the strategies used by the Japanese auto industry to upstage the leaders in their export markets?

■ NOTES

1. See Robert V. L. Wright, *A System for Managing Diversity* (Cambridge, Mass: Arthur D. Little, December 1974).

2. See Jordan P. Yale, "The Strategy of Nylon's Growth," *Modern Textiles Magazine*, February 1964, pp. 32 ff. Also see Theodore Levitt, "Exploit the Product Life Cycle," *Harvard Business Review*, November-December 1965, pp. 81-94.

3. See Eric von Hippel, "A Customer-Active Paradigm for Industrial Product Idea Generation," working paper, Sloan School of Management, MIT, Cambridge, Mass., May 1977.

4. Sun Tsu, *The Art of War* (London: Oxford University Press, 1963); Miyamoto Mushashi, *A Book of Five Rings* (Woodstock, N.Y.: Overlook Press, 1974); Carl von Clausewitz, *On War* (London: Routledge & Kegan Paul, 1908); and B. H. Liddell-Hart, *Strategy* (New York: Praeger, 1967).

5. These six defense strategies, as well as the five attack strategies described on pp. 378-81, are taken from Philip Kotler and Ravi Singh, "Marketing Warfare in the 1980s," *Journal of Business Strategy*, Winter 1981, pp. 30-41. For additional reading, see Gerald A. Michaelson, *Winning the Marketing War: A Field Manual for Business Leaders* (Lanham, Md.: Abt Books, 1987); and Al Ries and Jack Trout, *Marketing Warfare* (New York: McGraw-Hill, 1986).

6. See Michael E. Porter, *Competitive Strategy* (New York: Free Press, 1980), Chap. 4.

7. See "The H. J. Heinz Company (A)," Harvard Business School case 9-569-011 M-357. Also see page 391 of this text.

8. *Relative market share* is the business's market share in its served market relative to the combined market share of its three leading competitors, expressed as a percentage. For example, if this business has 30 percent of the market and its three largest competitors have 20 percent, 10 percent, and 10 percent: $30/(20 + 10 + 10) = 75\%$.

9. Sidney Schoeffler, Robert D. Buzzell, and Donald F. Heany, "Impact of Strategic Planning on Profit Performance," *Harvard Business Review*, March-April 1974, pp. 137-45; and Robert D. Buzzell, Bradley T. Gale, and Ralph G. M. Sultan, "Market Share—A Key to Profitability," *Harvard Business Review*, January-February 1975, pp. 97-106.

10. See Buzzell et al., "Market Share," pp. 97, 100. The results represent a "best fit" to the data. There was some variance around the data; for example, some low-share competitors were highly profitable and some high-share companies had low profits. But the regression was statistically significant. It also help up in more recent PIMS studies where the data base now includes some 2600 business units in a wide range of industries. For a summary of the most recent findings, see Robert D. Buzzell and Bradley T. Gale, *The PIMS Principles: Linking Strategy to Performance* (New York: Free Press, 1987).

11. Richard G. Hamermesh, M. J. Anderson, Jr., and J. E. Harris, "Strategies for Low Market Share Businesses," *Harvard Business Review*, May-June 1978, pp. 95-102.

12. Carolyn Y. Woo and Arnold C. Cooper, "The Surprising Case for Low Market Share," *Harvard Business Review*, November-December 1982, pp. 106-113; also see their "Market-Share Leadership—Not Always So Good," *Harvard Business Review*, January-February 1984, pp. 2-4.

13. John D. C. Roach, "From Strategic Planning to Strategic Performance: Closing the Achievement Gap," *Outlook*, published by Booz, Allen & Hamilton, New York, Spring 1981, p. 21. This curve assumes that pretax return on sales is highly correlated with profitability and that company revenue is a surrogate for market share, Michael Porter, in his *Competitive Strategy*, p. 43, shows a similar V-shaped curve that makes the same point.

14. *Business Week*, November 17, 1986, p. 155.

15. Philip Kotler and Paul N. Bloom, "Strategies for High Market-Share Companies," *Harvard Business Review*, November-December 1975, pp. 63-72. Also see Michael E. Porter, *Competitive Advantage* (New York: Free Press, 1985), pp. 221-26.

16. Philip B. Crosby, *Quality is Free* (New York: McGraw-Hill, 1979).

17. See Robert J. Dolan, "Models of Competition: A Review of Theory and Empirical Evidence," in *Review of Marketing*, ed. Ben M. Enis and Kenneth J. Roering (Chicago: American Marketing Association, 1981), pp. 224-34.

18. For additional reading, see C. David Fogg, "Planning Gains in Market Share," *Journal of Marketing*, July 1974, pp. 30-38; and Bernard Catry and Michel Chevalier, "Market Share Strategy and the Product Life Cycle," *Journal of Marketing*, October 1974, pp. 29-34.

19. See "Stopping the Greasies," *Forbes*, July 9, 1979, p. 121.

20. "A 'Me-Too' Strategy That Paid Off," *Fortune*, August 27, 1979, p. 86.

21. Quoted in "Honeywell Information Systems" (case available from the Intercollegiate Case Clearing House, Soldiers Field, Boston, 1975), pp. 7-8.

22. Liddell-Hart, *Strategy*, p. 161.

23. See "Seiko's Smash," *Business Week*, June 5, 1978, p. 89.

24. See "The Changing of the Guard," *Fortune*, Sept. 24, 1979; "How to Be Happy Though No. Two," *Forbes*, July 15, 1976, p. 36.

25. Liddell-Hart, *Strategy*, p. 335.

26. Theodore Levitt, "Innovative Imitation," *Harvard Business Review*, September-October 1966, pp. 63 ff.

27. Donald K. Clifford and Richard E. Cavanagh, *The Winning Performance: How America's High- and Midsize Growth Companies Succeed* (New York: Bantam Books, 1985).

28. See Bro Uttal, "Pitching Computers to Small Business," *Fortune*, April 1, 1985, pp. 95-104. Also see Stuart Gannes, "The Riches in Market Niches," *Fortune*, April 27, 1987, pp. 227-30.

15

Designing Strategies for the Global Marketplace

Unless we can trade with the outside world our condition must be one of stagnation, with the standards of living falling to ever lower levels, and with increasing strains upon the bonds that keep our federation together.

J.W. Dafoe

The 1990s marks the first decade when companies around the world have to start thinking globally. Time and distance have been rapidly shrinking with the advent of faster communication, transportation, and financial flows. Products developed in one country—Gucci purses, McDonald's hamburgers, Japanese sushi, Pierre Cardin suits, German BMWs—are finding enthusiastic acceptance in other countries. A global village seems to be emerging.

True, many companies have been carrying on international activities for decades. Companies such as Shell, Bayer, Toshiba, and other multinationals are familiar to most consumers around the world. But today, global competition is intensifying, and Canadian companies which have never thought about foreign competition increasingly find new competitors in their backyard. Over the years, Canadian consumers have grown accustomed to the dominance of Japanese cameras and German luxury cars. Canadian producers' loss of the markets for inexpensive textiles to Taiwan and other third-world countries is more recent. Even high-status brands like Nike footwear are made in the Third World.

But the most imminent threat for Canadian companies comes from the U.S. With tariffs quickly disappearing as a consequence of the Free Trade Agreement (see Marketing Environment and Trends 15-1), Canadian producers must become more competitive to protect their domestic markets. This threat is intensified in the service sector by the deregulation of industries such as transportation and financial services. Now, Canadian truckers have to compete with American firms who, after making a delivery in Canada, can pick up Canadian freight for their backhaul.

Although some would stem the foreign invasion through protective legislation, protectionism in the long run only raises living costs and protects inefficient domestic firms. The right answer is that companies must learn how to enter foreign markets and increase their global competitiveness.

Marketing Environment and Trends 15-1

THE CHALLENGE OF FREE TRADE

Since exchange is a value-creating process (see Chapter 1), logic suggests that barriers to exchange should be eliminated wherever possible. One such barrier between nations is the tariff which is levied on imported goods. Its purpose is to discourage imports and protect domestic producers from foreign competition. Its effect is to deny consumers the benefits of lower prices and preferred products. When tariffs between countries are eliminated, two things should happen. In the short term, the removal of the tariff protection should force domestic producers to become more competitive. In the long term, the resulting increase in the amount of exchange should yield benefits for all parties.

Worldwide tariffs have gradually been reduced by the General Agreement on Tariffs and Trade (GATT), and Canadian exporters have gradually benefited from the successive reductions. More dramatic benefits were realized by the Canada-U.S. Auto Pact, which allowed producers to move motor vehicles and parts across the border without any tariffs. Canadian plants and workers have benefited from a pro rata share of production, and Canadian consumers have benefited from lower prices on automobiles.

The recent Free Trade Agreement is intended to make virtually all trade between Canada and the U.S. subject to no tariffs. By the end of the nineties, the Canadian and U.S. economies should effectively be a customs union. Such a far-reaching arrangement could have a significant impact on certain industries and specific companies. The predicted short-term effects have already been observed: some plants have expanded, some have contracted, and some have moved to the U.S. The Economic Council of Canada has predicted that, as tariffs are phased out, some of the winning (+) and losing (–) industries will be:

☐ construction	+$2070 million
☐ food and accommodation	+ 586
☐ printing and publishing	+ 421
☐ primary metals	+ 337
☐ agriculture	+ 327
☐ business services	+ 171
☐ knitting mills	– 16
☐ electrical products	– 268

Critics of free trade point to the many short-term dislocations as companies adapt and workers have to find new jobs. Free-trade advocates argue that the long-term gain more than compensates for the short-term pain. They also claim that Canada really has no alternative, as the rest of the developed world reorganizes itself into trading blocs. Indeed, negotiations are proceeding to incorporate Mexico into the North American free-trade area, and ultimately, to extend a similar arrangement to the countries of Central and South America.

The challenge of free trade for marketers is to be adaptive. To survive and prosper, companies must regularly implement the strategic and marketing planning processes (see Chapters 2 and 3), and thereby adapt to the evolving opportunities and threats in an ever-broadening company environment.

Every country is trying to get more of its firms to internationalize. Every country wants to export more and import less. Export-promotion programs abound. Germany, the United Kingdom, and the Benelux and Scandinavian countries are now subsidizing marketing programs to help their firms move into export.[1] Denmark pays more than half the salary of marketing consultants to help small and medium-size Danish companies get into exports. Many countries go further and subsidize companies by granting preferential land and energy costs, and they even supply outright cash so that they can charge lower prices than their foreign competitors.

The more companies delay taking steps toward internationalizing, the more they risk being shut out of growing markets in Western Europe, Eastern Europe, the Far East, and elsewhere. The countries of the European Economic Community are stripping away barriers to the flow of goods, services, money, and people—they are deregulating business, privatizing some companies, and setting common commercial standards. New opportunities are proliferating in Eastern Europe as these countries struggle to convert from state-based economies to market-based economies.[2] Domestic businesses which thought they were safe now find companies from neighboring countries invading their markets. All companies will have to address some fundamental questions: What market position should we try to establish in our country, on our continent, and globally? Who will our competitors be and what are their strategies and resources? Where shall we produce or source our product? What strategic alliances should we form with other firms?

Ironically, while companies need to expand their foreign marketing, the risks are high. There are several major problems weighing on management's minds when they think of entering foreign markets:

1. *Huge Foreign Indebtedness:* Many countries with otherwise attractive markets have accumulated such high foreign indebtedness that they cannot even pay the interest on their foreign debt. Among these countries are Mexico, Brazil, and Poland.

2. *Unstable Governments:* High indebtedness, high inflation, and high unemployment in several countries have resulted in highly unstable governments that expose foreign firms to the risks of expropriation, nationalization, limits to profit repatriation, and so on.

3. *Foreign-Exchange Problems:* High indebtedness and economic and political instability force a country's currency to fluctuate or depreciate in value. Foreign firms want payment in hard currency with profit-repatriation rights, but that is not available in many markets. Foreign investors hesitate to hold much of the foreign currency, and this hesitancy limits trade.

4. *Foreign-Government Entry Requirements:* Governments place more regulations on foreign firms, such as requiring joint ownership with the majority share going to the domestic partner; a high number of nationals to be hired; technological transfer of trade secrets; and limits on profit repatriation;

5. *Tariffs and Other Trade Barriers:* Governments often impose high tariffs against imports in order to "subsidize" or protect their industries. They also resort to invisible trade barriers such as withholding or slowing down import approval and requiring adjustments in imported products to meet their standards.

6. *Corruption:* Officials in some countries require bribes before cooperating. Business is often awarded to the highest briber rather than the lowest bidder. Bribing officials is illegal for Canadian managers, whereas competitors from some other countries are subject to no such limitation.

7. *Technological Pirating:* A company locating its plant abroad worries about foreign managers learning how to make its product and breaking away to compete openly or clandestinely. This has happened in such diverse areas as machinery, electronics, chemicals, and pharmaceuticals.

8. *High Cost of Product and Communication Adaptation:* A company going abroad must study each foreign market carefully, become sensitive to its economics, politics, and culture, and make some adaptations in its products and communications to suit foreign tastes. Otherwise, it might make some serious blunders (see Marketing Strategies 15-1). It will bear higher costs and must be more patient in waiting for its profits to materialize.

GLOBAL MARKETING BLUNDERS

- Hallmark cards bombed in France. The French dislike syrupy sentiment and prefer writing their own cards.
- The Ronald McDonald promotion of McDonald's failed in Japan. White face means death.
- Philips only began to earn a profit in Japan only after it had reduced the size of its coffeemakers to fit into the smaller Japanese kitchens and its shavers to fit the smaller Japanese hands.
- Coca-Cola had to withdraw the two-litre bottle in Spain after discovering that few Spaniards owned refrigerators with large-enough compartments.
- General Foods's Tang initially failed in France because it was positioned as a substitute for orange juice at breakfast. The French drink little orange juice and almost none at breakfast.
- Kellogg's Pop-Tarts failed in Britain because the percentage of British homes with toasters was too small and the product was too sweet for British tastes.
- Crest initially failed in Mexico because Mexicans did not believe in or care about the decay prevention benefit, nor did scientifically oriented advertising appeal to them.
- General Foods squandered millions trying to introduce Japanese consumers to packaged cake mixes. The company failed to note that only 3 percent of Japanese homes were equipped with ovens.

One might conclude that companies are doomed whether they stay at home or go abroad. We would argue that companies selling in *global industries* have no choice but to internationalize their operations.

> A global industry *is an industry in which the strategic positions of competitors in major geographic or national markets are fundamentally affected by their overall global positions.*[3]

A *global firm* is therefore one that, in operating in more than one country, captures R&D, production, logistical, marketing, and financial advantages in its costs and reputation that are not available to purely domestic competitors. As an example, Ford's "world truck" has a European-made cab, a chassis built in Canada or the U.S., is assembled in Brazil, and brought back to North America for sale. Global firms plan, operate, and coordinate their activities on a worldwide basis.

Domestic firms in global industries must act before the window closes on them, since firms from other countries are globalizing at a rapid rate. This does not mean that small and medium-size firms must operate in over a dozen countries to succeed. These firms can practice global nichemanship, as many Scandinavian and Benelux companies do. A study of successful large and small multinationals would help firms in various countries proceed intelligently through the tangle of international business.

In this chapter, we will examine the following questions:

- What are the main features of the international marketing environment?
- What factors should a company consider in thinking about entering foreign markets?
- How can companies evaluate and select the right foreign markets to enter?
- What alternative ways are there for entering a foreign market?

□ To what extent should the company adapt its products and marketing program to the foreign country?

□ How should the company organize to handle its international activities?

APPRAISING THE GLOBAL MARKETING ENVIRONMENT

A company has to examine many issues before deciding whether and where to sell abroad. The company has to acquire a thorough understanding of the international marketing environment. The international marketing environment has undergone significant changes in the past two decades, creating new opportunities and new problems. The following are the most significant changes:

□ The globalization of the world economy reflected in the rapid growth of world trade and investment

□ The gradual erosion of some of Canada's traditional markets such as base metals, because of the ascendancy of Third-World producers

□ The rising economic power of Japan and several Far Eastern countries in world markets

□ The growing power of regional trade blocs, particularly the European Economic Community

□ The growth of global brands in autos, food, clothing, electronics, and many other categories

□ Rising trade barriers put up to protect domestic markets against foreign competition

□ The gradual opening up of major new markets, namely China, Eastern Europe, and the Arab countries

□ The severe debt problems of several countries, such as Mexico and Brazil, along with the increasing fragility of the international financial system

□ The increasing use of barter and countertrade to support international transactions

□ Movement in many countries toward "privatizing" publicly owned companies in order to make them more efficient

□ Increased forming of strategic alliances between major international companies from different countries—for example, General Motors and Toyota, GTE and Fujitsu, and Corning and Ciba-Geigy.

□ Substantial speedup of international transportation, communication, and financial transactions

The International Trade System

A company seeking to do business abroad needs to understand the international trade system. In attempting to sell to another country, a firm will face various trade restrictions. The most common is the *tariff*, which is a tax levied by the foreign government against designated imported products. The tariff may be designed to raise revenue (revenue tariff) or to protect domestic firms (protective tariff). The exporter might also face a *quota*, which sets limits on the amount of goods that the importing country will accept in certain product categories. The purpose of the quota is to conserve foreign exchange and protect local industry and employment. An *embargo* is the ultimate form of quota in that imports in prescribed categories are totally banned. Trade is also discouraged by *exchange control*, which regulates the amount of available foreign exchange and its exchange rate against other currencies. The company might also confront *nontariff barriers*, such as Japanese discrimination against Canadian company bids, and product standards that discriminate against Canadian product features. For example, the Dutch government bars tractors that run faster than sixteen kilometers per hour, which negates a product feature of the Massey-Ferguson tractors.

At the same time, certain forces seek to liberalize and foster trade between nations. The General Agreement on Tariffs and Trade (GATT) is an international agreement that has reduced the level of tariffs throughout the world on six different occasions. Today, however, GATT seems unable to preserve low tariffs against a growing wave of protectionism.

Several countries are joining economic communities, in which the member countries seek to eliminate tariffs between members while maintaining a common tariff against non-members. For a Canadian company, the most significant of these is clearly the evolving Canada-U.S.-Mexico community. Table 15-1 reveals that Canadian exports of goods to the U.S. in 1989 were $103.7 billion, or three-quarters of the total, and an increase of 130 percent over the previous decade. While exports to Mexico were much smaller, they were growing at an even faster rate.

Exports to European countries amounted to $12.5 billion. The European Economic Community currently consists of twelve Western European countries, and may soon be augmented by Austria, Switzerland, and the Scandinavian countries. Besides expanding business within the EEC, Canadian companies can anticipate opportunities to sell to countries in Eastern Europe. Some that have already done so include Bombardier, Alcan, Thomson, five chartered banks, and Northern Telecom. For example, Northern Telecom has joint ventures to convert telephone systems in Austria and Hungary.

The third major market for Canadian exports is Japan at $8.5 billion, plus the NIC's, or newly industrialized countries, of Asia at $4.8 billion. Trade with all of these countries is growing very rapidly, and it is anticipated that in time they will evolve into the world's third significant economic community, possibly including Australia and New Zealand.

Each national market has unique features which must be grasped. A nation's readiness to make or import different products and services and its attractiveness as a market to foreign firms depend on its economic, political-legal, cultural, and business environment.

Economic Environment

In considering foreign markets, the international marketer must study each country's economy. Three characteristics reflect a foreign country's attractiveness as an export market.

The first is the size of the country's *population*. Other things being equal, large countries are more attractive to exporters than small countries. Thus Turkey, with its fifty million people, is potentially a more attractive market for pharmaceutical products than Hungary, with its ten million people.

The second is the country's *industrial structure*. Four types of industrial structures can be distinguished:

1. *Subsistence Economies:* In a subsistence economy, the vast majority of people engage in simple agriculture. They consume most of their output and barter the rest for simple goods and services. They offer few opportunities for exporters.

2. *Raw-Material-Exporting Economies:* These economies are rich in one or more natural resources but poor in other respects. Much of their revenue comes from exporting these resources. Examples are Chile (tin and copper), Zaire (rubber), and Saudi Arabia (oil). These countries are good markets for extractive equipment, tools and supplies, materials-handling equipment, and trucks. Depending on the number of foreign residents and wealthy native rulers and landholders, they are also a market for Western-style commodities and luxury goods.

Table 15-1 Canada's Major Partners in Trade in Goods

	export value		import value	
	% change 1979-89	$ millions 1989	% change 1979-89	$ millions 1989
U.S.	+130	103 732	+110	93 322
EUROPE				
Switzerland	+290	719	+86	600
Norway	+127	635	+780	785
France	+103	1 260	+159	2 017
Belgium/Luxembourg	+84	1 231	+135	567
Sweden	+84	319	+145	939
Spain	+83	398	+220	567
Italy	+50	1 096	+216	2 012
Netherlands	+42	1 533	+227	823
Britain	+41	3 538	+145	4 604
West Germany	+30	1 777	+138	3 708
AUSTRALIA	+85	1 032	+34	618
JAPAN	+117	8 472	+291	8 262
NEWLY INDUSTRIALIZED ECONOMIES (NICs)				
Taiwan	+750	882	+350	2 352
Hong Kong	+637	1 014	+172	1 161
South Korea	+336	1 592	+427	2 441
Singapore	+112	243	+207	503
EMERGING NICs				
Indonesia	+371	295	+356	192
Thailand	+289	340	+1 224	420
Malaysia	+235	219	+232	320
Philippines	+159	219	+162	205
OTHER				
Mexico	+154	600	+706	1 680
China	+85	1 116	+606	1 182
Saudi Arabia	+34	337	-80	253
India	+32	297	+140	224
Brazil	+24	521	+261	1 130
U.S.S.R.	-11	685	+83	118
Algeria	-26	292	-66	30
TOTAL	+112	138 934	+120	134 255

Source: *The Financial Post 500*, Summer, 1990.

3. *Industrializing Economies:* In an industrializing economy, manufacturing begins to account for between 10 and 20 percent of the country's gross national product. Examples include India, Egypt, and the Philippines. As manufacturing increases, the country relies more on imports of textile raw materials, steel, and heavy machinery and less on imports of finished textiles, paper products, and automobiles. The industrialization creates a new rich class and a small but growing middle class, both demanding new types of goods, some of which can be satisfied only by imports.

4. *Industrial Economies:* Industrial economies are major exporters of manufactured goods and investment funds. They trade manufactured goods among themselves and also export them to other types of economies in exchange for raw materials and semifinished goods. The large and varied manufacturing activities of these industrial nations and their sizable middle class make them rich markets for all sorts of goods.

The third economic characteristic is the country's *income distribution.* Income distribution is related to a country's industrial structure but is also affected by the political system. The international marketer distinguishes countries with five different income-distribution patterns: (1) very low incomes, (2) mostly low incomes, (3) very low, very high incomes, (4) low, medium, high incomes, and (5) mostly medium incomes. Consider the market for Lamborghinis, an automobile costing more than fifty thousand dollars. The market would be very small in countries with type 1 or 2 income patterns. The largest single market for Lamborghinis turns out to be Portugal (income pattern 3), the poorest country in Europe, but one with enough wealthy status-conscious families to afford them.

Political-Legal Environment

Nations differ greatly in their political-legal environment. A company should consider four factors in deciding whether to do business in a particular country.

Attitudes Toward International Buying   Some nations are very receptive, indeed encouraging, to foreign firms, and others are very protectionistic. As an example of the former, Mexico for a number of years has been attracting foreign investment by offering investment incentives and site-location services. On the other hand, India in the past required the exporter to cope with import quotas, blocked currencies, local management requirements, and so on. IBM and Coca-Cola decided to leave India because of all the "hassles."

Political Stability   The country's future stability is another issue. Governments change hands, sometimes quite violently. Even without a change, a regime may decide to respond to populist feelings. The foreign company's property might be expropriated; or its currency holdings might be blocked; or import quotas or new duties might be imposed. Where political instability is high, international marketers might still find it profitable to do business in that country, but the situation will affect their mode of entry. They will prefer export marketing to direct foreign investment. They will keep their foreign stocks low. They will convert their currency rapidly. As a result, the people in the host country pay higher prices, have fewer jobs, and get less-satisfactory products.

Monetary Regulations   Sellers want to realize profits in a currency of value to them. In the best situation, the importer can pay in the seller's currency or a "hard" currency. Short of this, sellers might accept a blocked currency if they can buy needed goods in that country or goods that they can sell elsewhere for a needed currency. In the worst case, they have to take relatively unmarketable products that they can sell elsewhere only at a loss. (See the countertrade practices in Marketing Environment and Trends 15-2.) Besides currency restrictions, a fluctuating exchange rate also creates high risks for the exporter.

Government Bureaucracy   A fourth factor is the extent to which the host government runs an efficient system for assisting foreign companies: quick licensing procedures, efficient customs handling, adequate market information, and other factors conducive to doing business. Canadian companies have found it especially frustrating to do business with Eastern

HOW NATIONS HAVE BEEN MOVING BACK TO BARTER

Most international trade involves cash transactions. The buyer agrees to pay the seller in cash within a certain stated time period. Yet many nations today lack sufficient hard currency to pay for their purchases from other nations. They want to pay by trading other commodities. This practice is called countertrade. Its use in Eastern Europe diminished when the Communist bloc broke up, but it is still used by the less-developed countries. Although most vendors dislike countertrade deals, they may have no alternative if they want the business.

Countertrade takes several forms:

- *Barter:* Barter involves the direct exchange of goods, with no money and no third party involved. For example, the West Germans agreed to build a steel plant in Indonesia in exchange for Indonesian oil.

- *Compensation Deal:* Here the seller receives some percentage of the payment in cash and the rest in products. A British aircraft manufacturer sold planes to Brazil for 70 percent cash and the rest in coffee.

- *Buyback Arrangement:* The seller sells a plant, equipment, or technology to another country and agrees to accept as partial payment products manufactured with the equipment supplied. For example, a U.S. chemical company built a plant for an Indian company and accepted partial payment in cash and the remainder in chemicals to be manufactured at the plant.

- *Counterpurchase:* The seller receives full payment in cash but agrees to spend a substantial amount of money in that country within a stated time period. For example, Canada's armed forces bought Leopard tanks from Krauss-Maffei of West Germany under an arrangement which provided opportunities for Canadian subcontractors to provide components.

More complex countertrade deals involve more than two parties. For example, Daimler-Benz agreed to sell thirty trucks to Romania and accept in exchange 150 Romanian-made jeeps, which it sold in Ecuador for bananas, which in turn were sold to a West German supermarket chain for deutschmarks. Through this circuitous transaction, Daimler-Benz finally achieved payment in German currency. Various barter houses and countertrade specialists have emerged to assist the parties to these transactions. Everyone agrees that international trade would be more efficient if carried out in cash, but too many nations lack sufficient hard currency. Sellers have no choice but to learn the intricacies of countertrade, which is a growing phenomenon in world trade. (For further reading, see John W. Dizard, "The Explosion of International Barter," *Fortune*, February 7, 1983; and Leo G.B. Welt, *Trade without Money: Barter and Countertrade* [New York: Harcourt Brace Jovanovich, 1984].)

Bloc countries or the People's Republic of China. An executive even reported frustration in Portugal after his third month of waiting in Lisbon for the Ministry of International Trade to act on a proposal. A common shock to Canadians is the extent to which impediments to trade disappear if a suitable payment (bribe) is made to some official(s). (See Marketing Strategies 15-2.)

Cultural Environment

Each nation has its own values, customs, and taboos. Foreign businesspeople, if they are to be effective, must drop their ethnocentrism and try to understand the culture and business practices of their hosts, who often act on different concepts of time, space, and etiquette.

Marketing Strategies 15-2

MEGAMARKETING: BREAKING INTO BLOCKED MARKETS

It is one thing to want to do business in a particular country and another to be allowed in on reasonable terms. The problem of entering *blocked markets* calls for a *megamarketing approach*, defined as the strategic coordination of economic, psychological, political, and public-relations skills to gain the cooperation of a number of parties in order to enter and/or operate in a given market. Pepsi-Cola faced this problem in seeking to enter the Indian market:

> After Coca-Cola was asked to leave India, Pepsi began to lay plans to enter this huge market. Pepsi worked with an Indian business group to seek government approval for its entry over the objections of both domestic soft-drink companies and antimultinational legislators. Pepsi saw the solution to lie in making an offer that the Indian government would find hard to refuse. Pepsi offered to help India export its agro-based products in a volume that would more than cover the cost of importing soft-drink concentrate. Pepsi also promised to focus considerable selling effort on rural areas to help in their economic development. Pepsi further offered to transfer food-processing, packaging, and water-treatment tech-

nology to India. Clearly, Pepsi's strategy was to bundle a set of benefits that would win the support of various interest groups in India. ∎

Thus Pepsi's marketing problem was not the normal four Ps of operating effectively in a market, but rather the problem of getting in. Pepsi faced a six-P marketing problem, with *politics* and *public opinion* constituting the two additional Ps. Winning over the government and the public to gain admission is a much tougher challenge.

Once in, a multinational must be on its best behavior, since it is under great scrutiny, and critics abound. This task calls for well-thought-out *civic positioning* of the multinational. Olivetti, for example, enters new markets by building housing for workers, generously supporting local arts and charities, and hiring and training indigenous managers. In this way, it hopes to realize long-run profits by accepting high short-run costs.

Source: Philip Kotler, "Megamarketing," *Harvard Business Review*, March-April 1986, pp. 117-24.

The way foreign consumers perceive and use certain products must be checked out by the seller before planning the marketing program. Here is a sampling of some surprises in the consumer market:

- The average Frenchman uses almost twice as many cosmetics and beauty aids as does his wife.
- The Germans and the French eat more packaged, branded spaghetti than the Italians.
- Italian children like to eat a bar of chocolate between two slices of bread as a snack.
- Women in Tanzania will not give their children eggs for fear of making them bald or impotent.

Business Environment

Business norms and behavior also vary from country to country. Business executives need to be briefed before negotiating in another country. Here are some examples of foreign business behavior:

FIGURE 15-1
Major Decisions
in International
Marketing

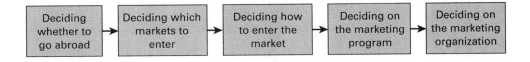

Each country (and even regional groups within each country) has cultural and business traditions, preferences, and taboos that the marketer must study.[4]

> Arab businessmen are accustomed to talking business in close physical proximity with other persons—in fact, almost nose to nose. They sometimes will take your hand and hold it as a sign of friendship. If the Canadian business executive retreats, the Arab is offended. ■
>
> In face-to-face communications, Japanese business executives rarely say no to a Canadian business executive. Canadians are frustrated and don't know where they stand. Canadians come to the point quickly. Japanese business executives find this offensive. ■
>
> In France, wholesalers don't care to promote a product. They ask their retailers what they want and deliver it. If a Canadian company builds its strategy around the French wholesaler cooperating in promotions, it is likely to fail. ■

Each country (and even regional groups within each country) has cultural and business traditions, preferences, and taboos that the marketer must study.[4]

We will now examine the five basic decisions that a company faces in international marketing (see Figure 15-1).

DECIDING WHETHER TO GO ABROAD

Most companies would prefer to remain domestic businesses if their domestic market were large enough. Managers would not need to learn another language, deal with strange and volatile currencies, face political and legal uncertainties and harassments, or redesign their products to suit quite different customer needs and expectations. Business would be easier and safer.

Yet there are several factors that might draw a company into the international arena. The company's domestic market might be attacked by global firms offering better products or lower prices (see Marketing Environment and Trends 15-3 for a partial explanation). The company might want to counterattack these competitors in their home markets to tie up their resources. The company might discover some foreign markets that present higher profit opportunities than the domestic market. The company might need an enlarged customer base in order to achieve economies of scale. The company might want to reduce its dependence on any one market so as to reduce its risk. The company's customers might be going abroad and require international servicing.

Before making a decision to go abroad, the company must weigh several risks. The company might not understand foreign-customer preferences and fail to offer a competitively attractive product. The company might not understand the foreign country's business culture and know how to deal effectively with foreign nationals. The company might underestimate foreign regulations and incur some unexpected costs. The company might realize that it lacks managers with international experience. The foreign country might change its commercial laws in an unfavorable way, might depreciate its currency or introduce exchange control, or might undergo a political revolution and expropriate foreign property.

Because of the competing advantages and risks, companies often don't act until some event thrusts them into the international arena. Someone—a domestic exporter, a foreign importer, a foreign government—solicits the company to sell abroad. Or the company is saddled with overcapacity and must find additional markets for its goods.

Marketing Environment and Trends 15-3

THE INTERNATIONAL PRODUCT LIFE CYCLE

One reason why domestic companies must pay attention to foreign market developments lies in the phenomenon of the *international product life cycle*. According to Wells, many products go through a trade cycle, during which the domestic company is initially an exporter, then loses its export markets, and may finally become an importer of the product, in the following four stages:

☐ *Domestic Producers Export Product:* An innovation is launched in the domestic market and succeeds. Eventually, domestic producers start exporting the product to other countries.

☐ *Foreign Production Starts:* As foreign producers become familiar with the product, some of them start producing it for their home market. They do this under licensing or joint-venture arrangement or simply by copying the product. Their government often abets their efforts by imposing tariffs or quotas on imports of the product.

☐ *Foreign Production Becomes Competitive in Export Markets:* By now, foreign producers have gained production experience, and with their lower costs, they start exporting the product to other countries.

☐ *Import Competition Begins:* The foreign producers' growing volume and lower costs enable them to compete with, and export to, the domestic market of the original producers.

Thus the product has moved from a *new product* (stage 1) to a *mature product* (stage 2) to a *stan-*

dardized product (stages 3 and 4). The implication is that the producer's sales in the domestic market will eventually decline as foreign markets start producing the product and ultimately export it to the domestic market. The domestic producer's best defense is to become a global marketer and open production and distribution facilities in other countries with large markets and/or lower costs. Global marketers are able to stretch the product life cycle of any product form by taking it to the countries that are getting ready to use it.

Source: See Louis T. Well, Jr., "A Product Life Cycle for International Trade?" *Journal of Marketing*, July 1968, pp. 1-6. The original formulation was stated in Raymond Vernon, "International Investment and International Trade in the Product Cycle," *Quarterly Journal of Economics*, May 1966, pp. 190-207. The international product life cycle describes past developments in such markets as office machinery, consumer durables, and synthetic materials. Some critics feel that it has less validity today because multinational enterprises now operate vast global networks through which they might innovate new products anywhere in the world and move them through various countries not necessarily in the sequence predicted by the original formulation of the international PLC. See Ian H. Giddy, "The Demise of the Product Cycle Model in International Business Theory," *Columbia Journal of World Business*, Spring 1978, p. 92; and Raymond Vernon, "The Product Cycle Hypothesis in a New International Environment," *Oxford Bulletin of Economics and Statistics*, November 1979, pp. 255-67.

DECIDING WHICH MARKETS TO ENTER

In deciding to go abroad, the company needs to define its *international marketing objectives and policies*. What *proportion of foreign to total sales* will it seek? Most companies start small when they venture abroad. Some plan to stay small, viewing foreign operations as a small part of their business. Other companies will have more-grandiose plans, seeing foreign business as ultimately equal to, or even more important than, their domestic business.

The company must decide whether to market in a *few countries* or *many countries*. The Bulova Watch Company made the latter choice and expanded into over one hundred countries. It spread itself too thin, made profits in only two countries, and lost around $40 million.

Generally speaking, it makes sense to operate in fewer countries with a deeper commitment and penetration in each. Ayal and Zif argued that a company should enter fewer countries when

☐ Market entry and market control costs are high;

☐ Product and communication adaptation costs are high;

☐ Population and income size and growth are high in the initial countries chosen; and

☐ Dominant foreign firms can establish high barriers to entry.[5]

The company must also decide on the *types of countries* to consider. Country attractiveness is influenced by the product, geographical factors, income and population, political climate, and other factors. The seller might have a predilection for certain groups of countries or parts of the world. Kenichi Ohmae, for example, argues that only the "triad powers"—the United States, Europe, and Japan—are worth pursuing as markets (see Marketing Strategies 15-3).

Suppose a company has assembled a list of potential export markets. How does it chose among them? Many companies opt for selling to neighboring countries because they understand those countries better, and distribution and control costs are lower because of the proximity. Thus it is not surprising that Canada's largest market is the U.S., or that Swedish companies first sold their goods to their Scandinavian neighbors. Sometimes, societal proximity rather than geographical proximity determines choices. Consider the following example:

> CMC's market research in the computer field revealed that England, France, West Germany, and Italy offer us significant markets. England, France, and Germany are about equal-size markets, while Italy represents about two-thirds the potential of any one of those countries. . . . Taking everything into consideration, we decided to set up first in England because its market for our products is as large as any and its language and laws are similar to ours. England is different enough to get your feet wet, yet similar enough to the familiar U.S. business environment so that you do not get in over your head.[6]

Yet one can question whether the reason for selecting England—the compatibility of its language and culture—should have been given this prominence. The candidate countries should be initially rated on three major criteria, namely, *market attractiveness, competitive advantage*, and *risk*. Here is an example:

> The International Hough Company manufacturers mining equipment and is evaluating China and four Eastern European countries as possible market opportunities. It first rates the market attractiveness of each country, looking at such indicators as GNP/capita, work force in mining, imports of machinery, and population growth. It then rates its own potential competitive advantage in each country, looking at such indicators as prior business dealings, whether it would be a low-cost producer, whether its senior management can work comfortably in that country. Finally it rates the risk level of each country, looking at such indicators as political stability, currency stability, and repatriation rules (see Marketing Concepts and Tools 15-1). By indexing, weighing, and combining the various numbers, it arrives at the picture shown in Figure 15-2. China appears to present the best opportunity insofar as it rates high on market attractiveness and competitive advantage, and low on risk. Romania, on the other hand, ranks low on market attractiveness, medium on competitive advantage, and high on risk. ∎

This approach provides an initial ranking of the candidate countries according to their overall attractiveness. China is first, followed by Czechoslovakia and East Germany. Now International Hough must prepare a financial analysis of these three countries to see what it could expect to earn on its investment. It could turn out that none of the countries promises

Marketing Strategies 15-3

SHOULD MULTINATIONALS RESTRICT THEIR TRADE TO THE TRIAD MARKETS?

Some trade strategists have argued that it is not worthwhile to sell in the Third World; the lucrative markets are in the United States, Europe, and Japan. Kenichi Ohmae, the head of McKinsey's office in Tokyo, argues this view in his *Triad Power*. He notes that

> opportunities are great in booming states such as California, which is bigger than Brazil (in economic terms), and Texas, whose gross state product is bigger than the combined GNP of the Association of Southeast Asian Nations.

He goes on to say:

> The "triad" of Japan, Europe, and U.S. represents not only the major and fastest growing market for most products but also an increasingly homogeneous one. Gucci bags, Sony Walkmans, and McDonald's hamburgers are seen on the streets of Tokyo, Paris, and New York.

Ohmae would advise multinationals to pull out of low-income countries and put more resources in the triad markets. He also thinks multinationals make a mistake rushing to Third World countries to produce components just because the wages are lower. Low wages do not necessarily spell lower costs if the labor is inefficient or product quality is poorer. With growing automation, labor costs are becoming smaller anyway.

Ohmae also sees multinationals as taking too much time to introduce their new products into foreign markets. As a result, swift competitors copy their products and capture leadership in these foreign markets. His solution: A multinational should form longstanding strategic alliances (licenses, joint ventures, consortia, and so forth) with companies that operate in each triad market, so that the multinational could introduce its new products in all triad markets simultaneously and establish market leadership. This strategy would provide a sufficient-size market to justify larger initial plant investment and lower unit costs. In addition, the multinational need not worry about being kept out by trade barriers, since its partners would be "insiders" in the foreign markets.

While Ohmae's position makes short-run sense—that is, profits are likely to be better in the triad regions—it can spell a disastrous policy for the world economy in the long run. Although the triad markets possess most of the world's purchasing power, they do not represent most of the world's latent demand. The triad markets are rich but mature: Companies have to strain their creativity to find growth opportunities in these markets. In contrast, the unmet needs of the developing world represent an ocean of opportunity. They are huge potential markets for food, clothing, shelter, consumer electronics, appliances, and other goods that triad markets take for granted. Unless purchasing power is somehow put into the Third World, the industrial world will remain saddled with excess productive capacity and a very slow growth rate; and the developing economies will be stuck with excess consumer needs that they are unable to satisfy. Somehow various governments and multinationals must find ways to link these two worlds together dynamically and synergistically in a mutually beneficial relationship.

Source: See Kenichi Ohmae, *Triad Power* (New York: Free Press, 1985).

a sufficient return, or that they all do. Five steps are involved in estimating the probable rate of return on investment:

1. *Estimate of Current Market Potential:* The first step is to estimate total industry sales in each market. This task calls for using published data and data collected through company surveys.

Marketing Concepts and Tools 15-1

Assessing Country Risk

The daily news is so filled with reports of unstable governments and faltering economies that business firms are of course hesitant to put their investment at risk in another country. If seemingly secure governments like the shah's regime in Iran and Marcos's regime in the Philippines could topple, can any country be depended on? Since 1960, over fifteen hundred companies were expropriated in 511 separate actions by seventy-six nations. Even short of expropriation, a company could lose its investment because of strikes, currency devaluation, blocked currency, and so on.

Analysts distinguish between two types of country risk. The first is *asset protection/investment recovery risk*, which arises from direct action taken by the government or the people that results in destroying, expropriating, or limiting transfer of invested resources. The second is *operational profitability/cash-flow risk*, which arises from economic downturns, currency depreciation, strikes, and so on. Some analysts think of the former risk as political risk and the latter risk as economic risk, but both types often intermingle.

No wonder then that companies are large buyers of *political-risk-assessment reports*. Supplied by a number of specialist firms, they include Business International's (BI) Country Assessment Service, which surveys seventy-one countries twice a year; BERI, which surveys forty-five countries three times a year; and Frost & Sullivan's World Political Risk Forecasts, which summarizes sixty countries monthly. Using somewhat different models and measurement techniques, these services come up with numerical ratings showing each country's current risk level and, in some cases, their expected risk level three years from now.

Many companies find these estimates interesting, but inadequate. They measure the *macrorisk* affecting all foreign companies but not the *microrisk* facing any particular company or industry. For example, a country may present little macrorisk but might be planning to nationalize foreign oil companies. Consequently, companies need to supplement macrorisk estimates with other methods of gaining insight into the risk they would face. General Motors and Caterpillar use advisory councils of prominent foreign experts. Gulf Oil has its own political-risk-assessment office staffed with area experts. Many companies send their senior officers on periodic grand tours to various countries where they have or are planning major investments, to talk to government officials and their own staff about recent and expected developments.

Sources: For further reading, see Stephan Kobrin, "Political Risk: A Review and Reconsiderations," *Journal of International Business Studies*, November 1980; R. J. Rummel and D. A. Heenan, "How Multinationals Analyze Political Risk," *Harvard Business Review*, January-February, 1978; and Louis Kraar, "The Multinationals Get Smarter about Political Risks," *Fortune*, March 24, 1980.

2. *Forecast of Future Market Potential and Risk:* The firm also needs to forecast future industry sales, a difficult task. It requires predicting economic and political developments and their impact on industry sales.

3. *Forecast of Sales Potential:* Estimating the company's sales requires forecasting its probable market share based on its competitive advantage, another difficult task.

4. *Forecast of Costs and Profits:* Costs will depend on the company's contemplated entry strategy. If it exports or licenses, its costs will be spelled out in the contracts. If it locates manufacturing facilities in the country, its cost estimation will require understanding local labor conditions, taxes, trade practices, and so on. The company subtracts estimated costs

FIGURE 15-2

Evaluating Which Markets to Enter

Market Attractiveness

	High	Medium	Low	
H	China			
M		Czech.		L
L	East Germany			
H		Poland		
M			Romania	H
L				

Competitive Advantage

Risk

from estimated sales to derive company profits for each year of the planning horizon.

5. *Estimate of Rate of Return On Investment:* The forecasted income stream should be related to the investment stream to derive the implicit rate of return. This should be high enough to cover the company's normal target return on its investment and the risk of marketing in that country.[7]

DECIDING HOW TO ENTER THE MARKET

Once a company decides to target a particular country, it has to determine the best mode of entry. Its broad choices are *indirect exporting, direct exporting, licensing, joint ventures,* and *direct investment.* Each succeeding strategy involves more commitment, risk, control, and profit potential. The five market-entry strategies are shown in Figure 15-3 and examined on the following pages.

Indirect Export

The normal way to get involved in a foreign market is through export. *Occasional exporting* is a passive level of involvement where the company exports from time to time on its own or in response to unsolicited orders from abroad. *Active exporting* takes place when the company makes a commitment to expand exports to a particular market. In either case, the company produces all of its goods in the home country. It might or might not adapt them to the foreign market. Exporting involves the least change in the company's product lines, organization, investments, or mission.

FIGURE 15-3

Five Modes of Entry Into Foreign Markets

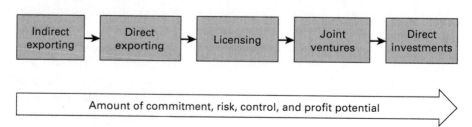

Amount of commitment, risk, control, and profit potential

Companies typically start with *indirect exporting*, that is, they work through independent middlemen. Four types of middlemen are available to the company:

- *Domestic-Based Export Merchant:* This middleman buys the manufacturer's product and sells it abroad on its own account.
- *Domestic-Based Export Agent:* This agent seeks and negotiates foreign purchases and is paid a commission. Included in the group are trading companies.
- *Cooperative Organization:* A cooperative organization carries on exporting activities on behalf of several producers and is partly under their administrative control. This form is often used by producers of primary products—fruits, nuts, and so on.
- *Export-Management Company:* This middleman agrees to manage a company's export activities for a fee.

Indirect export has two advantages. First, it involves less investment. The firm does not have to develop an export department, an overseas salesforce, or a set of foreign contacts. Second, it involves less risk. International-marketing middlemen bring know-how and services to the relationship, and the seller will normally make fewer mistakes.

Direct Export

Companies eventually undertake handling their own exports. The investment and risk are somewhat greater, but so is the potential return. The company can carry on direct exporting in several ways:

- *Domestic-Based Export Department or Division:* An export sales manager carries on the actual selling and draws on market assistance as needed. It might evolve into a self-contained export department performing all the activities involved in export and operating as a profit center.
- *Overseas Sales Branch or Subsidiary:* An overseas sales branch allows the manufacturer to achieve greater presence and program control in the foreign market. The sales branch handles sales distribution and might handle warehousing and promotion as well. It often serves as a display center and customer-service center.
- *Traveling Export Sales Representatives:* The company can send home-based sales representatives abroad to find business.
- *Foreign-Based Distributors or Agents:* The company can hire foreign-based distributors or agents to sell the goods on behalf of the company. They might be given exclusive rights to represent the manufacturer in that country or only general rights.

Licensing

Licensing represents a simple way for a manufacturer to become involved in international marketing. The licensor enters an agreement with a licensee in the foreign market, offering the right to use a manufacturing process, trademark, patent, trade secret, or other item of value for a fee or royalty. The licensor gains entry into the market at little risk; the licensee gains production expertise or a well-known product or name without having to start from scratch. Gerber introduced its baby foods in the Japanese market through a licensing arrangement. Coca-Cola carries out its international marketing by licensing bottlers around the world—or, more technically, franchising bottlers—and supplies them with the syrup needed to produce the product.

Licensing has potential disadvantages in that the firm has less control over the licensee than if it had set up its own production facilities. Furthermore, if the licensee is very successful, the firm has foregone profits, and if and when the contract ends, it might find that it has created a competitor. To avoid creating a future competitor, the licensor usually supplies some ingredients or components needed in the product. But the main hope is for the licensor to lead in innovation so that the licensee will continue to depend on this licensor.

Companies can enter foreign markets on other bases. A company can sell a *management contract* in which it offers to manage a hotel, an airport, a hospital, or other organization in return for a fee. In this case, the firm is exporting a service instead of a product. Management contracting is a low-risk method of getting into a foreign market, and it yields income from the beginning. The arrangement is especially attractive if the contracting firm is given an option to purchase some share in the managed company within a stated period. On the other hand, the arrangement is not sensible if the company can put its scarce management talent to better uses or if there are greater profits to be made by undertaking the whole venture. Management contracting prevents the company from setting up its competing companies for a period of time.

Another entry method is *contract manufacturing*, where the firm engages local manufacturers to produce the product. When Sears opened department stores in Mexico and Spain, Sears found qualified local manufacturers to produce many of its products. Contract manufacturing has the drawback of less control over the manufacturing process and the loss of potential profits on manufacturing. On the other hand, it offers the company a chance to start faster, with less risk, and with the opportunity to form a partnership or buy out the local manufacturer later.

Joint Ventures

In joint ventures, foreign investors join with local investors to create a new company in which they share joint ownership and control. Forming a jointly owned venture might be necessary or desirable for economic or political reasons. The foreign firm might lack the financial, physical, or managerial resources to undertake the venture alone. Or the foreign government might require joint ownership as a condition for entry.

Joint ownership has certain drawbacks. The partners might disagree over investment, marketing, or other policies. One partner might want to reinvest earnings for growth, and the other partner might want to take out these earnings. Furthermore, joint ownership can hamper a multinational company from carrying out specific manufacturing and marketing policies on a worldwide basis.[8]

Direct Investment

The ultimate form of foreign involvement is direct ownership of foreign-based assembly or manufacturing facilities. The foreign company can buy part or full interest in a local company or build its own facilities. As a company gains experience in export, and if the foreign market appears large enough, foreign production facilities offer distinct advantages. First, the firm could secure cost economies in the form of cheaper labor or raw materials, foreign-government investment incentives, freight savings, and so on. Second, the firm will gain a better image in the host country because it creates jobs. Third, the firm develops a deeper relationship with government, customers, local suppliers, and distributors, enabling it to adapt its products better to the local marketing environment. Fourth, the firm retains full control over the investment and therefore can develop manufacturing and marketing policies that serve its long-term international objectives.

The main disadvantage is that the firm exposes its large investment to risks such as blocked or devalued currencies, worsening markets, or expropriation. The firm will find it expensive to reduce or close down its operations, since the host country might require substantial severance pay to the employees. The firm, however, has no choice but to accept these risks if it wants to operate on its own in the host country.

The Internationalization Process

Many companies show a distinct preference for a particular mode of entry. One company might prefer exporting because it minimizes its risk. Another company might prefer licensing because it is an easy way to make money. Another company might favor direct investment because it wants full control. Yet insisting on one mode of entry is too limiting. Some countries will not permit imports of certain goods nor allow direct investment but will only accept a joint-owned venture with a foreign national. Consequently, companies must learn and master all of these entry methods. Even though a company might have preferences, it needs to adapt to each situation. Most sophisticated multinationals manage several different entry modes simultaneously.

The problem facing most countries is that too few of their companies participate in foreign trade. This keeps the country from earning sufficient foreign exchange to pay for needed imports. Consequently, governments have turned to aggressive export promotion. Yet export-promotion programs rarely achieve their goals. They are not based on a deep understanding of how companies become internationalized.

Johanson and his associates have studied the *internationalization process* among Swedish companies.[9] They see firms moving through four stages:

1. No regular export activities
2. Export via independent representatives (agents)
3. Establishment of one or more sales subsidiaries
4. Establishment of production facilities abroad

The first task is to get companies to move from stage 1 to stage 2. This move is helped by studies of how other firms made their first export decisions.[10] Most firms work with an independent agent, usually in a country posing low psychic barriers to entry. A company then engages further agents to enter additional countries. Later, it establishes an export department to manage its agent relationships. Still later, the company replaces its agents with sales subsidiaries in its larger export markets. This increases the company's investment and risk but also increases its earning potential. To manage these sales subsidiaries, the company replaces the export department with an international department. If certain markets continue to be large and stable, or if the host country insists on local production, the company takes the next step of locating production facilities in those markets, representing a still larger commitment and still larger potential earnings. By this time, the company is operating as a multinational company and reconsidering the best way to organize and manage its global operations.

DECIDING ON THE MARKETING PROGRAM

Companies that operate in one or more foreign markets must decide how much to adapt their marketing-strategy mix to local conditions. At one extreme are companies that use a *standardized marketing mix* worldwide. Standardization of the product, advertising, distribution channels, and other elements of the marketing mix promises the lowest costs because no major changes have been introduced. At the other extreme is the idea of an *adapted marketing mix*, where the producer adjusts the marketing-mix elements to each target market, bearing more costs but hoping for a larger market share and profit return. Between these two extremes, many possibilities exist. The debate is described more fully in Marketing Strategies 15-4. Here we will examine potential adaptations that firms might make of their product, promotion, price, and distribution as they enter foreign markets.

Product

Keegan distinguished five adaptation strategies of product and promotion to a foreign market (see Figure 15-4).[11]

Straight extension means introducing the product in the foreign market without any change. Top management instructs its people: "Take the product as it is and find customers for it." The first step, however, should be to determine whether the foreign consumers use that product. Deodorant usage among men ranges from 80 percent in North America, to 55 percent in Sweden to 28 percent in Italy to 8 percent in the Philippines. Many Spaniards do not use such common products as butter and cheese.

Straight extension has been successful with cameras, consumer electronics, many machine tools, and so on, but a disaster in other cases. General Foods introduced its standard powdered Jell-O in the British market only to find that British consumers prefer the solid wafer or cake form. Campbell Soup lost an estimated $30 million in introducing its condensed soups in England; the consumers saw the small-size cans and did not realize that water was to be added. Straight extension is tempting because it involves no additional R&D expense, manufacturing retooling, or promotional modification. But it can be costly in the long run.

Product adaptation involves altering the product to meet local conditions or preferences. There are several levels of adaptation. A company can produce a *regional version* of its product, such as a Western European version, a North American version, and so on. Or it can produce a *country version*. In Japan, Mister Donut's coffee cup is smaller and lighter to fit the finger size of the average Japanese consumer; even the doughnuts are a little smaller. In Australia, Heinz sells a baby food made from strained lamb brains; and in the Netherlands, a baby food made from strained brown beans. General Foods blends different coffees for the British (who drink their coffee with milk), the French (who drink their coffee black), and Latin Americans (who want a chicory taste). A company can produce a *city version* of its product, for instance, a beer to meet Munich tastes or Tokyo tastes. Finally, a company can produce *middleman versions* of its product, such as a coffee brew for the Migros chain store and another for the Cooperative chain store, both in Switzerland.

FIGURE 15-4
Five International Product and Promotion Strategies

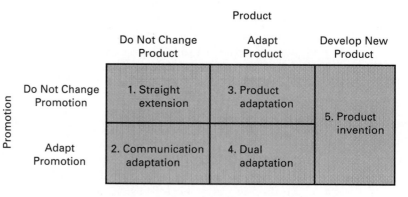

Marketing Strategies 15-4

GLOBAL STANDARDIZATION OR ADAPTATION?

Traditional supporters of the marketing concept hold that consumers vary in their needs and that marketing programs will be more effective if tailored to each customer target group. Since this applies within a country, it should apply even more cogently in foreign markets where economic, political, and cultural conditions vary widely.

Yet many multinationals are bothered by what they see as an excessive amount of adaptation. Consider Gillette:

> Gillette sells over eight hundred products in more than two hundred countries. It has fallen into a situation where different brand names are used for the same product in different countries, and where the same brand is formulated differently in different countries. Gillette's Silkience shampoo is called Soyance in France, Sientel in Italy, and Silience in Germany; and its formula is the same in some cases but varies in others. Its advertising messages and copy are also varied because each Gillette country manager proposes several changes that he or she thinks will increase sales. Headquarters management feels at a loss to think that it might know more about the local situation than the country managers. ■

As a result, Gillette and other companies have been anxious to impose more standardization, globally or at least regionally. They see this as a way to save costs and to build up global brand power.

And along have come the British advertising firm of Saatchi & Saatchi and Professor Theodore Levitt of Harvard to help them. Saatchi & Saatchi has won several new advertising accounts on the strength of their claim that they can build single advertising campaigns that will work globally. Meanwhile, Professor Levitt supplied the intellectual rationale for global standardization. He wrote:

> The world is becoming a common marketplace in which people—no matter where they live—desire the same products and lifestyles. Global companies must forget the idiosyncratic differences between countries and cultures and instead concentrate on satisfying universal drives.

Levitt believes that new communication and transportation technologies have created a more homogeneous world market. People around the world want the same basic things—things that make life easier and increase their discretionary time and buying power. This convergence of needs and wants has created global markets for standardized products.

According to Levitt, traditional multinational corporations focus on differences between specific markets. They cater to superficial preference differences and produce a proliferation of highly adapted products. Adaptation results in less efficiency and higher prices to consumers.

In contrast, the global corporation sells the same product the same way to all consumers. It focuses on similarities across world markets and aggressively works to "sensibly force suitably standardized products and services on the entire globe." These global marketers realize substantial economies through standardization of production, distribution, marketing, and management. They translate their efficiency into greater value for consumers by offering high quality and more-reliable products at lower prices.

Levitt would advise an auto company to make a world car, a shampoo company to make a world shampoo, and a tractor company to make a world tractor. In fact, some companies have successfully marketed global products: Coca-Cola, McDonald's hamburgers, A. T. Cross pens and pencils, Sony Walkmans, and so on. Some products are more global and require less adaptation on the whole. Yet even in these cases, some adaptation takes place. Coca-Cola is less sweet or less carbonated in certain countries; McDonald's uses chili sauce instead of ketchup on its hamburgers in Mexico; and Cross pens and pencils have different advertising copy and messages in some countries.

Professor Levitt assumes that global standardization will save a lot of cost, will lead to lower prices, and cause more goods to be snapped up by price-sensitive consumers. But these assumptions are debatable. A company needs to think in terms of incremental revenue versus incremental cost. Consider the following:

> Mattel Toys had successfully sold its Barbie doll in dozens of countries without modification. But in Japan, Barbie did not sell well. Takara, its Japanese licensee, surveyed eighth-grade girls and they (and their parents) thought the doll's breasts were too big and legs were too long. Mattel, however, was reluctant to modify the doll, because this would require additional production, packaging, and advertising costs. Finally, Takara prevailed, and within two years, Takara sold some two million of the modified Barbie doll. Clearly, the incremental revenue far exceeded the incremental cost. ■

Rather than assuming that the company's product can be introduced as is in another country, the company should review all possible adaptation elements and determine which adaptations would add more revenue than cost. The adaptation elements include product features and other marketing mix elements:

Product features	Colors
Name	Materials
Labeling	Advertising themes
Advertising media	Prices
Advertising execution	Packaging
Sales promotion	

One study showed that companies made one or more marketing-mix adaptations in 80 percent of their foreign-directed products and that the average number of adaptations was four. It should also be recognized that some host countries require adaptations, independent of whether the company wants to make them. The French do not allow children to be used in ads; the Germans ban the use of the word *best* to describe a product, and so on.

Thus global standardization is not an all-or-nothing proposition but a matter of degree. Companies are certainly justified in looking for more standardization, regionally if not globally. Goodyear, for example, is trying to bring regional uniformity into its logos, corporate advertising, and product lines in continental Europe so that it will have a more coherent presence. Resistance typically arises from country managers because regional standardization puts more power into the hands of the regional manager and less in each country manager. And country managers might have been excessive in the changes they ask for. Yet, all said, companies must remember that while standardization might save some costs, competitors are always ready to offer more of what the customers in each country want, and the company might pay dearly for replacing long-run marketing thinking with short-run financial thinking. Global marketing, yes; global standardization, not necessarily.

Sources: Theodore Levitt, "The Globalization of Markets," *Harvard Business Review,* May-June 1983, pp. 92-102. For an example of the work involved in building a single global campaign, see "Playtex Kicks Off a One-Ad-Fits-All Campaign," *Business Week,* December 16, 1985, pp. 48-49. For a negative assessment of global standardization attempts, see "Marketers Turn Sour on Global Sales Pitch Harvard Guru Makes," *Wall Street Journal,* May 12, 1988, p. 1. For a well-balanced approach, see John A. Quelch and Edward J. Hoff, "Customizing Global Marketing," *Harvard Business Review,* May-June 1986, pp. 59-68.

International companies often develop a product version to meet *basic needs* in developing economies. Ciba-Geigy has set up a specific product line for these markets, distinguished by a narrower and more-focused range (stressing, for example, antibiotics) and by "no-frills" packaging, allowing a reduced price. This concept, close to a branded generics line, is equally applicable to other areas, such as the food and beverage industry.

Product invention is creating something new. It can take two forms. *Backward invention* is reintroducing earlier product forms that are well adapted to a foreign country's needs. The National Cash Register Company reintroduced its crank-operated cash register at half the price of a modern cash register and sold substantial numbers in the Orient, Latin America, and Spain. That illustrates the *international product life cycle* where countries stand at different stages of readiness to accept a particular product. *Forward invention* is creating a new product to meet a need in another country. There is an enormous need in less-developed countries for low-cost, high-protein foods. Companies like Quaker Oats, Swift, and Monsanto are researching the nutrition needs of these countries, formulating new foods, and developing advertising campaigns to gain product trial and acceptance. Product invention is a costly strategy, but the payoffs can also be great.

A growing part of international trade is taking place in services in addition to goods. In fact, the world market for services is growing at double the rate of world merchandise trade. The largest firms in such service businesses as accounting, advertising, banking, communications, construction, insurance, law, and management consulting are pursuing global expansion. Service companies like American Express, Citicorp, Club Med, Hilton, and Thomas Cook are known worldwide. At the same time, many countries have erected barriers to entry or regulations that make the exporting of services difficult. Brazil requires all accountants to possess a professional degree from a Brazilian university. Some European countries limit the importation of television programs. The objectives of GATT are to encourage more free trade in services, but negotiations are proceeding very slowly.

Promotion

Companies can either run the same advertising-and-promotion campaign used in the home market or change it for each local market.

Consider the message. The company can change the message at three different levels. The company can use one message around the world by varying only the language, name, and colors. Exxon used "Put a tiger in your tank" with minor variations and gained international recognition. Colors were changed to avoid taboos in some countries. Purple is associated with death in most of Latin America; white is a mourning color in China and Korea; and green is associated with disease in countries with dense, green jungle. Even names and headlines have to be modified. In Germany, *mist* means "manure," and *scotch* (scotch tape) means "schmuck"; in Spain, Chevrolet's *Nova* translates as no va, which means "it doesn't go"! An Electrolux vacuum cleaner ad, translated from Swedish into English was run in a Korean magazine reading "Nothing sucks like Electrolux." And a laundry soap ad claiming to wash "really dirty parts" was translated in French-speaking Quebec to read "a soap for washing 'private parts.'"

The next possibility is to use the same theme globally but adapt the copy to each local market:

> A Camay soap commercial showed a beautiful woman bathing. In Venezuela, a man was seen in the bathroom; in Italy and France, only a man's hand was seen; and in Japan, the man waited outside. ∎

Finally, some companies encourage their ad agencies to make a full adaptation of theme and execution to the local market. Consider the following two examples:

> Kraft uses different ads for Cheez Whiz in different countries, given that household penetration is 95 percent in Puerto Rico, where the cheese is put on everything; 65 percent in Canada, where it is spread on toast in the morning breakfast; and 35 percent in the United States, where it is considered a junk food. ∎

> Renault advertises its car differently in different countries. In France, Renault is described as a little "supercar," which is fun to drive on highways and in the city. In Germany, Renault emphasizes safety, modern engineering, and interior comfort. In Italy, Renault emphasizes road handling and acceleration. And in Finland, Renault emphasizes solid construction and reliability. ∎

The use of media also requires international adaptation because media availability varies from country to country. Commercial radio or TV is not even available in some Scandinavian countries and Middle Eastern countries. In Germany, advertisers have access to commercial TV only during a few preannounced short time blocks, none of which interrupt the program. As a result, viewership of these commercial time blocks is low. Yet companies complain that they must buy time months in advance and have little control over when their ads will be broadcast. Certain countries add restrictions as to what can be advertised, often not allowing cigarette or alcoholic-beverage advertising on TV. The rapid growth of VCR usage in Europe has cut further into the size of TV audiences. Another medium, magazines, varies in its effectiveness; magazines play a major role in Italy and a minor one in Austria. Newspapers have a national reach in the United Kingdom, but the advertiser can buy only local newspaper coverage in Spain.

Marketers must also adapt their sales-promotion techniques to different markets. Germany and Greece, for example, prohibit coupons, whereas coupons are the leading form of consumer sales promotion in Canada. France prohibits games of chance and limits premiums and gifts to 5 percent of product value. The result of these varying restrictions is that international companies generally assign sales promotion as a responsibility of local management.

Price

Multinationals face a number of problems in setting their international prices. In setting a global pricing policy, companies have three choices:

1. *Setting a Uniform Price Everywhere:* Thus Coca-Cola might want to charge forty cents everywhere in the world. But this would be too high a price in poor countries and not high enough in rich countries.

2. *Setting a Market-Based Price in Each Country:* Here Coca-Cola would charge what each country would bear. But this ignores differences in the actual cost from country to country. Also it would lead to a situation where middlemen in low-price countries transhipped their Coca-Cola to high-price countries.

3. *Setting a Cost-Based Price in Each Country:* Here Coca-Cola would use a standard markup of its costs everywhere. But this might price Coca-Cola out of the market in certain countries where its costs are high.

Regardless of their choice, companies' foreign prices are likely to be higher than their domestic prices (unless they subsidize the foreign prices). The reason lies in the *price-escalation phenomenon.* A Gucci handbag may sell for $120 in Italy and $240 in Canada. Why? Gucci has to add the cost of transportation, tariffs, importer margin, wholesaler margin, and retailer margin to its factory price. Depending on these added costs, as well as the currency-fluctuation risk, the product might have to sell for two to five times as much in another country to make the same profit for the manufacturer.

Another problem arises when a company sets a *transfer price* for goods that it ships to its foreign subsidiaries. Consider the following:

> The Swiss pharmaceutical company Hoffman-Laroche charged its Italian subsidiary only $22 a kilo for librium in order to make high profits in Italy where the corporate taxes were lower. It charged its British subsidiary $925 per kilo for the same librium in order to make high profits at home instead of in Britain where the corporate taxes were high. The British Monopoly Commission sued Hoffman-LaRoche for back taxes and won. ∎

If the company charges too high a price to a subsidiary, it ends up paying higher tariff duties, although it may pay lower income taxes in the foreign country. If the company charges too low a price to its subsidiary, it can be charged with *dumping*. Dumping is indicated when a company either charges less than its costs or less than it charges in its home market. Thus Zenith accused Japanese television manufacturers of dumping their TV sets in North America. When the government finds evidence of dumping, it can levy a dumping tariff. Various governments are watching for abuses and often force companies to charge the *arm's-length price*, namely, the price charged by other competitors for the same or similar product.

Last but not least, many multinationals are plagued by the *gray market* problem. For example:

> Minolta sold its cameras to dealers in Hong Kong for a lower price than in Germany because of lower transportation costs and tariffs. The Hong Kong dealers worked on smaller margins than the German retailers, who preferred high markups to high volume. Minolta's cameras ended up selling at retail for $174 in Hong Kong and $270 in Germany. Some Hong Kong wholesalers noticed this price difference and shipped Minolta cameras to German dealers for less than they were paying the German distributor. The German distributor couldn't sell his stock and complained to Minolta. ■

Very often a company finds some enterprising distributors buying more than they can sell in their own country and transshipping goods to another country in competition with the established distributor in order to take advantage of price differences. Multinationals try to prevent gray markets by policing the distributors, or by raising their prices to lower-cost distributors, or by altering the product characteristics for different countries.

Distribution Channels

The international company must take a *whole-channel* view of the problem of distributing its products to the final users. Figure 15-5 shows the three major links between the seller and ultimate user. In the first link, *seller's international marketing headquarters*, the export department or international division makes decisions on channels and other marketing-mix elements. The second link, *channels between nations*, gets the products to the borders of the foreign nations. It consists of decisions on the types of intermediaries (agents, trading companies, and the like), the type of transportation (air, sea, and so on), and the financing and risk arrangements. The third link, *channels within foreign nations*, get the products from their foreign entry point to the final buyers and users. Too many Canadian exporters think their job is done once the product leaves their factory. They should pay attention to how the product moves within the foreign country.

Within-country channels of distribution vary considerably among countries. There are striking differences in the *number* and *types of middlemen* serving each foreign market. To get soap into Japan, Procter & Gamble has to work through what is probably the most complicated distribution system in the world. It must sell to a *general wholesaler*, who sells to a

FIGURE 15-5
Whole-Channel Concept for International Marketing

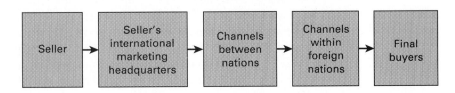

Seller → Seller's international marketing headquarters → Channels between nations → Channels within foreign nations → Final buyers

product wholesaler, who sells to a *product-specialty wholesaler*, who sells to a *regional wholesaler*, who sells to a *local wholesaler*, who finally sells to *retailers*. All these distribution levels can result in the doubling or tripling of the consumers' price over the importer's price.[12] If P&G takes the same soap to tropical Africa, the company might sell to an *import wholesaler*, who sells to several *jobbers*, who in turn sell to *petty traders* (mostly women) working in local markets.

Another difference lies in the *size and character of retail units* abroad. Where large-scale retail chains dominate the Canadian scene, most foreign retailing is in the hands of many small independent retailers. In India, millions of retailers operate tiny shops or sell in open markets. Their markups are high, but the real price is brought down through price haggling. Supermarkets would conceivably bring down prices, but they are difficult to start because of many economic and cultural barriers.[13] People's incomes are low, and they must shop daily for small amounts and are limited to whatever quantity can be carried home on foot or on a bicycle. Also, there is a lack of storage and refrigeration space to keep food for several days. Packaging costs are kept low in order to keep the prices low. In India, cigarettes are often bought singly (instead of in packs). Breaking bulk remains an important function of middlemen and helps perpetuate the long channels of distribution that are a major obstacle to the expansion of large-scale retailing in developing countries.

DECIDING ON THE MARKETING ORGANIZATION

Companies manage their international marketing activities in at least three ways.

Export Department

A firm normally gets into international marketing by simply shipping out the goods. If its international sales expand, the company organizes an export department consisting of a sales manager and a few assistants. As sales increase further, the export department is expanded to include various marketing services so that the company can go after business more aggressively. If the firm moves into joint ventures or direct investment, the export department will no longer be adequate to manage international operations.

International Division

Many companies become involved in several international markets and ventures. A company might export to one country, license another, have a joint-ownership venture in a third, and own a subsidiary in a fourth. Sooner or later it will create an international division to handle all its international activity. The international division is headed by an international-division president, who sets goals and budgets and is responsible for the company's growth to the international market.

International divisions are organized in a variety of ways. The international division's corporate staff consists of specialists in marketing, manufacturing, research, finance, planning, and personnel; they plan for, and provide services to, various operating units. The operating units can be organized according to one or more of three principles. They can be *geographical organizations*. Reporting to the international-division president might be regional vice-presidents for North America, Latin America, Europe, Africa, the Middle East, and the Far East. Reporting to the regional vice-presidents are country managers who are responsible for a salesforce, sales branches, distributors, and licensees in the respective countries. Or the operating units may be *world product groups*, each with an international vice-president responsible for worldwide sales of each product group. The vice-presidents may draw on corporate-staff area specialists for expertise on different geographical areas. Finally, the operating units may be *international subsidiaries*, each headed by a president. The various subsidiary presidents report to the president of the international division.

Many multinationals shift between these three types of organizations because each creates some problems. The history of Westinghouse's international operations is illustrative:[14]

> Before 1960, Westinghouse had several foreign subsidiaries that were loosely linked through an international division. To achieve more coordination, Westinghouse established in 1960 a strong international division with regional and country managers. However, several of Westinghouse's product groups found it frustrating to work through the international division, and they pressed for global control over planning and implementation. The corporation acceded in 1971 and disbanded the international division and gave 125 division managers worldwide responsibility. However, the results were not uniformly good. Many product groups did not pay sufficient attention to the international opportunities, since most of their business was domestic; they lacked international expertise; and they failed to coordinate their international operations with each other. Not surprisingly, in 1979 Westinghouse established a matrix organization consisting of an international vice-president who managed four regional managers, who in turn managed country managers, along with an overlay of international managers from the various product groups. The matrix solution promised to be sensitive both to local area needs and to global product strategy but at greater cost and greater management conflict along the way. ■

Global Organization

Several firms have passed beyond the international-division stage and have become truly global organizations. They have stopped thinking of themselves as national marketers who have ventured abroad and now think of themselves as global marketers. The top corporate management and staff plan worldwide manufacturing facilities, marketing policies, financial flows, and logistical systems. The global operating units report directly to the chief executive or executive committee, not to the head of an international division. Executives are trained in worldwide operations, not just domestic or international. Management is recruited from many countries; components and supplies are purchased where they can be obtained at the least cost; and investments are made where the anticipated returns are greatest.

Nonglobally organized companies must go more global if they hope to compete. As foreign companies invade the domestic market, Canadian companies will have to move more aggressively into foreign markets (see Companies and Industries 15-1).

Many multinationals have evolved from narrow *ethnocentric* thinking, where they view things only from their culture, to *polycentric* thinking, where they view things from the perspective of host cultures. Still, a polycentric orientation means a highly decentralized approach to building global sales. Polycentric multinationals give a high degree of autonomy to their country managers. Their managers work hard to be good citizens in the host country, and they advocate local production and product and marketing adaptations to win local favor. Yet the multinational's fate might depend more on its ability to shape a global competitive strategy and capture system-level advantages through design/production/marketing coordination and some degree of standardization. To succeed, planning and power must be more centralized at the regional and headquarters level. Today's multinationals are increasingly reestablishing more centralized control through *geocentric* planning, or at least *regiocentric* planning.[15]

THE WORLD'S CHAMPION MARKETERS: THE JAPANESE?

Few dispute that the Japanese have performed an economic miracle since World War II. In a relatively short time, they have achieved global market leadership in industries thought to be "mature" and dominated by impregnable giants: autos, motorcycles, watches, cameras, optical instruments, steel, shipbuilding, musical instruments, zippers, radios, television, video recorders, hand calculators, and so on. Japanese firms are currently moving into the number-two position in computers and construction equipment and making strong inroads into the chemical, rubber tires, pharmaceutical, and machine-tool industries. They are building a stronger position in designer clothing and cosmetics and slowly moving into aircraft manufacture.

Many theories have been offered to explain Japan's global successes. Some point to its unique business practices, such as lifetime employment, quality circles, consensus management, and just-in-time production. Others point to the supportive role of government policies and subsidies, the existence of powerful trading companies, and businesses' access to low-cost bank financing. Still others view Japan's success as based on low wage rates, unfair dumping practices, protected markets, and almost-zero defense industry costs.

One of the main keys to Japan's performance is its skill in marketing-strategy formulation and implementation. The Japanese first learned their marketing from Western companies, but now excel in implementing marketing principles. The Japanese know how to select a market, enter it in the right way, build their market share, and protect their leadership position against competitors' attacks.

Selecting Markets

The Japanese government and companies work hard to identify attractive global markets. They favor industries that require high skills, high labor intensity, and only small quantities of natural resources. Candidates include consumer electronics, cameras, watches, motorcycles, and pharmaceuticals. They prefer product markets that are in a state of technological evolution. They identify product markets where consumers are dissatisfied. They look for industries where the market leaders are complacent or underfinanced.

Entering Markets

The Japanese send study teams into the target country to spend several weeks or several months evaluating the market and figuring out a strategy. They often enter by first selling their products to a private brander, that might be a retail chain or a manufacturer. Later, they will introduce their own brand—a low-price, stripped-down product, or a product as good as the competitions' but priced lower, or a product exhibiting higher quality or new features or designs. The Japanese proceed to line up good distribution in order to provide reliable service to their customers. They rely on advertising to bring their products to the public's attention. A key characteristic of their entry strategy is to build market share rather than early profits. The Japanese are patient capitalists who will wait even a decade before realizing their profits.

Building Market Share

Once Japanese firms gain a market foothold, they direct their energies toward expanding their market share. They rely on product-development strategies and market-development strategies. They pour money into product improvement, product upgrading, and product proliferation, so that they can offer more and better things than the competition. They spot new opportunities through market segmentation and sequence market development across a number of countries, with the aim of building a network of world markets and production locations.

Protecting Market Share

Once the Japanese achieve market domination, they find themselves in the role of defenders rather than attackers. The Japanese defense strategy is a good offense through continuous product development and refined market segmentation. Japanese firms use two market-oriented principles to maintain their leadership. The first is "zero-customer-feedback time," whereby they survey recent customers to find out how they like the product and what improvements they would suggest. The second is "zero-product-improvement time," whereby they add worthwhile product improvements continuously, so that the product remains the leader.

Responding to the Japanese Competitors

Most Western firms were slow responding to Japanese inroads, but many of them are now mounting counteroffensives. IBM is adding new products, automatizing its factories, sourcing components from abroad, and entering strategic partnerships with others. Black & Decker is closing product-line gaps, increasing product quality, streamlining manufacturing and pricing more aggressively. More companies are copying Japanese practices that work—quality control, quality circles, consensus management, just-in-time production—when they fit the company culture. And more companies are entering the Japanese market to compete on their soil. Although getting in and operating successfully in Japan takes a considerable amount of money and patience, several companies have done an outstanding job, including Coca-Cola, McDonald's, Max Factor, Xerox, IBM, and Warner-Lambert.

Source: For further discussion, see Philip Kotler, Liam Fahey, and Somkid Jatusripitak, *The New Competition* (Englewood Cliffs, N.J., Prentice-Hall, 1985).

SUMMARY

Companies today can no longer pay attention only to their domestic market, no matter how large it is. Many industries are global industries, and their leading firms achieve lower costs and higher brand awareness. Protectionist measures can only slow down the invasion of superior goods; the best company defense is a sound global offense.

At the same time, global marketing is risky because of fluctuating exchange rates, unstable governments, protectionist barriers, high product- and communication-adaptation costs, and several other factors. Yet the international product life cycle suggests that comparative advantage in many industries will move from high-cost to low-cost countries, and companies cannot simply stay domestic and expect to maintain their markets. Given the potential gains and risks of international marketing, companies need a systematic way to make sound international marketing decisions.

The first step is to understand the international marketing environment, particularly the international trade system. In considering a particular foreign market, its economic, political, legal, and cultural characteristics must be assessed. Second, the company must consider what proportion of foreign to total sales to seek, whether to do business in a few or many countries, and what types of countries to enter. The third step is to decide which particular markets to enter, and this calls for evaluating the probable rate of return on investment against the level of risk. Fourth, the company has to decide how to enter each attractive market. Many companies start as indirect or direct exporters and then move to licensing, joint ventures, and finally direct investment; this company evolution has been called the internationalization process. Companies must next decide on the extent to which their products, promotion, price, and distribution should be adapted to individual foreign markets. Finally, the company must develop an effective organization for pursuing international marketing. Most firms start with an export department and graduate to an international division. A few become global companies, which means that top management plans and organizes on a global basis.

■ QUESTIONS

1. "The benefits for trading in the Canadian domestic market far outweigh the risks involved in doing business overseas." Discuss this statement citing specific examples in industry to support your arguments.

2. Select one of the following companies—Procter & Gamble, McDonald's or Hyundai—and analyze its strategies in reaching its overseas markets. How might the company have increased its effectiveness?

3. "While cigarette sales decline or stagnate in many industrialized nations . . . the Third World is where the growth is. Tobacco companies operate unburdened by many of the restraints they face in the West." Discuss the pros and cons of this "marketing opportunity."

4. Joint ventures between international partners have become an increasingly popular means of penetrating new markets. Find an example of an international joint venture and describe the motivation of the parties to enter into the venture, problems that had to be overcome, and expected effect on the relevant market.

5. It has been alleged that some of the negotiations to sell the Canadian Candu reactor abroad have been marred by the offering of bribes to government officials in the purchasing country. The bribing of government officials is illegal in Canada. Should these same standards be required of the domestic middlemen who handle the negotiations on behalf of the Canadian crown corporation?

6. Discuss the relevant aspects of the political-legal environ-

ment that might affect K mart's decision to open or retain outlets in Italy.

7. What product-strategy possibilities might Hershey's consider in marketing its chocolate bars in South American countries?

8. Which type of international marketing organization would you suggest for the following companies? (a) Raleigh bicycles in planning to sell three models in the Far East; (b) a small manufacturer of toys about to market its products in Europe; and, (c) Dodge in contemplating selling its full line of cars and trucks in Kuwait.

9. A Canadian heavy-equipment manufacturer operating in Western Europe has been using Canadians as salespeople. The company feels that it could reduce its costs by hiring and training nationals for salespeople. What are the advantages and disadvantages of using Canadians versus nationals for selling abroad?

10. A large company decided to enter the French tire market some years ago. The company produced tires for medium-sized trucks designed to meet the official rear-axle weight. Its subsequent experience was bad, with many of its tires blowing out. The company acquired a poor image in France as a result. What went wrong?

11. Select one of the following nations—Italy, Japan, or China—and describe its marketing institutions and practices.

12. Discuss the similarities and dissimilarities in marketing that might be experienced between planned and market economies.

■ NOTES

1. See "European States Subsidize Marketing Aid," *Business Marketing*, November 1986, pp. 27-28.

2. See John A. Quelch, Robert D. Buzzell, and Eric R. Salama, *The Marketing Challenge of 1992* (Boston: Addison-Wesley, 1990).

3. Michael E. Porter, *Competitive Strategy* (New York: Free Press, 1980), p. 275.

4. See David A. Ricks, Marilyn Y. C. Fu, and Jeffrey S. Arpan, *International Business Blunders* (Columbus, Ohio: Grid, 1974). For an account of negotiating styles in different countries, see Gavin Kennedy, *Negotiate Anywhere!* (London: Hutchinson Business, 1985).

5. Igal Ayal and Jehiel Zif, "Market Expansion Strategies in Multinational Marketing," *Journal of Marketing*, Spring

1979, pp. 84-94.

6. James K. Sweeney, "A Small Company Enters the European Market," *Harvard Business Review*, September-October 1970, pp. 127-28.

7. See David S. R. Leighton, "Deciding When to Enter International Markets," in *Handbook of Modern Marketing*, ed. Victor P. Buell (New York: McGraw-Hill, 1970), sec. 20, pp. 23-28.

8. However, see J. Peter Killing, "How to Make a Global Joint Venture Work," *Harvard Business Review*, May-June 1982, pp. 120-27.

9. See Jan Johanson and Finn Wiedersheim-Paul, "The Internationalization of the Firm," *Journal of Management Studies*, October 1975, pp. 305-22.

10. See Stan Reid, "The Decision Maker and Export Entry and Expansion," *Journal of International Business Studies*, Fall 1981, pp. 101-12; Igal Ayal, "Industry Export Performance: Assessment and Prediction," *Journal of Marketing*, Summer 1982, pp. 54-61; and Somkid Jatusripitak, *The Exporting Behavior of Manufacturing Firms* (Ann Arbor: University of Michigan Press, 1986).

11. Warren J. Keegan, *Multinational Marketing Management*, 4th ed. (Englewood Cliffs, N.J.: Prentice Hall, 1989), pp. 378-81.

12. See William D. Hartley, "How Not to Do It: Cumbersome Japanese Distribution System Stumps U.S. Concerns," *Wall Street Journal*, March 2, 1972.

13. See Arieh Goldman, "Outreach of Consumers and the Modernization of Urban Food Retailing in Developing Countries," *Journal of Marketing*, October 1974, pp. 8-16.

14. See Christopher A. Bartlett, "How Multinational Organizations Evolve," *Journal of Business Strategy*, Summer 1982, pp. 20-32. Also see Christopher A. Bartlett and Sumantra Ghoshal, *Managing Across Borders: The Transnational Solution* (Boston: Harvard Business School Press, 1989).

15. See Yoram Wind, Susan P. Douglas, and Howard V. Perlmutter, "Guidelines for Developing International Marketing Strategies," *Journal of Marketing*, April 1973, pp. 14-23.

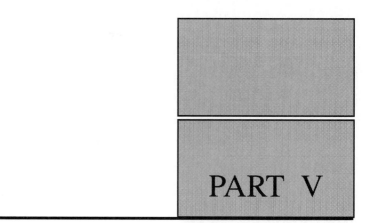

PART V

Planning Marketing Programs

Managing Product Lines, Brands, and Packaging

We are not manufacturers merely of articles of wood and stone, and iron and cotton and wool, and so on; we manufacture enthusiasms, we manufacture Canadian sentiment, we manufacture a feeling of pride.

Cyrus A. Birge

We are now ready to examine each marketing-mix element in some detail. We will begin with product, the most important element in the marketing mix. We will address the following questions in this chapter:

☐ What is a product?

☐ How can a company build and manage its product mix and product lines?

☐ How can a company make better brand decisions?

☐ How can packaging and labeling be used as a marketing tool?

WHAT IS A PRODUCT?

We define product as follows:

> A product *is anything that can be offered to a market for attention, acquisition, use, or consumption that might satisfy a want or need.*

Most products are physical goods, such as automobiles, toasters, shoes, eggs, and books. But services—such as haircuts, concerts, and vacations are also products (sometimes called service products). We can also think of persons as products. A celebrity like Anne Murray can be marketed, not in the sense that we "buy" her, but in the sense that we give her attention, buy her records, and attend her concerts. A *place* like Whistler, B.C. can be marketed, in the sense of either buying a condominium or taking a vacation there. An *organization* like the Red Cross can be marketed, in the sense that we feel positive toward it and will support it. Even an *idea* can be marketed, such as family planning or safe driving, in the sense that we might adopt the behavior associated with the idea. Thus we say that products consist broadly of anything that can be marketed, including physical objects, services, persons, places, organizations, and ideas.

Five Levels of a Product

In planning its market offer or product, the marketer needs to think through five product levels (see Figure 16-1).[1] The most fundamental level is the *core benefit*, namely the fundamental service or benefit that the customer is really buying. The hotel guest renting a room is really buying a good night's rest. The woman buying cosmetics is really buying self-esteem or hope. And the handyman buying a quarter-inch drill is really buying quarter-inch holes.

The marketer has to turn the core benefit into a *generic product*, namely a basic version of the product. Thus a hotel consists of a building that has a front desk and rooms to rent. In the same way, we can recognize other generic products—a toaster, a sheet of steel, a concert, a dental examination.

At the third level, the marketer prepares an *expected product*, namely a set of attributes and conditions that buyers normally expect and agree to when they purchase this product. Hotel guests, for example, expect a clean bed, soap and towels, plumbing fixtures, a telephone, clothes closet, and a relative degree of quiet. Since most hotels can meet this minimum expectation, the traveler normally will have no preference and will settle for whichever hotel is most convenient.

At the fourth level, the marketer prepares an *augmented product*, namely one that includes additional services and benefits that distinguish the company's offer from competitors' offers.

FIGURE 16-1
Five Product Levels

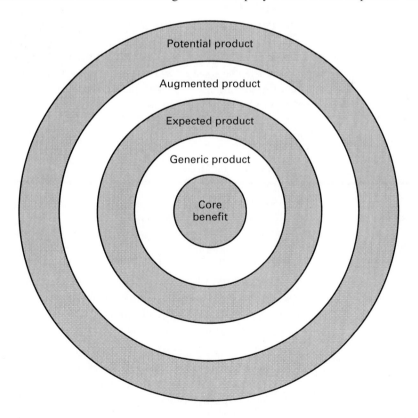

A hotel, for example, can augment its product by including a television set, shampoo, fresh flowers, rapid check-in, express checkout, fine dining and room service, and so on. Elmer Wheeler once observed, "Don't sell the steak—sell the sizzle."

Today's competition essentially takes place at the product-augmentation level. (In less-developed countries, competition takes place mostly at the expected product level.) Product augmentation leads the marketer to look at the buyer's total *consumption system*: "The way a purchaser of a product performs the total task of whatever it is that he or she is trying to accomplish when using the product."[2] In this way, the marketer will recognize many opportunities for augmenting its offer in a competitively effective way. According to Levitt:

> The *new competition* is not between what companies produce in their factories, but between what they add to their factory output in the form of packaging, services, advertising, customer advice, financing, delivery arrangements, warehousing, and other things that people value.[3]

However, some things should be noted about product-augmentation strategy. First, each augmentation costs the company money. The marketer has to ask whether customers will pay enough to cover the extra cost. Second, augmented benefits soon become expected benefits. Thus hotel guests now expect a television set, shampoo, and other amenities in their room. This means that competitors will have to search for still further features and benefits to add to their offer. Third, as companies raise the price of their augmented product, some competitors can revert to offering an expected product at a much lower price. Thus alongside the growth of fine hotels like Hyatt and Westin, we see the emergence of lower-cost hotels like Journey's End catering to clients who simply want the expected product.

At the fifth level stands the *potential product*, namely all of the augmentations and transformations that this product might ultimately undergo in the future. Whereas the augmented product describes what is included in the product today, the potential product points to its possible evolution. Here is where companies search aggressively for new ways to satisfy customers and distinguish their offer. The recent emergence of all-suite hotels where the guest occupies a set of rooms represents an innovative transformation of the traditional hotel product.

Some of the most successful companies add benefits to their offer that not only *satisfy* the customer but also *delight* the customers. Delighting is a matter of adding *unexpected surprises* to the offer. Thus the hotel guest finds candy on the pillow, or a bowl of fruit, or a videorecorder with optional videotapes. The company is saying that we want to treat you in a special way.

Product Hierarchy

Each product is related to certain other products. Product hierarchies stretch from basic needs to particular items that satisfy those needs. We can identify seven levels of the product hierarchy. Here they are defined and illustrated for life insurance:

1. *Need Family:* The core need that underlies the product family. Example: security.

2. *Product Family:* All the product classes that can satisfy a core need with more or less effectiveness. Example: savings and income.

3. *Product Class:* A group of products within the product family that are recognized as having a certain functional coherence. Example: financial instruments.

4. *Product Line:* A group of products within a product class that are closely related because they function in a similar manner or are sold to the same customer groups or are marketed through the same types of outlets or fall within given price ranges. Example: life insurance.

5. *Product Type:* Those items within a product line that share one of several possible forms of the product. Example: term life.

6. *Brand:* The name associated with one or more items in the product line that is used to identify the source or character of the item(s). Example: Prudential.

7. *Item:* A distinct unit within a brand or product line that is distinguishable by size, price, appearance, or some other attribute. The item is called a stockkeeping unit, or product variant. Example: Prudential renewable term life insurance.

Another example: the need "hope" gives rise to a product family called toiletries and a product class within that family called cosmetics, of which one line is lipstick, which has different product forms, such as tube lipstick, which is offered as a brand called Revlon in a particular type, such as "frosted."

Two other terms frequently arise. A *product system* is a group of diverse but related items that function in a compatible manner. For example, the Nikon Company sells a basic 35mm camera along with an extensive set of lenses, filters, and other options that constitute a product system. A *product mix* (or product assortment) is the set of all products and items that a particular seller makes available to the buyers.

Product Classifications

Marketers have traditionally classified products on the basis of differing product characteristics. Each product type should have an appropriate strategy and marketing mix. The Marketing Concepts and Tools 16-1 exhibit presents the major classifications of consumer and industrial goods and their marketing-strategy implications.

With this background, we are ready to examine company decisions regarding the product mix, product lines, and individual products.

Marketing Concepts and Tools 16-1

PRODUCT CLASSIFICATIONS AND THEIR MARKETING-STRATEGY IMPLICATIONS

Durable Goods, Nondurable Goods, and Services

Products can be classified into three groups according to their durability or tangibility:

- *Nondurable Goods:* Nondurable goods are tangible goods that normally are consumed in one or a few uses. Examples include beer, soap, and salt. Since these goods are consumed fast and purchased frequently, the appropriate strategy is to make them available in many locations, charge only a small markup, and advertise heavily to induce trial and build preference.

- *Durable Goods:* Durable goods are tangible goods that normally survive many uses. Examples include refrigerators, machine tools, and clothing. Durable products

normally require more personal selling and service, command a higher margin, and require more seller guarantees.

- *Services:* Services are activities, benefits, or satisfactions that are offered for sale. Examples include haircuts and repairs. Services are intangible, inseparable, variable, and perishable. As a result, they normally require more quality control, supplier credibility, and adaptability. (For further discussion of services, see Chapter 17.)

Consumer-Goods Classification

Consumers buy a vast number of goods. A useful way to classify these goods is on the basis of *consumer shopping habits*, because those habits have implications for marketing strategy. We can distinguish

---

between convenience, shopping, specialty, and unsought goods.

- □ *Convenience Goods.* Goods that the customer usually purchases frequently, immediately, and with the minimum of effort in comparison and buying. Examples include tobacco products, soaps, and newspapers.

Convenience goods can be further divided into staples, impulse goods, and emergency goods. *Staples* are goods that consumers purchase on a regular basis. For example, one buyer might routinely purchase Heinz ketchup, Crest toothpaste, and Ritz crackers. *Impulse goods* are purchased without any planning or search effort. These goods are usually available in many places, because consumers do not normally look for them. Thus candy bars and magazines are placed next to checkout counters, because shoppers may not have thought of buying them until they spotted them. *Emergency goods* are purchased when a need is urgent—umbrellas during a rainstorm, boots and shovels during the first winter snowstorm. Manufacturers of emergency goods will place them in many outlets so as to capture the sale when the customer needs these goods.

- □ *Shopping Goods.* Goods that the customer, in the process of selection and purchase, characteristically compares on such bases as suitability, quality, price, and style. Examples include furniture, clothing, used cars, and major appliances.

Shopping goods can be divided into homogeneous and heterogeneous goods. The buyer sees homogeneous shopping goods as similar in quality but different enough in price to justify shopping comparisons. The seller has to "talk price" to the buyer. But in shopping for clothing, furniture, and more heterogeneous goods, product features are often more important to the consumer than the price. If the buyer wants a pinstriped suit, the cut, fit, and look are likely to be more important than small price differences. The seller of heterogeneous shopping goods must therefore carry a wide assortment to satisfy individual tastes and must have well-trained sales personnel to provide information and advice to customers.

- □ *Specialty Goods.* Goods with unique characteristics and/or brand identification for which a significant group of buyers are habitually willing to make a special purchasing effort. Examples include specific brands and types of fancy goods, cars, stereo components, photographic equipment, and men's suits.

A Mercedes, for example, is a specialty good because buyers will travel far to buy one. Specialty goods do not involve the buyer in making comparisons; buyers invest time only to reach dealers carrying the wanted products. The dealers do not need convenient locations; however, they must let prospective buyers know their locations.

- □ *Unsought Goods.* Goods that the consumer does not know about or knows about but does not normally think of buying. New products, such as smoke detectors and food processors, are unsought goods until the consumer is made aware of them through advertising. The classic examples of known but unsought goods are life insurance, cemetery plots, and encyclopedias.

Unsought goods require substantial marketing effort in the form of advertising and personal selling. Some of the most sophisticated personal-selling techniques have developed from the challenge to sell unsought goods.

Industrial-Goods Classification

Organizations buy a vast variety of goods and services. A useful industrial-goods classification would suggest appropriate marketing strategies in the industrial market. Industrial goods can be classified in terms of *how they enter the production process and their relative costliness.* We can distinguish three groups: materials and parts, capital items, and supplies and services.

- □ *Materials and Parts.* Goods that enter the manufacturer's product completely. They fall into two classes: raw materials and manufactured materials and parts.

Raw materials fall into two major classes: *farm products* (e.g., wheat, cotton, livestock, fruits, and vegetables) and *natural products* (e.g., fish, lumber, crude petroleum, iron ore). Each is marketed somewhat differently. *Farm products* are supplied by many producers; who turn them over to marketing intermediaries; who provide assembly, grading, storage, transportation, and selling services. Farm products are somewhat expandable in the long run but not in the short run. Farm products' perishable and seasonal nature gives rise to special marketing practices. Their commodity character results in relatively little advertising and promotional activity, with some exceptions. From time to time, commodity groups will launch campaigns to promote the consumption of their product—potatoes, prunes, milk. And some producers brand their product—Sunkist oranges, Chiquita bananas.

Natural products are highly limited in supply. They usually have great bulk and low unit value and require substantial transportation to move them from producer to user. There are fewer and larger producers, who often market them directly to industrial users. Because the users depend on these materials, long-term-supply contracts are common. The homogeneity of natural materials limits the amount of demand-creation activity. Price and delivery reliability are the major factors influencing the selection of suppliers.

Manufactured materials and parts are exemplified by *component materials* (e.g., iron, yarn, cement, wires) and *component parts* (e.g., small motors, tires, castings). *Component materials* are usually fabricated further—for example, pig iron is made into steel, and yarn is woven into cloth. The standardized nature of component materials usually means that price and supplier reliability are the most important purchase factors. *Component parts* enter the finished product completely with no further change in form, as when small motors are put into vacuum cleaners, and tires are put on automobiles. Most manufactured materials and parts are sold directly to industrial users, with orders often placed a year or more in advance. Price and services are the major marketing considerations, and branding and advertising tend to be less important.

□ *Capital Items.* Goods that enter the finished product partly. They include two groups: installations and accessory equipment.

Installations consist of *buildings* (e.g., factories and offices) and *fixed equipment* (e.g., generators, drill presses, computers, elevators). Installations are major purchases. They are usually bought directly from the producer, with the typical sale preceded by a long negotiation period. The producers use a topnotch salesforce, which often includes sales engineers. The producers have to be willing to design to specification and to supply postsale services. Advertising is used but is much less important than personal selling.

Accessory equipment comprises *portable factory equipment and tools* (e.g., hand tools, lift trucks) and *office equipment* (e.g., typewriters, desks). These types of equipment do not become part of the finished product. They simply help in the production process. They have a shorter life than installations but a longer life than operating supplies. Although some accessory-equipment manufacturers sell direct, more often they use middlemen, because the market is geographically dispersed, the buyers are numerous, and the orders are small. Quality, features, price, and service are major considerations in vendor selection. The salesforce tends to be more important than advertising, although the latter can be used effectively.

□ *Supplies and Services.* Items that do not enter the finished product at all.

Supplies are of two kinds: *operating supplies* (e.g., lubricants, coal, typing paper, pencils) and *maintenance and repair items* (paint, nails, brooms). Supplies are the equivalent of convenience goods in the industrial field, as they are usually purchased with a minimum effort on a straight rebuy basis. They are normally marketed through intermediaries because of the great number of customers, their geographical dispersion, and the low unit value of these goods. Price and service are important considerations, since suppliers are quite standardized, and brand preference is not high.

Business services include *maintenance and repair services* (e.g., window cleaning, typewriter repair) and *business advisory services* (e.g., legal, management consulting, advertising). Maintenance and repair services are usually supplied under contract. Maintenance services are often provided by small producers, and repair services are often available from the manufacturers of the original equipment. Business advisory services are normally new taskbuying situations, and the industrial buyer will choose the supplier on the basis of the supplier's reputation and personnel.

Thus we see that a product's characteristics will have a major influence on marketing strategy. At the same time, marketing strategy will also depend on other factors, such as the product's life-cycle stage, competitors' strategies, and economic conditions.

Source: For definitions, see *Marketing Definitions: A Glossary of Marketing Terms* (Chicago: American Marketing Association, 1960). Also see Patrick E. Murphy and Ben M. Enis, "Classifying Products Strategically," *Journal of Marketing*, July 1986, pp. 24-42.

PRODUCT-MIX DECISIONS

We will first consider product-mix decisions.

> A product mix (*also called* product assortment) *is the set of all product lines and items that a particular seller offers for sale to buyers.*

Avon's product mix consists of three major product lines: cosmetics, jewelry, and household items. Each product line consists of several sublines: for example, cosmetics breaks down into lipstick, blusher, powder, and so on. Each line and subline contains many specific items.

Altogether, Avon's product mix includes 1300 items. A large supermarket handles more than 10 000 items; a typical K Mart stocks 15 000 items; and General Electric manufactures as many as 250 000 items.

A company's product mix will have a certain breadth, length, depth, and consistency. These concepts are illustrated in Table 16-1 for selected Procter & Gamble consumer products.

The *breadth* of P&G's product mix refers to how many different product lines the company carries. Table 16-1 shows a product-mix width of five lines. (In fact, P&G produces many additional lines—hair-care products, health-care products, personal-hygiene products, beverages, food, and so on.)

The *length* of P&G's product mix refers to the total number of items in its product mix. In Table 16-1, it is twenty-six. We can also talk about the average length of a line at P&G. This is obtained by dividing the total length (here 26) by the number of lines (here 5), or 5.2. The average product line at P&G, as represented in Table 16-1, consists of 5.2 brands.

The *depth* of P&G's product mix refers to how many variants are offered of each product in the line. Thus if Crest comes in three sizes and two formulations (regular and mint), Crest has a depth of six. By counting the number of variants within each brand, the average depth of P&G's product mix can be calculated.

The *consistency* of the product mix refers to how closely related the various product lines are in end use, production requirements, distribution channels, or some other way. P&G's product lines are consistent insofar as they are consumer goods that go through the same distribution

Table 16-1 Product-Mix Breadth and Product-Line Depth for Procter & Gamble Products

	Product-Mix Breadth				
	Detergents	Toothpaste	Bar Soap	Disposable Diapers	Paper Tissue
Product-Line Depth	Ivory Snow 1930	Gleem 1952	Ivory 1879	Pampers 1961	Charmin 1928
	Dreft 1933	Crest 1955	Kirk's 1885	Luvs 1976	White Cloud 1958
	Tide 1946	Denquel 1980	Lava 1893		Puffs 1960
	Cheer 1950		Camay 1926		Banner 1982
	Oxydol 1952		Zest 1952		
	Dash 1954		Safeguard 1963		
	Bold 1965		Coast 1974		
	Gain 1966				
	Era 1972				
	Solo 1979				

channels. The lines are less consistent insofar as they perform different functions for the buyers.

These four dimensions of the product mix provide the means for defining the company's product strategy. The company can expand its business in four ways. The company can add new product lines, thus broadening its product mix. The company can lengthen each product line. The company can add more product variants to each product and deepen its product mix. Finally, the company can pursue more product-line consistency or less, depending upon whether it wants to acquire a strong reputation in a single field or participate in several fields.

Product-mix planning is largely the responsibility of the company's strategic planners. They must assess, with information supplied by the company marketers, which product lines to grow, maintain, harvest, and divest. We have already reviewed the various analytical approaches to this task in Chapter 2.

PRODUCT-LINE DECISIONS

A product mix is made up of various product lines.

> A product line *is a group of products that are closely related because they perform a similar function, are sold to the same customer groups, are marketed through the same channels, or make up a particular price range.*

Each product line within a company is usually managed by some executive. In General Electric's Consumer Appliance Division, there are product-line managers for refrigerators, stoves, washing machines, dryers, and other appliances. At Queen's University, there are separate academic deans for the medical school, law school, business school, engineering school and liberal arts.

Product-Line Analysis

Product-line managers need two types of information. First, they must know the sales and profits of each item in the line. Second, they must know how their product line compares with competitors' product lines.

Product-Line Sales and Profits   The product-line manager needs to know the percentage of total sales and profits contributed by each item in the line. An example is shown for a five-item product line in Figure 16-2.

The first item accounts for 50 percent of total sales and 30 percent of total profits. The first two items account for 80 percent of total sales and 60 percent of total profits. If these two items were suddenly hurt by a competitor, the product line's sales and profitability would collapse. A high concentration of sales in a few items means line vulnerability. These items must be carefully monitored and protected. At the other end, the last item constitutes only 5 percent of the product line's sales and profits. The product-line manager may even want to consider dropping this slow-selling item from the line.

Product-Line Market Profile   The product-line manager must also review how the product line is positioned against competitors' product lines. Consider a paper company with a product line consisting of paper board.[4] Two of the major attributes of paper board are paper weight and finish quality. Paper weight is usually offered at standard levels of 90, 120,

FIGURE 16-2

Product-Item Contributions to a Product Line's Total Sales and Profits

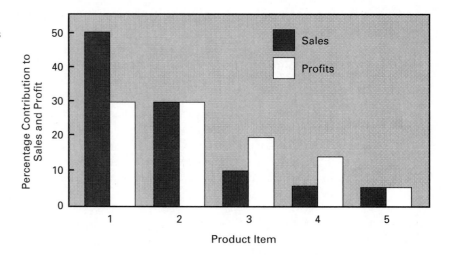

150, and 180 weight. Finish quality is offered at three standard levels. Figure 16-3 shows the location of the various product-line items of company X and four competitors, A, B, C, and D. Competitor A sells two product items in the extra-high weight class ranging from medium to low finish quality. Competitor B sells four items that vary in weight and finish quality. Competitor C sells three items in which the greater their weight, the greater their finish quality. Competitor D sells three items, all lightweight but varying in finish quality. Finally, company X offers three items that vary in weight and finish quality.

This product-item mapping is useful for designing product-line marketing strategy. It shows which competitors' items are competing against company X's items. For example, company X's low-weight/medium-quality paper competes against competitor D's paper. But its high-weight/medium-quality paper has no direct competitor. The map also reveals locations for new-product items. For example, no manufacturer offers a high-weight/low-quality paper. If company X estimates a strong unmet demand and can produce and price this paper right, it should consider adding this item to its line.

Another benefit of product mapping is that it identifies market segments. Figure 16-3 shows the types of paper, by weight and quality, preferred by the general printing industry, the point-of-purchase display industry, and the office-supply industry, respectively. The map shows that company X is well positioned to serve the needs of the general printing industry

FIGURE 16-3

Product Map for a Paper-Product Line

Source: Benson P. Shapiro, *Industrial Product Policy: Managing the Existing Product Line* (Cambridge, Mass.: Marketing Science Institute, September 1977), p. 101.

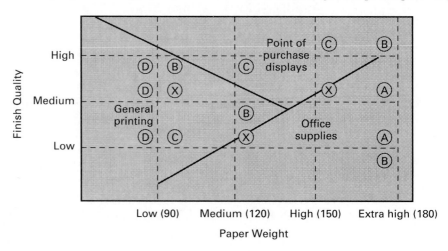

but is less effective in serving the other two industries and should consider bringing out more paper types that meet these needs.

Product-Line Length

An issue facing product-line managers is optimal product line length. A product line is too short if the manager can increase profits by adding items; the line is too long if the manager can increase profits by dropping items.

The issue of product-line length is influenced by company objectives. Companies seeking high market share and market growth will carry longer lines. They are less concerned when some items fail to contribute to profits. Companies that emphasize high profitability will carry shorter lines consisting of "cherry-picked" items.

Product lines tend to lengthen over time. Excess manufacturing capacity puts pressure on the product-line manager to develop new items. The salesforce and distributors also pressure for a more complete product line to satisfy their customers. The product-line manager will add items in pursuit of greater sales and profits.

But as items are added, several costs rise: design and engineering costs, inventory-carrying costs, manufacturing-changeover costs, order-processing costs, transportation costs, and new-item promotional costs. Eventually someone calls a halt to the mushrooming product line. Top management may freeze things because of insufficient funds or manufacturing capacity. The controller may question the line's profitability and call for a study. The study will probably show a large number of money-losing items. These items will be dropped in a major effort to increase profitability. A pattern of undisciplined product-line growth followed by massive product pruning will repeat itself many times.

A company can enlarge the length of its product line in two ways: by line stretching and line filling.

Line-Stretching Decision

Every company's product line covers a certain part of the total possible range. For example, BMW automobiles are located in the high price range of the automobile market. *Line stretching* occurs when a company lengthens its product line beyond its current range. The company can stretch its line downward, upward, or both ways.

Downward Stretch   Many companies initially locate at the high end of the market and subsequently stretch their line downward.

> IBM historically operated in the large-mainframe end of the computer market, leaving minicomputer manufacture to other firms, such as Digital Equipment and Data General. However, the slowdown in growth of the large-batch-oriented data-processing units led IBM to enter minicomputer manufacture as an avenue to further growth. IBM's interest in minicomputers was further stimulated by its growing interest in computer networks and distributed data-processing systems. This led IBM to stretch further downward into manufacturing microcomputers. ■

Companies often add models to the lower end of their line in order to advertise their brand as starting at a low price. Thus Sears may advertise room air conditioners "starting at $399," and General Motors may advertise a new Chevrolet at $8999. These "fighter" or "promotional" models are used to draw in customers on a price basis. The customers, upon seeing the better models, often trade up. This strategy must be used carefully. The "promotional" brand, although stripped, must support the brand's quality image. The seller must also stock the promotional model when it is advertised. Consumers object to "bait-and-switch" tactics.

A company might stretch downward for any of the following reasons:

☐ The company is attacked at the high end and decides to counterattack by invading the low end.

☐ The company finds that slower growth is taking place at the high end.

☐ The company initially entered the high end to establish a quality image and intended to roll downward.

☐ The company adds a low-end unit to plug a market hole that would otherwise attract a new competitor.

In making a downward stretch, the company faces some risks. The new low-end item might *cannibalize* higher-end items, leaving the company worse off. Consider the following:

> General Electric's Medical Systems Division is the market leader in catscanners, those expensive diagnostic machines used in hospitals. GE learned that a Japanese competitor was planning to attack their market. GE's guess was that the Japanese model would be smaller, more electronic, and less expensive. The best GE defense would be to introduce a similar machine before the Japanese model entered the market. But some GE executives were concerned that this lower price version would hurt the sales and higher profit margin on their large catscanner. But one manager settled the issue by saying: "Aren't we better off to cannibalize ourselves than to let the Japanese do it?" ∎

Or the low-end item might provoke competitors to counteract by moving into the higher end. Or the company's dealers may not be willing or able to handle the lower-end products because they are less profitable or dilute their image. Harley Davidson's dealers neglected the small motorcycles that Harley finally designed to compete with the Japanese.

One of the major miscalculations of several domestic producers has been their unwillingness to plug holes in the lower end of their markets. General Motors resisted building smaller cars, and Xerox resisted building smaller copying machines. Japanese companies spotted a major opening and moved in quickly.

Upward Stretch Companies in the lower end of the market might contemplate entering the higher end. They might be attracted by a higher growth rate, higher margins, or simply the chance to position themselves as full-line manufacturers.

An upward-stretch decision can be risky. Not only are the higher-end competitors well entrenched, but they may counterattack by going downmarket. Prospective customers may not believe that the newcomer can produce quality products. Finally, the company's sales representatives and distributors may lack the talent and training to serve the higher end of the market.

Two-Way Stretch Companies in the middle range of the market might decide to stretch their line in both directions. Texas Instruments' strategy in the hand-calculator market is an example. Before Texas Instruments (TI) entered this market, the market was dominated primarily by Bowmar at the low-price/low-quality end and Hewlett-Packard at the high-price/high-quality end. TI introduced its first calculators in the medium-price/medium-quality end of the market. Gradually, it added more calculators at each end. It offered better calculators at the same price or a lower price than Bowmar, ultimately destroying that company; and it designed high-quality calculators selling at lower prices than Hewlett-Packard calculators, taking away a good share of HP's sales at the high end. This two-way stretch won TI early market leadership in the hand-calculator market.

The Marriott Hotel group also has performed a two-way stretch of its hotel product line. Alongside its medium-price hotels, it added the Marriott Marquis line to serve the upper end of the market, the Courtyard line to serve a lower end of the market, and Fairfield Inns to serve the economy end of the market. Each branded hotel line is aimed at a different target market. Marriott Marquis aims to attract and please top executives; Marriotts, middle managers; Courtyards, salespeople; and Fairfield Inns, vacationers and others on a low travel budget. (See Figure 16-4). The major risk with this strategy is that some travelers will trade down after finding the lower-price hotels in the Marriott chain have pretty much everything they want.

Line-Filling Decision

A product line can also be lengthened by adding more items within the present range of the line. There are several motives for line filling: reaching for incremental profits; trying to satisfy dealers who complain about lost sales because of missing items in the line; trying to utilize excess capacity; trying to be the leading full-line company; and trying to plug holes to keep out competitors.

Line filling is overdone if it results in cannibalization and customer confusion. The company needs to differentiate each item in the consumer's mind. Each item should possess a *just-noticeable difference*. According to Weber's law, customers are more attuned to relative than to absolute differences.[5] They will definitely perceive the difference between packages weighing one and two kilograms, but may not perceive the difference between packages weighing eleven and twelve kilograms. Management should make sure that new products are noticeably different.

The company should check that the proposed item meets a market need and is not being added simply to satisfy an internal need. The famous Edsel automobile, on which Ford lost $350 million, met Ford's internal positioning needs but not the market's needs. Ford noticed that Ford owners would trade up to General Motors cars like Oldsmobile or Buick rather than step up to Ford's Mercury or Lincoln. Ford decided to create a steppingstone car to fill its line. The Edsel was created, but it failed to meet a market need because many similar cars were available, and many buyers were turning to smaller cars.

FIGURE 16-4
Two-Way Product-Line Stretch:
Marriott Hotels

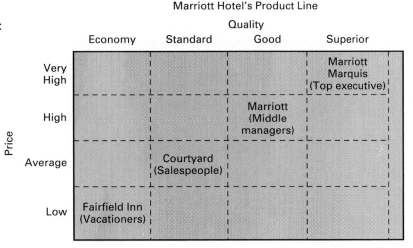

Once the product-line manager decides to add another item to sell at a certain price, the design task is turned over to the company engineers. The planned price will dictate how the item is designed, rather than the design's dictating the price that will be charged.

Line-Modernization Decision

Even when produce-line length is adequate, the line might need to be modernized. For example, a company's machine tools might have a 1950s look and lose out to newer-styled competitors' lines.

The issue is whether to overhaul the line piecemeal or all at once. A piecemeal approach allows the company to see how customers and dealers take to the new style. Piecemeal modernization is less draining on the company's cash flow. A major disadvantage of piecemeal modernization is that it allows competitors to see changes and start redesigning their own line.

In rapidly changing high-tech-product markets, product modernization is carried on continuously. Although Apple personal computers are only a decade old, the line has already migrated through Apple 1, Apple 2, Apple 3, Lisa, and McIntosh. Because competitors are constantly upgrading their equipment, each company must redesign its own equipment. Companies plan product improvements to include *customer migration* to higher-valued, higher-priced items. A major issue is timing the product improvements so they do not come out too early (thus damaging sales of the current product line) or too late (after competition has established a strong reputation for more-advanced equipment).

Line-Featuring Decision

The product-line manager typically selects one or a few items in the line to feature. Sometimes managers feature low-end promotional models to serve as "traffic builders." Thus Sears will announce a special low-price sewing machine to attract customers. And Rolls Royce announced an economy model selling for only $49 000—in contrast to its high-end model selling for $108 000—to bring people into its showrooms. Once the customers arrive, salespeople may try to persuade them to buy higher-end models.

At other times, managers will feature a high-end item to lend prestige to the product line. Stetson promotes a man's hat selling for $150, which few men buy but which acts as a "flagship" or "crown jewel" to enhance the whole line.

Sometimes a company finds one end of its line selling well and the other end poorly. The company may try to boost demand for the slower sellers, especially if they are produced in a factory that is idled by the lack of demand. This situation faced Honeywell when its medium-size computers were not selling as well as its large computers. But things are not this simple. It could be argued that the company should promote the items that sell well rather than trying to prop up weak demand.

Line-Pruning Decision

Product-line managers must periodically review items for pruning. There are two occasions for pruning. One is when the product line includes deadwood that is depressing profits. The weak items can be identified through sales and cost analysis. RCA cut down its color television sets from 69 to 44 models, and a chemical company cut down its products from 217 to the 93 with the largest volume, the largest contribution to profits, and the greatest long-term potential. Many companies have implemented major prunings to achieve stronger long-term profits.

The other occasion for product pruning is when the company is short of production capacity. The manager should concentrate on producing the higher-margin items. Companies typically shorten their lines in periods of tight demand and lengthen their lines in periods of slow demand.

BRAND DECISIONS

In developing a marketing strategy for individual products, the seller has to confront the branding decision. Branding is a major issue in product strategy. On the one hand, developing a branded product requires a great deal of long-term investment spending, especially for advertising, promotion, and packaging. It would be easier for manufacturers to make the product for others to brand. That was the course taken by Taiwanese manufacturers, who make a great amount of the world's clothing, consumer electronics, and computers but not under Taiwanese brand names.

On the other hand, these manufacturers eventually learn that the power lies with the brand-name companies. Brand-name companies can replace their Taiwanese manufacturing sources with cheaper sources in Malaysia and elsewhere. Meanwhile, Japanese and South Korean companies did not make this mistake. They spent liberally to build up brand names for their products, brand names such as Sony, Toyota, Goldstar, Samsung, and so on. Even when these companies can no longer afford to manufacture their products in their homeland, the brand names continue to command customer loyalty.

A powerful brand name is said to have *consumer franchise*. This is evidenced when a sufficient number of customers demand that brand and refuse a substitute, even if the price is somewhat lower. Mercedes has it; Chevy doesn't. Maytag has it; General Electric doesn't. IBM has it; Radio Shack doesn't. Companies that develop a brand with a strong consumer franchise are somewhat insulated from competitors' promotional strategies.

Companies such as Procter & Gamble, Caterpillar, IBM, and Sony have achieved impressive *company brand strength*. This is measured by the proportion of product/markets where the company is the brand leader or co-leader. Thus P&G's impressive marketing reputation rests on the fact that it is the leader in such a high proportion of its served product/markets.

Before going further, we should become familiar with the language of branding.[6]

☐ *Brand:* A name, term, sign, symbol, or design, or a combination of them, intended to identify the goods or services of one seller or group of sellers and to differentiate them from those of competitors.

☐ *Brand Name:* That part of a brand which can be vocalized—the utterable. Examples are Avon, Chevrolet, and Ski-doo.

☐ *Brand Mark:* That part of a brand which can be recognized but is not utterable, such as a symbol, or distinctive coloring or lettering. Examples are the Royal Bank lion and Canadian Tire's inverted red triangle.

☐ *Trademark:* A brand or part of a brand that is given legal protection because it is capable of exclusive appropriation. A trademark protects the seller's exclusive rights to use the brand name and/or brand mark.

☐ *Copyright:* The exclusive legal right to reproduce, publish, and sell the matter and form of a literary, musical, or artistic work.

Branding poses challenging decisions to the marketer. The key decisions are shown in Figure 16-5 and discussed below.

FIGURE 16-5

An Overview of Branding Decisions

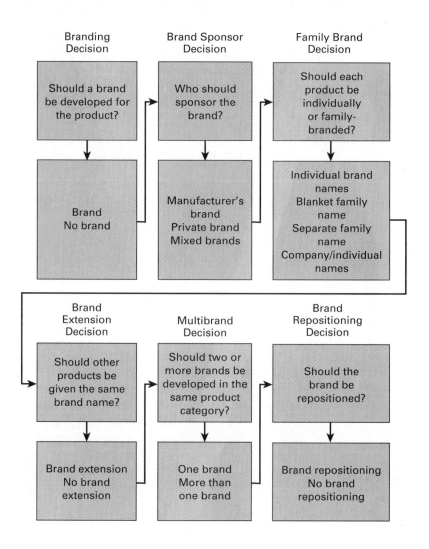

Branding Decision

The first decision is whether the company should put a brand name on its product. In the past, most products went unbranded. Producers and middlemen sold their goods out of barrels, bins, and cases, without any supplier identification. Buyers would have to depend on the seller's integrity. The earliest signs of branding were in the efforts of medieval guilds to require craftspeople to put trademarks on their products to protect themselves and consumers against inferior quality. In the fine arts, too, branding began with artists signing their works.

The earliest brand promoters were the patent-medicine makers. But branding's real growth occurred with the growth of national firms and national advertising media. Some of the early brands still survive, such as Borden's Condensed Milk, Quaker Oats, Vaseline, and Ivory Soap.

Today, branding is such a strong force that hardly anything goes unbranded. Salt is packaged in distinctive manufacturers' containers, fruit is stamped with growers' names, common nuts and bolts are packaged in cellophane with a distributor's label, and automobile components—spark plugs, tires, filters—bear separate brand names from the auto makers.

In some cases, there has been a return to "no branding" of certain staple consumer goods and pharmaceuticals. Loblaws introduced a line of "No-Name" generic products in 1978 that have since become the industry leader. *Generics* are unbranded, plainly packaged, less-expensive versions of common products purchased in supermarkets, such as spaghetti, paper towels, and canned peaches. They offer standard or lower quality at a price that may be as much as 30 to 50 percent lower than nationally advertised brands and 10 to 15 percent lower than retailer private label items. The lower price is made possible by lower-quality ingredients, lower-cost labeling and packaging, and minimal advertising. Nevertheless, generics are sufficiently satisfying that over 70 percent of consumers who have purchased generics said they would buy them again. Generic products in the food, household goods, and pharmaceutical industries present a major challenge to high-priced brands and weaker brands.

National brands have fought generics in a number of ways. Ralston-Purina increased its quality and targeted pet owners who identified strongly with their pets and cared most about quality. Generics also faced price competition from the nationals' "fighter" brands and from some grocery chains' private-label brands. After several years of rapid growth in the early eighties, sales of generics have stabilized at 15 percent of supermarket sales.[7]

Why do sellers prefer to brand their products when it clearly involves a cost—packaging, labeling, legal protection—and a risk if the product should prove unsatisfying to the user? It turns out that branding gives the seller several advantages.

First, the brand name makes it easier for the seller to process orders and track down problems. Thus John Labatt receives an order for one hundred cases of Classic beer instead of an order for "some of your better beer." Furthermore, the seller finds it easier to trace the order if it is misshipped or to determine why the beer was rancid if consumers complain.

Second, the seller's brand name and trademark provide legal protection of unique product features, which would otherwise be copied by competitors.

Third, branding gives the seller the opportunity to attract a loyal and profitable set of customers. Brand loyalty gives sellers some protection from competition and greater control in planning their marketing mix.

Fourth, branding helps the seller segment markets. Instead of P&G selling a simple detergent, it can offer eight detergent brands, each formulated somewhat differently and aimed at specific benefit-seeking segments.

Fifth, good brands help build the corporate image. By carrying the company's name, they help advertise the quality and size of the company.

There is evidence that distributors want brand names as a means of making the product easier to handle, identifying suppliers, holding production to certain quality standards, and increasing buyer preference. Consumers want brand names to help them identify quality differences and shop more efficiently. In Russia, consumers look for identification marks on television receivers to find out which factory produced them, since the factories have different reputations for reliability.

Brand-Sponsor Decision

In deciding to brand a product, the manufacturer has several options with respect to brand sponsorship. The product may be launched as a *manufacturer brand* (sometimes called a national brand). Or it may be launched as a *licensed name brand* (see Marketing Strategies 16-1). Or the manufacturer may supply the product to middlemen, who put on a *distributor brand* (also called retailer, store, or private brand). Or the manufacturer may produce some output under its own name and some under distributor labels. Kellogg's, Bombardier, and IBM produce virtually all of their output under their own brand names. Laura Secord makes some products like pudding both for its own brand and for sale as a generic product. In the clothing industry, brands like Christian Dior and Pierre Cardin are licensed to a number of Canadian manufacturers.

Marketing Strategies 16-1

LICENSING BRAND NAMES FOR ROYALTIES

A manufacturer or retailer may take years and spend millions to develop consumer preference for a new brand name. Or, it can "rent" names that already hold magic for consumers names or symbols created by other manufacturers, the names of well-known people, characters from popular movies and books. For a fee, any of these can give a product an instant and familiar brand name.

Name and character licensing has become a big business in recent years. Manufacturers pay out millions each year to use popular names and characters on their products, and these products generate billions each year in retail sales.

Clothing sellers are the largest users of licensing. Producers and retailers pay large royalties to adorn their products with the names of fashion innovators. Calvin Klein, Pierre Cardin, Gucci, and others license their names or initials for items ranging from blouses to ties and linens to luggage. Such names can be expensive—in 1981, Pierre Cardin reaped a reported $50 million in royalties on products that generated about $1 billion of wholesale business for 540 licensees. In recent years, designer labels have become so common that many retailers are dropping them in favor of their own store brands in order to regain exclusivity, pricing freedom, and higher margins.

Sellers of children's toys, games, food, and other products also do a lot of name and character licensing. The list of characters attached to children's clothing, toys, school supplies, linens, dolls, lunchboxes, cereals, and other items is almost endless—from such classics as Disney, Peanuts, and Flintstones characters to E.T. and the latest Star Wars heroes. And from the ageless Raggedy Ann and Andy to Pac Man, the Shirt Tales, Cabbage Patch Kids, and Pound Puppies.

Licensed names or characters can quickly make a new product familiar and can set it apart from competitors' products. Customers choosing between two similar products will most likely reach for the one containing a familiar name. In fact, consumers often seek out products that carry their favorite names or characters.

Almost everyone is getting into licensing these days. Harley-Davidson is licensing its name to toys and even chocolate and cologne. Porsche is licensing its name to skis, sunglasses, and other products needing an instant prestige image. And Maxim's is licensing its name to products from tuxedos to prune juice.

For further reading, see John A. Quelch, "How to Build a Product Licensing Program," *Harvard Business Review*, May-June 1985, pp. 186 ff.

Manufacturers' brands tend to dominate the Canadian scene. Consider such well-known brands as Campbell's soup and Heinz tomato ketchup. In recent times, however, large retailers and wholesalers have developed their own brands. Sears has created several names—Diehard batteries, Craftsman tools, Kenmore appliances—that command brand preference and even brand insistence. An increasing number of department stores, service stations, clothiers, drugstores, and appliance dealers are launching store brands.

Why do middlemen bother with sponsoring their own brands? They have to hunt down qualified suppliers who can deliver consistent quality. They have to order large quantities and tie up their capital in inventories. They have to spend money promoting their private label. They have to take the chance that if their private-label product is not good, the customer will develop a negative attitude toward their other products.

In spite of these potential disadvantages, middlemen develop private brands because they can be profitable. They search for manufacturers with excess capacity who will produce the private label at a low cost. Other costs, such as advertising and physical distribution, may also be low. This means that the private brander is able to charge a lower price and often make a higher profit margin. The private brander may be able to develop some strong store brands that draw traffic into its stores.

The competition between manufacturers' and middlemen's brands is called the *battle of the brands*. In this confrontation, middlemen have many advantages. Retail shelf space is scarce, and many manufacturers, especially the newer and smaller ones, cannot introduce products into distribution under their own name. Middlemen take special care to maintain the quality of their brands, thus building consumers' confidence. Many shoppers know that the store brand is often manufactured by one of the larger manufacturers anyway. Store brands are often priced lower than comparable manufacturers' brands, thus appealing to budget-conscious shoppers, especially in times of inflation. But for shoppers that want more than the low price of its No Name generic products, Loblaws promotes its President's Choice brand as a premium quality product. Prominent display and well-stocked shelves further strengthen house brands. Some commentators predict that such tactics will eventually eliminate all but a few of the strong manufacturers' brands.

Manufacturers of national brands are very frustrated. Their inclination is to spend a lot of money on consumer-directed advertising and promotion to maintain strong brand preference. Their price has to be somewhat higher to cover this promotion. At the same time, the mass distributors put considerable pressure on them to put more of their promotional money into trade allowances and deals if they want adequate shelf space. Once manufacturers start giving in, they have less to spend on consumer promotion, and their brand leadership starts slipping. This is the national brand manufacturers' dilemma.

Family-Brand Decision

Manufacturers who brand their products face further choices. Four brand-name strategies can be distinguished:

1. *Individual brand names:* This policy is followed by Procter & Gamble (Tide, Bold, Dash, Cheer, Gain, Oxydol, Duz) and Canada Packers (Maple Leaf, York, Devon).

2. *A blanket family name for all products:* This policy is followed by Heinz and General Electric.

3. *Separate family names for all products:* This policy is followed by Sears (Kenmore for appliances, and Craftsman for tools).

4. *Company trade name combined with individual product names:* This policy is followed by Kellogg's (Kellogg's Rice Krispies and Kellogg's Raisin Bran) and John Labatt (Labatt's Blue and Labatt's Classic).

Competitors within the same industry will often adopt different brand-name strategies. In the soap industry, Procter & Gamble favors individual brand names. P&G will use its name with new products during the first six weeks of television promotion and then deemphasize it. P&G wants each product to make it on its own. Colgate, on the other hand, makes much use of the phrase "the Colgate family" to help its individual products along.

What are the advantages of an individual-brand-names strategy? A major advantage is that the company does not tie its reputation to the product's acceptance. If the product fails or appears to have low quality, it does not compromise the manufacturer's name. A manufacturer of good-quality watches, such as Seiko, can introduce a lower-quality line of watches (called Pulsar) without diluting the Seiko name. The individual-brand-names strategy permits the firm to search for the best name for each new product. A new name permits the building of new excitement and conviction.

Using a blanket family name for the company's products also has some advantages. The cost of introducing the product is less because there is no need for "name" research or for heavy advertising expenditures to create brand-name recognition and preference. Furthermore, sales will be strong if the manufacturer's name is good. Thus Campbell's introduces new soups under its brand name with extreme simplicity and instant recognition. On the other hand, Philips in Europe used its name on all of its products, but since its products vary in quality, most people expect only average quality in a Philips product. This hurts the sales of its superior products; here is a case where individual branding might be better, or the company might avoid putting its own name on its weaker products.

Where a company produces quite different products, it is not possible to use one blanket family name. Swift and Company developed separate family names for its hams (Premium) and fertilizers (Vigoro). When Mead Johnson developed a diet supplement for gaining weight, it created a new family name, Nutriment, to avoid confusion with its family-brand weight-reducing products, Metrecal. Companies will often invent different family names for different quality lines within the same product class. Thus A&P food stores sell a first-grade, second-grade, and third-grade set of brands—Ann Page, Sultana, and Iona, respectively.

Finally, some manufacturers tie their company name with an individual brand name for each product. The company name legitimizes, and the individual name individualizes, the new product. Thus Quaker Oats in *Quaker Oats Cap'n Crunch* taps the company's reputation in the breakfast-cereal field, and Cap'n Crunch individualizes and dramatizes the new product.

The brand name should not be a casual afterthought but an integral reinforcer of the product concept. Among the desirable qualities for a brand name are the following:

1. *It should suggest something about the product's benefits.* Examples: Coldspot, Beautyrest, Craftsman, Accutron.

2. *It should suggest product qualities such as action or color.* Examples: Duz, Sunkist, Spic and Span, Firebird.

3. *It should be easy to pronounce, recognize, and remember.* Short names help. Examples: Tide, Crest, Puffs.

4. *It should be distinctive.* Examples: Mustang, Kodak, Xerox.

Marketing research firms have developed elaborate name-research procedures, including *association tests* (What images come to mind?), *learning tests* (How easily is the name pronounced?), *memory tests* (How well is the name remembered?), and *preference tests* (Which names are preferred?). One of the best-known specialists in the "name game" is NameLab, Inc., which uses a technique known as constructional linguistics to help clients find effective names. NameLab is responsible for such recent product names as Acura, Compaq, and Zapmail. There are even computer programs available to help firms find names.

Many firms strive to build a unique brand name that will eventually become identified with the product category. Such brand names as Frigidaire, Kleenex, Levis, Jell-O, Scotch Tape, and Fiberglas have succeeded in this way. However, their very success may threaten the exclusive rights to the name. Cellophane and shredded wheat are now names in the common domain.

Brand-Extension Decision

A brand-extension strategy is any effort to extend a successful brand name to launch new or modified products or lines. After Quaker Oats's success with Cap'n Crunch dry breakfast cereal, the company used the brand name and cartoon character to launch a line of ice-cream bars, T-shirts, and other products. Armour used its Dial brand name to launch a variety of new products that would not easily have obtained distribution without the strength of the Dial name. Honda Motor Company used its name to launch its new power lawnmower.

As a strategy, brand extension offers a number of advantages. A strong brand name gives a new product instant recognition. The company saves all the advertising cost involved in familiarizing consumers with a new name. Thus people would ordinarily respond positively to Pierre Cardin wine or Porsche sunglasses.

At the same time, brand-extension strategy involves some risk. Such brand extensions as Bic pantyhose and Life Savers gum met early deaths. The brand name might be put on a product that disappoints the consumer, hurting the consumer's regard for the company's other products. The brand name may be inappropriate to the new product, even if it is well made and satisfying—consider buying Sunoco ketchup or Drano milk. And the brand name may lose its special positioning in the consumer's mind through its overuse. Ries and Trout call this the "line-extension" trap.[8] They do not think that the Scott Paper Company benefited from naming its various paper products ScotTowels, ScotTissues, Scotties, Scotkins, and BabyScott diapers. The Scott name lost meaning, and the individual products lacked personality compared with rivals having distinctive names like Pampers and Luvs.

Multibrand Decision

In a *multibrand strategy*, the seller develops two or more brands in the same product category. This marketing practice was pioneered by P&G when it introduced Cheer detergent as a competitor for its already successful Tide. Although Tide's sales dropped slightly, the combined sales of Cheer and Tide were higher. P&G now markets eight detergent brands.

Manufacturers adopt multibrand strategies for several reasons. First, manufacturers can gain more shelf space, thus increasing the retailer's dependence on their brands. Second, few consumers are so loyal to a brand that they will not try another. The main way to capture the "brand switchers" is to offer several brands. Third, creating new brands develops excitement and efficiency within the manufacturer's organization. Managers in P&G and General Motors compete to outperform each other. Fourth, a multibrand strategy positions each brand to capture a different market segment.

In deciding whether to introduce another brand, the manufacturer should consider such questions as:

☐ Can a unique story be built for the new brand?

☐ Will the unique story be believable?

☐ How much will the new brand cannibalize the manufacturer's other brands versus competitors' brands?

☐ Will the new brand's sales cover the cost of product development and promotion?

A major pitfall in introducing multibrand entries is that each might obtain only a small market share, and none may be particularly profitable. The company will have dissipated its resources over several brands instead of building a few brands to a highly profitable level. These companies should weed out the weaker brands and establish tighter screening procedures for choosing new brands. Ideally, a company's brands should cannibalize the competitors' brands and not each other. Or at least the net profits or net cash flow with the multibrand strategy should be larger even if some cannibalism occurs.[9]

Brand-Repositioning Decision

However well a brand is positioned in a market, the company may have to reposition it later. A competitor may launch a brand next to the company's brand and cut into its market share. Or customer preferences may shift, leaving the company's brand with less demand.

A classic story of successful brand repositioning is the Seven-Up campaign. Seven-Up was one of several soft drinks and was bought primarily by older people who wanted a bland, lemon-flavored drink. Research indicated that while a majority of soft-drink consumers preferred a cola, they did not prefer it all the time, and many other consumers were noncola drinkers. Seven-Up went for leadership in the noncola market by executing a brilliant campaign, calling itself the Uncola. The Uncola was featured as a youthful and refreshing drink, the one to reach for instead of a cola. Seven-Up created a new way for consumers to view the soft-drink market, as consisting of colas and uncolas, with Seven-Up leading the uncolas.

The problem of repositioning a brand can be illustrated by the beer market. Figure 16-6 shows beer brand perceptions and taste preferences on two attributes: lightness and mildness. The dots show the perceived positions of the brands, and the circles represent locations of consumer preference. The larger circles represent more-intense preference. This map reveals that Brand A is not meeting the preferences of any distinct segment.

To remedy this problem, Brand A needs to identify the best preference cluster in which to reposition. Preference cluster #1 would be a poor choice, because Brand C and Brand D are serving this segment. Preference cluster #2 seems like a good choice because of its size and the presence of only one competitor, Brand B. Preference cluster #9 would be another possibility, although it is relatively small. Brand A can also think about a long-shot repositioning toward the supercluster #3, #5, and #8 or the supercluster #4 and #6.

Management must weigh two factors in making its choice. The first is the cost of shifting the brand to that segment. The cost includes changing the product's qualities, packaging, advertising, and so on. In general, the repositioning cost rises with the repositioning distance. The more radically the brand image has to be modified, the greater the required investment. Brand A would need more money to reposition in segment #8 than in segment #2. Management would be better off creating a new brand for segment #8 than repositioning its present brand.

FIGURE 16-6

Distribution of Perceptions and Preferences in the Beer Market

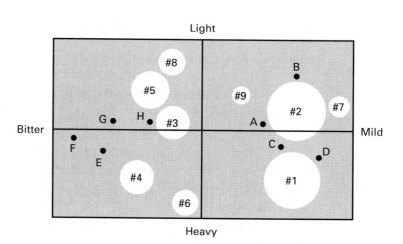

The other factor is the revenue that the brand would earn in the new position. The revenue depends on the number of consumers in the preference segment, their average purchase rate, the number and strength of competitors in that segment, and the price charged by brands in that segment. Management must make its decision by comparing likely revenues and costs of each repositioning alternative.

PACKAGING AND LABELING DECISIONS

Many physical products going to the market have to be packaged and labeled. Packaging can play a minor role (e.g., inexpensive hardware items) or a major role (e.g., cosmetics). Some packages—such as the Coke bottle and the L'eggs container—are world famous. Many marketers have called packaging a fifth P, along with price, product, place, and promotion. Most marketers, however, treat packaging as an element of product strategy.

We define *packaging as the activities of designing and producing the container or wrapper for a product.* The container or wrapper is called the package. The package might include up to three levels of material. The *primary package* is the product's immediate container. Thus the bottle holding Old Spice After-Shave Lotion is the primary package. The *secondary package* refers to material that protects the primary package and is discarded when the product is about to be used. The cardboard box containing the bottle of after-shave lotion is a secondary package and provides additional protection and promotion opportunity. The *shipping package* refers to packaging necessary for storage, identification, or transportation. Thus a corrugated box carrying six dozen bottles of Old Spice After-Shave Lotion is a shipping package. Finally, *labeling* is part of packaging and consists of printed information that describes the product, appearing on or with the package.

In recent times, packaging has become a potent marketing tool. Well-designed packages can create convenience value for the consumer and promotional value for the producer. Various factors have contributed to packaging's growing use as a marketing tool:

- *Self-Service:* An increasing number of products are sold on a self-service basis at supermarkets and discount houses. The package must perform many of the sales tasks. It must attract attention, describe the product's features, give the consumer confidence, and make a favorable overall impression.

- *Consumer Affluence:* Rising consumer affluence means consumers are willing to pay a little more for the convenience, appearance, dependability, and prestige of better packages.

- *Company and Brand Image:* Companies are recognizing the power of well-designed packages to contribute to instant recognition of the company or brand. Every film buyer immediately recognizes the familiar yellow packaging of Kodak film.

- *Innovation Opportunity:* Innovative packaging can bring large benefits to consumers and profits to producers. Toothpaste pump dispensers have captured 12 percent of the toothpaste market because for many consumers, they are more convenient and less messy. Chesbrough-Pond's increased its overall nail-polish sales by 22 percent after introducing its novel Aziza Polishing Pen for fingernails. Kraft is testing retort pouches, which are foil-and-plastic containers, as a successor to cans. The first companies to put their soft drinks in pop-top cans and their liquid sprays in aerosol cans attracted many new customers. Now wine makers are experimenting with pop-top cans and bag-in-the-carton forms of packaging.

Developing an effective package for a new product requires several decisions. The first task is to establish the *packaging concept*. The packaging concept defines what the package should basically *be* or *do* for the particular product. Should the package's main function(s) be to offer superior product protection, introduce a novel dispensing method, suggest certain qualities about the product or the company, or something else?

> General Foods developed a new dog-food product in the form of meatlike patties. Management decided that the unique and palatable appearance of these patties demanded maximum visibility. *Visibility* was defined as the basic packaging concept. Management considered various alternatives and finally chose a tray with a film covering. ∎

Decisions must be made on additional packaging elements—*size, shape, materials, color, text,* and *brand mark.* Decisions must be made on much or little text, cellophane or other transparent films, a plastic or a laminate tray, and so on. The various packaging elements must be harmonized. Size interacts with materials, colors, and so on. The packaging elements must also be harmonized with decisions on pricing, advertising, and other marketing elements.

After the packaging is designed, it must be tested. *Engineering tests* are conducted to ensure that the package stands up under normal conditions; *visual tests,* to ensure that the script is legible and the colors harmonious; *dealer tests,* to ensure that dealers find the packages attractive and easy to handle; and *consumer tests,* to ensure favorable consumer response.

In spite of these precautions, a packaging design occasionally gets through with some basic flaw:

> Warner-Lambert tested Fizzies, an effervescent soft drink tablet, in three cities. Fortunately, the temperatures in the test cities were high enough to reveal that the cardboard packaging did not provide sufficient protection against hot weather. The company switched to an aluminum foil package and avoided a costly mistake.[10] ∎

Developing effective packaging may cost a few hundred thousand dollars and take from a few months to a year. The importance of packaging cannot be overemphasized, considering the functions it performs in attracting and satisfying customers. Companies must pay attention, however, to the growing environmental concerns about packaging and make decisions that serve society's interests as well as immediate customer and company objectives.

Sellers must label their products. The label may be a simple tag attached to the product or an elaborately designed graphic that is part of the package. The label might carry only the brand name or a great deal of information. Even if the seller prefers a simple label, the law may require additional information.

Labels perform several functions. The label *identifies* the product or brand, for instance, the name Sunkist stamped on oranges. The label might also *grade* the product; thus canned peaches are grade labeled A, B, and C. The label might *describe* the product: who made it, where it was made, when it was made, what it contains, how it is to be used, and how to use it safely. Finally, the label might *promote* the product through its attractive graphics. Some writers distinguish between identification labels, grade labels, descriptive labels, and promotional labels.

Labels eventually become outmoded and need freshening up. The label on Ivory soap has been redone eighteen times since the 1890s, with gradual changes in the size and design of the letters. The label on Orange Crush soft drink was substantially changed when its competitors' labels began to picture fresh fruits, thereby pulling in more sales. Orange Crush developed a label with new symbols to suggest freshness and with much stronger and deeper colors.

There has been a long history of legal concerns surrounding labels. Formerly labels could mislead customers or fail to describe important ingredients or fail to include sufficient safety warnings. As a result, legislation was enacted to protect users. The most prominent is the federal *Consumer Packaging and Labeling Act*. Labeling practices have been affected in recent times by *unit pricing* (stating the price per unit of standard measure), *open dating* (stating the expected shelf life of the product), and *nutritional labeling* (stating the nutritional values in the product). Sellers should make sure that their labels contain all the required information before launching new products, including French language information as mandated by the province of Quebec.

SUMMARY

Product is the first and most important element of the marketing mix. Product strategy calls for making coordinated decisions on product mixes, product lines, brands, packaging, and labeling.

A product can be looked at on five levels. The core benefit is the essential service or benefit that the buyer is buying. The generic product is the basic product recognized as such. The expected product is the set of attributes and conditions that the buyer normally expects in buying the product. The augmented product is additional services and benefits that the seller adds to distinguish the offer from competitors. The potential product is the set of possible new features and services that might eventually be added to the offer.

All products can be classified according to their durability (nondurable goods, durable goods, and services). Consumer goods are usually classified according to customer shopping habits (convenience, shopping, specialty, and unsought goods). Industrial goods are classified according to how they enter the production process (materials and parts, capital items, and supplies and services).

Most companies handle more than one product. Their product mix can be described as having a certain breadth, length, depth, and consistency. The four dimensions of the product mix are the tools for developing the company's product strategy. The various lines making up the product mix have to be periodically evaluated for profitability and growth potential. The company's better lines should receive disproportionate support; weaker lines should be phased down or out; and new lines should be added to fill the profit gap.

Each product line consists of product items. The product-line manager should study the sales and profit contributions of each product item as well as the way the items are positioned against competitors' items. This provides information needed for making several product-line decisions. Line stretching involves the question of whether a particular line should be extended downward, upward, or both ways. Line filling raises the question of whether additional items should be added within the present range of the line. Line modernization raises the question of whether the line needs a new look and whether the new look should be installed piecemeal or all at once. Line featuring raises the question of which items to feature in promoting the line. Line pruning raises the question of how to detect and remove weaker product items from the line.

Companies have to develop brand policies for the individual product items in their lines. They must decide whether to brand at all, whether to do manufacturing or private branding, whether to use family brand names or individual brand names, whether to extend the brand name to new products, whether to put out several competing brands, and whether to reposition any of the brands.

Physical products require packaging decisions to create such benefits as protection, economy, convenience, and promotion. Marketers have to develop a packaging concept and test it functionally and psychologically to make sure it achieves the desired objectives and is compatible with public policy. Physical products also require labeling for identification and possible grading, description, and promotion of the product. The law requires sellers to present certain minimum information on the label to inform and protect consumers.

■ QUESTIONS

1. Use the "levels of the product concept" and compare the following vehicles: a Porsche, a Ford pick-up, and a Toyota Tercel.

2. Several companies are planning to put their brand names on fresh food, and many of their initial forays will be in produce. Discuss the problems that the companies might face, and suggest how these problems might be overcome.

3. The courts have ruled that Parker Bros.' game "Monopoly" is a generic trademark. The ruling was based on a market survey of buyers' motivations submitted by the makers of another board game "Antimonopoly," which revealed that 65 percent of the people surveyed would buy Monopoly if it were produced by any manufacturer. What implications does this ruling have for trademark protection by marketers?

4. Both North American Watch (marketers of Piaget, Corum, and Concord brands) and Timex have changed from advertising their products as accurate timepieces to promoting them as jewelry that tells time. What changes have taken place in the five product levels, and what are the respective companies' chances for success with the new strategy?

5. Define the primary want-satisfying purpose(s) of the following goods: (a) cars; (b) bread; (c) oil; (d) pillows; (e) pens; (f) novels; (g) textbooks; (h) uniforms; (i) detergents.

6. Offer a definition of the basic business of each of the following large companies: (a) General Motors; (b) Bayer's (maker of aspirin); (c) Investors' Syndicate (a mutual fund); (d) Sears; and (e) *Time* magazine.

7. Most firms prefer to develop a diversified product line to avoid overdependence on a single product. Yet there are certain advantages that accrue to the firm that produces and sells one product. Name them.

8. "As a firm increases the number of its products arithmetically, management's problems tend to increase geometrically." Do you agree?

9. Does the ranking of a company's products according to their relative profit contribution indicate the best way to allocate the marketing budget to these products? If yes, how should the budget be allocated to the products? If no, why?

10. A marketing consultant advised a large consumer packaged goods company that its product line should consist of (1) a top-quality national brand, (2) private-label brands for supermarket chains, and (3) a generic brand. Discuss the advantages and risks of this product-line strategy.

■ NOTES

1. This discussion is adapted from Theodore Levitt, "Marketing Success through Differentiation—of Anything," *Harvard Business Review*, January-February 1980, pp. 83-91. The first level, core benefit, has been added to Levitt's discussion.

2. See Harper W. Boyd, Jr., and Sidney J. Levy, "New Dimensions in Consumer Analysis," *Harvard Business Review*, November-December 1963, pp. 129-40.

3. Theodore Levitt, *The Marketing Mode* (New York: McGraw-Hill, 1969), p. 2.

4. This illustration is found in Benson P. Shapiro, *Industrial Product Policy: Managing the Existing Product Line* (Cambridge, Mass.: Marketing Science Institute, September 1977), pp. 3-5, 98-101.

5. See Steuart Henderson Britt, "How Weber's Law Can Be Applied to Marketing," *Business Horizons*, February 1975, pp. 21-29.

6. The first four definitions can be found in *Marketing Definitions: A Glossary of Marketing Terms* (Chicago: American Marketing Association, 1960).

7. For further reading, see Brian F. Harris and Roger A. Strang, "Marketing Strategies in the Age of Generics," *Journal of Marketing*, Fall 1985, pp. 70-81.

8. Al Ries and Jack Trout, *Positioning: The Battle For Your Mind* (New York: McGraw-Hill, 1981)

9. See Mark B. Taylor, "Cannibalism in Multibrand Firms," *Journal of Business Strategy*, Spring 1986, pp. 69-75.

10. "Product Tryouts: Sales Tests in Selected Cities Help Trim Risks of National Marketing," *Wall Street Journal*, August 10, 1962.

17

Managing Service Businesses and Ancillary Services

There are no such things as service industries. There are only industries whose service components are greater or less than those of other industries. Everybody is in service.

Theodore Levitt

It is wrong to imply that services are just like products except for intangibility. . . . Intangibility is not a modifier; it is a state.

Lynn Shostack

Marketing developed initially in connection with selling physical products or goods such as toothpaste, cars, and machinery. Yet one of the major megatrends in Canada has been the phenomenal growth of services. Service jobs now account for more than two-thirds of the GNP and of all existing jobs, and a much larger proportion of new jobs. Service jobs are everywhere, including not only persons working in service industries (hotels, airlines, banks, etc.) but also persons providing services within goods-based industries (corporate lawyers, medical staff, trainers, etc.). The growing demand for services is a consequence of rising affluence, more leisure time, and the increasing complexity of products. As a result, the typical Canadian worker is no longer a "hewer of wood and drawer of water," but a member of the post-industrial service economy. This has led to a greater interest in the special challenges of marketing services.[1]

Service industries are quite varied. The *government sector*, with its courts, employment services, hospitals, loan agencies, military services, police and fire departments, post office, regulatory agencies, and schools, is in the service business. The *private nonprofit sector*, with its museums, charities, churches, colleges, foundations, and hospitals, is in the service business. A good part of the *business sector*, with its airlines, banks, computer-service bureaus, hotels, insurance companies, law firms, management consulting firms, medical practices, motion picture companies, plumbing-repair companies, and real-estate firms, is in the service business. Many workers in the *manufacturing sector* are really service providers, such as the computer operators, accountants, and legal staff. In fact, they make up a "service factory" providing services to the "goods factory."

Not only are there traditional service industries, but new types keep popping up all the time:

> For a fee, there are now companies that will balance your budget, babysit your philodendron, wake you up in the morning, drive you to work or find you a new home, job, car, wife, clairvoyant, cat

feeder, or gypsy violinist. Or perhaps you want to rent a garden tractor? A few cattle? Some original paintings? Or maybe some hippies to decorate your next cocktail party? If it is business services you need, other companies will plan your convention and sales meetings, design your products, handle your data processing, or supply temporary secretaries or even executives.[2]

In this chapter, we will examine the following questions:

- How are services defined and classified?
- What are the distinctive characteristics of services as opposed to goods?
- How can service firms improve their differentiation, quality, and productivity?
- How can goods-producing companies improve their customer-support services?

NATURE AND CLASSIFICATION OF SERVICES

We define a service as follows:

> A service *is any act or performance that one party can offer to another that is essentially intangible and does not result in the ownership of anything. Its production may or may not be tied to a physical product.*

A company's offer to the marketplace usually includes some services. The service component can be a minor or a major part of the total offer. In fact, the offer can range from a pure good on the one hand to a pure service on the other. Four categories of offer can be distinguished:

1. *A Pure Tangible Good:* Here the offer consists primarily of a tangible good such as soap, toothpaste, or salt. No services accompany the product.

2. *A Tangible Good with Accompanying Services:* Here the offer consists of a tangible good accompanied by one or more services to enhance its consumer appeal. For example, an automobile manufacturer sells an automobile with a warranty, service and maintenance instructions, and so on. Levitt observes that "the more technologically sophisticated the generic product (e.g., cars and computers), the more dependent are its sales on the quality and availability of its accompanying customer services (e.g., display rooms, delivery, repairs and maintenance, application aids, operator training, installation advice, warranty fulfillment). In this sense, General Motors is probably more service intensive than manufacturing intensive. Without its services, its sales would shrivel."[3]

3. *A Major Service with Accompanying Minor Goods and Services:* Here the offer consists of a major service along with some additional services and/or supporting goods. For example, airline passengers are buying transportation service. They arrive at their destinations without anything tangible to show for their expenditure. However, the trip includes some tangibles, such as food and drinks, a ticket stub, and an airline magazine. The service requires a capital-intensive good called an airplane for its realization, but the primary item is a service.

4. *A Pure Service:* Here the offer consists primarily of a service. Examples include psychotherapy and massages. The psychoanalyst gives a pure service, with the only tangible elements an office and a couch.

As a consequence of this varying goods-to-service mix, it is difficult to generalize about services unless some further distinctions are made.

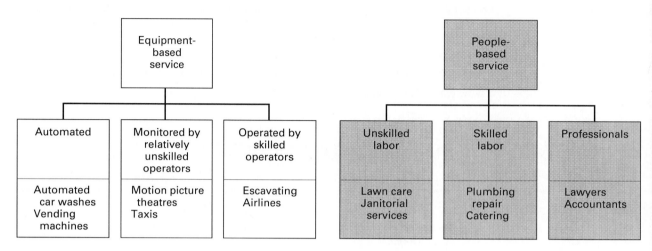

First, services vary as to whether they are *people based* or *equipment based*. Equipment-based services vary in turn depending on whether they are automated or monitored by unskilled or by skilled operators. People-based services also vary by whether they are provided by unskilled, skilled, or professional workers. Figure 17-1 shows several industries that cluster in each group.

Some, but not all services require the *client's presence*. Thus brain surgery involves the client's presence, but a car repair does not. If the client must be present, the service provider has to be considerate of his or her needs. Thus beauty shop operators will invest in their shop's decor, play background music, and engage in light conversation with the client.

Services differ as to whether they meet a *personal* need (personal services) or a *business* need (business services). Service providers typically develop different marketing programs for personal and business markets. For example, different service fees may be charged for individuals and for large corporations. Thus, the T-D Bank targeted its Green Line discount brokerage service at institutions.

Finally, *service providers differ in their objectives* (profit or nonprofit) and *ownership* (private or public). These two characteristics, when crossed, produce four quite different types of service organizations. The marketing needs of the Royal Bank (profit/private) are quite different from those of the Federal Business Development Bank (nonprofit/public), although both are in the same industry.[4]

CHARACTERISTICS OF SERVICES AND THEIR MARKETING IMPLICATIONS

Services have four major characteristics that greatly affect the design of marketing programs.

Intangibility

Services are intangible. Unlike physical products, they cannot be seen, tasted, felt, heard, or smelled before they are bought. The person getting a "face lift" cannot see the results before the purchase, and the patient in the psychiatrist's office cannot predict the outcome.

To reduce uncertainty, the buyer will look for signs or evidence of the service quality. They will draw inferences about the quality of the service from the place, people, equipment, communication material, symbols, and price that they see.

Therefore the service provider's task is to "manage the evidence," to "tangibilize the intangible."[5] Whereas product marketers are challenged to add abstract ideas, service marketers are challenged to put physical evidence and imagery on their abstract offers. Consider the following tangible images: "You are in good *hands* with Allstate"; "I've got a piece of the *Rock*." (Prudential).

Suppose a bank wants to convey the idea that its service is quick and efficient. It could "tangibilize" this positioning strategy through a number of tools:

1. *Place:* The bank's physical setting must connote quick and efficient service. The bank's exterior and interior should have clean lines. The layout of the desks and the traffic flow should be planned carefully. Queues should not seem overly long. Customers waiting for a loan officer should have plenty of seating. The background music should reinforce the concept of efficient service.

2. *People:* The bank's personnel should be busy. They should wear appropriate clothing, not be dressed in blue jeans or other apparel that would lead to negative inferences about the personnel and service.

3. *Equipment:* The bank's equipment—computers, copying machines, desks—should look "state of the art." A customer would think twice if all the typewriters were 1940-vintage Remingtons.

4. *Communication Material:* The bank's communication material should suggest efficiency. Pamphlets should have clean lines and avoid clutter. Photos should be chosen carefully. Lending proposals should be typed neatly. Ads should communicate the bank's positioning.

5. *Symbols:* The bank should choose a name and a tangible symbol for its service. For example, it could adopt the name Mercury Service and use the Greek god Mercury as a pictorial symbol.

6. *Price:* The bank's pricing of its various services should be kept simple and clear at all times.

Inseparability

Services are typically produced and consumed at the same time. This is not true of physical goods that are manufactured, put into inventory, distributed through multiple resellers, and consumed still later. If the service is rendered by a person, then the person is part of the service. Since the client is also present as the service is produced, provider-client interaction is a special feature of services marketing. Both the provider and the client affect the service outcome.

In the case of entertainment and professional services, buyers are highly interested in who the provider is. It is not the same service if an announcer at an Anne Murray concert says that Murray is indisposed and will be replaced by k. d. lang. Regardless of the relative merits of the entertainers, each has her loyal followers who have different preferences. When clients have strong provider preferences, price is used to ration the limited supply of the preferred provider's time.

Several strategies exist for getting around this limitation. The service provider can learn to work with larger groups. Psychotherapy has evolved from one-on-one therapy, to small-group therapy, to groups of over three hundred in a large hotel ballroom who are getting "therapized." The service provider can learn to work faster—the psychotherapist can spend thirty minutes with each patient instead of fifty minutes and can see more patients. The service organization can train more service providers and build up client confidence, as H&R Block has done with its national network of trained tax consultants.

Variability

Services are highly variable, since they depend on who provides them and when and where they are provided. A Dr. Christiaan Barnard heart transplant was believed to be of higher quality than one performed by a less-experienced surgeon. And Dr. Barnard's heart transplants varied with his energy and mental set at the time of each operation. Service buyers are aware of this high variability and frequently talk to others before selecting a service provider.

Service firms can take three steps toward quality control. The first is investing in good personnel selection and training. Airlines, banks, and hotels spend substantial sums to train their employees in providing good service. Thus one should find the same friendly and helpful personnel in every Hyatt Hotel.

The second step is standardizing the service-performance process throughout the organization. Figure 17-2 charts the performance process of a nationwide floral-delivery organization.[6] The customer's experience is limited to dialing the phone, making choices, and placing an order. Behind the scenes, the floral organization gathers the flowers, places them in a vase, delivers them, and collects payment.

The third step is monitoring customer satisfaction through suggestion and complaint systems, customer surveys, and comparison shopping, so that poor service can be detected and corrected.[7]

Perishability

Services cannot be stored. The reason many doctors charge patients for missed appointments is that the service value existed only at the point when the patient should have shown up. The perishability of services is not a problem when demand is steady, because it is easy to staff the services in advance. When demand fluctuates, service firms have difficult problems. For example, public-transportation companies have to own much more equipment because of rush-hour demand than they would if demand were even throughout the day.

Sasser has described several strategies for producing a better match between demand and supply in a service business.[8]

On the demand side:

☐ *Differential pricing* will shift some demand from peak to off-peak periods. Examples include low early-evening movie prices and weekend discount prices for car rentals.

☐ *Nonpeak demand can be cultivated.* McDonald's opened its Egg McMuffin breakfast service, and hotels developed their minivacation weekends.

☐ *Complementary services* can be developed during peak time to provide alternatives to waiting customers, such as cocktail lounges to sit in while waiting for a table and automatic tellers in banks.

FIGURE 17-2

A Service-Performance-Process Map: Nationwide Floral Delivery

Source: G. Lynn Shostack, "Service Positioning through Structural Change," *Journal of Marketing*, January 1987, p. 39.

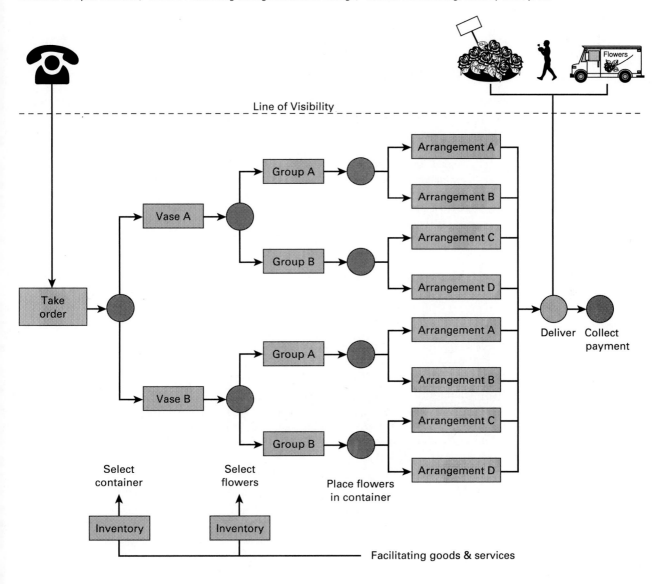

□ *Reservation systems* are a way to manage the demand level, and airlines, hotels, and physicians employ them extensively.

On the supply side:

□ *Part-time employees* can be hired to serve peak demand. Colleges add part-time teachers when enrolment goes up, and restaurants call in part-time waitresses when needed.

□ *Peak-time efficiency routines* can be introduced. Employees perform only essential tasks during peak periods. Paramedics assist physicians during busy periods.

□ *Increased consumer participation* in the tasks can be encouraged, as when consumers fill out their own medical records or bag their own groceries.

□ *Shared services* can be developed, as when several hospitals share medical-equipment purchases.

□ *Facilities for future expansion* can be developed, as when an amusement park buys surrounding land for later development.

MARKETING STRATEGIES FOR SERVICE FIRMS

Until recently, service firms lagged behind manufacturing firms in their use of marketing. George and Barksdale surveyed four hundred service and manufacturing firms and concluded that

> in comparison to manufacturing firms, service firms appear to be: (1) generally less likely to have marketing-mix activities carried out in the marketing department, (2) less likely to perform analysis in the offering area, (3) more likely to handle their advertising internally rather than go to outside agencies, (4) less likely to have an overall sales plan, (5) less likely to develop sales training programs, (6) less likely to use marketing research firms and marketing consultants, and (7) less likely to spend as much on marketing when expressed in a percentage of gross sales.[9]

There are several reasons why service firms neglected marketing in the past. Many service businesses are small (shoe repair, barbershops) and do not use formal management or marketing techniques. There are also service businesses (law and accounting firms) that formerly believed it was unprofessional to use marketing. Other service businesses (universities, lawyers) faced so much demand until recently that they saw no need for marketing.

Furthermore, service businesses are more difficult to manage using only a *traditional marketing* approach. In a goods business, the product is fairly standardized and sits on a shelf, waiting for the customer to reach for it, pay, and leave. In a service business, there are more elements (see Figure 17-3). Consider a customer A visiting a bank to get a loan (service X). Customer A sees other customers waiting for this and other services. Customer A also sees a physical environment consisting of a building, interior, equipment, furniture and so on. Customer A also sees contact personnel and deals with a loan officer. All this is visible to customer A. Not visible is a whole "backroom" production process and organization system that supports the visible serviced business. Thus the service outcome is highly influenced by a host of highly variable elements.

In view of this complexity, Gronroos has argued that service marketing requires not only 4P traditional external marketing but two other marketing thrusts, namely, internal marketing and interactive marketing (see Figure 17-4).[10] *External marketing* describes the normal work done by the company to prepare, price, distribute, and promote the service to customers. *Internal marketing* describes the work done by the company to train and motivate its *internal customers*, namely its customer-contact employees and supporting service personnel, to work as a team to provide customer satisfaction. Everyone must practice a customer orientation, or else a high and consistent level of service would not be forthcoming. Berry has argued that the most important contribution the marketing department can make is to be "exceptionally clever in getting everyone else in the organization to practice marketing."[11] (See Marketing Strategies 17-1.)

Interactive marketing describes the employees' skill in handling customer contact. In services marketing, the service quality is enmeshed with the service deliverer. This is especially true of professional services.[12] The client judges service quality not only by its *technical quality* (e.g., Was the surgery successful?) but also by its *functional quality* (e.g., Did the

FIGURE 17-3

Elements in a
Service Encounter

Source: Slightly modi-
fied from P. Eiglier and E.
Langeard, "A Conceptual
Approach of the Service
Offering," in *Proceedings
of the EAARM X Annual
Conference*, ed. H. Hartvig
Larsen and S. Heede,
Copenhagen School of
Economics and Business
Administration, 1981.

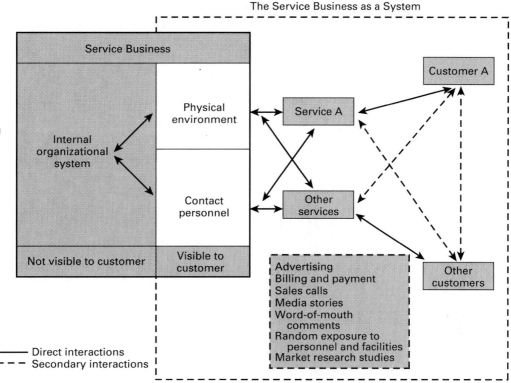

surgeon show concern and inspire confidence?).[13] Professionals cannot assume that they
will satisfy the patient simply because they provide good technical service. Therefore the
professional has to master the skills of interactive marketing.

In fact, there are some services that the customer cannot judge the technical quality of, after
they have been received! Figure 17-5 arrays various products and services according to their
difficulty of evaluation.[14] At the left are goods high in *search qualities*, namely, characteristics
that the buyer can evaluate before purchase. In the middle are goods and services high in
experience qualities, namely characteristics that the buyer can evaluate after purchase. At

FIGURE 17-4

Three Types of Marketing
in Service Industries

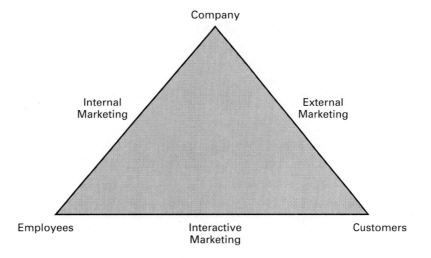

the right are goods and services high in *credence qualities*, namely characteristics that the buyer normally finds hard to evaluate even after consumption.

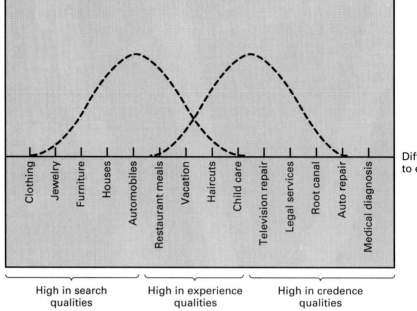

FIGURE 17-5

Continuum of Evaluation for Different Types of Products

Source: Valarie A. Zeithaml, "How Consumer Evaluation Processes Differ between Goods and Services," in *Marketing of Services*, ed. James H. Donnelly and William R. George (Chicago: American Marketing Association, 1981).

Easy to evaluate — Clothing, Jewelry, Furniture, Houses, Automobiles, Restaurant meals, Vacation, Haircuts, Child care, Television repair, Legal services, Root canal, Auto repair, Medical diagnosis — Difficult to evaluate

High in search qualities | High in experience qualities | High in credence qualities

---

Marketing Strategies 17-1

MOTIVATING EMPLOYEES TO CARE FOR THE CUSTOMER: THE CHALLENGE FACING CANADA'S HOSPITALS

Hospital patients have enough problems with their illnesses not to have to cope with poor service quality as well. It has been said that "quality begins in the boardroom." Nowhere is the dependence of service quality on top management support more evident than in the contrast between privately-funded hospitals and those funded by the government. In the U.S., private hospitals are turning to guest-room programs to train and motivate physicians, nurses, and other employees in hospitality. The Radford Hospital is among the latest of several hospitals to add a further wrinkle—a "guaranteed services" program. Radford set up a fund of $10 000 out of which they pay patients who have a justified complaint ranging from cold food to overlong waits in the emergency room. Any money not paid out of the fund by the end of the year is divided among the hospital's employees. With this incentive for the staff to treat the patients well, in the first six months of the plan the hospital had to pay out only $300.

Most of Canada's hospitals are funded by the provincial governments and any competition for patients is minimal. Lacking market incentives to provide high quality service, it is not surprising to encounter long queues in hospital waiting rooms, and to hear stories of cold meals and indifferent staff. But change may be coming, if only very slowly. Toronto's Doctors Hospital recently advertised an opening for a Vice-President of Patient Services!

Since services are generally higher in experience and credence qualities, consumers feel more risk in their purchase. That has several consequences. First, consumers generally rely more on word of mouth than on service-firm advertising. Second, they rely heavily on price, personnel, and physical cues to judge the service quality. Third, they are highly loyal to the service provider when satisfied.

As services competition intensifies, more marketing sophistication will be needed. One of the main agents of change will be product marketers who move into service industries. Sears moved into services marketing years ago—insurance, banking, income-tax consulting, car rentals. Gerber Products runs nursery schools and insurance companies.[15]

Service companies face three tasks—increasing their *competitive differentiation*, their *service quality*, and their *productivity*. Although these interact to some extent, we will examine each separately.

Managing Differentiation

Service marketers frequently complain about the difficulty of differentiating their services from those of competitors. The deregulation of regulated service industries like transportation permits intense competition. Travelers who care more about cost than service are forcing even established companies like Air Canada to reappraise their marketing mix.

Lacking a differentiated service, Air Canada has to offer periodic seat sales to defend its market share. Similarly, as financial services are deregulated, the success of the discount brokerage service shows that many customers have little loyalty to the more-established brokerage houses when they can save money. To the extent that customers view a service as fairly homogeneous, they care less about the provider than the price.

The solution to price competition is to develop a differentiated offer and image. The service company can add *innovative features* to distinguish its offer. What the customer expects is called the *primary service package*, and to this can be added *secondary service features*. In the airline industry, various carriers have introduced such innovations as movies on board, advanced seating, merchandise for sale, air-to-ground telephone service, and frequent-flyer award programs to augment the offer. Thus, Air Canada's Aeroplan program provides awards for the use of hotels and car rentals, as well as air travel. Airlines today talk about adding suit-pressing and shoe-shining services, a library of best-selling books, laptop computers, and so on.

The only problem is that most service innovations are easily copied. Few of them are pre-emptive in the long run. Still, the service company that regularly researches and develops service innovations will gain a succession of temporary advantages over its competitors, and through earning an innovative reputation, may retain customers who want to go with the best. The Toronto-Dominion enjoys the reputation as a *lead innovator* in the banking industry in aggressively creating or furthering such innovations as automatic teller machines and other services.

The service company can differentiate its service *delivery* in three ways, namely, through people, through physical environment, and through process. (Some have suggested that services marketing requires adding these 3Ps to the traditional 4Ps of marketing.) A service company can distinguish itself by having more able and reliable customer-contact people than its competitors. A service company can develop a superior physical environment in which the service product is delivered. Finally, a service company can design a superior delivery process. For example, home banking might be a superior way to deliver banking services rather than having customers drive, park, and wait in line.

Service companies can also work on differentiating their image, specifically through symbols and branding. The Royal Bank adopted a traditional lion symbol to convey an image of solid reliability. In contrast, Canada Trust adopted the name of Johnny Cash to popularize its automatic teller machines, and advise those who might otherwise queue-up for a live teller, not to "walk the line."

Managing Service Quality

One of the major ways to differentiate a service firm is to deliver consistently higher-quality service than competitors. The key is to meet or exceed the target customers' service-quality expectations. Their expectations are formed by their past experiences, word of mouth, and service firm advertising. The customers choose providers on this basis and after receiving the service, they compare the *perceived service* with the *expected service*. If the perceived service falls below the expected service, customers lose interest in the provider. If the perceived service meets or exceeds their expectations, they are apt to use the provider again.

Therefore, the service provider needs to identify target customers' wants in the way of service quality. Unfortunately, service quality is harder to define and judge than product quality. It is harder to get agreement on the quality of a haircut than on the quality of a hair dryer. Yet customers will make judgments about service quality, and service providers need to know customer expectations in order to design effective services.

Clearly, customers will be satisfied if they get what they want, when they want it, where they want it, and how they want it. Still, it is necessary to research the specific customer criteria for any specific service. Thus bank customers may expect on a trip to a bank that they will not wait in line more than five minutes; the teller will be courteous, knowledgeable and accurate; and that the computer will not break down. Service providers must do their best to identify the expectations of their target customers with respect to each specific service.

This does not mean that the service provider will be able to meet the customers' wishes. The service provider faces tradeoffs between customer satisfaction and company profitability. What is important is that the service provider clearly defines and communicates the service level that will be provided, so that the employees know what they must deliver and the attracted customers know what they will get.

Parasuraman, Zeithaml, and Berry formulated a service-quality model that highlights the main requirements for delivering the expected service quality.[16] The model, shown in Figure 17-6, identifies five gaps that cause unsuccessful service delivery. They are described below.

1. *Gap Between Consumer Expectation and Management Perception:* Management does not always perceive correctly what customers want or how customers judge the service components. Thus hospital administrators might think that patients judge hospital service by the food quality, whereas patients may be more concerned with nurse responsiveness.

2. *Gap Between Management Perception and Service-Quality Specification:* Management might set no quality standards, unclear standards, unrealistic standards, or if they are clear and realistic, management might not be fully committed to enforcing this quality level. For example, an airline's management may want phones to be answered within ten seconds of ringing but not provide enough operators nor do much about it when service falls below this level.

3. *Gap Between Service-Quality Specifications and Service Delivery:* Many factors affect service delivery. The personnel might be poorly trained or overworked. Their morale might be low. There might be equipment breakdowns. Those handling operations typically drive for efficiency, and sometimes this runs counter to a drive for customer satisfaction. Consider

FIGURE 17-6

Service-Quality Model

Source: A. Parasuraman, Valarie A.
Zeithaml, and Leonard L. Berry, "A
Conceptual Model of Service Quality
and Its Implications for Future
Research," *Journal of Marketing*, Fall
1985, p. 44.

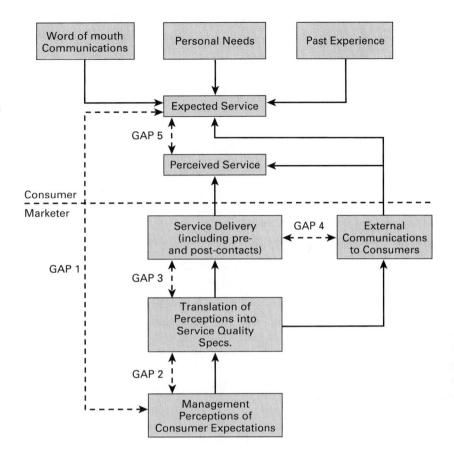

the cross-pressures on the bank teller who is told by the operations department to work fast and by the marketing department to be courteous and friendly to each customer.

4. *Gap Between Service Delivery and External Communications:* Consumer expectations are affected by promises made by the service provider's communications. If a resort hotel's brochure shows a gorgeous room but the guest arrives and finds the room to be cheap and tacky looking, then the fault lies in the expectations created by the external communications.

5. *Gap Between Perceived Service and Expected Service:* This gap results when one or more of the previous gaps occur. It becomes clear why service providers have a hard time delivering the expected service quality.

The same researchers developed a list of the major *determinants of service quality*. They found that consumers use basically similar criteria regardless of the type of service. The criteria follow.

1. *Access:* The service is easy to obtain in convenient locations at convenient times with little waiting.

2. *Communication:* The service is described accurately in the consumer's language.

3. *Competence:* The employees possess the required skill and knowledge.

4. *Courtesy:* The employees are friendly, respectful and considerate.

5. *Credibility:* The company and employees are trustworthy and have the customer's best interests at heart.

6. *Reliability:* The service is performed with consistency and accuracy.

7. *Responsiveness:* The employees respond quickly and creatively to customers' requests and problems.

8. *Security:* The service is free from danger, risk, or doubt.

9. *Tangibles:* The service tangibles correctly project the service quality.

10. *Understanding/Knowing the Customer:* The employees make an effort to understand the customer's needs and provide individual attention.

Various studies of excellently managed service companies show that they share a number of common practices with respect to service quality. Among them are the following:

1. *A strategic concept:* Top service companies have a clear sense of their target market and the customer needs they are trying to satisfy. They have developed a distinctive strategy for satisfying these needs that wins enduring customer loyalty.

2. *A history of top management commitment to quality:* Companies such as Marriott, and McDonald's have thorough commitments to quality. Their management looks not only at financial performance on a monthly basis but also at service performance. Ray Kroc of McDonald's insisted on continually measuring each McDonald's outlet on its conformance to QSCV; namely, quality, service, cleanliness, and value. Franchisers that failed to conform were dropped.

3. *The setting of high standards:* The best service providers set high service-quality standards. Swissair, for example, aims for having 96 percent or more of its passengers rate its service as good or superior; otherwise it takes action.

4. *Systems for monitoring service performance:* The top service firms audit service performance, both their own and competitors', on a regular basis. They use a number of devices to measure performance: *comparison shopping, ghost shopping, customer surveys*, and *suggestion and complaint forms*. A manufacturer sends out thousands of response cards a year to households to rate its service people's performance. A bank checks continuously on measures of ART, namely, accuracy, responsiveness, and timeliness. It does "ghost shopping" to check on its employees' delivering good service. The Marketing Concepts and Tools 17-1 exhibit outlines a useful system for rating the various elements of the service bundle and identifying what actions are required.

5. *Systems for satisfying complaining customers:* Well-run service businesses respond quickly and generously to customer complaints. An auto dealer who doesn't repair a car right the first time drives a "loaner" to the customer and picks up the customer's car at no charge. When the customer's ear is ready, the customer receives a complimentary gift. A restaurant set down these guidelines: "When guests have to wait more than ten minutes beyond their reservation time, but less than twenty, we suggest free drinks. If they wait more than twenty minutes, the entire meal may be free. If the bread arrives more than five minutes after the guests sit down, we suggest free chowder."[17]

6. *Satisfying the employees as well as the customers:* Excellently managed service companies believe that employee relations will reflect on customer relations. Management carries out internal marketing and creates an environment of employee support and rewards for good service performance. Management regularly audits employees' satisfaction with their jobs.

Marketing Concepts and Tools 17-1

MARKET-PERFORMANCE ANALYSIS

Services can be usefully rated according to their *customer importance* and *company performance*. The accompanying table shows how customers rated fourteen service elements (attributes) of an automobile dealer's service department on importance and performance.

Importance was rated on a four-point scale of "extremely important," "important," "slightly important," and "not important." Dealer performance was rated on a four-point scale of "excellent," "good," "fair," and "poor." For example, "Job done right the first time" received a mean importance rating of 3.83 and a mean performance rating of 2.63, indicating that customers felt it was highly important but was not being performed well.

The ratings of the fourteen elements are displayed in the figure and are divided into four sections. Quadrant A shows important service elements that are not being performed at the desired levels; they include elements 1, 2, and 9. The dealer should concentrate on improving the service department's performance on these elements. Quadrant B shows important service elements where the department is performing well; its job is to maintain the high performance. Quadrant C shows minor service elements that are being delivered in a mediocre way but do not need any attention, since

they are not very important. Quadrant D shows that a minor service element, "Send out maintenance notices," is being performed in an excellent manner, a case of possible overkill. Measuring service elements according to their importance and performance tells marketers where to focus their efforts.

Source: John A. Martilla and John C. James, "Importance-Performance Analysis," *Journal of Marketing*, January 1977, pp. 77-79.

Attribute Number	Attribute Description	Mean Importance Rating*	Mean Performance Rating**
1	Job done right the first time	3.83	2.63
2	Fast action on complaints	3.63	2.73
3	Prompt warranty work	3.60	3.15
4	Able to do any job needed	3.56	3.00
5	Service available when needed	3.41	3.05
6	Courteous and friendly service	3.41	3.29
7	Car ready when promised	3.38	3.03
8	Perform only necessary work	3.37	3.11
9	Low prices on service	3.29	2.00
10	Clean up after service work	3.27	3.02
11	Convenient to home	2.52	2.25
12	Convenient to work	2.43	2.49
13	Courtesy buses and cars	2.37	2.35
14	Send out maintenance notices	2.05	3.33

* Ratings obtained from a four-point scale of "extremely important," "important," "slightly important," and "not important."
** Ratings obtained from a four-point scale of "excellent," "good," "fair," and "poor." A "no basis for judgment" category was also provided.

WALT DISNEY ENTERPRISES— A HIGHLY RESPONSIVE ORGANIZATION

Service companies—hotels, hospitals, colleges, banks, and others—are increasingly recognizing that their marketing mix consists of five Ps, that is, product, price, place, promotion, people. And people may be the most important P! The organization's employees are in constant contact with consumers and can create good or bad impressions.

Organizations are eager to learn how to "turn on" their inside people (employees) to serve their outside people (customers). Here is what the Disney organization does to market "positive customer attitudes" to its employees:

1. The staff at Disney's personnel department extends a special welcome to new applicants. Those who are hired are given written instructions on what to expect—where to report, what to wear, and how long each training phase will be.

2. On the first day, new employees report to Disney University for an all-day orientation session. They sit four to a table, receive name tags, and enjoy coffee, juice, and pastry while they introduce themselves and get acquainted. The result is that each new employee immediately knows three other people and feels part of a group.

3. The employees are introduced to the Disney philosophy and operations through the latest audiovisual presentations. They learn that they are in the entertainment business. They are "cast members" whose job it is to be enthusiastic, knowledgeable, and professional in serving Disney's "guests." Each division is described, and the new employees learn how they will each play a role in producing the "show." Then they are treated to lunch, tour the park, and are shown the recreational area set aside for the employees' exclusive use. That area consists of a lake, recreation hall, picnic area, boating and fishing facilities, and a large library.

4. The next day, the new employees report to their assigned jobs, such as security hosts (police), transportation hosts (drivers), custodial hosts (street cleaners), or food-and-beverage hosts (restaurant workers). They will receive a few days of additional training before they go "on stage." When they have learned their function, they receive their "theme costumes" and are ready to perform.

5. The new employees receive additional training on how to answer questions guests frequently ask about the park. When they don't have the answer, they can dial switchboard operators who are armed with thick fact books and stand ready to answer any question.

6. The employees receive a Disney newspaper called *Eyes and Ears*, which features news of activities, employment opportunities, special benefits, educational offerings, and so on. Each issue contains a generous number of pictures of smiling employees.

7. Each Disney manager spends a week each year in "cross-utilization," namely, giving up the desk and heading for the front line, such as taking tickets, selling popcorn, or loading or unloading rides. In this way, management stays in touch with running the park and maintaining quality service to satisfy the millions of visitors. All managers and employees wear name badges and address each other on a first-name basis, regardless of rank.

8. All exiting employees answer a questionnaire on how they felt about working for Disney and any dissatisfactions they might have. In this way, Disney's management can measure its success in producing employee satisfaction and, ultimately, customer satisfaction.

No wonder the Disney people are so successful in satisfying their "guests." Management's attention to its employees helps the latter feel important and personally responsible for the "show." The employees' sense of "owning this organization" spills over to the millions of visitors with whom they come in contact.

Source: See N. W. Pope, "Mickey Mouse Marketing," *American Banker*, July 25, 1979; and "More Mickey Mouse Marketing," *American Banker*, September 12, 1979.

The Companies and Industries 17-1 exhibit illustrates how one great service marketer, Disney, combines a number of excellent practices that provide a continuing high level of customer satisfaction with its theme parks.

Managing Productivity

Service firms are under great pressure to increase productivity. Since service businesses are highly labor intensive, costs have been rising rapidly. There are six approaches to improving service productivity.

The first is to have service providers work harder or more skillfully. Working harder is not a likely solution, but working more skillfully can occur through better selection and training procedures.

The second is to increase the quantity of service by surrendering some quality. Dentists employ hygienists to provide some treatments, thus handling more patients and giving less time to each patient.

The third is to "industrialize the service" by adding equipment and standardizing production. Levitt recommended that companies adopt a "manufacturing attitude" toward producing services as represented by McDonald's assembly-line approach to fast-food retailing, culminating in the "technological hamburger."[18] Shouldice Hospital near Toronto, operates only on hernia patients and has reduced patient stay from the typical seven days to only $3\frac{1}{2}$ days by industrializing the service. Although its doctors are paid less than in private practice and its nurses attend more patients than in a normal hospital, patient satisfaction is unbelievably high.[19]

The fourth is to reduce or make obsolete the need for a service by inventing a product solution, the way television substituted for out-of-home entertainment, the wash-and-wear shirt reduced the need for commercial laundries, and certain antibiotics reduced the need for tuberculosis sanitariums.

The fifth is to design a more effective service. How-to-quit-smoking clinics and jogging may reduce the need for expensive medical services later on. Hiring paralegal workers reduces the need for expensive legal professionals.

The sixth is to present customers with incentives to substitute their own labor for company labor. For example, business firms that are willing to sort their own mail before delivering it to the post office pay lower postal rates. A restaurant that features a self-service salad bar is replacing "waitering" work with customer work.[20]

Companies must avoid pushing productivity so hard that it reduces perceived quality. Some productivity steps, by standardizing quality, increase customer satisfaction. Other productivity steps lead to too much standardization and rob the customer of customized service. "High touch" is replaced by "high tech." Burger King successfully challenged McDonald's with its "Have it your way" campaign, where customers could get a "customized" hamburger even though this reduced Burger King's productivity somewhat.

MANAGING PRODUCT SUPPORT SERVICES

Thus far we have focused our attention on service industries. No less important are product-based industries that must provide a service bundle to their customers. Manufacturers of equipment—small appliances, office machines, tractors, mainframes, airplanes—all have to provide the buyers with *product support services*. In fact, product support service is becoming a major arena in the battle for competitive advantage.

Table 17-1 Contribution of Service Quality to Relative Performance

	High Third in Service Quality	Low Third in Service Quality	Difference in % Points
Price index relative to competition	7%	−2%	+9%
Change in market share per annum	6%	−2%	+8%
Sales growth per annum	17%	8%	+9%
Return on sales	12%	1%	+11%

Source: Phillip Thompson, Glenn Desourza, and Bradley T. Gale, "The Strategic Management of Service and Quality," *Quality Progress*, June 1985, p. 24.

Firms that provide high-quality service will undoubtedly outperform their less-service-oriented competitors. Table 17-1 provides evidence. The Strategic Planning Institute selected several industries and sorted out the top third and the bottom third of the business units according to customer ratings of "relative perceived service quality." The table shows that the high-service businesses managed to charge more, grow faster, and make more profits on the strength of their superior service quality. Clearly, manufacturers have to think through their presale and postsale service strategy.

Presale Service Strategy

An equipment manufacturer must design its equipment and service to meet the expectations of its target customers. Granted, the manufacturer cannot meet the customers' ideal of equipment that performs fast and at low cost, never breaks down, and lasts forever. The manufacturer can only promise certain levels of performance on these various customer objectives. The promised levels of performance become the manufacturer's positioning strategy vis-à-vis competitors. For example, Caterpillar has achieved a lead over many competitors by guaranteeing forty-eight-hour delivery of parts anywhere in the world—or else the customer gets the parts free.

A necessary step requires the manufacturer to identify the services that customers value most and their relative importance. In the case of expensive equipment, such as medical imaging equipment, manufacturers have to offer a minimum number of *facilitating* services:

1. *Architectural Services* to design the special facility for housing the equipment
2. *Installation Services* to install the equipment
3. *Training Services* to enable the staff to operate the equipment
4. *Equipment Maintenance* and Repair Services
5. *Financing Services*

Even supplies and minor equipment products require product support services. These typically consist of information about the availability and application of the product. A business buyer will want to know at least the price and delivery promise before placing an order. Products that are used in production processes may require information concerning application and performance. Intermediaries like wholesalers and retailers need to know how to sell the product against its competition. By supplying the various kinds of information when they are needed, manufacturers can gain a significant advantage for their products.

Companies need to plan their product design and service-mix decisions in tandem. Design and quality-assurance managers should be part of the new-product team from the beginning.

Good product design will reduce the amount of subsequent servicing needed. The Canon home copier uses a disposable toner cartridge that greatly reduces the need for service calls. Kodak and 3M are designing equipment that allow the user to "plug in" to a central diagnostic facility that performs tests, locates the trouble, and fixes the equipment over the telephone lines. Thus a key to successful service strategy is to design the products so that they rarely break down and, if they do, are easily and rapidly fixable with minimal service expense.

Postsale Service Strategy

Equipment manufacturers must decide how they want to offer aftersales service to customers, including maintenance and repair services, training services, and the like. They have four alternatives:

1. The manufacturer could provide these services.
2. The manufacturer could make arrangements with distributors and dealers to provide these services.
3. The manufacturer could leave it to independent service-specialist firms to provide these services.
4. The manufacturer could leave it to their customers to service their own equipment.

Consider the case of maintenance and repair services. Manufacturers usually start out adopting the first alternative. They want to stay close to the equipment and know its problems. They also find it expensive to train others, and this takes time. They also discover that they can make good money running the parts-and-service business. As long as they are the only supplier of the needed parts, they can charge a premium price. In fact, many equipment manufacturers price their equipment low in order to sell it and compensate by charging high prices for parts and service. Some equipment manufacturers make over half of their profits in aftersale service. This also explains why competitors emerge who manufacture the same or similar parts and sell them to customers or middlemen for less. Manufacturers warn customers of the danger of using competitor-made parts, but they are not always convincing.

Over time, manufacturers switch more of the maintenance and repair service to authorized distributors and dealers. These middlemen are closer to the customers, operate in more locations, and can offer quicker if not better service. Manufacturers still make a profit on selling the parts but leave the servicing profit to their middlemen.

Still later, independent third-party service firms emerge. Over 40 percent of auto service work is now done outside the franchised automobile dealerships, by independent garages and chains such as Midas Muffler and Canadian Tire. Independent service organizations have emerged to handle mainframes, telecommunications equipment, and a variety of other equipment lines. They typically offer lower cost and/or faster service than the manufacturer or authorized middlemen.

Ultimately, some large customers take over responsibility for handling their own maintenance and repair services. Thus a company with several hundred personal computers, printers, and related equipment might find it cheaper to have its own service personnel on site. These companies typically press the manufacturer for an "unbundled" price, since they are providing their own services.

Lele has noted the following major trends in the product support area:

1. Equipment manufacturers are building more reliable and more easily fixable equipment. One reason is the shift from electromechanical equipment to electronic equipment, which has fewer breakdowns and is more repairable. Also, companies are adding modularity and disposability to facilitate self-servicing.

2. Customers are becoming more sophisticated about buying product-support services and are pressing for "services unbundling." They want separate prices quoted for each service element and the right to shop for the service elements they want.

3. Customers increasingly dislike having to deal with a multitude of service providers handling their different types of equipment. Some third-party service organizations now service a greater range of equipment.[21]

4. Service contracts are an "endangered species." Because of the increase in disposable and/or never-fail equipment, customers are less inclined to pay anywhere from 2 to 10 percent of the purchase price every year for a service.

5. Customer service choices are increasing rapidly, and this is holding down prices and profits on service. Equipment manufacturers increasingly have to figure out how to make money on pricing their equipment independent of service contracts.[22]

SUMMARY

As Canada moves increasingly toward a service economy, marketers need to know more about marketing service products. Services are activities or benefits that one party can offer to another that are essentially intangible and do not result in the ownership of anything. Services are intangible, inseparable, variable, and perishable. Each characteristic poses problems and requires strategies. Marketers have to find ways to "tangibilize" the intangible; to increase the productivity of providers who are inseparable from the product; to standardize the quality in the face of variability; and to influence demand movements and supply capacities better in the face of service perishability.

Service industries have typically lagged behind manufacturing firms in adopting and using marketing concepts, but this is now changing. Services marketing strategy calls not only for external marketing but also for internal marketing, to motivate the employees, and interactive marketing, to create skills in the service providers. Customers will use technical and functional criteria to judge the quality of services. To succeed, service marketers must create competitive differentiation, offer high service quality, and find ways to increase service productivity.

Even product-based companies must provide and manage a service bundle for their customers; in fact, their services bundle may be more critical than the product in winning customers. The service mix includes presale services such as technical advice and dependable delivery, as well as postsale services such as prompt repair, and personnel training. The marketer has to decide on the mix, quality, and source of various product-support services that customers require.

■ QUESTIONS

1. What is interactive marketing? What is its function? What is its importance and relevance to the marketing of services?

2. Discuss factors that contributed to the adoption of marketing concepts and practices by service industries.

3. Select an airline and suggest how it might increase its competitive differentiation, service quality, and productivity.

4. The following terms used by the health-care industry were reported by *Marketing News*:

   □ Advertising and public relations are referred to as "improved community awareness."

   □ Marketing research becomes "needs assessment."

   □ Salesmanship is called "persuasive interpersonal communication."

□ Sales or advertising success may be described as "improved community utilization."

What does this "unmarket speak" suggest about the health-care industry's perceptions of marketing? How should marketing professionals relate to these attitudes and perceptions?

5. Computer software technology is moving rapidly to develop "expert systems." These are software programs that capture a person's expertise in a given area and make it available on the computer for a fraction of the original cost. What are the implications for service industries?

6. Select any nearby firm offering a service. Survey its target customers. Identify the main services that these customers value and their relative importance to them. (Describe your methodology in your answer.) Develop a list of recommendations from your findings.

7. What is the role of the marketer's personal values in the marketing of a social cause? Should the marketer bring only technical competence to the problem?

8. Discuss the differences and similarities that exist between services and tangible goods marketing.

9. Identify the core need fulfilled by, and service characteristics of (a) the Canadian Forces, (b) organized religion, and (c) a life insurance company.

10. An Ontario branch of the Victorian Order of Nurses would like to increase public awareness of the home-visiting services provided by its nurses. Design a low-budget communications program that will achieve the VON's objective.

11. The GE multifactor portfolio approach (Chapter 2) uses market attractiveness and competitive position as the two dimensions for locating business on the matrix. Discuss the relevant dimensions for a college to use in locating academic departments on a GE matrix.

■ NOTES

1. See G. Lynn Shostack, "Breaking Free from Product Marketing," *Journal of Marketing*, April 1977, pp. 73-80; Leonard L. Berry, "Services Marketing Is Different," *Business*, May-June 1980, pp. 24-30; Eric Langeard, John E. G. Bateson, Christopher H. Lovelock, and Pierre Eiglier, *Services Marketing: New Insights from Consumers and Managers* (Cambridge, Mass.: Marketing Science Institute, 1981); Karl Albrecht and Ron Zemke, *Service America! Doing Business in the New Economy* (Homewood, Ill.: Dow-Jones-Irwin, 1985); and Karl Albrecht, *At America's Service* (Homewood, Ill., Dow-Jones-Irwin, 1988); and William H. Davidow and Bro Uttal, *Total Customer Service: The Ultimate Weapon* (New York: Harper & Row, 1989).

2. "Services Grow While the Quality Shrinks," *Business Week*, October 30, 1971, p. 50.

3. Theodore Levitt, "Production-Line Approach to Service," *Harvard Business Review*, September-October 1972, pp. 41-42.

4. Further classifications of services are described in Christopher H. Lovelock, *Services Marketing* (Englewood Cliffs, N.J.: Prentice-Hall, 1984). Also see John E. Bateson, *Managing Services Marketing: Text and Readings* (Hinsdale, Ill.: Dryden Press, 1989).

5. See Theodore Levitt, "Marketing Intangible Products and Product Intangibles," *Harvard Business Review*, May-June 1981, pp. 94-102; and Berry, "Services Marketing Is Different."

6. See G. Lynn Shostack, "Service Positioning through Structural Change," *Journal of Marketing*, January 1987, pp. 34-43.

7. For a good discussion of quality-control systems at the Marriott Hotel chain, see G. M. Hostage, "Quality Control in a Service Business," *Harvard Business Review*, July-August 1975, pp. 98-106.

8. See W. Earl Sasser, "Match Supply and Demand in Service Industries," *Harvard Business Review*, November-December 1976, pp. 133-40.

9. William R. George and Hiram C. Barksdale, "Marketing Activities in the Service Industries," *Journal of Marketing*, October 1974, p. 65.

10. Christian Gronroos, "A Service Quality Model and Its Marketing Implications," *European Journal of Marketing*, 18, no. 4 (1984), pp. 36-44. Gronroos's model is one of the most thoughtful contributions to service-marketing strategy.

11. Leonard Berry, "Big Ideas in Services Marketing," *Journal of Consumer Marketing*, Spring 1986, pp. 47-51.

12. See Philip Kotler and Paul N. Bloom, *Marketing Professional Services* (Englewood Cliffs, N.J.: Prentice-Hall, 1984).

13. Gronroos, "Service Quality Model," pp. 38-39.

14. See Valarie A. Zeithaml, "How Consumer Evaluation Processes Differ between Goods and Services," in *Marketing of Services*, ed. James H. Donnelly and William

R. George (Chicago: American Marketing Association, 1981), pp. 186-90.

15. The argument that product-based companies face substantial opportunities in the service sector is presented in Irving D. Canton, "Learning to Love the Service Economy," *Harvard Business Review*, May-June 1984, pp. 89-97.

16. A. Parasuraman, Valarie A. Zeithaml, and Leonard L. Berry, "A Conceptual Model of Service Quality and Its Implications for Future Research," *Journal of Marketing*, Fall 1985, pp. 41-50.

17. Timothy W. Firnstahl, "My Employees Are My Service Guarantee," *Harvard Business Review*, July-August 1989, pp. 29-34.

18. Theodore Levitt, "Production-Line Approach to Service," *Harvard Business Review*, September-October 1972, pp. 41-52; also see his "Industrialization of Service," *Harvard Business Review*, September-October 1976, pp. 63-74.

19. See William H. Davidow and Bro Uttal, "Service Companies: Focus or Falter," *Harvard Business Review*, July-August 1989, pp.77-85.

20. Christopher H. Lovelock and Robert F. Young, "Look to Consumers to Increase Productivity," *Harvard Business Review*, May-June, 1979.

21. However, see Ellen Day and Richard J. Fox, "Extended Warranties, Service Contracts, and Maintenance Agreement—A Marketing Opportunity?" *Journal of Consumer Marketing*, Fall 1985, pp. 77-86.

22. Milind M. Lele, "How Service Needs Influence Product Strategy," *Sloan Management Review*, Fall 1986, pp. 63-70.

18

Designing Pricing Strategies and Programs

A cheap article ain't always the best: if you want a real right down first chop, genuwine thing, you must pay for it.

T. C. Haliburton

All profit organizations and many nonprofit organizations set prices on their products or services. Price goes by many names:

> Price is all around us. You pay *rent* for your apartment, *tuition* for your education, and a *fee* to your physician or dentist. The airline, railway, taxi, and bus companies charge you a *fare*; the local utilities call their price a *rate*; and the local bank charges you *interest* for the money you borrow. The price for driving your car on a . . . parkway is a *toll*, and the company that insures your car charges you a *premium*. The guest lecturer charges an *honorarium* to tell you about a government official who took a *bribe* to help a shady character steal *dues* collected by a trade association. Clubs or societies to which you belong may make a special *assessment* to pay unusual expenses. Your regular lawyer may ask for a *retainer* to cover her services. The "price" of an executive is a *salary*, the price of a salesperson may be a *commission*, and the price of a worker is a *wage*. Finally, although economists would disagree, many of us feel that *income taxes* are the price we pay for the privilege of making money.[1]

How are prices set? Through most of history, prices were set by buyers and sellers negotiating with each other. Sellers would ask for a higher price than they expected to receive, and buyers would offer less than they expected to pay. Through bargaining, they would arrive at an acceptable price.

Setting one price for all buyers is a relatively modern idea. It was given impetus by the development of large-scale retailing at the end of the nineteenth century. F. W. Woolworth and others advertised a "strictly one-price policy" because they carried so many items and supervised so many employees.

Through most of history, price has operated as the major determinant of buyer choice. That is still the case in poorer nations, among poorer groups, and with commodity-type products.

However, nonprice factors have become relatively more important in buyer-choice behavior in recent decades. Yet price still remains one of the most important elements determining company market share and profitability.

Price is the only element in the marketing mix that produces revenue; the other elements produce costs. Furthermore, pricing and price competition was rated as the number-one problem facing marketing executives in the mid-1980s.[2] Yet many companies do not handle pricing well. The most common mistakes are these: Pricing is too cost oriented; price is not revised often enough to capitalize on market changes; price is set independent of the rest of the marketing mix rather than as an intrinsic element of market-positioning strategy; and price is not varied enough for different product items and market segments.

Companies handle pricing in a variety of ways. In small companies, prices are often set by top management rather than by the marketing or sales department. In large companies, pricing is typically handled by division and product-line managers. Even here, top management sets the general pricing objectives and policies and often approves the prices proposed by lower levels of management. In industries where pricing is a key factor (aerospace, railroads, oil companies), companies will often establish a pricing department to set prices or assist others in determining appropriate prices. This department reports either to the marketing department, finance department, or top management. Others who exert an influence on pricing include sales managers, production managers, finance managers, and accountants.

This chapter will examine three questions: How should a price be set on a product or service for the first time? How should the price be adapted over time and space to meet varying circumstances and opportunities? When should the company initiate a price change, and how should it respond to a competitor's price change?

SETTING THE PRICE

Pricing is a problem when a firm has to set a price for the first time. This happens when the firm develops or acquires a new product, when it introduces its regular product into a new distribution channel or geographical area, and when it enters bids on new contract work.

The firm must decide where to position its product on quality and price. Figure 18-1 shows nine possible price-quality strategies. The diagonal strategies 1, 5, and 9 can all coexist in the same market; that is, one firm offers a high-quality product at a high price, another firm offers an average-quality product at an average price, and still another firm offers a low-quality product at a low price. All three competitors can coexist as long as the market consists of three groups of buyers, those who insist on quality, those who insist on price, and those who balance the two considerations.

Positioning strategies 2, 3, and 6 represent ways to attack the diagonal positions. Strategy 2 says, "our product has the same high quality as product 1 but we charge less." Strategy 3 says the same thing and offers an even greater saving. If quality-sensitive customers believe these competitors, they will sensibly buy from them and save money (unless firm 1's product has acquired snob appeal).

Positioning strategies 4, 7, and 8 amount to overpricing the product in relation to its quality. The customers will feel "taken" and will probably complain or spread bad word of mouth about the company. These strategies should be avoided by professional marketers.

The firm has to consider many factors in setting its pricing policy. In the following paragraphs, we will describe a six-step procedure for price setting: (1) selecting the pricing objective, (2) determining demand, (3) estimating costs, (4) analyzing competitors' prices and offers, (5) selecting a pricing method, and (6) selecting the final price.

FIGURE 18-1
Nine Price/Quality Strategies

	High	**Medium**	**Low**
High	1. Premium strategy	2. High-value strategy	3. Superb-value strategy
Medium	4. Overcharging strategy	5. Medium-value strategy	6. Good-value strategy
Low	7. Rip-off strategy	8. False economy strategy	9. Economy strategy

Price (columns), *Product Quality* (rows)

Selecting the Pricing Objective

The company first has to decide what it wants to accomplish with the particular product. If the company has selected its target market and market positioning carefully, then its marketing-mix strategy, including price, will be fairly straightforward. For example, if a recreational-vehicle company wants to produce a luxurious truck camper for affluent customers, this implies charging a high price. Thus pricing strategy is largely determined by the prior decision on market positioning.

At the same time, the company might pursue additional objectives. The clearer a firm's objectives, the easier it is to set price. Each possible price will have a different impact on such objectives as profits, sales revenue, and market share. This is shown in Figure 18-2 for a hypothetical product. If the company wants to maximize pretax profits, it should charge $97. If it wants to maximize sales revenue, it should charge $86. If it wants to maximize market share, it should set an even lower price.

FIGURE 18-2
Relation Between Price, Revenue, Market Share, and Profits

Source: *Decision Making in Marketing* (New York: The Conference Board, 1971). Figure is by Franz Edelman.

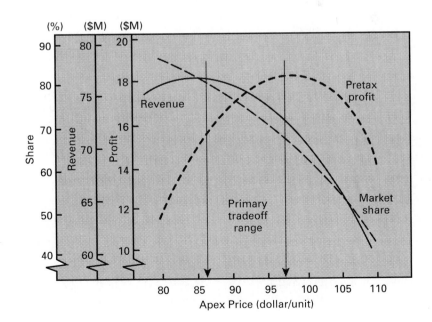

A company can pursue any of six major objectives through its pricing.

Survival Companies pursue survival as their major objective if plagued with overcapacity, intense competition, or changing consumer wants. To keep the plant going and the inventories turning over, they will often cut prices. Profits are less important than survival. As long as prices cover variable costs and some fixed costs, the companies stay in business. However, survival is only a short-run objective. In the long run, the firm must learn how to add value or face extinction.

Maximum Current Profit Many companies try to set the price that will maximize current profits. They estimate the demand and costs associated with alternative prices and choose the price that produces maximum current profit, cash flow, or rate of return on investment. (See Marketing Concepts and Tools 18-1 for theory of profit-maximization pricing.)

Marketing Concepts and Tools 18-1

FINDING THE PROFIT-MAXIMIZING PRICE

Economists have worked out a simple model for pricing to maximize current profits. The model assumes that the firm has knowledge of its demand and cost functions for the product in question. The demand function describes the estimated quantity (Q) that would be purchased per period at various prices (P) that might be charged. Suppose the firm determines through statistical demand analysis that its *demand equation* is

$$Q = 1000 - 4P \qquad (18\text{-}1)$$

This equation expresses the law of demand—less will be bought per period at higher prices.

The cost function describes the total cost (C) of producing any quantity per period (Q). In the simplest case, the total cost function is described by the linear equation $C = F + cQ$ where F is total fixed cost and c is unit variable cost. Suppose the company estimated the following *cost equation* for its product:

$$C = 6000 + 50Q \qquad (18\text{-}2)$$

Management is almost in a position to determine the current profit-maximizing price. It needs only two more equations, both definitional. First, *total revenue* (R) is equal to price times quantity sold—

that is,

$$R = PQ \qquad (18\text{-}3)$$

Second, *total profits* (Z) is the difference between total revenue and total cost—that is,

$$Z = R - C \qquad (18\text{-}4)$$

The company can now determine the relationship between profits (Z) and price (P) by starting with the profit equation (18-4) and going through the following derivation:

$$Z = R - C$$
$$Z = PQ - C$$
$$Z = PQ - (6000 + 50Q)$$
$$Z = P(1000 - 4P) - 6000 - 50(1000 - 4P)$$
$$Z = 1000P - 4P^2 - 6000 - 50\,000 + 200P$$
$$Z = -56\,000 + 1200 - 4P^2$$

Total profits turn out to be a second-degree function of price. It is a hatlike figure (a parabola), and profits reach their highest point ($34 000) at a price of $150. The optimal price of $150 can be found by drawing the parabola with some sample prices and locating the high point, or by using calculus.

There are some problems associated with current profit maximization. It assumes that the firm has knowledge of its demand and cost functions; in reality, they are difficult to estimate. Also, the company is emphasizing current financial performance rather than long-run performance. Finally, the company is ignoring the effects of other marketing-mix variables, competitors' reactions, and legal restraints on price.

Maximum Current Revenue   Some companies will set a price to maximize sales revenue. Revenue maximization requires only estimating the demand function. Many managers believe that revenue maximization will lead to long-run profit maximization and market-share growth.

Maximum Sales Growth   Other companies want to maximize unit sales. They believe that a higher sales volume will lead to lower unit costs and higher long-run profit. They set the lowest price, assuming the market is price sensitive. This is called *market-penetration pricing*. Texas Instruments (TI) is a prime practitioner of market-penetration pricing. TI will build a large plant, set its price as low as possible, with a large market share, experience falling costs, and cut its price further as costs fall.

The following conditions favor setting a low price: (1) the market is highly price sensitive, and a low price stimulates more market growth; (2) production and distribution costs fall with accumulated production experience; and (3) a low price discourages actual and potential competition.

Maximum Market Skimming   Many companies favor setting high prices to "skim" the market. Du Pont is a prime practitioner of *market-skimming pricing*. With each innovation—cellophane, nylon, Teflon, and so on—it estimates the highest price it can charge given the comparative benefits of its new product versus the available substitutes. The company sets a price that makes it just worthwhile for some segments of the market to adopt the new material. Each time sales slow down, Du Pont lowers the price to draw in the next price-sensitive layer of customers. In this way, Du Pont skims a maximum amount of revenue from the various market segments. As another example, Polaroid also practices market skimming. It first introduces an expensive version of a new camera and gradually introduces simpler, lower-price models to draw in new segments.

Market skimming makes sense under the following conditions: (1) a sufficient number of buyers have a high current demand; (2) the unit costs of producing a small volume are not so much higher that they cancel the advantage of charging what the traffic will bear; (3) the high initial price does not attract more competitors; (4) the high price supports the image of a superior product.

Product-Quality Leadership   A company might aim to be the product-quality leader in the market. Maytag, a prime example, builds high-quality washing machines and prices them at roughly $100 more than competitors' washing machines. Maytag uses the slogan "Built to last longer," and its ads feature "Ol' Lonely," the Maytag repairman, who doesn't have enough to do. This strategy earned Maytag over a 30 percent return on stockholder's equity in 1987.

Determining Demand

Each price that the company might charge will lead to a different level of demand and will therefore have a different impact on its marketing objectives. The relation between the current price charged and the resulting current demand is captured in the familiar *demand schedule* (see Figure 18-3[a].) The demand schedule shows the number of units the market will buy in a given time period at alternative prices that might be charged during the period. In the normal case, demand and price are inversely related, that is, the higher the price, the lower the demand (and conversely).

In the case of prestige goods, the demand curve is sometimes positively sloped. A perfume company found that by raising its price, it sold more perfume rather than less! Consumers take the higher price to signify a better or more expensive perfume. However, if too high a price is charged, the level of demand will be lower.

Factors Affecting Price Sensitivity   The demand curve shows the market's overall reaction to alternative prices that might be charged. It sums the reactions of many individuals who have different price sensitivities. The important first step is to understand the factors that affect buyers' price sensitivity. Nagle has identified nine factors:

1. *Unique-Value Effect:* Buyers are less price sensitive when the product is more unique.
2. *Substitute-Awareness Effect:* Buyers are less price sensitive when they are less aware of substitutes.
3. *Difficult-Comparison Effect:* Buyers are less price sensitive when they cannot easily compare the quality of substitutes.
4. *Total-Expenditure Effect:* Buyers are less price sensitive the lower the expenditure is as a proportion of their income.
5. *End-Benefit Effect:* Buyers are less price sensitive the less the expenditure is to the total cost of the end product.
6. *Shared-Cost Effect:* Buyers are less price sensitive when part of the cost is borne by another party.
7. *Sunk-Investment Effect:* Buyers are less price sensitive when the product is used in conjunction with assets previously bought.
8. *Price-Quality Effect:* Buyers are less price sensitive when the product is assumed to have more quality, prestige or exclusiveness.
9. *Inventory Effect:* Buyers are less price sensitive when they cannot store the product.[3]

Methods of Estimating Demand Schedules   Most companies make some attempt to measure their demand schedules. In researching the demand schedule, the investigator needs to make assumptions about competitive behavior. There are two ways to estimate demand. One is to assume that competitors' prices remain constant regardless of the price charged by the

FIGURE 18-3
Inelastic and Elastic
Demand

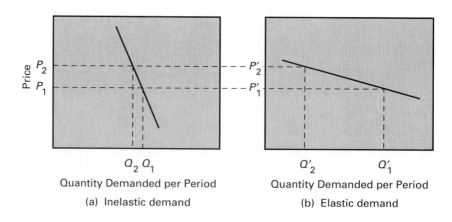

(a) Inelastic demand

(b) Elastic demand

company. The other is to assume that competitors charge a different price for each price the company might set. We will assume the former and defer the question of competitors' price reactions until later.

To measure a demand schedule requires varying the price. A study can be done in a laboratory setting asking subjects to state how many units they would buy at different possible prices.[4] Bennett and Wilkinson used an in-store method of estimating the demand schedule. They systematically varied the prices of several products sold in a discount store and observed the results.[5]

In measuring the price/demand relationship, the market researcher must control or allow for other factors that might affect demand. If a company increased its advertising expenditures at the same time that it lowered its price, we would not know how much of the increased demand was due to the lower price versus the increased advertising. Economists show the impact of nonprice factors on demand by shifts of the demand curve rather than movements along the demand curve. Nagle has presented an excellent summary of the various methods used to measure price sensitivity and demand.[6]

Price Elasticity of Demand Marketers need to know how responsive demand would be to a change in price. Consider the two demand curves in Figure 18-3. In (a), a price increase from P_1 to P_2 leads to a relatively small decline in demand from Q_1 to Q_2. In (b), the same price increase leads to a substantial drop in demand from Q_1 to Q_2. If demand hardly changes with a small change in price, we say the demand is inelastic. If demand changes considerably, demand is elastic. Specifically, the price elasticity of demand is given by the following formula:[7]

$$\text{Price elasticity of demand} = \frac{\%\ \text{Change in quantity demanded}}{\%\ \text{Change in price}}$$

Suppose demand falls by 10 percent when a seller raises the price by 2 percent. Price elasticity of demand is therefore −5 (the minus sign confirms the inverse relation between price and demand). If demand falls by 2 percent with a 2 percent increase in price, then elasticity is −1. In this case, the seller's total revenue stays the same. The seller sells fewer items but at a higher price that preserves the same total revenue. If demand falls by 1 percent when price is increased by 2 percent, then elasticity is $-\frac{1}{2}$. The less elastic the demand, the more it pays for the seller to raise the price.

What determines the price elasticity of demand? Demand is likely to be less elastic under the following conditions: (1) There are few or no substitutes or competitors; (2) buyers do not readily notice the higher price; (3) buyers are slow to change their buying habits and search for lower prices; (4) buyers think the higher prices are justified by quality improvements, normal inflation, and so on.

If demand is elastic rather than inelastic, sellers will consider lowering the price. A lower price will produce more total revenue. This makes sense as long as the costs of producing and selling more units does not increase disproportionately.

Various studies of price elasticity have been reported; for example, the price elasticity of automobiles, −1.0 to −2.2; coffee, −5.3; yogurt, −1.2; and confectionary, −2.0.[8] But one must be careful in using these estimates. Price elasticity depends on the magnitude and direction of the contemplated price change. It may be negligible, with a small price change, and substantial, with a large price change. It may differ for a price cut versus a price increase. Finally, long-run price elasticity is apt to differ from short-run elasticity. Buyers may continue with their current supplier after a price increase, because they do not notice the increase, or the increase is too small, or they are distracted by other concerns, or find choosing a new supplier takes time, but they may eventually switch suppliers. In this case, demand is more elastic in the long run than in the short run. Or the reverse may happen: Buyers drop a supplier after being notified of a price increase but return later. The distinction between short-run and long-run elasticity means that sellers will not fully know of the total effect of their price change.[9]

Estimating Costs

Demand largely sets a ceiling to the price that the company can charge for its product. And company costs set the floor. The company wants to charge a price that covers its cost of producing, distributing, and selling the product, including a fair return for its effort and risk.

Types of Costs   A company's costs take two forms, fixed and variable. *Fixed costs* (also known as overhead) are costs that do not vary with production or sales revenue. Thus a company must pay bills each month for rent, heat, interest, executive salaries, and so on, whatever the company's output. Fixed costs go on irrespective of the production level.

Variable costs vary directly with the level of production. For example, each hand calculator produced by Texas Instruments (TI) involves a cost of plastic, microprocessing chips, packaging, and the like. These costs tend to be constant per unit produced. They are called variable because their total varies with the number of units produced.

Total costs consist of the sum of the fixed and variable costs for any given level of production. Management wants to charge a price that will at least cover the total production costs at a given level of production.

Cost Behavior at Different Levels of Production per Period   To price intelligently, management needs to know how its costs vary with different levels of production.

Take the case where a company such as TI has built a fixed-size plant to produce 1000 hand calculators a day. Figure 18-4(a) shows the typical U-shaped behavior of the short-run average cost curve (SRAC). The cost per unit is high if few units are produced per day. As production approaches 1000 units per day, average cost falls. The reason is that the fixed costs are spread over more units, with each one bearing a smaller fixed cost. TI can try to produce more than 1000 units per day but at increasing costs. Average cost increases after 1000 units, because the plant becomes inefficient: Workers have to queue for machines, machines break down more often, and workers get in each other's way.

If TI believes that it could sell 2000 units per day, it should consider building a larger plant. The plant will use more efficient machinery and work arrangements, and the unit cost of producing 2000 units per day will be less than the unit cost of producing 1000 units per day. This is shown in the long-run average cost curve in Figure 18-4(b). In fact, a 3000-capacity

FIGURE 18-4
Cost per Unit at Different Levels of Production per Period

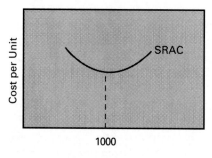

Quantity Produced per Day
(a) Cost behaviour in a fixed-size plant

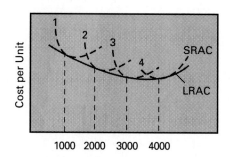

Quantity Produced per Day
(b) Cost behaviour over different-size plants

plant would be even more efficient according to Figure 18-4(b). But a 4000-daily production plant would be less efficient because of increasing diseconomies of scale: There are too many workers to manage, paperwork slows things down, and so on. Figure 18-4(b) indicates that a 3000-daily production plant is the optimal size to build, if demand is strong enough to support this level of production.

Cost Behavior as a Function of Accumulated Production   Suppose TI runs a plant that produces 3000 hand calculators per day. As TI gains experience producing hand calculators, it learns how to do it better. The workers learn shortcuts, the flow of materials is improved, procurement costs are cut, and so on. The result is that average cost tends to fall with accumulated production experience. This is shown in Figure 18-5. Thus the average cost of producing the first 100 000 hand calculators is $10 per calculator. When the company has produced the first 200 000 calculators, the average cost has fallen to $9. After its accumulated production experience doubles again to 400 000, the average cost is $8. This decline in the average cost with accumulated production experience is called the *experience curve* (sometimes *learning curve*).

Now suppose three firms compete in this industry, TI, A, and B. TI is the lowest-cost producer at $8, having produced 400 000 units in the past. If all three firms sell the calculator for $10, TI makes $2 profit per unit, A makes $1 and B breaks even. The smart move for TI would be to lower its price to $9. This will drive B out of the market, and even A will consider leaving. TI will pick up the business that would have gone to B (and possibly A). Furthermore, price-sensitive customers will enter the market at the lower price. TI's costs will drop still further and faster and more than restore its profits, even at a price of $9. TI has used this aggressive pricing strategy repeatedly to gain market share and drive others out of the industry. Experience-curve pricing nevertheless carries some major risks. The aggressive pricing might give the product a cheap image: This might have happened with TI's personal computers where it ran the price down from $950 in 1980 to $99 by 1983. The strategy also assumes that the competitors are weak and not willing to fight it out. Finally, the strategy leads the company into building more plants to meet the demand while a competitor might innovate a lower-cost technology and obtain lower costs than the market leader, who is now stuck with the old technology.

Most experience-curve pricing has focused on the behavior of manufacturing costs. But all costs, including marketing costs, are subject to learning improvements. Thus if three firms are each investing a large sum of money trying out telemarketing, the firm that has used it the longest might achieve the lowest telemarketing costs. This firm can charge a little less for its product and still earn the same return, all other costs being equal.[10]

FIGURE 18-5
Cost per Unit as a Function of Accumulated Production: The Experience Curve

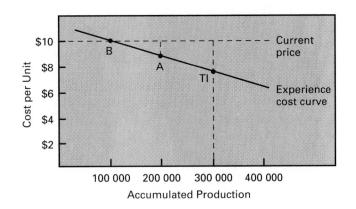

Analyzing Competitors' Prices and Offers

While market demand might set a ceiling and costs set a floor to pricing, competitors' prices and possible price reactions help the firm establish where its prices might be set. The company needs to learn the price and quality of each competitor's offer. That can be done in several ways. The firm can send out comparison shoppers to price and compare competitors' offers. The firm can acquire competitors' price lists and buy competitors' equipment and take it apart. The firm can ask buyers how they perceive the price and quality of each competitor's offer.

Once the company is aware of competitors' prices and offers, it can use them as an orienting point for its own pricing. If the firm's offer is similar to a major competitor's offer, then the firm will have to price close to the competitor or lose sales. If the firm's offer is inferior, the firm will not be able to charge more than the competitor. If the firm's offer is superior, the firm can charge more than the competitor. The firm must be aware, however, that competitors might change their prices in response to the firm's price. Basically, the firm will use price to position its offer vis-à-vis competitors.

Selecting a Pricing Method

Given the three Cs—the *customers' demand schedule*, the *cost* function, and *competitors'* prices—the company is now ready to select a price. The price will be somewhere between one that is too low to produce a profit and one that is too high to produce any demand. Figure 18-6 summarizes the three major considerations in price setting. Costs set a floor to the price. Competitors' prices and the price of substitutes provide an orienting point that the company has to consider in setting its price. Customers' assessments of unique product features in the company's offer establish the ceiling price. The three pricing considerations have been compared to the legs of a tripod that collectively support the price decision. All three are essential if the price decision is to be sustained.

But in practice, managers resolve the pricing question with methods that may emphasize only one or two of the pricing considerations at a time. Their simplified pricing methods will lead to a specific price, which can then be verified using the missing consideration(s). We will examine the following price-setting methods: markup pricing, target-return pricing, perceived-value pricing, going-rate pricing, and sealed-bid pricing.

Markup Pricing The most elementary pricing method is to add a standard markup to the cost of the product. Construction companies submit job bids by estimating the total project cost and adding a standard markup for profit. Lawyers, accountants, and other professionals typically price by adding a standard markup to their costs. Some sellers tell their customers they will charge their cost plus a specified markup; for example, aerospace companies price this way to the government.

To illustrate markup pricing, suppose a toaster manufacturer had the following costs and sales expectations:

FIGURE 18-6
The Three-Cs Model for Price Setting

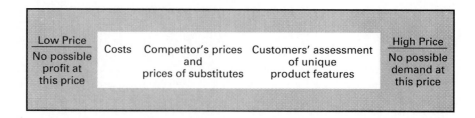

Low Price	Costs	Competitor's prices and prices of substitutes	Customers' assessment of unique product features	High Price
No possible profit at this price				No possible demand at this price

Variable cost	$10
Fixed cost	$300 000
Expected unit sales	50 000

Therefore the manufacturer's unit cost is given by:

$$\text{Unit cost} = \text{variable cost} + \frac{\text{fixed costs}}{\text{unit sales}} = \$10 + \frac{\$300\ 000}{50\ 000} = \$16$$

Now assume the manufacturer wants to earn a 20 percent markup on sales. The manufacturer's markup price is given by:

$$\text{Markup price} = \frac{\text{unit cost}}{(1 - \text{desired return on sales})} = \frac{\$16}{1 - .2} = \$20$$

The manufacturer would charge dealers $20 per toaster and make a profit of $4 per unit. The dealers in turn will mark up the toaster. If dealers want to earn 50 percent on sales, they will mark up the toaster to $40. This is equivalent to a cost markup of 100 percent (= $20/20).

Markups vary considerably among different goods. Some common markups (on price, not cost) in supermarkets are 9 percent on baby foods, 14 percent on tobacco products, 20 percent on bakery products, 27 percent on dried foods and vegetables, 37 percent on spices and extracts, and 50 percent on greeting cards.[11] Quite a lot of dispersion is found around the averages. Within the spices-and-extracts category, for example, markups on retail price range from a low of 19 percent to a high of 56 percent. Markups are generally higher on seasonal items (to cover the risk of not selling), specialty items, slower moving items, items with high storage and handling costs, and demand-inelastic items.

Does the use of standard markups to set prices make logical sense? Generally, no. Any pricing method that ignores current demand, perceived value and competition is not likely to lead to the optimal price. Suppose the toaster manufacturer above charged $20 but only sold 30 000 toasters instead of 50 000. Then the manufacturer's unit cost would have been higher, since the fixed costs are spread over fewer units, and its realized percentage markup on sales would have been lower. Markup pricing works only if that price actually brings in the expected level of sales.

Companies introducing a new product often price it high hoping to recover their costs as rapidly as possible. But a high-markup strategy could be fatal if a competitor is pricing low. This happened to Philips in pricing its videodisc players. Philips wanted to make a profit on each videodisc player. Meanwhile, Japanese competitors priced low and succeeded in building their market share rapidly, which in turn pushed down their costs substantially.

Still, markup pricing remains popular for a number of reasons. First, sellers have more certainty about costs than about demand. By tying the price to cost, sellers simplify their own pricing task; they do not have to make frequent adjustments as demand changes. Second, where all firms in the industry use this pricing method, their prices tend to be similar. Price competition is therefore minimized, which would not be the case if firms paid attention to demand variations when they priced. Third, many people feel that cost-plus pricing is fairer to both buyers and sellers. Sellers do not take advantage of buyers when the latter's demand becomes acute; yet the sellers earn a fair return on their investment.

Target-Return Pricing   Another cost-pricing approach is *target-return pricing*. The firm determines the price that would yield its target rate of return on investment (ROI).

Target pricing is used by General Motors, which prices its automobiles to achieve a 15 to 20 percent ROI. This pricing method is also used by public utilities that are constrained to make a fair return on their investment.

Suppose the toaster manufacturer above has invested $1 million in the business and wants to set price to earn a 20 percent ROI, namely $200 000. The target-return price is given by the following formula:

$$\text{Target-return price} = \text{unit cost} + \frac{\text{desired return} \times \text{invested capital}}{\text{unit sales}}$$

$$= \$16 + \frac{.20 \times \$1\,000\,000}{50\,000} = \$20$$

The manufacturer will realize this 20 percent ROI provided its costs and estimated sales turn out to be accurate. But what if sales do not reach 50 000 units? The manufacturer can prepare a *break-even chart* to learn what would happen at other sales levels. Figure 18-7 shows the break-even chart. Fixed costs are $300 000 regardless of sales volume. Variable costs are superimposed on the fixed costs and rise linearly with volume. The total revenue curve starts at zero and rises linearly with each unit sold. The slope of the total revenue curve reflects the price of $20 per unit.

The total revenue and total cost curve cross at 30 000 units. This is the *break-even volume*. It can be verified by the following formula:

$$\text{Break-even volume} = \frac{\text{fixed cost}}{\text{price} - \text{variable cost}} = \frac{\$300\,000}{\$20 - \$10} = 30\,000$$

The manufacturer, of course, is hoping that the market will buy 50 000 units at $20, in which case it earns $200 000 on its $1 million investment. But much depends on the price elasticity and competitors' prices. Unfortunately, target-return pricing tends to ignore these considerations. The manufacturer should consider different prices and estimate their probable impacts on sales volume and profits. The manufacturer should also search for ways to lower its fixed and/or variable costs, because lower costs will lower its required break-even volume.

Perceived-Value Pricing   An increasing number of companies are basing their price on the product's *perceived value*. They see the buyers' perceptions of value, not the seller's

FIGURE 18-7
Break-Even Chart for Determining Target Return Price and Break-Even Volume

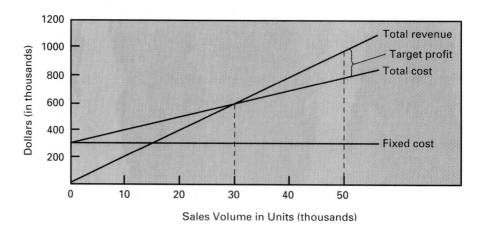

cost, as the key to pricing. They use the nonprice variables in the marketing mix to build up perceived value in the buyers' minds. Price is set to capture the perceived value.[12]

Perceived-value pricing fits in well with product-positioning thinking. A company develops a product concept for a particular target market with a planned quality and price. Then management estimates the volume it hopes to sell at this price. The estimate indicates the needed plant capacity, investment, and unit costs. Management then figures out whether the product will yield a satisfactory profit at the planned price and cost. If the answer is yes, the company goes ahead with product development. Otherwise, the company drops the idea.

Two major practitioners of perceived-value pricing are Du Pont and Caterpillar. When Du Pont developed its new synthetic fiber for carpets, it demonstrated to carpet manufacturers that they could afford to pay Du Pont as much as $1.40 per pound for the new fiber and still make their current profit. Du Pont calls this the *value-in-use price*. Du Pont recognized, however, that pricing the new material at $1.40 per pound would leave the market indifferent. So it set the price lower than $1.40, the amount depending on the rate of market penetration it wanted. Du Pont did not use its unit-manufacturing cost to set the price but only to judge whether there was enough profit to go ahead in the first place.

Caterpillar uses perceived value to set prices on its construction equipment. It might price its tractor at $100 000, although a similar competitor's tractor might be priced at $90 000. And Caterpillar will get more sales than the competitor! When a prospective customer asks a Caterpillar dealer why he should pay $10 000 more for the Caterpillar tractor, the dealer answers:

$ 90 000	is the tractor's price if it is only equivalent to the competitor's tractor
$ 7 000	is the price premium for superior durability
$ 6 000	is the price premium for superior reliability
$ 5 000	is the price premium for superior service
$ 2 000	is the price premium for the longer warranty on parts
$ 110 000	is the price to cover the value package
–$ 10 000	discount
$ 100 000	final price

This stunned customer learns that although he is asked to pay a $10 000 premium for the Caterpillar tractor, he is actually getting a $10 000 discount! He ends up choosing the Caterpillar tractor because he is convinced that its *lifetime operating costs* will be smaller.

The key to perceived-value pricing is to accurately determine the market's perception of the offer's value. Sellers with an inflated view of their offer's value will overprice their product. And sellers with an underestimated view will charge less than they could. Market research is needed to establish the market's perception of value as a guide to effective pricing. Methods for estimating perceived value are described in Marketing Concepts and Tools 18-2. Methods for estimating a price around the estimated perceived value are described in Marketing Concepts and Tools 18-3.

Going-Rate Pricing   In *going-rate pricing*, the firm bases its price largely on competitors' prices, with less attention paid to its own cost or demand. The firm might charge the same, more, or less than its major competitor(s). In oligopolistic industries that sell a commodity such as steel, paper, or fertilizer, firms normally charge the same price. The smaller firms "follow the leader." They change their prices when the market leader's prices change rather than when their own demand or cost changes. Some firms may charge a slight premium or slight discount, but they preserve the amount of difference. Thus minor gasoline retailers usually charge a few cents less than the major oil companies, without letting the difference increase or decrease.

Marketing Concepts and Tools 18-2

METHODS OF ESTIMATING PERCEIVED VALUE— AN ILLUSTRATION

Three companies, A, B, and C, produce rapid-relay switches. Industrial buyers are asked to examine and rate the respective companies' offers. Here are three alternative methods:

- *Direct Price-Rating Method:* Here the buyers estimate a price for each switch that they think reflects the total value of buying the switch from each company. For example, they may assign $2.55, $2.00, and $1.52, respectively.

- *Direct Perceived-Value-Rating Method:* Here the buyers allocate 100 points to the three companies to reflect the total value of buying the switch from each company. Suppose they assign 42, 33, and 25, respectively. If the average market price of a relay switch is $2.00, the three firms could charge, respectively, $2.55, $2.00, and $1.52, to reflect the variation in perceived value.

- *Diagnostic Method:* Here the buyers rate the three offers on a set of attributes. They allocate 100 points to the three companies with regard to each attribute. They also allocate 100 points to reflect the relative importance of the attributes. Suppose the results are as follows:

Importance Weight	Attribute	Products		
		A	B	C
25	Product durability	40	40	20
30	Product reliability	33	33	33
30	Delivery reliability	50	25	25
15	Service quality	45	35	20
100	(Perceived value)	(41.65)	(32.65)	(24.9)
	(Equilibrium price)	$2.55	$2.00	$1.52

By multiplying the importance weights against each company's ratings, we find that company A's offer is perceived to be above average (at 42), company B's offer is average (at 33), and company C's offer is below average (at 25).

Company A can set a high price for its switches because buyers perceive a better offer. If A wants to price proportionally to its perceived value, it can charge around $2.55 (= $2.00 for an average quality switch × 42/33). If all three companies set their price proportional to their perceived value, they will all enjoy some market share, since they all offer the same perceived value-to-price.

If a company prices at less than its perceived value, it will gain a higher-than-average market share because buyers will be getting extra value for their money. This is illustrated in the accompanying figure.

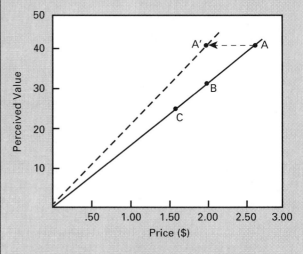

The three offers, A, B, and C, initially lie on the same value/price line. Respective market shares will depend on the relative density of ideal points (not shown) surrounding the three offers. Now suppose company A lowers its price to A′. Its value/price will be on a higher line (the dashed line), and it will pull market share away from both B and C, particularly B, because it offers more value at the same price as B. In self-defense, B will either lower its price or raise its perceived value by adding more service reliability, and so on. If the cost of increasing its perceived value is less than the revenue loss resulting from a lower price, B should strengthen its perceived value.

Marketing Concepts and Tools 18-3

METHODS FOR ESTABLISHING A PRICE AROUND A PERCEIVED VALUE

Companies cannot always depend on their customers' recognizing the value of their offer against their competitors' offers. Sophisticated industrial companies use a tool called *economic value to the customer* (EVC) to build up their customers' perception of value. EVC is calculated by comparing their product's total costs against the benefits of the product the customer is currently using (reference product). This is an effective way of analyzing pricing policy for industrial goods where the purchase price represents only a portion of the lifetime costs to the customer.

The accompanying figure illustrates how EVC is determined. Suppose a company is developing two products, Y and Z, to compete with product X, currently being used by the customer.

New product Y performs the same function as the reference product X, but its start-up and postpurchase costs are only $400, yielding a $300 savings. Because the customer's current product X has life-cycle costs of $1000, the economic value that new product Y offers the customer is $600 ($1000 minus $400). Thus the customer might be willing to pay up to $600 for product Y.

New product Z has more features or performance characteristics than product X or Y. These extra-features Zs have a perceived incremental value of $300 when compared with the reference product. So compared to the current product, Z saves $100 in postpurchase costs and has an incremental value of $300, resulting in an economic value of $700 to the customer. Thus Z provides a higher EVC than Y despite its higher postpurchase costs, because it provides additional customer value.

The firm should set its price at a point between its costs and the EVC that is perceived by the customer. If the firm priced Y at $400, the customer would save $200 compared with X, despite paying $100 more for Y. The firm's profit depends on its cost of supplying Y. If Y costs $250 to supply, the firm will make $150 (= $400 – $250).

The firm can use EVC to determine which market segments to enter. It should enter segments where its price would create more economic value than the customers are getting from their current product.

Source: This exhibit was condensed by the author from John L. Forbis and Nitin T. Mehta, "Economic Value to the Customer," *McKinsey Staff Paper* (Chicago: McKinsey & Co., Inc., February 1979), pp. 1-10.

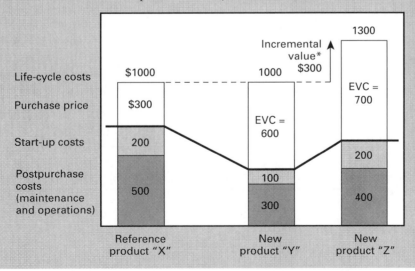

Going-rate pricing is quite popular. Where costs are difficult to measure, or competitive response is uncertain, firms feel that the going price represents a good solution. The going price is thought to reflect the industry's collective wisdom as to the price that would yield a fair return and not jeopardize industrial harmony.

Sealed-Bid Pricing   Competitive-oriented pricing is common where firms bid for jobs. The firm bases its price on expectations of how competitors will price rather than on a rigid relation to the firm's costs or demand. The firm wants to win the contract, and winning normally requires submitting a lower price than competitors.

Yet the firm cannot set its price below a certain level. It cannot price below cost without worsening its position. On the other hand, the higher it sets its price above its costs, the lower its chance of getting the contract.

The net effect of the two opposite pulls can be described in terms of the bid's *expected profit* (see Table 18-1). Suppose a bid of $9500 would yield a high chance of getting the contract, say .81, but only a low profit, say $100. The expected profit with this bid is therefore $81. If the firm bid $11 000, its profit would be $1600, but its chance of getting the contract might be reduced, say to .01. The expected profit would be only $16. One logical bidding criterion would be to bid the price that would maximize the expected profit. According to Table 18-1, the best bid would be $10 000, for which the expected profit is $216.

Using expected profit as a criterion for setting price makes sense for the firm that makes many bids. In playing the odds, the firm will achieve maximum profits in the long run. The firm that bids only occasionally or that needs a particular contract badly will not find it advantageous to use the expected-profit criterion. This criterion, for example, does not distinguish between a $1000 profit with a 0.10 probability and a $125 profit with an 0.80 probability. Yet the firm that wants to keep production going would prefer the second contract to the first.

Selecting the Final Price

The preceding pricing methods narrow the price range from which to select the final price. In selecting the final price, the company must consider some additional factors.

Psychological Pricing   Sellers should consider the psychology of prices in addition to their economics. Many consumers use price as an indicator of quality. When Fleischmann raised its price of gin from $4.50 to $5.50, its liquor sales went up, not down. Image pricing is especially effective with ego-sensitive products such as perfumes and expensive cars. A $100 bottle of perfume might contain $10 worth of scent, but giftgivers pay $100 to communicate their high regard for the receiver.

Table 18-1 Effect of Different Bids on Expected Profit

Company's Bid	Company's Profit	Probability of Getting Award with this Bid (Assumed)	Expected Profit
$ 9 500	$ 100	0.81	$ 81
10 000	600	0.36	216
10 500	1 100	0.09	99
11 000	1 600	0.01	16

A study of the relationship between price and quality perceptions of cars found the relationship to be operating in a reciprocal manner.[13] Higher-priced cars were perceived to possess (unwarranted) high quality. Higher-quality cars were likewise perceived to be higher priced than they actually were. When alternative information about true quality is available, price becomes a less significant indicator of quality.[14] When this information is not available, price acts as a quality signal.

Sellers often manipulate *reference prices* in pricing their product. Buyers carry in their minds a reference price when looking at a particular product. The reference price might have been formed by noticing current prices, past prices, or the buying context. For example, a seller can place its product among expensive products to imply that it belongs in the same class. Department stores will display women's apparel in separate departments differentiated by price; dresses found in the more expensive department are assumed to be of better quality. Reference price thinking is also created by stating a high manufacturer's suggested price, or by indicating that the product was priced much higher originally, or by pointing to a competitor's high price.

Many sellers believe that prices should end in an odd number. Newspaper ads are dominated by prices ending in odd numbers. Thus a stereo amplifier is priced at $299 instead of $300. Many customers see this as a price in the $200 range rather than $300 range. Another explanation is that odd endings convey the notion of a discount or bargain. But if a company wants a high-price image instead of a low-price image, it should avoid the odd-ending tactic.

The Influence of Other Marketing-Mix Elements on Price   The final price must take into account the brand's quality and advertising relative to competition. Farris and Reibstein examined the relationship between relative price, relative quality, and relative advertising for 227 consumer businesses and found the following results:

1. Brands with average relative high quality but high relative advertising budgets were able to charge premium prices. Consumers apparently were willing to pay higher prices for known products than for unknown products.

2. Brands with high relative quality and high relative advertising obtained the highest prices. Conversely, brands with low quality and low advertising charged the lowest prices.

3. The positive relationship between high prices and high advertising held most strongly in the later stages of the product life cycle, for market leaders, and for low-cost products.[15]

Company Pricing Policies   The contemplated price must be consistent with company pricing policies. Many companies set up a pricing department to develop pricing policies and establish or approve pricing decisions. Their aim is to insure that the salespeople quote prices that are reasonable to customers and profitable to the company.

Impact of Price on Other Parties   Management must also consider the reactions of other parties to the contemplated price. How will the *distributors and dealers* feel about it? Will the *company salesforce* be willing to sell at that price or complain that the price is too high? How will *competitors* react to this price? Will *suppliers* raise their prices when they see the company's price? Will the *government* intervene and prevent this price from being charged? In the last case, marketers need to know the laws affecting price and make sure that their pricing policies are defensible.

ADAPTING THE PRICE

Companies do not set a single price, they set a pricing structure that covers different products and items and that reflects variations in geographical demand and costs, market-segment variations, purchase timing, and other factors. We will examine several price-adaptation strategies: geographical pricing, price discounts and allowances, promotional pricing, discriminatory pricing, and product-mix pricing.

Geographical Pricing

Geographical pricing involves the company in deciding how to price its products to customers in different locations. Should the company charge higher prices to distant customers to cover the higher shipping costs and risk losing their business? Or should the company charge the same to all customers regardless of location? Companies have evolved five different approaches to geographical pricing, and they are described in Marketing Strategies 18-1.

Marketing Strategies 18-1

FIVE GEOGRAPHICAL PRICING STRATEGIES

We will examine five major geographical pricing strategies in connection with the following hypothetical situation:

> The Steel Company of Canada (Stelco) is located in Hamilton, Ontario and sells steel products to customers all over Canada. The cost of freight is high and can affect which suppliers will be used by customers in different locations. Stelco needs a geographical pricing policy. Let us consider the implications of alternative ways of pricing a nominal order of $100 to be shipped to three hypothetical customers. A is located in Toronto, B is in Cornwall, Ontario and C is in Halifax, Nova Scotia.

FOB Origin Pricing

Stelco can ask each customer to pay the shipping cost from the Hamilton factory to the specific destination. All three customers would pay the same factory price of $100, with customer A paying, say $10 additional shipping, customer B paying $15 additional, and customer C paying $25 additional. Called FOB origin pricing, it means that the goods are placed free on board a carrier, at which point the title and responsibility passes to the customer, who pays the freight from the factory to the destination.

Advocates of FOB pricing feel that it is the most equitable way to allocate freight charges, because each customer picks up his own cost. The disadvantage, however, is that Stelco will be a high-cost firm to distant customers. If Stelco's main competitor is Sysco Steel in Sydney, N.S., this competitor will outsell Stelco in Halifax. In fact, Sysco will outsell Stelco in all of the Atlantic Provinces while Stelco will dominate Ontario. A vertical line could be drawn on a map connecting the cities where the two companies' price plus freight will just be equal. Stelco will have the price advantage west of this line, and its competitor will have the price advantage east of this line.

Uniform Delivered Pricing

Uniform delivered pricing is the exact opposite of FOB pricing. Here the company charges the same price plus freight to all customers regardless of their location. It is called "postage stamp pricing" after the fact that the Canadian government sets a uniform delivered price on first class mail anywhere in the country. The freight charge is set at the average freight cost. Suppose this is $15. Uniform delivered pricing therefore results in a high charge to the Toronto customer (who pays $15 freight instead of $10) and a subsidized charge to the Halifax customer (who pays $15 instead of $25). The Toronto customer would prefer to buy from another local company that uses FOB origin pricing. On the other hand, Stelco has a better chance to win the Halifax customer. Other advantages are that uniform delivered pricing is relatively easy to administer and allows the firm to maintain a nationally advertised price.

Zone Pricing

Zone pricing falls between FOB origin pricing and uniform delivered pricing. The company establishes two or more zones. All customers within a zone pay the same total price; and this price is higher in the more distant zones. Stelco might set up an Ontario zone and charge $10 freight to all customers in this zone, a Quebec zone and charge $15, and an Atlantic zone and charge $25. In this way, the customers within a given price zone receive no price advantage from the company; thus customer A in Toronto and customer B in Cornwall pay the same total price to Stelco. The complaint, however, is that the Toronto customer is subsidizing the freight cost of the Cornwall customer. In addition, a customer just west of the line dividing Ontario and Quebec pays substantially less than one just on the east side of the line, although they may be within a few miles of each other.

Basing-Point Pricing

Basing-point pricing allows the seller to designate some city as a basing point and charge all customers the freight cost from that city to the customer location regardless of the city from which the goods are actually shipped. For example, Stelco might establish Montreal as the basing point and charge all customers $100 plus the appropriate freight from Montreal to their destination. This means that Toronto customers pay the freight cost from Montreal to Toronto though the goods may be shipped from Hamilton. They are paying a "phantom charge." In its favor, using a basing-point location other than the factory raises the total price to customers near the factory and lowers the total price to customers far from the factory.

If all the sellers used the same basing-point city, delivered prices would be the same for all customers, and price competition would be eliminated. Such industries as sugar, cement, steel, and automobiles used basing-point pricing for years, but this method is less popular today.

Some companies establish multiple basing points to create more flexibility. They would quote freight charges from the basing-point city nearest to the customer.

Freight-Absorption Pricing

The seller who is anxious to do business with a particular customer or geographic area might absorb all or part of the actual freight charges in order to get the business. Sellers might reason that if they can get more business, their average costs will fall and more than compensate for the extra freight costs. Freight-absorption pricing is used for market penetration and also to hold on to increasingly competitive markets.

Price Discounts and Allowances

Most companies will modify their basic price to reward customers for such acts as early payment, volume purchases, and off-season buying. These price adjustments—called discounts and allowances—are described below.

Cash Discounts   A cash discount is a price reduction to buyers who promptly pay their bills. A typical example is, "2/10, net 30," which means that payment is due within thirty days but the buyer can deduct 2 percent by paying the bill within ten days. The discount must be granted to all buyers who meet these terms. Such discounts are customary in many industries and serve the purpose of improving the sellers' liquidity and reducing credit-collection costs and bad debts.

Quantity Discounts   A quantity discount is a price reduction to buyers who buy large volumes. A typical example is, "$10 per unit for less than 100 units; $9 per unit for 100 or more units." Quantity discounts must be offered equally to all customers and must not exceed the cost savings to the seller associated with selling large quantities. These savings include reduced expenses of selling, inventory, and transportation. They can be offered on a noncumulative basis (on each order placed) or a cumulative basis (on the number of units ordered over a given period). Discounts provide an incentive to the customer to order more from a given seller rather than buying from multiple sources.

Functional Discounts   Functional discounts (also called trade discounts) are offered by the manufacturer to trade-channel members if they will perform certain functions, such as selling, storing, and record keeping. Manufacturers may offer different functional discounts to different trade channels because of their varying functions, but manufacturers must offer the same functional discounts within each trade channel.

Seasonal Discounts   A seasonal discount is a price reduction to buyers who buy merchandise or services out of season. Seasonal discounts allow the seller to maintain steadier production during the year. Ski manufacturers will offer seasonal discounts to retailers in the spring and summer to encourage early ordering. Hotels, motels, and airlines will offer seasonal discounts in their slow selling periods.

Allowances   Allowances are other types of reductions from the list price. For example, *trade-in allowances* are price reductions granted for turning in an old item when buying a new one. Trade-in allowances are most common in the automobile industry and are also found in some other durable-goods categories. *Promotional allowances* are payments or price reductions to reward dealers for participating in advertising and sales-support programs.

Promotional Pricing

Under certain circumstances, companies will temporarily price their products below the list price and sometimes even below cost. Promotional pricing takes several forms.

- *Loss-Leader Pricing:* Supermarkets and department stores may drop the price on well-known brands to stimulate additional store traffic. But manufacturers typically disapprove of their brands being used as loss leaders because this can dilute the brand image. Since manufacturers rarely have enough clout to control retailers' selling prices, some have tried to sell direct. After Hurtig Publishers experienced heavy discounting of Volume 1 of the *Canadian Encyclopedia* by Coles and W H Smith book stores, they sold Volume 2 directly using newspaper advertisements.

- *Special-Event Pricing:* Sellers will establish special prices in certain seasons to draw in more customers. Thus linens are promotionally priced every January to attract shopping-weary customers into the stores.

- *Cash Rebates:* Consumers are offered cash rebates to encourage their purchasing the manufacturer's product within a specified time period. The rebates can help the manufacturer clear inventories without cutting the list price. Auto manufacturers have offered rebates several times in recent years to stimulate sales. The initial rebates were effective but when repeated, they seemed to lose their effectiveness. They may have given a price break to those who intended to buy a car without stimulating others to think about buying a car. Rebates also appear in consumer-packaged-goods marketing. They stimulate sales without costing the company as much as would cutting the price. The reason is that many buyers buy the product but fail to mail in the coupon for a refund.

□ *Low-Interest Financing:* Instead of lowering the price, the company can offer customers low-interest financing. This is attractive to those auto buyers who finance their purchase. Automakers may offer rates several percent below commercial rates and occasionally as low as zero percent. Although low-interest financing attracts customer to auto showrooms, many don't buy when they learn that a large down payment is required; the loan must be paid back in thirty months instead of sixty months; the car price is not discounted much with this kind of loan; and the loan may apply only to expensive cars.[16]

□ *Warranties and Service Contracts:* The company can promote sales by adding a free warranty offer or service contract, or offering it at a reduced price. Sears offers special service contracts to buyers of major appliances in the hope that the customer will renew the contract annually at a more favorable price.

□ *Psychological Discounting:* This involves putting an artificially high price on a product and then offering it at substantial savings; for example, "Was $359, now $299." Illegitimate discount tactics are fought by government regulators and Better Business bureaus. On the other hand, discounts from normal prices are a legitimate form of promotional pricing.

Companies must research these promotional pricing tools and make sure that they do not contravene federal or provincial laws. But if they work, they can easily be copied by competitors so the initiating company loses its advantage. If they do not work, they waste company money that would have been put into longer-impact marketing tools, such as building up product quality and service and improving the product image through advertising.

Discriminatory Pricing

Companies will often modify their basic price to accommodate differences in customers, products, locations, and so on. *Discriminatory pricing* occurs when a company sells a product or service at two or more prices that do not reflect a proportional difference in costs. Discriminatory pricing takes several forms:

□ *Customer-Segment Pricing:* Here different customer groups are charged different prices for the same product or service. Museums will charge a lower admission fee to students and senior citizens.

□ *Product-Form Pricing:* Here different versions of the product are priced differently but not proportionately to their respective costs. SCM Corporation prices its most expensive Proctor-Silex steamdry iron at $54.95, $5 above its next most expensive iron. The top model has a light that signals when the iron is ready. Yet the extra feature costs less than $1 to make. As another example, mineral water can be bought as a beverage at less than $1 per 750 ml bottle. It can also be bought as a skin moisturizer spray at $5 for a fraction of that amount. Through product-form pricing, the supplier is able to increase the price while decreasing the quantity sold.

□ *Image Pricing:* Some companies will price the same product at two different levels based on image differences. Thus a perfume manufacturer can put the perfume in one bottle, give it a name and image, and price it at $10 an ounce; and in a fancier bottle with a different name and image and price it at $30 an ounce.

□ *Location Pricing:* Here different locations are priced differently even though the cost of offering each location is the same. A theater varies its seat prices according to audience preferences for different locations.

□ *Time Pricing:* Here prices are varied by season, day, or hour. Public utilities vary their energy rates to commercial users by time of day and weekend versus weekday.

For price discrimination to work, certain conditions must exist. First, the market must be segmentable, and the segments must show different intensities of demand. Second, members of the lower price segment must not be able to resell the product to the higher price segment. Third, competitors must not be able to undersell the firm in the higher price segment. Fourth, the cost of segmenting and policing the market must not exceed the extra revenue derived from price discrimination. Fifth, the practice must not breed customer resentment and ill will. Sixth, the particular form of price discrimination must not be illegal.

As a result of deregulation in several industries, competitors have increased their use of discriminatory pricing. An airline, for example, will charge different fares to passengers on the same flight depending on the seating class; the time of day (morning or night coach); the day of the week (workday or weekend); the season; the person's company, past business or status (youth, military, senior citizen); and so on. Airlines call this system *yield management*, which is an exercise in trying to realize as much revenue as possible while filling the plane's seats.

Product-Mix Pricing

Price-setting logic has to be modified when the product is part of a product mix. In this case, the firm searches for a set of prices that maximize the profits on the total product mix. Pricing is difficult, because the various products have demand and cost interrelationships and are subject to different degrees of competition. We can distinguish six situations.

Product-Line Pricing   Companies normally develop product lines rather than single products. For example, Panasonic offers five different color video sound cameras, ranging from a simple lightweight camera to a larger camera having more sophisticated controls like auto focusing, fade control and special lenses. Each successive camera offers additional features, permitting *premium pricing*. Management must decide on the *price steps* to establish between the various cameras. The price steps should take into account cost differences between the cameras, customer evaluations of the different features, and competitors' prices. If the price difference between two successive cameras is small, buyers will buy the more advanced camera, and this will increase company profits if the price difference is greater than the cost difference. If the price difference is large, customers will buy the less advanced camera.

In many lines of trade, sellers use well-established *price points* for the products in their line. Thus men's clothing stores might carry men's suits at three price levels: $150, $220, and $310. The customers will associate low-, average-, and high-quality suits with the three price "points." Even if the three prices are all raised, men will normally buy suits at their preferred price point. The seller's task is to establish perceived-quality differences that justify the price differences.

Optional-Feature Pricing   Many companies offer optional products or features along with their main product. The automobile buyer can order electric window controls, defoggers, and light dimmers. However, pricing these options is a sticky problem. Automobile companies must decide which items to include in the price and which to offer as options. General Motors's normal pricing strategy is to advertise a stripped-down model for $8000 to pull people into the showrooms and devote most of the showroom space to feature-loaded cars at $10 000 or up. The economy model is stripped of so many comforts and features that most buyers will reject it. When GM launched its new front-wheel-drive J-cars, it took a clue from the Japanese auto makers and included in the sticker price a number of popular options. Now the advertised price represented a well-equipped car. Unfortunately, the price was high, and many car shoppers balked.

Restaurants face a similar pricing problem. Restaurant customers can order liquor in addition to the meal. Many restaurants price their liquor high and their food low. The food revenue covers the food and other restaurant costs, and the liquor produces the profit. This explains why waiters press hard to get customers to order drinks. Other restaurants price their liquor low and food high to draw in a drinking crowd.

Captive-Product Pricing   Some products require the use of ancillary or captive products. Examples of captive products are razor blades and camera film. Manufacturers of the main products (razors and cameras) often price them low and set high markups on the supplies. Thus Kodak prices its cameras low, because it makes its money on selling film. Those camera makers who do not sell film have to price their cameras higher in order to make the same overall profit.

There is a danger, however, in pricing the captive product too high. Caterpillar, for example, makes high profits in the aftermarket by pricing high its parts and service. It marks up its equipment by 30 percent and its parts sometimes by 300 percent. This has given rise to "pirates," who counterfeit these parts and sell them to "shady tree" mechanics, who install them, sometimes without passing on the cost savings to the customers. Meanwhile Caterpillar loses these sales. Caterpillar attempts to control this problem by exhorting equipment owners to use only authorized dealers if they want guaranteed performance. But clearly the problem is created by the high prices that manufacturers charge for their aftermarket products.

Two-Part Pricing   Service firms often charge a fixed fee plus a variable usage fee. Thus telephone users pay a minimum monthly fee plus charges for calls beyond the minimum number. Amusement parks charge an admission fee plus fees for rides over a certain minimum. The service firm faces a problem similar to captive-product pricing, namely, how much to charge for the basic service and how much for the variable usage. The fixed fee should be low enough to induce purchase of the service, and the profit can be made on the usage fees.

Byproduct Pricing   In producing processed meats, petroleum products, and other chemicals, there are often byproducts. If the byproducts have little value and are in fact costly to dispose of, that will affect the pricing of the main product. The manufacturer should accept any price that covers more than the cost of disposing of them. If the byproducts have value to some customer group, then they should be priced on their value. Any income earned on the byproducts will make it easier for the company to charge a lower price on its main product if forced to by competition.

Product-Bundling Pricing   Sellers will often bundle their products at a set price. Thus an auto manufacturer might offer an option package at less than the cost of buying all the options separately. A theater company will price a season subscription at less than the cost of buying all the performances separately. Since customers may not have planned to buy all of the components, the savings on the price bundle must be substantial enough to induce them to buy the bundle.[17]

INITIATING AND RESPONDING TO PRICE CHANGES

After developing their price strategies and structures, companies will face situations where they will want to cut or raise prices.

Initiating Price Cuts

Several circumstances might lead a firm to cut its price, even though it might provoke a price war. One circumstance is *excess capacity.* Here the firm needs additional business and cannot generate it through increased sales effort, product improvement, or other measures. It may abandon "follow-the-leader" pricing and resort to "aggressive" pricing to boost its sales. But in initiating a price cut, the company might face a price war, as competitors try to hold on to their market shares.

Another circumstance is a *falling market share* in the face of vigorous price competition. Several industries—automobiles, consumer electronics, cameras, watches, and steel—have been losing market share to Japanese competitors. Zenith, General Motors, and other companies have resorted to more-aggressive pricing action. General Motors, for example, cut its subcompact car prices by 10 percent where Japanese competition is strongest.

Companies will also initiate price cuts in a *drive to dominate the market through lower costs.* Either the company starts with lower costs than its competitors or it initiates price cuts in the hope of gaining market share, which would lead to falling costs through larger volume. People Express waged an aggressive low-price strategy and gained a large market share. But this strategy also involves some high risks.

1. *Low-Quality Trap:* Consumers will assume that the quality is below that of the higher-priced competitors.

2. *Fragile-Market-Share Trap:* A low price buys market share but not market loyalty. Customers will shift to the next lower-price firm that comes along.

3. *Shallow-Pockets Trap:* The higher-priced competitors may cut their prices and have longer staying power because of deeper cash reserves.

People Express some years later fell into these traps.

Companies will consider cutting prices in a period of *economic recession.* Fewer consumers are willing to buy higher-price versions of a product. Marketing Strategies 18-2 shows several ways in which sellers can adjust their price and marketing mix in facing a declining demand situation.

Marketing Strategies 18-2

ANALYZING THE MARKETING-MIX ALTERNATIVES FACING A FIRM IN AN ECONOMIC RECESSION

Here we will describe an actual but disguised situation involving two competing appliance manufacturers. Company A's appliances are perceived to be of higher quality and higher prices than company B's appliances. The perceived positions of the two brands are shown in Figure (a) along the dimensions of *perceived value* and *price.* Note that the two brands lie on the same value-to-price line. This means that consumers feel they would get approximately the same value per dollar whether they bought brand A or B. Those who want more total value would buy A if they could afford it. Those who want to spend less would buy B.

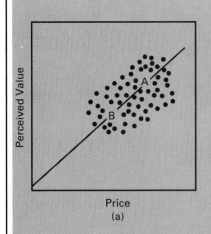

Price
(a)

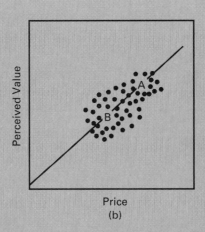

Price
(b)

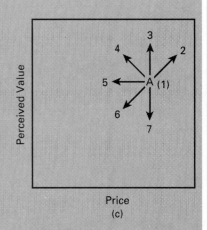

Price
(c)

The dots in Figure (a) represent the preferences of potential buyers for value/price combinations. Buyers whose preferences are nearest to A will buy A; the same goes for B. Clearly, each brand has a substantial market, and both are likely to enjoy good market shares.

An economic recession now occurs. There are fewer buyers and their preferences shift toward the cheaper appliance B (see Figure (b)). The number of buyers willing to buy the higher-price appliance diminishes. If company A does nothing about this, its market share will shrink.

Company A must identify its marketing alternatives and choose among them. At least seven marketing alternatives exist. They are illustrated in Figure (c) and described below.

STRATEGIC OPTIONS	REASONING	CONSEQUENCES
1. Maintain price and perceived value. Engage in selective customer pruning.	Firm has high customer loyalty. It is willing to lose poorer customers to competitors.	Smaller market share. Lower profitability.
2. Raise price and perceived value.	Raise price to cover rising costs. Improve quality to justify higher prices.	Smaller market share. Maintained profitability.
3. Maintain price and raise perceived value.	It is cheaper to maintain price and raise perceived value.	Smaller market share. Short-term decline in profitability. Long-term increase in profitability.
4. Cut price partly and raise perceived value.	Must give customers some price reduction but stress higher value of offer.	Maintained market share. Short-term decline in profitability. Long-term maintained profitability.
5. Cut price fully and maintain perceived value.	Discipline and discourage price competition.	Maintained market share. Short-term decline in profitability.
6. Cut price fully and reduce perceived value.	Discipline and discourage price competition and maintain profit margin.	Maintained market share. Maintained margin. Reduced long-term profitability.
7. Maintain price and reduce perceived value.	Cut marketing expenses to combat rising costs.	Smaller market share. Maintained margin. Reduced long-term profitability.

Here are some observations:

- Company A should consider launching an economy model located close to company B's model so that it can capture the increased number of economy-minded customers (a modification of alternative 6). By offering a prestige and an economy model, company A can hold or increase its market share.

- If company A is forced to raise its price, it should raise its perceived value at the same time (alternative 2). Perceived value can be increased by quality, feature,

and style improvements; better customer service; and more effective advertising.

- The choice of a marketing strategy hinges on a number of considerations, including company A's current market share, current and planned capacity, market growth rate, customer price sensitivity and perceived-value sensitivity, market-share/profitability relationship, and competitors' probable strategic responses and initiatives. The company needs to forecast the impact of each marketing strategy on its sales, market share, costs, profit, and long-run investment.

Initiating Price Increases

Many companies need to raise their prices; they know, however, that the price increases will be resented by customers, dealers, and the company's own salesforce. Yet a successful price increase can increase profits considerably. For example, if the company's profit margin is 3 percent of sales, a 1 percent price increase will increase profits by 33 percent if sales volume is unaffected. This is illustrated below, where we assume that a company charged $10 and sold 100 units and had costs of $970, leaving a profit of $30, or 3 percent on sales. By raising its price by 10¢ (1 percent price increase), it boosted its profits by $33\frac{1}{3}$ percent, assuming the same sales volume.

A major circumstance provoking price increases is *cost inflation*. Rising costs unmatched by productivity gains squeeze profit margins and lead companies to regular rounds of price increases. Companies often raise their prices by more than the cost increase in anticipation of further inflation or government price controls; this is called *anticipatory pricing*. Companies hesitate to make long-run price commitments to customers, fearing that cost inflation will erode their profit margins.

Another factor leading to price increases is *overdemand*. When a company cannot supply all of its customers, it can raise its prices, put customers on allocation, or both. The "real" price can be increased in several ways, each with a different impact on buyers. The following price adjustments are common:

- *Adoption of Delayed Quotation Pricing:* The company does not set its final price until the product is finished or delivered. Delayed quotation pricing is prevalent in industries with long production lead times, such as industrial construction and heavy-equipment manufacture.

- *Use of Escalator Clauses:* The company requires the customer to pay today's price and all or part of any inflation increase that takes place before delivery. An escalator clause in the

	Before	After
Price	$ 10	$10.10 (a 1% price increase)
Units sold	100	100
Revenue	$1000	$ 1010
Costs	–970	–970
Profit	$ 30	$ 40 (a 33 1/3% profit increase)

contract bases price increases on some specified price index, such as the cost-of-living index. Escalator clauses are found in many contracts involving industrial projects of long duration.

☐ *Unbundling of Goods and Services:* The company maintains its price but removes or prices separately one or more elements that were part of the former offer, such as free delivery or installation. IBM, for example, now offers training as a separately priced service. Many restaurants have shifted from dinner pricing to à la carte pricing. A joke in Argentina is that the current price of a car no longer includes the tires and steering wheel.

☐ *Reduction of Discounts:* The company instructs its salesforce not to offer its normal cash and quantity discounts.

A company might also have to decide whether to raise the price sharply on a one-time basis or to raise it by small amounts several times. For example, when costs rose for Supercut stores (a franchised chain of hairdressers), management debated between raising the price immediately from $6 to $8 or raising the price to $7 this year and $8 the following year. Generally, consumers prefer small price increases on a regular basis to sharp price increases. In passing price increases on to customers, the company needs to avoid the image of a price gouger. Customer memories are long, and they will turn against the price gougers when the market softens. The price increases should be accompanied by company communications explaining why prices are being increased. The company's salesforce should help customers find ways to economize.

There are other ways that the company can respond to high costs or demand without raising prices. The possibilities include the following:

☐ Shrinking the amount of product instead of raising the price. (At one time, Hershey Foods maintained its fifteen-cent candy bar but trimmed its size. Nestlé, on the other hand, maintained its old size but raised the price to twenty cents.)

☐ Substituting less-expensive materials or ingredients. (Many candy-bar companies substituted synthetic chocolate for real chocolate to fight the price increases in cocoa. Auto manufacturers have replaced metal with plastic wherever possible.)

☐ Reducing or removing product features to reduce cost. (Sears engineered down a number of its appliances so they could be priced competitively with those sold in discount stores.)

☐ Removing or reducing product services, such as installation, free delivery, or long warranties.

☐ Using less-expensive packaging material or promoting larger package sizes to keep down the relative cost of packaging.

☐ Reducing the number of sizes and models offered.

☐ Creating new economy brands. (For example, Loblaws introduced its generic items selling at 10 to 30 percent less than national brands to offer to price-conscious consumers.)

The best action to take is not always obvious. Quaker Oats produces the successful cereal called Harvest Crunch in Canada, which contains several ingredients, such as almonds and raisins, whose prices jumped during a recent inflation. Quaker Oats saw two choices, namely, raising the price, or cost reducing the ingredients by including fewer almonds and raisins, or finding cheaper substitutes. It decided against changing the ingredients and raised the price. But the price elasticity was high, and sales fell. This forced the company to reconsider ways to cost reduce the ingredients, knowing that such a move would involve a great risk.

Customers' Reactions to Price Changes

Any price change can affect customers, competitors, distributors, and suppliers and may interest government as well. Here we will consider customers' reactions.

Customers do not always put a straightforward interpretation on price changes.[18] A price cut can be interpreted in the following ways: The item is about to be replaced by a new model; the item is faulty and is not selling well; the firm is in financial trouble and may not stay in business to supply future parts; the price will come down even further, and it pays to wait; or the quality has been reduced.

A price increase, which would normally deter sales, may carry some positive meanings to customers: The item is "hot" and might be unobtainable unless it is bought soon; the item represents an unusually good value; or the seller is greedy and is charging what the traffic will bear.

Customers' reactions to price changes also vary with their perception of the product's cost in relation to their total expenditures. Customers are most price sensitive to products that cost a lot and/or are bought frequently, whereas they hardly notice higher prices on low-cost items that they buy infrequently. In addition, some buyers are less concerned with the product's *price* than the *total costs* of obtaining, operating, and servicing the product over its lifetime. A seller can charge more than the competition and still get the business if the customer can be convinced that the total lifetime costs are lower.

Competitors' Reactions to Price Changes

A firm contemplating a price change has to worry about competitors' as well as customers' reactions. Competitors are very likely to react where the number of firms is small, the product is homogeneous, and the buyers are highly informed.

How can the firm anticipate the likely reactions of its competitors? Assume that the firm faces one large competitor. The competitor's reaction can be estimated from two vantage points. One is to assume that the competitor reacts in a set way to price changes. In this case, its reaction can be anticipated. The other is to assume that the competitor treats each price change as a fresh challenge and reacts according to self-interest at the time. In this case, the company will have to figure out what lies in the competitor's self-interest. The competitor's current financial situation should be researched, along with recent sales and capacity, customer loyalty, and corporate objectives. If the competitor has a market-share objective, it is likely to match the price change. If it has a profit-maximization objective, it may react on some other strategy front, such as increasing the advertising budget or improving the product quality. The challenge is to read the competitor's mind by using inside and outside sources of information.

The problem is complicated, because the competitor can put different interpretations on, say, a company price cut: The competitor can surmise that the company is trying to steal the market, that the company is doing poorly and trying to boost its sales, or that the company wants the whole industry to reduce prices to stimulate total demand.

When there are several competitors, the company must estimate each close competitor's likely reaction. If all competitors behave alike, this estimate amounts to an analysis of a typical competitor. If the competitors do not react uniformly because of critical differences in size, market shares, or policies, then separate analyses are necessary. If some competitors will match the price change, there is good reason to expect that the rest will also match it. Marketing Concepts and Tools 18-4 shows how a major chemical company analyzed the probable reactions of various parties to a contemplated price reduction.

Marketing Concepts and Tools 18-4

HOW A LARGE CHEMICAL COMPANY USED DECISION THEORY TO ASSESS PROBABLE COMPETITORS' REACTIONS TO A CONTEMPLATED PRICE CUT

A large chemical company had been selling a plastic substance to industrial users for several years and enjoyed a 40 percent market share. The management became worried about whether its current price of $1.00 per pound could be maintained for much longer. The main source of concern was the rapid buildup of capacity by its three competitors and the possible attraction of further competitors by the current price. Management saw that the solution to possible oversupply lay in further market expansion. The key opportunity for market expansion lay in an important market segment that was closely held by a substitute plastic product produced by six firms. This substitute product was not as good, but it was priced lower. Management thought of displacing the substitute product through a price reduction. If it could penetrate this segment, there was a good chance it could also penetrate three other segments.

The first task was to develop a decision model for the problem. This required defining the objectives, price alternatives, and key uncertainties. The chosen objective was to maximize the present value of future profits over the next five years. Management considered four price alternatives: maintaining the price at $1.00 or reducing the price to 93¢, 85¢, and 80¢. The key uncertainties were the following:

☐ How much penetration in the key segment would take place without a price reduction?

☐ How would the six firms producing the substitute plastic react to each possible price reduction?

☐ How much key-segment penetration would take place for each possible price reaction by the suppliers of the substitute plastic?

☐ How much would key-segment penetration speed up penetration of the other three segments?

☐ If the key segment was not penetrated, what is the probability that the company's competitors would initiate a price reduction soon?

☐ How would a price reduction affect the decision of existing competitors to expand their capacity and potential competitors to enter the industry?

The data-gathering phase consisted in asking sales personnel to place subjective probabilities on the possible states of the key uncertainties. For example, one question asked for the probability that the substitute product producers would retaliate if the company reduced its price to 93¢ per pound. On the average, the sales personnel felt that there was a 5 percent probability of a full match, a 60 percent probability of a half match, and a 35 percent probability of no retaliation. They were also asked for probabilities if price were reduced to 85¢ and to 80¢. The sales personnel indicated, as expected, that the probability of retaliation increased with the size of the price reduction.

The next step was to estimate the payoff associated with each price alternative. A decision-tree analysis revealed over four hundred possible outcomes. The results indicated that all price reductions had a higher expected payoff than no price reduction, and a price reduction to 80¢ had the highest expected payoff. To check the sensitivity of these results, they were recomputed for alternative assumptions about the rate of market growth and the cost of capital. The ranking of the strategies was not affected by changes in assumptions. The analysis confirmed the desirability of a price reduction.

Source: See Paul E. Green, "Bayesian Decision Theory in Pricing Strategy," *Journal of Marketing*, January 1963, pp. 5-14.

Responding to Price Changes

Here we reverse the question and ask how a firm should respond to a price change initiated by a competitor. In markets characterized by high product homogeneity, the firm has little choice but to meet a competitor's price cut. The firm should search for ways to enhance its augmented product, but if it cannot find any, it will have to meet the price reduction.

When a competitor raises its price in a homogeneous-product market, the other firms might not match it. They will comply if the price increase will benefit the industry as a whole. But if one firm does not think that it or the industry would gain, its noncompliance can make the leader and the others rescind the price increases.

In nonhomogeneous-product markets, a firm has more latitude in reacting to a competitor's price change. Buyers choose the vendor on a multiplicity of considerations: service, quality, reliability, and other factors. These factors desensitize buyers to minor price differences.

Before reacting, the firm needs to consider the following issues: (1) Why did the competitor change the price? Is it to steal the market, to utilize excess capacity, to meet changing cost conditions, or to lead an industrywide price change? (2) Does the competitor plan to make the price change temporary or permanent? (3) What will happen to the company's market share and profits if it does not respond? Are other companies going to respond? and (4) What are the competitor's and other firms' responses likely to be to each possible reaction?

Market leaders frequently face aggressive price cutting by smaller firms trying to build market share. Using price, Fuji attacks Kodak, Bic attacks Gillette, and Datril attacks Tylenol. IBM's personal computers are under great attack today from much lower priced computers such as Leading Edge and Amstrad (both made in South Korea at much lower costs). When the attacking firm's product is comparable to the leader's, its lower price will cut into the leader's share. The leader at this point has several options.

☐ *Maintain Price:* The leader might maintain its price and profit margin, believing that (a) it would lose too much profit if it reduced its price; (b) it would not lose much market share; and (c) it could regain market share when necessary. The leader believes that it could hold on to good customers, giving up the poorer ones to the competitor. The argument against price maintenance is that the attacker gets more confident as its sales increase, the leader's sales force gets demoralized, and the leader loses more share than expected. The leader panics, lowers price to regain share, and finds it more difficult and costly than expected.

☐ *Raise Perceived Quality:* The leader could maintain price but strengthen the value of its offer. It could improve its product, services, and communications. It could stress the relative quality of its product over that of the low-price competitor. The firm may find it cheaper to maintain price and spend money to improve its perceived quality than to cut price and operate at a lower margin.

☐ *Reduce Price:* The leader might drop its price to the competitor's price. It might do so because (a) its costs fall with volume; (b) it would lose market share because the market is price sensitive; and (c) it would be hard to rebuild market share once it is lost. This action will cut its profits in the short run. Some firms will reduce their product quality, services, and marketing communications to maintain profits but this will ultimately hurt their long-run market share. The company should try to maintain its quality as it cuts prices.

☐ *Increase Price and Improve Quality:* The leader might raise its price and introduce some new brands to bracket the attacking brand. Heublein, Inc., used this strategy when its Smirnoff's vodka, which had 23 percent of the vodka market, was attacked by another brand, Wolfschmidt, priced at one dollar less a bottle. Instead of lowering the price of

FIGURE 18-8

Price-Reaction Program for Meeting a Competitor's Price Cut

Source: Redrawn, with permission, from an unpublished paper by Raymond J. Trapp, Northwestern University, 1964.

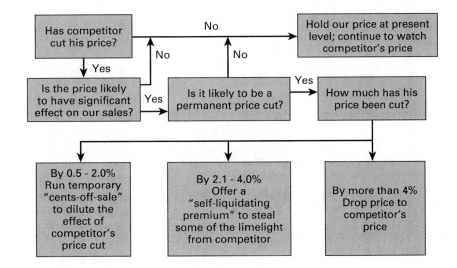

Smirnoff by one dollar, Heublein raised the price by one dollar and put the increased revenue into its advertising. Heublein introduced another brand, Relska, to compete with Wolfschmidt and still another, Popov, to sell for less than Wolfschmidt. This strategy effectively bracketed Wolfschmidt and gave Smirnoff an even more elite image.

☐ *Launch Low-Price Fighter Line:* One of the best responses is to add lower-price items to the line or to create a separate lower-price brand. This is necessary if the particular market segment being lost is price sensitive, since it will not respond to arguments of higher quality.

The best response varies with the particular situation. The company under attack has to consider the product's stage in the life cycle, its importance in the company's product portfolio, the intentions and resources of the competitor, the price and value sensitivity of the market, the behavior of costs with volume, and the company's alternative opportunities.

An extended analysis of company alternatives is not always feasible when the attack occurs. The competitor might have spent considerable time in preparing this decision, but the company may have to react decisively within hours or days. About the only way to reduce price-reaction time is to anticipate possible competitors' price changes and to prepare contingent responses. Figure 18-8 shows a company price-reaction program to be used if a competitor cuts prices. Reaction programs for meeting price changes find their greatest application in industries where price changes occur with some frequency and where it is important to react quickly. Examples can be found in the meat-packing, lumber, and oil industries.

SUMMARY

In spite of the increased role of nonprice factors in the modern marketing process, price remains a critical element and is especially challenging in markets characterized by monopolistic competition or oligopoly.

In setting the price of a product, the company follows a six-step procedure. First, the company carefully establishes its marketing objective(s), such as survival, maximum current profit, maximum current revenue, maximum sales growth, maximum market skimming, or product-quality leadership. Second, the company determines the demand schedule, which shows the probable quantity purchased per period at alternative price levels. The more inelastic the demand, the higher the company can set its price. Third, the company estimates how its costs vary at different output levels and with different levels of accumulated production experience. Fourth, the company examines competitors' prices as a basis for positioning its own price. Fifth, the company selects one of the following pricing methods: markup pricing, target-return pricing, perceived-value pricing, going-rate pricing, and sealed-bid pricing. Sixth, the company selects its final price, expressing it in the most effective psychological way, coordinating it with the other market-mix elements, checking that it conforms to company pricing policies, and making sure it will find acceptance with distributors and dealers, company salesforce, competitors, suppliers, and government.

Companies adapt the price to varying conditions in the marketplace. One is geographical pricing, where the company decides on how to price to distant customers. A second is price discounts and allowances, where the company establishes cash discounts, quantity discounts, functional discounts, seasonal discounts, and allowances. A third is promotional pricing, where the company decides on loss-leader pricing, special-event pricing, cash rebates, low-interest financing, and psychological discounting. A fourth is discriminatory pricing, where the company establishes different prices for different customer segments, product forms, brand images, places, and times. A fifth is product-mix pricing, where the company decides on the price zones for several products in a product line and on the pricing of optional features, captive products, byproducts, and product bundles.

When a firm considers initiating a price change, it must carefully consider customers' and competitors' reactions. Customers' reactions are influenced by the meaning customers see in the price change. Competitors' reactions flow from either a set reaction policy or from a fresh appraisal of each situation. The firm initiating the price change must also anticipate the probable reactions of suppliers, middlemen, and government.

The firm facing a price change initiated by a competitor must try to understand the competitor's intent and the likely duration of the change. If swiftness of reaction is desirable, the firm should preplan its reactions to different possible price actions by competitors.

■ QUESTIONS

1. A prominent Canadian university is planning to introduce a part-time MBA program that is targeted at public-sector executives. It is anticipated that the tuition will be paid by the students' employers, who are typically government departments. Discuss the issues involved in setting a price for this product.

2. Discount car dealers who have set prices at "$49 over invoice" have encountered long delivery delays and anonymous hate mail. What factors have they ignored in developing their pricing strategy?

3. What is price elasticity? Differentiate between elasticity, inelasticity, long-run elasticity, and short-run elasticity. Provide examples from industry.

4. Under what circumstances would a manufacturer initiate price cuts?

5. In an effort to stimulate sales during a recessionary period, small-appliance manufacturers offered rebates, and auto

makers offered low-interest-rate loans. What are the respective advantages and disadvantages of these two methods of price reduction?

6. Predatory pricing, defined as pricing below cost to damage or destroy a competitor, is illegal. But it is not clear whether "cost" should be defined as total cost or average variable cost. What would be the consequences for large versus small companies, of adopting one or the other of the cost definitions?

7. A major steel company has developed a new process for galvanizing steel sheets so that they can be painted (previously not possible) and used in car-body parts to prevent rust. What factors should the company consider in setting a price for this product?

8. A firm might set a low price on a product to discourage competitors from entering the market. Are there any situations when a firm might deliberately want to attract

competitors into a new market and set a high price for this reason?

9. Xerox developed an office-copying machine called 914. The machine was more expensive than competitive machines but offered the user superior copy and lower variable costs—1 cent per copy as opposed to between 4 cents and 9 cents for competing processes. The machine costs $2500 to produce, and management considered pricing it at either $3500 or $4500. How could management estimate unit sales at the two alternative price levels?

10. In principle, a reduction in price is tantamount to an increase in marketing effort. How can price reduction be monetized into its equivalent in increased marketing effort?

11. Four companies, W, X, Y, and Z, produce electric can openers. Consumers were asked to allocate 100 points among the companies' products for each of four attributes. The results are shown below:

Importance Weight	Attribute	Company Products			
		W	X	Y	Z
0.35	Durability	30	15	40	15
0.15	Attractiveness	20	20	30	30
0.25	Noiselessness	30	15	35	20
0.25	Safety	25	25	25	25

An average electric can opener sells for $20. What should company W do about the pricing of its product if company Y charges $22?

NOTES

1. David J. Schwartz, *Marketing Today: A Basic Approach*, 3rd ed. (New York: Harcourt Brace Jovanovich, 1981), p. 271.

2. See "Segmentation Strategies Create New Pressure among Marketers," *Marketing News*, March 28, 1986, p. 1.

3. Thomas T. Nagle, *The Strategy and Tactics of Pricing* (Englewood Cliffs, N.J.: Prentice Hall, 1987), Chap. 3. This is an excellent reference book for making pricing decisions.

4. John R. Nevin, "Laboratory Experiments for Estimating Consumer Demand—A Validation Study," *Journal of Marketing Research*, August, 1974, pp. 261-68.

5. See Sidney Bennett and J. B. Wilkinson, "Price-Quantity Relationships and Price Elasticity under In-Store Experimentation," *Journal of Business Research*, January 1974, pp. 30-34.

6. Nagle, *Strategy and Tactics of Pricing*, Chap. 11.

7. In summary:

$$Eqp = \frac{(Q_1 - Q_0)/\frac{1}{2}(Q_0 + Q_1)}{(P_1 - P_0)/\frac{1}{2}(P_0 + P_1)}$$

where:

Eqp = elasticity of quantity sold with respect to a change in price

Q_0, Q_1 = quantity sold per period before and after price change

P_0, P_1 = old and new price

Suppose a company lowers its price from $10 to $5, and its sales rise from 100 units to 150 units.

$$\frac{(150 - 100)/\frac{1}{2}(100 + 150)}{(\$5 - \$10)/\frac{1}{2}(\$10 + \$5)} = \frac{.40}{-.67} = -.60$$

Thus the demand elasticity is less than −1, or inelastic, and we know that total revenue will fall. Checking this, we note that the total revenue fell from $1000 to $750.

8. For a summary of elasticity studies, see Dominique M. Hanssens, Leonard J. Parsons, and Randall L. Schultz, *Market Response Models: Econometric and Time Series Analysis* (Boston: Kluwer Academic Publishers, 1990), pp. 187-91.

9. For methods of estimating elasticity, see Leonard J. Parsons and Randall L. Schultz, *Marketing Models and Econometric Research* (New York: North-Holland, 1976).

10. See William W. Alberts, "The Experience Curve Doctrine Reconsidered," *Journal of Marketing*, July 1989, pp. 36-49.

11. "Supermarket 1984 Sales Manual," *Progressive Grocer*, July 1984.

12. See Daniel A. Nimer, "Pricing the Profitable Sale Has a Lot to Do with Perception," *Sales Management*, May 19, 1975, pp. 13-14.

13. Gary M. Erickson and Johny K. Johansson, "The Role of Price in Multi-Attribute Product-Evaluations," *Journal of Consumer Research*, September 1985, pp. 195-99.

14. George J. Szybillo and Jacob Jacoby, "Intrinsic versus Extrinsic Cues as Determinants of Perceived Product Quality," *Journal of Applied Psychology*, February 1974, pp. 74-78.

15. Paul W. Farris and David J. Reibstein, "How Prices, Expenditures, and Profits Are Linked," *Harvard Business Review*, November-December 1979, pp. 173-84.

16. See "Finance Deals Aren't Helping Sales of Autos," *Wall Street Journal*, March 17, 1983.

17. See Gerald J. Tellis, "Beyond the Many Faces of Price: An Integration of Pricing Strategies," *Journal of Marketing*, October 1986, pp. 146-60, here p. 155. This excellent article also analyzes and illustrates other pricing strategies.

18. For an excellent review, see Kent B. Monroe, "Buyers' Subjective Perceptions of Price," *Journal of Marketing Research*, February 1973, pp. 70-80.

19

Selecting and Managing Marketing Channels

So long as the St. Lawrence flows into the sea, so long will the tide of commerce fall into and follow its natural declivity.

William F. Coffin

In today's economy, most producers do not sell their goods directly to the final users. Between them and the final users stand a host of marketing intermediaries performing a variety of functions and bearing a variety of names. Some intermediaries—such as wholesalers and retailers—buy, take title to, and resell the merchandise; they are called *merchant middlemen*. Others—such as brokers, manufacturers' representatives, and sales agents—search for customers and may negotiate on behalf of the producer but do not take title to the goods; they are called *agent middlemen*. Still others—such as transportation companies, independent warehouses, banks, and advertising agencies—assist in the performance of distribution but neither take title to goods nor negotiate purchases or sales; they are called *facilitators*.

Marketing-channel decisions are among the most critical decisions facing management. *The company's chosen channels intimately affect all the other marketing decisions.* The company's pricing depends on whether it uses mass merchandisers or high-quality boutiques. The firm's salesforce and advertising decisions depend on how much training and motivation the dealers need. In addition, the company's channel decisions *involve relatively long-term commitments to other firms.* When an auto maker signs up independent dealers to sell its automobiles, the auto maker cannot buy them out the next day and replace them with company-owned outlets. When a drug manufacturer relies on independent retail druggists to sell its products, the drug manufacturer must heed them when they object to its selling through mass-distribution outlets. Corey observed:

A distribution system . . . is a key *external* resource. Normally it takes years to build, and it is not easily changed. It ranks in importance with key *internal* resources such as manufacturing, research, engineering, and field sales personnel and facilities. It represents a significant corporate commitment to large numbers of independent companies whose business is distribution— and to the particular markets they serve. It represents, as well, a commitment to a set of policies and practices that constitute the basic fabric on which is woven an extensive set of long-term relationships.[1]

Thus there is a powerful inertial tendency in channel arrangements. Therefore management must choose channels with an eye on tomorrow's likely selling environment as well as today's.

In this chapter, we address the following questions: What is the nature of marketing channels? What decisions do companies face in designing, managing, evaluating, and modifying their channels? What trends are taking place in channel dynamics? How can channel conflict be managed? In the next chapter we will examine marketing-channel issues from the perspective of retailers, wholesalers, and physical-distribution agencies.

THE NATURE OF MARKETING CHANNELS

Most producers work with marketing intermediaries to bring their products to market. The marketing intermediaries make up a *marketing channel* (also called trade channel or distribution channel). We will use Stern and El-Ansary's definition of a marketing channel:

> Marketing channels *can be viewed as sets of interdependent organizations involved in the process of making a product or service available for use or consumption.*[2]

Why Are Marketing Intermediaries Used?

Why is the producer willing to delegate some of the selling job to intermediaries? The delegation means relinquishing some control over how and to whom the products are sold. The producer appears to be placing the firm's destiny in the hands of intermediaries.

Since producers could sell directly to final customers, they must feel they gain certain advantages in using middlemen. These advantages are described below.

Many producers lack the financial resources to carry out direct marketing. For example, General Motors sells its automobiles through more than ten thousand dealer outlets; even General Motors would be hard pressed to raise the cash to buy out its dealers.

Direct marketing would require many producers to become middlemen for the complementary products of other producers in order to achieve mass-distribution economies. For example, the Wm. Wrigley Jr. Company would not find it practical to establish small retail gum shops throughout the country or to sell gum door to door or by mail order. It would have to sell gum along with many other small products and would end up in the drugstore and grocery store business. Wrigley finds it easier to work through the extensive network of privately owned distribution institutions.

Producers who can afford to establish their own channels can often earn a greater return by increasing their investment in their main business. If a company earns a 20 percent rate of return on manufacturing and foresees only a 10 percent return on retailing, it will not want to undertake its own retailing.

Some producers, however, will set up a partially owned distribution system. Thus McDonald's owns over one-fourth of all its outlets. The advantage is that the company learns a lot about managing retail outlets and about the performance it can expect from operator-owned outlets. The disadvantage is that operator-owned outlets may resent the competition coming from company-owned outlets. Dual distribution often creates channel conflict.

The use of middlemen largely boils down to their superior efficiency in making goods widely available and accessible to target markets. Marketing intermediaries, through their contacts, experience, specialization, and scale of operation, offer the firm more than it can usually achieve on its own.

From the point of view of the economic system, the basic role of marketing intermediaries is to transform the heterogeneous supplies found in nature into assortments of goods that people want to buy. According to Stern and El-Ansary:

> Intermediaries smooth the flow of goods and services. . . . This procedure is necessary in order to bridge the discrepancy between the assortment of goods and services generated by the producer and the assortment demanded by the consumer. The discrepancy results from the fact that manufacturers typically produce a large quantity of a limited variety of goods, whereas consumers usually desire only a limited quantity of a wide variety of goods.[3]

Wroe Alderson made the same point: "The goal of marketing is the matching of segments of supply and demand."[4]

Figure 19-1 shows one major source of economies effected by using middlemen. Part (a) shows three producers, each using direct marketing to reach three customers. This system requires nine different contacts. Part (b) shows the three producers working through one distributor, who contacts the three customers. This system requires only six contacts. In this way, middlemen reduce the amount of work that must be done.

Marketing-Channel Functions and Flows

A marketing channel performs the work of moving goods from producers to consumers. It overcomes the time, place, and possession gaps that separate goods and services from those who would use them. Members in the marketing channel perform a number of key functions and participate in the following marketing flows:

- *Information:* The collection and dissemination of marketing research information about potential and current customers, competitors, and other actors and forces in the marketing environment.

- *Promotion:* The development and dissemination of persuasive communications about the offer designed to attract customers.

FIGURE 19-1
How a Distributor Effects an Economy of Effort

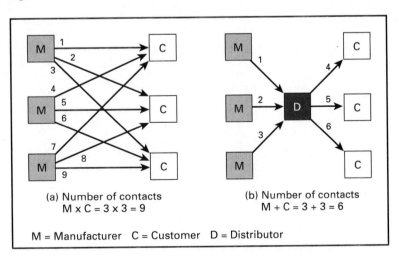

(a) Number of contacts
M x C = 3 x 3 = 9

(b) Number of contacts
M + C = 3 + 3 = 6

M = Manufacturer   C = Customer   D = Distributor

- □ *Negotiation:* The attempt to reach final agreement on price and other terms so that transfer of ownership or possession can be effected.
- □ *Ordering:* The backward communication of intentions to buy by the marketing-channel members to the manufacturer.
- □ *Financing:* The acquisition and allocation of funds required to finance inventories at different levels of the marketing channel.
- □ *Risk Taking:* The assumption of risks connected with carrying out the channel work.
- □ *Physical Possession:* The successive storage and movement of physical products from raw materials to the final customers.
- □ *Payment:* Buyers paying their bills through banks and other financial institutions to the sellers.
- □ *Title:* The actual transfer of ownership from one organization or person to another.

These functions and flows are listed in the normal order in which they arise between any two channel members. Some of these flows are *forward flows* (physical, title, and promotion); others are backward flows (ordering and payment); and still others move in *both directions* (information, negotiation, finance, and risk taking). Five of these flows are illustrated in Figure 19-2 for the marketing of forklifts. If all of these flows were superimposed in one diagram, the tremendous complexity of even simple marketing channels would be apparent.

FIGURE 19-2

Five Different Marketing Flows in the Marketing Channel for Forklift Trucks

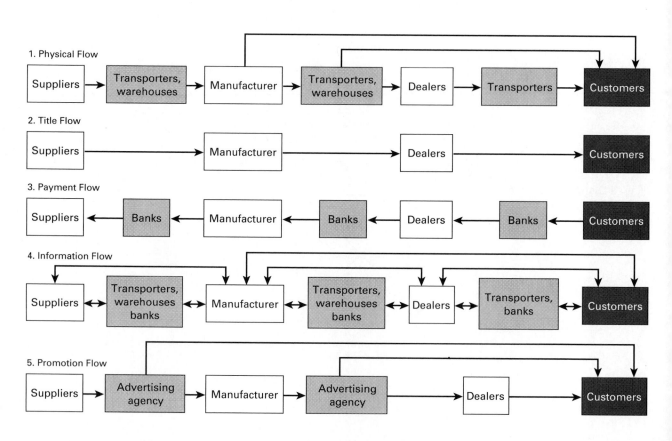

The question is not *whether* these functions need to be performed—they must be—but rather *who* is to perform them. All of the functions have three things in common: They use up scarce resources; they can often be performed better through specialization; and they are shiftable among channel members. To the extent that the manufacturer performs the functions, the manufacturer's costs go up, and its prices must be higher. When some functions are shifted to middlemen, the producer's costs and prices are lower, but the middlemen must add a charge to cover their work. If the middlemen are more efficient than the manufacturer, the prices faced by consumers should be lower. Consumers might decide to perform some of the functions themselves, in which case they should enjoy lower prices. The issue of who should perform various channel tasks is one of relative efficiency and effectiveness.

Marketing functions, then, are more basic than the institutions that at any given time perform them. Changes in channel institutions largely reflect the discovery of more efficient ways to combine or separate economic functions that must be carried on to provide meaningful assortments of goods to target customers.

Number of Channel Levels

Marketing channels can be characterized by the number of channel levels. Each middleman that performs some work in bringing the product and its title closer to the final buyer constitutes a *channel level*. Since the producer and the final customer both perform some work, they are part of every channel. We will use the number of *intermediary levels* to designate the *length* of a channel. Figure 19-3(a) illustrates several consumer-goods marketing channels of different lengths.

A *zero-level channel* (also called a *direct-marketing channel*) consists of a manufacturer selling directly to the final customer. The four major ways of direct marketing are door to door, home parties, mail order, and manufacturer-owned stores. Avon's sales representatives sell cosmetics to women on a door-to-door basis; Tupperware representatives sell kitchen goods through home parties; *Maclean's* sells magazine subscriptions through mail order; and Bata sells shoes through company-owned stores.

A *one-level channel* contains one selling intermediary, such as a retailer. A *two-level channel* contains two intermediaries. In consumer markets, they are typically a wholesaler and a retailer. A *three-level channel* contains three intermediaries. For example, in the meat-packing industry, wholesalers sell to jobbers, who sell to small retailers.

Higher-level marketing channels are also found but with less frequency. From the producer's point of view, the problem of obtaining information about the end users and exercising control increases with the number of channel levels, even though the manufacturer typically deals only with the adjacent level.

Figure 19-3(b) shows channels commonly used in industrial marketing. An industrial-goods manufacturer can use its salesforce to sell directly to industrial customers. Or it can sell to industrial distributors who sell to the industrial customers. Or it can sell through manufacturer's representatives or its own sales branches directly to industrial customers, or use them to sell through industrial distributors. Thus zero-, one-, and two-level marketing channels are quite common in industrial marketing channels.

Channels normally describe a forward movement of products. One can also talk about *backward channels*. According to Zikmund and Stanton:

> The recycling of solid wastes is a major ecological goal. Although recycling is technologically feasible, reversing the flow of materials in the channel of distribution—marketing trash through a "backward" channel—presents a challenge. Existing backward channels are primitive, and financial incentives are inadequate. The consumer must be motivated to undergo a role change and become a producer—the initiating force in the reverse distribution process.[5]

FIGURE 19-3
Consumer and Industrial Marketing Channels

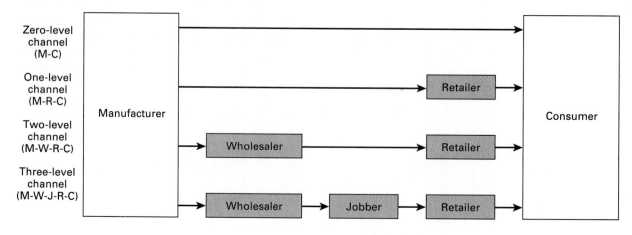

(a) Consumer marketing channels

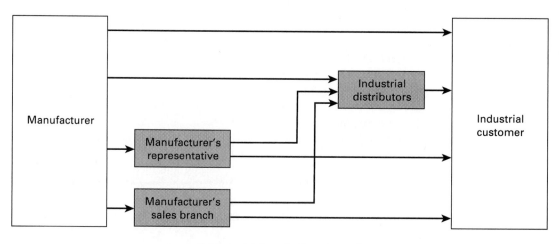

(b) Industrial marketing channels

The backward channel for recycling can be relatively simple for high-volume products. For example, Laidlaw Waste Systems' recycling division provides a distribution channel for products like cans and glass containers, that they collect from households for end-user companies like Dofasco, Alcan, and Consumers Glass. But other products like newsprint and cardboard may require the services of a broker. Other potential middlemen include recycling centers, processing warehouses, and specialists like Brewers' Retail stores that accept used beer bottles in Ontario.

Channels in the Service Sector

The concept of marketing channels is not limited to the distribution of physical goods. Producers of services and ideas also face the problem of making their output *available* and *accessible* to target populations. They develop "educational-dissemination systems" and "health-delivery systems." They must figure out agencies and locations for reaching a spatially distributed population:

> Hospitals must be located in geographic space to serve the people with complete medical care, and we must build schools close to the children who have to learn. Fire stations must be located to give rapid access to potential conflagrations, and voting booths must be placed so that people can cast their ballots without expending unreasonable amounts of time, effort, or money to reach the polling stations.[6]

Marketing channels also are used in "person" marketing. Before 1940, professional comedians could reach audiences through seven channels: vaudeville houses, special events, nightclubs, radio, movies, carnivals, and theatres. In the 1950s, television emerged as a strong channel, and vaudeville disappeared. Politicians also must find cost-effective channels—mass media, rallies, coffee hours—for distributing their messages to voters.[7]

CHANNEL-DESIGN DECISIONS

We will now examine several channel-decision problems facing manufacturers. In designing marketing channels, manufacturers have to struggle between what is ideal, what is feasible, and what is available. A new firm typically starts as a local operation selling in a limited market. Since it has limited capital, it usually uses existing middlemen. The number of middlemen in any local market is apt to be limited: A few manufacturer's sales agents, a few wholesalers, several established retailers, a few trucking companies, and a few warehouses. Deciding on the best channels might not be a problem. The problem might be to convince one or a few available middlemen to handle their line.

If the new firm is successful, it might branch out to new markets. Again, the manufacturer will tend to work through the existing intermediaries, although that might mean using different types of marketing channels in different areas. In the smaller markets, the firm might sell directly to retailers; in the larger markets, it might sell through distributors. In rural areas, it might work with general-goods merchants; in urban areas, with limited-line merchants. In one part of the country, it might grant exclusive franchises, because the merchants normally work this way; in another, it might sell through all outlets willing to handle the merchandise. Thus the manufacturer's channel system evolves in response to local opportunities and conditions.

Designing a channel system calls for analyzing customer needs, establishing channel objectives, identifying the major channel alternatives, and evaluating them.

Analyzing Service Output Levels Desired by Customers

Understanding what, where, why, when, and how target customers buy is the first step in designing the marketing channel. The marketer must understand the *service output levels* desired by the target customers. Channels produce five service outputs:

☐ *Lot Size:* The lot size is the number of units that the marketing channel permits a typical customer to buy on a buying occasion. In buying cars for its fleet, Tilden prefers a channel from which it can buy a large lot size; and a household wants a channel that would permit buying a lot size of one. Obviously different channels must be set up for fleet car buyers and household buyers. The smaller the lot size, the greater the service output level that the channel must provide.

- □ *Waiting Time:* Waiting time is the average time that customers of that channel wait for receipt of the goods. Customers normally prefer fast delivery channels. Faster service requires a great service output level.

- □ *Spatial Convenience:* Spatial convenience expresses the degree to which the marketing channel makes it easy for customers to purchase the product. Chevrolet, for example, offers greater spatial convenience than Cadillac, in that there are a much greater number of Chevrolet dealers. Chevrolet's greater market decentralization helps customers save on transportation and search costs in buying and repairing an automobile. Spatial convenience is being further augmented by the use of direct marketing.

- □ *Product Variety:* Product variety represents the assortment breadth provided by the marketing channel. Normally customers prefer greater assortment breadth because it increases the chance of exactly meeting their need. Thus car buyers would rather buy from a dealership carrying multiple manufacturer brands than only one manufacturer's brand.

- □ *Service Backup:* Service backup represents the add-on services (credit, delivery, installation, repairs) provided by the channel. The greater the service backup, the greater the work provided by the channel.[8]

The marketing-channel designer must know the service outputs desired by the target customers. Providing increased levels of service outputs means increased costs for the channel and higher prices for customers. The success of discount stores indicates that many consumers are willing to accept lower-service outputs when this translates into lower prices.

Establishing the Channel Objectives and Constraints

The channel objectives should be stated in terms of targeted service output levels. According to Bucklin, under competitive conditions, channel institutions should arrange their functional tasks so as to minimize total channel costs with respect to some desired levels of service outputs.[9] Usually, several segments can be identified that desire differing service output levels. Effective channel planning requires manufacturers to determine which market segments to serve and the best channels to use in each case. Each producer develops its channel objectives in the face of constraints stemming from products, intermediaries, competitors, company policies, the environment, and the level of service outputs desired by the target customers.

Product Characteristics   *Perishable* products require more direct marketing because of the dangers associated with delays and repeated handling. *Bulky* products, such as building materials or soft drinks, require channels that minimize the shipping distance and the number of handlings in the movement from producer to consumers. *Nonstandardized* products, such as custom-built machinery and specialized business forms, are sold directly by company sales representatives because middlemen lack the requisite knowledge. Products requiring installation and/or maintenance services are usually sold and maintained by the company or exclusively franchised dealers. *High unit value* products are often sold through a company salesforce rather than through middlemen.

Middlemen Characteristics   Channel design reflects the strengths and weaknesses of different types of intermediaries in handling various tasks. For example, manufacturers' representatives are able to contact customers at a low cost per customer because the total cost is shared by several clients. But the selling effort per customer is less intense than if the company's sales representatives did the selling. In general, marketing intermediaries differ in their aptitude for handling promotion, negotiation, storage, contact, and credit.

Competitive Characteristics   Channel design is influenced by the competitors' channels. The producers may want to compete in or near the same outlets carrying the competitors' products. Thus food processors want their brands to be displayed next to competitive brands; and Burger King wants to locate next to McDonald's. In other industries, producers may want to avoid the channels used by competitors. Avon decided not to compete with other cosmetics manufacturers for scarce space in retail stores and established instead a profitable door-to-door selling operation.

Company Characteristics   Company characteristics play an important role in channel design. The company's channel design is affected by its long-run objectives, resources, product mix, and marketing strategy.

Environmental Characteristics   When *economic conditions* are depressed, producers want to move their goods to market in the most economical way. This means using shorter channels and dispensing with non-essential services that add to the final price of the goods. *Legal regulations and restrictions* also affect channel design. The law looks unfavorably upon channel arrangements that "may tend to substantially lessen competition or tend to create a monopoly."

Identifying the Major Channel Alternatives

After a company has defined its target market and desired positioning, it should identify its channel alternatives. A channel alternative is described by three elements: the *types of business intermediaries*, the *number of intermediaries*, and the *terms and responsibilities of each channel participant*.

Types of Intermediaries   The firm should identify the types of intermediaries available to carry on its channel work. Here are two examples:

A test-equipment manufacturer developed an audio device for detecting poor mechanical connections in machines with moving parts. The company executives felt that this product would sell in all industries where electric, combustion, or steam engines were used, such as aviation, automobiles, railroads, food canning, construction, and oil. The company's salesforce was small. The problem was how to reach these diverse industries effectively. The following channel alternatives were identified: ■

☐ *Company Salesforce:* Expand the company's direct salesforce. Assign sales representatives to territories to contact all prospects in the area. Or develop separate salesforces for the different industries.

☐ *Manufacturer's Agency:* Hire manufacturer's agencies in different regions or end-use industries to sell the new test equipment.

☐ *Industrial Distributors:* Find distributors in the different regions and/or end-use industries who will buy and carry the audio device. Give them exclusive distribution, adequate margins, product training, and promotional support. ■

A consumer electronics company produces FM car radios. It identified the following channel alternatives:

☐ *Manufacturer Market:* The company could sell its radios to automobile original-equipment-manufacturers (OEMs) to be installed as original equipment.

☐ *Auto-Dealer Market:* The company could sell its radios to auto dealers for replacement sales when they service cars.

□ *Retail Automotive-Parts Dealers:* The company could sell its radios to retail automotive-parts dealers. They could reach these dealers through a direct salesforce or through distributors.

□ *Mail-Order Market:* The company could advertise its radios in mail-order catalogs. ■

Companies should also search for innovative marketing channels. The Conn Organ Company merchandised organs through department and discount stores, thus drawing more attention than organs ever enjoyed in small music stores. The Book-of-the-Month Club merchandised books through the mails. Other sellers followed with record-of-the-month clubs, candy-of-the-month clubs, and dozens of others.

Sometimes a company has to develop a channel other than the one it prefers because of the difficulty or cost of working with the preferred channel. The decision sometimes turns out extremely well. For example, the Timex people originally tried to sell their inexpensive watches through regular jewelry stores. But most jewelry stores refused to carry them. The company looked for other channels and managed to get its watches into mass-merchandise outlets. This turned out to be a great decision because of the rapid growth of mass merchandising. Similarly, Avon chose to do door-to-door cosmetics selling as a result of not being able to break into regular department stores. It not only mastered door-to-door selling but made more money than most cosmetics firms that sold through department stores.

Number of Intermediaries   Companies have to decide on the number of middlemen to use at each channel level. Three strategies are available.

Intensive Distribution   Producers of convenience goods and common raw materials typically seek *intensive distribution*—that is, stocking their product in numerous outlets. These goods must have place utility. Cigarettes, for example, are sold by many thousands of retailers to create maximum consumer convenience.

Selective Distribution   Between intensive and exclusive distribution stands *selective distribution*—the use of more than one but less than all of the intermediaries who are willing to carry a particular product. It is used both by established companies and by new companies seeking to obtain distributors by promising them selective distribution. The company does not have to dissipate its efforts over many outlets, including many marginal ones. It can develop a good working relation with the selected middlemen and expect a better than average selling effort. Selective distribution enables the producer to gain adequate market coverage with more control and less cost than intensive distribution.

Exclusive Distribution   Some producers limit the number of intermediaries handling their products. The extreme form is *exclusive distribution*, where only certain dealers can distribute the company's products. It often goes with *exclusive dealing*, where these dealers must not carry competing lines. Exclusive distribution is found in the distribution of new automobiles, some major appliances, and some women's apparel brands. Through granting exclusive distribution, the manufacturer hopes to obtain more aggressive and knowledgeable selling and more control over intermediaries' policies on prices, promotion, credit, and various services. Exclusive distribution tends to enhance the product's image and allow higher markups.

Terms and Responsibilities of Channel Members   The producer must determine the conditions and responsibilities of the participating channel members. The main elements in the "trade-relations mix" are *price policies, conditions of sale, territorial rights*, and *specific services to be performed by each party*.

Price policy calls for the producer to establish a price list and schedule of discounts. The middlemen must see these as equitable and sufficient.

Conditions of sale refer to payment terms and producer guarantees. Most producers grant cash discounts to their distributors for early payment. Producers might also guarantee distributors against defective merchandise or price declines. A guarantee against price declines induces distributors to buy larger quantities.

Distributors' territorial rights are another element in the trade-relations mix. Distributors want to know where the producer will enfranchise other distributors. They would also like to receive full credit for all sales taking place in their territory, whether or not they did the selling.

Mutual services and responsibilities must be carefully spelled out, especially in franchised and exclusive-agency channels. Canadian Tire, for example, provides its franchisees with a building, promotional and administrative support, training, and quick access to competitively-priced merchandise. In return, franchisees are expected to purchase an adequate level of inventory, and satisfy company standards regarding physical facilities, employee training and promotional programs.

Evaluating the Major Channel Alternatives

Suppose a producer has identified several channel alternatives and wants to determine the best one. Each alternative needs to be evaluated against *economic, control*, and *adaptive criteria*. Consider the following situation:

> A Winnipeg furniture manufacturer wants to sell its line to retailers in the Atlantic provinces. The manufacturer is trying to decide between two alternatives:
>
> 1. One alternative calls for hiring two new *sales representatives*, who would operate out of a sales office in Halifax. They would receive a base salary plus commissions based on their sales.
>
> 2. The other alternative would use a Halifax manufacturer's *sales agency* that has extensive contacts with retailers. The agency has six sales representatives, who would receive a commission based on their sales. ■

Economic Criteria   Each channel alternative will produce a different level of sales and costs. The first question is whether more sales will be produced through a company salesforce or through a sales agency. Most marketing managers believe that a company salesforce will sell more. Company sales representatives concentrate entirely on the company's products; they are better trained to sell the company's products; they are more aggressive, because their future depends on the company's success; they are more successful, because many customers prefer to deal directly with the company.

On the other hand, the sales agency could conceivably sell more than a company salesforce. First, the sales agent has six sales representatives, not just two. Second, the agency's salesforce might be just as aggressive as a direct salesforce. That depends on how much commission the company offers. Third, some customers prefer dealing with agents who represent several manufacturers rather than with salespersons from one company. Fourth, the agency has extensive contacts, whereas a company salesforce would have to build them from scratch.

The next step is to estimate the costs of selling different volumes through each channel. The cost schedules are shown in Figure 19-4. The fixed costs of engaging a sales agency are lower than those of establishing a company sales office. But costs rise faster through a sales agency, because sales agents get a larger commission than company salespeople.

FIGURE 19-4
Break-Even Cost Chart for the
Choice between a Company
Salesforce and a Manufacturer's
Sales Agency

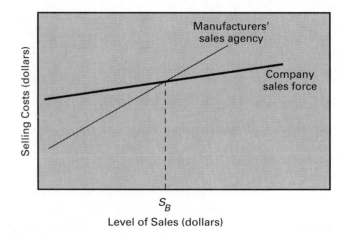

There is one sales level (S_B) at which selling costs are the same for the two channels. The sales agency is the preferred channel for any sales volume below S_B, and the company sales branch is preferred at any volume higher than S_B. Not surprisingly, sales agents tend to be used by smaller firms, or by large firms in their smaller territories wherever the sales volume is too low to warrant a company salesforce.

Control Criteria   Channel evaluation must be broadened to include control issues. Using a sales agency poses a control problem. A sales agency is an independent business firm seeking to maximize its profits. The agents may concentrate on the customers who buy the most, not necessarily of the manufacturer's goods. Furthermore, the agents might not master the technical details of the company's product or handle its promotion materials effectively.

Adaptive Criteria   Each channel involves some duration of commitment and loss of flexibility. A manufacturer seeking a sales agency might have to offer a five-year contract. During this period, other means of selling, such as direct mail, might become more effective, but the manufacturer is not free to drop the sales agency. A channel requiring a long commitment needs to be greatly superior on economic or control grounds to be considered.

CHANNEL-MANAGEMENT DECISIONS

After a company has chosen a channel alternative, individual middlemen must be *selected*, *motivated*, and *evaluated*. Also, channel arrangements must be modified over time.

Selecting Channel Members

Producers vary in their ability to attract qualified middlemen within the chosen channel. Some producers have no trouble recruiting middlemen. For example, Ford was able to attract twelve hundred new dealers for its ill-fated Edsel. In some cases, the promise of exclusive or selective distribution will draw a sufficient number of applicants.

At the other extreme are producers who have to work hard to get qualified middlemen. When Polaroid started, it could not get photographic-equipment stores to carry its new cameras and was forced to use mass-merchandising outlets. Small food producers normally find it hard to get grocery stores to carry their products. Equipment manufacturers often find it hard to locate qualified distributors and dealers (see the exhibit Companies and Industries 19-1).

Whether producers find it easy or difficult to recruit middlemen, they should at least determine what characteristics distinguish the better middlemen. They will want to evaluate the middlemen's number of years in business, the other lines carried, growth and profit record, solvency, cooperativeness, and reputation. If the middlemen are sales agents, producers will want to evaluate the number and character of other lines carried and the size and quality of the salesforce. If the middlemen are department stores that want exclusive distribution, the producer will want to evaluate the stores' locations, future growth potential, and type of clientele.

Companies and Industries 19-1

BUILDING A DISTRIBUTOR TEAM FOR EPSON PRODUCTS

Japan's Epson Corporation, a leading manufacturer of computer printers, was preparing to expand its product line to include computers. Not happy with its current distributors nor trusting their ability to sell to new types of retail outlets, Epson's general manager, Jack Whalen, decided to secretly recruit new distributors to replace the existing ones. Whalen hired Hergenrather & Company, a recruiting company, and gave the following instructions:

- Search for applicants who have two-step distribution experience (factory to distributor to dealer) in either brown goods (TVs, and so on) or white goods (refrigerators, etc.).

- The applicants have to be CEO types who would be willing and able to set up their own distributorships.

- They will be offered $80 000 yearly salary plus bonus, $375 000 to help them set up in business; each will add $25 000 of his own money, and each would get equity in the business.

- They will handle only Epson products but may stock other companies' software. Each distributor would have a training manager and a fully equipped service center.

The recruiting firm had a hard time finding qualified and motivated prospects. Their want ads in business newspapers (which did not mention the company's name) pulled almost seventeen hundred letters but mostly from unqualified people looking for jobs. Then the firm used the Yellow Pages to get the names of present distributors and phoned the second-in-command managers. It arranged interviews and, after much work, produced a list of highly qualified individuals. Whalen interviewed them and chose the twelve most-qualified candidates for his twelve distributor areas. The recruiting agency was paid $250 000 for its recruiting effort.

The final step called for terminating Epson's existing distributors. These distributors had no inkling of this development, since the recruitment was conducted in secrecy. Jack Whalen gave them a ninety-day notice of the changeover. They were of course shocked, having worked with Epson as its first distributors. But they had no contracts. Whalen knew they lacked the ability to handle Epson's expanded computer product line and reach the required new distribution channels. He saw no other way to do this.

Source: Arthur Bragg, "Undercover Recruiting: Epson America's Sly Distributor Switch," *Sales and Marketing Management*, March 11, 1985, pp. 45-49.

Motivating Channel Members

Middlemen must be continuously motivated to do their best job. The terms that lead them to join the channel provide some motivation, but these must be supplemented by training, supervision, and encouragement. The producer must not only sell *through* the middlemen but also *to* them.

Stimulating channel members to top performance must start with understanding of the middlemen's needs and wants. McVey listed the following propositions to help understand middlemen:

> [The middleman often acts] as a purchasing agent for his customers and only secondarily as a selling agent for his suppliers. . . . He is interested in selling any product which these customers desire to buy from him. . . .
>
> The middleman attempts to weld all of his offerings into a family of items which he can sell in combination, as a packaged assortment, to individual customers. His selling efforts are directed primarily at obtaining orders for the assortment, rather than for individual items. . . .
>
> Unless given incentive to do so, middlemen will not maintain separate sales records by brands sold. . . . Information that could be used in product development, pricing, packaging, or promotion planning is buried in nonstandard records of middlemen, and sometimes purposely secreted from suppliers.[10]

Producers vary greatly in how they manage their distributors. Essentially, they can draw on different types of power to gain cooperation (see Marketing Concepts and Tools 19-1). They can aim for achieving a relationship based on *cooperation, partnership*, or *distribution programming*.[11]

Most producers see the problem as that of gaining middlemen *cooperation*. They will use the carrot-and-stick approach. They will use positive motivators, such as higher margins, special deals, premiums, cooperative advertising allowances, display allowances, and sales contests. At times they will apply negative sanctions, such as threatening to reduce the margins, slow down delivery, or terminate the relationship. The weakness of this approach is that the producer has not really studied the middlemen's needs, problems, strengths, and weaknesses. Instead, the producer applies miscellaneous motivators based on crude stimulus-response thinking. McCammon notes that many manufacturer programs "consist of hastily improvised trade deals, uninspired dealer contests, and unexamined discount structures."[12]

More sophisticated companies try to forge a long-term *partnership* with their distributors. The manufacturer develops a clear sense of what it wants from its distributors in the way of market coverage, inventory levels, marketing development, account solicitation, technical advice and services, and marketing information. The manufacturer seeks distributor agreement with these policies and may introduce a *functional compensation plan* for adhering to the policies:

> A dental supply company, instead of paying a straight 35 percent sales commission to its distributors, pays 20 percent for carrying out its basic sales work, another 5 percent for carrying a 60-day inventory, another 5 percent for paying its bills on time, and another 5 percent for reporting customer purchase information. ∎

Distribution programming is the most advanced arrangement. McCammon defines this as building a planned, professionally managed, vertical marketing system that incorporates the needs of both the manufacturer and the distributors.[13] The manufacturer establishes a department within the company called distributor-relations planning, and its job is to identify the

Marketing Concepts and Tools 19-1

FIVE BASES OF POWER FOR MANAGING CHANNEL RELATIONSHIPS

Manufacturers need to draw on some source of power to gain middleman cooperation. *Power* is the ability of one channel member to get another channel member to do something that might not be done otherwise. French and Raven distinguished among five bases of power: coercive, reward, legitimate, expert, and referent.

Coercive power would be represented by the manufacturer's threatening to withdraw some resource or terminate the relationship if the middlemen fail to cooperate. This power is quite effective if the middlemen are highly dependent upon the manufacturer. But the exercise of coercive power produces resentment and can lead the middlemen to organize countervailing power. While coercive power may be effective in the short run, it is usually the least effective type of power to use in the long run.

Reward power would occur if the manufacturer offers some extra benefit for the performance of specific acts by middlemen. Reward power typically produces better results than coercive power but can be overrated. The middlemen are conforming to the manufacturer's wishes not out of intrinsic conviction but because of an external benefit. They will grow to expect a reward every time the manufacturer wants a certain behavior to occur. If the reward is later withdrawn, the middlemen feel cheated.

Legitimate power is wielded when the manufacturer requests a behavior as warranted by the hierarchical relationship and contract. Thus General Motors may insist that its dealers carry certain inventory levels as part of the franchise agreement. The manufacturer feels it has this right and the middleman has this obligation. As long as the middlemen view the manufacturer as a legitimate leader, legitimate power works.

Expert power can be applied by the manufacturer, who has special knowledge that is valued by the middlemen. For example, a manufacturer may have a sophisticated system for locating leads for middlemen or giving expert training to the middlemen's salesforces. This is an effective form of power, since the middlemen would perform poorly if they couldn't get this help from the manufacturer. The problem is that once the expertise is passed on to the middlemen, this basis of power weakens. The solution is that the manufacturer must continue to develop new expertise so that the middlemen will be eager to continue cooperating with the manufacturer.

Referent power occurs when the manufacturer is so highly respected that middlemen are proud to be identified with him. Companies such as IBM, Caterpillar, Procter & Gamble, and Xerox have high referent power, and middlemen are normally ready to go along with their wishes.

To the extent possible, manufacturers will gain cooperation best if they cultivate referent power, expert power, legitimate power, and reward power, in that order, and generally avoid the use of coercive power.

Source: These bases of power were first identified in John R. P. French and Bertram Raven, "The Bases of Social Power," in Dorwin Cartwright, ed. *Studies in Social Power* (Ann Arbor: University of Michigan Press, 1959) pp. 150-67.

---

distributors' needs and build up merchandising programs so each distributor operates as close to optimal as possible. This department and the distributors jointly plan the merchandising goals, inventory levels, space and visual merchandising plans, sales-training requirements, and advertising and promotion plans. The aim is to convert the distributors from thinking that they make their money primarily on the buying side (through tough negotiation with the manufacturer) to seeing that they make their money on the selling side by being part of a sophisticated vertical marketing system.

Too many manufacturers think of their distributors and dealers as their customers rather than their working partners. Marketing Strategies 19-1 describes the various mechanisms progressive manufacturers use to convert their distributors into partners.

Evaluating Channel Members

The producer must periodically evaluate middlemen's performance against such standards as sales-quota attainment, average inventory levels, customer delivery time, treatment of damaged and lost goods, cooperation in promotional and training programs, and middlemen services owed to the customer.

The producer will discover on occasion that too much is being paid to particular middlemen for what they are actually doing. One manufacturer discovered that he was compensating a distributor for holding inventories in his warehouse but the inventories were actually being held in a public warehouse at the manufacturer's expense. Producers must periodically review whether they are overcompensating certain middlemen or channels for the actual services they are rendering.

Underperforming middlemen need to be counseled. They may need more training or motivation. If they do not shape up, however, it might be better to terminate their services.

Marketing Strategies 19-1

TURNING INDUSTRIAL DISTRIBUTORS INTO BUSINESS PARTNERS

Narus and Anderson interviewed several manufacturers who enjoyed excellent working relations with their distributors to discover the channel attitudes and practices that contributed to the successful relations. Here are some of the partner-building practices they found:

1. Timken Corporation (roller bearings) has its sales representatives make *multilevel calls* on distributors, including their general managers, purchasing managers, and sales personnel.

2. Square D (circuit breakers, switchboards) has its sales representatives spend a day with each distributor, "*working the counter*" in order to understand the distributor's business.

3. Du Pont has established a *Distributor Marketing Steering Committee*, which meets to regularly discuss problems and trends.

4. Dayco Corporation (engineered plastics and rubber products) runs an *annual week-long retreat* with twenty young distributors' executives and twenty young Dayco executives interacting in seminars and outings.

5. Parker Hannifin Corporation (fluid-power products) sends out an *annual mail survey* asking its distributors to rate the corporation's performance on key dimensions. It also informs its distributors about new products and applications through *newsletters and videotapes.* It collects and analyzes *photocopies of distributors' invoices* and advises distributors on how to improve their sales.

6. Cherry Electrical Products (electrical switches and electronic keyboards) appointed a distributor marketing manager who works with distributors to produce *formal distributor marketing plans.* The company also operates a *rapid response system* to distributor calls by assigning two inside sales people to each distributor.

These are a few ways that progressive manufacturers have successfully turned their distributors into working partners.

Source: See James A. Narus and James C. Anderson, "Turn Your Industrial Distributors into Partners," *Harvard Business Review,* March-April 1986, pp. 66-71.

Modifying Channel Arrangements

A producer must do more than design a good channel system and set it into motion. The system will require periodic modification to meet new conditions in the marketplace. Modification becomes necessary when consumer buying patterns change, markets expand, products mature, new competition arises, and new, innovative distribution channels emerge (see Marketing Strategies 19-2).

This fact struck a large appliance manufacturer who had been marketing exclusively through franchised dealers and was losing market share. Several distribution developments had taken place since the original channel was designed:

☐ An increasing share of branded major appliances was being merchandised through discount houses.

☐ An increasing share of unbranded major appliances was being sold by department stores as private brands.

☐ Tract home builders increasingly wanted to buy directly from manufacturers.

☐ Door-to-door selling and direct mail were increasingly being used by dealers and competitors.

☐ The only strong independent dealers were located in small towns, but rural families were increasingly making their purchases in large cities.

These developments led this manufacturer to undertake a major overhaul of his channels.

Three levels of channel modification can be distinguished. The change could involve *adding or dropping individual channel members, adding or dropping particular market channels,* or *developing a totally new way to sell goods in all markets.*

Adding or dropping specific middlemen requires an incremental analysis. What would the firm's profits look like with and without this middleman? An automobile manufacturer's decision to drop a dealer would require subtracting the dealer's sales and estimating the possible loss or gain of sales to the manufacturer's other dealers.

Sometimes a producer contemplates dropping all middlemen whose sales are below a certain amount. Thus, a truck manufacturer noted that 5 percent of its dealers were selling fewer than three or four trucks a year. It cost the company more to service these dealers than their sales were worth. However, the decision to drop these dealers could have large repercussions on the system as a whole. The unit costs of producing trucks would be higher, since the overhead would be spread over fewer trucks; some employees and equipment would be idled; some business in these markets would go to competitors; and other dealers might become insecure. All of this would have to be taken into account.

The most difficult decision involves revising the overall channel strategy.[14] For example, an automobile manufacturer might replace independent dealers with company-owned dealers; a soft-drink manufacturer might consider replacing local franchised bottlers with centralized bottling and direct sales. These decisions would require revising most of the marketing mix and would have profound consequences (see Marketing Concepts and Tools 19-2).

CHANNEL DYNAMICS

Distribution channels do not stand still. New wholesaling and retailing institutions emerge, and new channel systems evolve. Here we will look at the recent growth of vertical, horizontal, and multichannel marketing systems and see how these systems cooperate, conflict, and compete.

How Companies Change Their Marketing Channels Over the Product Life Cycle

No marketing channel can be trusted to remain competitively dominant over the whole product life cycle. Early adopters might be willing to pay for high value-added channels, but later buyers will switch to lower-cost channels. Thus small office copiers were first sold by manufacturers' direct salesforces, later through office-equipment dealers, still later through mass merchandisers, and now by mail-order firms. Insurance companies that persist in using independent agents and auto companies that use independent dealers will face strong competition from new, lower-cost channels, and their reluctance to change might prove fatal in the long run.

Miland Lele developed the following grid to show how marketing channels have changed for PCs and designer clothing at different stages in the product life cycle:

□ *Introductory Stage:* Radically new products or fashions tend to enter the market through specialist channels (such as hobbyist shops, boutiques) that spot trends and attract early adopters.

□ *Rapid Growth Stage:* As buyers' interest grows, higher-volume channels appear (dedicated chains, department stores) that offer services but not as many as the previous channels offered.

□ *Maturity Stage:* As growth slows down, some competitors move their product into lower-cost channels (mass merchandisers).

□ *Decline Stage:* As the decline begins, even lower-cost channels emerge (mail-order houses, off-price discounters).

The earliest channels face the challenge of market creation; they are high cost because they must search for and educate buyers. They are followed by channels that expand the market and offer sufficient services. In the maturity stage, many buyers want lower costs, and they patronize lower value-added channels. Finally, the remaining potential buyers can be reached only by creating very low prices in low, value-added channels.

Source: See Miland M. Lele, "Change Channels during Your Product's Life Cycle," *Business Marketing*, December 1986, p. 64.

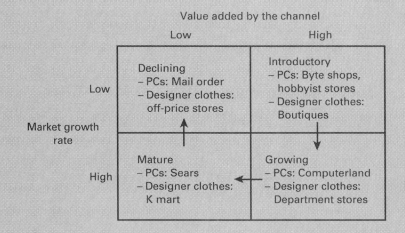

Marketing Concepts and Tools 19-2

MODIFYING EXISTING DISTRIBUTION SYSTEMS TOWARD THE IDEAL

Distribution channels can become outmoded with the passage of time. A gap arises between a seller's *existing distribution system* and the *ideal system* that would satisfy target customers' needs and desires. Examples of this abound: Avon's door-to-door system for selling cosmetics had to be modified as more women entered the workforce; IBM's exclusive reliance on a field salesforce had to be modified with the introduction of low-valued personal computers.

Yet distribution systems, in contrast to advertising budgets, prices, and sales-promotion programs, are very difficult to change. The company has built up long-standing relations with distributors and dealers, and replacing them is bound to meet resistance if not sabotage. To deal with this problem, Stern and Sturdivant have outlined an eight-step process for moving an obsolescent distribution system closer to target customers' ideal system.

The first step calls for finding out what target customers want in the way of channel services if no constraints existed. Customers would specify the lot size, convenience, amount of time they were willing to wait, product variety, and service backup they want. They would indicate the importance of various services and the tradeoffs they would make.

Step two consists of designing alternative distribution systems that would provide these services. Thus investors might be asked to evaluate buying stock through brokers, over the phone, through a computer linkup, and so on. Their responses will provide a picture of which distribution systems are favored by which customer segments.

Step three requires evaluating the feasibility and cost of the contending ideal distribution systems. It might be discovered, for example, that offering a computer-linked system of stock trading would cost too much or be unsupportable by current technologies.

Step four involves gathering company executives' objectives for the company's distribution system. At this point, some executives will insist on certain principles that must be observed: a brokerage company should not offer discount brokerage; an auto company should not compromise independent franchised dealerships; a paper company should not circumvent long-standing relationships with paper merchants in order to sell directly to discount chains.

Step five calls for comparing the available options given management's criteria on the one hand and the customer ideal distribution system on the other. One of three situations could emerge. The best would be where the ideal system, the management-bounded system, and the existing system closely resemble each other, in which case any customer dissatisfaction is probably the fault of poor implementation rather than poor distribution-system design. A second possibility is that the existing and management-bounded systems are similar but differ substantially from the ideal. If the gap is to be closed, then management must reconsider its constraints. A third possibility is that all three systems may differ substantially. In this case, there are two gaps to close before the distribution system can become customer driven.

The sixth step is to ask management and selected experts to review management's key assumptions. Management should know the costs of their assumptions and constraints as well as the gains and risks of changing them.

The seventh step calls for asking management to confront the gap between the existing and the ideal management system and to agree on what changes they are willing to make.

Step eight involves preparing a plan to implement the agreed-upon changes. If possible, changes on a small scale might be introduced to identify any positive or negative effects that might have been overlooked.

This eight-step process will not necessarily lead to modifying the company's existing distribution system.

Growth of Vertical Marketing Systems

One of the most significant recent channel developments consists of *vertical marketing systems*, which have emerged to challenge *conventional marketing channels*. A conventional marketing channel comprises an independent producer; wholesaler(s), and retailer(s). Each is a separate business entity seeking to maximize its own profits, even if it is at the expense of maximizing the profits for the system as a whole. No channel member has complete or substantial control over the other members. McCammon characterizes conventional channels as "highly fragmented networks in which loosely aligned manufacturers, wholesalers, and retailers have bargained with each other at arm's length, negotiated aggressively over terms of sale, and otherwise behaved autonomously."[15]

A vertical marketing system (VMS), by contrast, comprises the producer, wholesaler(s), and retailer(s) acting as a unified system. Either one channel member owns the others or franchises them or has so much power that they all cooperate. The vertical marketing system can be dominated by the producer, the wholesaler, or the retailer. McCammon characterizes VMSs as "professionally managed and centrally programmed networks, pre-engineered to achieve operating economies and maximum market impact."[16] VMSs came into being to control channel behavior and eliminate the conflict that results from independent channel members pursuing their own objectives. They achieve economies through their size, bargaining power, and elimination of duplicated services. VMSs have become the dominant mode of distribution in the consumer marketplace, serving between 70 and 80 percent of the total market.

We will now examine three major types of VMSs, those shown in Figure 19-5.

Corporate VMS   A *corporate VMS* combines successive stages of production and distribution under single ownership. Vertical integration is favored by companies that desire a high level of control over the channels. Vertical integration can be achieved by backward or forward integration. Consider some examples. Sears obtains over 50 percent of the goods it sells from companies that it partly or wholly owns. Sherwin-Williams makes paint but also owns and operates two thousand retail outlets.

A lesser-known example of the corporation VMS is the conglomerate which contains the Loblaws stores. Loblaws is much more than a retail chain of grocery supermarkets. First, it is the main retail channel for the bakery products of its majority owner George Weston Limited. Second, it contains a product development company International Merchants, which is responsible for developing its President's Choice and No Name product lines. Production contracts are maintained with the many food processors who make these products. Third, Loblaws also performs a wholesaling function for these private labels, which are sold to independent grocers in Canada and the U.S. Thus, the Loblaws organization is involved in all levels of the manufacturer-wholesaler-retailer channel.[17]

FIGURE 19-5

Conventional and Vertical
Marketing Channels

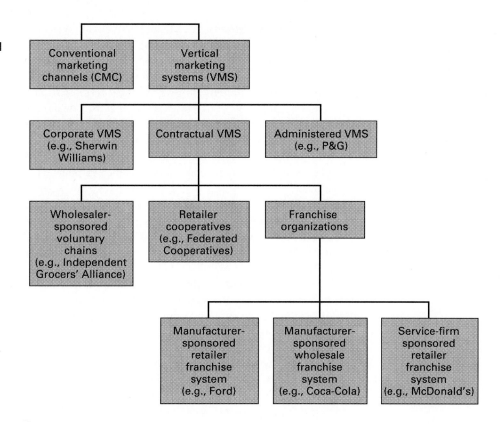

Administered VMS An *administered VMS* coordinates successive stages of production and distribution not through common ownership but through the size and power of one of the parties. Manufacturers of a dominant brand are able to secure strong trade cooperation and support from resellers. Thus Kodak, Gillette, Procter & Gamble, and Campbell Soup are able to command unusual cooperation from their resellers in connection with displays, shelf space, promotions, and price policies.

Contractual VMS A *contractual VMS* consists of independent firms at different levels of production and distribution integrating their programs on a contractual basis to obtain more economies and/or sales impact than they could achieve alone. Contractual VMSs have expanded the most in recent years and constitute one of the most significant developments in the economy. Contractual VMSs are of three types.

Wholesaler-Sponsored Voluntary Chains Wholesalers organize voluntary chains of independent retailers to help them compete with large chain organizations. The wholesaler develops a program in which independent retailers standardize their selling practices and achieve buying economies that enable the group to compete effectively with chain organizations.

Retailer Cooperatives Retailers might take the initiative and organize a new business entity to carry on wholesaling and possibly some production. Members concentrate their purchases through the retailer co-op and plan their advertising jointly. Profits are passed back to members in proportion to their purchases. Nonmember retailers might also buy through the co-op but do not share in the profits.

Franchise Organizations A channel member called a franchiser might link several successive stages in the production-distribution process. Franchising has been the fastest-growing and most interesting retailing development in recent years. Although the basic idea is an old one, some forms of franchising are quite new. Three forms of franchises can be distinguished.

The first is the *manufacturer-sponsored retailer franchise system*, exemplified by the automobile industry. Ford, for example, licenses dealers to sell its cars, the dealers being independent businesspeople who agree to meet various conditions of sales and services.

The second is the *manufacturer-sponsored wholesaler franchise system*, which is found in the soft-drink industry. Coca-Cola, for example, licenses bottlers (wholesalers) in various markets who buy its syrup concentrate and then carbonate, bottle, and sell it to retailers in local markets.

The third is the *service-firm-sponsored retailer franchise system*. Here a service firm organizes a whole system for bringing its service efficiently to consumers. Examples are found in auto rentals (Hertz, Avis, and Tilden), hospitality (Holiday Inn and Best Western), and fast food (McDonald's and Pizza Hut). This type of franchising system is discussed further in Chapter 20.

Many independent retailers, if they have not joined VMSs, have developed specialty stores that serve market segments that are not attractive to the mass merchandisers. The result is a polarization in retailing between large vertical marketing organizations, on the one hand, and specialty independent stores, on the other. This development creates a problem for manufacturers. They are strongly tied to independent middlemen, whom they cannot easily give up. But they must eventually realign themselves with the high-growth vertical marketing systems on less-attractive terms. Vertical marketing systems constantly threaten to bypass large manufacturers and set up their own manufacturing. *The new competition in retailing is no longer between independent business units but between whole systems of centrally programmed networks (corporate, administered, and contractual) competing against each other to achieve the best cost economies and customer response.*

Growth of Horizontal Marketing Systems

Another channel development is the readiness of two or more nonrelated companies to put together resources or programs to exploit an emerging marketing opportunity. Each company lacks the capital, know-how, production, or marketing resources to venture alone; or it is afraid of the risk; or it sees a substantial synergy in joining with another company. The companies might work with each other on a temporary or permanent basis or create a separate company. Adler calls this *symbiotic marketing*.[18] Here are several examples:

> Pillsbury and Kraft Foods Company set up an arrangement where Pillsbury makes and advertises its line of refrigerated dough products while Kraft uses its expertise to sell and distribute these products to the stores. ∎

> Coca-Cola and Joseph E. Seagram & Sons, Inc. formed a joint venture to produce and market a line of soft-drink mixers under the Seagram label. ∎

> Beecham Products, Inc., and Johnson & Johnson Company have jointly sponsored combined sales promotions of the former's Aqua-Fresh toothpaste and the latter's Reach toothbrush. ∎

All said, symbiotic marketing arrangements have increased dramatically in recent years, and the end is nowhere in sight.[19]

Growth of Multichannel Marketing Systems

In the past, many companies sold to a single market through a single channel. Today, with the proliferation of customer segments and channel possibilities, more and more companies have adopted multichannel marketing. *Multichannel marketing* occurs when a single firm uses two or more marketing channels to reach one or more customer segments.[20] Here are some examples:

General Electric sells large home appliances through independent retailers (department stores, discount houses, catalog houses) and also directly to large housing-tract builders, thus competing to some extent with the retailers. ■

IBM managed to put its new personal computers into twenty-five hundred stores in quick order by using a multichannel approach. ■

Some insurance companies sell through outside agents, exclusive agents, and their own telemarketing and direct-mail systems. ■

The good news is that the multichannel marketer gains volume with each new channel. The bad news is that the different channels may compete and create disruptive channel conflict. Some channels may refuse to work with the manufacturer if the latter does not limit the channel competition or recompense them in some way.

When IBM introduced the personal computer, it needed to supplement its salesforce with additional channels that could profitably handle smaller sales volumes. In addition to opening its own IBM Product Centers, it signed contracts with Sears, Computerland, and an assortment of other computer stores, office-product dealers, and value-added resellers. It also sold its computers to colleges at heavy discounts, causing complaints from retailers. Even the IBM salespeople complained when dealers sought large orders from major companies in a salesperson's territory. The salesperson wanted dealers to restrict themselves to small-lot-size situations or wanted sales credit when the dealers sold to companies in their territory. On the one hand, IBM did not want to pay double commission to dealers and the IBM salesforce; on the other hand, IBM did not want to severely restrict each party to a certain range of sales volume. Over the years, IBM managed to harmonize relations between the different channels so that they worked as partners, not adversaries.

Multichannel marketing shows less conflict when the multiple channels are all owned by the same company. The Hudson's Bay Company operates department stores, mass-merchandising stores, and specialty stores. Tillman has labeled such operations *merchandising conglomerates* and defined them as "a multiline merchandising empire under central ownership, usually combining several styles of retailing with behind-the-scenes integration of some distribution and management functions."[21] Here there is no conflict with outside channels, but the merchandising conglomerate might face internal conflict over how much financial support each channel deserves. (See Marketing Strategies 19-3 for more on multichannel retailing.)

Roles of Individual Firms in a Channel

Vertical, horizontal, and multichannel marketing systems underscore the dynamic and changing nature of channels. Each firm in an industry has to define its role in the channel system. McCammon has distinguished five roles:

- □ *Insiders* are members of the dominant channel, who enjoy access to preferred sources of supply and high respect in the industry. They want to perpetuate the existing channel arrangements and are the main enforcers of the industry code.

- □ *Strivers* are firms seeking to become insiders. They have less access to preferred sources of supply, which can handicap them in periods of short supply. They adhere to the industry code because of their desire to become insiders.

- □ *Complementors* are not part of the dominant channel. They perform functions not normally performed by others in the channel, or serve smaller segments of the market, or handle smaller quantities of merchandise. They usually benefit from the present system and respect the industry code.

- □ *Transients* are outside the dominant channel and do not seek membership. They go in and out of the market and move around as opportunities arise. They have short-run expectations and little incentive to adhere to the industry code.

Marketing Strategies 19-3

THE CASE FOR MULTICHANNEL MARKETING

Companies that persist in employing a single channel to sell different products to different customers will find themselves increasingly vulnerable to companies that build more appropriate channels. This can be illustrated with the *offering grid* shown in Figure (a) below.

The bottom of the grid shows products ranging from commodities to customized products; the vertical axis shows levels of distribution value-added service ranging from low to high. Thus pension fund management is located at the upper left: Pension funds are customized and require a high level of personal service, information, and execution. At the other extreme is Trade-Plus, a service of C.D. Anderson, which permits a person to trade directly at home using a personal computer; in this case, the product is extremely simple, and there is hardly any value added by the channel.

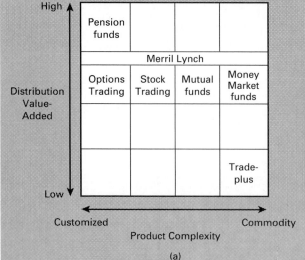

(a)

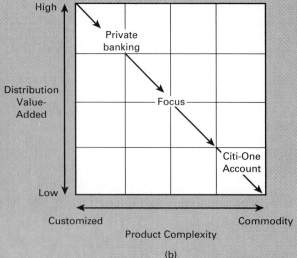

(b)

Now consider Merrill Lynch's offerings, which fall horizontally on the offering grid. Merrill Lynch offers several services through a fairly high value-added, full-service brokerage distribution channel consisting of its local-office account executives and home-office researchers. By sticking with only one channel, Merrill Lynch has allowed other competitors to appear. For example, the Toronto-Dominion Green Line discount brokerage service executes orders but provides little investment advice. It would be located near the middle of Figure (a).

The point is that each cell represents a potential opportunity if the demand is large enough. Companies that use only one channel for several products and customer groups will inevitably face increased competition. As customers become more knowledgeable about a service and as technology permits further mechanization, more channels will open up in the lower-right-hand cells of the grid, presenting competition to higher distribution-value-added channels.

The commercial banks are gradually providing financial services to exploit that opportunity. The upper-left corner of Figure (b) represents a customized banking service provided in gracious surroundings to satisfy the asset-management needs of wealthy customers. The lower-right corner represents a self-service form of banking in which the customer can receive a limited variety of standardized services by operating an automatic teller machine. Between these extremes, other services offer varying combinations of value-added and customization.

Source: This discussion is adapted from *Distribution: A Competitive Weapon*, published in 1985 by The MAC Group, 1430 Massachusetts Avenue, Cambridge, Mass. 02138, pp. 14-18.

- □ *Outside Innovators* are the real challengers and disrupters of the dominant channels. They develop a new system for carrying out the marketing work of the channel; if successful, they force major channel realignments. They are companies like McDonald's, Avon, and Holiday Inn, which doggedly develop new systems to challenge the old.[22]

Another important channel role is that of *channel captain*. The channel captain is the dominant member of a particular channel, the one who leads it. For example, General Motors is the channel captain of a system consisting of a huge number of suppliers, dealers, and facilitators. The channel captain is not always a manufacturer, as the examples of McDonald's and Sears indicate. Some channels do not have a channel captain in that each firm proceeds on its own.

CHANNEL COOPERATION, CONFLICT, AND COMPETITION

No matter how well channels are designed and managed, there will be some conflict, if only because the interests of independent businesses don't always coincide. Here we examine three questions: What types of conflict arise in channels? What are the major causes of channel conflict? What can be done to resolve situations of conflict?

Types of Conflict and Competition

Suppose a manufacturer sets up a vertical channel consisting of wholesalers and retailers. The manufacturer hopes for channel cooperation. Cooperation normally produces greater total channel profits than if each channel member acted only on self-interest. By cooperating, the channel members can more effectively sense, serve, and satisfy the target market.

Yet vertical, horizontal, and multichannel conflict can occur. *Vertical channel conflict* exists when there is conflict between different levels within the same channel. For example,

General Motors came into conflict with its dealers some years ago in trying to enforce policies on service, pricing, and advertising. And Coca-Cola came into conflict with those of its bottlers who agreed to also bottle another brand.

Horizontal channel conflict exists when there is conflict between members at the same channel level. In cities having more than one Ford dealer, some dealers complained that others were advertising too aggressively. And some Pizza Inn franchisees complained about other Pizza Inn franchisees cheating on the ingredients, maintaining poor service, and hurting the overall Pizza Inn image. In these cases, the *channel captain* must establish clear and enforceable policies and take quick action to control this type of conflict.

Multichannel conflict exists when the manufacturer has established two or more channels that compete with each other in selling to the same market. When Levi Straus agreed to distribute its jeans through department stores in addition to its normal specialty-store channel, it was highly resented by the specialty stores. When several clothing manufacturers who had been selling through department stores opened their own stores, the department stores who carried their clothes were mad. When Zenith agreed to sell its television sets through some mass merchandisers, it was resented by its independent radio and TV appliance stores. Multichannel conflict is likely to be especially intense when the members of one channel either get a lower price (based on larger volume purchases) or are willing to work with a lower margin.

Causes of Channel Conflict

It is important to distinguish the different causes that might produce channel conflict. Some causes are easy to resolve, others more difficult.

A major cause is *goal incompatibility*. For example, the manufacturer may want to achieve rapid market growth through a low-pricing policy. The dealers, on the other hand, may prefer to work with high margins and pursue short-run profitability. This is a hard type of conflict to solve.

Sometimes the conflict arises from *unclear roles and rights*. IBM sells personal computers to large accounts through its own salesforce, and its licensed dealers are also trying to sell to large accounts. Territory boundaries, credit for sales, and so forth, are confused and cause conflict.

The conflict can also stem from *differences in perception*. The manufacturer may be optimistic about the near-term economic outlook and want dealers to stock up on inventory. But the dealers may be pessimistic about the near-term outlook.

The conflict might arise because of the *great dependence* of the middlemen on the manufacturer. Exclusive dealers, such as auto dealers, have their fortunes intimately affected by the product design and pricing decisions of the manufacturer. This creates a high potential for conflict.

Managing Channel Conflict

Some amount of channel conflict can be constructive. It can lead to more dynamic adaptation to a changing environment. At the same time, too much conflict is dysfunctional. The problem is not one of eliminating conflict but of managing it better. There are several mechanisms for effective conflict management.[23]

Perhaps the most important solution is the adoption of *superordinate goals*. The channels members somehow come to an agreement on the fundamental goal they are jointly seeking, whether it is survival, market share, high quality, or customer satisfaction. This often takes place when the channel faces an outside threat, such as a more efficient competing channel, an adverse piece of legislation, or a shift in consumer desires. Working closely together might eliminate the threat. There is also the chance that the intense cooperation might have taught the parties a permanent lesson on the value of working toward the same end.

A useful conflict management device is the *exchange of persons* between two or more channel levels. For example, General Motors executives might agree to work in some dealerships, and some dealership owners might work at General Motors in their dealer policy area. Presumably, each side will grow to appreciate the other side's point of view and carry more understanding when returning to their position.

Co-optation is an effort by one organization to win the support of the leaders of another organization by including them in advisory councils, boards of directors, and the like, so that they feel that their opinions are being heard. As long as the initiating organization treats the leaders of the other organization seriously, cooptation can work to reduce conflict. But the initiating organization also pays a price in that it may have to compromise its policies and plans if it is to win the support of the other side.

Much can be accomplished by encouraging *joint membership in and between trade associations*. For example, there is good cooperation between the Grocery Manufacturers association and the Food Marketing Institute representing most of the food chains; this cooperation led to the development of the Universal Product Code. Presumably, the associations can consider issues between the food manufacturers and retailers and put them through an orderly process of resolution.

When conflict is chronic or acute, the parties may have to resort to diplomacy, mediation, or arbitration. *Diplomacy* takes place when each side sends a person or group to meet with their counterpart from the other side to resolve the conflict. It makes sense to assign diplomats to work more or less continuously with each other to avoid the flaring up of conflicts. *Mediation* means resorting to a neutral third party who brings skills in conciliating the interests of the two parties. *Arbitration* occurs when the two parties agree to present their arguments to a third party (one or more arbitrators) and accept the arbitration decision.

Given the potential for channel conflict in all channel arrangements, channel members would be wise to develop in advance agreed-upon methods of resolving channel conflict.

SUMMARY

Marketing-channel decisions are among the most complex and challenging decisions facing the firm. Each channel system creates a different level of sales and costs. Once a firm chooses a marketing channel, it must usually remain with it for a substantial period. The chosen channel will significantly affect and be affected by the other elements in the marketing mix.

Middlemen are used when they are able to perform channel functions more efficiently than the manufacturers can. The most important channel functions and flows are information, promotion, negotiation, ordering, financing, risk taking, physical possession, payment, and title. These marketing functions are more basic than the particular retail and wholesale institutions that may exist at any time.

Manufacturers face many channel alternatives for reaching a market. They can sell direct or use one, two, three or more intermediary-channel levels. Channel design calls for determining the service outputs (lot size, waiting time, spatial convenience, product variety, service backup), establishing the channel objectives and constraints, identifying the major channel alternatives (types and number of intermediaries, specifically intensive, exclusive, or selective distribution), and the channel terms and responsibilities. Each channel alternative has to be evaluated according to economic, control, and adaptive criteria.

Channel management calls for selecting particular middlemen and motivating them with a cost-effective trade-relations mix. The aim is to build a "partnership" feeling and joint-distribution programming. Individual channel members must be periodically evaluated against their own past sales and other channel members' sales. Channel modification must be performed periodically because of the continuously changing marketing environment. The company has to evaluate adding or dropping individual middlemen or individual channels and possibly modifying the whole channel system.

Marketing channels are characterized by continuous and sometimes dramatic change. Three of the most significant trends are the growth of vertical, horizontal, and multichannel marketing systems.

All channel systems have a potential for vertical, horizontal and multichannel conflict stemming from such sources as goal incompatibility, unclear roles and rights, differences in perception, and high dependence. Managing these conflicts can be sought through superordinate goals, exchange of persons, cooptation, joint membership in trade associations, diplomacy, mediation, and arbitration.

■ QUESTIONS

1. Marketing channels can be viewed as a set of interdependent organizations with high potential for conflict. Why would any business choose to become part of a channel system?

2. What are some of the factors involved in setting up a marketing channel? Illustrate your answer with examples from industry.

3. Describe the multichannel marketing systems used by record manufacturers. To what extent does each channel member participate in the marketing flows and functions discussed in the chapter?

4. Can any benefit be derived from applying channel management to service industries? How might the key functions and flows differ for a service industry?

5. "The auto-retailing industry could be transformed by new mega-dealers who each sell upwards of a dozen different brands of cars made by different manufacturers at up to thirty locations." If this trend becomes the norm, how will channel structures and relationships be affected? Who might become the channel captain?

6. When dealing with conflict, what is the goal of channel management? How might this goal be accomplished?

7. There is often conflict between manufacturers and retailers. Discuss the differing types of conflict. What does each party really want from the other, and why does this give rise to conflict?

8. Suggest some alternative channels for (a) a small firm that has developed a radically new harvesting machine, (b) a small plastic manufacturer that has developed a picnic pack for keeping bottles and food cold, and (c) a tankless, instant water heater. What would be the advantages and disadvantages of each channel alternative?

9. Sears acquired Dean Witter Reynolds, the fifth largest stock brokerage firm, in order to capitalize on the growing demand for financial services. Sears has opened financial service centers in its stores, offering money market funds, casualty and life insurance, credit cards, auto and boat installment loans, and so on. What forces are working for and against the success of such a venture?

10. In a market consisting of five producers and five customers, how many contacts would have to be made (a) without a middleman? (b) with a middleman? What are the general formulas?

11. Explain how the characteristics of peaches and cement affect the channels for each of them.

12. "Middlemen are parasites." This charge has been made by many observers over the centuries. Is this likely to be the case in a competitive economic system? Why or why not?

■ NOTES

1. E. Raymond Corey, *Industrial Marketing: Cases and Concepts* (Englewood Cliffs, N.J.: Prentice-Hall, 1976), p. 263.

2. Louis W. Stern and Adel I. El-Ansary, *Marketing Channels*, 3rd ed. (Englewood Cliffs, N.J.: Prentice Hall, 1988), p. 3.

3. *Ibid.*, pp. 6-7.

4. Alderson, "The Analytical Framework for Marketing," *Proceedings—Conference of Marketing Teachers from Far Western States* (Berkeley: University of California Press, 1958).

5. William G. Zikmund and William J. Stanton, "Recycling Solid Wastes: A Channels-of-Distribution Problem," *Journal of Marketing*, July 1971, p. 34.

6. Ronald Abler, John S. Adams, and Peter Gould, *Spatial Organizations: The Geographer's View of the World* (Englewood Cliffs, N.J.: Prentice-Hall, 1971), pp. 531-32.

7. See Irving Rein, Philip Kotler, and Martin Stoller, *High Visibility* (New York: Dodd, Mead, 1987).

8. Louis P. Bucklin, *Competition and Evolution in the Distributive Trades* (Englewood Cliffs, N.J.: Prentice-Hall, 1972).

9. Louis P. Bucklin, *A Theory of Distribution Channel Structure* (Berkeley: Institute of Business and Economic Research, University of California, 1966).

10. Phillip McVey, "Are Channels of Distribution What the Textbooks Say?" *Journal of Marketing*, January 1960, pp. 61-64.

11. See Bert Rosenbloom, *Marketing Channels: A Management View* (Hinsdale, Ill.: Dryden Press, 1983), pp. 228-40.

12. Bert C. McCammon, Jr., "Perspectives for Distribution Programming," in *Vertical Marketing Systems*, ed. Louis P. Bucklin (Glenview, Ill.: Scott, Foresman, 1970), p. 32.

13. *Ibid.*, p. 43.

14. For an excellent report on this issue, see Howard Sutton, *Rethinking the Company's Selling and Distribution Channels*, research report no. 885, Conference Board, 1986, 26 pp.

15. McCammon, "Perspectives for Distribution Programming," pp. 32-51.

16. *Ibid.*

17. Terry Brodie, "Loblaw's super growth strategy," *Financial Times*, January 12, 1987, p. 1.

18. Lee Adler, "Symbiotic Marketing," *Harvard Business Review*, November-December 1966, pp. 59-71.

19. See P. "Rajan" Varadarajan and Daniel Rajaratnam, "Symbiotic Marketing Revisited," *Journal of Marketing*, January 1986, pp. 7-17.

20. See Robert E. Weigand, "Fit Products and Channels to Your Markets," *Harvard Business Review*, January-February 1977, pp. 95-105.

21. Rollie Tillman, "Rise of the Conglomerchant," *Harvard Business Review*, November-December 1971, pp. 44-51.

22. Bert C. McCammon, Jr., "Alternative Explanations of Institutional Change and Channel Evolution," in *Toward Scientific Marketing*, ed. Stephen A. Greyser (Chicago: American Marketing Association, 1963), pp. 477-90.

23. This section draws heavily on Stern and El-Ansary, *Marketing Channels*, Chap. 6.

20

Managing Retailing, Wholesaling, and Physical-Distribution Systems

Canada has been adding sides to her hopper for a long time, but has neglected to enlarge the spout.

Sir William Van Horne

In the preceding chapter, we examined marketing intermediaries from the viewpoint of manufacturers who wanted to build and manage marketing channels. In this chapter, we view these intermediaries—retailers, wholesalers, and physical-distribution organizations—as requiring and forging their own marketing strategies. Some of these intermediaries are so large and powerful that they dominate the manufacturers who deal with them. Many are increasingly using modern strategic planning and marketing tools. They are measuring performance more on a return-on-investment basis than on a profit-margin basis. They are segmenting their markets better and improving their market targeting and positioning. They are aggressively pursuing market expansion and diversification strategies.

We will ask the following questions about each sector (retailers, wholesalers, and physical-distribution firms): What is the nature and importance of this sector? What major types of organizations occupy this sector? What marketing decisions do organizations in this sector make? and What are the major trends in this sector?

RETAILING

Nature and Importance of Retailing

Retailing includes all the activities involved in selling goods or services directly to final consumers for their personal, nonbusiness use. Any organization that does this selling—whether a manufacturer, wholesaler, or retailer—is doing retailing. It does not matter *how* the goods or services are sold (by person, mail, telephone, or vending machine) or *where* they are sold (in a store, on the street, or in the consumer's home). On the other hand, a *retailer* or *retail store* is any business enterprise whose sales volume comes primarily from retailing.

Retailing is one of the major industries in Canada. The industry is composed of more than 227 000 establishments employing 1.8 million people, or 13 percent of the labor force. Retail trade exceeds $181 billion and is growing at seven percent annually.[1] There is great variation in the sizes of the many types of retail outlets. At one extreme, the giant department store chains (Sears, Zellers, Eaton's, The Bay, Woolco, K mart) account for ten percent of retail volume. Grocery store chains (Loblaws, A&P, Steinberg, Provigo, Safeway) are even more concentrated. At the other extreme are the 4800 tiny convenience stores (Becker, Mac's, 7-Eleven) that collectively account for little more than one percent of the total.

Types of Retailers

Retail organizations exhibit great variety, and new forms keep emerging. Several classifications have been proposed. For our purposes, we will discuss (1) store retailers, (2) nonstore retailers, and (3) retail organizations.

Store Retailers Consumers today can shop for goods and services in a wide variety of stores. Marketing Environment and Trends 20-1 describes the most important retail-store types.

Marketing Environment and Trends 20-1

MAJOR RETAILER TYPES

Here are brief descriptions of the most important store types.

Specialty Store

A specialty store carries a narrow product line with a deep assortment within that line. Examples of specialty retailers are apparel stores, sporting-goods stores, furniture stores, florists, and bookstores. Specialty stores can be subclassified by the degree of narrowness in their product line. A clothing store would be a *single-line store*; a men's clothing store would be a *limited-line store*; and a men's custom-shirt store would be a *superspecialty store*. Some analysts contend that in the future, superspecialty stores will grow the fastest to take advantage of increasing opportunities for market segmentation, market targeting, and product specialization. Some of the successful current examples are Computerland (computers), The Pant Loft (jeans), and Foot Locker (sports shoes).

Department Store

A department store carries several product lines, typ-ically clothing, home furnishings, and household goods, where each line is operated as a separate department managed by specialist buyers or merchandisers. Examples of well-known department stores are Eaton's, Sears, The Bay, and Woodward's. *Specialty department* stores are also found, carrying only clothing, shoes, cosmetics, gift items, and luggage; Holt Renfrew is an example.

Many observers believe that department stores are in the declining stage of the *retail life cycle*. They point to the increased competition among department stores; the increased competition coming from other types of retailers, particularly discount houses, specialty-store chains, and warehouse retailers; and the heavy traffic, poor parking, and deterioration of central cities, which have made downtown shopping less appealing.

Department stores are waging a "comeback" war. Many have opened branches in suburban shopping centers, where there are better parking facilities and higher family incomes. Others are running more frequent sales to meet the discount threat. Still others are remodeling their stores, including "going boutique."

Some are leasing departments to outsiders. Some are experimenting with mail-order and telemarketing. Some department stores are retrenching on the number of employees, product lines, and customer services, such as delivery and credit, but this strategy may hurt their major appeal, namely, better service.

Supermarket

A supermarket is a relatively large, low-cost, low-margin, high-volume, self-service operation designed to serve the consumer's total needs for food, laundry, and household-maintenance products. There is intense competition among Canadian supermarkets, with the result that many of them earn an operating profit of barely 1 percent on their sales and 10 percent on their net worth.

Supermarkets have been hit hard by a number of innovative competitors, such as convenience food stores, discount food stores, and superstores. The food market is becoming more segmented, and no longer is it likely to be dominated by one major type of food retailer. Another challenge has been the rapid growth of out-of-home eating, with Canadians now spending nearly 40 percent of their food budgets outside the food stores.

Supermarkets have moved in several directions to improve their competitiveness. They have opened *larger stores*, with today's selling space occupying more than 2000 square meters. Supermarkets carry a large *number and variety of items*, typically over 12 000 items. The largest increase has been in nonfood items, which now account for 25 percent of total supermarket sales. Many supermarkets are moving into prescriptions, appliances, records, sporting goods, hardware, garden supplies, and even cameras, hoping to find high-margin lines to improve profitability. Supermarkets are also *upgrading their facilities* through more expensive locations, larger parking lots, carefully planned architecture and decor, longer store hours and Sunday openings, and a wide variety of customer services, such as cheque cashing, restrooms, and background music. Supermarkets have also increased their *promotional budgets*. They have also moved heavily into *private brands* to reduce their dependence on national brands and increase their profit margins.

"Supermarketing" as a method of doing business has recently spread to other types of business, particularly in the drug, home-improvement, toy, and sporting-goods fields.

Convenience Store

Convenience food stores are relatively small stores that are located near residential areas, open long hours and seven days a week, and carry a limited line of high-turnover convenience products. Examples are Becker Milk and Mac's Convenience Stores. Their long hours and their use by consumers mainly for "fill-in" purchases make them relatively high-price operations. Yet they fill an important consumer need, and people seem willing to pay for the convenience.

Superstore, Combination Store, and Hypermarché

Superstores are larger than the conventional supermarket, with more than 3000 square meters and they aim at meeting the consumers' total needs for routinely purchased food and nonfood items. They usually offer services such as laundry, dry cleaning, shoe repair, cheque cashing and bill paying, and bargain lunch counters. *Combination stores* represent a diversification of the supermarket store into the growing drug and prescription field. Combination food and drug stores average 5000 square meters of selling space. Hypermarchés are even larger than combination stores, ranging between 7500 and 20 000 square meters. The hypermarché combines supermarket, discount, and warehouse retailing principles. Its product assortment goes beyond routinely purchased goods and includes furniture, heavy and light appliances, clothing items, and many other things. The basic approach is bulk display and minimum handling by store personnel, with discounts offered to customers who are willing to carry heavy appliances and furniture out of the store.

Discount Store

A discount store sells standard merchandise at lower prices than conventional merchants by accepting lower margins and working on higher volume. A true discount store exhibits these elements: (1) the store regularly sells its merchandise at lower prices; (2) the store emphasizes national brands, so that low price does not suggest inferior quality; (3) the store operates on a self-service, minimum-facilities basis; and (4) the location tends to be a low-rent area, and the store draws customers from relatively long distances.

In recent years, intense competition among discount houses and between discount houses and department stores has led many discount retailers to trade up. They have improved their decor, added new lines such as wearing apparel, added more services such as cheque cashing and easy returns, and opened new branches in suburban shopping centers, all leading to higher costs and forcing higher prices. Furthermore, department stores often cut their prices to compete with the discounters, with the distinction between the two growing progressively blurred.

Discount retailing has moved beyond general merchandise into specialty merchandise stores, such as discount sporting goods stores, discount electronics stores, and discount bookstores.

Off-Price Retailers

When the major discount stores traded up, a new wave of off-price retailers moved in to fill the low-price, high-volume gap. Ordinary discounters buy at regular wholesale prices and accept lower margins to keep prices down. Off-price retailers, on the other hand, buy at less than regular wholesale prices and charge consumers less than retail. They tend to carry a changing and unstable collection of higher-quality merchandise, often leftover goods, overruns, and irregulars obtained at reduced prices from manufacturers or other retailers. Off-price retailers have made their biggest inroads in clothing, accessories, and footwear. But they can be found in all areas, from no-frills banking and discount brokerages to food stores and electronics.

There are three main types of off-price retailers— factory outlets, independents, and warehouse clubs.

Factory outlets are owned and operated by manufacturers and normally carry the manufacturer's surplus, discontinued, or irregular goods. Examples are the factory outlet stores of Glenayr Knitting Mills in Perth and of Highland Queen in Oshawa. Like the first factory outlets, these were located near their factories, but such locations were often inconvenient for shoppers. An emerging trend is for a number of factory outlets to group together in a factory outlet mall. The prospect of low prices on a wide range of merchandise is sufficient to draw shoppers from considerable distances.

Independent off-price retailers either are owned and operated by entrepreneurs or are divisions of larger retail corporations. Although many off-price operations are run by small independents, most of the large off-price retailers are owned by big retail chains. An example is K mart's ownership of Designer Depot.

Warehouse clubs, sometimes called wholesale clubs, sell a limited selection of brand-name appliances, furniture, clothing, groceries, or other merchandise. Members pay an annual fee of $25 to $50 for the privilege of receiving deep discounts on their purchases. While relatively new to Canada, examples of this type of outlet include Price Club Canada which is expanding westward from Montreal, and Costco Wholesale which is expanding eastward from Vancouver.

Warehouse stores operate from similar no-frills facilities, but do not charge a membership fee. Like discount stores, they operate on low margin and rely on high volume to generate profits. One variation is the furniture showroom warehouse, which adds an attractive showroom where shoppers choose their furniture. By the time payment has been made, the merchandise is ready to be picked up by the customer at the loading dock. A well-known example is Leon's.

Catalog Showroom

A catalog showroom applies catalog and discounting principles to a wide selection of high-markup, fast-moving, brand-name goods. These include jewelry, power tools, luggage, cameras, and photographic equipment. These stores have become one of retailing's hottest new forms, even posing a threat to the traditional discounter. Catalog showrooms issue four-color catalogs, often five hundred pages long, and supplement them with smaller seasonal editions. Each item's list price and discount price are shown. The customer can order an item over the phone and pay delivery charges or drive to the showroom, examine it firsthand, and buy it out of stock. Consumers Distributing is a catalog showroom.

For further reading, see Anthony Ramirez, "Department Stores Shape Up," *Fortune*, September 1, 1986, pp. 50-52; Julie Liesse Erickson, "Supermarket Chains Work to Fill Tall Order," *Advertising Age*, April 28, 1986, pp. S1-S2; Teresa Carson, "Karl Eller's Big Thirst for Convenience Stores," *Business Week*, June 13, 1988, pp. 86-87; and Todd Mason, "The Return of the Amazing Colossal Store," *Business Week*, August 22, 1988, pp. 59-61.

Retail store types, like products, pass through stages of growth and decline that can be described as the *retail life cycle*.[2] A retail store type emerges, enjoys a period of accelerated growth, reaches maturity, and then declines. Older retail forms took many years to reach maturity, but newer retail forms reach their maturity much earlier. This change is dramatically illustrated in Table 20-1. The department store took eighty years to reach maturity, whereas warehouse retail outlets, a more modern form, reached their maturity in ten years.

The table also shows that some well-known types (e.g., general stores and variety stores) have entered a stage of decline. This means that more units of these store types will be closed than opened in the coming years. Clearly, some well-located and well-run general stores and variety stores will survive because they serve their customers well and have adopted modern marketing and management practices. But as store types, they suffer competitive disadvantages in their operating costs and/or customer-value-generating ability.

One reason that new store types emerge to replace old store types is given by the *wheel-of-retailing* hypothesis.[3] Conventional store types typically offer many services to their customers and price their merchandise to cover the cost. This provides an opportunity for new store forms to emerge—for example, discount stores—which offer lower prices, less service, and less status but have lower operating costs. An increasing number of shoppers use the conventional stores for deciding what to buy and then drive to the discount stores to make the actual purchase. As these discount stores increase their market share, they offer more services and upgrade their facilities. Their increased costs, however, force them to raise their prices until they start to resemble the conventional outlets they displaced. As a consequence, they become vulnerable to newer types of low-cost, low-margin operations. This hypothesis partly explains the initial success and current troubles of department stores and, more recently, discount stores.

New store types emerge to meet widely different consumer preferences for service levels and specific services. Thus, in the past, most consumers purchased shoes in shoe stores, where they were waited on by fitters. Today, most shoes are bought in mass-merchandise outlets where consumers take them off the shelf, and an increasing number of shoes are purchased through the mail. It turns out that retailers in most product categories can position themselves as offering one of four levels of service:

☐ *Self-Service Retailing:* Used in many retailing operations, especially for obtaining convenience goods and, to some extent, shopping goods. Self-service is the cornerstone of all discount operations. Many customers are willing to carry out their own locate-compare-select process to save money.

☐ *Self-Selection Retailing:* Involves customers in finding their own goods, although they can ask for assistance. Customers complete their transactions by finding a salesperson to take the money for the item. Self-selection organizations have higher operating expenses than self-service operations because of the additional staff requirements.

☐ *Limited-Service Retailing:* Provides more sales assistance because these stores carry more shopping goods, and customers need more information. The stores also offer services, such as credit and merchandise-return privileges, not normally found in less service-oriented stores and hence they have higher operating costs.

☐ *Full-Service Retailing:* Provides salespeople who are ready to assist in every phase of the locate-compare-select process. Customers who like to be waited on prefer this type of store. The high staffing cost, along with the higher proportion of specialty goods and slower-moving items (fashions, jewelry, cameras), the more liberal merchandise-return policies, various credit plans, free delivery, home servicing of durables, and customer facilities such as lounges and restaurants, results in high-cost retailing.

Table 20-1 The Evolution of Today's Retail Institutions

Institutional Type	Period of Fastest Growth	Period from Inception to Maturity (years)	Stage of Life Cycle	Representative Firms
General store	1800-1840	100	Declining	A local institution
Single-line store	1820-1840	100	Mature	Maher Shoes
Department store	1860-1940	80	Mature	Eaton's
Variety store	1870-1930	50	Declining	Kresge
Mail order house	1915-1950	50	Mature	Sears
Corporate chain	1920-1930	50	Mature	Peoples Jewellers
Discount store	1955-1975	20	Mature	K mart
Supermarket	1935-1965	35	Mature/ declining	A&P
Shopping center	1950-1965	40	Mature	Yorkdale
Cooperative	1930-1950	40	Mature	Mountain Equipment
Gasoline station	1930-1950	45	Mature	Imperial Oil
Convenience store	1965-1975	20	Mature	Becker Milk
Fast-food outlet	1960-1975	15	Late growth	McDonald's
Home improvement center	1965-1980	15	Late growth	Beaver Lumber
Super specialists	1975-1985	10	Late growth	Mark's Work Wearhouse
Warehouse retailing	1970-1980	10	Maturity	The Brick
Personal computer stores	1980-	?	Early growth	Computerland

Source: Adapted from J. Barry Mason and Hazel F. Ezell, *Marketing* (Plano, Tex.: Business Publications, 1987), p. 517.

By combining these different service levels with different assortment breadths, we can distinguish four broad positioning strategies available to retailers. They are shown in Figure 20-1.

1. Holt Renfrew typifies stores that feature a broad product assortment and high value added. Stores in this quadrant pay close attention to store design, product quality, service, and image. Their profit margin is high, and if they are fortunate enough to have high volume, they will be very profitable.

2. Birks typifies stores that feature a narrow product assortment and high value added. Such stores cultivate an exclusive image and tend to operate on a high margin and low volume.

3. Bata Shoe typifies stores that feature a narrow line and low value added. Such stores, often referred to as specialty mass merchandisers, appeal to price-conscious consumers. They keep their costs and prices low through designing similar stores and centralizing buying, merchandising, advertising, and distribution.

4. K mart typifies stores that feature a broad line and low value added. They focus on keeping prices low so that they have an image of being a place for good buys. They make up for their low margin by achieving a high volume.

FIGURE 20-1

Retail Positioning Map

Source: Adapted from William T. Gregor and Eileen M. Friars, "Money Merchandising: Retail Revolution in Consumer Financial Service" (Cambridge, Mass.: The MAC Group, 1982).

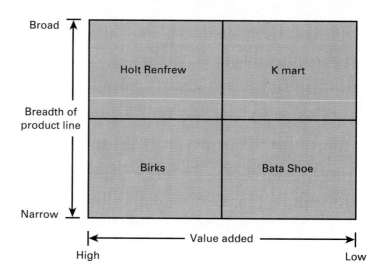

Nonstore Retailers Although the overwhelming majority of goods and services are sold through stores, *nonstore retailing* has been growing much faster than store retailing, amounting to more than 12 percent of all consumer purchases. Some observers foresee as much as a third of all general-merchandise retailing being done through nonstore channels by the end of the century. Here we will examine *direct selling, automatic vending*, and *buying service. Direct marketing* will be examined in Chapter 23.

Direct Selling Direct selling—which started centuries ago with itinerant peddlers—has burgeoned into an industry employing 200 000 Canadians engaged in selling *door to door, office to office*, or at *home sales parties*. The pioneers include the Fuller Brush Company (brushes, brooms, and the like), Electrolux (vacuum cleaners), Reader's Digest (magazines) and Encyclopaedia Britannica (encyclopedias). Door-to-door selling improved considerably with Avon's entry into the industry, with the concept of the homemaker's friend and beauty consultant—the Avon lady. Avon's phenomenal success has spawned several imitators, including Mary Kay, Lady Finelle, and Beauty Counsellors. Amway and Shaklee also sell cosmetics door-to-door as part of a broader product line. Tupperware, developed the home-sales parties method of selling, in which several friends and neighbors are invited to a party in someone's home where Tupperware products are demonstrated and sold.

Direct selling is expensive (the salesperson gets a 20 to 50 percent commission), and there are the costs of hiring, training, managing, and motivating the salesforce. The salesforces are recruited by local "sales directors," who can earn lavish prizes when their groups achieve sales targets. Typical rewards are jewelry and vacation trips, and even pink Cadillacs for Mary Kay people. The future of direct selling is uncertain as more women take employment outside the home. The salesperson may gradually be replaced by electronic shopping.

Automatic Vending Automatic vending through coin-operated machines has been a major post-World War II growth area. By 1988, total sales had grown to $360 million. Automatic vending has been applied to a considerable variety of merchandise, including impulse goods with high convenience value (cigarettes, soft drinks, candy, newspapers, hot beverages) and other products (hosiery, cosmetics, food snacks, hot soups and food, paperbacks, record albums, film, T-shirts, insurance policies, shoeshines, and even fishing worms). Vending machines are found in factories, offices, large retail stores, gasoline stations, and even railway dining cars.

Vending machines offer customers the advantages of twenty-four-hour selling, self-service, and unhandled merchandise. At the same time, automatic vending is a relatively expensive channel, and prices of vended merchandise are often 15 to 20 percent higher. Vendor costs are high because of frequent restocking at widely scattered locations, frequent machine breakdowns, and the high pilferage rate in certain locations. For the customer, the biggest irritations are machine breakdowns, out-of-stocks, and the fact that merchandise cannot be returned.

Vending machines are increasingly supplying entertainment services—pinball machines, slot machines, juke boxes, and electronic computer games. A highly specialized machine is the *automatic teller*, which allows bank customers twenty-four-hour service on checking, savings, withdrawals, and transfer of funds from one account to another. Industry trends include cashless "debit card" vending, and downsized machines for serving locations with smaller customer populations.

Buying Service A buying service is a storeless retailer serving specific clienteles—usually the employees of large organizations, such as schools, hospitals, unions, and government agencies. The organization's members become members of the buying service and are entitled to buy from a selective list of retailers who have agreed to give discounts to buying service members. Thus a customer seeking a video camera would get a form from the buying service, take it to an approved retailer, and buy the appliance at a discount. The retailer would then pay a small fee to the buying service. Comp-U-Card operates a variation of this service, which provides members with telephone price quotations, and then accepts telephone orders that are charged to the members' Master Card accounts.

Retail Organizations

Although many retail stores are independently owned, an increasing number are falling under some form of corporate retailing. The five types of corporate retailing are *corporate chains, voluntary chain and retailer cooperatives, consumer cooperatives, franchise organizations*, and *merchandising conglomerates*.

Corporate Chain The chain store is one of the most important retail developments of this century. *Chain stores* are two or more outlets that are commonly owned and controlled, employ central buying and merchandising, and sell similar lines of merchandise. Corporate chains appear in all types of retailing, but they are strongest in department stores, variety stores, food stores, drugstores, shoe stores, and women's clothing stores.

Corporate chains gain many advantages over independents. Their size allows them to buy in large quantities at lower prices. They can afford to hire corporate-level specialists to deal with such areas as pricing, promotion, merchandising, inventory control, and sales forecasting. Chains gain promotional economies, because their advertising costs are spread over many stores and a large sales volume. And some chains permit their units freedom to meet variations in consumer preferences and competition in local markets.

Voluntary Chain and Retailer Cooperative The growing competition from the chains triggered a competitive reaction from independents, which began to form two types of associations. One is the *voluntary chain*, which consists of a wholesaler-sponsored group of independent retailers engaged in bulk buying and common merchandising. Examples include the Independent Grocers Alliance (IGA) in groceries and Home Hardware in hardware. The other is the *retailer cooperative*, which consists of independent retailers who set up a central buying organization and conduct joint promotion efforts. Federated Co-operatives is the main supplier for 322 independent retailers in Western Canada.

Consumer Cooperative A consumer cooperative (or co-op) is any retail firm owned by its customers. Consumer co-ops are started by community residents who feel that local retailers are not serving them well, either charging too high prices or providing poor-quality products. The residents contribute money to open their own store, and they vote on its policies and elect a group to manage it. The store might set its prices low or, alternatively, set normal prices with members receiving a patronage dividend based on their individual level of purchases. The Mountain Equipment Co-op serves 200 000 members from stores in Vancouver, Calgary, and Toronto, as well as by a big mail-order operation.

Franchise Organization A franchise organization is a contractual association between a franchiser (a manufacturer, wholesaler, or service organization) and franchisees (independent business people who buy the right to own and operate one or more units in the franchise system). Franchise organizations are normally based on some unique product, service, or method of doing business, or on a trade name, or patent, or on goodwill that the franchiser has developed. Franchising has been prominent in fast foods, video stores, health/fitness centers, hair cutting, auto rentals, motels, travel agencies, real estate, and dozens of other product and service areas.[4]

The franchiser's compensation can consist of the following elements: an initial fee, a royalty on gross sales, rental and lease fees on equipment and fixtures supplied by the franchiser, a share of the profits, and sometimes a regular license fee. In a few cases, franchisers have also charged management consulting fees, but usually the franchisee is entitled to this service as part of the total package.

> One of the most successful franchise systems of all time is McDonald's. McDonald's charges franchisees an initial fee of $22 500 and receives a 3.5 percent service fee and a rental charge of 8.5 percent of the franchisee's monthly gross sales. It also requires its new franchisees to attend "Hamburger University" for three weeks to learn how to manage the business. The franchisees must also adhere to certain procedures in buying raw materials and in preparing and selling the product. In 1985 there were approximately 9400 outlets in 45 countries with sales of $11.1 billion. McDonald's opens a new store every 15 hours. In January 1990, the first outlet was opened in Moscow as a result of a long-term selling effort by McDonald's of Canada. A 700-seat establishment, it rang up 30 000 meals on 27 cash registers, breaking the opening-day record for McDonald's worldwide.[5] ∎

McDonald's and other fast-food franchisers are currently facing rising labor costs and food costs, forcing them to raise their prices. New competitors continue to emerge, popularizing ethnic foods, such as tacos and gyros. Some major franchisers are now opening units in smaller towns, where there is less competition. Others are moving into large factories, office buildings, colleges, and even hospitals. Others are experimenting with new products that they hope will appeal to consumers and be profitable to the firm.

Merchandising Conglomerate Merchandising conglomerates are free-form corporations that combine several diversified retailing lines and forms under central ownership, along with some integration of their distribution-and-management function.[6] For example, Dylex is a conglomerate that operates a dozen different retail chains having a total of 1352 stores across Canada. Most of them are specialty clothing stores, some catering to the needs of different types of women, others targeted at different types of men, and still others intended to meet the clothing needs of the family. With the typical shopping mall containing several specialized Dylex stores, there is ample opportunity for integrating the conglomerate's distribution and management functions. In the future, diversified retailing is likely to be adopted by more corporate chains. The major question is whether diversified retailing produces superior management systems and economies that benefit all of the separate retail lines.

Retailer Marketing Decisions

Retailers today are anxious to find new marketing strategies to attract and hold customers. In the past, they held customers by having special or unique assortments of goods, by offering greater or better services than competitors, and by offering store credit cards to enable their buyers to buy on credit. All of this has changed. Today, many stores offer similar assortments: National brands such as Calvin Klein, Izod, and Levi are found not only in most department stores but in mass-merchandise outlets and in off-price discount stores. The national brand manufacturers, in their drive for volume, placed their branded goods everywhere. The result was that stores looked more and more alike; they became homogenized. In any city, a shopper could find many stores but only a few assortments.

As for service differentiation among retailers, this too eroded. Many department stores trimmed their services, and many discounters increased their services. Customers became smarter shoppers and more price sensitive. They did not see a reason for paying more for identical brands, especially when service differences were diminishing. Nor did they need to get credit from a particular store, as bank credit cards became increasingly accepted by all stores. For all these reasons, many retailers today are rethinking their marketing strategy.[7]

We will now examine the marketing decisions faced by retailers in the areas of target market, product assortment and services, price, promotion, and place.

Target-Market Decision   A retailer's most important decision concerns the target market. Should the store focus on upscale, midscale, or downscale shoppers? Do the target shoppers want variety, assortment depth, or convenience? Until the target market is defined and profiled, the retailer cannot make consistent decisions on product assortment, store decor, advertising messages and media, price levels, and so on.[8]

Too many retailers have not clarified their target market or are trying to satisfy too many markets, satisfying none of them well. Even Sears, which serves so many different people, must define better which groups to make its major target customers so that it can fine tune its product assortment, prices, locations, and promotion to these groups.

Some retailers define their markets well at the outset. Ikea, the Swedish furniture store started their North American operations in Halifax. They targeted "the younger buyer who shops for value, likes the contemporary look, and doesn't mind assembling it once he gets home." So successful is their line of modular furniture that their major problem is keeping it in stock. Ikea's major competitor acknowledged "They've figured out what they want to do, and they're doing it very, very well."[9]

Other retailers are forced by circumstances to change their market definition. During the 1970s, Simpsons Ltd. became dowdy and unprofitable. After losing $82.7 million during 1982-84, new management was brought in. The new strategy was to replace slow-moving stock with fashion merchandise, because "Simpsons was . . . the store of our parents, but it is the yuppies who have the money."[10]

Retailers should conduct periodic marketing research to ensure that they are reaching and satisfying their target customers. Consider a store that seeks to attract affluent consumers but whose image is shown by the solid line in Figure 20-2. The store's image does not appeal to its target market. The store has to either serve the mass market or redesign itself into a "classier store." Suppose it decides on the latter. Some time later, the store interviews customers again. The store image is now shown by the dashed line in Figure 20-2. The store has succeeded in realigning its image closer to its target market.

FIGURE 20-2

A Comparison Between the Old and New Image of a Store Seeking to Appeal to a Class Market

Source: Adapted from David W. Cravens, Gerald E. Hills, and Robert B. Woodruff, *Marketing Decision Making: Concepts and Strategy* (Homewood, Ill.: Richard D. Irwin, 1976), p. 234. © 1976 by Richard D. Irwin, Inc.

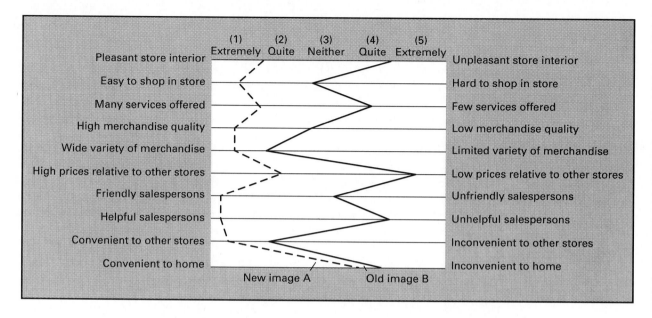

Product-Assortment-and-Services Decision   Retailers have to decide on three major "product" variables that help position their store to their target market, namely, product assortment, services mix, and store atmosphere.

The retailer's *product assortment* must match the shopping expectations of the target market. In fact, it becomes a key element in the competitive battle among similar retailers. The retailer has to decide on product-assortment *breadth* (narrow or wide) and *depth* (shallow or deep). Thus in the restaurant business, a restaurant can offer a narrow and shallow assortment (small lunch counters), a narrow and deep assortment (delicatessen), a broad and shallow assortment (cafeteria), or a broad and deep assortment (large restaurants). Another product-assortment dimension is the quality of the goods. The customer is interested not only in the range of choice but also in the quality of the product.

The retailer's real challenge begins after the store's product assortment and quality level have been defined. There will always be competitors with similar assortments and quality. The challenge is to develop a product-differentiation strategy. Wortzel suggests several product-differentiation strategies for retailers:

1. *Feature some exclusive national brands which are not available at competing retailers:* Thus Holt Renfrew may get exclusive rights to carry the dresses of a well-known international designer.

2. *Feature mostly private branded merchandise:* Thus Roots designs most of the clothes carried in its stores.

3. *Feature blockbuster distinctive merchandise events:* Harrod's will run long shows featuring the goods of another country, such as India or China, throughout its store.

4. *Feature surprise or ever-changing merchandise:* Honest Ed's offers surprise assortments of distress merchandise, overstocks, and closeouts.

5. *Feature the latest or newest merchandise first:* The Sharper Image will lead other retailers in introducing the newest or latest electronic appliances from around the world.

6. *Offer merchandise customizing services:* Tip Top Tailors will make custom-tailored suits for customers, in addition to its ready-made men's wear.

7. *Offer a highly targeted assortment:* Pennington's carries goods for the mature, larger woman.

Retailers must also decide on the *services mix* to offer customers. The old "mom and pop" grocery stores offered home delivery, credit, and conversation, services that today's supermarkets have completely eliminated. Table 20-2 lists some major services that full-service retailers can offer. The services mix is one of the key tools for differentiating one store from another.

The *store's atmosphere* is a third element in its product arsenal. Every store has a physical layout that makes it hard or easy to move around. Every store has a "look"; one store is dirty, another is charming, a third is palatial, a fourth is somber. The store must embody a planned atmosphere that suits the target market and draws them toward purchase. A funeral parlor should be quiet, somber, and peaceful, and a discotheque should be bright, loud, and vibrating. The Ikea furniture stores encourage young families to shop there by providing supervised play areas for young children and creating a family atmosphere. Supermarkets have found that varying the tempo of music affects the average time spent in the store and the average expenditures. Currently supermarkets are exploring ways to release aromas through sticker displays on store shelves to stimulate hunger or thirst. Some fine department stores vaporize perfume fragrances in certain departments. "Packaged environments" are designed by creative people who know how to combine visual, aural, olfactory, and tactile stimuli to produce the desired effect.[11]

Price Decision   The retailer's prices are a key positioning factor and must be decided in relation to the target market, the product-and-service assortment mix, and competition. All retailers would like to charge high markups and achieve high volumes, but usually the two do not go together. Most retailers fall into the *high-markup, lower-volume group* (fine specialty stores) or the *low-markup, higher-volume group* (mass merchandisers and discount stores). Within each of these groups, there are further gradations. Thus, Loblaws emphasizes

Table 20-2 Typical Retail Services

Prepurchase Services	Postpurchase Services	Ancillary Services
1. Accepting telephone orders	1. Delivery	1. Cheque cashing
2. Accepting mail orders (or purchases)	2. Regular wrapping (or bagging)	2. General information
		3. Free parking
3. Advertising	3. Gift wrapping	4. Restaurants
4. Window display	4. Adjustments	5. Repairs
5. Interior display	5. Returns	6. Interior decorating
6. Fitting rooms	6. Alterations	7. Credit
7. Shopping hours	7. Tailoring	8. Restrooms
8. Fashion shows	8. Installations	9. Baby-attendant service
9. Trade-ins	9. Engraving	
	10. COD delivery	

Source: Carl M. Larson, Robert E. Weigand, and John S. Wright, *Basic Retailing,* 2nd ed. (Englewood Cliffs, N.J.: Prentice-Hall, 1976), p. 384. Reprinted by permission of Prentice-Hall, Inc., Englewood Cliffs, N.J.

its yellow-label "no-name" products to convey an image of value for money. Yet in the same store, shoppers can choose between pre-packaged cold cuts at the self-serve meat counter, or at a slightly higher price they can order freshly-sliced cold cuts from the Ziggy's deli counter.

Retailers must also pay attention to pricing tactics. Most retailers will put low prices on some items to serve as *traffic builders* or *loss leaders*. They will run storewide sales on some occasions. They will plan markdowns on slower-moving merchandise: for example, shoe retailers expect to sell 50 percent of their shoes at the normal markup, 25 percent at a 40 percent markup, and the remaining 25 percent at cost. (For more on price decision, see Marketing Strategies 20-1.)

Promotion Decision   The retailer must use promotion tools that support and reinforce its image positioning. Fine stores will place full-page tasteful ads in magazines such as *Vogue* and *Harper's*. Discount retailers will place loud ads on radio, television, and newspapers touting low prices and specials. Fine stores will carefully train their salespeople in how to greet customers, interpret their needs, and handle their doubts and complaints. Discounters will use less well-trained salespeople and use a whole range of sales promotion tools to generate traffic.

Place Decision   Retailers are accustomed to saying that the three keys to success in retailing are "location, location, and location." The retailer's choice of location is a key competitive factor in its ability to attract customers. For example, customers primarily choose the bank that is nearest to them. Department-store chains, oil companies, and fast-food franchisers are particularly careful in selecting locations. The problem breaks down into selecting regions of the country in which to open stores, then particular cities, and then particular sites. A supermarket chain, for example, may decide to operate in B.C. and Alberta; within Alberta in the cities of Edmonton and Calgary; and within Edmonton, in fourteen locations, mostly suburban.

Large retailers must wrestle with the problem of whether to locate several small stores in many locations or larger stores in fewer locations. Generally speaking, the retailer should locate enough stores in each city to gain promotion and distribution economies. The larger the individual stores, the greater their trading area or reach.

Retailers have a choice of locating their stores in the central business district, a regional shopping center, a community shopping center, or a shopping strip.

□ *Central business districts* represent the oldest and most heavily trafficked city area, often known as "downtown." Store and office rents are normally high. But a number of downtowns have been hit by a flight to the suburbs with resulting deterioration of downtown retailing facilities and a changing shopper composition.

□ *Regional shopping centers* are large suburban malls containing forty to over one hundred stores and drawing from an eight-to-sixteen kilometer radius. Typically, the malls feature one or two nationally known anchor stores, such as The Bay and Zellers, and a great number of smaller stores, many of them under franchise operation. Malls are attractive because of generous parking, one-stop shopping, restaurants, and recreational facilities. Successful malls charge high rents but in return generate high shopper density.

□ *Community shopping centers* are smaller malls with typically one anchor store and between twenty and forty smaller stores.

□ *Shopping strips* contain a cluster of stores serving a neighborhood's normal needs for groceries, hardware, laundry, and gasoline. They serve people within a five-to-ten-minute driving range.

DOES AN "EVERYDAY-LOW-PRICES" STRATEGY MAKE MORE SENSE THAN A "PROMOTIONAL-PRICING" STRATEGY?

Many companies charge list prices and then run price-off sales from time to time. In this way, most of their customers pay the full price while deal-prone customers willing to wait for sales pay less than the full price. The full-price customers essentially subsidize the promotional-price customers (assuming that there are no economies of scale).

Sears used this traditional pricing strategy. But Sears and other companies have recently had to reconsider their pricing strategy in the face of discounters. Historically, Sears set its prices lower than upscale department stores and attracted almost everyone to its stores to buy something. Sears ran frequent sales on seasonal items, special-purchased items, and items accumulating in inventory.

In recent years, Sears has seen growing competition from discount merchants such as K mart who feature *everyday low prices* and run far fewer sales. A growing number of Sears customers have been switching many of their purchases to these discount merchants.

Sears found itself facing a critical pricing-strategy decision. In the spring of 1989, it announced the biggest pricing change in its 102-year history. Scrapping its weekly-sales approach, Sears adopted an *everyday low-price* strategy. Sears closed all of its stores for forty-two hours and retagged every piece of merchandise, slashing prices by as much as 50 percent! During the next three weeks, Sears aired its biggest-ever advertising campaign to announce: "We've lowered our prices on over 50 000 items!"

Sears expected to benefit in a number of ways. It would retain its present customers and attract some old customers back; the higher volume would compensate for the reduced margins. Sears would save the high advertising, inventory and personnel costs involved in running weekly sales.

A year later, Sears found that its everyday-low-price strategy did not seem to be working. Their volume was not building up and their margins were lower. Sears apparently did not lower its prices significantly; many shoppers reported that Sears's "low" prices were still higher than competitors'. One reason was that Sears's selling and administrative expenses ran about 30 percent of sales, as compared with about 23 percent at rival K mart. In order to be successful with everyday low *prices*, Sears first had to achieve everyday low *costs*. Another problem was that Sears's customers were conditioned to "hold out" for its traditional price-off sales and still expected them. Recently, Sears has begun to run price-off sales again and it is not clear whether they will maintain the claim of everyday low prices.

Coughlan and Vilcassim believe that in a duopolistic retail market with no real differentiation, a promotional-price retailer will eventually be forced to change to everyday low prices if facing a competitor who runs everyday low prices. Both firms would be unable to make above-normal profits because of competitive price pressures. Both firms will be tempted to run occasional sales in the hope of gaining a temporary advantage.

See Anne T. Coughlan and Naufel J. Vilcassim, "Retail Marketing Strategies: An Investigation of Everyday Low Pricing vs. Promotional Pricing Policies," working paper, Northwestern University, Kellogg Graduate School of Management, December 1989.

In view of the tradeoff between high traffic and high rents, retailers must decide on the most advantageous locations for their outlets. They can use a variety of methods to assess locations, including traffic counts, surveys of consumer shopping habits, analysis of competitive locations, and so on.[12] Several models for site location have also been formulated.[13]

Retailers can assess a particular store's sales effectiveness by looking at four indicators:

1. Number of people passing by on an average day
2. Percentage who enter the store
3. Percentage of those entering who buy
4. Average amount spent per sale.

A store that is doing poorly might be in a poorly trafficked location; or not enough passerbys drop in; or too many drop-ins browse but do not buy; or the buyers do not buy very much. Each problem can be remedied. Traffic is remedied by a better location; drop-ins are increased by better window displays and sales announcements; and the number buying and the amount purchased are largely a function of merchandise quality, prices, and salesmanship.

Trends in Retailing

At this point, we can summarize the main developments that retailers need to take into account as they plan their competitive strategies:

1. *New Retail Forms:* New retail forms constantly emerge to threaten established retail forms. For example, the Pop Shoppe developed decentralized bottling stores to serve people who want to buy low-price soft drinks in quantity. They located some of them in the vacant service bays of service stations that had been converted from full-service to self-service. This encouraged motorists who stop for gas to impulse-buy some soft drinks without making another stop.

2. *Cross-Border Shopping:* The traditional attraction of border-city Canadians to nearby U.S. shopping malls has intensified in recent years. A strong exchange rate has combined with reaction against the Goods and Service Tax, to persuade even residents in more distant cities like Toronto, to make regular cross-border shopping trips. Across Canada, the annual drain from Canadian merchants is estimated to be near $2 billion.

3. *Nonstore Retailing:* Over the past decade, mail-order sales increased at twice the rate of in-store sales. The electronic age has significantly increased the growth for nonstore retailing. Consumers receive sales offers over their televisions, computers, and telephones to which they can immediately respond by calling a toll-free number.

4. *Increasing Intertype Competition:* Competition today is increasingly intertype or between different types of outlets. Thus we see competition between in-store and nonstore retailers. Discount stores, catalog showrooms, and department stores all compete for the same consumers.

5. *Polarity of Retailing:* Increasing intertype competition has produced retailers positioning themselves on extreme ends of the number of product lines carried. High profitability and growth have been achieved by mass merchandisers like K mart and specialty stores like Radio Shack and Toys 'R' Us.

6. *Changing Definition of One-Stop Shopping:* Specialty stores in "malls" are becoming increasingly competitive with large department stores by offering "one-stop shopping." Customers park once and have a variety of specialty shops available to them.

7. *Growth of Vertical Marketing Systems:* Marketing channels are increasingly becoming professionally managed and programmed. As large corporations extend their control over marketing channels, independent small stores are being squeezed out.

8. *Portfolio Approach:* Retail organizations are increasingly designing and launching new store formats targeted to different lifestyle groups. They are not sticking to one format, such as department stores, but are moving into a mix of businesses that appear promising.

9. *Growing Importance of Retail Technology:* Retail technologies are becoming critically important as competitive tools. Progressive retailers are using computers to produce better forecasts, control inventory costs, order electronically from suppliers, send electronic mail between stores, and even sell to customers within stores. They are adopting checkout scanning systems, electronic funds transfer, in-store television, and improved merchandise-handling systems.[14]

WHOLESALING

Nature and Importance of Wholesaling

Wholesaling includes *all activities involved in selling goods or services to those who buy for resale or business use.* A retail bakery selling pastry to a local hotel is engaged in wholesaling at that point. We will use the term *wholesalers*, however, to describe firms that are engaged primarily in wholesaling activity. It excludes manufacturers and farmers, because they are engaged primarily in production, and it excludes retailers. About 627 000 Canadians are employed in wholesaling, and wholesaling costs represent about 10 percent of every consumer dollar.[15]

Wholesalers differ from retailers in a number of ways. First, wholesalers pay less attention to promotion, atmosphere, and location, because they are dealing with business customers rather than final consumers. Second, wholesale transactions are usually larger than retail transactions, and wholesalers usually cover a larger trade area than retailers. Third, the government deals with wholesalers and retailers differently in regard to legal regulations and taxes.

Why are wholesalers used at all? Manufacturers could bypass them and sell directly to retailers or final consumers. The answer lies in several efficiencies that wholesalers bring about. First, small manufacturers with limited financial resources cannot afford to develop direct-selling organizations. Second, even manufacturers with sufficient capital might prefer to use their funds to expand production rather than carry out wholesaling activities. Third, wholesalers are likely to be more efficient at wholesaling because of their scale of operation, their wider number of customer contacts, and their specialized skills. Fourth, retailers who carry many lines often prefer to buy assortments from a wholesaler rather than buy directly from each manufacturer.

Thus retailers and manufacturers have reasons to use wholesalers. Wholesalers are used when they are more efficient in performing one or more of the following functions:

☐ *Selling and Promoting:* Wholesalers provide a salesforce enabling manufacturers to reach many small customers at a relatively low cost. The wholesaler has more contacts and is often more trusted by the buyer than is the distant manufacturer.

☐ *Buying and Assortment Building:* Wholesalers are able to select items and build assortments needed by their customers, thus saving the customers considerable work.

☐ *Bulk Breaking:* Wholesalers achieve savings for their customers through buying in carload lots and breaking the bulk into smaller units.

☐ *Warehousing:* Wholesalers hold inventories, thereby reducing the inventory costs and risks to suppliers and customers.

□ *Transportation:* Wholesalers provide quicker delivery to buyers, because they are closer than the manufacturer.

□ *Financing:* Wholesalers finance their customers by granting credit, and they finance their suppliers by ordering early and paying their bills on time.

□ *Risk Bearing:* Wholesalers absorb some risk by taking title and bearing the cost of theft, damage, spoilage, and obsolescence.

□ *Market Information:* Wholesalers supply information to their suppliers and customers regarding competitors' activities, new products, price development, and so on.

□ *Management Services and Counseling:* Wholesalers often help retailers improve their operations by training their sales clerks, helping with stores' layouts and displays, and setting up accounting and inventory-control systems. They may help their industrial customers by offering training and technical services.

Growth and Types of Wholesaling

Wholesale trade amounting to $257.7 billion was handled by some 50 000 Canadian establishments in 1987.[16] Recent year-to-year increases of more than nine percent have been experienced. A number of factors have contributed to wholesaling's growth: the growth of larger factories located some distance from the principal buyers; the growth of production in advance of orders rather than in response to specific orders; an increase in the number of levels of intermediate producers and users; and the increasing need for adapting products to the needs of intermediate and final users in terms of quantities, packages, and forms.

Wholesalers fall into four groups, namely, *merchant wholesalers, brokers and agents, manufacturers' and retailers' branches and offices*, and *miscellaneous wholesalers* (see Marketing Environment and Trends 20-2).

Marketing Environment and Trends 20-2

MAJOR WHOLESALER TYPES

The major types of wholesalers are *merchant wholesalers, brokers and agents, manufacturers' and retailers' branches and offices*, and *miscellaneous wholesalers*. They are described below.

Merchant Wholesalers

Merchant wholesalers are independently owned businesses that take title to the merchandise they handle. In different trades they are called jobbers, distributors, or mill-supply houses. The various types of merchant wholesalers account for 85 percent of all wholesaling (in sales volume and in number of establishments). Merchant wholesalers can be subclassified into full-service wholesalers and limited-service wholesalers.

FULL-SERVICE WHOLESALERS Full-service wholesalers provide such services as carrying stock, maintaining a salesforce, offering credit, making deliveries, and providing management assistance. They include two types: wholesale merchants and industrial distributors.

Wholesale Merchants Wholesale merchants sell primarily to retailers and provide a full range of services. They vary mainly in the breadth of their product line. General-merchandise wholesalers carry several merchandise lines to meet the needs of both general-merchandise retailers and single-line retailers. General-line wholesalers carry one or two lines of

---

merchandise in a greater depth of assortment. Major examples are hardware wholesalers, drug wholesalers, and clothing wholesalers. Specialty wholesalers specialize in carrying only part of a line in great depth. Examples are health-food wholesalers, seafood wholesalers, and automotive-item wholesalers. They offer customers the advantage of deeper choice and greater product knowledge.

Industrial Distributors Industrial distributors are merchant wholesalers who sell to manufacturers rather than to retailers. They provide several services, such as carrying stock, offering credit, and providing delivery. They may carry a broad range of merchandise (often called a mill supply house), a general line, or a specialty line. Industrial distributors may concentrate on such lines as MRO items (maintenance, repair, and operating supplies), OEM items (original-equipment supplies such as ball bearings, motors), or equipment (such as hand and power tools, fork trucks).

LIMITED-SERVICE WHOLESALERS Limited-service wholesalers offer fewer services to their suppliers and customers. There are several types of limited-service wholesalers.

Cash-and-Carry Wholesalers Cash-and-carry wholesalers have a limited line of fast-moving goods and sell to small retailers for cash and normally do not deliver. A small fish-store retailer, for example, normally drives at dawn to a cash-and-carry fish wholesaler and buys several crates of fish, pays on the spot, and drives the merchandise back to the store and unloads it.

Truck Wholesalers Truck wholesalers (also called truck jobbers) perform a selling and delivery function primarily. They carry a limited line of semiperishable merchandise (such as milk, bread, snack foods), which they sell for cash as they make their rounds of supermarkets, small groceries, hospitals, restaurants, factory cafeterias, and hotels.

Drop Shippers Drop shippers operate in bulk industries, such as coal, lumber, and heavy equipment. They do not carry inventory or handle the product. Once an order is received, they find a manufacturer, who ships the merchandise directly to the customer on the agreed terms and time of delivery. The drop shipper assumes title and risk from the time the order is accepted to its delivery to the customer. Because drop shippers do not carry inventory, their costs are lower, and they can pass on some savings to customers.

Rack Jobbers Rack jobbers serve grocery and drug retailers, mostly in the area of nonfood items. These retailers do not want to order and maintain displays of hundreds of nonfood items. The rack jobbers send delivery trucks to stores, and the delivery person sets up toys, paperbacks, hardware items, health and beauty aids, and so on. They price the goods, keep them fresh, set up point-of-purchase displays, and keep inventory records. Rack jobbers sell on consignment, which means that they retain title to the goods and bill the retailers only for the goods sold to consumers. Thus they provide such services as delivery, shelving, inventory carrying, and financing. They do little promotion, because they carry many branded items that are highly advertised.

Producers' Cooperatives Producers' cooperatives are owned by farmer members and assemble farm produce to sell in local markets. Their profits are distributed to members at the end of the year. They often attempt to improve product quality and promote a co-op brand name, such as Sun Maid raisins, Sunkist oranges, or Diamond walnuts.

Mail-Order Wholesalers Mail-order wholesalers send catalogs to retail, industrial, and institutional customers featuring jewelry, cosmetics, specialty foods, and other small items. Their main customers are businesses in small outlying areas. No salesforce is maintained to call on customers. The orders are filled and sent by mail, truck, or other efficient means of transportation.

Brokers and Agents

Brokers and agents differ from merchant wholesalers in two ways: They do not take title to goods, and they perform only a few functions. Their main function is to facilitate buying and selling. Their commission ranges from 2 percent up to 15 percent for demanding functions. Like merchant wholesalers, they generally specialize by product line or customer type. They account for 15 percent of total wholesale trade.

BROKERS The chief function of a broker is to bring buyers and sellers together and assist in negotiation. They are paid by the party who hired them. They do not carry inventory, get involved in financing, or assume risk. The most familiar examples are food brokers, real-estate brokers, insurance brokers, and security brokers.

AGENTS Agents represent either buyers or sellers on a more permanent basis. There are several types.

Manufacturers' Agents Manufacturers' agents (also called manufacturers' representatives) are more numerous than other types of agent wholesalers. They represent two or more manufacturers of complementary lines. They enter into a formal written agreement with each manufacturer covering pricing policy, territories, order-handling procedure, delivery service and warranties, and commission rates. They know each manufacturer's product line and use their wide contacts to sell the manufacturer's products. Manufacturers' agents are used in such lines as apparel, furniture, and electrical goods. Most manufacturers' agents are small businesses, with only a few employees, who are skilled salespeople. They are hired by small manufacturers who cannot afford to maintain their own field salesforces and by large manufacturers who want to use agents to open new territories or to represent them in territories that cannot support full-time salespeople.

Selling Agents Selling agents are given contractual authority to sell a manufacturer's entire output. The manufacturer either is not interested in the selling function or feels unqualified. The selling agent serves as a sales department and has significant influence over prices, terms, and conditions of sale. The selling agent normally has no territorial limits. Selling agents are found in such product areas as textiles, industrial machinery and equipment, coal and coke, chemicals, and metals.

Purchasing Agents Purchasing agents generally have a long-term relationship with buyers and make purchases for them, often receiving, inspecting, warehousing, and shipping the merchandise to the buyers. One type consists of resident buyers in major apparel markets, who look for suitable lines of apparel that can be carried by small retailers located in small cities. They are knowledgeable and provide helpful market information to clients as well as obtaining the best goods and prices available.

Commission Merchants Commission merchants (or houses) are agents who take physical possession of products and negotiate sales. Normally, they are not employed on a long-term basis. They are used most often in agricultural marketing by farmers who do not want to sell their own output and do not belong to producers' cooperatives. A commission merchant would take a truckload of commodities to a central market, sell it for the best price, deduct a commission and expenses, and remit the balance to the producer.

Manufacturers' and Retailers' Branches and Offices

Some manufacturers and retailers perform wholesaling functions like maintaining inventories. Since the functions are not performed by wholesalers, they are not included in the wholesaling statistics, but are a significant part of the wholesaling function. There are two types.

SALES BRANCHES AND OFFICES Manufacturers often set up their own sales branches and offices to improve inventory control, selling, and promotion. *Sales branches* carry inventory and are found in such industries as lumber and automotive equipment and parts. Sales offices do not carry inventory and are most prominent in dry-goods and notions industries.

PURCHASING OFFICES Major retailers need to be represented in large cities where suppliers are located. Construction contractors need buying offices at jobsites. Such facilities function like brokers or agents, except that they are part of the buyer's organization.

Miscellaneous Wholesalers

A few specialized types of wholesalers are found in certain sectors of the economy, such as agricultural assemblers, petroleum bulk plants and terminals, and auction companies.

Wholesaler Marketing Decisions

Wholesaler-distributors have experienced mounting competitive pressures in recent years. They have faced new sources of competition, demanding customers, new technologies, and more direct-buying programs by large industrial, institutional and retail buyers. As a result, they have had to develop appropriate strategic responses. One major drive has been to increase asset productivity by managing better their inventories and receivables. And they have had to improve their strategic decisions on target markets, product assortment and services, pricing, promotion, and place.

Target-Market Decision   Wholesalers need to define their target markets and not try to serve everyone. They can choose a target group of customers according to size criteria (e.g., only large retailers), type of customer (e.g., convenience food stores only), need for service (e.g., customers who need credit), or other criteria. Within the target group, they can identify the more profitable customers and design stronger offers and build better relationships with them. They can propose automatic reordering systems, set up management-training and advisory systems, and even sponsor a voluntary chain. They can discourage less-profitable customers by requiring larger orders or adding surcharges to smaller ones.

Product-Assortment-and-Services Decision   The wholesalers' "product" is their assortment. Wholesalers are under great pressure to carry a full line and maintain sufficient stock for immediate delivery. But this can kill profits. Wholesalers today are reexamining how many lines to carry and are choosing to carry only the more profitable ones. They are grouping their items on an ABC basis, with A standing for the most-profitable items and C for the least profitable. Inventory-carrying levels are varied for the three groups. Wholesalers are also examining which services count most in building strong customer relationships and which ones should be dropped or charged for. The key is to find a distinct mix of services valued by their customers.

Pricing Decision   Wholesalers usually mark up the cost of goods by a conventional percentage, say 20 percent, to cover their expenses. Expenses may run 17 percent of the gross margin, leaving a profit margin of approximately 3 percent. In grocery wholesaling, the average profit margin is often less than 2 percent. Wholesalers are beginning to experiment with new approaches to pricing. They might cut their margin on some lines in order to win important new customers. They will ask suppliers for a special price break when they can turn it into an opportunity to increase the supplier's sales.

Promotion Decision   Wholesalers rely primarily on their salesforce to achieve promotional objectives. Even here, most wholesalers see selling as a single salesperson talking to a single customer instead of a team effort to sell, build, and service major accounts. As for nonpersonal promotion, wholesalers would benefit from adopting some of the image-making techniques used by retailers. They need to develop an overall promotion strategy involving trade advertising, sales promotion, and publicity. They also need to make greater use of supplier promotion materials and programs.

Place Decision   Wholesalers typically locate in low-rent, low-tax areas and put little money into their physical setting and offices. Often the materials-handling systems and order-processing systems lag behind the available technologies. To meet rising costs, progressive wholesalers have been making time and motion studies of materials-handling procedures. The ultimate development is the *automated warehouse*. Orders are fed into a computer and items are picked up by mechanical devices and conveyed on a belt to the shipping platform, where they are assembled. This type of mechanization is progressing rapidly, and so is the mechanization of many office activities. Most wholesalers now use computers to carry out accounting, billing, inventory control, and forecasting. An interesting variation is the CAR system provided by the Canadian Automobile Recycling Association for its 65 auto-wrecker members. When a service station needs a part that is no longer manufactured, a local wrecker can draw on inventories at other wreckers from Ottawa to Winnipeg who are interconnected by telex and fax machines. This has greatly reduced search time by service stations and boosted the wreckers' sales.

Trends in Wholesaling

Manufacturers always have the option of bypassing wholesalers or of replacing inefficient wholesalers with better ones. Manufacturers' major complaints against wholesalers are as follows: They do not aggressively promote the manufacturer's product line, acting more like order takers; they do not carry enough inventory and therefore fail to fill customers' orders fast enough; they do not supply the manufacturer with up-to-date market and competitive information; they do not attract high-caliber managers and bring down their own costs; and they charge too much for their services.

Progressive wholesaler-distributors, on the other hand, are those who adapt their services to meet the changing needs of their suppliers and target customers. They recognize that the rationale for their existence comes from adding value to the channel. They are constantly improving their services and/or reducing their costs. (See Marketing Strategies 20-2 for core strategies used by high-performance wholesaler-distributors.)

Narus and Anderson interviewed leading industrial distributors and identified four ways they strengthened their relationships with manufacturers:

1. They sought a clear agreement with their manufacturers about their expected functions in the marketing channel.
2. They gained insight into the manufacturers' requirements by visiting their plants and attending manufacturer association conventions and trade shows.
3. They fulfilled their commitments to the manufacturer by meeting the volume targets, promptly paying their bills, and feeding back customer information to their manufacturers.
4. They identified and offered value-added services to help their suppliers.[17]

A recent Arthur Andersen & Company study concluded that wholesale-distributors will need to undergo "aggressive restructuring" in the 1990s:

> Competitive pressures will keep sales prices in check, resulting in stable or, in many instances, shrinking gross margins. Consolidation will reduce significantly the number of firms in the industry, while the remaining larger firms will use new technology-driven services to increase market share and technology-driven operating techniques to improve productivity. Wholesaler-distributors will need new sources of capital to fund these investments in technology and market expansion. The challenge for companies in the industry will be to generate and balance the investment needed to capture growth in a maturing market with those needed to improve value-added services.[18]

PHYSICAL DISTRIBUTION

Producers engage the services of physical-distribution organizations to help them stock and move goods so that they will be available to customers at the right time and place. Customer

STRATEGIES OF HIGH-PERFORMANCE WHOLESALER-DISTRIBUTORS

McCammon, Lusch and their colleagues studied ninety-seven high-performance wholesaler-distributors to uncover their core strategies for gaining a sustained competitive advantage. The study identified the following twelve core strategies that were transforming the structure of distribution.

1. *Mergers and Acquisitions:* At least a third of the sampled wholesalers made new acquisitions which were aimed at entering new markets, at strengthening their position in existing markets, and/or at diversifying or vertically integrating.

2. *Asset Redeployment:* At least twenty of the ninety-seven wholesalers sold or liquidated one or more marginal operations in order to strengthen their core businesses.

3. *Corporate Diversification:* Several wholesalers diversified their respective portfolio of businesses in order to reduce their firm's cyclical exposure.

4. *Forward and Backward Integration:* Several wholesalers increased their vertical integration in order to improve their margins. For example, Super Valu integrated forward into retailing and Genuine Parts increased its backward integration into manufacturing.

5. *Proprietary Brands:* A third of the companies increased their proprietary-brand programs.

6. *Expansion into International Markets:* At least twenty-six wholesalers operated on a multinational basis and planned to increase their penetration into Western Europe and East Asia.

7. *Value-Added Services:* Most wholesalers increased their value-added services including "red flag" delivery service, customized packaging operations, and computerized management information systems. As an example of the latter, McKesson, the large drug wholesaler, established direct computer links with thirty-two drug manufacturers, a computerized accounts-receivable program for pharmacists, and computer terminals for drug stores for ordering inventories.

8. *Systems Selling:* More wholesalers offered turnkey merchandising programs to their buyers, posing a threat to those wholesalers who remained off-the-shelf suppliers.

9. *New Game Strategies:* Some wholesalers spotted new customer groups and created new turnkey merchandising programs for them.

10. *Niche Marketing:* Some wholesalers have specialized in one or few product categories, carrying extensive inventories, and in high service and rapid delivery, to satisfy special markets neglected by larger competitors.

11. *Multiplex Marketing:* Multiplex marketing occurs when firms manage to simultaneously serve multiple market segments in a cost-effective and competitively superior way. Several wholesalers have added new market segments to their core segments, hoping to achieve larger economies of scale and competitive strength. Thus membership warehouse clubs, in addition to wholesaling to small and medium-size business customers, obtain additional sales from consumers. Some drug wholesalers, in addition to serving hospitals, have created programs for doctor clinics, ethical pharmacies, and health maintenance organizations.

12. *New Technologies of Distribution:* High-performance wholesalers have improved their systems for computerized order entry, inventory control, and warehouse automation. In addition, they are making increased use of direct-response marketing and telemarketing.

Source: See Bert McCammon, Robert F. Lusch, Deborah S. Coykendall, and James M. Kenderdine, *Wholesaling in Transition* (Norman: University of Oklahoma, College of Business Administration, 1989).

attraction and satisfaction are highly influenced by the seller's physical-distribution capabilities and decisions. We will examine the nature, objectives, systems, and organizational aspects of physical distribution.

Nature of Physical Distribution

Physical distribution *involves planning, implementing, and controlling the physical flows of materials and final goods from points of origin to points of use to meet customer needs at a profit.*

Physical distribution involves several activities (see Figure 20-3). The first is sales forecasting, on the basis of which the company schedules production and inventory levels. The production plans indicate the materials that the purchasing department must order. These materials arrive through inbound transportation, enter the receiving area, and are stored in raw-material inventory. Raw materials are converted into finished goods. Finished-goods inventory is the link between the customers' orders and the company's manufacturing activity. Customers' orders draw down the finished-goods inventory level, and manufacturing activity builds it up. Finished goods flow off the assembly line and pass through packing, in-plant warehousing, shipping-room processing, outbound transportation, field warehousing, and customer delivery and servicing.

Management has become concerned about the total cost of physical distribution, which amounts to about 8 percent of sales revenue. Considering that advertising costs less than 3 percent of sales, marketing executives would undoubtedly be well rewarded if they could find ways to reduce physical-distribution costs. Lowered physical-distribution costs will permit lower prices or yield higher profit margins.

The main elements of total physical-distribution costs are transportation (37 percent), inventory carrying (22 percent), warehousing (21 percent), and order processing/customer service/distribution administration (20 percent).[19] Experts believe that substantial savings can be effected in the physical-distribution area, which has been described as "the last frontier for cost economies" and "the economy's dark continent."

Physical distribution is not only a cost; it is a potent tool in competitive marketing. Companies can attract additional customers by offering better service or lower prices through physical-distribution improvements. Companies lose customers when they fail to supply goods on time. In the summer of 1976, Kodak launched its national advertising campaign for its new instant camera before it had delivered enough cameras to the stores. Customers found that it was not available and bought Polaroids instead.

Traditional physical-distribution thinking starts with goods at the plant and tries to find low-cost solutions to get them to customers. Marketers prefer *market logistics* thinking that starts with the marketplace and works backward to the factory. Here is an example of market logistics thinking:

> German consumers typically purchase separate bottles of soft drinks. A soft-drink manufacturer decided to test a six-pack. Consumers responded positively to the convenience aspect of carrying a six-pack home. Retailers responded positively because the bottles could be loaded faster on the shelves, and more bottles would be purchased per occasion. The manufacturer designed the six-packs to fit comfortably on the store shelves. Then cases and pallets were designed for bringing these six-packs efficiently to the store's receiving rooms. Factory operations were redesigned to produce the new six-packs. The purchasing department let out bids for the new needed materials. Once implemented, this new packaging of soft drinks was an instant hit with consumers, and the manufacturer's market share rose substantially. ∎

The Physical-Distribution Objective

Many companies state their physical-distribution objective as *getting the right goods to the right places at the right time for the least cost.* Unfortunately, this provides little actual

FIGURE 20-3

Major Activities Involved in Physical Distribution

Source: Redrawn, with modifications, from Wendell M. Stewart, "Physical Distribution: Key to Improved Volume and Profits," *Journal of Marketing*, January 1965, p. 66.

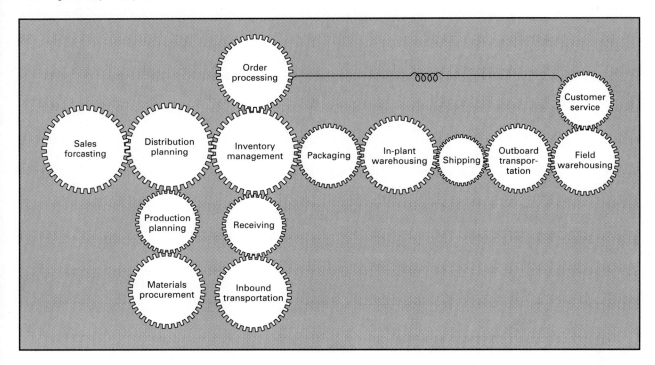

guidance. No physical-distribution system can simultaneously maximize customer service and minimize distribution cost. Maximum customer service implies large inventories, premium transportation, and multiple warehouses, all of which raise distribution cost. Minimum distribution cost implies cheap transportation, low stocks, and few warehouses.

A company cannot achieve physical-distribution efficiency by asking each physical-distribution manager to minimize his or her own costs. Physical-distribution costs interact, often in an inverse way:

> The traffic manager favors rail shipment over air shipment whenever possible. It reduces the company's freight bill. However, because the railroads are slower, rail shipment ties up working capital longer, delays customer payment, and might cause customers to buy from competitors offering faster service. ■

> The shipping department uses cheap containers to minimize shipping costs. This leads to a high rate of damaged goods in transit and customer ill will. ■

> The inventory manager favors low inventories to reduce inventory cost. However, this policy increases stockouts, back orders, paperwork, special production runs, and high-cost fast-freight shipments. ■

Given that physical-distribution activities involve strong tradeoffs, decisions must be made on a total system basis.

The starting point for designing the physical-distribution system is to study what the customers want and what competitors are offering. Customers are interested in several things:

on-time delivery, supplier willingness to meet customer emergency needs, careful handling of merchandise, supplier willingness to take back defective goods and resupply them quickly, and supplier willingness to carry inventory for the customer.

The company has to research the relative importance of these services to customers. For example, service-repair time is very important to buyers of copying equipment. Xerox therefore developed a service-delivery standard that can put a disabled machine anywhere in Canada back into operation within four hours after receiving the service request. Xerox runs a service division consisting of two thousand service and parts personnel.

The company must look at competitors' service standards in setting its own. It will normally want to offer at least the same level of service as competitors. But the objective is to maximize profits, not sales. The company has to look at the costs of providing higher levels of service. Some companies offer less service but charge a lower price. Other companies offer more service than competitors and charge a premium price to cover their higher costs.

The company ultimately has to establish physical-distribution objectives to guide its planning. For example, Coca-Cola wants to "put Coke within an arm's length of desire." Companies go further and define standards for each service factor. One appliance manufacturer has established the following service standards: to deliver at least 95 percent of the dealer's orders within seven days of order receipt, to fill the dealer's orders with 99 percent accuracy, to answer dealer inquiries on order status within three hours, and to ensure that damage to merchandise in transit does not exceed 1 percent.

Given a set of physical-distribution objectives, the company is ready to design a physical-distribution system that will minimize the cost of achieving these objectives. Each possible physical-distribution system implies a total distribution cost given by the expression

$$D = T + FW + VW + S \tag{20-1}$$

where:

D = total distribution cost of proposed system

T = total freight cost of proposed system

FW = total fixed warehouse cost of proposed system

VW = total variable warehouse costs (including inventory) of proposed system

S = total cost of lost sales due to average delivery delay under proposed system

Choosing a physical-distribution system calls for examining the total distribution cost associated with different proposed systems and selecting the system that minimizes total distribution cost. Alternatively, if it is hard to measure S in (20-1), the company should aim to minimize the distribution cost T + FW + VW of reaching a *target level of customer service*.

We will now examine the following major decision issues: (1) How should orders be handled? (*order processing*); (2) Where should stocks be located? (*warehousing*); (3) How much stock should be held? (*inventory*); and (4) How should goods be shipped? (*transportation*).

Order Processing

Physical distribution begins with a customer order. The order department prepares multicopy invoices and dispatches them to various departments. Items out of stock are back ordered. Shipped items are accompanied by shipping and billing documents, with copies going to various departments.

The company and customers benefit when these steps are performed quickly and accurately. Ideally, sales representatives send in their orders every evening, increasingly through computer hookups. The order department processes them quickly. The warehouse sends the goods out as soon as possible. Bills go out as soon as possible. The computer is used to expedite the order-shipping-billing cycle.

Industrial engineering studies of how sales orders are processed can help shorten this cycle. Some of the key questions are: What happens when the company receives a customer purchase order? How long does the customer credit check take? What procedures are used to check inventory, and how long does this take? How soon does manufacturing hear of new stock requirements? How long does it take for sales managers to get a complete picture of current sales?

Companies are making great progress in speeding up order handling, thanks to computers. General Electric operates a computer-oriented system that upon receipt of a customer's order, checks the customer's credit standing and whether and where the items are in stock. The computer issues an order to ship, bills the customer, updates the inventory records, sends a production order for new stock, and relays the message back to the sales representative that the customer's order is on its way—all in less than fifteen seconds.

Warehousing

Every company has to store its goods while they wait to be sold. A storage function is necessary, because production and consumption cycles rarely match. Many agricultural commodities are produced seasonally, whereas demand is continuous. The storage function overcomes discrepancies in desired quantities and timing.

The company must decide on a desirable number of stocking locations. More stocking locations means that goods can be delivered to customers more quickly. Warehousing costs go up, however. The number of stocking locations must strike a balance between customer-service levels and distribution costs.

Some company stock is kept at or near the plant, and the rest is located in warehouses around the country. The company might own *private warehouses* and rent space in *public warehouses*. Companies have more control in owned warehouses, but they tie up their capital and face some inflexibility if desired locations change. Public warehouses, on the other hand, charge for the rented space and provide additional services (at a cost) for inspecting goods, packaging them, shipping them, and invoicing them. In using public warehouses, companies have a broad choice of locations and warehouse types, including those specializing in cold storage, commodities only, and so on.

Companies use storage warehouses and distribution warehouses. *Storage warehouses* store goods for moderate to long periods of time. *Distribution warehouses* receive goods from various plants and suppliers and move them out as soon as possible. For example, a regional discount-store chain operates four distribution centers. One center covers 37 000 square meters on a 38-hectare site. The shipping department loads fifty to sixty trucks daily, delivering merchandise on a twice-weekly basis to its retail outlets. This is less expensive than supplying each retail outlet from each plant directly. Distribution centers are used in grocery distribution by Loblaws and Safeway, and in hardware distribution by Canadian Tire and Home Hardware.

The older multistoried warehouses with slow elevators and inefficient materials-handling procedures are receiving competition from newer single-storied *automated warehouses* with advanced materials-handling systems under the control of a central computer. The computer reads store orders and directs lift trucks and electric hoists to gather goods, move them to loading docks, and issue invoices. These warehouses have reduced worker injuries, labor costs, pilferage, and breakage and have improved inventory control.

Inventory

Inventory levels represent a major physical-distribution decision affecting customer satisfaction. Marketers would like their companies to carry enough stock to fill all customer orders immediately. However, it is not cost effective for a company to carry this much inventory. *Inventory cost increases at an increasing rate as the customer-service level approaches 100 percent.* Management would need to know by how much sales and profits would increase as a result of carrying larger inventories and promising faster order-fulfillment times.

Inventory decision making involves knowing when to order and how much to order. As inventory draws down, management must know at what stock level to place a new order. This stock level is called the *order (or reorder) point.* An order point of twenty means reordering when the stock falls to twenty units. The order point should be higher, the higher the order lead time, the usage rate, and the service standard. If the order lead time and customer-usage rate are variable, the order point should be set higher to provide a *safety stock.* The final order point should balance the risks of stockout against the costs of overstock.

The other decision is how much to order. The larger the quantity ordered, the less frequently an order has to be placed. The company needs to balance order-processing costs and inventory-carrying costs. Order-processing costs for a manufacturer consist of *setup costs* and *running costs* for the item. If setup costs are low, the manufacturer can produce the item often, and the cost per item is quite constant and equal to the running costs. If setup costs are high, however, the manufacturer can reduce the average cost per unit by producing a long run and carrying more inventory.

Order-processing costs must be compared with inventory-carrying costs. The larger the average stock carried, the higher the inventory-carrying costs. These carrying costs include storage charges, cost of capital, taxes and insurance, and depreciation and obsolescence. Inventory-carrying costs might run as high as 30 percent of inventory value. This means that marketing managers who want their companies to carry larger inventories need to show that the larger inventories would produce incremental gross profit that would exceed incremental inventory-carrying costs.

The optimal order quantity can be determined by observing how order-processing costs and inventory-carrying costs sum up at different order levels. Figure 20-4 shows that the order-processing cost per unit decreases with the number of units ordered, because the order costs are spread over more units. Inventory-carrying charges per unit increase with the number of units ordered, because each unit remains longer in inventory. The two cost curves are summed vertically into a total-cost curve. The lowest point on the total-cost curve is projected down on the horizontal axis to find the optimal order quantity Q*.[20]

The growing interest in *just-in-time production methods* promises to change inventory-planning practices. Just-in-time production consists of arranging for supplies to come into the factory at the rate that they are needed. If the suppliers are dependable, then the manufacturer can carry much lower levels of inventory and still meet customer-order-fulfillment standards.

Transportation

Marketers need to be concerned with their company's transportation decisions. Transportation choices will affect the pricing of the products, on-time delivery performance, and the condition of the goods when they arrive, all of which will affect customer satisfaction.

FIGURE 20-4
Determining Optimal Order
Quantity

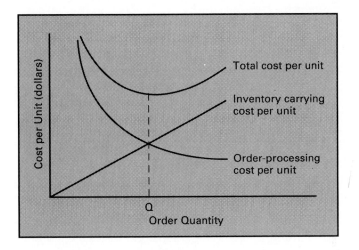

In shipping goods to its warehouses, dealers, and customers, the company can choose among the five transportation modes shown in Marketing Environment and Trends 20-3. Shippers consider such criteria as *speed, frequency, dependability, capability, availability*, and *cost*. If a shipper seeks speed, air and truck are the prime contenders. If the goal is low cost, then water and pipeline are the prime contenders. Trucks stand high on most of the criteria, and that accounts for their growing share.

Shippers are increasingly combining two or more transportation modes, thanks to containerization. *Containerization* consists of putting the goods in boxes or trailers that are easy to transfer between two transportation modes. *Piggyback* describes the use of rail and trucks; *fishyback*, water and trucks; *trainship*, water and rail; and *airtruck*, air and trucks. Each coordinated mode of transportation offers specific advantages to the shipper. For example, piggyback is cheaper than trucking alone and yet provides flexibility and convenience.

In choosing transportation modes, shippers can decide between private, contract, and common carriers. If the shipper owns its own truck or air fleet, the shipper becomes a *private carrier*. A *contract carrier* is an independent organization selling transportation services to others on a contract basis. A *common carrier* provides services between predetermined points on a schedule basis and is available to all shippers at standard rates.

Transportation decisions must consider the complex tradeoffs between various transportation modes and their implications for other distribution elements, such as warehousing and inventory. As transportation costs change over time, companies need to reanalyze their options in the search for optimal physical-distribution arrangements.[21]

Organizational Responsibility for Physical Distribution

We see that decisions on warehousing, inventory, and transportation require the highest degree of coordination. A growing number of companies have set up a permanent committee composed of managers responsible for different physical-distribution activities. This committee meets periodically to develop policies for improving overall distribution efficiency. Some companies have appointed a vice-president of physical distribution, who reports to the marketing or manufacturing vice-president or the president. Here are two examples:

> The Burroughs Corporation organized the Distribution Services Department to centralize control over its physical-distribution activities. This department reported to the marketing vice-president because of the great importance Burroughs attached to good customer service. Within two and

one-half years following the reorganization, the company achieved savings of over $2 million annually, and provided a higher level of service to field branches and customers. ∎

Heinz created a new department of comparable stature with marketing and production, which was headed by a vice-president of distribution. Heinz felt that this arrangement would guarantee respect for the department, develop a greater degree of professionalism and objectivity, and avoid partisan domination by marketing or production. ∎

Marketing Environment and Trends 20-3

FIVE MAJOR TRANSPORTATION MODES

Rail

In spite of a shrinking share of total transportation, railroads remain the nation's largest transportation carrier, accounting for 37 percent of total cargo moved. Railroads are one of the most cost-effective modes for shipping carload quantities of bulk products—coal, sand, minerals, farm and forest products—over long land distances. The rate costs for shipping merchandise are quite complex. The lowest rate comes from shipping carload rather than less-than-carload quantities. Manufacturers will attempt to combine shipments to common destinations to take advantage of lower carload rates. Railroads have begun to increase customer-oriented services. They have designed new equipment to handle special categories of merchandise, provided flatcars for carrying truck trailers by rail (piggyback), and provided in-transit services such as goods diversion to other destinations en route and goods processing en route.

Water

A substantial amount of goods move by ships and barges on coastal and inland waterways. Water transportation is low cost for shipping bulky, low-value, nonperishable products such as sand, coal, grain, oil, and metallic ores. On the other hand, water transportation is the slowest transportation mode and is dependent on climatic conditions.

Truck

Motor trucks have steadily increased their share of transportation and now account for 25 percent of total cargo. They account for the largest portion of intracity as opposed to intercity transportation. Trucks are highly flexible in their routing and time schedules. They can move merchandise door to door, saving shippers the need to transfer goods from truck to rail and back again at a loss of time and risk of theft or damage. Trucks are an efficient mode of transportation for short hauls of high-value merchandise. Their rates are competitive with railway rates in many cases, and trucks can usually offer faster service.

Pipeline

Pipelines are a specialized means of shipping petroleum, coal, and chemicals from sources to markets. Pipeline shipment of petroleum products is less expensive than rail shipment, although more expensive than waterway shipment. Most pipelines are used by their owners to ship their own products, although they are technically available for use by any shipper.

Air

Air carriers transport less than 1 percent of the nation's goods, but are becoming more important as a transportation mode. Although air freight rates are considerably higher than rail or truck freight rates, air freight is ideal where speed is essential and/or distant markets have to be reached. Among the most frequently air-freighted products are perishables (e.g., fresh fish, cut flowers) and high-value, low-bulk items (e.g., technical instruments, jewelry). Companies find that air freight reduces their required inventory levels, number of warehouses, and costs of packaging.

The location of the physical-distribution department within the company is a secondary concern. The important thing is that the company coordinates its physical-distribution and marketing activities in order to create high market satisfaction at a reasonable cost.

SUMMARY

Retailing and wholesaling consists of many organizations involved in bringing goods and services from the point of production to the point of use.

Retailing includes all the activities involved in selling goods or services directly to final consumers for their personal, nonbusiness use. Retailing is one of the major industries in Canada. Retailers can be classified in terms of store retailers, nonstore retailers, and retail organizations.

Store retailers include many types, such as specialty stores, department stores, supermarkets, convenience stores, superstores/combination stores/hypermarchés, discount stores, warehouse stores, and catalog showrooms. These store forms have had different longevities and are at different stages of the retail life cycle. Depending on the wheel of retailing, some will go out of existence because they cannot compete on a quality, service, or price basis.

Nonstore retailing is growing more rapidly than store retailing. It includes direct marketing, direct selling (door-to-door, party selling), automatic vending, and buying services.

Much of retailing is in the hands of retail organizations such as corporate chains, voluntary chain and retailer cooperatives, consumer cooperatives, franchise organizations, and merchandising conglomerates. More retail chains are willing to sponsor diversified retailing lines and forms instead of sticking to one form, such as the department store.

Retailers, like manufacturers, must prepare marketing plans that include decisions on target markets, product assortment and services, pricing, promotion, and place. Retailers are showing strong signs of improving their professional management and their productivity, in the face of such trends as shortening retail life cycles, new retail forms, increasing intertype competition, new retail technologies, and so on.

Wholesaling includes all the activities involved in selling goods or services to those who are buying for the purpose of resale or for business use. Wholesalers help manufacturers deliver their products efficiently to the many retailers and industrial users across the nation. Wholesalers perform many functions, including selling and promoting, buying and assortment building, bulk breaking, warehousing, transporting, financing, risk bearing, supplying market information, and providing management services and counseling. Wholesalers fall into four groups: merchant wholesalers; agents and brokers; manufacturers' and retailers' branches and offices; and miscellaneous wholesalers.

Wholesalers, too, must make decisions on their target market, product assortment and services, pricing, promotion, and place. Wholesalers who fail to carry adequate assortments and inventory and provide satisfactory service are likely to be bypassed by manufacturers. Progressive wholesalers, on the other hand, are adapting marketing concepts and streamlining their costs of doing business.

The marketing concept calls for paying increased attention to physical distribution. Physical distribution is an area of potentially high cost savings and improved customer satisfaction. When order processors, warehouse planners, inventory managers, and transportation managers make decisions, they affect each other's costs and demand-creation capacity. The physical-distribution concept calls for treating all these decisions within a unified framework. The task becomes that of designing physical-distribution arrangements that minimize the total cost of providing a desired level of customer service.

■ QUESTIONS

1. Create a matrix of differing service levels and assortment breadths. Discuss the broad positioning strategies that result from these combinations. Identify major retailers in each of these categories.

2. Discuss the environmental factors that facilitate the growth of nonstore retailing.

3. State who is being targeted by each of the following retailing strategies: (a) "Big retailers adopt specialty stores' marketing tactics"; (b) "Retailers that target low-income shoppers are growing rapidly."

4. The physical-distribution concept calls for treating a host of decisions within a unified framework that provides a desired level of customer service for a minimal cost. What does consumer service mean in the context of physical distribution, and what is its relationship to the marketing concept?

5. Many camera stores now have film-developing machines which provide the option of fast, on-site service. A similar choice is being offered to purchasers of prescription eyeglasses, with the advent of franchised stores containing production facilities. What is the marketing mix of such stores?

6. Wholesalers typically do not invest much in the promotional part of their marketing mix. Why has this been a weak area for wholesalers?

7. Does it follow that the company offering high customer service bears high physical-distribution costs in relation to sales?

8. What are the two inventory-production policy alternatives facing a seasonal producer?

9. A company's inventory-carrying cost is 30 percent. A marketing manager wants the company to increase its inventory investment from $400 000 to $500 000, believing this would lead to increased sales of $120 000 because of greater customer loyalty and service. The gross profit on sales is 20 percent. Does it pay the company to increase its inventory investment?

10. You are the marketing manager of a medium-sized manufacturing company. The president has just made the following statement: "The distribution activity is not a concern of the marketing department. The function of the marketing department is to sell the product . . . let the rest of the company handle production and distribution." How would you reply to this statement?

11. Why would manufacturers and retailers use wholesalers? What functions are the latter expected to perform?

■ NOTES

1. Statistics Canada, *Annual Retail Trade 1988.*

2. William R. Davidson, Albert D. Bates, and Stephen J. Bass, "Retail Life Cycle," *Harvard Business Review* (November-December 1976), pp. 89-96.

3. Malcolm P. McNair, "Significant Trends and Developments in the Postwar Period," in *Competitive Distribution in a Free, High-Level Economy and Its Implication for the University*, ed. A. B. Smith (Pittsburgh: University of Pittsburgh Press, 1958), pp. 1-25. Also see the critical discussion by Stanley C. Hollander, "The Wheel of Retailing," *Journal of Marketing*, July 1960, pp. 37-42.

4. See Ralph Raffio, "Double-Decker Franchising," *Venture*, November 1986, pp. 50-67.

5. Here are the investment costs (exclusive of real-estate cost) required by other well-known franchisers: Godfather's Pizza, $200 000; Baskin-Robbins, $50 000; Dunkin' Donuts, $45 000; AAMCo Transmissions, $101 000; and Southland Corp. (7-Eleven convenience markets), $37 000. See *The Wall Street Journal*, May 19, 1986, p. 14D.

6. See Rollie Tillman, "Rise of the Conglomerchant," *Harvard Business Review*, November-December 1971, pp. 44-51.

7. For a fuller discussion, see Lawrence H. Wortzel, "Retailing Strategies for Today's Marketplace," *Journal of Business Strategy*, Spring 1987, pp. 45-56.

8. See Roger D. Blackwell and W. Wayne Talarzyk, "Life-Style Retailing: Competitive Strategies for the 1980s," *Journal of Retailing*, Winter 1983, pp. 7-26.

9. Colin Lanquedoc, "Ikea plotting expansion in fun furniture outlets," *Financial Post*, July 27, 1987, p. 13.

10. Ann Walmsley, "The glamorous return of an old lady," *Maclean's*, January 20, 1986, p. 34.

11. For more discussion, see Philip Kotler, "Atmospherics as a Marketing Tool," *Journal of Retailing*, Winter 1973-74, pp. 48-64; and "Beautiful Ways to Shop," *Newsweek*, November 10, 1986.

12. R.L. Davies and D.S. Rogers, eds., *Store Location and Store Assessment Research* (New York: John Wiley, 1984).

13. David L. Huff, "Defining and Estimating a Trading Area," *Journal of Marketing*, July 1964, pp. 34-38; David A. Gautschi, "Specification of Patronage Models for Retail Center Choice," *Journal of Marketing Research*, May 1981, pp. 162-74; Sara L. McLafferty, *Location Strategies for Retail and Service Firms* (Lexington, Mass.: Lexington Books, 1987).

14. For further discussion of retail trends, see Eleanor G. May, C. William Ress, and Walter J. Salmon, *Future Trends in Retailing* (Cambridge, Mass.: Marketing Science Institute, February 1985); and Louis W. Stern and Adel I. El-Ansary, *Marketing Channels* (Englewood Cliffs, N.J.: Prentice Hall 1988).

15. Statistics Canada, *Wholesale Trade Statistics 1987*.

16. Statistics Canada, *Labour Force Annual Averages 1990*.

17. James A. Narus and James C. Anderson, "Contributing as a Distributor to Partnerships with Manufacturers," *Business Horizons*, September-October 1987. Also see James D. Hlavecek and Tommy J. McCuistion, "Industrial Distributors—When, Who, and How," *Harvard Business Review*, March-April 1983, pp. 96-101.

18. Arthur Andersen & Co., *Facing the Forces of Change: Beyond Future Trends in Wholesale Distribution* (Washington, D.C.: Distribution Research and Education Foundation, 1987), p. 7. This report is an excellent source of information on the wholesaling industry.

19. See "Know Your Distribution Costs," *Distribution*, April 1987, p. 36.

20. The optimal order quantity is given by the formula $Q^* = 2DS/IC$ where D = annual demand, S = cost to place one order, and I = annual carrying cost per unit. Known as the economic-order quantity formula, it assumes a constant ordering cost, a constant cost of carrying an additional unit in inventory, a known demand, and no quantity discounts. For further reading on this subject, see Charles D. Mecimore, *Techniques in Inventory Management and Control* (Montvale, N.J.: National Association of Accountants, 1987).

21. See the report prepared by A. T. Kearney, management consultants, entitled *Logistics Productivity: The Successful Companies* (National Council of Physical Distribution Management, 1984). Also see Ronald H. Ballou, *Basic Business Logistics*, 2nd ed. (Englewood Cliffs, N.J.: Prentice Hall, 1987).

Designing Communication and Promotion-Mix Strategies

. . . in operational and practical fact, the medium is the message.

Marshall McLuhan

Modern marketing calls for more than developing a good product, pricing it attractively, and making it accessible to target customers. Companies must also communicate with their present and potential customers. Every company is inevitably cast into the role of communicator and promoter.

What is communicated, however, should not be left to chance. To communicate effectively, companies hire advertising agencies to develop effective ads; sales-promotion specialists to design sales-incentive programs; and public-relations firms to develop the corporate image. They train their salespeople to be friendly and knowledgeable. For most companies, the question is not whether to communicate but rather what to say, to whom, and how often.

A modern company manages a complex marketing communications system. The company communicates with its middlemen, consumers, and various publics. Its middlemen communicate with their consumers and various publics. Consumers engage in word-of-mouth communication with other consumers and publics. Meanwhile, each group provides communication feedback to every other group.

The marketing communication mix (also called the promotion mix) consists of four major tools:

☐ *Advertising:* Any paid form of nonpersonal presentation and promotion of ideas, goods, or services by an identified sponsor.

☐ *Sales Promotion:* Short-term incentives to encourage purchase or sale of a product or service.

☐ *Public Relations:* A variety of programs designed to improve, maintain, or protect a company or product image.

Table 21-1 Some Common Communication/Promotion Tools

Advertising	Sales Promotion	Public Relations	Personal Selling
Print and broadcast ads	Contests, games, sweepstakes, lotteries	Press kits	Sales presentations
Packaging—outer		Speeches	Sales meetings
Packaging inserts	Premiums and gifts	Seminars	Telemarketing
Mailings		Annual reports	Incentive programs
Catalogs	Sampling	Charitable donations	Samples
Motion pictures	Fairs and trade shows	Sponsorships	Fairs and trade shows
House magazines		Publications	
Brochures and booklets	Exhibits	Community relations	
Posters and leaflets	Demonstrations	Lobbying	
Directories	Couponing	Identity media	
Reprints of ads	Rebates		
Billboards	Low-interest financing		
Display signs	Entertainment		
Point-of-purchase displays	Trade-in allowances		
Audiovisual material	Trading stamps		
Symbols and logos	Tie-ins		

☐ *Personal Selling:* Oral presentation in a conversation with one or more prospective purchasers for the purpose of making sales.[1]

Numerous specific tools, such as those listed in Table 21-1, fall within these categories. At the same time, communication goes beyond these specific communication/promotion tools. The product's styling, its price, the package's shape and color, the salesperson's manner and dress—all communicate something to the buyers. The whole marketing mix, not just the promotional mix, must be orchestrated for maximum communication impact.

This chapter examines three major questions: How does communication work? What are the major steps in developing an effective marketing communications program? Who should be responsible for marketing communication planning? Chapter 21 deals with advertising; Chapter 22, with direct-marketing sales promotion and public relations; and Chapter 23, with the salesforce.

THE COMMUNICATION PROCESS

Marketers need to understand how communication works. According to Lasswell, a communication model answers (1) who (2) says what (3) in what channel (4) to whom (5) with what effect.[2] Figure 21-1 shows a communication model with nine elements. Two elements represent the major parties in a communication—*sender* and *receiver*. Two represent the major communication tools—*message* and *media*. Four represent major communication functions—*encoding, decoding, response*, and *feedback*. The last element is *noise* in the system. These elements are defined as follows:

- *Sender:* The party sending the message to another party (also called the source or communicator)
- *Encoding:* The process of putting thought into symbolic form
- *Message:* The set of symbols the sender transmits
- *Media:* The communication channels through which the message moves from sender to receiver
- *Decoding:* The process by which the receiver assigns meaning to the symbols transmitted by the sender
- *Receiver:* The party receiving the message sent by another party (also called the audience or destination)
- *Response:* The set of reactions the receiver has after being exposed to the message
- *Feedback:* The part of the receiver's response that the receiver communicates back to the sender
- *Noise:* Unplanned static or distortion during the communication process

The model underscores the key factors in effective communication. Senders must know what audiences they want to reach and what responses they want. They encode their messages in a way that takes into account how the target audience usually decodes messages. The source must transmit the message through efficient media that reach the target audience. Senders must develop feedback channels so that they can know the receiver's response to the message.

For a message to be effective, the sender's encoding process must mesh with the receiver's decoding process. Schramm sees messages essentially as signs that must be familiar to the receiver. The more the sender's field of experience overlaps with that of the receiver, the more effective the message is likely to be. "The source can encode, and the destination can decode, only in terms of the experience each has had."[3] This puts a burden on communicators from one social stratum (such as advertising people) who want to communicate effectively with another stratum (such as factory workers).

The sender's task is to get his or her message through to the receiver. There is considerable noise in the environment—people are bombarded by several hundred commercial messages a day. The target audience may not receive the intended message for any of three reasons. The first is *selective attention* in that they will not notice all of the stimuli. The second is *selective*

FIGURE 21-1

Elements in the Communication Process

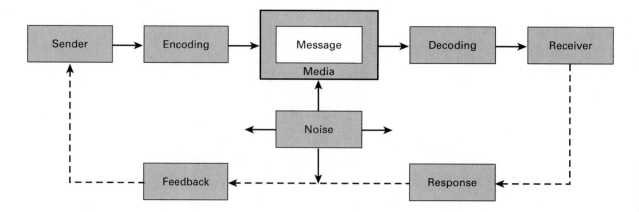

distortion in that they will twist the message to hear what they want to hear. The third is *selective recall* in that they will retain in permanent memory only a small fraction of the messages that reach them.

The communicator must design the message to win attention in spite of surrounding distractions. The likelihood that a potential receiver will pay attention to a message is given by:[4]

$$\frac{\text{Likelihood}}{\text{of attention}} = \frac{\text{Perceived reward strength} - \text{Perceived punishment strength}}{\text{Perceived expenditure of effort}}$$

Selective attention explains why ads with bold headlines promising something, such as "How to Make a Million," along with an arresting illustration and little copy, have a high likelihood of grabbing attention. For very little effort, the receiver might gain a great reward.

As for selective distortion, receivers have set attitudes, which lead to expectations about what they will hear or see. They will hear what fits into their belief system. As a result, receivers often add things to the message that are not there (*amplification*) and do not notice other things that are there (*leveling*). The communicator's task is to strive for message simplicity, clarity, interest, and repetition, to get the main points across to the audience.

As for selective recall, the communicator aims to get the message into the receiver's long-term memory. Long-term memory holds all the information one has ever processed. In entering the receiver's long-term memory, the message can modify the receiver's beliefs and attitudes. But first the message has to enter the receiver's short-term memory, which is a limited-capacity store that processes incoming information. Whether the message passes from the receiver's short-term memory to his or her long-term memory depends on the amount and type of *message rehearsal* by the receiver. Rehearsal is not simply message repetition; rather, the receiver elaborates on the meaning of the information in a way that brings related thoughts from the receiver's long-term memory into his or her short-term memory. If the receiver's initial attitude toward the object is positive and he or she rehearses support arguments, the message is likely to be accepted and have high recall. If the receiver's initial attitude is negative and the person rehearses counterarguments, the message is likely to be rejected but to stay in long-term memory. Counterarguing inhibits persuasion by making an opposing message available. Much of persuasion requires the receiver's rehearsal of his or her own thoughts. Much of what is called persuasion is self-persuasion.[5]

Communicators have been looking for audience traits that correlate with their degree of persuasibility. People of high education and/or intelligence are thought to be less persuasible, but the evidence is inconclusive. Women have been found to be more persuasible than men, although this is mediated by a woman's acceptance of the prescribed female role. Women who value traditional sex roles are more influenceable than women who are less accepting of the traditional roles.[6] Persons who accept external standards to guide their behavior and who have a weak self-concept appear to be more persuasible. Persons who are low in self-confidence are also thought to be more persuasible. However, research by Cox and Bauer showed a curvilinear relation between self-confidence and persuasibility, with those moderate in self-confidence being the most persuasible.[7] The communicator should look for audience traits that correlate with persuasibility and use them to guide message and media development.

Fiske and Hartley have outlined some factors that moderate the effect of a communication:

1. The greater the monopoly of the communication source over the recipient, the greater the change or effect in favor of the source over the recipient.

2. Communication effects are greatest where the message is in line with the existing opinions, beliefs, and dispositions of the receiver.

3. Communication can produce the most effective shifts on unfamiliar, lightly felt, peripheral issues, which do not lie at the center of the recipient's value system.

4. Communication is more likely to be effective where the source is believed to have expertise, high status, objectivity, or likability, but particularly where the source has power and can be identified with.

5. The social context, group, or reference group will mediate the communication and influence whether or not it is accepted.[8]

STEPS IN DEVELOPING EFFECTIVE COMMUNICATIONS

We will now examine the major steps in developing a total communication and promotion program. The marketing communicator must (1) identify the target audience, (2) determine the communication objectives, (3) design the message, (4) select the communication channels, (5) allocate the total promotion budget, (6) decide on the promotion mix, (7) measure the promotion's results, and (8) manage and coordinate the total marketing communication process.

Identifying the Target Audience

A marketing communicator must start with a clear target audience in mind. The audience could be potential buyers of the company's products, current users, deciders, or influencers. The audience could be individuals, groups, particular publics, or the general public. The target audience will critically influence the communicator's decisions on what to say, how to say it, when to say it, where to say it, and to whom to say it.

Image Analysis   A major part of audience analysis is to assess the audience's current image of the company, its products, and its competitors. People's attitudes and actions toward an object are highly conditioned by their beliefs about the object. *Image* is the *set of beliefs, ideas, and impressions that a person holds of an object.*

The first step is to measure the target audience's knowledge of the object, using the following *familiarity scale:*

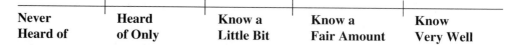

| Never Heard of | Heard of Only | Know a Little Bit | Know a Fair Amount | Know Very Well |

If most respondents circle only the first two categories, then the company's task will be to build greater awareness.

Respondents who are familiar with the product should be asked how they feel toward it, using the following *favorability scale:*

| Very Unfavorable | Somewhat Unfavorable | Indifferent | Somewhat Favorable | Very Favorable |

If most respondents check the first two categories, then the organization must overcome a negative image problem.

The two scales can be combined to develop insight into the nature of the communication challenge. To illustrate, suppose area residents are asked about their familiarity with and

FIGURE 21-2
Familiarity-Favorability Analysis

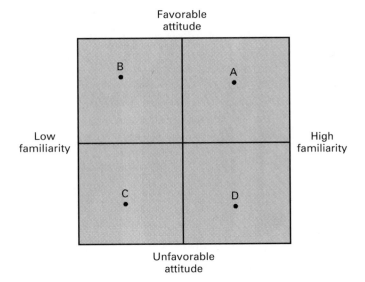

attitudes toward four local hospitals, A, B, C, and D. Their responses are averaged and shown in Figure 21-2. Hospital A has the most positive image: Most people know it and like it. Hospital B is less familiar to most people, but those who know it like it. Hospital C is viewed negatively by those who know it, but fortunately for the hospital, not too many people know it. Hospital D is seen as a poor hospital, and everyone knows it!

Clearly, each hospital faces a different communication task. Hospital A must work at maintaining its good reputation and high community awareness. Hospital B must gain the attention of more people, since those who know it consider it a good hospital. Hospital C must find out why people dislike it and must take steps to improve its performance while keeping a low profile. Hospital D should lower its profile (avoid news), improve its quality, and then seek public attention again.

Each hospital needs to go further and research the specific content of its image. The most popular tool for this research is the *semantic differential*.[9] It involves the following steps:

1. *Developing a Set of Relevant Dimensions:* The researcher asks people to identify the dimensions they would use in thinking about the object. People could be asked, "What things do you think of when you consider a hospital?" If someone suggests "quality of medical care," this would be turned into a bipolar adjective scale—say, "inferior medical care" at one end and "superior medical care" at the other. It could be rendered as a five- or seven-point scale. A set of additional dimensions for a hospital are shown in Figure 21-3.

2. *Reducing the Set of Relevant Dimensions:* The number of scales should be kept small to avoid respondent fatigue from having to rate several objects on many scales. Respondents seem to use three rating criteria that should be measured: evaluation (measured by good-bad scales); potency (measured by strong-weak scales); activity (measured by active-passive scales). Using these criteria as a guide, the researcher can avoid using scales that fail to add much information.

3. *Administering the Instrument to a Sample of Respondents:* The respondents are asked to rate one object at a time. The bipolar adjectives should be randomly arranged so as not to list all of the unfavorable adjectives on one side.

4. *Averaging the Results:* Figure 21-3 shows the results of averaging the respondents' pictures of hospitals A, B, and C (hospital D is left out). Each hospital's image is represented by

FIGURE 21-3
Images of Three
Hospitals (Semantic
Differential)

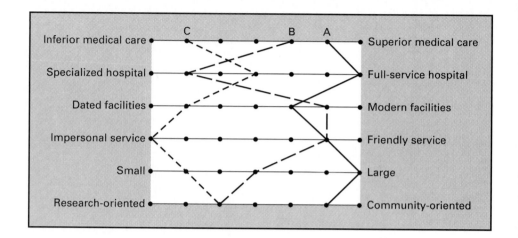

the zig-zag profile that summarizes the average perception of that hospital. Thus hospital A is seen as a large, modern, friendly, and superior hospital. Hospital C, on the other hand, is seen as a small, dated, impersonal, and inferior hospital.

5. *Checking on the Image Variance:* Since each image profile is a line of means, it does not reveal how variable the image actually is. Did everyone see hospital B exactly as shown, or was there considerable variation? In the first case, we would say that the image is highly *specific*; and in the second case, highly *diffused*. An organization might not want a very specific image. Some organizations prefer a diffused image so that different groups will see the organization in different ways.

The management should now propose a *desired image* in contrast to the *current image*. Suppose hospital C would like the public to view more favorably the quality of the hospital's medical care, facilities, friendliness, and so on. Management must decide which image gaps it wants to close first. Is it more desirable to improve the hospital's friendliness (through staff training programs) or the quality of its facilities (through renovation)? Each image dimension should be reviewed in terms of the following questions:

☐ What contribution to the organization's overall favorable image would be made by closing that particular image gap to the extent shown?

☐ What strategy (combination of real changes and communication changes) would help close the particular image gap?

☐ What would be the cost of closing that image gap?

☐ How long would it take to close that image gap?

An organization seeking to improve its image must have great patience. Images are "sticky." They persist long after the organization has changed. Thus a famous hospital's medical care might have deteriorated, and yet it continues to be highly regarded in the public mind. Image persistence is explained by the fact that once people have a certain image of an object, they selectively perceive further data. They perceive what is consistent with their image. It will take highly disconfirming information to raise doubts and open them to new information. Thus an image enjoys a life of its own, especially when people do not have continuous or new first-hand experiences with the changed object.

Determining the Communication Objectives

Once the target market and its characteristics are identified, the marketing communicator must decide on the desired audience response. The ultimate response, of course, is purchase and satisfaction. But purchase behavior is the end result of a long process of consumer decision making. The marketing communicator needs to know how to move the target audience to higher states of readiness to buy.

The marketer can be seeking a *cognitive, affective*, or *behavioral* response from the target audience. That is, the marketer might want to put something into the consumer's mind, change the consumer's attitude, or get the consumer to act. Even here, there are different models of consumer-response stages. Figure 21-4 shows the four best known *response hierarchy models*.

The *AIDA model* shows the buyer as passing through the stages of attention, interest, desire, and action. The *hierarchy-of-effects model* shows the buyer as progressing through awareness, knowledge, liking, preference, conviction, and purchase. The *innovation-adoption model* shows the buyer as passing through awareness, interest, evaluation, trial, and adoption. The *communications model* shows the buyer as progressing through exposure, reception, cognitive response, attitude, intention, and behavior. Most of these differences are semantic.

All of these models assume that the buyer passes through a cognitive, affective, and behavioral stage, in that order. This sequence is the "learn-feel-do" sequence and is appropriate when the audience has high involvement with a product category perceived to have high differentiation, as is the case in purchasing an automobile. An alternative sequence is the "do-feel-learn" sequence, when the audience has high involvement but perceives little or no differentiation within the product category, as in purchasing aluminum siding. Still a third sequence is the "learn-do-feel" sequence, when the audience has low involvement and

FIGURE 21-4

Response Hierarchy Models

Sources: (a) E. K. Strong, *The Psychology of Selling* (New York: McGraw-Hill, 1925), p. 9; (b) Robert J. Lavidge and Gary A. Steiner, "A Model for Predictive Measurements of Advertising Effectiveness," *Journal of Marketing*, October 1961, p. 61; (c) Everett M. Rogers, *Diffusion of Innovations* (New York: Free Press, 1962), pp. 79-86; (d) various sources.

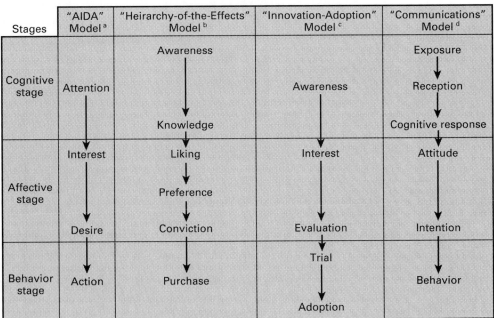

perceives little differentiation within the product category, as is the case in purchasing salt. By understanding the appropriate sequence, the marketer can do a better job of planning communications.

Here we will assume that the buyer has high involvement with the product category and perceives high differentiation within the category. Therefore we will work with the "hierarchy-of-effects" model (learn, feel, do) and describe the six buyer-readiness states—awareness, knowledge, liking, preference, conviction, and purchase.[10]

Awareness   If most of the target audience is unaware of the object, the communicator's task is to build awareness, perhaps just name recognition. This can be accomplished with simple messages repeating the name. Even then, building awareness takes time. Suppose a small private school in Calgary seeks applicants from Vancouver, but has little name recognition there. And suppose there are thirty thousand parents in Vancouver who might potentially be interested in sending their children to the school. The administration might set the objective of making 70 percent of these parents aware of the school within one year.

Knowledge   The target audience might be aware that private schools exist but not know much more. The school may want its target audience to know that it is a co-educational school with quality academic programs serving grades 6 to 12. The school thus needs to learn how many people in the target audience have little, some, or much knowledge about the school. The school may then decide to select knowledge of its name and programs as its communication objective.

Liking   Once target parents know about the school, how do they feel about it? If the parents look unfavorably on the school, the communicator has to find out why and then develop a communication campaign to shore up favorable feelings. If the unfavorable view is based on real problems of the school, then a communication campaign alone cannot do the job. The school will have to fix its problems and then communicate its renewed quality. Good public relations calls for "good deeds followed by good words."

Preference   Parents who come to like the school might not prefer it to others. In this case, the communicator must try to build consumer preference. The communicator will promote the programs' quality, value, performance, and other features. The communicator can check on the campaign's success by measuring audience preferences again after the campaign.

Conviction   Some of the target parents might prefer the school but not yet be convinced because of guilt about sending their children away to school. The communicator's job is to build conviction that doing so will be good for their children. For example, testimonials from satisfied parents might be used.

Purchase   Finally, some members of the target audience might have conviction but not quite get around to taking action. They may wait for more information or plan to act later. The communicator must lead these consumers to take the final step by finding out why the parents are hesitating. If tuition cost is a problem, scholarships might be offered. If unfamiliarity is a problem, they might be invited to visit the school, look at the facilities, and possibly let the children attend some classes.

Determining the target response is critical in developing a communication program. Marketing Concepts and Tools 21-1 shows how the communicator can determine simultaneously both the target audience and the target response.

Marketing Concepts and Tools 21-1

DETERMINING THE TARGET AUDIENCE AND SOUGHT RESPONSE

Communication objectives depend heavily on how many people already know about a product and may have tried it. Ottesen developed a device called a *market map* to be used in choosing the target audience and eliciting the sought response. The market map is shown below.

The horizontal dimension shows the current percentage of the market that know the brand, here 90 percent. The vertical dimension shows the percentage of the market that have tried the brand, here 80 percent. From these two measures, we know that the brand is mature. The knowers-triers further divide into those who prefer (23 percent), are indifferent (39 percent), and have rejected (18 percent) the brand. The knowers-nontriers can also be assumed to divide into those who have a positive, indifferent, and negative attitude toward the brand.

The task is to set communication objectives for this brand. Since 90 percent of the target market already know the brand, it would not make sense to build awareness in the remaining 10 percent. The 10 percent who do not know this brand consist of persons who are unaware of many things and probably do not have much income. It is expensive to reach these people and is seldom worth it.

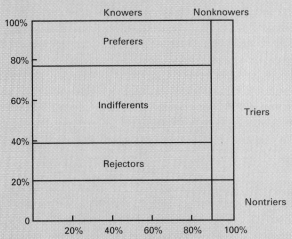

What about getting more knowers-nontriers to try the product? That is a worthwhile objective and can best be accomplished through sales promotion (free samples, cents-off coupons, and so on) rather than through additional advertising or personal selling. Since 25 percent of the current triers prefer the brand, we cannot expect that more than 25 percent of the new triers will stay with the brand. The marketer should calculate whether achieving this number of new-trier preferers would be worth the cost of the sales-promotion campaign.

Another plausible communication objective is to increase the proportion of triers who prefer this brand to other brands. This is difficult because consumer attitude is a function of how the consumer experiences the brand's performance and price of the brand. If the company wants to increase preference, what is required is product improvement and lower prices rather than more advertising.

The following conclusions can be drawn about the three trier groups. Communication to those who already prefer the brand is usually not very productive unless there is high consumer forgetfulness or a high level of competitors' expenditure aimed at preferers. Communication directed to the rejectors is probably wasted because the rejectors are not likely to pay attention to the advertising and probably would not retry the brand. Communication directed to the indifferents will probably be effective in attracting some proportion of their purchases, especially if the advertising makes some strong point to this audience.

Thus the communication objectives depend very much on the state of the market. When a brand is new, there are few knowers and triers, and communication can be very effective in increasing their number. When the brand is mature, it makes sense to try to convert nontriers into triers through sales promotion and to fight for a normal share of the indifferent triers; it makes less sense to try to increase the percentage of knowers to reinforce preferers, or to try to get rejectors to retry the brand.

Source: See Otto Ottesen, "The Response Function," in *Current Theories in Scandinavian Mass Communications Research*, ed. Mie Berg (Grenaa, Denmark: G.M.T., 1977).

Designing the Message

Having defined the desired audience response, the communicator moves to developing an effective message. Ideally, the message should gain *attention*, hold *interest*, arouse *desire*, and elicit *action* (AIDA model). In practice, few messages take the consumer all the way from awareness through purchase, but the AIDA framework suggests the desirable qualities.

Formulating the message will require solving four problems: what to say (*message content*), how to say it logically (*message structure*), how to say it symbolically (*message format*), and who should say it (*message source*).

Message Content   The communicator has to figure out what to say to the target audience to produce the desired response. This process has been variously called the *appeal, theme, idea*, or *unique selling proposition* (USP). It amounts to formulating some kind of benefit, motivation, identification, or reason why the audience should think about or investigate the product. Three types of appeals can be distinguished. *Rational appeals* appeal to the audience's self-interest. They show that the product will produce the claimed benefits. Examples would be messages demonstrating a product's quality, economy, value, or performance. It is widely believed that industrial buyers are most responsive to rational appeals. They are knowledgeable about the product class, trained to recognize value, and accountable to others for their choice. Consumers, when they buy certain big-ticket items, also tend to gather information and compare alternatives. They will respond to quality, economy, value, and performance appeals.

Emotional appeals attempt to stir up some negative or positive emotions that will motivate purchase. Communicators have worked with *fear, guilt*, and *shame appeals* in getting people to do things they should (e.g., brushing teeth, taking an annual health checkup) or stop doing things they shouldn't (e.g., smoking, overimbibing, drug abuse, overeating). Fear appeals are effective up to a point, but if the audience anticipates too much fear in the message, they will avoid it (see Marketing Strategies 21-1). Communicators also use positive emotional appeals such as *humor, love, pride*, and *joy*. Evidence has not established that a humorous message, for example, is necessarily more effective than a straight version of the same message. Humorous messages probably attract more attention and create more liking and belief in the sponsor, but humor can also detract from comprehension.[11]

Moral appeals are directed to the audience's sense of what is right and proper. They are often used to exhort people to support social causes, such as a cleaner environment, better race relations, equal rights for women, and aid to the disadvantaged. An example is the March of Dimes appeal: "God made you whole. Give to help those He didn't." Moral appeals are less often used in connection with everyday products.

Some advertisers believe that messages are maximally persuasive when they are moderately discrepant with what the audience believes. Messages that only state what the audience believes attract less attention and at best only reinforce audience beliefs. But if the messages are too discrepant with the audience's beliefs, they will be counterargued in the audience's mind and be disbelieved. The challenge is to design a message that is moderately discrepant and avoids the two extremes.

Message Structure   A message's effectiveness depends on its structure as well as its content. Hovland's research has shed much light on conclusion drawing, one- versus two-sided arguments, and order of presentation.

Conclusion drawing raises the question as to whether the communicator should draw a definite conclusion for the audience or leave it to them. Some early experiments supported the greater efficacy of stating conclusions for the audience. Recent research, however, indicates

DO FEAR APPEALS WORK?

Fear appeals have been studied more than any other emotional appeal, not only in marketing communication but also in politics and child rearing. For many years marketing communicators believed that a message's effectiveness increased with the level of fear produced. Actually study findings indicate that neither extremely strong nor extremely weak fear appeals are as effective as moderate ones in producing adherence to a recommendation. Ray and Wilkie explained the finding by hypothesizing two types of effects as fear increases:

> First, there are the facilitating effects that are most often overlooked in marketing. If fear can heighten drive, there is the possibility of greater attention and interest in the product and message than if no drive were aroused. . . . But fear also brings the important characteristic of inhibition into the picture. . . . If fear levels are too high, there is the possibility of defensive avoidance of the ad, denial of the threat, selective exposure or distortion of the ad's meaning, or a view of the recommendations as being inadequate to deal with so important a fear.

Source credibility moderates the effectiveness of a fear appeal. When source credibility is high, a fear appeal induces attitude change. American Express, a high-credibility source, uses a fear appeal in its campaign to admonish consumers to carry American Express traveler's checks. If the fear message is to be effective, the communication should promise to relieve, in a believable and efficient way, the fear it arouses: otherwise buyers will ignore or minimize the threat.

Source: Michael L. Ray and William L. Wilkie, "Fear: The Potential of an Appeal Neglected by Marketing," *Journal of Marketing*, January 1970, pp. 55-56; Brian Sternthal and C. Samuel Craig, "Fear Appeals: Revisited and Revised," *Journal of Consumer Research*, December, 1974, pp. 22-34; John J. Burnett and Richard L. Oliver, "Fear Appeal Effects in the Field: A Segmentation Approach," *Journal of Marketing Research*, May 1979, pp. 181-90; and Lynette S. Unger and James M. Stearns, "The Use of Fear and Guilt Messages in Television Advertising: Issues and Evidence," in *1983 Educators' Proceedings*, ed. Patrick E. Murphy (Chicago: American Marketing Association, 1983), pp. 16-20.

that the best ads ask questions and allow readers and viewers to come to their own conclusions.[12] Conclusion drawing might cause negative reactions in the following situations:

- ☐ If the communicator is seen as untrustworthy, the audience might resent the attempt to influence them.
- ☐ If the issue is simple or the audience is intelligent, they might be annoyed at the attempt to explain the obvious.
- ☐ If the issue is highly personal, the audience might resent the communicator's attempt to draw a conclusion.

Drawing too explicit a conclusion can limit a product's acceptance. If Ford had hammered away on the point that the Mustang was for young people, this strong definition might have blocked other age groups who were attracted to it. *Stimulus ambiguity* can lead to a broader market definition and more spontaneous uses of certain products. Conclusion drawing seems better suited for complex or specialized products where a single and clear use is intended.

One- or two-sided arguments raises the question of whether the communicator should only praise the product or also mention some of its shortcomings. One would think that one-sided presentations would be the most effective. Yet the answer is not clear-cut. Here are some findings:[13]

- One-sided messages work best with audiences that are initially predisposed to the communicator's position, and two-sided arguments work best with audiences who are opposed.
- Two-sided messages tend to be more effective with better-educated audiences.
- Two-sided messages tend to be more effective with audiences that are likely to be exposed to counterpropaganda.

Order of presentation raises the question of whether a communicator should present the strongest arguments first or last. In the case of a one-sided message, presenting the strongest argument first has the advantage of establishing attention and interest. This is important in newspapers and other media where the audience may not pay attention to the whole message. However, it means an anticlimactic presentation. With a captive audience, a climactic presentation might be more effective. In the case of a two-sided message, the issue is whether to present the positive argument first (*primacy effect*) or last (*recency effect*). If the audience is initially opposed, the communicator might start with the other side's argument. This will disarm the audience and allow concluding with his or her strongest argument. Neither the primacy nor recency effect dominates in all situations.[14]

Message Format   The communicator must develop a strong format for the message. In a print ad, the communicator has to decide on the headline, copy, illustration, and color. If the message is to be carried over the radio, the communicator has to carefully choose words, voice qualities (speech rate, rhythm, pitch, articulation), and vocalizations (pauses, sighs, yawns). The "sound" of an announcer promoting a used automobile has to be different from one promoting a new Cadillac. If the message is to be carried on television or in person, then all of these elements plus body language (nonverbal clues) have to be planned. Presenters have to pay attention to their facial expressions, gestures, dress, posture, and hair style. If the message is carried by the product or its packaging, the communicator has to pay attention to color, texture, scent, size, and shape.

> Color plays an important communication role in food preferences. When women sampled four cups of coffee that had been placed next to brown, blue, red, and yellow containers (all the coffee was identical, unknown to the women), 75 percent felt that the coffee next to the brown container tasted too strong; nearly 85 percent judged the coffee next to the red container to be the richest; nearly everyone felt that the coffee next to the blue container was mild and that the coffee next to the yellow container was weak. ∎

Message Source   Messages delivered by attractive sources achieve higher attention and recall. Advertisers often use celebrities as spokespeople, such as Michael J. Fox for Pepsi-Cola and O.J. Simpson for Hertz. Celebrities are likely to be effective when they personify a key product attribute of the product because this gives them credibility. Since O.J. Simpson is known for his speed, his claim that Hertz has fast service was also credible. In contrast, William Shatner's role in *Star Trek* did not provide a credible basis for his brief stint as spokesperson for Loblaws. Credibility is important because messages delivered by highly credible sources are more persuasive. Pharmaceutical companies want doctors to testify about their products' benefits, because doctors have high credibility. Antidrug crusaders will use ex-drug addicts to warn high school students against drugs, because ex-addicts have higher credibility than teachers.

But what factors underlie source credibility? The three factors most often identified are expertise, trustworthiness, and likability.[15] *Expertise* is the specialized knowledge the communicator appears to possess that backs the claim. Doctors, scientists, and professors rank high on expertise in their respective fields. *Trustworthiness* is related to how objective and honest the source is perceived to be. Friends are trusted more than strangers or salespeople. *Likability* describes the source's attractiveness to the audience. Such qualities as candor, humor, and naturalness make a source more likable. The most highly credible source, then, would be a person who scored high on all three dimensions.

If a person has a positive attitude toward a source and a message, or a negative attitude toward both, a state of congruity is said to exist. What happens if the person holds one attitude toward the source and the opposite toward the message? Suppose a homemaker hears a likable celebrity praise a brand that she dislikes. Osgood and Tannenbaum posit that *attitude change will take place in the direction of increasing the amount of congruity between the two evaluations.*[16] The homemaker will end up respecting the celebrity somewhat less and respecting the brand somewhat more. If she encounters the same celebrity praising other disliked brands, she will eventually develop a negative view of the celebrity and maintain her negative attitudes toward the brands. The *principle of congruity* says that communicators can use their good image to reduce some negative feelings toward a brand but in the process might lose some esteem with the audience.

Selecting the Communication Channels

The communicator must select efficient channels of communication to carry the message. Communication channels are of two broad types, *personal* and *nonpersonal*.

Personal Communication Channels   Personal communication channels involve two or more persons communicating directly with each other. They might communicate face to face, person to audience, over the telephone, or through the mails. Personal communication channels derive their effectiveness through the opportunities for individualizing the presentation and feedback.

A further distinction can be drawn between advocate, expert, and social channels of communication. *Advocate channels* consist of company salespeople contacting buyers in the target market. *Expert channels* consist of independent experts making statements to target buyers. *Social channels* consist of neighbors, friends, family members, and associates talking to target buyers. This last channel, known as *word-of-mouth influence*, is the most persuasive in many product areas. The Companies and Industries 21-1 exhibit illustrates how dentists can use word of mouth to expand their client base.

Personal influence carries great weight, especially in the following two situations:

☐ *Where the Product Is Expensive, Risky, or Purchased Infrequently:* Here buyers are likely to be high information seekers. They will go beyond mass-media information and seek the opinions of knowledgeable and trusted sources.

☐ *Where the Product Has a Significant Social Status:* Such products as automobiles, clothing, and even beer and cigarettes have significant brand differentiation that implies something about user status or taste. Consumers are likely to choose brands acceptable to their groups.

Companies can take several steps to stimulate personal influence channels to work on their behalf:

☐ *Identify Influential Individuals and Companies and Devote Extra Effort to Them:* In industrial selling, the entire industry might follow a single lead company in adopting new innovations. Early sales efforts should focus on this company.

DENTISTS USE WORD OF MOUTH TO DRAW MOUTHS TO THEIR PRACTICE

Many professionals find that a substantial number of their new clients come to them through word of mouth. These professionals therefore need to know how to get their present clients to recommend new ones. Here are some approaches that dentists have used:

1. Ask patients for names of friends and acquaintances to send brochures to, or ask them to tell friends about the practice.

2. Keep a poster in the outer office that says:

Satisfied customers are our best customers
If you are happy with us, tell your friends

3. When completing a patient's treatment, ask if he or she is satisfied. If yes, say that you hope that you can satisfy the patient's friends too. Hand the patient a useful brochure about dental care along with some extra copies for the patient's friends.

4. Ask each new patient how he or she was referred. Put the new patient's name on the card of the old patient. When the old patient comes again, thank him or her for recommending the new patient.

□ *Create Opinion Leaders by Supplying Certain People with the Product on Attractive Terms:* A new tennis racket might be offered initially to members of high school tennis teams at a special low price. The company would hope that these star high school tennis players would "talk up" their new racket to other high schoolers.

□ *Work Through Community Influentials Such as Local Disc Jockeys, Class Presidents, and Presidents of Women's Organizations:* When the Ford Thunderbird was introduced, invitations were sent to executives offering them a free car to drive for the day. Of the fifteen thousand who took advantage of the offer, 10 percent indicated that they would become buyers, while 84 percent said they would recommend it to a friend.

□ *Use Influential People in Testimonial Advertising:* The past performance of Wayne Gretzky and Michael Jordan makes them influential endorsers of athletic products, so they command big endorsement fees.

□ *Develop Advertising That Has High "Conversation Value":* Wendy's "Where's the Beef?" campaign (showing an elderly lady named Clara questioning where the hamburger was hidden in all that bread) created high conversation value.[17]

Nonpersonal Communication Channels   Nonpersonal communication channels carry messages without personal contact or interaction. They include media, atmospheres, and events.

Media consist of print media (newspapers, magazines, direct mail), broadcast media (radio, television), electronic media (audiotape, videotape, videodisc), and display media (billboards, signs, posters). Most nonpersonal messages come through paid media.

Atmospheres are "packaged environments" that create or reinforce the buyer's leanings toward product purchase. Thus law offices are decorated with oriental rugs and oak furniture to communicate "stability" and "experience."[18] A luxury hotel will incorporate elegant chandeliers, marble columns, and other tangible signs of luxury.

Events are occurrences designed to communicate particular messages to target audiences. Public-relations departments arrange news conferences, grand openings, and sport sponsorships to achieve specific communication effects with a target audience.

Although personal communication is often more effective than mass communication, mass media might be the major means to stimulate personal communication. Mass communications affect personal attitudes and behavior through a *two-step flow-of-communication process*. "Ideas often flow from radio and print to opinion leaders and from these to the less active sections of the population."[19]

This two-step communication flow has several implications. First, the influence of mass media on public opinion is not as direct, powerful, and automatic as supposed. It is mediated by *opinion leaders*, persons who belong to primary groups and whose opinions are sought in one or more product areas. Opinion leaders are more exposed to mass media than those they influence. They carry messages to people who are less exposed to media, thus extending the influence of the mass media; or they may carry altered messages or none at all, thus acting as *gatekeepers*.

Second, the hypothesis challenges the notion that people's consumption styles are primarily influenced by a "trickle-down" effect from higher-status classes. To the contrary, people primarily interact within their own social class and acquire their fashion and other ideas from people like themselves who are opinion leaders.[20]

A third implication is that mass communicators would be more efficient by directing their messages specifically to opinion leaders, letting the latter carry the message to others. Thus pharmaceutical firms try to promote their new drugs to the most influential physicians first. More recent research indicates that both opinion leaders and the general public are affected by mass communication. Opinion leaders are prompted by the mass media to spread information, while the general public seeks information from the opinion leaders.

Communication researchers are moving toward a social-structure view of interpersonal communication.[21] They see society as consisting of *cliques*, small social groups whose members interact with each other more frequently than with others. Clique members are similar, and their closeness facilitates effective communication but also insulates the clique from new ideas. The challenge is to create more system openness whereby cliques exchange more information with others in the society. This openness is helped by persons who function as liaisons and bridges. A *liaison* is a person who connects two or more cliques without belonging to either. A *bridge* is a person who belongs to one clique and is linked to a person in another clique. Word-of-mouth communications flow most readily within cliques, and the problem is to facilitate communication between cliques and to create a diffusion network.

Establishing the Total Promotion Budget

One of the most difficult marketing decisions facing companies is how much to spend on promotion. John Wanamaker, the department-store magnate, said, "I know that half of my advertising is wasted, but I don't know which half."

Thus it is not surprising that industries and companies vary considerably in how much they spend on promotion. Promotional expenditures might amount to 30 to 50 percent of sales in the cosmetics industry and only 10 to 20 percent in the industrial equipment industry. Within a given industry, low- and high-spending companies can be found. For example, Nabisco Brands is a high-promotion-spender in the packaged-goods industry. The low spenders in the same industry are the producers of generic products and house brands for grocery chains like A&P and Loblaws.

How do companies decide on their promotion budget? We will describe four common methods used to set a promotion budget.

Affordable Method   Many companies set the promotion budget at what they think the company can afford. One executive explained this method as follows: "Why it's simple. First, I go upstairs to the controller and ask how much they can afford to give us this year. He says a million and a half. Later, the boss comes to me and asks how much we should spend and I say 'Oh, about a million and a half.'"[22]

This method of setting budgets completely ignores the role of promotion as an investment and the immediate impact of promotion on sales volume. It leads to an uncertain annual promotion budget, which makes long-range market planning difficult.

Percentage-of-Sales Method   Many companies set their promotion expenditures at a specified percentage of sales (either current or anticipated) or of the sales price. A railroad company executive said: "We set our appropriation for each year on December 1 of the preceding year. On that date we add our passenger revenue for the next month, and then take 2 percent of the total for our advertising appropriation for the new year."[23] Automobile companies typically budget a fixed percentage for promotion based on the planned car price. Oil companies set the appropriation at some fraction of a cent for each gallon of gasoline sold under their own label.

A number of advantages are claimed for the percentage-of-sales method. First, it means that promotion expenditures would vary with what the company can "afford." This satisfies the financial managers, who feel that expenses should bear a close relation to the movement of corporate sales over the business cycle. Second, it encourages management to think in terms of the relationship between promotion cost, selling price, and profit per unit. Third, it encourages competitive stability to the extent that competing firms spend approximately the same percentage of their sales on promotion.

In spite of these advantages, the percentage-of-sales method has little to justify it. It uses circular reasoning in viewing sales as the cause of promotion rather than as the result. It leads to a budget set by the availability of funds rather than by market opportunities. It discourages experimenting with countercyclical promotion or aggressive spending. The promotion budget's dependence on year-to-year sales fluctuations interferes with long-range planning. The method does not provide a logical basis for choosing the specific percentage, except what has been done in the past or what competitors are doing. Finally, it does not encourage building up the promotion budget by determining what each product and territory deserves.

Competitive-Parity Method   Some companies set their promotion budget to achieve *share-of-voice* parity with their competitors. This thinking is illustrated by the executive who asked a trade source, "Do you have any figures which other companies in the builders' specialties field have used which would indicate what proportion of gross sales should be given over to advertising?"[24] This executive believes that by spending the same percentage of his sales on advertising as his competitors, he will maintain his market share.

Two arguments are advanced for this method. One is that the competitors' expenditures represent the collective wisdom of the industry. The other is that maintaining a competitive parity helps prevent promotion wars.

Neither argument is valid. There are no grounds for believing that competition knows better what should be spent on promotion. Company reputations, resources, opportunities, and objectives differ so much that their promotion budgets are hardly a guide. Furthermore, there is no evidence that budgets based on competitive parity discourage promotional wars from breaking out.

Objective-and-Task Method   The objective-and-task method calls upon marketers to develop their promotion budgets by defining their specific objectives, determining the tasks that must be performed to achieve these objectives, and estimating the costs of performing these tasks. The sum of these costs is the proposed promotion budget.

Suppose a soft-drink producer wants to establish an advertising budget for a new soft drink called Forest, which is packaged in individual biodegradable plastic bottles. The steps in using the objective-and-task method are:

1. *Establish the Market-Share Goal:* The company wants 8 percent of the market. Of 5 million soft-drink users, the company wants 400 000 to drink Forest.

2. *Determine the Percent of the Market That Should be Reached:* The advertising should make 80 percent (i.e., 4 million) of soft-drink users aware of Forest.

3. *Determine the Percent of Trial Within the Aware Market:* If 25 percent of the aware soft-drink users (i.e., 1 million) try Forest, it is estimated that 40 percent of them (i.e., 400 000) will become loyal users. That is the goal.

4. *Determine the Number of Advertising Impressions Per 1 Percent Trial Rate:* The advertiser estimates that 40 advertising impressions (exposures) for every 1 percent of the target population will produce a 25 percent trial.

5. *Determine the Number of Gross Rating Points That Will Have to Be Purchased:* Since 1 GRP is defined as 1 exposure to 1 percent of the target population, to achieve 40 exposures of Forest to 80 percent of the population will require a purchase of $(40 \times 80 =)$ 3200 GRP.

6. *Determine the Cost of the Advertising to Produce the Necessary GRPs:* If the cost of 1 exposure to 1 percent of the target population (i.e., 40 000) averages $800 for the media being considered, then the advertising budget for 3200 GRPs should be $(800 \times 3200 =)$ $2 560 000 for Forest's first year.

This method has the advantage of requiring management to spell out its assumptions about the relationship between dollars spent, exposure levels, trial rates, and regular usage.

A major question is how much weight should promotion receive in the total marketing mix (as opposed to product improvement, lower prices, more services, and so on). The answer depends on where the company's products are in their life cycles, whether they are commodities or highly differentiable products, whether they are routinely needed or have to be "sold," and other considerations. In theory, the total promotional budget should be established where the marginal profit from the last promotional dollar just equals the marginal profit from the last dollar in the best nonpromotional use. Implementing this principle, however, is not easy.

Deciding on the Promotion Mix

Companies face the task of distributing the total promotion budget over the four promotion tools of advertising, sales promotion, public relations, and salesforce. Within the same industry, companies can differ considerably in how they allocate their promotional budget. Avon concentrates its promotional funds on personal selling (its advertising is only 1.5 percent of sales), while Revlon spends heavily on advertising (about 7.0 percent of sales). In selling vacuum cleaners, Electrolux spends heavily on a door-to-door salesforce, while Hoover relies more on advertising. Thus it is possible to achieve a given sales level with various mixes of advertising, personal selling, sales promotion, and publicity. (Marketing Strategies 21-2 shows the promotional mix of business-to-business marketers.)

Companies are always searching for ways to gain efficiency by substituting one promotional tool for another as its economics become more favorable. Many companies have

Marketing Strategies 21-2

THE PROMOTIONAL MIX OF BUSINESS-TO-BUSINESS MARKETERS

Business Marketing magazine published a comprehensive study of the expenditure levels on major promotional tools by business-to-business marketers. It estimated that business-to-business marketers spent their 1985 promotion budgets in the following percentages:

Advertising	9.4%	Business and consumer publications, radio and TV, directories, yellow pages, outdoors, and ad production
Direct marketing	33.7%	Direct mail and telemarketing
Trade shows	23.0%	Show costs and exhibitor travel and entertainment
Sales promotion	8.3%	Collateral, audiovisual and point of sale
Incentives	16.5%	Merchandise incentives, travel incentives and sweepstakes
Salesforce management	6.5%	Training and meetings (excluding selling costs)
Public relations	2.6%	Publicity

replaced some field sales activity with ads, direct mail, and telemarketing. Other companies have increased their sales-promotion expenditures in relation to advertising, to gain quicker sales. The substitutability among promotional tools explains why marketing functions need to be coordinated in a single marketing department.

Designing the promotion mix is further complicated when one tool can be used to promote another. Thus when McDonald's decides to run a Million Dollar Sweepstakes program in its fast-food outlets (a form of sales promotion), it has to take out newspaper ads to inform the public. When General Mills develops a consumer advertising campaign to launch a new cake mix, it has to also develop a trade-channel campaign to win their support.

Is there a logical sequence for building up the promotion budget? Usually the salesforce cost is established first because much of this is a fixed cost. Then there is the question of whether to set the sales-promotion budget or the advertising budget next. Brand managers in consumer package goods companies increasingly set the trade-promotion budget first, because the trade is powerful enough to demand a certain amount of trade-promotion money. Then they set the consumer-promotion budget to make sure that consumers come in and buy enough of the promoted products. Finally, they decide on the advertising budget. This is a reverse order from the past, when leading manufacturers had more power over the trade.

Many factors influence the marketer's choice and mix of promotional tools. We will examine these factors in the following paragraphs.

Nature of Each Promotional Tool Each promotional tool—advertising, personal selling, sales promotion, and publicity—has its own unique characteristics and costs. Marketers have to understand these characteristics in selecting them.

Advertising Because of the many forms and uses of advertising, it is difficult to make all-embracing generalizations about its distinctive qualities as a component of the promotional mix. Yet the following qualities can be noted:

☐ *Public Presentation:* Advertising is a highly public mode of communication. Its public nature confers a kind of legitimacy on the product and also suggests a standardized offering. Because many persons receive the same message, buyers know that their motives for purchasing the product will be publicly understood.

☐ *Pervasiveness:* Advertising is a pervasive medium that permits the seller to repeat a message many times. It also allows the buyer to receive and compare the messages of various competitors. Large-scale advertising by a seller says something positive about the seller's size, popularity, and success.

☐ *Amplified Expressiveness:* Advertising provides opportunities for dramatizing the company and its products through the artful use of print, sound, and color. Sometimes, however, the tool's very success at expressiveness may dilute or distract from the message.

☐ *Impersonality:* Advertising cannot be as compelling as a company sales representative. The audience does not feel obligated to pay attention or respond. Advertising is able to carry on only a monologue, not a dialogue, with the audience.[25]

On the one hand, advertising can be used to build up a long-term image for a product (Coca-Cola ads), and on the other, to trigger quick sales (a Sears ad for a weekend sale). Advertising is an efficient way to reach numerous geographically dispersed buyers at a low cost per exposure. Certain forms of advertising, such as TV advertising, can require a large budget, while other forms, such as newspaper advertising, can be done on a small budget. Advertising might have an effect on sales simply through its presence. Consumers might believe that a heavily advertised brand must offer "good value"; otherwise, why would advertisers spend so much money touting the product?

Personal Selling Personal selling is the most effective tool at certain stages of the buying process, particularly in building up buyers' preference, conviction, and action. The reason is that personal selling, when compared with advertising, has three distinctive qualities:

☐ *Personal Confrontation:* Personal selling involves an alive, immediate, and interactive relationship between two or more persons. Each party is able to observe each other's needs and characteristics at close hand and make immediate adjustments.

☐ *Cultivation:* Personal selling permits all kinds of relationships to spring up, ranging from a matter-of-fact selling relationship to a deep personal friendship. Effective sales representatives will normally keep their customers' interests at heart if they want long-run relationships.

☐ *Response:* Personal selling makes the buyer feel under some obligation for having listened to the sales talk. The buyer has a greater need to attend and respond, even if the response is a polite "thank you."[26]

These distinctive qualities come at a cost. A salesforce represents a greater long-term cost commitment than advertising. Advertising can be turned on and off, but the size of a salesforce is more difficult to alter.

Sales Promotion Although sales-promotion tools—coupons, contests, premiums, and the like—are highly diverse, they have three distinctive characteristics:

□ *Communication:* They gain attention and usually provide information that may lead the consumer to the product.

□ *Incentive:* They incorporate some concession, inducement, or contribution that gives value to the consumer.

□ *Invitation:* They include a distinct invitation to engage in the transaction now.

Companies use sales-promotion tools to create a stronger and quicker response. Sales promotion can be used to dramatize product offers and to boost sagging sales. Sales-promotion effects are usually short run, however, and not effective in building long-run brand preference.

Public Relations The appeal of public relations is based on its three distinctive qualities:

□ *High Credibility:* News stories and features seem more authentic and credible to readers than ads do.

□ *Off Guard:* Public relations can reach many prospects who might avoid salespeople and advertisements. The message gets to the buyers as news rather than as a sales-directed communication.

□ *Dramatization:* Public relations has, like advertising, a potential for dramatizing a company or product.

Marketers tend to underuse public relations or use it as an afterthought. Yet a well-thought-out public-relations program coordinated with the other promotion-mix elements can be extremely effective.

Factors in Setting the Promotion Mix   Companies consider several factors in developing their promotion mix. These factors are examined below.

Type of Product Market The rated importance of promotional tools varies between consumer and industrial markets (see Figure 21-5). Consumer-goods companies rate advertising, sales promotion, personal selling, and public relations in that order. Industrial-goods companies rate personal selling, sales promotion, advertising, and public relations in that order. In general, personal selling is more heavily used with complex, expensive, and risky goods and in markets with fewer and larger sellers (hence, industrial markets).

FIGURE 21-5
Relative Importance of Promotion Tools in Consumer versus Industrial Markets

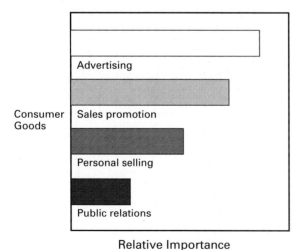

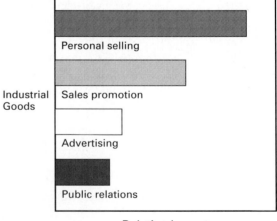

While advertising is less important than sales calls in industrial markets, it still plays a significant role. Advertising can perform the following functions:

- *Awareness Building:* Prospects who are not aware of the company or product might refuse to see the sales representative. Furthermore the sales representative might have to use up a lot of time describing the company and its products.

- *Comprehension Building:* If the product embodies new features, some of the burden of explaining them can be effectively undertaken by advertising.

- *Efficient Reminding:* If prospects know about the product but are not ready to buy, reminder advertising would be more economical than sales calls.

- *Lead Generation:* Advertisements carrying return coupons are an effective way to generate leads for sales representatives.

- *Legitimation:* Sales representatives can use tear sheets of the company's ads in leading magazines to legitimatize their company and products.

- *Reassurance:* Advertising can remind customers how to use the product and reassure them about their purchase.

Advertising's important role in industrial marketing is underscored in a number of studies. Morrill showed in his study of industrial-commodity marketing that advertising combined with personal selling increased sales 23 percent over what they werewith no advertising. The total promotional cost as a percentage of sales was reduced by 20 percent.[27] Freeman developed a formal model for dividing promotional funds between advertising and personal selling on the basis of the selling tasks that each performs more economically.[28] Levitt's

---

Marketing Strategies 21-3

ROLE OF CORPORATE ADVERTISING IN INDUSTRIAL MARKETING

Professor Theodore Levitt sought to determine the relative contribution of the company's reputation (built mainly by advertising) and the company's sales presentation (personal selling) in producing industrial sales. Purchasing agents were shown filmed sales presentations of a new but fictitious technical product for use as an ingredient in making paint. The variables were the quality of the sales presentation and whether the salesperson came from a well-known company, a less-known but creditable company, or an unknown company. Purchasing-agent reactions were collected after viewing the films and again five weeks later. The findings were as follows:

1. A company's reputation improves the chances of getting a favorable first hearing and an early adoption of the product. Therefore, corporate advertising that can build up the company's reputation (other factors also shape its reputation) will help the company's sales representatives.

2. Sales representatives from well-known companies have an edge in getting the sale if their sales presentations are adequate. If a sales representative from a lesser-known company makes a highly effective sales presentation, that can overcome the disadvantage. Smaller companies should use their limited funds to select and train good sales representatives rather than spend the money on advertising.

3. Company reputations help most where the product is complex, the risk is high, and the purchasing agent is less professionally trained.

Source: Theodore Levitt, *Industrial Purchasing Behavior: A Study in Communication Effects* (Boston: Division of Research, Harvard Business School, 1965).

research also showed the important role that advertising can play in industrial marketing (see Marketing Strategies 21-3). Lilien carried out a series of investigations in a project called ADVISOR in which he sought to determine and critique the practices used by industrial marketers to set their marketing communication budgets (see Marketing Concepts and Tools 21-2).

Conversely, personal selling can make a strong contribution in consumer-goods marketing. Some consumer marketers play down the role of the salesforce, using them mainly to collect weekly orders from dealers and to see that sufficient stock is on the shelf. The common feeling is that "salespeople put products on shelves and advertising takes them off." Yet even here an effectively trained salesforce can make three important contributions:

☐ *Increased Stock Position:* Sales representatives can persuade dealers to take more stock and devote more shelf space to the company's brand.

☐ *Enthusiasm Building:* Sales representatives can build dealer enthusiasm for a new product by dramatizing the planned advertising and sales-promotion backup.

Marketing Concepts and Tools 21-2

THE ADVISOR PROJECT PROBES INTO HOW INDUSTRIAL MARKETERS SET THEIR MARKETING BUDGETS

Professor Gary L. Lilien directed a five-year study called the ADVISOR project, which examined how industrial marketers set their advertising budgets. ADVISOR ultimately consisted of two projects— ADVISOR 1 and ADVISOR 2.

Data on various marketing factors were collected on sixty-six industrial products from twelve companies. The study sought to develop marketing expenditure norms for industrial marketers. Industrial marketers tended to make a two-step decision in setting their advertising budgets. They decided, first, how much to spend on total marketing as a percentage of sales (the M/S ratio) and, second, how much to spend on advertising as a percentage of the marketing budget (the A/M ratio). When these ratios are multiplied, they give the A/S ratio, namely the advertising-to-sales ratio.

The data yielded the following norms:

	Advertising	A/S	M/S	A/M
Median	$92 000	0.6%	6.9%	9.9%
Range for 50% of products:	$16 000-$272 000	0.1%-1.8%	3%-14%	5%-19%

Thus the average industrial company in the sample spent $92 000 on advertising each product, and in 50 percent of the cases, this figure ranged from $16 000 to $272 000. The average industrial company spent only 0.6 percent of its sales on advertising; it budgeted about 7 percent of its sales for total marketing; and it budgeted about 10 percent of its total marketing budget for advertising. The table also shows the 50 percent ranges for each ratio.

A company could use this table to check whether its M/S and A/M ratios are within a 50 percent range of most companies. If one or both ratios are outside of the range, either too low or too high, then management should ask why. If good reasons cannot be found, the advertising and marketing budgets should be revised.

There could be good reasons for spending outside of the typical range. Lilien investigated a large number of factors suggested by marketing managers that would lead them to spend more or less than the normal amount on advertising and/or marketing. He found six factors that had a major influence on marketing budgets: stage in life cycle; frequency of purchase; product quality, uniqueness, and identification with the company; market share; concentration of sales; and growth rate of customers. Here are some findings:

- The M/S ratio fell as the product life cycle progressed.
- The higher the purchase frequency, the greater the A/M.
- The higher the product quality or uniqueness, the higher the A/M.
- The higher the market share, the lower the M/S.
- The higher the customer concentration, the lower the MS ratio.
- The higher the customer growth rate, the higher the M/S and A/M ratios.

Next ADVISOR investigated how industrial companies allocated their advertising budgets to the following four media:

- *Space:* trade, technical press, and house journals (41 percent)
- *Direct Mail:* leaflets, brochures, catalogs, and other direct-mail pieces (24 percent)
- *Shows:* trade shows and industrial films (11 percent)
- *Promotion:* sales promotion (24 percent)

The numbers show the median percentage that industrial companies spent on the four media. Lilien tested four variables that influence the allocation per-

centages, namely sales volume, life cycle, sales concentration, and number of customers. Here are some conclusions:

- The higher the sales volume, the more the use of shows and sales promotion and the less the use of space and direct mail.
- Products in later stages of the life cycle spend more on direct mail and less on sales promotion.
- The higher the customer concentration, the more for sales promotion and the less for trade shows.
- The greater the number of customers, the less the use of direct mail.

Subsequently ADVISOR 2 was launched with a larger sample, and it confirmed the earlier results. ADVISOR 2 led to the building of some optimization models for setting marketing and advertising budgets.

Sources: Gary L. Lilien and John D. C. Little, "The ADVISOR Project: A Study of Industrial Marketing Budgets," *Sloan Management Review*, Spring 1976, pp. 17-31, by permission of the publisher. Copyright © 1976 by the Sloan Management Review Association. All rights reserved; and Gary L. Lilien, "ADVISOR 2: Modeling the Marketing Mix Decision for Industrial Products," *Management Science*, February 1979, pp. 191-204. Copyright © 1979 The Institute of Management Science.

- *Missionary Selling:* Sales representatives can sign up more dealers to carry the company's brands.

Push Versus Pull Strategy The promotional mix is heavily influenced by whether the company chooses a push or pull strategy to create sales. The two strategies are contrasted in Figure 21-6. A *push strategy* involves manufacturer marketing activities (primarily sales-force and trade promotion) directed at channel intermediaries to induce them to order and carry the product and promote it to end users. A *pull strategy* involves marketing activities (primarily advertising and consumer promotion) directed at end users to induce them to ask intermediaries for the product and thus induce the intermediaries to order the product from the manufacturer. Companies in the same industry may differ in their emphasis on push or pull. For example, Lever Brothers relies more heavily on push, and Procter & Gamble on pull.

Buyer-Readiness Stage Promotional tools vary in their cost effectiveness at different stages of buyer readiness. Figure 21-7 shows the relative cost effectiveness of three promotional tools. Advertising and publicity play the most important roles in the awareness stage, more than is played by "cold calls" from sales representatives or by sales promotion. Customer comprehension is primarily affected by advertising and personal selling. Customer conviction is influenced mostly by personal selling and less by advertising and sales promotion. Closing the sale is influenced mostly by personal selling and sales promotion. Reordering is

FIGURE 21-6
Push versus Pull Strategy

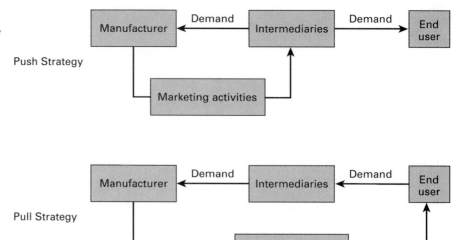

Push Strategy

Pull Strategy

also affected mostly by personal selling and sales promotion, and somewhat by reminder advertising. Clearly, advertising and publicity are most cost effective at the early stages of the buyer decision process, and personal selling and sales promotion are most effective at the later stages.

Product-Life-Cycle Stage Promotional tools also vary in their cost effectiveness at different stages of the product life cycle. Figure 21-8 offers a speculative view of their relative effectiveness.

In the introduction stage, advertising and publicity have high cost effectiveness, followed by sales promotion to induce trial and personal selling to gain distribution coverage.

In the growth stage, all the tools can be toned down, because demand has its own momentum through word of mouth.

In the maturity stage, sales promotion, advertising and personal selling all grow more important, in that order.

In the decline stage, sales promotion continues strong, advertising and publicity are reduced, and salespeople give the product only minimal attention.

FIGURE 21-7

Cost Effectiveness of Different Promotional Tools at Different Buyer-Readiness Stages

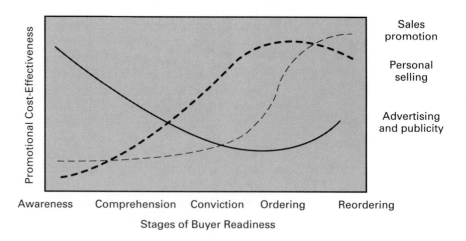

FIGURE 21-8

Cost Effectiveness of Different Promotional Tools at Different Stages of Product Life Cycle

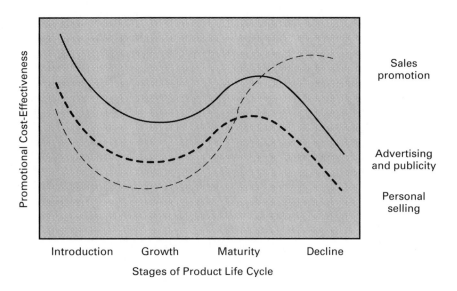

Measuring Promotion's Results

After implementing the promotional plan, the communicator must measure its impact on the target audience. This involves asking the target audience whether they recognize or recall the message, how many times they saw it, what points they recall, how they felt about the message, and their previous and current attitudes toward the product and company. The communicator would also want to collect behavioral measures of audience response, such as how many people bought the product, liked it, and talked to others about it.

Figure 21-9 provides an example of good feedback measurement. Looking at brand A, we find that 80 percent of the total market are aware of brand A, 60 percent have tried it, and only 20 percent who have tried it are satisfied. This indicates that the communication program is effective in creating awareness, but the product fails to meet consumer expectations.

FIGURE 21-9

Current Consumer States for Two Brands

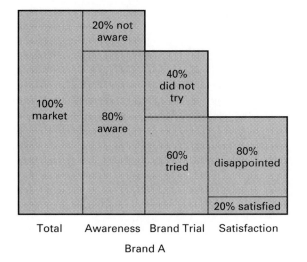

On the other hand, only 40 percent of the total market are aware of brand B, and only 30 percent have tried it, but 80 percent of those who have tried it are satisfied. In this case, the communication program needs to be strengthened to take advantage of the brand's satisfaction-generating power.

Managing and Coordinating the Marketing Communication Process

The wide range of communication tools and messages makes it imperative that they be coordinated. Otherwise, the messages might be ill timed in terms of the availability of goods; they may lack consistency; or they might not be cost effective. Left alone, each manager of a communication resource will fight for more budget irrespective of the relative merits of each tool. The sales manager will want to hire two extra sales representatives for $80 000, while the advertising manager will want to spend the same money on a prime-time television commercial. The public-relations manager wants more money for publicity. Little thought will be given to telemarketing and direct-mail programs unless they have their internal advocates.

Today, some companies are moving toward the concept of *integrated marketing communications*. This concept calls for

- ☐ Appointing a marketing communications director who has overall responsibility for the company's persuasive communications efforts
- ☐ Working out a philosophy of the role and the extent to which the different promotional tools are to be used
- ☐ Keeping track of all promotional expenditures by product, promotional tool, stage of product life cycle, and observed effect, as a basis for improving further use of these tools
- ☐ Coordinating the promotional activities and their timing when major campaigns take place

Integrated marketing communication will produce more consistency in the company's meaning to its buyers and publics. It places a responsibility in someone's hand—where none existed before—to unify the company's image as it comes through thousands of company activities. It leads to a total marketing communication strategy aimed at showing how the company and its products can help customers solve their problems.

SUMMARY

Marketing communication is one of the major elements of the company's marketing mix. Marketers must know how to use advertising, sales promotion, public relations, and personal selling to communicate the product's existence and value to the target customers.

The communication process itself consists of nine elements: sender, receiver, encoding, decoding, message, media, response, feedback, and noise. Marketers must know how to get through to the target audience in the face of the audience's tendencies toward selective attention, distortion, and recall.

Developing the promotion program involves eight steps. The communicator must first identify the target audience and its characteristics, including the image that the audience has of the product. Next the communicator has to define the communication objective, whether it is to create awareness, knowledge, liking, preference, conviction, or purchase. Then a message must be designed containing an effective content, structure, format, and source. Then communication channels—both personal and nonpersonal—must be selected. Next the total promotion budget must be established. Four common methods are the affordable method, the percentage-of-sales method, the competitive-parity method, and the objective-and-task method. The promotion budget must be divided among the main promotional tools, as affected by such factors as push versus pull strategy, buyer-readiness stage, and product-life-cycle stage. The communicator must then monitor to see how much of the market becomes aware of the product, tries it, and is satisfied in the process. Finally, all of the communication must be managed and integrated for consistency, good timing, and cost effectiveness.

■ QUESTIONS

1. The K.C. Corporation sells shoes. They have just recently conducted a test of advertising effectiveness for their K shoe versus four other competitors' models. Compare the results of their product (Case 5 in the table below) with those of the other four products (Cases 1 to 4). Use the communication process model to analyze and discuss.

	Case 1	Case 2	Case 3	Case 4	Case 5
Number of consumers	5000	5000	5000	5000	5000
Number of consumers for whom there was:					
Exposure to the brand	1200	4000	4000	4000	4000
Recall of the brand	450	1000	3000	3000	3000
Favorable attitude to the brand	75	220	675	1550	350
Trial of the brand	15	44	135	310	210

2. Using the dimensions of familiarity-favorability, select three businesses in your local area or three academic departments in your school. With a sample size of 10, do a familiarity-favorability analysis, plotting your results in a matrix as shown in Figure 21-2.

3. Expand your study and do a more careful analysis of the specific content of their image. (See Figure 21-3.) Present your recommendations for improving the images of your organizations.

4. Discuss the factors that may prevent someone from receiving *the* message intended by the communicator. What strategies can be employed to minimize this possibility?

5. You are faced with the following problems. Recommend an appropriate strategy and give reasons for your choice.
   (a) The target audience for your product has reservations

about it. What personal qualities would you recommend that the spokesperson for your message possess?

(b) State which appeal strategies would be the most effective for the following products or services, and why: disposable diapers, detergent, cigarettes, seat belts, United Way, and life insurance.

6. A firm can choose to establish the size of its promotion budget on the basis of an arbitrary-decision rule or a strategy-informed rule. What are the merits of each? Give examples.

7. Based on your understanding of the communication process, suggest some guidelines for the effective use of visual and verbal content in the creation of both print and broadcast advertising.

8. Lite Beer commercials by Miller were the most-often noticed, remembered, and liked ads on TV. Oscar Meyer commercials ranked twelfth on the list of most-remembered commercials. Can we claim that Miller ads were considerably more successful than Oscar Meyer ads? Why or why not?

9. Apply the four major tools in the marketing communication mix to professional sports teams.

10. The major mass media—newspapers, magazines, radio, television, and outdoor media—show striking differences in their capacity for dramatization, credibility, attention getting, and other valued aspects of communication. Describe the special characteristics of each media type.

11. Develop a set of thematic guidelines that laundry detergent companies might follow in preparing ads aimed at upper-class, lower-class, and lower-middle-class homemakers in the 25-to-45-age bracket.

12. What types of consumer responses should be aimed at in communication strategies for the following products: legal services, frozen pizza, veterinarian services, sewing machines, pianos, telephone-answering services, hammers?

NOTES _____

1. The definitions of advertising and personal selling are from *Marketing Definitions: A Glossary of Marketing Terms* (Chicago: American Marketing Association, 1960).

2. Harold D. Lasswell, *Power and Personality* (New York: W. W. Norton, 1948), pp. 37-51.

3. Wilbur Schramm, "How Communication Works," in *The Process and Effects of Mass Communication*, ed. Wilbur Schramm and Donald F. Roberts (Urbana: University of Illinois Press, 1971), p. 4.

4. *Ibid.*, p. 32

5. See Brian Sternthal and C. Samuel Craig, *Consumer Behavior, an Information Processing Perspective* (Englewood Cliffs, N.J.: Prentice-Hall, 1982), pp. 97-102.

6. See Alice H. Eagly, "Sex Differences in Influenceability," *Psychological Bulletin*, January 1978, pp. 86-116.

7. Donald F. Cox and Raymond A. Bauer, "Self-confidence and Persuasibility in Women," *Public Opinion Quarterly*, Fall 1964, pp. 453-66; and Raymond L. Horton, "Some Relationships between Personality and Consumer Decision-Making," *Journal of Marketing Research*, May 1979, pp. 233-46.

8. See John Fiske and John Hartley, *Reading Television*, (London: Methuen, 1980), p. 79.

9. The semantic differential was developed by C. E. Osgood, C. J. Suci, and P. H. Tannenbaum, *The Measurement of Meaning* (Urbana: University of Illinois Press, 1957).

10. See Michael L. Ray, *Advertising and Communications Management* (Englewood Cliffs, N.J.: Prentice-Hall, 1982).

11. See Brian Sternthal and C. Samuel Craig, "Humor in Advertising," *Journal of Marketing*, October 1973, pp. 12-18; and John Koten, "After the Serious '70's, Advertisers Are Going for Laughs Again," *Wall Street Journal*, February 23, 1984, p. 31.

12. See James F. Engel, Roger D. Blackwell, and Paul W. Minard, *Consumer Behavior*, 5th ed. (Hinsdale, Ill.: Dryden Press, 1986), p. 477.

13. See C. I. Hovland, A. A. Lumsdaine, and F. D. Sheffield, *Experiments on Mass Communication*, vol. 3 (Princeton, N.J.: Princeton University Press, 1948), Chap. 8. For an alternate viewpoint, see George E. Belch, "The Effects of Message Modality on One- and Two-Sided Advertising Messages," in *Advances in Consumer Research*, ed. Richard P. Bagozzi and Alice M. Tybout (Ann Arbor, Mich.: Association for Consumer Research, 1983), pp. 21-26.

14. See Sternthal and Craig, *Consumer Behavior*, pp. 282-84.

15. Herbert C. Kelman and Carl I. Hovland, "Reinstatement of the Communication in Delayed Measurement of Opinion Change," *Journal of Abnormal and Social Psychology* 48 (1953), 327-35.

16. C. E. Osgood and P. H. Tannenbaum, "The Principles of Congruity in the Prediction of Attitude Change," *Psychological Review* 62 (1955), 42-55.

17. Also see Thomas S. Robertson, *Innovative Behavior and Communication* (New York: Holt, Rinehart & Winston, 1971), Chap. 9; and Peter H. Reingen and Jerome B. Kernan, "Analysis of Referral Networks in Marketing: Methods and Illustration," *Journal of Marketing Research*, November 1986, pp. 370-78.

18. See Philip Kotler, "Atmospherics as a Marketing Tool," *Journal of Retailing*, Winter 1973-74, pp. 48-64.

19. P. F. Lazarsfeld, B. Berelson, and H. Gaudet, *The People's Choice*, 2nd ed. (New York: Columbia University Press, 1948), p. 151.

20. See George P. Moschis, "Social Comparison and Informal Group Influence," *Journal of Marketing Research*, August 1976, pp. 237-44.

21. See Everett M. Rogers, *Diffusion of Innovations*, 3rd ed. (New York: Free Press, 1983).

22. Quoted in Daniel Seligman, "How Much for Advertising?" *Fortune*, December 1956, p. 123. For a good discussion of setting promotion budgets, see Michael L. Rothschild, *Advertising* (Lexington, Mass.: D. C. Heath, 1987), Chap. 20.

23. Albert Wesley Frey, *How Many Dollars for Advertising?* (New York: Ronald Press, 1955), p. 65.

24. *Ibid.*, p. 49.

25. See Sidney J. Levy, *Promotional Behavior* (Glenview, Ill.: Scott, Foresman, 1971), Chap. 4.

26. *Ibid.*

27. *How Advertising Works in Today's Marketplace: The Morrill Study* (New York: McGraw-Hill, 1971), p. 4.

28. Cyril Freeman, "How to Evaluate Advertising's Contribution," *Harvard Business Review*, July-August 1962, pp. 137-48.

22

Designing Effective Advertising Programs

Advertising may be described as the science of arresting the human intelligence long enough to get money from it.

Stephen Leacock

Advertising is one of the four major tools companies use to direct persuasive communications to target buyers and publics. We define *advertising* as any paid form of nonpersonal presentation and promotion of ideas, goods, or services by an identified sponsor. In 1990, $10.86 billion was spent on advertising in Canada. The spenders included not only businesses but professionals, advocacy groups, and others who advertise their causes to various publics. In fact, the third-largest advertising spender in 1990 was the federal government.

Advertising expenditures were distributed unevenly, with a small number of organizations accounting for a disproportionate amount of the total. The five largest advertisers were (in millions): Thomson Group ($76), General Motors Canada ($68), Government of Canada ($67), Procter & Gamble ($67), and Sears Canada ($64). Advertising as a percentage of sales also varied greatly, with spending being higher for consumer, than for industrial, products. Among consumer products, packaged goods (laundry, personal care, food) tended to have higher advertising:sales ratios than consumer durables like automobiles.[1]

The advertising dollars support various media: magazine and newspaper space; radio and television; outdoor displays (posters, billboards, signs, skywriting); direct mail; novelties (matchboxes, pens, calendars); tear pads (car, bus); catalogs; directories (Yellow Pages); and circulars. And advertising has many purposes: long-term buildup of the organization's corporate image (*institutional advertising*), long-term buildup of a particular brand (*brand advertising*), information dissemination about a sale, service, or event (*classified advertising*), announcement of a special sale (*sale or promotional advertising*), and advocacy of a particular cause (*advocacy advertising*).

Although advertising is primarily a private-enterprise marketing tool, it is used in all the countries of the world, including socialist countries. Advertising is a cost-effective way to disseminate messages, whether it is to build brand preference for Coca-Cola or to motivate a developing nation's consumers to drink milk or to practice birth control.

Organizations obtain their advertising in different ways. In small companies, advertising is handled by someone in the sales or marketing department, who works with an advertising agency. Large companies set up their own advertising departments, whose managers report to the vice-presidents of marketing. The advertising department's job is to develop the total budget, approve advertising agency ads and campaigns, and handle direct-mail advertising, dealer displays, and other forms of advertising not ordinarily performed by the agency. Most companies use an outside advertising agency to help them create advertising campaigns and to select and purchase media (see the Companies and Industries 22-1 exhibit).

In developing an advertising program, marketing managers must always start by identifying the *target market* and *buyer motives*. Then they can proceed to make the five major decisions in developing an advertising program, known as the five Ms:

☐ What are the advertising objectives? (*mission*)

☐ How much can be spent? (*money*)

☐ What message should be sent? (*message*)

☐ What media should be used? (*media*)

☐ How should the results be evaluated? (*measurement*)

These decisions are further described in Figure 22-1 and in the following sections.

SETTING THE ADVERTISING OBJECTIVES

The first step in developing an advertising program is to set the advertising objectives. These objectives must flow from prior decisions on the target market, market positioning, and marketing mix. The marketing-positioning and marketing-mix strategies define the job that advertising must do in the total marketing program.

Many specific communication and sales objectives can be assigned to advertising. Colley lists fifty-two possible advertising objectives in his well-known *Defining Advertising Goals for Measured Advertising Results*.[2] He outlines a method called DAGMAR (after the book's title) for turning advertising objectives into specific measurable goals. An *advertising goal* is a specific communication task and achievement level to be accomplished with a specific audience in a specific period of time. Consider the following example:

FIGURE 22-1
Major Decisions in Advertising Management

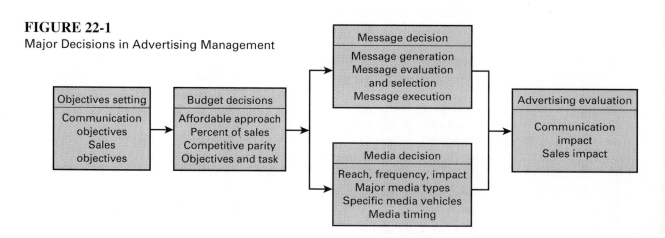

HOW DOES AN ADVERTISING AGENCY WORK?

Although familiar with advertisements, few consumers know much about the agencies that design and produce them, and arrange for the ads to be run in various media. Many agencies are concentrated in Toronto and Montreal, but most large cities have at least one agency. The three largest Canadian ad agencies are McKim, MacLaren Lintas, and Cossette. Each had revenues of $33 million in 1989.

Even companies with strong advertising departments use advertising agencies. Agencies employ specialists who can often perform advertising tasks better than a company's own staff. Agencies also bring an outside point of view to solving a company's problems, along with years of experience from working with different clients and situations. Agencies are paid partly from media discounts and often cost the firm very little. And because the firm can drop its agency at any time, an agency works hard to do a good job.

Advertising agencies usually have four departments: *creative*, which develops and produces ads; *media*, which selects media and places ads; *research*, which studies audience characteristics and wants; and *business*, which handles the agency's business activities. Each account is supervised by an account executive, and people in each department are usually assigned to work on one or more accounts.

Agencies often attract new business through reputation or size. Generally, however, a client invites a few agencies to make a presentation for its business and then selects one of them.

Ad agencies have traditionally been paid through commissions and some fees. Under this system, the agency usually receives 15 percent of the media cost as a rebate. Suppose the agency buys $60 000 of magazine space for a client. The magazine bills the advertising agency for $51 000 ($60 000 less 15 percent), and the agency bills the client for $60 000, keeping the $9000 commission. If the client bought space directly from the magazine, it would have paid $60 000, because commissions are paid only to recognized advertising agencies.

However, both advertisers and agencies have become more and more unhappy with the commission system. Larger advertisers complain that they pay more for the same services received by smaller ones simply because they place more advertising. Advertisers also believe that the commission system drives agencies away from low-cost media and short advertising campaigns. Agencies are unhappy, because they perform extra services for an account without getting any more pay. As a result, the trend is now toward paying either a straight fee or a combination commission and fee. And some large advertisers are tying agency compensation to the performance of the agency's advertising campaigns. General Foods, for example, is happy to work with a 15 percent commission if the advertising campaign is excellent; if the campaign is only good, the agency should get 13 percent; and if the campaign is poor, the agency should get 13 percent and a warning. The problem with incentive compensation is how to judge whether the campaign is excellent, good, fair, or poor. Measures of sales and communication effects can be misleading.

Another trend in recent years is that, as advertisers become multinationals, their Canadian operations prefer to deal with the branches of multinational ad agencies. To offset this, some independent Canadian ad agencies have combined with agencies having branches in other countries.

Worldwide, ad agencies have entered into combinations as a growth strategy. The largest such "supergroup" is Saatchi & Saatchi Plc, which consists of several large agencies having combined revenues of $13.5 billion. Other agencies have grown by diversifying into related marketing services, including sales promotion, public relations, marketing research, and direct marketing.

Sources: See Walecia Konrad, "A Word from the Sponsor: Get Results—Or Else," *Business Week*, July 4, 1988, p. 66; Anthony Ramirez, "Do Your Ads Need a Superagency?" *Fortune*, April 27, 1987, pp. 84-89; and "U.S. and Foreign Advertising Agency Income Report," a special issue of *Advertising Age*, March 29, 1989.

To increase among three million homemakers who own automatic washers the number who identify brand X as a low-sudsing detergent and who are persuaded that it gets clothes cleaner—from 10 percent to 40 percent in one year. ∎

Note the four goal elements:

☐ *Target:* Three million homemakers who own automatic washers
☐ *Communication Objective:* the ability to identify brand X as a low-sudsing detergent and be persuaded that it gets clothes cleaner
☐ *Desired Change:* from 10 to 40 percent
☐ *Time Horizon:* one year

Advertising objectives can be classified as to whether their aim is to inform, persuade, or remind. Table 22-1 lists examples of these objectives.

Informative advertising figures heavily in the pioneering stage of a product category, where the objective is to build *primary demand.* Thus the yogurt industry initially had to inform consumers of yogurt's nutritional benefits and many uses.

Persuasive advertising becomes important in the competitive stage, where a company's objective is to build *selective demand* for a particular brand. Most advertising falls into this category. For example, Crown Royal tries to persuade consumers that it delivers more status than any other rye. Some persuasive advertising has moved into the category of *comparison advertising*, which seeks to establish the superiority of one brand through specific comparison with one or more other brands in the product class.[3] Comparison advertising has been used in such product categories as deodorants, fast-food hamburgers, toothpastes, tires, and automobiles.

The Burger King Corporation successfully developed comparison advertising for its franchise when it battled McDonald's in a burger war over flame broiling versus frying hamburgers. In using comparison advertising, a company should make sure that it can prove its claim of superiority and that it cannot be counterattacked in an area where the other brand is stronger.

Table 22-1 Possible Advertising Objectives

To Inform

Telling the market about a new product	Describing available services
Suggesting new uses for a product	Correcting false impressions
Informing the market of a price change	Reducing consumers' fears
Explaining how the product works	Building a company image

To Persuade

Building brand preference	Persuading customer to purchase now
Encouraging switching to your brand	Persuading customer to receive a sales
Changing customer's perception of	call
product attributes	

To Remind

Reminding consumers that the product may be needed in the near future	Keeping it in their minds during off seasons
Reminding them where to buy it	Maintaining its top-of-mind awareness

Reminder advertising is highly important in the mature stage of the product to keep the consumer thinking about the product. Expensive four-color Coca-Cola ads in magazines have the purpose not of informing or persuading but of reminding people to purchase Coca-Cola. A related form of advertising is *reinforcement advertising*, which seeks to assure current purchasers that they have made the right choice. Automobile ads will often depict satisfied customers enjoying some special feature of their new car.

The choice of the advertising objective should be based on a thorough analysis of the current marketing situation. For example, if the product class is mature, and the company is the market leader, and if brand usage is low, the proper objective should be to stimulate more brand usage. On the other hand, if the product class is new, and the company is not the market leader, but its brand is superior to the leader, then the proper objective is to convince the market of the brand's superiority.

DECIDING ON THE ADVERTISING BUDGET

After determining advertising objectives, the company can proceed to establish its advertising budget for each product. The role of advertising is to shift the product's demand curve upward. The company wants to spend the amount required to achieve the sales goal. But how does a company know if it is spending the right amount? If the company spends too little, the effect is insignificant, and the company is, paradoxically, spending too much. On the other hand, if the company spends too much on advertising, then some of the money could have been put to better use. Some critics charge that large consumer-packaged-goods firms tend to overspend on advertising, and industrial companies generally underspend on advertising:[4]

> Large consumer-packaged-goods companies use image advertising extensively and are uncertain about its effect, since it doesn't produce immediate sales. They overspend as a form of "insurance" against not spending enough. In addition, their advertising agencies have a vested interest in convincing the companies to put most of their promotional funds into advertising. Finally, the companies get low efficiency out of their dollars by doing too little front-end work (marketing research and strategic positioning) and too much back-end work (copy testing). ■

> Industrial companies rely heavily on their salesforces to bring in orders. They do not spend enough on advertising to build customer awareness and comprehension. They underestimate the power of company and product image in preselling industrial customers. ■

A possible counterargument to the charge that consumer-packaged-goods companies spend too much is that advertising has a carryover effect that lasts beyond the current period. Although advertising is treated as a current expense, part of it is really an investment that builds up an intangible value called goodwill. When $5 million is spent on capital equipment, it is treated as, say, a five-year depreciable asset and only one-fifth of the cost is written off in the first year. When $5 million is spent on advertising to launch a new product, the entire cost must be written off in the first year. This treatment of advertising as a complete expense limits the number of new-product launches that a company can undertake in any one year.

How much impact does advertising really have on inducing brand switching or brand loyalty? Recently, Tellis analyzed household purchases of twelve key brands of a frequently purchased consumer product. Here are his conclusions:

Advertising appears effective in increasing the volume purchased by loyal buyers but less effective in winning new buyers. For loyal buyers, high levels of exposure per week may be unproductive because of a leveling off of ad effectiveness. . . . Advertising appears unlikely to have some cumulative effect that leads to loyalty. . . . Features, displays, and especially price have a stronger impact on response than does advertising.[5]

These findings did not sit well with the advertising community, and several people attacked his data and methodology. The whole subject of advertising effectiveness is still poorly understood and awaiting evidence from further carefully designed empirical studies.

Four commonly used methods for setting the advertising budget were described earlier in Chapter 21. We favored the *objective-and-task method*, because it requires the advertiser to define the advertising campaign's specific objectives and then to estimate the costs of the activities needed to achieve these objectives. Here we will describe some specific factors to consider when setting the advertising budget:[6]

☐ *Stage in the Product Life Cycle:* New products typically receive large advertising budgets to build awareness and to gain consumer trial. Established brands usually are supported with smaller budgets as a percentage of sales.

☐ *Market Share and Consumer Base:* High-market-share brands usually require smaller advertising budgets as a percentage of sales to maintain their share. To build share by increasing market size or market share requires larger advertising budgets. Additionally, on a cost-per-impression basis, it is less expensive to reach consumers of a widely used brand than to reach consumers of low-share brands.

☐ *Competition and Clutter:* In a market with a large number of competitors and high advertising spending, a brand must advertise more heavily to be heard above the noise in the market. Even simple clutter from advertisements not directly competitive to the brand creates a need for heavier advertising.

☐ *Advertising Frequency:* The number of repetitions needed to put across the brand's message to consumers also determines the advertising budget.

☐ *Product Substitutability:* Brands in a commodity class (e.g., cigarettes, beer, soft drinks) require heavy advertising to establish a differential image. Advertising is also important when a brand can offer unique physical benefits or features.

Marketing scientists have built a number of advertising-expenditure models that take into account these and other factors. One of the best early models was developed by Vidale and Wolfe.[7] Essentially, the model called for a larger advertising budget, the higher the sales-response rate, the higher the sales-decay rate (i.e., the rate at which customers forget the advertising and brand), and the higher the untapped sales potential. On the other hand, this model leaves out other important factors, such as the rate of competitive advertising and the effectiveness of the company's ads.

Professor John Little proposed an adaptive-control method for setting the advertising budget.[8] Suppose the company has set an advertising-expenditure rate based on its most current information on the sales-response function. It spends this rate in all markets except some randomly-chosen test markets. Advertising is at a lower rate in half of the test markets and at a higher rate in the other half. This will yield information on the average sales created by low, medium, and high rates of advertising that can be used to update the parameters of the sales-response function. The updated function is used to determine the best advertising-expenditure rate for the next period. If this experiment is conducted each period, advertising expenditures will closely track optimal advertising expenditures.[9]

DECIDING ON THE MESSAGE

Many studies of the sales effect of advertising expenditures neglect the message creativity factor. Some analysts argue that all large advertising agencies are equally creative, and therefore differences in individual campaigns "wash out." But it is precisely the differences in individual campaigns that advertisers seek. As William Bernbach observed: "The facts are not enough . . . Don't forget that Shakespeare used some pretty hackneyed plots, yet his message came through with great execution." Consider the following: [10]

> McDonald's spent $21 million on advertising in 1986, over twice the spending rate of its rival, Burger King. Yet viewers said they remembered Burger King ads better and preferred them to McDonald's. ■

> The best-known and best-liked advertising on TV in 1983 was Miller Lite beer commercials showing sports figures and celebrities arguing over whether Miller's advantage was "great taste" or "less filling." This campaign outperformed all the other beer commercials even though several spent more money. ■

By leaving out the creative factor, a substantial part of market-share differences are unexplained. One study found that the effect of the creativity factor in a campaign is more important than the number of dollars spent. Only after gaining attention can a commercial help to increase the brand's sales.[11] Differences and variety in creative strategy are undoubtedly very important in advertising success. Advertisers go through the following steps to develop a creative strategy: message generation, message evaluation and selection, and message execution.

Message Generation

In principle, the product's message (theme, appeal) should be decided as part of developing the product concept; it expresses the major benefit that the brand offers. Yet even within this concept, there may be latitude for a number of possible messages. And over time, the marketer might want to change the message without even changing the product, especially if consumers are seeking new "benefits" from the product.

Creative people use several methods to generate possible advertising appeals. Many creative people proceed *inductively* by talking to consumers, dealers, experts, and competitors. Consumers are the major source of good ideas. Their feelings about the strengths and shortcomings of existing brands provide important clues to creative strategy. Leo Burnett advocates "in-depth interviewing where I come realistically face to face with the people I am trying to sell. I try to get a picture in my mind of the kind of people they are—how they use this product and what it is."[12] A leading hair-spray company carries out continuous consumer research to determine consumer satisfaction with existing brands. If consumers want stronger holding power, the company considers reformulating its product and using this new appeal.

Some creative people use a *deductive* framework for generating advertising messages. Maloney proposed one framework (see Table 22-2).[13] He saw buyers as expecting one of four types of reward from a product: *rational, sensory, social,* or *ego satisfaction*. And buyers might visualize these rewards from *results-of-use experience, product-in-use experience,* or *incidental-to-use experience*. Combining the four types of rewards with the three types of experience generates twelve types of advertising messages.

The advertiser can generate a theme for each of the twelve cells as possible messages for the product. For example, the appeal "gets clothes cleaner" is a rational-reward promise

Table 22-2 Examples of Twelve Types of Appeals

Types of Potentially Rewarding Experience with a Product	Potential Type of Reward			
	Rational	Sensory	Social	Ego Satisfaction
Results-of-Use Experience	1. Get clothes cleaner	2. Settles stomach upset completely	3. When you care enough to serve the best	4. For the skin you deserve to have
Product-in-Use Experience	5. The flour that needs no sifting	6. Real gusto in a great light beer	7. A deodorant to guarantee social acceptance	8. The store for the young executive
Incidental-to-Use Experience	9. The plastic pack keeps the cigarette fresh	10. The portable television that's lighter in weight, easier to lift	11. The furniture that identifies the home of modern people	12. Stereo for the man with discriminating taste

Source: Adapted from John C. Maloney, "Marketing Decisions and Attitude Research," in *Effective Marketing Coordination*, ed. George L. Baker, Jr. (Chicago: American Marketing Association, 1961) pp. 595-618.

following results-of-use experience; and the phrase "real gusto in a great light beer" is a sensory-reward promise connected with product-in-use experience.

How many alternative ad themes should the advertiser create before making a choice? The more ads created, the higher the probability that the agency will develop a first-rate appeal. Yet the more time it spends creating ads, the higher the costs. There must be some optimal number of alternative ads that an agency should create and test for the client. Under the present commission system, typically 15 percent, the agency does not like to go to the expense of creating and pretesting many ads. In an ingenious study, Gross concluded that agencies generally create too few ad alternatives for their clients.[14] He estimates that advertising agencies spend from 3 to 5 percent of their media income on creating and testing ads, whereas he believes they should spend closer to 15 percent. He even proposes that a company hire competing advertising agencies to create ads, from which the best one is selected.

Message Evaluation and Selection

The advertiser needs to evaluate the alternative messages. A good ad normally focuses on one central selling proposition without trying to give too much product information, which dilutes the ad's impact. Twedt suggested that messages be rated on *desirability, exclusiveness*, and *believability*.[15] The message must first say something desirable or interesting about the product. The message must also say something exclusive or distinctive that does not apply to every brand in the product category. Finally, the message must be believable or provable.

For example, the March of Dimes searched for an advertising theme to raise money for its fight against birth defects.[16] Several messages came out of a brainstorming session. A group of young parents were asked to rate each message for interest, distinctiveness, and believability, assigning up to 100 points for each (see Figure 22-2). For example, "Seven hundred children are born each day with a birth defect" scored 70, 60, and 80 on interest, distinctiveness, and believability, while "Your next baby could be born with a birth defect" scored 58, 50, and 70. The first message outperformed the second and was preferred for advertising purposes.

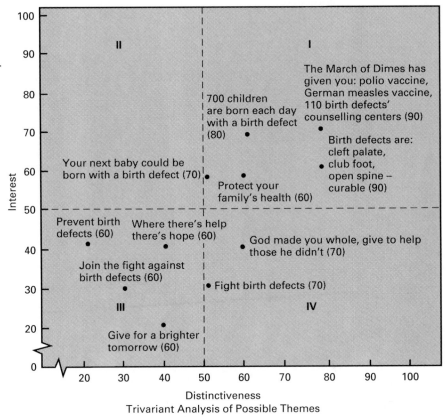

FIGURE 22-2

Advertising Message Evaluation

Source: William A. Mindak and H. Malcolm Bybee, "Marketing's Application to Fund Raising," *Journal of Marketing*, July 1971, pp. 13-18.

Distinctiveness

Trivariant Analysis of Possible Themes

The advertiser should pretest with the hope of determining which appeal has the strongest behavioral impact. For example, Transport Canada was trying to determine which of three messages would be the most effective in informing motorists of the dangers of driving without using seatbelts. They pretested three different advertisements in matched pairs of Canadian cities, using newspapers, radio, and television. Telephone surveys conducted before and after the advertisements measured people's recall and comprehension of the three messages.[17]

Message Execution

The message's impact depends not only upon what is said but also on how it is said. Some ads aim for *rational positioning* and others for *emotional positioning*. In our society, ads typically present an explicit feature or benefit designed to appeal to the rational mind: "Gets clothes cleaner," "Brings relief faster," and so on. Japanese ads are more indirect and appeal to the emotional mind: an example was Nissan's Infiniti car ad, which showed not the car but beautiful scenes from nature that produced an emotional association and response.

The choice of headlines, copy and so on, can make a difference in the ad's impact:

Lalita Manrai reported a study in which she created two ads for the same car. The first ad carried the headline "A New Car"; the second, the headline "Is This Car for You?" The second headline utilized an advertising strategy called labeling, in which the consumer is labeled as the type of person who is interested in that type of product. The two ads also differed in that the first ad described the car's features and the second described the car's benefits. In the test, the second ad far outperformed the first ad in terms of overall impression of the product, reader interest in buying the product, and likelihood of recommending it to a friend.[18]   ∎

Message execution can be decisive for those products that are highly similar, such as detergents, cigarettes, coffee, and beer. The advertiser usually prepares a *copy strategy statement* describing the objective, content, support, and tone of the desired ad. Here is the strategy statement for a Pillsbury product called 1869 Brand Biscuits:

> The *objective* of the advertising is to convince biscuit users that now they can buy a canned biscuit that's as good as homemade—Pillsbury's 1869 Brand Biscuits. The *content* consists of emphasizing the following product characteristics: they look like homemade biscuits; they have the same texture as homemade biscuits; and they taste like homemade biscuits. *Support* for the "good as homemade" promise will be twofold: (1) 1869 Brand Biscuits are made from a special kind of flour (soft wheat flour) used to make homemade biscuits but never before used in making canned biscuits, and (2) the use of traditional biscuit recipes. The *tone* of the advertising will be a news announcement, tempered by a warm, reflective mood emanating from a look back at traditional baking quality.   ∎

Creative people must now find a *style, tone, words,* and *format* for executing the message. All of these elements must deliver a cohesive image and message. Since few people read body copy, the picture and headline must summarize the selling proposition.

Any message can be presented in different *execution styles:*

☐ *Slice-of-Life:* This shows one or more persons using the product in a normal setting. A family seated at the dinner table might express satisfaction with a new biscuit brand.

☐ *Lifestyle:* This emphasizes how a product fits in with a lifestyle. A Scotch ad shows a handsome middle-aged man holding a glass of Scotch in one hand and steering his yacht with the other.

☐ *Fantasy:* This creates a fantasy around the product or its use. Revlon's ad for Jontue features a barefoot woman wearing a chiffon dress. She comes out of an old French barn, crosses a meadow, and confronts a handsome young man on a white steed, who carries her away.

☐ *Mood or Image:* This builds an evocative mood or image around the product, such as beauty, love, or serenity. No claim is made about the product except through suggestion. Many cigarette ads create moods.

☐ *Musical:* This uses background music or shows one or more persons or cartoon characters singing a song involving the product. Many cola ads have used this format.

☐ *Personality Symbol:* This creates a character that personifies the product. The character might be *animated* (Jolly Green Giant, Pillsbury Doughboy) or *real* (Ronald McDonald, Morris the Cat).

☐ *Technical Expertise:* This shows the company's expertise and experience in making the product. Coffee ads show company buyers carefully selecting coffee beans, and wine ads emphasize the wine makers' years of experience.

☐ *Scientific Evidence:* This presents survey or scientific evidence that the brand is preferred to or outperforms one or more other brands. For years, Crest toothpaste has featured scientific evidence to convince toothpaste buyers of Crest's superior cavity-fighting properties.

☐ *Testimonial Evidence:* This features a highly credible, likable, or empathetic source endorsing the product. It could be a celebrity like Michael J. Fox (Pepsi Cola) or ordinary people saying that they prefer the product (see the Marketing Strategies 22-1 exhibit).

Marketing Strategies 22-1

CELEBRITY ENDORSEMENTS AS A STRATEGY

Marketers have used celebrities from time immemorial to endorse their products. A well-chosen celebrity can at the very least draw attention to a product or brand, as when Ed McMahon promotes Alpo dog food or Publishers Clearing House. Or the celebrity's mystique can transfer over to the brand—Catherine Deneuve in an ad for Chanel No 5. Or the celebrity's expertise and authority transfers to the brand—Chris Evert endorsing a Wilson tennis racquet.

The choice of the right celebrity is critical. The celebrity should have high recognition, high positive affect, and high appropriateness to the product. Howard Cossell has high recognition but negative affect among many groups. Sylvester Stallone has high recognition and high positive affect but might not be appropriate for advertising a World Peace Conference. Alan Alda, Paul Newman, and Bill Cosby could successfully advertise a large number of products, because they have extremely high ratings for well-knownness and likability (known as the Q factor in the entertainment industry).

Athletes are a particularly effective endorsing group, especially for athletic products, beverages, and apparel. Joe Namath advertises Brut and Joe Montana advertises Pepsi. Michael Jordan, star of the Chicago Bulls, earns about $4 million a year endorsing Nike, Wilson, Coca-Cola, Johnson Products, and McDonald's. Nike sold $110 million worth of "Air Jordan" basketball shoes and apparel in its first year with Jordan as its representative. Not only does the celebrity's image appear in ads but the message is multiplied in the sales of T-shirts, toys and games, and hundreds of additional merchandise items.

The marketer's chief worry in selecting a celebrity is that the additional sales more than cover the costs. The marketer also hopes that the celebrity won't endorse too many other products and wear thin. Beyond this, they pray that the celebrity doesn't get involved in a scandal (as when Pepsi dropped Madonna because of an anti-Christian song), get sick, injured, or die. They cover these last risks with insurance.

Source: See Irving Rein, Philip Kotler, and Martin Stoller, *High Visibility: How Executives, Politicians, Entertainers, Athletes, and Other Professionals Create, Market, and Achieve Successful Images* (New York: Dodd, Mead, 1987).

The communicator must also choose an appropriate *tone* for the ad. Procter & Gamble is consistently positive in its tone; its ads say something superlatively positive about the product. Humor is avoided so as not to take attention away from the message. On the other hand, Volkswagen's ads for its famous "Beetle" typically took on a humorous and self-deprecating tone ("the Ugly Bug").

Memorable and attention-getting *words* must be found. The themes listed below on the left would have had much less impact without the creative phrasing on the right:[19]

Theme	Creative Copy
7-Up is not a cola.	*"The Un-Cola"*
Let us drive you in our bus instead of driving your car.	*"Take the bus, leave the driving to us."*
Shop by turning the pages of the telephone directory.	*"Let your fingers do the walking."*
We don't rent as many cars, so we have to do more for our customers.	*"We try harder."*

Creativity is especially required for headlines. There are six basic types of headlines: *news* ("New Boom and More Inflation Ahead . . . and What You Can Do About It"); *question* ("Have You Had It Lately?"); *narrative* ("They Laughed When I Sat Down at the Piano, but When I Started to Play"); *command* ("Don't Buy Until You Try All Three"); 1-2-3 ways ("12 Ways to Save on Your Income Tax"); and *how-what-why* ("Why They Can't Stop Buying"). Consider the care exercised by airlines to find the right way to describe their planes as safe. Instead of mentioning safety, they use confidence-building phrases like "The Wings of Man" and "The World's Most Experienced Airline."

Format elements such as ad size, color, and illustration will make a difference in an ad's impact as well as its cost. A minor rearrangement of mechanical elements within the ad can improve its attention-getting power. Larger-size ads gain more attention, though not necessarily by as much as their difference in cost. Four-color illustrations instead of black and white increase ad effectiveness and ad cost. By planning the relative dominance of different elements of the ad, optimal delivery can be achieved. New electronic eye movement studies show that consumers can be led through an ad by strategic placement of the ad's dominant elements.

A number of researchers into print advertisements report that the *picture, headline,* and *copy* are important, in that order. The reader first notices the picture, and it must be strong enough to draw attention. Then the headline must be effective in propelling the person to read the copy. The copy itself must be well composed. Even then, a really outstanding ad will be noted by less than 50 percent of the exposed audience; about 30 percent of the exposed audience might recall the headline's main point; about 25 percent might remember the advertiser's name; and less than 10 percent will have read most of the body copy. Ordinary ads, unfortunately, do not achieve even these results.

An industry study listed the following characteristics for ads that scored above average in recall and recognition: innovation (new product or new uses), "story appeal" (as an attention-getting device), before-and-after illustration, demonstrations, problem solution, and the inclusion of relevant characters that become emblematic of the brand (these may be cartoon figures, such as the Jolly Green Giant, or actual people, including celebrities).[20]

The questions are often raised: Why do so many ads look alike? Why aren't advertising agencies more creative? Norman W. Brown, head of the advertising agency of Foote, Cone & Belding, answers that in many cases the advertisers, and not their agencies, are to blame. When his agency develops a highly creative campaign, the brand manager or higher management levels worry about the risk and either reject it or ask for so many modifications that it loses its force. His conclusion: "Many ads aren't creative because many companies want comfort, not creativity."

DECIDING ON THE MEDIA

The advertiser's next task is to choose advertising media to carry the advertising message. The steps are deciding on desired reach, frequency, and impact; choosing among major media types; selecting specific media vehicles; and deciding on media timing.

Deciding on Reach, Frequency, and Impact

Media selection is the *problem of finding the most cost-effective media to deliver the desired number of exposures to the target audience.* But what do we mean by the desired number of exposures? Presumably, the advertiser is seeking a certain response from the target audience, for example, a certain level of *product trial.* Now the rate of product trial will depend,

FIGURE 22-3

Relationship between
Trial, Awareness,
and the
Exposure Function

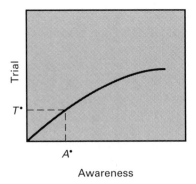

Awareness

(a) Relationship between product
trial rate and audience
awareness level

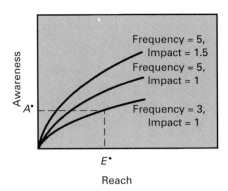

Reach

(b) Relationship between audience
awareness level and exposure
reach and frequency

among other things, on the level of audience brand awareness. Suppose the rate of product trial increases at a diminishing rate with the level of audience awareness, as shown in Figure 22-3(a). If the advertiser seeks a product trial rate of (say) T*, it will be necessary to achieve a brand awareness level of A*.

The next task is to find out how many exposures, E*, will produce a level of audience awareness of A*. The effect of exposures on audience awareness depends on the exposures' reach, frequency, and impact:

☐ *Reach (R):* The number of different persons or households exposed to a particular media schedule at least once during a specified time period.

☐ *Frequency (F):* The number of times within the specified time period that an average person or household is exposed to the message.

☐ *Impact (I):* The qualitative value of an exposure through a given medium (thus a food ad in *Good Housekeeping* would have a higher impact than in the *Police Gazette*).

Figure 22-3(b) shows the relationship between audience awareness and reach. Audience awareness will be greater, the higher the exposure's reach, frequency, and impact. The media planner recognizes important tradeoffs between reach, frequency, and impact. Suppose the media planner has an advertising budget of $1 000 000 and the cost per thousand exposures of average quality is $20. This means that the advertiser can buy 50 000 000 exposures (= $1 000 000 ÷ 20/1000). If the advertiser seeks an average exposure frequency of 10, then the advertiser can reach 5 000 000 people (= 50 000 000 ÷ 10) with the given budget. Now if the advertiser wants higher-quality media costing $25 per thousand exposures, the advertiser will be able to reach only 4 000 000 people unless it is willing to lower the desired exposure frequency.

The relationship between reach, frequency, and impact is captured in the following concepts:

☐ *Total Number of Exposures (E):* This is the reach times the average frequency, that is, $E = R \times F$. This measure is referred to as the *gross rating points* (GRP). If a given media schedule reaches 80 percent of the homes with an average exposure frequency of 3, the media schedule is said to have a GRP of 240 (= 80×3). If another media schedule has a GRP of 300, it is said to have more weight, but we cannot tell how this weight breaks up into reach and frequency.

☐ *Weighted Number of Exposures (WE):* This is the reach times average frequency times average impact, that is $WE = R \times F \times I$.

The media planning tradeoff is as follows. With a given budget, what is the most cost-effective combination of reach, frequency, and impact? *Reach* is more important when launching new products or flanker brands, or going after an undefined target market. *Frequency* is more important where there are strong competitors, a complex story to tell, high consumer resistance or a frequent-purchase cycle.[21] Suppose the media planner is willing to use average-impact media. It would make sense to settle the issue of frequency first. How many exposures does an average member of the target audience need for the advertising to trigger behavior? Once this target frequency is decided, then reach will be determined.

Many advertisers believe that a target audience needs a large number of exposures for the advertising to work. Too few repetitions can be a waste, since they will hardly be noticed. Others doubt the value of high ad frequency. They feel that after people see the same ad a few times, they either act on it, get irritated by it, or stop noticing it. Krugman asserted that three exposures to an advertisement might be enough:

> The first exposure is by definition unique. As with the initial exposure to anything, a "What is it?" type of cognitive response dominates the reaction. The second exposure to a stimulus . . . produces several effects. One may be the cognitive reaction that characterized the first exposure, if the audience missed much of the message the first time around. . . . More often, an evaluative "What of it?" response replaces the "What is it?" response. . . . The third exposure constitutes a reminder, if a decision to buy based on the evaluations has not been acted on. The third exposure is also the beginning of disengagement and withdrawal of attention from a completed episode.[22]

Krugman's thesis favoring three exposures has to be qualified. He means three actual *advertising exposures*—i.e., the person actually sees the ad three times. This should not be confused with *vehicle exposures*, namely, the number of times the person has been exposed to the vehicle carrying the ad. If only half the readers look at magazine ads, or if the readers look at ads only every other issue, then the advertising exposure is only half of the vehicle exposures. Most research services estimate only vehicle exposures, not ad exposures. A media strategist would have to buy more vehicle exposures than three in order to achieve Krugman's three "hits."[23]

Another factor arguing for some advertising repetition is that of forgetting. The job of advertising repetition is partly to put the message back into memory. The higher the forgetting rate associated with that brand, product category, or message, the higher the warranted level of repetition.

Choosing Among Major Media Types

The media planner has to know the capacity of the major media types to deliver reach, frequency, and impact. The major advertising media along with their costs, advantages, and limitations are profiled in Table 22-3. The major media types, in order of their advertising volume, are *telephone, newspapers, television, direct mail, radio, magazines*, and *outdoor*.

Media planners make their choice among these media categories by considering several variables, the most important ones being the following:

☐ *Target-Audience Media Habits:* For example, radio and television are the most effective media for reaching teenagers.

☐ *Product:* Women's dresses are best shown in color magazines, and Polaroid cameras are best demonstrated on television. Media types have different potentials for demonstration, visualization, explanation, believability, and color.

Table 22-3 Profiles of Major Media Types

Medium	1990 Spending $000 000	%	Example of Cost (1990)	Advantages	Limitations
Newspapers (all types)	2923	30.2	$47 430 for 1/3 page B/W ad in 3 major cities	Flexible, timely, local coverage, broad acceptance	Short duration, poor quality, low pass-along
Direct mail & catalog	2204	22.7	Consult Canadian Direct Marketing Association	Selective, can be personalized, no competition	High cost per contact, "junk-mail" image
Television	1465	15.1	$15 500 for 30-second spot on 16 CTV stations	High attention, good reach, good sensory appeal	Clutter, costly, not selective, fleeting
Directories	1109	11.4	$8124 for 1/4 page in Toronto *Yellow Pages*	Very timely, high repeat exposure	Not selective, not variable, poor quality
Outdoor	764	7.9	$31 807 for 25 panels, 4 weeks, 3 major cities	Flexible, repeat exposure, low cost	Not selective, short exposures
Radio	751	7.8	$20 000 for five spots on four Toronto stations	Can be selective, reasonable cost, flexible	Low attention, fleeting
Periodicals	477	4.9	$22 950 for full page, four color ad in *Maclean's*	Pass-along, high quality, durable selective	Long lead time, no assurance of position, waste

Sources: *Canadian Media Directors' Council Media Digest 1990/91; Marketing,* May 20, 1991, p. 1; Radio Marketing Bureau of Canada.

□ *Message:* A message announcing a major sale tomorrow will require radio or newspapers. A message containing a great deal of technical data might require specialized magazines or mailings.

□ *Cost:* Television is very expensive, whereas newspaper advertising is inexpensive. What counts is the cost-per-thousand exposures rather than the total cost.

Ideas about media impact and cost must be reexamined regularly. For a long time, television enjoyed the dominant position in the media mix, and other media were neglected. Then media researchers began to notice television's reduced effectiveness, which was due to increased commercial clutter (advertisers beamed shorter and more numerous commercials at the television audience, resulting in poorer audience attention and impact), increased "zipping and zapping" of commercials, and lowered commercial TV viewing owing to the growth in cable TV and VCRs. Furthermore, television advertising costs rose faster than other media costs. Several companies found that a combination of print ads and television commercials often did a better job than television commercials alone. This illustrates that advertisers must periodically review the different media to determine their best buys. Another reason for review is the continuous emergence of *new media* (see the exhibit Marketing Environment and Trends 22-1).

Given the abundant media and their characteristics, the media planner must decide on how to allocate the budget to the major media types. For example, Pillsbury might decide in

Marketing Environment and Trends 22-1

THE CEASELESS SEARCH FOR NEW MEDIA

As mass-media costs rise and market segments narrow, advertisers are driven to invent or discover new targeted promotional media. One promising media site is the store itself. Older promotional in-store vehicles, such as end-aisle displays and special price tags, are being supplemented by a flurry of new media vehicles. Some supermarkets are selling space on their tiled floors for company logos. They are experimenting with talking shelves, where shoppers get information as they pass certain food sections. One company has introduced the videocart, which contains a computerized screen that carries consumer-benefit information ("cauliflower is rich in vitamin C") 70 percent of the time and advertiser promotions ("20 cents off on White Star Tuna this week") 30 percent of the time.

New media are also being created for other special locations. The most inventive media creator is Chris Whittle, who has targeted both physician waiting rooms and school lunchrooms. His company places copies of *Special Reports* in cooperating doctors' waiting rooms, which carry feature articles on family, health, and money matters along with full-page ads from Kraft, P&G, and other major advertisers.

He seeks agreement from physicians to carry no more than two other magazines in their waiting rooms and boasts of twenty-five million readers who, he claims, are four times more likely to remember ads in *Special Reports* than those in traditional women's service magazines. He also donates television sets to school lunchrooms, provided they carry his Channel One news show, which also carries commercials of special interest to young people. In this area, he has met a lot of resistance.

Whittle and others are also pushing for ads to appear in bestselling paperback books and in movie videotapes. Written material such as annual reports, data sheets, catalogs, and newsletters are increasingly carrying ads. Many companies sending out monthly bills (credit card companies, department stores, oil companies, airlines, and the like) are including inserts in the envelope that advertise products. As the productivity of more standard media declines, the search for new media will grow unabated.

Sources: Betsy Sharkey, "Shopping Cart Videos: A New Medium for Ads?" *Adweek*, January 8, 1990; "Whittle's Advertisers Are Getting Tired of Waiting," *Business Week*, January 22, 1990, p. 33.

---

launching its new biscuit to allocate $3 million to daytime network television, $2 million to women's magazines, and $1 million to daily newspapers in twenty major markets.

Selecting Specific Media Vehicles

Now the media planner searches for the most cost-effective media vehicle. The media planner faces an incredible number of choices:

> If consumer magazines are preferred, there are 82 English and 33 French magazines having circulation over 30 000. Only four of them have circulation over one million (*Chatelaine, Homemaker's, Reader's Digest,* and *TV Times*). Since most are small and specialized, advertisers can reach special-interest groups, like the 110 147 readers of *Hockey News*. But it is hard to reach large general-interest consumers through magazines. For this, newspapers or television are preferred. In the newspaper field, there are 110 daily newspapers excluding supplements and weekend papers. There are three national TV networks, each having numerous stations (41 CBC, 20 Radio Canada, 16 CTV), plus 8 regional networks, and 10 specialty networks (e.g.,

MuchMusic and TSN). Within each network and station, the media planner must consider specific time slots and programs as media vehicles. The same is true of the radio medium, of which there are 385 AM stations and 302 FM stations in Canada.[24] ■

All of this means a condition of extreme media fragmentation, which may allow advertisers to reach special-interest groups more effectively, but raises the cost of reaching general audiences for standard household products. ■

Thus even after choosing one of the major media types—magazines, newspapers, television, or radio—the advertiser is still left with a complex choice. For example, if television is the medium, should the vehicles be network or local? prime time or late night? sitcom or drama? How does the media planner make a choice among the rich set of programs? The media planner relies on media-measurement services that provide estimates of audience size, composition, and media cost. Audience size has several possible measures:

☐ *Circulation:* The number of physical units through which advertising is distributed.

☐ *Audience:* The number of people who are exposed to the vehicle. (If the vehicle has pass-on readership, then the audience is larger than circulation.)

☐ *Effective Audience:* The number of people with the target's characteristics who are exposed to the vehicle

☐ *Effective Ad-Exposed Audience:* The number of people with the target's characteristics who actually saw the ad.

The Cost-per-Thousand Criterion   Media planners calculate the *cost per thousand persons reached* by a particular vehicle. If a full-page, four-color advertisement in *Maclean's* costs $22 950 and *Macleans'* estimated readership is 645 000 people, the cost of reaching each one thousand persons is approximately $36. The same advertisement in *Equinox* may cost $7550 but reach only 156 000 persons, at a cost per thousand of $48. The media planner would rank the various magazines according to cost per thousand and favor those magazines with the lowest cost per thousand.

Several adjustments have to be applied to this initial measure. First, the measure should be adjusted for *audience quality*. For a baby lotion advertisement, a magazine read by one million young mothers would have an exposure value of one million, but if read by one million old men it would have a zero exposure value. Second, the exposure value should be adjusted for the *audience-attention probability*. Readers of *Vogue*, for example, pay more attention to ads than do readers of *Newsweek*. Third, the exposure value should be adjusted for the *editorial quality* (prestige and believability) that one magazine might have over another. Fourth, the exposure value should be adjusted for the magazine's ad placement policies and extra services (such as regional or occupational editions and lead time requirements).

Media planners are increasingly using more sophisticated measures of media effectiveness and employing them in mathematical models for arriving at the best media mix. Many advertising agencies use a computer program to select the initial media and then make further improvements based on subjective factors omitted in the model.[25]

Deciding on Media Timing

The advertiser faces a macroscheduling problem and a microscheduling problem.

Macroscheduling Problem   The advertiser has to decide how to schedule the advertising in relation to seasonal and business-cycle trends. Suppose 70 percent of a product's sales occur between June and September. The firm has three options. The firm can vary its advertising expenditures to follow the seasonal pattern, to oppose the seasonal pattern, or to be constant throughout the year. Most firms pursue a policy of seasonal advertising. Yet consider this:

> Some years ago, one of the soft-drink manufacturers put more money into off-season advertising. This resulted in increased nonseasonal consumption of its brand, while not hurting the brand's seasonal consumption. Other soft-drink manufacturers started to do the same, with the net result that a more-balanced consumption pattern occurred. The previous seasonal concentration of advertising had created a self-fulfilling prophecy. ∎

Forrester has proposed using his "industrial dynamics" methodology to test cyclical advertising policies.[26] He sees advertising as having a lagged impact on consumer awareness; awareness has a lagged impact on factory sales; and factory sales have a lagged impact on advertising expenditures. These time relationships can be studied and formulated mathematically into a computer-simulation model. Alternative timing strategies would be simulated to assess their varying impacts on company sales, costs, and profits. Rao and Miller also developed a lag model to relate a brand's share to advertising and promotional expenditures on a market-by-market basis. They tested their model successfully with five Lever brands in fifteen districts relating market share to dollars spent on TV, print, price-off and trade promotions.[27]

Kuehn developed a model to explore how advertising should be timed for frequently purchased, highly seasonal, low-cost grocery products.[28] Kuehn showed that the appropriate timing pattern depends on the *degree of advertising carryover* and the *amount of habitual behavior in customer brand choice. Carryover* refers to the rate at which the effect of an advertising expenditure wears out with the passage of time. A carryover of 0.75 per month means that the current effect of a past advertising expenditure is 75 percent of its level in the previous month. *Habitual behavior* indicates how much brand holdover occurs independent of the level of advertising. High habitual purchasing, say 0.90, means that 90 percent of the buyers repeat their brand choice in the next period.

Kuehn found that when there is no advertising carryover or habitual purchasing, the decision maker is justified in using a percentage-of-sales rule to budget advertising. The optimal timing pattern for advertising expenditures coincides with the expected seasonal pattern of industry sales. But if there is advertising carryover and/or habitual purchasing, the percentage-of-sales budgeting method is not optimal. It would be better to time advertising to lead sales. Advertising expenditures should peak before sales peak. Lead time should be greater, the higher the carryover. Furthermore the advertising expenditures should be steadier, the greater the habitual purchasing.

Microscheduling Problem   The microscheduling problem calls for allocating advertising expenditures within a short period to obtain the maximum impact. Suppose the firm decides to buy thirty radio spots in the month of September.

Figure 22-4 shows several possible patterns. The left side shows that advertising messages for the month can be concentrated in a small part of the month ("burst" advertising), dispersed continuously throughout the month, or dispersed intermittently throughout the month. The top side shows that the advertising messages can be beamed with a level, rising, falling, or alternating frequency.

The most effective pattern depends upon the communication objectives in relation to the nature of the product, target customers, distribution channels, and other marketing factors. Consider the following cases:

FIGURE 22-4

Classification of Advertising Timing Patterns

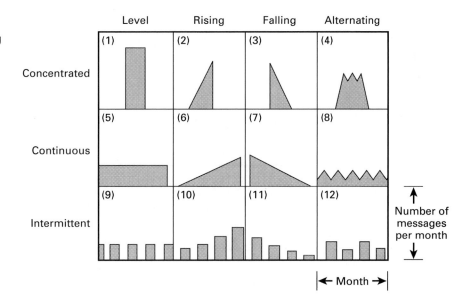

A *retailer* wants to announce a preseason sale of ski equipment. She recognizes that only certain people are interested in skis. She thinks that the target buyers need to hear the message only once or twice. Her objective is to maximize reach, not frequency. She decides to concentrate the messages on sale days at a level rate but to vary the time of day to avoid the same audiences. She uses pattern (1). ∎

A *muffler manufacturer-distributor* wants to keep his name before the public. Yet he does not want his advertising to be too continuous because only 3 to 5 percent of the cars on the road need a new muffler at any given time. He chooses to use intermittent advertising. Furthermore, he recognizes that Fridays are paydays, so he sponsors a few messages on a midweek day and more messages on Friday. He uses pattern (12). ∎

The timing pattern should consider three factors. *Buyer turnover* expresses the rate at which new buyers enter the market; the higher this rate, the more continuous the advertising should be. *Purchase frequency* is the number of times during the period that the average buyer buys the product; the higher the purchase frequency, the more continuous the advertising should be. The *forgetting rate* is the rate at which the buyer forgets the brand; the higher the forgetting rate, the more continuous the advertising should be.

In launching a new product, the advertiser has to choose between ad continuity, concentration, flighting, and pulsing. *Continuity* is achieved by scheduling exposures evenly throughout a given period. But high advertising costs and seasonal variations in sales discourage continuous advertising. Generally, advertisers use continuous advertising in expanding market situations, with frequently purchased items, and in tightly defined buyer categories. *Concentration* calls for spending all the advertising dollars in a single period. This makes sense for products with only one selling season or holiday. *Flighting* calls for advertising for some period, followed by a hiatus with no advertising, and then followed by a second flight. It is used when funding is limited, the purchase cycle is relatively infrequent, or with seasonal items. *Pulsing* is continuous advertising at low weight levels reinforced periodically by waves of heavier activity. Pulsing draws upon the strength of continuous advertising and flights to create a compromise scheduling strategy. Those who favor pulsing feel that the audience will learn the message more thoroughly, and money can be saved.

Research indicated that Budweiser could suspend advertising in a particular market and experience no adverse sales effect for at least a year and a half.[29] Then the company could introduce a six-month burst of advertising and restore the previous growth rate. Although the research was based on flighting, Budweiser adopted a less risky pulsing advertising strategy. ■

EVALUATING ADVERTISING EFFECTIVENESS

Good planning and control of advertising depend critically on measures of advertising effectiveness. Yet the amount of fundamental research on advertising effectiveness is appallingly small. According to Forrester:

> I doubt that there is any other function in industry where management bases so much expenditure on such scanty knowledge. The advertising industry spends 2 or 3 percent of its gross dollar volume on what it calls "research," and even if this were really true research, the small amount would be surprising. However, I estimate that less than a tenth of this amount would be considered research plus development as these terms are defined in the engineering and product research departments of companies . . . probably no more than 1/5 of 1 percent of total advertising expenditure is used to achieve an enduring understanding of how to spend the other 99.8 percent.[30]

Most of the measurement of advertising effectiveness is of an applied nature, dealing with specific ads and campaigns. Most of the money is spent by agencies on *pretesting* the given ad, much less is spent on *postevaluating* its effects. Many companies develop an advertising campaign, put it into the national market, and then evaluate its effectiveness. It would be better to put the campaign into one or a few towns first and evaluate what is happening before rolling a campaign throughout the country with a very large budget. When a company tested its new campaign first in one city, the campaign bombed and the company saved all the money that it would have spent going national.

Most advertisers try to measure the *communication effect* of an ad, that is, its potential effect on awareness, knowledge, or preference. They would like to measure the *sales effect* but often feel it is too difficult to measure. Yet both can be researched.

Communication-Effect Research

Communication-effect research seeks to determine whether an ad is communicating effectively. Called *copy testing*, it can be done before an ad is put into media and after it is printed or broadcast.

There are three major methods of advertising pretesting. The first is a *direct rating method*, which asks consumers to rate alternative ads. These ratings are used to evaluate an ad's attention, read-through, cognitive, affective, and behavior strengths (see Figure 22-5). Although an imperfect measure of an ad's actual impact, a high rating indicates a potentially more effective ad. *Portfolio tests* ask consumers to view and/or listen to a portfolio of advertisements, taking as much time as they need. Consumers are then asked to recall all the ads and their content, aided or unaided by the interviewer. Their recall level indicates an ad's ability to stand out and to have its message understood and remembered. *Laboratory tests* use equipment to measure consumers' physiological reactions—heartbeat, blood pressure, pupil dilation, perspiration—to an ad. These tests measure an ad's attention-getting power but reveal nothing about its impact on beliefs, attitudes, or intentions. (The exhibit Marketing Concepts and Tools 22-1 describes some specific ad research techniques.)

FIGURE 22-5
Rating Sheet for Ads

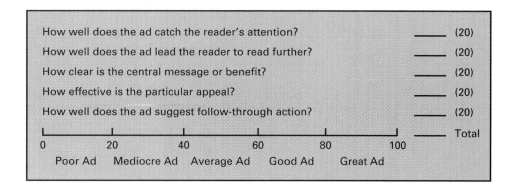

How well does the ad catch the reader's attention? _____ (20)

How well does the ad lead the reader to read further? _____ (20)

How clear is the central message or benefit? _____ (20)

How effective is the particular appeal? _____ (20)

How well does the ad suggest follow-through action? _____ (20)

_____ Total

0	20	40	60	80	100
	Poor Ad	Mediocre Ad	Average Ad	Good Ad	Great Ad

Marketing Concepts and Tools 22-1

SOME ADVERTISING RESEARCH TECHNIQUES

There are several methods of ad pretesting.

Print

Daniel Starch (Canada) Ltd. offers a widely used print pretesting service in which some test ads are placed into magazines. The magazines are then circulated to consumers. These consumers are contacted later and interviewed concerning the magazines and their advertising. Recall and recognition tests are used to determine advertising effectiveness. Three readership scores are prepared by Starch: (a) *noted*, the percentage of readers who recall seeing the ad in the magazine; (b) *seen/associated*, the percentage who correctly identify the product and advertiser with the ad; and (c) *read most*, the percentage who say they read more than half of the written material in the ad. Starch also furnishes adnorms showing the average scores for each product class for the year, and separately for men and women for each magazine, to enable advertisers to compare their ad's impact to competitors' ads.

Broadcast Services

Four broadcast pretest methods are available:

☐ *In-Home Tests:* A small-screen projector is taken into the homes of target consumers. These consumers then view the commercials. The technique gains a subject's complete attention but creates an unnatural viewing situation.

☐ *Trailer Tests:* To get closer to the consumers' actual decision point, pretesting is conducted in a trailer in a shopping center. Shoppers are shown the test products and given an opportunity to select a series of brands in a simulated shopping situation. Consumers then view a series of commercials. They are then given coupons to be used in the shopping center. By evaluating redemption, advertisers can estimate the commercial's influence on purchase behavior.

☐ *Theater Tests:* Consumers are invited to a theater to view a potential new television series along with some commercials. Before the show begins, the consumers indicate their preferred brands in different categories. After the viewing, consumers are again asked to choose their preferred brands in various categories. Preference changes are assumed to measure the persuasive power of the commercials.

☐ *On-Air Tests:* These tests are conducted on a regular TV channel. Respondents are recruited to watch the program during the test commercial or are selected based on their having viewed the program. They are asked questions about their commercial recall. This technique creates a real-world atmosphere in which to evaluate commercials.

Advertisers are also interested in measuring the overall communication impact of a completed advertising campaign. To what extent did the ad campaign increase brand awareness, brand comprehension, stated brand preference, and so on? Assuming that the advertiser had measured these levels before the campaign, the advertiser can draw a random sample of consumers after the campaign to assess the communication effects. If a company hoped to increase brand awareness from 20 percent to 50 percent and only succeeded in increasing it to 30 percent, then something is wrong: the company is not spending enough, its ads are poor, or some other factor is missing.

Sales-Effect Research

Communication-effect advertising research helps advertisers assess advertising's communication effects but reveals little about its sales impact. What sales are generated by an ad that increases brand awareness by 20 percent and brand preference by 10 percent?

Advertising's sales effect is generally harder to measure than communication effect. Sales are influenced by many factors besides advertising, such as the product's features, price, availability and competitors' actions. The fewer or more controllable these other factors are, the easier it is to measure advertising's effect on sales. The sales impact is easiest to measure in direct-marketing situations and hardest to measure in brand or corporate-image-building advertising.

Companies are generally interested in finding out whether they are overspending or underspending on advertising. One approach is to work with the following formulation:

$$\frac{\text{Share of}}{\text{expenditure}} = \frac{\text{Share of}}{\text{voice}} = \frac{\text{Share of}}{\text{mind and heart}} = \frac{\text{Share of}}{\text{market}}$$

In other words, a company's share of advertising expenditures produces a share of voice that earns a share of their minds and hearts and ultimately a share of market. Peckham studied the relationship between share of voice and share of market for several consumer products over a number of years and found a 1-to-1 ratio for established products and a 1.5-2.0 to 1.0 ratio for new products.[31] Using this information, suppose we observed the following data for three well-established firms selling an almost identical product at an identical price:

	Advertising Expenditure	Share of Voice	Share of Market	Advertising Effectiveness
A	$2 000 000	57.1	40.0	70
B	1 000 000	28.6	28.6	100
C	500 000	14.3	31.4	220

Firm A spends $2 000 000 of the industry's total expenditures of $3 500 000; so its share of voice is 57.1 percent. Yet its share of market is only 40 percent. By dividing its share of market by its share of voice, we get an advertising-effectiveness ratio of 70, suggesting that firm A is either overspending or misspending. Firm B is spending 28.6 percent of total advertising expenditures and has a 28.6 market share; the conclusion is that it is spending its money efficiently. Firm C is spending only 14.3 percent of the total and yet achieving a market share of 31.4 percent; the conclusion is that it is spending its money superefficiently and should probably increase its expenditures.

Researchers try to measure the sales impact through analyzing either historical or experimental data. The *historical approach* involves correlating past sales to past advertising expenditures on a current or lagged basis using advanced statistical techniques. Palda studied the effect of advertising expenditures on the sales of Lydia Pinkham's Vegetable Compound between 1908 and 1960.[32] He calculated the short-term and long-term marginal sales effects of advertising. The marginal advertising dollars increased sales by only fifty cents in the short term, suggesting that Pinkham spent too much on advertising. But the long-term marginal sales effect was three times as large. Palda calculated a posttax marginal rate of return on company advertising of 37 percent over the whole period.

Montgomery and Silk estimated the sales effectiveness of three communication tools used in the pharmaceutical industry.[33] A drug company spent 38 percent of its communication budget on direct mail, 32 percent on samples and literature, and 29 percent on journal advertising. Yet the sales-effects research indicated that journal advertising, the least-used communication tool, had the highest long-run advertising elasticity, here .365; samples and literature had an elasticity of .108; and direct mail had an elasticity of only .018. They concluded that the company spent too much on direct mail and too little on journal advertising.

Other researchers use *experimental design* to measure the sales impact of advertising. Instead of spending the normal percentage of advertising to sales in all territories, the company spends more in some territories and less in others. These tactics are called *high-spending tests* and *low-spending tests*. If the high-spending tests produce substantial sales increases, it appears that the company has been underspending. If they fail to produce more sales and if low-spending tests do not lead to sales decreases, then the company has been overspending. These tests, of course, must be accompanied by good experimental controls and last sufficiently long to capture lagged effects of changed advertising-expenditure levels.

Du Pont was one of the first companies to design advertising experiments. Du Pont's paint division divided fifty-six sales territories into high, average, and low market-share territories.[34] Du Pont spent the normal amount for advertising in one-third of the group; in another third, two and one-half times the normal amount; and in the remaining third, four times the normal amount (see Figure 22-6.) At the end of the experiment, Du Pont estimated how much extra sales was created by higher levels of advertising expenditure. Du Pont found that higher advertising expenditure increased sales at a diminishing rate, and that the sales increase was weaker in Du Pont's high market-share territories. ∎

Another approach to allocating an advertising budget geographically is to use a model that considers the differences between geographic areas in terms of their market size, advertising response, media efficiency, competition, and profit margins. Urban developed a media allocation model that relies upon these geographic variables to allocate the advertising budget.[35]

FIGURE 22-6

Experimental Design for Testing the Effect of Three Levels of Advertising Expenditure on Market Share

Source: From p. 166, *Mathematical Models and Marketing Management*, by Robert Buzzell. Boston: Division of Research, Graduate School of Business Administration, Harvard University, 1968. Reprinted by permission.

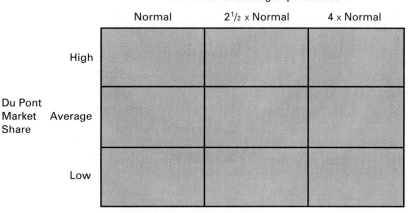

In general, a growing number of companies are striving to measure the sales effect of advertising expenditures instead of settling only for communication-effect measures.

SUMMARY

Advertising—the use of paid media by a seller to communicate persuasive information about its products, services, or organization—is a potent promotional tool. Advertising takes on many forms (national, regional, local; consumer, industrial, retail; product, brand, institutional; and so on) designed to achieve a variety of objectives (immediate sales, brand recognition, preference, and so on).

Advertising decision making is a five-step process consisting of objectives setting, budget decision, message decision, media decision, and ad-effectiveness evaluation. Advertisers need to establish clear goals as to whether the advertising is supposed to inform, persuade, or remind buyers. The advertising budget can be established on the basis of what is affordable, as a percentage of sales, on the basis of competitors' expenditures, or on the basis of objectives and tasks; and more advanced decision models are available. The message decision calls for generating messages, evaluating and selecting among them, and executing them effectively. The media decision calls for defining the reach, frequency, and impact goals; choosing among major media types; selecting specific media vehicles; and scheduling the media. Finally, campaign evaluation calls for evaluating the communication and sales effects of advertising, before, during, and after the advertising.

■ QUESTIONS

1. "If I had my way I would confine all advertising to a recitation of the facts about the product and no more." Discuss this philosophy of advertising. Say why you agree or disagree.

2. "It is not important that the objectives and goals of an advertising campaign be stated. Management only needs to know that advertising's fundamental goal is to generate sales and profits." Discuss this statement. Say whether you agree or disagree with it. Give reasons for your position.

3. An executive recently recommended allocating advertising expenditures to various markets in proportion to sales in those markets. His reasons were as follows. In the absence of further company advertising, a fixed (but unknown) percentage of sales in each market would be lost to competitors. The role of advertising is to maintain the present level of customers. Therefore the promotional level in each market should be proportional to the sales level. Do you agree?

4. Examine current copies of two magazines (e.g., *TV Guide* and *Harrowsmith*). Classify the execution styles used by the full-page ads in each of these issues. Comment on differences of style, tone, and format of the ads found in each magazine. What factors might contribute to these differences?

5. Discuss the strengths and weaknesses of both communication-effects research and sales-effects research. Assess the concerns that you have for each of the techniques used under these two research approaches.

6. Consumer protection is one of the major rationales used for regulating advertising around the world. What other global forces should be monitored for their potential impact on advertising regulation?

7. Advertisers often do research to test for the effectiveness of an ad before it is placed in the media. Suggest some principles that should be followed when testing ad copy.

8. Consider the following two statements: "The purpose of advertising is to create sales." "The purpose of advertising is to improve the buyer's disposition toward the company's products." Which comes closer to the truth?

9. The advertising manager of a large firm asks the executive committee to approve a $100 000 increase in the advertising budget. She submits that this extra money will probably increase company sales by $500 000 over what they would otherwise be. What other information would you want in order to judge the budget request?

10. A canned dog-food manufacturer is trying to choose between media A and B. Medium A has 10 000 000 readers and charges $20 000 for a full-page ad ($2 per 1000). Medium B has 15 000 000 readers and charges $25 000 for a full-page ad ($1.67 per 1000). Is there any other calculation that might be made before assuming that B is the better medium?

11. A large oil company allocates its advertising budget to its territories according to current territorial sales. The adver-

tising manager justifies using a constant advertising-to-sales ratio by saying that the company loses a certain percentage of its customers in each market each year and that advertising's most important job is to get new customers to replace them. What assumptions underlie this reasoning?

12. Discuss the value of emotional appeals in advertising. Are there any advantages to affective or emotional advertising?

■ NOTES

1. See Stan Sutter, "Advertising Revenues Continue to Climb..." *Marketing*, May 20, 1991, p. 1, and Marina Strauss, "Advertising spending up only 3%," *The Globe and Mail*, April 2, 1991, p. B12.

2. See Russell H. Colley, *Defining Advertising Goals for Measured Advertising Results* (New York: Association of National Advertisers, 1961).

3. See William L. Wilkie and Paul W. Farris, "Comparison Advertising: Problem and Potential," *Journal of Marketing*, October 1975, pp. 7-15.

4. For a good discussion, see David A. Aaker and James M. Carman, "Are You Overadvertising?" *Journal of Advertising Research*, August-September 1982, pp. 57-70.

5. Gerald J. Tellis, "Advertising Exposure, Loyalty, and Brand Purchase: A Two-Stage Model of Choice," *Journal of Marketing Research*, May 1988, pp. 134-44.

6. See Donald E. Schultz, Dennis Martin, and William P. Brown, *Strategic Advertising Campaigns* (Chicago: Crain Books, 1984), pp. 192-97.

7. M. L. Vidale and H. R. Wolfe, "An Operations-Research Study of Sales Response to Advertising," *Operations Research*, June 1957, pp. 370-81.

8. John D. C. Little, "A Model of Adaptive Control of Promotional Spending," *Operations Research*, November 1966, pp. 1075-97.

9. For additional models for setting the advertising budget, see Gary L. Lilien and Philip Kotler, *Marketing Decision Making: A Model-Building Approach* (New York: Harper & Row, 1983), pp. 490-501.

10. See John Koten, "Creativity, Not Budget Size, Is Vital to TV-Ad Popularity," *Wall Street Journal*, March 1, 1984, p. 25.

11. *Ibid.*

12. See "Keep Listening to That Wee, Small Voice," in

Communications of an Advertising Man (Chicago: Leo Burnett Co., 1961), p. 61.

13. John C. Maloney, "Marketing Decisions and Attitude Research," in *Effective Marketing Coordination*, ed. George L. Baker, Jr. (Chicago: American Marketing Association, 1961), pp. 595-618.

14. Irwin Gross, "An Analytical Approach to the Creative Aspect of Advertising Operations" (Ph.D. dissertation, Case Institute of Technology, November 1967).

15. Dik Warren Twedt, "How to Plan New Products, Improve Old Ones, and Create Better Advertising," *Journal of Marketing*, January 1969, pp. 53-57.

16. See William A. Mindak and H. Malcolm Bybee, "Marketing Application to Fund Raising," *Journal of Marketing*, July 1971, pp. 13-18.

17. Ruth M. Heron, "Evaluation of the Canadian Seat Belt Campaign: Methodological Considerations," *Proceedings of the Canadian Psychological Association*, Vancouver, June 1977.

18. Lalita Manrai, "Effect of Labeling Strategy in Advertising: Self-Referencing versus Psychological Reactance" (Ph.D. dissertation, Northwestern University, 1987).

19. L. Greenland, "Is This the Era of Positioning?" *Advertising Age*, May 29, 1972.

20. David Ogilvy and Joel Raphaelson, "Research on Advertising Techniques That Work—and Don't Work," *Harvard Business Review*, July-August 1982, pp. 14-18.

21. Schultz et al., *Strategic Advertising Campaigns*, p. 340.

22. See Herbert E. Krugman, "What Makes Advertising Effective?" *Harvard Business Review*, March-April 1975, pp. 96-103, here p. 98.

23. See Peggy J. Kreshel, Kent M. Lancaster, and Margaret A. Toomey, "Advertising Media Planning: How Leading Advertising Agencies Estimate Effective Reach and

Frequency" (Urbana: University of Illinois, Department of Advertising, paper no. 20, January 1985). Also see Jack Z. Sissors and Lincoln Bumba, *Advertising Media Planning*, 3rd ed. (Lincolnwood, Ill: NTC Business Books), Chap. 9.

24. *Canadian Media Directors' Council Media Digest 1990/91*

25. See Roland T. Rust, *Advertising Media Models: A Practical Guide* (Lexington, Mass.: Lexington Books, 1986).

26. See Jay W. Forrester, "Advertising: A Problem in Industrial Dynamics," *Harvard Business Review*, March-April 1959, pp. 100-110.

27. See Amber G. Rao and Peter B. Miller, "Advertising/Sales Response Functions," *Journal of Advertising Research*, April 1975, pp. 7-15.

28. See Alfred A. Kuehn, "How Advertising Performance Depends on Other Marketing Factors," *Journal of Advertising Research*, March 1962, pp. 2-10.

29. Philip H. Dougherty, "Bud 'Pulses' the Market," *New York Times*, February 18, 1975.

30. Forrester, "Advertising," p. 102.

31. See J. O. Peckham, *The Wheel of Marketing* (Scarsdale, N.Y.: privately printed, 1975), pp. 73-77.

32. Kristian S. Palda, *The Measurement of Cumulative Advertising Effect* (Englewood Cliffs, N.J.: Prentice-Hall, 1964), p. 87.

33. David B. Montgomery and Alvin J. Silk, "Estimating Dynamic Effects of Market Communications Expenditures," *Management Science*, June 1972, pp. 485-501.

34. See Robert D. Buzzell, "E. I. Du Pont de Nemours & Co.: Measurement of Effects of Advertising," in his *Mathematical Models and Marketing Management* (Boston: Division of Research, Graduate School of Business Administration, Harvard University, 1964), pp. 157-79.

35. See Glen L. Urban, "Allocating Ad Budgets Geographically," *Journal of Advertising Research*, December, 1975, pp. 7-16.

23

Designing Direct Marketing, Sales-Promotion, and Public-Relations Programs

In science the credit goes to the man who convinces the world, not the man to whom the idea first occurs.

Sir William Osler

In this chapter, we will examine the nature and purpose of direct marketing, sales promotion, and public relations and the decisions involved in using them. These tools are often viewed as secondary to the major ones of advertising and personal selling. Yet they can contribute strongly to marketing performance and are playing a growing role. Direct marketing, sales promotion, and public relations are not well understood by marketing practitioners, nor are marketing departments typically organized to handle them effectively. The first companies in their industries to learn to use these tools more effectively will gain a substantial competitive edge.

DIRECT MARKETING

Most companies rely primarily on advertising, sales promotion, and personal selling to move their products and services. They use advertising to create awareness and interest, sales promotion to provide a reason to buy now, and personal selling to close the sale. Direct-marketing attempts to compress these elements to lead to a direct sale without using an intermediary. The person exposed to an ad—in a catalog, direct-mail piece, phone call, magazine, newspaper, or radio program—can call a toll-free 800 number and charge the order to a credit-card number, or respond by mail and either write the credit card number or enclose a check.

Although direct marketing first emerged in the form of direct mail and mail-order catalogs, it has taken on several more forms in recent years, including telemarketing, direct-response radio and television, electronic shopping, and the like. What is common to these diverse marketing vehicles is that they are used to obtain direct orders from targeted customers or prospects. This is in contrast to mass advertising, which reaches an unspecified number of people, most of whom are not in the market for the product and will not make a purchase decision at a retail outlet until some future occasion.

Although direct marketing has boomed in recent years, a large number of companies still relegate it to a minor role in their promotion mix. The company's advertising, sales-promotion, and salesforce departments receive most of the promotion dollars and jealously guard their budgets (although some of these budgets are used for direct marketing). Many advertising agencies still don't offer direct-marketing services, because they are unfamiliar with this new discipline or believe they can make more money developing and running advertising campaigns. Still, most large advertising agencies have acquired direct-marketing capabilities and are increasingly offering their clients more varied communication resources. The total number of Canadian direct marketers is unknown, but the Toronto *Yellow Pages* lists 118 direct-mail advertising agencies, as well as 41 telemarketing service bureaus. There are also an estimated 400-500 catalog companies.

The salesforce tends to resist direct marketing for reasons given by Roman:

> If salespeople hear "direct marketing," they instinctively feel that their turf is threatened and that accounts will be taken away from them by direct writing of orders. Even if the program is as benign as lead generation and qualification to produce better leads, and hence higher sales, for the field sales force, there is likely to be resentment based on a perceived loss of control of the selling process.[1]

But many companies have embraced direct marketing as a means of improving market communications and building profitable relationships with their customers. Procter & Gamble, General Foods, and Colgate-Palmolive have used direct marketing to sample products and retain loyal customers or switch users of competing brands. Retailers like Consumer's Distributing and Canadian Tire regularly send out catalogs to stimulate their in-store sales. however, most direct marketers do not have stores so rely on mail orders, typically from a more specialized product line; for example Barnes & Noble (books), Mary Maxim (needlework), and Day-Timers (work diaries).

Here we will consider the nature, growth, and advantages of direct marketing, the trend toward integrated direct marketing, the development of a marketing database system, and the major decisions in direct marketing.

Nature, Growth, and Advantages of Direct Marketing

The term *direct marketing* has taken on new meanings over the years. Originally, it was simply a form of marketing in which products or services moved from producer to consumer without an intermediate channel of distribution. In this sense, companies that use salespeople to sell direct to end users or that operate factory outlets are using direct marketing. Later, the term described marketing done through the mails, whether catalog marketing or direct-mail marketing. As the telephone and other media came into heavy use to promote offers directly to customers, direct marketing was redefined by the Direct Marketing Association (DMA):

> Direct marketing *is an interactive system of marketing which uses one or more advertising media to effect a measurable response and/or transaction at any location.*

In this definition, the emphasis is on marketing undertaken to get a measurable response, typically an order from a customer. (It can be called *direct-order marketing*.)

Today, many users of direct marketing visualize it as playing a broader role (which can be called *direct-relationship marketing*).[2] These direct marketers use *direct-response advertising media* to make a sale and learn about a customer whose name and profile is entered in a *customer database*, which is used to build a continuing and enriching *relationship*. The emphasis is on building preferred customer relationships. Airlines, hotels, and others are building strong customer relationships through award programs and are using their customer database to match more carefully their offers to individual customers. They are approaching a stage where offers are sent only to those customers and prospects most able, willing, and ready to buy the product or service. To the extent that they succeed, they will gain much higher response rates to their promotions.

Sales produced through direct-marketing channels have been growing at a rapid rate. The Canadian Direct Marketing Association estimates that industry sales were $7.8 billion in 1990. In spite of a slump in the retail sector, direct sales to consumers have been growing at 7 percent annually.[3] Marketing Concepts and Tools 23-1 describes the popular methods used in direct marketing.

Marketing Concepts and Tools 23-1

MAJOR TOOLS OF DIRECT MARKETING

Direct marketing was responsible for sales of $7.8 billion of Canadian products in 1990. Of this total, consumer goods accounted for 37 percent, consumer services for 19 percent, nonprofit fundraising for 13 percent and business products for 31 percent. The average Canadian consumer bought $170 of goods and services in response to several types of direct marketing that are described below.

Catalog Marketing

Each year, Canada's catalog marketers mail out 500 000 catalogs. Their annual sales of $2.2 billion are growing at more than 10 percent annually. About 71 percent of the catalogs are sent to homes and 29 percent are sent to businesses. The average purchase size is $84.

Retailers that send out catalogs include the large full-line merchandisers like Sears, as well as specialty stores like Tilley Endurables. Several large companies have catalog divisions—Xerox (children's books), Avon (women's apparel), General Foods (needlework kits). But the greatest number of catalogs comes from the hundreds of catalog houses that sell the more specialized products. These businesses develop appealing product assortments and illustrate them in attractive four-color layouts. Not only mail-order forms are provided, but also credit-card terms

and toll-free 24-hour telephone service. They range in size from small specialty houses like Comforts of Home to the Philatelic Service of Canada Post.

The success of a mail-order business depends greatly on the company's ability to manage its mailing and customer lists, to control its inventory carefully, to offer quality merchandise, and to project a distinctive customer-benefiting image. Some catalog companies distinguish themselves by adding literary or information features to their catalog, sending swatches of materials, operating a special hotline to answer questions, sending gifts to the best customers, and offering to donate a percent of profits to good causes.

A current trend, as the industry grows, is for the more successful catalog houses to experiment with different media. Thus, Sears is trying videotape "catalogs" which can be targeted to their better customers.

Direct-Mail Marketing

This is the largest part of the direct marketing industry. It accounts for more than half of the industry's sales, and a quarter of Canada Post's revenues. Direct mail takes several forms—letters, flyers, foldouts, and other "salespeople on wings." Recently, some direct marketers have been mailing audiotapes, videotapes, and even computer diskettes. An exercise-equipment

---

company mails a videotape to inquirers demonstrating the use and health advantages of an expensive home exercise machine called the Nordic Track Cardiovascular Exerciser. Ford sends out a computer diskette called a Disk Drive Test Drive to consumers responding to its car ads in computer publications. The diskette's menu allows the consumer to read persuasive copy, get technical specifications, view attractive graphics about the car, and get answers to frequently asked questions.

In general, direct-mail marketers hope to sell a product or service, collect or qualify leads for the salesforce, communicate some interesting news, or reward loyal customers with a gift. The names might be selected from a list compiled by the company or from lists purchased from mailing-list brokers. These brokers are able to sell lists of any description—the superwealthy, mobile-home owners, classical-music lovers, and so on. Direct marketers typically buy a subsample of names from a potential list and do a test mailing to see if the response rate is high enough.

Direct mail is becoming increasingly popular, because it permits high target-market selectivity, can be personalized, is flexible, and allows testing and measuring of results. While the cost per thousand people reached is higher than with mass media, the people reached are much better prospects. Over 30 percent of recipients purchased something through direct mail in 1987. Direct mail has proved very successful in promoting books, magazine subscriptions, and insurance and is increasingly being used to sell novelty and gift items, clothing, gourmet foods, and industrial items. Direct mail is also used heavily by charities.

Telemarketing

Telemarketing has recently become a significant direct-marketing tool, producing revenues of $1 billion. It began to blossom in the late 1960s with the introduction of inbound and outbound Wide Area Telephone Service (WATS). With IN WATS, marketers can offer customers and prospects toll-free 800 numbers to place orders for goods or services stimulated by print or broadcast ads, direct mail or catalogs, or to make complaints and suggestions. With OUT WATS, they can use the phone to sell directly to consumers and businesses, generate or qualify sales leads, reach more distant buyers, or service current customers or accounts.

Some telemarketing systems are fully automated. For example, automatic-dialing and recorded-message players (ADRMPs) can dial numbers, play a voice-activated advertising message, and take orders from interested customers on an answering-machine device or by forwarding the call to an operator. Telemarketing is increasingly used in business marketing as well as consumer marketing. For example, Raleigh Bicycles used telemarketing to reduce the amount of personal selling needed for contacting its dealers. In the first year, salesforce travel costs were reduced by 50 percent, and sales in a single quarter were up 34 percent.

Television Direct-Response Marketing

Television is a growing medium for direct marketing both through network and cable channels. Television is used in two ways to market products directly to consumers. The first is through *direct-response advertising*. Direct-response marketers air television spots, often 60 or 120 seconds long, that persuasively describe a product and give customers a toll-free number for ordering. Direct-response advertising works well for magazines, books, small appliances, records and tapes, collectibles, and many other products. One of the best examples is Dial Media's ads for Ginsu knives, which ran for seven years and sold almost three million sets of knives worth over $40 million in sales. Recently, some companies have prepared thirty-minute "informercials," which resemble documentaries—on quitting smoking, curing baldness, or losing weight—and carry testimony from satisfied users of the product or service, and include a toll-free number for ordering or getting further information.

Another television marketing approach is *home shopping channels* where an entire television program—or whole channel—is dedicated to selling goods and services. The Canadian Home Shoppers Club (CHSC) is a cable TV service. The program's hosts offer bargain prices on products ranging from jewely, lamps, and clothing, to power tools and consumer electronics—usually obtained by CHSC at closeout prices. Viewers call an 800 number to order goods. At the other end, dozens of operators enter orders directly into computer terminals. The goods are typically shipped within a few days.

Radio, Magazine, and Newspaper Direct-Response Marketing

Magazines, newspapers, and radios are also used to present direct response offers to customers. The person hears or reads about an offer and dials a toll-free number to place an order.

Kiosk Shopping

Some companies have designed "customer-order-placing machines" (in contrast to vending machines) and placed them in stores, airports, and other locations. For example, the Florsheim Shoe Company includes a machine in several of their stores on which the customer indicates the type of shoe he wants (dress, sport), and the color and size. Pictures of Florsheim shoes appear on the screen that meet his criteria. If the particular shoes are not available in the store, the customer can dial an attached phone and type in his credit-card information and where the shoes should be delivered.

Electronic Shopping

Electronic shopping takes two forms. The first, videotex, is a two-way system that links consumers' television sets with the seller's computer data banks by cable or telephone lines. The videotex service makes up a computerized catalog of products offered by producers, retailers, banks, travel organizations, and others. Consumers use an ordinary television set that has a special keyboard device connected to the system by two-way cable.

The other form involves the use of personal computers with a modem through which consumers dial a service such as Prodigy or CompusServe. For a monthly charge or usage charge, these services allow consumers to order goods from local or national retailers; do their banking with local banks; book airline, hotel, and car rental reservations; get headline news and movie reviews; and send messages to others. The number of users of electronic home shopping is still quite small but is likely to grow as more consumers acquire cable television and personal computers.

Sources: For more reading, see Jancie Steinberg, "Cacophony of Catalogs Fill All Niches," *Advertising Age*, October 26, 1987, pp. S1-2; Rudy Oetting, "Telephone Marketing: Where We've Been and Where We Should Be Going," *Direct Marketing*, February 1987, p. 8; Arthur Bragg, "TV's Shopping Shows: Your New Move?" *Sales & Marketing Management*, October 1987, pp. 85-89; Alison Fahey, "Prodigy Videotex Expands Its Reach," *Advertising Age*, April 24, 1989, p. 75.

All kinds of organizations use direct marketing: manufacturers, retailers, service companies, catalog merchants, nonprofit organizations. Its growth in the consumer market is largely a response to the "demassification" of the market, in which there is an ever-multiplying number of minimarkets with highly individualized needs and preferences. People in these markets have credit cards and known mailing addresses and telephone numbers, which facilitate reaching and transacting with them. Households have less time to shop because of the substantial number of women who have entered the workforce. The higher costs of driving, traffic congestion, parking headaches, the shortage of retail sales help and queues at the checkout counter all encourage *in-home shopping*. In addition, many chain stores have dropped slower-moving specialty items, thus creating an opportunity for direct marketers to promote these items. The development of toll-free phone numbers and the willingness of direct marketers to accept telephone orders at night or on Sundays have boosted this form of selling. Another major factor is the growth of twenty-four-hour and forty-eight-hour delivery via Federal Express, Airborne, DHL, and other carriers. Finally, the growth of computer power has allowed direct marketers to build enhanced customer databases from which they can single out the best prospects for any product they wish to advertise.

Direct marketing has also grown rapidly in business-to-business marketing. A major reason is the high and increasing costs of reaching business markets through the salesforce.

Table 23-1 Typical Cost per Contact of Reaching Business Markets with Different Media Vehicles

Personal sales calls	$250	(out of town)
	52	(local)
Seminars, trade show exhibits	40	
Salesperson writes a single letter	25	
Showroom or counter selling	16	
Yellow Pages large display ad	16	
Telephone order desk	9	(800 number)
	6	(local)
Mass phoning program	8	(national with WATS)
	4	(local)
Direct mail	.30-3	
Selective media	.15	(ad in trade publication)
Mass media	.01-.05	(radio, newspaper, TV)

Source: John Klein & Associates, Inc. 1988.

Table 23-1 shows the typical cost per contact in reaching business markets with different media. Clearly, if out-of-town personal sales calls cost $250 per contact, they ought to be made only to customers and prospects who are virtually ready to buy. Lower cost-per-contact media, such as telemarketing, direct mail, and selective and mass advertising, should be used to identify and prime these prospects before visiting them.

Direct marketing provides a number of benefits to customers. Consumers who buy from mail-order channels say that mail-order shopping is fun and a convenient and hassle-free method of shopping. It saves them time. They can do comparative shopping from their armchairs by browsing through their catalogs. It introduces them to a larger selection of merchandise and to new lifestyles. They can order gifts to be sent directly to intended recipients without having to leave their homes. Industrial customers also attest to a number of advantages, specifically learning about many products and services without tying up time in meetings with salespeople.

Direct marketing provides a number of advantages to sellers. It allows greater prospect *selectivity*. A direct marketer can buy a mailing list containing the names of almost any group: left-handed people, overweight people, millionaires, newborn babies, and so on. The message can be *personalized* and *customized*. Eventually, according to Pierre Passavant, "We will store hundreds . . . of messages in memory. We will select ten thousand families with twelve or twenty or fifty specific characteristics and send them very individualized laser-printed letters."[4] Furthermore, the direct marketer can build a *continuous relationship* with each customer. The mother of the newborn baby will receive regular mailings describing new clothes, toys, and other goods that the growing baby will need. Direct marketing can be *timed* more precisely to reach prospects at the right moment. Direct-marketing material receives *higher readership*, since it reaches more interested prospects. Direct marketing permits *testing* of alternative media and messages (headlines, salutations, benefits, prices, and the like) in the search for the most cost-effective approach. Direct marketing permits *privacy* in that the direct marketer's offer and strategy is not visible to competitors. Finally, the direct marketer knows whether the campaign has been profitable because of *response measurement*.

The Development of Integrated Direct Marketing

Most direct marketers rely on a single advertising vehicle and a "one-shot" effort to reach and sell a prospect. An example of a *single vehicle, single-stage campaign* would be sending a one-time mailing offering a cookware item. A *single vehicle, multiple-stage campaign* would involve sending successive mailings to a prospect to trigger purchase. Magazine publishers, for example, send about four notices to a household to get reluctant subscribers to renew.

A more powerful approach is to execute a *multiple vehicle, multiple-stage campaign*. Roman calls this technique *integrated direct marketing (IDM)*. Consider the following sequence:

Paid ad with a response mechanism $\longrightarrow$	Direct mail $\longrightarrow$	Outbound telemarketing $\longrightarrow$	Face-to-face sales call $\longrightarrow$	Ongoing communication

The paid ad creates product awareness and stimulates inquiries. The company then sends direct mail to those who inquired. Within forty-eight to seventy-two hours following mail receipt, the company phones, seeking an order. Some prospects will place an order; others might request a face-to-face sales call. Even if the prospect is not ready to buy, there is ongoing communication. Roman says that this use of *response compression*, whereby multiple media are deployed within a tightly defined time frame increases impact and awareness of the message. The underlying idea is to deploy select media with precise timing to generate greater incremental sales, while offsetting incremental costs.

As an example, Roman cites a bank's campaign to market home equity loans. Instead of using only mail and an 800 number, the bank added a coupon, outbound telemarketing, and print advertising. Although the campaign cost increased, it resulted in a 15 percent increase in the number of new accounts.

Roman concluded:

> When a mailing piece which might generate a 2 percent response on its own is supplemented by a tollfree 800-number ordering channel, we regularly see response rise by 50-125 percent. A skillfully integrated outbound telemarketing effort can add another 500 percent lift in response. Suddenly our 2 percent response has grown to 13 percent or more by adding interactive marketing channels to a "business as usual" mailing. The dollars and cents involved in adding media to the integrated media mix is normally marginal on a cost-per-order basis because of the high level of responses generated. . . . Adding media to a marketing program will raise total response . . . because different people are inclined to respond to different stimuli.[5]

Rapp and Collins developed a very useful model—they call it *maximarketing*—that makes direct marketing techniques the driving force in the general marketing process.[6] Their model recommends the creation of a customer database and advocates making direct-contact marketing a full partner in the marketing process. Maximarketing consists of a comprehensive set of steps for reaching the prospect, making the sale, and developing the relationship. The maximarketing concept is an approach that can be followed as well by the mass marketer with retail distribution as by the marketer selling direct (see Marketing Concepts and Tools 23-2).

Developing a Marketing Database System

In order to successfully implement integrated direct marketing, companies need to invest in a marketing database system:

Marketing Concepts and Tools 23-2

THE "MAXIMARKETING" MODEL FOR INTEGRATED MARKETING

Rapp and Collins's maximarketing model consists of the nine steps shown here and described below.

1. *Maximized targeting* calls upon the marketer to define and identify the best target prospects for the offer. The marketer either buys appropriate mailing lists or searches the customer database for characteristics that point to high interest, ability to pay, and readiness to buy. Additional "best customer" criteria include those who buy with some frequency, don't return many orders, don't complain, and pay on time. Mass marketers can go "fishing" for prospects with direct-response advertising in such mass media as television, newspaper supplements, and magazine insert cards.

2. *Maximized media* leads the direct marketer to examine the exploding variety of media and choose those which allow for convenient two-way communication and measurement of results.

3. *Maximized accountability* calls for evaluating campaigns on the basis of cost per prospect response rather than cost per thousand exposures as is used in mass advertising.

4. *Maximized awareness* involves searching for messages that will break through the clutter and reach the hearts and minds of the prospects by means of "whole brain" advertising, appealing to a person's rational and emotional sides.

5. *Maximized activation* emphasizes that advertising must trigger purchase or at least advance prospects to a measurably higher stage of buying readiness. Activation devices include statements like "Send for

more information" and "Reply coupon must be returned by September 30."

6. *Maximized synergy* involves finding ways of doing double duty with the advertising, for instance, combining awareness building with direct response, promoting other distribution channels, and sharing costs with other advertisers.

7. *Maximized linkage* calls for linking the advertising to the sale by concentrating on the better prospects and spending more of the total budget to convert them, rather than spending money simply to send an awareness message to the world at large.

8. *Maximized sales* through database building calls upon the marketer to continue to market directly to known customers by cross-selling, upgrading, and introduction of new products. The marketer keeps enhancing the customer database with more customer information and ends up with a rich private advertising medium. Many marketers today are getting as interested in the loyalty-building process as they are in the customer-acquisition process, with the aim of maximizing "lifetime customer value."

9. *Maximized distribution* involves the marketer in building additional channels to reach prospects and customers—for instance, when the direct marketer opens retail stores or obtains shelf space in existing retail stores, or when the retailer issues a catalog or a manufacturer such as General Foods decides to sell a high-ticket brand of coffee directly to the consumer.

Source: Stan Rapp and Thomas L. Collins, *Maximarketing* (New York: McGraw-Hill, 1987).

A marketing database *is an organized collection of data about individual customers, prospects, or suspects that is accessible and actionable for such marketing purposes as lead generation, lead qualification, sale of a product or service, or maintenance of customer relationships.*

Most companies have not yet built an effective marketing database system. Mass marketers generally know little about individual customers. Retailers know a lot about their charge-account customers but almost nothing about their cash or other credit-card customers. Banks develop customer databases in each separate product area but typically fail to tie this information together in a complete profile of the customer that could be used for cross-selling purposes or relationship pricing.

Building a marketing database involves investing in central and remote computer hardware, data-processing software, information-enhancement programs, communication links, personnel to capture data, user-training costs, design of analytical programs, and so forth. The system should be user friendly and available to various marketing groups, such as those in product and brand management, new-product development, advertising and promotion, direct mail, telemarketing, field sales, order fulfillment, and customer service. Building a marketing database takes time and involves much cost, but when it runs properly, the selling company will achieve much higher marketing productivity. Consider the following:

A General Electric customer database indicates each customer's geodemographics, psychographics, mediagraphics, appliance purchasing history, and so on. GE direct marketers can determine which past customers might be ready to replace their washing machines, for instance, those who bought their GE washing machines six years ago and have large families. They can determine which customers would be interested in a new GE videorecorder based on their history of buying other GE consumer electronic products. They can identify the heaviest past GE purchasers and send them $30 gift certificates to apply against their next purchase of a GE appliance. Clearly, a rich customer database allows a company to anticipate customer needs, locate good prospects, and reward loyal customers. ∎

Major Decisions in Direct Marketing

In preparing a direct-marketing campaign, marketers must decide on their objectives, targets, offer strategy, various tests, and measures of campaign success. Here we will review these decisions.

Objectives The direct marketer normally aims to secure immediate purchases from prospects. The campaign's success is judged by the response rate. A response rate of 2 percent is normally considered good in direct-marketing sales campaigns. Yet this rate also implies that 98 percent of the campaign effort was wasted.

That is not necessarily the case. The direct marketing presumably had some effect on awareness and intention to buy at a later date. Furthermore, not all direct marketing aims to produce an immediate sale. One major use of direct marketing is to produce prospect leads for the salesforce. Direct marketers also send communications to strengthen brand image and company preference; examples include banks that mail birthday greeting cards to their best customers and department stores that send gifts to their best customers. Some direct marketers run campaigns to inform and educate their customers to prepare them for later purchase; thus Ford sends out booklets on "How to Take Good Care of Your Car." Given the variety of direct-marketing objectives, the direct marketer needs to carefully spell out the campaign objectives.

Target Customers Direct marketers need to figure out the characteristics of customers and prospects who would be most able, willing, and ready to buy. Bob Stone recommends applying the R-F-M formula (recency, frequency, monetary amount) for rating and selecting customers from a list.[7] The best customer targets are those who bought most recently, who buy frequently, and who spend the most. Points are established for varying R-F-M levels, and each customer is scored; the higher the score, the more attractive the customer.

Direct marketers can use segmentation criteria in targeting prospects. Good prospects can be identified on the basis of such variables as age, sex, income, education, previous mail-order purchases, and so forth. Occasions also provide a good segmentation departure point. New mothers will be in the market for baby clothes and baby toys; college freshmen will buy typewriters, computers, television sets, and clothing; and newly marrieds will be looking for housing, furniture, appliances, and bank loans. Another good segmentation departure point is consumer lifestyles. There are consumers who are computer buffs, cooking buffs, outdoor buffs, and so forth; some successful catalog marketers have targeted these groups and won their hearts and minds.

Once the target market is defined, the direct marketer needs to obtain names of good prospects in the target market. Here is where *list acquisition and management skills* come into play. The direct marketer's best list is typically the house list of past customers who have bought the company's products. The direct marketer can buy additional lists from list brokers. Names on these lists are priced at so much a name. But external lists have problems, including name duplication, incomplete data, obsolete addresses, and so on. The better lists include overlays of demographic and psychographic information, in addition to simple addresses. The main point is that the direct marketer needs to test lists in advance to know their worth.

Offer Strategy   Direct marketers have to figure out an effective offer strategy to meet the target market's needs. Nash sees the offer strategy as consisting of five elements—the product, the offer, the medium, the distribution method, and the creative strategy.[8] Fortunately, all of these elements can be tested.

Each medium has its own rules for effective use. Consider direct mail. In developing a package mailing, the direct marketer has to decide on five components. Each component can help or hurt the overall response rate. The *outside envelope* will be more effective if it contains an illustration, preferably in color, and/or a catchy reason to open the envelope, such as the announcement of a contest, premium, or benefit to the recipient. Outside envelopes are more effective—but more costly—when they contain a colorful commemorative stamp, when the address is handtyped or handwritten, and when the envelope differs in size or shape from standard envelopes. (However, in business-to-business marketing, the most effective outer envelope is often the one with no promotional copy at all.)

The *sales letter* should use a personal salutation and start with a headline in bold type in the form of a newslead, a how/what/why statement, a narrative, or a question to gain attention. The letter should be printed on good-quality paper and run for as many pages as are necessary to make the sale, with some indented paragraphs and underlining of pertinent phrases and sentences. A computer-type letter usually outpulls a printed letter, and the presence of a pithy P.S. at the letter's end increases the response rate, as does the signature of someone whose title is appropriate and impressive. A colorful *circular* accompanying the letter will also increase the response rate in most cases by more than its cost. The *reply form* should feature an 800 toll-free number and contain a perforated receipt stub and guarantee of satisfaction. The inclusion of a postage-free *reply envelope* will dramatically increase the response rate.

Consider, on the other hand, a telemarketing campaign. Effective telemarketing depends on choosing the right telemarketers, training them well, and motivating them. Telemarketers should have pleasant voices and project enthusiasm. Women are more effective than men for many products. The telemarketers should initially train with a script and eventually move toward more improvisation. The opening lines are critical: They should be brief and lead with a good question that catches the listener's interest. The telemarketer needs to know how to end the conversation if the prospect seems to be a poor one. The call should be made at the right time, which is late morning and afternoon to reach business prospects, and the evening hours of 7:00 to 9:00 to reach households. The telemarketing supervisor can build up telemarketer enthusiasm by offering prizes to the first one who gets an order or to the top performer. Given the higher cost per contact for telemarketing, and privacy issues, precise list selection and targeting is critical.

Clearly, other media, such as catalog mail order, TV home shopping, and so on, have their own rules for effective use.

Testing Direct-Marketing Elements   One of the great advantages of direct marketing is the ability to test under real marketplace conditions the efficacy of different components of the offer strategy. Direct marketers can test product features, copy, prices, media, mailing lists, and the like. Although direct-marketing response rates are at the single-digit level, testing these components can add substantially to the overall response rate and profitability.

The response rate of a direct-marketing campaign typically understates the long-term impact of the campaign. Suppose only 2 percent of recipients of a direct-mail advertisement for Samsonite luggage placed an order. A much larger percentage became aware (direct mail has high readership), and some percentage formed an intention to buy at a later date (the purchase will occur at a retail outlet). Furthermore, some percentage of the audience may mention Samsonite luggage to others as a result of seeing the promotion. Some companies are now measuring the impact of direct marketing on awareness, intention to buy, and word of mouth to derive a larger estimate of the promotion's impact than is measured by the response rate alone.

Measuring the Campaign's Success   By adding up the planned campaign costs, the direct marketer can figure out in advance the needed break-even response rate. This rate must be net of returned merchandise and bad debts. Returned merchandise can kill an otherwise effective campaign. The direct marketer needs to analyze the main causes of returned merchandise, such as late arrival, defective merchandise, damage in transit, product not as advertised, incorrect order fulfillment.

By carefully analyzing past campaigns, direct marketers can steadily improve their performance. Even when a specific campaign fails to break even, it might still be profitable.

> Suppose a membership organization spends $10 000 on a new-member campaign and attracts one hundred new members, each paying $70. It appears that the campaign has lost $3000 (= $10 000 – $7000). But if 80 percent of new members renew their membership in the second year, the organization gets another $5600 without any effort. It has now received $12 600 (= $7000 + $5600) for its investment of $10 000. To figure out the long-term break-even rate, one needs to figure out not only the initial response rate but the percentage who renew each year and for how many years they renew. In addition, with long-term payouts, the direct marketer must factor in the cost of money. (In the case of product campaigns, break-even analysis will have to include backend costs, returns, and so forth.) ■

This example introduces the concept of the *lifetime value of a customer*. The ultimate value of a customer is not revealed by the customer's purchase during a particular mailing. Rather the customer's ultimate value is the profit made on all the customer's purchases over time less the customer acquisition and maintenance costs. Direct marketers are working hard to develop measures of customer lifetime value, so that they can focus their communication efforts on the more attractive customers. These efforts include sending communications that may not even sell the customer anything—but maintain the customer's interest in the company and its products. Such communications include free newsletters, tips, and birthday greetings, all serving to build a stronger customer relationship.

Direct marketing has spawned a growing body of theory, measurement, and competent practice. It adds a number of communication concepts and capabilities to the marketers' toolbox. When tied to a carefully developed customer database, it can increase sales and profit yields and strengthen customer relationships. It can provide more accurate prospect leads and trigger new sales at a lower cost. Ultimately, marketers will make direct marketing an integral part of their marketing strategy and planning.

SALES PROMOTION

Sales promotion consists of a diverse collection of incentive tools, mostly short-term, designed to stimulate quicker and/or greater purchase of particular products/services by consumers or the trade. Examples are found everywhere:

> A coupon in the Sunday newspaper clearly indicates a forty-cent savings on brand X coffee. The end-of-the-aisle display confronts an impulse buyer with a wall of snack foods. A family buys a camcorder and gets a free traveling case or buys a car and gets a check for a $500 rebate. An appliance retailer is given a 10 percent manufacturer discount on January's orders if the retailer advertises the product in the local newspaper.[9] ∎

Whereas advertising offers a *reason* to buy, sales promotion offers an incentive to buy. Sales promotion includes tools for *consumer promotion* (e.g., samples, coupons, cash refund offers, prices off, premiums, prizes, patronage rewards, free trials, warranties, demonstrations, contests); *trade promotion* (e.g., buying allowances, free goods, merchandise allowances, cooperative advertising, advertising and display allowances, push money, dealer sales contests); and *salesforce promotion* (e.g., bonuses, contests, sales rallies).

Sales-promotion tools are used by most organizations, including manufacturers, distributors, retailers, trade associations, and nonprofit organizations. As examples of the last, churches often sponsor bingo games, theater parties, testimonial dinners, and raffles.

Rapid Growth of Sales Promotion

Traditionally, sales promotion commanded a smaller proportion of the marketing budget than advertising. But sales promotion spending has been growing at a faster rate than advertising spending, at least in some industries. In the Canadian packaged-goods industry, the ratio of sales promotion to advertising is currently estimated to be 64:36. However, there is evidence that total Canadian spending on sales promotion still lags behind advertising, in contrast to the U.S., where they are approximately equal. Yokom estimated that total Canadian spending on sales promotion in 1989 was only $3.5 billion, of which the packaged-goods industry accounted for one third. This is considerably less than the rule-of-thumb of 10 percent of the $100 billion spent in the U.S., and if true, would imply that the above ratio is much lower outside the packaged-goods industry.[10]

Several factors contributed to the growth of sales promotion, particularly in consumer markets.[11] Internal factors include the following: Promotion is now more accepted by top management as an effective sales tool; more product managers are qualified to use sales-promotion tools; and product managers are under greater pressure to increase their current sales. External factors include the following: The number of brands has increased; competitors use promotions frequently; many brands are at parity; consumers are more deal oriented; the trade has demanded more deals from manufacturers; and advertising efficiency has declined because of rising costs, media clutter, and legal restraints.

The rapid growth of sales-promotion media (coupons, contests, and the like) has created a situation of *promotion clutter*, similar to advertising clutter. There is a danger that consumers will start tuning out, in which case coupons and other media will weaken in their ability to trigger purchase. Manufacturers will have to find ways to rise above the clutter, for instance, by offering larger coupon-redemption values or using more dramatic point-of-purchase displays or demonstrations.

Purpose of Sales Promotion

Sales-promotion tools vary in their specific objectives. A free sample stimulates consumer trial, while a free management-advisory service cements a long-term relationship with a retailer.

Sellers use incentive-type promotions to attract new triers, to reward loyal customers, and to increase the repurchase rates of occasional users. New triers are of three types—users of another brand in the same category, users in other categories, and frequent brand switchers. Sales promotions often attract the brand switchers, because users of other brands and categories do not always notice or act on a promotion. Brand switchers are primarily looking for low price, good value, or premiums. Sales promotions are unlikely to turn them into loyal brand users. Sales promotions used in markets of high brand similarity produce a high sales response in the short run but little permanent gain in market share. In markets of high brand dissimilarity, sales promotions can alter market shares more permanently.

Sellers often think of sales promotion as designed to break down brand loyalty, and advertising as designed to build up brand loyalty. Therefore, an important issue for marketing managers is how to divide the budget between sales promotion and advertising. Ten years ago marketing managers would decide what they needed to spend on advertising and put the rest into sales promotion. Today, marketing managers first estimate what they need to spend in trade promotion, then what they need to spend in consumer promotion, and whatever is left they will budget for advertising.

There is a danger, however, in letting advertising take a back seat to sales promotion. When a brand is price promoted too much of the time, the consumer begins to think of it as a cheap brand and often will only buy it on deal. No one knows when this happens, but there is risk in putting a well-known brand leader on promotion more than 30 percent of the time.[12] Dominant brands use dealing infrequently, since most of it would only subsidize current users.

Most observers feel that dealing activities do not build long-term consumer loyalty, as does advertising. Brown's study of twenty-five hundred instant coffee buyers concluded that:

- Sales promotions yield faster responses in sales than advertising does.
- Sales promotions do not tend to yield new, long-term buyers in mature markets because they attract mainly deal-prone consumers who switch among brands as deals become available.
- Loyal brand buyers tend not to change their buying patterns as a result of competitive promotion.
- Advertising appears to be capable of increasing the "prime franchise" of a brand.[13]

There is also evidence that price promotions do not permanently build total category volume. They usually build short-term volume that is not maintained. Small-share competitors find it advantageous to use sales promotion, because they cannot afford to match the large advertising budgets of the market leaders. Nor can they obtain shelf space without offering trade allowances or stimulate consumer trial without offering consumer incentives. Price competition is often used by a small brand seeking to enlarge its share, but it is less effective for a category leader whose growth lies in expanding the entire category.[14]

The upshot is that many consumer-packaged-goods companies feel that they are forced to use more sales promotion than they would like. Kellogg, Kraft, and some other market leaders have announced that they will put a growing emphasis on the pull side of the business and increase their advertising budgets. They blame the heavy use of sales promotion for causing decreasing brand loyalty, increasing consumer price sensitivity, brand-quality-image dilution, and a focus on short-run marketing planning.

Farris and Quelch, however, dispute this.[15] They argue that the heavy use of sales promotion is a symptom and not a cause of these problems. They point to more fundamental causes, such as slower population growth, more educated consumers, industry overcapacity, the diminishing effectiveness of advertising, the growth of trade power, and the great pressure for short-run profit performance.

Farris and Quelch counter that sales promotion provides a number of benefits that are important to manufacturers as well as consumers. Sales promotions enable manufacturers to adjust to short-term variations in supply and demand. They enable manufacturers to charge a higher list price to test "how high is up." They induce consumers to try new products instead of never straying from their current ones. They lead to more varied retail formats, such as the everyday-low-price store and the promotional-pricing store, giving consumers more choice. They promote greater consumer awareness of prices. They permit manufacturers to sell more than they would normally sell at the list price, and to the extent that there are economies of scale, this reduces the unit costs. They help the manufacturer adapt programs to different consumer segments. Consumers themselves enjoy some satisfaction from being smart shoppers when they take advantage of price specials.

Major Decisions in Sales Promotion

In using sales promotion, a company must establish the objectives, select the tools, develop the program, pretest the program, implement and control it, and evaluate the results. We will examine these steps in the following paragraphs.

Establishing the Sales-Promotion Objectives   Sales-promotion objectives are derived from broader *promotion objectives*, which are derived from more basic *marketing objectives* developed for the product. The specific objectives set for sales promotion will vary with the type of target market. For *consumers*, objectives include encouraging purchase of larger-size units, building trial among nonusers, and attracting switchers away from competitors' brands. For *retailers*, objectives include inducing retailers to carry new items and higher levels of inventory, encouraging off-season buying, encouraging stocking of related items, offsetting competitive promotions, building brand loyalty of retailers, and gaining entry into new retail outlets. For the *salesforce*, objectives include encouraging support of a new product or model, encouraging more prospecting, and stimulating off-season sales.

Selecting the Sales-Promotion Tools   Many sales-promotion tools are available to accomplish these objectives. The promotion planner should take into account the type of market, sales-promotion objectives, competitive conditions, and cost effectiveness of each tool. We will now consider the main sales-promotion tools used for consumer promotion, trade promotion, and business promotion.

Consumer-Promotion Tools The main consumer-promotion tools are listed in Marketing Concepts and Tools 23-3. We can distinguish between *manufacturer promotions* and *retailer promotions* to consumers. The latter includes price cuts, feature advertising, retailer

Marketing Concepts and Tools 23-3

MAJOR CONSUMER-PROMOTION TOOLS

Samples

Samples are offers of a free amount or a trial of a product for consumers. The sample might be delivered door to door, sent in the mail, picked up in a store, found attached to another product, or featured in an advertising offer. Sampling is the most effective and most expensive way to introduce a new product. For example, Vick Chemical sampled nearly a million Quebec homes with its Oil of Olay beauty lotion, and won more than 100 000 new users of the product.

Coupons

Coupons are certificates entitling the bearer to a stated saving on the purchase of a specific product. Coupons can be mailed, enclosed in other products or attached to them, or inserted in magazine and newspaper ads. The redemption rate varies with the mode of distribution; newspaper coupons are redeemed about 2 percent of the time, direct-mail-distributed coupons about 8 percent of the time, and pack-distributed about 17 percent of the time. Coupons can be effective in stimulating sales of a mature brand and inducing early trial of a new brand. Experts believe that coupons should provide a 15-to-20-percent saving to be effective. Canadian households received 3.9 billion cents-off coupons in 1990, an average of 410 coupons per family. Redemptions totalled 248 million coupons (6.4 percent) worth an average of 53 cents per coupon.

Cash Refund Offers (Rebates)

Cash refund offers provide a price reduction after the purchase rather than at the retail shop. The consumer sends a specified "proof of purchase" to the manufacturer, who "refunds" part of the purchase price by mail. Toro ran a clever preseason promotion on specific snowblower models, offering a rebate if the snowfall in the buyer's market area was below average; competitors were not able to match this offer on such short notice. On the other hand, automobile rebates have become so common that many car buyers postpone purchasing until a rebate is announced. Since most auto companies match each other on the rebates, little is gained. The money could be better spent on advertising to build a stronger brand image.

Price Packs

Price packs (also called cents-off deals) are offers to consumers of savings off the regular price of a product, flagged on the label or package. They can take the form of a *reduced-price pack*, which is single packages sold at a reduced price (such as two for the price of one), or a *banded pack*, which is two related products banded together (such as a toothbrush and toothpaste). Price packs are very effective in stimulating short-term sales, even more than coupons.

Premiums

Premiums (or gifts) are merchandise offered at a relatively low cost or free as an incentive to purchase a particular product. A *with-pack premium* accompanies the product inside (in-pack) or on (on-pack) the package. Quaker Oats ran a promotion where it inserted $5 million in gold and silver coins in bags of Ken-L Ration dog food. The package itself, if a *reusable container*, can serve as a premium. A *free in-the-mail premium* is an item mailed to consumers who send in a proof of purchase, such as a box top. A *self-liquidating premium* is an item sold below its normal retail price to consumers who request it. Manufacturers now offer consumers all kinds of premiums bearing the company's name: The Budweiser fan can order T-shirts, hot-air balloons, and hundreds of other items with Bud's name on them.

Prizes (Contests, Sweepstakes, Games)

Prizes are offers of the chance to win cash, trips, or merchandise as a result of purchasing something. A *contest* calls for consumers to submit an entry—a jingle, estimate, suggestion—to be examined by a panel of judges who will select the best entries. A *sweepstake* calls for consumers to submit their names in a drawing. A *game* presents consumers with something every time they buy—bingo numbers, missing letters—which might or might not help them win a prize. All of these tend to gain more attention than do coupons or small premiums. The prizes in a contest by Gabriel of Canada, were sports cars for both the customers and the garages that install their automotive shock absorbers. The prize is sometimes a person, as when Canada Dry offered its winner the choice of a $1 million cash prize or dinner with actress Joan Collins (The cash won!).

Patronage Awards

Patronage awards are values in cash or in other forms that are proportional to one's patronage of a certain vendor or group of vendors. Air Canada's frequent-flyer plan offers points for miles travelled that can be used for free air fares, car rentals, and hotel accomodations. Hotel chains offer similar incentives. Cooperatives pay their members dividends, based on their purchases. Trading stamps also represent patronage rewards in that customers receive stamps when they buy from certain merchants and can redeem them for merchandise at stamp redemption centers or through mail-order catalogs.

Free Trials

Free trials consist of inviting prospective purchasers to try the product without cost in the hope that they will buy the product. Thus auto dealers encourage free test drives to stimulate purchase interest.

Product Warranties

Product warranties are an important promotional tool, especially as consumers become more quality sensitive. When Chrysler offered a five-year car warranty, substantially longer than GM's or Ford's, customers took notice. They inferred that Chrysler quality must be good. And Sears's offer of a lifetime warranty on its auto batteries certainly screams quality to the buyers. Companies must make a number of decisions before featuring a warranty. Is the product quality high enough? Should the product quality be improved further? Can competitors offer the same warranty? How long should the warranty be? What should it cover (replacement, repair, cash)? How much should be spent to advertise the warranty so that potential consumers know about it and consider it? Clearly, companies must carefully estimate the sales-generating value of the proposed warranty against its potential costs.

Tie-in Promotions

Tie-in promotions involve two or more brands or companies that team up on coupons, refunds, and contests to increase their pulling power. Companies pool funds with the hope of broader exposure, while several salesforces push these promotions to retailers, giving them a better shot at extra display and ad space.

Point-of-Purchase (POP) Displays and Demonstrations

POP displays and demonstrations take place at the point of purchase or sale. A 1.5-meter-high cardboard figure of Cap'n Crunch, himself, next to Cap'n Crunch cereal boxes or at the end of an aisle is an example. Unfortunately, many retailers do not like to handle the hundreds of displays, signs, and posters they receive from manufacturers. Manufacturers are responding by creating better POP materials, tying them in with television or print messages, and offering to set them up. The L'eggs pantyhose display is one of the most creative in the history of POP materials and a major factor in the success of this brand.

coupons, retailer contests/premiums, and so on. We can also distinguish between those sales-promotion tools that are "consumer-franchise building" and those that are not. The former imparts a selling message along with the deal, as in the case of free samples, coupons when they include a selling message, and premiums when they are related to the product. Sales-promotion tools that are not consumer-franchise building include price-off packs, consumer premiums not related to a product, contests and sweepstakes, consumer refund offers, and trade

Marketing Concepts and Tools 23-4

MAJOR TRADE-PROMOTION TOOLS

Price-Off

A price-off (also called off-invoice or off-list) is a straight discount off the list price on each case purchased during a stated time period. The offer encourages dealers to buy a quantity or carry a new item that they might not ordinarily buy. The dealers can use the buying allowance for immediate profit, advertising, or price reductions.

Allowance

An allowance is an amount offered in return for the retailer's agreeing to feature the manufacturer's products in some way. An *advertising allowance* compensates retailers for advertising the manufacturer's product. A *display allowance* compensates them for carrying a special product display.

Free Goods

Free goods are offers of extra cases of merchandise, to middlemen who buy a certain quantity or who feature a certain flavor or size. Manufacturers might offer *push money*, which is cash or gifts to dealers or their salesforce to push the manufacturer's goods. Manufacturers might offer free *specialty advertising items* to the retailers that carry the company's name, such as pens, pencils, calendars, paperweights, matchbooks, memo pads, ashtrays, and yardsticks.

---

allowances. Sellers should use consumer-franchise-building promotions, because they reinforce the consumer's brand understanding.

Sales promotion seems most effective when used together with advertising. "In one study, point-of-purchase displays related to current TV commercials were found to produce 15 percent more sales than similar displays not related to such advertising. In another, a heavy sampling approach along with TV advertising proved more successful than either TV alone or TV with coupons in introducing a product."[16]

Many large companies have a sales-promotion manager whose job is to help brand managers choose the right promotional tool. The following example shows how one firm determined the appropriate sales-promotion tool:

> A firm has launched a new product and achieved a 20 percent market share within six months. Its penetration rate is 40 percent (i.e., the percentage of the target market that purchased the brand at least once). Its repurchase rate is 10 percent (the percentage of the first-time triers who repurchased the brand one or more times). This firm needs to create more loyal users. An in-pack coupon would be appropriate to build more repeat purchase. But if the repurchase rate had been high, say 50 percent, then the company should try to attract more new triers. Here a media-mailed coupon might be appropriate. ∎

Trade-Promotion Tools   The types of promotions that manufacturers offer to the trade are described in Marketing Concepts and Tools 23-4. In some industries, the proportion of promotional spending may be higher for the trade than for consumers. This is especially true for Canadian packaged-goods (where the proportion has been estimated as high as 77:23), because of the concentration and channel power of the large grocery chains.[17]

1. *Trade promotion can persuade the retailer or wholesaler to carry the brand*: Shelf space is so scarce that manufacturers often have to offer price-offs, allowances, buy-back guarantees, free goods, or outright payments (called slotting allowances) to get on the shelf, and once there, to stay on the shelf.

2. *Trade promotion can persuade the retailer or wholesaler to carry more goods than the normal amount*: Manufacturers will offer volume allowances to get the trade to carry more in their warehouses and stores. Manufacturers believe that the trade will work harder when they are "loaded" with the manufacturer's product.

3. *Trade promotion can induce the retailers to promote the brand by featuring, display, and price reductions*: Manufacturers might seek an end-of-aisle display or increased shelf facings or price reduction stickers and obtain them by offering the retailers allowances paid on "proof of performance."

4. *Trade promotion can stimulate retailers and their sales clerks to push the product*: Manufacturers compete for retailer sales effort by offering push money, sales aids, recognition programs, premiums, and sales contests.

Manufacturers probably spend more on trade promotion than they would freely choose to spend. The increased concentration of buying power in the hands of fewer and larger retailers has increased the trade's ability to demand manufacturers' financial support at the expense of consumer promotion and advertising. In fact, the trade has come to depend on promotion money from the manufacturers: It is estimated that the trade received $866 million in 1989 from the packaged-goods producers, which was a significant proportion of the trade's profits. If this money were withdrawn, trade margins would have to rise. Nor can any manufacturer unilaterally stop offering trade allowances without losing channel support. In some countries, the retailers have become the major advertisers, using mostly the promotional allowances extracted from their suppliers.

Food retailers strongly prefer trade deals to consumer deals. They are unhappy about the amount of consumer deals they have to handle. According to Chevalier and Curhan:

> Retailers view promotional efforts initiated by manufacturers as encouraging profitless brand switching rather than increasing sales or profits. Manufacturers, on the other hand, complain that retailer-initiated promotions sometimes damage brand franchises which have been carefully and expensively nurtured over many years. Worse yet, manufacturers complain that retailers frequently take advantage of them by "absorbing" deals without passing their benefits along to consumers.[18]

As the number of competitive sales promotions have increased, friction has been created between the company's salesforce and its brand managers. The salesforce says that the retailers will not keep the company's products on the shelf unless they receive more trade-promotion money, while the brand managers want to spend the limited funds on consumer promotion and advertising. Some company sales vice-presidents are insisting that they control the budget for consumer promotion and especially trade promotion, since they know the local market better than a brand manager sitting at headquarters. Some companies have given a substantial part of the sales-promotion budget to the salesforce or local marketing managers to handle.

Manufacturers have other problems with trade promotions. First, they find it difficult to police retailers to make sure that they are doing what they agreed to do. Retailers do not always convert the buying allowances into reduced prices for consumers, and they might not provide extra shelving or display even after receiving merchandise or display allowances. Manufacturers are increasingly insisting on proof of performance in paying these allowances. Second, more retailers are doing "forward buying," namely, buying a greater quantity of the brand during the deal period than they can sell during the deal period. Retailers might respond to a 10 percent off-case allowance by buying a twelve-week or longer supply. The manufacturer finds that it has to schedule more production than planned and bear the costs of extra work shifts and overtime.

Third, retailers are doing more "diverting," namely, buying more cases than needed in a region in which the manufacturer offered a deal and shipping the surplus to nondeal regions. Manufacturers are trying to handle forward buying and dealing by limiting the amount they will sell at a discount, or producing and delivering less than the full order in an effort to smooth production.[19]

Business-Promotion Tools Companies spend billions of dollars on business promotion, the main tools of which are described in Marketing Concepts and Tools 23-5. These tools are used for such purposes as gathering business leads, impressing and rewarding customers, and stimulating the salesforce to greater effort. Companies typically develop budgets which stay fairly close from year to year for each business-promotion tool.

Developing the Sales-Promotion Program
The marketer must make further decisions to define the full promotion program. The marketer has to determine the *size of the incentive* to offer. A certain minimum incentive is necessary if the promotion is to succeed. A higher incentive level will produce more sales response but at a diminishing rate. *Conditions for participation* have to be established. Incentives might be offered to everyone or to select groups. A premium might be offered only to those who turn in box tops or proof-of-purchase seals. Sweepstakes might not be offered in certain provinces or to families of company personnel or to persons under a certain age.

The marketer has to decide on the *duration of promotion*. If the sales-promotion period is too short, many prospects will not be able to take advantage, since they might not be repurchasing at the time. If the promotion runs too long, the deal will lose some of its "act now" force. According to one researcher, the optimal frequency is about three weeks per quarter, and optimal duration is the length of the average purchase cycle.[20] Of course, the optimal promotion cycle varies by product category and even by specific product.

The marketer must choose a *distribution vehicle*. A fifteen-cents-off coupon can be distributed in the package, store, mail, or advertising media. Each distribution method involves a different level of reach and cost.

The *timing of promotion* must be established. For example, brand managers develop calendar dates for the annually planned promotions. The dates are used by production, sales, and distribution. Some on-the-spot promotions will also be needed and will require cooperation on a short notice.

Finally, the marketer must determine the *total sales-promotion budget*. The sales-promotion budget can be developed in two ways. It can be built from the ground up, where the marketer chooses the individual promotions and estimates their total cost. The cost of a particular promotion consists of the *administrative cost* (printing, mailing, and promoting the deal) and the *incentive cost* (cost of premium or cents-off, including redemption costs), multiplied by the *expected number of units* that will be sold on the deal.

> Suppose a brand of after-shave lotion will be marked down $.09 for a limited period. The item regularly sells for $1.09, of which $.40 represents a contribution to the manufacturer's profit before marketing expense. The brand manager expects a million bottles to be sold under this deal. Thus the incentive cost of the deal will be $90 000 (= 0.09 × 1 000 000). Suppose the administrative cost is estimated at $10 000. Then the total cost is $100 000. In order to break even on this deal, the company will have to sell 250 000 (= $100 000 ÷ 0.40) more units than would have occurred over the same period without the deal. ■

MAJOR BUSINESS-PROMOTION TOOLS

Trade Shows and Conventions

Industry associations organize annual trade shows and conventions. Firms selling products and services to the particular industry buy space and set up displays to demonstrate their products at the trade show. Hundreds of trade shows take place every year, drawing millions of attendees. Trade show attendance can range from a few thousand to tens of thousands in the case of large shows held by the hospitality industry. The participating vendors expect several benefits, including generating new sales leads, maintaining customer contacts, introducing new products, meeting new customers, selling more to present customers, and educating customers with publications, motion pictures, and audiovisual materials. Here are some findings:

> Trade shows help companies reach many prospects not reached through their salesforces. About 90 percent of a trade show's visitors see a company salesperson for the first time. ■

> The average attendee spends 7.8 hours viewing exhibits over a two-day period and spends an average of 22 minutes at each exhibit. Eighty-five percent of the attendees make a final purchase decision for one or more products displayed. ■

> The average cost per visitor reached (including exhibits, personnel travel, living and salary expenses, and preshow promotion costs) is $200. The Trade Show Bureau estimates that this is much lower than the cost of generating a sale from a sales call. ■

Business marketers may spend as much as 35 percent of their annual promotion budget on trade shows. They face a number of decisions, including which trade shows to participate in, how much to spend on each trade show, how to build dramatic exhibits that attract attention, and how to effectively follow up on sales leads. Trade show preparation and participation is an area in which professional management promises to squeeze more efficiency out of the trade show budget.

Sales Contests

A *sales contest* is a contest involving the salesforce or dealers, aimed at inducing them to increase their sales results over a stated period, with prizes going to those who succeed. A majority of companies sponsor annual or more frequent sales contests for their salesforce. Called incentive programs, they serve to motivate and to give recognition to good company performance. The good performers may receive trips, cash prizes, or gifts. Some companies award points for performance, which the receiver can turn into any of a variety of prizes. An unusual though not very expensive prize may often work better than much more costly prizes. Incentives work best when they are tied to measurable and achievable sales objectives (such as finding new accounts, reviving old accounts) where employees feel they have an equal chance. Otherwise, employees who do not think the goals are reasonable will not take up the challenge.

Specialty Advertising

Specialty advertising consists of useful, low-cost items given by salespeople to prospects and customers bearing the giver's name and address and sometimes an advertising message. Common items are ballpoint pens, calendars, cigarette lighters, and memo pads. The item keeps the company's name before the prospect and creates goodwill because of the utility of the item.

Sources: For trade shows, see Thomas V. Bonoma, "Get More Out of Your Trade Shows," *Harvard Business Review*, January-February 1983, pp. 75-83; and Jonathan M. Cox, Ian K. Sequeira, and Lori L. Bock, "Show Size Grows: Audience Quality Stays High, *Business Marketing*, May 1988, pp. 84-88. For sales contests, see C. Robert Patty and Robert Hite, *Managing Sales People*, 3rd ed., (Englewood Cliffs, N.J.: Prentice Hall, 1988), pp. 313-27. For specialty advertising, see George M. Zinkham and Lauren A. Vachris, "The Impact of Selling Aids on New Prospects," *Industrial Marketing Management* 13 (1984), 187-93

In the case of a coupon deal, the cost would take into account the fact that only a fraction of the consumers will redeem the coupons. In the case of an in-pack premium, the deal cost must include the costs of procurement and packaging of the premium, offset by any price increase on the package.

The more common way to develop the sales-promotion budget is to use a conventional percentage of the total promotion budget. For example, toothpaste might get a sales-promotion budget of 30 percent of the total promotion budget, whereas shampoo might get 50 percent. These percentages vary for different brands in different markets and are influenced by the stages of the product life cycle and competitive expenditures on promotion.

Multiple-brand companies should coordinate their sales-promotion activities, such as making single mailings of multiple coupons to consumers. Strang, in his study of company sales-promotion practices, found three major budgeting inadequacies:

- [ ] Lack of consideration of cost effectiveness.

- [ ] Use of simplistic decision rules, such as extensions of last year's spending, percentage of expected sales, maintenance of a fixed ratio to advertising, and the "left-over approach," where promotion gets what is left after advertising is set.

- [ ] Advertising and promotional budgets being prepared independently.[21]

Pretesting the Sales-Promotion Program   Although sales-promotion programs are designed on the basis of experience, pretests should be conducted to determine if the tools are appropriate, the incentive size optimal, and the presentation method efficient. A survey by the Premium Advertisers Association indicated that fewer than 42 percent of premium offerers ever tested their effectiveness.[22] Strang maintains that promotions can usually be tested quickly and inexpensively and that some large companies test alternative strategies in selected market areas with each of their national promotions.[23]

Sales promotions directed at consumer markets can be readily pretested. Consumers can be asked to rate or rank different possible deals. Or trial tests can be run in limited geographical areas.

Implementing and Controlling the Sales-Promotion Program   Implementation and control plans should be prepared for each individual promotion. Implementation planning must cover lead time and sell-in time. Lead time is the time necessary to prepare the program prior to launching it.

> It covers initial planning, design, and approval of package modifications or material to be mailed or distributed to the home, preparation of conjunctive advertising and point-of-sale materials, notification of field sales personnel, establishment of allocations for individual distributors, purchasing and printing of special premiums or packaging materials, production of advance inventories and staging at distribution centers in preparation for release at a specific date, and finally, the distribution to the retailer.[24]

Sell-in time begins with the launch and ends when approximately 95 percent of the deal merchandise is in the hands of consumers, which can take one to several months, depending on the deal duration.

Evaluating the Sales-Promotion Results   Evaluation is a crucial requirement, and yet, according to Strang, "evaluation of promotion programs receives . . . little attention. Even where an attempt is made to evaluate a promotion, it is likely to be superficial. . . . Evaluation in terms of profitability is even less common."[25]

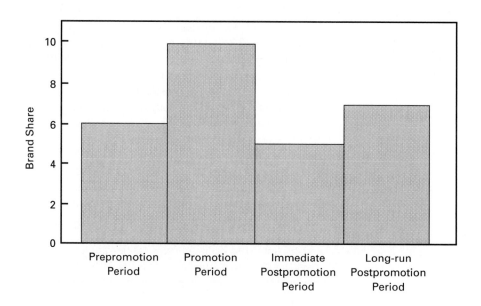

FIGURE 23-1

Effect of Consumer Deal on Brand Share

Manufacturers can use four methods to measure sales-promotion effectiveness. The most common method is to examine the *sales data* before, during, and after a promotion. Suppose a company has a 6 percent market share in the prepromotion period, which jumps to 10 percent during the promotion, falls to 5 percent immediately after the promotion, and rises to 7 percent in the postpromotion period (see Figure 23-1). The promotion evidently attracted new triers and also stimulated more purchasing by existing customers. After the promotion, sales fell as consumers worked down their inventories. The long-run rise to 7 percent indicates that the company gained some new users. Sales promotions work best, in general, when they attract competitors' customers to try a superior product.

If the company's product is not superior, the brand's share is likely to return to its prepromotion level. The sales promotion only altered the time pattern of demand rather than the total demand. The promotion may have covered its costs but more likely did not. Some experts think that less than 20 percent of all sales promotions prove profitable.

Consumer-panel data would reveal the kinds of people who responded to the promotion and what they did after the promotion.[26] If more information is needed, *consumer surveys* can be conducted to learn how many recall the promotion, what they thought of it, how many took advantage of it, and how the promotion affected their subsequent brand-choice behavior. Sales promotions can also be evaluated through *experiments* that vary such attributes as incentive value, duration, and distribution media.

Beyond these methods of evaluating the results of specific promotions, management must recognize other potential costs and problems. First, promotions might decrease long-run brand loyalty by making more consumers deal prone rather than advertising prone. Second, promotions can be more expensive than they appear. Some are inevitably distributed to the wrong consumers (nonswitchers, always switchers, and the company's own customers, who get a free subsidy). Furthermore, there are hidden costs of special production runs, extra salesforce effort, and handling requirements. Third, certain promotions irritate retailers, and they demand extra trade allowances or refuse to cooperate in the promotion.

In spite of these problems, sales promotion will continue to play a growing role in the total promotion mix. Its effective use will require defining the sales-promotion objectives, selecting the appropriate tools, constructing the sales-promotion program, pretesting it, implementing it, and evaluating the results.[27]

PUBLIC RELATIONS

Public relations (PR) is another important marketing tool, which until recently, was treated as a marketing stepchild. The public-relations department is typically located at corporate headquarters; and its staff is so busy dealing with various publics—stockholders, employees, legislators, community leaders—that PR support for product marketing objectives tends to be neglected. PR departments perform the following five activities, not all of which feed into direct product support:

□ *Press Relations*: The aim of press relations is to place newsworthy information in the news media to attract attention to a person, product, or service.

□ *Product Publicity*: Product publicity involves various efforts to publicize specific products.

□ *Corporate Communication*: This activity covers internal and external communications and promotes understanding of the organization.

□ *Lobbying*: Lobbying involves dealing with legislators and government officials to promote or defeat legislation and regulation.

□ *Counseling*: Counseling involves advising management about public issues and company positions and image.[28]

In addition, marketing managers and PR practitioners do not always talk the same language. One major difference is that marketing managers are much more bottom-line oriented, whereas PR practitioners see their job as disseminating communications. But this is changing in two ways. First, companies are calling for more *market-oriented PR*. They want their PR department to manage their PR activities to contribute toward marketing the company and improving the bottom line. Second, companies are setting up a *marketing PR group* to directly support corporate/product promotion and image making. Thus marketing PR, like financial PR and community PR, would serve a special constituency, namely the marketing department.

The old name for marketing PR was *publicity*, which was seen as the task of securing editorial space—as opposed to paid space—in print and broadcast media to promote or "hype" a product, place, or person. But marketing PR goes beyond simple publicity. Marketing PR can contribute to the following tasks:

□ *Assist in the Launch of New Products*: The amazing commercial success of Cabbage Patch Kids was due not so much to the paltry advertising budget of $500 000 but to clever publicity, including donating the dolls to children in hospitals, sponsoring Cabbage Patch Kids adoption parties for schoolchildren, and so on.

□ *Assist in Repositioning a Mature Product*: Petro-Canada's takeovers created an image of a government-run bureaucracy, so it sponsored the Olympic torch relay to improve its corporate image and halt further decline in market share.

□ *Build Up Interest in a Product Category*: The Insurance Bureau of Canada distributed videos on crime and fire prevention to local fire chiefs and service clubs, who made presentations at schools to stimulate awareness of the issues.

□ *Influence Specific Target Groups*: McDonald's raised sufficient funds for eleven Ronald McDonald Houses across Canada, to provide accommodations in connection with the treatment of children stricken with cancer.

□ *Defend Products That Have Encountered Public Problems*: Johnson & Johnson's masterly use of PR was a major factor in saving Tylenol from extinction.

□ *Build the Corporate Image in a Way That Projects Favorably on Its Products*: Iaccoca's speeches and his autobiography created a whole new winning image for the Chrysler Corporation.

As the power of mass advertising weakens owing to rising media costs, increasing clutter, and smaller audiences, marketing managers are turning more to PR. In a survey of 286 marketing managers, three-fourths reported that their companies were using marketing PR. They found it particularly effective in building awareness and brand knowledge, for both new and established products. In several cases, PR proved more cost effective than advertising. Nevertheless, it must be planned jointly with advertising. PR needs a larger budget than it used to, and the money might have to come from advertising.[29]

Marketing managers will need to acquire more skill in using PR resources. The Gillette company requires each brand manager to have a budget line for PR and to justify *not* using it if they do not. A brand manager might ask the PR professional how many cases $100 000 for PR would move. But that is a hard question to answer. PR is even more difficult to evaluate than advertising. Advertising is much more under the control of the company, and the measurement tools are better developed. Therefore, PR people find it hard to recommend a budget level; much depends on coming up with good PR ideas and then convincing others that the favorable results would far exceed their cost.

Clearly, public relations can make a memorable impact on public awareness at a fraction of the cost of advertising. The company does not pay for the space or time obtained in the media. It pays for a staff to develop and circulate the stories and manage certain events. If the company develops an interesting story, it could be picked up by all the news media and be worth millions of dollars in equivalent advertising. Furthermore, it would have more credibility than advertising. Some experts say that consumers are five times more likely to be influenced by editorial copy than by advertising.

Major Decisions in Marketing PR

In considering when and how to use marketing PR, management should establish the marketing objectives, choose the PR messages and vehicles, and evaluate the PR results. The main tools of marketing PR are described in Marketing Concepts and Tools 23-6.

Establishing the Marketing Objectives   Marketing PR can contribute to the following objectives:

□ *Build Awareness*: PR can place stories in the media to bring attention to a product, service, person, organization, or idea.

□ *Build Credibility*: PR can add credibility by communicating the message in an editorial context.

□ *Stimulate the Salesforce and Dealers*: PR can help boost salesforce and dealer enthusiasm. Stories about a new product before it is launched will help the salesforce sell it to retailers.

□ *Hold Down Promotion Costs*: PR costs less than direct mail and media advertising. The smaller the company's promotion budget, the stronger the case for using PR to gain share of mind.

Objectives should be set for every PR campaign. Procter & Gamble established an educational services program that was designed for the needs of Canadian schools. The objectives were to help position P&G as a consumer-oriented company, socially responsible, and

Marketing Concepts and Tools 23-6

MAJOR TOOLS IN MARKETING PR

Publications

Companies rely extensively on communication materials to reach and influence their target markets. These include annual reports, brochures, articles, audiovisual materials, and company newsletters and magazines. Chrysler's annual report almost serves as a sales brochure, promoting each new car to the stockholders. Brochures can play an important role in informing target customers about what a product is, how it works, and how it is to be assembled. Thoughtful articles written by company executives can draw attention to the company and its products. Company newsletters and magazines can help build up the company's image and convey important news to target markets. Audiovisual material, such as films, slides-and-sound, and video and audio cassettes, are coming into increasing use as promotion tools. The cost of audiovisual materials is usually greater than the cost of printed material, but so is the impact. Some cities that want to attract new industry hire a professional firm to prepare an attractive video to be sent to companies that are considering opening a new plant.

Events

Companies can draw attention to new products or other company activities by arranging special events. These include news conferences, seminars, outings, exhibits, contests and competitions, anniversaries, and sport and cultural sponsorships that will reach the target publics. Sponsoring a sports event, such as the Molson Public Challenge golf tournament or the Volvo International Tennis Tournament, gives these companies a chance to invite and host their suppliers, distributors, and customers as well as to bring repeated attention to their name and products.

News

One of the major tasks of PR professionals is to find or create favorable news about the company, its products, and its people. News generation requires skill in developing a story concept, researching it, and writing a press release. But the PR person's skill must go beyond preparing news stories. Getting the media to accept press releases and attend press conferences calls for marketing and interpersonal skills. A good PR media director understands the press's needs for stories that are interesting and timely and for press releases that are well written and attention getting. The media director needs to gain the favor of editors and reporters. The more the press is cultivated, the more likely it is to give more and better coverage to the company.

Speeches

Speeches are another tool for creating product and company publicity. Iaccoca's charismatic talks before large audiences helped Chrysler sell its cars. Increasingly, company executives must field questions from the media or give talks at trade associations or sales meetings, and these appearances can build or hurt the company's image. Companies are choosing their spokespersons carefully and using speech writers and coaches to help improve the public speaking of those spokespersons.

Public-Service Activities

Companies can improve public goodwill by contributing money and time to good causes. A large company typically will ask executives to support community affairs where their offices and plants are located. In other instances, companies will offer to donate a certain amount of money to a specified cause out of consumer purchases. Called *cause-related marketing*, it is used by a growing number of companies to build public goodwill. General Foods offered to pay five cents to the Muscular Dystrophy Association for every redeemed General Foods cents-off coupon and ten cents to Mothers against Drunk Driving for every redeemed Tang coupon. Procter & Gamble and

Publishers' Clearing House jointly coordinated a promotion to aid the Special Olympics. Product coupons were included in the Publishers' Clearing House mailing, and Procter & Gamble donated ten cents per coupon redeemed to the Special Olympics program.

Identity Media

Normally, a company's materials acquire separate looks, which creates confusion and misses an opportunity to create and reinforce a corporate identity. In an overcommunicated society, companies have to compete for attention. They should strive to create a visual identity that the public immediately recognizes. The visual identity is carried by the company's logos, stationery, brochures, signs, business forms, business cards, buildings, uniforms and dress codes, and rolling stock.

Sources: For further reading on cause-related marketing, see P. Rajan Varadarajan and Anil Menon, "Cause-Related Marketing: A Co-Alignment of Marketing Strategy and Corporate Philanthropy," *Journal of Marketing*, July 1988, pp. 58-74.

responsive to the Canadian consumer. After surveying teachers and officials of the relevant teaching associations to determine their needs, P&G prepared kits containing booklets, posters, games, hand-outs, and overhead masters. The kits were advertised to teachers and school boards, and distributed for use in the Fall term. Attempts to evaluate the success of the program were hampered by the difficulty of identifying and interviewing students who had used the kits. However, teachers' usage of the kits and attitudes toward P&G could be monitored as proxy measures of success.[30]

Choosing the PR Messages and Vehicles   The PR practitioner next identifies or develops interesting stories to tell about the product. Suppose a small regional university wants more visibility. The PR practitioner will search for possible stories. Do any faculty members have unusual backgrounds, or are any working on unusual projects? Are any new and unusual courses being taught? Are any interesting events taking place on campus? Usually this search will uncover scores of stories that can be fed to the press. The chosen stories should reflect the image this university wants.

If the number of stories is insufficient, the PR practitioner should propose newsworthy events that the college could sponsor. Here the challenge is to *create news* rather than *find news*. PR ideas include hosting major academic conventions, inviting celebrity speakers, and developing news conferences. Each event is an opportunity to develop a multitude of stories directed at different audiences.

Event creation is a particularly important skill in publicizing fund-raising drives for nonprofit organizations. Fundraisers have developed a large repertoire of special events, including *anniversary celebrations, art exhibits, auctions, benefit evenings, bingo games, book sales, cake sales, contests, dances, dinners, fairs, fashion shows, parties in unusual places, phonathons, rummage sales, tours,* and *walkathons*. No sooner is one type of event created, such as a walkathon, than competitors spawn new versions, such as readathons, bikathons, and jogathons.

For-profit organizations also use various events to call attention to their products and services. Perhaps the best-known example is the Goodyear blimp, which has been present at major sporting events and other notable occasions for several decades. So successful has that been that in recent years, the Fuji Photo Film Company has been flying its own blimp on similar occasions.

PR practitioners are able to find or create stories on behalf of even mundane products. Here are two examples:

Some years ago the Potato Board financed a publicity campaign to encourage more potato consumption. A national attitude-and-usage study indicated that many consumers perceived potatoes as fattening, non-nutritious, and a poor source of vitamins and minerals. These attitudes were disseminated by various opinion leaders, such as food editors, diet advocates, and doctors. Actually, potatoes have far fewer calories than most people imagine, and they contain several important vitamins and minerals. The Potato Board decided to develop separate publicity programs for consumers, doctors and dieticians, nutritionists, home economists, and food editors. The consumer program consisted of disseminating many stories about the potato for network television and women's magazines, developing and distributing *The Potato Lover's Diet Cookbook*, and placing articles and recipes in food editors' columns. The food editors' program consisted of food-editor seminars conducted by nutrition experts. ■

One of the top brands of cat food is Star-Kist Foods' 9-Lives. Its brand image revolves around Morris the Cat. The advertising agency of Leo Burnett, which created Morris for its ads, wanted to make him more of a living, breathing, real-life feline to whom cat owners and cat lovers could relate. It hired a public-relations firm, which then proposed and carried out the following ideas: (1) launch a Morris "look-alike" contest in nine major markets; (2) write a book called *Morris, an Intimate Biography*; (3) establish a coveted award called The Morris, a bronze statuette given to the owners of award-winning cats at local cat shows; (4) sponsor an "Adopt-a-Cat Month," with Morris as the official "spokescat"; and (5) distribute a booklet called "The Morris Method" on cat care. These publicity steps strengthened the brand's market share in the cat-food market. ■

Implementing the Marketing PR Plan   Implementing publicity requires care. Take the matter of placing stories in the media. A great story is easy to place. But most stories are less than great and might not get past busy editors. One of the chief assets of publicists is their personal relationship with media editors. Public-relations practitioners are often ex-journalists who know many media editors and know what they want. PR people look at media editors as a market to satisfy so that these editors will continue to use their stories.

Publicity requires extra care when it involves staging special events, such as testimonial dinners, news conferences, and national contests. PR practitioners need a good head for detail and for coming up with quick solutions when things go wrong.

Evaluating the PR Results   PR's contribution is difficult to measure, because it is used along with other promotion tools. If it is used before the other tools come into action, its contribution is easier to evaluate.

Exposures The easiest measure of PR effectiveness is the number of *exposures* created in the media. Publicists supply the client with a clipping book showing all the media that carried news about the product and a summary statement such as the following:[31]

> Media coverage included 3500 column inches of news and photographs in 350 publications with a combined circulation of 79.4 million; 2500 minutes of air time on 290 radio stations and an estimated audience of 65 million; and 660 minutes of air time on 160 television stations with an estimated audience of 91 million. If this time and space had been purchased at advertising rates, it would have amounted to $1 047 000.

This exposure measure is not very satisfying. There is no indication of how many people actually read, heard, or recalled the message and what they thought afterward. There is no information on the net audience reached, since publications overlap in readership. Because publicity's goal is reach, not frequency, it would be useful to know the number of unduplicated exposures.

Awareness/Comprehension/Attitude Change A better measure is the change in product *awareness/comprehension/attitude* resulting from the PR campaign (after allowing for the effect of other promotional tools). For example, how many people recall hearing the news item? How many told others about it (a measure of word of mouth)? How many changed their minds after hearing it? The Potato Board learned, for example, that the number of people who agreed with the statement "Potatoes are rich in vitamins and minerals" went from 36 percent before the campaign to 67 percent after the campaign, a significant improvement in product comprehension.

Sales-and-Profit Contribution Sales-and-profit impact is the most satisfactory measure, if obtainable. For example, 9-Lives sales had increased 43 percent by the end of the Morris the Cat PR campaign. However, advertising and sales promotion had also been stepped up, and their contribution has to be allowed for. Suppose total sales have increased $1 500 000, and management estimates that PR contributed 15 percent of the total sales increase. Then the return on PR investment is calculated as follows:

Total sales increase	$1 500 000
Estimated sales increase due to PR (15%)	225 000
Contribution margin on product sales (10%)	22 500
Total direct cost of PR program	– 10 000
Contribution margin added by PR investment	12 500
Return on PR investment ($12 500/$10 000)	125%

In the years ahead, we can expect more joint strategy planning of advertising, PR, and the other promotional tools. Major advertising agencies have recognized the growing leverage obtained from PR by recently acquiring major PR firms. The acquired PR firms will benefit from the highly disciplined methods of the ad agencies, and the ad agencies will benefit from the expanded areas of creativity afforded by PR.

SUMMARY

Direct marketing, sales promotion, and public relations are three tools of growing importance in marketing planning.

Direct marketing is an interactive system of marketing, which uses one or more advertising media (direct mail, catalogs, telemarketing, electronic shopping, and so forth) to effect a measurable response and/or transaction at any location. It has been growing at a more rapid rate than store marketing and is used by manufacturers, retailers, service companies and other types of organizations. Among its advantages are selectivity, personalization, continuity, better timing, high readership, testability, and privacy. There are strong trends toward integrated direct marketing, maximarketing, and database marketing.

Sales promotion covers a wide variety of short-term incentive tools designed to stimulate consumer markets, the trade, and the organization's own salesforce. Expenditures on sales promotion are less than on advertising, but they are growing faster. Consumer-promotion tools include samples, coupons, cash refund offers, price packs, premiums, prizes, patronage awards, free trials, product warranties, tie-in promotions, and point-of-purchase displays and demonstrations. Trade-promotion tools include price-off, advertising and display allowances, free goods, push money, and specialty advertising items. Business-promotion tools include trade shows/conventions, sales contests, and specialty advertising. Sales-promotion planning calls for establishing the sales-promotion objectives, selecting the tools, developing, pretesting and implementing the sales-promotion program, and evaluating the results.

Public relations is another important communication/promotion tool. Although less utilized, it has great potential for building awareness and preference in the marketplace, repositioning products, and defending them. The major PR tools are publications, events, news, speeches, public-service activities, written material, audiovisual material, corporate-identity media, and telephone information services. Public-relations planning involves establishing the PR objectives, choosing the appropriate messages and vehicles, and evaluating the PR results.

■ QUESTIONS

1. What impact has the "demassification" of the market, and the lack of personal time had on promotional activities?

2. You are developing a business to sell personal computers. Because of limited resources, you have been advised to use a direct-marketing approach. What are the major-decision steps that you need to take in establishing an effective promotional direct-marketing strategy?

3. What are the possible tradeoffs a manager should consider when deciding between sales promotion and advertising strategies and direct marketing?

4. Of the 3.9 billion cents-off coupons distributed to Canadian households in 1990, only 248 million coupons were redeemed. What factors influence the rate of coupon redemption?

5. What psychological and business factors have contributed to "promotion clutter? How might a manager best respond to this problem?

6. Companies spend millions of dollars on trade shows each year. What quesitons should marketing managers ask themselves when determining how much of the advertising budget to allocate to trade shows?

7. Joe Pringle, a product manager at the XYZ Snacks Company, is concerned about falling sales in recent months. His inventory is high. He is contemplating a sales promotion to reverse the sales trend and reduce inventories. Joe is thinking of offering a case allowance to the trade. He expects sales to be 40 000 cases in the absence of promotion. The case price is $10, and the gross profit contribution is 40 percent. He is currently thinking of offering a $1/case allowance. Joe expects increased sales of 20 000 cases during the promotion period. The estimated cost of developing this promotion is $412 000. (a) Will he make a profit on this promotion? (b) What is the break-even sales increase that will justify this case allowance? (c) If he offers only a $.50/case allowance, he expects additional net sales of 12 000. Should he offer a $1/case or a $.50/case allowance?

8. A major basketball team experienced a decline in home-game attendance. The team's owner decided to hire a marketer to stimulate attendance. What are some of the steps that can be taken?

9. Select a product or service and recommend which sales promotion tools should be used to build its consumer franchise.

10. Much of the public relations work done by business firms consists of miscellaneous and unrelated activities. Can you suggest an underlying public relations orientation a company could adopt that would provide a focus for many publicity activities?

11. If top management were considering a proposal to establish a public relations department outside the marketing department, what would your response be to the proposal? Give reasons for the position you have taken.

12. Review three recent crises in business or government in which credibility was threatened. In each case, how was the damage to the entity's image managed from a public relations perspective? Can you suggest a strategy for damage control from these experiences?

13. What is meant by a "public? Do organizations serve more than one public? If yes, say why and give examples. How might a public relations program be influenced by the existence of several publics?

■ NOTES ———————————————————————

1. Ernan Roman, *Integrated Direct Marketing*, (New York: McGraw-Hill, 1989), p. 108.

2. The terms *direct-order marketing and direct-relationship marketing* were suggested as subsets of direct marketing by Stan Rapp and Tom Collins in *The Great Marketing Turnaround* (Englewood Cliffs, N.J.: Prentice-Hall, 1990).

3. Personal communication with *Canadian Direct Marketing Association*, August 1991.

4. Pierre A. Passavant, "Where Is Direct Marketing Headed in the 1990's?" an address in Philadelphia, May 4, 1989.

5. Roman, *Integrated Direct Marketing*, p. 3. As another illustration, LaTour and Manrai reported the following results for the percentage of people who came to a blood drive: no direct mail, no telephone, 2.0 percent; direct mail only, 4.4 percent; telephone only, 7.4 percent; direct mail followed by telephone, 21.9 percent. See Stephen A. LaTour and Ajay K. Manrai, "Interactive Impact of Informational and Normative Influence on Donations," *Journal of Marketing Research*, August 1989, pp. 327-35.

6. Stan Rapp and Thomas L. Collins, *Maximarketing* (New York: McGraw-Hill, 1987).

7. Bob Stone, *Successful Direct Marketing Methods* (Chicago: Crain Books, 1979), pp. 323-325.

8. Edward Nash, Direct Marketing, 2nd ed. (New York: McGraw-Hill, 1986), p. 16.

9. From Robert C. Blattberg and Scott A. Neslin, *Sales Promotion: Concepts, Methods, and Strategies* (Englewood Cliffs, N.J.: Prentice Hall, 1990). This text provides the most comprehensive and analytical treatment of sales promotion to date.

10. Ken Riddell, "New study shows sales promotion spending estimates may be inflated," *Marketing*, April 23, 1990, p. 1.

11. Roger A. Strang, "Sales Promotion—Fast Growth, Faulty Management," *Harvard Business Review*. July-August 1976, pp. 115-24, here pp. 116-19.

12. For a good summary of the research on whether promotion erodes the consumer franchise of leading brands, see Blattberg and Neslin, *Sales Promotion*, pp. 471-75.

13. Robert George Brown, "Sales Response to Promotions and Advertising," *Journal of Advertising Research*, August 1974, pp. 33-39, here pp. 36-37.

14. F. Kent Mitchel, "Advertising/Promotion Budgets: How Did We Get Here, and What Do We Do Now?" *Journal of Consumer Marketing*, Fall 1985, pp. 405-47.

15. See Paul W. Farris and John A. Quelch, "In Defense of Price Promotion," *Sloan Management Review*, Fall 1987, pp. 63-69.

16. Strang, "Sales Promotion," p. 124.

17. Canadian packagd goods spending in 1989 was estimated to be 52% trade promotion, 12% consumer promotion, and 36% advertising. See John Yokom, "Skeptical look at industry figures," *Marketing*, April 23, 1990, p. 11.

18. See Michel Chevalier and Ronald C. Curhan, *Temporary Promotions as a Function of Trade Deals: A Descriptive Analysis* (Cambridge, Mass.: Marketing Science Institute, 1975), p. 2.

19. See "Retailers Buy Far in Advance to Exploit Trade Promotions," *Wall Street Journal*, October 9, 1986, p. 35.

20. Arthur Stern, "Measuring the Effectiveness of Package Goods Promotion Strategies" (Paper presented to the Association of National Advertisers, Glen Cove, N.Y., February 1978).

21. Strang, "Sales Promotion," p. 119.

22. Russell D. Bowman, "Merchandising and Promotion Grow Big in Marketing World," *Advertising Age*, December 1974, p. 21.

23. Strang, "Sales Promotion," p. 120.

24. Kurt H. Schaffir and H. George Trenten, *Marketing Information Systems* (New York: Amacom, 1973), p. 81.

25. Strang, "Sales Promotion," p. 120.

26. See Joe A. Dodson, Alice M. Tybout, and Brian Sternthal, "Impact of Deals and Deal Retraction on Brand Switching," *Journal of Marketing Research*, February 1978, pp. 72-81. They found that deals generally increase brand switching, the rate depending on the type of deal. Media-distributed coupons induce substantial switching, cents-off deals induce somewhat less switching, and package coupons hardly affect brand switching. Furthermore, consumers generally return to their preferred brands after the deal.

27. Recent books on sales promotion include John A. Quelch, *Sales Promotion Management* (Englewood Cliffs, N.J.: Prentice Hall, 1989); and John C. Totten and Martin P. Block, *Analyzing Sales Promotion: Text and Cases* (Chicago: Commerce Communications, 1987). For an expert systems approach to sales promotion, see John W. Keon and Judy Bayer, "An Expert Approach to Sales Promotion Management," *Journal of Advertising Research*, June/July 1986, pp. 19-26.

28. Adapted from Scott M. Cutlip, Allen H. Center, and Glen

M. Brown, *Effective Public Relations*, 6th ed. (Englewood Cliffs, N.J.: Prentice-Hall, 1985), pp. 7-17.

29. Tom Duncan, *A Study of How Manufacturers and Service Companies Perceive and Use Marketing Public Relations* (Muncie, Ind.: Ball State University, December 1985).

30. Proctor & Gamble (B), a case written by L. Markle and R. E. Vosburgh, University of Guelph.

31. Arthur M. Merims, "Marketing's Stepchild: Product Publicity," *Harvard Business Review*, November-December 1972, pp. 111-12. Also see Katerine D. Paine, "There Is a Method for Measuring PR," *Marketing News*, November 6, 1987, p. 5.

24

Managing the Salesforce

Hail to the huckster! Knight errant of our time! Proudly he rides to war for the barons of soap, perpetually storming the castles of the home.

F.R. Scott

Robert Louis Stevenson observed that "everyone lives by selling something." In 1989, 1.2 million Canadians were involved in sales and related occupations.[1] While not quite Stevenson's "everyone," this figure is an impressive ten percent of Canada's workforce. Salesforces are found in non-profit and for-profit organizations. Recruiters are the university's salesforce for attracting new students. Churches use membership committees to attract new members. The Ontario Ministry of Natural Resources has forestry specialists who show owners of country properties how to manage them as woodlots. Charitable organizations use fund raisers to contact and raise money from donors. Selling is one of the world's oldest occupations.

People who sell are called by various names: saleswomen and salesmen, sales representatives, salespersons, account executives, sales consultants, sales engineers, field representatives, agents, service representatives, and marketing representatives. The public tends to carry many stereotypes about salespeople. *Salesman* can conjure up an image of Arthur Miller's pitiable Willy Loman in *Death of a Salesman* or Meredith Wilson's cigar-smoking, back-slapping, joke-telling Harold Hill in *The Music Man.* Sales representatives are typically pictured as loving sociability—although many sales representatives actually dislike it. They are criticized for foisting goods on people—although buyers often search out sales representatives.

Actually the term *sales representative* covers a broad range of positions in our economy, where the differences are often greater than the similarities. McMurry devised the following classification of sales positions:

1. *Deliverer:* Positions where the salesperson's job is predominantly to deliver the product (e.g., milk, bread, fuel, oil)

2. *Order Taker:* Positions where the salesperson is predominantly an inside order taker (e.g., the haberdashery salesperson standing behind the counter) or outside order taker (e.g., the soap salesperson calling on the supermarket manager)

FIGURE 24-1

Steps in Designing and Managing the Salesforce

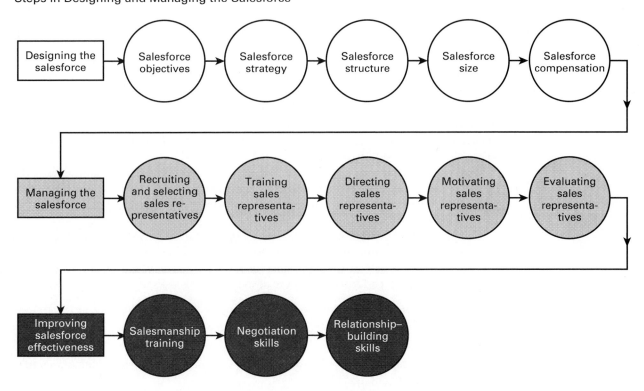

3. *Missionary:* Positions where the salesperson is not expected or permitted to take an order but is called on only to build goodwill or to educate the actual or potential user (e.g., the medical "detailer" representing an ethical pharmaceutical house)

4. *Technician:* Positions where the major emphasis is placed on technical knowledge (e.g., the engineering salesperson who is primarily a consultant to the "client" companies)

5. *Demand creator:* Positions that demand the creative sale of tangible products (e.g., vacuum cleaners, refrigerators, siding, and encyclopedias) or of intangibles (e.g., insurance, advertising services, or education)[2]

The positions range from the least to the most creative types of selling. The first jobs call for servicing accounts and taking new orders, while the latter require seeking prospects and influencing them to buy. Our discussion will focus on the more creative types of selling.

This chapter examines three major questions related to the salesforce: What decisions do companies make in designing a salesforce? How can the planned salesforce be implemented and managed? What tools can the salesforce use to improve its sales effectiveness? The components of these decisions are shown in Figure 24-1 and discussed below.

DESIGNING THE SALESFORCE

Sales personnel serve as the company's personal link to the customers. The sales representative is the company to many of its customers and in turn brings back to the company much needed intelligence about the customer. Therefore, the company needs to give its deepest thought to issues in salesforce design, namely, developing salesforce objectives, strategy, structure, size, and compensation.

Salesforce Objectives

Salesforce objectives must be based on the character of the company's target markets and the company's desired position in these markets. The company must consider the unique role that personal selling can play in the marketing mix to serve customer needs in a competitively effective way. Personal selling happens to be the most expensive contact and communication tool used by the company. According to McGraw-Hill, the cost of an industrial sales call in 1987 was $250.[3]

On the other hand, personal selling is also the most effective tool at certain stages of the buying process, such as the buyer-education, negotiation, and sales-closing stages. It is important that the company carefully consider when and how to use sales representatives to facilitate the marketing task.

Companies typically set different objectives for their salesforces. IBM's sales representatives are responsible for *selling, installing*, and *upgrading* customer computer equipment; Bell Canada sales representatives are responsible for *developing, selling*, and *protecting* accounts. Sales representatives perform one or more of the following tasks for their companies:

☐ Prospecting: Sales representatives find and cultivate new customers.

☐ *Communicating:* Sales representatives skillfully communicate information about the company's products and services.

☐ *Selling:* Sales representatives know the art of "salesmanship"—approaching, presenting, answering objections, and closing sales.

☐ *Servicing:* Sales representatives provide various services to the customers—consulting on their problems, rendering technical assistance, arranging financing, and expediting delivery.

☐ *Information Gathering:* Sales representatives conduct market research and intelligence work and fill in call reports.

☐ *Allocating:* Sales representatives are able to evaluate customer quality and allocate scarce products during product shortages.

Companies typically define their salesforce objectives and activities more tightly. One company wants its sales representatives to spend 80 percent of their time with current customers and 20 percent with prospects, and 85 percent of their time on established products and 15 percent on new products. If norms are not established, sales representatives tend to spend most of their time selling established products to current accounts and neglect new products and new prospects.

The sales representative's mix of tasks varies with the state of the economy. During product shortages, sales representatives find themselves with nothing to sell. Some companies jump to the conclusion that fewer sales representatives are needed. But this thinking overlooks the salesperson's other roles—allocating the product, counseling unhappy customers, communicating company plans on remedying shortages, and selling the company's other products that are not in short supply.

As companies move toward a stronger market orientation, their salesforces need to become more market focused and customer oriented. The traditional view is that salespeople should worry about volume and sell, sell, sell, and that the marketing department should worry about marketing strategy and profitability. The newer view is that salespeople should know how to produce customer satisfaction and company profit. They should know how to analyze sales data, measure market potential, gather market intelligence, and develop marketing strategies and plans. Sales representatives need analytical marketing skills, and this becomes especially critical at the higher levels of sales management. Marketers believe that salesforces will be more effective in the long run if they understand marketing as well as selling.

Salesforce Strategy

Companies compete with each other to get orders from customers. They must deploy their salesforces strategically so that they call on the right customers at the right time and in the right way. Sales representatives can reach customers in several ways:

- *Sales Representative to Buyer:* A sales representative talks to a prospect or customer in person or over the phone.
- *Sales Representative to Buyer Group:* A sales representative makes a sales presentation to a buying group.
- *Sales Team to Buyer Group:* A sales team (such as a company officer, a sales representative, and a sales engineer) makes a sales presentation to a buying group.
- *Conference Selling:* The sales representative brings resource people from the company to meet with one or more buyers to discuss problems and mutual opportunities.
- *Seminar Selling:* A company team conducts an educational seminar for a technical group in a customer company about state-of-the-art developments.

Thus today's sales representative often acts as the "account manager," who arranges contacts between various people in the buying and selling organizations. Selling increasingly calls for teamwork, requiring the support of other personnel, such as *top management*, which is increasingly involved in the sales process, especially when *national accounts*[4] or *major sales*[5] are at stake; *technical people*, who supply technical information and service to the customer before, during, or after product purchase; *customer-service representatives*, who provide installation, maintenance, and other services to the customer; and an *office staff*, consisting of sales analysts, order expediters, and secretaries.

Once the company decides on a desirable selling approach, it can use either a direct or a contractual salesforce. A *direct (or company) salesforce* consists of full- or part-time paid employees who work exclusively for the company. This salesforce includes *inside sales personnel*, who conduct business from their office using the telephone and receiving visits from prospective buyers, and *field sales personnel*, who travel and visit customers. A *contractual salesforce* consists of manufacturers' reps, sales agents, or brokers, who are paid a commission based on their sales.

Salesforce Structure

The salesforce strategy will have implications for structuring the salesforce. If the company sells one product line to one end-using industry with customers in many locations, the company would use a territorial salesforce structure. If the company sells many products to many types of customers, it might need a product or market salesforce structure. These alternative salesforce structures are discussed below. (See the Companies and Industries 24-1 exhibit for an example of the work involved in setting up a new salesforce.)

Companies and Industries 24-1

BUILDING A SALESFORCE FROM SCRATCH: THE CASE OF WILKINSON

The North American division of Wilkinson Sword had a 7.9 percent market share of the razor blade market in 1974, but its share had fallen to 0.7 percent by 1984. The parent company had cut down its advertising, preferring to spend the money in Europe, and sales had plummeted. In addition, the division did not have its own sales force but used manufacturer's reps for drugstores and brokers for food stores, with the result that its product had little push.

In 1984, the company was reorganized and president Norman R. Proulx was given a large budget to revive the company. He budgeted $23.5 million to run a two-year advertising campaign and used most of the rest of the budget to build a Wilkinson sales force for the first time. Ronald E. Mineo, Wilkinson's sales vice-president, proceeded to build a 34-person salesforce by taking the following steps:

1. The first step was account identification. Wilkinson identified 25 leading chains in the food store, drugstore, and mass-merchandise business and established them as national accounts to be handled in the divisional headquarters by two national account managers. Then several regional accounts were identified and assigned to area sales managers. Finally, smaller accounts were assigned to sales representatives.

2. The second step was setting up geographical regions. The country was partitioned into three regions. Each region was sliced into roughly five areas, and each area was further sliced into a few territories.

3. The third step was staffing the positions. Mineo said that "organizing is the easy part. The hard part is finding the people." He looked primarily for people with at least five years of selling experience in top health-and-beauty-aids companies. He offered a package at least as good as the competition's. It cost Wilkinson over half-a-million dollars in the first year's recruiting, training, salaries, bonuses, etc., to build the salesforce.

4. The fourth step was hiring a vice-president of trade relations who would be a critical appointment. Wilkinson also began hiring retail merchandisers to support the salespeople by reducing out-of-stocks, building incremental facings and displays, and monitoring pricing.

Now that these steps are in place, we will learn in a few years if Wilkinson has achieved its goal of winning over 10 percent of the wet-shave market. Its ultimate goal is to become the number-two razor blade company in North America. One of its managers said: "We've opened the doors. Now we need to kick the doors down."

Source: Rayna Skolnik, "The Birth of a Sales Force," *Sales and Marketing Management*, March 10, 1986, pp. 42-44.

Territorial-Structured Salesforce   In the simplest sales organization, each sales representative is assigned an exclusive territory in which to represent the company's full line. This sales structure has a number of advantages. First, it results in a clear definition of the salesperson's responsibilities. As the only salesperson working the territory, he or she bears the credit or blame for area sales to the extent that personal selling effort makes a difference. Second, territorial responsibility increases the sales representative's incentive to cultivate local business and personal ties. These ties contribute to the sales representative's selling effectiveness and personal life. Third, travel expenses are relatively small, since each sales representative travels within a small geographical area.

Territorial sales organization is often supported by many levels of sales-management positions. For example, Campbell Soup has changed from a product salesforce structure to a territorial one in which each salesperson is responsible for selling all Campbell Soup products. Starting at the bottom of the organization, *sales merchandisers* report to *sales representatives*, who report to *retail supervisors*, who report to *directors of retail sales operations*, who report to one of twenty-two *regional sales managers*. Regional sales managers are headed by one of four *general sales managers* for the four main regions, who report to a *vice-president and general sales manager*.[6]

Each higher-level sales manager takes on increasing marketing and administrative work in relation to the time available for selling. In fact, sales managers are paid for their management skills rather than their selling skills. The new sales trainee, in looking ahead, can expect to become a sales representative and then a district manager and, depending on his or her ability and motivation, may move to higher levels of sales or general management.

In designing territories, the company seeks certain territorial characteristics: The territories are easy to administer; their sales potential is easy to estimate; they reduce total travel time; and they provide a sufficient and equitable workload and sales potential for each sales representative. These characteristics are achieved through decisions about the size and shape of territorial units.

Territory Size Territories can be designed to provide either *equal sales potential* or *equal workload*. Each principle offers advantages at the cost of some dilemmas.

Territories of *equal potential* provide each sales representative with the same income opportunities and provide the company with a means to evaluate performance. Persistent differences in sales yield by territory are assumed to reflect differences in ability or effort of individual sales representatives. Salespersons are encouraged to work at their top capacity.

But because customer density varies by territory, territories with equal potential can vary widely in size. The potential for selling office copiers in Toronto is larger than in all of the Western provinces. A sales representative assigned to Toronto can cover the same sales potential with much less effort than the sales representative who sells in the West.

The sales representative assigned to the larger and sparser territory is going to end up with either fewer sales and less income for equal effort or equal sales through extraordinary effort. One solution is to pay the Western sales representatives more compensation for the extra effort. But this reduces the profits on sales in the western territories. Another solution is to acknowledge that territories differ in attractiveness and assign the better or more senior sales representatives to the better territories.

Alternatively, territories could be designed to *equalize the sales workload*. Each sales representative can then cover his or her territory adequately. This principle, however, results in some variation in territory sales potentials. That does not concern a salesforce on straight salary. But where sales representatives are compensated partly on their sales, territories will vary in their attractiveness even though their workloads are equal. A lower compensation rate can be paid to sales representatives in the territories with the higher sales potential, or the territories with the better potential can go to the higher performers.

Territory Shape Territories are formed by combining smaller units, such as counties or census tracts, until they add up to a territory of a given sales potential or workload. Territorial design must take into account the location of natural barriers, the compatibility of adjacent areas, the adequacy of transportation, and so forth. Many companies prefer a certain territory shape because the shape can influence the cost and ease of coverage and the sales representatives' job satisfaction. Most common are circular, cloverleaf, and wedge-shaped territories. Today, companies can use computer programs to design sales territories that optimize such criteria as compactness, equalization of workload or sales potential, and minimal travel time.[7]

Product-Structured Salesforce   The importance of sales representatives' knowing their products, together with the development of product divisions and product management, has led many companies to structure their salesforces along product lines. Product specialization is particularly warranted where the products are technically complex, highly unrelated, or very numerous. For example, Kodak uses different salesforces for its film products and its industrial products. The film-products salesforce deals with simple products that are intensively distributed, while the industrial-products salesforce deals with complex products that require technical understanding. The film salesforce is paid by salary, which permits management to centralize the direction of its selling effort. The industrial salesforce must tailor its selling efforts to localized demand, so compensation is partly based on commission, which provides localized incentives.

The mere existence of different company products, however, is not a sufficient argument for specializing the salesforce by product. Such specialization might not be the best course if the company's separate product lines are bought by the same customers. For example, Westinghouse Canada sells most of its products through a full-line salesforce. This permits customers to purchase most of their needs for electrical products from one salesperson. Only the more technical products like turbines have specialized salesforces. For such products, the extra costs of sales specialization are offset by the need to provide technical service.

Market-Structured Salesforce   Companies often specialize their salesforces to serve different markets. Separate salesforces may be set up for different industries and even different customers. For example, IBM recently set up a separate sales office for finance and brokerage customers, and two separate automotive sales offices for General Motors and for Ford.

The most obvious advantage of market specialization is that each salesforce can become knowledgeable about specific customer needs. At one time, General Electric's sales representatives specialized in products (fan motors, switches, and so forth), but it later changed to specialization in industries, such as the air-conditioning industry and auto industry, because that is how customers saw the purchase of fan motors, switches, and so forth. A market-specialized salesforce can sometimes reduce total salesforce costs. A pump manufacturer at one time used highly trained sales engineers to sell to both original-equipment manufacturers (who needed to deal with technical representatives) and jobbers (who did not need to deal with technical representatives). Later, the company split its salesforce and staffed the jobber salesforce with lower-paid, less-technical sales personnel. The major disadvantage of market-structured salesforces arises when the various types of customers are scattered throughout the country. This means extensive travel by each of the company's salesforces.

Complex Salesforce Structures   When a company sells a wide variety of products to many types of customers over a broad geographical area, it often combines several principles of salesforce structure. Sales representatives can be specialized by territory-product, territory-market, product-market, and so on. A sales representative might then report to one or more line managers and staff managers. One of the most interesting developments is the growth of national account-management divisions (see Marketing Strategies 24-1).

Companies need to rethink their salesforce structure as market and economic conditions change. Xerox is a good case in point:

> Xerox managed several salesforces, the main one selling copier/duplicator equipment, and others selling typewriters, printing systems, office systems, and so on. With the move to the electronic office, Xerox decided to merge salesforces so that different Xerox salespeople would not all call upon the same customers and confuse them with arguments for different office products and systems. Xerox divided the new salesforce into four groups:

Marketing Strategies 24-1

NATIONAL ACCOUNT MANAGEMENT— WHAT IT IS AND HOW IT WORKS

When a company sells to many small accounts, it uses a territory-based salesforce. However, large accounts (called key accounts, major accounts, house accounts) are often singled out for special attention and handling. If the account is a large company with many divisions operating in many parts of the country and subject to many buying influences (such as Sears or General Motors), it is likely to be handled as a *national account* and assigned to a specific individual or sales team. If the company has several such accounts, it is likely to organize a *national account management (NAM) division.* The company will then sell to these larger customers through this division. A company such as Xerox handles about 250 national accounts through its NAM division.

National account management is growing for a number of reasons. As buyer concentration increases through mergers and acquisitions, fewer buyers account for a larger share of a company's sales. Thus the largest 10 percent of accounts might account for more than 50 percent of a company's sales. Another factor is that many buyers are centralizing their purchases of certain items instead of leaving those purchases to the local units. This gives them more bargaining power with the sellers. The sellers in turn need to devote more attention to these major buyers. Still another factor is that as products become more complex, more groups in the buyer's organi-

zation become involved in the purchase process, and the typical salesperson might not have the skill, authority, or coverage to be effective in selling to the large buyer.

In organizing a national account program, a company faces a number of issues, including how to select national accounts; how to manage them; how to develop, manage, and evaluate national account managers; how to organize a structure for national account management; and where to locate national account management in the organization.

Essentially a company wants its national account managers to be good at a number of things. They must be able to reach all of the buying influences in the buyer's organization. They must be able to reach all the groups in their own organization—salespeople, R&D staff, manufacturing people, and so on— to coordinate them in meeting the buyer's requirements. Thus national account managers link all the parts of their company with all the parts of the buying company. In many organizations they are, in fact, called "relationship managers."

Sources: For further discussion, see the working papers on National Account Management prepared by Benson P. Shapiro and Rowland T. Moriarty under the sponsorship of the Marketing Science Institute, Cambridge, Mass., published in 1980-83. Also see Linda Cardillo Platzer, *Managing National Accounts* (New York: Conference Board, 1984), report no. 850.

- ☐ *NAMs:* national account managers serving major companies with dispersed multiple locations
- ☐ *MAMs:* major account managers serving major accounts with one or two other accounts in the region
- ☐ *ARs:* account representatives serving standard commercial accounts with potential of $5000-$10 000
- ☐ *MRs:* marketing representatives serving all others

Each group faces a different selling cycle and is rewarded under a different compensation plan. In taking this step, Xerox put its salesforce through a deep and long sales retraining program because each sales rep needed to learn how to represent all of Xerox's product lines to the customer. At the same time, each sales rep could call in Xerox experts in particular product lines to help make the sale. Xerox used a team approach to sell which they called Team Xerox.[8]   ∎

Salesforce Size

Once the company clarifies its salesforce strategy and structure, it is ready to consider salesforce size. Sales representatives are one of the company's most productive and expensive assets. Increasing their number will increase both sales and costs.

Salesforce size is partly determined by how much use the company makes of other marketing tools, such as telemarketers, distributors, and agents. Suppose the company uses its salesforce to reach all customers regardless of their size or profit potential. The cost is shown by sales-cost line A in Figure 24-2, which rises for larger customers. Now suppose the company divides its pool of customers into large, medium, and small (urban and rural) customers. The salesforce visits large customers; telemarketers phone medium-size customers for orders; distributors are used for small urban customers; and agents are used for small rural customers. This arrangement results in sharply reducing the selling cost of serving smaller customers, as shown by selling-cost line B. Now there is more profit available from each customer group. The main thing the company has to worry about is possible multichannel conflict between its salesforce and the other sales channels.

Once the company establishes the number of customers it wants to reach with its salesforce, it often uses a *workload approach* to establish salesforce size. This method consists of the following steps:

1. Customers are grouped into size classes according to their annual sales volume.

2. The desirable call frequencies (number of sales calls on an account per year) are established for each class. They reflect how much call intensity the company seeks in relation to competitors.

FIGURE 24-2
The Effect of Sales
Channel on Sales Cost

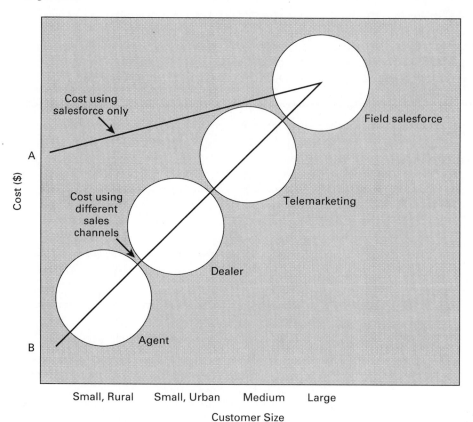

3. The number of accounts in each size class is multiplied by the corresponding call frequency to arrive at the total workload for the country, in sales calls per year.

4. The average number of calls a sales representative can make per year is determined.

5. The number of sales representatives needed is determined by dividing the total annual calls required by the average annual calls made by a sales representative.

Suppose the company estimates that there are one thousand A accounts and two thousand B accounts required in the nation; and A accounts require thirty-six calls a year and B accounts twelve calls a year. This means the company needs a salesforce that can make sixty thousand sales calls a year. Suppose the average sales representative can make one thousand calls a year. The company would need sixty full-time sales representatives.

Salesforce Compensation

To attract sales representatives, the company has to develop an attractive compensation package. Sales representatives would like income regularity, extra reward for an above-average performance, and fair payment for experience and longevity. On the other hand, management would like to achieve control, economy, and simplicity. Management objectives, such as economy, will conflict with sales representatives' objectives, such as financial security. No wonder that compensation plans exhibit a tremendous variety among industries and even within the same industry.

Management must determine the level and components of an effective compensation plan. The *level of compensation* must bear some relation to the "going market price" for the type of sales job and required abilities. For example, the average earnings of an experienced salesperson in 1988 amounted to \$38 900.[9] If the market price for salespeople is well defined, the individual firm has little choice but to pay the going rate. To pay less would bring forth less than the desired quantity or quality of applicants, and to pay more would be unnecessary. The market price for salespeople, however, is seldom well defined. For one thing, sales compensation plans differ in the importance of fixed and variable salary elements, fringe benefits, and expense allowances. And data on the average take-home pay of competitors' sales representatives can be misleading because of significant variations in the average seniority and ability levels of the competitors' salesforces. Published data on industry salesforce compensation levels are infrequent and generally lack sufficient detail.

The company must next determine the *components of compensation*—a fixed amount, a variable amount, expenses, and fringe benefits. The *fixed amount*, which might be salary or a drawing account, is intended to satisfy the sales representatives' need for some stability of income. The *variable amount*, which might be commissions, bonus, or profit sharing, is intended to stimulate and reward greater effort. *Expense allowances* enable the sales representatives to meet the expenses involved in travel, lodging, dining, and entertaining. And *fringe benefits*, such as paid vacations, sickness or accident benefits, pensions, and life insurance, are intended to provide security and job satisfaction.

Sales management must decide on the relative importance of these components in the compensation plan. A popular rule favors making about 70 percent of the salesperson's total income fixed and allocating the remaining 30 percent among the other elements. But the variations around this average are so pronounced that it can hardly serve as a guide. Fixed compensation receives more emphasis in jobs with a high ratio of nonselling to selling duties and in jobs where the selling task is technically complex and involves teamwork. Variable compensation receives more emphasis in jobs where sales are cyclical or depend on salesforce initiative.

Fixed and variable compensation give rise to three basic types of salesforce compensation plans—straight salary, straight commission, and combination salary and commission. A recent study of salesforce compensation plans showed that about 14 percent paid straight salary, 19 percent paid straight commission, 37 percent paid salary plus commission, 26 percent paid salary plus bonus, and 10 percent paid salary plus commission plus bonus.[10] The advantages and disadvantages of each plan and component are described in Marketing Concepts and Tools 24-1.

Marketing Concepts and Tools 24-1

SALES PLANS AND COMPONENTS

Straight Salary

This plan pays sales representatives a fixed salary and expenses. Occasionally there is additional compensation through discretionary bonuses or sales-contest prizes. Among the advantages are these: Management can alter sales duties without strong objection; straight salary plans are easier to explain and administer; they simplify the task of projecting the sales payroll for the coming year; and finally, by providing the sales force with a stable income, they can lead to higher salesforce morale. Among the weaknesses are these: The straight salary plan does not stimulate the salesforce to do a better-than-average selling job; they constitute an inflexible selling-expense burden during business downswings; during upswings, sales representatives will not have sufficient incentive to exploit the increased business potential; thorny questions arise in salary adjustment for ability, living cost differences, and length of service; and straight salary plans do not attract or hold the more aggressive sales representatives.

Straight Commission

This plan pays sales representatives some fixed or sliding rate related to their sales or profit volume. The *commission base* can be gross sales volume, net sales after returns, gross margins, or net profits. (Most researchers say that basing commission on gross margin is superior to basing it on gross sales, although the latter base is used more often; see source below.) The *commission rates* can be identical for all sales or differentiated by customers and/or products. The *commission starting point* can be the first sale or sales over a minimum quota. Straight commission plans are prominent in the selling of insurance and investment securities, furniture, office equipment, small office machines, and clothing; in the textile and shoe industries; and in drug and hardware wholesaling. Their advantages are these: They stimulate sales representatives to work at maximum capacity; they tie selling expenses to current revenue; and they allow setting different commissions on different products and sales tasks, thereby influencing how the salespersons spend their time. Their weaknesses include these: The salesforce resists performing activities that do not generate immediate income, such as following up leads, filling out reports, or providing customer service; they can stimulate high-pressure tactics or price discounting; they are more costly to administer; and they provide little income security and cause morale to drop when sales fall through no fault of the salesforce.

Combination Salary and Commission

The great majority of firms pay a combination of salary and commission, in the hope of achieving the advantages of each while avoiding the disadvantages. The most common split is 70 percent salary and 30 percent commission. The combination plan is appropriate where sales volume depends on the sales representative's motivation and yet management wants some control over nonselling duties performed by the sales representative. The plan means that during downswings, the company is not stuck with inflexible selling costs, and sales representatives do not lose their whole income.

Bonus

Bonuses are noncontractual payments for extra effort, merit, or results. They reward sales representatives for performing tasks that are desirable but not rewardable through commissions, such as preparing prompt reports, supplying useful selling ideas, and developing unusual product or market knowledge. The main problem with bonuses is that managerial judgment enters into their determination, and sales representatives can raise questions of fairness.

Other Costs

The company's selling costs include the following additional elements: *selling expenses* (travel, lodging, telephone, entertainment, samples promotion, and office and/or clerical expenses); *fringe benefits* (hospitalization insurance, life insurance, pension plan, association memberships, and moving expenses); *special incentives* (contests, service awards); and *staff backup costs* (cost of technical and customer-service people, sales analysts, computer time, and sales-training programs). Thus the cost of running a salesforce adds up to much more than the direct-compensation elements alone.

Source: For further reading, see Anne T. Coughlan and Subrata K. Sen, "Salesforce Compensation: Theory and Managerial Implications," *Marketing Science*, Fall 1989, pp. 324-42.

MANAGING THE SALESFORCE

Having established the salesforce's objectives, strategy, structure, size, and compensation, the company has to move to recruiting, selecting, training, directing, motivating, and evaluating sales representatives. Various policies and procedures guide these decisions.

Recruiting and Selecting Sales Representatives

Importance of Careful Selection   At the heart of a successful salesforce operation is the selection of effective sales representatives. The performance difference between an average and a top sales representative can be considerable. One survey revealed that the top 27 percent of the salesforce brought in over 52 percent of the sales. Beyond the differences in sales productivity are the great wastes in hiring the wrong persons. The average annual salesforce turnover rate for all industries is almost 20 percent. When a salesperson quits, the costs of finding and training a new salesperson—plus the costs of lost sales—can run as high as $50 000 to $75 000. And a salesforce with a lot of new people is less productive.[11]

The financial loss due to turnover is only part of the total cost. The new sales representative who remains with the company receives a direct income averaging around half of the direct selling cost. If he or she receives $20 000 a year, another $20 000 goes into fringe benefits, expenses, supervision, office space, supplies, and secretarial assistance. Consequently, the new sales representative needs to produce sales on which the gross margin at least covers the selling expenses of $40 000. If the gross margin is 10 percent, the new salesperson will have to sell at least $400 000 for the company to break even.

What Makes a Good Sales Represntative?   Selecting sales representatives would be simple if one knew what traits to look for. One good starting point is to ask customers what traits they like and prefer in salespeople. Most customers say they want the sales representative to be honest, reliable, knowledgeable, and helpful. The company should look for these traits when selecting candidates.

Another approach is to look for traits common to the most successful salespeople in the company. If the successful sales representatives were outgoing, aggressive, and energetic, these characteristics could be checked in applicants. But many successful sales representatives are introverted, mild mannered, and far from energetic. Successful sales representatives include men and women who are tall and short, articulate and inarticulate, well-groomed and slovenly.

Nevertheless, the search continues for the magic combination of traits that spells surefire sales ability. Numerous lists have been drawn up. McMurry wrote: "It is my conviction that the possessor of an *effective* sales personality is a *habitual 'wooer,' an individual who has a compulsive need to win and hold the affection of others.*"[12] He listed five additional traits of the super salesperson: "A high level of energy, abounding self-confidence, a chronic hunger for money, a well-established habit of industry, and a state of mind that regards each objection, resistance, or obstacle as a challenge."[13]

Mayer and Greenberg offered one of the shortest lists of traits.[14] They concluded that the effective salesperson has at least two basic qualities: (1) *empathy*, the ability to feel as the customer does; and (2) *ego drive*, a strong personal need to make the sale. Using these two traits as criteria led to fairly good predictions of the subsequent performance of applicants for sales positions in three different industries.

The company should also consider the nature of the sales job. Is there a lot of paperwork? Does the job call for much travel? Will the salesperson confront a high proportion of rejections?

Recruitment Procedures   After management develops its selection criteria, it must recruit. The personnel department seeks applicants by various means, including soliciting names from current sales representatives, using employment agencies, placing job ads, and contacting university students. But few university students want a career in selling.[15] Even business school graduates prefer positions in product management to selling. The reluctant ones say "Selling is a job not a profession," "It calls for deceit if the person wants to succeed," and "There is insecurity and too much travel." To counter these objections, company recruiters emphasize starting salaries, income opportunities, and the fact that one-fourth of the presidents of large corporations started out in marketing and sales.

Applicant-Rating Procedures   Recruitment procedures, if successful, will attract many applicants, and the company will need to select the best ones. The selection procedures can vary from a single informal interview to prolonged testing and interviewing, not only of the applicant but of the applicant's spouse.[16]

Many companies give formal tests to sales applicants. Although test scores are only one information element in a set that includes personal characteristics, references, past employment history, and interviewer reactions, they are weighted quite heavily by such companies as IBM, Procter & Gamble, and Gillette. Gillette claims that tests have reduced turnover by 42 percent and have correlated well with the subsequent progress of new sales representatives in the sales organization.

Training Sales Representatives

Many companies send their new sales representatives into the field almost immediately after hiring them. They are supplied with samples, order books, and a description of their territory. And much of their selling is ineffective. A vice-president of a major food company spent one week watching fifty sales presentations to a busy buyer for a major supermarket chain. Here is what he observed:

I watched a soap company representative come in to the buyer. He had three separate new promotional deals to talk about with six different dates. He had nothing in writing. . . . After the salesman left, the buyer looked at me and said, "It will take me fifteen minutes to get this straightened out."

I watched another salesman walk in to the buyer and say, "Well, I was in the area, and I want you to know that we have a great new promotion coming up next week." The buyer said, "That's fine. What is it?" He said, "I don't know. . . . I'm coming in next week to tell you about it." The buyer asked him what he was doing there today. He said, "Well, I was in the area."

Another salesman came in and said, "Well, it's time for us to write that order now . . . getting ready for the summer business." The buyer said. "Well, fine, George, how much did I buy last year in total?" The salesman looked a little dumbfounded and said, "Well, I'll be damned if I know. . . ."

The majority of salesmen were ill prepared, unable to answer basic questions, uncertain as to what they wanted to accomplish during the call. They did not think of the call as a studied professional presentation. They didn't have a real idea of the busy retailer's needs and wants.[17]

It is true that training programs are costly. They involve large outlays for instructors, materials, and space; paying a person who is not yet selling; and losing opportunities because he or she is not in the field. Yet they are essential. Today's new sales representatives may spend a few weeks to several months in training. The median training period is twenty-eight weeks in industrial-products companies, twelve in service companies, and four in consumer-products companies.[18] Training time varies with the complexity of the selling task and the type of person recruited into the sales organization. At IBM, new sales representatives are not on their own for two years! And IBM expects its sales representatives to spend 15 percent of their time each year in additional training.

The annual sales-training bill for major corporations runs into millions of dollars. Yet sales management sees training as adding more value than cost. Today's sales representatives are selling to more cost- and value-conscious buyers. Furthermore, they are selling technically complex products. The company wants and needs mature and knowledgeable sales representatives.

The training programs have several goals:

☐ *Sales representatives need to know and identify with the company:* Most companies devote the first part of the training program to describing the company's history and objectives, the organization and lines of authority, the chief officers, the company's financial structure and facilities, and the chief products and sales volumes.

☐ *Sales representatives need to know the company's products:* Sales trainees are shown how the products are produced and how they function in various uses.

☐ *Sales representatives need to know customers' and competitors' characteristics:* Sales representatives learn about the different types of customers and their needs, buying motives, and buying habits. They learn about the company's and competitors' strategies and policies.

☐ *Sales representatives need to know how to make effective sales presentations:* Sales representatives receive training in the principles of selling. In addition, the company outlines the major sales arguments for each product and may provide a sales script.

☐ *Sales representatives need to understand field procedures and responsibilities:* Sales representatives learn how to divide time between active and potential accounts; how to use the expense account, prepare reports, and route effectively.

New methods of training are continually emerging. Among the instructional approaches are role playing, sensitivity training, cassette tapes, videotapes, programmed learning, and films on selling and on company products.

One of the latest training methods is exemplified by a self-study system that IBM uses called Info-Window. Info-Window combines a personal computer and a laser videodisc. A sales trainee can practice sales calls with an on-screen actor who portrays a manager in a particular industry. The actor responds differently depending on what the sales trainee says. The trainee is filmed during this interactive session on a VCR linked to Info-Window.[19]

Training departments need to collect evidence of the effect of different training approaches on sales performance. There should be a measurable impact on salesforce turnover, sales volume, absenteeism, average sale size, calls-to-close ratio, customer complaints and compliments, new accounts per time unit, and volume of returned merchandise. The substantial costs of company training programs raise the question of whether a company could do better by hiring experienced sales representatives away from other companies. The gain is often illusory, however, because the experienced salesperson is brought in at a higher salary. Some of the representatives' specific training and company experience is wasted when they transfer to other companies. Within some industries, companies tacitly agree not to hire sales personnel away from each other.

Directing Sales Representatives

New sales representatives are given more than a territory, a compensation package, and training—they are given supervision. Supervision is the fate of everyone who works for someone else. It is the expression of the employers' natural and continuous interest in the activities of their agents. Through supervision, employers hope to direct and motivate the salesforce to do a better job. Marketing Environment and Trends 24-1 indicates that much work still needs to be done.

Companies vary in how closely they direct their sales representatives. Sales representatives who are paid mostly on commission generally receive less supervision. Those who are salaried and must cover definite accounts are likely to receive substantial supervision.

Developing Norms for Customer Calls   In 1989, the average salesperson made 4.2 sales calls a day.[20] This was down from 5 daily sales calls in the early 1980s. The downward trend is due to the increased use of the phone and fax machines, the increased reliance on automatic ordering systems, and the drop in cold calls owing to better market research information for pinpointing prospects.

Companies also decide on how many calls to make a year on particular-size accounts. Most companies classify customers into A, B, and C accounts, reflecting the sales volume, profit potential, and growth potential of the account. A accounts might receive nine calls a year; B, six calls; and C, three calls. The call norms depend on competitive call norms and expected account profitability.

The real issue is how much sales volume could be expected from a particular account as a function of the annual number of calls. Magee described an experiment where similar accounts were randomly split into three sets.[21] Sales representatives were asked to spend less than five hours a month with accounts in the first set, five to nine hours a month with those in the second set, and more than nine hours a month with those in the third set. The results demonstrated that additional calls produced more sales, leaving only the question of whether the magnitude of sales increase justified the additional cost.

Developing Norms for Prospect Calls   Companies often specify how much time their salesforces should spend prospecting for new accounts. Spector Freight wants its sales representatives to spend 25 percent of their time prospecting and to stop calling on a prospect after three unsuccessful calls.

Companies set up prospecting standards for a number of reasons. If left alone, many sales representatives will spend most of their time with current customers. Current customers are better-known quantities. Sales representatives can depend upon them for some business, whereas a prospect might never deliver any business. Unless sales representatives are rewarded for opening new accounts, they might avoid new-account development. Some companies rely on a missionary salesforce to open new accounts.

Using Sales Time Efficiently   Sales representatives need to know how to use their time efficiently. One tool is the *annual call schedule* showing which customers and prospects to call on in which months and which activities to carry out.

> Sales representatives of Bell Telephone companies plan their calls and activities around three concepts. The first is *market development*—various efforts to educate customers, cultivate new business, and gain greater visibility in the buying community. The second is *sales-generating activities*—direct efforts to sell particular products to customers on particular calls. The third is *market-protection activities*—various efforts to learn what competition is doing and to protect relations with existing customers. The salesforce aims for some balance among these activities, so that the company does not achieve high current sales at the expense of long-run market development. ∎

Another tool is *time-and-duty analysis*. The sales representative spends time in the following ways:

- ☐ *Travel:* In some jobs, travel time amounts to over 50 percent of total time. Travel time can be cut down by using faster means of transportation—recognizing, however, that this will increase costs. Companies encourage air travel for their salesforce, to increase their ratio of selling to total time.

□ *Food and Breaks:* Some portion of the salesforce's workday is spent in eating and taking breaks.

□ *Waiting:* Waiting consists of time spent in the outer office of the buyer. This is dead time unless the sales representative uses it to plan or to fill out reports.

□ *Selling:* Selling is the time spent with the buyer in person or on the phone. It breaks down into "social talk" and "selling talk."

□ *Administration:* This consists of the time spent in report writing and billing, attending sales meetings, and talking to others in the company about production, delivery, billing, sales performance, and other matters.

No wonder actual face-to-face selling time can amount to as little as 25 percent of total working time![22] If it could be raised from 25 percent to 30 percent, this would be a 20 percent improvement. Companies are constantly seeking ways to use salesforce time effectively. Their methods take the form of training sales representatives in the use of "phone power," simplifying record-keeping forms, using the computer to develop call and routing plans, and supplying marketing research reports on customers.

To reduce time demands on their *outside salesforce*, many companies have increased the size and responsibilities of their *inside salesforce*. In a survey of 135 electronics distributors, Narus and Anderson found that an average of 57 percent of the salesforce members were inside salespeople.[23] Managers gave as reasons the escalating cost of outside sales calls and the growing use of computers and innovative telecommunications equipment. These managers think the proportion of inside salesforce members will reach two-thirds by 1990.

Inside salespeople include three types. There are *technical-support persons*, who provide technical information and answers to customers' questions. There are *sales assistants*, who provide clerical backup for the outside salespersons. They call ahead and confirm appointments, carry out credit checks, follow up on deliveries, and answer customers' questions when they cannot reach the outside sales rep. And there are *telemarketers*, who use the phone to find new leads, qualify them, and sell to them. A telemarketer can call up to fifty customers a day compared to the four that an outside salesperson can contact. They can be effective in the following ways:

□ Cross-selling compatible products

□ Upgrading orders

□ Introducing new company products

□ Opening new accounts and reactivating former accounts

□ Giving more attention to neglected accounts

□ Following up and qualifying direct-mail leads

The inside salesforce frees the outside sales reps to spend more time selling to major accounts, identifying and converting new major prospects, placing electronic ordering systems in customers' facilities, and obtaining more blanket orders and systems contracts. Meanwhile, the inside salespeople spend more time in checking inventory, following up orders, phoning smaller accounts, and so on. The outside sales reps are paid largely on an incentive-compensation basis, and the inside reps on a salary or salary plus bonus pay.

Another dramatic breakthrough in improving salesforce productivity is provided by new technological equipment—desktop and laptop computers, videocassette recorders, videodiscs, automatic dialers, electronic mail, fax machines, teleconferencing. The salesperson has truly gone "electronic." Not only is sales and inventory information transferred much faster, but specific computer-based decision support systems have been created for sales managers and sales representatives (see Marketing Environment and Trends 24-2).

Motivating Sales Representatives

Some sales representatives will put forth their best effort without any special coaching from management. To them, selling is the most fascinating job in the world. They are ambitious and self-starters. But the majority of sales representatives require encouragement and special incentives to work at their best level. This is especially true of field selling, for the following reasons:

Marketing Environment and Trends 24-2

SALESPEOPLE USE COMPUTERS AS A PRODUCTIVITY TOOL

Companies have been struggling with the twin problems of containing salesforce costs and improving information distribution between headquarters and field offices. *Sales automation* has been making inroads on both problems. The key idea is to help salespeople improve the speed with which they can find and qualify leads, gather information prior to a customer presentation, reduce their paperwork, and report sales results back to the company. The laptop computer has provided the answer. Although many salespeople initially resisted the computer—they couldn't type, they didn't have time to learn the software, and so on—many today don't know how they can operate without it.

Here is how sales automation worked at a large chemical company, which developed a laptop-computer-based software package consisting of several applications. Some applications had more initial appeal to the salesforce than others. The salesforce first responded to the *automatic-expense-statement* program because they could more easily and accurately record expenses and get reimbursed sooner. Soon the salesforce increased their use of the *sales-inquiry* function, which allowed them to retrieve the latest account-specific information, including phone numbers, addresses, recent developments and prices. No longer did they have to rely on clerical-staff assistance or obsolete data. *Electronic mail* allowed the

sales reps to rapidly receive and send messages to others. Various *corporate forms*, such as territory work plans and sales call reports could be filled out faster and sent electronically. The salesforce automation package also included an *appointment-calendar* function, a *to-do list* function, a *spreadsheet* function, and a *graphics software* package, which proved very helpful for salespeople to prepare charts and graphs for customer presentations.

Many of the large companies that have equipped their salesforces with laptops report sharp increases in the productivity of their sales reps. Some companies report increases of 5 to 10 percent in a salesperson's selling time because of less travel and paperwork, better call planning, and more effective calls. An insurance company believes that as much as 50 percent of its recent sales gains may be attributable to their salesforce's use of their laptop-computer-based sales-support system.

Sources: See Kate Bertrand, "Sales Management Software Tackles Toughest Customers," *Business Marketing*, May 1988, pp. 57-64; "Computer-Based Sales Support: Shell Chemical's System" (New York: Conference Board, Management Briefing: Marketing, April-May 1989), pp. 4-5; *Computers and the Sales Effort* (New York: Conference Board), August 1986; Thayer C. Taylor, "Computers in Sales and Marketing: S & MM's Survey Results," *Sales & Marketing Management*, May 1987, pp. 50-53; and "If Only Willy Loman Had Used a Laptop," *Business Week*, October 12, 1987, p. 137.

☐ *The Nature of the Job:* The selling job is one of frequent frustration. Sales representatives usually work alone; their hours are irregular; and they are often away from home. They confront aggressive, competing sales representatives; they have an inferior status relative to the buyer; they often do not have the authority to do what is necessary to win an account; they lose large orders that they have worked hard to obtain.

☐ *Human Nature:* Most people operate below capacity in the absence of special incentives, such as financial gain or social recognition.

☐ *Personal Problems:* Sales representatives are occasionally preoccupied with personal problems, such as sickness in the family, marital discord, or debt.

The problem of motivating sales representatives has been studied by Churchill, Ford, and Walker.[24] The basic model is shown below.

This says that the higher the salesperson's motivation, the greater his or her effort; greater effort will lead to greater performance; greater performance will lead to greater rewards; greater rewards will lead to greater satisfaction; and greater satisfaction will produce still greater motivation. This model implies the following:

1. *Sales managers must be able to convince salespeople that they can sell more by working harder or by being trained to work smarter.* But if sales are determined largely by economic conditions or competitive actions, this linkage is somewhat undermined.

2. *Sales managers must be able to convince salespeople that the rewards for better performance are worth the extra effort.* But if the rewards seem to be set arbitrarily or are too small or of the wrong kind, this linkage is undermined.

The researchers went on to measure the importance of different possible rewards. The reward with the highest value was *pay*, followed by *promotion, personal growth*, and *sense of accomplishment*. The least-valued rewards were *liking and respect, security*, and *recognition*. In other words, salespeople are highly motivated by pay and the chance to get ahead and satisfy their intrinsic needs, and less motivated by strokes and security. But the researchers also found that the importance of motivators varied with the salespersons' demographic characteristics:

1. Financial rewards were mostly valued by older, longer-tenured salespeople and those who had large families.

2. Higher-order rewards (recognition, liking and respect, sense of accomplishment) were more valued by young salespeople who were unmarried or had small families and usually more formal education.

We discussed compensation as a motivator earlier. Here we will examine sales quotas and some supplementary motivators.

Sales Quotas   Many companies set sales quotas prescribing what their sales representatives should sell during the year and by product. Compensation is often tied to the degree of quota fulfillment.

Sales quotas are developed from the annual marketing plan. The company first prepares a sales forecast. This forecast becomes the basis for planning production, workforce size, and financial requirements. Then management establishes sales quotas for its regions and territories, which typically add up to more than the sales forecast. Sales quotas are set higher than the sales forecast in order to stretch sales managers and salespeople to perform at their best level. If they fail to make their quotas, the company nevertheless might make its sales forecast.

Each area sales manager divides the area's quota among the area's sales representatives. There are three schools of thought on quota setting. The *high-quota school* sets quotas higher than what most sales representatives will achieve but that are attainable. Its adherents believe that high quotas spur extra effort. The *modest-quota school* sets quotas that a majority of the salesforce can achieve. Its adherents feel that the salesforce will accept the quotas as fair, attain them, and gain confidence. The *variable-quota school* thinks that individual differences among sales representatives warrant high quotas for some, modest quotas for others. According to Heckert:

> Actual experience with sales quotas, as with all standards, will reveal that sales representatives react to them somewhat differently, particularly at first. Some are stimulated to their highest efficiency, others are discouraged. Some sales executives place considerable emphasis upon this human element in setting their quotas. In general, however, good men will in the long run respond favorably to intelligently devised quotas, particularly when compensation is fairly adjusted to performance.[25]

Quotas can be set on dollar sales, unit volume, margin, selling effort or activity, and product type. One general view is that a salesperson's quota should be at least equal to the person's last year's sales plus some fraction of the difference between territory sales potential and last year's sales, the fraction being higher, the more the salesperson reacts favorably to pressure.

Supplementary Motivatiors Companies use additional motivators to stimulate salesforce effort. Periodic *sales meetings* provide a social occasion, a break from routine, a chance to meet and talk with "company brass," and a chance to air feelings and to identify with a larger group. Sales meetings are an important communication and motivational tool.[26]

Companies also sponsor *sales contests* to spur the salesforce to a special selling effort above what would normally be expected. The awards could be cars, vacations, fur coats, cash, or recognition. The contest should present a reasonable opportunity for enough salespeople to win. At IBM, about 70 percent of the salesforce makes their 100% Club. Their reward is a three-day trip that includes a recognition dinner and a blue and gold pin. If only a few salespersons can win or almost everyone can win, it will fail to spur additional effort. The sales contest period should not be announced in advance, or else some salespersons will defer some sales to the beginning of the period; also some may pad their sales during the period with customer promises to buy that do not materialize after the contest period ends.

Evaluating Sales Representatives

We have been describing the *feed-forward* aspects of sales supervision—how management communicates what the sales representatives should be doing and motivates them to do it. But good feed-forward requires good *feedback*. And good feedback means getting regular information from sales representatives to evaluate their performance.

Sources of Information Management obtains information about its sales representatives in several ways. The most important source is sales reports. Additional information comes through personal observation, customers' letters and complaints, customer surveys, and conversations with other sales representatives.

Sales reports are divided between *activity plans* and *writeups of activity results*. The best example of the former is the *salesperson's work plan*, which sales representatives submit a week or month in advance. The plan describes intended calls and routing. This report leads the salesforce to plan and schedule their activities, informs management of their whereabouts, and provides a basis for comparing their plans and accomplishments. Sales representatives can be evaluated on their ability to "plan their work and work their plan." Occasionally management contacts individual sales representatives after receiving their plans to suggest improvements.

Many companies require their sales representatives to develop an annual *territory marketing plan* in which they outline their program for developing new accounts and increasing business from existing accounts. This type of report casts sales representatives into the role of market managers and profit centers. Their sales managers study these plans, make suggestions, and use them to develop sales quotas.

Sales representatives write up their completed activities on call reports. Call reports inform sales management of the salesperson's activities, indicate the status of specific customer accounts, and provide useful information for subsequent calls. Sales representatives also submit expense reports, new-business reports, lost-business reports, and reports on local business and economic conditions.

These reports provide raw data from which sales managers can extract key indicators of sales performance. The key indicators are (1) average number of sales calls per salesperson per day, (2) average sales call time per contact, (3) average revenue per sales call, (4) average cost per sales call, (5) entertainment cost per sales call, (6) percentage of orders per hundred sales calls, (7) number of new customers per period, (8) number of lost customers per period, and (9) salesforce cost as a percentage of total sales. These indicators answer several useful questions: Are sales representatives making too few calls per day? Are they spending too much time per call? Are they spending too much on entertainment? Are they closing enough orders per hundred calls? Are they producing enough new customers and holding on to the old customers?

Formal Evaluation of Performance   The salesforce's reports along with other observations supply the raw materials for evaluating members of the salesforce. Formal evaluation procedures lead to at least three benefits. First, management has to communicate their standards for judging sales performance. Second, management needs to gather comprehensive information about each salesperson. And third, sales representatives know they will have to sit down one morning with the sales manager and explain their performance or failure to achieve certain goals.

Salesperson-to-Salesperson Comparisons   One type of evaluation is to compare and rank the sales performance of the various sales representatives. Such comparisons, however, can be misleading. Relative sales performances are meaningful only if there are no variations in territory market potential, workload, competition, company promotional effort, and so forth. Furthermore, current sales are not the only success indicator. Management should also be interested in how much each sales representative contributes to current net profits; this requires examining each sales representative's mix of products sold and sales expenses. Even more important is finding out how satisfied the salesperson's customers are with his or her service.

Current-to-Past Sales Comparisons   A second type of evaluation is to compare a sales representative's current performance and past performance. An example is shown in Table 24-1.

The sales manager can learn many things about John Smith from this table. Smith's total sales increased every year (line 3). This does not necessarily mean that Smith is doing a better job. The product breakdown shows that he has been able to push the sales of product B further than the sales of product A (lines 1 and 2). According to his quotas for the two products (lines 4 and 5), his success in increasing product B sales could be at the expense of product A sales. According to gross profits (lines 6 and 7), the company earns more selling A than B. Smith might be pushing the higher-volume, lower-margin product at the expense of the more profitable product. Although he increased total sales by $1100 between 1989 and 1990 (line 3), the gross profits on his total sales actually decreased by $580 (line 8).

Sales expense (line 9) shows a steady increase, although total expense as a percentage of total sales seems to be under control (line 10). The upward trend in Smith's total dollar expense does not seem to be explained by any increase in the number of calls (line 11), although it might be related to his success in acquiring new customers (line 14). There is a possibility that in prospecting for new customers, he is neglecting present customers, as indicated by an upward trend in the annual number of lost customers (line 15).

The last two lines show the level and trend in Smith's sales and gross profits per customer. These figures become more meaningful when they are compared with overall company averages. If John Smith's average gross profit per customer is lower than the company's average, he could be concentrating on the wrong customers or not spending enough time with each customer. A review of his annual number of calls (line 11) shows that Smith might be making fewer annual calls than the average salesperson. If distances in his territory are similar to other territories, this could mean that he is not putting in a full workday, he is poor at sales planning and routing, or he spends too much time with certain accounts.

Table 24-1 Form for Evaluating Sales Representative's Performance

	Territory: Midland Sales Representative: John Smith			
	1987	1988	1989	1990
1. Net sales product A	$251 300	$253 200	$270 000	$263 100
2. Net sales product B	$423 200	$439 200	$553 900	$561 900
3. Net sales total	$674 500	$692 400	$823 900	$825 000
4. Percent of quota product A	95.6	92.0	88.0	84.7
5. Percent of quota product B	120.4	122.3	134.9	130.8
6. Gross profits product A	$ 50 260	$ 50 640	$ 54 000	$ 52 620
7. Gross profits product B	$ 42 320	$ 43 920	$ 55 390	$ 56 190
8. Gross profits total	$ 92 580	$ 94 560	$109 390	$108 810
9. Sales expense	$ 10 200	$ 11 100	$ 11 600	$ 13 200
10. Sales expense to total sales (%)	1.5	1.6	1.4	1.6
11. Number of calls	1 675	1 700	1 680	1 660
12. Cost per call	$ 6.09	$ 6.53	$ 6.90	$ 7.95
13. Average number of customers	320	324	328	334
14. Number of new customers	13	14	15	20
15. Number of lost customers	8	10	11	14
16. Average sales per customer	$2 108	$2 137	$2 512	$2 470
17. Average gross profit per customer	$289	$292	$334	$326

Customer-Satisfaction Evaluation   John Smith might be quite effective in producing sales but not rate high with his customers. Perhaps he is slightly better than the competitors' salespeople, or his product is better, or he keeps finding new customers to replace others who don't like to deal with him. An increasing number of companies are measuring customer satisfaction not only with their product and customer-support service but with their salespeople. The customers' opinion of the salesperson, product, and service can be measured by mail questionnaires or telephone calls. Company salespeople who score high on satisfying their customers receive special recognition, awards, or bonuses.

Qualitative Evaluation of Sales Representatives   Evaluations also take into account the salesperson's knowledge of the company, products, customers, competitors, territory, and responsibilities. Personality characteristics can be rated, such as general manner, appearance, speech, and temperament. The sales manager can also review any problems in motivation or compliance. The sales manager should check that the sales representative knows and observes the law. Each company must decide what would be most useful to know. It should communicate these criteria to the sales representatives so that they know how their performance is judged and can make an effort to improve it.

PRINCIPLES OF PERSONAL SELLING

We turn now from designing and managing a salesforce to the purpose of a salesforce, namely, to sell. Personal selling is an ancient art. It has spawned a large literature and many principles. Effective salespersons have more than instinct; they are trained in a method of analysis and customer management. Selling today is a profession that involves mastering and applying a whole set of principles. There are many different styles of personal selling, some consistent with the marketing concept and some antithetical to the spirit of the marketing concept. We will examine three major aspects of personal selling: salesmanship, negotiation, and relationship management.

Selling

Today's companies spend millions of dollars each year to train their salespeople in the art of selling. Over a million copies of books, cassettes and videotapes on selling are purchased annually, with such tantalizing titles as *How to Outsell the Born Salesman, How to Sell Anything to Anybody, How Power Selling Brought Me Success in 6 Hours, Where Do You Go from No. 1?* and *1000 Ways a Salesman Can Increase His Sales.* One of the most enduring books is Dale Carnegie's *How to Win Friends and Influence People.*

All of the sales-training approaches try to convert a salesperson from being a passive *order taker* to an active *order getter. Order takers* operate on the following assumptions: Customers know their needs; they resent attempts at influence; and they prefer courteous and self-effacing salespersons. An example of an order-taking mentality would be a Fuller Brush salesperson who knocks on dozens of doors each day, simply asking consumers if they need any brushes.

In training salespersons to be *order getters*, there are two basic approaches, a *sales-oriented approach* and a *customer-oriented approach*. The first one trains the salesperson in *high-pressure selling techniques*, such as those used in selling encyclopedias or automobiles. The techniques include exaggerating the product's merits, criticizing competitive products, using a slick presentation, selling yourself, and offering some concession to get the order on the spot.

This form of selling assumes that the customers are not likely to buy except under pressure, that they are influenced by a slick presentation and ingratiating manners, and that they will not be sorry after signing the order, or if they are, it doesn't matter.

The other approach trains salespeople in *customer problem solving*. The salesperson learns how to listen and question in order to identify customer needs and come up with good product solutions. Presentation skills are made secondary to need analysis skills. The approach assumes that customers have latent needs that constitute company opportunities, that they appreciate constructive suggestions, and that they will be loyal to sales representatives who have their long-term interests at heart. The problem solver is a much more compatible image for the salesperson under the marketing concept than the hard seller or order taker.

No sales approach works best in all circumstances (see Marketing Concepts and Tools 24-2). Yet most sales-training programs agree on the major steps involved in any effective sales process. These steps are shown in Figure 24-3 and discussed below.[27]

Prospecting and Qualifying   The first step in the selling process is to identify prospects. Although the company will try to supply leads, sales representatives need skill in developing their own leads. Leads can be developed in the following ways:

☐ Asking current customers for the names of prospects

☐ Cultivating other referral sources, such as suppliers, dealers, noncompeting sales representatives, bankers, and trade association executives

☐ Joining organizations to which prospects belong

☐ Engaging in speaking and writing activities that will draw attention

☐ Examining data sources (newspapers, directories) in search of names

☐ Using the telephone and mail to track down leads

☐ Dropping in unannounced on various offices (cold canvassing)

Sales representatives need skill in screening out poor leads. Prospects can be qualified by examining their financial ability, volume of business, special requirements, location, and likelihood of continuous business. The salesperson might phone or write to prospects before deciding whether to visit them. The leads can be categorized as hot leads, warm leads, and eventual leads.

Preapproach   The salesperson needs to learn as much as possible about the prospect company (what it needs, who is involved in the purchase decision) and its buyers (their personal characteristics and buying styles). The salesperson can consult standard sources (*Moody's, Standard and Poor's, Dun and Bradstreet*), acquaintances, and others to learn about the company. The salesperson should set *call objectives*, which might be to qualify the prospect or gather information or make an immediate sale. Another task is to decide on the best *approach*, which might be a personal visit, a phone call, or a letter. The best *timing* should be thought out because many prospects are busy at certain times. Finally, the salesperson should plan an *overall sales strategy* for the account.

FIGURE. 24-3
Major Steps in Effective Selling

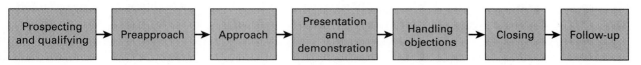

Marketing Concepts and Tools 24-2

THE VARIETY OF SELLING STYLES AND BUYING STYLES

Blake and Mouton distinguish selling styles along two dimensions, the salesperson's *concern for the sale* and *concern for the customer*. These two dimensions give rise to the *sales grid* shown below, which describes five types of salespersons. Type 1, 1 is very much the order taker and 9, 1 is the hard seller. Type 5, 5 is a soft seller, while the 1, 9 is "sell myself." Type 9, 9 is the problem-solving mentality, which is most consistent with the marketing concept.

Blake and Mouton argue that no one selling style is effective with all buyers. Furthermore, buying styles are just as varied. Buyers vary in their concern for the purchase and concern for the salesperson. Some buyers couldn't care less; some are defensive; some will only listen to salespersons from well-known companies.

Effective selling depends on matching the seller's style to the buyer's style. Evans sees selling as a *dyadic process*, where the outcome depends on the match of *buyer and seller characteristics* as well as on *buying and selling styles*. He found that people bought insurance from people very much like themselves in such factors as age, height, income, political opinions, religious beliefs, and smoking. What mattered was the perceived similarity more than the actual similarity. Evans proposed that insurance companies should hire all types of salespersons if they want to achieve broad market penetration. The only requirement is that they exhibit the intelligence and abilities effective in selling insurance.

Source: Robert R. Blake and Jane S. Mouton, *The Grid for Sales Excellence: Benchmarks for Effective Salesmanship* (New York: McGraw-Hill, 1970), p. 4. For additional reading, see Franklin B. Evans, "Selling as a Dyadic Relationship—a New Approach," *American Behavioral Scientist*, May 1963, pp. 76-79, at pp. 76 and 78. Also see Harry L. Davis and Alvin J. Silk, "Interaction and Influence Processes in Personal Selling," *Sloan Management Review*, Winter 1972, pp. 59-76; and Barton A. Weitz, Harish Sujan, and Mita Sujan, "Knowledge, Motivation, and Adaptive Behavior: A Framework for Improving Selling Effectiveness," Marketing Science Institute, working paper, November 1985.

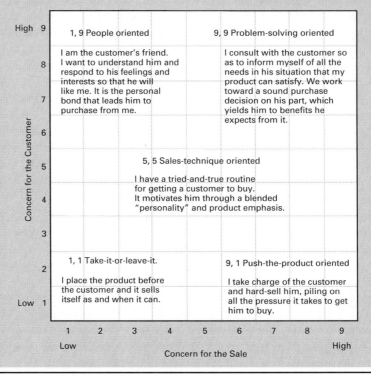

Approach   The salesperson should know how to greet the buyer to get the relationship off to a good start. This involves the salesperson's appearance, the opening lines, and the follow-up remarks. The salesperson might consider wearing clothes similar to what buyers wear (the construction industry dresses less formally than the banking industry); showing courtesy; avoiding distracting mannerisms, such as pacing the floor or staring at the customer. The opening line should be positive; for example, "Mr. Smith, I am Alice Jones from the ABC Company. My company and I appreciate your willingness to see me. I will do my best to make this visit profitable and worthwhile for you and your company." This might be followed by some key questions and active listening to understand the buyer and his or her needs better.

Presentation and Demonstration   The salesperson now tells the product "story" to the buyer, following the AIDA formula of gaining *attention*, holding *interest*, arousing *desire*, and obtaining *action*. The salesperson emphasizes throughout customer benefits, bringing in product features as evidence of these benefits. A benefit is any advantage, such as lower cost, less work, or more profit for the buyer. A feature is a product characteristic, such as weight or size. A common selling mistake is to dwell on product features (a product orientation) instead of customer benefits (a marketing orientation).

Companies have developed three different styles of sales presentation. The oldest is the *canned approach*, which is a memorized sales talk covering the main points. It is based on stimulus-response thinking; that is, the buyer is passive and can be moved to purchase by the use of the right stimulus words, pictures, terms, and actions. Thus an encyclopedia salesperson might describe the encyclopedia as "a once-in-a-lifetime buying opportunity" and focus on some beautiful four-color pages of sports pictures, hoping to trigger desire for the encyclopedia. Canned presentations are used primarily in door-to-door and telephone selling. The *formulated approach* is also based on stimulus-response thinking but identifies early the buyer's needs and buying style and then uses a formulated approach to this type of buyer. The salesperson initially draws the buyer into the discussion in a way that reveals the buyer's needs and attitudes. Then the salesperson moves into a formulated presentation that shows how the product will satisfy the buyer's needs. It is not canned but follows a general plan.

The *need-satisfaction approach* starts with a search for the customer's real needs by encouraging the customer to do most of the talking. This approach calls for good listening and problem-solving skills. The salesperson takes on the role of a knowledgeable *business consultant* hoping to help the customer save money or make more money. It is well described by an IBM sales representative: "I get inside the business of my key accounts. I uncover their key problems. I prescribe solutions for them, using my company's systems and even, at times, components from other suppliers. I prove beforehand that my system will save money or make money for my accounts. Then I work with the account to install the system and make it prove out."[28]

Sales presentations can be improved with demonstration aids such as booklets, flip charts, slides, movies, audio and video cassettes and actual product samples. To the extent that the buyer can see or handle the product, he or she will better remember its features and benefits. During the demonstration, the salesperson can draw on five influence strategies:[29]

☐ *Legitimacy:* The salesperson emphasizes the reputation and experience of his or her company.

☐ *Expertise:* The salesperson shows deep knowledge of the buyer's situation and company's products, doing this without being overly "smart."

☐ *Referent Power:* The salesperson builds on any shared characteristics, interests, and acquaintances.

☐ *Ingratiation:* The salesperson provides personal favors (a free lunch, promotional gratuities) to strengthen affiliation and reciprocity feelings.

☐ *Impression Management:* The salesperson manages to convey favorable impressions of himself or herself.

Handling Objections   Customers almost always pose objections during the presentation or when asked for the order. Their resistance can be psychological or logical. *Psychological resistance* includes resistance to interference, preference for established supply sources or brands, apathy, reluctance to giving up something, unpleasant associations about the other person, predetermined ideas, dislike of making decisions, and neurotic attitude toward money. *Logical resistance* might consist of objections to the price, delivery schedule, or certain product or company characteristics. To handle these objections, the salesperson maintains a positive approach, asks the buyer to clarify the objection, questions the buyer in a way that the buyer has to answer his or her own objection, denies the validity of the objection, or turns the objection into a reason for buying. The salesperson needs training in the broader skills of negotiation, of which handling objections is a part.

Closing   Now the salesperson attempts to close the sale. Some salespeople do not get to this stage or do not do it well. They lack confidence or feel uncomfortable about asking for the order or do not recognize the right psychological moment to close the sale. Salespersons need to know how to recognize closing signals from the buyer, including physical actions, statements or comments, and questions. Salespersons can use one of several closing techniques. They can ask for the order, recapitulate the points of agreement, offer to help the secretary write up the order, ask whether the buyer wants A or B, get the buyer to make minor choices such as the color or size, or indicate what the buyer will lose if the order is not placed now. The salesperson might offer the buyer specific inducements to close, such as a special price, an extra quantity at no charge, or a token gift.

Follow-Up   This last step is necessary if the salesperson wants to ensure customer satisfaction and repeat business. Immediately after closing, the salesperson should complete any necessary details on delivery time, purchase terms, and other matters. The salesperson should schedule a follow-up call when the initial order is received, to make sure there is proper installation, instruction, and servicing. This visit would detect any problems, assure the buyer of the salesperson's interest, and reduce any cognitive dissonance that might have arisen.

Negotiation

Much of business-to-business selling involves negotiating skills. The two parties need to reach agreement on the price and the other terms of sale. Salespersons need to win the order without making deep concessions that will hurt profitability.

Negotiation Defined   Marketing is concerned with exchange activities and the manner in which the terms of exchange are established. In *routinized exchange*, the terms are established by administered programs of pricing and distribution. In *negotiated exchange*, price and other terms are set via bargaining behavior. Arndt observed that a growing number of markets are coming under negotiated exchange, in which two or more parties negotiate long-term binding agreements (e.g., joint ventures, franchises, subcontracts, vertical integration). These markets are moving from being highly competitive to being highly "domesticated," that is, being less available to competitors.[30]

Although price is the most frequently negotiated issue, other issues include contract completion time; quality of goods and service offered; purchase volume; responsibility for financing, risk taking, promotion, and title; and product safety. The number of negotiation issues is virtually unlimited.

Bargaining, or *negotiation*, which we will use interchangeably, has the following features:

- [ ] At least two parties are involved.
- [ ] The parties have a conflict of interest with respect to one or more issues.
- [ ] The parties are at least temporarily joined together in a special kind of voluntary relationship.
- [ ] Activity in the relationship concerns the division or exchange of one or more specific resources and/or the resolution of one or more intangible issues among the parties or among those they represent.
- [ ] The activity usually involves the presentation of demands or proposals by one party and evaluation of these by the other, followed by concessions and counter proposals. The activity is thus sequential rather than simultaneous.[31]

Marketers who find themselves in bargaining situations need certain traits and skills to be effective. The most important traits are preparation and planning skill, knowledge of subject matter being negotiated, ability to think clearly and rapidly under pressure and uncertainty, ability to express thoughts verbally, listening skill, judgment and general intelligence, integrity, ability to persuade others, and patience. These will help the marketer in knowing when to negotiate and how to negotiate.[32]

When to Negotiate   Lee and Dobler have listed the following circumstances where negotiation is an appropriate procedure for concluding a sale:

1. When many factors bear not only on price, but also on quality and service.
2. When business risks cannot be accurately predetermined.
3. When a long period of time is required to produce the items purchased.
4. When production is interrupted frequently because of numerous change orders.[33]

Negotiation is appropriate whenever a *zone of agreement* exists.[34] A zone of agreement exists when there are simultaneously overlapping acceptable outcomes for the parties. This concept is illustrated in Figure 24-4. Suppose two parties are negotiating a price, and each privately establishes a *reservation price*. The seller has a reservation price, s, which is the minimum he will accept. Any final-contract value, x, that is below s is worse than not reaching an agreement at all. For any $x > s$, the seller receives a surplus. Obviously, the seller desires as large a surplus as possible while maintaining good relations with the buyer. Likewise, the buyer has a reservation price, b, that is the *maximum* he will pay; any x above b is worse than no agreement. For any $x < b$, the buyer receives a surplus. If the seller's reservation price is below the buyer's, that is, $s < b$, then a zone of agreement exists, and the final price will be determined through bargaining.

There is an obvious advantage in knowing the other party's reservation price and in making one's own reservation price seem higher (for a seller) or lower (for a buyer) than it really is. However, the openness with which buyers and sellers reveal their reservation prices depends upon the bargainers' personalities, the negotiation circumstances, and the expectation about future relations.

FIGURE 24-4

The Zone of Agreement

Source: Reprinted by permission
of the publishers from
*The Art and Science of
Negotiation*, by Howard
Raiffa, Cambridge, Mass.: the
Belknap Press of Harvard
University Press, copyright
© 1982 by the President and
Fellows of Harvard College.

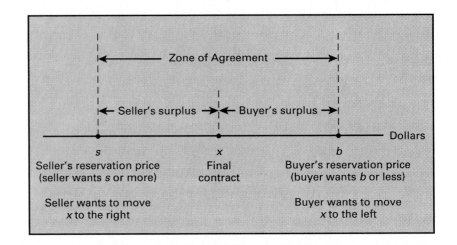

Formulating a Bargaining Strategy   Bargaining involves preparing a strategic plan before bargaining begins and making good tactical decisions during the bargaining sessions.

> A bargaining strategy *can be defined as a commitment to an overall approach that has a good chance of achieving the negotiator's objectives.*

For example, some negotiators pursue a "hard" strategy with opponents, while others maintain that a "soft" strategy yields more favorable results. Fisher and Ury propose another strategy, that of "principled negotiation."[35] They claim that this strategy will result in outcomes favorable to its adopter regardless of the strategy selected by the other party. The strategy of principled negotiation is

> to decide issues on their merits rather than through a haggling process focused on what each side says it will and won't do. It suggests that you look for mutual gains wherever possible, and that where your interests conflict, you should insist that the results be based on some fair standards independent of the will of either side. The method of principled negotiations is hard on the merits, soft on the people.[36]

Marketing Concepts and Tools 24-3 describes the four basic points of the principled-negotiation strategy.

Bargaining Tactics During Negotiations   Negotiators use a variety of tactics when bargaining.

> *Bargaining tactics can be defined as maneuvers to be made at specific points in the bargaining process.*

Threats, bluffs, last-chance offers, hard initial offers, and other tactics occur in bargaining. Advice includes "Don't tip your hand too early" and "Negotiate on your home ground whenever possible" (see Marketing Strategies 24-2).

Fisher and Ury have offered some tactical advice that is consistent with their strategy of principled negotiation. Their first piece of tactical advice concerns what should be done if the other party is more powerful. The best tactic is to know one's BATNA—Best Alternative to a Negotiated Agreement. By identifying one's alternatives if a settlement is not reached, it sets a standard against which any offer can be measured. It protects one from being pressured into accepting unfavorable terms from a more powerful opponent.

Marketing Concepts and Tools 24-3

THE PRINCIPLED-NEGOTIATION APPROACH TO BARGAINING

In a research program known as the Harvard Negotiation Project, Roger Fisher and William Ury arrived at four points for conducting "principled negotiations."

1. *Separate the People from the Problem:* Because people are involved in the bargaining, it is easy for emotions to become entangled with the objective merits of the issue being negotiated. Framing negotiation issues in terms of the personalities involved rather than the interests of the parties can lead to ineffective bargaining. Negotiation deteriorates when it becomes a test of wills instead of a joint problem-solving activity. Separating the people from the problem first involves making accurate perceptions. Each party must understand empathetically the opponent's viewpoint and try to feel the level of emotion with which they hold it. Second, emotions brought into or evolving out of negotiations should be made explicit and acknowledged as legitimate. Openly discussing emotions of both parties while not reacting to an emotional outburst helps keep negotiations from degenerating into unproductive name-calling sessions. Third, clear communications must exist between parties. Listening actively, acknowledging what is being said, communicating about problems rather than the opponent's shortcomings, and directly addressing interests will improve the chances of reaching a satisfactory solution.

2. *Focus on Interests, Not Positions:* The difference between positions and interests is that one's position is something one decided upon, while one's interests are what caused one to adopt the position. Thus a bargaining *position* may be that a contract must include a stiff penalty for late shipment; but the party's *interest* is to maintain an unbroken flow of raw materials. Reconciling interests works better because for every interest there usually exist several possible positions that could satisfy that interest.

3. *Invent Options for Mutual Gain:* Inventing options for mutual gain involves searching for a larger pie rather than arguing over the size of each slice. Looking for options that offer mutual gain helps identify shared interests.

4. *Insist on Objective Criteria:* When an opposing negotiator is intransigent and argues his position rather than his interests, a good strategy is to insist that the agreement must reflect some fair objective criteria independent of the position of either side. By discussing objective criteria instead of stubbornly held positions, neither party is yielding to the other; both are yielding to a fair solution. Such objective criteria may be market value, depreciated book value, competitive prices, replacement costs, wholesale price index, and so on.

Source: Adapted from Roger Fisher and William Ury, *Getting to Yes: Negotiating Agreement Without Giving In* (Boston: Houghton Mifflin Co., 1981), p. 57.

Another tactic comes into play when the opposing party insists on arguing his *position* instead of his *interests* and attacks one's proposals or person. While the tendency is to push back hard when pushed, the better tactic is to deflect the attack from the person and direct it against the problem. Look at the interests that motivated the opposing party's position and invent options that can satisfy both parties' interests. Invite the opposing party's criticism and advice ("If you were in my position, what would you do?").

Another set of bargaining tactics are responses to opposition tactics that are intended to deceive, distort, or otherwise influence the bargaining to their own advantage. What tactic should be used when the other side uses a threat, or a take-it-or-leave-it tactic, or seats the other party on the side of the table with the sun in his eyes? A negotiator should recognize the tactic, raise the issue explicitly, and question the tactic's legitimacy and desirability—in

SOME CLASSIC BARGAINING TACTICS

Here are several standard bargaining tactics:

☐ *Acting Crazy:* Put on a good show by visibly demonstrating your emotional commitment to your position. This increases your credibility and may give the opponent a justification to settle on your terms.

☐ *Big Pot:* Leave yourself a lot of room to negotiate. Make high demand at the beginning. After making concessions, you'll still end up with a larger payoff than if you started too low.

☐ *Get a Prestigious Ally:* The ally can be a person or a project that is prestigious. You try to get the opponent to accept less because the person/object he or she will be involved with is considered "prestigious."

☐ *The Well Is Dry:* Take a stand and tell the opponent you have no more concessions to make.

☐ *Limited Authority:* You negotiate in good faith with the opponent, and when you're ready to sign the deal, you say, "I have to check with my boss."

☐ *Whipsaw/Auction:* You let several competitors know you're negotiating with them at the same time. Schedule competitors' appointments with you for the same time and keep them all waiting to see you.

☐ *Divide and Conquer:* If you're negotiating with the opponent's team, sell one member of the team on your proposals. That person will help you sell the other members of the team.

☐ *Get Lost/Stall for Time:* Leave the negotiation completely for a while. Come back when things are getting better and try to renegotiate then. Time period can be long (say you're going out of town) or short (go to the bathroom to think).

☐ *Wet Noodle:* Give no emotional or verbal response to the opponent. Don't respond to his or her force or pressure. Sit there like a wet noodle and keep a "poker face."

☐ *Be Patient:* If you can afford to outwait the opponent, you'll probably win big.

☐ *Let's Split the Difference:* The person who first suggests this has the least to lose.

☐ *Play the Devil's Advocate:* Argue against the opponent's proposal by stating, "Before I say yes or no, let's look at all the bad things that could possibly happen if we did what you want." This lets you show the opponent your better way of achieving his or her objectives without directly opposing the opponent's viewpoint.

☐ *Trial Balloon:* You release your decision through a so-called reliable source before the decision is actually made. This enables you to test reaction to your decision.

☐ *Surprises:* Keep the opponent off balance by a drastic, dramatic, sudden shift in your tactics in general. Never be predictable—keep the opponent from anticipating your moves.

Source: From a list of over two hundred tactics prepared by Professor Donald W. Hendon of the University of Hawaii in his seminar "How to Negotiate and Win."

other words, negotiate over it. Negotiating the use of the tactic follows the same principled negotiation procedure: Question the tactic, ask why the tactic is being used, or suggest alternative courses of action to pursue. If this fails, resort to one's BATNA and terminate the negotiation until the other side ceases to employ these tactics. Meeting these tactics by defending principles is more productive than counterattacking with tricky tactics.

Relationship Management

The principles of personal selling and negotiation are *transaction oriented*, that is, their aim is to help marketers close a specific sale with a customer. There is a larger concept, however, that should guide the seller's dealings with customers, that of *relationship management*. The seller who knows how to build and manage strong relationships with key customers will have plenty of future sales from these customers. Relationship management is a key skill needed by marketers.

Relationship management is most appropriate with those customers who can most affect the company's future. For many companies, the top 20 percent of the customers account for a disproportionate share of the company's sales. Salespeople working with key customers must do more than call when they think customers might be ready to place orders. They should call or visit at other times, taking customers to dinner, making useful suggestions about their business, and so on. They should monitor these key accounts, know their problems, and be ready to serve them in a number of ways.

Here are two examples:

> The marketing vice-president of a Vancouver construction firm has as a major account a large fast-food franchiser headquartered in Hamilton. When he travels to Hamilton, he always contacts the marketing vice-president of the fast-food franchising firm and takes him out to dinner or a show. He also invites this manager on skiing trips and golf outings. He rarely asks the fast-food franchiser for any business. Some people have called this LGD marketing: "lunch, golf, and dinner marketing." ■

> A major consulting firm observed that it had repeat business from certain clients and no repeat business from others. It discovered that some of its consultants were good at managing relationships and getting repeat business, and others were good at managing projects but not relationships. The consulting firm identified its key clients and made sure that consultants skilled in relationship building were assigned to them. ■

Relationship management will undoubtedly play an increasing role in the future. Companies are recognizing that they earn a higher return from repeat sales from current customers than from spending money to attract new customers. Companies are recognizing more cross-selling opportunities with their current customers. More companies are forming strategic partnerships, and skilled relationship management is essential. And for customers who buy large, complex products—such as cement factories, robotic equipment, or large computer systems—the sale is only the beginning of the relationship. Levitt sees a growing movement toward relationship marketing (see Table 24-2).[37] Barbara Jackson agrees, although she does not think relationship marketing is appropriate in all situations. (See Marketing Strategies 24-3.)

Table 24-2 The Movement Toward Relationship Marketing

Category	Past	Present	Future
Item	Product	Augmented product	System contracts
Sale	Unit	System	System/time
Value	Feature advantage	Technology advantages	System advantages
Lead time	Short	Long	Lengthy
Service	Modest	Important	Vital
Delivery place	Local	National	Global
Delivery phase	Once	Frequently	Continuous
Strategy	Sales	Marketing	Relationship

Source: Theodore Levitt, *The Marketing Imagination* (New York: Free Press, 1983), p. 116.

WHEN—AND HOW—TO USE RELATIONSHIP MARKETING

Barbara Jackson argues that relationship marketing is not effective in all situations but is extremely effective in the right situations. She sees transaction marketing as more appropriate with customers who have a short time horizon and low switching costs, such as buyers of commodities. A customer buying steel can buy from one of several steel suppliers and choose the one offering the best terms. The fact that one steel supplier has been particularly attentive or responsive does not automatically earn it the next sale; its terms have to be competitive. Jackson calls these always-a-share customers.

On the other hand, relationship marketing investments pay off handsomely with customers who have long time horizons and high switching costs, such as buyers of office automation systems. Presumably, the customer for a major system carefully researches the competing suppliers and chooses one to work with from whom it can expect good long-term service and state-of-the-art technology. Both the customer and the supplier invest a lot of money and time in the relationship. The customer would find it costly and risky to switch to another vendor, and the seller would find that losing this customer would be a major loss. Jackson calls these lost-for-good customers, and here relationship marketing has the greatest payoff.

In "lost-for-good" situations, the challenge is different for the in-supplier versus out-supplier. The in-supplier's strategy is to make switching difficult for the customer. The in-supplier will develop product systems that are incompatible with competitive products and will install proprietary ordering systems that facilitate inventory management and delivery. On the other hand, the out-supplier will design product systems that are compatible with the customer's system, are easy to install and learn, save the customer a lot of money, and promise to improve through time.

Anderson and Narus believe that transaction versus relationship marketing is not so much an issue of the type of industry as it is an issue of the wishes of the particular customer. Some customers value a high service bundle and will stay with that supplier for a long time. Other customers want to cut their costs and will switch suppliers for lower costs. In this case, the company can still try to retain the customer by agreeing to reduce the price provided the customer is willing to accept fewer services; for example, the customer may forego free delivery, some training, and so on. This customer would be treated on a transaction basis rather than on a relationship-building basis. As long as the company cuts its own costs by as much or more than its price reduction, the "transaction-oriented" customer will still be profitable.

Clearly, relationship marketing is not appropriate with all customers in that heavy relationship investments will not always pay off. But it is extremely effective with the right type of customers, who get heavily committed to a specific system and expect consistent and timely service.

Sources: Barbara Bund Jackson, *Winning and Keeping Industrial Customers: The Dynamics of Customer Relationships* (Lexington, Mass.: Heath, 1985); and James C. Anderson and James A. Narus, "Value-Based Segmentation, Targeting and Relationship-Building in Business Markets," ISBM report no. 12, 1989, Institute for the Study of Business Markets, Pennsylvania State University, University Park, 1989.

Here are the main steps in establishing a relationship management program in a company:

- ☐ *Identify the key customers meriting relationship management:* The company can choose the five or ten largest customers and designate them for relationship management. Additional customers can be added who show exceptional growth or who pioneer new developments in the industry, and so on.

Table 24-3 Actions Affecting Buyer-Seller Relationships

Things Affecting Relationships	
Good Things	Bad Things
Initiate positive phone calls	Make only callbacks
Make recommendations	Make justifications
Candor in language	Accommodative language
Use phone	Use correspondence
Show appreciation	Wait for misunderstandings
Make service suggestions	Wait for service requests
Use "we" problem-solving language	Use "owe-us" legal language
Get to problems	Only respond to problems
Use jargon/shorthand	Use long-winded communications
Personality problems aired	Personality problems hidden
Talk of "our future together"	Talk about making good on the past
Routinize responses	Fire drill/emergency responsiveness
Accept responsibility	Shift blame
Plan the future	Rehash the past

Source: Theodore Levitt, *The Marketing Imagination* (New York: Free Press, 1983), p. 119.

☐ *Assign a skilled relationship manager to each key customer:* The salesperson who is currently servicing the customer should receive training in relationship management or be replaced by someone who is more skilled in relationship management. The relationship manager should have characteristics that match or appeal to the customer.

☐ *Develop a clear job description for relationship managers:* It should describe their reporting relationships, objectives, responsibilities, and evaluation criteria. The relationship manager is responsible for the client, is the focal point for all information about the client, and is the mobilizer of company services for the client. Each relationship manager will have only one or a few relationships to manage.

☐ *Appoint an overall manager to supervise the relationship managers:* This person will develop job descriptions, evaluation criteria, and resource support to increase relationship managers' effectiveness.

☐ *Each relationship manager must develop long-range and annual customer-relationship plans:* The annual relationship plan will state objectives, strategies, specific actions, and required resources.

When a relationship management program is properly implemented, many aspects of dealing with customers will change (see Table 24-3). The organization will begin to focus as much on managing its customers as on managing its products.

SUMMARY

Most companies use sales representatives, and many companies assign them the pivotal role in the marketing mix. Sales people are very effective in achieving certain marketing objectives. At the same time, they are very costly. Management must carefully design and manage its personal-selling resources.

Salesforce design calls for decisions on objectives, strategy, structure, size, and compensation. Salesforce objectives include prospecting, communicating, selling and servicing, information gathering, and allocating. Salesforce strategy involves deciding what types and mix and selling approaches are most effective (solo selling, team selling, and so on). Salesforce structure involves organizing by territory, product, market, or some hybrid combination and developing the right territory size and shape. Salesforce size involves estimating the total workload and how many sales hours—and hence salespersons—would be needed. Salesforce compensation involves determining pay level and pay components, such as salary, commission, bonus, expenses, and fringe benefits.

Managing the salesforce involves recruiting and selecting sales representatives and training, directing, motivating, and evaluating them. Sales representatives must be recruited and selected carefully to hold down the high costs of hiring the wrong persons. Sales-training programs familiarize new salespeople with the company's history, its products and policies, the characteristics of the market and competitors, and the art of selling. Salespeople need direction on such matters as developing customer and prospect targets and call norms and using their time efficiently. Salespeople need encouragement through economic and personal rewards and recognition, because they must make tough decisions and are subject to many frustrations. The key idea is that appropriate salesforce motivation will lead to more effort, better performance, higher reward, higher satisfaction, and more motivation. The last management step calls for periodically evaluating each salesperson's performance to help the person do a better job.

The purpose of the salesforce is to sell, and selling is an art. Selling is a seven-step process: prospecting and qualifying, preapproach, approach, presentation and demonstration, handling objections, closing, and follow-up. Another aspect of selling is negotiation, the art of arriving at transaction terms that satisfy both parties. A third aspect is relationship management, the art of creating a closer working relation and interdependence between the people in two organizations.

■ QUESTIONS

1. Describe the functions that might be fulfilled by a salesperson. Give examples for each of these functions.

2. Review the six tasks of the salesperson. Are these tasks performed (and by whom) in (a) a hospital? (b) a university?

3. Discuss and evaluate the purpose of each of the following procedures used as standards for evaluation: salesperson-to-salesperson comparisons, current-to-past-sales comparisons, qualitative evaluations, and key indicators.

4. Describe the major variations in salesforce structure. Assume you had a salesforce of eighty people selling four major product groups to four types of retailers. How would the selling function be managed under each variation? What factors would you consider in evaluating each structure?

5. Apart from personal-selling skills, what other factors can help or hinder a salesperson's performance?

6. In what ways has the customer been viewed in the buying-selling transaction? What perspective does Levitt say should form the buyer-seller transaction? What rights do you think customers would be entitled to under this concept?

7. Select a bargaining situation between a marketing agent and another party (internal or external to the firm) and discuss how the principled-negotiation approach could be used successfully to reach agreement for both parties.

8. You are a member of a marketing team negotiating with a potential customer over a robotics system for her production line. The other party is attempting to use the "divide and conquer" tactic described in Marketing Strategies 24-2. What is your response to this tactic?

9. A district sales manager voiced the following complaint at a sales meeting: "The average salesperson costs our company $40 000 in compensation and expenses. Why can't we buy a few less $40 000 full-page advertisements in *Maclean's* and use the money to hire more people? Surely

one individual working a full year can sell more products than a one-page ad in one issue of *Maclean's*." Evaluate this argument.

10. A sales manager wants to determine how many sales calls per month the salesforce should make to average-size accounts. Describe how an experiment might be set up to answer the question.

11. A sales manager is trying to figure out the most that should be spent to win a particular account. This account would produce sales of $10 000 a year; the company's profit margin on sales is 15 percent. The company wants its various investments to earn 8 percent. What is the most that the company should spend to win this account?

12. Suppose a salesperson can make 1600 calls a year. If he or she has been writing $420 000 worth of business a year, how many calls can the salesperson make to a $10 000-a-year account without diluting the total business written during the year?

13. Describe several types of selling situations where a straight salary plan seems appropriate.

14. Should sales representatives participate in the establishment of sales quotas for their territories? What would be the advantages and disadvantages of their participation?

■ NOTES

1. Statistics Canada, *Catalogue 12-565E*, 1989.

2. Adapted from Robert N. McMurry, "The Mystique of Super-Salesmanship," *Harvard Business Review*, March-April 1961, p. 114. For a study of other classifications, see William C. Moncrief, III, "Selling Activity and Sales Position Taxonomies for Industrial Salesforces," *Journal of Marketing Research*, August 1986, pp. 261-70.

3. The McGraw-Hill cost includes salespeople's salaries, commissions, bonuses, and travel and entertainment expenses. However, the Dartnell Corporation disputes this figure. Their survey puts the cost of a sales call (compensation, field expenses, and benefits) at $65 in 1989, but their figure does not distinguish between industrial and other sales calls or between out-of-town and in-town sales calls. (Dartnell's study shows the average varying greatly by industry; for example, the average cost of a sales call to sell instruments was $226.) Dartnell's study adds that the average business-to-business sale takes 3.6 sales calls to close. Using their numbers, a company spends an average of $234 (= $65 × 3.6) to make a sale. See *Sales Force Compensation* (Chicago, Ill.: Dartnell's 25th Survey, 1989), p. 13.

4. Roger M. Pegram, *Selling and Servicing the National Account* (New York: Conference Board, 1972).

5. William H. Kaven, *Managing the Major Sale* (New York: American Management Association, 1971); Benson P. Shapiro and Ronald S. Posner, "Making the Major Sale," *Harvard Business Review*, March-April 1976, pp. 68-78; and Mack Hanan, *Key Account Selling* (New York: Amacom 1982).

6. See Rayna Skolnik, "Campbell Stirs Up Its Salesforce," *Sales & Marketing Management*, April 1986, pp. 56-58.

7. Andris A. Zoltners and Prabhakant Sinha, "Sales Territory Alignment: A Review and Model," *Management Science*, November 1983, pp. 1237-56; and Leonard M. Lodish, "Sales Territory Alignment to Maximize Profits," *Journal of Marketing Research*, February 1975, pp. 30-36.

8. See Thayer C. Taylor, "Xerox's Sales Force Learns a New Game," *Sales & Marketing Management*, July 1, 1986, pp. 48-51; and Taylor, "Xerox's Makeover," *Sales & Marketing Management*, June 1987, p. 68.

9. "1989 Survey of Selling Costs," *Sales and Marketing Management*, February 20, 1989, p. 16.

10. *Ibid*. The percentages total to more than 100 percent, because some companies use more than one type of plan.

11. George H. Lucas, Jr., A. Parasuraman, Robert A. Davis, and Ben M. Enis, "An Empirical Study of Salesforce Turnover," *Journal of Marketing*, July 1987, pp. 34-59.

12. McMurry, "Super-Salesmanship," p. 117.

13. *Ibid.*, p. 118.

14. David Mayer and Herbert M. Greenberg, "What Makes a Good Salesman?" *Harvard Business Review*, July-August 1964, pp. 119-25.

15. John C. Crawford and James R. Lumpkin, "The Choice of Selling as a Career," *Industrial Marketing Management*, October 1983, pp. 257-61.

16. James M. Comer and Alan J. Dubinsky, *Managing the Successful Sales Force* (Lexington, Mass.: Lexington Books, 1985), pp. 5-25.

17. From an address given by Donald R. Keough at the twenty-seventh annual conference of the Super-Market Institute, Chicago, April 26-29, 1964.

18. "Double-Digit Hikes in 1974 Sales Training Costs," *Sales and Marketing Management*, January 6, 1974, p. 54.

19. Patricia Sellers, "How IBM Teaches Techies to Sell," *Fortune*, June 6, 1988, pp. 141 ff.

20. *Sales Force Compensation*.

21. See John F. Magee, "Determining the Optimum Allocation of Expenditures for Promotional Effort with Operations Research Methods," in *The Frontiers of Marketing Thought and Science*, ed. Frank M. Bass (Chicago: American Marketing Association, 1958), pp. 140-56.

22. "Are Salespeople Gaining More Selling Time?" *Sales and Marketing Management*, July 1986, p. 29.

23. James A. Narus and James C. Anderson, "Industrial Distributor Selling: The Roles of Outside and Inside Sales," *Industrial Marketing Management* 15 (1986), 55-62.

24. See Gilbert A. Churchill, Jr., Neil M. Ford, and Orville C. Walker, Jr., *Sales Force Management: Planning, Implementation and Control* (Homewood, Ill.: Irwin, 1985).

25. J. B. Heckert, *Business Budgeting and Control* (New York: Ronald Press, 1946), p. 138.

26. Richard Cavalier, *Sales Meetings That Work* (Homewood, Ill.: Dow Jones-Irwin, 1983).

27. Some of the following discussion is based on W. J. E. Crissy, William H. Cunningham, and Isabella C. M. Cunningham, *Selling: The Personal Force in Marketing* (New York: John Wiley, 1977), pp. 119-29.

28. Mark Hanan, "Join the Systems Sell and You Can't Be Beat," *Sales and Marketing Management*, August 21, 1972, p. 44. Also see Hanan, James Cribbin, and Herman Heiser, *Consultative Selling* (New York: American Management Association, 1970).

29. See Rosann L. Spiro and William D. Perreault, Jr., "Influence Use by Industrial Salesmen: Influence Strategy Mixes and Situational Determinants," paper, Graduate School of Business Administration, University of North Carolina, 1976.

30. Johan Arndt, "Toward a Concept of Domesticated Markets," *Journal of Marketing*, Fall 1979, pp. 69-75.

31. Jeffrey Z. Rubin and Bert R. Brown, *The Social Psychology of Bargaining and Negotiation* (New York: Academic Press, 1975), p. 18.

32. For additional reading, see Howard Raiffa, *The Art and Science of Negotiation* (Cambridge, Mass.: Harvard University Press, 1982); Samuel B. Bacharach and Edward J. Lawler, *Bargaining: Power, Tactics, and Outcome* (San Francisco: Jossey-Bass, 1981); Herb Cohen, *You Can Negotiate Anything* (New York: Bantam Books, 1980); and Gerard I. Nierenberg, *The Art of Negotiating* (New York: Pocket Books, 1984).

33. Lamar Lee and Donald W. Dobler, *Purchasing and Materials Management* (New York: McGraw-Hill, 1977), pp. 146-47.

34. This discussion of zone of agreement is fully developed in Raiffa, *Art and Science of Negotiation*.

35. Roger Fisher and William Ury, *Getting to Yes: Negotiating Agreement without Giving In* (Boston: Houghton Mifflin, 1981).

36. *Ibid.*, p. xii.

37. Theodore Levitt, *The Marketing Imagination* (New York: Free Press, 1983), Chap. 6, "Relationship Management," pp. 111-26.

PART VI

Organizing Implementing, and Controlling Marketing Effort

25

Organizing and Implementing Marketing Programs

It is not enough to have good principles; we must have organization also. Principles without organization may lose, but organization without principles may often win.

Sir Wilfrid Laurier

We now turn from the *strategic* and *tactical* sides of marketing to the *administrative* side to examine how firms organize, implement, and control their marketing activities. In this chapter, we will ask: What trends are occurring in company organization? How is marketing organized in various companies? What is the marketing department's relation to each key business function? What steps can a company take to build a stronger market orientation? How can a company improve its marketing-implementation skills? In the next chapter, we will examine concepts and tools for evaluating and controlling marketing performance.

COMPANY ORGANIZATION

Companies need fresh concepts on how to organize their business and marketing in response to significant changes that have occurred in the business environment in recent years. Advances in computers and telecommunication, global competition, increasing buyer sophistication, the growing importance of service, and several other forces are requiring companies to reconsider how to organize their business.

In response to these changes, companies have restructured along several lines. Companies are increasingly focusing on their core businesses or at least closely related businesses. In the 1960s and 1970s, many companies diversified into totally unrelated industries. Although the industries looked promising, the companies lacked the strength and knowledge to compete. Examples are K-tel's venture in the oil and gas business, and Lavalin's diversification beyond engineering projects.

Managers of large companies learned that making existing businesses grow was not the same as starting successful new businesses. Small entrepreneurs did the latter. So companies began to cultivate "intrapreneurship" by giving more freedom to their executives to produce ideas and take some risk. If 3M could do it, so could they.

Companies also reduced the number of organizational levels in order to get closer to the customer. One large utility's organization had 19 levels. Clearly, top management was too far removed from customers to fully understand what was happening in their markets. One corrective was to advise managers at all levels to do more "managing by walking around." But a more fundamental corrective was to flatten the organization. Tom Peters proposed that no well-managed organization would have more than five hierarchical levels. The implication was that each manager needed to manage more people. The key to doing this was to teach more employees to be self-managers.

Hierarchy also has been giving way to networking. With more companies using computers, electronic mail, and fax machines, messages increasingly pass between people at different levels of the organization. Companies encourage more teamwork as the key to improving performance.

In more traditional companies, the process of building and delivering value follows the flow shown in Figure 25-1(a). The process starts with the R&D department's searching for new ideas, screening them, and developing the more promising ones. Purchasing orders the parts, and manufacturing makes the product. Finance prices the product, marketing sells, advertises, and distributes it, and customer service provides the service.

Although the flow sounds logical, it has several weaknesses. The R&D staff often falls in love with new ideas that don't fit the interest or purchasing power of customers. They develop prototypes without consulting manufacturing, only to learn at a subsequent stage that manufacturing costs are too high and some redesign work is necessary. This results in higher costs and greater delays. The manufacturing department might take shortcuts that hurt quality, or they might resist adding features that marketing believes will help sell the product. Marketing inherits a product to sell on which it had minimum influence, and yet it is held responsible when the product doesn't sell well. The customer is seen as the end of the process rather than the beginning, and little is done to collect and use customer feedback to improve the product and the process.

FIGURE 25-1

Two Views of Creating Value

Source: Michael J. Lanning and Edward G. Michaels, "A Business Is a Value Delivery System," McKinsey staff paper, no. 41, June 1988. (McKinsey & Co., Inc.).

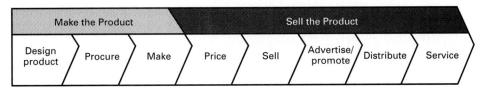

(a) Traditional Physical Process Sequence

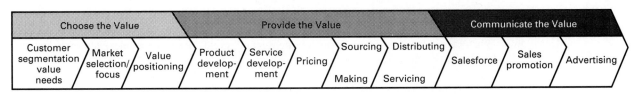

(b) The Value Creation and Delivery Sequence

What is missing from the traditional model is the concept of starting with the customer and applying teamwork throughout the process. Figure 25-1(b) shows the process, which starts with choosing the right value for the customer. This step is implemented by the company's marketing department, which collects value-building ideas from customers and other sources. The key departments participate in evaluating and selecting the better ideas. They work as a team to provide the value. Then marketing takes primary responsibility for communicating the value through its salesforce, sales promotion, and advertising.

The Japanese have further developed this view of the value-creation-and-delivery process by adding the following concepts:

☐ *Zero Customer Feedback Time*: Customer feedback should be continuously collected after purchase to learn how to improve the product and its marketing.

☐ *Zero Product-Improvement Time*: The company should evaluate all the customers' improvement ideas, as well as employee ideas, and introduce the most valued and feasible improvements as soon as possible.

☐ *Zero Purchasing Time*: The company should receive the required parts and supplies continuously through just-in-time arrangements with suppliers. By lowering its inventories, the company can reduce its costs.

☐ *Zero Setup Time*: The company should be able to manufacture any of its products as soon as they are ordered, without facing high setup costs or time.

☐ *Zero Defects*: The products should be of high quality and free of flaws.

In this context, we will now look at how marketing departments are organized.

MARKETING ORGANIZATION

Over the years, marketing has evolved from a simple sales function to a complex group of activities, not always well-integrated themselves or in relation to the firm's nonmarketing activities. Questions abound concerning the relationship between marketing managers at headquarters and salespeople in the field; about the future of brand management; about the need for a corporate vice-president of marketing; about marketing's relations to manufacturing, R&D, and finance; and so on. To gain some understanding, we will examine how marketing departments evolved in companies, how they are organized, and how they interact with other company departments.

The Evolution of the Marketing Department

The modern marketing department is the product of a long evolution. At least five stages can be distinguished, and some companies are still found in each stage.

Simple Sales Department   All companies start out with five simple functions. Someone must raise and manage capital (finance), hire people (personnel), produce the product or service (operations), sell it (sales), and keep the books (accounting). The selling function is headed by a sales vice-president, who manages a salesforce and also does some selling. When the company needs some marketing research or advertising, the sales vice-president also handles those functions [see Figure 25-2(a)].

Sales Department with Ancillary Marketing Functions   As the company expands to serve new types of customers or new geographical areas, it needs to strengthen certain

FIGURE 25-2
Stages in the Evolution of the Marketing Department

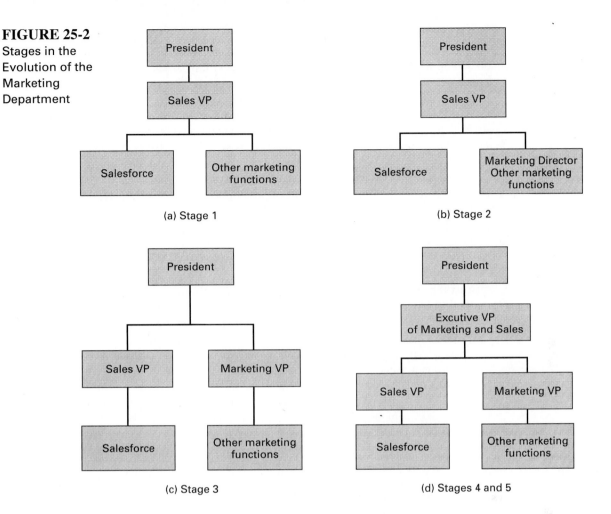

(a) Stage 1

(b) Stage 2

(c) Stage 3

(d) Stages 4 and 5

marketing functions other than sales. For example, an Ontario firm that plans to open in Quebec will first have to conduct marketing research to learn about customer needs and market potential. If it opens business in Quebec, it will have to advertise its name and products in the area. The sales vice-president will need to hire specialists to handle these these activities on a more expert basis. The sales vice-president may also decide to hire a *marketing director* to manage these functions [see Figure 25-2(b)].

Separate Marketing Department   The continued growth of the company increases the productive potential of investments in other marketing functions—marketing research, new-product development, advertising and sales promotion, customer service—relative to salesforce activity. Yet the sales vice-president normally continues to give disproportionate time and resources to the salesforce. The marketing director will appeal for more resources but will usually get less than needed. Some marketing directors will quit out of frustration.

Eventually the company president will see the advantage of establishing a separate marketing department [see Figure 25-2(c)]. The marketing department will be headed by a marketing vice-president, who reports, along with the sales vice-president, to the president or executive vice-president. At this stage, sales and marketing are separate functions in the organization that are expected to be working closely together.

This arrangement is used by many industrial companies. It permits the company president to get a more balanced view of company opportunities and problems. Suppose sales are falling and the company president asks the sales vice-president for solutions. The sales vice-president might recommend hiring more salespeople, raising sales compensation, running a sales contest, providing more sales training, or cutting the price so that the product will be easier to sell. The company president then asks the marketing vice-president for solutions. The marketing vice-president is less ready to suggest immediate price and salesforce solutions. The marketing vice-president will see the question more from the customer's point of view. Is the company going after the right customers? How do the target customers see the company and its products relative to competitors? Are there changes in product features, styling, packaging, services, distribution, other forms of promotion, and so on, that are warranted? In general, there will be more effort to understand the problem rather than going after it with a pure selling push.

Modern Marketing Department   Although the sales and marketing vice-presidents are supposed to work harmoniously, their relationship is occasionally strained and marked by distrust. The sales vice-president resents efforts to make the salesforce less important in the marketing mix; and the marketing vice-president seeks a larger budget for nonsalesforce activities. The sales vice-president is short-run oriented and preoccupied with achieving current sales. The marketing vice-president is more long-run oriented and preoccupied with planning the right products and marketing strategy to meet the customers' long-run needs.

If there is too much disharmony between sales and marketing, the company president might place marketing activities back under the sales vice-president, or instruct the executive vice-president to handle conflicts that arise, or place the marketing vice-president in charge of everything, including the salesforce. This last solution forms the basis of the modern marketing department, a department headed by a marketing and sales executive vice-president with managers reporting from every marketing function, including sales management [see Figure 25-2(d)].

Modern Marketing Company   A company can have a modern marketing department and yet not operate as a modern marketing company. The latter depends upon how the other company managers view the marketing function. If they view marketing as primarily a selling function, they are missing the point. If they point to the marketing department and say, "They do the marketing," they are missing the point. All the departments must work for the customer. Everyone is in marketing. Marketing is not only a department but a thorough-going company philosophy. Only then does a company turn into a modern marketing company.

Ways of Organizing the Marketing Department

Modern marketing departments take on numerous forms. All marketing organizations must accommodate four dimensions of marketing activity: *functions, geographical areas, products,* and *customer markets*.

Functional Organization   The most common form of marketing organization consists of functional-marketing specialists reporting to a marketing vice-president, who coordinates their activities. Figure 25-3 shows five specialists. Additional specialists might include a customer-service manager, a marketing-planning manager, and a physical-distribution manager.

The main advantage of a functional-marketing organization is its administrative simplicity. On the other hand, this form loses effectiveness as the company's products and markets

FIGURE 25-3
Functional Organization

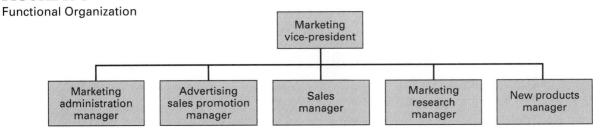

increase. First, there is inadequate planning for specific products and markets, since no one has full responsibility for any product or market. Products that are not favored by anyone are neglected. Second, each functional group competes to gain more budget and status vis-à-vis the other functions. The marketing vice-president has to constantly weigh the claims of competing functional specialists and faces a difficult coordination problem.

Geographical Organization   A company selling in a national market often organizes its salesforce (and sometimes other functions) along geographical lines. The national sales manager may supervise four regional sales managers, who each supervise six zone managers, who in turn supervise eight district sales managers, who supervise ten salespeople. The span of control increases as we move from the national sales manager down toward the district sales managers. Shorter spans allow managers to give more time to subordinates and are warranted when the sales task is complex, the salespersons are highly paid, and the salesperson's influence on profits is substantial.

Several companies are now adding *area market specialists* (regional or local marketing managers) to support the sales efforts in high-volume, distinctive markets. The local market specialist for Vancouver, for example, would know Vancouver's customer and trade makeup in great detail, and would help headquarters marketing managers adjust their marketing mix for Vancouver to take maximum advantage of the opportunities. The local market specialist would prepare annual and long-range plans for selling all the company's products in Vancouver, and would act as liaison between the headquarters marketing staff and the local salesforce (see Marketing Environment and Trends 25-1).

Product and Brand Management Organization   Companies producing a variety of products and brands often establish a product, or brand, management organization. The product management organization does not replace the functional management organization but serves as another layer of management. The product management organization is headed by a senior executive, who supervises several group product managers, each supervising several product (or brand) managers.

A product management organization makes sense if the products are quite different, or if the sheer number of products exceeds the ability of a functional-marketing organization to handle.

Product management first appeared in the Procter & Gamble Company in 1927. A new company soap, Camay, was not doing well, and one of the young executives, Neil H. McElroy (later president of P&G), was assigned to give his exclusive attention to developing and promoting this product. He did it successfully, and the company soon added other product managers.

Since then, many firms have established product management organizations. General Foods, for example, uses a product management organization in its Post Division. There are separate product group managers in charge of cereals, pet food, and beverages. Within the

Marketing Environment and Trends 25-1

REGIONALIZATION—A PASSING FAD OR THE NEW MARKETING ERA?

For most of this century, major consumer-products companies have held fast to two mass-marketing principles—product standardization and national brand identification. They have marketed the same set of products in about the same way all across the country. But recently, Campbell Soup, Procter & Gamble, General Foods, H. J. Heinz, and other companies have tried a new approach—regionalization. Instead of marketing in the same way nationally to all customers, they are tailoring their products, advertising, sales promotions, and personal selling efforts to suit the needs and tastes of specific regions, cities, and even neighborhoods.

Several factors have fueled the move toward regionalization. First, the mass market for many products has gradually broken down into smaller segments—teens, Westerners, single parents, francophones—the list goes on. Market fragmentation is everywhere, and marketers find it increasingly difficult to create a single product or program that appeals to all of these diverse groups. Second, improved information and marketing research technologies have also spurred regionalization. For example, data from retail-store scanners allow instant tracking of product sales from store to store, helping companies pinpoint local problems and opportunities that might call for localized marketing actions. A third important factor is the increasing power of retailers. Scanners give retailers mountains of market information, and this information gives them power over manufacturers. Furthermore, competition has increased dramatically in recent years for the precious shelf space controlled by retailers. The average supermarket now carries over three hundred thousand stock-keeping units, and about ten new products are introduced each day. Retailers are often lukewarm about large, national marketing campaigns aimed at masses of consumers. They strongly prefer local programs tied to their own promotion efforts and aimed at consumers in their own cities and neighborhoods. Thus, to keep retailers happy and to get shelf space for their products, manufacturers must now allot more and more of their marketing budgets to local, store-by-store promotions.

Campbell Soup, a pioneer in regionalization, has jumped in with both feet. For starters, Campbell has created many successful regional brands like Ranchero beans and Creole soup. These and other brands appealing to regional tastes add substantially to Campbell's annual sales. But perhaps more significantly, Campbell has reorganized its entire marketing operation to suit its regional strategy. Each of its regions has new responsibilities for planning local marketing programs, and each has its own advertising and promotion budgets. Currently, up to 20 percent of Campbell's marketing budget is allocated to the regions, but that may eventually increase to 50 percent.

Within each region, Campbell sales managers and salespeople now have the authority to create advertising and promotions geared to local market needs and conditions. They use local appeals and choose whatever local advertising media work best in their areas, ranging from newspapers and radio to parking meters, shopping carts, and church bulletins. And they work closely with local retailers on displays, coupon offers, price specials, and local promotional events. For example, one sales manager recently offered Campbell's Pork & Beans at a fifty-year-old price (five cents) to help a local retailer celebrate its fiftieth anniversary. Such localized efforts win retailer support and boost consumer sales.

Although regionalization offers much promise, it also presents some problems. Offering many different regional products and programs results in higher manufacturing and marketing costs. And letting area sales staffs make local marketing decisions causes some quality, planning, and control problems. Salespeople will need a lot of training and guidance.

Regionalization is still in its infancy—even Campbell has yet to implement the strategy fully. Some marketers view it as just a fad—they think

Sources: See Christine Dugas, Mark N. Vamos, Jonathan B. Levine, and Matt Rothmann, "Marketing's New Look," *Business Week*, January 26, 1987, pp. 64-69; Al Urbanski, "Repackaging the Brand Manager," *Sales & Marketing Management*, April 1987, pp. 42-45; Scott Hume, "Execs Favor Regional Approach," *Advertising Age*, November 2, 1987, p. 36; "National Firms Find that Selling to Local Tastes Is Costly, Complex," *Wall Street Journal*, February 9, 1987, p. B1; and Joe Schwartz, "Rock Soup," *American Demographics*, April 1989, p. 66.

cereal product group, there are separate product managers for nutritional cereals, children's presweetened cereals, family cereals, and miscellaneous cereals. In turn, the nutritional-cereal product manager supervises brand managers.[1]

The product manager's role is to develop product plans, see that they are implemented, monitor the results, and take corrective action. This responsibility breaks down into six tasks:

☐ Developing a long-range and competitive strategy for the product

☐ Preparing an annual marketing plan and sales forecast

☐ Working with advertising and merchandising agencies to develop copy, programs, and campaigns

☐ Stimulating support of the product among the salesforce and distributors

☐ Gathering continuous intelligence on the product's performance, customer and dealer attitudes, and new problems and opportunities

☐ Initiating product improvements to meet changing market needs

These basic functions are common to both consumer- and industrial-product managers. Yet there are some differences in their jobs and emphases. Consumer-product managers typically manage fewer products than industrial-product managers. They spend more time on advertising and sales promotion. They spend more time working with others in the company and various agencies and little time with customers. They are often younger and more educated. Industrial-product managers, by contrast, think more about the technical aspects of their product and possible design improvements. They spend more time with laboratory and engineering personnel. They work more closely with the salesforce and key buyers. They pay less attention to advertising, sales promotion, and promotional pricing. They emphasize rational product factors over emotional ones.

The product management organization introduces several advantages. First, the product manager develops a cost-effective marketing mix for the product. Second, the product manager can react more quickly to problems in the marketplace than a committee of specialists. Third, smaller brands are less neglected, because they have a product advocate. Fourth, product management is an excellent training ground for young executives, for it involves them in almost every area of company operations (see Figure 25-4).

But a price is paid for these advantages. First, product management creates some conflict and frustration.[2] Typically, product managers are not given enough authority to carry out their responsibilities effectively. They have to rely on persuasion to get the cooperation of advertising, sales, manufacturing, and other departments. They are told they are "minipresidents" but are often treated as low-level coordinators. They are burdened with a great amount of "housekeeping" paperwork. They often have to go over the heads of others to get something done.

FIGURE 25-4

The Product Manager's Interactions

Source: Adapted from "Product Managers: Just What Do They Think?"
Printer's Ink, October 28, 1966, p. 15.

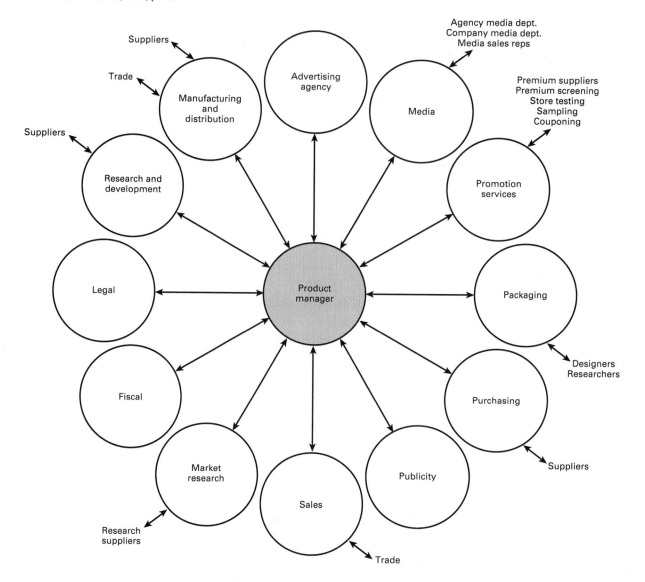

Second, product managers become experts in their product but rarely become experts in any functions. They vacillate between posing as experts and being cowed by real experts. This is unfortunate when the product depends on a specific type of expertise, such as advertising.

Third, the product management system often turns out to be costlier than anticipated. Originally, one person is appointed to manage each major product. Soon product managers are appointed to manage even minor products. Each product manager, usually overworked, pleads for and gets an *associate brand manager*. Later, both overworked, they persuade management to give them an *assistant brand manager*. With all these people, payroll costs climb. In the meantime, the company continues to increase its functional specialists in copy, packaging, media, sales promotion, market surveys, statistical analysis, and so on. The company becomes saddled with a costly structure of product management people and functional specialists.

Fourth, brand managers normally manage their brand for only a short time. Either product managers move up in a few years to another brand or product, or they transfer to another company, or they leave product management altogether. Their short-term involvement with the brand leads to short-term marketing planning and plays havoc with building up the brand's long-term strengths.

Pearson and Wilson have suggested five steps to make the product management system work better:[3]

□ *Clearly delineate the limits of the product manager's role and responsibility for the product*: (They are essentially proposers, not deciders.)

□ *Build a strategy-development-and-review process to provide an agreed-to framework for the product manager's operations*: (Too many companies allow product managers to get away with shallow marketing plans featuring a lot of statistics but little strategic rationale.)

□ *Take into account areas of potential conflict between product managers and functional specialists when defining their respective roles*: (Clarify which decisions are to be made by the product manager, which by the expert, and which will be shared.)

□ *Set up a formal process that forces to the top all conflict-of-interest situations between product management and functional line management*: (Both parties should put the issues in writing and forward them to general management for settlement.)

□ *Establish a system for measuring results that is consistent with the product manager's responsibilities*: (If product managers are accountable for profit, they should be given more control over the factors that affect their profitability.)

A second alternative is to switch from a product-manager to a product-team approach. In fact, there are three types of product-team structures in product management (see Figure 25-5).

□ *Vertical Product Team*: This consists of a product manager, associate product manager, and product assistant [Figure 25-5(a)]. The product manager is the leader and primarily deals with other executives to gain their cooperation. The associate product manager assists in these tasks and also does some paper work. The product assistant does most of the paperwork and routine analysis.

FIGURE 25-5
Three Types of Product
Teams

(a) Vertical
product team

(b) Triangular
product team

(c) Horizontal
product team

PM = product manager, APM = associate product manager,
PA = product assistant, R = market researcher,
C = communication specialist, S = sales manager,
D = distribution specialist, F = finance/accounting specialist
E = engineer

□ *Triangular Product Team*: This consists of a product manager and two specialized product assistants, one who takes care of (say) marketing research and the other, marketing communications [(Figure 25-5(b)]. Hallmark, the greeting card company, uses a "marketing team" type of organization, with each item consisting of a market manager (the leader), a marketing manager, and a distribution manager.

□ *Horizontal Product Team*: This consists of a product manager and several specialists from marketing and other functions [Figure 25-5(c)]. Thus the 3M Company divided its commercial tape division into nine business-planning teams, each team consisting of a team leader and representatives from sales, marketing, laboratory, engineering, accounting, and marketing research. Instead of a product manager's bearing the entire responsibility of product planning, he or she shares it with representatives from key parts of the company. Their input is critical in the marketing-planning process, and furthermore each team member can bring influence to bear in his or her own department. The ultimate step after a horizontal product team is to form a product division around the product.

A third alternative is to eliminate product-manager positions for minor products and assign two or more products to each remaining product manager. This is feasible especially where two or more products appeal to a similar set of needs. Thus a cosmetics company does not need separate product managers, because cosmetics serve one major need—beauty—whereas a toiletries company needs different managers for headache remedies, toothpaste, soap, and shampoo, because these products differ in their use and appeal.

Product management systems are undergoing several important changes.[4] Marketing Environment and Trends 25-2 discusses current developments affecting the future of brand management.

Market Management Organization

Many companies sell their products to a diverse set of markets. For example, Smith Corona sells its electric typewriters to consumer, business, and government markets. When customers fall into different user groups with distinct buying preferences and practices, a market management organization is desirable. A *markets manager* supervises several *market managers* (also called market development managers, market specialists, or industry specialists). The market managers draw upon functional services as needed. Market managers of important markets might even have some functional specialists reporting to them.

Market managers are staff, not line, people, with duties similar to those of product managers. Market managers develop long-range and annual plans for their markets. They must analyze where their market is going and what new products their company should offer to this market. Their performance is often judged by their contribution to market-share growth rather than to current profitability in their market. This system carries many of the same advantages and disadvantages of product-management systems. Its strongest advantage is that the marketing activity is organized to meet the needs of distinct customer groups rather than focusing on marketing functions, regions, or products per se.

Many companies are reorganizing along market lines. Hanan calls these companies *market-centered organizations* and argues that "the only way to ensure being market-oriented is to put a company's organizational structure together so that its major markets become the centers around which its divisions are built."[5] Alcan's organization targets its marketing efforts to the consumer market (aluminum foil), the contractor market (aluminum siding), and the industrial market (aluminum extrusions).

One of the most dramatic changes to market centeredness has occurred at the Heinz Company. Heinz was organized around a brand management system, with separate brand

Marketing Environment and Trends 25-2

WHAT'S THE FUTURE OF BRAND MANAGEMENT?

Brand management has become a well-established fixture in consumer-packaged-goods companies. Yet the environment in which it was created and thrived is drastically altered today, and observers are questioning whether it provides the best system for managing brands in the new environment.

Today's brand managers are in a double bind: they are under great pressure to produce increased profits while being given less latitude for achieving them. Top management wonders if they need all the group brand managers, brand managers, associate brand managers, and assistant brand managers. Companies are facing three new environmental forces that are calling into question the whole concept of brand managers:

1. *Growing Bargaining Power of the Distribution Channels and Growing Importance of Sales Promotion:* The major distributors of consumer packaged goods—supermarket chains and mass merchandisers—are growing more powerful and are demanding better terms from consumer-packaged-goods companies in exchange for scarce shelf space. These distributors are primarily interested in generating more store traffic, and they are pressing manufacturers for more trade deals. The heat is felt by the manufacturers' salesforces, who tell the brand managers that they cannot get shelf space without more trade deals. The result is that the brand managers shift more money into sales promotion and have less funds to build their brand franchises.

   Furthermore, giant retailers are demanding more multibrand and multicategory promotion deals from each manufacturer. They want customized multibrand deals that would enable them to compete better. These deals have to be worked out at higher levels of management than the brand level. But the brand managers have to be taxed to support these deals, sometimes by giving up about 25 percent of their budget. Brand managers are being left with less control over their sales-promotion funds.

   As sales promotion becomes more important, the manufacturers are realizing that they are not organized to handle it efficiently. Originally, sales promotion was handled individually by each brand manager. Some companies later appointed a sales-promotion specialist to help brand managers choose good premiums and couponing schemes for consumer sales promotion. Meanwhile, the company's salesforce keeps pressing for more trade-promotion money. The question becomes, How much should be spent on sales promotion out of the total budget and how should this money be split between trade and consumer promotion? Unfortunately, the decisions are being made politically rather than rationally.

2. *Declining Cost Effectiveness of Mass Advertising:* Brand managers are finding that they have less money to spend on advertising, the one tool they know best. Furthermore, mass advertising—particularly network television—is becoming less cost effective. There are fewer people watching network television, and many are not in the market for the advertised products. The money can be spent more effectively by studying category and brand interest levels market by market. But brand managers do not know the individual markets that well. Companies are increasingly developing area marketing plans through area specialists.

3. *Declining Level of Customer Brand Loyalty:* Consumers have been exposed to so much dealing that a growing number are deal prone rather than brand prone. The consumers' set of acceptable brands is increasing. As more consumers switch their brands each week depending on the deals, brand shares become more volatile. A brand's weekly or monthly market share means less and becomes less useful in deciding how much money to allocate to each brand. Higher levels of management have to decide how much funds to allocate to each brand.

These developments are forcing consumer-packaged-goods companies to rethink how they should develop and manage their brands. There are two competing solutions:

1. *Changing the Job Emphasis of the Brand Manager:* One line of thought is that the brand manager should spend less time creating the promotion plans and become more involved in product improvement and production. Normally, the brand manager has little time to think about creating flankers and brand extensions,

and this has forced companies to appoint new-product specialists within brand or category groups to do this work. And the brand manager does not become very involved in knowing the production and logistics steps and how to find cost improvements. Therefore, it might be argued that brand managers should have their responsibilities shifted more to product improvement and production/distribution efficiency concerns.

2. *Introducing Category Management*: Another line of thought is that a company should introduce a strong category focus in managing its brands. P&G found too much internal competition among its own brands within each category: Its Puritan and Crisco oils both fought for a budget increase, although one deserved it more than the other; its Cheer brand started to copy the same claim as its Tide brand, thus diluting Tide's positioning. P&G's answer: The brand managers are now accountable to a new corps of category managers, who resolve conflicts, protect positionings, allocate budgets, and develop new brands for the category. Nabisco took a different route. Instead of several cookie brand managers, it has three cookie-category management teams: adult rich cookies, children's cookies, and nutritional cookies. Each category team manages several brands with specialists handling advertising, sales promotion, packaging, line extension, and business development. The net result is to reduce the number of middle managers, thus creating a leaner organization.

In reducing the number of brand managers, their counterparts in advertising agencies—namely, account executives—might also be reduced. Many consumer-packaged-goods companies are pressing advertising agencies to lower their costs, especially considering the reduced effectiveness of mass advertising. These companies normally prepare their own brand marketing plans and simply want a good creative plan and media plan from their advertising agency. They wonder why they have to work through account executives and their assistants. Some companies are telling their advertising agencies they are going to pay less or else switch agencies, thus forcing these agencies to reconsider their own organizing patterns and the role of the account executives.

Making changes in the brand management system will not be easy. Everyone involved in brand management will fight changes, since these changes will destroy the normal promotion ladder in the organization. Any company that is rumored to be thinking about abandoning brand management will lose some of its best people before it can reorganize, and the transition will be difficult.

Yet changes are called for. The fact is that brand management is a sales-driven, not a customer-driven, system. Brand managers focus on pushing out their brands to anyone and everyone. Category management simply shifts the emphasis to a broader definition of product (cookie vs Oreo). Colgate recently has moved from *brand management* (Colgate toothpaste) to *category management* (toothpaste) to a new stage, *customer-need management* (oral health). This last step finally gets the organization to focus on a customer need.

Sources: For further reading, see Robert Dewar and Don Schultz, "The Product Manager, An Idea Whose Time Has Gone," *arketing Communications*, May 1989, pp. 28-35; and "The Marketing Revolution at Procter & Gamble," *Business Week*, July 25, 1988, pp. 72-76.

managers for soups, condiments, puddings, and so on. Each brand manager was responsible for both grocery sales and institutional sales. Then Heinz created a separate marketing organization for institutional sales, because institutional sales were growing faster than grocery sales but were not as well understood by the brand managers. Later, Heinz created three broad market groups: groceries, commercial restaurants, and institutions. Each group contains further market specialists. For example, the institutional division contains market specialists for schools, universities, hospitals, and prisons.

The prison market manager's job is to visit prison kitchen managers and learn about their food needs and budgets. Then this manager proposes reformulations of Heinz ketchup, soup, mustard, and other products to make them cost effective and competitive with the offers of other suppliers. Thus Heinz will use a lower grade of tomato and package its ketchup in bulk in order to compete for prison business, which happens to be a growth market as well as a "captive" market! ■

Product Management/Market Management Organization Companies that produce many products flowing into many markets face a dilemma. They could use a product management system, which requires product managers to be familiar with highly divergent markets. Or they could use a market management system, which means that market managers would have to be familiar with highly divergent products bought by their markets. Or they could install both product and market managers, that is, a *matrix organization.*

Du Pont as a company has done the latter (see Figure 25-6).[6] Its textile fibers department consists of separate product managers for rayon, acetate, nylon, orlon, and dacron; and separate market managers for men's wear, women's wear, home furnishings, and industrial markets. The product managers plan the sales and profits of their respective fibers. Their aim is to expand the use of their fiber. They ask market managers to estimate how much of their fiber they can sell in each market. The market managers, on the other hand, are more interested in meeting the needs of their market rather than pushing a particular fiber. In preparing their market plans, they ask each product manager about planned prices and availabilities of the different fibers. The final sales forecasts of the market managers and the product managers should add to the same grand total.

A matrix organization would seem desirable in a multiproduct, multimarket company. The problem is that this system is costly and conflictual. There is the cost of supporting both types of managers. There are also questions about where authority and responsibility should reside. Here are two of many dilemmas:

☐ *How should the salesforce be organized?* Should there be separate salesforces for rayon, nylon, and the other fibers? Or should the salesforces be organized according to men's wear, women's wear, and other markets? Or should the salesforce not be specialized?

☐ *Who should set the prices for a particular product/market?* Should the nylon product manager have final authority for setting nylon prices in all markets? What happens if the men's-wear market manager feels that nylon will lose out in this market unless special price concessions are made on nylon?

Most managers feel that only the more important products and markets justify separate managers. Some are not upset about the conflicts and cost and believe that the benefits of product and market specialization outweigh the costs.[7]

Corporate/Divisional Organization As multiproduct companies grow in size, they often turn their larger product groups into separate divisions. The divisions set up their own departments and services. This raises the question of what marketing services and activities should be retained at corporate headquarters.

FIGURE 25-6
Product-Market Management System

	Market Managers			
	Men's wear	Women's wear	Home furnishings	Industrial markets
Rayon				
Acetate				
Product Managers Nylon				
Orlon				
Dacron				

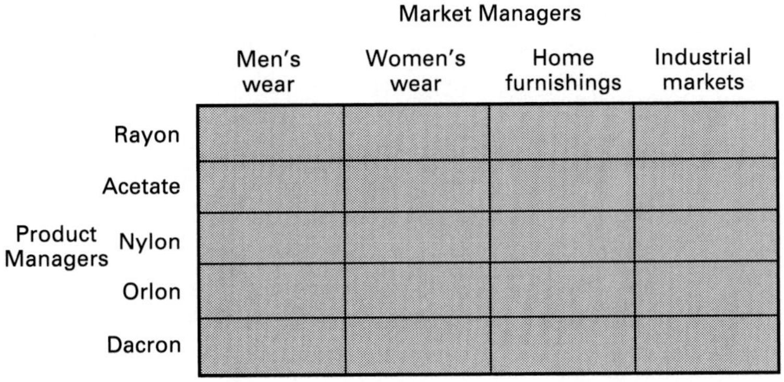

Divisionalized companies have reached different answers to this question. Corporate marketing staffs follow one of three models:

- *No Corporate Marketing*: Some companies lack a corporate marketing staff: They don't see any useful function for marketing to perform at the corporate level. Each division has its own marketing department.

- *Moderate Corporate Marketing*: Some companies have a small corporate marketing staff that performs a few functions, primarily (a) assisting top management with overall opportunity evaluation, (b) providing divisions with consulting assistance on request, (c) helping divisions that have little or no marketing, and (d) promoting the marketing concept to other departments of the company.

- *Strong Corporate Marketing*: Some companies have a corporate marketing staff that in addition to the preceding activities, also provides various marketing services to the divisions. The corporate marketing staff might provide specialized *advertising services* (e.g., coordination of media buying, institutional advertising, review of division advertising from a taste and image standpoint, auditing of advertising expenditures), *sales-promotion services* (e.g., companywide promotions, central buying of promotional materials), *marketing research services* (e.g., advanced mathematical analysis, research on marketing development cutting across divisional lines), *sales-administration services* (e.g., counsel on sales organization and sales policies, development of common sales-reporting systems, management of salesforces selling to common customers), and some miscellaneous services (e.g., counseling of marketing planning, hiring, and training of marketing personnel).[8]

The question arises as to whether companies favor one of these models of the corporate marketing department. The answer is no. Some companies have recently installed a corporate marketing staff for the first time; others have expanded their corporate marketing department; others have reduced its size and scope; and still others have eliminated it altogether.

The potential contribution of a corporate marketing staff varies in different stages of the company's evolution. Most companies begin with weak marketing in their divisions and often establish a corporate marketing staff to bring stronger marketing into the divisions through training and other services. Some members of the corporate marketing staff might be hired by divisions to head marketing departments. As the divisions become strong in their marketing, corporate marketing has less to offer them. Some companies might decide that corporate marketing has done its job and proceed to eliminate the department.

A corporate marketing staff generally has three justifications. The first is to serve as a corporate focus for review and leadership of overall company marketing activities and opportunities. The second is to offer certain marketing services that can be provided more economically on a centralized basis than by being duplicated in the different divisions. The third is to take responsibility for educating divisional managers, sales managers, and others in the company on the need for, and implementation of, the marketing concept.[9]

Marketing's Relations with Other Departments

In principle, business functions should interact harmoniously to pursue the overall objectives of the firm. In practice, interdepartmental relations are often characterized by deep rivalries and distrust. Some interdepartmental conflict stems from differences of opinion as to what is in the company's best interests, some from real tradeoffs between departmental well-being and company well-being, and some from unfortunate departmental stereotypes and prejudices.

In the typical organization, each department has an effect on customer satisfaction through its activities and decisions. Under the marketing concept, all departments need to "think customer" and work together to satisfy customer needs and expectations. The marketing department must drive this point home. The marketing vice-president has two tasks: to coordinate the internal marketing activities of the company and to coordinate marketing with finance, operations, and the other company functions, in the interests of the customers.

Yet there is little agreement on how much influence and authority marketing should have over other departments to bring about coordinated marketing. Generally speaking, the marketing vice-president must work through persuasion rather than authority.

> This situation is well illustrated in the case of the marketing vice-president of a major European airline. His mandate is to build up his airline's market share. Yet he has no authority over other functions that affect customer satisfaction:
>
> ☐ He can't hire or train the cabin crew (personnel department).
>
> ☐ He can't determine the type or quality of food (catering department).
>
> ☐ He can't enforce cleanliness standards on the plane (maintenance department).
>
> ☐ He can't determine schedules (operations department).
>
> ☐ He can't establish the fares (finance department).
>
> What does he control? He controls marketing research, the salesforce, and advertising and promotion. But he must work through the other departments to shape key factors that affect customer travel comfort. ■

Other departments often resist bending their efforts to meet the customers' interests. Just as marketing stresses the customer's point of view, other departments stress the importance of their tasks. Inevitably, departments define company problems and goals from their point of view. As a result, conflicts of interest are unavoidable. Table 25-1 summarizes the main differences in orientation between marketing and other departments. We will briefly examine the typical concerns of each department.

R&D   The company's drive for successful new products is often thwarted by poor working relations between R&D and marketing. In many ways, these groups represent two different cultures in the organization. The R&D department is staffed with scientists and technicians who pride themselves on scientific curiosity and detachment, like to work on challenging technical problems without much concern for immediate sales payoffs, and prefer to work without much supervision or accountability for research costs. The marketing/sales department is staffed with business-oriented persons who pride themselves on a practical understanding of the world, like to see many new products with sales features that can be promoted to customers, and feel compelled to pay attention to costs. Each group often carries negative stereotypes of the other group. Marketers see the R&D people as impractical, long-haired, sometimes mad-scientist types who do not understand business, while R&D people see marketers as gimmick-oriented hucksters who are more interested in sales than in the technical features of the product. These stereotypes get in the way of productive teamwork.

Companies tend to be technology driven, market driven, or balanced. In *technology-driven companies*, the R&D staff researches fundamental problems, looks for major breakthroughs, and strives for technical perfection in product development. R&D expenditures are high, and the new-product success rate tends to be low, although R&D occasionally comes up with clever new products.

In *market-driven companies*, the R&D staff designs products for specific market needs, much of it involving product modification and the application of existing technologies. A

Table 25-1 Summary of Organizational Conflicts between Marketing and Other Departments

Department	Their Emphasis	Marketing's Emphasis
R&D	Basic research	Applied research
	Intrinsic quality	Perceived quality
	Functional features	Sales features
Engineering	Long design lead time	Short design lead time
	Few models	Many models
	Standard components	Custom components
Purchasing	Narrow product line	Broad product line
	Standard parts	Nonstandard parts
	Price of material	Quality of material
	Economical lot sizes	Large lot sizes to avoid stockouts
	Purchasing at infrequent intervals	Immediate purchasing for customer needs
Manufacturing	Long production lead time	Short production lead time
	Long runs with few models	Short runs with many models
	No model changes	Frequent model changes
	Standard orders	Custom orders
	Ease of fabrication	Aesthetic appearance
	Average quality control	Tight quality control
Finance	Strict rationales for spending	Intuitive arguments for spending
	Hard and fast budgets	Flexible budgets to meet changing needs
	Pricing to cover costs	Pricing to further market development
Accounting	Standard transactions	Special terms and discounts
	Few reports	Many reports
Credit	Full financial disclosures by customers	Minimum credit examination of customers
	Long credit risks	Medium credit risks
	Tough credit terms	Easy credit terms
	Tough collection procedures	Easy collection procedures

higher ratio of new products succeed, but they represent mainly product modifications with relatively short product lives.

A *balanced technology- and market-driven company* is one in which R&D and marketing share responsibility for successful market-oriented innovation. The R&D staff takes responsibility not for invention alone but for successful innovation. The marketing staff takes responsibility not for new sales features alone but also for helping identify new ways to satisfy needs.

Gupta, Raj, and Wilemon concluded that a balanced R&D-marketing coordination is strongly correlated with innovation success.[10] R&D-marketing cooperation can be facilitated in several ways:[11]

☐ Joint seminars are sponsored to build understanding and respect for each other's goals, working styles, and problems.

- Each new project is assigned to an R&D person and a marketing person, who work together through the life of the project. R&D and marketing should jointly establish the goals of the development and marketing plan early in the project.

- R&D's participation continues into the selling period, including involvement in preparing technical manuals, participating in trade shows, carrying out some post-introductory marketing research with customers, and even doing some selling.

- Conflicts are worked out by higher management, following a clear procedure. In one company, R&D and marketing both report to the same vice-president.

Engineering   Engineering is responsible for finding practical ways to design new products and new production processes. Engineers are interested in achieving technical quality, cost economy, and manufacturing simplicity. They come into conflict with marketing executives when the latter want several models to be produced, often with product features requiring custom rather than standard components. Engineers see marketers as wanting "bells and whistles" on the products rather than intrinsic quality. These problems are less pronounced in companies where marketing executives have engineering backgrounds and can communicate effectively with engineers.

Purchasing   Purchasing executives are responsible for obtaining materials and components in the right quantities and quality at the lowest possible cost. They see marketing executives pushing for several models in a product line, which requires purchasing small quantities of many items rather than large quantities of a few items. They think that marketing insists on too high a quality of ordered materials and components. They dislike marketing's forecasting inaccuracy; it causes them to place rush orders at unfavorable prices and at other times to carry excessive inventories.

Manufacturing   Manufacturing people are responsible for the smooth running of the factory to produce the right products in the right quantities at the right time for the right cost. They have spent their lives in the factory, with its attendant problems of machine breakdowns, inventory stockouts, and labor disputes and slowdowns. They see marketers as having little understanding of factory economics or politics. Marketers will complain about insufficient plant capacity, delays in production, poor quality control, and poor customer service. Yet marketers often turn in inaccurate sales forecasts, recommend product features that are difficult to manufacture, and promise more factory service than is reasonable.

Marketers do not see the factory's problems, but rather they see the problems of their customers, who need the goods quickly, who receive defective merchandise, and who cannot get factory service. Marketers often don't show enough concern for the extra factory costs involved in helping a customer. The problem is not only poor communication but an actual conflict of interest.

Companies settle these conflicts in different ways. In *manufacturing-driven companies*, everything is done to ensure smooth production and low costs. The company prefers simple products, narrow product lines, and high-volume production. Sales campaigns calling for a hasty production buildup are kept to a minimum. Customers on back order have to wait.

Other companies are *marketing driven*, in that the company goes out of its way to satisfy customers. In one large toiletries company, the marketing personnel call the shots, and the manufacturing people have to fall in line, regardless of overtime costs, short runs, and so on. The result is high and fluctuating manufacturing costs, as well as variable product quality.

Companies need to develop a *balanced manufacturing/marketing orientation*, in which both sides codetermine what is in the best interests of the company. Solutions include joint seminars to understand each other's viewpoint, joint committees and liaison personnel, personnel exchange programs, and analytical methods to determine the most profitable course of action.[12]

Company profitability is greatly dependent on achieving successful manufacturing-marketing working relations. Marketers need to understand the marketing implications of new manufacturing strategies—the flexible factory, automation and robotization, just-in-time production, quality circles, and so on. If the company wants to win through being the low-cost producer, that will call for one manufacturing strategy; if the company wants to win through excelling at high quality or high variety or high service, each calls for different manufacturing strategies. Manufacturing design and capacity decisions must take their cues from the manufacturing targets set by marketing strategy with respect to planned output, cost, quality, variety, and service.

Manufacturing is also a tool of marketing after the product is produced. Before they choose a vendor, buyers often want to visit the plant to assess how well it is managed. Thus manufacturing personnel and plant layout become important marketing tools.

Finance   Financial executives pride themselves on being able to evaluate the profit implications of different business actions. When it comes to marketing expenditures, they feel frustrated. Marketing executives ask for substantial budgets for advertising, sales promotions, and salesforce, without being able to prove how many sales will be produced by these expenditures. Financial executives suspect that the marketers' forecasts are self-serving. They think that marketing people do not spend enough time relating expenditures to sales and shifting their budgets to more profitable areas. They think that marketers are too quick to slash prices to win orders, instead of pricing to make a profit.

Marketing executives, on the other hand, often see financial people as controlling the purse strings too tightly and refusing to invest funds in long-term market development. Financial people see all marketing expenditures as expenses rather than investments. They seem overly conservative and risk averse, causing many opportunities to be lost. The solution lies in giving marketing people more financial training and giving financial people more marketing training. Financial executives need to adapt their financial tools and theories to support strategic marketing.

Accounting   Accountants see marketing people as lax in providing their sales reports on time. They dislike the special deals that salespeople make with customers, because these require special accounting procedures. Marketers, on the other hand, dislike the way accountants allocate fixed-cost burdens to different products in the line. Brand managers may feel that their brand is more profitable than it looks, the problem being high overhead assigned to it. They would also like accounting to prepare special reports on sales and profitability by different channels, territories, order sizes, and so on.

Credit   Credit officers evaluate the credit standing of potential customers and deny or limit credit to the more doubtful ones. They think that marketers will sell to anyone, including those from whom payment is doubtful. Marketers, on the other hand, often feel that credit standards are too high. They think that "zero bad debts" really means that the company lost a lot of sales and profits. They feel they work too hard to find customers to hear that they are not good enough to sell to.

Strategies for Building a Companywide Marketing Orientation

Only a handful of companies, like Procter & Gamble and McDonald's, are truly market- and customer-driven. Most companies are either sales driven, or product driven or technology driven. These companies sooner or later experience some market shock. They may lose a major market, experience slow growth or low profitability, or find themselves facing formidable competitors.

> General Motors's substantial market-share decline is largely attributed to its chronic sales orientation. In the past, it produced a variety of cars and sold them successfully primarily because it had twice as many sales and service dealerships as its next largest competitor. But it didn't pay attention to a changing market of smaller cars, higher-quality foreign cars, more service-minded competitor dealerships, and so on. Its management was inside focused, not outside focused.[13] ∎

Companies like GM eventually take steps to become "market driven." Yet in many cases, they don't succeed. Why?

In some companies, their CEOs do not really understand marketing and confuse it with promotion. They want their organizations to sell and advertise more aggressively and miss the point that promotion is wasted if their products and prices don't give value to their target customers.

Some CEOs oversimplify the task of changing their company's culture. They think that making speeches about everyone "working for the customer" and running marketing training seminars are sufficient to produce the desired results. They underestimate the resistance to change, especially in the absence of new incentives. When performance doesn't improve within a year or two, they lose patience and turn their attention to another theme, such as a companywide productivity drive.

What steps must a company take if it hopes to successfully grow a marketing culture? Here are the main steps:

1. *Top management must want better marketing and understand it*: The CEO's leadership and commitment are key. The CEO must convince the company's top managers that better marketing is needed. The CEO must give frequent speeches to employees, suppliers and distributors about the importance of delivering quality and value to customers. The CEO must personally exemplify strong customer commitment and reward those in the organization who do likewise.

2. *Appoint a marketing task force*: The CEO should appoint a high-level marketing task force to develop programs for bringing modern marketing practices into the company. The task force should include the CEO, and the vice-presidents of sales, R&D, purchasing, manufacturing, finance, personnel, and a few other key individuals. They should set objectives, anticipate problems and develop an overall strategy. Some high-level person should be given the authority to implement the programs. For the next few years, this committee should meet frequently to measure progress and take new initiatives.

3. *Get outside help and guidance*: The marketing task force would benefit from outside consulting assistance in building a company marketing culture. Consulting firms have considerable experience in helping companies move toward a marketing orientation.

4. *Change the reward structures in the company*: The company will have to change department reward structures if it expects departmental behavior to change. As long as purchasing and manufacturing get rewarded for keeping costs low, they will resist accepting some costs required to serve customers better. As long as finance focuses on short-term profit performance, finance will oppose major marketing investments designed to build more satisfied and loyal customers.

5. *Hire strong marketing talent*: The company should consider hiring well-trained marketing talent from outside, preferably from leading marketing companies. When the banks got

serious about marketing, they hired many of their marketers from packaged food companies. The company will need a strong marketing vice-president who not only manages the marketing department but gains respect and influence with the other vice-presidents. A multidivision company would benefit from establishing a strong corporate marketing department to consult and strengthen divisional marketing programs.

6. *Develop strong in-house marketing training programs*: The company should design well-crafted marketing training programs for top corporate management, divisional general managers, marketing and sales personnel, manufacturing personnel, R&D personnel, and so on. These programs should deliver marketing knowledge, skills, and attitudes to company managers and employees.

7. *Install a modern marketing-planning system*: An excellent way to train managers in marketing thinking is to install a modern market-oriented planning system. The planning format will require managers to think first about the market environment, marketing opportunities, competitive trends, and other outside forces. Then marketing strategies and sales forecasts can be developed on a sound marketing database.

One company that successfully moved from an inward-looking to an outward-looking culture is Du Pont. Under Richard Heckert's CEO leadership, a number of initiatives were undertaken to build a "marketing community." Several divisions were reorganized along market lines more than product lines; for example, Du Pont created a new automotive-products department located near the car makers, which brought together all groups that were selling to the auto industry with little coordination. Du Pont also launched a series of marketing management training seminars, which were ultimately attended by three hundred senior people, two thousand middle managers and fourteen thousand employees. Du Pont established a corporate marketing recognition program and honored thirty-two Du Pont employees from around the world who had developed innovative marketing strategies, service improvements, and so on.[14]

Another major company, Hewlett-Packard, undertook a successful drive to become more market oriented. Hewlett-Packard conducted deep studies of customer need and satisfaction; introduced a major total-quality-improvement program; developed better links and teamwork between marketing and other departments; and created a system of measurements of market-oriented performance.

SAS (Scandinavian Airlines), British Airways, Ford, and some other major companies also showed that achieving a marketing culture is both possible and profitable. It takes a great amount of planning and patience to get managers to accept the fact that customers are the foundation of the company's business and future. But it can be done.

MARKETING IMPLEMENTATION

We now turn to the question of how marketing managers can effectively implement marketing plans. A brilliant strategic marketing plan counts for little if it is not implemented properly. Consider the following example:

A chemical company decided that customers were not getting good service from any of the competitors. The company decided that it would make customer service its strategic thrust. When this strategy failed, a postmortem revealed a number of implementation failures. The customer-service department continued to be held in low regard by top management; it was undermanned; and it was used as a dumping ground for weak managers. Furthermore, the company's reward system continued to focus on cost containment and current profitability. The company had failed to make the changes required to carry out its strategy. ■

We define marketing implementation as follows:

> *Marketing implementation* is the process that turns marketing plans into action assignments and ensures that such assignments are executed in a manner that accomplishes the plan's stated objectives.

Whereas strategy addresses the *what* and *why* of marketing activities, implementation addresses the *who, where, when*, and *how*. Strategy and implementation are closely related in that one "layer" of strategy implies certain tactical implementation assignments at a lower level. For example, top management's strategic decision to "harvest" a product must be translated into specific actions and assignments.

Bonoma identified four skills related to the effective implementation of marketing programs:

- [ ] Skills in recognizing and diagnosing a problem
- [ ] Skills in assessing the company level where the problem exists
- [ ] Skills in implementing plans
- [ ] Skills in evaluating implementation results[15]

We will examine these skills in the following paragraphs.

Diagnostic Skills

The close interrelationship between strategy and implementation can pose difficult diagnostic problems when marketing programs do not fulfill their expectations. Was the low sales rate the result of poor strategy or poor implementation? Moreover, is the issue to determine what the problem *is* (diagnosis) or what should be *done* about it (action)? Each problem calls for different management tools and solutions.

Company Levels

Marketing implementation problems can occur at three levels. One level is that of carrying out a *marketing function* successfully. For example, how can the company get more creative advertising from its advertising agency? Another level is that of implementing a *marketing program* that has to blend marketing functions into a coherent whole. This problem arises in launching a new product into the marketplace. A third level is that of implementing a *marketing policy*. For example, the company might want every employee to treat the customer as number one.

Marketing Implementation Skills

A set of skills must be practiced at each company level—functions, programs, policies—to achieve effective implementation. The four skills are allocating, monitoring, organizing, and interacting.

Allocating skills are used by marketing managers in budgeting resources (time, money, and personnel) to functions, programs, and policies. For example, determining how much money to spend on trade shows (functions level) or what warranty work to perform on "marginal" products (policies level) are problems requiring allocation skills.

Monitoring skills are used in managing a system of controls to evaluate the results of marketing actions. Controls can be of four types: annual-plan control, profitability control, efficiency control, and strategic control (see Chapter 26).

Organizing skills are used in developing an effective working organization. Understanding the informal as well as formal marketing organization is important to carrying out effective implementation.

Interacting skills refer to the ability of managers to get things done by influencing others. Marketers must not only motivate the company's own people but must also motivate outsiders—marketing research firms, ad agencies, dealers, wholesalers, agents—whose objectives might differ from the company's. Managing conflict within a distribution channel also demands a high level of interaction skill.

Implementation-Evaluation Skills

Good performance in the marketplace does not necessarily prove that there was good marketing implementation. Evidence of effective marketing implementation practice would include positive responses to the following questions:

☐ Is there a clear marketing strategy, strong marketing leadership, and a culture that promotes excellence?

☐ Do the company's marketing programs integrate and deliver marketing activities in a focused fashion to various customer groups?

☐ How good is marketing management at interacting with the marketing staff, other functions in the company, and customers and distributors?

☐ Does management have good monitoring systems for observing customers, competitors, and distributors?

☐ How good is management at allocating time, money, and people to marketing tasks?

Assessing the relative influence of strategy and implementation on sales results will always be a difficult task. Clearly, companies must do their best to excel at both strategy and implementation.

SUMMARY

This chapter examined how marketing is organized, how it relates to other company functions, and how marketing strategies must be implemented to succeed in the marketplace.

The modern marketing department evolved through several stages. It started as a sales department and later took on ancillary functions, such as advertising and marketing research. As the ancillary functions grew in importance, many companies created a separate marketing department to manage them. Sales and marketing people generally worked well together. Eventually, the two departments were merged into a modern marketing department headed by a marketing and sales vice-president. A modern marketing department, however, does not automatically create a modern marketing company unless all the other departments and employees accept and practice a customer orientation.

Modern marketing departments are organized in a number of ways. A functional marketing organization is one in which marketing functions are headed by separate managers reporting to the marketing vice-president. A product management organization is one in which products are assigned to product managers, who work with functional specialists to develop and implement their plans. A market management organization is one in which major markets are assigned to market managers, who work with functional specialists to develop and implement their plans. Some large companies use a combined product and market management organization called a matrix organization. Finally, multidivision companies have to decide whether to establish a corporate marketing department as well as divisional marketing departments.

Marketing must work harmoniously with the other company departments. In its pursuit of customers' interests, marketing often comes into conflict with R&D, engineering, purchasing, manufacturing, inventory, finance, accounting, credit, and other functions. These conflicts can be reduced when the company president commits the company to a customer orientation and when the marketing vice-president learns to work effectively with the other officers. Acquiring a modern marketing orientation requires presidential support, a marketing task force, outside marketing consulting help, a corporate marketing department, in-house marketing seminars, marketing talent hired from the outside and promoted inside, and a market-oriented marketing-planning system.

Those responsible for the marketing function must develop effective strategies and also implement them successfully. Marketing implementation is the process of turning plans into action assignments describing who does what, when, and how. Effective implementation requires skills in allocating, monitoring, organizing, and interacting at the level of marketing functions, programs, and policies.

■ QUESTIONS

1. Is it necessary for companies to change the organization of their marketing activities? If yes, why? If no, why not?

2. Describe the various ways of organizing the marketing department. Discuss these designs in terms of their ability to respond to changing conditions.

3. Discuss the advantages and limitations of brand management as an organizational arrangement.

4. You have been asked to develop a marketing organizational design for a distributor of tankless water heater units ($10 million in sales). What kind of information would you need so that you might select an appropriate organizational design for the company?

5. What advantages and what problems do you anticipate in having a financial analyst as a member of the marketing department? What would be the purpose of such an appointment? How else might this purpose be achieved?

6. Choose a product or service and list some strategy-stage issues and some implementation-stage issues.

7. For the product or service discussed in Question 6, indicate some specific problems of diagnosis and problems of action that could occur at the strategy and implementation stages.

8. For the product or service discussed in Question 6, give an example of the problems that could arise at the function, program, and policy levels when implementing a marketing strategy.

9. In order to carry out a proposed national sales promotion, describe some of the departments whose efforts must be coordinated with those of the marketing department. Through what kind of planning device might these efforts be integrated?

10. Does it make organizational sense to combine the company's marketing department and public relations department under one vice-president?

11. A major airline's marketing department is now organized on a functional basis—advertising, field sales, customer services, and so on. The airline is considering setting up a route-manager organization, with a manager, who would be to a route what a brand manager is to a brand, assigned to each major route. Do you think this is a good idea?

12. The General Electric Company does not have a corporate vice-president of marketing. Its vice-presidents of marketing are found in various sectors, groups, and divisions. General Electric does have a corporate vice-president of strategic planning. Do you think a corporate vice-president of marketing should be added?

13. Show from your reading of the chapter how marketing strategy shapes the structure of the organization. Where possible illustrate with examples from industry.

14. What factors generally predispose a firm to adopt a marketing orientation? What are some key steps that must be taken to ensure success?

■ NOTES

1. For details, see "General Food Corporation: Post Division," in *Organization Strategy: A Marketing Approach*, ed. E. Raymond Corey and Steven H. Star (Boston: Division of Research, Graduate School of Business Administration, Harvard University, 1971), pp. 201-30.

2. See David J. Luck, "Interfaces of a Product Manager," *Journal of Marketing*, October 1969, pp. 32-36.

3. Andrall E. Pearson and Thomas W. Wilson, Jr., *Making Your Organization Work* (New York: Association of National Advertisers, 1967), pp. 8-13.

4. See Richard M. Clewett and Stanley F. Stasch, "Shifting Role of the Product Manager," *Harvard Business Review*, January-February 1975, pp. 65-73; Victor P. Buell, "The Changing Role of the Product Manager in Consumer Goods Companies," *Journal of Marketing*, July 1975, pp. 3-11; "The Brand Manager: No Longer King," *Business Week*, June 9, 1973; Joseph A. Morein, "Shift from Brand to Product Line Marketing," *Harvard Business Review*, September-October 1975, pp. 56-64; and Thomas D. Giese and T. M. Weisenberger, "Product Manager in Perspective," *Journal of Business* Research 10 (1982), 267-77.

5. Mark Hanan, "Reorganize Your Company around Its Markets," *Harvard Business Review*, November-December 1974, pp. 63-74.

6. For details, see Corey and Star, *Organization Strategy*, pp. 187-96.

7. See B. Charles Ames, "Dilemma of Product/Market Management," *Harvard Business Review*, March-April 1971, pp. 66-74.

8. See Watson Snyder, Jr., and Frank B. Gray, *The Corporate Marketing Staff: Its Role and Effectiveness in Multi-Division Companies* (Cambridge, Mass.: Marketing Science Institute, April 1971).

9. For further reading on marketing organization, see Nigel Piercy, *Marketing Organization: An Analysis of Information Processing, Power and Politics* (London: George Allen & Unwin, 1985); Robert W. Ruekert, Orville C. Walker, and Kenneth J. Roering, "The Organization of Marketing Activities: A Contingency Theory of Structure and Performance," *Journal of Marketing*, Winter 1985, pp. 13-25; and Tyzoon T. Tyebjee, Albert V. Bruno, and Shelby H. McIntyre, "Growing Ventures Can Anticipate Marketing Stages," *Harvard Business Review*, January-February 1983, pp. 2-4.

10. Askok K. Gupta, S. P. Raj, and David Wilemon, "A Model for Studying R&D-Marketing Interface in the Product Innovation Process," *Journal of Marketing*, April 1986, pp. 7-17.

11. See William E. Souder, *Managing New Product Innovations* (Lexington, Mass.: Heath, 1987), Chaps. 10-11; and William L. Shanklin and John K. Ryans, Jr., "Organizing for High-Tech Marketing," *Harvard Business Review*, November-December 1984, pp. 164-71.

12. See Benson P. Shapiro, "Can Marketing and Manufacturing Coexist?" *Harvard Business Review*, September-October 1977, pp. 104-14. Also see Robert W. Ruekert and Orville C. Walker, Jr., "Marketing's Interaction with Other Functional Units: A Conceptual Framework and Empirical Evidence," *Journal of Marketing*, January 1987, pp. 1-19.

13. See J. Patrick Wright, *On a Clear Day You Can See General Motors* (New York: Avon Books, 1979), Chap. 8.

14. Edward E. Messikomer, "Du Pont's 'Marketing Community,'" *Business Marketing*, October 1987, pp. 90-94.

15. Thomas V. Bonoma, *The Mareting Edge: Making Strategies Work* (New York: Free Press, 1985). Much of this section is based on Bonoma's work.

26

Evaluating and Controlling Marketing Performance

Not a mortal in the universe but has said to himself "I will" and in the evening we are aware of determinations unfulfilled.

Bliss Carman

The marketing department's job is to plan and control marketing activity. Because many surprises will occur during the implementation of marketing plans, the marketing department has to continuously monitor and control marketing activities. In spite of this need, many companies have inadequate control procedures. This conclusion was reached in a study of seventy-five companies of varying sizes in different industries. The main findings were these:

☐ Small companies have poorer controls than large companies. They do a poorer job of setting clear objectives and establishing systems to measure performance.

☐ Fewer than half of the companies know the profitability of their individual products. About one-third of the companies have no regular review procedures for spotting and deleting weak products.

☐ Almost half of the companies fail to compare their prices with competition, to analyze their warehousing and distribution costs, to analyze the causes of returned merchandise, to conduct formal evaluations of advertising effectiveness, and to review their salesforce call reports.

☐ Many companies take four to eight weeks to develop control reports, and they are occasionally inaccurate.

Four types of marketing control can be distinguished (Table 26-1).

In *annual-plan control*, managers check ongoing performance against the annual plan and take corrective action when necessary. *Profitability* control consists of determining the actual profitability of different products, territories, end-use markets, and trade channels. *Efficiency control* involves searching for ways to improve the productivity of different marketing tools and expenditures. *Strategic control* consists of periodically reviewing whether the

Table 26-1 Types of Marketing Control

Type of Control	Prime Responsibility	Purpose of Control	Approaches
I. Annual-plan control	Top management Middle management	To examine whether the planned results are being achieved	Sales analysis Market-share analysis Sales-to-expense ratios Financial analysis Attitude tracking
II. Profitability control	Marketing controller	To examine where the company is making and losing money	Profitability by: product territory customer group trade channel order size
III. Efficiency control	Line and staff management Marketing controller	To evaluate and improve the spending efficiency and impact of marketing expenditures	Efficiency of: sales force advertising sales promotion distribution
IV. Strategic control	Top management Marketing auditor	To examine whether the company is pursuing its best opportunities with respect to markets, products, and channels	Marketing-effectiveness rating instrument Marketing audit

company's basic strategies are well matched to its opportunities and resources. We now turn to these four types of marketing control.

ANNUAL-PLAN CONTROL

The purpose of annual-plan control is to ensure that the company achieves the sales, profits, and other goals established in its annual plan. The heart of annual-plan control is *management by objectives*. Four steps are involved (see Figure 26-1). First, management sets monthly or quarterly goals. Second, management monitors its performance in the marketplace. Third, management determines the causes of serious performance deviations. Fourth, management takes corrective action to close the gaps between its goals and performance. This could require changing the action programs or even changing the goals.

This control model applies to all levels of the organization. Top management sets sales and profit goals for the year. These goals are elaborated into specific goals for each lower level of management. Thus each product manager is committed to attaining specified levels of sales and costs. Each regional and district sales manager and each sales representative is also committed to specific goals. Each period, top management reviews and interprets the results and ascertains whether any corrective action is needed.

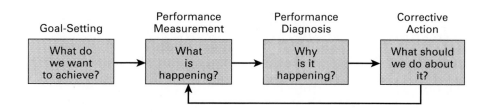

FIGURE 26-1
The Control Process

Goal-Setting	Performance Measurement	Performance Diagnosis	Corrective Action
What do we want to achieve?	What is happening?	Why is it happening?	What should we do about it?

Managers use five tools to check on plan performance: sales analysis, market-share analysis, marketing expense-to-sales analysis, financial analysis, and customer-attitude tracking.

Sales Analysis

Sales analysis consists of measuring and evaluating actual sales in relation to sales goals. There are two specific tools in this connection.

Sales-variance analysis measures the relative contribution of different factors to a gap in sales performance. Suppose the annual plan called for selling 4000 widgets in the first quarter at $1 per widget, or $4000. At quarter's end, only 3000 widgets were sold at $.80 per widget, or $2400. The sales performance variance is $1600, or 40 percent of expected sales. The question arises, How much of this underperformance is due to the price decline and how much to the volume decline? The following calculation answers this question:

$$\text{Variance due to price decline} \quad = (\$1.00 - \$.80)(3000) = \$\ 600 \quad 37.5\%$$

$$\text{Variance due to volume decline} = (\$1.00)(4000 - 3000) = \$1000 \quad 62.5\%$$

$$\overline{}$$

$$\$1600 \quad 100.0\%$$

Almost two-thirds of the sales variance is due to a failure to achieve the volume target. The company should look closely into why its expected sales volume was not achieved.[1]

Micro-sales analysis may provide the answer. Micro-sales analysis looks at specific products, territories, and so forth, that failed to produce their expected share of sales. Suppose the company sells in three territories and expected sales were 1500 units, 500 units, and 2000 units, respectively, adding up to 4000 widgets. The actual sales volume was 1400 units, 525 units, and 1075 units, respectively. Thus territory 1 showed a 7 percent shortfall in terms of expected sales; territory 2, a 5 percent surplus; and territory 3, a 46 percent shortfall! Territory 3 is causing most of the trouble. The sales vice-president can check into territory 3 to see which hypothesis explains the poor performance: Territory 3's sales representative is loafing or has a personal problem; a major competitor has entered this territory; or business is generally depressed in this territory.

Market-Share Analysis

Company sales do not reveal how well the company is performing relative to competitors. Suppose a company's sales increase. The increase could be due to improved economic conditions benefiting all companies. Or it could be due to improved company performance relative to competitors. Management needs to track its market share (see Marketing Concepts and Tools 26-1). If the company's market share goes up, the company is gaining on competitors; if it goes down, the company is losing relative to competitors.

Marketing Concepts and Tools 26-1

DEFINING AND MEASURING MARKET SHARE

The first step in using market-share analysis is to define which measure(s) of market share will be used. Four different measures are available.

- *Overall Market Share*: The company's overall market share is its sales expressed as a percentage of total industry sales. Two decisions are necessary to use this measure. The first is whether to use unit sales or dollar sales to express market share. Any changes in unit market share reflect volume changes among competitors, whereas changes in dollar market share reflect a combination of volume and price changes.

    The other decision has to do with defining the total industry. For example, suppose Harley Davidson wants to measure its share of the Canadian motorcycle market. If motor scooters and motorized bikes are included, then Harley Davidson's market share will be lower, since it does not produce these. The issue hinges on whether consumers perceive lighter cycles to be highly substitutable for standard motorcycles.

- *Served Market Share*: The company's served market share is its sales expressed as a percentage of the total sales to its served market. Its served market is the market that would be interested in the company's offering and is reached by the company's marketing effort. If Harley Davidson only markets its expensive motorcycles in Eastern Canda, its served market share would be its sales as a percentage of the total sales of expensive motorcycles sold in Eastern Canada. A company's served market share is always larger than its overall market share. A company could have close to 100 percent of its served market and yet a relatively small percentage of the overall market. A company's first task is to try to get the lion's share of its served market. As it approaches this goal, it should add new product lines and territories to enlarge its served market.

- *Relative Market Share (to Top Three Competitors):* This involves expressing the company's sales as a percentage of the combined sales of the three largest competitors. For example, if this company has 30 percent of the market, and the next two largest competitors have 20, and 10 percent, then this company's relative market share is 50 percent (= 30/60). If each of the three companies had one third of the market, then any company's relative market share would be one third. Relative market shares above one third are considered to be strong.

- *Relative Market Share (to Leading Competitor)*: Some companies track their shares as a percentage of the leading competitor's sales. A relative market share greater than 100 percent indicates a market leader. A relative market share of exactly 100 percent means that the firm is tied for the lead. A rise in the company's relative market share means that it is gaining on its leading competitor.

After choosing which market-share measure(s) to use, the company must find the necessary data. Overall market share is normally the most available measure, since it requires only total industry sales, and these are often available in government or trade association publications. Estimating served market share is harder in that the company will have to keep track of its served market, which will be affected by changes in the company's product line and geographical market coverage, among other things. Estimating relative market shares is still harder because the company will have to estimate the sales of specific competitors, who guard these figures. The company has to use indirect means, such as learning about competitors' purchase rate of raw materials or the number of shifts they are operating. In the consumer-goods area, individual brand shares are available through syndicated store and consumer panels.

customer selectivity at 75 percent, and price selectivity at 130 percent. Clearly, the market-share decline was due mainly to a loss of some customers (fall in customer penetration) who normally made larger-than-average purchases (fall in customer selectivity). The manager can now investigate why these customers were lost.

These conclusions from market-share analysis, however, are subject to certain qualifications:

☐ *The assumption that outside forces affect all companies in the same way is often not true*: The government's report on the harmful consequences of cigarette smoking caused total cigarette sales to falter but not equally for all companies. Companies with a reputation for better filters were hurt less.

☐ *The assumption that a company's performance should be judged against the average performance of all companies is not always valid*: A company's performance should be judged against the performance of its closest competitors.

☐ *If a new firm enters the industry, then every existing firm's market share might fall*: A decline in a company's market share might not mean that the company is performing any worse than other companies. A company's share loss will depend on the degree to which the new firm hits the company's specific markets.

☐ *Sometimes a market-share decline is deliberately engineered by a company to improve profits*: For example, management might drop unprofitable customers or products to improve its profits.

☐ *Market share can fluctuate for many minor reasons*: For example, market share can be affected by whether a large sale is made on the last day of the period or at the beginning of the next period. Not all shifts in market share have marketing significance.[2]

Managers must carefully interpret market-share movements by product line, customer type, region, and other breakdowns. A useful way to analyze market-share movements is in terms of the following four components:

$$\frac{\text{Overall}}{\text{market share}} = \frac{\text{Customer}}{\text{penetration}} \times \frac{\text{Customer}}{\text{loyalty}} \times \frac{\text{Customer}}{\text{selectivity}} \times \frac{\text{Price}}{\text{selectivity}} \qquad (26\text{-}1)$$

where:

☐ *Customer penetration* is the percentage of all customers who buy from this company.

☐ *Customer loyalty* is the purchases from this company by its customers expressed as a percentage of their total purchases from all suppliers of the same products.

☐ *Customer selectivity* is the size of the average customer purchase from the company expressed as a percentage of the size of the average customer purchase from an average company.

☐ *Price selectivity* is the average price charged by this company expressed as a percentage of the average price charged by all companies.

Now suppose the company's dollar market share falls during the period. Equation (26-1) provides four possible explanations. The company lost some of its customers (lower customer penetration). Existing customers are buying a smaller share of their total supplies from this company (lower customer loyalty). The company's remaining customers are smaller in size (lower customer selectivity). The company's price has slipped relative to competition (lower price selectivity).

By tracking these factors through time, the company can diagnose the underlying cause of market-share changes. Suppose at the beginning of the period, customer penetration was 60 percent; customer loyalty, 50 percent; customer selectivity, 80 percent; and price selectivity, 125 percent. According to equation (26-1), the company's market share was 30 percent. Suppose that at the end of the period, the company's market share fell to 27 percent. In checking, the company finds customer penetration 55 percent, customer loyalty at 50 percent,

Marketing Expense-to-Sales Analysis

Annual-plan control requires making sure that the company is not overspending to achieve its sales goals. The key ratio to watch is *marketing expense-to-sales*. In one company, this ratio was 30 percent and consisted of five component expense-to-sales ratios: *salesforce-to-sales* (15 percent); *advertising-to-sales* (5 percent); *sales promotion-to-sales* (6 percent); *marketing research-to-sales* (1 percent); and *sales administration-to-sales* (3 percent).

Management needs to monitor these marketing-expense ratios. They will normally exhibit small fluctuations that can be ignored. But fluctuations outside of the normal range are a cause for concern. The period-to-period fluctuations in each ratio can be tracked on a *control chart* (Figure 26-2). This chart shows that the advertising expense-to-sales ratio normally fluctuates between 8 and 12 percent, say ninety-nine out of one hundred times. In the fifteenth period, however, the ratio exceeded the upper control limit. One of two hypotheses can explain this occurrence:

☐ *Hypothesis A*: The company still has good expense control, and this situation represents one of those rare chance events.

☐ *Hypothesis B*: The company has lost control over this expense and should find the cause.

If hypothesis A is accepted, no investigation is made to determine whether the environment has changed. The risk in not investigating is that some real change might have occurred, and the company will fall behind. If hypothesis B is accepted, the environment is investigated at the risk that the investigation will uncover nothing and be a waste of time and effort.

The behavior of successive observations even within the control limits should be watched. Note that the level of the expense-to-sales ratio rose steadily from the ninth period onward. The probability of encountering six successive increases in what should be independent events is only one in sixty-four.[3] This unusual pattern should have led to an investigation sometime before the fifteenth observation.

When an expense-to-sales ratio gets out of control, disaggregative data are needed to track down the problem. An *expense-to-sales deviation chart* can be used. Figure 26-3 shows the performances of different sales districts in terms of their sales-quota attainment and

FIGURE 26-2
The Control-Chart Model

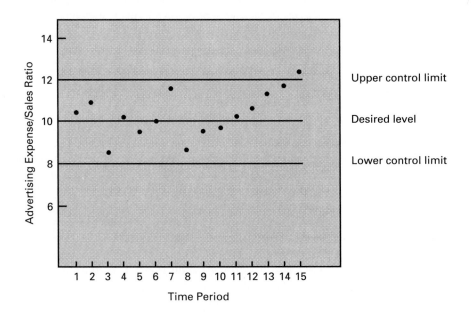

FIGURE 26-3

Comparison of Expense and
Revenue Deviations by District

Source: Adapted from D.M. Phelps
and J.H. Westing, *Marketing
Management*, 3rd ed.
(Homewood, Ill.: Richard D. Irwin, Inc.,
1968), p. 754. © 1968 by
Richard D. Irwin Inc.

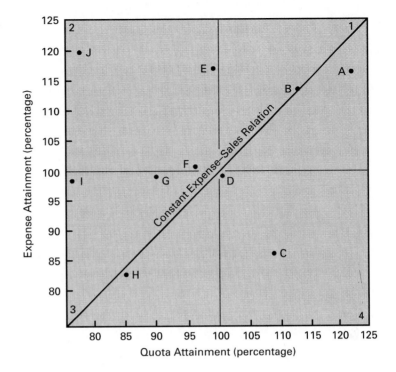

expense attainment in percentages. For example, district D achieved its sales quota close to
the expected expense level. District B exceeded its quota, and its expenses are proportionately
higher. The most troubling districts are in the second quadrant. For example, district J achieved
less than 80 percent of its quota, and its expenses are disproportionately high. The next step
is to prepare a chart for each deviant district showing sales representatives' standings. Within
district J, for example, the poor performance might be associated with one or a few specific
sales representatives.

Financial Analysis

The expenses-to-sales ratios should be analyzed in an overall financial framework to determine how and where the company is making its money. Marketers are increasingly using
financial analysis to find profitable strategies and not just sales-building strategies.

Financial analysis is used by management to identify the factors that affect the company's
rate of return on net worth.[4] The main factors are shown in Figure 26-4, along with some
illustrative numbers for a large chain-store retailer. The retailer is earning a 12.5 percent return
on net worth. Many retailers would argue that retail organizations need at least a 15 percent
return to satisfy their profit requirements. Some successful retailers routinely earn over 20
percent.

The return on net worth is the product of two ratios, the company's *return on assets* and
its *financial leverage*. To improve its return on net worth, the company must either increase
the ratio of its net profits to its assets or increase the ratio of its assets to its net worth. The company should analyze the composition of its assets (i.e., cash, accounts receivable, inventory,
and plant and equipment) and see if it can improve its asset management.

The return on assets is the product of two ratios, namely, the *profit margin* and the *asset
turnover*. The profit margin seems low, while the asset turnover is more normal for retailing.

FIGURE 26-4
Financial Model of Return on Net Worth

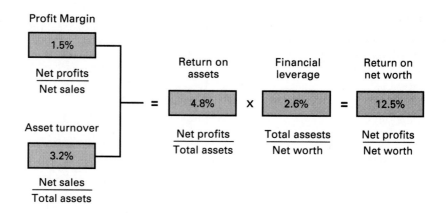

The marketing executive can seek to improve performance in two ways: (1) to increase the profit margin by increasing sales or cutting costs; and (2) to increase the asset turnover by increasing sales or reducing the assets (e.g., inventory, receivables) that are held against a given level of sales.[5]

Customer-Satisfaction Tracking

The preceding control measures are largely financial and quantitative in character. They are important but not sufficient. Needed are qualitative measures that provide early warnings to management of impending market-share changes. Alert managers set up systems to monitor the attitudes and satisfaction of customers, dealers, and other marketing-system participants. By monitoring changing levels of customer preference and satisfaction before they affect sales, management can take earlier action. The main customer-satisfaction tracking systems are the following:

☐ *Complaint and Suggestion Systems*: Market-oriented companies record, analyze, and respond to written and oral complaints that come from customers. The complaints are tabulated, and management attempts to correct whatever is causing the most frequent types of complaints. Many retailers, such as hotels, restaurants, and banks, provide suggestion cards to encourage customer feedback. Market-oriented companies try to maximize the opportunities for consumer complaining so that management can get a more complete picture of customer reactions to their products and services.[6]

☐ *Customer Panels*: Some companies run panels of customers who have agreed to communicate their attitudes periodically through phone calls or mail questionnaires. These panels are more representative of the range of customer attitudes than customer complaint and suggestion systems.

☐ *Customer Surveys*: Some companies periodically mail questionnaires to a random sample of customers to evaluate the friendliness of the staff, the quality of the service, and so on. The customers answer these questions on a five-point scale (very dissatisfied, dissatisfied, neutral, satisfied, very satisfied). The responses are summarized and go to both local managers and corporate management, as illustrated in Figure 26-5. Local managers see how their service components were rated in the current period as compared to the last period, to the average of all the local units, and to the standard. This system improves the staff's motivation to provide good customer service given that the ratings will be reviewed by corporate management.[7]

FIGURE 26-5

A Consumer-Survey Feedback System

Source: Arthur J. Daltas, "Protecting Service Markets with Consumer Feedback," *Cornell Hotel and Restaurant Administration Quarterly*, May 1977, pp. 73-77.

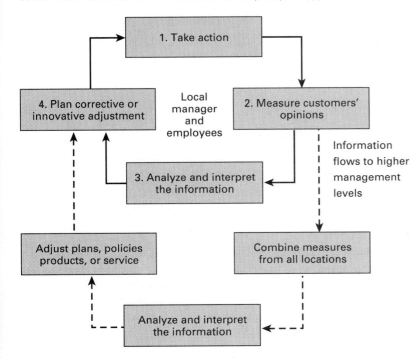

1. Local managers and employees service customers' needs on a daily basis, using locally modified procedures along with general corporate policies and procedures.
2. By means of a standardized and locally sensitive questionnaire, determine the needs and attitudes of customers on a regular basis.
3. Comparing financial data, expectations, and past attitude information, determine strengths and weaknesses and their probable causes.
4. Determine where and how effort should be applied to correct weaknesses and preserve strengths. Repeat the process by taking action—Step 1—and maintain it to attain a steady state or to evolve in terms of customer changes.
5. A similar process can take place at higher levels, using aggregated data from the field and the existing policy flows of the organization.

Corrective Action

When performance deviates too much from the plan's goals, management needs to undertake corrective action. Normally the company adopts some minor corrective actions, and if they fail to work, the company adopts more drastic measures. When a large fertilizer company's sales continued to decline, because of excess capacity and rampant price cutting by competitors, the company resorted to an increasingly drastic set of remedies. First the company ordered cutbacks in production. Then it cut its prices selectively. Next it put more pressure on its salesforce to meet their quotas. The company then cut the budgets for personnel hiring and training, advertising, public relations, and research and development. Soon it introduced personnel cuts through layoffs and early retirement. Then it undertook fancy bookkeeping to produce a better picture of its situation. Investment in plant and equipment was cut next. The company then sold some of its businesses to other companies. Finally, the company looked for and found a buyer.

PROFITABILITY CONTROL

Here are some disconcerting findings from a recent study:

We have found that anywhere from 20 to 40 percent of an individual institution's products are unprofitable, and up to 60 percent of their accounts generate losses.

Our research has shown that in most firms, more than half of all customer relationships are not profitable, and 30 to 40 percent are only marginally so. It is frequently a mere 10 to 15 percent of a firm's relationships that generate the bulk of its profits.

Our profitability research into the branch system of a regional bank produced some surprising results . . . 30 percent of the bank's branches were unprofitable.[8]

Besides annual-plan control, companies need to measure the profitability of their various products, territories, customer groups, trade channels, and order sizes. This information will help management determine whether any products or marketing activities should be expanded, reduced, or eliminated.

Methodology of Marketing-Profitability Analysis

We will illustrate the steps in marketing-profitability analysis with the following example:

The marketing vice-president of a lawnmower company wants to determine the profitability of selling its lawnmower through three types of retail channels: hardware stores, garden supply shops, and department stores. Its profit-and-loss statement is shown in Table 26-2. ∎

Step 1: Identifying the Functional Expenses   Assume that the expenses listed in Table 26-2 are incurred to sell the product, advertise it, pack and deliver it, and bill and collect for it. The first task is to measure how much of each expense was incurred in each activity.

Suppose that most salary expense went to sales representatives and the rest went to an advertising manager, packing and delivery help, and an office accountant. Let the breakdown of the $9300 be $5100, $1200, $1400, and $1600, respectively. Table 26-3 shows the allocation of the salary expense to these four activities.

Table 26-3 also shows the rent account of $3000 as allocated to the four activities. Since the sales representatives work away from the office, none of the building's rent expense is assigned to selling. Most of the expenses for floor space and rented equipment are in connection with packing and delivery. A small portion of the floor space is used by the advertising manager and office accountant.

Finally, the supplies account covers promotional materials, packing materials, fuel purchases for delivery, and home-office stationery. The $3500 in this account is reassigned to the functional uses made of the supplies. Table 26-3 summarizes how the natural expenses of $15 800 were translated into functional expenses.

Step 2: Assigning the Functional Expenses to the Marketing Entities   The next task is to measure how much functional expense was associated with selling through each type

Table 26-2 A Simplified Profit-and-Loss Statement

Sales		$60 000
Cost of goods sold		39 000
Gross margin		$21 000
Expenses		
Salaries	$9 300	
Rent	3 000	
Supplies	3 500	
		15 800
Net profit		$ 5 200

Table 26-3 Mapping Natural Expenses into Functional Expenses

Natural Accounts	Total	Selling	Advertising	Packing and Delivery	Billing and Collecting
Salaries	$ 9300	$5100	$1200	$1400	$1600
Rent	3000	—	400	2000	600
Supplies	3500	400	1500	1400	200
	$15 800	$5500	$3100	$4800	$2400

of channel. Consider the selling effort. The selling effort is indicated by the number of sales made in each channel. This number is found in the selling column of Table 26-4. Altogether, 275 sales calls were made during the period. Since the total selling expense amounted to $5500 (see Table 26-4), the selling expense per call averaged $20.

Advertising expense can be allocated according to the number of ads addressed to the different channels. Since there were one hundred ads altogether, the average ad cost $31.

The packing and delivery expense is allocated according to the number of orders placed by each type of channel; this same basis was used for allocating billing and collection expense.

Step 3: Preparing a Profit-and-Loss Statement for Each Marketing Entity   A profit-and-loss statement can now be prepared for each type of channel. The results are shown in Table 26-5. Since hardware stores accounted for one-half of total sales ($30 000 out of $60 000), this channel is charged with half the cost of goods sold ($19 500 out of $39 000). This leaves a gross margin from hardware stores of $10 500. From this must be deducted the proportions of the functional expenses that hardware stores consumed. According to Table 26-4, hardware stores received 200 out of 275 total sales calls. At an imputed value of $20 a call, hardware stores have to be charged with a $4000 selling expense. Table 26-4 also shows that hardware stores were the target of fifty ads. At $31 an ad, the hardware stores are charged with $1550 of advertising. The same reasoning applies in computing the share of the other functional expenses to charge to hardware stores. The result is that hardware stores gave rise to $10 500 of the total expenses. Subtracting this from the gross margin, the profit of selling through hardware stores is only $450.

This analysis is repeated for the other channels. The company is losing money in selling through garden supply shops and makes virtually all of its profits in selling through depart-

Table 26-4 Bases for Allocating Functional Expenses to Channels

Channel Type	Selling	Advertising	Packing and Delivery	Billing and Collecting
	No. of Sales Calls in Period	No. of Advertisement	No. of Orders Placed in Period	No. of Orders Placed in Period
Hardware	200	50	50	50
Garden supply	65	20	21	21
Department stores	10	30	9	9
	275	100	80	80
Functional expense	$5500	$3100	$4800	$2400
No. of units	275	100	80	80
Expense/Unit	$20	$31	$60	$30

Table 26-5 Profit-and-Loss Statements for Channels

	Hardware	Garden Supply	Dept. Stores	Whole Company
Sales	$30 000	$10 000	$20 000	$60 000
Cost of goods sold	19 500	6 500	13 000	39 000
Gross margin	$10 500	$ 3 500	$ 7 000	$21 000
Expenses				
Selling ($20 per call)	$ 4 000	$ 1 300	$ 200	$ 5 500
Advertising ($31 per advertisement)	$ 1 550	620	930	3 100
Packing and delivery ($60 per order)	3 000	1 260	540	4 800
Billing ($30 per order)	1 500	630	270	2 400
Total expenses	$10 050	$ 3 810	$ 1 940	$15 800
Net profit (or loss)	$ 450	$ (310)	$ 5 060	$ 5 200

ment stores. Notice that the gross sales through each channel are not a reliable indicator of the net profits being made in each channel.

Determining the Best Corrective Action

It would be naive to conclude that garden supply shops and possibly hardware stores should be dropped in order to concentrate on department stores. The following questions would need to be answered first:

☐ To what extent do buyers buy on the basis of the type of retail outlet versus the brand? Would they seek out the brand in those channels that were not eliminated?

☐ What are the trends with respect to the importance of these three channels?

☐ Have company marketing strategies directed at the three channels been optimal?

On the basis of the answers, marketing management can evaluate a number of alternative actions:

☐ *Establish a special charge for handling smaller orders to encourage larger orders*: This move assumes that small orders are a cause of the relative unprofitability of dealing with garden supply shops and hardware stores.

☐ *Give more promotional aid to garden supply shops and hardware stores*: This assumes that the managers of these stores could increase their sales with more training or promotional materials.

☐ *Reduce the number of sales calls and the amount of advertising going to garden supply shops and hardware stores*: This assumes that some costs can be saved without seriously reducing sales to these channels.

☐ *Do nothing*: This assumes that current marketing efforts are optimal and either that marketing trends point to an imminent profit improvement in the weaker channels or that dropping any channel would reduce profits because of repercussions on production costs or on demand.

☐ *Don't abandon any channel as a whole but only the weakest retail units in each channel*: This assumes that a detailed cost study would reveal many profitable garden shops and hardware stores whose profits are concealed by the poor performance of other stores in these categories.

In general, marketing-profitability analysis indicates the relative profitability of different channels, products, territories, or other marketing entities.[9] It does not prove that the best course of action is to drop the unprofitable marketing entities, nor does it capture the likely profit improvement if these marginal marketing entities are dropped.

Direct versus Full Costing

Like all information tools, marketing-profitability analysis can lead or mislead marketing executives, depending upon the degree of their understanding of its methods and limitations. The example showed some arbitrariness in the choice of bases for allocating the functional expenses to the marketing entities being evaluated. Thus the "number of sales calls" was used to allocate selling expenses, when in principle, "number of sales working-hours" is a more accurate indicator of cost. The former base was used because it involves less record keeping and computation. These approximations might not involve too much inaccuracy, but marketing executives should be aware of this judgmental element in determining marketing costs.[10]

Far more serious is another judgmental element affecting profitability analysis. The issue is whether to allocate *full costs* or only *direct and traceable costs* in evaluating the performance of a marketing entity. The example above sidestepped this problem by assuming only simple costs that fit in with marketing activities. But the question cannot be avoided in the actual analysis of profitability. Three types of costs have to be distinguished:

☐ *Direct Costs*: These are costs that can be assigned directly to the proper marketing entities. For example, sales commissions are a direct cost in a profitability analysis of sales territories, sales representatives, or customers. Advertising expenditures are a direct cost in a profitability analysis of products to the extent that each advertisement promotes only one company product. Other direct costs for specific purposes are salesforce salaries, supplies, and traveling expenses.

☐ *Traceable Common Costs*: These are costs that can be assigned only indirectly, but on a plausible basis, to the marketing entities. In the example, rent was analyzed in this way. The company's floor space was needed for three different marketing activities, and an estimate was made of how much floor space supported each activity.

☐ *Nontraceable Common Costs*: These are costs whose allocation to the marketing entities is highly arbitrary. Consider "corporate image" expenditures. To allocate them equally to all products would be arbitrary, because all products do not benefit equally from corporate image making. To allocate them proportionately to the sales of the various products would be arbitrary because relative product sales reflect many factors besides corporate image making. Other typical examples of difficult-to-assign common costs are top management salaries, taxes, interest, and other types of overhead.

No one disputes including direct costs in marketing cost analysis. There is a small amount of controversy about including traceable common costs. Traceable common costs lump together costs that would change with the scale of marketing activity and costs that would not change. If the lawn mower company drops garden supply shops, it will probably continue to pay the same rent for contractual reasons. In this event, its profits would not rise immediately by the amount of the present loss in selling to garden supply shops ($310). The profit figures are more meaningful when traceable costs can be eliminated.

The major controversy concerns whether the nontraceable common costs should be allocated to the marketing entities. Such allocation is called the *full-cost approach*, and its advocates argue that all costs must ultimately be imputed in order to determine true profitability. But this argument confuses the use of accounting for financial reporting with its use for managerial decision making. Full costing has three major weaknesses:

☐ The relative profitability of different marketing entities can shift radically when one arbitrary way to allocate nontraceable common costs is replaced by another. This weakens confidence in the tool.

☐ The arbitrariness demoralizes managers, who feel that their performance is judged adversely.

☐ The inclusion of nontraceable common costs could weaken efforts at real cost control. Operating management is most effective in controlling direct costs and traceable common costs. Arbitrary assignments of nontraceable common costs can lead them to spend their time fighting the arbitrary cost allocations rather than managing their controllable costs well.

EFFICIENCY CONTROL

Suppose a profitability analysis reveals that the company is earning poor profits in connection with certain products, territories, or markets. The question is whether there are more efficient ways to manage the sales force, advertising, sales promotion, and distribution in connection with these poorer-performing marketing entities.

Salesforce Efficiency

Sales managers should keep track of the following key indicators of salesforce efficiency in their territory:

☐ Average number of sales calls per salesperson per day

☐ Average sales-call time per contact

☐ Average revenue per sales call

☐ Average cost per sales call

☐ Entertainment cost per sales call

☐ Percentage of orders per one hundred sales calls

☐ Number of new customers per period

☐ Number of lost customers per period

☐ Salesforce cost as a percentage of total sales

These indicators raise such useful questions as the following: Are sales representatives making too few calls per day? Are they spending too much time per call? Are they spending too much on entertainment? Are they closing enough orders per hundred calls? Are they producing enough new customers and holding onto the old customers?

When a company starts investigating salesforce efficiency, it can often find areas for improvement. General Electric reduced the size of one of its divisional salesforces after discovering that its salespeople were calling on customers too often. When a large airline found that its salespeople were both selling and servicing, they transferred the servicing function to lower-paid clerks. Another company conducted time-and-duty studies and found ways to reduce the ratio of idle-to-productive time.

Advertising Efficiency

Many managers feel that it is almost impossible to measure what they are getting for their advertising dollars. But an effort should be made to keep track of at least the following statistics:

- Advertising cost per thousand target buyers reached by media category and media vehicle
- Readership estimates of print advertisements, based on percentages of readers who noted, saw, associated, and read most of them in each media-vehicle
- Consumer opinions on the ad content and effectiveness
- Before-after measures of attitude toward the product
- Number of inquiries stimulated by the ad
- Cost per inquiry

Management can undertake a number of steps to improve advertising efficiency, including doing a better job of positioning the product, defining advertising objectives, pretesting messages, using the computer to guide the selection of advertising media, looking for better media buys, and doing advertising post-testing.

Sales-Promotion Efficiency

Sales promotion includes dozens of devices for stimulating buyer interest and product trial. To improve sales-promotion efficiency, management should record the costs and sales impact of each sales promotion. Management should watch the following statistics:

- Percentage of sales sold on deal
- Display costs per sales dollar
- Percentage of coupons redeemed
- Number of inquiries resulting from a demonstration.

If a sales-promotion manager is appointed, that manager can analyze the results of different sales promotions and advise product managers on the most cost-effective promotions to use.

Distribution Efficiency

Management needs to search for distribution economies. Several tools are available for improving inventory control, warehouse locations, and transportation modes. Improvement of local delivery costs is also possible, as the following example shows:

> *Wholesale bakers* face increased competition from *chain-store bakers*. They are especially at a disadvantage in the physical distribution of bread. The wholesale bakers must make more stops and deliver less bread per stop. Furthermore, the driver typically loads each store's shelf, while the chain bakery leaves the bread at the chain's unloading platform to be placed on the shelf by store personnel. This led the bakers' association to investigate whether more efficient bread-handling procedures were achievable. A systems engineering study was conducted. The bread delivery operation was studied in minute detail from the time of truck loading to the time of shelving. As a result of riding with the drivers and observing procedures, the engineers recommended several changes.

Economies could be secured from more scientific routing; from a relocation of the truck's door from the back of the trailer to the driver's side; and from the development of preshelved racks. These economies were always available but not recognized until competitive pressure increased the need for improved efficiency. ■

STRATEGIC CONTROL

From time to time, companies need to undertake a critical review of their overall marketing effectiveness. Marketing is an area where rapid obsolescence of objectives, policies, strategies, and programs is a constant possibility. Each company should periodically reassess its overall approach to the marketplace. Two tools are available, namely, a *marketing-effectiveness rating review* and a *marketing audit*.

Marketing-Effectiveness Rating Review

Here is an actual situation.

The president of a major industrial-equipment company reviewed the annual business plans of various divisions and found several division plans lacking in marketing substance. He called in the corporate vice-president of marketing and said:

I am not happy with the quality of marketing in our divisions. It is very uneven. I want you to find out which of our divisions are strong, average, and weak in marketing. I want to know if they understand and are practicing customer-oriented marketing. I want a marketing score for each division. For each marketing-deficient division, I want a plan for improving its marketing effectiveness over the next several years. I want evidence next year that each marketing-deficient division is making progress toward a marketing orientation.

The corporate marketing vice-president agreed, recognizing that it was a formidable task. His first inclination was to base the evaluation of marketing effectiveness on each division's performance in sales growth, market share, and profitability. His thinking was that high-performing divisions had good marketing leadership and poor-performing divisions had poor marketing leadership. ■

Marketing effectiveness is not necessarily revealed by current sales and profit performance. Good results could be due to a division's being in the right place at the right time, rather than having effective marketing management. Improvements in that division's marketing might boost results from good to excellent. Another division might have poor results in spite of excellent marketing planning. Replacing the present marketing managers might only make things worse.

The marketing effectiveness of a company or division is reflected in the degree to which it exhibits five major attributes of a marketing orientation: *customer philosophy, integrated marketing organization, adequate marketing information, strategic orientation*, and *operational efficiency*. Each attribute can be measured. Table 26-6 presents a *marketing-effectiveness rating instrument* based on these five attributes. This instrument is filled out by marketing and other managers in the division. The scores are then summarized.

The instrument has been tested in a number of companies, and very few achieve scores within the superior range of twenty-six to thirty points. The few include well-known master marketers such as Procter & Gamble, McDonald's, IBM, and General Electric. Most companies and divisions receive scores in the fair-to-good range, indicating that their own managers see room for marketing improvement. Low attribute scores indicate that the attribute needs

Table 26-6 Marketing-Effectiveness Rating Instrument (Check One Answer to Each Question)

Customer Philosophy

A. *Does management recognize the importance of designing the company to serve the needs and wants of chosen markets?*

Score

0 □ Management primarily thinks in terms of selling current and new products to whoever will buy them.

1 □ Management thinks in terms of serving a wide range of markets and needs with equal effectiveness.

2 □ Management thinks in terms of serving the needs and wants of well-defined markets chosen for their long-run growth and profit potential for the company.

B. *Does management develop different offerings and marketing plans for different segments of the market?*

0 □ No.

1 □ Somewhat.

2 □ To a good extent.

C. *Does management take a whole marketing system view (suppliers, channels, competitors, customers, environment) in planning its business?*

0 □ No. Management concentrates on selling and servicing its immediate customers.

1 □ Somewhat. Management takes a long view of its channels although the bulk of its effort goes to selling and servicing the immediate customers.

2 □ Yes. Management takes a whole marketing systems view recognizing the threats and opportunities created for the company by changes in any part of the system.

Integrated Marketing Organization

D. *Is there high-level marketing integration and control of the major marketing functions?*

0 □ No. Sales and other marketing functions are not integrated at the top and there is some unproductive conflict.

1 □ Somewhat. There is formal integration and control of the major marketing functions but less than satisfactory coordination and cooperation.

2 □ Yes. The major marketing functions are effectively integrated.

E. *Does marketing management work well with management in research, manufacturing, purchasing, physical distribution, and finance?*

0 □ No. There are complaints that marketing is unreasonable in the demands and costs it places on other departments.

1 □ Somewhat. The relations are amicable although each department pretty much acts to serve its own power interests.

2 □ Yes. The departments cooperate effectively and resolve issues in the best interest of the company as a whole.

F. *How well-organized is the new product process?*

0 □ The system is ill-defined and poorly handled.

1 □ The system formally exists but lacks sophistication.

2 □ The system is well-structured and professionally staffed.

Adequate Marketing Information

G. *When were the latest marketing research studies of customers, buying influences, channels, and competitors conducted?*

0 □ Several years ago.

1 □ A few years ago.

2 □ Recently.

H. *How well does management know the sales potential and profitability of different market segments, customers, territories, products, channels, and order sizes?*
0 □ Not at all.
1 □ Somewhat.
2 □ Very well.

I. *What effort is expended to measure the cost effectiveness of different marketing expenditures?*
0 □ Little or no effort.
1 □ Some effort.
2 □ Substantial effort.

Strategic Orientation

J. *What is the extent of formal marketing planning?*
0 □ Management does little or no formal marketing planning.
1 □ Management develops an annual marketing plan.
2 □ Management develops a detailed annual marketing plan and a careful long-range plan that is updated annually.

K. *What is the quality of the current marketing strategy?*
0 □ The current strategy is not clear.
1 □ The current strategy is clear and represents a continuation of traditional strategy.
2 □ The current strategy is clear, innovative, data-based, and well-reasoned.

L. *What is the extent of contingency thinking and planning?*
0 □ Management does little or no contingency thinking.
1 □ Management does some contingency thinking although little formal contingency planning.
2 □ Management formally identifies the most important contingencies and develops contingency plans.

Operational Efficiency

M. *How well is the marketing thinking at the top communicated and implemented down the line?*
0 □ Poorly.
1 □ Fairly.
2 □ Successfully.

N. *Is management doing an effective job with the marketing resources?*
0 □ No. The marketing resources are inadequate for the job to be done.
1 □ Somewhat. The marketing resources are adequate but they are not employed optimally.
2 □ Yes. The marketing resources are adequate and are deployed efficiently.

O. *Does management show a good capacity to react quickly and effectively to on-the-spot developments?*
0 □ No. Sales and market information is not very current and management reaction time is slow.
1 □ Somewhat. Management receives fairly up-to-date sales and market information; management reaction time varies.
2 □ Yes. Management has installed systems yielding highly current information and fast reaction time.

Total Score

The instrument is used in the following way. The appropriate answer is checked for each question. The scores are added—the total will be somewhere between 0 and 30. The following scale shows the level of marketing effectiveness:

attention. Divisional management can then establish a plan for correcting its major marketing weaknesses.[11]

The Marketing Audit

Those companies and divisions that discover marketing weakness through applying the marketing-effectiveness rating review should undertake a more thorough study known as a *marketing audit*.[12] We define *marketing audit* as follows:

> A marketing audit *is a* comprehensive, systematic, independent, *and* periodic *examination of a company's—or business unit's—marketing environment, objectives, strategies, and activities with a view to determining problem areas and opportunities and recommending a plan of action to improve the company's marketing performance.*

Let us examine the marketing audit's four characteristics:

☐ *Comprehensive*: The marketing audit covers all the major marketing activities of a business, not just a few trouble spots. It would be called a functional audit if it covered only the salesforce or pricing or some other marketing activity. Although functional audits are useful, they sometimes mislead management as to the real source of its problem. Excessive salesforce turnover, for example, could be a symptom not of poor salesforce training or compensation but of weak company products and promotion. A comprehensive marketing audit usually is more effective in locating the real source of the company's marketing problems.

☐ *Systematic*: The marketing audit involves an orderly sequence of diagnostic steps covering the organization's marketing environment, internal marketing system, and specific marketing activities. The diagnosis is followed by a corrective-action plan involving both short-run and long-run proposals to improve the organization's overall marketing effectiveness.

☐ *Independent*: A marketing audit can be conducted in six ways: self-audit, audit from across, audit from above, company auditing office, company task-force audit, and outsider audit. Self-audits, where managers use a checklist to rate their own operations, can be useful, but most experts agree that self-audits lack objectivity and independence.[13] The 3M Company has made good use of a corporate auditing office, which provides marketing audit services to divisions on request.[14] Generally speaking, however, the best audits are likely to come from outside consultants who have the necessary objectivity and independence, broad experience in a number of industries, some familiarity with this industry, and the undivided time and attention to give to the audit.

☐ *Periodic*: Typically, marketing audits are initiated only after sales have turned down, salesforce morale has fallen, and other company problems have occurred. Ironically, companies are thrown into a crisis partly because they failed to review their marketing operations during good times. A periodic marketing audit can benefit companies in good health as well as those in trouble. "No marketing operation is ever so good that it cannot be improved. Even the best can be made better. In fact, even the best must be better, for few if any marketing operations can remain successful over the years by maintaining the status quo."[15]

Marketing Audit Procedure   A marketing audit starts with a meeting between the company officer(s) and the marketing auditor(s) to work out an agreement on the objectives, coverage, depth, data sources, report format, and the time period for the audit. A detailed plan as to who is to be interviewed, the questions to be asked, the time and place of contact, and so on, is carefully prepared so that auditing time and cost are kept to a minimum. The cardinal rule in marketing auditing is, don't rely solely on the company's managers for data and opinion. Customers, dealers, and other outside groups must be interviewed. Many companies do not really know how their customers and dealers see them, nor do they fully understand customer needs.

When the data-gathering phase is over, the marketing auditor presents the main findings and recommendations. A valuable aspect of the marketing audit is the process that the managers go through to assimilate, debate, and develop new concepts of needed marketing action.

Components of the Marketing Audit   The marketing audit examines six major components of the company's marketing situation. The six components are described below, and the major auditing questions are listed in Table 26-7.

☐ *Marketing-Environment Audit*: This audit analyzes major macroenvironment forces and trends in the key components of the company's task environment: markets, customers, competitors, distributors; and dealers, suppliers, and facilitators.

☐ *Marketing-Strategy Audit*: This audit reviews the company's marketing objectives and marketing strategy to appraise how well these are adapted to the current and forecasted marketing environment.

☐ *Marketing-Organization Audit*: This audit evaluates the capability of the marketing organization for implementing the necessary strategy for the forecasted environment.

☐ *Marketing-Systems Audit*: This audit assesses the quality of the company's systems for analysis, planning, and control.

☐ *Marketing-Productivity Audit*: This audit examines the profitability of different marketing entities and the cost effectiveness of different marketing expenditures.

☐ *Marketing-Function Audits*: These audits make in-depth evaluations of major marketing-mix components, namely, products, price, distribution, salesforce, advertising, promotion, and publicity.

Table 26-7 Components of a Marketing Audit

Part I. Marketing-Environment Audit	
	MACROENVIRONMENT
A. Demographic	1. What major demographic developments and trends pose opportunities or threats to this company?
	2. What actions has the company taken in response to these developments and trends?
B. Economic	1. What major developments in income, prices, savings, and credit will affect the company?

2. What actions has the company been taking in response to developments and trends?

C. Ecological
1. What is the outlook for the cost and availability of natural resources and energy needed by the company?
2. What concerns have been expressed about the company's role in pollution and conservation, and what steps has the company taken?

D. Technological
1. What major changes are occurring in product technology? In process technology? What is the company's position in these technologies?
2. What major generic substitutes might replace this product?

E. Political
1. What laws are being proposed that could affect marketing strategy and tactics?
2. What federal, provincial, and local actions should be watched? What is happening in the areas of pollution control, equal employment opportunity, product safety, advertising, price control, and so forth, that affects marketing strategy?

F. Cultural
1. What is the public's attitude toward business and toward the products produced by the company?
2. What changes in consumer and business lifestyles and values have a bearing on the company?

TASK ENVIRONMENT

A. Markets
1. What is happening to market size, growth, geographical distribution, and profits?
2. What are the major market segments?

B. Customers
1. How do customers and prospects rate the company and its competitors on reputation, product quality, service, salesforce, and price?
2. How do different customer segments make their buying decisions?

C. Competitors
1. Who are the major competitors? What are their objectives and strategies, their strengths and weaknesses, their sizes and market shares?
2. What trends will affect future competition and substitutes for this product?

D. Distribution and Dealers
1. What are the main trade channels for bringing products to customers?
2. What are the efficiency levels and growth potentials of the different trade channels?

E. Suppliers
1. What is the outlook for the availability of key resources used in production?
2. What trends are occurring among suppliers in their pattern of selling?

F. Facilitators and Marketing Firms
1. What is the cost and availability outlook for transportation service?
2. What is the cost and availability outlook for warehousing facilities?
3. What is the cost and availability outlook for financial resources?

4. How effective are the company's advertising agencies and marketing research firms?

G. Publics

1. What publics represent particular opportunities or problems for the company?
2. What steps has the company taken to deal effectively with each public?

Part II. Marketing-Strategy Audit

A. Business Mission

1. Is the business mission clearly stated in market-oriented terms? Is it feasible?

B. Marketing Objectives Goals

1. Are the corporate and marketing objectives stated in the form of clear goals to guide marketing planning and performance and measurement?
2. Are the marketing objectives appropriate, given the company's competitive position, resources, and opportunities?

C. Strategy

1. Is management able to articulate a clear marketing strategy for achieving its marketing objectives? Is the strategy convincing? Is the strategy appropriate to the stage of the product life cycle, competitors' strategies, and the state of the economy?
2. Is the company using the best basis for market segmentation? Does it have sound criteria for rating the segments and choosing the best ones? Has it developed accurate profiles of each target segment?
3. Has the company developed a sound positioning and markeking mix for each target segment? Are marketing resources allocated optimally to the major elements of the marketing mix—i.e., product quality, service, salesforce, advertising, promotion, and distribution?
4. Are enough resources or too many resources budgeted to accomplish the marketing objectives?

Part III. Marketing-Organization Audit

A. Formal Structure

1. Does the marketing officer have adequate authority over, and responsibility for, company activities that affect the customer's satisfaction?
2. Are the marketing activities optimally structured along functional, product, end-user, and territorial lines?

B. Functional Efficiency

1. Are there good communication and working relations between marketing and sales?
2. Is the product management system working effectively? Are product managers able to plan profits or only sales volume?
3. Are there any groups in marketing that need more training, motivation, supervision, or evaluation?

C. Interface

1. Are there any problems between marketing and manufacturing, Efficiency R&D, purchasing, finance, accounting, and legal that need attention?

Part IV. Marketing-Systems Audit

A. Marketing Information System	1. Is the marketing intelligence system producing accurate, sufficient, and timely information about marketplace developments with respect to customers, prospects, distributors and dealers, competitors, suppliers, and various publics?
	2. Are company decision makers asking for enough marketing research, and are they using the results?
	3. Is the company employing the best methods for market and sales forecasting?
B. Marketing Planning Systems	1. Is the marketing planning system well conceived and effective?
	2. Is sales forecasting and market potential measurement soundly carried out?
	3. Are sales quotas set on a proper basis?
C. Marketing Control System	1. Are the control procedures adequate to ensure that the annual-plan objectives are being achieved?
	2. Does management periodically analyze the profitability of products, markets, territories, and channels of distribution?
	3. Are marketing costs periodically examined?
D. New-Product-Development System	1. Is the company well organized to gather, generate, and screen new-product ideas?
	2. Does the company do adequate concept research and business analysis before investing in new ideas?
	3. Does the company carry out adequate product and market testing before launching new products?

Part V. Marketing-Productivity Audit

A. Profitability Analysis	1. What is the profitability of the company's different products, markets, territories, and channels of distribution?
	2. Should the company enter, expand, contract, or withdraw from any business segments and what would be the short-and long-run profit consequences?
B. Cost-Effectiveness Analysis	1. Do any marketing activities seem to have excessive costs? Can cost-reducing steps be taken?

Part VI. Marketing-Function Audits

A. Products	1. What are the product-line objectives? Are these objectives sound? Is the current product line meeting the objectives?
	2. Should the product line be stretched or contracted upward, downward, or both ways?
	3. Which products should be phased out? Which products should be added?
	4. What is the buyers' knowledge and attitude toward the company's and competitors' product quality, features, styling, brand names, etc.? What areas of product strategy need improvement?
B. Price	1. What are the pricing objectives, policies, strategies, and procedures? To what extent are prices set on cost, demand, and competitive criteria?

2. Do the customers see the company's prices as being in line with the value of its offer?

3. What does management know about the price elasticity of demand, experience curve effects, and competitors' prices and pricing policies?

4. To what extent are price policies compatible with the needs of distributors and dealers, suppliers, and government regulation?

C. Distribution
1. What are the distribution objectives and strategies?
2. Is there adequate market coverage and service?
3. How effective are the following channel members: distributors, dealers, manufacturers' representatives, brokers, agents, etc.?
4. Should the company consider changing its distribution channels?

D. Advertising, Sales Promotion, and Publicity
1. What are the organization's advertising objectives? Are they sound?
2. Is the right amount being spent on advertising? How is the budget determined?
3. Are the ad themes and copy effective? What do customers and the public think about the advertising?
4. Are the advertising media well chosen?
5. Is the internal advertising staff adequate?
6. Is the sales-promotion budget adequate? Is there effective and sufficient use of sales-promotion tools such as samples, coupons, displays, sales contests?
7. Is the publicity budget adequate? Is the public-relations staff competent and creative?

E. Salesforce
1. What are the organization's salesforce objectives?
2. Is the salesforce large enough to accomplish the company's objectives?
3. Is the salesforce organized along the proper principles of specialization (territory, market, product)? Are there enough (or too many) sales managers to guide the field sales representatives?
4. Does the sales-compensation level and structure provide adequate incentive and reward?
5. Does the salesforce show high morale, ability, and effort?
6. Are the procedures adequate for setting quotas and evaluating performances?
7. How does the company's salesforce compare to competitors' salesforces?

Example of a Marketing Audit[16]   O'Brien Candy Company is a medium-size candy company. In the past two years, its sales and profits have barely held their own. Top management feels that the trouble lies with the salesforce; they don't "work hard or smart enough." To correct the problem, management plans to introduce a new incentive-compensation system and hire a salesforce trainer to train the salesforce in modern merchandising and selling techniques. Before doing this, however, they decide to hire a marketing consultant to do a marketing audit. The auditor interviews managers, customers, sales representatives, and dealers and examines various data. Here is what the auditor finds:

The company's product line consists primarily of eighteen products, mostly candy bars. Its two leading brands are mature and account for 76 percent of total sales. The company has looked at the fast-developing markets of chocolate snacks and candies but has not made any moves yet. ∎

The company recently researched its customer profile. Its products appeal especially to lower-income and older people. Respondents who were asked to assess O'Brien's chocolate products in relation to competitors' products described them as "average quality and a bit old-fashioned." ∎

O'Brien sells its products to candy jobbers and large chains. Its salesforce calls on many of the small retailers reached by the candy jobbers, to fortify displays and provide ideas; its salesforce also calls on many small retailers not covered by jobbers. O'Brien enjoys good penetration of small retailing, although not in all segments, such as the fast-growing restaurant area. Its major approach to middlemen is a "sell-in" strategy: discounts, exclusively contracts, and stock financing. At the same time O'Brien does not do well in penetrating the various chains. Its competitors rely more heavily on mass consumer advertising and store merchandising and are more successful with the large chains. ∎

O'Brien's marketing budget is set at 15 percent of its total sales, compared with competitors' budgets of close to 20 percent. Most of the marketing budget supports the salesforce, and the remainder supports advertising; consumer promotions are very limited. The advertising budget is spent primarily in reminder advertising for the company's two leading products. New products are not developed often, and when they are, they are introduced to retailers by using a "push" strategy. ∎

The marketing organization is headed by a sales vice-president. Reporting to the sales vice-president is the sales manager, the marketing research manager, and the advertising manager. Having come up from the ranks, the sales vice-president is partial to salesforce activities and pays less attention to the other marketing functions. The salesforce is assigned to territories headed by area managers. ∎

The marketing auditor concluded that O'Brien's problems would not be solved by actions taken to improve its salesforce. The salesforce problem was symptomatic of a deeper company malaise. The auditor prepared and presented a report to management consisting of the findings and recommendations shown in Table 26-8.

THE MARKETING CONTROLLER CONCEPT

We have examined how an outside marketing auditor can contribute to strategic control. Some companies have established inside positions known as *marketing controllers* to monitor marketing expenses and activities. Marketing controllers are persons working in the controller office who have specialized in the marketing side of the business. In the past, controller offices concentrated on watching manufacturing, inventory, and financial expenses and did not include staff that understood marketing very well. The new marketing controllers are trained in finance and marketing and can perform a sophisticated financial analysis of past and planned marketing expenditures. A survey by Goodman showed that

Large sophisticated companies, such as General Foods, Du Pont, and Johnson & Johnson, have all instituted financial control positions which directly oversee advertising and, in some selected cases, merchandising policies. The major functions of these individuals are to verify

Table 26-8 Summary of Marketing Auditor's Findings and Recommendations for O'Brien Candy Company

Findings

The company's product lines are dangerously unbalanced. The two leading products accounted for 76 percent of total sales and have no growth potential. Five of the eighteen products are unprofitable and have no growth potential.

The company's marketing objectives are neither clear nor realistic.

The company's strategy is not taking changing distribution patterns into account or catering to rapidly changing markets.

The company is run by a sales organization rather than a marketing organization.

The company's marketing mix is unbalanced, with too much spending on salesforce and not enough on advertising.

The company lacks procedures for successfully developing and launching new products.

The company's selling effort is not geared to profitable accounts.

Short-Term Recommendations

Examine the current product line and weed out marginal performers with limited growth potential.

Shift some marketing expenditures from supporting mature products to supporting the more recent ones.

Shift the marketing-mix emphasis from direct selling to national advertising, especially for new products.

Conduct a market-profile study of the fastest growing segments of the candy market and develop a plan to break into these areas.

Instruct the salesforce to drop some of the smaller outlets and not to take orders for under twenty items. Also, cut out the duplication of effort of sales representatives and jobbers calling on the same accounts.

Initiate sales-training programs and an improved compensation plan.

Medium-to-Long-Term Recommendations

Hire an experienced marketing vice-president from the outside.

Set formal and operational marketing objectives.

Introduce the product manager concept in the marketing organization.

Initiate effective new-product-development programs.

Develop strong brand names.

Find ways to market its brands to the chain-stores more effectively.

Increase the level of marketing expenditures to 20 percent of sales.

Reorganize the selling function by specializing sales representatives by distribution channels.

Set sales objectives and base sales compensation on gross profit performance.

Source: Adapted with permission from Dr. Ernst A. Tirmann, "Should Your Marketing Be Audited?" *European Business*, Autumn 1971.

advertising bills, ensure the optimization of agency rates, negotiate agency contracts, and perform the audit function regarding the client's agency and certain of the suppliers.[17]

Goodman feels that this step is in the right direction and advocates an even fuller role for the marketing controller. The marketing controller would maintain a record of adherence to profit plans; maintain close control of media expense; prepare brand managers' budgets; advise on optimum timing for strategies; measure the efficiency of promotions; analyze media production costs; evaluate customer and geographic profitability; present sales-oriented financial reports; assist direct accounts in optimizing purchasing and inventory policies; and educate the marketing area to financial implications of decisions.

The Nestlé Company took a step in this direction when a specific segment of the controller operation was made available for marketing planning and control. Marketing-service analysts were assigned to each of Nestle's six marketing divisions to work for the marketing head. They carried out diverse assignments designed to improve marketing efficiency and performance. Their reports proved helpful, and the position served as a training ground for future general managers because of their exposure to marketing, production, and finance.

The marketing-controller position is desirable, particularly in organizations where marketing is still oriented toward sales rather than profits. The marketing controller can help analyze how and where the company is making its money. As future marketing managers acquire greater financial training, they can do more of this work themselves, with marketing controllers providing primarily a monitoring function of marketing expenditures.

SUMMARY

Marketing control is the natural sequel to marketing planning, organization, and implementation. Companies need to carry out four types of marketing control.

Annual-plan control consists of monitoring the current marketing effort and results to ensure that the annual sales and profit goals will be achieved. The main tools are sales analysis, market-share analysis, marketing expense-to-sales analysis, financial analysis, and customer-attitude tracking. If underperformance is detected, the company can implement several corrective measures, including cutting production, changing prices, increasing salesforce pressure, and cutting fringe expenditures.

Profitability control calls for determining the actual profitability of the firm's products, territories, market segments, and trade channels. Marketing-profitability analysis reveals the weaker marketing entities, although it does not indicate whether the weaker units should be bolstered or phased out.

Efficiency control is the task of increasing the efficiency of such marketing activities as personal selling, advertising, sales promotion, and distribution. Managers must watch certain key ratios that indicate how efficiently these functions are being performed.

Strategic control is the task of ensuring that the company's marketing objectives, strategies, and systems are optimally adapted to the current and forecasted marketing environment. One tool, known as the marketing-effectiveness rating instrument, profiles a company's or a division's overall marketing effectiveness in terms of customer philosophy, marketing organization, marketing information, strategic planning, and operational efficiency. Another tool, known as the marketing audit, is a comprehensive, systematic, independent, and periodic examination of the organization's marketing environment, objectives, strategies, and activities. The purpose of the marketing audit is to determine marketing problem areas and recommend a corrective short-run and long-run action plan to improve the organization's overall marketing effectiveness.

A growing number of companies have established marketing controller positions to monitor marketing expenditures and develop improved financial analyses of the effect of these expenditures.

■ QUESTIONS

1. "Successful marketing is really creativity in action. One cannot control creativity. To control it is to lose it." Do you agree with this statement?

2. In what ways are the "planning" and "control" of marketing strategy similar, and in what ways are they different?

3. There are four types of marketing control. Compare and contrast their objectives and purposes. How does each contribute to assessing the marketing effectiveness of the firm?

4. Discuss any major problems that confront attempts to control and evaluate marketing activities.

5. What reasons can you offer to justify doing a marketing audit for a very successful manufacturer and distributor of power boats designed for the upscale end of the market?

6. In many instances, marketing control requires comparison of a performance measure with an established standard of measurement. Suggest some steps that marketing managers could take to establish a performance standard.

7. What are the relative advantages and disadvantages of customer-satisfaction tracking when compared with other annual plan control approaches?

8. A sales manager examined his company's sales by region and noted that the Western region's sales were about 2 percent below the quota. To probe further, the sales manager examined district sales figures. He discovered that the Calgary sales district within the Western region was responsible for most of the underachievement. He then examined the individual sales of the four sales people in the Calgary sales district. This examination revealed that the top salesman, Roberts, had filled only 69 percent of his quota for the period. Is it safe to conclude that Roberts is loafing or having personal problems?

9. Suppose a company's market share falls for a couple of periods. The marketing vice-president, however, refuses to take any action, calling it a random walk. What does he mean? Is he justified?

10. Company XYZ produces five products, and its salespeople represent the full product line on each sales call. In order to determine the profit contribution of each product, sales representatives' costs (salary, commission, and expenses) have to be allocated among the five products. How should this be done?

11. A large manufacturer of industrial equipment has a salesperson assigned to each major city. Regional sales managers supervise the sales representatives in several cities. The chief marketing officer wants to evaluate the profit contribution of the different cities. How might each of the following costs be allocated to the cities: (a) billing, (b) district sales manager's expenses, (c) national magazine advertising, (d) marketing research?

12. A company conducts a marketing cost study to determine the minimum-size order for breaking even. After finding that size, should the company refuse to accept orders below it? What issues and alternatives should be considered?

13. The idea of treating the marketing department as a profit center raises some difficult problems. Name them and suggest possible solutions.

14. What is the difference between the job of a marketing auditor and that of a marketing controller?

15. Why is marketing control viewed as the natural sequel to the three other tasks of planning, organization, and implementation?

■ NOTES

1. For further discussion, see James M. Hulbert and Norman E. Toy, "A Strategic Framework for Marketing Control," *Journal of Marketing*, April 1977, pp. 12-20.

2. See Alfred R. Oxenfeldt, "How to Use Market-Share Measurement," *Harvard Business Review*, January-February 1969, pp. 59-68.

3. There is a one-half chance that a successive observation will be higher or lower. Therefore the probability of finding six successively higher values is given by $(1/2)^6 = 1/64$.

4. Alternatively, companies need to focus on the factors affecting *shareholder value*. The goal of marketing planning is to take the steps that will increase shareholder value. Shareholder value is the *present value* of the future income stream created by the company's present actions. *Rate-of-return analysis* usually focuses on only one year's results. See Alfred Rappaport, *Creating Shareholder Value* (New York: Free Press, 1986), pp. 125-30.

5. For additional reading on financial analysis, see Peter L. Mullins, *Effective Financial Management for Wholesaler-Distributors* (Washington, D.C.: National Association of Wholesaler-Distributors, 1979); and Peter L. Mullins,

Measuring Customer and Product Line Profitability (Washington, D.C.: Distribution Research and Education Foundation, 1984).

6. See Claes Fornell, "Complaint Management and Marketing Performance," (Paper, Graduate School of Management, Northwestern University, Evanston, Ill., October 1978).

7. For an application to a hotel chain, see Arthur J. Daltas, "Protecting Service Markets with Consumer Feedback," *Cornell Hotel and Restaurant Administration Quarterly*, May 1977, pp. 73-77.

8. The MAC Group, *Distribution: A Competitive Weapon* (Cambridge, Mass.: 1985), p. 20.

9. For another example, see Leland L. Beik and Stephen L. Buzby, "Profitability Analyses by Market Segments," *Journal of Marketing*, June 1973, pp. 48-53.

10. For common bases of allocation, see Charles H. Sevin, *Marketing Productivity Analysis* (New York: McGraw-Hill, 1965).

11. For further discussion of this instrument, see Philip Kotler, "From Sales Obsession to Marketing Effectiveness," *Harvard Business Review*, November-December 1977, pp. 67-75.

12. See Philip Kotler, William Gregor, and William Rodgers, "The Marketing Audit Comes of Age," *Sloan Management Review*, Winter 1977, pp. 25-43.

13. However, useful checklists for a marketing self-audit can be found in Aubrey Wilson, *Aubrey Wilson's Marketing Audit Checklists* (London: McGraw-Hill, 1982); and Mike Wilson, *The Management of Marketing* (Westmead, Eng.: Gower Publishing, 1980).

14. Kotler, Gregor, and Rodgers, "Marketing Audit Comes of Age," p. 31.

15. Abe Shuchman, "The Marketing Audit: Its Nature, Purposes, and Problems," in *Analyzing and Improving Marketing Performance*, ed. Alfred Oxenfeldt and Richard D. Crisp (New York: American Management Association, 1950), report no. 32, pp. 16-17.

16. This case is adapted with permission from the excellent article by Dr. Ernst A. Tirmann, "Should Your Marketing Be Audited?" *European Business*, Autumn 1971, pp. 49-56.

17. Sam R. Goodman, *Increasing Corporate Profitability* (New York: Ronald Press, 1982), Chap. 1.

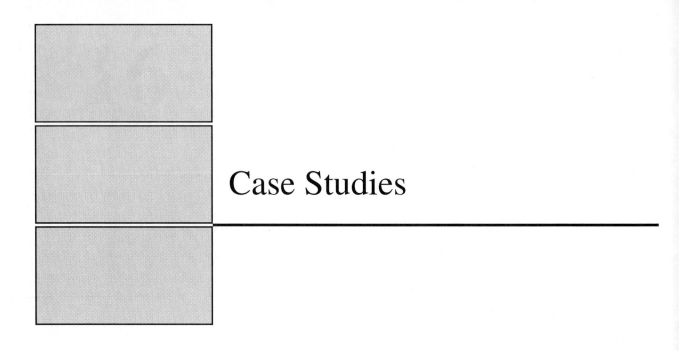

Case Studies

CASE NAME	RELEVANT CHAPTERS
A. Millie's Hand Cooked Potato Chips	Managing the Marketing Process and Marketing Planning (3) Identifying Market Segments and Selecting Target Markets (10)
B. St. Lawrence College	Managing Information Systems and Marketing Research (4) Marketing Strategies for Differentiating and Positioning the Marketing Offer (11)
C. The Detergents Industry: Green Marketing	Analyzing the Marketing Environment (5)
D. Ted Rummel Rides on Michelins	Analyzing Consumer Markets (6)
E. Atomic Energy of Canada: The 3-D Viewing System	Measuring and Forecasting Market Demand (9) Developing, Testing, and Launching New Products and Services (12)
F. E.D. Smith & Sons Ltd	Analyzing Competitors (8) Managing Product Lines, Brands and Packaging (16)
G. Sperry/MacLennan	Designing Strategies for the Global Marketplace (15) Managing Service Businesses and Ancillary Services (17)
H. Dominion Tanking	Designing Pricing Strategies and Programs (18) Analyzing Business Markets and Organizational Buying Behaviour (7)
I. Sobers of Ontario	Selecting and Managing Marketing Channels (19) Managing Retailing, Wholesaling, and Physical Distribution Systems (20)
J. Atlantic Canada Plus	Designing Communication and Promotion-Mix Strategies (21) Designing Effective Advertising Programs (22)
K. London Life Insurance	Managing the Salesforce (24) Evaluating and Controlling Marketing Performance (26)

A MILLIE'S HAND COOKED POTATO CHIPS*

In March 1990 John Miles and John Potter, equal partners in the Toronto-based food brokerage firm Betmar, purchased the assets and trademarks of Millie's Hand Cooked Potato Chips from a receiver. When the deal closed, Miles returned to his native Nova Scotia to re-establish the business. He expected to be able to have the unique chips back on the Nova Scotia market in six weeks. In order to turn the business around quickly, Miles needed to determine what had gone wrong. How could Millie's sales have increased from $500 000 to $3 million in three years and the company still have gone out of business?

John Miles had a wealth of experience in the confectionary business, having spent 23 years with Nabisco Brands as a sales manager and national account representative. After leaving Nabisco, Miles started Betmar with John Potter who came from the sales promotion company Nash Potter. Potter was the idea man and Miles made things happen.

Betmar was the successful bidder for the assets of Millie's: the machinery, a computer, the trademarks and a few supplies. The plant was not in working order, as the packaging machine had been repossessed in January 1989 due to a default on payments. In addition, the registration of the trademarks had never been completed, so the brand names were not legally protected. Betmar was to be a source of working capital for the first year.

Upon arriving at the plant, Miles discovered that there were no records or files and that he would have to try to understand what had gone wrong using only limited information. Based upon recent newspaper articles, previous conversations with Brian Shore (the former owner of Millie's), and interviews with former employees and retailers, Miles was able to piece together the following chronology of events.

Millie's was founded in 1984 by Brian Shore, a 38-year-old law school drop-out who was a natural salesman. Shore had a history of entrepreneurial activity including building and selling prefabricated homes and producing New York-style soft pretzels which he sold from vending carts. The new company was set up under Mazel Mining Co., an existing Shell company. This would enable Shore to use what little cash he had for the downpayment on a delivery vehicle, a '79 Oldsmobile with the rear seat removed. Shore had been looking for a product which would generate revenue even in hard economic times. He turned to snack foods, stating: "When people don't have a lot of money, they buy a bag of chips and a six-pack of beer and go home and watch the hockey game rather than go out to a nightclub." Financing had been through a $30 000 loan from a silent partner (who left the business in March 1985), a $64 000 loan from the Toronto Dominion Bank (five other banks refused) and a $100 000 federal government small business loan.

Canadian retail potato chip sales in 1984 were $500 million and had been experiencing an annual growth rate of 5%. The highly competitive industry was dominated by three national producers: Hostess Food Products (General Foods), Humpty Dumpty (American Brands) and Frito-Lay (Pepsi-Cola Canada). Shore commented, "I thought if I could get 2% of the industry, I would have a hell of a business."

The Millie's chip was based on a 75-year-old Pennsylvania Mennonite recipe which Shore altered to suit his taste. Conventional chip production used a continuous process where the potatoes were peeled using caustic soda, sliced, then dipped in a chemical bath or boiling water to bleach out the color and finally fried in oil. Millie's used a batch process, slicing the chips directly into an open vat fryer and cooking them at a lower temperature for a longer time. The chips were hand stirred and the cooking time was determined by sight. "Our people get used to knowing when they're ready," said Philip Morris, Millie's production manager. No preservatives or monosodium glutamate were added and sunflower oil was used to make the chips cholesterol free. The result was a thicker, crispier, more nutritious and flavorful chip. Millie's was the only company with a hand cooked chip on the Canadian market.

The name "Millie's" came from Shore's partner's wife. Said Shore, "I liked the sound of the name and the look of the double l's." Shore designed the white, red and blue package which pictured a woman with piled hair wearing a long dress and apron, stirring a cooking kettle with a ladle. The bag boasted "Natural Ingredients"

*This case was prepared by Professor Scott B. Follows at Acadia University for the Atlantic Entrepreneurial Institute as a basis for classroom discussion, and is not meant to illustrate either effective or ineffective management.

and stated, "Millie's Hand Cooked Chips are made the old-fashioned way—hand cooked one batch at a time. This original method produces a potato chip that is golden crisp and crunchy with that tremendous natural potato flavor." Said Shore, "'Naturals,' like Millie's, have become a 'yuppie' product—they've developed a cult following." And, "I just figured that if I made a different potato chip, I'd get a niche in the market."

Millie's chips cost about 20% more to produce than conventional chips, but Shore felt, "If people like a product, they'll willingly pay a premium for it." The suggested price to the consumer was similar to national producers' prices but Millie's packages were smaller.

1984—The Beginning

Shipments from the 325-square-meter north-end Halifax plant, described by Shore as "a dump with a leaky roof," began in November 1984. Millie's offered three varieties: regular, Bar-B-Q and no salt. Two package sizes were available: a 32 gram snack pack (national producers used 48 grams) and the regular 180 gram bag (national producers used 200 grams). Shore spent no money on advertising but gave a lot of chips away hoping to generate word-of-mouth: "We don't need all the new and improved hoopla. If the people like it, they'll buy it, and they'll create the demand." The only promotion of Millie's chips was Shore's sales efforts. Said Shore, "We're purposely being unsophisticated, not hiring marketing guys and whatever."

1985—Modest Growth

Shore sold to health food stores, student pubs, and independent grocery and convenience stores in the Halifax-Dartmouth area because he had difficulty getting his product into the large grocery and convenience chain stores. He felt the chain stores should be obligated to stock a local product, and refused to negotiate shelf allowances in order to get listings. It was common trade practice for grocery retailers to expect incentive payments from manufacturers. Allowances lowered a retailer's costs and paid for in-store promotions and store advertising which featured the manufacturer's product. Shore fought tradition because he believed allowances discriminated against smaller companies with limited financial resources. Unable to achieve wide distribution, he began to look beyond the Maritime region for opportunities. In early 1985, Shore thought of producing a kosher chip for the annual Jewish religious holiday,

Passover. He approached Steinberg in Montreal, one of Quebec's largest grocery chains, and received a $30 000 order. By the end of 1985, Millie's was shipping chips throughout Nova Scotia and New Brunswick, and ended the year with sales of $500 000 and a profit of almost $20 000.

1986—Rapid Growth

The year 1986 brought tremendous consumer acceptance for the chips and growth for Millie's. Listings were obtained in the large grocery chains: Sobey's, The Food Group and IGA. This move expanded distribution to Prince Edward Island and Newfoundland. In order to increase volume, Shore positioned Millie's as the low-priced competitor. Moreover, prices were occasionally reduced further during selected promotional periods, and Millie's was often used by some retailers as a low price promotion.

Due to the large number of retail accounts in Nova Scotia and New Brunswick, Millie's contracted with independent general-line wholesalers to merchandise its product in major markets outside the Halifax-Dartmouth area (Fredericton, Moncton, and Saint John in New Brunswick; Truro, Bridgewater, Sydney, and the Annapolis Valley in Nova Scotia). Merchandising entails order taking, delivering the chips, placing them on the rack in a presentable fashion and rotating the older chips to the front. The wholesalers received minimal direction and attention from Millie's. In contrast to Millie's, national producers used company vehicles operated by trained company employees.

Millie's made a number of changes in response to the growing demand for the product. It installed a new $200 000 form-filled packaging machine to speed up production. The product line was broadened to include "salt and vinegar" and "sour cream and onion," and the original snack bag was increased in size to 42 grams. In spite of $2 million in annual sales, Millie's barely broke even in 1986.

1987—Expansion

In 1987, Millie's received its first large national order. It was unexpected, and had been prompted by a small order to a local store in the Zellers chain which had put Millie's on the supplier's list. A few months later, the president of Zellers sent a letter to all suppliers soliciting funds for a charity. Shore replied with product samples and a letter stating if he had a contract he would be able to afford a donation. This resulted in an order for 500 000 bags and many of the stores sold out in two weeks. Internationally, Millie's received an order from a Taiwanese food importer whose representatives visited the plant and then ordered a container of chips (40 000 bags) six months later.

The sale of the building rented by Millie's provided an opportunity for expansion. Based on Shore's forecasted sales of $20-15 million in the next two years, Millie's moved into a $1.3 million, 1600-square-meter plant across the harbor in Dartmouth's Burnside Industrial Park. The move was financed by a $250 000 loan from the Small Business Development Corporation, and accomplished during a two-month summer shutdown caused by a potato shortage.

Shore perceived the need to compete in the conventional potato chip market, so the company launched a thinner chip called "Archie's." It gained wide distribution and was pegged at a price lower than the national producers' products. By the end of the year, Shore had appeared on the CBC's business program "Venture," and was negotiating a national contract with Boots Drug Stores, and was looking at the European and Asian markets. The company's annual sales were $3 million and it employed 35 people.

1988—The Demise

In 1988, consumer loyalty for the locally produced chip remained strong even though the chips had become increasingly greasy. Millie's had been trying to maximize the use of the frying oil to reduce costs, but had no way of testing the oil's quality.

By mid-year sales had slowed. The situation worsened when Millie's became caught in the crossfire of a price war between the national producers. Stated Shore, "If they want to shoot cannons at a mosquito they can, but they will make a mess of the wall." In addition, the federal government introduced a sales tax on snack foods which increased the price of chips to the consumer.

Distribution in the Maritimes became spotty when some of the wholesalers dropped the product due to falling sales. Shore continued to look for expansion in the Ontario market and approached John Miles to act as the Ontario broker. After a number of meetings, a tentative agreement was reached between the two parties. By year end, Shore was not returning Miles's phone calls and by January 1989, no one was answering at Millie's until one day Miles's call was answered by a representative of Touche Ross, the receiver.

■ QUESTIONS

1. Why did Millie's fail?

2. What recommendations would you make to John Miles?

B ST. LAWRENCE COLLEGE[*]

George MacIvor leaned back in his chair and thought about the assignment he had just received from the Principal.

> "I know that we conducted this survey to help develop new programs. But I want you to look at the data we collected, and see if there is anything else we might be doing to keep our students satisfied with their experience at St. Lawrence."

With that charge, the Principal handed George a copy of a recent report titled *Responding to the New Competition*, which documented the results obtained from a survey conducted by outside consultants on behalf of the College. MacIvor had mixed feelings. He was eager to examine the report, but doubtful that much could be done to satisfy today's students, who seemed more restive and demanding than those of the past.

The Environment of Adult Education

It was common knowledge in 1988 that the adult-education environment in Ontario was experiencing rapid change. Government funding was being re-channelled through agencies that encouraged the growth of new

*This case was written for class discussion by Patrick G. Buckley, Tom Mahaffey and Ronald E. Turner. Names of case characters are disguised.
Copyright © 1991, School of Business, Queen's University, Kingston, Ontario.

adult-education providers, such as computer vendors who offered programming courses. Curriculum changes in the province's secondary schools that would soon phase out grade 13, created uncertainty concerning the number of graduates who would be available to start college or university. At the same time, job opportunities upon graduation were changing as growth in the service sector outpaced that in the traditional "smokestack" industries. Consequently, many of the students who enroled in adult-education programs were increasingly anxious about job expectations. Those who became less than satisfied with their programs had a greater tendency to drop out before finishing. To minimize that problem, the College administration was making every effort to ensure that St. Lawrence's academic programs delivered what they promised.

The Mandate of St. Lawrence College

St. Lawrence College is one of Ontario's 23 colleges of applied arts and technology, whose mandate is to "provide students with the opportunity to develop the skills necessary to prepare for rewarding careers in business, the applied arts, technology, and health sciences." Most academic programs lead to either a diploma over two to three years, or a certificate over one year or less. Located in the eastern Ontario city of Kingston, St. Lawrence competes for students with the continuing education programs of both Queen's University and the Frontenac County Board of Education. The Kingston-area population is approximately 120 000 permanent residents. Local employment opportunities are provided by a mixture of light industry and government institutions. Additional job opportunities exist in Ottawa, Toronto, and Montreal, each of which is less than a three-hour drive from Kingston.

St. Lawrence's faculty and administration believe that the College should be sensitive to the education needs and wants of adults in the Kingston area. Thanks to a series of workshops held in the early eighties, they also recognize that the best way to identify those needs and wants is to employ a marketing approach to planning. That marketing management perspective led to the decision in 1987 to conduct a market survey.

The Survey

The survey was part of a study whose purpose was to identify educational needs among current and potential

students, for which St. Lawrence "could make an appropriate response." This response was expected to be the development of new educational programs. To realize these broad objectives, the research design employed several data-collection procedures, including interviews with students registered in programs at St. Lawrence. A questionnaire was developed consisting of 28 questions covering a variety of topics concerning peoples' awareness, perceptions, and preferences for adult-education institutions and their academic programs. It was administered to 117 St. Lawrence students.

As George MacIvor read the questionnaire, his attention focused on questions 3 and 4 which asked the students:

☐ to indicate on a five-point scale the importance of each of 27 attributes of educational institutions; the responses ranged from "not at all important" (coded 1) to "very important" (coded 5).

☐ to rate on a five-point scale the extent of their agreement with statements that St. Lawrence possessed each of the 27 attributes; the responses ranged from "strongly agree" (coded 1) to "strongly disagree" (coded 5).

The number of attributes and their identities had been determined by exploratory research of two kinds. First, a search was made of reports based on past studies of similar educational institutions, and a composite list of attributes was produced. Second, in a series of exploratory interviews with St. Lawrence faculty members and administrators, the list was discussed and some attributes were added while others were deleted. The outcome of that process was the list shown in Table B.1, in which the 27 attributes are partitioned into seven groups of similar-appearing attributes.*

Table B.1 also contains the arithmetic means for the scale values of each of the attributes, averaged over the 117 St. Lawrence students. The first column of means labeled "Importance" is derived from the responses to question 3. The second column labeled "Performance" contains the means obtained from the responses to question 4.

Student Satisfaction

Since the analysis of new program opportunities was being pursued as a separate activity, the main question facing George MacIvor was whether the data contained in Table B.1 might reveal any evidence of student dissatisfaction. He assumed that the root cause of dissatisfaction occurs when students' expectations are not realized. MacIvor also wondered whether Table B.1 might indicate how the limited resources available to the administration of St. Lawrence might be re-allocated to increase the level of student satisfaction most efficiently.

He was aware that sometimes only a simple retabulation of data is needed to reveal new meaning. At other times, it may be necessary to re-analyze the data, perhaps using some kind of model of market behavior. But perhaps the answer was right in front of him, if only he could recognize it. As he studied Table B.1, MacIvor wondered how much and what kind of additional analysis would be necessary to answer the question raised by the Principal.

■ QUESTIONS

1. Suggest two or more methods of analysis of the data contained in Table B.1 that George MacIvor should consider.

2. Choose one of the methods and re-analyze the data.

3. Based on your re-analysis, what recommendations should MacIvor make to the Principal?

*In the questionnaire, the attributes were ordered randomly. The partitioning shown in Table B.1 was done after the data were collected, using a technique called factor analysis.

Table B.1: Importance and Performance on Attributes of Educational Institutions

Attribute	Importance[†]	Performance[†]
Institutional access		
□ personal attention by faculty	3.84	4.19
□ easy to talk to recruitment personnel	3.29	4.01
□ reasonably priced courses	4.22	4.10
□ safe grounds at night	4.03	3.92
□ courses with the content you want	4.74	4.32
Extra-curricular activities		
□ opportunity for extra-curricular activities	3.60	4.01
□ good athletic facilities	2.88	3.57
□ good intercollegiate teams	3.08	3.76
□ attractive campus grounds	3.07	3.88
Sociable atmosphere		
□ a good social life	2.92	3.95
□ courteous students	4.07	3.77
□ friendly campus atmosphere	4.06	3.91
Facilities		
□ a good library	4.15	3.82
□ modern equipment in classes and labs	4.70	3.87
□ comfortable classrooms	3.44	3.34
□ a variety of programs	4.07	4.19
□ lots of parking	3.84	3.41
Quality of education		
□ competent graduates	4.16	4.00*
□ high-quality students	3.81	3.67
□ knowledgeable teachers	4.59	4.21
□ good-quality programs	4.82	4.23
Easy access		
□ convenient location	3.49	4.20

☐ ease of registration	3.64	3.96
☐ courses at convenient times	4.07	4.05
Applied emphasis		
☐ courses that lead to employment	4.24	4.48
☐ programs needed in the community	3.67	4.17
☐ employment assistance to students	3.92*	4.10

† *Importance was measured on a five-point scale on which:*
1 = not at all important .... 5 = very important

Performance was measured on a five-point scale on which:
1 = strongly disagree .... 5 = strongly agree (that attribute is provided)

* *Median value of the mean ratings for all attributes in the column.*

C THE DETERGENTS INDUSTRY: GREEN MARKETING*

In Canada, public interest in the environment increased dramatically in 1989. Several polls were conducted to determine the magnitude of consumer demand for environmentally friendly products. A June 1989 poll conducted by Telepoll Research Inc. reported that 51% of respondents said that they regularly bought environmentally friendly products. The percentage of shoppers who consciously looked for environmentally safe products was 65% in Quebec, 54% in B.C., 46% in Ontario and the Atlantic provinces, and 42% in the Prairies.

A survey conducted by the Grocery Products Manufacturers of Canada in November 1989 indicated that 29% of shoppers surveyed were definitely willing to pay a premium for environmentally friendly products and that a further 51% were somewhat willing to pay more. The poll also revealed that 36% of shoppers surveyed would look for recyclable biodegradable packaging on a household product.

The catalyst that accelerated interest in Green products, was the introduction of the "Green" line of environmentally friendly products by Loblaws, a major Ontario based grocery chain, on June 3, 1989. This line of products joined Loblaws' two other private label brands, President's Choice and No Name. The Green line of products contained such items as re-refined motor oil, phosphate free laundry detergent, and disposable diapers made of pulp fluff, bleached without chlorine. This launch of environmentally friendly products was backed by a $3 million television and print ad campaign. The "Insider's Report," an in-house flyer, featured different products on a bi-monthly basis. The slogan, "Something Can Be Done," heralded the Green line of products.

David Nichol, president of Loblaw International Merchants, outlined the objective for the new line of products. "These products are merely a single step in the long journey toward a cleaner, healthier environment. Until now we had considered that environmental problems are too big for one person to tackle. If Green products do nothing more than teach Canadians something can be done . . . even by individuals to help improve our environment . . . they will have made a positive contribution."

Cleaning products were one of the principal categories identified by Loblaws. Loblaws introduced a green 100% phosphate free laundry detergent and a complete line of "Ecover" biodegradable detergents and cleaning products from Belgium. Although the introduction of these products posed no immediate threat to the major laundry detergent manufacturer's market shares, the message was clear. Environmentally friendly products presented a marketing opportunity.

Loblaws worked with environmental groups such as Pollution Probe and Friends of the Earth to develop many of the products. In some cases, specific products were developed which some of the environmental groups endorsed. Loblaws received the endorsement of Pollution Probe for some of the Green products, including a new line of green diapers. The executive director of Pollution Probe, Colin Isaacs, appeared in a television commercial with David Nichol endorsing Loblaws' environmentally friendly diapers.

Many Pollution Probe members disagreed with such actions, which led to internal fighting within the organization. This resulted in the resignation of Colin Isaacs. Some members felt that the organization should not support a company that marketed "less than perfect" products as the Green products were only less harmful to the environment, not environmentally pure. Others felt that endorsement would compromise the integrity and independence of the whole organization. After all, David Nichol was only after a buck. David Nichol summed up the affect of this controversy on other manufacturers. "Because of the nonsense and the tempest in a tea pot that's been going on, given how conservative Canadian businessmen are, I'm sure that nobody will follow us in terms of a line of products. And I'm sure that manufacturers will just back away from dealing with issues that have to do with the environment."

The detergent manufacturers had already been developing environmental products because of the success of similar products in Europe. The public's immediate positive response to Loblaws' campaign speeded up the product and packaging development process for the Canadian market. Procter & Gamble was the first manufacturer to respond.

Procter & Gamble

In October 1989, Procter & Gamble introduced a new form of refill packaging called Enviro-Pak for a number of its market leading cleaning products. These market leading brands included such brands as Liquid Tide laundry detergent, Mr. Clean household cleaner, Ivory Liquid dishwashing detergent, and Downy Liquid fabric softener. The consumer would buy the Enviro-Pak and then pour the contents into a plastic bottle. It was a lightweight pouch made of laminated, double-film plastic combining low density polyethylene and polyester. The Enviro-Pak reduced the amount of plastic packaging by 70% per unit on Liquid Tide, Mr. Clean, and Ivory Liquid. The reduction in packaging materials on Downy was 85% per unit.

"We developed Enviro-Pak to meet a growing consumer need for products that reduce solid waste. It's a practical way for consumers to make a difference by reducing the amount of plastic they throw out," said Procter & Gamble President, E. Douglas Grindstaff. "Enviro-Pak will cut by about five million the number of plastic bottles thrown away each year in Canada."

The introduction of the Enviro-Pak on the Canadian market was backed by a substantial advertising program. Television advertising for the Enviro-Pak featured all four brands in each advertisement. The Enviro-Paks were priced at a level that was up to 15% less than an equivalent rigid plastic bottle. However, lower prices on Enviro-Pak were not necessarily reflected at the shelf level. Trade promotion support behind Enviro-Pak was significantly less than competitive brands. As a result, it was rarely feature priced in the store. It would usually be possible to purchase a competitive brand at a comparable or lower price as the categories were heavily promoted.

Procter & Gamble encountered a few other problems after introducing the Enviro-Pak. The process used to manufacture the packages used 70-85% less plastic; however, the plastic used to manufacture the pouches was a multilaminate plastic that could not be recycled using existing technology. The flexibility of the pouches created two additional problems. They were not easy to stack on the shelf. Also, the company had to reinforce the cardboard packing containers (requiring the cutting down of more trees) in order to protect the Enviro-Pak from the stock boy's knife when the packages were opened.

Other environmental initiatives included Procter & Gamble's use of 100% recycled paper for its packaging and shipping containers. The company also reduced the amount of material used to manufacture its disposable diapers. The bulky cellulose core of the disposable diaper was replaced with a nonbulky absorbent material that reduced the disposable diaper volume going into landfills by 50%.

In December 1989, Procter & Gamble relaunched Unscented Tide as Tide Free. Unscented Tide, had been promoted as not containing perfumes. The relaunched brand, Tide Free, did not contain perfumes, dyes, or phosphates. The regular brand of Tide continued to be formulated with 5% phosphates.

Church & Dwight

One company, Church & Dwight, was fortunate to be already marketing products that were enthusiastically endorsed by environmental groups. Church & Dwight manufactures such brands as Cow Brand Baking Soda, Arm & Hammer Super Washing Soda, Arm & Hammer Heavy Duty Detergent, and Cow Brand Carpet and Room Deodorizer.

"I believe that our products are a part of the real solution to major environmental issues. This is a growing field of concern and, if it's handled right by companies like ourselves, we can educate consumers to displace products for safer products that are more beneficial to the environment," said Donald Bowman, the Canadian president. He was referring to the fact that the majority of Church & Dwight's products contained baking soda, a product considered friendly to the environment. Baking soda and washing soda, both manufactured by Church & Dwight, were listed by many environmental groups as alternatives to household cleaners which released chemicals into the water systems.

Church & Dwight recognized the potential role of its products in an increasingly environmentally concerned marketplace. The company responded to this growing concern by placing an environmentally friendly symbol on the packaging of its baking soda and by developing point-of-sale material to indicate to the consumer that the product was environmentally friendly.

The company also introduced a new two kilogram box of baking soda under the American brand name "Arm & Hammer." This large box of baking soda was introduced to satisfy the growing demand for baking soda as consumers discovered the wide variety of environmentally friendly uses for baking soda. The second brand provided the opportunity for retailers to shelve a baking soda product in the cleaning products section of the store.

In response to other detergent manufacturers' environmental initiatives, Church & Dwight removed phosphates from its Arm & Hammer Heavy Duty Detergent during this period.

"What we are talking about is a very small part of a solution to a much bigger problem, but it's a part that our company is responding to. Companies will respond when they see a commercial advantage," said Bowman. "They may be driven by some noble aspirations, but there has to be a payoff." Other companies, like Bristol Myers, were watching developments very carefully.

Bristol Myers

Bristol Myers is a multinational manufacturer of drug, personal, and household products. The Canadian household division has dominated the bleach market with Javex and has been a major factor in the fabric softener market with Fleecy. In addition, it markets the products of its parent U.S. affiliate, Drackett Company, such as Windex and Vanish. The Javex and Fleecy brands were sold to Colgate-Palmolive in the first half of 1990.

"The cleaning products industry in general has been

under suspicion without it being under attack. We have been checking every ingredient and every element that we use for any effect that could be undesirable," said Stephen Ader, Vice President Marketing, Bristol Myers. "We want to ensure that our packaging is recyclable and that it is actually being recycled. It's more of a defensive strategy to avoid criticism.

Bristol Myers' environmental initiatives during this period included using recycled paper for its packaging and using a percentage of recycled plastics to manufacture its plastic bottles. The company also introduced superconcentrated forms of its products to reduce packaging. It introduced a one liter package of superconcentrated Fleecy fabric softener that contained as much fabric softener as the normal five liter plastic bottle of Fleecy. An environmentally friendly flash promoting the fact that the packaging saved plastic was placed on the new form of packaging; however, the sales of Fleecy did not increase as a result. "Not enough people have understood that this is the best environmental choice you can make when buying a fabric softener. We simply cannot advertise this fact because the brand is such a small seller," said Ader.

Stephen Ader pointed out the difficulty that manufacturers face when they try to determine how environmentally friendly their products really are. "We are not entirely sure what environmental impact any one of our products has. I think anyone that tells you the contrary is lying," said Ader. We are not prepared to just throw something on the marketplace. Whatever steps we take must be good for the environment. They can't be pretense products."

Lever Detergents

Lever Detergents is the Canadian cleaning products subsidiary of Unilever, a worldwide conglomerate headquartered in London and Rotterdam, manufacturing primarily packaged goods such as edible oils, frozen foods, tea, soups, and household products.

In Canada, its cleaning products franchise centers on the Sunlight family. This includes a detergent in both powdered and liquid forms which is the number two brand in the market, the leading dishwashing liquid, a glass cleaner, dishwasher detergent, and the original toilet soap. These products are positioned as good value products providing effective cleaning, often reinforced with the imagery of lemon, at a price marginally below the premium priced products in their respective categories.

In 1990, Lever Detergents introduced a $20 million dollar environmental action plan. As part of this plan, Lever introduced 100% Phosphate Free Sunlight Laundry Detergent. This product was a reformulation of its premier brand, Sunlight Detergent, as a phosphate free product.

"Phosphate Free Sunlight will provide consumers with parity cleaning performance to current Sunlight at a parity price, but will not expel phosphates into Canada's water systems. The main objective of this move is to minimize any adverse impact that Lever products may have on environment," said Peter Elwood, Lever's Vice President of Marketing.

"The relaunch of Sunlight as a 100% phosphate free detergent is intrinsically tied to the brand's image. Sunlight has always had a psychological aspect of its positioning that has to do with being friendly and nice. This psychological positioning is the key to evolving Sunlight into a green brand."

"The introduction of phosphate free Sunlight will be backed by radio and newspaper advertising, as well as a poster campaign. The overall campaign will be very subtle, reflecting the "friendly" and "nice" nature of the brand, while at the same time associating Sunlight with nature and environmental friendliness. A clean wash is important and so is a clean conscience. The Sunlight package will also be redesigned to include an environmentally friendly flash and a side panel listing Sunlight's environmentally friendly features."

Research indicated that consumers believed that Sunlight without phosphates would clean as effectively as before due to the fact that Sunlight was a major national brand. The statement "If Sunlight's doing it, I'm sure it cleans just as well" showed up during many interviews. The move to a phosphate free formula would result in a marginal increase in costs, however, this price increase was small enough to absorb without passing the price increase on to the consumer. Even though initial marketing research relating to green marketing indicated that the consumer would pay more for an environmentally friendly product, Elwood did not believe this was true due to the highly price sensitive nature of the laundry detergent category.

The rest of the Sunlight family contained no phosphates with one exception. Sunlight powdered dishwashing detergent, like its competitors, contained 40% phosphates. To remove them would significantly diminish the product's cleaning capabilities. R&D were working on the problem but no satisfactory alternative formulation had been developed.

"It's simply not enough to talk about a change in product and packaging," said Marc Rudolph, Lever's environmental consultant. "You can have a company and a product associated with that company that is environmentally sound, but if the company itself, in an environmental sense, doesn't have a leg to stand on, the true green consumer isn't going to buy the product."

The environmental program would be guided by the following mission statement: "As a responsible corporate entity, Lever Brothers has an obligation to minimize and eventually eliminate any adverse impact that our company or its products have on the environment. To do so, we will take a holistic approach to this issue. We will evaluate the effect that our plant, our offices and our products have on the Canadian environment, and then take action for improvement. We are committed to dealing with these issues in an open and cooperative fashion with government bodies, consumers, and environmental groups. We will continue to invest funds into projects that will allow us to establish Lever Brothers as a leading, environmentally responsible corporation."

The company's environmental program included a number of initiatives. The plan specified using recycled paperboard in product cartons and proposed that Lever start funding research to manufacture plastic bottles using recycled plastic. One of the key elements of the policy was Lever's support for recycling programs across the country.

Lever examined its manufacturing processes to determine the environmental friendliness of its operations. Audits were carried out to examine water and air emissions from the factory and programs were implemented to upgrade already existing programs that recycled chemicals and packaging materials back into the production process.

The plan also led to an enhanced office recycling program. All office paper was sent to a recycler and Lever began purchasing only recycled paper. Lever estimated that this effort alone would remove 10 tonnes of paper out of the waste stream each year. In Lever's offices, every employee was issued with a ceramic mug to eliminate paper cups. Plastic cups that were placed in boxes of Sunlight to measure the detergent were replaced by paper cups that would biodegrade.

In order to assist the general public to understand environmental problems and issues, Lever developed a chemistry module and educational videos for the Ontario high school curriculum. This educational program explained how household cleaners and detergents were manufactured and their effect on the environment.

1. What is an environmentally friendly product?

2. What obligation do these companies have to provide environmentally friendly products?

3. Should companies be environmentally pro-active if they continue to be subject to criticism?

D TED RUMMEL RIDES ON MICHELINS*

The sky was low and heavy at 7:00 p.m. on January 19, 1987. In the darkness pierced by the misty glow of overhead lights, the snowflakes were falling thick and furious and nearly every parked car was hidden under a blanket of fresh snow. Ted Rummel waded through the curtain of snow to his Honda Civic, barely able to identify it on his company's parking lot in Hamilton, Ontario. The 39-year-old employee, hired just two weeks earlier as a senior analyst, was on his way home to Guelph, 50 km away. While he brushed the snow off the windshield, he noticed that cars were sliding and fishtailing their way out of their parking spots as they headed toward the exit. Ted could sense that this was a full-blown snowstorm. "What will the roads be like?" he wondered. As he gently let out the clutch, his car lurched forward a touch, then the wheels began to spin and the car slipped sideways to a halt. He was stuck. Panic! He got out and called to a couple who were approaching their car. "Could you please give me a push while I get behind the wheel?" he pleaded.

He got his car moving and gingerly made his way out to the street, but this incident had already unnerved him. His mind raced back to the day, four weeks earlier, when he had gone to the Honda dealership in Guelph to pick up his brand new Civic. "What kind of tires did they sell me? I bet they are summer tires," he thought in annoyance. "How could they do such a thing, knowing what Ontario winters are like?" By now, Ted was on Highway 403, a six-lane freeway linking Hamilton to Toronto and leading to Highway 6 to Guelph. Traffic was crawling at a snail's pace. It looked hopeless: all the way to the horizon, he could see headlights and taillights bumper to bumper; it would obviously be several hours of nervous driving before he reached Guelph. Nearing an exit to downtown Hamilton, he decided that this was his last chance to get out of the traffic mess ahead of him and to head into the city to look for a place to stay until the morning, by which time the roads would be cleared and he could drive straight to work.

Downtown Hamilton was in utter chaos, he discovered. It took him another hour to travel 1.5 km and at the sight of the very first motel sign, he decided he had taken enough. At the Town Manor Motor Hotel on Main Street West, he turned into their parking lot and checked in at the front desk. There was still enough time before drug stores closed at 10 o'clock, so he walked down the street to a Shopper's Drug Mart to buy shaving cream, razors, toothpaste, and a toothbrush. After eating at a fast-food place, he turned in for the night. Total cost of this overnight diversion: $53.

Ted Rummel prided himself on his driving skills. In his younger days, he had been an amateur race driver in a local automobile club and had also driven in many car rallies, some of them over roads that were far worse than most drivers ever encounter. He reckoned he still was, by any measure, a skilled driver who should not be deterred by snow on the roads, since he felt confident he could control a car—even after it got into a skid. In fact, after a heavy snowfall, he would sometimes go alone to the large, empty parking lots at shopping malls and practice skid controls and 360° handbrake turns in his car to sharpen his driving skills under slippery conditions. He would practise this way until he could put his car into a spin and recover it perfectly so that it was still moving ahead in the original direction.

Ted had bought his car to commute to Hamilton. It was a 1987 Honda Civic 1500 S hatchback, a sporty version of the standard Civic hatchback, with a slightly larger, peppier engine. Ted used to confide to his wife and closest friends that "This is my little red Ferrari." He was so delighted with the car, that, seven months after he bought it, he wrote a glowing letter directly to Mr.

*Copyright © 1991 by Thomas E. Muller, This case was written by Professor Thomas E. Muller, School of Business, McMaster University, Hamilton, Canada L8S 4M4.

Tadashi Kume, president of Honda Motor Company in Japan, praising the car for being "a sure-footed goat in cheetah's clothing."

His Honda Civic was indeed fitted with Bridgestone radial-ply summer tires. Summer tires have a smoother tread profile (narrower grooves and tighter tread pattern) and generally give a quieter ride, but are unsuitable for deep snow because the tread has less of a grip on the snow surface. Winter tires, on the other hand, are designed with wide grooves and large, claw-like tread blocks to grip the snow, but this makes them rather noisy when driving on a hard, smooth surface, so most motorists switch to summer tires when the winter is over. Tire makers also manufacture all-season tires. These have special tread patterns that make them quiet on smooth, dry road surfaces yet safe for driving in all but the worst winter conditions. Their major merit is that one can drive on such tires all year round.

Two days after the snowstorm, Ted decided to equip himself with tire chains, which, when mounted on the summer tires, would give them more traction in the event of another snowstorm. After work that day, he drove to the Canadian Tire store on Stone Road in Guelph and bought two tire chains, at $19.99 each, which were meant for the front wheels of his front-wheel drive Honda. While in the store, he noticed that a brand of emergency auto kits for winter driving was being promoted at a special price of $13.99. As he examined its contents, Ted had visions of being stuck with the car somewhere on the side of Highway 6 in the middle of another snowstorm waiting to be rescued and needing to keep himself warm with the emergency food, aluminized mylar blanket, and paraffin heater supplied in the kit. Since his wife drove their second car, a Mazda 626, he bought two of these kits. Ted also picked up some lock de-icer for his Honda which he saw displayed on a rack near the cashier, and his bill totalled $76.99.

In late March, about two months after this incident, an overnight snowstorm hit Southern Ontario again when Ted wanted to drive to work in the morning, he first had to shovel a path for the car out of the garage. Several important meetings would be awaiting him at work that day. Although the tire chains were sitting in the trunk of his car and he could have mounted them on the wheels to improve their traction, he did not bother to do this and drove to Hamilton on the same summer tires that had given him trouble in the previous snowstorm. Ted did, however, arrive three hours late.

Throughout the following summer, the question of tires receded to the back of Ted's mind, but as fall approached and the prospects of another winter of commuting between Guelph and Hamilton became more real, he again began to evaluate his options. One late-September morning while waiting to have his car serviced at the Olympic Honda dealership in Guelph where he had purchased the Civic, he spotted a promotional floor stand with Nokia Rollster winter tires, manufactured in Finland. Studying the accompanying promotional brochure, he discovered that Finnish tire makers did a lot of research and development to come up with the most advanced winter tires, since, by law, cars in Finland must be fitted with such tires in winter. He fingered the profile of the Nokia tire and was impressed by its solid-looking tread and overall design which made it ruggedly handsome: it was wider than his summer tires and looked to Ted like something that could conquer the elements and take on any snowstorm. The price of $80 per tire seemed very reasonable and, after some discussion about the tire's performance with the service manager, Ted decided to buy a set of four and had them installed right away on the Civic. Meanwhile, the summer tires were taken home to be stored until the following summer.

During the next two and a half years, Ted was less than fully satisfied with his Nokia winter tires. He felt they were excellent in the snow and gave a very secure grip on wet roads, but the car constantly needed to be taken in for wheel balancing in order to get rid of high speed vibrations (apparently due to the tires' out-of-roundness, according to the mechanic) which made the steering wheel jiggle in his hands when driving at high speeds. Also, they were extremely noisy on dry tarmac. As well, every spring he had the additional hassle and expense of switching to the summer tires, only to change back to the Nokias at the start of the winter season. Wheel balancing was costing him about $10 per wheel, and every seasonal changeover of tires, including balancing, would come to between $40 and $65.

Ted was quite well aware of all-season tires. In fact, within a year of buying the Nokia winter tires, he became interested in the Michelin Sport EP-X, a high-performance all-season tire. He found it to be a visually pleasing tire and a smart, sporty look; its wide grooves and large triangular blocks in the centre of the tread made it look like a racing tire. He talked to a Guelph tire dealer who handled the Michelin line and was very disappointed to find out that Michelin didn't make the EP-X for the smaller 13-inch wheel rims of the Honda Civic.

Ted had known about Michelin tires since boyhood—his earliest memory being their trademark, the white, balloon-like Michelin Man fashioned out of the tires. To

Ted, the Michelin name meant a very high standard in tire design (Michelin invented the radial tire in 1948). He was also familiar with Michelin's national advertising campaign supported by the slogan "Because so much is riding on your tires," a slogan that he found clever and thought-provoking. He noticed that many of the print ads from his campaign featured a naked baby, sitting in stark, pink contrast next to a big, black Michelin tire. Even individual tire dealers had picked up the "Michelin Baby" theme for their advertisements in local newspapers and entertainment guides.

In March of 1990, Ted was on a business trip in Vancouver and, after work one day, had accompanied a friend to the Woolco department store at the Capilano Mall, on Marine Drive in North Vancouver. While the friend was shopping in one part of the store, Ted wandered over to the tire section at the back. There he spotted a Michelin tire display and a large wall poster for the Michelin XA4, with the bold headline: "The positively durable, positively all-season radial." His attention now riveted, he studied the remainder of the poster which described the fine points of the XA4's tread design and drew attention to the pattern of tread blocks shaped like popped champagne corks that gave added traction under wet and snowy road conditions. From a nearby rack, he picked out a small brochure describing the Michelin passenger tire line and in it found further details on the XA4. Ted studied the entire brochure, carefully comparing the characteristics of each tire described, against that of the XA4. He then took out his pen and marked an "X" in the brochure next to the XA4. He examined the XA4 sitting in the floor rack and ran his fingers over the "champagne corks" and along the grooves, pinching the rubber to judge its stiffness. He then removed it from the rack, rolled it along the floor for a few feet, and bounced it a few times. When a salesman finally appeared, Ted did not ask his opinion of the tire, but questioned him about the price, since there were no price tags on any of the tires displayed. The salesman consulted his master price list and told Ted that the XA4 in the 175/70R13 size (a narrower width than his Nokia winter tires) was on special at $72, reduced, for a limited time, from the list price of $107. Ted noted this on his brochure and, after the salesman disappeared again, he continued to review the entire line of displayed tires. He had now been at the Woolco tire department for over an hour and the friend he came in with, unable to find Ted, got the store's staff to page him over the public address system.

Ted was not sure whether there were Woolco stores in Ontario, but he made a mental note to find out upon his return home. That never happened.

By this time, he had moved to Burlington, 25 km to the west of Hamilton and much closer to his office. In the early spring of 1990, Ted was driving home along one of Burlington's busiest streets, when he spotted a city bus straight ahead with an advertisement of Remco Tire Distributors painted on its side. The back of the bus was painted with a huge Michelin Man, leaning out the back window with a magnifying glass in his hand. Ted raced forward to draw up alongside the bus and had just enough time to catch the Remco name, before the bus drove off.

In early May, a promotional flyer from Tires Only, a Burlington tire distributor, was delivered to his home. It featured promotional prices on Michelin, Firestone, Pirelli and B.F. Goodrich tires, and included coupons for "tire tune-ups" and wheel alignments. On the weekend, Ted telephoned the sore to ask about the availability of Michelin XA4s for the Honda Civic, confirm the advertised $99.86 price for the 185/70R13 size (a wider size than the one he had priced at Woolco, but the same width as his Nokia winter tires), and ask about a trade-in allowance for his four Nokia winter tires. He was told that Tires Only was not offering any trade-ins for used winter tires.

Following this call, Ted wanted a comparison price for the XA4s from a second tire dealer. He remembered the Michelin tire ad he had spotted on the sides of the Burlington city bus, but could no longer recall the dealer's name. To jog his memory, he scanned the Yellow Pages listing under tire dealers until he saw an ad for Remco and recognized the name. A telephone call revealed that they were selling the same sized tire for $97.65 and would give Ted a trade-in allowance. Ted made an appointment right away and brought in his car later that morning to have the new tires fitted. The Remco dealer inspected the four winter tires and offered Ted a $60 trade-in allowance, which he accepted. He paid a total of $408.88, including taxes and a $28 charge for wheel balancing, once the four new tires had been installed.

Almost immediately, Ted could feel the differences between his new Michelins and the Nokia winter tires he had replaced. The ride felt softer and more cushioned, and going over bumps in the road felt more rubbery or spongy. The new tires were certainly more quiet. About a week after his purchase, Ted noticed a set of Michelin MXV high-performance tires on a visitor's Acura parked next to his Civic at work. It was a type he had never seen before and he was somewhat upset that he hadn't come across this sports tire at the time he was evaluating other Michelin tires. He decided to keep an eye out for it, while reasoning that the tire was probably not available for the 13-inch diameter wheel of the Civic.

A month later, in June, he was again on a business trip in Vancouver. At the first opportunity he could find, he borrowed a friend's car and drove to the Woolco store at Capilano Mall in North Vancouver where he had seen the Michelin display in March. He walked straight to the back of the store where the tires were, and found a Michelin brochure for their high-performance passenger car tire line. Sure enough, there was the Michelin MXV that he had spotted on the Acura. It was available for 13-inch wheels like those of the Honda Civic.

However, nowhere in the brochure did it explicitly say that the MXV was an all-season tire. Ted Rummel could sense his tension easing. He left the store, treating himself to a mental sigh of relief.

■ QUESTIONS

1. What motivated Ted Rummel to do something about the tires on his brand-new Honda Civic?

2. Analyze the information-gathering and decision-process steps Ted took, prior to and following each purchase decision.

3. Why did Ted buy Michelin tires?

4. Why did it take him so long to get all-season tires?

5. If Ted Rummel were typical of many buyers of new tires, what implications does his consumption behavior have for tire makers and retailers?

E ATOMIC ENERGY OF CANADA LIMITED: THE 3-D VIEWING SYSTEM*

Gnawing frustration was evident on Rudy Allen's face as he slammed a heavy cost report onto a growing pile of paper on his otherwise orderly desk. "Garbage in, garbage out," he muttered as he quickly scanned last month's financial statement for his branch. He had long since given up on promises to improve the "system," relying on his own tailor made spreadsheet programs for status on crucial projects. Glancing up, he saw Ted Valiant sauntering past his open door.

"Hey Ted, . . . how'd it go?" Rudy called out eagerly. Ted, Rudy's top mechanical development engineer, had just returned from giving a site demonstration of a new closed-circuit television (CCTV) system to a group of utility operators. Rudy and Ted had a solid working relationship based on a mutual respect for each other's abilities. Rudy's strong drive to succeed being suitably tempered by Ted's practical view of reality. But this time, even Ted seemed excited.

"Great!" Ted responded beaming. "Everyone was positive about the system. At one point, I had one of the operators use a crane to pick up an eighteen-foot waste can to align and insert it into a five-inch vacuum collar." Pausing for effect, Ted pulled a comb out of his back pocket, drew it once over his shiny bald spot and returned it to its home before continuing. "They had been having problems inserting the can using their current 2-D TV system and kept slicing off the rubber seal on the collar. Anyhow, using 3-D, the guy did it first time with no trouble in less than ten minutes. Using 2-D, he never even came close and after half-an-hour he just gave up in frustration, "I'm telling you, I think I could have sold three systems right there on the spot after that."

"That's what I wanted to hear," exclaimed Rudy punching Ted's shoulder, "so where do we go from here?" Snatching a market research study from his secretary's desk, Rudy grabbed Ted's elbow with his free hand and together they hurried off to Ted's sunny office at the end of the hall from some peace and quiet and a chance to plan some strategy.

The Company

Atomic Energy of Canada Limited was a crown corporation established in 1952 by the Government of Canada for the primary purpose of carrying out research and development into the peaceful uses of atomic energy. The corporation consisted of several sister organizations

---

*© 1990, Faculty of Administration, University of Ottawa. This case was written by Charles A. Kittmer and Leo P. Buckley under the supervision of David S. Litvack.

offering products and services for health care, for cancer therapy, for nuclear power stations and for research and development. In May 1985, the federal government embarked on a program to transfer a share of the cost burden for nuclear R&D to those receiving the benefits. AECL responded to the resulting budget cuts with various cost-cutting measures.

The division Rudy's branch was in performed well during this period of constraint. Previous diversification and experience with commercial contracts facilitated rapid adjustment to the new environment. Within two years, the revenues of all 100% federally-funded programs had doubled since 1987 to $3.2 million in 1989. Rudy emphasized the importance of a commercial orientation in running his branch. "If it doesn't make sense outside the fence, then it shouldn't be applied here either." Overall, his staff of twenty top-notch engineers and technologists bought into this concept. Morale, productivity, and individual ownership continued on a high level.

Since taking over the Mechanical Equipment Development (MED) Branch in 1986, Rudy had continually emphasized the need for an MED product. It was hard to generate much revenue selling R&D manhours on the open market, particularly when high nuclear overheads severely limited the profit potential. Anything above 10% markup on labour, while still competitive with other R&D labs, priced AECL out of the market. There was more leniency with developed products where the product price related to its value in service and was marked up according to whatever the market would bear (typical values from similar labs ranged from around 20% to 30%). The resultant profit was then used to recapture R&D costs associated with the development. However, past history in AECL had demonstrated the dangers of technology push (a plethora of high quality products based on nuclear knowhow that nobody seemed to want or was willing to buy). The answer had to lie in market pull, but something with a direct link to MED's strong background in research and in design and development of complex mechanisms and remote tooling.

The Product

Three-dimensional television was not a "new" product. Various 3-D viewing systems had been around for ten years or more, but the poor quality of picture had severely restricted application and acceptance of this technology within both the consumer and industrial markets. In the industrial market, 3-D viewing was particularly helpful in remote handling tasks involving ballistic movement, recognition of unfamiliar scenes, analysis of three dimensionally complex scenes and the accurate placement of manipulators or tools within such scenes. The perception of three dimensions results from the various visual depth cues such as motion, light and shadow, size, interposition, haziness of distant objects and convergence. However, most of the commercially available technology in stereoscopic TV systems was based on binocular retinal parallax, the difference between the images seen by each eye of a person viewing a given object. This binocular viewing principal—a separate view for each eye—carried over to most 3-D TV systems with two cameras set side-by-side. For ideal results, the resultant TV images must be exactly the same in every respect except parallax.

Rudy had tried each of the techniques that were available commercially. In fact, he had been involved with a small cooperative effort with the University of Waterloo to produce a low cost version of LCD-based spectacles for 3-D computer aided design five years previously. The most recent experience had been at a remote maintenance conference in England where he had tried out a 3-D stereographic TV system developed by Harwell in the UK. The technology had been developed to the stage where the picture quality was claimed to be unsurpassed, and certainly was the very best that Rudy had seen.

The development work at Harwell was aimed at facilitating the widespread acceptance of 3-D TV within the nuclear plant. In interacting with end-users, Harwell had identified three factors that had been having an adverse affect on 3-D performance:

☐ Fundamental limitations of the method of display which subjected the operators to abnormal or unexpected viewing conditions.

☐ Poor matching of the two pictures for size, geometry, and contrast.

☐ The attempt to reproduce excessive depth of field.

All factors were addressed in the Harwell development program and were reflected in the resultant product. In particular, a method was developed to graphically display picture magnification and distortion to assist in design of the stereoscopic system. Points were plotted on a graph to show how far the image points appeared from the viewer for a given convergence distance. An ellipse was drawn around the point to show the width and depth magnifications in relation to the original scene. The shape and size of each ellipse thus showed the magnification and distortion (shape ratio) for each point. In this manner it was possible to establish limits on the amount of parallax used in reproducing acceptable 3-D images with minimal operator discomfort. The results of this work had been then proven out in actual field trials within the nuclear industry in the UK.

The Opportunity

Seated in Ted's office, Rudy leaned forward in his chair. "What bothers me is getting a handle on the market. How's your report coming?" Ted had been doing an evaluation of the economics of using 2-D versus 3-D systems for remote operation.

Ted picked up a file of handwritten pages. "The figures don't lie, . . . there's a saving of two or four times using 3-D over 2-D, but don't forget the other benefits as well, like improved operator performance, reduced task training time, fewer accidents and tool breakage, . . . " As Ted elaborated on each of the benefits, Rudy couldn't help but remember the amazed look on those senior managers' faces when he switched from 2-D to 3-D and they saw how wrong they had been in lining things up, and how much easier the simple task was under 3-D.

"Two to four times" ran around in Rudy's head. If a typical outage ran three to four weeks, with energy replacement costs of $250 000/day, and assuming that remote operations took up about half of that time, then the savings to the utilities in energy replacement power alone would be in the range $1–$3 million. They could buy twenty units and still be ahead of the game, just for one outage! He had better work up a "value in use" analysis right away.

Rudy tuned in again to hear Ted say, "I figure we'll need three guys part-time over the next year . . . a hustler on the road, a TV repairman-type to handle simple mods and repairs, and a smart-cookie to handle the technical side of things. That's about $100 thousand for our labour, plus the cost of the demo unit. How is Harwell doing at getting the price down? $100 thousand a shot isn't chicken feed, but then the sites spend three to four times that just getting their monitoring systems installed."

"I was talking to Andrew this morning," Rudy replied, "about the distributorship. It looks like it's a go from their side, and they're gearing up to go into production. He figures they can cut the price by about 20 percent. He also mentioned that they were figuring to offer us a 10 percent commission as distributors. But let's not lose sight of why we're here. It's the added-value resale that

we're after! There isn't much risk we'll lose money selling 3-D TVs. We have that R&D program next year to cover the cost of the demo unit, and we can easily reallocate the manpower if things go belly up. But it's the accessories, the remote arms, the special and effectors…that's where the money is for us, and everything we do on this should be aimed at that goal. Now, how are we going to position ourselves in this?" With that, Ted reached for his scratch pad, and replied with a twinkle in his eye. "Thought you'd never ask . . . "

The Market

The slowdown in nuclear construction in North America was expected to continue for the short term. However, despite the oil shortage of the seventies and early eighties, there had been an overall increase in the world demand for energy, electrical energy in particular. Potentially doubling the world's population by the year 2050 would bring massive demands for increased energy supply, especially in large urban and industrialized settings. Environmental concerns which had worked against nuclear power in the past could turn favorable with increased public awareness and concern over increased pollution in the form of acid rain and greenhouse gases, caused by the combustion of fossil fuels. In discussing nuclear power, sustainability and environmental acceptability were now being emphasized along with the commercial safety and economic criteria.

The need to maintain the current nuclear capacity would directly affect the demand for remote inspection in order to carry out maintenance or repair operations in high radiation fields. Similarly, as nuclear plants reach their design lifetimes, decommissioning activities would also sustain the demand for remote operations and vision capability. The same was true for operation in any hazardous environment. As such, potential buyers could include nuclear utilities, research establishments, CCTV suppliers, manufacturers of remote inspection/tooling as original equipment manufacturers (OEM), remote inspection services, chemical process industries and oil and gas extraction and refining. A preliminary estimate of market size was given as:

End Users—Nuclear Utilities	50
Nuclear Research Establishments	15
Oil and Gas, Chemical Processing	75
OEMs	75
Service companies	35
Total	175-250

Within the nuclear industry, the utilities could be classified as either leaders or followers. The leaders tended to be more innovative, always looking to initiate changes to their mode of operation in an attempt to maximize efficiency, output and profit, and carried out their own R&D programs. Generally speaking, they bought-in equipment and used their own maintenance crews and staff to plan, resource and carry out all activities on site. The central procurement department (individual procurement officers acting on behalf of one of several sites) hired-in outside contractors for specialized services that they did not feel the need to develop in-house. The three to four utilities that fit in this category generally demanded immediate response to their needs and were willing to pay a premium for quality services and goods. Once on their list of qualified suppliers, you were guaranteed an opportunity to bid, as long as you continued to supply top quality goods on a demand schedule. Occasionally, for extensive outages planned well in advance (once per site per year), more time was available to supply goods and services; however, this was more the exception than the rule. Each site tended to have its own set of tooling and equipment so as to avoid being "caught" with long-term tooling commitments elsewhere and an immediate need on site.

The remaining utilities tended to follow the example of the leaders on a more limited scale. Generally smaller in size, they maintained a skeleton crew for site operation and hired-in (via a site procurement department) manpower and equipment to perform major outage functions under their direction (serving as a prime market for the service groups and OEMs). General-use equipment would be purchased for site use during smaller scale outage activities. The smaller utilities were generally more cost-conscious than the leaders (although still willing to "pay the price" if required), and participated in cost-sharing arrangements within the industry wherever possible. In this manner, the followers could implement actions defined by the leaders, but with significantly reduced overheads.

The petrochemical industry followed a similar breakdown for the nuclear utilities with respect to leaders and followers, and maintenance habits. While some of the maintenance activities were performed on the same components as for the nuclear application, the radiation hazard was replaced by toxic fumes and a highly flammable and corrosive environment. As such, product requirements dealt with explosion-proof casings and corrosion resistance, in place of radiation tolerance and decontamination specifications. Approximately 10% of the firms could be classified as industry leaders. Overall, without the penalty of man-rem radiation exposure costs associated with nuclear maintenance activities, the petrochemical industry tended to be more sensitive to product costs, and was less willing to pay the premium associated with high quality products.

The Competition

There were four major players in the 3-D TV market in North America: Stereographics Corporation, International Telepresence Corporation, Toshiba, and Metron Optics. Except for Metron Optics, the competition products were based on LCD-shutter technology. NV Philips held a patent on a lenticular screen approach but had taken no action on it.

The Metron Optics product was a single-operator-only device that appeared to have been developed as an accessory to a binocular microscope inspection device for electronic component manufacture. Metron Optics cameras were listed at $7000 with a complete system costing around $15 000. Toshiba had just released a very low-cost LCD-shutter device (a 3-D Camcorder) but it suffered from poor picture quality due to too low a shutter frequency and was having limited success in the consumer market (value-added retailers had also tried to sell it to industry.) List price for the Camcorder was only $4000 with a complete system selling for around $8000.

Both Harwell and Stereographics had been successful in supplying units to the nuclear utilities. However, according to one source in the remote inspection service industry, the Stereographics system used at Three Mile Island had been short-lived and not very successful. A basic black and white Stereographics system cost less than $10 000, with a complete high-resolution color system in the range $30 000 to $50 000. The Harwell system had been supplied to a nuclear utility in the United Kingdom. Preliminary feedback indicated that they were entirely satisfied with the performance of the system with respect to picture quality and functionality.

A Toshiba Camcorder, the first one sold in North America, had been bought on a limited trial basis by Hydro-Quebec in Canada. Ted Valiant had arranged to obtain the Camcorder on load to perform a comparison test with the Harwell system. Unfortunately, although the Camcorder had worked well initially, it had developed a malfunction after one day of use and had to be sent back to the manufacturer for repairs. Eventual testing confirmed initial concerns with poorer picture and lower manufacturing quality.

An estimate of the market volume based on published sales information is given in Table E.1.

Table E.1

	Unit Sales	Sales (k$)	Market Share in: Units	Market Share in: Sales
Competitor				
ITC	7	200	18%	29%
Toshiba	13	100	33%	14%
Metron Optic	7	100	18%	14%
Stereographics	7	200	18%	29%
Others	5	100	13%	14%
Totals	38	700	100%	100%

Competitive Market Analysis
3-D TV Systems — Sales to Industry

Distribution

Products were sold directly to the customer and also by value-added retailers who supplied complete systems, and in some cases, associated remote tooling, robotic inspection, etc. The recent improvements in picture quality had attracted some market attention for 3-D stereographic vision technology; however, too few systems had been sold as yet to develop much in the way of business in servicing or replacement parts.

Service companies and established retailers offered significant advantage for the introduction of a new product in that they had already established contacts and a knowledge of their client needs and interests. This was particularly attractive for breaking into the U.S. market. Conversely, 3-D vision could be just one more product in an established portfolio of products, or of limited interest to a firm that specialized in routine maintenance tasks with an intensive labour content. Because of the maintenance practices of the nuclear utilities, selection of either one or the other of these options would cover only a portion of the potential market (the hire-in and we let you do everything, versus the buy-in and we do everything ourselves approach). In order to maximize market coverage, both approaches could be required.

D&D Distribution in Toronto had expressed interest in handling 3-D vision for AECL. They were a small firm established three years earlier with a mandate to service nuclear utility needs. Young and energetic, they prided themselves on fast turnaround response to pretty well anything and everything that was asked of them. Low overheads kept them ahead of their competition; in fact, they were asking only 6% commission as distributors. However, in line with their philosophy to keep overheads to a minimum, they were prepared to treat this on a flow-through basis only, refusing to accept commitment to purchase even one system for demonstration purposes. They had not provided a formal strategy as yet, but it appeared to be based on loading a vision system in the back of a van and touring up and down Ontario, hitting all the thermal and nuclear generating stations, as well as any chemical processing plants and oil refineries along the way. They were looking to AECL to provide them with initial technical support and training to get them started, as well as any promotional literature that was available. They talked a good story, and getting that first sale as soon as possible certainly was attractive.

Strategy

"All in all, it looks like we have more questions here than answers," said Rudy, scratching his head with his pencil. "Even if we stay with the nuclear industry at first, who do we target? And how do we make the jump into supplying remote tooling systems and not just vision?"

"One step at a time, Rudy," replied Ted patiently. "We have to establish the vision business first, and build from there, . . . one step at a time. We haven't even established a price yet!"

"I know Ted, I know" said Rudy, wincing good-naturedly at the mock sarcasm, "but time's running out." Glancing at his watch, Rudy stood up abruptly. "I've got a meeting to go to for eleven thirty, so let's pick this up again right after lunch."

■ QUESTIONS

1. What should be the target market for this product? Develop a market strategy for this product including price, distribution, promotion and market position alternatives. How would this strategy change with time?

2. Is this a business that AECL should be in?

F   E.D. SMITH AND SONS LIMITED

Chris Powell and Lee Ann Jessop of E.D. Smith and Sons Limited, reviewed the history of the firm's line of jam and jelly products. As Marketing/Sales Manager-Grocery Products and Product Manager, respectively, they determined the company strategic plan for the product line. The hundred-year-old company based in Winona, Ontario would have to respond to the potential of a free trade agreement with the United States, a recent lack of advertising support for the product line and trade rumors that shelf space for all jam, jelly, and marmalade products was about to decrease. As they gazed at the lush agricultural lands of the Niagara Escarpment on this warm June day, the plan of action for the remainder of 1988 and 1989 was far from certain.

Company Background

In 1882, Ernest D'Israeli Smith was a fruit farmer in the fertile Niagara Escarpment area of Ontario known as Winona. Growing raspberries, black currants, grapes, apples, and cherries, E.D. Smith was dissatisfied with shippers' taking part of the grower's profit. His solution was to ship his own fruit directly to the wholesaler. He was so successful that demand overtook his own farm's supply and he bought and shipped other farmers' fruit as well. At the turn of the century, this entrepreneur was faced with a glut of fruit in successive seasons which had caused a price drop and excess fruit left unsold. E.D. Smith decided to start making jams and jellies.

Up to 1903, all pure jams sold in Canada were imported from England. E.D. Smith's was the first pure jam ever produced commercially in Canada. Starting in the basement of the fruit house, the first products were so great a success that in 1905 a factory was built and the company went into full scale jam production.

In 1910, the company expanded production into tomato ketchup and purée. In the Depression of the 1930s, demand for fruit products declined. Tomato purée grew to become an important product especially in export markets. One company with whom they had a contract, H.P. Sauce Limited in Great Britain, responded by allowing E.D. Smith to sell their products in Canada. In 1942, the Second World War reduced commercial trans-Atlantic shipping to a trickle and H.P. sales were severely reduced. H.P. licensed E.D. Smith to make their sauce in Canada using a secret formula a deal sealed with only a handshake. In 1948, H.P. acquired Lea and Perrins which, in turn, allowed E.D. Smith to manufacture the famous Worcestershire Sauce.

In that same year, E.D. Smith died at the age of 95. Among his achievements was a ten year term as Member of Parliament for Wentworth South and a seat in the Senate granted in 1913. He fought for, and won, better transportation facilities for fruit in railways and steamships. He also inspired improvements to mechanical loading and unloading of ships at dockside. He was a strong advocate of women's rights, in particular, a woman's right to vote.

Returning from active service in the War, Armand Smith, E.D. Smith's son, became President of the company. The return of servicemen and the increased flow of immigrants to Canada brought a renewed demand for processed food products. Plant operations had to be expanded to process fruit pie fillings and a host of new tomato-based products. Armand Smith remained as President until 1956 when E. Llewellyn G. Smith, grandson of the founder, succeeded him.

From 1956 to 1981, the company went through a major expansion plan that enabled them to compete with multinational food corporations in the Canadian market. A company organization based on the functional areas of business—marketing, sales, manufacturing, finance, and data processing—was adopted. Diet products, bulk pie fillings and, in 1969, Garden Cocktail vegetable juice were all introduced. In 1968, E.D. Smith purchased Ware Foods Limited of Hamilton which produced a broad line of institutional products for the growing food service industry. In 1976, the company acquired McLarens Foods Limited of Hamilton whose olives, pickles, and selected specialty products had an excellent reputation within Canada.

In 1986, a fourth generation of Smiths became President with the appointment of Llewellyn S. Smith. E.D. Smith remained, over one hundred years later, a wholly Canadian controlled and operated company.

Company Operations

The company had kept pace with changing markets and new taste trends by means of a modern, efficient manufacturing capability, progressive management, and a dedicated group of over 200 employees. With the exception of sales offices, the entire E.D. Smith company operated from Winona, Ontario. The company continued to handle its own shipping. Products were carried by rail to Atlantic and western Canada while in Ontario and Quebec, the E.D. Smith fleet of transport trailers handled deliveries.

Grocery products accounted for a major proportion of the Food Division business. Not mentioned previously, E.D. Smith marketed chili sauce relish under their own name, H.P. Sauce and Lea & Perrins. Sales of these products were handled primarily by the 20 person national grocery salesforce who worked in all provinces except the Atlantic provinces where a broker was retained.

Although the company's markets were mostly domestic, the firm had limited sales outside North America. Wherever possible, Canadian products were purchased as raw materials. Raspberries from British Columbia, blueberries from the Maritimes, rhubarb from Quebec, and apples and cherries from Ontario were examples of Canadian sourcing. In fact, the company was working to establish a Canadian source of strawberries that met its specifications.

People were a key ingredient to E.D. Smith's success. A team spirit was promoted and an open door policy was maintained to ensure good labor relations. Employees were encouraged to participate in "speak-up sessions" and in the company newsletter, *The Homestead*, which provided a forum for suggestions on maintaining and improving the company's standards. Employees were also encouraged to participate in subsidized courses both on and off the premises.

Automation and innovation had streamlined the production process. Modern methods preserved the products' natural goodness and ensured quality standards while maintaining stable prices. Computers assisted management in controling operations from receipt of ingredients to order assembly for customer deliveries. While the company was busiest in the fall, production continued year-round with frozen and fresh fruit imported from the United States, British Columbia, and Europe. The seasonality and variety of products necessitated a complex scheduling system to ensure maximum efficiency and cost control.

The Jam, Jelly, and Marmalade Market

Marketing research indicated that when consumers were asked what image the name E.D. Smith conjured in their mind, the answer most often given was jam. After all, E.D. Smith was the first company to sell "pure" jam in Canada. Any product called "pure" jam had to contain a minimum of 45% fruit. The remainder of the product could contain sugar and natural preservatives such as citric acid. No additives, no artificial colours and no chemicals could be added to "pure" jams.

E.D. Smith sold 80-85% of its pure jams and jellies in Ontario. Sales in Quebec were negligible due mostly to Quebecers liking of sweeter, less thick jams. Likewise sales in Canada's west were nearly negligible. The Maritimes accounted for the remainder of E.D. Smith's jam and jelly sales. Due to the concentration of sales in Ontario, Lee Ann and Chris decided to narrow their focus to this market.

In Ontario, the top six brands of jam, jelly and marmalade accounted for 50.7% of the sales. (See Table F.1 for a comparison of the top six companies.) This was a highly fragmented market with many companies vying for market share. Even foreign companies had some market share though their jams were not classified as "pure" jams and were of low quality containing large quantities of pectin (a natural substance used to "solidify" a jam, jelly or marmalade). Yet heavy competition was surprising since demand for both jam and jelly had not grown in the last five years (annual changes in demand fluctuated between +1% and –1%) and demand for marmalade was declining at the rate of 8% per year.

Theories to explain the competition were plentiful. Perhaps more and more people were not eating breakfast, or at least not eating breakfast in the home, but breakfast cereal and microwaveable breakfast sales were growing. Perhaps consumers had turned away from jam, jelly, and marmalade in favor of honey, peanut butter, and other breakfast spreads but these products had not shown any appreciable growth in sales. Certainly, people had not turned to making their own jam. The amount of homemade jam produced in Canada had been on a steady decline for the past 20 years.

The top selling brand in Ontario was Kraft with 13.7% of the market. In fact, it was the best selling brand in Canada. Typical consumers of Kraft's products were children who used the spread with peanut butter in a sandwich. Kraft was a large, diversified, processed food company which used a family branding approach. They started selling jam, jelly, and marmalade in the 1920s. With a large advertising budget, they were able to establish and maintain the brand name in the consumer's mind. Their position, as the only jam, jelly, and marmalade producer, was solidified by a product relaunch in 1988. Kraft had changed the packaging (from a round glass jar to a square glass jar), and labelling (giving new emphasis to the fruit).

The number two brand was Laura Secord with 9.5% of the market. Laura Secord only sold "pure" jams and marmalades. A division of Catelli foods, the company started selling jam and marmalade in 1977 making it the newest market entrant. Typical consumers of Laura Secord jams were "discriminating" shoppers. They were looking for a better product with a better taste. Independent taste tests indicated their flavor was better than Kraft's and equal to E.D. Smith's. The Laura Secord name was also a family brand which was used for ice

Table F.1 Comparison of the Top Six Jam, Jelly, and Marmalade Producers

	Kraft	Laura Secord	Aylmer	E.D. Smith	Welchs	Shirriff
Market Share	13.7%	9.5%	9.3%	7.6%	5.3%	5.3%
Typical Retail Selling Price	$2.19	$2.19	$2.29	$2.19	$2.09	$2.09
Jam (250 ml)						
Strawberry	X	X	X	X		
Raspberry	X	X	X	X		
Peach	X	X	X	X		
Apricot	X	X		X		
Cherry	X	X	X	X		
Grape	X				X	
Damson Plum	X		X	X		
Blueberry	X			X		
Black Currant		X	X	X		
Other Jam Flavors	Pineapple Red Currant	Kiwi Fieldberry	Red Plum	Seedless Raspberry		
Jelly (250 ml)						
Grape	X			X	X	
Mint				X		X
Apple	X		X	X		
Lemon Spread				X		
Other Jelly Flavors	Raspberry Strawberry Red Current Cherry					
Marmalade	Crabapple					
Orange	X	X				X
Three Fruit	X	X				X
Pineapple						X
Seville Orange						X
Flavors						
Available in 500 ml jars	Raspberry Strawberry Apricot	Raspberry Strawberry Orange Marmalade	*	Raspberry Strawberry Lemon Spread	Grape Jam and Jelly	Orange Three Fruit

* All of Aylmer's products were sold only in 500 ml jars.

cream, chocolate, and pudding products. Rumors were afoot that Catelli's parent company, John Labatt Ltd., was preparing to sell the Catelli division. These rumors were reinforced when it was announced that the Laura Secord name had been sold to Nestlé. Nestlé was interested in continuing the chocolate and milk products line but did not seem to have any interest in continuing the jam line. Catelli could soon begin a process of selling the jam production facilities and closing out this business.

The number three brand was Aylmer with 9.3% of the market. This company sold mostly pectin jam and apply jelly. The former had far less fruit and far more pectin. Like Laura Secord and Kraft, Aylmer was a family brand spread over several product lines including canned vegetables and soups. The typical consumers of this product were children and the value-conscious consumer.

E.D. Smith was fourth in the market with 7.6% of the market. Like Laura Secord, typical E.D. Smith consumers were looking for a better product with better flavor. The diet line of jams, introduced in 1978, accounted for 53% of E.D. Smith's market share figure. The diet jams contained no sugar but were sweetened with Sorbitol—a natural sweetener suitable for use in a low sugar diet. The Diet product line, including Apricot, Blueberry, Raspberry and Strawberry/Rhubarb, had recently been reformulated using juice concentrates as sweeteners. The only competition in the "diet" line was Weight Watchers but E.D. Smith's market share was 66% greater. Overall, E.D. Smith sold jam, diet jam, jelly, and a unique lemon spread that was especially popular in the Maritimes.

One quarter of the jam packaged at E.D. Smith used private labeling—the packaging of E.D. Smith product using another firm's jars and labels. Typically, private labeling was done for a grocery store which possessed a house brand (like Top Valu, Domino, President's Choice, etc.). In recent months, private labels had requested a change in the glass jars from the round shape used by E.D. Smith to a squarer shape similar to that used by Kraft. Kraft had never engaged in any private labeling.

Tied for fifth position were Welch's and Shirriff at 5.3% of the market each. Welch's competed in a narrower niche—grape jams and jellies. In fact, Welch's was the number one seller in that niche. The Welch's family brand extended to grape juice and grape drinks in frozen concentrate, glass jar and tetra-brick (cardboard box) forms. Shirriff was responsible for the "Good Morning" product line consisting of marmalades and

mint jelly. In 1987, Shirriff Good Morning Marmalade was sold to Smuckers of the United States.

The Situation at Hand

In 1983, E.D. Smith sold 250 000 cases of jam and jelly in Ontario—a $3.5 million business. By 1988, that figure had declined to 163 000 cases—an annual sales decrease of 11%. Without realizing it, E.D. Smith had been "milking a cash cow" for, at one time, they had been the market leader. The steady decline had been halted only twice during the last twenty years—the introduction of diet jam in 1978 and a relaunch of the product in 1974. The relaunch consisted of a change in label design (emphasizing the fruit) accompanied by a couponing campaign on a newspaper/magazine insert. In recent years, the jam line was given no advertising support as E.D. Smith had focused advertising dollars on other product opportunities.

During the recession of the early 1980s, E.D. Smith undertook cost-cutting moves which saw the amount of fruit used in the pure jam reduced to the minimum. Only a small quantity of fruit could be supplied by the E.D. Smith farms so, with purchasing budgets cut back, the quality of the imported fruit also suffered. A final cost-cutting measure saw the substitution of cheaper fructose sugar for glucose sugar—a savings of thirty-six cents per case of twelve jars. A side effect of using fructose in cooking the jam was a slight-browning of the mixture. Glucose sugar not only improved the color of the mixture but improved the flavor as well.

The market was highly price sensitive and E.D. Smith was a price taker or follower. Their strategy was simply to match Kraft's pricing policy which had been a $2.19 price for the 250 ml container on the retail store shelf. This parity pricing policy was also followed by Laura Secord. Occasionally, to help move a volume of product, one of the three firms used a feature price of $1.99 at the retail store. However, it was not unusual to find all three brands moving to that price once one took the lead. E.D. Smith expected the regular price, set by Kraft, to increase soon as there had been no price increase during the previous three years.

Chris and Lee Ann were concerned with rumors/suggestions from wholesalers and retailers that the amount of shelf space devoted to jam, jelly, and marmalade in retail stores was about to be reduced. The argument made by the trade was that sales of these products had been declining and thus did not deserve as much exposure as they currently had. This meant either that the number of varieties carried by each store of each type of jam, jelly, and marmalade would be reduced or some brand(s) would have to be eliminated. Both Aylmer and Laura Secord appeared to be vulnerable.

The possible approval of the Free Trade agreement between the United States and Canada would bring another set of problems. Smuckers, the number one producer of jam, jelly, and marmalade in the United States, had been trying to enter the Canadian market for some time. Though not prohibited from exporting product to Canada, Smuckers had not pursued that Canadian market because of perceived bureaucratic problems. With the Free Trade Agreement in place, a new openness in terms of American investment in Canada, and the acquisition of Shirriff, Smuckers would likely succeed in opening a new Canadian operation.

The Possibilities for E.D. Smith

Lee Ann and Chris could take a defensive posture and eliminate some of the varieties of jam and jelly produced by E.D. Smith. Three varieties (strawberry, raspberry, and lemon spread) accounted for nearly 80% of the sales. These three could be kept in two sizes (250 ml and 500 ml). A different posture would be a flanking maneuver which positioned the jam and jelly line as a product used in cooking/baking rather than as a breakfast spread. Jam could be used in cakes as a filling, in jelly rolls, on ice cream, over waffles, in tarts, in dessert treats, in Christmas baking, as a sauce ingredient, or in muffins.

A different flanking maneuver would be to focus on "peculiar" or unique flavors of specialty jams and jellies. At a current average price of $17.00 per case, a new flavor had to generate sales of at least 4000 cases to break even. Coupled with this could be a price increase to establish a premium image. Though sales volume would likely fall, the profit margin on each jar would be greater and, presumably, profits could rise. A more offensive move would be to relaunch or even reformulate the product. In a relaunch, a company could change the packaging, the labeling or the promotion of the product in such a way that it had a fresh, new image. Reformulation would mean a change in the basic product itself either through a new jam recipe, a change in fruit, or a change in sugar. If a relaunch or reformulation were undertaken,

how similar or dissimilar should the packaging, label, promotion, or recipe be to the other products on the market? Should the price be changed? Should E.D. Smith try to become the price leader?

Another offensive move would be to launch the product line in the United States. Informally, E.D. Smith liked to concentrate the firm's efforts within an 80 mile [130 kilometer] radius of Winona. Shipping costs increased price to a nearly non-competitive level outside of that area. Nonetheless, including the United States, 125 million people lived within an 800 mile [1300 kilometer] radius of Winona.

Twenty years ago, E.D. Smith stopped selling Orange and Three Fruit marmalade. Perhaps the line could be revitalized. The ultimate offensive move would be the launch of a second E.D. Smith jam and jelly line. Like "New Coke" and "Classic Coke," E.D. Smith could have a regular and premium/old-fashioned line of jams and jellies. These two lines would have different price points, packages, labels, and recipes and would require separate promotional support to build awareness and separation in the minds of the consumer.

The Decision

The costing of the many options would have to come later. For now, Chris and Lee Ann were screening the alternatives from a strategic viewpoint. Equally of concern was the tactical plan that would have to be developed for any chosen strategies. Chris loosened his tie and Lee Ann took off her jacket. There was plenty of work to be done.

■ QUESTIONS _____

1. Using any brain-storming technique, try to develop as many different strategic directions that E.D. Smith may take with the jam/jelly line.

2. Using any technique, try to assess the riskiness of each of the strategies developed previously, taking into account the company resources and activities in the environment.

3. Recommend a strategy, giving your reasons for choosing it, and highlight a brief tactical plan showing key activities and time frames.

G SPERRY/MACLENNAN: ARCHITECTS AND PLANNERS*

In August of 1988, Mitch Brooks, a junior partner and director of Sperry/MacLennan (S/M), a Dartmouth, N.S. architectural practice specializing in recreational facilities, is in the process of developing a plan to export his company's services. He intends to present the plan to the other directors at their meeting the first week of October. The regional market for architectural services is showing some signs of slowing and S/M realizes that it must seek new markets. As Sheila Sperry, the office manager and one of the directors, said at their last meeting: "You have to go wider than your own backyard. After all, you can only build so many pools in your own backyard."

About the Company

Drew Sperry, one of the two senior partners in Sperry/MacLennan, founded the company in 1972 as a one-man architectural practice. After graduating from the Nova Scotia Technical College (now the Technical University of Nova Scotia) in 1966, Sperry worked for six years for Robert J. Flinn before deciding that it was time to start his own company. By then he had cultivated a loyal clientele and a reputation as a good design architect and planner. In the first year, the business was supported part-time by a contract with the Province of Prince Edward Island Department of Tourism to undertake parks planning and the design of parks facilities from park furniture to interpretive centers. At the end of its first year, the company was incorporated as H. Drew Sperry and Associates; by then Sperry had added three junior architects, a draftsman and a secretary. One of those architects was John MacLennan, who would later become a senior partner in Sperry/MacLennan.

Throughout the 1970s, the practice grew rapidly as the local economy expanded, even though the market for architectural services was competitive. The architectural program at the Nova Scotia Technical College (TUNS) was graduating more architects wishing to stay in the Maritimes than could be readily absorbed. But that was not the only reason why competition was stiff; there was a perception among businesspeople and local government personnel that, if you wanted the best, you had to get it from Toronto or New York. The company's greatest challenge throughout this period was persuading the local authorities that they did not have to go to central Canada for first-class architectural expertise.

With the baby boom generation entering the housing market, more than enough business came their way to enable Sperry's to develop a thriving architectural practice, and by 1979 the company had grown to 15 employees and had established branch offices in Charlottetown and Fredericton. These branch offices had been established to provide a local market presence and meet licensing requirements during their aggressive growth period. The one in Charlottetown operated under the name of Allison & Sperry Associates, with Jim Allison as the partner while in Fredericton, partner Peter Fellows was in charge.

But the growth could not last. The early 1980s were not an easy time for the industry and many architectural firms found themselves unable to stay in business through a very slow period in 1981-82. For Sperry/MacLennan, it meant a severe reduction in staff and it also marked the end of the branch offices. Financially stretched and with work winding down on a multipurpose civic sports facility, the Dartmouth Sportsplex, the company was asked to enter a design competition for an aquatics center in Saint John, New Brunswick. it was a situation where they had to win or close their doors. The company laid off all but the three remaining partners, Drew, Sheila Sperry and John MacLennan. However, one draftsman and the secretary refused to leave, working without pay for several months in the belief that the company would win; their faith in the firm is still appreciated today.

Their persistence and faith was rewarded. In 1983, Sperry won the competition for the aquatics facility for the Canada Games to be held in Saint John. The clients in Saint John wanted to build a new aquatic center which would house the Canada Games competition *and* provide a community facility which was self-supporting after the Games were over. The facility needed to reflect a forward-thinking image to the world and act as a linchpin in the downtown revitalization plan. Therefore, it

*This case has been prepared by Dr. Mary R. Brooks of Dalhousie University, as a basis for classroom discussion rather than to illustrate effective or ineffective handling of an administrative situation. The assistance of the Secretary of State, Canadian Studies Program in developing the case is gratefully acknowledged.

was paramount that the facility adhere to all technical competition requirements and the design include renovation details for its conversion to a community facility sporting a new Sperry design element, the "indoor beach." The Saint John Canada Games Society decided to use Sperry's for the contract and were very pleased with the building, the more so since the building won two design awards in 1985, the Facility of Merit Award for its "outstanding design" from *Athletics Business* and the Canadian parks and Recreation Facility of Excellence Award. Sperry's had gained national recognition for its sports facility expertise and their reputation as a good design firm specializing in sports facilities was secured.

From the beginning, the company found recreational facilities work to be fun and exciting. To quote Sheila Sperry, this type of client "wants you to be innovative and new. It's a dream for an architect because it gives him an opportunity to use all the shapes and colours and natural light. It's a very exciting medium to work in." So they decided to focus their promotional efforts to get more of this type of work and consolidate their "pool designer" image by associating with Creative Aquatics on an exclusive basis in 1984. Creative Aquatics provided aquatics programming and technical operations expertise (materials, systems, water treatment, safety, and so on) to complement the design and planning skills at Sperry's.

The construction industry rebounded in 1984; declining interest rates ushered in a mini building boom which kept everyone busy for the 1984-87 period. Jim Reardon joined the company through its inevitable expansion. John MacLennan, by then a senior shareholder in the firm, wanted to develop a base in the large Ontario market and establish an office in Toronto. Jim Reardon was able to take over John's activities with very little difficulty as he had been working very closely with John in the recreational facilities aspect of the business. Reardon became a junior partner in 1986.

With John MacLennan's move to Toronto in 1985, the company changed its name to Sperry/MacLennan in hopes that the name could be used for both offices. But the Ontario Association of Architects ruled that the name could not include "Sperry" because Drew Sperry was not an Ontario resident, and the Toronto office was required to operate under the name of MacLennan Architects. The Ontario office gradually became self-supporting and the company successfully entered a new growth phase.

Mitch Brooks joined the practice in 1987. He had graduated from TUNS in 1975 and had been one of the small number in his class to try and make a go of it in

Halifax. The decision to add Brooks as a partner, albeit a junior one, stemmed from their compatibility. Brooks was a good production architect and work under his supervision came in on budget and on time, a factor compatible with the Sperry/MacLennan emphasis on customer service. The company's fee revenue amounted to approximately $1.2 million in the 1987 fiscal year; however, salaries are a major business expense and profits after taxes (but before employee bonuses) accounted for only 4.5 percent of revenue.

Now it is late August, and with the weather cooling Mitch Brooks reflects on his newest task, planning for the coming winter's activities. The company's reputation in the Canadian sports facility market is secure. The company has completed or has in construction 5 sports complexes in the Maritimes and 5 in Ontario, and 3 more facilities are in design. The awards have followed and, just this morning, Drew was notified of their latest achievement—the company has won the $10 000 *Canadian Architect* Grand Award for the Grand River Aquatics and Community Center near Kitchener, Ontario. This award is a particularly prestigious one as it is given by fellow architects in recognition of design excellence. Last week Sheila Sperry received word that the Amherst, N.S., YM-YWCA won the American National Swimming Pool and Spa Gold Medal for pool design against French and Mexican finalists, giving them international recognition. Mitch Brooks is looking forward to his task ahead. The partners anticipate a slight slowdown in late 1988 and economists are predicting a recession for 1989. With 19 employees to keep busy and a competitor on the west coast, they decided this morning that it is time to consider exporting their hard-won expertise.

The Architecture Industry

In order to practice architecture in Canada, an architect must graduate from an accredited school and serve a period of apprenticeship with a licensed architect, during which time he or she must experience all facets of the practice. At the end of this period, the would-be architect must pass an examination similar to that required of U.S. architects.

Architects are licensed provincially and these licenses are not readily transferable from province to province. Various levels of reciprocity are in existence. For this reason, joint ventures are not that uncommon in the business. In order to "cross" provincial boundaries, architecture firms in one province often enter into a joint venture arrangement with a local company. For example, the well-known design firm of Arthur Erickson of Vancouver/Toronto often engages in joint ventures with local production architects, as was the case for their design of the new Sir James Dunn Law Library on the campus of Dalhousie University in Halifax.

In the U.S., Canadian architects are well-respected. The primary difficulty in working in the U.S. has been founded in immigration policies, which limit the movement of staff and provide difficulties in securing contracts. These policies will be eliminated with the Free Trade Agreement and the reciprocity accord signed between the American Institute of Architects and the Royal Architectural Institute of Canada, a voluntary group representing the provincial associations.

As architects in Nova Scotia are ethically prohibited from advertising their services, an architect's best advertisement is a good project, well done and well-received. The provincial association (Nova Scotia Association of Architects—NSAA) will supply potential clients with basic information about licensed firms, their area of specialization, and so on. NSAA guidelines limit marketing to announcements of new partners, presentations to targeted potential clients, advertisements of business card size with "business card" information, and participation in media events.

The provincial association also provides a minimum schedule of fees, although many clients view this as the maximum they should pay. Although architects would like to think that the client chooses to do business with them because they like their past work, the price of the service is often the decision point. Some developers prefer to buy services on a basis other than the published fee schedule, such as a lump sum amount or a per square foot price. Although fee cutting is not encouraged by the professional organization, it is a factor in winning business, particularly when interest rates are high and construction slow.

As the "product" of an architecture firm is the service of designing a building, the marketing of the "product" centers on the architect's experience with a particular building type. Therefore, it is imperative that the architect convince the client that he has the necessary experience and capability to undertake the project and complete it satisfactorily. S/M has found with its large projects that the amount of time spent meeting with the client requires some local presence, although the design need not be done locally.

The process of marketing architectural services is one of marketing ideas. Therefore, it is imperative that the architect and the client have the same objectives and ultimately the same vision. Although that vision may be constrained by the client's budget, part of the marketing process is one of communicating with the client to ensure these common objectives exist.

Architects get business in a number of ways. "Walk-in" business is negligible and most of S/M's contracts are a result of one of the following five processes:

1. By referral from a satisfied client.

2. A juried design competition will be announced. (S/M has found that these prestigious jobs, even though they offer "runners-up" partial compensation, are not worth entering except to WIN as costs are too high and the compensation offered other entrants too low. Second place is the same as last place. The Dartmouth Sportsplex and the Saint John Aquatic Center were both design competition wins.)

3. A client will publish a "Call for Proposals" or a "Call for Expressions of Interest" as the start of a formal selection process. (S/M rates these opportunities; unless they have a 75 percent chance of winning the contract, they view the effort as not worth the risk.)

4. A potential client invites a limited number of architectural firms to submit their qualifications as the start of a formal selection process. (S/M has a prepared qualification package which it can customize for a particular client.)

5. S/M hears of a potential building and contacts the client, presenting its qualifications.

The fourth and fifth processes are most common in buildings done for institutions and large corporations. As the primary buyers of sports facilities tend to be municipalities or educational institutions, this is the way S/M acquires a substantial share of its work. While juried competitions are not that common, the publicity possible from success in landing this work is important to S/M. The company has found that its success in securing a contract is often dependent on the client's criteria and the current state of the local market, with no particular pattern evident for a specific building type.

After the architect signs the contract, there will be a number of meetings with the client as the concept evolves and the drawings and specifications develop. On a large sports facility project, the hours of contract can run into the hundreds. Depending on the type of project, client meetings may be held weekly or every two weeks; during the development of working drawings and specifications for a complex building, meetings may be as often as once a day. Therefore, continuing client contact is as much a part of the service sold as the drawings, specifications, and site supervision and, in fact, may be the key factor in repeat business.

Developers in Nova Scotia are often not loyal buyers, changing architects with every major project or two. Despite this, architects are inclined to think the buyer's loyalty is greater than it really is. Therefore S/M scrutinizes buyers carefully, interested in those that can pay for a premium product. S/M's philosophy is to provide "quality products with quality service for quality clients," and thus produce facilities which will reflect well on the company.

The Opportunity

In 1987, the Department of External Affairs and the Royal Institute of Canada commissioned a study of exporting opportunities for architects on the assumption that free trade in architectural services would be possible under the Free Trade Agreement. The report, entitled *Precision, Planning, and Perseverance: Exporting Architectural Services to the United States*, identified eight market niches for Canadian architects in the U.S., one of which was educational facilities, in particular post-secondary institutions.

This niche, identified by Brooks as most likely to match S/M's capabilities, is controlled by state governments and private organizations. Universities are known not to be particularly loyal to local firms and so present a potential market to be developed. The study reported that "post-secondary institutions require design and management competence, whatever the source: (p. 39). Athletic facilities were identified as a possible niche for architects with mixed-use facility experience. Finally, the study concluded that ". . . there is an enormous backlog of capital maintenance and new building requirements facing most higher education institutions . . . " (p. 38).

In addition to the above factors, the study indicated others Brooks felt were of importance:

1. The U.S. has 30 percent fewer architectural firms per capita than Canada.
2. The market shares many Canadian values and work practices.
3. The population shift away from the Northeast to the sunbelt is beginning to reverse.
4. Americans are demanding better buildings.

Although Brooks knows that Canadian firms have always had a good reputation internationally for the quality of their buildings, he is concerned that American firms are well ahead of Canadian ones in their use of CADD (computer-assisted design and drafting) for everything from conceptual design to facility management. S/M, in spite of best intentions, has been unable to get CADD off the ground but is in the process of applying to the Atlantic Canada Opportunities Agency for financial assistance in switching over to CADD.

Finally, the study cautions that "joint ventures with a U.S. architectural firm may be required but the facility managers network of the APPA [Association of Physical Plant Administrators of Universities and Colleges] should also be actively pursued" (p. 41).

Under free trade, architects will be able to freely engage in trade in services. Architects will be able to travel to the U.S. and set up an architectural practice without having to become qualified under the American Institute of Architects; as long as they are members of their respective provincial associations and have passed provincial licensing exams and apprenticeship requirements, they will be able to travel and work in the U.S., and import staff as required.

Where to Start?

In a meeting in Halifax in January 1988, the Department of External Affairs had indicated that trade to the U.S. in architectural services was going to be one positive benefit of the Free Trade Agreement to come into force in January 1989. As a response, S/M targeted New England for their expansion, because of its geographical proximity to S/M's home base in the Halifax/Dartmouth area, and also because of its population density and similar climatic conditions. However, with all the hype about free trade and the current focus on the U.S., Brooks is quite concerned that the company might be overlooking some other very lucrative markets for his company's expertise. As part of his October presentation to the Board, he wants to identify and evaluate other possible markets for S/M's services. Other parts of the U.S., or the affluent countries of Europe where recreational facilities are regularly patronized and design is taken seriously, might provide a better export market, given their string of design successes at home and the international recognition afforded by the Amherst facility design award. Brooks feels that designing two sports facilities a year in a new market would be an acceptable goal.

As part of searching for leads, Brooks notes that the APPA charges $575 for a membership which provides access to their membership list once a year. But this is only one source of leads. And of course there is the U.S. Department of Commerce, Bureau of the Census, as another source of information for him to tap. He wonders what other sources are possible.

S/M looks to have a very good opportunity in the New England market with all of its small universities and colleges. After a decade of cutbacks on spending, corporate donations and alumni support for U.S. universities has never been so strong, and many campuses have sports facilities which are outdated and have been poorly maintained. But Mitch Brooks is not sure that the New England market is the best. After all, a seminar on exporting that he attended last week indicated that the most geographically close market, or even the most psychically close one, may not be the best choice for long-run profit maximization and/or market share.

■ QUESTIONS

1. What types of information will Brooks need to collect before he can even begin to assess the New England market? Develop a series of questions you feel are critical to this assessment.

2. What selection criteria do you believe will be relevant to the assessment of any alternative markets? What preliminary market parameters are relevant to the evaluation of S/M's *global* options?

3. Assuming that S/M decides on the New England market, what information will be needed to implement an entry strategy?

H DOMINION TANKING LIMITED*

On March 1, 1985, Brock Preston, London, Ontario Branch Manager for Dominion Tanking Limited, was preparing the company's bid for a trucking contract. The bid, to deliver liquid fertilizer for Natural Fertilizers Limited, also of London, was due in two weeks and he expected intense competition. Dominion Tanking won the last bid, five years ago, and had operated under that contract, in London, to only serve Natural Fertilizers. Brock knew that if this bid was unsuccessful, the Head Office would close his branch.

Company Background

Dominion Tanking Limited, a subsidiary of Canadian Hughes Trucking, was comprised of a series of Ontario branches administered through a head office in Toronto. The branch office in London consisted of eight truck drivers and the Branch Manager who operated out of a rented office inside the Natural Fertilizers Plant. The drivers were all members of the Teamsters Union, Local 141, and were paid on a combined basis of kilometers driven and time spent on delivery. Their average wage was approximately $13.29 per hour for a 44 hour regular work week. The drivers were paid time and a half for

overtime (any hours worked over and above the 44 hour work week). Benefits such as Ontario Health Insurance Protection, Canada Pension Plan, Unemployment Insurance, Vacation Pay, etc. were equal to 10% of regular wages and were paid over and above the weekly wages. No benefits were paid on overtime wages. The union agreement was coming up for renegotiation on January 1, 1986. Brock was paid a straight annual salary plus benefits and was not a part of the union.

The company transported liquid fertilizer in eight stainless steel tank trucks ranging in capacity from 15 000 liters to 26 000 liters. The truck portion of each rig was leased from the RYDER Truck Company while Dominion owned the tanker trailers. The lease for the trucks was scheduled to expire on the anniversary of the trucking contract with Natural Fertilizers (i.e., January 1, 1986).

Dominion's tankers delivered an average of eight to nine loads of liquid fertilizer a day, five days a week. Though many deliveries were local, drivers were expected to deliver loads of fertilizer throughout Ontario and to near northern states. As could be expected, spring was a peak season for deliveries while the winter months experienced a decline in demand. In these months, drivers were allowed to take their holidays and the tanker trailers were serviced.

The London branch of the company existed solely to serve the delivery needs of Natural Fertilizers. Brock knew the company would not allow him to solicit outside

*This case was written by Marvin Ryder. Case material is prepared as a basis for classroom discussion only. Copyright © 1985 by Marvin Ryder, Faculty of Business, McMaster University. This case is not to be reproduced in whole or in part by any means without the express written consent of the author.

contracts to increase revenue. Further, should Natural Fertilizers go out of business, or should Dominion Tanking lose its delivery contract, the branch would have no other source of business and the branch would be closed. Brock knew closure was possible as a Sarnia branch had been closed, under similar circumstances, a year ago.

Competition

Dominion Tanking experienced competition from two other trucking companies: Ellsworth Transport of Port Colborne, Ontario and Billings Equipment Leasing of Woodstock, Ontario. Both of these companies offered comparable service but with lower "per kilometer" rates than Dominion Tanking. One reason for the lower rate was the use of non-union labour by the two companies. Billings was the more aggressive company of the two. It had been formed little more than a year before and was operating with new equipment. Billings wanted the Natural Fertilizers trucking contract to give it more credibility. Management there could be expected to put in a low bid.

Natural Fertilizers also had the option of rejecting all submitted bids and purchasing their own trucks for delivery. Tanker prices varied from $80 000 for the 15 000 liter size to $120 000 for the 26 000 liter size. The truck or cab portion could either be leased or purchased. Prices for transport trucks varied, depending on options, from $60 000 to $80 000. The company would also have to hire and train drivers and a dispatcher. Brock estimated that it would take at least one year to make a new fleet of trucks run efficiently.

The Bidding Process

Natural Fertilizers subcontracted delivery of their liquid fertilizer, to trucking firms, on a five year basis. Over the period of the contract, the winner of the bidding process would be given first priority for all delivery assignments. If more fertilizer had to be shipped than the trucking company could handle, Natural Fertilizers was free to hire extra trucks as needed to make those deliveries. This institution often arose in the spring and summer months when drivers were working overtime to meet as many delivery schedules as possible yet they were still unable to meet them all.

While the sealed bids would be received on March 15, the actual contract would commence on January 1, 1986 and run for five years. In soliciting bids, Natural

Fertilizers had made it clear to the three trucking firms that it wanted to lower its delivery costs from the $1.37 charge per kilometer that it currently paid. Each firm was attempting to come up with the lowest bid while maintaining adequate profit margins. Though timely delivery, friendly drivers and good service were important, the winning bid would be the lowest rate charged but only if that rate was acceptable to Natural Fertilizers.

The Problem

Dominion Tanking had been associated with Natural Fertilizers for 20 years, having won four consecutive contracts, yet Brock knew that loyalty would only be a small factor in deciding the winning bid. Looking at a breakdown of the company's revenues and costs (Table H.1), he felt that the company's bid should be from 10 to 20% lower than the current rate to be competitive. The problem was further compounded by the uncertainty surrounding the bids of the other companies. His job depended on his coming up with a bid that attempted to maintain past margins and would win the five year contract.

Table H.1 Dominion Tanking Limited

Revenue and Costs Analysis for Dominion Tanking London Office—Fiscal Year 1984

Revenues		
Fillings to Natural Fertilizers		$1 054 363
Costs		
Truck Drivers Wages & Benefits	$357 042	
Fuel	$117 111	
Leasing Costs	$142 612	
Tanker Maintenance	$102 754	
Depreciation on Tankers	$ 51 317	
Administration & General Overhead	$ 60 915	
Total Costs		$ 831 751
Gross Profit from London Operations		$ 222 612

■ QUESTIONS

1. In terms of dollars per kilometer, what bid should Brock Preston submit to win the Natural Fertilizer contract? Why?

2. What activities can be undertaken by Brock to improve his chances of winning the bid?

3. Should any provisions be made in the bid to match a lower competitive bid or to increase the bid should all of the competitive bids be much higher?

I SOBERS OF ONTARIO

Mr. D. McMurray, the President and owner of Sobers of Ontario was contemplating his response to the changing distribution system and the nature of competition in the Canadian small jewelry industry. While comparing his company's sales figure of 1987 with that of 1986, he observed a leveling off phenomenon. He wondered what actions were called for in order to regain his company's usual annual sales growth rate and to adapt to such changes.

Company Background

Sobers of Ontario was founded by the grandfather of Mr. D. McMurray. Except for a brief period of time when the company was owned by a partnership between his father and his father's brother-in-law, Sobers of Ontario has been a one-man-owned enterprise located in a moderate sized city in southwestern Ontario. The company's products were sold all over Canada. The product line consisted of small jewelry, primarily wedding, engagement, and anniversary rings and approximately 65% to 75% of such rings had diamonds in them.

Marketing

Sobers of Ontario, though selling its products nationally, had in the last two years done well mainly in the Prairies as well as small towns and rural areas of Ontario, places which were somewhat geographically isolated. For both 1986 and 1987 total sales had been around $3 million.

Despite the fact that special occasion rings were considered to be luxury items, branding played no role in consumer choice. The major influences on consumers' decision to purchase a particular ring were the store image, store loyalty, price, and the appearance of the product (quality, finish, and size of the precious stone).

Distribution

The distribution system in the small jewelry industry had undergone significant changes in the previous 2 to 3 years. Sobers of Ontario and most of its competing manufacturers bought diamonds through importers. Thereafter, the finished product was sold to jewelry retailers in Canada using independent sales agents who were compensated by commission of 8% to 10% of Sobers selling price to the retailers. This provided Sobers with a reasonable mark-up and the business was quite profitable.

Over the years Sobers had used the independent sales agents to implement its push strategy at the retail level. The company was also well known in the industry for providing very effective point-of-purchase displays and other services to the retailers, for example, credit facilities.

During the past 2-3 years the importers of diamonds from Europe had also started manufacturing rings and selling the rings and/or diamonds directly to the jewelry retailers in Canada. The industry had also seen some basement manufacturers spring up to manufacture rings for those retailers who did not have their own manufacturing facilities. As a result prices of rings dropped somewhat at the retail level.

To counteract the above development in the channel, Sobers started importing diamonds directly from sources in Europe. However, in view of their reputation and the previously successful distribution strategy, Sobers still used their usual independent sales agents and continued to pay them the usual commission of 8-10% on their selling price to the retailer. Sobers continued to employ five such commissioned sales representatives, each one of which sold to about 200 retailers.

Pricing and Legal Aspects

The inroads made by diamond importers and small basement operators into Sobers' established market resulted

This case was written by Raz Haque of the University of Windsor during the 1988 Case Writing Workshop at the University of Western Ontario.

in a steady decline in the selling price of diamond rings to the retailers. The problem was further complicated by the fact that manufacturers of diamond rings had to charge a 12% federal sales tax and a 10% excise tax on all sales to retailers as diamond rings were classified as luxury goods. Most of the small basement type manufacturers had found ways to avoid paying such taxes by accepting cash only payments from the retailers and not issuing invoices. This situation was becoming increasingly widespread among suppliers to smaller retailers who were Sobers's primary customers.

Industry Response

The industry had been slow to respond to the developments in the distribution channel. The only significant step taken by Sobers's competitors was to reduce the rate of commission they paid to independent sales agents from 8–10% to 3–5%, with a resulting higher turnover rate among such sales agents. Sobers has so far resisted taking any such steps. As a result most of the well-established retailers who were customers of Sobers had been putting pressure on Mr. D. McMurray to let them deal directly with Sobers, thereby eliminating the independent salesmen whose commission resulted in an added cost of 8–10% on their buying cost. In their view, this would result in a significant cost reduction, thereby making their relationship with Sobers more profitable.

Conclusion

Mr. McMurray felt that he had to respond to such developments very soon. Otherwise he was afraid of a decline in the profitability of his business. He was quite convinced that small (basement type) manufacturers could not match the quality of his product nor match his well-established business in consistency of quality or service. He knew he would soon either have to follow competitors, reduce the commission rate of his independent sales agents, or reduce his own profit margin.

■ QUESTIONS ────────

1. How would you describe the company's current situation, including its strengths and weaknesses?

2. What alternatives, if any, are available to the company from a legal standpoint?

3. What recommendations would you make to Mr. McMurray?

J ATLANTIC CANADA PLUS

In May 1990, Aubrey Palmeter, Executive Director, and Lorna Bremner, Promotions Manager of Atlantic Canada Plus (ACP) were preparing their presentation for the June 1990 Board of Directors meeting. The Board had drafted a revised mission statement and had charged Aubrey and Lorna with the responsibility of developing a promotional plan that would fulfill this mission. The mission statement read: "To create opportunities in Atlantic Canada by promoting and marketing goods and services produced in the region."

The Inception of Atlantic Canada Plus

Harvey Webber, a retail merchant from Sydney, Nova Scotia, founded ACP in 1977. Harvey's enthusiasm inspired other businesspeople who shared his vision of the problems and opportunities of business in the Atlantic Canadian provinces—Nova Scotia, Newfoundland, Prince Edward Island, and New Brunswick.

Harvey's message was simple and straightforward:

> The Atlantic Canada market has a potential 2.2 million consumers to purchase competitive products and services made regionally . . . if more Atlantic Canadians bought what is produced . . . what we grow, catch, package, assemble or manufacture . . . in the region, it would create jobs here and make it possible for future generations to stay in Atlantic Canada and find jobs . . . .

In presenting the self-help aspect to Atlantic Canadians, ACP supporters believed that they were going directly to what they perceived to be the root of the frustration experienced by many Atlantic Canadians— "Atlantic inferiority"—the attitude that Atlantic manufacturers could not produce a product at par with

---

outsiders. The ACP movement gave a voice to Atlantic Canadian pride. To them, the real impact of Atlantic Canada Plus was on people's values and self-image.

Organization of Atlantic Canada Plus

The prototype organization for Atlantic Canada Plus was the Irish Goods Council, a marketing organization funded by the Irish government with the mandate of promoting the purchase of Irish goods.

In the late 1970s, membership in ACP grew very fast. At first membership consisted primarily of regional manufacturers, but it eventually expanded to include retail business and professional service industries, large and small. It became obvious that to truly influence the purchase of Atlantic goods and services in the region, the whole distribution network—manufacturing, processing, distributing, retailing and service sectors—had to be integrated. At its high point in 1986-87, there were 600 members in the organization.

ACP operated with a board of directors and the aid of several volunteer committees. From 1977 to 1989, ACP had only a small core administrative staff. In 1990 though, Atlantic Canada Plus was able to obtain the financial support of the Atlantic Canada Opportunities Agency (ACOA), a regional economic development program, to establish the Supplier Development Services (SDS). The five year, $9 million dollar program, designed to help local suppliers sell to government (primarily to the Federal government), presented many opportunities for ACP. The Supplier Development Services (SDS) had offices in the four provinces and in Ottawa, and brought the total number of employees in the new ACP/SDS organization close to thirty.

ACP's revenues were derived from an annual management fee paid by SDS; the support from the four Atlantic Provinces (the Newfoundland provincial government began supporting ACP in 1989); and membership fees. Total expected revenues for ACP in 1990 were over a quarter of a million dollars.

Past Marketing Strategies

Advertising and Promotions   The goal Atlantic Canada Plus had set for itself was to ask Atlantic Canadians to buy regionally-made products and services in order to create jobs in the area. The campaigns had to appeal to three different types of consumers: shoppers, government purchasing agents and business people, each

with a different set of needs and each requiring a specific approach. Given that the ability of ACP to mount high impact promotional campaigns was related directly to government funding, which fluctuated significantly from year to year, ACP promotional efforts lacked consistency and stability, and occurred in a somewhat erratic fashion throughout its fourteen year history.

Early efforts to establish Atlantic Canada Plus crystallized in a program that involved *awareness* and *identification*.

Awareness, involved making consumers in Atlantic Canada realize that buying "locally made" products and services was a direct benefit to them. The campaign also had to convince Atlantic Canadians that local products and services were competitive in quality, price, service and consumer appeal.

Identification, had to work a more concrete level. A region-wide study conducted by ACP showed that 97 percent of the people surveyed would buy Atlantic Canadian products, if the price and quality were equal to products from outside the region. However, only 36 percent of the shoppers checked to see where the product was made. ACP staff believed that one of the simplest and most effective techniques for arousing consumer interest and product identification had been the development of the ACP logo (see Figure J.1). The logo was put into circulation on products, as well as on letterhead, T-shirts, packaging, billboards, trucks, advertising—anywhere where the ACP staff thought it could make a difference. As one member of the marketing committee put it: "The ACP logo had to be as familiar to Atlantic Canadians as Coke and Pepsi." Committee members hoped that recognition of the logo would result in the purchase of a product or service marked by the logo.

FIGURE J.1
ACP Logo

The marketing committee also conducted member opinion and consumer reaction polls; designed posters for public display, contests, mall displays and store displays; made presentations to business and government groups; canvassed local business people encouraging them to become members; and conducted a massive public advertising campaign which eventually topped a million dollars.

Results from this early campaign were mixed. Research indicated that in short term, there was a rise in sales of a product that used the logo in its advertising or on the product itself. Unfortunately, ACP staff discovered that purchase habits did not change in the long-run. "Buy Atlantic is a good idea, (but) many do not put the idea into practice. . . It's easier to change ideas than habits."

During 1982-84 period, ACP renewed its promotional efforts. In 1982 and 1983 ACP implemented two annual PlusPak promotions—direct mailouts to households in the region presenting Atlantic products directly to the consumer under the ACP umbrella. It included coupons of the member companies and was supported by a heavy media campaign. The ambitious project, while successful on many counts, required extraordinary effort. The cost of the campaign exceeded the expected returns, and weakened ACP's financial position. In 1984, as part of the national "Shop Canadian" campaign, ACP mounted a campaign using radio, television and print media promotion.

In 1986-87, DRIE, a government economic development program, awarded ACP approximately $280 000 to mount a campaign, with the provision that the motifs connected with the concurrent federal "Think Canadian" campaign be clearly incorporated. The new campaign, as the ACP creative group envisioned it, was designed to make an impression on approximately 75 percent of the region's consumers. The objective was to educate consumers about the benefits of purchasing Atlantic-made. A second objective was to persuade the member businesses that there was an advantage in marketing from that perspective. The region-wide campaign reached consumers with the logo and several themes including: "The sign that we've made it. Buy Atlantic Canadian. Bring home quality and jobs."

The media used for this campaign were busboards, shopping carts, newspapers and magazines for an intense three-month period, March through May of 1987. The kingpin element was a direct mail offer sent to 100 000 households which also allowed for a great deal of participation by ACP member companies. Atlantic consumers were offered a free set of four historical prints in return for sending in a logo from anywhere in the marketplace. Members of ACP were invited to prepare for this incentive with advertising, poster, decals, shelf talkers, banners, and other point-of-purchase material that could influence shoppers, at the moment of choice.

The campaign was considered a success with a four percent response rate, for the direct mail component, an exceptionally strong rate for this type of direct mail promotion. ACP promotions staff believed that "what this campaign points out is that many Atlantic Canadian consumers are highly aware," and that there was "much loyalty." In addition, ACP enjoyed its largest membership roster ever (600 members) as a result of this renewed awareness.

From 1987 to 1990, ACP consumer promotions activities were drastically reduced, Harry Lockhurst, president from 1988 to 1989, concentrated his efforts on reducing ACP's deficit and on increasing membership through personal sales and public relations. He was able to strengthen ACP's financial position, but the promotional cutback, administrative problems within the staff, and the overhead costs associated with the direct sales effort, resulted in a declining public profile and a loss of membership. ACP staff worried that the budgetary constraints might mean that future campaigns would not have the necessary follow-up to maintain top of mind awareness and consumer confidence in the ACP mission.

Advocacy and Public Relations   Despite its limited staff, ACP was able to participate as player and a spokesman in major events. Newspaper and magazine articles even lauded it as a "love child of the media."

With the aim of increasing the economies of scale of local firms, representatives of ACP also embarked in the early 1980s on advocacy campaigns aimed at increasing the number of purchases of Atlantic products by national chains (e.g., Zellers, The Bay) and by government agencies. Since the majority of chain stores depend on the initiative of the manufacturers to present their products to them, ACP brought manufacturers and purchasers together in trade fairs. According to ACP staff, the response to these efforts had been erratic with some chains willing to cooperate more than others. "Food store chains have been the most supportive and flexible, because their buying offices are local."

In 1979, with support from ACP, the premiers of Nova Scotia, Prince Edward Island, and New Brunswick introduced the Maritime Purchasing Policy. The new policy for provincial purchasing agents was that, if price and quality were similar, they should buy first in the province, second in the region, and third in Canada. Unfortunately, the implementation of this program met with much resistance.

Problems—Where Did All the Logos Go? Research conducted by ACP during the late 1980s showed that even though ACP's mission of Atlantic economic self-help was still dear to many consumers and businesspeople, the organization itself was regarded as having lost some of its effectiveness.

Membership declined in the late 1980s, and producers were no longer as enthusiastic about using the logo as a promotional scheme. "There was a time when everywhere you looked you saw the stickers and promos," said the director of merchandising for a large food retailer. "Our suppliers are no longer asking to be identified with the logo," he added. In addition, many of the large companies did not want to use the logo because a considerable portion of their production was destined for export markets where the "Buy Atlantic Canadian" exhortation would not apply. Research conducted in 1989 showed that many of the members did not perceive a tangible benefit from belonging to the organization. Few used the logo. Nevertheless, the members were still enthusiastic about the mission of the organization and would be willing to recommend other businesses for membership.

Surveys showed that the ACP logo was familiar and everybody was in favor of its cause. But buying habits had not changed to match that approval. As Harvey Webber put it "Starting out from scratch, we've done wonders in awakening the consciousness of the consumer, business and government about buying form ourselves. But we can't stop there, people have to convert that awareness into action."

An additional problem for ACP promotional campaigns was that consumers confused Atlantic Canada Plus with the A-Plus Lottery based in Moncton, New Brunswick. The 1977 design of the logo also gave it a tired and outmoded look.

Some possible explanations for the lower profile of the organization and for the serious decline in ACP membership given in 1990 by the Board of Directors and the management of ACP were that:

1. There was no field force pressing for membership fees.

2. There was no apparent benefit to being an ACP member.

3. There were cloudy membership issues, such as methods for determining membership fees, important businesses being excluded from membership, and problems in determining what represents a service organization.

4. ACP's concentration on consumer aspects required grants of funds to help promotion.

5. ACP should have been responsible for telling consumers about the logo, rather than leaving that responsibility to its members.

6. There was too much emphasis on protectionism. Today's business environment concentrates on "free trade" and being able to sell everywhere. A more international export focus was important.

7. There was too much competition with other associations such as Boards of Trade, Chambers of Commerce. ACP had to offer something different.

A New Direction for Atlantic Canada Plus

In 1990, ACP still had to appeal to three different types of target markets: government purchasing agents, the private sector and consumers.

Government Purchasing Agents The Supplier Development Services concentrated on serving this market. Even though Aubrey and Lorna's mandate did not include the promotion of SDS, the program was expected to raise the profile of ACP considerably. It had a presence in all four Atlantic provinces and in Ottawa, provided a tangible benefit to participants (streamline access to government purchasing), was expected to be an effective vehicle for obtaining government contracts, and would provide a good opportunity for public speaking engagements and media coverage. ACP also saw an opportunity for a cost-effective awareness campaign in SDS's promotional program aimed at encouraging businesses to register on the service. Since SDS was a well-funded, highly visible and powerful program, the appropriate relationship between SDS and ACP in terms of organization, management, and public image also had to be carefully determined.

The Private Sector and Consumers *Membership*: Aubrey and Lorna had to find a way to provide members with more tangible benefits by more clearly defining the kinds of activities that the organization should sponsor. These activities had to be in tandem with the organization's objectives and were expected to not duplicate the efforts of other private and public sector organizations (e.g., Chambers of Commerce, Board of Trade, etc.).

Since ACP had been involved in many types of activities in the past, the Board had suggested that the first step should be to carry out a telephone survey, asking present members and previous members what they wanted from ACP. The cost of this research ($10 000) and the follow-up activities related to marketing development ($6000) were added to the 1990 budget.

In 1990, a salesperson was hired to solicit more members. The sales commission and expense for 1990 were budgeted at $38 000. Up until now, no particular industries or regions had been targeted for recruitment. Aubrey and Lorna felt that it was up to the new salesperson to decide if this shotgun approach was still best. A possible strategy was to use the existing membership roster to recruit new members.

Consumer promotions: ACP staff felt that one of the most important benefits ACP provided to its members was consumer promotions. In 1990, approximately $75 000 was budgeted from promotional campaigns: $40 000 ($20 000 for production and $20 000 for media) provided by the four Atlantic Provinces on an equal share basis, and a $35 000 general promotional budget. The provincial money was earmarked specifically for a T.V. testimonial campaign by local celebrities. Even though this might not have been the most efficient use of these funds, Aubrey and Lorna were concerned with losing the provincial commitments if they changed the campaign concept.

The target market for this campaign was quite broad. ACP officials believed that designing marketing campaigns to appeal to a particular consumer segment (e.g., encouraging people to buy Nova Scotia strawberries in the summer) would alienate ACP member companies from other industry sectors (e.g., industrial adhesives) or provinces. This constraint, combined with the limited funds available for promotional campaigns, had always resulted in the development of mass market campaigns with general, across-the-board appeals, to buy Atlantic-made products.

Aubrey and Lorna felt that a strength of the organization was that the membership roster included several large, powerful, and committed companies which could be of great help by providing free access to the media (public service announcements, editorials, regular columns) and inclusion of the logo and promotional messages in their own promotional vehicles (e.g., supermarket fliers, package inserts, shelf talkers, POP displays, print ads, etc.). The leverage that these companies could

offer in terms of free promotional vehicles, presented Aubrey and Lorna with the opportunity to create more targeted campaigns. This new campaign could be developed inexpensively with the cooperation of these members. Their involvement in the campaign could also serve as a way to strengthen their commitment to the goals of ACP.

The Task at Hand

Aubrey and Lorna had only two months to work on the promotional campaign. In this time, they had to come up with a creative concept for the campaign, develop a media plan, and prepare a general sales and promotional plan for approval. Once approved by the Board of Directors, they could then call local media production and promotional design houses to get quotes on the estimated costs of their new campaign. Time was running out.

Altogether, Aubrey Palmeter and Lorna Bremner faced a difficult task in 1990—with limited time and human and financial resources, their promotional plan had to find a way to reposition ACP as a distinct and dynamic organization that would deliver the promised benefits. They had to "revive" the organization in the eyes of its members, government purchasing agents, Atlantic businesses and consumers, and make the relationship to SDS clear. Aubrey and Lorna had to communicate that Atlantic Canada Plus was very much alive.

■ QUESTIONS ───────

1. How should ACP be positioned in the coming decade, particularly in terms of SDS?

2. What services and activities should the organization be involved in?

3. What promotional plan (target markets, objectives, creative strategies, promotional activities, media plan, budgets, costs and evaluation methods and criteria) should it develop in order to implement these strategies?

K LONDON LIFE INSURANCE COMPANY*

Ralph G. Simmons, Regional Manager at the Toronto Branch of London Life Insurance Company, was reviewing the monthly activity reports for four of his salespeople. It was May, 1988, and he was trying to determine what, if any, action was needed to improve the selling performance for the four salespeople. A friend had told him about the three R's as applied to sales staff problems—retrain, relocate, replace. He remembered these as he thought about what could be done to help the salespeople achieve their full capabilities.

Company Background

Founded in London, Ontario, in 1874, London Life operated, in 1988, in all parts of Canada through a network of regional offices in major cities. Policies were sold and personal contacts were maintained by a sales and management team of over 2700 professional representatives. This was the largest salesforce among insurance companies in Canada and the field operations were supported by over 2600 administrative staff members.

London Life sold a comprehensive range of personalized financial security products and services including: life, health, and disability insurance; retirement savings; annuities; and pension policies and contracts. More than two million London Life policies and contracts were owned by Canadians, making the company the number one provider of insurance in the country. They also sold and managed group benefit plans for more than 16 000 businesses coast to coast.

The company was highly computerized with a national network for handling policy applications, processing claims, managing mortgages, loans and investments, and maintaining instant communications among all London Life people to ensure a high level of service to customers.

London Life was a stock insurance company operating under a federal charter. They were a member company of the Trilon Financial Corporation group, and 98 percent of the company's stock was owned by Lonvest Corporation, of Toronto, the insurance arm of Trilon. Through their affiliation with Royal Trust, Royal LePage real estate services, Wellington Insurance for homes and automobiles, Triathlon, a leasing company, Trilon Bancorp and the Holden Group of insurance companies in the United States, they were able to network and develop business referrals of financial services to their customers.

London Life had a very good year in 1987. Total income, for the first time in company history, exceeded $2.0 billion, double the company's 1981 revenue, while earnings, assets and shareholder income showed healthy increases. With assets of $8.5 billion, they were a major investor in residential and commercial mortgages, real estate, financial markets, and an extensive range of Canadian resource and transportation companies. Their dividend rate to participating policyowners and their level of return to shareholders were among the highest in the industry.

The Corporate Mission Statement was re-written in 1987 to reflect trends in their markets and changing needs of their customers. It now said: "Our Corporate Mission is to be the leader in meeting the needs of Canadians for personalized financial security. We recognize that corporate integrity and superior service are essential in serving our individual and business customers. Everything we do supports our mission."

In the past five years, they had changed their product mix significantly. Sales of savings, investment and retirement products had grown substantially, augmenting strong increases in sales of their traditional individual and group insurance product lines. New technology, much of it in the hands of the sales representatives, was helping to maintain the personalized sales approach which they considered a vital customer service advantage of their company.

The Insurance Industry

At the end of 1987, Canadians owned $819 billion of life insurance, an increase of $79 billion in the past year and nearly seven times the amount owned in 1970. The industry administered 14.2 million individual life insurance policies in Canada and almost 94 000 group life

*This case was written by Marvin Ryder. Case material is prepared as a basis for classroom discussion only. The author gratefully acknowledges the support of the Life Underwriters Association of Canada Research Grant which funded this work. Copyright © 1988 by Marvin Ryder, Faculty of Business, McMaster University and the Life Underwriters Association of Canada. This case is not to be reproduced in whole or in part by any means without the express written consent of the author.

insurance policies, covering 29.4 million certificates at the end of 1987.

Individual life insurance could be broken down into two basic types of protection—whole life (permanent) and term insurance. Whole life insurance offered more than death protection. Unlike term policies, it built cash value that could help families meet financial emergencies, pay for special goals, or provide retirement income. Cash value of whole life insurance policies was a by-product of the level premium system. As the mortality rate increased with age, the cost of life insurance increased. Under the level premium approach, the annual premium remained the same, despite the increased risk of death.

Although the premium charged in a whole life policy's earlier years was higher than the actual cost of the insurance, in later years, it was substantially lower than the actual cost of protection. In the early years, the excess amount of each premium was held in reserve, which, along with interest earned and future level premiums, assured that funds would be available to cover the increased risk of death as the policyholder grew older. The policyholder who decided to give up the protection by surrendering the policy was entitled to a share of the company's reserves. The measure of this share was the cash value plus policy dividends.

Term insurance policies offered protection only and most did not build up cash value. The premiums were initially lower than whole life policies of the same amounts but increased with each renewal of the term policy, reflecting higher mortality rates at older ages.

One form of individual life insurance that had come into use in recent years was mass-marketed insurance. It was sold on an individual basis to members of a group, usually as term life insurance policies with automatic renewal provisions. In contrast, group life insurance was issued in the form of a master policy, under which certificates were issued to the individuals covered.

People bought life insurance for many reasons, but mainly to provide financial protection for their families in the event they themselves should die prematurely. A person created an estate, or added to one, with a life insurance policy, and the future of this estate was protected as the policy was maintained over the years.

During 1987, Canadians purchased $135 billion of life insurance, $14.9 billion more than the amount bought in 1986 and over nine times the 1970 amount. Of that total, 61 percent of new life insurance protection purchased in Canada was bought on an individual basis—that is, by personal or family decision usually through a life insurance agent. Although the market share of individual

insurance was down from 1986 when it registered 65 percent, purchases of individual life insurance totalled $83 billion, an increase of five percent for the year.

A study of the individual life insurance policies bought by Canadians during 1987 showed that 54 percent were bought by people with incomes under $25 000. Three in four policies were bought by persons aged 15 to 44, one in three by those 25 to 34. Compared to earlier years, more women were buying life insurance. In 1987, 40 percent of policies covered females, compared to 29 percent in 1970. The face amount of these policies on females was 29 percent of the 1987 total, compared to 13 percent in 1970.

There were 169 active life insurance companies in Canada: 80 Canadian incorporated, 67 United States, 10 British, and 12 from Continental Europe. Of the 169 companies, 145 were registered under federal laws and 24 were provincial. Federally registered companies provided 93 percent of the total life insurance in force at the end of 1987. Mutual life insurance companies, which had no shareholders and whose entire boards of directors were elected by their policyholders, provided 55 percent of life insurance in force at the end of 1987. Stock life insurance companies, owned by their shareholders, accounted for 45 percent of life insurance in force.

For over a hundred years, Canadian governments had supervised the life insurance business in Canada to ensure commitments to policyholders were provided for and met. Each year, every life insurance company doing business in Canada had to obtain government certification of its right to continue to do business.

At the end of 1987, 60 600 people were working in the life insurance business in Canada. Of these, 37 100 were engaged in administrative work and 23 500 were in sales. Of the administrative employees, 28 800 were in company head offices and 38 300 worked in branch offices of the companies located throughout the country. Of those in sales, 20 500 were full-time agents and 3000 were supervisory personnel.

Sales Activities at the Toronto Branch

There were two sources of salespeople for the Toronto Branch. Each year universities were visited by representatives from the London Life head office. Local managers would join these representatives to conduct first interviews and screen potential candidates. While students in Commerce or Business programs were usually recruited for sales positions, it was not unusual to interview students from Humanities or Social Sciences as well. A second source of salespeople was referral from agents and other managers both from within London Life and from other insurance companies. Some salespeople work better in some environments than in others. Moving people from one branch to another or from one company to another might help them reach their full selling potential. At no time were salespeople solicited through an ad in the newspaper.

When recruiting a potential salesperson, Mr. Simmons looked for seven key factors:

1. An interest in people—concern, caring, being able to relate to someone's feeling, and ability to establish trust;

2. Good, sound judgment—when to act, when to listen;

3. Ability to handle rejection—not consider rejection to be personal when someone isn't interested in a product;

4. Imagination—someone needs imagination to turn the intangible benefits of insurance into something tangible, and good verbal communication skills to express these benefits;

5. Motivation—in some ways this is the spirit of entrepreneurialism yet it should not be "greed" driven—he looked for people who wanted to achieve goals;

6. Intelligence—not measured in grades achieved while taking courses but seen as common sense—"street smart";

7. Ethics/Morals—insurance is a product that people cannot really understand so one needs an agent who will not take advantage of someone's ignorance—as well when people need the product, they are usually facing a crisis and could be easily preyed upon.

Mr. Simmons realized that there was a difference between working for an insurance company and other financial institutions. Insurance involved a personal interaction between the salesperson and the client. It was important that the salesperson understand a client's feelings and interests and then translate these into financial opportunities. It required more than simply "niceness." Salespeople could be nice yet not have someone's basic interests at heart. As Mr. Simmons often said, "An ounce of interest was worth a pound of niceness."

According to Mr. Simmons, salespeople had to keep one overriding objective in mind. London Life existed to help people achieve the financial security or freedom to allow them to do what they want. Mr. Simmons saw this as three basic freedoms: freedom to do; freedom to become; and freedom to belong. Salespeople worked to help clients achieve this freedom on their own terms.

The Toronto branch had approximately 30 salespeople. London Life tried to keep a ratio of one manager for every eight salespeople. This did not imply that a manager "managed" a specific eight salespeople. "Telling people what to do is not managing them." Rather each of the four managers were specialists in recruiting, training, advancement, and motivation.

All salespeople and managers attended a monthly meeting. Each person's activity report for the month was displayed for the group to see and someone was chosen to make constructive, but critical (if necessary), comments. These comments were not meant to be judgmental—criticism did not help motivate either. While quotas were set by Head Office for each agency, these were not directly translated into quotas for each salesperson. Activity targets were set on a personal basis taking into account each person's strengths and goals.

The Monthly Activity Reports

Mr. Simmons was examining the monthly activity reports for the four salespeople (see Table K.1). The first section of the report looked at telephone activity. The first column within the section listed the number of telephone numbers dialed fro the month. The next column listed the number of completed calls. From statistical evidence, one of every three calls should be completed. The third and fourth columns listed the number of appointments that were made. "New appointments were people with whom the agent had no previous contact while with "old" appointments the agent had some previous contact with the people. As a rule of thumb, one of every two completed calls should result in an appointment.

The second section of the report looked at lunch time activity. After hours selling was frequently associated with this industry but Mr. Simmons did not believe in it. He felt the hours after work belonged to the agent and he or she should spend that time with family and friends. Instead, he suggested that many of the sales contacts should be made at lunchtime. In fact, London Life served lunch in their offices in downtown Toronto. Over some sandwiches and soft drinks, the agents could talk with their contacts.

In this section of the report the first column showed the number of lunchtime appointments (contacts) that were made. Not all contacts were prospective purchasers. Those contacts who were prospective purchasers were called suspects. The second column showed the number of suspects that were determined from the lunchtime meeting. The third column showed the number of fact sheets that were completed. A fact sheet took roughly an hour to complete and listed a lot of personal information about a suspect. The fourth column showed the number of open cases while the fifth column showed the number of closed cases. An open case was a suspect with whom the agent had ongoing relations. An open case might mean a suspect was considering the purchase of life insurance, an agent was still putting together a presentation for that person or that they had simply agreed to meet and talk again. A closed case indicated that the agent and suspect had finished their transaction. This might mean that some insurance had been sold or instead that the person had decided not to purchase any insurance.

The next section of the report detailed the same information, summed over all time periods including lunch. In other words, the number of suspects shown under "All Activities" included those suspects "From Lunches." The final section listed an agent's "Efficiency Points." To determine this number, an agent received one point for a lunch appointment, one point for a completed fact sheet, one point for open cases, one point for closed cases and a half point for suspects. As a rule of thumb, an agent should generate 5 efficiency points per working day or roughly 100 efficiency points each month. It should be noted that this was a measure of efficiency and not effectiveness. Effective agents did more than simply "process" suspects and generate sales.

The Four Salespeople

Roy Girard joined the company eight months ago after graduating with a Bachelor of Commerce degree from the University of Toronto. In the summer of 1987, he went to Europe and travelled for four months before starting work in September. Roy was very athletic. He played slo-pitch and coached a junior girl's softball team in the summer. In the winter, he played racquetball three times a week and was a forward with a hockey team in a corporate "No-Body-Contact" league. In February, Roy became engaged to his long-time fiancée. She was a public health nurse in London, Ontario. They planned to be married in May, 1989.

Linda McCallum joined the company twenty-two months ago after graduating with a Bachelor or Arts degree in Economics from Queen's University. As far as Mr. Simmons knew, she led a rather quiet life. She was quite fond of the symphony and was also interested in antiques. When she took a vacation in 1987, she travelled through New England. She returned with six new goblets for her early Victorian glass collection. Linda was engaged to be married but Mr. Simmons knew very little about her fiancé or when she planned to be married.

Donald Widner joined the company three years ago after working for two years with an investment company. He had a community college diploma in Marketing and Sales Management. For the past eighteen months, Donald had been the top salesperson in the branch. Intensely competitive, he seemed to thrive on the demands of personal selling. He often stated that "he would do whatever it took" to remain number one. Donald was a member of two service clubs (Rotary and Lions) and an elder with his church. His wife was a neurosurgeon at the Hospital for Sick Children in Toronto. They lived in a beautiful penthouse condominium in downtown Toronto and they also had a cabin in northern Ontario, though they did not seem to visit it often. They had no children.

David Southcott was one of the senior salespeople within the company. He joined the company after getting his Bachelor of Commerce degree in 1978 from the University of Toronto. He had been offered promotions to Assistant Sales Manager but he had turned them down as they would have meant leaving the Toronto agency. Many people felt that he was waiting for a vacancy within the agency before accepting a promotion. He was active in the community, serving on the Boards for the United Way and for Big Brothers. He also helped organize the annual corporate fitness challenge which London Life had won last year. His wife had been a public school teacher but she currently chose to stay at home and help raise their three children. David's oldest son had just finished his first season of hockey. David never missed one of his son's games.

The Problem

The activity reports showed salesperson efficiency. Effectiveness could be measured by the volume of life insurance sold. All four salespeople were candidates for the Million Dollar Round Table. To qualify for membership in the Round Table, a life insurance salesperson had to sell $4 000 000 worth of whole life insurance during the year. For example, a salesperson would qualify for the Round Table if he or she sold forty people whole life insurance policies with a face value of $100 000 each. The Round Table was an independent organization that promoted the life insurance industry. If an individual qualified for membership, for a fee of $50, he or she could join. Upon joining he or she received a plaque, a magazine, and the opportunity to attend conferences and seminars on such topics as motivation and selling skills. In a given year, approximately 25 percent of the salespeople in the life insurance industry qualified for membership in the Round Table.

Like most companies in the industry, London Life paid their salespeople on the basis of sales performance. The salespeople received a combination of commissions and bonuses and no base salary. The commission rate was one percent of the value of a whole life policy. For example, the sale of a $100 000 whole life policy translated into a commission of $1000. Bonuses were based on the commissions received for the year and increased on a sliding scale from five to fifteen percent. As shown in Table K.2, a salesperson earning $25 000 in commissions received a five percent bonus while a salesperson earning commissions of $150 000 (or more) received a fifteen percent bonus. While salespeople earned the one percent commission on a new policy, if that policy was renewed by the customer in the next year, the salesperson received a reduced commission on the renewal. The commission structure on renewals was as follows: 0.5 percent of first year renewal, 0.25 percent second year, 0.15 percent third year, 0.12 percent fourth year, 0.08 percent fifth year, and 0.05 percent thereafter.

Mr. Simmons estimated that if the four salespeople continued their current level of sales performance for the year that Roy Girard would receive approximately $39 000 in commissions and bonuses while Linda McCallum would receive approximately $45 000. Virtually all of their commissions and bonuses would be the result of new business. Donald Widner would earn between $75 000 and $80 000 with a small portion of the commission and bonus coming from renewal business. David Southcott would earn about $60 000 for the year with a significant portion of that in renewal commissions.

As Ralph Simmons examined the activity reports he wondered what recommendations, if any, he should make to these salespeople.

Table K.1 Monthly Activity Reports for the Four Employees

Roy Girard	Telephoning				From Lunches					All Activities				
	Dialed	Reached	New	Old	No.	Suspects	Fact Sheets	Cases Open	Closed	Suspects	Fact Sheets	Cases Open	Closed	Effic. Points
January	455	143	30	39	16	11	7	9	10	32	20	30	24	106
February	401	126	27	31	14	10	8	6	9	28	18	26	26	98
March	375	130	28	37	13	8	5	6	7	22	17	29	20	90
April	362	134	25	29	10	7	5	3	6	24	18	24	19	83
Linda McCallum	Dialed	Reached	New	Old	No.	Suspects	Fact Sheets	Cases Open	Closed	Suspects	Fact Sheets	Cases Open	Closed	Effic. Points
January	500	117	19	26	10	7	4	8	11	28	15	29	30	98
February	464	92	15	25	8	5	4	9	10	34	19	27	30	101
March	525	97	15	27	11	8	6	10	8	36	16	35	28	108
April	517	102	13	24	8	6	4	12	8	30	19	34	22	98
Donald Widner	Dialed	Reached	New	Old	No.	Suspects	Fact Sheets	Cases Open	Closed	Suspects	Fact Sheets	Cases Open	Closed	Effic. Points
January	830	280	91	48	15	12	9	12	13	58	41	51	49	185
February	793	270	85	55	18	14	11	9	9	66	45	57	51	200
March	801	265	88	46	16	13	9	13	12	62	39	48	49	180
April	824	290	86	62	18	15	12	11	11	70	51	62	57	223
David Southcott	Dialed	Reached	New	Old	No.	Suspects	Fact Sheets	Cases Open	Closed	Suspects	Fact Sheets	Cases Open	Closed	Effic. Points
January	351	108	22	37	15	8	5	11	12	28	13	32	31	105
February	275	83	14	30	8	3	3	5	4	36	13	28	28	95
March	409	130	24	39	16	9	3	11	12	48	14	29	23	106
April	346	115	21	34	8	6	5	6	1	44	16	30	24	98

Table K.2 London Life Bonus Structure

Salesperson Commission	Bonus (%)	Bonus ($)	Total Commission and Bonus
$25 000	5%	$1250	$26 250
$50 000	7%	$3500	$53 500
$75 000	9%	$6750	$81 750
$100 000	11%	$11 000	$111 000
$125 000	13%	$16 250	$141 250
$150 000	15%	$22 500	$172 500

■ QUESTIONS

1. Evaluate each of the salespeople based on your knowledge of their background and the activity chart. Should any actions be taken?

2. How effective is the activity chart and its publication as a sales motivation tool?

3. As a sales manager, should a salesperson's private life have any bearing on your evaluation of his/her performance?

Name Index

Aaker, David, 633, 653 n4

Abell, Derek F. 40, 61, 63 nn10, 18; 299

Abelson, Herbert, I., 112, 124 n8

Abler, Ronald, 545, 567 n6

Abrams, Bill, 159, 163 n24

Achenbaum, Alvin A., 357, 358, 369 n27

Ackoff, Russell, L., 88, 96 n2; 262, 275 n2

Adams, John S., 545, 567 n6

Adler, Lee, 560, 567 n18

Aguilar, Francis Joseph, 104, 123 n2

Alberts, William W., 513, 537 n10

Albrecht, Karl, 19, 32 n20; 484, 503 n1

Alda, Alan, 639

Alderson, Wroe, 541, 567 n4

Alexander, Ralph S., 220, 386, 396 n18

Alford, Charles L., 339, 368 n12

Alpert, Mark L., 194, 202 n26; 206

Alter, Stewart, 170, 201 n2

Ames, B. Charles, 294, 306 n12; 737, 748 n7

Amstutz, Arnold E., 127, 134 n2

Anderson, James C., 105, 123 n3; 220, 231 n21; 554, 588, 599 n17; 702, 718, 722 n23

Anderson, M.J., Jr., 406, 423 n11

Andreasen, Alan R., 284, 306 n2

Ansoff, H. Igor, 47, 370, 396 n1

Arbeit, Stephen P., 279, 306 n1

Arndt, Johan, 712, 722 n30

Arnold, John, 338, 368 n10

Arpan Jeffery S., 435, 454 n4

Ashcraft, Laurie, 178

Assael, Henry, 188, 189, 202 n21

Athos, Anthony G., 58, 63 n16

Austin, Nancy, 3, 30 n2

Ayal, Igal, 437, 454, 455 nn5, 10

Bacharach, Samuel B., 713, 722 n32

Bachman, Randy, 370

Backhaus, Klaus, 221, 231 n22

Bailey, Earl, 332, 368 n3

Ballachey, Egerton L., 187, 202 n20

Ballou, Ronald H., 595, 599 n21

Barksdale, Hiram C., 490, 503 n9

Barnard, Christiaan, 488

Bartlett, Christopher A., 451, 455 n14

Bass, Frank M., 130, 134 n14; 292, 306 n10; 351

Bass, Stephen J., 572, 598 n2

Bates, Albert D., 598, 572 n2

Bateson, John E.G., 484, 486, 503 nn1, 4

Bauer, Raymond A., 159, 163 n25; 196, 202 n33; 603, 628 n7

Bayer, Judy, 122, 124 n16; 676, 684 n27

Bayus, Barry L., 198, 203 n38

Beatles, 159

Beckman, M.D., 111, 124 n7

Behrens, William W., III, 145, 163 n6

Beik, Leland L., 761, 777 n9

Belch, George E., 612, 628 n13

Belk, Russell W., 284, 306 n2

Bell, David E., 277

Bell, Martin L. 28, 32 n25

Bennett, Sidney, 511, 537 n5

Benson, Lissa, 28, 32 n26

Berelson, Bernard, 185, 202 n18; 615, 628 n19

Bernbach, William, 635

Berning, Carol K., 199, 203 n43

Bernstein, Peter, W., 183

Berry, Leonard, L., 3, 32 n4; 320, 329 n5; 484, 487, 490, 494, 495, 503, 504, nn1, 5, 11, 16

Bertrand, Kates, 703

Best, Roger J., 271, 275 n9

Bettman, James R., 191, 202 n23

Biggadike, Ralph, 421

Birge, Cyrus A., 458

Bishop, William S., 209, 231 n3

Blackwell, Roger D., 116, 124 n9; 191, 202 n24; 577, 598 n8; 611, 628 n12

Blake, Robert R., 710

Blattberg, Robert C., 350, 369 n21; 666, 667, 684 nn9, 12

Block, Martin P., 676, 684 n27

Bloom, Paul N., 29, 33 n27; 144, 408, 424 n15; 490, 503 n12

Bock, Lori L., 674

Bonoma, Thomas V., 24, 32 n23; 293, 294, 306 n12; 674, 745 n15

Borch, Fred J., 17, 32 n18

Borden, Neil H., Jr., 224, 237 n25

Boulding, Kenneth, 150

Bowman, Russell D., 675, 684 n22

Boyd, Harper W., Jr., 91, 96 n5; 181, 196, 201, 202 n12, 30; 355, 369 n25; 460, 482 n2

Bragg, Arthur, 551, 659

Bramel, Dana, 197, 203 n37

Brinberg, David, 177, 201 n5

Britt, Steuart Henderson, 469, 482 n5

Brodie, Terry, 558, 567 n17

Brooks, John, 178, 201 n9

Brown, Bert R., 713, 722 n31

Brown, George H., 292, 306 n11

Brown, Glen M., 667, 677, 685 n28

Brown, James R., 208, 231 n2

Brown, Norman W., 640

Brown, Rex V., 130, 134 n14

Brown, Robert George, 667, 684 n13

Brown, William P., 634, 653 n6

Bruning, Edward R., 125, 133 n2

Bruno, Albert B., 738, 748 n9

Bucklin, Louis P., 546, 567 nn8, 9

Buell, Victor P., 734, 748 n4

Bultez, Alain V., 126, 134 n6

Bumba, Lincoln, 642, 654 n23

Burdick, Richard K., 212, 231 n10

Burke, Raymond, 122, 124 n15

Burnett, John H., 157, 163 n21

Burnett, John J., 611

Burnett, Leo, 601, 681

Buzby, Stephen L., 761, 777 n9

Buzzell, Robert D., 322, 373, 377, 396 nn5, 14, 15, 16; 406, 409, 423 nn9, 10; 427, 454 n2; 651, 654 n34

Bybee, H. Malcolm, 636, 637, 653 n16

Cacioppo, John T., 196, 202 n30

Calder, Bobby J., 187, 202 n19

Cannon, Hugh M., 267

Canton, Irving D., 492, 504 n15

Cardozo, Richard N., 222, 231 n24; 294, 306 n12

Cardwell, John J., 96, 97 n10

Carlson, Chester, 341

Carlzon, Jan, 22, 23

Carman, Bliss, 749

Carman, James M., 633, 653 n4

Carnegie, Dale, 708

Carson, Rachel, 143, 150

Carson, Teresa, 571

Cash, Johnny, 320

Catry, Bernard, 409, 424 n18

Cattin, Philippe, 126, 133 n4

Cavalier, Richard, 705, 722 n26

Cavanaugh, Richard E., 3, 32 n4; 420, 424 n27

Center, Allen H., 677, 684 n28

Chapin, Marian, 278

Cheng, Joyce, 107, 108, 123 n5

Chevalier, Michel, 409, 424 n18; 672, 684 n18

Choate, Robert, 143

Chou, Ya-Lun, 271, 275 n10

Churchill, Gilbert A., Jr., 210, 231 n8; 704, 722 n24

Clark, Bruce H., 24, 32 n23

Clausewitz, Carl von, 402, 423 n4

Clemons, Eric K., 217

Clewett, Richard M., 734, 748 n4

Clifford, Donald K., Jr., 3, 32 n4; 420, 424 n27

Coffin, William F., 539

Cohen, Herb, 713, 722 n32

Cohen, Joel B., 195, 202 n29

Cohen, William, 238

Coleman, Richard P., 176, 288, 306 n5

Colley, Russell H., 630, 653 n2

Collins, Joan, 670

Collins, Thomas L., 661, 662, 656, 684 nn2, 6

Colombo, John Robert, 135

Comer, James M., 698, 721 n16

Conway, David, 107, 108, 123 n5

Cook, Victor, 373, 396 n4

Cooper, Arnold, 406, 424 n12

Corey, E. Raymond, 295, 539, 540, 567 n1; 737, 748 n6

Cosby, Bill, 639

Cossell, Howard, 639

Coughlan, Anne T., 581, 697

Cox, Donald F., 603, 628 n7

Cox, Jonathan M., 674

Cox, William E., Jr., 373, 374, 396 n8

Coykendall, Deborah S., 589

Craig, C. Samuel, 603, 610, 611, 612, 628; nn5, 11, 14

Cravens, David W., 578

Crawford, C. Merle, 374, 396 n8

Crawford, John C., 698, 721 n15

Cribbin, James, 711, 722 n28

Crissy, W.J.E., 709, 722 n27

Crosby, Philip B., 408, 424 n16

Cross, James, 220

Crutchfield, Richard S., 187, 202 n20

Cunningham, Isabella C.M., 709, 722 n27

Cunningham, William H., 709, 722 n27

Curhan, Ronald C., 672, 684 n18

Cutlip, Scott M, 677, 684 n18

Dafoe, J.W., 425

Dalkey, Norman, 271, 275 n9

Daltas, Arthur J., 756, 757, 777 n7

Darmon, Rene Y., 323, 329 n9

Darwin, Charles, 130
Davidow, William H., 484, 503
   n1; 499, 504 n19
Davidson, William R., 572, 598 n2
Davies, R.L., 581, 598 n12
Davis, Harry L., 177, 201 n8; 710
Davis, Robert A., 697, 721 n11
Davis, Robert T., 90, 96 n5
Davis, Stanley M., 60, 63 n17;
   281, 282
Dawson, Leslie M., 28, 32 n26
Day, Ellen, 502, 504 n21
Day, George, 44, 311, 329 n1
Day, Ralph L., 197, 198, 203 n36;
   301, 306 n19
Deal, Terrence, E., 60, 63 n17
Dempsey, William A., 219, 231
   nn18, 19
Denenberg, Herbert S., 143
Deneuve, Catherine, 639
Derrick, Frederick W., 180
Desia, Padma, 30, 33 n29
Desourza, Glenn, 500
Dewar, Robert, 736
Dhalla, Nariman K., 390, 397 n23
Dichter, Ernest, 183, 184, 202
   n15; 213, 231 n13
Dickinson, Roger A., 225, 231 n26
Dietvorst, Thomas F., 199, 203 n43
Dillon, William R., 125, 133 n2
Dizard, John, 433
Dobler, Donald W., 713, 722 n33
Dodson, Joe A., 676, 684 n26
Dolan, Robert J., 409, 424 n17
Donnelly, James H., Jr., 198, 203
   n42
Dorfman, Robert, 93, 97 n7
Dougherty, Philip H., 648, 653
   n29
Douglas, Susan P., 451, 455 n15
Dowst, Somerby, 217
Doyle, Peter, 210, 231 n7; 390
Drucker, Peter F., 2, 16, 37, 61,
   63 n5; 73, 84 n2; 135, 162
   n1
Dubinsky, Alan J., 698, 721 n16
Dugas, Christine, 731
Dumaine, Brian, 319
Duncan, Tom, 678, 685 n29
Dunphy, Dermot, 321

Eagly, Alice H., 603, 628 n6
Edelman, Franz, 507
Ehrlich, Paul R., 150
Eiglier, Pierre, 484, 491, 503 n1
El-Ansary, Adel I., 540, 541, 567
   n2; 564 n23; 583, 599 n14
Eliashberg, Jehoshua, 122, 124 n15
Elrich, A., 356, 369 n26
Ely, E.S., 4, 32 n6
Emerson, Ralph Waldo, 15, 32 n13
Emery, Albert W., 233

Emery, C. William, 28, 32 n25
Emshoff, James R., 88, 96 n2;
   191, 202 n24
Engle, Ernest, 149
Engle, James F., 159, 202 n24;
   611, 628 n12
Enis, Ben M., 463, 697, 721 n11
Eovaldi, Thomas L., 210, 231 n4
Erickson, Gary M., 521, 537 n13
Erickson, Julie Liesse, 571
Erlichs, the, 150
Evans, Franklin B., 289, 306 n6;
   710
Evert, Chris, 639

Fahey, Alison, 659
Fahey, Liam, 453
Faris, Charles W., 210, 215, 218,
   231 nn6, 17
Farris, Paul W., 521, 538 n15; 632,
   653 n3; 667, 668, 684 n15
Feick, Lawrence F., 177, 201 n5
Feinstein, Selwyn, 118, 124 n10
Feldman, Laurence P., 28, 32
   n25; 388, 397 n22
Fenn, Dan H., Jr., 159, 163 n25
Ferber, Robert, 92, 97 n6
Fern, Edward F., 208, 231 n2
Festinger, Leon, 197, 198, 203
   nn37, 39
Firnstahl, Timothy W., 496, 504
   n17
Fishbein, Martin, 195, 202 n29;
   196 n32
Fisher, Roger, 714, 715, 722 n35
Fisk, George, 28, 32 n26
Fiske, John, 603, 604, 628 n8
Flax, Steven, 247
Fogg, C. David, 409, 424 n18
Forbis, John L., 519
Ford, Henry, 14, 278, 284, 341,
   403, 408
Ford, Neil M., 704, 722 n24
Fornell, Claes, 379, 756, 777 n6
Forrester, Jay W., 133, 134 n17;
   646, 648, 654 nn26, 30
Foster, David, 416
Foster, George, 238, 253 n5
Fourt, Louis A., 351
Fox, Michael J., 612, 638
Fox, Richard J., 502, 504 n21
Free, Valerie, 122, 124 n13
Freeman, Cyril, 621, 628 n28
French, John R.P., 553
Freud, Sigmund, 130, 183
Frey, Albert Wesley, 70, 84 n1;
   219, 616, 628 nn23, 24
Frey, John B., 379, 380, 396 n17
Friars, Eileen M., 574
Frons, Marc, 360
Fry, Joseph, 107
Fu, Marilyn Y.C., 435, 454 n4

Fuld, Leonard M., 233, 253 n1

Gafin, Arniram, 196, 202 n33
Galbraith, John Kenneth, 143
Gale, Bradley T., 322, 406, 423
   nn9, 10; 500
Gannes, Stuart, 422, 424 n28
Gardner, Burleigh, 301, 306 n18
Garreau, Joel, 148, 163 n10
Garvin, David A., 313, 329 n2
Gaskin, S.P., 402
Gatignon, Hubert, 367, 369 n34
Gaudet, H., 615, 628 n19
Gautschi, David A., 581, 599 n13
Gelb, Betsy D., 360
Gelb, Gabriel M., 360
George, Weston, 490, 503 n9
George, William R., 490, 503 n9
Ghoshal, Sumantra, 451, 455 n14
Giddy, Ian H., 436
Giese, Thomas D., 734, 748 n4
Gilbert, J., 178
Gilly, Mary C., 198, 203 n41
Golanty, John, 350, 369 n21
Goldman, Arieh, 375, 450, 455 n13
Goldstein, Matthew, 125, 133 n2
Goldstucker, Jac L., 373, 396 n5
Goligoski, Bob, 122, 124 n14
Gonik, Jacob, 270, 275 n8
Goodman, Charles S., 207
Goodman, Sam R., 773, 774, 777
   n17
Gorbachev, Mikhail, 30
Gordon, William, J. J., 340
Gould, Peter, 545, 567 n6
Graham, John L., 209, 231 n3
Gray, Frank B., 738, 748 n8
Green, Paul E., 194, 202 n28;
   206, 346-48, 533
Greenberg, Herbert M., 698, 721
   n14
Greenland, Leo, 639, 653 n19
Gregor, William T., 574, 767, 777
   nn12, 14
Gretzky, Wayne, 614
Greyser, Stephen A., 144
Griffiths, Frances, 64
Groeneveld, Leonard, 221, 231 n22
Gronroos, Christian, 490-91
   nn10, 13
Gross, Irwin, 636, 653 n14
Gubar, George, 180
Gupta, Askok K., 740, 748 n10
Guzzardi, Walter, Jr., 215, 231 n16

Haines Jr., George, 107, 108, 123
   n5
Haire, Mason, 119, 124 n12
Haley, Russell I., 290, 358, 369
   n28
Haliburton, T.C., 505

Hall, William G.,356, 369 n26
Hall, William K., 59
Hamelman, Paul W., 387, 396 n19
Hamermesh, Richard G., 373, 396
   n6; 406, 423 n11
Hanan, Mark, 342, 369 n18; 711,
   722 n28; 734, 748 n5
Haneland, Peter, 154, 163 n16
Hansen, Richard W., 198, 203 n41
Hanssens, Dominique M., 88, 96
   n1; 537, 571 n8
Harding, Murray, 213, 231 n13
Hardy, Kenneth, 107
Harrell, Steve, 36, 63 n2
Harrigan, Kathryn Rudie, 237,
   253 n2; 387, 396 nn20, 21
Harris, Brian F., 473, 482 n7
Harris, J.E., 406, 423 n11
Hartley, John, 603, 604, 628 n8
Hartley, William D., 450, 455 n12
Hartvig Larsen, H., 491
Harvey, Michael, 352, 369 n22
Hauser, John R., 126, 134 n5; 402
Heany, Donald F., 423
Heckert, J.B., 705, 722 n25
Heckert, Richard, 744
Heede, S., 491
Heenan, D.A., 439
Heidrick, 4
Heinzl, John, 301, 306 n20
Heiser, Herman, 711, 722 n20
Heldey, B., 41
Helmer, Olaf, 271, 275 n9
Henderson, Bruce, 245, 246, 253
   n8
Hendon, Donald W., 176, 201 n4;
   716
Henion, Karl E., III, 152, 163 n12
Henkoff, R., 412
Hensel, James S., 116, 124 n9
Heron, Ruth M., 653, 637 n17
Hertz, David B., 353, 369 n24
Herzberg, Frederick, 183, 184,
   202 n17
Hill, Harold, 686
Hill, Richard, 220
Hills, Gerald E., 578
Hindin, Russell, 210, 231 n5
Hippel, Eric A. von, 337, 339, 340,
   368 nn9, 14; 400, 423 n3
Hirschman, Albert O., 198, 203
   n40
Hise, Richard T.,387, 396 n19
Hite, Robert, 674
Hlavac, T.E., Jr., 126, 134 n6
Hlavacek, James D., 294, 306
   n12; 588, 599 n17
Hoff, Edward J., 446
Hollander, Stanley C., 572, 598 n3
Honomichi, Jack, 360
Hopkins, David S., 332, 335, 368
   nn3, 7
Hormer, La Rue T., 45

Hornby, William H., 27, 32 n24
Horton, Raymond L., 603, 628 n7
Hostage, G.M., 488, 503 n7
Houston, Franklin S., 28, 32 n25
Hout, Thomas, 319
Hovland, Carl I., 610, 612, 628 nn13, 15
Howard, John A., 188, 191, 193, 202 nn21, 24, 25
Huff, David L., 581, 599 n13
Hughes, David, 358, 369 n28
Hugo, Victor, 330
Hulbert, James M., 731, 776 n1
Hume, Scott, 731
Hutton, Beth, 111

Iaccoca, Lee, 678, 679
Irwin, Richard D., 299, 755
Ivancevich, John M., 198, 203 n42

Jackson, Barbara Bund, 717-18
Jackson, Donald W., Jr., 212, 231 n10
Jacoby, Jacob, 199, 203 n43; 521, 538 n14
James, John C., 497
Jatusripitak, Somkid, 453, 443, 455 n10
Jobs, Steve, 3
Johanson, Jan, 443, 454 n9
Johansson, Johny K., 443, 454 n9; 521, 537 n13
Johnson, Richard M., 323, 329 n10
Johnson, S.C., 48, 63 n14
Jones, Conrad, 48, 63 n14
Jones, Michael H., 209, 231 n3
Jordan, Michael, 614, 639

Kalwani, Manohar U., 285, 306 n3
Kanuk, Leslie Lazar, 173, 201 n13
Kassarjian, Harold H., 181, 201 n13
Katz, Elihu, 366, 369 n33
Katz, Gerald M., 126, 134 n5
Kaven, William H., 689, 721 n5
Kearney, A.T., 595, 599 n21
Keefer, Bill, 338
Keegan, Warren J., 444, 455 n11
Keenye, Ralph L., 277
Keith, Janet E., 212, 231 n10
Keith, Robert J., 17, 32 n18
Kelley, Bill, 412
Kelly, Eugene J., 70, 84 n1
Kelman, Herbert C., 612, 628 n15
Kelvin, Lord, 100
Kenderine, James M., 589
Kennedy, Allan A., 60, 63 n17
Kennedy, Gavin, 435, 454 n4
Keon, John W., 122, 124 n16; 676, 684 n27

Keough, Donald R., 6699, 721 n17
Kerin, Roger A., 41, 63 n11; 352, 369 n22
Kernan, Jerome H., 614, 628 n17
Kidd, Kenneth, 150, 163 n11
Killing, J. Peter, 442, 454 n8
Kindel, Stephen, 170, 201 n2
Kinnear, Thomas C., 105, 123 n5; 125, 133 n1
Klompmaker, Jay E., 358, 369 n28
Kobrin, Stephen, 439
Konrad, Walecia, 631
Koopman-Iwerna, Agnes M., 184, 202 n17
Koschnick, Wolfgang J., 30, 33 n29
Koten, John, 610, 628 n11; 635, 653 nn10, 11
Kotler, Philip, 12, 29, 33 n27; 88, 90 nn3, 4; 133, 134 n18; 138, 142, 145, 162, 163 nn2, 3, 7; 317, 329 n3; 197, 202 n34; 277, 282, 362, 369 n30; 387, 388, 396 nn19, 22; 403, 408, 423, 424 nn5, 15; 434, 453, 490, 503 n12; 545, 567 n7; 579, 598 n11; 614, 628 n18; 634, 639, 653 n9; 767, 777 nm11, 12, 14
Kovacic, Mary L., 125, 133 n2
Kraar, Louis, 439
Krech, David, 187, 202 n20
Kreshel, Peggy J., 642, 653 n23
Kroc, Ray, 496
Krugman, Herbert E., 190, 202 n22; 642, 653 n22
Kuehn, Alfred A., 301, 306 n19; 646, 654 n28
Kurland, Mark A., 233, 244, 253 n1

La Barbera, Priscilla A., 197, 203 n35
Lafleur, Guy, 323
lang, k.d., 488
Lambin, Jean-Jacques, 88, 96 n1
Lancaster, Kent M., 642, 653 n23
Land, Edwin H., 338
Landon, E. Laird, 198
Langeard, Eric, 484, 491, 503 n1
Lanning, Michael J., 725
Lanquedoc, Colin, 577, 598 n9
Larson, Carl M., 579
Lasswell, Harold D., 601, 628 n2
LaTour, Stephen A., 661, 684 n5
Laurier, Sir Wilfrid, 724
Lavidge, Robert J., 130, 134 n16; 356, 369 n26; 607
Lawler, Edward J., 713, 722 n32
Lazarsfeld, Paul F., 366, 369 n33; 615, 628 n19
Lazer, William, 70, 84 n1

Leacock, Stephen, 629
Learner, David B., 127, 134 n11
Lecor, Tex, 323
Lee, Lamar, 713, 722 n33
Lehmann, Donald R., 110, 124 n6; 219, 231 n20
Leigh, Thomas W., 126, 134 n11
Leighton, David S.R., 107, 440, 454 n7
Lele, Milind M., 3, 32, n4; 501, 502, 504 n22; 556
Lepisto, Lawrence, 179, 201 n10
Lerreche, Jean-Claude, 126, 134 n10
Levine, Jonathan B., 731
Levinson, Horace C., 119, 124 n11
Levitt, Theodore, 6, 17, 32 nn10, 19; 39, 63 n8; 321, 329 n8; 346, 369 n20; 374, 396 n9; 400, 418, 423, 424 nn2, 26; 445, 446, 459, 460, 482 nn1,3; 484, 485, 487, 499, 503, 504 nn3, 5, 18; 621, 717, 719, 722 n37
Levy, Sidney J., 12, 138, 162 n2; 181, 201 nn11, 12; 301, 306 n18; 460, 482 n2; 619, 628 n25, 26
Liddell-Hart, B.H., 402, 415, 416, 423, 424, 425 nn4, 22
Lilien, Gary L., 88, 96 n4; 133, 134 n18; 277, 622, 623, 634, 653 n9
Lincoln, John W., 340, 368 nn16, 17
Linda, Gerald, 267
Lindbergh, Charles, 325
Linfield, Alane E., 180
Little, Arthur D., 398
Little, John D.C., 126, 134 nn6, 8, 9; 277, 623, 634, 653 n8
Lodish, Leonard M., 126, 134 nn7, 8; 691, 721 n7
Loman, Willy, 686
Lonsdale, Ronald T., 292, 306 n10
Lorenz, Christopher, 317, 329 n3
Lovelock, Christopher H., 484, 486, 499, 503, 504 nn1, 4, 20
Lucas, George H., Jr., 697, 721 n11
Luce, R., Duncan, 130, 134 n15
Luck, David J., 731, 748 n2
Lumpkin, James R., 698, 721 n15
Lumsdaine, A.A., 612, 628 n13
Lusch, Robert F., 589

MacKay, David B., 126, 134 n4
Madonna, 639
Magee, John F., 700, 722 n21
Magrath, A.J., 319, 329 n4
Mahajan, Vijay, 41, 63 n11
Mahaloo, W.H., 107

Maidique, Modesto A., 333, 337, 368 n8
Makridakis, S., 272, 275 n11
Maloney, John C., 635, 636, 653 n13
Manoochehri, G.H., 217
Manrai, Ajay K., 661, 684 n5
Manrai, Lalita, 637, 638, 653 n18
Mantrala, Murali K., 197, 202 n34
Markin, Rom J., 193, 202 n25
Markle, L., 680, 685 n30
Marriott, Bill, Jr., 21
Marriott, J. Willard, Sr., 3
Marschner, Donald C., 94, 97 n8
Martilla, John A., 497
Martin, Dennis, 634, 653 n6
Marx, Karl, 130
Maslow, Abraham, 183, 184, 202 n16; 394
Mason, Joseph Barry, 302, 306 n22; 339, 368 n12
Mason, Todd, 571
Mathews, H. Lee, 221, 231 n22
May, Eleanor G., 583, 599 n14
Mayer, David, 698, 721 n14
Mazursky, David, 197, 203 n35
Mazze, Edward M., 387, 396 n19
McAlister, Leigh, 194, 202 n28
McCammon, Bert C., Jr., 552, 558, 561, 567 nn12, 13, 15, 16; 563 n22; 589
McCann, John M., 133, 134 n18
McCarthy, E. Jerome, 70-71, 84 n1
McCuistion, Tommy J., 588, 599 n17
McElroy, Neil H., 729
McFarlan, F. Warren, 217
McGinniss, Joseph, 16, 32 n16
McIntyre, Shelby H., 738, 748 n9
McKitterick, John B., 17, 32 n18
McLafferty, Sara L., 581, 599 n13
McLaughlin, Robert L., 271, 275 n10
McMahon, Ed, 639
McMurry, Robert N., 686, 687, 698, 721 nn2, 12, 13
McNair, Malcolm P., 572, 598 n3
McVey, Philip, 552, 567 n10
Meadows, Dennis L., 145, 150, 163 n6
Meadows, Donella H., 145, 150, 163 n6
Mecimore, Charles D., 594, 599 n20
Mehta, Nitin T., 519
Meidan, Arthur, 126, 134 n7
Menon, Anil, 680
Merims, Arthur M., 681, 685 n31
Messikomer, Edward E., 744, 748 n14
Michaels, Edward G., 725
Michaelson, Gerald A., 403, 423 n5

Miller, Arthur, 686
Miller, Herman, 316
Miller, Peter B., 646, 654 n27
Milner, Brian, 320, 329 n6
Mindak, William, 142, 162 n3;
    636, 637, 653 n16
Mineo, Ronald E., 690
Miniard, Paul W., 191, 195, 202
    nn24, 29; 611, 628 n12
Mirvish, Ed, 308
Mitchel, F. Kent, 667, 684 n14
Mitchell, Arnold, 160, 163 n26;
    182
Mitchell, Paul, 210, 231 n7
Mograth, A.J., 319, 329 n4
Moncreif, William C., III, 687,
    721 n2
Monroe, Kent B., 532, 538 n18
Montana, Joe, 639
Montgomery, David B., 106, 126,
    134 nn10, 13; 651, 654 n33
Moore, Thomas, 267
Moore, William L., 250, 253 n11
Morein, Joseph A., 734, 748 n4
Moriarty, Rowland T., 214, 231
    n15; 693
Morrill, John E., 621, 628 n28
Morrison, Donald G., 285, 306 n3
Moschis, George P., 177, 201 n6;
    615, 628 n20
Mouton, Jane S., 710
Muller, E., 375
Mullins, Peter L., 756, 776 n5
Murray, Anne, 82, 320, 458, 487,
    488
Murphy, Patrick E., 180, 463
Mushashi, Miyamoto, 400, 402,
    423 n4
Myers, James H., 194, 202 n26;
    206

Nader, Ralph, 143
Naert, Philippe A., 126, 134 n6
Nagle, Thomas T., 510, 511, 537
    nn3, 6
Naisbitt, John, 160-61
Namath, Joe, 639
Narayana, Chem L., 193, 202 n25
Narus, James A., 105, 123 n3;
    220, 231 n21; 554, 588, 599
    n17; 702, 718, 722 n23
Nash, Edward, 664, 684 n8
Nash, Laura, 339, 63 n7
Neslin, Scott A., 666-67, 684 nn9,
    12
Neugartens, the, 287
Nevin, John R., 511, 537 n4
Newman, Paul, 639
Nicosia, Francesco M., 191, 202
    n24
Nierenberg, Gerard I., 713, 722
    n32

Nimer, Daniel A., 517, 537 n12

Oberdick, Larry E., 125, 133 n2
Oetting, Rudy, 659
Ogilvy, David, 640, 653 n20
Ohmae, Kenichi, 437, 438
O'Keefe, Frank R., Jr., 35
Oliver, Richard L., 611
O'Meara, John T., Jr., 342, 369 n19
Orr, Bobby, 323
Osborn, Alex F., 339, 340, 368
    nn11, 15
Osgood, C.E., 605, 613, 628 nn9,
    16
O'Shaughnessy, John, 219, 231
    n20
Osler, Sir William, 655
Ostrom, Lonnie L., 222, 231 n23
Ottesen, Otto, 609
Oxenfeldt, Alfred R., 250, 253
    n11; 753, 776 n2
Ozanne, Urban B., 210, 211, 231
    n8

Packard, David, 20
Packard, Vance, 143
Page, Albert L., 214, 231 n15;
    388, 397 n22
Paine, Katerine D., 681, 685 n31
Palda, Kristian S., 154, 163 nn16,
    18; 273, 275 n12; 651, 654
    n32
Panas, Jerold, 341
Panat, Charles, 153, 163 n15
Parasuraman, A., 3, 32 n4; 320,
    329 n5; 387, 396 n19; 494-
    95, 504 n16; 697, 721 n11
Parsons, Leonard J., 88, 96 n1;
    511, 512, 537 nn8, 9
Pascale, Richard Tanner, 58, 63
    n13
Passavant, Pierre A., 660, 684 n4
Patel, Peter, 46, 63 n13
Patty, C. Robert, 674
Pazderka, Bohumir, 154, 163 n18
Pearson, Andrall E., 733, 748 n3
Peckham, J.O., 650, 654 n31
Pegram, Roger M., 689, 721 n4
Perlmutter, Howard V., 451, 455
    n15
Perreault, William D., Jr., 711,
    722 n29
Peters, Thomas J., 3, 31 nn1, 2;
    58, 60, 63 n16; 725
Peterson, Don, 338
Peterson, Esther, 29
Petty, Richard E., 196, 202 n30
Phelps, D.M., 755
Phillips, Michael B., 116, 124 n9
Piercy, Nigel, 738, 748 n9
Platzer, Linda Cardillo, 693

Plimpton, Linda, 177, 201 n5
Plummer, Joseph T., 182
Pol, Louis G., 144, 162 n4
Polli, Rolando, 372-73, 396 n4
Polli, N.W., 498
Popper, Ed, 76, 84 n3
Porter, Michael E., 57-58, 63 n15;
    237, 243, 248, 253 nn3, 4,
    7, 9, 10; 297, 298, 306
    nn14, 15; 311, 329 n1; 404,
    407, 408, 423, 424, nn5, 13,
    15; 428, 454 n3
Posner, Ronald S., 609, 721 n5
Presley, Elvis, 159
Price, Linda L., 177, 201 n5
Proulx, Norman R., 690
Punj, Girish, 126, 133 n3

Quelch, John A., 427, 446, 454
    n2; 474, 668, 684 nn15, 27

Raffio, Ralph, 576, 598 n4
Raia, Ernest, 217
Raiffa, Howard, 130, 134 n15;
    713-14, 722 nn32, 34
Rainwater, Lee P., 176
Raj, S.P., 740, 748 n10
Rajaratnam, Daniel, 560, 567 n19
Ramirez, Anthony, 571, 631
Randers, Jorgen, 145, 163 n6
Rangaswamy, Arvind, 122, 124
    n15
Rankin, Deborah, 29, 33 n28
Rao, Amber G., 646, 654 n27
Raphaelson, Joel, 640, 653 n20
Rapp, Stan, 656, 661, 662, 684
    nn2, 6
Rappaport, Alfred, 755, 776 n4
Raven, Bertram, 553
Ray, Michael L., 196, 202 n30;
    608, 611, 628 n10
Reeves, Rosser, 324, 329 n11
Reibstein, David J., 521, 538 n15
Reid, Stan, 443, 455 n10
Rein, Irving J., 16, 32 n15; 545,
    567 n7; 639
Reingen, Peter H., 614, 628 n17
Rejans, Adrian B., 128, 134 n13
Resnik, Alan J., 302, 306 n22
Ress, C. Williams, 583, 599 n14
Reynolds, William H., 376, 396
    n11
Rice, Faye, 412
Richman, Barry M., 343
Ricks, David A., 435, 454 n4
Riddell, Ken, 666, 684 n10
Ries, Al., 233, 253 n1; 324-26,
    329 n12; 403, 423 n5; 477,
    483 n8
Rink, David R., 374, 396 n8
Roach, John D.C., 406, 407, 424

n13
Roberto, Eduardo, 145, 163 n7
Roberts, Alan A., 300, 306 nn16,
    212
Robertson, Thomas S., 367, 369
    n34; 614, 628 n17
Robinson, Dwight E., 376, 396 n12
Robinson, Patrick J., 210, 215,
    218, 231 nn6, 17
Robinson, S.J.Q., 46, 63 n13
Robinson, William, 379
Rodgers, Frank "Buck", 3
Rodgers, William, 767, 777 nn12,
    14
Roering, Kenneth J., 738, 748 n9
Rogers, D.S., 581, 598 n12
Rogers, Everett M., 198, 203 n39;
    364-66, 369 nn31, 32; 607,
    615, 628 n21
Roman, Ernan, 656, 661, 684
    nn1, 5
Ronald, Marilyn, 150, 123 n5
Root, Ann, 105, 123 n5
Rosenbloom, Bert, 552, 567 n11
Rotenberg, Ronald, 111
Rothe, James T., 28, 32 n26; 352,
    369 n22
Rothmann, Matt, 731
Rothschild, Michael L., 616, 628
    n22
Rothschild, William E., 240-41,
    253 n6
Rubin, Jeffrey Z., 713, 722 n31
Ruekert, Robert W., 738, 742,
    748 nn9, 12
Rummel, R.J., 439
Rust, Roland T., 645, 654 n25
Ryans, John K., Jr., 740, 748 n11

Salama, Eric, 427, 454 n2
Salancik, Gerald R., 158
Salmon, Walter J., 583, 599 n14
Sammon, William L., 233, 244,
    253 n1
Sasieni, Maurice, 93
Sasser, W.Earl, 488, 503 n8
Schaffir, Kurt H., 675, 684 n24
Scherer, F.M., 235
Schiedt, Marsha A., 211, 231 n9
Schiffman, Leon G., 125, 133 n2;
    173, 201 n3
Schiller, Zachary, 35, 63 n1
Schoeffler, Sidney, 406, 423 n9
Schramm, Wilbur, 602, 603, 628
    nn3, 4
Schultz, Donald E., 634, 642, 653
    nn6, 21; 736
Schultz, Randall L., 88, 96 n1;
    126, 134 n10; 511, 512, 537
    nn8, 9
Schwartz, David J., 505, 537 n1
Schwartz, Joe, 731

Scott, F.R., 686
Scredon, Scott, 360
Scully, John, 4
Seligman, Daniel, 616, 628 n22
Sellers, Patricia, 700, 722 n19
Sen, Subrata K., 697
Sequeira, Jan K., 674
Sevin, Charles H., 761, 777 n9
Sexton, Donald E., Jr., 88, 96 n1
Shakespeare, William, 635
Shanklin, William L., 740, 748 n11
Shapiro, Benson P., 214, 231 n15;
    293, 294, 306 n12; 465,
    466, 482 n4; 693, 689, 721
    n5; 742, 748 n12
Sharkey, Betsy, 644
Shatner, William, 612
Sheffet, Mary Jane, 181, 201 n13
Sheffield, F.D., 612, 628 n13
Sheth, Jagdish N., 3, 31 n4; 188,
    191, 193, 196, 202 nn21,
    24, 25, 31
Shiskin, Julius, 271, 275 n10
Shocker, Allan D., 356, 369 n26
Shostack, G. Lynn, 484, 488, 489,
    503 nn1, 6
Shruggles, B., 4
Shuchman, Abe, 768, 777 n15
Shugan, Steve M., 402
Silk, Alvin J., 356, 369 n26; 651,
    654 n33; 710
Silk, Steven B., 373, 396 n6
Simpson, O.J., 612
Sinatra, Frank, 323
Singh, Ravi, 403, 423 n5
Sinha, Prabhakant, 126, 134 n7;
    691, 721 n7
Sirgy, M. Joseph, 181, 201 n14
Sissors, Jack Z., 642, 654 n23
Skolnik, Rayna, 690, 691, 721 n6
Smith, Adam, 309
Smith, Fred, 318
Smith, Lee, 15, 32 n14
Smith, Wendell R., 300, 306
    nn16, 17
Smythe, Robert J., 295, 296, 306
    n13
Snyder, Watson, Jr., 738, 748 n8
Souder, William E., 740, 748 n11
Spiro, Rosann L., 177, 201 n7;
    711, 722 n29
Spitalnic, Robert, 233, 244, 253 n1
Sproles, George B., 376, 396 n13
Stalk, George, Jr., 319
Stallone, Sylvester, 639
Stanbury, W.T., 156, 163 n20
Stanton, William J., 543, 567 n5
Staples, William A., 180
Star, Steven H., 737, 748 n6
Starzinger, Page Hill, 282
Stasch, Stanley F. 734, 748 n4
Stearns, James M., 611
Steinberg, Janice, 659

Steiner, Gary A., 130, 134 n16;
    185, 202 n18; 607
Steiner, Peter O., 93, 97 n7
Steklasa, Robert, 154, 163 n17
Stern, Arthur, 673, 684 n20
Stern, Louis W., 210, 231 n4;
    540, 541, 557, 558, 564,
    567 nn2, 3, 23; 583, 599
    n14
Sternthal, Brian, 116, 124 n9;
    187, 202 n19; 603, 610,
    611, 612, 628 nn5, 11; 676,
    684 n26
Stevenson, Robert Louis, 686
Stevenson, Thomas H., 214, 231
    n15
Stewart, David W., 126, 133 n3
Stewart, Wendell M., 591
Stoller, Martin, 545, 567 n7; 639
Stone, Bob, 266, 275 n5; 663, 664
    n7
Stonich, Paul J., 94, 97 n9
Strang, Roger A., 473, 482 n7;
    666, 668, 671, 675, 684
    nn11, 16, 21, 23, 25
Strauss, Marina, 653
Strong, E.K., 607
Strong, Edward C., 196, 202 n30
Sturdivant, Frederick D., 557, 558
Suci, C.J., 605, 628 n9
Sujan, Harish, 710
Sujan, Mita, 710
Sultan, Ralph G.M., 406, 423 n9
Summers, John O., 126, 134 n4
Sun Tsu, 402, 423 n4
Sutter, Stan, 653
Sutton, Howard, 555, 567 n14
Swan, John E., 211, 231 n9; 374,
    396 n8
Sweeney, James K., 437, 454 n6
Sweitzer, Robert W., 157, 163 n21
Szybillo, George J., 521, 538 n14

Talarzyk, W. Wayne, 5577, 598
    n8
Tannenbaum, P.H., 605, 613, 628
    nn9, 16
Tauber, Edward M., 339, 368
    nn12, 13
Taylor, James R., 125, 133 n1
Taylor, James W., 196, 202 n33
Taylor, Mark B., 478, 483 n9
Taylor, Thayer C., 693, 703, 721
    n8
Tellis, Gerald J., 374, 396 n8;
    527, 538 n17; 633, 634, 653
    n5
Temple, Paul, 157, 163 n21
Thierry, Henk, 184, 202 n17
Thomas, Dan R.E., 486
Thomas, Robert J., 361, 369 n29
Thompson, Donald W., 107

Thompson, Phillip, 500
Tigert, Douglas J., 292, 306 n10
Tillman, Rollie, 561, 567 n21;
    576, 598 n6
Tirmann, Ernst A., 772, 774, 777
    n16
Toffler, Alvin, 135, 153, 162 nn1,
    13, 14
Toomey, Margaret A., 642, 653
    n23
Torrance, George W., 196, 202 n33
Totten, John C., 676, 684 n27
Toy, Norman E., 711, 732 n1
Trapp, Raymond J., 535
Trawick, Fredrick T., 211, 231 n9
Trenten, H. George, 675, 684 n24
Trout, Jack, 233, 253 n1; 324,
    325, 326, 329 n10; 403, 423
    n5; 477, 483 n8
Tsu, Sun, See Sun Tsu
Turney, Peter B.B., 302, 306 n22
Twedt, Dik Warren, 105, 123 n4;
    291, 636, 653 n15
Tybout, Alice M., 187, 202 n19;
    676, 684 n26
Tyebjee, Tyzoon T., 738, 748 n9

Unger, Lynette S., 611
Upah, Gregory D., 158
Urban, Glen L., 126, 134 n5; 356,
    369 n26; 651, 654 n35
Urbanski, Al., 731
Ury, William, 714, 715, 722
    nn35, 36
Uttal, Bro, 422, 424 n28; 484,
    499, 503, 504 nn1, 19

Vachris, Lauren A., 674
Vamos, Mark N., 731
Van Horne, Sir William, 398, 568
Varadarajan, P. Rajan, 41, 63 n11;
    560, 567 n19; 680, 731
Venkatesh, Alladi, 170, 201 n2
Verdoorn, P.J., 92, 97 n6
Vernon, Raymond, 436
Vidale, M.L., 634, 653 n7
Vilcassim, Naufel J., 581
Viswanathan, R., 387, 396 n19
Vizza, Robert, 701
Vosburgh, E., 685

Walker, Orville C., Jr., 704, 722
    n24; 738, 742, 748 nn9, 12
Walmsley, Ann, 577, 598 n10
Wanamaker, John, 615
Ward, Scott, 76, 84 n3
Wasson, Chester R., 372, 374,
    376, 390, 396 nn3, 10
Waterman, Robert H., Jr., 3, 31
    n1; 58, 60, 63 n16

Weber, John A., 385, 386, 390,
    469
Webster, Frederick E., Jr., 207,
    212, 213, 231 nn1, 11, 12,
    14
Weidersheim-Paul, Finn, 454
Weigand, Robert E., 561, 567 n20
Weinberg, Charles B., 106
Weisenberger, T.M., 734, 748 n4
Weiss, Doyle L., 88, 96 n1
Weitz, Barton A., 710
Well, Louis T., Jr., 436
Wells, William D., 180, 183, 436
Welt, Leo G.B., 433
Wensley, Robin, 311, 329 n1
Westfall, Ralph, 289, 306 n7;
    355, 369 n25
Westing, J.H., 755
Whalen, Jack, 551
Wheeler, Elmer, 460
Wheelwright, S.C., 272, 275 n11
White, 4, 32 n5
Whittle, Chris, 644
Whittle, Jack, 281, 282
Wiedersheim-Paul, Finn, 443,
    454 n9
Wiersema, Frederick D., 409
Wieters, C. David, 222, 231 n23
Wilemon, David, 740, 748 n10
Wilkie, William L., 611, 632 n3
Wilkinson, J.B., 511, 537 n5
Wilson, Aubrey, 767, 777 n13
Wilson, David T., 221, 231 n22
Wilson, Meredith, 686
Wilson, Mike, 733, 767, 777 n13
Wilson, Thomas W., Jr., 733, 748
    n3
Wind, Jerry, 122, 124 n15
Wind, Yoram J., 194, 202 n28;
    206, 207, 210, 212, 213,
    215, 218, 231 nn1, 6, 11,
    12, 14, 17; 294, 306 n12;
    346-48
Winer, Leon, 56
Wittink, Dick R., 126, 133 n4
Wolfe, H.R., 634, 653 n7
Woo, Carolyn Y., 406, 424 n12
Wood, Wally, 116, 124 n9
Woodlock, Joseph N., 351
Woodruff, Robert B., 578
Woodside, Arch G., 210, 231 n7
Woolworth, F.W., 505
Wortzel, Lawrence H., 177, 201
    n7; 577, 578, 598 n7
Wright, J. Patrick, 743, 748 n13
Wright, John S., 373, 396 n5; 579
Wright, Robert V.L., 398, 423 n1

Yale, Jordan P., 374, 396 n9; 405,
    423 n2
Yankelovich, Daniel, 4, 32 n5;
    290, 306 n9

Yokom, John, 671, 684 n17
Young, Robert F., 499, 504 n20
Young, Shirley, 289, 306 n8
Younger, Michael, 46, 63 n13
Yuspeh, Sonia, 390, 397 n23

Zaltman, Gerald, 362, 369 n30
Zeithaml, Valarie A., 3, 32 n4;
    320, 329 n5; 491, 493-95,
    503, 504 nn14, 16
Zemke, Ron, 19, 32 n20; 484,

503 n1
Zif, Jehiel, 437, 454 n5
Zikmund, William G., 543, 567 n5
Zinkham, George M., 674
Zirger, Billie Jo, 337, 368 n8

Zoltners, Andris A., 126, 134
    nn7, 10; 691, 721 n7
Zufryden, Fred S., 126, 134 n5

Company/Brand Index

A&P (Great Atlantic & Pacific
    Tea Company), 74, 224,
    476, 569, 573, 615
Accutron, 476
A.C. Neilson, 105, 106, 224, 242,
    266, 373
Acura, 476
Adidas shoes, 136
Advertising Age, 325
Age of Discontinuity, 135
Agree, 414
Aim, 290
Airborne, 659
Air Canada, 114, 115, 492-93, 670
"Air Jordan" basketball shoes, 639
Air Ontario, 37
Alabe Products, 287
Alcan, 391, 393, 430, 544, 734
Allegro stereo line, 75-76, 78-82,
    89, 94
Allen-Bradley Company, 242, 339
Allstate, 487
Alpo dog food, 639
American Express, 447, 611
Amstrad, 534
Amway, 574
Ann Page, 476
Apple Computer Company, 3, 4,
    136, 172, 184, 186, 187,
    191, 216, 419, 470
Aquafresh toothpaste, 302, 324,
    560
Arm & Hammer, 374, 382, 400
Armour, 477
Armstrong Cork, 405
Armstrong Rubber, 35-36, 58
Arthur Andersen & Company, 588
A.T. Cross, 420, 445
AT&T, 241
Atari, 16, 136, 416
Atlantic Canada Plus, 778, 808-12
Atlas typewriter, 65-74
Atomic Energy of Canada
    Limited, 778, 791-95
Automobile Protection
    Association, 143
Avanti, 316
Avis, Inc., 325, 401, 418, 560

Avon Products, Inc., 22, 136,
    320, 418, 464, 471, 543,
    547, 548, 557, 574, 617,
    657
Aziza Polishing Pen, 479

BabyScott diapers, 477
Bang & Olufsen, 316
Banner, 464
Bantron, 388
Barbie doll, 446
Barnes & Noble, 656
Bata Shoe, 543, 573-74
Bausch and Lomb, 248
Bay, The, 569, 580
Bayer Aspirin, 313, 399, 425
Beatles, 159
Beauty Counsellors, 574
Beautyrest, 476
Beaver Lumber, 573
Bechtel, 211
Becker Milk Co. Ltd., 139, 569-
    70, 573
Beckton-Dickenson Company, 281
Beecham, 4, 30, 238, 302, 324,
    411, 560
Beefeater gin, 181
BehaviorScan, 118
Bell Canada, 24, 318, 688
Bell Northern Research, 154, 321
Bell Telephone, 701
BERI surveys, 439
Best Western, 560
Better Business Bureau, 525
Betty Crocker, 27
Bic Corporation, 401, 412, 477,
    534
BIC pens, 136
Birks, 573-74
Bissell Company, 346, 354
Biway, 301
Black & Decker Mfg. Company,
    453
Black's, 318
Block, H&R, 128, 457
BMW automobiles, 327, 425, 467
Boeing 747, 136

Bold detergent, 464, 475
Bombardier, 136, 280, 430, 473
Book-of-the-Month Club, 548
Booz, Allen & Hamilton, 330-31,
    333, 334, 337
Borden, Inc., 225, 472
Boston Consulting Group (BCG),
    39, 58, 232, 292
Bounty towels, 472
Bowmar, 379, 468
Brador, 323
Braemar, 301
Brand Biscuits (Pillsbury), 638
Breck, 414
Brewer's Retail, 544
Brick, The, 573
Bridgestone, 35
Brim, 296
Bristol-Myers Company, 388,
    402, 786
British Airways, 744
British Design Council, 317
British Monopoly Commission,
    448
Brooks Brothers, 181
Brut, 639
Budweiser beer, 648, 669
Buick, 216, 234, 278, 284, 469
Bulova Watch Company, 436
Burger King Corporation, 401,
    499, 547, 632, 635
Burroughs Corporation, 595
Business International (BI)
    Country Assessment
    Service, 439
Business Marketing, 618
Business Quarterly, 111

Cabbage Patch Kids, 474, 677
Cadillac, 5, 143, 284, 287, 314-
    16, 405, 418, 546, 574, 612
Calvin Klein, 474, 577
Camay soap, 287, 387, 447, 464,
    729
Campbell Soup Company, 379,
    406, 444, 474, 476, 559,
    690-91, 730

Campbell's Pork & Beans, 730
Canada Commerce, 111
Canada Dry, 670
Canada Packers, 475
Canada Post, 236, 657
Canada Trust, 320, 494
Canadian Banker, 111
Canadian Commercial
    Corporation, 227
Canadian Consumer, 111
Canadian Federation of
    Independent Business, 269
Canadian Home Shopping Club
    (CHSC), 658
Canadian Imperial Bank of
    Commerce, 320
Canadian Pacific, 39, 399
Canadian Tire, 103, 405, 471,
    501, 549, 593, 656
Canon, 58, 234, 501
Cap'n Crunch, 476, 477, 670
Carrier Corp, 39
Cascade detergent, 410
Caterpillar, Inc., 8, 22, 38, 58,
    214, 309, 310, 319, 399,
    409-12, 439, 477, 500, 517,
    527, 553
CBC, 644
C.D. Anderson, 562
Chanel No. 5, 639
Charlie Perfume, 136
Charmin toilet tissue, 410, 464, 477
Chase Econometric, 271
Chatelaine, 644
Cheer detergent, 464, 475, 477,
    736
Cheez Whiz, 447
Cherry Coke, 360
Cherry Electrical Products, 554
Chesbrough-Ponds, 479
Chevrolet, 19, 125, 197, 248, 284,
    287, 289, 314, 315, 447,
    467, 471, 546
Chicago Bulls, 639
Chiquita, 463
Chivas Regal Scotch, 178
Christian Dior, 473
Chrysler Corporation, 24, 58, 74,

152, 213, 284, 326, 328, 404, 670, 678-79
Church & Dwight, 785-86
Ciba Geigy, 429, 446
Citicorp (Citibank), 447
Clairol, 414
Claritas Corp., 267
Clark Equipment, 412
Classic beer, 473
Clearasil, 405
Club Med, 136, 447
Club Monaco, 301
CMC International, 440
Coast soap, 464
Coca-Cola Company, 29, 234, 300, 304, 325, 359, 379, 383, 399, 401, 403, 428, 432, 434, 441, 445, 448, 453, 559, 560, 564, 592, 619, 630, 633, 639
Coke, 325, 479, 592
Coke Classic, 359
Coldspot, 476
Coleman, 287
Coles, 524
Colgate-Palmolive Company, 238, 357, 409, 411, 414, 416, 475, 656, 736
Colgate toothpaste, 290, 292, 736
Compaq, 172, 476
Comp-U-Card, 575
Compusearch, 267
Compuserve, 659
Computerland, 136, 191, 561, 569, 573
Conference Board, 268
Conn Organ Company, 548
Consumer Interest, 111
Consumer's Distributing, 571, 656
Consumers Association of Canada, 155
Consumers Glass, 544
Construction Safety Association of Ontario, 292
Coop, The, 139
Corfam, 332
Corning, 429
Corvair automobile, 143
Cossette, 631
Costco Wholesale, 571
Courtyard, 469
Craftsman tools, 474, 475, 476
Cray Research, 250
Creole soup, 730
Cressida, 284
Crest toothpaste, 136, 190, 290, 291, 292, 324, 392, 393, 410, 462, 464, 476, 638
Crib Jiminy, 287
Crisco oil, 736
Crispy Crunch, 140-41
Crispy Fry, 358
Crown Royal, 632

CTV, 644
Cuticura, 388
Cycle 1-4 dog food, 287

Daimler-Benz, 4, 433
Daniel Starch (Canada) Ltd., 649
Dash detergent, 464, 475
Data General Corp., 314, 467
Data Resources, 271
Datril, 402, 534
Day-Timers, 656
Dayco Corporation, 554
Death of a Salesman, 686
DEC, 241, 407
Deere & Company, 406, 411
Del Monte Corp., 406
Deluxe Check Printers, Inc., 317
Denquel toothpaste, 464
Department of Industry Trade and Commerce, 269
Department of National Health and Welfare, 154, 156
Designer Depot, 571
Devoir, Le, 323
Devon, 475
DHL, 659
Dial Media, 658
Dial soap, 327, 477
Diamond Crystal Salt, 417
Diamond walnuts, 585
Diehard batteries, 473
Digital Equipment Corp., 314, 467
Direct Marketing Association (DMA), 656, 657
Disney Enterprises, Walt, 319, 474, 498, 499
Disney University, 498
Doan's Pills, 388
Dodge, 284
Dofasco, 399, 544
Dominion Tanking Limited, 778, 805-7
Domino's Pizza, 319, 399
Dow Chemical Company, 24, 38, 336
Downy fabric softener, 410
Doyle Dane Bernbach, 159
Drano, 477
Dreft detergent, 464
DuMaurier, 321
DuPont, 15, 38, 139, 154, 213, 244, 289, 332, 335, 400, 509, 517, 554, 651, 737, 744, 773
Duz detergent, 475, 476
Dylex Limited, 301, 576

Eaton's, 320, 409, 569, 573
E.D. Smith and Sons, 778, 796-800
Edmonton Oilers, 176

Edsel automobile, 332, 469, 550
EG&G, 420
Egg McMuffin (McDonald's), 488
1869 Brand Biscuits, 638
Electrolux, 447, 574, 617
Electrophonic, 77
Elgin National Watch Company, 14-15
Encyclopedia Britannica, 39, 574
Epson Corporation, 551
Equinox, 645
Era Detergent, 464
Erickson, 4
Erlichs, the, 150
E.T., 474
Evian, 525
Excedrin, 402
Export cigarettes, 373
Exxon Corp, 447

Fab detergent, 416
Fairchild, 61, 371
Fairfield Inns, 469
Fairweather, 301
Federal Business Development Bank, 486
Federal Express, Inc., 318, 659
Federal Trade Commission, 525
Federated Co-operatives, 559, 575
Fiberglas, 476
Financial Post, 105, 111, 323
Financial Times of Canada, 111
Firebird, 476
Firestone, 35
Fizzies, 480
Fleischmann, 520
Flintstones, 474
Florsheim Shoe Company, 659
Folger coffee, 296
Food Marketing Institute (FMI), 226, 565
Foote, Cone & Belding, 640
Foot Locker, 569
Forbes, 414
Ford Motor Company, 35, 38, 59, 125, 213, 234, 248, 278, 279, 284, 287, 289, 317, 318, 332, 338, 401, 404, 409, 428, 469, 550, 559, 560, 564, 611, 614, 658, 663, 670, 692, 744
Fortune, 247
Fortune 1000, 420
Freightliner, 59
French Concorde, 332
Frigidaire, 476
Frost & Sullivan's World Political Risk Forecasts, 439
Fuji Corporation, 233, 401, 417, 534, 680
Fujitsu, 241, 250, 429

Fuller Brush Company, 574, 708
Future Shock, 135, 153
Futures Group, 269

Gabriel of Canada, 670
Gain detergent, 464, 475
Gazette, The, 323
General Electric (GE) 29, 36, 40, 41, 43, 52, 60, 61, 77, 238, 269, 317, 371, 406, 413, 464, 465, 468, 471, 475, 561, 593, 663, 692, 762, 764
General Foods Corp., 125, 287, 321, 335, 353, 358, 386, 428, 444, 480, 631, 656, 657, 662, 679, 729, 730, 773
General Mills, Inc., 27, 85, 125, 336, 406, 618
General Motors (GM) Corp., 15, 19, 22, 29, 52, 59, 61, 143, 215-17, 234, 278, 281, 284, 300, 301, 316, 318, 342, 399, 401, 404, 406, 420, 429, 439, 467, 468, 469, 477, 485, 526, 528, 540, 553, 563, 564, 565, 629, 670, 692, 693, 743 Genuine Parts, 589
George Weston Limited, 558
Gerber Products Company, 38, 145, 300, 441, 492
Giant Foods, Inc., 28
Gillette Company, 399, 401, 412, 413, 414, 445, 534, 559, 658, 678, 698
Ginsu Knives, 658
Girl Guides, 37
Gleem toothpaste, 464
Glenayr Knitting Mills, 571
Globe and Mail, The, 105, 111, 285
Glory, 346
Goldstar, 471
Good Housekeeping, 641
Goodyear Tire & Rubber Co., 35, 208, 229, 446, 680
Gould Corporation, 242, 333
Government of Canada, 629
Gray Research, 250
Green Giant, 638, 640
Green Line, 486, 563
Greenpeace, 150
Grocery Manufacturers of America, 565
GTE, 429
Guardian Oil Company, 94
Gucci, 425, 438, 448, 474
Gulf Oil Corp., 439

H&R Block, 136, 488

Hallmark Company, 379, 428, 734
Hamburger University, 317, 576
Hamm's beer, 478, 479
Hardee's, 405
Harley Davidson, 24, 217, 468, 474, 752
Harper's, 580
Harrod's of London, 578
Harry Rosen, 301
Harvest Crunch, 531
Head & Shoulders shampoo, 401, 410, 414
Health & Welfare Canada, 154, 156
Heinz Company, H.J., 404, 406, 414, 416, 418, 444, 475, 596, 730, 734, 736
Heinz ketchup, 462, 736
Helene Curtis, 414
Hell's Angels, 158
Hendry Corporation, 285
Hergenrather & Company, 557
Herman Miller, 315
Hershey Foods Corporation, 137-42, 164, 325, 531
Hershey Kisses, 137
Hertz Rent-a-Car, 325, 401, 418, 560, 612
Hesston, 406
Heublein, Inc., 534-35
Hewlett-Packard Company, 3, 20, 22, 239, 299, 420, 468, 744
Highland Queen, 571
High Point Coffee, 296
Hills Brothers, 296
Hilton, 447
Hitachi, 4, 241
Hockey News, 644
Hoffman-Laroche, 448
Holiday Inns, Inc., 39-40, 560, 563
Holt-Renfrew, 569, 573, 574, 578
Home Hardware, 575, 593
Homemaker's, 644
Honda Motor Company, 136, 187, 234, 259, 284, 477
Honest Ed's, 578
Honeywell, Inc., 241, 414, 470
Hoover Vacuum Cleaner Company, 617
Hudson Institute, 269
Hudson's Bay Company, 561
Hunt's Foods, 404, 415, 416, 418
Hurtig Publishers, 524
Hyatt Hotel, 460, 488
Hyundai, 279

IBM Corporation, 18, 19, 20, 22, 58, 65, 66, 67, 106, 172, 181, 186, 187, 241, 250, 293, 300, 301, 317, 319, 320, 328, 341, 399, 401, 407, 409, 410, 413, 414, 418, 432, 453, 467, 471, 473, 531, 534, 553, 557, 561, 564, 688, 692, 698, 699, 700, 705, 711, 764
IBM Product Centers, 561
IBM Selectric, 65
Ikea, 577, 579
Imasco, 405
Imperial Oil, 39, 573
Imperial Tobacco, 157, 405
Independent Grocers Alliance (IGA), 559, 575
Info-Window, 700
Information Resources, Inc., 118
Instamatic camera, 16
Institute for the Future, 269
Intel, 136
Intellivision, 416
International Harvester Company, 24, 58, 59, 74, 216, 412
International Hough Company, 437
International Merchants, 559
"Interprovincial Telephone", 56
Iona, 476
Ipana toothpaste, 388
Irish Spring, 287
Ivory Snow detergent, 464
Ivory Soap, 374, 387, 464, 472, 480
Izod, 577

Jack Daniels bourbon, 181
Jaguar, 248, 316
J-cars, 526
Jeffrey Martin, Inc., 388
Jell-O, 374, 382, 444, 476
J.I. Case, 406, 411
John Deere, 411
John Klein & Associates, Inc., 661
John Labatt, 473, 475
Johnson & Johnson, 145, 248, 302, 335, 383, 400, 419, 560, 677, 773
Johnson & Johnson Baby Shampoo, 414
Johnson Products, 639
Johnson & Sons, S.C., 414
Johnny Cash, 494
Jontue, 638
Journey's End, 460

Kao Company of Japan, 342
Kasle Steel, 216
Kellogg Company, 428, 473, 475, 668
Ken-L Ration, 669
Kenmore appliances, 474, 475
Kentucky Fried Chicken, 359
Kettle Creek, 578
Kevlar, 15

Kimberly-Clark, 411
Kirk's soap, 464
Kleenex, 476
K mart Corp., 136, 464, 569, 571, 573, 574, 581, 582
Knotts Berry Farm, 536
Kodak film, 16, 213, 223, 229, 234, 337, 341, 379, 399, 400, 401, 417, 476, 479, 501, 527, 534, 559, 590, 692
Komatsu, 309, 310, 411, 412
Kool-Aid, 385-86
Kraft Foods Company, 447, 479, 560, 644, 668
Krauss-Maffei, 433
Kresge, 573
K-tel, 724

Labatt, 323. See John Labatt
Labatt's Blue, 475
Labatt's Classic, 475
Lady Finelle, 574
Laidlaw Waste Systems, 544
Lamborghinis, 432
Landis Group, 339
Laura Secord, 473
Lava Soap, 464
Lavalin, 211, 725
Lavoris, 353
Leading Edge, 534
L'eggs, 136, 479, 670
Lens Crafters, 318
Leon's, 572
Lenox china, 325
Lever Detergents, 786-88
Lever Brothers, 238, 411, 623
Levi Strauss Company, 58, 136, 318, 476, 564, 577
Life Savers, 477
Limits to Growth, 143
Lincoln (car), 284, 469
Lincoln Electric, 220
Lintas, 631
Lisa computer, 470
Listerine, 353
L.L. Bean, Inc., 20
Loblaws, 139, 151, 403, 404, 472, 5312, 558, 569, 593, 612, 615
Ziggy's, 580
London Life Insurance Company, 778, 813-18
Luvs, 464, 477
Lux, 287
Lydia Pinkham's Vegetable Compound, 273, 651

McDonald's Corporation, 3, 22, 37, 58, 136, 146, 174, 279, 317, 319, 359, 399, 401, 410, 425, 428, 438, 445, 453, 488, 496, 499, 540, 547, 559, 560, 563, 573, 576, 618, 635, 639, 677, 742, 764
McGraw-Hill, 688
McIntosh computer, 470
McKesson, 589
McKid's, 146
McKim, 631
McKinsey & Company, 58, 318, 438
Mack Truck, 59, 322
MacLaren Lintas, 631
Macleans, 511, 611
Maclean's toothpaste, 290
Mac's Convenience Stores, 139, 569, 570
Madique, 333
Magnavox Consumer Electronics, 77, 79
Maher Shoes, 573
Maple Leaf Mills, 319, 475
March of Dimes, 610, 636, 637
Marketing, 111
Mark's Work Warehouse, 573
Marriott Hotels, 3, 21, 22, 469, 496
Marriott Marquis, 469
Mary Kay Cosmetics, 574
Mary Maxim, 656
Massey-Ferguson, Inc., 39, 406, 411, 430
Mastercard, 575
Matsushita, 333
Mattel Toys, 446
Max Factor & Company, 453
Maxim's, 474
Maxwell House, 296, 353
Maytag Company, 238, 471, 509
Mazda automobiles, 16, 316
Mead Johnson, 476
Mercedes-Benz, 59, 234, 279, 284, 324, 405, 407, 418, 462, 471
Mercury, 289, 469
Merrill Lynch, 562-63
Metrecal, 476
Michelin Tire Company, 35, 401, 409, 778, 788-91
Micrin, 353
Midas Muffler, 501
Migros, 139, 444
Milky Way candy, 325
Miller Beer, 418
Miller Brewing Company, 415, 418
Miller Lite beer, 412, 635
Millie's Hand Cooked Potato Chips, 778, 779-81
Minolta, 449
Mister Donut, 444
Mitsubishi, 316
Mmmarvelous Mmmuffins, 318
Model T Ford, 278

Molson, 292, 323, 679
Molson Public Challenge Golf
    Tournament, 679
Monsanto Company, 327, 447
Morris the Cat, 638, 681, 682
Morton Salt, 313, 417
Mothers Against Drunk Driving,
    321, 679
Mother's Pizza, 362, 399
Motorola, 316
Mountain Equipment Coop, 573,
    576
Much Music, 645
Muscular Dystrophy Association,
    679
Music Man, The, 686
Mustang, 279, 287, 327, 476, 611

Nabisco, 615, 736
NameLab, Inc., 476
National Bureau of Economic
    Research, 269
National Car Rental, 325
National Cash Register Company,
    446
National Lead, 270
Nautilus, 136
Navistar International, 59, 322
Needham, Harper, and Steers, 182
Neilson, 140, 148
Nescafe, 296
Nestle Company, 30, 289, 531, 775
Neugarten's, 287
New Coke, 359
Newsweek, 645
Nike, 136, 639
Nikon Company, 461
9-Lives cat food, 681, 682
Nissan Motor, 284, 316, 637
Nixdorf, 30
No-Name, 404, 472, 475, 558
Nordic Track Cardiovascular
    Exerciser, 658
Northern Telecom, 430
Nova (car), 447
Nutriment, 476

O'Brien Candy Company, 772-74
Oil of Olay, 669
Oldsmobile, 278, 284, 469
Old Spice After-Shave Lotion, 479
Olivetti Corporation of America,
    30, 66, 186, 316, 434, 479
Olivetti ET121, 66
Ontario Hydro, 236
Ontario Ministry of Natural
    Resources, 247, 686
OPEC, 151
Orange Crush, 480
Oreo cookies, 736
Osborne computers, 379

Oster blenders, 315
Ovaltine, 382
Oxy-5, 405
Oxydol detergent, 464, 475

Paccar, 59
PacMan, 136, 473
Pampers, 135, 410, 464, 477
Panasonic Company, 77, 526
Pant Loft, The, 569
Parker Hannifin Corporation 104,
    105, 554
Peanuts, 474
Pennington's, 578
Penthouse magazine, 400
People's Drug Store, 405
People Express, 528
Peoples Jewellers, 573
Pepsi, 325, 359
PepsiCo, Inc. (Pepsi-Cola), 4,
    151, 234, 304, 383, 401,
    409, 434, 612, 638, 639
Perdue Farms, 22
Perrier, 136
Petro Canada, 679
Philips Industries, 4, 428, 476,
    515
Phillips Petroleum Company, 476
Picturevision, 321
Pierre Cardin, 5, 425, 473, 474,
    477
Pillsbury Company, 5, 425, 560,
    638, 643
Pillsbury Doughboy, 638
PIMS. See Profit Impact of
    Management Strategies
Pininfarina, 316
Pinto, 404
Pizza Hut, 560
Pizza Inn, 564
Playboy Enterprises, Inc., 136,
    159, 323, 400
Plymouth, 284
Polaroid Corp., 321, 338, 362,
    418, 509, 550, 590, 642
Polarvision, 321, 338
Police Gazette, 641
Pollution Probe, 150, 152
Pontiac, 278, 284
Popov vodka, 535
Pop Shoppe, 582
Porsche, 38, 279, 282, 315, 325,
    474, 477
Post Division of General Foods,
    729
Potato Board, 681, 682
Potato Lover's Diet Cookbook,
    The, 681
Pound Puppies, 474
Premium Advertisers
    Association, 675
Premium ham, 476

President's Choice, 404, 475, 558
Price-Club, 571
Prince tennis racquets, 136
Pringles, 410
Procter & Gamble Company
    (P&G), 3, 22, 58, 105, 108,
    234, 238, 245, 314, 317,
    328, 387, 392, 393, 399,
    401, 409, 410, 411, 414,
    416, 449, 464, 471, 475,
    477, 553, 559, 623, 629,
    639, 644, 656, 678, 679,
    680, 698, 729, 730, 736,
    742, 764, 785
Proctor-Silex, 525
Prodigy, 659
Profit Impact of Management
    Strategies, 407, 409
Provigo, 569
Prudential, 461, 487
Public Citizen, 143
Publishers' Clearing House, 639,
    680
Puffs, 464, 476
Purchasing Management
    Association of Canada, 209
Pulsar, 476
Purex Corporation, 388
Puritan oil, 736
Pylon Electric, 393

Quaker Oats, 85, 139, 361, 447,
    472, 476, 477, 531, 669
Quaker Oats Natural, 532
Quasar division of Motorola, 316
Queen's University, 465

Radford Hospital, 492
Radio Canada, 644
Radio Shack, 172, 241, 471, 582
Ragedy Ann & Andy, 474
Raisin Bran, 475
Raleigh Bicycles, 658
Ralston-Purina, 473
Ranchero beans, 730
RCA Corporation, 3, 241, 332,
    341, 371, 413, 470
RC Cola, 325
Reach toothbrush, 560
Reader's Digest, 574, 644
Red Cross, 458
Reese's candy, 137
Relska vodka, 535
Remington typewriters, 487
Renault, 234, 447
Rent-a-Wreck, 420
Report on Business, 111
Revlon, Inc., 39, 355, 461, 617,
    638
Reynolds Pen, 379, 248
Rice Krispies, 475

Ritz crackers, 462
Rolex Watches, 419
Rolls-Royce, 314, 470
Roots, 578
Royal 5010, 66
Royal Bank, 26, 320, 471, 486,
    494
Royal Doulton, 325
Royale, 410
Rubik's Cube, 136
Russell Reynolds Associates, 4
RX-7 (Mazda), 16

Saab, 284, 338
Saatchi & Saatchi, 445, 631
Safeguard soap, 464
Safeway Stores, Inc., 569, 593
Sales and Marketing
    Management, 264
SAMI/Burke, 106
Samsonite luggage, 665
Samsung, 471
Sanka coffee, 296
SAS (Scandinavian Airlines), 22,
    23, 744
Saturn, 265
Schering-Plough, 248
S.C. Johnson, 414
SCM Corporation, 525
Scotch Tape, 476
Scotkins, 477
Scotties, 477
ScotTissues, 477
ScotTowels, 477
Scott Paper Company, 477
Seagram & Sons, Joseph E., 560
Sears, 52, 146, 151, 224, 238,
    292, 399, 420, 467, 470,
    475, 492, 531, 558, 561,
    563, 569, 573, 577, 581,
    619, 629, 657, 670, 693
Seiko, 404, 415, 476
7-11 convenience stores, 569
Seven-Up Company, 325, 478,
    639
Seville, 405
Shaklee, 574
Sharper Image, 579
Shell Chemical Company, 46,
    425
Sherwin-Williams, 558-59
Shirt Tails, 474
Shoppers Drug Mart, 405
Shouldice Hospital, 499
Siemens, 241
Silkience, 445
Simpsons Ltd., 3, 569, 577, 612
Singapore Airlines, 319
Singer Company, 24, 74, 149
Ski-doo, 471
Smirnoff vodka, 534-35
Smith Corona, 66, 734

Sobers of Ontario, 778, 807-9
Softsoap, 136
Solo Detergent, 464
Sony Corporation, 4, 30, 77, 79, 234, 235, 333, 438, 445, 471
Soyance, 445
Special Olympics, 679
Spector Freight, 700
Spectra, 362
Sperry Corporation, 241
Sperry/Maclennan, 778, 801-5
Sperry-New Holland Company, 406
Spic and Span, 476
Square D, 554
SRI International, 182
St. Lawrence College, 29, 778, 781-84
Star-Kist Foods, 681
Star Wars, 474
Statistics Canada, 263
Steel Company of Canada (Stelco), 399, 522, 523
Steelcase, Inc., 293
Steinberg, 139, 569
Stetson, 470
Steuben, 324
Stew Leonard's Supermarket, 3
Strategic Planning Institute, 313, 500
Suave shampoo, 414
Sultana, 476
Sunbeam, 316
Sunkist, 463, 476, 480, 585
Sun Maid raisins, 585
Sunoco, 477
Suntory Liquors, 287
Supercut stores, 530
Super Valu, 589
Supply and Services Canada, Department of, 227, 228
Suzy Shier, 301
Sweet Marie, 140, 141

Swift and Company, 447, 476
Swissair, 496
Sysco Steel, 522

Takara, 446
Talky Rattle, 287
Tang, 428, 679
Taster's Choice, 296
Taurus, 318, 338
Texas Instruments (TI), 14, 32 n12; 53, 57, 61, 239, 242, 332, 371, 404, 408, 414, 417, 468, 509, 512, 513
TG Magazine, 171
Third Wave, The, 153
Thrifty's, 301
Thomas Cook, 447
Thomson, 430
Thomson Group, 629
3M Company, 3, 19, 38, 336, 412, 501, 725, 734, 767
Thunderbird, 279, 614
Tide detergent, 410, 416, 464, 475, 476, 477, 736
Tilden, 545, 560
Tilley Endurables, 657
Timex, 290, 418, 547
Timken Corporation, 554
Tip Top Tailors, 301, 579
Toni, 414
Topol, 238
Toro, 669
Toronto Dominion Bank, 320, 486, 493, 563
Toronto Yellow Pages, 656
Toshiba Corporation, 4, 241, 425
Town & Country, 301
Toyota Motors, 30, 197, 217, 234, 284, 304, 337, 429, 471
Toys 'R' Us, 146, 582
Trade-Plus, 562
Trade Show Bureau, 674
Transitron, 61, 371

Transport Canada, 637
Travelers Insurance Company, 106
Trend Report, 161
TSN, 645
Tupperware, 543, 575
TV Times, 644
Tylenol, 136, 399, 402, 534, 677

Ultra Brite toothpaste, 290
Unilever, 4, 30, 38
Uniroyal Goodrich, 35-37
University of Toronto, 37
UTDC, 280

Vancouver Symphony, 29
Vaseline, 472
Vega, 61, 404
Via Rail, 29, 108, 110, 111, 112, 113, 116, 119
Viceroy homes, 157
Vick Chemical, 669
Victor Talking Machine Company, 341
Vigoroham, 476
Vogue, 580, 645
Volkswagen, 61, 284, 289, 299, 639
Volvo, Inc., 30, 59, 284, 315, 324, 679
Volvo International Tennis Tournament, 679

Walkman, 135, 235, 438, 445
Warner Electric Brake and Clutch, 338
Warner-Lambert Company, 453, 480
WATS (Wide Area Telephone System), 658
Wendy's, 614

Westinghouse Canada Inc., 692
Westinghouse Electric Corp., 336, 409, 451
Westin Stamford, 321, 460
W.H. Smith, 524
Wharton Econometric, 271
Whirlpool Corporation, 238
White Cloud, 464
White Motor, 59
White Star Tuna, 644
Wilkinson Sword USA, 690
Wilson tennis racquet, 639
Winston's Restaurants, 174
Wolfschmidt, 534-35
Woolco, 569
Wondra, 387
Woodwards, 569
Woolworth & Company, F.W., 505
Wrigley Jr. Company, Wm., 540

Xerox Corporation, 24, 39, 66, 320, 338, 341, 379, 399, 401, 412, 413, 418, 468, 476, 553, 592, 657, 692, 693

Yellow Pages, 551, 629, 643, 656, 660
Yokom, 666-67
York, 475
Yorkdale, 573
Yugo, 234

Zapmail, 476
Zellers, 569, 580
Zenith Corporation, 24, 37, 75-82, 89, 94, 241, 449, 528, 564
Zest, 464
"Zeus, Inc.", 65, 66
Ziggy's, 404, 580

Subject Index

Accelerated test marketing, 354-56
Acceleration principle, 210
Access barriers, 258
Accessory equipment, 463
Accounting, 137
Accounting department, 742
Accumulated production, cost behavior as function of, 513-14
Acquisition of new product, 330
Acquisitions, 589, 693

Action programs, marketing plan, 75, 81-82
Activities, interests, and opinions (AIO) framework, 182
Actual self-concept, 181
Adaptation of price, 522-27
Adaptation strategies for foreign market, 443-48
Administered vertical marketing system, 559

Adoption process, 362-66
Advertising, 600, 629-651; budget for, 622-23; buyer-readiness stage and, 623-24; carryover effect, 634, 646; as component of promotional mix, 618-19; defined, 629; evaluating effectiveness of, 634, 647-51; major decisions in, 630; measur-

ing consumer response to, 118; media for, 629, 640-45; media timing, 645-47; message, deciding on, 635-40; objectives, setting, 630, 633; role in industrial markets, 620-23; sales promotion and, 667; tools of, 602; types of, 614, 629, 630-33, 638, 658, 674, 735

Advertising agencies, 629, 631, 635, 656, 736
Advertising allowance, 671
Advertising as percentage of marketing budget (A/M ratio), 622, 623
Advertising department, 629
Advertising efficiency, 763
Advertising elasticities, 93
Advertising exposures, 640-42
Advertising frequency, 634
Advertising goal, 630
Advertising promotion, 418
Advertising research, 106, 648-51
Advertising-to-sales-promotion ratio, 666-67
Advertising-to-sales ratio (A/S ratio), 622, 623
ADVISOR project, 621, 622
Advocacy advertising, 629
Affordable promotion budget method, 615
Age: consumer behavior and, 179; segmentation by, 287
Age-group growth trends, 146
Age of Discontinuity (Drucker), 135
Agent middlemen, 138, 212, 539, 550, 586
Aging of Canada's population, 146, 171
AIDA (attention, interest, desire, action) model, 607, 610, 709
Air carrier transport, 596
Allocating skills, 746
Allocations, strategic, 72
Allowances, 523, 524; trade-promotion, 671-72
Aluminum market, 294
Ambiguity, stimulus, 611
Annual call schedule, 701
Annual-plan control, 73, 749, 750-57
Annual Survey of Buying Power, 264
Appeals, types of, 610, 611, 635, 636
Arbitration, 565
Area market potential, 263-67
Area market specialists, 729
Arm's-length price, 449
Arranged interviews, 116-17
Arthur D. Little model, 46
Aspirational groups, 174
Asset redeployment, 589
Asset turnover, 755
Assets, return to, 755
Assortment strategies, 223
Atmosphere, 320, 580, 614
Attack strategies, 409-18
Attention: heightened, 192; selective, 185, 602
Attitude: consumer behavior and,

186-88; cultural values reflected in, 159-60; toward international buying, 432; of others, influence of, 196; segmentation by, 292
Attraction, customer, 18
Attribute competition, dynamics of, 393-94
Attribute listing, 338
Attributes, product. See Product attributes
Audit, marketing, 73, 767-74
Augmented product, 459-60
Automated warehouse, 586-88, 589, 593
Automatic teller, 575
Automatic vending, 575
Automobile industry, 178, 284, 287, 524-25, 526, 559
Available market, 257, 258
Average sales response, 94
Awareness, 608, 641, 677-78

Backward channels, 544
Backward integration strategy, 48, 589
Balanced manufacturing/marketing orientation, 741
Balanced technology and market-driven company, 739
Bank marketing, 26-28
Bargaining power, 298; of marketing channels, 735
Barriers: access, 258; entry, 235; exit, 235-36, 387; mobility, 235; shrinkage, 236; tariff, 429-30; trade, 427
Barter, 7, 433
Basing-point pricing, 523
BATNA-Best Alternative to a Negotiated Agreement, 715, 716
Battle of the brands, 475
Bayesian decision theory, 129
Beer market, 291, 292, 478
Begging, 6
Behavioral response, 7
Behavioral segmentation, 290
Beliefs, buying behavior and, 186, 194-95
Benchmarking, 338
Benefit segmentation, 290
Better Business bureaus, 525
"Better-mousetrap" fallacy, 14
Bibliographies, 111
Bids, expected profit and, 520
Biogenic needs, 183
Birthrate, slowdown in Canada, 145-46
Blanket contracts, 220
Blocked markets, 434
Bonuses, 696

Boston Consulting Group approach, 41-43
Brainstorming, 339-41
Brand(s), 460, 471-79; advantages from branding, 473; communication objectives for, 609; defined, 471; evaluation of alternative, 204-5; ideal, 204-5; national, 473; private, 473-75; proprietary, 589; strategies for, 471-79; *See also* Product life cycle (PLC)
Brand advertising, 521, 629
Brand beliefs and image, 194-95, 479, 681
Brand competitors, 140, 141
Brand concept, 345
Brand conviction, 189
Brand development index, 265
Brand-dominant hierarchy, 284
Brand-extension strategy, 477
Brand familiarity, 189
Brand life cycle, 371, 373
Brand loyalty, 291-92, 667-68, 735
Brand-management organization, 729-36
Brand managers, 672
Brand mark, 471
Brand name, 373, 471; family, 475-77
Brand personalities, 289
Brand-positioning map, 345
Brand repositioning strategy, 478-79
Brand-sponsor decision, 473, 475
Brand switching, 634, 667
Break-even analysis, 351, 665-66
Break-even chart, 515, 550
Broadcast services, 649
Broadcasting Act, 157
Brokers, 586
Budget: advertising, 622-23, 633-35; R&D, 153; sales, 261; total promotion, 615-17; total sales-promotion, 673
Bundling of products, 527
Bureaucracy, government, 433
Business analysis for new product, 349-53
Business domain, defining, 40-41
Business economics and corporate research, 107
Business environment of foreign market, 434-35
Business markets, 67
Business market. See Industrial market
Business Marketing magazine, 618
Business portfolio, evaluating current, 41-46
Business-promotion tools, 673-74
Business sector, 29, 484

Business services, 463
Business strategic planning, 49-61; external environment analysis, 51-53; feedback and control, 60-61; goal formulation, 56-57; implementation, 58-60; internal environment analysis, 53-56; mission, 49-51; strategy and program formulation, 57-58
Business-to-business marketing, 618, 658-59
Business unit strategic plan, 36
Buyback arrangement, 433
Buyclasses, 210, 218
Buyer, 188
Buyer behavior. See Consumer behavior; Industrial market
Buyer group, 689
Buyer, industrial, 213
Buyer readiness, 292, 607-8, 623-34
Buyer-seller relationships, management of, 716-19
Buyer turnover, 647
Buyers' intentions, survey of, 269
Buygrid framework, 217
Buying centers, 212-13, 220
Buying decisions and decision process: alternative methods of evaluation, 204-5; for consumer, 188-99; for government, 227-28; for industrial buyers, 210-23; for resellers, 223-26
Buying patterns, 24
Buying roles, 188
Buying service, retail, 575
Buying styles, 710
Buyphases model, 217-23
Bypass attack, 416
Byproduct pricing, 527

Calls, sales representative, 701, 706, 709
Canada Agriculture Products Standard Act, 157
Canada-U.S. Auto Pact, 426
Canadian Commercial Corporation, 227
Canadian Direct Marketing Association, 656
Canadian Federation of Independent Business polls, 269
Canadian Home Shoppers Club (CHSC), 658
Canned sales approach, 709
Cannibalized income, 352
Capital items, 463
Captive-product pricing, 527

Carryover effect, advertising, 634, 646
Cash-and-carry wholesalers, 585
Cash cows (growth-share cell), 41, 42
Cash discounts, 524
Cash refund offers (rebates), 524-25, 669
Catalog marketing, 656, 657
Catalog showroom, 572
Category development index, 265
Category management, 735-36
Cause-related marketing, 679
Celebrity endorsements, 612-13
Census of Population, 111
Central business districts, 581
Centralized purchasing, 215
Cents-off deal, 669
CEOs, 743
Chain-ratio method, 262
Chain stores, 559, 576
Challengers, market, 409-18
Channel captain, 563
Channels, communication, 613-15
Channels, marketing. *See* Marketing channels
Cheaper-goods strategy, 418
Children age-group, growth trend in, 146
Citizen-action publics, 142
Class, social. *See* Social class
Cliques, 615
Closed-end questions, 114
Closing of sale, 711
Cluster analysis, 126, 284
Coercion, 6
Coercive power, 551
Cold War, thawing of, 2
Combination store, 570
Commercialization, 360-62
Commission merchants, 586
Commission system, 631, 696
Common-stock security ratio, 243
Communication(s): of company's positioning strategy, 327-28; determining objectives of, 607-10; integrated marketing, 626-27; steps in developing effective, 604-27
Communication channels, selecting, 613-15
Communication-effect research, 648-49
Communication process, 602-4; elements in, 602; managing and co-ordinating, 626-27
Communications mix: deciding on, 617-24; major tools of, 600, 602, 618-20; *See also* Advertising; Personal selling; Public relations (PR); Sales promotion
Communications model, 607

Community influentials, 613-14
Community shopping centers, 582
Company: channel design and characteristics of, 547; history, 37; internal microenvironment of, 136-37; objectives and resources of, 298-99, 343
Company brand strength, 471
Company demand and demand function, 261
Company organization, 725-26
Company orientations toward marketplace, 13-28, 250-51, 742-44; marketing concept, 3, 16-27; product concept, 14-15; production concept, 12-13; selling concept, 15-16, 17; societal marketing concept, 26-28
Company potential, 262
Company pricing policies, 521
Company sales forecast, 261
Comparison advertising, 630-33
Compendiums of Statistics, 111
Compensation deal, 433
Compensation, salesforce, 695-97, 696, 704
Competences, distinctive, 37, 51, 53-55
Competition Act, 154, 157
Competition: advertising budget and, 634; channel, 563; channel design and, 515; differentiation and, tools for, 312-320; industry concept of, 234-37; intertype, 582; market concept of, 237; monopolistic, 236; pure, 236; in retailing, 560; in services, 492-93
Competitive advantage, 52, 53-55, 249, 311-12, 323
Competitive attack strategies, 409-18
Competitive cycle, stages of, 380
Competitive depositioning, 196
Competitive environment, 140
Competitive equilibrium, 245
Competitive intelligence system, designing, 245-48
Competitive-parity promotion budget method, 616
Competitive position, 43-44; classification of, 398-422
Competitive scopes, 37-38
Competitive situation, marketing plan, 77-78
Competitor-centered company, 250-51
Competitor myopia, 233-34
Competitors, 233-251; choosing, 409-12; identifying, 233-

37; identifying strategies of, 238-40; intelligence gathering on, 245-48; Japanese, 24, 453; objectives of, determining, 240-41; prices and offers, analyzing, 514; product life cycle stages and, 376, 381-82; reaction patterns of, estimating, 245; reactions to price changes, 532-33; responding to price changes of, 532-35; as source of new-product ideas, 337-38; strengths and weaknesses of, assessing, 242-45, 248; types of, 140-41, 245, 248-50
Complaint and suggestion systems, 496, 755
Complex buying behavior, 188
Complex salesforce structures, 693
Composite of salesforce opinions, 270
Computer workstations, 120
Computers; planning effective resource allocation using, 85-95; salesforce productivity and, 702-3; warehousing and, 586, 588, 593
Concentrated marketing, 299, 303
Concentric diversification strategy, 49
Concept development, 343-44
Concept selling, 348
Concept testing, 345, 348
Conclusion drawing, 611
Conference Board of Canada, 269
Conference selling, 689
Conflict, channel, 563-65
Conformance, 315
Conglomerate diversification strategy, 49
Conjoint analysis, 126
Conjunctive model, 205
Constant-budget line, 91
Constant-mix line, 91
Consulting services, 317-19
Consumer(s): changing spending patterns of, 149; need/problem identification by, 339; regulation to protect, 154-56
Consumer-adoption process, 362-66
Consumer base, advertising budget and, 634
Consumer behavior, alternative brand evaluation, 204-5; buying decision process, 188; major factors influencing, 172-88; model of, 171-72; roles and, 188; types of, 188-90
Consumer cooperative, 576

Consumer credit, 149-50
Consumer-goods classification, 461
Consumer-goods market testing, 356-59
Consumer involvement, 189-90
Consumer market, 67, 139, 171; bases for segmenting, 9, 171, 258, 284-92, 294; promotion mix in, 620, 621; *See also* Consumer behavior
Consumer marketing channels, 543, 544
Consumer Packaging and Labelling Act, 157
Consumer-panel data, 677
Consumer preferences, measuring, 349-50, 354
Consumer-product managers, 731
Consumer promotion, 82, 666, 668, 669-71
Consumer testing, 354
Consumerism, Impact of, 143, 145
Consumers Association of Canada, 156
Consumption system, 459
Contact methods, research, 116-17
Contests, 669, 674, 706
Contingency plans, 82
Contract manufacturing, 442
Contraction defense, 405
Contracts: blanket, 220; long-term, 215; management, 442; negotiated, 228; service, 525
Contractual vertical marketing system, 559-60
Control, 28, 60-61, 750-74; annual-plan, 73, 749-57; efficiency, 73, 749-50, 763-64; evaluating channel alternatives on basis of, 550; in marketing plan, 75, 82; product life cycle concept as tool in, 389; profitability, 73, 749-50, 758-62; for sales-promotion program, 675; strategic, 749-50, 764-773, 774
Control chart, 754
Controlled test marketing, 357, 360
Controllers, marketing, 773-75
Convenience goods, 461
Convenience stores, 570
Conventions trade, 674
Conviction state of buyer readiness, 608
Cooperation: channel, 563
Cooperatives, 559, 576, 586
Co-ordination, 565
Co-ordinated marketing, 19-21
Copyright Act, 157
Copy strategy statement, 638
Copy testing, 648-49

Copyright, 471
Copy benefit, 459
Corporate chain, 576
Corporate diversification, 589
Corporate headquarters, 64
Corporate responsibility research, 107
Corporate retailing, types of, 575-77
Corporate strategic planning, 36-49; corporate mission, 36-38; evaluating current business portfolio, 41-46; new business plan, 46-49; strategic business unit identification, 38-41
Corporate vertical marketing system, 558-59
Corporate/divisional marketing organization, 698
Corrective action, 757, 760
Corruption of foreign officials, 427
Cost(s), 6; choice of media and, 642; differentiated marketing and, 301; direct vs. full, 760-62; estimating, 512-14; evaluating channel alternatives on basis of, 550, 694, 695; of information, value and, 119; inventory-carrying, 594; new-product, estimating, 350-53; order-processing, 594; physical-distribution objective for, 590, 592; in profit equation, 85; total sales promotion, 673; types of, 512
Cost equation, 508
Cost inflation, 528
Cost-per-thousand criterion, 645
Cost-plus pricing, 515
Cost reduction strategy, 35
Cost structures of industry, 236-37
Counterarguments, 602-4
Counteroffensive defense, 404
Counter purchase, 433
Countersegmentation, 303
Countertrade, 433
Country risk assessing, 439-40
Coupons, 669, 673
Creativity: in advertising message execution, 637-40; research, 119; techniques for, 338-41; See also New-product development
Credibility, source, 611, 612-13
Credit, consumer, 149-50
Credit department, 742
Criminal Code, 157
Cross-elasticity of demand, 234
Cross-impact analysis, 269
Cultural environment, 158-61, 434
Cultural Mosaic, 148

Culture, consumer behavior and, 173-74
Current demand, estimating, 262-68
Current marketing situation, 75-78
Current-to-past sales comparisons, 706-8
Custom marketing research firms, 107
Customer(s): central importance of, 3; economic value to, 519; lifetime value of, 666; ratings of competitors on key success factors, 242; reactions to price changes, 532; service output levels desired by, 546-47; as source of new-product ideas, 337
Customer-added value, determinants of, 309-10
Customer attraction, 18
Customer calls, 701, 706, 709
Customer-centered company, 251
Customer group, defining business by, 40
Customer is key, The (Lele, Sheth), 3
Customer market, 11, 139-40
Customer-need management, 736
Customer orientation, 17-20, 23, 25, 251
Customer panels, 755
Customer philosophy, 765
Customer problem solving, 708
Customer retention, 18
Customer satisfaction, 6, 20, 708, 755-57; customer retention and, 18; postpurchase, 197, 198
Customer-segment pricing, 525
Customer segment profile, 294-95
Customer service, target level of, 592
Customer surveys, 677, 757
Customer training, 317
Customer value analysis, 248, 249
Customized marketing, 278, 280, 281

Data analysis, 117
Data-collection methods, 117
Data sources, 110-12
Database, marketing, 661-62
Debt, consumer, 149-50
Decider, 188
Decision making: consumer buying decision process, 188-99; global marketing and, 435-52; industrial buying decisions, 210-23; marketing decision support system

(MDSS) and, 120-21, 125-33
Decision-making unit, 188
Decision models, 128-32, 133, 533
Decision-tree diagram, 133
Decline stage: in market evolution, 393; in product life cycle, 372, 386-88, 556, 624
Decoding, 602
Defender model, 378
Defensive strategies, 401-5
Defining Advertising Goals for Measured Advertising Results (Colley), 630
Delayed quotation pricing, 528
Delivered value, 309
Delivering Quality Service (Zeithaml, Parasuraman, Berry), 3
Delivery: differentiation by, 317; service, 493-95
Demand, 5; company, 261; determining, 509-12; high cross-elasticity of, 234; for industrial goods, 208-10; law of, 87; market. See Market demand; measurement of, 257-272; price elasticity of, 510-12; for services, 488-90; states of, 12-13
Demand equation, 508
Demand management, 11
Demand schedule, 509, 510
Demand/hazard forecasting, 269
Demand/technology life cycle, 370-71, 391
Demarketing, 13
Demographic environment, 141-148
Demographic segmentation, 9, 285-88, 294
DEMON model, 127
Demonstration aids, 711
Department stores, 569, 570
Dependent variable, 125
Depositioning, competitive, 196
Deregulation, 526
Descriptive models, 126-27
Design, product, 317
Desire competitors, 140
Determinance model of consumer choice, 205
Deterministic model, 133
Diagnostic skills, 746
Dialectical theory, 394
Differential calculus, 128-32
Differentiated marketing, 301
Differentiated oligopoly, 236
Differentiation, 57, 578; degree of, 234-35; positioning and, 68-69; of services, 317-19, 492-94, 577; tools for competitive, 312-20

Diffusion process, 364
Diplomacy, 565
Direct costs, 762
Direct export, 440-42
Direct investment, 443
Direct mail, 656, 657, 663-65
Direct mail advertising, 643
Direct marketing, 656-66; defined, 656; development of integrated, 661-62; major decisions in, 662-66; major tools of, 657-59; nature, growth and advantages of, 656-61; response rate to, 663, 665
Direct Marketing Association (DMA), 656
Direct-marketing channel, 543
Direct product profitability (DPP), 226
Direct purchasing, 210
Direct rating method, 648
Direct-response advertising, 658
Direct selling, 574-75
Directories, 111, 643
Discount stores, 570, 581
Discounts, 523-24, 525, 530
Discriminant analysis, 125
Discrimination, learning, 186
Discriminatory pricing, 525-26
Disjunctive model, 205
Display allowance, 671
Dissociative groups, 174
Dissonance, postpurchase, 189, 197, 198
Distinctive competences, 37, 51, 53-55
Distortion, selective, 185, 602
Distribution: exclusive, 548; intensive, 548; physical, 588-96; selective, 548; speeding up, 317-19
Distribution channels. See Marketing channels
Distribution efficiency, 764
Distribution-innovation strategy, 418
Distribution programming, 551-54
Distribution situation, current, 78
Distributor and dealer display rooms, 360
Distributor brand, 473-75
Diversification growth strategy, 35, 47, 49
Divesting strategy, 43, 387, 388
Division of labor, 9
Division plan, 36
Divisionalized companies, 737
Dogs (growth-share cell), 41, 42
Dragalong income, 352
Drives, 186
Drop decision, 388
DROP error, 341-42

Drop shipper, 585
Dumping, 449
Duns and Bradstreet, 709
Dun's Market Identifiers, 264
Durability, product, 315
Durable goods, 461
Dynamic model, 133, 269

Early-adopter theory, 362
Early supplier involvement, 217
Eastern Europe, 2
Economic circumstances, consumer behavior and, 179
Economic communities, 429-30
Economic Council of Canada, 426
Economic marketing environment, 148-50; channel design and, 547; international, 429-32
Economic value to customer (EVC), 519
Education of workforce, 148
Edwards Personal Preference test, 289
Effective marketing-resource allocation, theory of, 85-95
Effectiveness, reviewing marketing, 764-67
Efficiency control, 73, 749, 750, 763-64, 766
Elasticity: advertising, 93; of demand, price, 510-12
Electronic cottage, 153
Electronic mail, 703
Electronic shopping, 659
Embargo, 429-30
Emergence stage in market evolution, 391-92
Emotional appeals, 610, 611
Emotional positioning, 637
Employee relations in service firms, 496, 498
Employees, new-product ideas from, 337
Encirclement attack, 415-16
Encoding, 602
Endorsements, celebrity, 612, 613, 639
Energy, increased cost of, 150-52
Engineering department, 739-41
Entry barriers, 235
Environment: channel design and characteristics of, 547; competitive, 140; external environment analysis, 51-53; feedback and control to monitor, 60-61; industrial buying and, 213; internal environment analysis, 53-56; market, 37; marketing audit of, 768-70; opportunities/threats analysis and, 51-

53, 79; See also Marketing environment
Environment protection, governmental, 152
Environmental forecasting, 268, 269
Environmentalism, impact of, 151
Equilibrium, competitive, 245
Errors in screening ideas, 341-42
Escalator clauses, use of, 530
Ethics, 247
European Common Market, 233, 425
European Economic Community (EEC), 429-30
Events: as communication channel, 614; creating, 678-81; sponsoring, 320
Excess capacity, price cuts and, 527-28
Exchange control, 429-30
Exchange, 6, 7-8; of persons, 565
Exchange economy, structure of flows in modern, 9-10
Exclusive club strategy, 327
Exclusive dealing, 548
Exclusive distribution, 548
Executive summary, 76
Exit barriers, 235-36, 387
Expectancy-value model of consumer choice, 195, 204
Expectations: postpurchase satisfaction and, 197; service-quality, 494-95
Expected product, 459
Expected profit, 520
Expenditures, marketing, 24, 70; advertising, 622-23, 633-35, 651; promotional, 615-17, 626; sales-promotion, 667; sales volume and, 87-88
Expense-to-sales analysis, marketing, 754-55
Expense-to-sales deviation chart, 755
Expenses, functional, 758
Experience-curve pricing, 513-14
Experimental design sales-effect research, 651
Experimental method of estimating sales-response function, 88
Experimental research, 112-13
Expert power, 551
Expertise or expert opinion, 269, 270, 612, 711
Exponential smoothing, 271-272
Export department, 450
Exports, direct or indirect, 440-42
Exposure: advertising, 640-42, 646-47; as measure of PR effectiveness, 645-46

External environment analysis, 51-53
External marketing, 21, 490
Eye cameras, 115

Facilitating services, 500
Facilitators, 539
Factor analysis, 125-26, 284
Fads, 376
Falling demand, 12
Familiarity scale, 604-5
Family: Canadian household, 146-47; consumer behavior and, 177-78; life cycle stage of, 179, 180
Family-brand decision, 475-77
Fashion life cycle, 374
Fear appeals, 611
Features and feature strategies, 313, 383-84, 470-71
Feedback, 60-61, 602; from sales representatives, 706-8; See also Control
Feedback-system diagram, 131, 133
Final price, selecting, 521-22
Finance department, 742
Financial analysis, 755; to evaluate foreign markets, 439-40
Financial intermediaries, 139
Financial leverage, 755
Financial management, 137
Financial objectives, 80
Financial publics, 141-42
Financial ratios, 243
Financing, low-interest, 525
Finite resources, 150
First-time sales, estimating, 350, 351
Fixed costs, 512
Flank attack, 414-15
Flanking defense, 403-4
FOB origin pricing, 522
Focus-group research, 112
Focus strategy, 57-58; See also Positioning
Follower strategies, 418-19
Follow-up on sale, 711, 713
Food & Drugs Act, 157
Food Marketing Institute (FMI), 226
Force, principle of, 414
Forced relationships, 338-39
Forecasts and forecasting: company, 261; environmental, 268, 269; future demand, 268-72; market, 259; shape and duration of product life cycle, 375
Foreign marketing. See Global markets and marketing
Forgetting rate, 27, 647

Format for message, 612
Formulated sales approach, 709
Forward buying, 672-74
Forward integration strategy, 49, 589
Fragmented industry, 312
Franchise organizations, 559-60, 576-77
Free goods, trade promotion with, 671
Free Trade Agreement, 425-26
Free trials, 670
Freight-absorption pricing, 523
French Canadian consumers, 171
Frequency of ad exposure, 641-42, 646-47
Freudian motivation theory, 183-84
Frontal attack, 412-14
Full-cost approach, 762
Full demand, 13
Full market coverage, 300
Full profile approach to preference measurement, 346-47
Full-service retailing, 572-74
Full-service wholesalers, 585
Functional compensation plan, 551
Functional discounts, 524
Functional expenses, 758
Functional-marketing organization, 727
Functional-relationship diagram, 131, 133
Functional tests, 353
Fundamental theorem of market-share determination, 276
Fund-raising drives, nonprofit, 678-81
Future demand, estimating, 268-72
Future Shock (Toffler), 135, 153
Futurist research firms, 269

Galvanometers, 115
Game theory, 129-32
Games, 669-70
Gatekeepers, 213, 615
General Agreement on Tariff and Trade, 426, 429-30, 444
General Electric approach, 43-46
General public, 142
Generalization, 186
Generic competitors, 140
Generics, 459, 473
Geodemographic analysis, 267
Geographical marketing organization, 728
Geographical marketing plans, 147-48
Geographical scope, 38, 51
Geographic markets, 9
Geographic segmentation, 284-85; commercialization and,

361; pricing strategy, 522-23; shifts in population and, 147-48

Gifts, 669

Glasnost, 30

Global industries, 237, 427

Global interdependence, 161

Global markets and marketing, 4, 140, 400-25; blunders, 428; choosing markets to target, 436-39; decision to go abroad, 435-36; environment, appraising, 428-35; Japanese performance in, 452-53; market-entry strategies, 440-43, 452-53; marketing strategy mix for, 443-50; organization for, 450-52; risks in, 426-27, 439, 440

Global organization, 451-52

Goals: formulation of, 56-57; in mission statements, 37; superordinate, 565; *See also* Objectives

GO error, 342

Going-rate pricing, 520

Goodwill, 679

Government catalogues, 111

Government: constraints, 333; environmental protection role of, 152; foreign, global marketing and, 426-27; regulation, 154-57

Government market, 10, 139-40, 227-28

Government publics, 142

Government sector, 484

Graphical models, 131, 132-33

Gray-maket problem, 449

Greenhouse effect, 150

Gross contribution margin per unit, 85-86

Gross profit function, 89

Growth: diversification, 47, 49; integrative, 47, 48-49; intensive; market growth rate, 42

Growth-share matrix, 41-43

Growth stage: in market evolution, 392; in product life cycle, 372, 381, 556, 624

Guerrilla attack, 416-18

Habitual buying behavior, 189, 646

Hard selling, 15

Harper's magazine, 580

Harvesting strategy, 43, 387-88

Hazardous Products Act, 157

Heart share, rating competitors, 243

Heightened attention, 192

Heuristic model, 128

Hierarchy: of attributes, 284; of needs, 184; of objectives, 56

Hierarchy-of-effects model, 607-8

High-pressure selling techniques, 708

Historical approach to sales impact, 651

Historical base, 90

Historical product data, 77

History, company, 37

Holding objective, SBU, 43

Home sales parties method of selling, 574-75

Home shopping channels, 658

Horizontal channel conflict, 563

Horizontal diversification strategy, 49

Horizontal integration strategy, 49

Horizontal marketing systems, 560

Horizontal product team, 734

Hospital services, 492

Household, changing Canadian, 146-47

How to Win Friends and Influence People (Carnegie), 708

Hypermarket, 570

IBM Way, The (Rodgers), 3

Ideal-brand model, 204-5

Ideal business, 53

Ideal product, 6

Ideal self-concept, 181

Ideas: generation of, 337-41; screening of, 341-44; *See also* New product development

Identity media, 679

Image: brand, 479, 681; store, 577

Image analysis, 604-7

Image differentiation, 320, 494

Image persistence, 607

Image pricing, 525

Impact, 641

Implementation, marketing, 58-60, 72-73, 744-46

Import quotas, 429-30

Impression management, 711

Improved-services strategy, 418

Income, changes in, 149

Income distribution, 432

Income market segmentation, 258, 287-88

Incumbent firms, strategies for entering markets held by, 421

Independent variable, 125

Index method, 264-65

Indexing services, 111

Indirect export, 440

Industrial Design & Union Label Act, 157

Industrial distributors, 547, 585

Industrial economies, 432

Industrial-goods classification, 462

Industrial-goods market testing, 360

Industrial market, 139, 207-23; advertising role in, 620-23; bases for segmenting, 294; buying decisions in, 210-23; characteristics of, 208-10; influences on buyers in, 213-16; participants in buying process, 212-13

Industrial marketing channels, 543-44

Industrial-organization analysis, model of, 235

Industrial-product manager, 731

Industrializing economies, 432

Industry: defined, 234; global, 237; market and, 9; service, 484; structure of, 234-37, 311-12, 429-32

Industry sales, estimating, 268

Industry scope, 37

Industry Trade & Commerce, Department of, 271

Infinite resource, 150

Inflation, cost, 528

Influence strategies, 711

Influencer, 188

Information-based society, shift to, 161

Information search, consumer buying and, 192-94

Information systems. *See* Marketing Information systems (MIS)

Informative advertising, 630

Ingratiation, 711

Ingredient labeling, 156

In-home shopping, 658

In-home tests, 649

Initiator, 188

Innovation, 26-28, 35, 364; balanced R&D-marketing coordination and, 739; continuous, 401; in packaging, 479; service, 493; speeding up, 317; *See also* New-product development

Innovation-adoption model, 607

Innovativeness, individual differences in, 364-66

In Search of Excellence (Peters and Waterman), 3

Inseparability of services, 488

Inside-out perspective, 17

Inside salesforce, 702

Installation, 317, 463

Institutional advertising, 629

Institutional market, 227

Intangibility of services, 486-88

Integrated direct marketing (IDM), 661; marketing database system for, 661-62

Integrated marketing communications, 626-27

Integrated marketing organization, 765-66

Integrative growth, 47, 48-49

Intelligence system: competitive, designing, 245-48; marketing, 51, 103-5

Intensive distribution, 548

Intensive growth, 47-48

Interacting skills, 746

Interactive marketing, 490

Intercept interviews, 117

Interdepartmental relations, 738-42

Interdepartmental strengths and weaknesses, assessing, 55-56

Interest, defining market by consumer, 258

Intermediaries, marketing, 138-39, 540-41, 547-48; *See also* Marketing channels; Middlemen; Physical distribution; Retailers; Wholesalers

Internal environment analysis, 53-56

Internal marketing, 21, 490

Internal marketing information systems committee, 103

Internal microenvironment, 136-37

Internal publics, 142

International division, 450-51

International marketing. *See* Global markets and marketing

International product life cycle, 436, 444

International sector, 30

International subsidiaries, 449, 451

International trade system, 429-30

Internationalization process, 443

Interpersonal factors in industrial buying, 215

Intertype competition, 582

Interviewing, types of, 112, 116-17

Intrapreneurship, 336, 725

Introduction stage in product life cycle, 372, 376-80, 556, 624

Introductory market strategy, 362

Introspective method, 190

Inventory, 594; *See also* Physical distribution

Investment, direct, 443

Involvement, consumer, 188, 189, 190

Irregular demand, 12-13

Issues analysis, 79

Item, 460

Japan: competitive strategy in, 24, 337-38, 453; contrasting

Canadian firms with firms in, 240; customized marketing in, 281; global marketing by, 452-53; organizational buying behavior in, 221; value-creation-and-delivery process in, 726-27
Joint ventures, 442-43
Judgmental method, 88
Just-in-time (JIT) production, 138, 216-17, 594
Just-noticeable difference, 470

Kiosk shopping, 558
Knowledge state of buyer readiness, 608

Labeling, 479, 480-81
Labeling (advertising strategy), 638
Labor market, 11
Laboratory test markets, 356-57
Laboratory tests, 648
Laid-back competitor, 245
Laptop computer, 703
Latent demand, 12
Latent market, 391
Law of demand, 87
Lead time, 675
Lead users, 337, 339
Leaders: market, 400-11, 533-35; opinion, 177, 613, 614-15
Leadership, product-quality, 509
Leads, developing, 708-9
Learning, slow, 27, 26-28
Learning curve, 514
Leasing, 210
Legal-political environment, 154-58, 430-34
Legislation, 154-57, 480-81
Legitimacy, 711
Legitimate power, 551
Leverage-capital-structure ratio, 243
Lexicographic model, 205
Licensed name brand, 473
Licensing, 442
Life-cycle stage, psychological, 179, 287
Life cycles. See also Family; Product life cycle (PLC); Retail life cycle
Lifestyle: classification of, 181-82; consumer behavior and, 179-82
Lifestyle segmentation, 289, 663
Lifetime value of customer, 666
Likability of source, 613
Liking state of buyer readiness, 608

Limited-service retailing, 572
Limited-service wholesalers, 585-86
Limits to Growth, The (Meadows, Meadows, Randers and Behrens), 143
Linear models, 133
Liquidity ratio, 243
Location pricing, 525
Location. See Place
Logical-flow diagram, 131-32
Logical resistance, 711
Long-term contracts, 215
Loss-leader pricing, 524
Loss leaders, 580
Lot size, 546
Low-interest financing, 525
Low involvement products, 189
Low-spending tests, 651
Loyalty, brand, 291-92, 634, 667-68, 735

McKinsey 7-S framework, 58, 60
Macroenvironment, forces in, 51, 67, 78, 136, 142-161; cultural environment, 158-61; demographic environment, 142-48; economic environment, 148-50, 429-32, 547; marketing audit of, 768-69; natural environment, 150-52; political environment, 154-58; technological environment, 152-54
Macromodel, 126
Macroscheduling problem in advertising, 645-46
Macrosegmentation, 294
Magazines, 643, 644, 645, 659
Mail Order, 586, 656, 657
Mail questionnaire, 116
Maintenance and repair services, 501
"Make or buy" decision, 139
Management: levels of, 137; of marketing channels, 550-56; of product support services, 499-501; relationship, 716-19; of sales-force, 697-708; of services industries, 492-99; top, 137, 333-34, 338, 496, 743; use of marketing research, 119-20
Management by objectives, 749
Management contract, 442
Managers, 11-12; product, 335, 336, 729-34
Manufactured materials and parts, 462-63
Manufacturer brand, 473, 475
Manufacturer promotions, 670

Manufacturer-sponsored retailer or wholesaler franchise system, 559
Manufacturer's agency and agents, 547, 586
Manufacturers, branches and offices, 586
Manufacturing, 137, 484
Manufacturing-cost-reduction strategy, 418
Manufacturing department, 741
Manufacturing-driven companies, 741
Mapping of marketing strategy, 164-69
Marginal sales response, 94
Market(s): concept of, 8-10; customer, types of, 11, 139-40; flows connecting, 9-10; latent, 391; types of, 9, 11, 257-59; See also Organizational markets; Target (served) market; Test markets
Market attractiveness, 43-46
Market broadening, 405
Market-buildup method, 263-64
Market-centered organizations, 736-37, 739
Market-challenger strategies, 409-18
Market demand, 257-272; current, estimating, 262-68; defined, 259; demand function, 259; future, estimating, 268-72; See also Demand
Market-development strategy, 47, 48
Market entry strategies, 440-43; Japanese, 452-53; market pioneer, 378-80; timing of, 361
Market environment, 37
Market evolution, 391-94
Market expansion strategy, 400
Market focus, 17
Market-follower strategies, 418-19
Market forecast, 259
Market-fragmentation stage, 392
Market growth rate, 42
Market-leader strategies, 400-11; price cutting in response to, 528, 533-35
Market logistics thinking, 590
Market management organization, 734-37
Market manager, 11, 734-37
Market map, 609
Market minimum, 259
Market modification, 383
Market-nicher strategies, 419-21
Market opportunities analyzing, 51-53, 66-67, 75, 78-79

Market opportunity index, 265
Market-penetration strategy, 47-48, 257, 258, 508
Market-performance analysis, 496, 497
Market pioneer, 378-80
Market potential, 259-61; area, 263-67; total, 262
Market-reconsolidation stage, 392-93
Market salesforce structure, 692-93
Market segmentation, 68, 126, 280-303; bases for consumer markets, 9, 171, 258, 284-92, 294; bases for industrial markets, 294; customer segment profile, 294-95; by direct marketer, 663; general approach to, 280-82; patterns of, 282; procedure, 282-84; requirements for effective, 295
Market segments: branding and, 473; evaluation of, 297-99, 303; identifying shifts in, 415; interrelationships between, 303; natural, 282; product mapping and, 466; scope of, 37-38, 51; segment-by-segment invasion plans, 303; selecting, 299-303
Market share: advertising budget and, 634; analysis of, 751-54; declining, 528; defending, 401-5; defining and measuring, 752; determinants of company, 276; estimating, 268; expansion strategies for, 405-9; Japanese strategies for building and protecting, 453; marketing mix and, 409; optimal, 409; rating competitors, 242, 243; relative, 42
Market-share-maximization model, 240
Market signals, 404
Market-skimming pricing, 508-9
Market specialization, 300
Market targeting, 280, 297-303; See also Target (served) market
Market testing, 270, 354-60
Marketer, 10, 22, 25
Marketing: analysis in, 28; core concepts of, 5-10; defined, 5
Marketing-allocation optimization, 91-95
Marketing as percentage of sales (M/S ratio), 622-23

Marketing audit, 73, 767-73, 774
Marketing budget-to-sales ratio, 70
Marketing channels, 539-32; allocating functional expenses to, 758; alternatives, 547-50, 694-95; channel-design decisions, 546-50; channel-management decisions, 550-56; conflict, cooperation, and competition in, 563-65; consumer and industrial, 543, 544; defined, 540; dynamics, 556-63; functions and flows, 541-43; global marketing and, 449-50; growing bargaining power of, 735; modification of, 555, 557; nature of, 540-46; number of levels, 543-44; profit-and-loss statement for, 758-60; roles of individual firms in, 561-63; in service sector, 544
Marketing concept, 3, 16-27; coordinated marketing, 19-21; customer orientation, 17-20, 23, 25, 251; defined, 16; market focus, 17; organized resistance to, 23-27; profitability, 21-24
Marketing control. See Control
Marketing controller concept, 773-74
Marketing database system, developing, 661-62
Marketing decision support system (MDSS), 120-21, 125-33; model bank, 126-33; statistical bank, 125-26
Marketing department, 726-44; evolution of, 726-28; relations with other departments, 738-42; strengths and weaknesses of, 53; ways of organizing, 728-34
Marketing driven company, 741
Marketing-effectiveness rating review, 764-67
Marketing environment, 135-69; cultural, 158-61, 434; defined, 136; demographic, 142-48; economic, 148-50, 429-32, 547; global, 428-35; macroenvironment, forces in, 51, 67, 78, 136, 142-61; in marketing system, 164-69; microenvironment, 51, 67, 136-42; natural, 150-52; political, 154-58; technological, 152-54
Marketing expense-to-sales analysis, 754-55
Marketing hyperopia, 405

Marketing implementation, 58-60, 72-73, 744-46
Marketing information center, 105
Marketing information systems (MIS), 100-33; concept and components of, 101; defined, 101; developments rendering need for, 100; internal records system, 102-3; marketing decision support system (MDSS), 120-21; marketing intelligence system, 51, 103-5; marketing research system, 66-67, 105-20
Marketing intelligence system, 51, 103-5
Marketing intermediaries, 138-39, 540-41, 547-48; See also Middlemen; Physical distribution; Retailers; Wholesalers
Marketing management, 11-12; defined, 11; process of, 64-74; rapid adoption of, 29-30; See also Control
Marketing mix, 71, 73; defined, 70; of entrants, 421; estimated sales and, 89-90; four Ps of, 70-72, 172; for global marketing, 443-50; influence on price, 521; interactions of, 93; market share and, 409; marketing function audits, 768; modification of, 384; optimization of, 90, 91; positioning strategy and, 324; in recession, 528; retailer decisions on, 578-82; trade, 166; See also Place; Price; Product(s); Promotion
Marketing myopia, 15, 403, 405
"Marketing Myopia" (Levitt), 38
Marketing network, 8
Marketing objectives, 80
Marketing-partitioning theory, 284
Marketing performance assessment, 24, 750-74
Marketing plan, 36, 64; implementation of, 72-73; nature and contents of, 74-82; tools and concepts to improve, 85-95
Marketing-plan simulator, 90
Marketing planning decisions, 11-12
Marketing-planning system, 743
Marketing process, 64-74; defined, 65; designing strategies, 68-70; opportunities/threats analysis, 51-53, 66-67, 75, 78-79; organizing, implementing

and controlling effort, 72-74; planning programs, 70-72; researching and selecting target markets, 67-68
Marketing-profitability analysis, 758-60
Marketing programs: organizing and implementing, 725-746; planning, 70-72
Marketing research, 66-67, 105-110; characteristics of good, 118-19; defined, 105; evolving techniques in, 109; management's use of, 119-20; process, 108-18; by retailers, 577; scope of, 106-8; suppliers of, 105-6; types of, 106
Marketing research department, 105
Marketing research firms, 105, 106, 269, 476
Marketing resources, 11
Marketing service agencies, 139
Marketing situation, 76-77
Marketing strategy(ies): of competitors, identifying, 238-40; defined, 70; designing, 68-70; factors influencing company, 73-74; for global marketing, 443-50; for introduction stage, 378-79; mapping of, 164-69; marketing audit of, 768, 770; in marketing plan, 75, 80-81; for new product, 348-49; by product life cycle stage, 381, 382-84, 387-88; for retailers, 577-82; for service firms, 490-99; of wholesalers, 586-88, 589
Marketing system: audit of, 768, 770; main actors and forces in modern, 10; strategy and environment interaction with, 164-69; vertical, 421, 551, 558-60, 582-83
Marketing vice-president, 11, 19-21, 72-73, 727
Markov-process model, 127
Markup pricing, 514-15
Mass advertising, 735
Mass customization, 281
Mass market, 148
Mass marketing, 278, 362
Mass media. See Media
Mass, principle of, 405, 412
Materials and parts, 462-63
Mathematical programming, 129
Matrix organization, 737
Maturity stage: in market evolution, 392; in product life cycle, 372, 381-86, 556, 624

Maximarketing, 661, 662
Maximum investment exposure, 352
Meat & Canned Food Act, 157
"Me society", 159
Media, 602; for advertising, 629; as communication channel, 614; identity, 679; international adaptation in use of, 448; new, 644; sales-promotion, 667; timing, 645-47; types of, 642-43; vehicles, 643-45; written and audiovisual, image and, 320
Media coverage, 682
Media-measurement services, 645
Media publics, 142
Mediation, 565
Megamarketing, 434
Megatrends, 484; See also Marketing environment
Megatrends: Ten New Directions Transforming Our Lives (Naisbitt), 161
Melting pot policy, 148
Merchandising conglomerates, 561, 577
Merchant (middlemen) wholesalers, 138, 539, 585
Mergers, 589
Message: advertising, 635-40; choice of media and, 642; in communication process, 602; designing, 610-13; international adaptation of, 445-48; public relations, choosing, 678-81; See also Communication(s)
Message rehearsal, 602
Microanalytic model, 126-27
Microbehavioral model, 127
Microcomputer industry, 223, 241
Microenvironment, company, 51, 67, 136-42
Micromarketing, 278
Micromarkets, 148
Microsales analysis, 751
Microscheduling, advertising, 646-47
Microsegmentation, 294
Middle age (early & late), growth trends in, 146
Middlemen, 138-39, 501; characteristics, 547; management of, 550-56; private brands developed by, 473-75; as source of new-product ideas, 338; types of, 138, 539, 585, 586; See also Marketing channels
Mind share, rating competitors, 242, 243

Minimarket testing, 357
Minimax criterion, 131-32
Mission: business, 49-51; corporate, 36-38
Mobile defense, 405
Mobility barriers, 235
Model bank, 126-33
Modernization, product-line, 470
Modified rebuy, 210
Monadic rating, 354
Monetary regulation, 432-33
Monetary transaction, 7
Money market, 11
Monitoring of service performance, 496; See also Control
Monitoring skills, 746
Monopolistic competition, 236
Monopoly, pure, 236
Moody's, 709
Moral appeals, 610
Morphologic analysis, 339
Motivation: of channel members, 550-54; corporate mission statement and, 38; of sales representatives, 702-6; theories of, 183-85
Motivational research, 183
Motives, 186
Multiattribute demographic segmentation, 288
Multibrand strategy, 477-78
Multichannel conflict, 563
Multichannel marketing systems, 560-61, 562
Multifactor portfolio matrix, 43, 46
Multinationals, 425, 438, 451-52; *See also* Global markets and marketing
Multiple-factor index method, 264-65
Multiple regression analysis, 125
Multiple scenarios, 269
Multiplex marketing, 589
Multivariate statistical techniques, 125

Name-research procedures, 476
Narcotic Control Act, 157
Nation-dominant hierarchy, 284
National account management (NAM) division, 693, 694; *See also* Relationship management
National brands, 473-75, 577
National Health & Welfare, Department of, 154
Nationality groups, 173
Nations, 11
Natural environment, 150-52
Natural market segments, 282
Natural products, 462

Nature, people's views of, 160
Need(s), 4-5; from customer point of view, 18; defining business by customer, 40; hierarchy of, 184, 394; identification, 192, 218, 339; theories of human motivation, 183-85; human, 5
Need family, 460
Need markets, 9
Need-satisfaction sales approach, 711
Need set, 6
Negative demand, 12
Negotiated contracts, 228
Negotiation, 8, 713-16
Net price, 85
Net profit curve, 89
Net worth, rate of return on, 755
Network-planning (critical path) diagram, 131, 132
New-business plan, corporate, 46-49
New Game Strategies, 589
New-product committees, 336
New-product department, 336
New-product development, 330-66; business analysis, 349-53; commercialization, 360-62; concept development and testing, 344-45; consumer-adoption process, 362-66; decision process summary for, 363; dilemma of, 332-33; effective organizational arrangements for, 333-37; idea generation, 337-41; idea screening, 341-44; investment cost of, 335; launching, 677; marketing strategy development, 346-49; marketing testing, 354-60; process, 69; product development, 47, 48, 353-54; strategic roles for new products, 333-34; types of new products, 330-32
New-product managers, 336
New-product venture teams, 336
New-task buying, 210, 217-23
New users and uses, developing, 400
News generation for public relations, 679
Newspapers, 27, 643, 659
Newsweek magazine, 111, 645
Nichemanship, 35
Niching strategies, 35, 282, 382, 419-21, 589
No demand, 12
Noise, 602
Nondurable goods, 461
Nonlinear models, 133

Nonmarketing variables, 93
Nonpersonal communication channels, 614-15
Nonprobability sampling, 116
Nonprofit sector, 15, 29, 139-40, 678-79
Nonstore retailers, 574-75
Nontariff barriers, 429-30
Nontraceable common costs, 762
Norms, call, 701
Nutritional labeling, 156

Objections, handling, 711
Objective-and-task promotion budget method, 616-17, 634
Objective, principle of the, 405, 409
Objectives: advertising, 630, 633; channel, 547; choosing strategic, 409-12; communication, determining, 607-10; company, evaluating idea in terms of, 343; company, market targeting and, 298-99; of competitors, determining, 240-41; direct marketing, 663; goal formulation, 56-57; hierarchy of, 56; in marketing plan, 75, 79-80; marketing public relations, 678; in physical distribution, 590-92; price, 507-9; research, defining, 108, 110; sales-promotion, establishing, 668-69; salesforce, 687-89; tradeoffs between, 57
Observational research, 112
Occasion segmentation, 289-90, 663
Occupation, consumer behavior and, 179
Off-invoice or off-list, 671
Off-price retailers, 570-72
Offer, categories of, 485
Offer mix, 71
Offer strategy in direct marketing, 663-65
Offering grid, 562
Office of the future, 66
Oil prices, 150
Older consumers, 171
Oligopoly, 236
On-air tests, 649
One or two-sided arguments, 611-12
Ontario's Business Practices Act, 156
Ontario Ministry of Natural Resources, 686
Open-bid buying, 228
Open dating, 156

Open-end questions, 114
Operating asset turnover, 245
Operating margin, 245
Operating variables, segmentation by, 294
Operational efficiency, 766
Opinion leaders, 177, 613, 614-15
Opportunities/threats analysis (O/T analysis), 51-53, 66-67, 75, 78-79
Optimal market share, 409
Optimal order quantity, 594
Optimization model, 128-32
Optional-feature pricing, 526-27
Order of presentation, 612
Order processing, 592-93; costs, 594
Order quantity, optimal, 594
Order (reorder) point, 594
Order-routine specification, 220-21
Order-shipping-billing system, 102
Order taker, 22
Organization(s), 11; company, 725-26; for global marketing, 450-52; marketing audit of, 768-70; for new-product, development, 333-37; orientation toward market-place, 12-28; people's views of, 160; rate of adoption by, 366; retail, 575-77
Organization of marketing effort, 72
Organizational buying, defined, 207
Organizational levels, 35-36
Organizational markets, 207-28; government markets, 10, 139-40, 227-28; reseller markets, 139, 223-26; *See also* Industrial market
Organizational resistance to marketing concept, 23-27
Organizing skills, 746
Others-self-concept, 181
Outdoor advertising, 643
Outside-in perspective, 17
Overall cost leadership strategy, 57
Overcapacity, selling concept used with, 15-16
Overdemand, 528
Overfull demand, 13
Overhead, 512

Packaging, 479-81
Pair-wise approach, 347
Paired-comparison method, 354
Paper-towel market, evolution of, 393
Partnership, producer-middlement, 551-52, 554

Passion for Excellence, A (Peters), 3
Patent Act, 157
Patronage awards, 670
Payback period, 351-52
Penetration strategies, 47-48, 257, 258, 378
Perceived risk, 196-97
Perceived value, 528
Perceived-value pricing, 516-20
Percentage-of-sales promotion budget method, 615-16
Perception: consumer behavior and, 185-86; psychological pricing and, 521; of quality, 327-28
Performance: marketing, tools to evaluate and control, 24, 750-74; product, 313-15
Performance evaluation: for industrial suppliers, 221-23; for sales representatives, 706-8
Performance-importance matrix, 53, 54
Periodic purchase orders, 220
Periodicals and books, 111, 643
Perishability of services, 488-90
Peristroika, 30
Personal communication channels, 613-14
Personal factors in consumer behavior, 179-81
Personal influence, 366, 403-4
Personal interviewing, 116-17
Personal selling, 600, 619, 686, 687, 708-19; buyer-readiness stage and, 623-24; in consumer market, 621; methods, 689; negotiation, 713-16; relationship management, 716-19; salesmanship, 708-713; tools of, 602; *See also* Salesforce
Personality: consumer behavior and, 181-82; effective sales, 698; segmentation by, 289, 294
Personnel differentiation, 320
Persuasability, 604
Persuasive advertising, 630-33
Pharmaceutical industry, 651
Physical distribution, 138, 588-96; major activities involved in, 591; nature of, 588-90; objectives in, 590-92; organizational responsibility for, 594-96
PIMS (Profit Impact of Market Strategy), 406, 407, 409
Pipelines, 596
Place, 70, 72; retailer's strategy for, 580-82; wholesaler's strategy for, 586-88

Plan, marketing. *See* Marketing plan
Planning, 28, 74-82; marketing programs, 70-72; product life cycle concept as tool in, 388-89; profit-optimization, 86-88; tools to improve, 85-95; *See also* Strategic planning
Point-of-purchase (POP) displays and demonstrations, 670
Political-action committee (PACs), 158
Political-legal environment, 154-58; in foreign market, 432-34
Political-problem products, 219
Political risk assessment reports, 439
Pollution, 152
Population growth, 142-48
Portfolio approach to retailing, 583
Portfolio-evaluation models, 41-46
Portfolio tests, 648
Position defense, 403
Positioning, 28, 67-68; communicating, 327; differentiation and, 68-69, 320-28; emotional, 637; four Cs of market, 141; price-quality strategies, 506; product-positioning map, 68, 69, 345; rational, 637; repositioning, 195; for retailers, 574; retailer's price strategy and, 580
Postpurchase behavior, consumer, 189, 197-99
Postsale service strategy, 500-1
Potential market, 258, 259
Potential product, 459, 460
Power, bases of, 552-54
Preapproach, sales, 709
Precious Metal Marketing Act, 157
Preemptive defense, 404
Preference segments, 282
Preference state of buyer readiness, 608
Preferences: diffused-preference market, 391; of management and owners, 37; measuring, 346-50, 354
Premium pricing, 526
Premiums, 669, 673
Presale service strategy, 500
Prescriptive method, 190
Presentation: order of, 612; of research findings, 117-18; sales, 709-11
Prestige-goods strategy, 418
Pretesting, sales-promotion, 675
Price, 70, 72, 505-35; adapting, 522-27; arm's length, 449;

buyer definition of value and, 309-10; demand and, 509-12; global marketing and, 448-49; in growth stage, 381; matrix organization and setting, 737; net, 85; price/quality strategies, 506; profit maximizing, 507, 508; reference, 521; reservation, 714; retailer's strategy for, 580, 581; sales volume and, 87; setting, 506-22; transfer, 449; wholesaler's strategy for, 586
Price-aggressive strategy, 414
Price changes, 527-35; competitors' reactions to, 532; customers' reactions to, 532, 533; price cuts, 527-28, 532, 532, 533-35; price increases, 530-32; responding to, 532-35
Price-discount strategy, 418
Price elasticity of demand, 510-12
Price-escalation phenomenon, 448-49
Price gouger, 530-32
Price-off, 671
Price-packs, 669
Price points, 526
Price sensitivity, 510, 532
Price steps, 526
Pricing: discriminatory, 525-26; experience curve, 513-14; geographical, 522-23; going-rate, 520; market penetration, 508; market-skimming, 508-9; markup, 514-15; perceived-value, 516-20; product-mix, 526-27; promotional, 524-25; psychological, 521; sealed-bid, 520; selecting method of, 514-19; selecting objective of, 514-19; target-return, 515-16
Primary data, 110, 112
Primary demand, 259
Primacy effect, 612
Primary groups, 174
Principled-negotiation approach to bargaining, 714-15
Print pretesting services, 649
Private brand, 473-75, 607
Private nonprofit sector, 484
Prizes, 669
PRIZM system, 267
Probability sampling, 116
Problem recognition, 217-18
Problem solving, customer, 708
Procedural-problem products, 219
Producer market. *See* Industrial market

Producers' cooperatives, 586
Product(s), 6, 7, 70, 72; adaptation or invention for foreign market, 444; adaptation strategies for foreign market, 443-444; choice of media and, 642; classifications of, 461-63; defined, 6, 459; ideal, 7; levels of, 459-60; substitute, 234, 298, 634; *See also* New-product development; Positioning
Product assortment, 578, 587
Product attributes, 194-95, 219, 547; competition dynamics, 393-94; hierarchy of, 284
Product-bundling pricing, 527
Product category, 372-73, 677
Product champion, 338
Product choice set, 6
Product class, 460
Product concept, 14-15
Product development strategy, 47, 48, 353-54; *See also* New-product development
Product-differentiation, 312-17, 578
Product fact book, 75
Product failures, 342
Product family, 460
Product-form competitors, 140
Product-form pricing, 525
Product-form life cycles, 371, 373
Product hierarchy, 460
Product-idea rating devices, 342-43
Product imitation, 418-19
Product-innovation strategy, 418
Product-item mapping, 466
Product ladder, 327
Product life cycle (PLC), 333, 370-91; advertising budget, 634; critique of, 388-91; estimating sales by, 349-50; international, 436, 444; rationale for, 376; stages and shapes in, 371-88, 556, 624
Product line, 460, 465-71
Product-line pricing, 526
Product-management organization, 729-36
Product management/market management organization, 737
Product manager, 335, 336, 729-34
Product market, 9; promotional mix and, 620-23
Product-mix decisions, 461-63; pricing, 526-27
Product modification, 383
Product positioning, 280; map of, 68, 69, 345; *See also* Niching strategies; Positioning

Product-proliferation strategy, 418
Product quality, 14-15, 315, 509
Product research, 107
Product salesforce structure, 692
Product situation, 77
Product specialization, 300
Product support services, managing, 499-501
Product-team approach, 733-34
Product testing, 360
Product trial, 640-41
Product type, 460
Product-use test, 360
Product-value analysis, 218-19
Product-variety marketing, 278, 546
Product warranties, 525, 670
Production: estimating cost of, 512-14; just-in-time, 138, 216-17, 594; self, 6
Production concept, 12-13
Productivity: marketing audit of, 768-70; of service firms, managing, 498-99
Product/market battlefield, 237, 241
Product/market expansion grid, 47, 68
Professional purchasing, 210
Professional service providers, 29
Professionals, marketing of, 490
Profile, developing customer segment, 294-95
Profit(s), 28; estimating new-product, 350-53; expected, 520; in growth stage, 381; product-line, 465
Profit-and-loss planning base, 90
Profit-and-loss statement, 75, 82, 758-60
Profit equation, 85-86
Profit forecasting and planning map, 169-70
Profit Impact of Market Strategy (PIMS), 406-9
Profit margin, 755
Profit optimization (maximization), 86-90, 240, 507-8
Profitability, 21-24; customer satisfaction and, 19-20; direct product, 226; evaluating market segment for, 297-98; market share and, 406-7; product performance and, 313-315
Profitability control, 73, 750, 749, 758-62
Profitability ratio, 243
Programs, 11, 58
Projected profit-and-loss statement, 75, 82
Projective techniques, 183
Promotion, 70, 72; adaptation for

global markets, 444-48; measuring results of, 624-26; retailer's strategy for, 580, 669; wholesaler's strategy for, 586; See also Sales promotion
Promotion budget, 615-17, 626
Promotion clutter, 667
Promotion mix, 71, 617-24; of business-to-business marketers, 618; factors in setting, 620-24; major tools of, 600, 602, 618-620
Promotional advertising, 418, 629
Promotional allowances, 524
Promotional pricing, 524-25
Proposal solicitation, 219
Proprietary brands, 589
Prospective method, 190
Prospects, sales, 659-61, 701, 708-9
Prototype, 353
Pruning decision, 471
Psychogenic needs, 183
Psychographic segmentation, 285, 288-89
Psychological discounting, 525
Psychological factors in consumer behavior, 183-88
Psychological life-cycle stages, 179, 287
Psychological pricing, 521
Psychological repositioning, 195
Psychological resistance, 711
Public Citizen group, 143
Public-interest groups, growth of, 158
Public interests, 28
Public relations (PR), 600, 602, 677-682; activities, 677; buyer-readiness stage and, 623-24; distinctive qualities of, 619-20; evaluating results of, 681-82; major decisions in, 678-79
Public-service activities, 679
Publications, public relations through, 679
Publicity, 677
Publics, 136, 141-42
Purchase decision, 196-97; See also Consumer behavior
Purchase frequency, 647
Purchase laboratories, 356-57
Purchase probability scale, 269
Purchase state of buyer readiness, 608
Purchasing: centralized, 215; direct, 210; performance evaluation, 215; segmentation by approach to, 294; stockless purchase plan, 220-21
Purchasing agents, 212, 586

Purchasing departments, 213-15, 741
Purchasing offices, 586
Pure competition, 236
Pure monopoly, 236
Pure oligopoly, 236
Push versus pull strategy, 621-22

Qualitative evaluation of sales representatives, 708
Quality: communicating, 327-28; improvement strategy for, 383; product, 14-15, 315, 509; service, managing, 494-98
Quality-control procedures, 216, 488
Quantity discounts, 524
Question marks (growth-share cell), 41, 42
Questionnaires, 113-15, 116
Queuing models, 127-28
Quiet Revolution, 148
Quotas: import, 429-30; sales, 261, 704-6

R-F-M formula (recency, frequency, monetary amount), 663
Racial population, 173
Rack jobbers, 585-86
Radio, 643, 644, 659
Rail transportation, 596
Rapid-penetration strategy, 378
Rapid-skimming strategy, 378
Rational appeals, 610
Rational positioning, 637
Raw-material-exporting economies, 429-32
Raw materials, 11, 150, 462
Reach, 641
Reaction profiles of competitors, 245
Real repositioning, 195
Rebates, 524-25, 669
Rebuy, straight or modified, 210, 221
Recall, selective, 602
Receiver, 602
Recency effect, 612
Recession, economic, 528
Reciprocity, 210
Records system, internal, 102-3
Recruitment of sales representatives, 697-98
Reference groups, 174-77
Reference prices, 521
Referent power, 551, 711
Regional shopping centers, 581
Regionalization, 729
Regression analysis, 125

Regulation government, 547; labeling, 480-81; legislation, 154-57; of technological change, 154
Reinforcement advertising, 633
Relationship management, 693, 716-719
Relationship marketing, 8, 217
Relative market share, 42
Reliability, differentiation through, 315
Religious groups, 173
Reminder advertising, 633
Repair service, 319
Repairability, differentiation through, 315
Repeat and replacement sales, 127, 350
Reports, internal, 102-3
Repositioning, 195, 325-27, 478-79, 677
Research, 107; advertising, 107, 648-51; business economics and corporate, 107; on buying decision process, 190-92; communication-effect, 648-49; creativity in, 119; defining objectives in, 108-10; motivational, 183; sales-wave, 356; on target markets, 67-68; See also Marketing research
Research-and-development management, 137
Research and development (R&D), 726; budgets, 153; marketing department relations with, 738-39; new-product development and, 330, 333, 334, 353
Research and development (R&D) department, 336, 353
Research instruments, 113-15
Research plan, developing, 110-117
Reseller market, 139, 223-26
Resellers, value-added, 421
Reservation price, 714
Resistance: from customer, 711; to marketing concept, 23-27
Resource markets, 9
Resources, 11, 37, 72, 298-99, 343; finite vs infinite, 150; theory of effective marketing-resource allocation, 85-95
Response, 602
Response hierarchy models, 607-8
Restaging of product, 388
Retail life cycle, 569, 570
Retail organizations, 575-77
Retailer brand, 473-75
Retailer cooperative, 559, 576

Retailer promotions, 580, 669
Retailers, 543, 568-83, 647, 729, 735; branches and offices, 586; defined, 568; marketing strategies of, 577-82; positioning strategies for, 574; sales-promotion objectives for, 668; trade promotion to, 671-74; types of, 568-577
Retailing: competition in, 560; multichannel, 561-62; service levels, 569-74; speeding up, 319; trends in, 582-83
Retention customer, 18; selective, 186
Retirees, 146
Retrospective method, 190
Return on investment (ROI), 59, 515-16, 682
Return on net worth rate of, 755
Return on operating assets (ROA), 245
Return to assets, 755
Revenue maximization, 508
Reward power, 551
Rewards: company, 704, 743; types of product, 636
Risk(s): analysis of, 353; in global marketing, 426-27, 439-40; new-product development and, 332-33; perceived, 196-97
Roles, consumer behavior and, 178-79, 188
Rollout marketing, 361
Routine-order products, 219
Royalties, licensing brand names for, 473
Rubber tire industry, 35
Runner-up firms, 409
Rural areas, 147

Safety stock, 594
Sale (promotional) advertising, 418, 629
Sales: branches and offices, 586; budget for, 261; comparing current-to-past, 706-8; decline in, 24; evaluating channel alternatives on basis of, 550; marketing as percentage of (M/S) ratio, 622-23; marketing mix and estimated, 89-90; new-product, estimating, 349-50; product-line, 465; repeat and replacement, 127, 350
Sales agency, 550
Sales analysis, 106, 749-51
Sales-and-profit contribution of public relations, 682

Sales assistants, 702
Sales automation, 703
Sales branches, 586
Sales contests, 674, 706
Sales department, 726
Sales-effect research, 649-651
Sales equation, 86
Sales maximization, 508
Sales meetings, 706
Sales promotion, 600, 666-677; buyer-readiness stage and, 623-24; distinctive characteristics, 619; efficiency control in, 764; evaluating results of, 118, 675-77; growing importance of, 735; major decisions in, 668-77; objectives, establishing, 668-69; percentage-of-sales promotion budget method, 615-16; purpose of, 667-68; rapid growth of, 666-67; tools of, 602, 669-73
Sales-promotion program, 81-82, 673-677
Sales quota, 261, 703-4
Sales reporting, 102, 706
Sales representatives, 686, 687; compensation for, 695, 697; directing, 700-2; evaluating, 706-8; marketing intelligence from, 105; motivation of, 702-6; recruiting and selecting, 696-98; as source of new product ideas, 338; tasks of, 689; training of, 698-700, 708; types of, 710
Sales-response function, 72, 86-88, 89, 94, 167-169, 261
Sales (selling) concept, 15-16, 17
Sales team, 689
Sales-variance analysis, 749-51
Sales vice-president, 727
Sales volume, 86, 87-88, 89
Sales-wave research, 356
Salesforce, 22, 547, 617, 619, 620, 686-719; classification of sales positions, 686; compensation of, 695-97, 696, 704; designing, 687-97; efficiency control of, 763; friction between brand managers and, 672; managing, 697-708; in matrix organization, 737; objectives of, 687-89; purpose of, 708-719; resistance to direct marketing, 656; sales promotion and, 666, 668-69; size of, 694-95; strategy for, 689; structuring, 689-94; See also Sales representatives

Salesforce opinions, composite of, 270
Salesmanship, 708-13
Salesperson-to-salesperson comparisons, 706
Salesperson's work plan, 706
Samples, promotional, 669
Sampling plan, 110, 115-16
Satisfaction, customer, 6, 18, 19, 20, 25, 197, 198, 708, 755-57
Savings, low rate of, 149-50
Scanners, 729
Scientific evidence, 638
Scientific method, 118-19
Scopes: business mission, 51; competitive, 37-38
Sealed-bid pricing, 520
Seasonal discounts, 524
Secondary data, 110-111
Secondary groups, 174
Segment-by-segment invasion plans, 303-4
Segmentation, segments. See Market segmentation; Market segments
Selective attention, 185, 602
Selective competitor, 245
Selective demand, 259
Selective distortion, 185, 602
Selective distribution, 548
Selective recall, 602
Selective retention, 186
Selective specialization, 300
Self-concept, consumer behavior and, 181
Self production, 6
Self-selection retailing, 572
Self-service, 479, 570
Sell-in time, 675
Sellers, number of, 234-35
Selling agents, 586
Selling and salesmanship, 708-713
Selling concept, 15-16, 17
Selling, personal. See Personal selling
Semantic differential, 605-6
Seminar selling, 689
Sender, 602
Sensations, 185
Served market. See Target (served) market
Service backup, 546
Service channels, 544
Service contracts, 525
Service-firm sponsored retailer franchise system, 560
Service industries, 484
Service output levels: analyzing, 546-47; retailing, 569-574
Service-performance-process map, 488
Service quality, managing, 494-98
Services, 6, 461, 484-501; busi-

ness, 463; characteristics of, 486-90; defined, 485; growth in, 484; marketing strategies for service firms, 490-99; nature and classification of, 485-86; physical-distribution objective for, 592; product support, 499-501; retailer decisions on services mix, 578-80; two-part pricing for, 527; types of businesses in, 486; value-added, 589; wholesalers definition of, 587
Services differentiation, 317-19, 492-94, 577
Seventh Day Adventists, 267
Sex segmentation, 287
Share-of-voice parity, 616
Shared values, 58
Shell directional-policy model, 46
Shipping, 596
Shopping goods, 461
Shopping strips, 582
Shrinkage barriers, 236
Simple-rank-order method, 354
Simulated store technique, 356-57
Single sourcing, 217
Skills, marketing implementation, 58, 746
Skimming strategies, 378, 508-9
Slow learning, 26-28
Slow-penetration strategy, 378
Slow-skimming strategy, 378
Small Loans Act, 148
Social class, 174, 175, 287-88
Social factors in consumer behavior, 174-79
Social marketing, 26-28, 143
Socialist economies, 30
Society, people's views of, 160
Soft-drink industry, 559
Software programs, 120-21
Source credibility, 611, 612-13
Source dominant hierarchy, 284
Spatial convenience, 546
SPC (Statistical process control), 216
Special Reports, 644
Specialization, 300, 421; See also Niching strategies
Specialized forecasting firms, 269
Specialized industry, 312
Specialty advertising, 674
Specialty goods, 461-62
Specialty-line marketing research firms, 107
Specialty store, 570
Speculative business, 570
Speeches, 679
SSWD group (single, separated, widowed, divorced), 147
Staffing, 58

Stalemated industry, 312
Standard and Poor, 709
Standard Industrial Classification System (SIC), 263-64
Standardization, 445-46, 488, 496
Stars (growth-share cell), 41, 42
Static model, 133
Statistical bank, 125-26
Statistical decision theory, 129
Statistical-demand analysis, 272
Statistical method, 88
Statistical process control (SPC), 216
Statistics Canada, 263
Status, consumer behavior and, 178-79
Status symbols, 179
Stimulus ambiguity, 611
Stochastic competitor, 245, 611
Stochastic model, 133-34
Stock level, 594
Stockless purchase plan, 220-21
Storage warehouses, 593
Store brand, 473-75
Store image, 577
Store retailers, 559, 569-74, 576, 577
STP (segmenting, targeting, and positioning) marketing, 278
Straight extension strategy, 443-44
Straight rebuy, 210, 221
Strategic business area (SBA), 371
Strategic business units (SBU), 38-46; business strategic planning, 49-61; corporate new-business plan, 46-49; evaluation of current portfolio, 41-46; identification, 38-41
Strategic control, 749, 750, 764-773, 774
Strategic fit with environment, 60-61
Strategic group, 58, 59, 238-40
Strategic marketing, 278
Strategic orientation, 766
Strategic planning, 34-63; business, 49-61; corporate, 36-49; defined, 35; key ideas underlying, 35-36; relationship between marketing and, 65
Strategic planning gap, 46-47
Strategic roles for new products, 335-36
Strategy formulation, 57-58, 80-81
Strengths/weaknesses analysis (S/W analysis), 53-56, 79; of competitors, assessing, 242-45, 248
Style differentiation, 315-17
Style improvement strategy, 384
Style life cycle, 374

Style, organizational, 58
Subcultures, 159, 173-74
Subdecisions, purchase, 197
Subsegmentation, 68
Subsidiaries, international, 449, 451
Subsistence economies, 429-30
Substitute products, 234, 298, 634
Suburbs, 147
Success probability, 51-52
Suggestion systems, 755
Supermarket, 570
Superordinate goals, 565
Supersegments, 303
Superstore, 570
Suppliers; bargaining power of, 298; in industrial market, 208, 219-23; physical distribution objectives and, 592; for resellers, 223, 226
Supplies, 463
Supply and Services, 227
Survey of Current Business, 269
Survey research, 112, 677, 757;
    See also Marketing research
Survival, pricing for, 507
Sweepstakes, 669
Switching-in and switching-out rate, 127
Symbiotic marketing, 560
Symbols, 320; status, 179
Syndicated-service research firm, 105-107
Synectics, 341
Systems buying and selling, 210-212, 589

Tachistoscope, 115
Target audience: advertising exposure of, 642, 646-47; choice of media and, 642; identifying, 604-7, 609; promotional impact on, 624-26
Target marketing, 278, 280, 362;
    See also Market segmentation; Product positioning; Target (served) market
Target-return pricing, 515-16
Target (served) market, 258; data on, 75-77; direct marketing decision on, 663; geodemographic analysis to identify, 267; global marketing and, 436-39; market-allocation optimization for, 91-95; prospects, 362; researching and selecting, 67-68, 299-304; retailer's definition of, 577; wholesaler's definition of, 587
Tariffs, 427, 429, 449

Task environment, marketing audit of, 768-70
Tasks, marketing, 12-13
Teamwork, 336-37, 726, 733-34
Technical-support persons, 702
Technological environment, 152-54
Technological leapfrogging, 416
Technological pirating, 427
Technology, 2; automated warehouse, 586-88; defining business by, 40; demand/technology life cycle, 370-71, 391; for measuring consumer response to advertising, 118; regionalization and, 729; retail, 583; salesforce productivity and, 702-3; telecommunications, 216-17
Technology-driven companies, 739
Teenage-Student Consumers, 171
Telecommunications, 216-17
Telemarketing, 658, 665, 702
Telephone interviewing, 116
Television, 241, 643, 644, 658
Terms of exchange, 6
Territorial-structured salesforce, 689-92
Territory marketing plan, 706
Test markets, 270, 357-58, 360
Testimonial advertising, 614, 638
Testing: concept, 345-48; copy, 648-49; of direct-marketing elements, 665; market, 270, 354-60; product, 353, 354;
    See also Research
Theater tests, 649
Third Wave, The (Toffler), 153
Threats, analysis of, 52-53, 75, 78-79, 297-98
Thriving on Chaos (Peters), 3
Tie-in promotions, 670
Tiger competitor, 245
Time-and-duty analysis, 701-2
Time pricing, 525
Time series analysis, 271
Timing: market-entry, 361; media, 645-47; of sales-promotion program, 673
Toothpaste market, 237, 290, 292, 393
Top management, 137, 333-34, 338, 496, 743
Total added value, 309-10
Total costs, 512
Total customer price, 289-90
Total customer value, 309
Total market, expanding, 400
Total market potential, 262
Total profits, 508
Total quality-improvement programs, 102

Total revenue, 508
TQC (total quality control), 216
Trade associations, 565
Trade barriers, 427
Trade channels. See Marketing channels
Trade-in allowances, 523
Trade in Goods, Canada's major partners in, 429-30
Trade marketing mix, 166
Trade Marks Act, 157
Trade promotion, 666, 671-74
Trade-relations mix, 548
Trade Show Bureau, 674
Trade shows and conventions, 360, 674
Trade system, international, 429-30; See also Global markets and marketing
Trademark, 471
Tradeoff approach, 347
Tradeoffs between objectives, 57
Traffic builders, 580
Trailer tests, 649
Training: customer, 317; in-house marketing, 743; of sales representatives, 698-99, 708
Transaction marketing, 7-8
Transfer, 7
Transfer price, 449
Transportation, 139, 594-96
Trend correlation and extrapolation, 269
Triad Power (Ohmae), 438
Triangular product team, 733-34
Troubled business, 53
Truck-manufacturing industry, 59
Truck transportation, 596
Truck wholesalers, 585
Trustworthiness of source, 612-13
Truth-in-lending, 156
Truth-in-advertising, 156
Turbomarketing, 317
Turbulent environment, 60
Turnkey solution, 210
Turnover ratio, 243
Two-factor theory of motivation, 184-85
Two-part pricing, 527
Two-step flow-of-communication process, 614

Unbundling of goods and services, 530
Underdeveloped world, 2
Undifferentiated marketing, 300-301, 303
Uniform delivered pricing, 522
Unique selling proposition (USP), 290, 324, 610
Unit pricing, 156
Universal Product Code, 118, 565

Universe, people's views of, 160
Unselling campaigns,13
Unsought goods, 462
Unwholesome demand, 13
Urban areas, 147
Urban renewal, 147-48
Usage rate, segmentation by, 291
User, 188
User-oriented reports system, designing, 102-3
User status, segmentation by, 291
Utility function, 194

Value, product, 7; added by channel, 556; buyer definition of, 309-10; perceived, 516-20, 528; process of building and delivering, 725-26; shareholder, 776 n4
Value-added resellers (VARS), 421
Value-added services, 589
Value analysis; customer, 248
Value-chain analysis, 311-12

Value-in-use price, 516
Value lifestyle groups (VALS) Value/price ratios, 181
Value/price ratios, 310
Values, cultural, 158-60
Variability of services, 488
Variable costs, 512
Variety-seeking buying behavior, 189-90
Vending machines, 575
Verbal models, 132
Vertical channel conflict, 563
Vertical integration, 237, 558
Vertical marketing system (VMS), 421, 551, 558-60, 582-83
Vertical product team, 733
Vertical scope, 38, 51
Vogue magazine, 580, 645
Volume, break-even, 515
Volume industry, 311-12
Volume segmentation, 291
Voluntary chain, 576

Waiting time, 546
Wants, consumer, 5-6, 8, 28
Warehousing, 139, 586-88, 589, 593
Warranties, 525, 670
Water transportation, 596
Weak products, identifying, 387
Weaknesses, analysis of, 79
Weighted-index method, 343-44
Weights & Measures Act, 157
Westward movement, 147
Wheel-of-retailing hypothesis, 569
White-collar population, 148
Whole channel concept for international marketing, 449-50
Wholesaler-sponsored voluntary chains, 559
Wholesalers, 543, 583; marketing strategies of, 587-88, 589; trade promotion to, 671-74; types of, 138, 539, 585-86, 588, 589
Wholesaling, 583-88
Wide Area Telephone Service (WATS), 658

Winning Performance (The), 3
Women: car buying and, 178; working, 147
Word-of-mouth influence, 613, 614
Workload approach salesforce size, 694-95
World population explosion, 141-43

Yankelovich Monitor, 159
Yield management, 526
Young adults, growth trends in, 146
Youths age group, growth trends in, 146
Yuppies (young urban professionals), 159, 288

Zero-based budgeting, 94, 95
Zero-level channel, 543
Zone of agreement, 713-14
Zone pricing, 523